103d Congress } JOINT COMMITTEE PRINT { S. Print 103–11
1st Session } { Vol. 2

THE FORMER SOVIET UNION IN TRANSITION

VOLUME 2

STUDY PAPERS

SUBMITTED TO THE

JOINT ECONOMIC COMMITTEE
CONGRESS OF THE UNITED STATES

MAY 1993

Printed for the use of the Joint Economic Committee

U.S. GOVERNMENT PRINTING OFFICE

57–372 WASHINGTON : 1993

For sale by the U.S. Government Printing Office
Superintendent of Documents, Congressional Sales Office, Washington, DC 20402
ISBN 0-16-040929-2

JOINT ECONOMIC COMMITTEE

[Created pursuant to sec. 5(a) of Public Law 304, 79th Cong.]

DAVID R. OBEY, Wisconsin, *Chairman*
PAUL S. SARBANES, Maryland, *Vice Chairman*

LETTER OF TRANSMITTAL

May 17, 1993.

To the Members of the Joint Economic Committee:

I am hereby transmitting for use by the Joint Economic Committee, Congress, and the public the second volume of a study assessing the economies of the newly independent states of the former Soviet Union entitled, *The Former Soviet Union in Transition.* The study contains papers prepared at the committee's request by a large number of government and private experts.

This volume contains analyses of key sectoral developments in energy, agriculture, the environment, science and transportation, defense and defense conversion, and human resource issues including health and education. Special emphasis is placed on economic developments in the 15 former Soviet Republics. There are economic assessments and profiles on each of the newly independent states.

The study was planned, directed, and edited by John P. Hardt, Associate Director of the Congressional Research Service of the Library of Congress, and Richard F Kaufman, General Counsel of the Joint Economic Committee. Phillip J. Kaiser acted as publications coordinator. We are grateful to the Congressional Research Service for making Dr. Hardt and others available to work on the project, and to the many authors who contributed papers.

Sincerely,

DAVID R. OBEY,
Chairman, Joint Economic Committee.

LETTER OF SUBMITTAL

THE LIBRARY OF CONGRESS,
CONGRESSIONAL RESEARCH SERVICE,
Washington, DC, April 30, 1993.

Hon. DAVID R. OBEY
Chairman, Joint Economic Committee
Congress of the United States
Washington, DC.

DEAR MR. CHAIRMAN: I am pleased to transmit to you the second volume of a collection of papers on the situation in the former U.S.S.R. entitled, "The Former Soviet Union in Transition." The study was directed by John P. Hardt, Associate Director and Senior Specialist in Soviet Economics of the Congressional Research Service and Richard F Kaufman, General Counsel of the Joint Economic Committee. Phillip J. Kaiser coordinated the publication with editing and production assistance from Karen Wirt, James Voorhees, Linda Kline, Mary Maddox, and John Bartoli. Many CRS and other Library of Congress personnel, as well as government and private specialists contributed significantly to the project.

We trust that the analyses and information contained in this study will be of value to the Joint Economic Committee, as well as the Congress in general and the broad audience of students of the former Soviet Union.

Sincerely,

JOSEPH E. ROSS,
Director.

CONTENTS

VIII

INTRODUCTION: TRANSITION AND INTEGRATION IN NEWLY INDEPENDENT STATES

By John P. Hardt and Richard F Kaufman *

The former Soviet Union is undergoing twin revolutions that are remarkable, unprecedented historical events. The first revolution—the transition to a pluralistic state with a market economy under the rule of law—was the subject of the first volume of this publication. The second revolution—the disintegration of the empire and its reconstruction into several newly independent states—provides a major theme for this volume.

Since the "mongol yoke" was lifted in the fourteenth century, there has been one dominant power in the region from Poland to the sea of Japan—Russia. Under the czars, russification—one czar, one language, and one religion—characterized a policy that placed all political, economic, social, and military power in the hands of the leaders in the Russian capital. Soviet leaders paid lip service to self determination and preservation of minorities but in effect reinforced this historical orientation toward the center with an emphasis on one party leadership, one Russian culture, and a Marxist-Leninist ideological substitute for religion.

The end of the Leninist-Stalinist system and the empire paradoxically came through an attempt to reinforce the traditional system of governance by reforming it. As Mikhail Gorbachev attempted to strengthen the party's central role with transformation to a socialist market, his reforms eroded the power of the party-dominated, command-economy system. Likewise while Gorbachev also acted as if the empire was eternal, his political reforms and glasnost eroded the cohesion of the Moscow-centered system and challenged the principle of geographic unity. By not enforcing the Brezhnev doctrine in Eastern Europe he weakened the glue of force that held together the Soviet bloc, and invited revolutions in Central and Eastern Europe. Just as Soviet tanks resolved challenges to Soviet domination in the Central European region in Berlin (1953), Budapest (1956), and Prague (1968), so the inhabitants of the Russian Federation and regions of the Soviet Union were bound together by the certainty that the Soviet military and police would enforce adherence to the dictates of Moscow. With the abortive Moscow coup in 1991, it became clear that the military and police force that had held together the old system and empire was unwilling to support

---

* John P. Hardt is Associate Director, Congressional Research Service, Library of Congress. Richard F Kaufman is General Counsel, Joint Economic Committee, U.S. Congress.

the overthrow of Gorbachev. Gorbachev, in turn, was unable to hold back the forces that led to the break up of the Soviet Union.

The Dilemma of Sovereignty and Integration

Yeltsin moved quickly to abolish the Communist Party and to begin the dismantlement of the command economy system. As the power of the party, military, and police proved unable to maintain the Stalinist system and the empire, the long repressed forces of ethnicity and nationalism surged forward. Free to choose, all republics took their own sovereignty in preference to subservience to Russia; many minority groups within newly sovereign states and between states likewise challenged the authority of the new states being formed. While the change from russification seemed irreversible, the new sovereignty based on self-determination was unstable as the networks of trade, investment, infrastructure, and other regional interrelationships were strained or ruptured, and old ethnic hostilities were let loose.

The creation of new sovereign states weakened the long-established economic integration of the region and thereby undermined economic recovery, development, and the transition to a market system. The heritage of Russian and Soviet development was a monopolized, highly centralized, military-oriented economy with a high degree of immutable interdependence. Every new independent political unit broke long-established interstate relations and so created economic bottlenecks for other states and regions. Moreover, the monetization of economies in transition and collapse of the ruble made interstate trade even more difficult. Many of the critical problems in food and energy supply, environment, and infrastructure were necessarily regional problems made worse by the disintegration of traditional economic ties.

The security problems of demilitarization, also regional, were complicated by the disintegration of the empire; weapons held in Ukraine, Kazakhstan, Belarus and other newly independent states could no longer be controlled or dismantled by order from Moscow. With the retrenchment of Soviet military power came a lack of control over weapons and forces and a reduced ability to relocate and reemploy the demobilized enlisted and officers' corps. Moreover, the control of residual forces and weapons was fragmented and contentious. While Russia led in agreeing to arms control in START 1 and 2, most of the best conventional forces and many of the critical nuclear weapons were outside Russia's borders.

Each ethnic group brought forward historical claims against the other groups, especially against the Russians. These suppressed ethnic and nationalistic claims had been exacerbated by Stalin's contentious nationalism policy, especially the forced resettlement of several ethnic groups during and after World War II. The mix of ethnicity and nationalism in a new, weak Commonwealth of Independent States has not been conducive to regional economic reintegration.

The new states need trade, investment, infrastructure, and the environment to act as centripetal forces for regional integration if they are to make effective transitions to market economies and if they are to join and compete successfully in the world economy.

Yet centrifugal nationalistic forces and the need to retain and build political independence continue to pull the new states apart. The new states are adopting and extending the old "country once removed" principle of Central and Eastern Europe, i.e., all alliances and good relations are with non-neighboring countries in the region. Russia is still a neighbor of everyone and the 25–28 million ethnic Russians outside Russia frequently bring that point home.

Most of the new states favor economic integration but not with their neighbors, especially Russia. Each newly independent state aspires to join a regional association and integrate into the global economy. But the regional association that attracts most of them is the European Community, not the Commonwealth of Independent States (CIS). While the International Monetary Fund, the World Bank, and the OECD draw the various independent states toward the global market system by stimulating openness and market-oriented discipline, the indirect conditionality they prescribe is not sufficient impetus for regional reintegration. The divorce from Russia, as the ruble zone ends and as other economic ties that bound the empire are broken, creates a fissure that will be hard to fill or repair. The rancor of divorce makes accommodation between Russia and the newly independent states today difficult if not impossible, even on specific issues that might seem to be easily resolvable such as who is liable for the Soviet debt, how the assets of the Soviet Union are to be dispersed, and how the interstate links in transportation and communication are to be cooperatively managed.

Objective leadership and a regional divorce counselor are needed. The historical conditions that made the Treaty of Rome and the Common Market possible are not present. There is no partnership analogous to the partnership between Germany's Adenauer and France's DeGaulle; Yeltsin and Kravchuk do not form an easy alliance. No Western umbrella covers the economic space as the overarching American presence did in Western Europe. Overriding ethnic, nationalistic and sovereignty barriers to integration are now omnipresent in what was the Soviet Union. They had faded in post-World War II Western Europe. While the international system of economic institutions may play a role in integration, it appears at best a marginal factor. The CIS, multilateral and regional organizations, and bilateral arrangements are all potential engines for integration. Private non-governmental institutions might play effective roles. One of those in particular, the "International Committee for Economic Reform," might be effective if taken over by the G-7. [1] The International Committee offers a multilateral, but nongovernmental framework for identifying practical opportunities for the use of international assistance—in full participation with countries of the region and properly coordinated with the efforts of countries themselves. By its first major meeting scheduled for Kiev, June 7–9, 1993, it is expected that up to 25 Eastern countries and all the larger Western countries will have already joined. The

---

[1] The Committee includes the major countries in the former Soviet Union and East Europe and the Western Industrial Countries; it offers a non-governmental, multilateral framework for dealing with regional issues. R. Martin Lees, Counsellor International of the Committee. Memo. March 10, 1993.

International Committee can complement and strengthen the present approach of the G–7 in the region by helping it to clarify priorities, strategies, and programs, and by helping to coordinate the assistance provided region-wide. The coordination of assistance on a country-by-country basis is necessary, but not sufficient.

Indeed, a key element of Western strategy will likely be to encourage cooperation among the countries of the former Soviet Union. This would promote economic reform and growth and help reduce tensions and the threat of confrontation. Incentives may be provided to encourage such cooperation, and a proportion of the assistance provided by the G–7 may be made available to promote it. This would create a sound foundation for partnership between East and West on key issues of economic reform and cooperation; and it could make a significant contribution to renewed growth, economic reform, stability and peace in Russia and in the region as a whole.

One of the more hopeful developments is the movement towards an international agreement on energy trade and investment. Discussion of a European Energy Charter among the former Cold War adversaries, have been underway since mid-1990. The basic agreement on the European Energy Charter may be reached by the July G–7 meeting. [2] It is designed to provide a legal and regulatory framework for the energy industries from the Atlantic to the Pacific and would provide a framework for meeting the needs of both Russian energy suppliers and energy importers of the former Soviet Union. Russians complain that by selling energy to former republics at below market prices they capture only a fraction of the income from the trade they would obtain if their energy products were sold on the world market. Ukrainians and others complain they cannot afford current Russian prices and that delivery is too often uncertain. Some regulatory framework and short term subsidies may be needed to weather the energy price shock. This could be provided from the IMF Systemic Transformation Facility. The energy agreement may include as many as 50 countries with the European Community, the United States, Russia and Kazakhstan representing the core. The Charter would include elements of a GATT-like Trade Agreement; an Investment Treaty; and a Third Party Dispute Settlement facility. Energy security by pipeline protection and supply discipline and creation of an investment friendly environment would be important to producers. While the EC seems inclined to make some exceptions to national treatment, they may accept more open access to their market, especially an opening of the gas market.

Such organizational and structural umbrellas as the International Committee and the Energy Charter could form a useful framework for interrelating security, political, and economic issues such as payments and environmental protection that Russia and the former Soviet Union republics seem to be unable to resolve either bilaterally or through the CIS.

---

[2] "The Energy Charter Negotiation: Time for Decision", discussion paper, Department of State, April 16, 1993.

xiii

New States in Transition: Some Are More Equal Than Others

Even with an effective set of regional and international umbrellas, the integration necessary for effective transition to market economies by individual countries and the region as a whole requires acceptance of the need for openness and integration, especially by the major economies of the region.

Some newly independent states have more assets and potential regional and global leverage for development. Military downscaling is essential. Demobilization is critical for the economic future of Russia because past military allocations have preempted the best natural resources, capital, and manpower to fulfill military objectives. Nuclear demobilization in the other newly independent states is unlikely without Russian leadership. A Russia that is less threatening to the region and that cooperates in peacekeeping efforts and crisis resolution throughout the world reduces the military burden on all states in the region.

Economically Russia is the behemoth of the newly independent region with its natural, human, and capital resource assets. Large-scale enterprises in the highly monopolized Soviet industrial sector were based in Russia. Moreover, Russia was and is the dominant market for all the newly independent states. Taking the Russian trunk out of the tree of the former Soviet economy would leave the branches and roots in a perilous state.

Issues of sovereignty, ethnic nationalism, and local identity have not been limited to the newly independent states, but are a central concern in the Russian Federation. The federative problem within Russia is similar to the drive for self-determination that broke up the empire. Autonomous regions of the Russian Federation, such as Tatarstan and Chechen-Ingushtia have opted for independence within or outside the Russian Federation. Other regions, such as East Siberia, Sakhalin, and Komi have pressed for more rights and less responsibility to the center. Even cities in the Russian Federation have reduced their ties to the Russian central government. Control of assets and the capture of revenue by the governmental treasuries from exports such as oil, financial and monetary discipline in revenue collection and credit creation are economic problems exacerbated by the federative problem. [3] New social structures such as new entrepreneurial groups have been slow to arise to fill voids created by the collapse of the party and the command economy system.

Fear of and antagonism toward Russia in the newly independent states and concern in Russia over the fate of the 25 million or more Russians outside Russia make Russian nationalism an issue. Russian nationalism will continue to assert itself as the Russians slough off their Soviet identity and seek a new one. Will the new identity take the form of an intolerant chauvinism, or of an inclusive patriotism? Vladimir Lukin, Russian Ambassador to the United States, has spoken of the difference between an inclusive "rossiisskii dom" and exclusive, narrow "russkii dom." Certainly

[3] Rolf J. Langhammer, Matthew J. Sagers and Matthias Lucke. Regional Distribution of the Russian Federation's Export Earnings Outside the Former Soviet Union and Its Implications for Regional Economic Autonomy. *Post-Soviet Geography*, December 1992, pp. 617–634.

there are many prominent voices from several points on the political spectrum who seem to be trying to construct a russkii dom, among them the extremist Zhirinovsky and the moderate Stankevich. But Dimitri Likhachev has reminded us that Russians have lived in a rossiisskii dom as well. [4] It is this "house" that will allow Russia to live at peace with its neighbors and take advantage of the united energies of all the people of the Russian Federation and the larger region of the former Soviet suzerainty. The alternative is conflict within and without the Russian borders. Conflict bedevils the attempts to reestablish open, healthy trade among the former Soviet states and to address regional problems of commerce, environment, security, and governance.

There are also subgroupings of newly independent states that promise some degree of cooperation and integration. Ukraine and Moldova are an example. The presence in Moldova of ethnic Russians in the Trans-Dniestr military district is a problem that Russia, Ukraine, and Moldova are coping with but threatens to escalate. Reestablishing economic ties will be difficult if ethnic and nationality concerns are not restrained.

Kazakhstan and the states of Central Asia make a regional grouping not only by common borders but in terms of ethnicity, culture, and religion. Uzbekistan, leading the Turkic group of nations, also has a claim to a regional leadership role. Kazakhstan, which has energy, wheat, and weapons, is by far the most powerful and geographically largest of these independent Muslim states and is capable of leadership in regional integration.

The Caucasus is an especially fractious region. Open hostility between Azerbaijan and Armenia is a running sore that threatens any cooperation and is an ever present threat to escalate into violence. Georgia is riven by controversy among different ethnic groups, families, and clans. Chechen-Ingushtia and other parts of the Caucasus bordering on the Russian Federation have unsettled sovereignty issues. Regional integration of the Caucasus will probably come, if it does, from outside forces or influence.

Baltic states such as Latvia promise effective market reform and openness to traditional trading partners. But like other new states, the Baltic states find that increased integration with West Europe and Scandinavia is more attractive than economic ties with the East. Regional integration may come simultaneously with or subsequent to integration with the West.

Local initiatives in cities such as Nizhnii Novgorod promise enterprise conversion, price liberalization, and entrepreneurship. However, even such reforming localities have not worked out their role with the center in such critical areas as taxation, property rights, monetary policy, foreign commerce, and other interregional issues. Local reform may be frustrated by regional instability in monetary, fiscal and infrastructure problems.

If destruction of the old command economy has opened the opportunity for a transition to the market, the manner in which the

---

[4] Dimitrii Sergeyevich Likhachev, The National Nature of Russian History, the Second annual W. Averell Harriman Lecture (New York: The W. Averell Harriman Institute for the Advanced Study of the Soviet Union, 1990). Vladimir Lukin at meeting on "America and the Russian Future", Russian Embassy, Washington, January 15, 1993. The Librarian of Congress, James H. Billington amplified this theme.

empire is disintegrating makes it more difficult to create the broader, regional, open economic space so important to successful reform within and among the newly sovereign states.

Ed A. Hewett

1942–1993

Ed A. Hewett, one of the nation's foremost experts on the economies of the former Soviet Union and Eastern Europe, died on January 15, 1993. Dr. Hewett was a senior fellow at the Brookings Institution from 1981 to 1991 when he joined the staff of the National Security Council and became an advisor to President Bush. He was a frequent contributor to studies of the Joint Economic Committee and an expert witness in committee hearings. His views were often sought after by policymakers in Congress and the Executive Branch. He gave his time generously to many members of Congress and their staffs. Dr. Hewett was held in the highest regard by all who knew him, his works, and his writings. His publications included *Energy, Economics and Foreign Policy in the Soviet Union* (1984), *Reforming the Soviet Union: Equality Versus Efficiency* (1988), and *Open for Business: Russia's Return to the Global Economy* (1992). These volumes are dedicated to his memory.

III. KEY SECTORAL DEVELOPMENTS

OVERVIEW

By Phillip J. Kaiser *

The selected sectors analyzed here are key either because of their positive or negative impact on economic transformation and development in the states of the former Soviet Union. The energy sector, important in every modern economy, is important not only for supplying domestic industrial and residential users, but may be the best bet for attracting foreign investment and earning hard currency in the near term, for those republics that have energy resources. The supply of agricultural products is a critical measure of living standards, and failure in this sector is likely to have important political implications. Improved transportation of all goods facilitates commerce, and the food losses in transit from farms to cities is an all too familiar problem. The Soviet science and space programs are considered world class by many, and provide the opportunity for trade and investment as many foreign countries would like to take advantage of the pool of talented scientists and engineers, as well as purchase advanced technology. On the negative side, the risk exists that militarily significant technology may more likely be sold in the current dire economic conditions and with the political situation in flux. The environment has been neglected for so long that there is now a severe impact on public health and productivity, and the states of the former Soviet Union must decide how to include environmental clean-up and protection in their economic development and investment policies. The contributors to this section analyze important issues regarding the present difficulties in these sectors and the ramifications of the disintegration of the Soviet Union.

THE ENERGY SECTOR

The Soviet Union, the world's leading oil producer since 1974, has experienced declining production in recent years and may never reach previous peak levels, according to Joseph Riva. The reasons for the decrease include the natural decline in older fields, reduced investment to replace outdated technology and equipment, ethnic conflict in areas that produce oil and oil field equipment, poor production methods and the fact that the easily accessible oil has been tapped, leaving further production to be found in more unfavorable environments which make it more difficult and expen-

---

* Phillip J. Kaiser is a Consultant with the Congressional Research Service.

sive to produce. Foreign investment and joint ventures can help remedy financial and technical problems, Riva notes, but cannot overcome the problems associated with ethnic strife, political instability, and labor unrest. In addition, the current chaotic tax situation may deter or reduce foreign investment plans. Over the next few years oil production is expected to continue to decline, with negative implications for export revenues, and for successor states dependent on oil imports. Although natural gas production declined slightly in 1991 for the first time since World War II, the former Soviet Union has a very large gas resource base—large enough to maintain the present level of exports well into the next century. Supply problems will be related to disintegrating infrastructure and political and ethnic unrest.

No former republic is entirely self-sufficient in energy, Jeffrey Schneider points out, and "no republic will be able to implement energy policies in isolation from its former Union partners." Energy producing republics are dependent on others for industrial inputs, energy equipment, and access to international markets for example, and energy importers are connected by pipelines and power grids to the former Soviet Union. While Russia dominates the energy sector with about 90 percent of oil and 77 percent of natural gas production in the former Soviet Union, it is a net importer of coal and major foods including meat, milk, grain, and vegetables, and its natural gas pipelines cross Ukraine on their route to Western Europe. Among the large republics, Schneider contends that Ukraine is in the most difficult situation due to rapidly falling coal production, shrinking electric energy capacity, and its requirement to import increasingly expensive oil and gas to support its energy-intensive heavy industry and mechanized farming. All republics are faced with escalating prices for oil, which will likely lead to tense relations between oil producers and importers. There will be a strong incentive for producers to export for hard currency, leaving importing republics at a disadvantage, and perhaps seeking alternative suppliers such as Ukraine has done with Iran.

THE AGRICULTURE SECTOR

It has been widely accepted among analysts of the Soviet agriculture sector that the primary problem has not been gross production, but storage, transport, distribution, and processing. The papers in this section reaffirm this assessment. In addition, the successor states face the problems associated with the collapse of central command and supply, inter-republic trade barriers, and reduced hard currency reserves and greater debt that make importing more difficult. Some economic reform policies also have had a negative effect on agriculture, as William Liefert points out. Macroeconomic imbalance, in particular the large increase in money income while maintaining low prices from 1985 to 1991, caused extreme inflationary pressure and undermined the ruble as a medium of exchange. This effective devaluation of the currency reduced incentives to produce and sell for rubles and has hindered the development of a money-based system of exchange. Price liberalization policies begun in January 1992 will restore macroeconomic balance only if the government implements strict fiscal and monetary policies that limit further inflation and restore value to the ruble, Liefert asserts.

Food availability in the former Soviet Union faces further deterioration, with particular impact in some regions and among vulnerable groups (e.g. those on fixed incomes), according to Allan Mustard and Christopher Goldthwait. The dismal Soviet record in agriculture is a result of the excessive focus on production (to the detriment of processing, storage, etc.), the desire for central control of food supplies that led to inadequate on-farm storage, the monopoly control of processing facilities, and the absence of a wholesale market. The lack of private ownership of food led to the careless and irresponsible treatment of it resulting in large losses. Mustard and Goldthwait cite three major obstacles to improvement: anti-reform bureaucracy and management, absence of privatized capital infrastructure and land, and the lack of capital to establish, operate, and expand private enterprises.

The successor states of the Soviet Union vary greatly in their capacities for agricultural production, reflecting differences in climate and soil, but also economic development patterns, according to Barbara Severin. Soviet policy created a substantial interdependence among the former republics especially regarding food. For example, what crops to produce and where processing facilities were located were determined by central managers. As the Soviet Union disintegrated, this interdependence caused a disruption of food availability. Severin states that interrepublic trade in food-stuffs has fallen by about half. Food consumption also varies among the former republics both in terms of per capita calories consumed and the composition of food consumed. She observes that in spite of an overall decline, average food consumption is well above that in many other developed countries. Nevertheless, some of the poorer former republics face further declines in the quality and quantity of food available, with some citizens facing malnutrition. The good news is that production appears to be increasing in the areas that have privatized, and higher prices are reducing waste.

The Soviet Union has been an important export market for U.S. feed grains, wheat, and soybean products. Remy Jurenas points out that historically the U.S.S.R. paid cash, but beginning in 1990 requested and was granted credit. U.S. extension of credit has been based on two factors, (1) the maintaining of agricultural sales and, (2) the support for democratic and market reforms in the Soviet Union. The primary form of credit has been export credit guarantees, which allowed the Soviets and now the successor states to obtain loans in the private sector to finance purchases, at market rates. Second, the United States has offered grant aid and long-term concessional credits. The United States has also offered technical assistance and training. Jurenas raises several important considerations regarding U.S. policy. Export credit guarantees, for example, are conditioned on creditworthiness. Questions have been raised about Russia and other successor states' ability to pay, considering current debt and payments problems. Some analysts have suggested that continued short-term lending is unwise and that repayment periods should be lengthened. Others argue that Western commodities may undermine the domestic producers and slow down the development of the market. A compromise may be to sell some U.S. imported grain through Russian commodity exchanges to help establish the domestic prices and market. If reform is successful, Jurenas notes, the successor states would be expected to increase production and the market for some U.S. products would be reduced. The composition of trade is likely to change from what it is today toward food processing equipment, agricultural technology, and oilseeds.

THE ENVIRONMENT

The extent of environmental degradation in the Soviet Union has become widely known only in the past few years. Murray Feshbach describes in detail the widespread pollution of the air, land, and water. The breadth of pollution is significant: radioactivity due to nuclear power accidents, poor handling of waste, and nuclear weapons testing; soil contaminated by excessive use of pesticides, herbicides, and fertilizers with erosion and runoff into the water supply; air pollution from industry and transportation virtually unrestrained by environmental considerations. The ramifications include an unhealthy work force with lower life expectancy, increased birth defects and the real possibility of damage to the gene pool. Feshbach concludes that the problem is unlikely to improve in the near term due to the enormous costs of clean up, while the country faces a severely deteriorating economy.

With the disintegration of the U.S.S.R. there will likely be 15 or more different structures to replace the central ministries that had responsibility for conservation and environmental protection, according to Philip Pryde. However, pollution does not stop at national or republic borders but flows down rivers and blows with the wind. Inter-republic cooperation will be essential if environmental concerns are to be adequately addressed. An example of logical cooperation would be among those states that border on the Caspian Sea and depend on the flow of the Volga River. The water resources of Central Asia could be cooperatively managed by an agreement similar to the Colorado River Compact of the southwestern United States. Other issues to be faced include the disposal of nuclear waste and nuclear and chemical weapons; and whether regulations for foreign investment will require environmentally responsible development. While not optimistic that the environment will be a top priority due to the poor economic situation, Philip Pryde argues that the environment should not be neglected further. He writes that, "[I]t must be understood that there is no such thing as a healthy economy built on top of a polluted environment, and that environmental degradation is merely the postponement of necessary costs of production, often at the cost of public health."

THE SCIENCE AND TRANSPORTATION SECTORS

The Soviet Union had more scientists and engineers, per million population, than any other country, and some areas such as fundamental science, military and space research are world class, according to William Boesman. For the most part these scientists and their facilities are located in Russia. This endowment of scientists and engineers provides both a domestic resource for economic development and a rich potential for foreign investment and trade. Boesman contends that the most serious problem facing science and technology in the former Soviet Union today is the lack of sufficient funds. The general economic decline is compounded by a reduction in the military share of the budget, which historically was the largest financial supporter of science and technology. While the current number of scientists and engineers may not be supportable in a market environment, excessive cutbacks could lead to the sale of sensitive military technology and the emigration of personnel capable of assisting weapons programs in states opposed to the interests of the West. Scientific facilities are deteriorating and the potential is for large numbers of scientists to emigrate, which would have a negative impact on domestic economic transformation as well.

U.S. scientific collaboration with the successor states aims to prevent the diversion of militarily significant technology and scientists by providing some retraining for former weapons scientists and some supplementary activities in research and educational exchange programs, according to Genevieve Knezo. She is not optimistic that these efforts are large enough or sufficiently well designed and coordinated to stem the "brain drain" of scientists, strengthen the scientific infrastructure in the former Soviet Union, or take full commercial advantage of advanced technology.

Marcia Smith assesses the post-Soviet space program, which may offer opportunities for trade and scientific advancement through the purchase of space products and technologies, but also poses the prospect of competition for commercial space launch services. In addition, there is the concern that sales of rocket technology may contribute to ballistic missile proliferation. While Russia is the most important successor state, with 80 percent of the scientific and manufacturing personnel and infrastructure for space, Kazakhstan and Ukraine are also important. Kazakhstan is the location of a launch site as well as facilities for research into space nuclear power and propulsion. Ukraine is the site of a major launch vehicle factory and an important tracking station. Smith concludes that economic problems and political instability in the former Soviet republics may undermine their commitment to continue the space program if it cannot be made economically viable.

Strong laws to enforce patent rights and protect intellectual property will be important for economic development and investment in the former Soviet Union. K. Malfliet points out that implementation of such legal protection is uncertain and the potential exists for 15 separate patent structures with the added obstacle of national language translations for each new state. However, an agreement of December 1991 among Russia, Ukraine, Armenia, Belarus, Moldova, and Tadjikistan provides for some provisional interstate patent coordination until a permanent system is established. There is some continuity with the previous system, as Russia has succeeded the U.S.S.R. in the World Intellectual Property Organization and has taken over the offices of Gospatent, the U.S.S.R. state patent office.

Holland Hunter describes a transportation system that provides poor passenger service and inefficient freight service, suffers from a deteriorating infrastructure of undermaintained railways and railcars, a declining stock of usable trucks and tractors, an overage merchant fleet that is increasingly unseaworthy and many decrepit ports. Of course there is great variation in the density of transport services such as hard surfaced roads and the railway network across the expanse of the former Soviet Union. For much of the former U.S.S.R. the population density is sparse and distances between population centers are long. This creates additional expenses for the transportation of goods between these areas, and implies that for the near term commercial relations may be most rationally fostered with neighboring areas. Shortages of key inputs for the transport sector such as fuel, steel, and spare parts, which have historically been a problem, have become more severe since 1988. This problem is partially the result of the erosion of the central command and the rise of regional autonomy. Additional problems may arise as republics seek to take control of rail lines, cars, terminals, and service facilities on their territories. Hunter indicates that improvement in freight traffic efficiency would result from the adoption of procedures such as cleaning coal before transporting it, cleaning and drying grain before transport, and introducing multimodal container transport as in the West.

A. Energy

THE PETROLEUM RESOURCES OF RUSSIA AND THE COMMONWEALTH OF INDEPENDENT STATES

By Joseph P. Riva, Jr.*

CONTENTS

SUMMARY

In the long history of petroleum production in Russia and the Commonwealth of Independent States (CIS), a normal development progression has occurred in which several prolific petroleum provinces have been discovered in sequence, have become dominant producers and then declined. The present drop in oil output from this vast region is partially the result of the natural decline of many of its large older fields, but also is due to recently reduced capital investments and to the reliance on outdated and inefficient exploration and development technology. Financial and technical problems can be remedied by joint ventures with foreign oil companies. Despite these limitations, the former Soviet Union led the world in oil production every year since 1974, often by a considerable margin.

---

* Joseph P. Riva, Jr., is a Specialist in Earth Sciences, Science Policy Research Division, with the Congressional Research Service.

In the process, the oil resource base has been "high graded" with much of the "easy" oil having been discovered and produced.

The exploration for and development of the remaining oil will be technically more difficult, since the new fields are likely to be smaller and in more unfavorable environments than those exploited in the past. In the short term, Russian and CIS oil output is expected to decline significantly. Political and economic instability, labor unrest, and ethnic strife are contributing to the decline, a problem not amenable to solution by foreign oil companies. Eventually, with outside technical and financial assistance, oil output may recover, but not necessarily to previous peak levels.

Russian and CIS natural gas production, which also leads the world, declined slightly last year for the first time since World War II, despite a huge gas resource base. Gas supply problems are related to the current economic and political instability, the ethnic unrest, and the disintegrating gas infrastructure, rather than to a lack of gas reserves or resources.

Oil and gas production is critical to the CIS, both for internal use and for exports to earn hard currency.

HISTORICAL OVERVIEW: OIL AND GAS DEVELOPMENT THROUGH THE 1980s

Russia and oil are intertwined. The history of the vast region that was the Soviet Union is linked to the great petroleum accumulations that have been exploited over the centuries. Early petroleum utilization is associated with the Baku region of Azerbaijan. This is the location of the eternal pillars of fire worshiped by the Zoroastrians, which were seepages of natural gas that had ignited. Marco Polo, in the thirteenth century, noted the oil seeps in the area that produced a substance good to burn, but not to eat.

THE CZAR'S PETROLEUM

Russian interest in petroleum intensified in the eighteenth century when expeditions from the St. Petersburg Imperial Academy of Science reported on Baku oil, and was further heightened in the early nineteenth century when the war with Persia brought most of the oil areas of the Caucasus under Russian sovereignty. In Baku, the czarist administration had a monopoly on oil exploitation, but its operations were inefficient. By the 1870s, however, the government monopoly was abolished and the Baku area was opened to competitive private enterprise. The result was an explosion of entrepreneurship.[1] Wells were drilled and discoveries made. By 1873 more than 20 small refineries were in business.

The great oil fields that made Russia a major oil producer in the last century were associated with the foothills region of the Caucasus Mountains, generally on the northern flank.[2] The tremendous yields of some of the early wells attracted important financial interests. In the search for foreign markets, a railroad was constructed west from Baku over the Caucasus to Batum, a port on the

---

[1] Yergin, Daniel. *The Prize: The Epic Quest for Oil, Money, and Power.* Simon & Schuster, New York, 1991, pp. 57–58.
[2] Tiratsoo, E. N. *Oilfields of the World.* Third Edition, Scientific Press, Ltd., Beaconsfield, England, 1984, pp. 117–118.

Black Sea. By 1884 crude oil production had increased dramatically; nearly 200 refineries were operating in an industrial suburb of Baku alone.

During the 1890s the rapid rise of Russian oil production, the struggle to establish new world markets, and the competition from foreign interests (with a substantial amount of oil discovered in Indonesia) led to a period known as the oil wars.

THE RUSSIAN REVOLUTION

At the turn of the century, in 1901, Russian oil output reached 84.5 million barrels (mb), 81 mb of which was from Azerbaijan.[3] Geological conditions were favorable for the rapid increase of production as relatively large fields were found close to the surface. The expansion, however, was not constant. With the empire in turmoil and the region a revolutionary hotbed, the oil industry provided a training ground for a number of future Bolshevik leaders. Strikes and worker agitation, a massive earthquake, and other social upheavals led to chaotic and haphazard drilling and production practices. Production capacity declined in the damaged fields around Baku, and Russian oil production, despite new discoveries, became unprofitable. Between 1904 and 1913 the Russian share of world oil exports fell from almost a third to less than 10 percent.

The czarist regime collapsed early in 1917 as World War I was being fought with machines powered by oil. The Germans hoped to control Baku to obtain much-needed oil for their war effort. In 1918 they ended hostilities with revolutionary Russia, but their allies, the Ottoman Turks, advanced on Baku. The Germans offered to try to restrain the Turks in exchange for oil. But the war dragged on, and the Germans did not obtain the oil in time to help their war machine. An exhausted Germany had ample iron and coal, but the victorious allies had oil. Russian oil production in 1918 was 27.2 million barrels (mb).

SOVIET PETROLEUM AND GAS FIELDS

Following World War I the Communist regime, beset with economic chaos and famine and in desperate need of foreign capital, announced a policy of offering concessions to foreign investors. Revitalized by infusions of Western technology, annual oil production in 1930 topped 100 mb. In the 1930s the growing volume of low-cost Soviet oil entered a saturated world oil market, but normal commercial considerations did not apply as the Soviets attempted to earn as much foreign currency as possible to buy machinery for industrialization.

As World War II began, many factors influenced Hitler's decision to attack the Soviet Union, but the central issue was oil. In 1940 Soviet oil production reached 223 mb, 163 mb of which came from the Baku region.[4] In the early 1940s, as the Germans drove through Russia major objectives were the Baku and Groznyy oil fields. The German army was stopped short of its goal and as the war ended, was reduced to having teams of oxen pull its trucks. Al-

---

[3] Elliot, Iain F. *The Soviet Energy Balance*. Praeger Publishers, New York, 1974, pp. 69–70.
[4] Dienes, Leslie, and Theodore Shabad. *The Soviet Energy System: Resource Use and Policies*. V. H. Winston & Sons, Washington, D.C. and John Wiley & Sons, New York, 1979, p. 50.

though the Baku and Groznyy fields were not occupied during World War II, wartime exploration lagged and oil production eventually declined. In 1945, 155 mb were produced.

In an effort to restore production following the war, the Soviets began exploration and development in the Caspian Sea. However, offshore oil development in the Baku region was not able to compensate for declining onshore production, and total Azerbaijan oil output continued to fall. As time has gone on, exploration for and development of remaining oil has become technically more difficult, since new fields are likely to be smaller and in more unfavorable environments than those exploited in the past.

Specifically, there have been a number of problems in the Baku region that adversely affected oil production in the 1980s: technological shortcomings and a continuing shortage of spare parts and equipment; fires and pipeline ruptures; and ethnic violence that disrupted the area's petroleum equipment manufacturing industry, refineries, petrochemical plants, and oil fields. Due to the violence and oil worker strikes, pipeline deliveries of crude oil from Groznyy and tanker shipments across the Caspian Sea were sharply reduced and Azerbaijan's oil output plummeted.[5] Baku and Groznyy currently provide only a small fraction of total Soviet oil production.

The gas fields of the Caucasus also have declined. In the late 1970s annual gas production from the important fields in the Stavropol and Krasnodar region was about 1.3 trillion cubic feet, and by the late 1980s it had further declined to about 765 billion cubic feet.

Expansion of oil production in the Volga-Urals region began to compensate for the declining Caucasus oil fields in the mid-1960s, but by the late 1980s, this region also became began to be depleted and production declined. The region is also rich in natural gas, however, and production has increased, yielding a huge gas resource base. Volga-Urals gas is accessible to industrial users and is exported to Europe. Throughout the 1980s annual gas production was about 2.4 trillion cubic feet.

Intensive exploration in West Siberia in the 1960s and 1970s led to gas and oil discoveries, and the region has been developed to increase production considerably. Other areas with petroleum and gas potential include the Timan-Pechora region north of the Volga-Urals on the Barents Sea (the Komi Republic), East Siberia, Central Asia (Kazakhstan, Turkmenistan, Uzbekistan, and Tadzhikistan), and Ukraine. Oil accumulations in smaller quantities have been recovered on the Kamchatka Peninsula and Sakhalin Island.

GLASNOST AND PERESTROIKA

In 1977, the U.S. Central Intelligence Agency projected that Soviet oil output would peak no later than the early 1980s, although most other observers had not yet recognized existing Soviet oil industry problems.[6] The CIA based its analysis on the premise

---

[5] "Civil Strife Worsens USSR's Petroleum Situation." *Oil and Gas Journal*, January 22, 1990, p. 29.

[6] Prospects for Soviet Oil Production. Central Intelligence Agency, ER 77–10270, April 1977, p. 9.

that large new oil fields could not be found quickly enough to provide sufficient reserves to sustain production and that the fields that provided most of the Soviet oil output were experiencing severe water encroachment. The Soviet government, however, was aware of the problems, and, perhaps even stimulated by the CIA assessment, acted vigorously. Leonid Brezhnev ordered that most oil industry resources be shifted to West Siberia along with additional money, manpower, and equipment. Soviet investment in oil more than doubled between 1976 and 1983 as did Ministry of Oil drilling nationwide. The petroleum industry accounted for 13 percent of total Soviet capital investment in 1980, some $11 billion. As a result, the production decline projected by the CIA did not occur as anticipated. Instead, yearly oil production increased from 3.833 billion barrels (bb) in 1976 to 4.398 bb in 1980, although estimated reserves declined from 78.1 bb to 63.0 bb. Production in 1981 was 4.409 bb, 4.453 bb in 1982, and 4.522 bb in 1983. The U.S.S.R. desperately needed the oil to continue its exports of some 1.8 million barrels per day (mb/d) to satellite countries and 1.7 mb/d to the West (which earned about $25 billion in 1983).

Much of the emergency effort concerned drilling and almost all of the drilling was for development rather than for exploration.[7] The drilling of 25,000 new production wells in West Siberia was mandated. Waterflooding (in which large volumes of water are injected at high pressure in the oil recovery process) also was increased to include about 230 fields that, together, accounted for over 85 percent of total Soviet oil output. While generally successful, the water displaced the oil in some wells, resulting in a decrease in productivity. The huge increase in development drilling put off the production decline for three years. The CIA had underestimated Soviet determination to prevent, at all costs, a decline in oil production, but the essence of the CIA analysis was sound. The decline (the first since World War II) came in 1984, with the production of 4.464 bb of oil. It continued into 1985, as Soviet output fell to 4.345 bb, less than in 1980. By 1985, estimated proved oil reserves had declined to 61.0 bb.

Then Mikhail Gorbachev came to power and promised a new deal: glasnost (openness) and perestroika (restructuring). Gorbachev visited the West Siberia oil region in September, 1985. His visit resulted in the early retirement of a number of oil industry managers and party bosses. He stated: "It has now become clear that the time of golden gushers, of easy oil is coming to an end. It is necessary to switch to forced extraction of oil, to move to more difficult areas with fields providing lower yields and to develop more complex deposits. ... management organizations in Tyumen province ... decided to compensate for their own shortcomings by increasing the producing burden on giant fields."[8] Tyumen Province produced about 22 bb of oil between 1964 and 1985, but about half of this output came from the super-giant *Samotlor* field, which was in decline. Initially, there was more glasnost than perestroika. Despite this candor, Gorbachev adopted tactics similar to those previ-

---

[7] Gustafson, Thane. "The Origins of the Soviet Oil Crisis, 1970–1985." *Soviet Economy*, April–June, 1985, p. 103–145.

[8] "Gorbachev Cites W. Siberia's Woes." *Oil and Gas Journal*, October 7, 1985, p. 66.

ously used by Brezhnev to increase oil production. Once again, oil output was temporarily rescued from a crisis by massive investment in development activities. The Ministry of Oil spent nearly 70 percent of its $14 billion budget in West Siberia, where new field wells were drilled, existing equipment was repaired, and shut-in wells reactivated. In the short term, as in the Brezhnev era, the tactics were successful. Soviet oil output increased in 1986 to 4.490 bb, but from a declining proved reserve estimated at 59.0 bb. Oil output from West Siberia increased twice as fast as total oil output, the region accounting for two-thirds of all oil produced. *Samotlor*, however, continued to decline.

The peak came the following year. With West Siberia contributing nearly 3 bb, total 1987 production reached 4.558 bb. West Siberia's output continued upward in 1988, to 3.022 bb, but with other oil provinces in decline, Soviet output fell slightly to 4.554 bb. Estimated proved oil reserves again declined, to 58.5 bb. The Ministry of oil drilled 18,200 wells in 1988, 40 percent more than in 1985, but the new discoveries most often were quite small and in complex reservoirs. Although drilling increased, oil production declined by 3 percent in 1989, to 4.435 bb, with West Siberia's output falling even faster. In 1990, with the effects of natural depletion of the older large fields becoming evident, the rate of decline quickened to over 5 percent, as 4.190 bb of oil were produced. Also, labor unrest and ethnic violence hampered oil production.

Natural gas has fared somewhat better than oil. The gas development policy of the U.S.S.R. favored the early exploitation of fields located in the vicinity of industrial areas, followed by the development of those fields in remote areas that proved large enough to support long-distance pipelines. Between 1950 and 1970, there was a vast increase in gas pipeline construction, as production and reserves continued to increase. In 1970, there were some 41,985 miles of gas pipelines in use. Gas production was 7.069 trillion cubic feet (tcf) from a reserve of 431.85 tcf. By the end of that decade gas production had doubled and reserves were estimated at 900.0 tcf. There were about 77,375 miles of gas pipelines on-line, the first major (600-mile, 40-inch) line to transport Middle-Ob associated gas having gone on-stream in 1977. In 1985, the Soviets completed the last of six 56-inch gas pipelines from West Siberia to European Russia, as natural gas production increased to 22.698 tcf from a proved reserve estimated at 1,500.0 tcf. By 1988, gas output had risen to 27.192 tcf, while proved reserves remained about level. Despite continued gains in production, the gas industry was accused of imposing excessive production levels in *Urengoy*, the Soviet's largest producing gas field, that caused reservoir damage. It appeared that the mistake of overproduction, which had led to premature reservoir deterioration in many oil fields, was being repeated by the gas industry. Although considerable attention has been given to utilizing associated gas, more than one-quarter (some 0.7 tcf) is flared. In 1988, this included 0.53 tcf flared in West Siberia.[9]

The 1989 output of 28.145 tcf was far below plan, and also represented the smallest annual production increase since 1952. The ex-

---

[9] Fueg, Jean-Christophe. "USSR." *World Oil*, August 1989, p. 85.

plosion of the liquid petroleum gas line, which killed several hundred train passengers near Ufa, deprived the gas industry of its main pipeline used to transport West Siberia associated gas to European Russia. Pipeline repair has been far behind schedule because of equipment shortages. Consequently, pipeline ruptures have become an almost daily occurrence. In 1990, gas production increased by only 2.2 percent (compared to an average yearly increase of nearly 7 percent in the 1980s), as the new gas fields being developed in West Siberia were mostly small. About 28.754 tcf of gas was produced from a proved reserve 1,600.0 tcf.

THE COMMONWEALTH OF INDEPENDENT STATES

Following a failed communist coup d'etat in August 1991, the Soviet Union finally unraveled. On Christmas day, President Mikhail Gorbachev resigned and the world acknowledged the legal existence of 12 new countries (not including the three Baltic states) and an 11-member Commonwealth of Independent States that had been created. In 1991, oil production in Russia and the Commonwealth (CIS) declined by more than 10 percent, to 3.760 bb from a proved reserve estimated at 57 bb (see tables 1 and 2). The Russian Federation produced 9.22 million barrels per day (mb/d), down about 11 percent from the previous year. For the CIS as a whole, the reserves/production (R/P) ratio of 15/1 represented a decline in recovery efficiency from the 14/1 R/P ratio achieved in 1990. In the United States, the R/P ratio is 10/1, with very intensive development. At similar exploitation efficiency, CIS oil production would average over 15 mb/d. Thus, Western assistance in development efficiency could result in gains in oil production. An estimated 16,000 CIS wells are reported idle due to a shortage of functioning production equipment and some giant fields cannot be developed because of a lack of modern technology. Also, the potential for field growth is substantial, with inferred reserves projected at 23 bb. Western investment and improved recovery technology may convert a portion of the inferred reserves to proved reserves, making large volumes of oil available for production.

In addition, there is good potential for new discoveries. Between 46 and 187 bb of undiscovered oil resources are estimated, with 101 bb the amount expected eventually to be discovered. However, this oil will be technically more difficult and more costly to find and recover, as the new fields mostly will be either comparatively small or in more difficult environments. Time and capital are necessary to find and exploit oil accumulations. In the United States, during more than 100 years of intensive oil development, an average of about 0.8 percent of the total original recoverable oil endowment has been converted to proved reserves each year. If this level of exploitation can be achieved in the CIS, current production levels could be sustained into the early years of the next century. This is a resource-based projection, assuming efficient Western-style exploration and development. Since conditions in the CIS oil industries are chaotic, the current production decline is expected to become even more severe. Because of declining oil production, exports have had to be reduced. Oil exports peaked in 1988 at 1.498 bb and since have declined, to 1.349 bb in 1989 and 1.157 bb in 1990. In 1991, an

TABLE 1. 1991 Petroleum Status.

Measure	Oil (Billions of Barrels)	Gas (Trillion cubic feet)
Cumulative Production	116	418
Proved Reserves	57	1,750
Inferred Reserves (field growth)	23	
Undiscovered Resources (range)	101 (46–187)	1,582 (739–2,861)
Total Petroleum Endowment	297	3,750
1991 Production	3.760	28.619
Reserves/Production Ratio (R/P)	15/1	61/1
Potential Maximum Production at R/P = 10/1.	5.7	175.0
Period to which current production could be sustained (with Western technology).	2000–2005	
Number of Producing Wells	148,900	
Oil production per Well	69.17 [a]	
Average Exports	2.093 (1991) [b]	10.668 (1990) [c]

Sources: Reserve and production data used in this report are derived from *Oil and Gas Journal*, December 30, 1991, p. 48; *Oil and Gas Journal*, March 9, 1992, p. 25; Masters, C.D., et. al., "Resource Constraints in Petroleum Production Potential," *Science*, July 12, 1991, p. 146–152; International Energy Statistical Review; and CIA, DI IESR 92–003, March 31, 1992, 17 p.

[a] Barrels per day.
[b] Millions of barrels per day.
[c] Billions of cubic feet per day.

TABLE 2. Estimated Oil Production and Reserves, by State, 1991.

State	Production (Millions of Barrels per Day)	Reserves (Billions of Barrels)
Russia	9.22	51.4
Kazakhstan and Turkmenistan	0.64	3.3
Azerbaijan and Armenia	0.23	1.2
Ukraine	0.10	0.5
Uzbekistan, Kirghizia & Tadzhikistan	0.06	0.3
Byelorussia and Baltic States	0.04	0.2
Georgia	0.01	0.1
Moldavia	a	a
Totals	10.30	57.0

Sources: Reserve and production data used in this report are derived from *Oil and Gas Journal*, December 30, 1991, p. 48; *Oil and Gas Journal*, March 9, 1992, p. 25; Masters, C.D., et. al., "Resource Constraints in Petroleum Production Potential," *Science*, July 12, 1991, p. 146–152; International Energy Statistical Review; and CIA, DI IESR 92–003, March 31, 1992, 17 p.

a Negligible.

even more significant drop occurred, to 764 mb, only about half the amount exported four years before. Although the amount of oil shipped to the United States is minimal, the CIS is a major world oil exporter. Thus, a significant drop in sales would have domestic as well as international ramifications.

In 1991, CIS natural gas production declined for the first time since the war. The decline was slight, to 28.619 tcf, and proved reserves increased to 1750 tcf. The gas production rate, R/P = 61/1, indicates that many more years of near current high volume gas

FIGURE 1. CIS CRUDE OIL PRODUCTION, 1920–1991

(BILLIONS OF BARRELS)

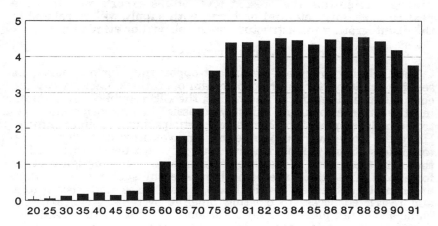

Source: Congressional Research Service

FIGURE 2. CIS NATURAL GAS PRODUCTION, 1930–1991.

(TRILLION CUBIC FEET)

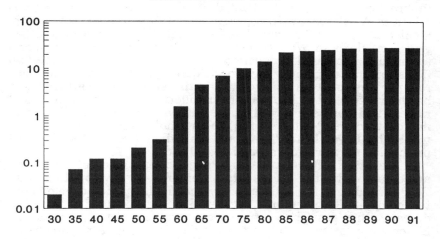

Source: Congressional Research Service.

production are possible. There is also a very significant (739–2,861 tcf) amount of gas estimated to remain undiscovered, with 1,582 tcf the amount expected to eventually be recovered. Thus, the CIS is well endowed with a very large natural gas resource base. Natural gas exports have significantly increased in recent years (from 8.657

bcf/d to 10.668 bcf/d), as gas has become a very important commodity and a major source of hard currency. As the resource base is sufficient to sustain the present level of gas exports well into the next century, any potential problems with supply will be related to the disintegrating infrastructure or to political or ethnic unrest.

JOINT VENTURES

The CIS may provide a significant opportunity for oil companies seeking crude oil for their downstream operations. Lacking capital, equipment, and technical knowledge, the CIS republics are requesting the international oil industry to assist in mitigating their petroleum development problems by participating in joint ventures. However, while over 50 petroleum joint ventures have been registered, less than 20 appear active and only two have progressed to the point that crude oil has become available to the foreign partner for export. The others are being hampered by such factors as high and complicated excess profits taxes, export taxes, and custom fees, and restricted access to existing pipeline systems. Also, a recent value-added tax plus runaway inflation have greatly increased production costs, which are largely ruble based. The oil companies need to insure that the rate of return is commensurate with the risks and the ventures are competitive with other opportunities around the world. Thus, it is necessary that the recovered petroleum be sold at market prices for convertible currency.

White Nights is a joint venture one-half of which is owned by VNG, a Russian enterprise, and one-half by Anglo-Suisse and Phibro Energy, Inc., of the United States. The venture began operations in April 1991, with a program of well workovers, redevelopment drilling, and horizontal wells in the *West Varyegan* and *Tagrinsk* oil fields in West Siberia. Using more advanced production techniques, increased production has been achieved from the two fields, but oil shipments have been quite small, below 50,000 barrels per day (b/d). In spite of the initial success of the venture it has been attacked in Pravda for "plundering Russia's underground riches" and has been forced to use Russian rather than U.S. drilling contractors.[10] The second operational joint venture is controlled by Royal Dutch/Shell and Canadian Fracmaster. Current production may average around 15,000 b/d.

In May 1992, after two years of negotiations, Chevron signed an agreement with the Kazakhstan Republic to develop the giant *Tengiz* field and the adjacent *Korolev* field. Special development technology will be required because of a high content of toxic hydrogen sulfide gas. The venture is expected to cost the partners $20 billion over the next 40 years. Chevron will have a 50 percent interest, but Kazakhstan will receive 80 percent of the income, after Chevron pays taxes and royalties on its share. The *Tengiz* project was generally viewed as a test case for foreign ventures in the Soviet Union prior to the collapse of the Communist regime. It became an object of intense contention between reformers and hardline Communists. The key issues were the division of revenue and jurisdictional authority between Moscow and Kazakhstan. The

---

10 "White Nights Rebuts Pravda Claims." *Oil and Gas Journal,* March 23, 1992, p. 130–131.

collapse of the Soviet Union left Chevron to deal only with Kazakhstan.

Amoco is involved in a joint venture to develop the huge *Azeri* gas field, located in the center of the Caspian Sea. This project, like *Tengiz,* will be very capital-intensive and require advanced recovery technology. Conoco is leading an international consortium to develop the massive *Shtokmanovskoye* gas and condensate accumulation located in the Barents Sea off the Kola Peninsula. Marathon Oil, McDermott International, and Mitsui have signed a long-delayed agreement to conduct a feasibility study of oil field development off Sakhalin Island in the Russian Far East.

The French oil companies (Total and Elf Aquitaine) have recently taken the initiative in promoting major onshore petroleum joint ventures in the CIS, while attempting to allay CIS fears of foreign exploitation. Izvestia has explained that Total and Elf will provide the Commonwealth with more oil and also will increase government revenues, giving the CIS a better chance of avoiding economic catastrophe. Total and Elf have openly discussed their plans, in contrast to the secrecy practiced by many other foreign firms, while at the same time bluntly criticizing Russian bureaucratic barriers. Total's major joint venture is a several-year effort to increase oil production from the super-giant *Romashkino* field in the Volga-Urals. The first incremental production increase is expected this year from the field that is now about 85 percent depleted. Total also has signed an agreement to increase oil production in the Komi Republic, a 25 to 30 year venture that may cost over $1 billion. Other Total joint ventures are in Tyumen Province, Azerbaijan, and Kazakhstan. Elf plans to invest about $1 billion in exploring areas in the Volga-Urals and Kazakhstan.[11]

Other U.S. ventures are of a more general nature. The University of Houston Law Center has assisted Russian officials develop an underground resource code and is working on oil and natural gas legislation that is compatible with world practice. Professional Geophysics of Houston, Texas, will provide seismic data acquisition and data processing services to foreign oil companies working in Russian territory.

CONCLUSIONS

The recent decline in Russian and Commonwealth oil and gas production can partially be attributed to reduced capital investment and reliance on outdated and inefficient exploration and production technology. Such problems can be ameliorated by joint ventures with foreign oil companies. However, political and economic instability, labor unrest, and ethnic violence also are hampering petroleum output. Such problems are not amenable to solution by foreign oil companies. Russia and the Commonwealth have a long history of successful oil and gas production in a variety of geologic basins, including some of the most prolific in the world. With a drilling rig fleet more than twice the size of that of the United States, the CIS has been systematically explored. Discoveries have

---

[11] "French Companies Lead the Pack in Promoting C.I.S. Joint Ventures." *Oil and Gas Journal,* April 6, 1992, p. 44–48. and "Elf Blows Past Chevron in Kazakhstan." *World Oil,* April 1992, p. 15.

been made throughout this vast region without regard to climate or geography. Giant oil and gas fields have been found above the Arctic Circle, beneath the Caspian Sea, on the continental shelves, and in the Central Asian deserts. Given the intensity of exploration over a long period of time and the fact that no region has been off limits to drilling, most of the very large fields have probably already been discovered. While there is a significant amount of petroleum thought to remain undiscovered, it likely to be reservoired in smaller fields that, while numerous, will be more difficult to find and develop than were the giants of the past.

Development has also been very intensive. The CIS has led the world in oil output since 1974 and in natural gas production since 1983, often by a wide margin. Both Brezhnev and Gorbachev realized the critical importance of high level petroleum output and mobilized major efforts to sustain the industry. Both efforts concentrated on output and included enhanced oil recovery projects, which now account for about 2 percent of production. They were successful in the short-term, but production has been so high for so long that sustaining it, even with foreign oil company assistance, will become ever more difficult. The petroleum resource base has been "high graded," with a large proportion of the "easy" oil and gas already discovered and produced. As the smaller oil fields are developed, the number of fields in production has increased (from 856 to 1,099 between 1986 and 1990), but the output from 80 percent of these fields is declining. The policy to maximize oil production in the short-term often resulted in improper reservoir management and severe reservoir damage, putting additional recovery at risk. With most of the older, larger fields in decline, oil production in the CIS is expected to continue to drop significantly. In 1992 it has slipped to about 9.6 mb/d, but exports were above last year's average. There is some concern that the inability to get shut-in wells back on-stream and the lack of drilling equipment could result in a decline to below 9 mb/d by the end of the year. Eventually, with outside help, CIS oil production may, at least partially, recover, but not necessarily to previous peak levels. Gas production has slightly decreased, although the CIS is endowed with a very large natural gas resource base. Thus, for many years, future supply problems will be related to the disintegrating infrastructure or to political or ethnic unrest, rather than to a lack of gas reserves or resources.

473

FIGURE 3. LOCATIONS OF MAJOR SOVIET OIL PROVINCES, 1991.

Source: Congressional Research Service.

APPENDIX A. CIS SUPER-GIANT * AND GIANT OIL AND GAS FIELDS,
1870 TO PRESENT

(Listed in order of size, from largest to smallest)

Oil	Gas

Baku/Caucasus/Azerbaijan/Kazakhstan

Malgobek (1915)	Severo Stavropol (1950)
Balakhano (1896)	Maykop (1909)
Bibieybatskoye (1871)	Tul'skiy (1969)
Neftyanyye Kamni (1949)	Bakhar (1968)
Sangachaly-Duvannyy (1963)	
Tengiz (1979)	
Uzen'skoye (1961)	
Zhetybayskoye (1961)	
Surakhanskoye (1870)	
Anastasiyevsko (1953)	
Peschanyy More (1952)	
Starogroznenskoye (1893)	
Karachukhur (1920)	
Ozeksuatskoye (1953)	
Azeri (1987)	

Volga-Urals

Romashkino * (1948)	Orenburg * (1966)
Arlanskoye (1955)	Mazunin (1960)
Mukhanovskoye (1945)	Korobkovskoye (1949)
Novo Elkhov (1955)	
Shkapovskoye (1944)	
Tuymazy (1937)	
Kuleshovskoye (1958)	
Yarino (1954)	

Komi

Usinskoye (1962)	Kyrtaiol'skoye * (1970)
Yozey (1972)	Vuktyl'skoye (1964)
Usanovskoye (1963)	Layavozhskoye (1965)

Central Asia

Kotur Tepe (1956)	Dauletabad * (1976)
Cheleken (1965)	Shatlyskoye * (1968)
	Gazlinskoye (1956)
	Bagadzhin (1971)
	Shurtanskoye (1976)
	Kirpichlin (1972)
	Naipskoye (1970)
	Achakskoye (1966)
	Kandymoskoye (1967)
	Gugurtlinskoye (1965)
	Zevardin (1968)
	Urtabulakskoye (1963)
	Uchkyrskoye (1961)
	Beurdeshik (1969)

APPENDIX A. CIS SUPER-GIANT * AND GIANT OIL AND GAS FIELDS, 1870 TO PRESENT—CONTINUED

(Listed in order of size, from largest to smallest)

Oil	Gas
Ukraine	
Prilukskoye (1959)	Shebelinka (1950)
	Zapadno (1968)
	Yefremovskoye (1965)
	Glynsko (1958)
East Siberia	
	Sredrebotnobin (1970)
	Verkhue (1975)
	Sredue Vilyuy
	Maastakh (1967)
West Siberia	
Samotlor * (1965)	Urengoy * (1966)
Fedorovskoye (1971)	Yamburg * (1969)
Sovetskoye (1962)	Bovanenkovo * (1971)
Ust'bakykskoye (1961)	Zapolyarnoye * (1965)
Zapadno-Surgutskoye (1962)	Arkticheskoye * (1968)
Mamontorskoye (1965)	Kytaiol'skoye * (1970)
Yuzhno Cheremshanskoye (1969)	Medvezh'ye * (1967)
Megionskoye (1961)	Kharasaveyskoye * (1974)
Bolshoye Chernogor (1970)	Kruzernshtern * (1976)
Pokachev (1970)	Severo Urengoy * (1971)
Agan (1966)	Sema Kovskoye (1971)
Severo Varyegan (1971)	Komsomolskoye (1966)
Salymskoye (1963)	Yamsovey Tyumen (1970)
Russkoye (1968)	Yubileynoye Tyumen (1968)
Vat'yegan (1971)	Messoyakhskoye (1967)
Kholmogor (1973)	Vyngapurovskoye (1968)
	Yuzhno Russkoye (1968)
	Yuzhno Samburg (1978)
	Sredneyamal'skoye (1970)
	Pelyatkinskoye (1969)
	Palyanovo (1972)
	Lyantor (1966)
	Myl'dzhino (1964)
	Antipayutin (1978)
	Novoportovskoye (1964)
	Tazovskoye (1964)
	Severo Komsomol (1969)
	Vostoclmo Tarkosalin (1971)
	Gydan (1978)
	Nakhodkinskoye (1974)

APPENDIX A. CIS SUPER-GIANT * AND GIANT OIL AND GAS FIELDS,
1870 TO PRESENT—CONTINUED

(Listed in order of size, from largest to smallest)

Oil	Gas
	Neytin (1975)
	Kharvutin (1976)
	Kazanskoye (1967)
	Luginetskoye (1967)
	Nyda (1967)
	Yetypurovskoye (1971)
	Zapadno Tarkosalin (1972)
	Yuzhnotambey (1974)
	Verkhnepurpey (1976)

* **Super-giant fields** originally contained the equivalent of at least 5 billion barrels of recoverable oil or 30 trillion cubic feet of recoverable natural gas.

Giant fields originally contained the equivalent of 500 million to 5 billion barrels of recoverable oil or 3 to 30 trillion cubic feet of recoverable natural gas.

Source: Congressional Research Service.

REPUBLIC ENERGY SECTORS AND INTER-STATE DEPENDENCIES OF THE COMMONWEALTH OF INDEPENDENT STATES AND GEORGIA

by Jeffrey W. Schneider *

CONTENTS

SUMMARY

Overall energy production exceeds the aggregate domestic consumption of the Commonwealth of Independent States (CIS) and Georgia, but all the former Soviet republics face rocky energy futures. Oil production is falling sharply in Russia, natural gas production is down in Turkmenistan, coal output is declining in Russia and Ukraine, and many CIS states face problems in their electric power industries. These production problems will lead to increased frictions between states with energy surpluses and those dependent on imports.

Nevertheless, the web of interdependencies spun by decades of Soviet planning will keep the energy sectors of the republics entan-

---

* Jeffrey W. Schneider is an Analyst with the Office of Slavic and Eurasian Analysis, Central Intelligence Agency.

gled; no republic will be able to implement energy policies in isolation from its former Union partners. Russian economic reforms, which include the sharp price increases for energy of May 1992 and plans for freeing energy prices in the future, will adversely affect the terms of trade of the energy-importing republics. As energy exporting republics such as Turkmenistan, Azerbaijan, and Uzbekistan follow Russia's price lead, republics that import most of the energy they consume—especially Moldova, Armenia, and Georgia—will be the hardest hit.

Among the large republics, Ukraine is in the most difficult situation because of its rapidly falling coal production, shrinking electric power generation capacity, and its need to import large amounts of increasingly expensive oil and gas. Even energy-rich Russia remains dependent on its former union partners for access to international markets, energy equipment, the integrity of its electric power grid, and uranium for its nuclear power program. Throughout the CIS economies, the iron and steel and electric power industries are the most affected by the upheavals in the energy sectors of the republics.

OVERALL TRENDS

Energy production in the former Soviet republics declined by about 6 percent in 1991 as a result of the maturation of the resource base, investment cuts, equipment supply disruptions, worker strikes, and general economic chaos. Lower output of oil and coal accounted for most of the decline in total energy, while supplies of natural gas and electric power were stagnant. Although the republics collectively continue to produce more energy than they consume, disruptions of traditional economic ties have forced political leaders of the successor states, many of whom are inexperienced in economic and energy matters, to grapple with energy uncertainties the likes of which were seldom experienced under the old Soviet system.

The collapse of the U.S.S.R. has clearly left Russia in the dominant energy position among the former Union republics (Figure 1). All the former Soviet republics except Turkmenistan and Azerbaijan are dependent on Russia for significant portions of their energy supplies, and their economies long were based on artificially low prices for Russian energy (Table 1). Russia, however, is no longer willing to subsidize its former union partners. While eager to maintain amicable relations with other republics, Russia's leadership now is playing the energy card both to improve the welfare of its citizens and to achieve other policy goals. Moreover, the Russian government probably will have a strong incentive to maintain critically needed hard currency exports by reducing oil deliveries to states within the CIS. The non-Russian republics are also being affected by Russia's efforts to reform its energy sector, particularly by policies to increase and eventually free energy prices and to allow Russian producers greater latitude to dispose of their output. Such reforms could decrease the amount of energy available for importing republics unable or unwilling to compete with hard currency buyers.

FIGURE 1. Energy Output in the Soviet Union and Russia, 1985–1991

Output Source	1985	1986	1987	1988	1989	1990	1991
Oil (million barrels per day)							
U.S.S.R.	11.9	12.3	12.5	12.5	12.1	11.4	10.3
Russia	10.8	11.2	11.4	11.4	11.0	10.3	9.2
Natural gas (billion cubic meters)							
U.S.S.R.	643	686	727	770	796	815	810
Russia	462	503	544	590	616	640	643
Coal (million metric tons)							
U.S.S.R.	726	751	760	772	740	703	629
Russia	395	408	415	425	410	395	353
Electric power (billion kilowatt-hours)							
U.S.S.R.	1,544	1,599	1,665	1,705	1,722	1,728	1,645
Russia	962	1,001	1,047	1,066	1,077	1,082	1,046

Source: Official Soviet data.

The decline in production has been compounded by the deterioration of the distribution and delivery system throughout the CIS and Georgia. The perennial shortages that characterized the U.S.S.R. have been aggravated since the collapse of Soviet power by the confusion that has resulted from the incomplete replacement of bureaucratic directives by market methods. Remnants of the central distribution system continue to provide priority supplies to traditional customers even when demand for their goods and services has fallen sharply. Meanwhile, smaller and weaker energy users who lack bureaucratic clout are left to fend for themselves, and new sources of supply outside bureaucratic channels such as commodity exchanges and licensed private retailers are relatively undeveloped and incapable of satisfying all of the new demand. The resulting maldistribution of energy supplies has led to hoarding, bartering, and black marketeering, and has caused energy consumption to remain high despite the reduction in industrial activity throughout the CIS. In 1991, for example, CIS GNP dropped a reported 17 percent, but oil consumption dropped only 2 percent.

The next few years should witness a contraction of energy use in all the republics of the CIS and in Georgia as energy prices rise and economic activity falls or stagnates. Higher oil prices and the continued drop in Russian oil output will lead to reduced oil consumption and prompt some energy consumers to switch to still plentiful natural gas, although here too, the major gas exporting republics—Russia and Turkmenistan—have begun driving harder bargains. Energy importing republics will also look to diversify energy suppliers, develop their own energy resources, and implement conservation measures. The energy rich republics, meanwhile, will find that the disastrous policies of past Soviet mismanagement will entail increasing expenditures to rebuild their energy industries.

TABLE 1. Relative Energy Self-Sufficiency of the CIS Republics and Georgia During the Soviet Period: Ratio of Indigenous Energy Production to Consumption, 1990 [1]

Republic	Ratio
Turkmenistan.....................................	555
Russia	140
Kazakhstan......................................	120
Azerbaijan	110
Uzbekistan......................................	80
Ukraine...	60
Tajikistan..	55
Kyrgyzstan	45
Georgia...	20
Byelarus..	5
Armenia...	<5
Moldova..	<1

Source: Official Soviet data.
[1] This ratio should not be interpreted literally as a measure of a republic's ability to do without imports. A given republic might produce more than it consumes overall, but still need to import specific types of energy products. Russia, for example, produces enough oil and gas to export, but must import coal.

SITUATION IN THE ENERGY SECTORS

OIL

Oil production in the former Soviet republics declined by about 10 percent in 1991; An even steeper decline is in store for 1992. It appears that overall output in 1992, however, will still be sufficient to cover the energy needs of the former Soviet republics if the major oil-producing republics—Azerbaijan, Kazakhstan, and most importantly Russia, which accounts for about 90 percent of CIS oil output—maintain interrepublic deliveries at or near agreed levels. Major oil consumers in the CIS and Georgia are the transportation sector, agriculture, and electric power generation.

The maturation and overproduction of Russian oilfields during the 1980s are the primary causes of the current difficulties. The former Soviet Union's myopic policies—particularly the emphasis on high rates of current production at the expense of total recovery—have caused Russian oil production to fall markedly since it reached a peak output of 11.4 million barrels per day (b/d) in 1987. Although a decline in oil production is inevitable over the next few years, the rate of decline probably could be moderated by a transition to Western methods of project management coupled with imports of Western equipment to develop small fields, boost drilling, and reduce the maintenance backlogs that have idled several thousand oilwells.

Large-scale participation by international firms, however, will require the creation of new working relationships in Russia. The days when a central ministry could dictate a plan of action to the industry are over. Oil production associations and, in some cases, the local governments of oil-producing regions now determine production policy in their areas and control a substantial portion of the hard currency that would be needed to acquire Western oilfield services. Moreover, many producers, local authorities, and republic officials are averse to large-scale Western participation because of traditional suspicion of foreigners, a low level of understanding of market economics and international business practices, and a fear that Western firms will displace Russian workers and suppliers.

Oil production in the two other significant oil-producing republics—Kazakhstan and Azerbaijan—is essentially stagnant at present, but both republics have substantial reserves that can be developed with Western technology. The agreement Kazakhstan signed with Chevron in May 1992 to develop the technically challenging Tengiz oilfield could, if successful, double the republic's oil output around the turn of the century. Similarly, Azerbaijan's award of an offshore tract in the promising South Caspian Sea to Amoco in 1991 could significantly boost that republic's oil production in years to come.

NATURAL GAS

Natural gas production in the former Soviet Union declined slightly in 1991, although Russian production—which accounted for almost 80 percent of Soviet production—registered a small increase. Turkmenistan, Uzbekistan, and Ukraine account for most of the remaining production. Physical output of natural gas in 1992 will be about the same as in 1991. It should be sufficient to satisfy aggregate demand in the former Soviet republics and maintain exports to Europe. Shortages could result, however, from problems unrelated to production, including trade disputes between republics such as the disagreement in early 1992 between Turkmenistan and Ukraine as a result of which Turkmenistan halted natural gas deliveries to Ukraine.

Gas supply is especially important for the electric power and heat sector, which relies on gas for over half of its fuel. Gas is also important to producers of iron and steel, chemicals, and building materials such as cement, glass, and prefabricated concrete. In addition, 80 percent of the former Union's population rely on gas for home heating or cooking. Republics that rely on imported gas to satisfy over 25 percent of their total energy needs include Ukraine, Georgia, Armenia, and Moldova. In general, the southern tier states of Central Asia and the Transcaucasus depend primarily on gas imports from Turkmenistan, while the European republics of Ukraine, Byelarus, and Moldova receive the bulk of their gas imports from Russia.

Although the gas industry is in better shape than the rest of the energy sector, it too has suffered from investment cuts and heavy taxes, gasfield equipment shortages, and skyrocketing increases in maintenance requirements on trunk pipelines. In coming years, the gas industry needs to achieve more thorough recovery and processing of gas condensates, to rebuild the entire natural gas pipeline system and its compressor stations to improve reliability and efficiency, to improve operations in Arctic regions with harsh climates and fragile ecologies, and to meter its customers to reduce consumption and encourage more efficient energy usage.

COAL

Coal production in the former Soviet republics declined by about 11 percent in 1991. About 55 percent of coal output came from Russia; Ukraine and Kazakhstan accounted for most of the remainder. As with oil and natural gas, coal output remains sufficient to satisfy overall domestic demand and to allow for international exports as well. The quality of coal has continued to decline, however. In addition periodic labor strikes and work stoppages often interrupt normal stockpiling efforts and have made deliveries increasingly unreliable.

The trouble in the coal industry is especially threatening to the electric power industry, which relies on coal for 24 percent of its energy, and to iron and steel producers, who consume over a quarter of all the coal produced in the former U.S.S.R. Russia, although the largest producer, must still import about 5 percent of the coal it consumes. Kazakhstan and Ukraine rely on coal for over a third of their energy needs and both produce more coal than they consume. In Kyrgyzstan and Moldova, coal accounts for over a quarter of total energy consumed, and both republics are net importers. The other republics are less dependent on coal, but all—except for Georgia—have to import coal from their one-time Union partners.

The coal industry is plagued by chronic material and supply shortages, obsolete equipment, and severe environmental challenges. Russia's Ministry of Fuel and Power has estimated that 70 percent of Russia's coal mines are in need of radical reconstruction and modernization. In addition to refurbishing existing facilities, Russia also would have to open 15 million metric tons of new mining capacity each year to stabilize coal production at current levels. Other coal-producing republics such as Ukraine, Kazakhstan, Kyrgyzstan, and Georgia face similar situations.

The coal industry also has a large, militant work force that has been in the forefront of labor movements over the past several years and has been willing to strike to achieve political and economic goals. Governments of coal-producing republics, therefore, will find it difficult politically to shift the industry onto an economically profitable and self-sustaining basis over worker opposition through the closure of uneconomic mines and the introduction of labor-saving technology.

ELECTRIC POWER

Electric power production in the former Soviet Union declined for the first time since World War II during 1991. Output in 1992, while likely to be sufficient to meet the needs of most of the republics, will be inadequate to prevent "brown-outs" and intermittent enforced conservation regimes. Widespread public opposition to building electric power plants of any type has crippled the power industry's plans to expand generating capacity over the last five years. Capacity reserves are now probably less than 4 percent— compared to Western reserves of 25 percent—leaving little margin to cover breakdowns and surges in demand. In recent years electricity shortages have been especially acute in fuel-deficient areas such as Ukraine and the countries of the Transcaucasus and in isolated regions such as Russia's Far East. When shortages do occur, industry, which consumes over half of all electricity, generally bears the brunt of the shortages.

Alleviating the problems of the power industry will pose major challenges. Breakdowns in the supply chain and the disintegration of trade relationships have caused critical shortages of spare parts for many aging power plants. In addition, growing safety and environmental concerns will continue to stymie power plant construction and operations, especially in the nuclear power sector. In Ukraine, for example, concerns about the safety of the troubled Chernobyl' nuclear power plant prompted Kiev to shut the station down a year ahead of schedule. If growing safety concerns prompt the shutdown of Ukraine's other nuclear power plants—which are of a different design than the Chernobyl' plant and considered to be safer—the state would lose one-fifth of its electricity output. Western training and equipment could help improve safety at CIS nuclear power plants, blunt public demands to shut down all nuclear plants, and allow power officials more time to develop alternative energy sources. Overall, the power sector in the former Soviet republics would also benefit from improved management training, increased meter use, and adoption of Western environmental standards.

ENERGY SITUATION IN THE REPUBLICS

Just as the problems of the energy sector vary greatly from branch to branch, so do they vary from republic to republic and from region to region (see Tables 2 and 3). These differences largely coincide with the different natural resource endowments of the Commonwealth republics and the regions within those republics.

TABLE 2. CIS and Georgia: Energy Consumption, by Fuel Percentage of Apparent Consumption Satisfied.

Republic	Oil	Gas	Coal	Primary Electricity [1]
Russia	32	39	22	7
Ukraine	26	35	34	4
Byelarus	74	16	4	4
Moldova	44	31	25	0
Armenia	33	60	2	5
Azerbaijan	48	50	—	2
Georgia	21	60	5	15
Kazakhstan	35	11	49	5
Kyrgyzstan	35	22	29	14
Tajikistan	36	16	5	43
Turkmenistan	42	55	3	0
Uzbekistan	26	70	3	1

Source: Official Soviet data.
[1] Nuclear power, hydro power, and imports.

TABLE 3. CIS and Georgia: Oil, Gas, and Coal Balance.

Republic	Crude Oil	Petroleum Products	Natural Gas	Coal
Russia	X	X	X	0
Ukraine	0	0	0	X
Byelarus	0	X	0	0
Moldova	—	0	0	0
Armenia	—	0	0	0
Azerbaijan	0	X	0	0
Georgia	0	0	0	=
Kazakhstan	X	0	0	X
Kyrgyzstan	—	0	0	=
Tajikistan	—	0	0	0
Turkmenistan	X	=	X	0
Uzbekistan	0	0	X	0

Source: Official Soviet data.
X = Net Exporter.
0 = Net Importer.
— Does not engage in crude oil trade.
= Production equals consumption.

RUSSIA

Russia is by far the dominant force on the energy scene of the former Soviet Union. Russia accounts for 90 percent of the oil and gas condensates and 77 percent of the natural gas produced in the CIS and Georgia. It was the largest producer of oil and of natural gas combined in the world in 1991. Last year, Russia produced crude oil and natural gas liquids at an average daily rate of 9.2 million b/d—compared to 1991 U.S. production of about 9 million b/d and Saudi Arabian production of about 8.5 million b/d. At the same time, Russia produced 643 billion cubic meters (bcm) of natural gas last year—compared to the 480 bcm of second place United States and the 100 bcm of third place Canada. Russia possesses enough refining capacity to satisfy domestic needs for petroleum products such as gasoline, diesel fuel, and heating oil and to export a variety of oil products.

Russia produces over half the CIS's coal, and its 1991 output of 353 million tons of coal made it the third largest producer in the world. Russia also has substantial primary electric power sources (hydroelectric and nuclear) which, combined with its fossil-fuel-fired plants, enable it to generate more electric power than it consumes.

With production so much larger than domestic consumption, Russia has enormous potential as an energy exporter. Were Russia not to supply the needs of the other republics, it could export 3 million b/d of oil—rivaling the best export years of the U.S.S.R.—and almost 250 bcm of natural gas—well over twice the U.S.S.R.'s best export total.

These large energy resource endowments notwithstanding, Russia's energy sector faces serious difficulties. Oil and coal production have been falling since 1988, and natural gas production registered its smallest increase ever in 1991. In addition, Russia's thermal electric power industry needs a major overhaul and the nuclear power industry has been stalled over safety concerns. Russian energy producers—especially oil and gas enterprises—are heavily dependent on other CIS republics such as Azerbaijan, Ukraine, and Georgia for equipment, and the disruption of interstate trade has severely retarded Russian oil and gas drilling and maintenance operations. Even without interstate trade difficulties, however, CIS and Russian equipment producers are no longer able to supply the amount of equipment needed to maintain production at existing oilfields, nor can they provide the advanced technology required to exploit the new oil and gas fields that are crucial to Russia's energy future.

Energy shortages in Russia tend to be especially prevalent in the North Caucasus and the Russian Far East, but all regions of Russia are susceptible to sudden, acute shortages of specific types of energy. Industry is very energy intensive in Russia, consuming almost two-thirds of Russian electricity and more than a third of total energy. Transportation is the second largest consumer of energy in Russia, accounting for about a third of total energy, but is underdeveloped by Western standards. Its consumption of energy should grow throughout the decade.

THE WESTERN REPUBLICS

Ukraine is a net exporter of coal and electricity but depends on Russia for nearly 40 percent of its energy needs. Ukraine is a major center of energy-intensive heavy industry, including iron and steel, machine building and metalworking, and chemicals production. It relies on mechanized farming to produce one-fifth of the former U.S.S.R.'s total agricultural output.

Coal from the Donets Basin in the eastern part of the republic is the backbone of the economy, satisfying one-third of total Ukrainian energy demand. Ukraine produces only 10 percent of its natural gas and 6 percent of its oil needs. Most of the remainder is imported from Russia. The republic's eight oil refineries have the combined capacity to produce 85 percent of Ukrainian oil product requirements, given sufficient availability of crude. The Ukrainian electric power system consists mostly of power plants fueled by locally produced coal, but it also has five nuclear power plants that in recent years have accounted for almost one-fourth of the electricity consumed in the republic. The shutdown of the Chernobyl' plant in May 1992 reduced this share to about one-fifth.

Ukraine's already tenuous energy situation has been compounded in recent years by coal shortages resulting from miners strikes and equipment shortfalls. Ukraine's energy vulnerabilities have led it to seek ways to lessen its dependence on allocation agreements with the Russian government. Ukraine has concluded barter deals directly with Russian oil producers and has successfully sought out non-Russian oil and gas suppliers, including Iran. Ukraine is also actively exploring ways of reducing its energy consumption through greater efficiency and improving its energy infrastructure—such as upgrading its refinery at Lisichansk—to make it more efficient and responsive to domestic needs.

Byelarus produces only 8 percent of the energy it consumes, primarily oil, peat, and a small quantity of natural gas. Its major energy consumers are the chemical, agricultural machinery, electronics, machine tool, and consumer goods industries. The republic's crop, livestock, and timber sectors use large amounts of gasoline and diesel fuel.

Byelarus depends on Russia for nearly all its oil and gas. Its two large oil refineries have the capacity to provide sufficient petroleum products to meet domestic needs and support sizable exports. Russian crude oil deliveries in 1992, however, will be cut from 800,000 b/d to 500,000 b/d. While this should be enough to satisfy domestic needs, it will be a major blow to Byelarus's efforts to earn hard currency by exporting refined products.

Virtually all the republic's electric generating capacity is fossil-fuel-fired, and its largest thermal power plant burns oil. Coal imported from Ukraine and Poland provides 4 percent of Byelarus's total energy needs.

Moldova imports all of its oil, natural gas, and coal from Ukraine and Russia. Coal is essential for its steel industry, which also consumes over 25 percent of its electric power. The republic's economy is dominated by agriculture, consumer goods, and electronics production.

Petroleum products provide about 60 percent of Moldova's energy needs, and all are brought in by rail or truck. Natural gas is imported from Ukraine via two pipelines. The State Regional Power Plant at Dnestrovsk—which burns coal and oil—generates enough power for deliveries to Ukraine, Romania, and Bulgaria and makes the republic a net exporter of electricity.

THE CAUCASUS

Armenia arguably has the bleakest energy outlook of all the former Soviet republics. With the exception of limited hydroelectric power resources, Armenia is totally dependent on imports for its energy needs. It is also surrounded by neighbors who are openly hostile, unsympathetic, or in turmoil, and it has an economy with little potential to obtain needed supplies through international trade. Armenia's major energy consuming industries are mining, chemicals and petrochemicals, electronics, machinery, and soft goods.

The bulk of Armenian energy imports—mainly natural gas from Turkmenistan and oil products from Russia—arrive via rail or pipeline through Azerbaijan, its neighbor to the east. Armenia relies on natural gas for 60 to 70 percent of its energy needs. All but one of its ten bread factories use this fuel. Early in 1992 a new pipeline was opened from Georgia, but the line's capacity can meet only one-third to one-half of Armenia's needs. Moreover, the new pipeline is not linked to the delivery system served by the pipeline from Azerbaijan and therefore can supply only a limited geographical area.

Armenia's energy vulnerabilities were graphically demonstrated in late 1991 and early 1992 when the Azeris cut off natural gas flows and blockaded deliveries of other fuels by rail. Industrial output dropped to 20 percent of normal (and on occasion ground to a near halt), normal social services such as schools were curtailed, and several persons died from exposure as a result of the lack of heat. Electric power was hit hard as major power stations at Razdan and Yerevan had to idle half or more of their generating capacity. Rotating blackouts and brownouts that lasted as long as six hours were employed by republic officials to force reductions in consumption.

Azerbaijan, by contrast, is in a fairly strong energy position because it is capable of satisfying all of its needs for crude oil and oil products and electric power. Azerbaijan can also meet most of its natural gas requirements from its own resources, but does have to import about 3 to 5 bcm of natural gas each year—about 20 percent of its requirements—from Russia, Turkmenistan, and Iran. Azerbaijan's access to multiple suppliers gives it some bargaining leverage. Azerbaijan also has refining capacity exceeding its own needs for products, which enables it to export substantial amounts of oil products although many of these product exports are refined from crude oil imported from other republics.

Georgia produces only about 20 percent of the energy needed by its economy and its major industries—mining, metallurgy, and textiles. The most important domestic energy resource is hydroelectric power, which satisfies about 40 percent of the country's electricity demand. Natural gas imported from Turkmenistan is the main source of energy for the Georgian economy. Next in importance is oil, of which Georgia imports over 90 percent. Only about 8 percent is produced indigenously, largely in the area around Tbilisi, the capital of the republic. Georgia's aged Batumi refinery cannot supply the required grades or amounts of transportation fuels, so Georgia must import 85 percent—about 30,000 b/d—of its gasoline supplies from the neighboring Russian Republic and Azerbaijan. Coal contributes only 5 percent of total Georgian energy consumption, and Tbilisi would like to expand the republic's indigenous coal industry.

KAZAKHSTAN AND CENTRAL ASIA

Kazakhstan has a fairly strong energy position because it is a net exporter of crude oil and coal, and is almost self-sufficient in natural gas. Kazakhstan, however, does not currently have enough refining or electric power capacity to satisfy its requirements and so must import petroleum products and about 15 percent of its electricity. It is expanding its refining capacity by upgrading a refinery at Pavlodar and building a new refinery in western Kazakhstan— where most Kazakh oil is produced—and should be self-sufficient in oil products in a few years.

Because former Soviet planners built energy facilities with little regard for republic borders, however, Kazakhstan is more dependent on other republics than its net export figures indicate. Most of its natural gas—primarily the sour gas from the Karachaganak field in the western part of the country—is exported by pipeline to a gas treatment plant in Russia. The gas is used regionally on both sides of the Russo-Kazakh border after being treated. Most domestic consumers of natural gas, however, are situated in central and eastern Kazakhstan and rely on imports through pipelines from Uzbekistan and Turkmenistan. Similarly, the crude oil pipeline system built by the Soviets forces Kazakhstan to export much of the oil it produces in the western part of the republic to Russia and to import oil from Siberia for its refineries in the east. Kazakhstan's electric power system faces a similar situation—northern Kazakhstan is part of an electric power grid controlled in Moscow, while the remainder of the republic is supplied by a grid controlled in Tashkent in neighboring Uzbekistan.

Kyrgyzstan produces only small quantities of oil and natural gas, but it is nearly self-sufficient in coal. The republic's hydroelectric power plants alone are capable of satisfying almost 90 percent of internal electricity demand and combined with its fossil-fuel-fired plants make Kyrgyzstan a net exporter of electricity. Major energy users include the electrical equipment, livestock machinery, and food-processing industries. Kyrgyzstan's agricultural sector also consumes substantial amounts of electricity.

Oil accounts for about 35 percent of the country's energy consumption. Because Kyrgyzstan has no oil refineries, all petroleum products must be imported from other republics, primarily Russia and Kazakhstan. Any shortage of gasoline or diesel fuel is especially threatening to Kyrgyzstan because trucks carry 98 percent of the republic's freight. Kyrgyzstan imports 95 percent of its natural gas from Turkmenistan and neighboring Uzbekistan. Power plants, including district heating stations, account for almost half the republic's gas consumption. Kyrgyzstan is well endowed with coal, but output has been declining because of poor mining practices and a lack of modern equipment and methods.

Tajikistan ranks last among the former Soviet republics in per capita energy consumption. Hydropower resources supply about 35 percent of its total energy needs, but the republic must still import 15 percent of its electric power from Turkmenistan and Uzbekistan, although actual amounts vary seasonally. Because hydropower depends upon the availability of water, Tajikistan exports electricity to Uzbekistan in spring and early summer as the mountain snows melt, and imports electricity from Uzbekistan in the winter. The aluminum industry is the biggest single consumer of energy in Tajikistan, accounting for almost half the republic's electricity use. Additional major energy consumers in the republic include other nonferrous metals industries (copper, lead, and zinc) and chemical and machinery producers.

After hydroelectric power, oil is the next most important energy source to the Tajik economy, satisfying roughly one-third of total energy demand. Although it produces about 15 percent of the oil it needs domestically, Tajikistan lacks an oil refinery, and all of its petroleum products must be brought in by truck or rail from Kazakhstan, Turkmenistan, and Russia. Agriculture accounts for about 40 percent of Tajik oil consumption, including 70 percent of Tajikistan's gasoline and diesel fuel. Maintaining supplies to this sector is a major concern of Tajik energy decisionmakers.

Natural gas is imported primarily from Turkmenistan although natural gas from Uzbekistan serves the Tajik capital, Dushanbe. Only 5 percent of Tajikistan's energy consumption consists of coal, about half of which comes from indigenous sources.

Turkmenistan is the only CIS country other than Russia that can satisfy almost all its own needs from domestic production and still export significant quantities of energy. Turkmenistan is a major natural gas producer and exports natural gas to six CIS republics, Georgia, and Europe. Production, however, has been declining recently and Turkmenistan's natural gas industry will need help from the West and the other republics to stabilize output. While Turkmenistan currently imports coal, the amount is small and coal accounts for only 3 percent of Turkmenistan's total energy consumption.

Uzbekistan obtains more than three-fourths of its energy requirements from indigenous resources. The republic's major industries are metallurgy and the production of agricultural machinery and chemicals to support its huge cotton-growing activity.

Natural gas is the cornerstone of the Uzbek energy economy, supplying 65 percent of the republic's total energy needs. While having sufficient production to satisfy its domestic needs in the aggregate, Uzbekistan actually imports almost as much gas as it exports because Uzbek gasfields, like those throughout Central Asia, are linked by pipeline to the other Central Asian republics and Russia.

Uzbekistan imports 68 percent of its crude oil needs from Russia and 40 percent of its oil product needs from Kazakhstan. Uzbekistan's oil future may be bright, however, if the oil well blowout that occurred in March 1992 at Mingbulak signifies the discovery of a giant oilfield. Uzbekistan's two refineries could meet three-fourths of internal demand for petroleum products if sufficient crude oil were available, but Russia plans to reduce crude oil deliveries from 120,000 b/d to 80,000 b/d in 1992.

Uzbekistan is a net exporter of electric power, 70 percent of which is produced from natural gas. Industry accounts for half of Uzbekistan's electric power consumption, while households and agriculture divide the remainder. Coal, most of which is produced domestically, provides only 6 percent of the republic's energy.

B. Agriculture

DISTRIBUTION PROBLEMS IN THE FOOD ECONOMY OF THE FORMER SOVIET UNION

By William M. Liefert *

CONTENTS

SUMMARY

The recent problems of the food economy of the former Soviet Union have mainly involved distribution and demand, not agricultural production and supply. During 1986–90, despite growing perceived consumer food shortages, average annual output of both grain and meat in the former Soviet Union was about 20 percent higher than during 1981–85. The two major causes of food distribution problems have been macroeconomic imbalance and the breakup of the Union.

From 1985 to 1991 per capita money income in the former Soviet Union rose over 150 percent, creating severe inflationary pressure. However, state prices for most consumer goods, including foods, remained controlled below market-clearing levels. The results were repressed inflation, excess consumer demand, not only for food but for most consumer goods, and a large overhang (surplus) of ruble money unspendable at existing controlled prices. Since selling for rubles became increasingly unattractive, ruble money broke down

* William M. Liefert is Acting Leader of the Former Soviet Union Section of the Economic Research Service, U.S. Department of Agriculture. The author thanks Kenneth Gray and David Sedik for helpful comments. The views expressed are the author's alone and do not in any way reflect official USDA views or policies.

in its main function as an accepted means of exchange. By 1991 much of the economy had reverted to crude barter as the dominant mode of exchange, especially at the regional and republic level. Disruption in the flow of inputs, as well as reduced incentives to work, produce, and sell for rubles, eventually affected production. In 1991 agricultural output fell by 7 percent (according to official Soviet figures; GDP is reported to have dropped 17 percent).

The dissolution of the Union in 1991 further aggravated the distribution problems. The system of central supply and distribution at the All-Union level died along with the Union. The weakness of the ruble as a means of exchange, however, hindered development of a substitute money-based market system of exchange.

The breakup of the Union and conditions that created macroeconomic imbalance combined in another way to hurt distribution, in this case specifically the interrepublic movement of foodstuffs. Price controls not only helped generate consumer "shortages," but also subsidized consumers who purchased at the controlled prices. To reduce the outflow of "scarce" foodstuffs, as well as prevent the export of consumer food subsidies, most republics by early 1992 had established quotas, or for some products complete bans, on food exports.

The main short-run objective of the ambitious economic reform program begun by Russia in January 1992, and followed to some degree by most other republics, is to restore macroeconomic balance and thereby reestablish the ruble as effective money. The key policy adopted to this end has been price liberalization, intended to eliminate the debilitating money overhang. Prices for most foods and other consumer goods have been freed. Price liberalization will succeed in restoring macro balance, though, only if the government prevents the further growth of inflationary pressure through fairly austere fiscal and monetary policies. Russian policy was strict from January through mid-April 1992. In response to strong opposition to the reform program, however, the Russian government made budget and credit concessions in late spring that will aggravate inflation.

Price liberalization has changed the mix and magnitude of monetary versus nonmonetary costs of obtaining food and other goods for different social groups. Nonetheless, Russia has sufficient food supplies in 1992 (with anticipated imports) such that market-clearing prices should not deprive the majority of people of a minimally acceptable diet.

THE EFFECT OF MACROECONOMIC IMBALANCE

During Gorbachev's first five years in power, the production of agricultural goods did not fall. From 1986 to 1990, average annual output of both grain and meat in the former Soviet Union was about 20 percent higher than during 1981–85, mainly because of more favorable weather. In the latter 1980s average annual grain and meat output equalled 212 and 19.3 million metric tons (mmt), respectively, compared to 180 and 16.2 mmt during the preceding five years (table 1). In 1990 the Soviets produced a near-record grain harvest of 235 mmt (the record was 237 mmt in 1978). Since labor productivity in agriculture in the republics is still only about one-tenth that in the United States, potential remains for large increases in efficiency, productivity, and output in primary agriculture. Nonetheless, the figures just given show that the reason consumer food shortages grew during the Gorbachev years is not that farm output fell.

Downstream agricultural activities—transportation, storage, and processing—have arguably been the most neglected and inefficient sectors in the former Soviet Union economy. Losses in handling could be as high as 30 percent for grain and 50 percent for potatoes and vegetables (though these figures probably include field and harvesting losses, not purely post-production waste). Elimination of these losses would go far to end any existing shortages. Yet, the weaknesses in these downstream operations have existed throughout the postwar period, and thus also fail to explain why food distribution problems worsened and consumer food shortages grew under Gorbachev.

TABLE 1. Grain and Meat Production, Net Imports, and Availability in the Former U.S.S.R., 1980–91.

(Millions of Metric Tons)

Year	Grain			Meat		
	Production [a]	Net Imports	Availability [b]	Production [c]	Net Imports	Availability [b]
1980	189	29	218	15.1	0.8	15.9
1981	158	43	201	15.2	0.9	16.1
1982	187	38	225	15.4	0.9	16.3
1983	192	32	224	16.4	1.0	17.4
1984	173	42	215	17.0	0.8	17.8
1985	192	44	236	17.1	0.8	17.9
1986	210	25	235	18.1	0.9	19.0
1987	211	29	240	18.9	0.8	19.7
1988	195	34	229	19.7	0.7	20.4
1989	211	36	247	20.1	0.7	20.8
1990	235 [d]	31	266	20.0	1.0	21.0
1991	175 [d]	38 [e]	213	18.6 [f]	1.0 [e]	19.6

Sources: *Narodnoe khoziaistvo SSSR, Vneshniaia torgovlia SSSR, Ekonomika i zhizn'*, no. 6, 1992, and ERS, *Former USSR Agriculture and Trade Report,* 1992.
[a] Bunkerweight (before cleaning and drying).
[b] Availability equals production plus net imports.
[c] Slaughterweight.
[d] Estimate of U.S. Dept. of Agriculture.
[e] Own estimate, supported by ERS, *Former USSR Agriculture and Trade Report,* 1992.
[f] Estimated mainly from data provided by Goskomstat U.S.S.R.

The explanation also cannot be found in decreasing agricultural imports. During 1986–90 former Soviet Union average annual net imports of grain equalled 31 mmt, compared to 40 mmt during 1981–85. Although grain imports fell, the drop was less than one-third the size of the rise in domestic grain production in the second half of the 1980s compared to the first. Average annual imports of meat from 1986 to 1990 were 0.83 mmt, only slightly less than the 0.88 mmt from 1981 to 1985. Thus, availability of both grain and meat increased during the Gorbachev years.

Levels of Soviet food consumption have not been that unfavorable compared even to developed countries. According to data released by the UN Economic Commission for Europe, during 1987–89 per capita red meat and poultry consumption in the former Soviet Union was about 62 kilograms, compared to 67 and 62 for Britain and Finland, respectively. [1]

The main cause of the food economy's worsening problems during the Gorbachev years was macroeconomic imbalance, caused by a combination of wage, price, budget, and monetary policies. Ironically, the harmful imbalance was largely a result of government attempts to improve economic performance. The main goal of the economic changes under Gorbachev was to motivate enterprises to become more efficient. This was to be achieved by increasing their decisionmaking power and making them more financially self-supporting. The 1987 Law on State Enterprises increased enterprises' freedom and responsibility to obtain input and sell output. Firms were to finance input purchases from their own sales revenue. Unfortunately, to help enterprises make these adjustments, the state did things that substantially increased the funds available to them. This directly negated the objective behind self-financing, which was to create an efficiency-raising "hard budget" constraint for enterprises. The main way by which the state boosted enterprise funds was by allowing firms to retain more of their earnings, mainly through a drop in the enterprise profit tax. [2] Also, enterprise assets and accounts were made more fungible, and thereby more easily convertible by firms into liquid money form. [3]

One of the areas in which enterprise freedom was increased most was wage-setting. Enterprises used this power, along with the funds that had become available, to raise workers' monetary wages in excess of productivity gains. This reaction was understandable, given enterprises' traditional worry that they will have insufficient inputs, including labor, to meet their mandated output targets. Further driving the increase in consumer purchasing power was continued high state spending on consumer subsidies and welfare-type payments.

From 1985 to 1990, per capita money income in the former Soviet Union increased 48 percent. [4] Labor productivity grew, however, only about 8 percent. [5] The result was strong demand-led inflationary pressure. Rather than face the political fallout from substantial open price inflation, the state opted for repressed inflation. The official index for retail prices in state stores and cooperatives rose in 1985–1990 by only 11 percent, with food prices rising 15 percent. [6]

---

[1] UN Economic Commission for Europe, *The Livestock and Meat Market*, vol. 4 of *Agricultural Review for Europe*, annual issues for 1987, 1988, and 1989. To obtain the former Soviet Union figure given, the Economic Commission for Europe discounts official Soviet consumption data for slaughter fat by 7 percent for beef, 15 percent for pork, and 4 percent for sheep meat.

[2] One author calculates that the profit tax rate for Soviet enterprises fell from 64 percent in 1985 to 40 percent in 1990. See Edward C. Cook, "How Fiscal Policy Fueled Inflation in the USSR," *CPE Agriculture Report*, Vol. 4, no. 1, January/February 1991, p. 13.

[3] For further discussion of Soviet financial policies, see IMF, World Bank, OECD, and EBRD, *A Study of the Soviet Economy*, 1991, vol. 1, chap. III.2.

[4] U.S.S.R., *Narodnoe khoziaistvo SSSR v 19—godu*, Moscow, various issues.

[5] U.S. Central Intelligence Agency, *Handbook of Economic Statistics*, 1991, Washington, D.C., U.S. Government Printing Office, 1991, p. 66.

[6] U.S.S.R., *Narodnoe khoziaistvo SSSR 1990*, p. 166.

Shortages grew in the sense that existing output could not satisfy steadily increasing consumer demand, fueled by the climbing money incomes. [7] Excess demand caused by income growth and low prices existed not only for food, but also other consumer products, such as shoes, clothing, medicine, and toiletries. Soviet consumers were simply earning more ruble income than they could spend at existing prices, creating a large overhang of unspendable rubles. [8]

To soak up excess purchasing power, the government in April 1991 tripled the prices for food and most other price-controlled consumer goods. Yet, money income in 1991 alone rose by about 90 percent. [9] The growth in consumer purchasing power negated much of the stabilizing effect of the April price increases. In summer 1991 the monetary overhang in the former Soviet Union was estimated still to be over 200 billion rubles. [10] By contrast, the value of all consumer goods produced in 1990 in retail prices was only 459 billion rubles. [11] Another indication of the degree of accumulated inflationary pressure is that in 1991 open inflation for those goods lacking price controls was over 100 percent.

The most serious consequence of the monetary overhang and related imbalances is that the domestic currency declined as an accepted means of exchange. Incentives to buy with rubles were very strong, but incentives to sell for rubles, particularly at low state prices, were correspondingly weak. If money breaks down as a means of exchange, barter will ensue. Barter, with its inevitable inefficiencies, grew throughout the economy—at the personal, enterprise, regional, and republic level. Many republics would surrender food only in return for other goods, not rubles.

A corollary development to barter is hoarding. In a barter economy, goods themselves become the means of exchange, and thus also the main store of value. Hence, hoarding. In the former Soviet Union in 1991 households would commonly acquire supplies of key foodstuffs that could last weeks, if not months. [12] Hoarding foodstuffs, however, exacerbates physical waste. Also, even if durable, goods of real use value should be consumed, not wasted as an ersatz money supply.

Under the system of central planning and supply, central agencies existed to procure foodstuffs from farms and distribute them to deficit areas. The large cities, such as Moscow and Leningrad, were particularly dependent on central food supplies. The unattractiveness of the ruble has made the purchasing of output from farms increasingly difficult. In 1991 the republics collectively purchased from farms only 53 percent of the original All-Union procurement

---

[7] In an unpublished manuscript, William M. Liefert, "An Elasticities Approach To Estimating Excess Demand in Price Controlled Markets," estimates are given for excess demand for meat in the U.S.S.R. during 1980–89. Excess demand in 1989 is calculated to be 5.8 mmt, such that 78 percent of total demand for meat was satisfied by purchase. The estimation procedure involves a supply and demand model in which excess demand is a function of price elasticities. For preliminary estimates for 1980–87, see William M. Liefert, "Estimates of Excess Demand in Soviet Meat and Grain Markets," *CPE Agriculture Report*, vol. 2, no. 4, July/August 1989, pp. 19–23.

[8] For a discussion of general problems in Soviet consumer markets through 1989, see Gertrude E. Schroeder, "'Crisis' in the Consumer Sector: A Comment," *Soviet Economy*, vol. 6, no. 1, 1990, pp. 56–64.

[9] *Ekonomika i zhizn'*, no. 6, 1992, p. 13.

[10] *Izvestiia*, July 24, 1991, p. 2.

[11] *Ekonomika i zhizn'*, no. 5, 1991, p. 10.

[12] *Rabochaia tribuna*, April 16, 1991, p. 2.

target for grain (41 of 77 mmt). [13] For grain, failure to achieve the planned target for domestic procurement, rather than production, has been the main factor in determining the size of imports. [14] USDA estimates that total grain imports by the former Soviet Union in 1991 equalled 38 mmt. [15] Even in 1990, despite a near-record grain harvest of 235 mmt, the state met only 79 percent of its procurement target (68 of 86 mmt). [16] Consequently, the country imported 33 mmt of grain.

This paper has argued that the main cause of the growing "shortages" of food and other consumer goods during the Gorbachev years was not reduced output. Yet, in 1991, for the first time under Gorbachev's leadership, Soviet production began to fall seriously, across the economy. According to the State Committee for Statistics of the former Union, in 1991 GDP dropped 17 percent. Industrial and agricultural output decreased 8 and 7 percent, respectively. [17] USDA estimates the 1991 grain harvest at 175 mmt, compared to 235 mmt in 1990.

One reason why output of some agricultural products fell in 1991 was less favorable weather compared to 1990. Yet, the weakening of the ruble as a means of exchange and accompanying distribution problems were to a large degree responsible for the economy-wide drop in output. The inefficient hoarding and barter that the weakened ruble encouraged seriously disrupted the flow of goods through the economy. Factories and farms failed to receive deliveries of needed inputs, mainly because suppliers were unwilling to part with their output unless they could get goods in return. [18]

Production of agricultural inputs in the former Union, such as machinery and fertilizers, is heavily concentrated. Since barter becomes more difficult to negotiate the greater the distance between trading partners, the concentration of agricultural input production creates another burden for farms. The enterprise "Rostsel'mash" in Rostov produces all the country's corn and sunflower seed combines, and about 85 percent of grain combines. [19] The enterprise "Khibiny" in the Murmansk area manufactures over half of all phosphate fertilizer, [20] while two enterprises (in Belorussia and the Urals) account for about 90 percent of potash output.

Output also dropped because the weakened ruble reduced incentives to work and produce. During a trip to the Soviet republics in fall 1991, this writer heard agricultural officials in a number of regions explain that attempts to stimulate farm output through higher prices had in fact backfired by motivating farms to produce

[13] *Ekonomika i zhizn'*, no. 6, 1992, p. 15.
[14] Economic Research Service (ERS), USDA, *USSR Agriculture and Trade Report*, RS–89–1, 1989, p. 49.
[15] USDA, *World Grain Situation and Outlook*, FG 5–92, May 1992, p. 15.
[16] *Ekonomika i zhizn'*, no. 5, 1991, p. 12.
[17] *Ekonomika i zhizn'*, no. 6, 1992, p. 13. The smaller (though still substantial) declines in industrial and agricultural output appear inconsistent with the large 17 percent drop in GDP. This suggests that the actual percentage decreases for the three variables might have been closer to each other and somewhere between 7 and 17 percent.
[18] *Izvestiia*, July 25, 1991, p. 1; *Sovetskaia Rossiia*, August 6, 1991, p. 1; *Pravda*, July 1, 1991.
[19] Interview with Yuri Peskov, *Pravda*, February 14, 1992.
[20] *Khimiia v sel'skom khoziaistve*, no. 5, 1985, p. 3. Heavy concentration is a feature of industrial production in general, not just for agricultural inputs. In 212 of the main 344 industrial product groups (62 percent) in the former Union in 1988, the largest single enterprise within the product group accounted for more than half of all the group's output. IMF, World Bank, OECD, EBRD, *A Study of the Soviet Economy*, 1991, vol. 2, p. 39.

less. Because the value of additional ruble income was judged so low, farms' objective was not to increase revenue or profit. Rather, the goal was to produce the minimum necessary to obtain a given level of revenue. Higher prices allowed farms to obtain the desired income level with less output. [21]

THE EFFECT OF THE UNION'S BREAKUP

The demise of the Union hurt the food economy in the short run mainly because it entailed the collapse of the system of central supply and distribution (at least at the All-Union level). In fact, the increasing assertiveness of the republics and decentralizing pressure of the reform movement had seriously weakened many All-Union economic agencies even before the abortive August 1991 coup. For example, the All-Union Fund responsible for the central purchase and distribution of grain stopped functioning in July 1991. [22]

It has been the combination of the dying central supply system and the ruble-weakening macroeconomic imbalance that has so paralyzed the economy and distribution system. The collapse of central planning and supply has necessitated the development of a substitute distribution system. The ruble's unattractiveness as a means of payment, though, impedes the creation of a well-functioning money-based market system of exchange. Crude barter is the unattractive though necessary alternative.

The weakened ruble in fact contributed to the Union's breakup by intensifying nationalist pressures for separatism. Regions and republics have felt that the sale of their output for rubles alone has been a subsidy to others at their expense. Such thinking has strengthened autarkic attitudes. Also, many republics lost hope that the All-Union government, given the increasing pressures put on it, would exercise the budgetary and monetary discipline necessary to restore and protect the ruble as effective money.

Another reason the ending of the Union has disrupted the former Soviet Union's food economy is that individual republics have established formal barriers to interrepublic flows of foodstuffs. As opposed to most trade restrictions in the developed Western countries, these measures mainly restrict exports, rather than imports. In 1991 and early 1992 most republics banned the export of certain foodstuffs, and established export quotas for others. For example, by January 1992 Russia had prohibited the export of about 60 types of food and other consumer products. Included were meat, butter, cheese, fish, flour, sugar, coffee, tea, tobacco, and wine. [23] A common "export restraint" concerning food has been preventing nonrepublic citizens from buying at republic state stores. The creation of quasi-currency coupons, in Ukraine and Byelarus, for example, has been an indirect way of preventing sale to nonrepublic "foreigners." The coupons are necessary for purchase of food and other designated goods within the republic. Cer-

---

[21] Other sectors of the economy have also suffered from this perverse negative relationship between output prices and production. *Rossiiskaia gazeta,* 3/18/92, p. 3.
[22] The author obtained this information during his 1991 visit to the former Union.
[23] TASS, 1253 GMT, January 10, 1992; *Rossiiskaia gazeta,* January 10, 1992, p. 4.

tain cities and oblasts have also issued coupons to protect their residents.

In some areas, serious supply shortfalls of certain foods, such as meat and milk, could well exist. The trade restrictions might therefore reflect concern by republics, as well as smaller jurisdictions, that their own population be adequately provided for before exports are allowed. Another motive for the export restraints, though, most likely exists. The main cause of consumer shortages has been the combination of rising money incomes and controlled prices. By lowering the prices consumers pay, controls that fix consumer prices below market-clearing levels subsidize consumers. If a republic allowed the price-controlled goods to be exported, or equivalently, sold to foreigners who come to buy, it would be subsidizing foreigners rather than natives. To prevent the export of subsidies, price controls require trade controls. [24]

A development that could further disrupt trade between the republics in all goods in the short term is if the non-Russian republics abandon the ruble and establish their own currencies. The new national currencies would in all likelihood not be immediately convertible. Leaving the ruble, then, would make financing trade between the republics more difficult. Although separate currencies would further disrupt interrepublic trade, a strong motive of republics for establishing them would be to acquire greater control over their national macroeconomic policies. As of May 1992, Ukraine, Byelarus, the Baltic States, and Moldova appeared committed to creating their own currencies (with Ukraine and Byelarus already having a quasi one with their coupon systems).

INTERREPUBLIC TRADE IN AGRICULTURE

Useful indicators of the degree to which distribution problems have disrupted the former Soviet Union's food economy would be the magnitude of interrepublic trade in agriculture and food in past years, and in particular, the decrease in interrepublic flows in 1991. Yet, this writer could obtain republic trade data for specific agricultural products for only a single year before 1991 (1990 for most goods; 1989 for grain). Such information can nonetheless be used to compute interrepublic flows for the given year. The data are also useful for identifying which particular republics should be markets for Western agricultural exports.

In 1990, total interrepublic trade equalled about 20 percent of Soviet GDP. Interrepublic flows in agricultural products, though, amounted to only 10 percent of agricultural output. [25] Trade in grain and meat was particularly low. In 1989 interrepublic flows of grain equalled 9.2 mmt, 4.7 percent of Soviet grain output (clean-weight). Foreign imports of grain were around four times as large as interrepublic trade. Interrepublic meat flows in 1990 were 0.9 mmt, 4.5 percent of meat production. Foreign meat imports were

---

[24] For further discussion of the relationship between price and trade policy, specifically for the former Council for Mutual Economic Assistance (CMEA) countries, see Franklyn D. Holzman, *The Economics of Soviet Bloc Trade and Finance*, Boulder, CO, Westview Press, 1987, Chap. 4, pp. 91–112; reprinted from *Comparative Economic Systems: Models and Cases*, edited by Morris Bornstein, Homewood, IL, Richard D. Irwin, 1985, pp. 367–386.

[25] ERS, USDA, *Former USSR Agriculture and Trade Report*, RS–92–1, 1992, p. 13.

TABLE 2. Imports and Exports of Grain, by Republic, 1989.

(Thousands of Metric Tons)

Republic	Production [a]	Imports [b]	Exports [c]	Net Imports [d]	Availability [e]	Net Imports as % of Availability [f]
Russia	104,800	21,544	1,162	20,382	125,182	16
Ukraine	51,200	4,180	5,029	−849	50,351	2
Byelarus	7,400	3,376	34	3,342	10,742	31
Moldova	3,300	746	60	686	3,986	17
Kazakhstan	18,800	586	2,935	−2,349	16,451	12
Uzbekistan	1,500	3,866	12	3,854	5,354	72
Kyrgyzstan	1,600	1,056	3	1,053	2,653	40
Tajikistan	300	1,386	—	1,386	1,686	82
Turkmenistan	400	742	—	742	1,142	65
Armenia	200	850	—	850	1,050	81
Azerbaijan	800	1,349	—	1,349	2,149	63
Georgia	500	1,722	—	1,722	2,222	77
Lithuania	3,300	1,381	11	1,370	4,670	29
Latvia	1,600	1,256	1	1,255	2,855	44
Estonia	1,000	1,093	—	1,093	2,093	52
Total	196,700	45,133	9,247	35,886	232,586	15

Sources: Production from *Narodnoe khoziaistvo SSSR 1990*, p. 471. Imports and exports obtained by author directly from Goskomstat U.S.S.R. in 1991.
[a] Cleanweight.
[b] Equal foreign imports plus inflows from other republics.
[c] Equal only outflows to other republics; exclude foreign exports.
[d] Since "Exports" column excludes foreign exports, net imports are overstated. Values for grain exports in Soviet foreign trade statistical yearbook include not only exports of domestically produced grain, but also foreign grain purchased for other countries' use. In its annual *USSR Agriculture and Trade Report*, ERS of USDA uses the figure 0.5 mmt for yearly exports of domestically produced grain throughout 1980's. Thus, values in the table for net imports and availability are overstated only slightly.
[e] Equals production plus net imports.
[f] If the republic is a net exporter, equals net exports as a percentage of production, not availability.

about as large as interrepublic trade. Goods whose production is more limited by climate naturally traded more heavily between republics, such as cotton, sugar, vegetable oil, tea, and citrus.[26] The relatively low volume of interrepublic agricultural trade mitigates the seriousness of distribution problems that specifically concern interrepublic flows. Yet, the gravest distribution problems affect movement not only between, but within, republics.

In 1989, with the exception of Ukraine and Kazakhstan, all the republics were net grain importers (table 2). Russia accounted for about 57 percent of the Union's net imports, which provided 16 percent of grain consumed by the republic. Most other republics imported from about one-third to two-thirds of all grain they consumed. In 1990, Russia and the Transcaucasus and Central Asian republics (again with the exception of Kazakhstan) were net im-

[26] Production from U.S.S.R., *Narodnoe khoziaistvo SSSR*, various years; foreign imports from USSR, *Vneshniaia torgovlia SSSR*, various years; interrepublic flows from Goskomstat, U.S.S.R., *Zavoz i vyvoz tovarov narodnogo potrebleniia v 1990 g.*, Moscow, 1991.

porters of meat; the remaining republics of the former Union net
exporters (table 3). Each net-importing republic, though, was more
self-sufficient in meat than grain. [27]

TABLE 3. Imports and Exports of Meat, by Republic, 1990.

(Thousands of Metric Tons)

Republic	Production	Imports [a]	Exports [b]	Net Imports	Availability [c]	Net Imports as % of Availability [d]
Russia	10,112	1,501	69	1,432	11,544	12
Ukraine	4,358	25	316	−291	4,067	7
Byelarus	1,181	9	185	−176	1,005	15
Moldova	366	—	54	−54	312	15
Kazakhstan	1,548	13	182	−169	1,379	11
Uzbekistan	484	206	—	206	690	30
Kyrgyzstan	254	2	1	1	255	—
Tajikistan	108	42	8	34	142	24
Turkmenistan	104	55	—	55	159	35
Armenia	93	60	—	60	153	39
Azerbaijan	176	70	—	70	246	28
Georgia	170	47	—	47	217	22
Lithuania	530	—	112	−112	418	21
Latvia	308	—	38	−38	270	12
Estonia	219	2	38	−36	183	16
Total	20,011	2,032	1,003	1,029	21,040	5

Sources: Production from *Narodnoe khoziaistvo SSSR 1990*, p. 503. Imports and exports from *Zavoz i vyvoz tovarov narodnogo potrebleniia v 1990 g.*, Goskomstat U.S.S.R., 1991.
[a] Equal foreign imports plus inflows from other republics.
[b] Equal foreign exports plus outflows to other republics.
[c] Equals production plus net imports.
[d] If the republic is a net exporter, equals net exports as a percentage of production, not availability.

Table 4 provides additional data on imports and exports of foodstuffs by republic in 1989. Though the source is not wholly clear,
the goods in question appear to be processed foods. Russia is a
major net importer, and Ukraine a major net exporter.

REFORM IN THE RUSSIAN REPUBLIC

After formally dissolving the U.S.S.R. in late December, the republics each began 1992 with at least an official commitment to decentralizing, if not radical, market-oriented economic reform.
Russia has led the way. The long-term objective of Russia's ambitious reform program is to create the institutional base for a
market capitalist system, the key being privatization. The immediate objective, though, is to restore macroeconomic balance and
thereby reestablish the ruble as effective money. Two policy moves
are necessary to achieve the latter. The first is that the govern-

---

[27] For imports and exports by republic of sugar, cotton, and vegetable oil, see ERS, *Former USSR Agriculture and Trade Report*, 1992, pp. 70, 73, and 76.

TABLE 4. Imports and Exports of Food, by Republic, 1989.

Republic	Millions of Rubles			Percent of Total	
	Imports [a]	Exports [b]	Net Imports	Imports	Exports
Russia..................	17,277	3,124	14,153	64.4	16.8
Ukraine..............	1,546	6,584	−5,038	5.8	35.4
Byelarus..............	802	1,494	−692	3.0	8.0
Moldova..............	176	1,123	−947	0.7	6.0
Kazakhstan..........	1,098	544	554	4.1	2.9
Uzbekistan...........	1,618	720	898	6.0	3.9
Kyrgyzstan...........	264	377	−113	1.0	2.0
Tajikistan............	454	149	305	1.7	0.8
Turkmenistan........	477	305	172	1.8	1.6
Armenia..............	713	138	575	2.7	0.7
Azerbaijan...........	860	464	396	3.2	2.5
Georgia..............	824	1,415	−591	3.1	7.6
Lithuania.............	308	879	−571	1.1	4.7
Latvia..................	183	672	−489	0.7	3.6
Estonia...............	242	589	−347	0.9	3.2
Total	26,842	18,577	8,265	100.0	100.0

Source: *Narodnoe khoziaistvo SSSR 1990*, p. 637.
[a] Equal foreign imports plus inflows from other republics.
[b] Equal foreign exports plus outflows to other republics.

ment must prevent the further growth of inflationary pressure. This requires reducing both the budget deficit and the growth of the money supply (which can be achieved mainly by the state banking system decreasing the flow of credit to enterprises). The Russian program has promised tough budget, money, and credit policies.

After stopping the growth, or "flow," of excess consumer purchasing power, the state must then mop up the existing "stock" of surplus rubles. The most direct way would be to free prices and thereby let them rise to their market-clearing level. On January 2 Russia began major price liberalization. Prices were wholly freed for most producer and consumer goods. Foodstuffs on the freed list included meat, potatoes, vegetables, and fruit. Controls were kept for bread, milk, sugar, vegetable oil, cooking salt, baby foods, vodka and other spirits. Prices for most of these foods initially tripled. Price controls were also retained for fuel, transport, and rent, with fuel prices also generally tripling. [28] More prices were decontrolled in spring. In January alone the price level increased about 250 percent, while the inflation rate in February, March, and April was 30–40 percent each month. [29] Such rates correspond to an inflation of 700–800 percent during the first third of 1992.

---

[28] *Rossiiskaia gazeta*, December 26, 1991, p. 3.
[29] *Financial Times*, April 22, 1992, p. 16.

Almost all the other republics responded to Russia's action on prices. Yet, most republics raised, rather than freed, food prices, most commonly tripling them. Some republics, such as the Ukraine, did so reluctantly, mainly out of fear that to not respond would risk being deluged by Russian consumers wanting to buy at the republics' lower prices.

The price liberalization will restore confidence in the ruble only if the large ensuing price rises are largely a one-shot affair. The risk is that the pressure for compensation will result in major increases in wages, pensions, and other income support that lead to a ruble-destroying inflationary spiral. Through March the government's commitment to stricter budget and monetary policies had prevented the large emission of funds required for substantial increases in compensation. Admittedly, in the first three months of 1992 aggregate money incomes (including retirees' pensions) about tripled. However, since the percentage growth in prices through March had significantly exceeded the percentage rise in money incomes, the threat of hyperinflation had been so far averted.

In April 1992, however, critics of the relatively austere reform program challenged the government's policies at a meeting of the Russian Congress of People's Deputies. The reformist ministers retained power and the determination to continue reform. Yet, the government compromised by increasing income compensation, financial support to agricultural producers, and credit to enterprises. The total credit growth from the decisions made in April alone should equal 700–800 billion rubles.[30] Such budgetary and monetary concessions raise the fear that inflation will remain so high that it threatens price liberalization, as well as other linchpins of the reform program, such as ruble convertibility.

THE EFFECT OF PRICE LIBERALIZATION

The Russian government hopes that price liberalization will increase farms' incentives to produce and sell, for two reasons. The money prices farms receive for their output will rise. Also, price liberalization, along with other measures that stabilize the macroeconomy and strengthen the monetary system, is intended to promote money-based market exchange. Yet, if freeing prices leads to chronic high inflation, the ruble will remain weak and scorned. If so, farms' aversion to producing and selling for currency will continue.

Also, the immediate effect of price liberalization on agricultural production has probably been negative, in that it has worsened agriculture's terms of trade. In Russia during the first couple months of 1992, prices for agricultural machinery rose 7 to 15 times.[31] Agricultural producer prices, however, increased only about 4 to 5 times. Price liberalization has allowed the heavily concentrated producers of machinery and other agricultural inputs to exploit their newly acquired market power by substantially raising prices.

Farms' ability to finance inputs has been harmed not only by suppliers' pricing behavior, but also by the elimination of many

---

[30] Ibid.
[31] ERS, *Former USSR Agriculture and Trade Report*, 1992, p. 28.

state input subsidies. The setting of high prices by enterprises with market power hurts economic efficiency, and is a problem the government must respond to. On the other hand, reforms that require farms and enterprises to pay prices that reflect full production costs, such as ending input subsidies and artificially low state-set prices, promote economic efficiency. A drop in agricultural output that results from decreased input use because input prices are rising closer to real cost is part of healthy restructuring of the economy. Also, many agricultural material inputs, such as machinery, appear to have low marginal productivity. [32] A decrease in input use would then have only a small effect on output. The impact of price liberalization and other reform measures on agricultural production and sale will be tested during the 1992 harvest year.

The area of the Russian food economy, though, where price liberalization has had the strongest immediate effect is consumer demand. Higher prices have reduced the amount of food, as well as other goods, people wish to buy. For most foods long lines in shops and hoarding have ended. Although food supplies in general are lower than last year, since goods are not now immediately bought up when made available, shops give the appearance of being better stocked.

The price liberalization has changed the nature of the food problem for individual consumers. Formerly the difficulty was finding available food to buy in barren state stores, with more rubles in one's pocket than one could find goods to spend them on. The problem now for many people is that food can be found in state stores, but at much higher prices. The price liberalization has changed the mix and magnitude of monetary versus nonmonetary costs of obtaining food and other goods for social groups. Some will benefit from the price rises, such as those with higher money incomes who can now outbid others for products through a flexible price mechanism. People on less variable incomes, though, will suffer.

Some Russian commentators have argued that as a result of the price increases most of the population has been, or soon will be, impoverished, such that they could face real hunger. [33] Such fears are exaggerated. Evidence indicates that price liberalization initially resulted in food prices in certain local markets overshooting the market-clearing price. The experience of the reforming Central European countries, such as Poland and Czechoslovakia, supports this conclusion. During the 1980s these countries suffered from the same macroeconomic problems as the former Soviet Union, and during the past few years liberalized prices have been the most effective way of restoring price and monetary balance. In these countries prices rose so high that consumer demand fell substantially. Although aggregate food supplies had in fact decreased, many

---

[32] Information provided by the CIA's annual *Handbook of Economic Statistics* (Washington, D.C., U.S. Government Printing Office) indicates that the average productivity (AP) of capital in both Soviet industry and the economy at large has been decreasing since the early 1960s. From macroeconomic data provided in the *Handbook* series, one can then also compute that the AP of capital in agriculture has also been steadily dropping. If the AP of capital is falling, the marginal product (MP) is also falling, and is below AP. Thus, steadily decreasing AP implies that the MP of agricultural capital is currently small.

[33] For example, see *Rossiia*, no. 8, February 19–25, 1992, p. 1.

shops soon had unsold surpluses. [34] Prices eventually moved down, though, toward market-clearing levels.

In some local food markets in Russia immediately after price liberalization, the price of a kilogram of beef or pork in state stores rose to a level about one-tenth of average monthly pay. [35] Data presented earlier show that in recent years per capita meat consumption in the former Soviet Union was on a par with Western countries such as Britain and Finland. Official Soviet statistics claim that in 1991 the drop in aggregate meat output for the former Soviet Union was only about 7 percent. [36] This means that given the total amount of meat available for consumption, prices at which meat is unaffordable to the majority of the Russian population cannot be sustainable market prices. At such prices demand will fall, requiring price decreases in order for shops to avoid unsold surpluses (as in Central Europe). Such an effect is already occurring in Russia.

Another effect of price liberalization is that as the republics that have most boldly freed prices move closer to market-clearing prices for foodstuffs, they begin relaxing controls on food exports. Price liberalization reduces both motives discussed earlier for export restrictions. Since higher prices discourage indiscriminate buying and hoarding of food, goods become easier for shoppers to find and thus appear less scarce. Price liberalization also ends the consumer subsidies that existed because price controls kept prices below production cost. The government no longer need worry about keeping consumer subsidies "within country." In May 1992, for example, Estonia, one of the faster reforming republics, ended quotas on outflows of farm products. Free trade was allowed in meat, milk, butter, potatoes, and vegetables. [37] As the rationale for export restrictions in the republics fades, the down-side of export controls, such as the negative effect on balance of payments, becomes more apparent.

Over the longer term, price liberalization will contribute to the regional restructuring of former Soviet Union agriculture along more rational lines. The Soviets used a system of differentiated prices for agricultural output, in order to extract differential rent from superior climate and soils. Low-cost producing regions received low prices, and high-cost regions high prices. The effect was to discourage specialization by regions that had natural advantages in the production of certain output. [38] By eliminating the differentiated producer price system, price liberalization should motivate greater regional and republic specialization and trade in agriculture based on comparative advantage. The differentiated price system helps explain the low volume of Soviet interrepublic agricultural trade discussed earlier.

Yet, the move over time to a more economically rational agricultural structure in the republics will be difficult and itself disrup-

[34] ERS, USDA, *Agricultural Policies and Performance in Central and Eastern Europe*, 1989–92 (ERS Staff Report forthcoming in summer 1992).
[35] *Rossiiskaia gazeta*, February 1, 1992, p. 2.
[36] *Ekonomika i zhizn'*, no. 6, 1992, p. 16.
[37] BBC, *Summary of World Broadcasts*, May 29, 1992, pp. C1/1–2.
[38] Kenneth R. Gray, "Soviet Agricultural Specialization and Efficiency," *Soviet Studies*, vol. 31, no. 4, October 1979, pp. 542–558; Kenneth R. Gray, "Soviet Agricultural Prices, Rent and Land Cadastres," *Journal of Comparative Economics*, vol. 5, no. 1, March 1982, pp. 43–59.

tive. A major reason for low labor productivity in former U.S.S.R. agriculture is that the sector has functioned as a social welfare system for the countryside. Shedding unproductive labor, as well as other inputs with low productivity, will create social and political problems and resistance. This reaction will buttress opposition to reform by other conservative agricultural interests, such as the state and collective farm management.

FOOD AVAILABILITY IN THE FORMER SOVIET UNION: A SUMMARY REPORT OF THREE MISSIONS LED BY THE U.S. DEPARTMENT OF AGRICULTURE

By Allan Mustard and Christopher E. Goldthwait *

CONTENTS

SUMMARY

Three missions to the Soviet Union in May, September, and October 1991 at the joint request of the Soviet government and the White House made four critical determinations that continue to shape the U.S. response to food supply problems in the former Soviet Union. The missions found, first, that the Soviet Union did not face a threat of widespread famine but did face deterioration in food availability; would encounter hardships on a regional basis; and needed to protect certain vulnerable groups. Second, they found that the root of most difficulties in supplying foodstuffs to the population was inefficiency in the food distribution system, not in production of agricultural commodities. Third, the missions determined that the keys to improvements in food availability are movement away from the collapsed command system and a successful move to a market economy, with establishment of private ownership and creation of free market incentives to manufacture, store, transport, and sell commodities critical elements of that effort.

Third, the missions found that the Soviet Union, traditionally a cash customer for U.S. agricultural products, needs extension of credit to maintain something approaching the historical level of food and feed imports, and that Soviet leaders preferred credit to outright grants of food aid.

---

* Allan Mustard is Deputy Coordinator, Eastern Europe and Soviet Secretariat; Christopher E. Goldthwait is Acting General Sales Manager and Associate Administrator. Both authors are with the Foreign Agricultural Service, U.S. Department of Agriculture.

BACKGROUND TO THE MISSIONS

In May 1991 Under Secretary of Agriculture Richard T. Crowder led a mission to the Soviet Union to follow up on President Bush's earlier offer of American expertise in the food distribution sector to President Gorbachev. This mission had four objectives: to assess the overall food situation, to determine how the distribution system was contributing to reduced availability of food, to determine what follow-up steps could be taken jointly to improve food availability, and to obtain information in analyzing a Soviet request for additional commodity credit guarantees. Mission participants visited farms; processing, storage, and transportation facilities; retail outlets; and met with individual citizens ranging from ordinary shoppers to President Gorbachev. The itinerary for this mission included the cities and environs of Kiev, Ukraine; Stavropol', Ufa, and Moscow, Russia.

A second mission was dispatched by the White House in the wake of the abortive coup d'etat in August 1991, arriving on September 7. In nine days this mission, also led by Under Secretary Crowder, visited six cities in four republics: Moscow and Yekaterinburg, Russia; Alma Ata, Kazakhstan; Tashkent and Samarkand, Uzbekistan; and Yerevan, Armenia. This mission visited many of the same type of establishments as the preceding one had, and in addition visited public welfare institutions such as orphanages and hospitals, private farms as well as state farms, and took pains to meet with private farm group leaders and nongovernmental agricultural and food sector experts.

The third mission, also at the request of the White House, was led by Secretary of Agriculture Edward Madigan in early October 1991. It included 12 private individuals who, travelling largely at their own expense, lent their professional expertise to an evaluation of the status of food availability and prospects for short-term improvement in food processing and manufacturing, transportation, storage, wholesaling and retailing. [1] This mission visited Moscow, Russia, and Kiev, Ukraine. The Secretary additionally visited St. Petersburg, Russia, where he met with local officials and assessed food availability in the second most populous city of the Soviet Union.

FOOD AVAILABILITY

All three missions determined that while food availability would be reduced in 1991 and 1992 relative to previous years, there was no threat of famine. Subsequent events, aided by the hindsight of evaluations as the winter of 1991 and spring of 1992 came to an end, have borne out this observation. The delegations noted, however, that pockets of hardship would exist in the large northern cities

---

[1] These twelve individuals were Mr. Eddie Moyer of Illinois Central Railroad, Chicago, Illinois; Mr. Robert Peyton of Conagra International Inc., Omaha, Nebraska; Mr. Russell Bragg of Grand Metropolitan, Minneapolis, Minnesota; Mr. Howard Gochberg of Land O' Lakes, Minneapolis, Minnesota; Mr. Maurice Gordon, private farmer from Rantoul, Illinois; Mr. Majid Gheissari of FMC Corporation; Mr. Mark Kuechler of Southland Distribution, Falmouth, Virginia; Mr. Chester McCorkle of the University of California, Davis; Mr. Karl Nigl of Pepsi-Cola International U.S.S.R.; Mr. Andrew Rafalat of Pizza Hut Eastern Europe; Mr. Gary Ray of George A. Hormel & Co., Austin, Minnesota; and Mr. Wayne Showers of Griffin and Brand, McAllen, Texas.

that have traditionally focused on defense-related industrial output, Russia east of the Urals, Armenia, and parts of Central Asia. This was in great part due to the collapse of the centralized allocation system, which administratively redistributed food from production areas to consumption areas. As this system collapsed, and as the ruble lost credibility as a unit of value, a barter system emerged. Those cities and other regions with little or nothing to offer for barter were left wanting. [2] Armenia was noted as a special case, for the problems of a barter economy it faced in common with other parts of the Soviet Union were compounded by its isolation in the face of hostile neighbors.

Food availability was generally better than expected and certainly better than the common wisdom prevailing in the West. The missions attributed this to two factors. First, there was a discernible if unquantifiable trend toward regional autarky. That is, each locale undertook to produce as much food as it could locally. City residents in large numbers were availing themselves of opportunities to grow food on private plots, resulting in increased self-sufficiency. These additions to the food supply could not be measured, but were significant. In addition, there was great reliance on personal connections between rural and urban dwellers, with city residents depending on relatives in production areas for food deliveries outside the normal system. Also of importance were high levels of hoarding by the population at large, about which the missions collected much anecdotal evidence.

In addition, local authorities and farm managers withheld deliveries of foodstuffs to central (i.e., Soviet) authorities. These deliveries to the "All-Union Fund" historically were accumulated at harvest time then redistributed to feed Moscow and other large cities as well as organizations subordinate to the central authorities (such as the military). One mission was told, as only one example, that state and collective farms in the Ukraine were refusing to deliver up to 25 million tons of grain under the centralized procurement system. This made more grain available for local use via the black market and other nontraditional marketing channels.

The second factor causing better-than-expected food availability was the rapid appearance of a horizontal (i.e., enterprise-to-enterprise) barter economy that circumvented the vertically oriented command apparatus. In Stavropol', for example, the May delegation met a farm manager bound for Irkutsk to negotiate a pork-for-timber deal. All three missions found primitive commodity exchanges functioning in which foodstuffs were being traded against other physical commodities ranging from computers to construction materials. Though cumbersome and inefficient by Western standards, barter continued to grow over the period of the missions' visits as a mechanism for assuring income of some sort to produc-

---

[2] The extremes were noted, for example, in the disparate food situations in Ufa and Yekaterinburg. Ufa, though a net food importer, faced few food problems since that city refined about 20 percent of the gasoline used in the Soviet Union. As the ruble collapsed, gasoline became a very liquid asset that could be bartered for anything the city needed. Yekaterinburg, where food supplies were noticeably tighter, had little to offer but heavy industrial and military goods for which food producers and processors had minimal use (though the Yekaterin oblast' government did manage to sign an emergency agreement with Kazakhstan for provision of milling quality wheat in return for some industrial goods).

ers and food supplies to those areas able to offer something of value in return.

During the visits of the three missions, the delegations found little recognition on the part of Soviet officials of the roles of local self-sufficiency or growing horizontal trade, and no apparent efforts to measure the impact they were having on food availability to the general population. The missions thus concluded that the U.S. Government needed to make an analysis of Soviet food import requirements that was independent of the Soviets' own assessments before the United States could respond to requests either for food assistance or credit to import food.

THE FOOD DISTRIBUTION SYSTEM

All three missions examined the Soviet food chain from field to consumer with an eye to identifying weaknesses that could be redressed in order to improve food supplies in the near term. All agreed that Soviet raw agricultural output was adequate, in the aggregate, to feed the population. On a per capita basis, according to Soviet data, grain and meat production was on a par with that of Western Europe, and per capita potato production, for example, was greater than in the United States. On the basis of information provided by official sources and informal observations made on the ground, the missions concluded that production should not be the focus of efforts to assist the Soviets in improving food availability.

Soviet official sources conceded, however, that grain losses reach as high as 20 to 30 percent of the harvest, roughly equal to the level of grain imports, and that vegetable and fruit losses are believed to range as high as 50 percent. These phenomenal levels of waste highlighted the fact that distribution, rather than production, is at the heart of the former U.S.S.R.'s food problems. [3]

The missions concluded that these maladies are rooted in both economic mismanagement and in shortcomings of physical infrastructure. Chief among the causes are:

- First, the physical plant is not structured properly. Some facilities are outdated, others are underutilized, and others are in the wrong location. There is simultaneously overinvestment and underinvestment in the food distribution system, which creates inefficiencies and bottlenecks;
- Second, there is no organized wholesale market. This is exacerbated by lack of confidence in the ruble as a medium of exchange, which excludes certain cities from participation in the growing barter economy;
- Third, there is not enough appreciation that part of the value of food products is created in the distribution system. This is evident in the overemphasis on production agriculture without commensurate investment in post-harvest food handling facilities. Even a normal harvest of any crop, let alone a record harvest, ensures astounding losses due to the poor location and in-

---

[3] For purposes of these missions, the term "distribution" was used in a very broad sense to encompass the activities of the entire post-harvest food chain, including farmgate marketing, wholesaling, processing, storage, transport, and retailing.

efficient use of storage infrastructure and inefficient use of processing facilities;

• Fourth, food moved through the state system is owned by nobody and is thus treated very carelessly.

An ideological focus on the importance of production, and a desire by the Soviet regime to control food supplies centrally, led directly to inadequate on-farm storage, monopoly control of regional storage and processing facilities, and the absence of a wholesale market in foodstuffs.

Absence of appropriate and adequate grain storage on the farm and the desire to control supplies has led to overbuilding of grain storage at centrally controlled mills. In Kiev, for example, the May mission saw one of the city's two flour mills, which each year accepts a year's needs immediately after the harvest and stores it all for the coming 12 months. On the other hand, the same mission saw on-farm grain storage in Stavropol', which consisted of a two-sided shed open to the weather on the other two sides. The missions saw plants operating at one-third to one-half of rated capacity due to shortages of a critical input or inefficiency somewhere else in the economy. Again in Kiev, an ultra-high temperature milk processing line imported at great expense was running at half capacity due to short supplies of the special cartons it requires.

The absence of a functional, currency-based wholesale market creates massive inefficiency in food distribution. Commodities moved through state procurement channels belong to the state and, in the words of one interviewee, "We know what we now produce belongs to nobody." The lack of care for commodities, loss of or damage to which results in no penalty to those responsible, contributes to massive losses.

Nevertheless, precursors of wholesale markets were in evidence in the form of primitive commodity exchanges. These were augmented by direct barter trade between food producers and manufacturers of consumer items and inputs. Though these channels are inefficient, they are more efficient than the central allocation system they are supplanting. Their ultimate development into genuine wholesale markets is hindered by slow public acceptance of middlemen who turn profits by reselling commodities they did not produce. Such activity until recently was a crime. Development of wholesale markets is also hamstrung by short supplies of capital for investment in facilities.

Continued "old thinking" on the part of many in the agricultural leadership was and remains a major obstacle to resolving problems in the food distribution system. There is almost no recognition that the value of food products can be created or augmented through processing, handling, and packaging. This is not surprising since much of the agricultural leadership of the new independent states of the former Soviet Union consists even today mostly of technically and production-oriented bureaucrats. Many began their careers as farm chairman and directors, concerned wholly with meeting production plan goals and having no need to care about marketing or other aspects of the food chain. These leaders clearly fail to realize that continued relative overinvestment in production agriculture will not only fail to solve the former Soviet states' food problems, it also will divert scarce and desperately needed capital from making economically rational improvements in processing, transportation, and storage.

With continued ideological focus primarily on production, and no appreciation of value added in distribution, it isn't surprising that food—once produced—is handled carelessly. Further, since in most instances even yet no one owns food during various steps in processing and distribution, no one has any incentive to preserve it or enhance its value. The delegations attributed much of the spillage, spoilage, waste, and poor quality the members saw to this lack of ownership.

Keys to Improving Food Availability

The missions determined that the keys to improvements in food availability are movement away from the collapsed command system and a successful move to a market economy. Interestingly, two of the major obstacles to this reform identified by the May mission were, while not eliminated, greatly reduced in the wake of the abortive August coup d'etat. The May mission identified the entrenched Communist Party bureaucracy, which controlled the middle and lower levels of government and actively sought to thwart reform, as the single greatest threat to successful reform. When asked what they would do if allowed to work only one miracle in support of reform, a majority of Soviet citizens asked by the May mission responded that they would break the Communist Party's stranglehold on government. Surprisingly, this view was shared even by some party members. And, though the grip of the old party bureaucracy was greatly weakened by the failure of the coup and the subsequent abolition of the Communist Party, many old party members remain in positions of considerable influence and continue to obstruct reforms. The October mission noted that despite enthusiasm for reform at the very top and at the grass roots level, there remains at the middle levels of government a significant and intransigent morass of bureaucracy that fears and is threatened by reform, and that actively seeks to hinder economic restructuring. Events since then have demonstrated that conservative elements in the national parliaments of several of the new independent states also seek to stymie reform.

The second major obstacle identified by the May mission was the absence of a privatization law. Since then, several of the new independent states have adopted decrees and laws to privatize capital infrastructure and, to a more limited extent, land. These remain subject in many cases to local bureaucracies dominated by conservative elements, however. They also continue to face obstructionism on the part of local officials and leaders of collective and state farms (even those being forcibly privatized).

The third major obstacle identified by the May mission remains, and that is a lack of capital that makes establishment, operation, and expansion of private enterprises exceedingly difficult. The shortage of ruble capital is critical. While a growing number of commercial banks are making small loans to entrepreneurs at high rates of interest, what is most vitally needed are sources of equity capital. This, of course, is tied closely to private ownership issues, and is compounded by the absence of capital markets.

THE FOCUS OF U.S. ASSISTANCE EFFORTS

The United States implemented several programs in the wake of the three missions to assist the Soviet Union in its transition to a market-oriented economy. Following the collapse of the Soviet Union in December 1991, the programs were continued within the framework of U.S. recognition of each individual state of the former Soviet Union.

Recognizing that the Soviet Union faced continuing cash-flow problems and could not maintain its desired level of agricultural imports on a cash basis, the United States extended commodity credit guarantees beginning in December 1990. Since the demise of the U.S.S.R., additional credit guarantees have been announced for 12 new independent states of the former Soviet Union. Though not a form of assistance, extension of credit guarantees in support of commercial sales assured continued movement of large quantities of U.S. agricultural commodities to the former Soviet Union.

Humanitarian food assistance began in December 1991 with airlifts of surplus Defense Department rations to cities in greatest need. These rations were specifically targeted for vulnerable groups, including occupants of orphanages, retirement homes, and other institutions. These were followed by deliveries of food assistance under authority of the Food for Progress program worth over $165 million to cities identified as severely food deficit. This latter program utilized private voluntary organizations to distribute food to vulnerable population groups in Russia, Armenia, Byelarus, Kazakhstan, and Turkmenistan.

In the longer term, however, improvements in food availability will be most dependent on reform of the food systems of the new independent states. Toward that end the United States Government has initiated several technical assistance projects intended to facilitate the difficult transition to a market economy.

Several themes developed by the missions are reflected in the choice of activities:

- Maximizing returns from existing resources through market-oriented management,
- A focus on the post-harvest part of the food chain, even in farmer-oriented activities,
- Demonstration efforts that can be duplicated or imitated elsewhere using resources available within the former Soviet Union, and
- Work that will have a measurable impact in the next crop cycle.

These include a model farm project in the St. Petersburg area, which focuses on marketing of agricultural products; a project to establish wholesale markets in Moscow and Kiev; establishment of an extension service in Armenia; and a program to loan American private sector executives to enterprises in the former Soviet Union to help them make better use of existing capital infrastructure. In addition, a farmer-to-farmer program is already under way and will be expanded over the next year to share U.S. knowledge of marketing, processing, storage, and transportation of agricultural commodities with the nascent agribusiness entrepreneurs of the new independent states. The Cochran Fellowship Program, a program of short-term training, will also be extended to the new independent states this year, supported by funding under the Emerging Democracies provisions of the 1990 Farm Bill.

DIFFERENCES IN FOOD PRODUCTION AND FOOD CONSUMPTION AMONG THE REPUBLICS OF THE FORMER SOVIET UNION

By Barbara S. Severin *

CONTENTS

SUMMARY

With the breakup of the former Soviet Union into 15 new states, the availability of food has become tremendously important to their leaders, eager to defend their newly won political powers and fearful of consumer unrest. Seven former republics—Ukraine, Byelarus, Kazakhstan, Moldova, Estonia, Latvia, and Lithuania—have

---

* Barbara S. Severin is a Senior Analyst with the Office of Slavic and Eurasian Analysis, Central Intelligence Agency.

(514)

accounted for larger shares of the former union's food production in recent years than they have of its population. Of these, Ukraine is by far the biggest producer of food per capita, producing more meat, milk, grain, and vegetables than it consumes and exporting these products to its former Union partners. The other food exporters lacked Ukraine's broad production capabilities, but their surplus output of some types of food provides them with the wherewithal for acquiring oil, gas, and industrial inputs via trade with other republics. Russia has been the largest food producer in absolute terms, but its need to import substantial amounts of food is one of its few vulnerabilities relative to the other former republics. Uzbekistan, Turkmenistan, and Tajikistan—the lowest consumers of food per capita of the former Soviet republics—are also the most dependent on imports for the food they consume. As such, they are the most at risk nutritionally as the former republics assert their independence.

The following discussion will briefly review differences among the various former republics in food production, in privatization as it relates to agricultural production, in food consumption, and in food processing and distribution, and it will discuss some of the implications of these differences. It will not address questions of potential republic self-sufficiency in food availability based on natural resources, either through production possibilities such as cropping pattern changes or through trade—with reciprocal products or in hard currency. In a world of highly economically interdependent states, as Schroeder so cogently points out: "The question of economic viability centers much less on the self-sufficiency of an economic territory than it does on the ability of that territory's population to perform within the larger global economy." [1]

At a cost—perhaps very high—any new nation-state can survive. The potential for doing so with trade and foreign investment is limited only by that nation-state's own policies and stability.

FOOD SUPPLIES: A NEAR-TERM AND LONG-TERM PROBLEM

After peaking in 1989, agricultural output in the former Soviet Union declined and food shortages, already widespread, worsened the country's chronic food-supply problem. Moreover, the gradual disintegration of the traditional centrally directed food distribution system meant that formerly favored areas, such as large industrial cities, bore the brunt of the production downturn while areas producing farm products benefited. Officials of many agricultural areas instituted bans against exports of foodstuffs to other regions to provide more abundant supplies for their constituents.

For several decades, providing the public with more and better food supplies had been a key goal of successive regimes, in part because the availability and quality of food have long been perceived as the most important determinants of living standards. [2] With the gradual breakup of the Union in 1991, availability of food became tremendously important to republic leaders, eager to defend their

---

[1] Schroeder, Gertrude E., "On the Economic Viability of New Nation States," *Journal of International Affairs*, Winter, 1992, vol. 45, no. 2, pp. 549–574.
[2] Numerous polls over the past decade have testified to this. For a recent example, see *Moscow News*, no. 38, 1991, p. 5.

newly won political powers and fearful of consumer backlash. Republic and local officials as well as consumers in general began worrying that serious food shortages, perhaps even famine, were likely during the winter. [3] With the aid of a relatively mild winter, stepped-up food imports—both donated and purchased with Western credits—and a massive price liberalization in Russia in January 1992 that was followed to a greater or lesser extent by the other states, the former republics suffered few ill effects throughout the winter of 1991/92. Many consumers used hoarded household stocks, others shifted buying patterns from more expensive meat and dairy products to milk- and grain-based products, the prices of which were still partially controlled. Less favored groups of the population—elderly pensioners, the chronically ill, and larger families with low incomes—may have experienced occasional hunger. There were reports of vitamin deficiencies among children. [4] Nonetheless, few instances of nutrition-related disease were reported. Ensuring reliable and adequate supplies of food for their populations remains one of the major challenges to the various former republics as they assert their political independence and try to overcome their traditional economic interdependence, a challenge that is likely to take years to resolve.

DIFFERENCES IN FOOD PRODUCTION

The 15 former Soviet republics have agricultural production profiles that, in part, reflect the differences in their climate, soil, and other natural resources, but that have also been heavily influenced by the previous regime's strategy for economic development. Only one-quarter of the former union's land mass is suitable for farm operations, and two-thirds of that area is only fit for permanent meadows and pastures. Most of the highly productive farmland is located in a broad band that encompasses most of Ukraine, Kazakhstan, and roughly one-quarter of Russia's oblasts. These are the only areas of the former U.S.S.R. that produce enough grain to meet their needs for food, feed, and seed use.

Even in these areas, agricultural production is constrained by a short growing season in the northern areas and by lack of moisture in the south. Grain production, for example, requires on average a 100-day growing season, which is not generally present north of 55°N. It also requires a minimum of 10 inches annual rainfall, which limits its southern extension in the absence of irrigation. Moreover, weather is subject to rapid, extreme, and damaging fluctuation. Precipitation and temperature vary widely from year to year and seasonal distribution is often unfavorable. In years of adequate rainfall, for example, torrential precipitation may greatly damage crops. Droughts occur over wide areas in two out of every five years on average. [5]

The impact of regional differences in soil and climate on production was magnified over the years by an economic development

---

[3] *Pravda*, 15 August 1991, p. 1, Moscow, Russian television network, 13 August 1991.
[4] *Argumenty i fakti*, no. 43, November 1991, p. 5.
[5] Based on CIA, *USSR Agriculture Atlas*, Washington, D. C., December 1974, CIA/ER 76-10577 U; CIA, *USSR: The Impact of Recent Climate Change on Grain Production*, Washington, D. C., October 1976, and World Meteorological Organization temperature and precipitation data.

strategy that placed little emphasis on efficiency and did not encourage republics and regions to grow sufficient food to provide for their residents. Rather, they were to specialize in production of industrial goods or certain key commodities and to depend on a complex set of trading relationships for food supplies. In Central Asia, for example, central planners stressed the need to produce cotton rather than food crops. [6]

As a result of this combination of geographic and policy factors, a substantial interdependence among the former republics developed, particularly with respect to food. During the period of the 1986–90 five-year plan, four republics and the three Baltic states generally accounted for a larger share of the former union's food production than they did of its population (see Table 1). Of these seven, however, only Ukraine exported all the major types of food to other republics, while the other leading food producers all required some imports to maintain their current diets (see Table 2). Estonia, Latvia, Lithuania, and Byelarus, for example, produced more food overall than they consumed, but depended on feedstuffs brought in from other republics or the West to support their high-value livestock production. These republics, in turn, shipped livestock products to other parts of the country.

Meanwhile, the Central Asian republics (excluding Kazakhstan), Georgia, Armenia, Azerbaijan, and vast areas of Russia produced far less grain and other foods than they consumed. Turkmenistan, Uzbekistan, Tajikistan, and Kyrgyzstan were also net importers of food, but, together with Moldova, produced one-fifth of the country's vegetables, one-quarter of its fruit, and over half of its grapes.

DIFFERENCES IN PRIVATIZATION

To some extent, these interrepublic differences in food production are changing as the planned economy gives way to the market. Privatization, in particular, is a powerful force for change. To date, however, the former republics also differ substantially among themselves in the extent to which food production is privatized. During 1986–91 about three-quarters of the former Soviet Union's agricultural output was produced on *sovkhozy* (state farms), *kolkhozy* (collective farms), and other state enterprises that had developed their own farms, primarily to supply their cafeterias and dining rooms. The remaining quarter came largely from the traditional private plots in rural areas, which averaged less than 1 acre in size, and from small garden plots in suburban areas, which averaged less than one-third of an acre. Over the past 5 years the number of garden plots has more than doubled. In 1990 nearly one-quarter of urban families had plots, and, according to official Soviet statistics, produced an estimated 3 million tons of potatoes, about 1 million tons of other vegetables, and over 500 thousand tons of fruit. [7] These were important supplements for urban diets.

---

[6] See, for example, Gertrude E. Schroeder, "Economic Relations Among the Soviet Republics," in Michael Claudon and Tamar Gutner, eds., *Investing in Reform: Doing Business in a Changing Soviet Union,* New York, New York University Press, 1991, pp. 19–38.

[7] Derived from *Narkhoz 1990,* p. 484 and *Statisticheskiy Bulletin,* no. 8, 1991, Goskomstat, Moscow.

TABLE 1. Shares of Food Production and Population in the Republics of the Former Soviet Union, 1986–90, Various Years.

(Percent)

Republic	Food Production [a]			Population [b]
	Total	Crops	Livestock products [c]	1 July 1988
Russia	49.2	46.5	50.9	51.5
Ukraine	24.0	26.1	22.7	18.1
Byelarus	6.4	7.0	6.1	3.6
Moldova	2.0	2.7	1.6	1.5
Kazakhstan	6.5	6.8	6.3	5.8
Kyrgyzstan	0.9	0.8	1.0	1.5
Tajikistan	0.6	0.6	0.6	1.8
Turkmenistan	0.4	0.3	0.4	1.2
Uzbekistan	2.3	2.2	2.3	6.8
Armenia	0.6	0.6	0.6	1.2
Azerbaijan	1.3	1.8	1.0	2.4
Georgia	1.1	1.4	0.9	1.9
Estonia	1.0	0.7	1.1	0.6
Latvia	1.5	1.0	1.8	1.0
Lithuania	2.3	1.6	2.8	1.3
Total	100.0	100.0	100.0	100.0

Sources: *Narodnoye khozyaystvo SSSR v 1990 g* and earlier editions, similar compilations published annually in the respective republics, and other official Soviet sources.
Italics indicate that the republic accounted for a larger share of food production than its total population.
[a] Average of 1986–1990, excludes nonfood farm products such as cotton, tobacco, wool, changes in livestock inventories, and seed and waste in grain and potatoes.
[b] Interpolated from data in *Narkhoz 1988*, p. 19, and *Narkhoz 1987*, p. 344.
[c] Includes feed used to produce product.

The average area and importance of private plots, both rural and urban, varied greatly among the republics (see Table 3). In Georgia, for example, private agriculture accounted for a large share of sown area and output, in part because collectivization was merely a formality for the numerous farms located in mountainous and remote areas. Private agriculture also accounted for a larger than average share of output in republics such as Ukraine and Byelarus, where the fertility of the soil and other growing conditions are conducive to production of vegetables, fruit, berries, and other crops that lend themselves to small-scale cultivation. In Turkmenistan, private agriculture had a low share of sown area but a surprisingly large share of output, which reflected the importance of grazing animals to the private farming sector.

In addition to these traditional types of private plots, beginning in 1989, the private sector in agriculture began to include a new form of production, the "peasant" or "farmer's" farm. These are independent farms operated by an individual, a family, or another small group to produce, process, and sell agricultural products. A peasant farmer has possession of his farm for life and can bequeath

TABLE 2. Surpluses or Deficits in the Supply of Selected Foods in the Republics of the Former Soviet Union, 1986–90.

Republic	Meat	Milk (including Butter)	Grain	Potatoes	Vegetables
Russia	−	−	−	−	−
Ukraine	+	+	+	+	+
Byelarus	+	+	−	+	+
Kazakhstan	+	+	+	even	−
Moldova	+	+	−	−	+
Armenia	−	−	−	+	+
Azerbaijan	−	−	−	−	+
Georgia	−	−	−	−	+
Kyrgyzstan	even	−	−	−	+
Tajikistan	−	−	−	even	−
Turkmenistan	−	−	−	−	−
Uzbekistan	−	−	−	−	+
Estonia	+	+	−	+	−
Latvia	+	+	−	+	−
Lithuania	+	+	−	+	even

Sources: Same as Table 1.
Notes: Based on official Soviet statistics from the annual republic yearbooks on quantities produced and consumed during 1986–90. Grain and potato statistics are adjusted for seed, feed, and waste. Pluses indicate that an area produces more than sufficient quantities based on historical data for consumption. Minuses indicate that an area produces less.

it to his heirs so long as it remains in agricultural use. By mid-1991, Soviet officials indicated that there were nearly 70,000 of these farms, occupying nearly four million acres. [8] Those in Kazakhstan and Kyrgyzstan—which concentrate primarily on pasturing cattle and sheep—were by far the largest, averaging nearly 1,000 acres and 400 acres respectively. Those in Georgia and Armenia, averaging less than one hectare, were the smallest. The number of peasant farms was increasing particularly rapidly in Russia and Uzbekistan, while between spring and December 1991, Armenia reportedly had transferred roughly 70 percent of its crop land and almost all vineyards and orchards from collective to private holdings. [9] As a result, almost no state and collective farms now operate in Armenia. By the end of 1991, the total number had increased to more than 200,000 peasant farms. [10]

Roughly three-quarters of peasant farms specialized in production of meat, milk, and eggs, while the remaining quarter produced only crops such as potatoes, other vegetables, and feedstuffs. [11] Although peasant farms produced too little to be reported in official

---

[8] *Glasnost'*, no. 41, 1991, p. 4, and *Goskomstat* press release no. 195, 8 July 1991.
[9] *Pravda*, 24 December 1991, p. 2.
[10] *APK: Ekonomika, upravleniye*, no. 1, 1992, p. 8.
[11] Interfax quoted by Grey and Markish in *Economies in Transition*, vol. 5, no. 1, 1992, p. 8.

TABLE 3. Measures of Private Agriculture by Republic of the
Former Soviet Union, 1986–88, Various Years.

Republic	Percent of Total Sown Area [a]	Percent of Total Output [b]
Russia	1.9	21.4
Ukraine	6.0	26.0
Byelorussia	7.4	26.0
Moldova	6.8	16.7
Kazakhstan	0.4	24.0
Kyrgyzstan	3.6	24.1
Tajikistan	3.5	23.1
Turkmenistan	0.3	19.2
Uzbekistan	2.9	22.0
Armenia	5.9	35.7
Azerbaijan	2.0	33.3
Georgia	12.0	45.4
Estonia	4.7	22.2
Latvia	4.7	24.1
Lithuania	9.4	28.6
Total	100.0	100.0

Sources: Same as Table 1.
[a] From republic statistical handbooks. Data for Lithuania are for 1986; data for Estonia and Uzbekistan are for 1988; and data for all other republics are for 1987. In 1990, area in private production for the entire country increased to 3.0 percent (*Narkhoz* 1990, p. 467). Data for the individual republics are not yet available.
[b] Annual average output for the 1986–88 period calculated from official data on production, expressed in 1983 prices. The share in 1988-90 increased slightly to 24.8 percent (*Narkhoz* 1990, p. 458). Data for all the individual republics are not yet available.

totals, anecdotal comments and survey results indicate that their productivity is higher than that on state and collective farms. [12] To judge from data on their number and size alone, peasant farms could have easily added close to 2 percent to total agricultural production in 1991. According to a Novosti newscast, their share in Russia was about 1 percent, and the 1991 report on economic results estimated that peasant farms produced 0.3 percent of total meat and milk output. [13]

Privatization—particularly the development of private farms—is now occurring at different rates in the former republics, with Armenia and Russia in the lead. In an effort to spur more rapid land reform in Russia, President Boris Yel'tsin issued a spate of decrees in late December 1991 ordering state and collective farms to reorganize into new forms and to give land to those who want to

---

[12] See, for example, *Pravda*, 24 December 1991, p. 2, for the effects in Armenia.
[13] *Novosti*, 3 February 1992.

become private farmers. [14] The move to reorganize state and collective farms is still in its early stages. Russian Agriculture Minister Khlystun told the People's Congress on 7 April 1992 that between January and March 3,600 of Russia's 24,000 profitable state and collective farms had reorganized: 390 into associations of private farms, over 2,000 into joint stock companies, and others into cooperatives. [15] At that time, the number of private farms had increased by 50 percent to 80,000. A few days earlier, parliament head Ruslan Khasbulatov was somewhat less optimistic at Russia's Supreme Soviet meeting, pointing out that some 2,700 Russian private farmers had given up their farms, undoubtedly because of obstruction on the part of local officials and the difficulties of acquiring needed inputs such as fuel and equipment, seed, and agrochemicals. [16] Nonetheless, in mid-May, *Izvestiya* reported that a total of 120,000 peasant farms—occupying nearly 5 million hectares or 2 percent of agricultural land—were in existence. [17] The goal of setting up 150,000 such farms by the end of 1992 is within reach. [18]

Land reform and the development of peasant farms are proceeding at a slower pace in all the other former republics. In the Baltic states the number of private farms is going more slowly than initially expected, partly because of complications associated with verifying ownership documents, but also because of the costs of setting up private farms. [19] In Lithuania, many workers and managers on state and collective farms sharply opposed breaking up existing farms. [20] In March Ukraine passed a decree aimed at speeding up land reform. [21] The decree specified a time table for completing land reform by 1995. Other republics have somewhat tighter deadlines, but all, even Russia, are facing serious difficulties in implementing their plans. [22] Kazakhstan, which does not include land ownership in its economic privatization program although it recognizes the validity of long-term leases and heritability, may face even more difficulties than the others. [23] Nonetheless, and despite problems with inputs, bureaucratic resistance, and so on, early returns indicate that productivity on private farms is sharply higher than it had been in the "socialized" sector. For example, in 1991 tomato yields on Armenian private farms were double the traditional yield, and milk yields on Russian private farms were 30–40 percent higher. [24]

DIFFERENCES IN FOOD CONSUMPTION

Just as the amounts and composition of agricultural production differ greatly from republic to republic, there also are interrepublic

---

[14] Resolution "On Procedure for Reorganization of Kolkhozes and Sovkhozes," signed on 29 December 1991 and published in *Sel'skaya zhizn'*, 7 January 1992. Decree "Land Reform Implementation," signed on 27 December 1991 and published in *RIA Official News*, 28 December 1991.
[15] Radio Rossii, 7 April 1992.
[16] Moscow TV, 2 April 1992.
[17] *Izvestiya*, 20 May 1992, p. 2.
[18] Moscow radio, 2 February 1992.
[19] *Ekho Litvy*, 4 December 1991, p. 3.
[20] *Pravda*, 24 May 1991, p. 1.
[21] *Holos Ukrayiny*, 24 March 1992, p. 14.
[22] *Rossiyskaya gazeta*, 1 April 1992, p. 1, outlines some of the abuses in Russia.
[23] *Kazakhstanskaya pravda*, 17 September 1991, p. 2.
[24] *Izvestiya*, 2 October 1991, p. 1.

differences in consumption. These result both from differences in the availability of food in local outlets and from differences in income. Even official Soviet statistics, which Western scholars have criticized as incomplete and flawed, show substantial differences in average consumption of food (see Table 4). In 1990, the latest year for which complete official data on all the republics are available, average reported per capita food consumption in the U.S.S.R. ranged from a high of over 3,500 calories per day in Ukraine, Bye-larus, and Moldova to a low of about 2,700 calories in Azerbaijan and Tajikistan, and about 2,800 in Turkmenistan and Uzbekistan. Starch-staple ratios—a quality measure based on the share of calories from potatoes and grain-based products—ranged from about 30 percent in Estonia (comparable to the United States), to roughly 40 percent in Russia, Ukraine, Byelarus, Lithuania, and Latvia, to over 50 percent in Uzbekistan, Georgia, Azerbaijan, and Turkmenistan, and nearly 60 percent in Tajikistan. Reported starch-staple ratios in the republics are generally inversely related to differences in average per capita income.[25] With increasing income, consumers shift their food spending from less expensive starchy foods to higher priced meats, dairy products, vegetables, and fruits to the extent they are available.

TABLE 4. Official Indicators of Dietary Quality in the Republics of the Former Soviet Union, 1980 and 1990.

Republic	Calories per Day [a]		Starch-Staple Ratio [b] (Percent)	
	1980	1990	1980	1990
Russia	3,215	3,355	42.5	38.1
Ukraine	3,485	3,614	45.2	42.2
Byelarus	3,470	3,585	47.5	40.9
Moldova	3,390	3,575	51.5	46.9
Kazakhstan	3,055	3,295	48.9	45.0
Kyrgyzstan	2,615	2,955	55.6	47.0
Tajikistan	2,740	2,695	60.9	58.5
Turkmenistan	2,695	2,840	57.0	54.3
Uzbekistan	2,760	2,835	60.0	56.2
Armenia	2,925	2,930	46.9	43.6
Azerbaijan	2,730	2,635	54.8	53.8
Georgia	3,285	3,150	55.0	55.0
Estonia	3,310	3,060	33.3	29.2
Latvia	3,270	3,390	37.1	35.6
Lithuania	3,290	3,495	39.3	37.3

Sources: Same as Table 1.
[a] Based on official statistics on consumption from *Torgovlya SSSR*, Moscow, 1989, pp. 24–25, and *Vestnik statistiki*, no. 10, 1991, pp. 54–56, converted to calories using coefficients developed by the U.S. Department of Agriculture.
[b] Percentage of calories derived from potatoes and grain products.

[25] Well over half the households in Tajikistan, Uzbekistan, Kyrgyzstan, Turkmenistan, and Azerbaijan had monthly per capita incomes of less than 100 rubles in 1988 compared with about one-quarter of all households in the U.S.S.R., while only 8 percent of households in Estonia had such low incomes. IMF, *A Study of the Soviet Economy*, vol. 2, p. 203, Paris, 1991.

Net farm output dropped roughly 8 percent in 1991. That drop, combined with the country's increasing inability to purchase foodstuffs abroad and the disarray throughout the republics in the traditional food production and distribution system, raised fears among the citizenship and in the West of imminent hunger and even raised the spector of famine. In the event, however, substantial increases in imports of products such as meat and soy oil (largely with Western credits) eased the impact. Per capita consumption (in terms of calories) on average dropped by only 5 percent while the starch-staple ratio increased by roughly the same percentage. [26] Per capita consumption of nearly all foodstuffs except potatoes and grain-based products declined. Meat consumption fell by about 8 percent to its lowest level since 1984 and sugar consumption was down by 7 percent. Even with these declines, *average* food consumption remains well above that in many other developed countries and roughly 20 percent above the average world level as calculated by the Food and Agricultural Organization of the United Nations. [27] Some of the decline in livestock product consumption arose from the April 1991 restructuring of retail prices, but more of it undoubtedly occurred in the second half of the year as the drop in farm output began to affect food supplies. [28] For example, survey data indicate that consumption of livestock products in the Transcaucasus republics had fallen by as much as 40 percent by midyear. [29]

Little data on 1991 consumption of food products in the various republics had been published by mid-1992. Clearly, however, republics that were major producers of farm products bore less of the brunt of the production shortfall. Protectionist measures played a role in improving the food situation in some areas while worsening it in others. Republic officials used their newfound authority to impose restrictions on the outflow of local products in short supply. Trade wars proliferated and became increasingly localized. In Siberia, for example, district governments prohibited export of food to other Siberian districts and established cordons to enforce the bans. [30] By mid-1991 nearly every republic had instituted some sort of control on shipment of foodstuffs beyond its border. Major cities, traditionally dependent on centrally supplied stocks for maintaining retail food sales, suffered particularly. Consumption of livestock products in cities such as Moscow, Yekaterinburg, and St. Petersburg dropped by some 15 to 30 percent. [31] Scattered data indicate that Kyrgyzstan, Tajikistan, and Azerbaijan, where meat consumption already was well below average, suffered the sharpest drop-off in meat consumption while Moldova and Ukraine had the largest decline in per capita milk consumption. [32]

In January 1992, most wholesale and retail prices for foodstuffs were freed in the 11 former republics that now constitute the Com-

[26] Calculated primarily from data in *Ekonomika stran chlenov sodruzhestvo nezavisimikh gosudarstv v 1991*, Moscow, 1992, p. 59.
[27] FAO *Production Yearbook 1989*, vol. 43, Rome, 1990, p. 106.
[28] *Vestnik statistiki*, no. 12, 1991, p. 13.
[29] *Ibid.*, p. 14.
[30] A prime example of this was reported in *Izvestiya*, 5 August 1991, p. 2.
[31] op. cit., *Vest. stat.*, no. 12, 1991, p. 15.
[32] op. cit., *Ekonomika stran*, p. 59.

monwealth of Independent States (CIS). These prices had been largely freed in the Baltic republics during the last half of 1991.[33] Again Russia took the initial action, effectively forcing the other former republics to go along or face the prospect of their goods flowing to Russia at the same time as Russians increasingly shopped across borders. With few subsidies remaining on foodstuffs, state-store food prices rose dramatically.[34] Consequently, consumers reduced purchases of some foods and stopped buying others entirely. State stores found previously scarce foods going unsold. Trade workers did not react by cutting prices to stimulate sales but returned goods to producers and cut orders for future deliveries. As unsold inventories began to accumulate, both state stores and food processors in Russia realized that they had priced themselves out of the market, and prices—although remaining high—began to decline. Some other former republics, however, reinstituted price ceilings on more products. These factors, combined with the continuing failure to observe interrepublic trade agreements, indicate that differences in the amounts and composition of foods consumed in the former republics are likely to be greater in 1992 than in 1991.

DIFFERENCES IN FOOD PROCESSING AND INTERREGIONAL TRADE

Food processing is an important industry in all the republics, but it is concentrated particularly in southern Russia, Ukraine, Moldova, and the Caucasus, which grow most of the raw material for producing sugar, vegetable oil, canned fruits, vegetables, and juices. Small-scale processing is carried out in tens of thousands of shops managed by farms across the country, but over three-quarters of industrial food processing is done in centralized large enterprises that are poorly equipped and are generally located in or near larger cites. Russia, for example, with about half the population of the 15 former republics, has about 60 percent of total industrial food-processing plants.[35] As a result of this concentration of production near large urban areas, long hauls of raw materials from farms to processors frequently occur with huge waste along the way.

In 1991 increasing republic autonomy compounded the difficulties of moving processed farm products to consumers. Ukraine's advantageous position in production and processing of sugar combined with its desire to supply local residents first, for example, exacerbated shortages in other republics. A former Russian Minister of Agriculture commented that his republic, which consumes 7.5 million tons of sugar annually, relies on Ukraine for about 15 percent of its needs.[36] Similarly, Central Asia's refusal to honor cotton-supply agreements with Russia led to a near shut-down of Russia's major textile processing center in Ivanovo in early 1992.[37]

[33] The maintenance of low, stable, subsidized food prices had long been a major drain on the state budget, requiring about 100 billion rubles in 1990. These prices had also stimulated demand for these foods far beyond the ability of the agricultural sector to fill. Severin, Barbara, "Solving the Soviet Livestock Feed Dilemma," in *Gorbachev's Economic Plans*, Joint Economic Committee, Washington, D. C., November 1987, pp. 45–61.
[34] *Delovoy mir*, no. 56, 21 March 1992, p. 6.
[35] Based on data in republic statistical handbooks.
[36] Radio Rossii, 5 September 1991.
[37] *Pravda*, 7 May 1992, p. 2, and Teleradiokompaniya Ostankino, 12 May 1992.

Although Central Asia produces most of the cotton used in the former republics, only preliminary processing is done there. Most of the intermediate and final processing is done in Russia, which in turn sent finished goods to the Central Asians.

Overall, for all the problems of the food processing and food distribution systems, interregional trade has historically provided residents of the less agriculturally favored republics and regions with substantial supplements to local food production. The Far East region of Russia, for example, imports more than one-half of the meat it consumes, and the Transcaucasian and Central Asian republics (except for Kyrgyzstan and Kazakhstan) import more than one-third of the meat they consume. [38] Meanwhile, vegetables, fruit, and grapes from the southern republics provide welcome variety in the diets of the rest of the country as well as raw material for the processing industry.

SHORT-TERM IMPLICATIONS

Now that the 15 former Soviet republics have become independent and interrepublic trade in foodstuffs has essentially fallen by about half, several republics such as Ukraine and Kazakhstan and parts of Russia face the happy prospect of improving food availability in terms of both quality and quantity. [39] Others, however, such as Tajikistan, Azerbaijan, Turkmenistan, and Armenia, face the dismal prospect of further declines in the near-term unless trade relations improve substantially and soon. Indeed, the Central Asian countries with already low per capita consumption may be hit with increasing malnutrition and all its sad consequences for the population's health and productivity. There are a few encouraging signs that interrepublic trade is beginning to recover and market factors are beginning to play a role in all the former republics. Russia and Lithuania have signed an agreement to exchange oil and meat. Kazakhstan has promised grain to Uzbekistan. In some regions, notably Central Asia, production patterns are already changing in ways that can help improve local food supplies. In Russia, farms are planting more sugar beets and sunflower seed. This should help increase republic supplies of sugar and vegetable oil products that are currently in short supply there. Moreover, weather conditions over the winter and into mid-1992 suggest that overall farm production of foodstuffs in all the new countries should increase this year. More of this year's production should be available to consumers as Western assistance with food processing, handling, and distribution is brought into play and chronically high waste and losses are reduced. Higher prices—both wholesale and retail—should encourage more careful handling. Finally, high retail prices have already reduced demand and curtailed waste as households have become more thrifty in their use of foodstuffs.

---

[38] Calculated by the author and based on official statistics on production and consumption within each republic and, in the case of Russia, each oblast.

[39] Based on 9-month interrepublic trade data, *Ekonomika i zhizn'*, no. 43, October 1991, p. 8.

APPENDIX A. FARM OUTPUT OF THE REPUBLICS

TABLE A-1. Russia: Selected Components of Farm Output, 1970–90.

Thousand Tons

Component	1970	1975	1980	1981	1982	1983	1984	1985	1986	1987	1988	1989	1990
Total Grain													
Bunker Weight	113,500.0	77,500.0	105,122.0	78,818.0	105,155.0	111,485.0	92,431.0	106,593.0	117,967.0	109,048.0	102,800.0	113,200.0	128,241.0
Clean Weight	NA	NA	97,300.0	NA	NA	NA	NA	98,600.0	107,500.0	98,600.0	93,700.0	104,800.0	116,700.0
Potatoes	53,993.0	51,102.0	36,971.0	32,108.0	40,665.0	42,094.0	43,421.0	33,840.0	43,076.0	38,028.0	33,692.0	33,760.0	30,848.0
Vegetables	10,066.0	10,600.0	11,101.0	11,104.0	12,662.0	12,813.0	12,940.0	11,131.0	11,729.0	11,155.0	11,481.0	11,154.0	10,328.0
Fruit, Berries and Grapes	3,045.0	3,293.0	2,884.0	3,518.0	3,314.0	3,972.0	3,963.0	3,400.0	3,709.0	3,086.0	3,327.0	3,322.0	2,978.0
Sugar Beets	23,903.0	19,226.0	24,130.0	16,215.0	23,000.0	26,772.0	27,972.0	31,450.0	29,200.0	34,156.0	32,824.0	37,378.0	31,091.0
Sunflower Seeds	3,066.0	2,192.0	1,995.0	2,031.0	2,493.0	2,552.0	1,942.0	2,621.0	2,363.0	3,067.0	2,958.0	3,789.0	3,427.0
Soybeans	595.0	766.0	441.0	394.0	429.0	424.0	349.0	357.0	575.0	541.0	675.0	738.0	700.0
Other Oil Crops	139.0	42.0	164.0	75.0	178.0	124.0	109.0	122.0	162.0	192.0	367.0	373.0	573.0
Total Oil Crops	3,800.0	3,000.0	2,600.0	2,500.0	3,100.0	3,100.0	2,400.0	3,100.0	3,100.0	3,800.0	4,000.0	4,900.0	4,700.0
Beef and Veal	2,883.0	3,341.0	3,274.0	3,240.0	3,243.0	3,488.0	3,577.0	3,575.0	3,756.0	3,991.0	4,150.0	4,256.0	4,329.0
Pork	2,195.0	2,810.0	2,579.0	2,600.0	2,686.0	2,955.0	3,033.0	2,978.0	3,093.0	3,264.0	3,399.0	3,499.0	3,480.0
Mutton and Kid	449.0	459.0	338.0	349.0	325.0	327.0	344.0	321.0	345.0	346.0	371.0	385.0	395.0
Poultry	554.0	787.0	1,134.0	1,190.0	1,299.0	1,420.0	1,483.0	1,532.0	1,621.0	1,712.0	1,776.0	1,831.0	1,801.0
Other Meat	132.0	151.0	102.0	96.0	94.0	737.0	104.0	81.0	101.0	119.0	117.0	111.0	107.0
Total Meat	6,213.0	7,548.0	7,427.0	7,475.0	7,647.0	8,927.0	8,541.0	8,487.0	8,916.0	9,432.0	9,813.0	10,082.0	10,112.0
Milk	45,400.0	48,100.0	46,823.0	45,500.0	47,400.0	50,200.0	50,400.0	50,169.0	52,217.0	52,880.0	54,535.0	55,742.0	55,715.0
Eggs (Million Eggs)	23,600.0	33,400.0	39,539.0	41,300.0	42,000.0	43,600.0	44,200.0	44,277.0	46,195.0	47,447.0	49,144.0	49,024.0	47,470.0
Honey	142.0	111.0	110.0	NA	NA	NA	NA	102.0	98.2	105.0	NA	NA	NA

Source: *Narodnoye khozyaystvo SSSR v 1990 g* and earlier editions, similar compilations published annually in the respective republics, and other official sources.
Excludes non-edible farm products such as cotton, tobacco, tea, and changes in livestock inventories.
NA—Not available.

TABLE A-2. Ukraine: Selected Components of Farm Output, 1970–90.

Thousand Tons

Component	1970	1975	1980	1981	1982	1983	1984	1985	1986	1987	1988	1989	1990
Total Grain													
Bunker Weight	36,391.8	33,803.0	38,100.0	36,056.0	41,905.0	36,488.0	41,711.0	40,495.0	43,063.0	50,183.0	47,388.0	53,186.0	53,125.0
Clean Weight	NA	NA	36,600.0	NA	NA	NA	NA	38,900.0	41,506.0	47,978.0	45,369.0	51,212.0	51,009.0
Potatoes	19,727.1	16,453.2	13,133.0	19,025.0	20,064.0	20,730.0	19,931.0	20,315.0	21,410.0	18,863.0	13,510.0	19,308.0	16,732.0
Vegetables	5,808.1	6,038.0	7,186.0	6,481.0	7,653.0	7,038.0	8,329.0	7,383.0	7,731.0	8,111.0	7,292.0	7,443.0	6,666.0
Fruit, Berries and Grapes	3,254.0	3,697.0	3,139.0	3,940.0	4,646.0	4,131.0	4,206.0	3,851.0	4,060.0	2,905.0	2,887.0	3,289.0	3,738.0
Sugar Beets	46,308.8	38,342.2	48,841.0	36,612.0	42,337.0	47,739.0	49,170.0	43,622.0	42,920.0	49,702.0	48,205.0	51,917.0	44,265.0
Sunflower Seeds	2,654.0	2,384.8	2,257.0	2,317.0	2,523.0	2,135.0	2,174.0	2,288.0	2,561.0	2,716.0	2,774.0	2,885.0	2,725.0
Soybeans	0.0	0.0	0.0	80.1	80.1	80.1	80.1	0.0	67.7	84.8	101.3	123.8	99.3
Other Oil Crops	0.0	0.0	0.0	0.0	0.0	0.0	0.0	0.0	68.3	107.2	142.7	139.2	144.7
Total Oil Crops	2,654.0	2,384.8	2,257.0	2,397.1	2,603.1	2,215.1	2,254.1	2,288.0	2,697.0	2,908.0	3,018.0	3,148.0	2,969.0
Beef and Veal	1,105.0	1,353.0	1,556.0	1,545.0	1,542.0	1,587.0	1,632.0	1,740.0	1,879.0	1,982.0	2,019.0	2,011.0	1,986.0
Pork	1,331.0	1,578.0	1,315.0	1,316.0	1,319.0	1,408.0	1,433.0	1,435.0	1,464.0	1,469.0	1,576.0	1,595.0	1,576.0
Mutton and Kid	43.0	41.0	29.0	29.0	28.0	33.0	35.0	35.0	38.0	42.0	44.0	44.0	46.0
Poultry	312.0	436.0	522.0	545.0	572.0	583.0	580.0	636.0	664.0	673.0	704.0	731.0	708.0
Other Meat	59.0	108.0	78.0	78.0	65.0	66.0	67.0	72.0	73.0	76.0	52.0	49.0	42.0
Total Meat	2,850.0	3,516.0	3,500.0	3,513.0	3,526.0	3,677.0	3,747.0	3,918.0	4,118.0	4,242.0	4,395.0	4,430.0	4,358.0
Milk	18,712.0	21,287.0	21,112.0	20,613.0	20,598.0	22,253.0	22,808.0	23,039.0	23,554.0	23,655.0	24,200.0	24,377.0	24,508.0
Eggs (Million Eggs)	9,202.0	12,429.0	14,606.0	15,252.0	15,561.0	16,122.0	16,344.0	16,645.0	17,297.0	17,425.0	17,672.0	17,393.0	16,287.0
Honey	35.6	28.5	33.4	NA	NA	NA	NA	43.7	45.8	47.6	NA	NA	NA

Sources: Same as Table A-1.
Excludes non-edible farm products such as cotton, tobacco, tea, and changes in livestock inventories.
NA—Not available.

TABLE A-3. Byelarus: Selected Components of Farm Output, 1970–90.

Thousand Tons

Component	1970	1975	1980	1981	1982	1983	1984	1985	1986	1987	1988	1989	1990
Total Grain													
Bunker Weight	4,239.5	5,121.0	5,009.0	5,812.0	5,516.0	5,796.0	7,230.0	6,754.0	7,041.0	9,281.0	6,922.0	8,700.0	8,235.0
Clean Weight	NA	NA	4,100.0	NA	NA	NA	NA	5,800.0	6,050.0	7,804.0	5,906.0	7,384.0	7,035.0
Potatoes	13,234.4	12,735.9	9,333.0	13,430.0	8,829.0	0.0	12,917.0	10,553.0	13,414.0	11,755.0	7,708.0	11,097.0	8,591.0
Vegetables	855.2	711.0	733.0	868.0	876.0	839.0	956.0	828.0	969.0	926.5	809.0	894.0	749.0
Fruit, Berries and Grapes	438.6	693.0	414.0	694.0	573.5	432.1	516.2	766.0	833.0	180.0	261.0	704.0	373.0
Sugar Beets	1,030.2	1,134.6	1,122.0	1,412.0	1,093.0	1,400.0	1,441.0	1,568.0	1,609.0	1,485.0	1,579.0	1,810.0	1,479.0
Sunflower Seeds	0.0	0.0	0.0	0.0	0.0	0.0	0.0	0.0	0.0	0.0	0.0	0.0	0.0
Soybeans	0.0	0.0	0.0	0.0	0.0	0.0	0.0	0.0	0.0	0.0	0.0	0.0	0.0
Other Oil Crops	0.0	0.0	0.0	0.0	0.0	0.0	0.0	0.0	0.0	0.0	0.0	0.0	0.0
Total Oil Crops	0.0	0.0	0.0	0.0	0.0	0.0	0.0	0.0	0.0	0.0	0.0	0.0	0.0
Beef and Veal	324.6	407.1	411.0	NA	NA	NA	430.7	470.0	505.0	538.0	572.9	NA	NA
Pork	310.6	361.2	350.0	NA	NA	NA	421.1	424.0	418.0	433.0	457.9	NA	NA
Mutton and Kid	8.9	6.0	4.0	NA	NA	NA	7.1	8.0	8.0	9.0	8.9	NA	NA
Poultry	34.5	58.9	87.0	NA	NA	NA	119.0	124.0	128.0	130.0	133.2	NA	NA
Other Meat	5.9	9.1	5.0	841.0	875.0	933.0	6.1	6.0	6.0	7.0	7.2	1,195.0	1,181.0
Total Meat	684.5	842.3	857.0	841.0	875.0	933.0	984.0	1,032.0	1,065.0	1,117.0	1,180.1	1,195.0	1,181.0
Milk	5,263.5	6,108.8	6,105.0	5,821.0	6,075.0	6,300.0	6,575.0	6,759.0	7,002.0	7,254.0	7,460.0	7,419.0	7,457.0
Eggs (Million Eggs)	1,669.2	2,631.2	3,034.0	3,119.0	3,241.0	3,331.0	3,379.0	3,363.0	3,406.0	3,495.0	3,572.0	3,651.0	3,657.0
Honey	4.4	3.6	2.3	NA	NA	NA	NA	3.1	3.6	2.8	NA	NA	NA

Sources: Same as Table A-1.
Excludes non-edible farm products such as cotton, tobacco, tea, and changes in livestock inventories.
NA—Not available.

TABLE A-4. Kazakhstan: Selected Components of Farm Output, 1970–90.

Thousand Tons

Component	1970	1975	1980	1981	1982	1983	1984	1985	1986	1987	1988	1989	1990
Total Grain													
Bunker Weight	22,240.4	12,007.4	27,506.0	23,838.0	19,516.7	23,236.0	15,840.0	24,164.0	28,306.0	27,444.0	22,560.0	19,200.0	30,319.0
Clean Weight	NA	NA	25,900.0	NA	NA	NA	NA	22,700.0	26,562.0	25,721.0	20,970.0	18,797.0	28,488.0
Potatoes	1,892.0	1,728.0	2,239.0	1,684.0	1,895.0	1,908.0	2,078.0	2,197.0	2,137.0	2,066.0	2,260.0	1,784.0	2,324.0
Vegetables	798.0	918.0	1,134.0	1,204.0	1,128.0	1,169.0	1,210.0	1,085.0	1,211.0	1,190.0	1,354.0	1,254.0	1,136.0
Fruit, Berries and Grapes	283.8	283.7	429.0	415.8	462.3	476.6	356.5	202.0	544.0	350.0	369.0	166.0	342.0
Sugar Beets	2,223.0	1,959.4	2,223.0	2,651.0	1,046.0	1,629.0	1,697.0	1,901.0	1,721.0	1,804.0	1,321.0	1,188.0	1,134.0
Sunflower Seeds	78.0	75.0	100.0	94.0	79.0	94.0	108.0	93.0	83.0	117.0	139.0	105.0	141.0
Soybeans	0.0	0.0	0.0	94.0	94.0	94.0	94.0	94.0	34.6	45.2	40.8	32.9	32.9
Other Oil Crops	0.0	0.0	0.0	0.0	0.0	0.0	0.0	0.0	21.4	19.8	36.2	29.1	0.0
Total Oil Crops	78.0	75.0	100.0	188.0	173.0	188.0	202.0	187.0	139.0	182.0	216.0	167.0	230.0
Beef and Veal	424.2	480.1	465.0	537.8	512.6	537.6	536.4	506.0	579.0	632.0	NA	NA	NA
Pork	126.6	206.4	195.0	218.5	184.7	203.5	196.7	185.0	219.0	245.0	NA	NA	NA
Mutton and Kid	272.0	252.1	231.0	224.6	211.2	226.0	233.8	221.0	253.0	258.0	NA	NA	NA
Poultry	41.9	80.3	126.0	133.8	139.0	155.0	158.8	166.0	191.0	197.0	NA	NA	NA
Other Meat	50.7	56.4	52.0	53.3	55.5	54.9	73.3	55.0	58.0	67.0	NA	NA	NA
Total Meat	915.4	1,075.3	1,069.0	1,168.0	1,103.0	1,177.0	1,199.0	1,133.0	1,300.0	1,399.0	1,493.0	1,573.0	1,548.0
Milk	3,932.2	4,045.0	4,597.0	4,652.0	4,511.0	4,582.0	4,635.0	4,763.0	5,040.0	5,185.0	5,321.0	5,563.0	5,642.0
Eggs (Million Eggs)	1,707.6	2,835.0	3,369.0	3,475.0	3,484.0	3,586.0	3,726.0	3,803.0	4,097.0	4,189.0	4,202.0	4,253.0	4,185.0
Honey	5.5	NA	10.9	NA	NA	NA	NA	10.4	11.5	12.8	0.0	0.0	0.0

Sources: Same as Table A-1.
Excludes non-edible farm products such as cotton, tobacco, tea, and changes in livestock inventories.
NA—Not available.

TABLE A-5. Moldova: Selected Components of Farm Output, 1970–90.

Thousand Tons

Component	1970	1975	1980	1981	1982	1983	1984	1985	1986	1987	1988	1989	1990
Total Grain													
Bunker Weight	2,438.0	2,677.0	2,815.0	2,290.0	2,813.0	2,154.0	2,031.0	2,373.0	2,044.0	2,011.0	3,052.0	3,400.0	2,577.0
Clean Weight	NA	NA	2,800.0	NA	NA	NA	NA	2,300.0	1,994.0	1,952.0	2,970.0	3,323.0	2,539.0
Potatoes	297.4	238.0	308.0	329.0	459.0	419.0	377.0	408.0	449.0	304.0	299.0	464.0	295.0
Vegetables	553.4	930.4	1,221.0	1,200.0	1,360.0	1,257.0	1,442.0	1,245.0	1,438.0	1,282.0	1,281.0	1,203.0	1,177.0
Fruit, Berries and Grapes	1,321.0	1,870.0	1,839.0	1,838.0	2,799.0	2,539.0	2,296.0	1,653.0	2,424.0	2,114.0	1,987.0	2,213.0	1,841.0
Sugar Beets	2,816.2	2,549.5	2,726.0	1,696.0	2,325.0	2,424.0	2,941.0	2,365.0	2,413.0	2,155.0	2,270.0	3,612.0	2,374.0
Sunflower Seeds	331.2	318.6	250.0	220.0	233.0	265.0	290.0	244.0	253.0	209.0	269.0	282.0	252.0
Soybeans	0.0	0.0	0.0	11.0	11.0	11.0	11.0	11.0	20.3	37.0	52.7	51.4	23.8
Other Oil Crops	1.0	0.0	0.0	0.0	0.0	0.0	0.0	0.0	0.7	0.0	1.3	-0.4	0.2
Total Oil Crops	332.2	318.6	250.0	231.0	244.0	276.0	301.0	255.0	274.0	246.0	323.0	333.0	276.0
Beef and Veal	NA	NA	86.0	68.5	73.9	82.3	89.5	93.0	103.0	103.0	NA	NA	NA
Pork	NA	NA	139.0	104.7	125.0	129.7	142.3	146.0	155.0	160.0	NA	NA	NA
Mutton and Kid	NA	NA	4.0	3.3	3.0	3.7	4.3	5.0	5.0	5.0	NA	NA	NA
Poultry	NA	NA	44.0	43.4	44.8	48.8	48.9	55.0	60.0	58.0	NA	NA	NA
Other Meat	176.5	230.0	2.0	2.2	1.9	3.2	3.4	4.0	4.0	5.0	339.0	356.0	366.0
Total Meat	176.5	230.0	275.0	222.1	248.6	267.7	288.4	303.0	327.0	331.0	339.0	356.0	366.0
Milk	792.0	1,035.0	1,194.0	1,174.0	1,097.0	1,234.0	1,318.0	1,402.0	1,398.0	1,421.0	1,490.0	1,548.0	1,512.0
Eggs (Million Eggs)	578.2	672.0	874.0	896.0	943.0	979.0	1,012.0	1,075.0	1,118.0	1,116.0	1,169.0	1,154.0	1,129.0
Honey	2.6	2.3	2.8	NA	NA	NA	NA	4.9	4.8	4.1	NA	NA	NA

Sources: Same as Table A-1.
Excludes non-edible farm products such as cotton, tobacco, tea, and changes in livestock inventories.
NA—Not available.

TABLE A-6. Armenia: Selected Components of Farm Output, 1970–90.

Thousand Tons

Component	1970	1975	1980	1981	1982	1983	1984	1985	1986	1987	1988	1989	1990
Total Grain													
Bunker Weight	252.0	296.0	236.0	319.0	253.0	248.0	283.0	284.0	331.0	274.0	374.0	230.0	300.0
Clean Weight	NA	NA	200.0	NA	NA	NA	NA	300.0	311.0	255.0	349.0	180.0	254.0
Potatoes	267.3	190.0	254.0	243.0	309.0	253.0	341.0	306.0	266.0	296.0	207.0	266.0	213.0
Vegetables	279.3	298.6	468.0	469.0	477.0	466.0	554.0	620.0	570.0	571.0	567.0	485.0	485.0
Fruit, Berries and Grapes	375.0	366.3	336.0	485.0	458.9	344.8	468.6	417.0	451.0	316.0	455.0	289.0	289.0
Sugar Beets	89.7	154.0	128.0	154.0	168.0	149.0	154.0	129.0	132.0	105.0	117.0	NA	NA
Mutton and Kid	14.7	14.3	17.0	16.0	17.7	14.8	13.1	15.0	14.0	12.0	0.0	0.0	0.0
Poultry	6.3	9.2	21.0	22.1	23.5	25.8	25.6	26.0	29.0	29.0	0.0	0.0	0.0
Other Meat	0.1	0.3	0.0	0.3	0.5	0.4	0.2	0.0	0.0	0.0	0.0	0.0	0.0
Total Meat	52.2	67.3	96.0	93.4	95.5	100.0	103.2	107.0	113.0	107.0	113.0	105.0	93.0
Beef and Veal	23.4	27.3	38.0	35.7	35.2	35.6	40.3	43.0	45.0	43.0	0.0	0.0	0.0
Pork	7.7	16.2	20.0	19.3	18.6	23.4	24.0	23.0	25.0	23.0	0.0	0.0	0.0
Mutton and Kid	14.7	14.3	17.0	16.0	17.7	14.8	13.1	15.0	14.0	12.0	0.0	0.0	0.0
Poultry	6.3	9.2	21.0	22.1	23.5	25.8	25.6	26.0	29.0	29.0	0.0	0.0	0.0
Other Meat	0.1	0.3	0.0	0.3	0.5	0.4	0.2	0.0	0.0	0.0	0.0	0.0	0.0
Total Meat	52.2	67.3	96.0	93.4	95.5	100.0	103.2	107.0	113.0	107.0	113.0	105.0	93.0
Milk	363.2	410.9	488.0	518.7	550.6	541.3	540.2	546.0	573.0	576.0	566.0	491.0	432.0
Eggs (Million Eggs)	238.4	352.9	467.0	478.4	498.0	546.7	562.3	573.0	609.0	637.0	618.0	561.0	518.0
Honey	1.3	1.8	0.9	NA	NA	NA	NA	0.8	0.8	1.1	0.0	0.0	0.0

Sources: Same as Table A-1.
Excludes non-edible farm products such as cotton, tobacco, tea, and changes in livestock inventories.
NA—Not available.

TABLE A-7. Azerbaijan: Selected Components of Farm Output, 1970–90.

Thousand Tons

Component	1970	1975	1980	1981	1982	1983	1984	1985	1986	1987	1988	1989	1990
Total Grain													
Bunker Weight	723.0	893.0	1,136.6	1,151.0	1,211.0	1,240.0	1,299.0	1,298.1	1,066.1	1,119.1	1,417.3	820.0	1,429.0
Clean Weight	NA	NA	1,100.0	NA	NA	NA	NA	1,200.0	1,024.0	1,073.0	1,356.0	832.0	1,364.0
Potatoes	130.6	88.8	172.0	124.0	184.0	203.0	218.0	220.0	189.0	202.0	165.0	184.0	185.0
Vegetables	409.3	603.8	824.0	850.0	917.0	875.0	940.0	871.0	896.0	855.0	880.0	915.0	856.0
Fruit, Berries and Grapes	508.9	858.1	1,759.0	1,943.0	2,161.0	2,017.0	2,478.0	2,134.0	1,940.0	1,878.0	1,677.0	1,534.0	1,515.0
Sugar Beets	0.0	0.0	0.0	0.0	0.0	0.0	0.0	0.0	0.0	0.0	0.0	0.0	0.0
Sunflower Seeds	0.0	0.0	0.0	0.0	0.0	0.0	0.0	0.0	0.0	0.0	0.0	0.0	0.0
Soybeans	0.0	0.0	0.0	0.0	0.0	0.0	0.0	0.0	0.0	0.0	0.0	0.0	0.0
Other Oil Crops	0.0	0.0	0.0	0.0	0.0	0.3	0.0	0.0	0.0	0.0	0.0	0.0	0.0
Total Oil Crops	0.0	0.0	0.0	0.0	0.0	0.0	0.0	0.0	0.0	0.0	0.0	0.0	0.0
Beef and Veal	49.5	56.2	62.0	NA	NA	NA	NA	76.0	79.0	80.0	NA	NA	NA
Pork	6.8	9.5	11.0	NA	NA	NA	NA	11.0	12.0	12.0	NA	NA	NA
Mutton and Kid	22.7	30.0	30.0	NA	NA	NA	NA	30.0	30.0	33.0	NA	NA	NA
Poultry	13.1	18.5	36.0	NA	NA	NA	NA	51.0	56.0	59.0	NA	NA	NA
Other Meat	1.8	0.6	0.0	147.0	151.0	158.0	162.0	0.0	0.0	0.0	185.0	188.0	188.0
Total Meat	93.9	114.8	139.0	147.0	151.0	158.0	162.0	168.0	177.0	184.0	185.0	188.0	188.0
Milk	478.1	658.1	796.0	836.0	871.0	900.0	925.0	951.0	1,032.0	1,062.0	1,067.0	1,054.0	970.0
Eggs (Million Eggs)	412.5	577.9	721.0	772.0	835.0	875.0	926.0	948.0	998.0	1,056.0	1,077.0	1,056.0	985.0
Honey	0.8	1.5	1.4	NA	NA	NA	NA	1.0	0.9	0.9	NA	NA	NA

Sources: Same as Table A-1.
Excludes non-edible farm products such as cotton, tobacco, tea, and changes in livestock inventories.
NA—Not available.

532

TABLE A-8. Georgia: Selected Components of Farm Output, 1970–90.

Thousand Tons

Component	1970	1975	1980	1981	1982	1983	1984	1985	1986	1987	1988	1989	1990
Total Grain													
Bunker Weight	620.9	715.0	636.0	518.0	604.0	557.0	687.0	640.0	638.0	664.0	714.2	510.0	700.0
Clean Weight	NA	NA	600.0	NA	NA	NA	NA	600.0	619.0	644.0	692.0	475.0	666.0
Potatoes	298.7	267.2	393.0	400.0	413.0	366.0	390.0	394.0	367.0	360.0	326.0	332.0	294.0
Vegetables	327.0	406.4	546.0	560.0	587.0	565.0	632.0	604.0	662.0	619.0	641.0	515.0	443.0
Fruit, Berries and Grapes	1,088.0	1,084.8	1,660.4	1,760.0	1,526.5	1,637.2	1,945.1	1,714.6	1,625.9	1,370.8	1,710.0	1,213.0	1,565.0
Sugar Beets	123.6	141.0	120.0	113.0	122.0	110.0	97.0	63.0	53.0	51.0	51.0	39.0	34.0
Sunflower Seeds	11.5	13.9	10.0	9.0	7.0	10.0	5.0	9.0	6.0	5.0	17.0	3.0	9.0
Soybeans	0.0	0.0	0.0	5.0	5.0	5.0	5.0	5.0	7.6	7.0	6.9	5.5	3.4
Other Oil Crops	0.0	0.0	0.0	0.0	0.0	0.0	0.0	0.0	0.0	0.0	0.0	0.0	0.0
Total Oil Crops	11.5	13.9	10.0	14.0	12.0	15.0	10.0	14.0	14.0	12.0	24.0	8.5	12.0
Beef and Veal	NA	NA	45.0	NA	NA	NA	NA	52.0	54.0	56.0	NA	NA	NA
Pork	NA	NA	64.0	NA	NA	NA	NA	70.0	71.0	68.0	NA	NA	NA
Mutton and Kid	NA	NA	10.0	NA	NA	NA	NA	8.0	9.0	9.0	NA	NA	NA
Poultry	NA	NA	23.0	NA	NA	NA	NA	36.0	37.0	41.0	NA	NA	NA
Other Meat	104.2	135.4	1.0	147.4	148.0	149.9	157.6	NA	1.0	0.0	172.0	179.0	170.0
Total Meat	104.2	135.4	143.0	147.4	148.0	149.9	157.6	167.0	172.0	174.0	172.0	179.0	170.0
Milk	518.1	574.9	642.0	645.9	639.2	647.6	663.0	684.0	722.0	724.0	731.0	712.0	660.0
Eggs (Million Eggs)	397.3	536.8	655.0	664.8	711.9	752.1	782.9	823.0	880.0	887.0	890.0	861.0	769.0
Honey	2.6	2.7	2.2	NA	NA	NA	NA	2.1	1.9	1.9	0.0	0.0	0.0

Sources: Same as Table A-1.
Excludes non-edible farm products such as cotton, tobacco, tea, and changes in livestock inventories.
NA—Not available.

TABLE A-9. Kyrgyzstan: Selected Components of Farm Output, 1970–90 [a]

Thousand Tons

Component	1970	1975	1980	1981	1982	1983	1984	1985	1986	1987	1988	1989	1990
Total Grain													
Bunker Weight	1,013.8	1,055.0	1,307.0	1,550.0	958.0	1,512.0	1,224.0	1,477.0	1,633.0	1,910.0	1,800.0	1,700.0	1,600.0
Clean Weight	NA	NA	1,300.0	NA	NA	NA	NA	1,400.0	1,568.0	1,827.0	1,676.0	1,601.0	1,503.0
Potatoes	288.8	280.4	293.0	297.0	100.0	309.3	294.6	306.0	329.0	287.0	333.0	324.0	365.0
Vegetables	193.9	309.4	400.0	426.0	368.0	457.9	505.0	445.0	512.0	491.0	553.0	585.0	487.0
Fruit, Berries and Grapes	106.5	244.6	240.0	259.5	266.7	294.1	236.4	103.0	259.0	125.0	173.0	115.0	184.0
Sugar Beets	1,684.9	1,798.4	956.0	812.0	204.0	347.0	228.0	NA	b	b	b	b	2.0
Sunflower Seeds	0.0	0.0	0.0	0.0	0.0	0.0	0.0	0.0	0.0	0.0	0.0	0.0	0.0
Soybeans	0.0	0.0	0.0	0.0	0.0	0.0	0.0	0.0	0.0	0.0	0.0	0.0	0.0
Other Oil Crops	0.0	0.0	0.0	0.0	0.0	0.0	0.0	0.0	0.0	0.0	0.0	0.0	0.0
Total Oil Crops	0.0	0.0	0.0	0.0	0.0	0.0	0.0	0.0	0.0	0.0	0.0	0.0	0.0
Beef and Veal	41.3	51.7	51.0	55.8	55.8	55.8	58.1	56.0	64.0	66.0	NA	NA	NA
Pork	15.8	24.7	25.0	28.1	27.0	28.7	24.4	23.0	28.0	32.0	NA	NA	NA
Mutton and Kid	63.8	63.0	61.0	57.2	58.8	60.7	63.8	59.0	66.0	67.0	NA	NA	NA
Poultry	8.2	10.6	15.0	14.5	16.3	18.3	19.0	23.0	25.0	30.0	NA	NA	NA
Other Meat	4.6	7.4	7.0	7.1	7.4	6.7	7.7	8.0	10.0	9.0	222.0	241.0	254.0
Total Meat	133.7	157.4	159.0	162.7	165.3	170.2	173.0	169.0	193.0	204.0	222.0	241.0	254.0
Milk	548.0	611.0	682.0	684.0	694.0	706.0	731.0	771.0	909.0	998.0	1,063.0	1,202.0	1,185.0
Eggs (Million Eggs)	268.0	361.2	416.0	434.9	428.1	460.4	498.3	532.0	573.0	612.0	666.0	704.0	714.0
Honey	2.7	3.8	7.0	NA	NA	NA	NA	11.1	11.6	12.7	NA	NA	NA

Sources: Same as Table A-1.
[a] Excludes non-edible farm products such as cotton, tobacco, tea, and changes in livestock inventories.
[b] Negligible.
NA—Not available.

TABLE A-10. Tajikistan: Selected Components of Farm Output, 1970-90.

Thousand Tons

Component	1970	1975	1980	1981	1982	1983	1984	1985	1986	1987	1988	1989	1990
Total Grain													
Bunker Weight	222.0	218.3	245.0	327.0	277.0	394.0	280.0	326.0	246.0	359.0	382.0	300.0	312.0
Clean Weight	NA	NA	200.0	NA	NA	NA	NA	300.0	238.0	345.0	365.0	293.0	303.0
Potatoes	66.2	113.8	153.0	162.0	160.0	158.0	161.0	185.0	199.0	192.0	183.0	217.0	207.0
Vegetables	206.5	284.8	381.0	383.0	414.0	410.0	447.0	473.0	505.0	511.0	556.0	567.0	528.0
Fruit, Berries and Grapes	240.7	423.2	371.0	459.0	416.3	480.9	372.2	411.0	439.0	338.0	390.0	367.0	406.0
Sugar Beets	0.0	0.0	0.0	0.0	0.0	0.0	0.0	0.0	0.0	0.0	0.0	0.0	0.0
Sunflower Seeds	0.0	0.0	0.0	0.0	0.0	0.0	0.0	0.0	0.0	0.0	0.0	0.0	0.0
Soybeans	0.0	0.0	0.0	0.0	0.0	0.0	0.0	0.0	0.0	0.0	0.0	0.0	0.0
Other Oil Crops	0.0	0.0	0.0	0.0	0.0	0.0	0.0	0.0	0.0	0.0	0.0	0.0	0.0
Total Oil Crops	0.0	0.0	0.0	0.0	0.0	0.0	0.0	0.0	0.0	0.0	0.0	0.0	0.0
Beef and Veal	NA	NA	47.0	NA	NA	NA	NA	53.0	54.0	57.0	NA	NA	NA
Pork	NA	NA	8.0	NA	NA	NA	NA	11.0	13.0	14.0	NA	NA	NA
Mutton and Kid	NA	NA	25.0	NA	NA	NA	NA	25.0	26.0	25.0	NA	NA	NA
Poultry	NA	NA	13.0	NA	NA	NA	NA	14.0	16.0	14.0	NA	NA	NA
Other Meat	63.9	83.5	2.0	97.8	98.8	102.0	104.0	2.0	1.0	2.0	113.0	113.0	108.0
Total Meat	63.9	83.5	95.0	97.8	98.8	102.0	104.0	105.0	110.0	112.0	113.0	113.0	108.0
Milk	284.9	382.6	499.0	509.9	516.1	528.0	538.5	547.0	571.0	567.0	574.0	580.0	575.0
Eggs (Million Eggs)	131.3	236.5	322.0	374.8	375.2	397.2	421.2	469.0	555.0	579.0	632.0	619.0	592.0
Honey	1.1	2.1	2.1	2.4	2.8	3.1	3.4	3.8	3.4	3.8	0.0	0.0	0.0

Sources: Same as Table A-1.
Excludes non-edible farm products such as cotton, tobacco, tea, and changes in livestock inventories.
NA—Not available.

TABLE A-11. Turkmenistan: Selected Components of Farm Output, 1970–90.

Thousand Tons

Component	1970	1975	1980	1981	1982	1983	1984	1985	1986	1987	1988	1989	1990
Total Grain													
Bunker Weight	68.6	224.0	276.0	303.0	271.0	312.0	337.0	322.0	320.0	353.0	435.0	430.0	430.0
Clean Weight	NA	NA	300.0	NA	NA	NA	NA	300.0	293.0	324.0	408.0	379.0	449.0
Potatoes	12.2	12.8	12.0	17.0	15.0	17.0	19.0	21.0	25.0	34.0	38.0	37.0	35.0
Vegetables	155.8	182.2	267.0	285.0	288.0	273.1	296.0	312.0	334.0	354.0	372.0	414.0	411.0
Fruit, Berries and Grapes	57.0	101.0	77.0	60.6	68.8	76.0	0.0	151.0	197.0	200.0	215.0	166.0	216.0
Sugar Beets	0.0	0.0	0.0	0.0	0.0	0.0	0.0	0.0	0.0	0.0	0.0	0.0	0.0
Sunflower Seeds	0.0	0.0	0.0	0.0	0.0	0.0	0.0	0.0	0.0	0.0	0.0	0.0	0.0
Soybeans	0.0	0.0	0.0	0.0	0.0	0.0	0.0	0.0	0.0	0.0	0.0	0.0	0.0
Other Oil Crops	0.0	0.0	0.0	0.0	0.0	0.0	0.0	0.0	0.0	0.0	0.0	0.0	0.0
Total Oil Crops	0.0	0.0	0.0	0.0	0.0	0.0	0.0	0.0	0.0	0.0	0.0	0.0	0.0
Beef and Veal	35.8	NA	36.0	NA	NA	NA	NA	37.0	41.0	44.0	NA	NA	NA
Pork	6.9	NA	7.0	NA	NA	NA	NA	8.0	10.0	10.0	NA	NA	NA
Mutton and Kid	29.3	NA	29.0	NA	NA	NA	NA	29.0	28.0	32.0	NA	NA	NA
Poultry	6.4	NA	6.0	NA	NA	NA	NA	7.0	8.0	7.0	NA	NA	NA
Other Meat	2.3	75.0	3.0	81.0	82.0	87.0	84.0	5.0	3.0	5.0	98.0	103.0	104.0
Total Meat	80.7	75.0	81.0	81.0	82.0	87.0	84.0	86.0	90.0	98.0	98.0	103.0	104.0
Milk	192.0	245.0	306.0	320.0	323.0	337.0	334.0	348.0	373.0	402.0	411.0	423.0	436.0
Eggs (Million Eggs)	122.0	194.0	248.0	216.0	276.0	311.0	281.0	275.0	301.0	319.0	328.0	328.0	327.0
Honey	NA	NA	NA	NA	NA	NA	NA	NA	NA	NA	NA	NA	NA

Sources: Same as Table A-1.
Excludes non-edible farm products such as cotton, tobacco, tea, and changes in livestock inventories.
NA—Not available.

TABLE A-12. Uzbekistan: Selected Components of Farm Output, 1970–90.

Thousand Tons

Component	1970	1975	1980	1981	1982	1983	1984	1985	1986	1987	1988	1989	1990
Total Grain													
Bunker Weight	979.6	1,078.9	2,518.0	2,902.0	2,784.0	3,354.0	1,671.0	1,541.0	1,248.0	1,822.0	2,200.0	1,600.0	2,000.0
Clean Weight	NA	NA	2,400.0	NA	NA	NA	NA	1,500.0	1,186.0	1,738.0	2,083.0	1,555.0	1,899.0
Potatoes	182.9	213.9	239.0	326.0	336.0	373.0	251.0	241.0	309.0	261.0	308.0	325.0	336.0
Vegetables	772.1	1,412.3	2,459.0	2,527.0	2,537.0	2,630.0	2,480.0	2,386.0	2,491.0	2,558.0	2,760.0	2,585.0	2,843.0
Fruit, Berries and Grapes	696.5	1,014.8	1,198.0	1,410.5	1,393.3	1,641.6	1,252.5	1,266.0	1,353.0	1,253.0	1,278.0	965.0	1,401.0
Sugar Beets	0.0	0.0	0.0	0.0	0.0	0.0	0.0	0.0	0.0	0.0	0.0	0.0	0.0
Sunflower Seeds	0.0	0.0	0.0	0.0	0.0	0.0	0.0	0.0	0.0	0.0	NA	NA	NA
Soybeans	0.0	0.0	0.0	0.0	0.0	0.0	0.0	0.0	0.0	0.0	NA	NA	NA
Other Oil Crops	0.0	0.0	0.0	0.0	0.0	0.0	0.0	0.0	0.0	0.0	NA	NA	NA
Total Oil Crops	0.0	0.0	0.0	0.0	0.0	0.0	0.0	0.0	0.0	0.0	NA	NA	NA
Beef and Veal	127.7	158.8	213.0	NA	NA	NA	NA	242.0	235.0	246.0	NA	NA	NA
Pork	14.8	25.7	27.0	NA	NA	NA	NA	38.0	41.0	45.0	NA	NA	NA
Mutton and Kid	51.0	62.0	61.0	NA	NA	NA	NA	59.0	59.0	56.0	NA	NA	NA
Poultry	12.4	17.0	27.0	NA	NA	NA	NA	44.0	47.0	54.0	NA	NA	NA
Other Meat	2.5	4.7	2.0	355.4	376.6	389.0	383.5	3.0	4.0	3.0	440.0	478.0	484.0
Total Meat	208.4	268.2	330.0	355.4	376.6	389.0	383.5	386.0	386.0	404.0	440.0	478.0	484.0
Milk	1,332.9	1,708.2	2,266.0	2,380.9	2,445.6	2,532.7	2,444.4	2,439.0	2,505.0	2,650.0	2,837.0	2,929.0	3,034.0
Eggs (Million Eggs)	859.8	1,247.1	1,461.0	1,585.8	1,726.7	1,751.0	1,837.4	1,948.0	2,042.0	2,218.0	2,334.0	2,429.0	2,453.0
Honey	2.1	2.2	5.1	NA	NA	NA	NA	10.9	11.4	14.6	NA	NA	NA

Sources: Same as Table A-1.
Excludes non-edible farm products such as cotton, tobacco, tea, and changes in livestock inventories.
NA—Not available.

TABLE A-13. Estonia: Selected Components of Farm Output, 1970–90.

Thousand Tons

Component	1970	1975	1980	1981	1982	1983	1984	1985	1986	1987	1988	1989	1990
Total Grain														
Bunker Weight	726.1	1,113.8	1,198.0	915.0	1,220.0	1,164.0	1,235.0	929.0	1,159.0	1,257.0	600.0	1,300.0	1,333.0
Clean Weight	NA	NA	1,000.0	NA	NA	NA	NA	700.0	915.0	906.0	447.0	967.0	954.0
Potatoes	1,414.4	1,215.9	1,146.0	704.0	980.0	934.0	1,200.0	833.0	1,146.0	728.0	716.0	864.0	617.0
Vegetables	138.1	106.6	125.0	117.0	125.0	126.0	138.0	124.0	163.0	116.0	129.0	144.0	105.0
Fruit, Berries and Grapes	42.8	29.1	30.0	64.9	28.3	62.4	37.4	39.0	49.0	31.0	22.0	-75.0	22.0
Sugar Beets	0.0	0.0	0.0	0.0	0.0	0.0	0.0	0.0	0.0	0.0	0.0	0.0	0.0
Sunflower Seeds	0.0	0.0	0.0	0.0	0.0	0.0	0.0	0.0	0.0	0.0	0.0	0.0	0.0
Soybeans	0.0	0.0	0.0	0.0	0.0	0.0	0.0	0.0	0.0	0.0	0.0	0.0	0.0
Other Oil Crops	0.0	0.0	0.0	0.0	0.0	0.0	0.0	0.0	0.0	0.0	0.0	0.0	0.0
Total Oil Crops	0.0	0.0	0.0	0.0	0.0	0.0	0.0	0.0	0.0	0.0	0.0	0.0	0.0
Beef and Veal	54.7	NA	73.0	NA	NA	NA	NA	77.0	77.0	78.0	NA	NA	NA
Pork	74.2	85.6	106.4	108.3	92.8	109.3	110.7	116.0	114.0	120.0	NA	NA	NA
Mutton and Kid	2.6	NA	4.0	NA	NA	NA	NA	4.0	4.0	3.0	NA	NA	NA
Poultry	3.5	NA	13.0	NA	NA	NA	NA	19.0	20.0	20.0	NA	NA	NA
Other Meat	1.0	76.3	0.0	89.7	80.5	91.3	98.4	0.0	0.0	1.0	228.0	229.0	219.0
Total Meat	136.0	161.9	196.4	198.0	173.3	200.6	209.1	216.0	215.0	222.0	228.0	229.0	219.0
Milk	1,024.6	1,181.4	1,169.0	1,145.6	1,116.1	1,195.5	1,246.6	1,260.0	1,267.0	1,290.0	1,289.0	1,277.0	1,208.0
Eggs (Million Eggs)	358.9	450.3	542.0	543.7	556.2	556.3	559.4	528.0	545.0	557.0	579.0	600.0	547.0
Honey	NA	NA	NA	NA	NA	NA	NA	NA	NA	NA	NA	NA	NA

Sources: Same as Table A-1.
Excludes non-edible farm products such as cotton, tobacco, tea, and changes in livestock inventories.
NA—Not available.

TABLE A-14. Latvia: Selected Components of Farm Output, 1970–90.

Thousand Tons

Component	1970	1975	1980	1981	1982	1983	1984	1985	1986	1987	1988	1989	1990
Total Grain													
Bunker Weight	1,322.7	1,243.0	1,054.0	1,178.0	1,472.0	1,494.0	2,007.0	1,610.0	1,850.0	2,086.0	1,686.0	2,100.0	2,106.0
Clean Weight	NA	NA	800.0	NA	NA	NA	NA	1,300.0	1,508.0	1,630.0	1,142.0	1,597.0	1,622.0
Potatoes	2,327.5	1,490.8	1,199.0	1,286.0	1,484.0	1,456.0	1,843.0	1,272.0	1,565.0	1,135.0	1,110.0	1,316.0	1,016.0
Vegetables	274.6	195.6	200.0	254.0	253.0	248.0	247.0	217.0	218.0	194.0	214.0	219.0	170.0
Fruit, Berries and Grapes	101.0	46.0	80.2	146.3	64.8	102.5	81.0	75.1	117.4	32.3	49.0	121.0	24.0
Sugar Beets	236.2	204.7	181.6	306.6	286.9	391.2	352.0	356.0	363.0	352.0	455.0	395.0	439.0
Sunflower Seeds	0.0	0.0	0.0	0.0	0.0	0.0	0.0	0.0	0.0	0.0	0.0	0.0	0.0
Soybeans	0.0	0.0	0.0	0.0	0.0	0.0	0.0	0.0	0.0	0.0	0.0	0.0	0.0
Other Oil Crops	0.0	0.0	0.0	0.0	0.0	0.0	0.0	0.0	0.0	0.0	0.0	0.0	0.0
Total Oil Crops	0.0	0.0	0.0	0.0	0.0	0.0	0.0	0.0	0.0	0.0	0.0	0.0	0.0
Beef and Veal	85.0	115.0	114.4	106.8	105.0	114.2	NA	127.0	132.0	133.0	NA	NA	NA
Pork	97.0	112.0	132.0	141.9	132.5	146.7	NA	152.0	155.0	157.0	NA	NA	NA
Mutton and Kid	8.0	7.0	4.1	4.1	3.9	4.1	NA	4.0	4.0	4.0	NA	NA	NA
Poultry	13.0	19.0	32.4	33.7	33.9	37.4	NA	40.0	40.0	43.0	NA	NA	NA
Other Meat	2.0	3.0	1.4	1.2	1.1	1.5	314.0	1.0	1.0	1.0	344.0	331.0	308.0
Total Meat	205.0	256.0	284.3	287.7	276.4	303.9	314.0	324.0	332.0	338.0	344.0	331.0	308.0
Milk	1,046.0	1,174.0	1,695.0	1,630.0	1,649.0	1,754.0	1,842.0	1,957.0	1,959.0	1,988.0	1,974.0	1,977.0	1,893.0
Eggs (Million Eggs)	331.0	477.0	730.0	739.0	748.0	823.0	861.0	880.0	923.0	921.0	920.0	890.0	819.0
Honey	3.0	2.9	1.4	NA	NA	NA	NA	1.1	1.4	1.3	0.0	0.0	0.0

Sources: Same as Table A-1.
Excludes non-edible farm products such as cotton, tobacco, tea, and changes in livestock inventories.
NA—Not available.

TABLE A-15. Lithuania: Selected Components of Farm Output, 1970–90.

Thousand Tons

Component	1970	1975	1980	1981	1982	1983	1984	1985	1986	1987	1988	1989	1990
Total Grain													
Bunker Weight	2,098.9	2,143.0	1,932.0	2,239.0	2,817.0	2,782.0	3,451.0	2,867.0	3,155.0	3,554.0	3,060.0	3,640.0	4,136.0
Clean Weight	NA	NA	1,600.0	NA	NA	NA	NA	2,500.0	2,756.0	3,063.0	2,688.0	3,272.0	3,265.0
Potatoes	2,721.4	2,547.2	1,178.0	2,004.0	2,055.0	1,627.0	2,068.3	1,851.0	2,312.0	1,397.0	1,850.0	1,927.0	1,573.0
Vegetables	365.7	355.2	265.0	369.0	348.5	318.0	366.5	331.0	354.0	317.0	370.0	326.0	295.0
Fruit, Berries and Grapes	130.7	231.0	191.0	262.0	163.0	154.0	198.0	183.0	204.0	65.0	127.0	253.0	87.0
Sugar Beets	526.4	801.4	559.0	871.0	772.0	884.0	1,148.6	938.0	906.0	838.0	1,212.0	1,075.0	912.0
Sunflower Seeds	0.0	0.0	0.0	0.0	0.0	0.0	0.0	0.0	0.0	0.0	0.0	0.0	0.0
Soybeans	0.0	0.0	0.0	0.0	0.0	0.0	0.0	0.0	0.0	0.0	0.0	0.0	0.0
Other Oil Crops	0.0	0.0	0.0	0.0	0.0	0.0	0.0	0.0	0.0	0.0	0.0	0.0	0.0
Total Oil Crops	0.0	0.0	0.0	0.0	0.0	0.0	0.0	0.0	0.0	0.0	0.0	0.0	0.0
Beef and Veal	NA	NA	174.0	NA	NA	NA	NA	223.0	234.0	229.0	NA	NA	NA
Pork	212.8	230.6	205.0	197.2	189.0	217.7	235.1	233.0	229.0	248.0	NA	NA	NA
Mutton and Kid	NA	NA	2.0	NA	NA	NA	NA	4.0	4.0	3.0	NA	NA	NA
Poultry	NA	NA	40.0	NA	NA	NA	NA	42.0	45.0	49.0	NA	NA	NA
Other Meat	176.9	207.1	1.0	212.9	212.1	229.7	258.0	2.0	2.0	2.0	545.0	534.0	530.0
Total Meat	389.7	437.7	422.0	410.1	401.1	447.4	493.1	504.0	514.0	531.0	545.0	534.0	530.0
Milk	2,490.4	2,702.4	2,524.0	2,492.8	2,557.4	2,742.0	2,891.0	2,973.0	3,051.0	3,122.0	3,209.0	3,235.0	3,157.0
Eggs (Million Eggs)	701.0	844.3	959.0	980.3	1,026.2	1,062.7	1,090.9	1,116.0	1,207.0	1,279.0	1,347.0	1,331.0	1,273.0
Honey	3.2	3.2	1.1	NA	NA	NA	NA	1.2	1.6	1.3	NA	NA	NA

Sources: Same as Table A-1.
Excludes non-edible farm products such as cotton, tobacco, tea, and changes in livestock inventories.
NA—Not available.

U.S. AGRICULTURAL EXPORTS AND ASSISTANCE TO THE FORMER SOVIET UNION

By Remy Jurenas *

CONTENTS

SUMMARY

The Soviet Union and its successor states for two decades have been a key export market for U.S. feed grains, wheat, and soybean meal. Large Soviet purchases of agricultural commodities have had noticeable impacts on U.S. commodity prices, exports, carryover stocks, and on the administration of domestic production policies and commodity programs. With the exception of the 1980–81 grain embargo imposed in response to the Soviet Union's invasion of Afghanistan, the U.S. Government's policy of supporting farm exports to this major overseas market successfully survived the ups and downs in U.S.-Soviet political and military rivalry as competing superpowers.

---

* Remy Jurenas is a Specialist in Agricultural Policy with the Congressional Research Service.

Although the Soviet Union historically purchased commodities from Western countries on a cash basis, declining hard currency reserves led the central Soviet Government in 1990 to request U.S. credit assistance to support continued purchases of U.S. grain. Congressional support for maintaining sales to this key market for American agriculture, and the Administration's objective to bolster then-President Gorbachev's reform efforts, led President Bush in December 1990 to offer U.S. Department of Agriculture (USDA) export credit guarantees.

The Bush Administration, starting in November 1991, expanded the scope of U.S. assistance in response to the poor 1991 Soviet harvest, food shortages reflecting continued economic and political chaos, and the dissolution of the Soviet Union into separate states. This included offering food aid to meet the needs of vulnerable groups in the population, and technical assistance and training programs targeted toward identified agricultural and food sector problems. From December 1990 through mid-November 1992, the U.S. Government offered to the Soviet Union and the new independent states $6.5 billion in various forms of agricultural assistance. Commodity sales backed by USDA credit guarantees accounted for 86 percent of this assistance, food aid for 13 percent, and technical assistance and exchanges represented 1 percent.

Current U.S. policy, as of November 1992, continues to support the twin objectives of maintaining agricultural sales to this important market, and helping the emerging democratic governments markedly boost food availability through farm and food sector reforms. However, U.S. programs in support of these objectives have implications for both the pace and outcome of the reforms themselves, and for the future of the former Soviet Union's 15 newly independent and diverse states as markets for U.S. agriculture.

Some observers are urging policymakers to take a closer look at whether or not USDA-guaranteed export sales to Russia and Ukraine are helping these countries develop more open agricultural markets. They recommend that U.S. grain sales be used creatively to help introduce price incentives that would encourage Russian farms to sell more of their output to the state. Others question whether the Administration's emphasis on short-term USDA guarantees is appropriate in light of Russia's difficulties in paying its foreign debt and its request for a comprehensive debt rescheduling. They identify other options that may have more promise in maintaining U.S. sales to meet Russia's food import needs, such as making available credit guarantees with longer repayment terms or facilitating barter transactions.

Other observers comment that U.S. policy, by virtue of the programmatic mix and proportions of agricultural assistance offered, reflects a short-term rather than long-term perspective. They urge that more U.S. resources be devoted toward technical assistance and training to help the new states develop market-oriented agricultural and food sectors. This would encourage U.S. agribusinesses to learn about this vast market and position themselves to take advantage of future trade and investment opportunities.

Some analysts foresee that the economic reforms, particularly as they affect the agricultural and food sectors, could significantly alter the nature and importance of this key market to U.S. agriculture. Likely changes in import needs could lead to reduced U.S. grain sales but to an increase in oilseed exports, and to increased U.S. exports of agricultural technology and food processing equipment to countries introducing policies intended to boost food supplies.

IMPORTANCE OF THE U.S.S.R. AS A MARKET FOR U.S. AGRICULTURE

To cover a substantial grain production shortfall due to a serious drought, the U.S.S.R. in 1972-73 purchased large amounts of U.S. grain. These purchases, together with the Soviet leadership's decision to expand the country's livestock sector to increase meat supplies, put the U.S.S.R. in the position of a substantial net importer in the world grain market for years to come. These initial purchases inaugurated a 20-year agricultural trading relationship between the United States and the Soviet Union. The importance of this relationship is reflected in the fact that U.S. agricultural exports accounted for almost three-quarters of total U.S. exports (farm, manufactured goods, and other) to the Soviet Union in the 1972 to mid-1992 period (Table 1).

To inject some predictability into this relationship, the United States and the Soviet Union, starting in 1976-77, entered into long-term grain agreements (LTA). These agreements committed the U.S.S.R. to purchase minimum levels of grain and soybeans from the United States each year, assured the Soviets access to U.S. supplies, and helped stabilize U.S. farm export sales by supporting the level of U.S. grain and soybean sales to that key market. For many years, Soviet purchases against LTA provisions were viewed as an important factor in contributing to the economic well-being of U.S. agriculture. [1]

The U.S.S.R. in most years since 1972 ranked among the top 10 leading markets (in value terms) for U.S. agricultural exports (Table 1). In 1989, the Soviet Union ranked second as an overseas market for U.S. farmers and agribusiness. U.S. agricultural exports to the U.S.S.R. that year reached a record $3.6 billion, and represented 9 percent of total U.S. farm exports to all destinations. Though U.S. farm exports to that market subsequently fell by more than one-third to $2.3 billion in 1990, largely due to the record grain crop harvested in the former Soviet Union that fall, 1991 exports recovered 10 percent to $2.5 billion. This 1991 increase reflected U.S. Government decisions to make USDA export credit guarantees available to the U.S.S.R., largely to maintain a export sales to this market and to meet food shortages caused by a poor harvest and related economic problems. Commercial sales supported by offers of USDA guarantees and food aid shipments under various programs are expected to maintain 1992 U.S. farm exports to all of the 15 former Soviet republics in the $2.6 billion to $2.8 billion range, about 8 percent higher than in 1991.

---

[1] With the dissolution of the Soviet Union in December 1991, the third LTA (covering 1991-95) is, practically speaking, no longer in effect. Though the U.S. Government's position is that all agreements with the former U.S.S.R. are "under review," future U.S. grain and oilseed sales to the new states will largely be dependent upon the availability of USDA credit guarantees and export subsidies.

TABLE 1. U.S. Agricultural Exports to the Former Soviet Union, Quantity and Value, 1972–92.

Calendar Year	Grains (Wheat and Feed Grains)		Soybeans & Products		Total Agricultural Exports	Agricultural Exports' Share of U.S. Agricultural Exports	U.S.S.R.'s Rank as U.S. Agricultural Export Market (Based on Value)
	Billion $	Million Metric Tons	Billion $	Million Metric Tons	Billion $	Percent	
1972	0.393	7.291	0.054	0.400	0.459	80.2	6
1973	0.917	14.331	0.087	0.550	1.017	79.0	3
1974	0.301	3.378	0.000	0.002	0.324	51.3	17
1975	1.140	7.619	0.003	0.015	1.170	62.5	4
1976 a	1.462	11.605	0.126	0.579	1.605	66.2	3
1977	0.853	6.860	0.154	0.565	1.053	64.3	5
1978	1.471	13.448	0.222	0.832	1.765	75.8	3
1979 b	2.394	18.870	0.517	1.887	3.000	80.0	2
1980 b	1.029	6.662	0.045	0.173	1.138	71.1	11
1981	1.574	9.652	0.008	0.034	1.685	68.8	8
1982	1.637	11.422	0.171	0.649	1.871	71.8	3
1983	1.205	7.868	0.159	0.569	1.473	73.6	7
1984	2.621	18.262	0.014	0.046	2.878	86.1	2
1985	1.719	14.233	0.027	0.040	1.924	78.2	2
1986	0.291	2.671	0.313	1.519	0.658	52.3	12
1987	0.786	10.167	0.100	0.492	0.938	62.9	8
1988	1.731	16.684	0.410	1.900	2.246	78.8	3
1989	3.057	24.762	0.471	1.714	3.597	81.5	2
1990	1.651	13.165	16.270	1.857	2.271	73.4	5
1991	1.660	0.403	0.719	3.132	2.495	68.9	4
Jan.–June:							
1991	0.825	8.158	0.241	1.133	1.115	65.8	4
1992 c	0.988	7.932	0.276	1.121	1.342	73.5	4
Total, 1972–1991 and Jan.–June 1992.	$28.880	—	$4.279	—	$34.909	73.5	—

Source: U.S. Department of Agriculture (USDA), Economic Research Service (ERS), *Foreign Agricultural Trade of the United States (FATUS)*, various annual issues; *USSR: Agriculture and Trade Report*, May 1991, p. 29; and unpublished FATUS data. U.S. Department of Commerce, Bureau of Census, "U.S. Merchandise Trade: 1991 Final Report," May 13, 1992, p. 18, and "U.S. Merchandise Trade: June 1992 - FT-900 Supplement," August 20, 1992, Exhibit 6.
Note: The former Soviet Union refers to all 15 former Soviet republics—the members of the Commonwealth of Independent States (Armenia, Belarus, Kazakhstan, Kyrgyzstan, Moldova, Russia, Tajikistan, Turkmenistan, Ukraine and Uzbekistan), Azerbaijan, Georgia, and the three Baltic states (Estonia, Latvia and Lithuania). 1972–78 agricultural exports to the U.S.S.R. are adjusted for grain and oilseed transshipments through Canada, West Germany, Belgium, and the Netherlands; 1979–92 agricultural exports adjusted for transshipments through Canada.
a The first U.S.-Soviet Long-Term Grain Agreement (LTA) went into effect October 1, 1976.
b President Carter on January 4, 1980, suspended all agricultural sales to the Soviet Union in excess of the 8 million metric tons of grain that the United States was committed to sell under the LTA. President Reagan lifted all agricultural export restrictions on April 24, 1981.
c Data are adjusted to reflect exports to the 15 new states that formerly constituted the Soviet Union.

Three commodities—wheat, corn, and oilseeds—have accounted for most U.S. agricultural exports to the Soviet Union since 1972. In 1991 alone, wheat and feed grains accounted for 67 percent of the value of farm exports to the Soviet Union. Sales of oilseeds (soybean meal and soybeans) constituted 29 percent of sales, followed by poultry products with a 3 percent share. In terms of quantities shipped, the U.S.S.R. since 1972 has been a critical sales outlet for U.S. agriculture in most years. Most years it ranked first or second as a market for U.S. corn, and first, second, or third for U.S. wheat. The Soviet Union in several years ranked among the top 10 markets for U.S. soybeans; and since 1987–88 has been among the top two markets for U.S. soybean meal (Table 2).

TABLE 2. U.S. Commodity Exports to the Former Soviet Union: Quantity, Share of Total Exports, and Market Rank, 1974–75 to 1991–92.

Marketing Year [a]	Corn			Wheat			Soybeans			Soybean Cake & Meal		
	Exports to U.S.S.R. (Thousand Metric Tons)	U.S.S.R.'s Share of Total Exports (Percent)	U.S.S.R.'s Rank as Market Export Destination	Exports to U.S.S.R. (Thousand Metric Tons)	U.S.S.R.'s Share of Total Exports (Percent)	U.S.S.R.'s Rank as Market Export Destination	Exports to U.S.S.R. (Thousand Metric Tons)	U.S.S.R.'s Share of Total Exports (Percent)	U.S.S.R.'s Rank as Market Export Destination	Exports to U.S.S.R. (Thousand Metric Tons)	U.S.S.R.'s Share of Total Exports (Percent)	U.S.S.R.'s Rank as Market Export Destination
1974–75	882.5	2.9	8	1,002.6	3.5	6	0.0	NA	—	0.0	NA	—
1975–76	11,846.8	26.9	1	3,924.6	13.3	2	287.5	1.8	11	0.0	NA	—
1976–77	3,051.7	7.0	3	2,616.6	10.8	2	889.3	5.5	5	0.0	NA	—
1977–78	11,075.7	22.5	1	3,438.5	11.9	1	805.1	4.2	7	0.0	NA	—
1978–79	11,387.9	20.9	1	2,604.0	8.5	3	1,187.2	5.7	6	27.0	0.5	24
1979–80 [b]	5,953.0	9.5	2	4,422.0	12.5	1	806.5	3.3	9	0.0	NA	—
1980–81	5,738.1	9.6	2	2,999.9	7.6	3	0.0	NA	—	0.0	NA	—
1981–82	7,772.6	15.1	4	6,538.8	13.9	2	709.6	2.7	9	0.0	NA	—
1982–83	3,207.7	6.7	2	3,373.6	8.8	3	198.6	0.8	19	0.0	NA	—
1983–84	6,476.5	13.7	2	4,141.2	11.7	1	416.2	2.0	13	0.0	NA	—
1984–85	15,750.1	34.3	1	6,339.1	17.7	1	0.0	NA	—	0.0	NA	—
1985–86	6,808.1	23.2	2	152.6	0.7	29	1,518.7	7.5	5	0.0	NA	—
1986–87	4,102.3	10.5	2	0.0	NA	—	68.2	0.3	25	0.0	NA	—
1987–88	5,184.0	11.8	2	12,374.6	30.5	1	830.7	3.8	8	1,319.8	22.1	1
1988–89	16,674.1	31.7	1	4,958.6	13.2	2	298.7	2.0	11	1,348.8	29.4	1
1989–90	16,486.2	28.1	1	4,312.6	13.2	2	342.3	2.0	12	1,373.8	31.5	1
1990–91	8,495.0	22.6	2	2,843.3	10.2	3	415.8	2.7	9	1,811.0	38.2	1
1991–92	7,054.0	18.1	2	7,050.3	22.0	1	661.6	3.5	8	427.9	7.6	2

Source: USDA, Foreign Agricultural Service (FAS). U.S. Exports of Reported Agricultural Commodities For 1974/75–1978/79 Marketing Years, January 1980; U.S. Exports of Reported Agricultural Commodities For 1975/76–1979/80 Marketing Years, April 1981; unpublished data maintained by FAS' Export Sales Reporting Branch; selected issues of FAS' weekly U.S. Export Sales.

Note: In recent years, the U.S.S.R. ranked fourth as a market for U.S. grain sorghum exports in 1988–89, third as a market for U.S. barley exports in 1991–92 and fourteenth in 1989–90, and fifth as a market for U.S. exports of wheat product (e.g., flour) in 1990–91.

[a] Marketing year for corn is September 1 to August 31; for wheat, June 1 to May 31; for soybeans, September 1 to August 31; for soybean cake and meal, October 1 to September 30. Marketing years were slightly different through 1984–85 for corn and through 1975–76 for wheat.

[b] The United States suspended agricultural sales to the U.S.S.R. on January 4, 1980, and allowed sales to resume on April 24, 1981.

NA—Not Applicable.

Because large purchases by the former U.S.S.R., and now Russia, Ukraine, and the other new states, or their lack of buying interest, do substantially influence domestic grain and soybean prices, U.S. farmers and futures markets carefully watch both rumored and actual buying activity. Large sales of U.S. grain and oilseeds to these customers also can have a significant economic impact on U.S. agribusiness, especially commodity exporters, whose profit margins are largely determined by export volumes. However, since late 1990, expectations on the amount and timing of credit guarantees that USDA might announce for use by these countries (rather than projected import needs) have become the deciding factor determining what sales to these states might mean for U.S. farmers and agribusiness.

To illustrate, the extension of a large amount of credit guarantees to such a major export market can noticeably affect U.S. commodity prices, the farm economy, and farm program spending. A CRS analysis compared the impacts of extending $1.5 billion in credit guarantees to the U.S.S.R. in late June 1991 (and distributed over a 14-month period) to a scenario where no guarantees were extended. [2] Projections showed that commodity prices would significantly strengthen with such extensive use of guarantees to maintain U.S. agricultural exports, notably wheat. The farm wheat price was projected to be 20 cents per bushel higher (up 7.5 percent) in the June 1991-May 1992 marketing year, and 34 cents higher in 1992-93 (up almost 14 percent). Farm corn prices were projected to be 5 cents higher per bushel in the September 1990-August 1991 marketing year (up more than 2 percent) and 18 cents in 1991-92 (about 9 percent). Soymeal prices were projected to be higher by $3 per short ton (up almost 2 percent) in the October 1990-September 1991 marketing year and by $5 (up 3 percent) in 1991-92. With higher market prices, Government deficiency payments (income subsidies) to producers participating in the USDA's 1991 wheat and corn price support programs were expected to be $1.3 billion lower compared to the no-guarantees scenario, and $1.8 billion lower for participants in both crops' 1992 programs. Lower deficiency payments, in turn, would represent Federal budgetary savings attributable to such a policy decision.

With respect to the bottom line for the entire farm sector, additional guarantees were projected to increase U.S. net farm income only by 1.3 percent ($500 million) in 1991 and by 2.2 percent ($800 million) in 1992. However, wheat and corn producers in particular would benefit from noticeably higher crop receipts associated with such a policy decision. At the same time, projected Federal farm program spending would show noticeable savings.

U.S. AGRICULTURAL ASSISTANCE PROGRAMS TO THE FORMER SOVIET UNION

The United States at present offers export credit guarantees to back privately financed agricultural export sales, export subsidies on sales of U.S. wheat and other commodities, grant food aid, long-

---

[2] A similar analysis for another time period is found in: Carol Brookins and Bill Bailey. *World Perspectives: Ag Review.* "Who Benefits from U.S. Agricultural Credits to the Soviet Union?" December 1, 1991. pp. 10–11.

term concessional credits, and technical assistance and training targeted to address problems in agricultural and food sectors of the new states that comprise the former Soviet Union. [3] Table 3 summarizes U.S. food and agricultural-related assistance in FY91, FY92, and assistance announced for FY93.

EXPORT CREDIT GUARANTEES

From December 1990 through October 1992 the United States offered $5.56 billion in USDA agricultural export credit guarantees to the former Soviet Union, and separately to Russia and Ukraine, to help them access private financing to purchase on a commercial basis U.S. agricultural commodities and food products. These guarantees represent almost 86 percent of the value of U.S. agricultural assistance made available to the 15 former Soviet republics since FY91 (Table 3). The guarantees are extended under the Commodity Credit Corporation's (CCC) [4] GSM-102 short-term export credit guarantee program. [5] This program's objective is to maintain and expand commercial agricultural exports to countries not able to secure normal trade financing for such purchases. With access to USDA guarantees, eligible creditworthy countries can repay guarantee-bank loans over a 3 year period. [6] The short-term GSM-102 and intermediate-term GSM-103 programs are administered by the Office of the General Sales Manager (OGSM) within USDA's Foreign Agricultural Service (FAS).

The U.S.S.R. in mid-1990 requested USDA credit guarantees to finance needed agricultural imports as the central Soviet Government faced declining hard currency reserves and the reluctance of commercial banks to extend any additional loans. Previously, the Soviet Union had purchased U.S. agricultural commodities on a cash basis or with short-term credits extended by U.S. exporters or their banks. With President Bush's decision to waive the Jackson-Vanik freedom of emigration requirements (which prohibited extending U.S. Government financial assistance, including credits of any form) with respect to the Soviet Union, the United States offered in December 1990 the first $1.0 billion in GSM-102 guarantees to the U.S.S.R. The Administration subsequently offered addi-

---

[3] There are four earlier instances where the United States extended food assistance to the Soviet Union. These were: (1) the famine relief efforts (under the auspices of the American Relief Administration's Russian Unit) in 1921–23 responding to the request of the new Bolshevik government for foreign assistance to meet the serious food shortfalls along the Volga River, (2) agricultural commodity and food shipments under the Lend-Lease Act during World War II to supply Soviet armies fighting on the eastern front, (3) USDA export subsidies made available on U.S. wheat sales in 1964 (in response to Soviet requests to ensure adequate bread supplies that winter) and again in 1972–73, and (4) the extension of $550 million in three-year direct credits under USDA's Export Credit Sales Program in fiscal year (FY) 1973 and FY74 to finance U.S. corn and wheat sales.

[4] A U.S. Government-owned and operated corporation responsible for financing major USDA programs, including price supports, domestic and foreign food assistance, and export sales programs. The CCC also maintains stocks of commodities obtained through administering various price support programs.

[5] In issuing credit guarantees to participating commercial banks, the CCC agrees to pay them if a foreign buyer's bank does not pay back its loans on schedule. By reducing lender risk, Russia and Ukraine now are able to obtain commercial bank financing that they otherwise would not be able to, and do so usually at near-market interest rates. Should either country in the future default, the CCC under its guarantee commitment is obligated to pay to banks missed payments.

[6] USDA guarantee-backed export sales that are repaid over three years are in contrast to agricultural export sales transacted on a cash basis or using short-term trade credits (financing extended usually for 90 to 180 days).

tional guarantees of $1.5 billion in June 1991 and $1.25 billion in November 1991 to the U.S.S.R.; $1.1 billion in April 1992 to the Commonwealth of Independent States (CIS), of which $700 million went to Russia and $110 million to Ukraine; $800 million to Russia in September 1992; and $200 million to Ukraine in October 1992.

TABLE 3. U.S. Agricultural Assistance to the Former Soviet Union, FY91–FY93.

(Millions of Dollars)

Form of Assistance/Program	FY91	FY92	FY93 [a]	Total, FY91–93	Share of FY91–93 Total (Percent)
Agricultural Export Credit Guarantees ..	$1,915.0	$2,645.0	$1,000.0 [b]	$5,560.0	85.5%
Food Aid	0.0	412.1	450.0	862.1	13.3%
Donations [c]	—	285.8	365.0 [d]	650.8	—
Credits [e]	—	74.0	30.0	104.0	—
Operation Provide Hope	—	52.3	55.0	107.3	—
Technical Assistance, Training and Exchanges [f]	1.05	36.925	40.2	78.2	1.2%
Total	$1,916.1	$3,094.0	$1,490.2	$6,500.3	100.0%
Addendum					
Export subsidies,	146.5	375.7	29.8	552.0	NA
Export Enhancement Program (EEP) [g]	146.5	369.1	29.8	545.4	NA
SOAP [h]	0.0	5.3	0.0	5.3	NA
DEIP [i]	0.0	1.24	0.04	1.3	NA

Source: Derived from press releases and program announcements issued by USDA's Foreign Agricultural Service, and available information from other U.S. Government agencies.

Note: The data include all 15 former Soviet republics. Fiscal years are October 1–September 30. Amounts for credit guarantees and food aid cover some costs for transporting commodities and food products.

NA—Not available.

[a] Preliminary; reflects status as of November 18, 1992. Should additional resources become committed during FY93 as circumstances change, the U.S. Government may announce additional offers of credit guarantees, food aid, export subsidies, and technical assistance, training, and exchanges.

[b] For FY93, allocations announced (Table 4) are less than the amount of guarantees offered through mid-November 1992 and shown here.

[c] Extended under the USDA's Section 416(b) and Food for Progress (FFP) programs using CCC's broad funding authority and P.L. 480 appropriated funds, respectively.

[d] Includes $250 million in food aid for Russia (of which USDA has announced the details of the first aid package of $134 million), $100 million in corn donations under FFP to any of the 15 former republics, and $15 million in other FFP donations.

[e] Long-term concessional credits under the USDA's P.L. 480 (Food for Peace) Title I program.

[f] Funding is based on available data provided by the USDA, the U.S. Agency for International Development (AID), and other agencies.

[g] EEP bonuses, or export subsidies, that the USDA paid to U.S. exporters in FY87–90 totaled $620.4 million.

[h] SOAP is the Sunflowerseed Oil Assistance Program.

[i] DEIP is the Dairy Export Incentive Program.

The other independent states' eligibility for GSM guarantees will depend on whether they meet program criteria. Most important is showing their ability to repay guaranteed credits that may be extended, or in other words, meet the statutory creditworthiness standard (see policy discussion below in the section entitled "Agricultural Import Financing and Creditworthiness of the Former Soviet Union"). The fact that the U.S. Government has extended concessional credits or food aid grants to 10 of the other new states in large part reflects their inability at this time to meet the GSM program criteria. Also, the U.S. response to future requests for

USDA credit guarantees from Russia or any of the new states will depend on how the United States and other major Western nations address the issue of Soviet foreign debt repayment within the context of the Paris Club. [7] Through mid-November 1992, Russia (having assumed the debt obligations of the former Soviet Union and on behalf of the CIS), had repaid all of the principal and interest owed on loans that USDA had earlier guaranteed.

Of the $5.56 billion in guarantees offered from 1990 through October 1992, USDA has made available almost $5.3 billion for use by the former U.S.S.R., Russia, and Ukraine to purchase specific U.S. agricultural commodities and food products. These countries have used 39 percent of the amount allocated to purchase corn, and 20 percent to buy soybeans and meal, for use as feed in their vulnerable livestock sectors. Wheat for bread accounts for 28 percent of the released guarantees, consumer-ready foodstuffs—5 percent, and freight costs—8 percent (Table 4). Together with these guarantees, USDA also made export subsidies available under the Export Enhancement Program and two smaller programs (see below) on sales of wheat and other designated commodities, to make U.S. prices competitive in those markets.

EXPORT SUBSIDIES

The 12 new states of the former Soviet Union are eligible for export subsidies under the Export Enhancement Program (EEP), the Sunflowerseed Oil Assistance Program (SOAP), and the Dairy Export Incentive Program (DEIP). The Baltics presently are eligible only under an EEP rice sales initiative for Eastern Europe. The former U.S.S.R. used, and now the new states have access to, these three USDA programs to purchase certain U.S. agricultural bulk and semi-processed commodities at lower prices than they might otherwise pay.

Though buyers benefit from such subsidized purchases, the intent of these programs is to challenge other countries' use of unfair trade practices, including export subsidies, and to make U.S. farm exports more price competitive in targeted foreign markets. [8] U.S. agricultural interests have viewed EEP as a useful tool to expand the U.S. share of this important wheat import market and to help maintain the income of U.S. wheat producers. Officials of the new states desire continued access to EEP because the program enables them to divert more of their scarce hard currency to purchase other needed imports. Other observers have contended that the amount the former Soviet Union saved in subsidized wheat and other commodity purchases constitutes a form of economic aid.

---

[7] The Paris Club is an informal group of officials of Western creditor governments who meet in Paris to reschedule the loans they have made to countries that are no longer able to repay them on schedule. These loans include direct government-to-government credits and officially guaranteed export credits.

[8] To accomplish this, USDA makes CCC-owned surplus commodity stocks or cash available to U.S. agricultural exporting firms to permit them to offer foreign buyers lower prices. The United States instituted these programs particularly to counter the European Community's (EC) practice of subsidizing its wheat and other agricultural exports and to prod the EC to negotiate the contentious agricultural export subsidy issue in the current multilateral trade negotiations held under General Agreement of Trade and Tariffs (GATT) auspices. USDA's targeting of the former Soviet republics responds to the EC's extensive use of export subsidies to expand and maintain its market share in that region.

TABLE 4. GSM-102 Export Credit Guarantee Allocations for the U.S.S.R., Russia and Ukraine, by Commodity, FY91-FY93.

Commodity or Food Product	Allocations Announced (Millions of Dollars)				Distribution of Allocations (Percent)			
	FY91	FY92	FY93 [a]	Total, FY91–93	FY91	FY92	FY93 [a]	Total, FY91–93
Feed grains [b]	$998.0	$681.18	$373.0	$2,052.18	52.1	25.8	51.4	38.8
Wheat and flour	252.5	990.60	229.0	1,472.10	13.2	37.5	31.6	27.9
Protein meals [c]	337.0	383.50	63.0	783.50	17.6	14.5	8.7	14.8
Poultry meat	33.5	15.00	30.0	78.50	1.7	0.6	4.1	1.5
Soybeans	128.0	120.60	NA	248.60	6.7	4.6	—	4.7
Almonds	9.0	4.75	—	13.75	0.5	0.2	—	0.3
Hops	2.0	4.75	NA	6.75	0.1	0.2	—	0.1
Vegetable oils	NA	66.20	NA	66.20	—	2.5	—	1.3
Rice	NA	11.92	NA	11.92	—	0.5	—	0.2
Tallow	NA	23.45	NA	23.45	—	0.9	—	0.4
Butter	NA	55.35	—	55.35	—	2.1	—	1.0
Pork	NA	NA	30.0	30.00	—	—	4.1	0.6
Subtotal, Commodities	1,760.0	2,357.3	725.0	4,842.3	91.9	89.1	100.0	91.6
Freight	155.0	287.7	0.0	442.7	8.1	10.9	—	8.4
Total	$1,915.0	$2,645.0	$725.0	$5,285.0	100.0	100.0	100.0	100.0
Addendum								
Bulk commodities [d]	$1,379.0	$1,804.3	$602.0	$3,784.8	72.0	68.2	83.0	71.6
High value commodities and processed food products [e]	382.0	553.0	123.0	1,057.5	19.9	20.9	17.0	20.0

Source: Derived from press releases and program announcements issued by USDA's Foreign Agricultural Service.
[a] Reflects activity through the latest announcement made on October 19, 1992. USDA's allocations by commodity with respect to the additional $275 million available to Russia for purchases during January–February 1993 are expected to be made by January 1, 1993.
[b] Corn, barley, sorghum, and oats.
[c] Soybean meal, cottonseed meal, linseed meal, and sunflower seed meal.
[d] Feed grains, wheat, soybeans, and rice.
[e] Soybean meal, poultry meat, almonds, hops, vegetable oils, tallow, butter, and pork.
NA—Not Available.

Since April 1987, when the U.S.S.R. first took advantage of EEP to purchase U.S. wheat, the USDA has announced other EEP initiatives to offer subsidies on U.S. exports of wheat flour (September 1990), vegetable oil (October 1991), barley and rice (November 1991), pork (August 1992), and barley malt (October 1992). EEP wheat sales to the U.S.S.R. and successor states accounted for 28 percent of the tonnage of all EEP-subsidized U.S. wheat exports shipped worldwide from 1985 through mid-November 1992. In dollar terms, the former U.S.S.R., and now the 12 states together, continue to be the prime worldwide EEP beneficiary. The U.S.S.R. and successor states through mid-November 1992 benefited from almost $1.2 billion in EEP subsidies used to purchase eligible commodities (Table 3, addendum).

SOAP and DEIP subsidize exports of U.S. sunflowerseed oil and dairy products, respectively, to make them competitive in selected overseas markets. Under SOAP, the USDA targeted the former Soviet Union in FY92 and FY93 to offer subsidies for exports of sunflowerseed oil. In FY92 and FY93, the USDA offered subsidies under DEIP on sales of milk powder and butterfat to the former U.S.S.R.

The new states' actual use of export subsidies under these three programs will largely depend on whether they are also eligible for credit guarantees or take advantage of a barter option that USDA announced in September 1992. Another factor is whether Russia, Ukraine, and other potentially eligible countries receive credit guarantee allocations for the commodities that the USDA is offering to subsidize.

FOOD AID

In FY92 and early FY93, the United States offered $862 million in food aid under several programs and statutory authorities to the new states. This food aid represents just over 13 percent of the value of U.S. agricultural assistance made available to the 15 former Soviet republics since FY91 (Table 3). The USDA tapped three programs, all administered by the USDA's Foreign Agricultural Service, to follow through on the Bush Administration's commitments to provide humanitarian aid to meet the needs of economically or nutritionally vulnerable groups and to enable certain countries to purchase U.S. commodities on very liberal credit terms. A separate initiative in early 1992 involved emergency shipments of Department of Defense food surpluses and selected USDA donations to cities scattered across the new states.

The USDA extended, and will likely continue to offer, grant food aid under: (1) the Section 416(b) [9] program that authorizes USDA to donate CCC-owned surplus commodities, as needed and available, to fill short-term deficits in foreign countries, and (2) the Food-for-Progress (FFP) Program that involves donating CCC-purchased commodities to countries that agree to enhance their private agricultural sectors. During FY92, the USDA under these two programs made available $198.7 million in humanitarian food aid for hard-hit food deficit regions in six of the new states for distribution through 11 U.S. private voluntary organizations (PVOs) and by the Russian Government. Donations were targeted primarily toward the more vulnerable groups (children, the elderly, and infirm) in Russia (Moscow, St. Petersburg, the Ural Mountain cities, Eastern Siberia), Armenia, Turkmenistan, Belarus, Kazakhstan, and Georgia. Donated food products included butter, butter oil, nonfat dry milk, bulgur wheat, flour, lentils (peas, beans, and others), rice, vegetable oil, and powdered infant formula. Initial assessments indicate that the PVOs for the most part effectively distributed this food aid. Under a separate government-to-government agreement, the USDA donated CCC butter stocks for distribution by the Russian Government.

For FY93, USDA has offered up to $250 million in food aid to Russia under various USDA humanitarian assistance programs. The mix of commodities and food products to be offered and the terms ("donational or concessional") will be announced as details are negotiated and finalized. On October 9, 1992, USDA announced the first aid package of $134 million, which includes rice, butter, corn, pork, wheat and wheat products, baby food, poultry, whole dry milk, and peanuts. The USDA expects some food aid will be

---

[9] Refering to the Agricultural Act of 1949, as amended.

programmed through the PVOs already present in Russia, and indicated proposals will be considered for projects involving additional resources, not just in Russia, but in the other new states.

In addition, in early 1992 the three Baltic states (Estonia, Latvia, and Lithuania) received $33 million (plus $7.6 million on shipping costs) in Section 416(b) donations of corn to help these countries maintain their livestock sectors. The recipient governments planned to sell the donated corn to private sector feed millers and to livestock and poultry producers for feed to maintain meat and dairy production. Sales proceeds were to be used to help private sector farms increase grain production, and to assist PVOs provide food aid to the needy.

For FY93, USDA plans to purchase U.S. corn worth about $100 million to donate under the FFP to the Baltics and the former Soviet republics. These donations are intended to avert a potential liquidation in livestock herds, to encourage their rebuilding, and to help ensure a future market for U.S. food grains. Recipient countries, though, will be responsible for covering the cost of transporting donated corn.

Under a third program, during the second half of FY92 the USDA extended food aid under agreements signed with governments of 10 of the new independent states. P.L. 480 (Food for Peace) Title I provides for commercial sales of U.S. agricultural commodities using long-term concessional credits extended by the CCC. Loans carry maximum repayment terms of 30 years and interest is charged at below-market rates. Title I is intended to serve as a market development tool to facilitate U.S. export sales to countries without the financial resources to purchase needed agricultural commodities. The USDA's decision to use Title I reflects assessments that these countries are not sufficiently creditworthy to be eligible for USDA credit guarantees but are in need of assistance to cover their immediate food and feed needs. Also, expectations exist that some of these countries may, once economic growth resumes, become commercial markets for U.S. agriculture.

In FY92, $120.5 million in Title I resources was extended as concessional credits and donated under provisions of the Food for Progress program. The USDA signed agreements to extend $74 million in long-term credits (financing commodity costs and shipping) to Belarus ($24 million), Moldova ($10 million), Tajikistan ($10 million), Estonia ($10 million), Latvia ($10 million) and Lithuania ($10 million). To illustrate the concessional nature of such agreements, Tajikistan will repay its loan over 30 years, with the interest rate set at 2 percent for the first 17 years, and then 3 percent for the balance of the period. [10] Under Food for Progress (FFP) agreements totaling $46.5 million (which also cover transportation costs), USDA will donate wheat to Armenia ($15 million), wheat and wheat flour to Georgia ($21.5 million), and wheat to Kyrgyzstan ($10 million). With FFP donations made to encourage agricultural reform, these three countries have agreed to carry out a number of measures to expand the role of the private sector and improve food supplies. For FY93, USDA (under Title I) has allocated $15 million

---

[10] Interfax News Service. "U.S. Extends Tajikistan $10 [M]l to Buy Grain." August 31, 1992.

in credits to Belarus, Moldova and Turkmenistan, and $5 million to each of the Baltic states. Also, $15 million in P.L. 480 resources is allocated for commodity donations to Armenia, Georgia, and Kyrgyzstan under prospective FFP agreements.

A fourth effort involved an emergency airlift and land shipment of food supplies left over from the Gulf War to 24 cities in the new states. President Bush announced Operation Provide Hope at an international conference on aid to the former Soviet republics held in Washington, D.C., on January 22, 1992. The Administration used $7.3 million (out of $100 million in available Department of Defense funds) to cover the cost of shipping surplus military food stocks valued at $45 million and USDA-donated nonfat dry milk in early 1992. In late 1992, the U.S. Government plans to ship $40 million in ready-to-eat meals and processed food targeted for needy individuals and families in Russia.

TECHNICAL ASSISTANCE, TRAINING, AND EXCHANGES

U.S. Government missions to the Soviet republics during 1991 identified the food processing and distribution systems as the weak links in their food systems. Their findings led both President Bush and Secretary of Agriculture Madigan to state their strong interest in involving both the U.S. Government and the private sector in helping the new states reduce harvesting and transportation losses in order to increase food supplies. Since then, the USDA, the U.S. Agency for International Development (AID), and the U.S. Trade and Development Program have made available about $78 million: (1) for various technical assistance efforts to help improve food processing, distribution, and storage methods; and (2) for related programs to train and expose farmers and agricultural/food sector professionals in the new states to American farming methods and agribusiness management (Table 3).

To aid in the longer-term restructuring of their food systems, USDA's technical assistance projects (funded by the CCC) include: (1) establishing a model demonstration farm on the outskirts of St. Petersburg, (2) helping to develop wholesale markets in Moscow, (3) assisting in USDA Extension Service projects in Armenia that focus on the needs of private farmers, (4) coordinating the placement of U.S. food industry and transportation executives at food processing and distribution facilities to offer advice on streamlining existing operations, and (5) sending two agricultural policy advisors to work in the Russian and Kazakh Ministries of Agriculture. USDA Cochran Fellowships will be offered in FY93 to agricultural and food sector professionals in Russia, Ukraine, Kazakhstan, and Belarus to enable them to visit the United States for short-term training.

AID is funding a farmer-to-farmer exchange program that will send 1,500 farm-experienced U.S. volunteers primarily to Russia, Kazakhstan, and Ukraine to advise and work with private farmers, and initiated a pilot effort to privatize and commercialize Estonia's dairy industry. AID also has under way food systems restructuring efforts in Russia and the other new states intended to increase the efficiency of supplying domestically produced food through privatization of the food sector. These include funding USDA's extension efforts in Armenia and placing an emphasis on improving agricultural storage facilities in the new states. AID's future focus will be to involve U.S. agribusiness and cooperatives in helping the emerging private sectors operate successfully within the changing food sector and to help the public sectors institute limited policy reform. The FY93 foreign operations appropriations act (P.L. 102–391) makes available additional foreign aid funds to expand these technical assistance and related efforts to address the agricultural and food sector problems in the new states. The Trade and Development Program in March 1992 awarded a $500,000 grant (matched by the State of Iowa and private firms) to develop agribusiness centers in Russia and Ukraine to train local farmers in ways to bring their product to market efficiently and profitably.

POLICY ISSUES

Current U.S. policy to extend agricultural assistance to the new states of the former Soviet Union is motivated by both domestic and foreign policy objectives. The first is to maintain access to an important export outlet for the U.S. agricultural sector. This objective is also politically important for farm state Members of Congress and incumbent administrations. The second goal is to aid the former Soviet Union in meeting its food needs in order to lessen social and political tensions that could undermine the emerging democratic governments and the introduction of market reforms. U.S. programs to help meet these objectives, though, pose implications for the pace of and possible outcome of the reform efforts in the new states, and also for U.S. agricultural trade prospects with the new states in light of the changes taking place.

RELATIONSHIP AMONG U.S. FOOD ASSISTANCE AND ECONOMIC REFORMS AND RESTRUCTURING IN THE FORMER SOVIET UNION

Some observers of agricultural sector developments in the former U.S.S.R. urge U.S. policymakers to evaluate whether or not U.S. Government-guaranteed agricultural credit sales to Russia and Ukraine facilitate the emergence of competitive agricultural markets. They argue that U.S. Government-backed commodity exports that do not meet this objective inadvertently thwart the introduction of additional agricultural reforms, particularly when imports of foreign grain account for a large share of the grain stocks these governments can make available for distribution to consumers.

Focusing on the grain sector, these observers view additional liberalization of the prices that governments offer farmers for harvested commodities as critical to ensuring the availability of adequate food supplies to the large cities and food deficit regions. Allowing fundamental supply and demand factors to determine the level of commodity prices would encourage collective and state farms to sell more of their grain to government-administered procurement agencies. [11] However, grain imported by Russia in late

---

[11] To ensure the distribution of adequate supplies to the cities and food-deficit regions, the military and health care facilities, the former Soviet government, and now the governments of the individual states set a "procurement," or purchase, target for each agricultural commodity. While the former U.S.S.R. mandated the quantity that each farm must sell at administratively

Continued

1992 is sold to end users (e.g., flour milling and mixed feed plants) at prices much below what Russian farms receive selling grain either through free market channels or to the state. With Russia's policy to subsidize the price that end users pay for imports of foreign grain, sales of imported U.S. grain (taking into account the dollar-ruble exchange rate) in effect significantly undercut the price that Russian farms receive from their government for their grain. [12] This policy is driven by the Russian Government's objective to keep bread prices low for consumers and to help subsidize the unprofitable livestock sector. However, some argue that these import subsidies do not allow consumer demand to force market adjustments, or create a market environment that would allow farms to respond to the incentive of world grain prices, which in ruble terms would be much higher than the government offers. Also, these subsidies have adverse implications for broader Russian macroeconomic stabilization in that they increase the Russian Government's budget deficit and make it more difficult to restrain inflation.

Some advocate that the U.S. Government could encourage a more realistic grain pricing policy in Russia by requiring that some portion of the U.S. grain purchased by Roskhleboprodukt (a Government stock company, which replaced the Russian Committee on Grain and Grain Products in October 1992) with USDA guarantees be resold through the commodity exchanges or other emerging market mechanisms at prices determined through auction sales. Supporters of this approach predict that the subsequent advertising of these market prices widely throughout Russia and the other new states would facilitate price discovery (enable farms to determine what the real value of their output is). If the Russian government then adjusted its procurement prices to reflect these market-set prices, or if other market mechanisms emerged to play a larger role in marketing commodities, farms would sell more grain, rather than wait for the government to raise its administered price. With prices set more by market forces, resulting in more grain flowing

---

set prices, the new states with the introduction of partial economic reforms have moved to raise procurement prices and offer other incentives in order to coax farms to sell to state authorities. To the extent, though, that farms do not respond to these policy decisions as planned, governments resort to seeking imports of foreign commodities and foodstuffs to cover the projected needs of the procurement system's intended beneficiaries.

[12] To illustrate, the Russian Government in mid-August 1992 announced it will pay farmers an average of 12,000 rubles per metric ton (MT) of grain harvested in 1992. At the same time, the very limited amount of grain marketed through the new commodity exchanges during August 1992 on average sold at about 13,300 rubles (before taxes) per ton (derived from *Interfax Agriculture Report*, September 4-11, 1992, p. 11) with some Russian experts forecasting that the exchange price will rise even further. Grain sold on either a barter basis or sold across former republic borders is priced even higher, with some reports indicating that Kazakhstan is seeking to sell surplus wheat to Russia at world market prices. With Russia's grain import subsidies equal to 80 percent of the world price expressed in dollars, U.S. wheat sold to Russia in July 1992 at a weighted average of $137.39 per MT was available in August to Russian flour mills at about 4,600 rubles (reflecting the average August dollar/ruble exchange rate of $1/168.2R), or at just above 6,000 rubles in September (when the rate of 220.5 rubles to the dollar applied). At these exchange rates, if the flour mills had paid the ruble equivalent of world market prices, they would have paid 23,109 rubles in August and 30,295 rubles in September. U.S. wheat sold to Russia at an average $118 MT in late August was available in October (when the higher 95 percent import subsidy went into effect) to Russian end users at almost 2,100 rubles ($1=354R) and at about 2,500 rubles ($1=423R) in November. Without subsidies, the world market price would have been 41,772 rubles in October and 49,914 rubles in November. Comparable calculations on the price paid by Russian mixed feed processors for U.S. corn and barley sold to Russia in September and October 1992 would also be much lower than the procurement price the Russian Government is offering farms for feed grains.

through procurement and other channels in the emerging non-state trading network, the amount of grain available to end users for processing would increase, these experts predict, and the Russian Government's ability to meet overall food needs would improve.

U.S. efforts to place such a condition on guaranteed-credit sales, though, would face opposition from Roskhleboprodukt and other Russian governmental institutions, which currently exercise monopoly powers in managing grain marketing. The existing bureaucracy would fear losing political control and influence if farms, responding to widely disseminated market prices, started to bypass the procurement agencies by selling larger amounts of grain through the commodity exchanges or on a barter basis. Furthermore, the Russian Government does fear allowing grain procurement prices to rise to market levels, and is concerned about the political implications of consumers paying much higher prices, particularly for bread. For this reason, some officials view continued access to Western credits as critical to maintaining food prices at levels acceptable to consumers. [13]

Other observers, though, argue that the easy availability of Western credits removes the need for the Russian and other Governments to make their grain procurement systems subject to market forces, and to allow for complementary marketing mechanisms to emerge. They assert that without the availability of Western-financed imported grain, Russia and the other new states would move more quickly to introduce mechanisms that allow for market forces to work. With the incentive of higher commodity prices, farms and others in the food chain would respond by reducing the current high level of losses and waste. This, in turn, would result in noticeably more abundant food supplies available to consumers, though at a higher price. Others suggest that, to address the politically-sensitive consumer price issue, the Russian Government should expand social safety net programs for the poor and elderly (which could be partially supported by Western assistance).

AGRICULTURAL IMPORT FINANCING AND CREDITWORTHINESS OF THE FORMER SOVIET UNION

The U.S. agricultural community since 1990 has generally viewed the availability of USDA credit guarantees as critical to maintaining agricultural exports to the former Soviet Union. To accomplish this, the Bush Administration tapped the existing GSM-102 guarantee program to help the former U.S.S.R. purchase needed commodities. Under this approach, offers of guarantees did not require any advance congressional authorization, and that there was no immediate budgetary impact associated with making guarantees available as compared to other alternatives to extend credit assistance that might have been contemplated. Members of Congress from farm states welcomed each announcement to offer credit guarantees, cognizant of the beneficial impact that these commodity sales would have on agricultural producers and the agribusiness community.

---

[13] *Journal of Commerce.* "Russian Official Expects Grain Buys To Go On Despite Strong Food Supply." September 29, 1992. p. 8A.

However, some Members of Congress have argued that the Administration was using USDA's export credit guarantees as a foreign aid program for the former Soviet Union. [14] The continuation of this policy, they feared, would jeopardize the program's overall credibility in promoting sales of U.S. agricultural exports to other markets in the long term.

These views reflected concerns that the U.S.S.R., and subsequently, the new independent states, may eventually not be able to repay the credits backed by GSM guarantees due to the continuing fall in their economic activity and in energy exports. Should Russia and Ukraine default on any repayments, the USDA would be obligated to pay any missed loan payments to banks. Under current policy, the USDA would also immediately suspend future sales backed by guarantees until the delinquent debt is repaid. Current law prohibits the USDA from making credit guarantees available for sales of agricultural commodities to any country that the Secretary of Agriculture determines cannot adequately service the debt associated with such sales. It also prohibits the use of these guarantees for foreign aid, foreign policy, or debt rescheduling purposes. [15]

Through mid-November 1992, Russia (on behalf of the former Soviet Union and now the Commonwealth of Independent States) has met scheduled principal and interest payments owed to banks that had extended USDA guarantee-backed credits. Russia has placed the highest priority in making these loan repayments, bypassing other creditors, in order to ensure continued access to USDA guarantees to cover future food import needs. [16] Top U.S. officials have also clearly indicated that Russia's access to future guarantees is dependent upon staying current in making payments.

Questions, though, still exist about Russia's ability to pay back over the next three years the approximately $4 billion in principal still owed. U.S. General Accounting Office (GAO) investigators analyzing the creditworthiness of the new states reportedly believe that Russia is nearly bankrupt and that its ability to service all of its debts is seriously in doubt. At the same time, they believe Russia will do everything possible to make payments on GSM-backed credits, since Russian officials fully comprehend that missed payments will likely lead to the termination of additional USDA credit guarantees and that this in turn would jeopardize their continued access to a critical source for needed food imports. [17] The future GSM repayment outlook depends largely on whether there is an easing in Russia's debt servicing requirements, an improvement in its balance of payments position, or both over the next few years. Particularly crucial will be: (1) the outcome of the current Paris Club negotiations on rescheduling government-to-

---

[14] USDA credit guarantees accounted for about 90 percent of all U.S. bilateral economic assistance (grants, credits, and guarantees) made available in FY91 and FY92 to the former Soviet Union.

[15] 7 U.S.C. 5622; section 202 of the Agricultural Trade Act of 1978, as amended.

[16] Knight-Ridder Financial. "Official says Russian bank hopes to clear foreign debt arrears." June 17, 1992.

[17] World Perspectives, Inc. Ag Perspectives. "GAO Brief on FSU Creditworthiness." July 17, 1992. For background on the foreign debt problems facing the former Soviet Union, see Congressional Research Service Report, *International Debt and the Ex-Soviet Republics: Mortgaging the Future*, by Pat Wertman. August 12, 1992.

government debt and the scope of the debt that will be included in any final agreement; (2) separate but related negotiations on how the former Soviet Union's debt to Western commercial banks will be serviced; (3) the pace of progress in Russian economic reforms, particularly as they affect the energy and mineral sectors, in generating hard currency earnings; and (4) the availability of IMF and World Bank financial assistance.

Other observers contend that a more appropriate U.S. policy to help meet the short-term food needs of the new independent states would be to offer guarantees that allow for loan repayment over a longer period of time and to establish other mechanisms that specifically address their unique circumstances in seeking to finance food purchases. They view recurring decisions to extend additional amounts of three-year guarantees an unrealistic policy, leading at a minimum to a likely rescheduling of these GSM-backed credits by 1994 or 1995. To head this off, some urge that USDA offer intermediate-term agricultural export guarantees rather than short-term guarantees. This GSM-103 program makes guarantees available for credits with repayment terms up to 10 years, compared to the maximum three years under the GSM-102 program exclusively used to date. This would give some states a longer period over which to spread out their repayments until their economies stabilize and start to grow and their debt servicing requirements become more manageable. Related options would be to extend medium-term direct or guaranteed credits of three to five years, or long-term concessional credits or donations under the USDA's P.L. 480 programs to some of the new states.

Another approach, recommended by a major grain exporter, would be to create a special revolving fund within the CCC to enable the new states to purchase U.S. agricultural commodities as they repay previously granted GSM-guaranteed debt. This fund could be capped at a set maximum amount, with repayments against previously extended guarantees credited toward issuing new guarantees. A fund, it is argued, "offers the disciplines necessary for the republics to develop" their food production and business management skills and allows their private sectors to emerge. The exporter argues that it would also create "a more predictable footing for their continued purchases of U.S. agricultural products, ... and if properly designed, create the kind of environment in which fledgling enterprises in the republics, operating independently from state-owned companies, have a greater chance to succeed." [18]

Others urge that the USDA be more flexible in administering all of its export programs so as to enable U.S. firms to respond easier to emerging trade possibilities, that barter transactions (e.g., involving the exchange of U.S. agricultural commodities for Russian oil and minerals) be encouraged as a way to facilitate sales to those states without sufficient hard currency reserves, and that some of the GSM guarantees offered be secured by the natural resource assets located in some of these countries.

---

[18] Whitney MacMillan. "Revolving Fund Would Aid Former Soviet States." *Cargill Bulletin.* June 1992. p. 2.

Recent USDA decisions on facilitating U.S. agricultural export sales to some of the new states incorporate some of the above suggested approaches, and reflect the evolution of a policy that acknowledges that there are substantial differences among the new states in their ability to purchase U.S. agricultural commodities. In September 1992, after a successful experiment, USDA announced that its export subsidy programs could be used to facilitate barter trade with the former Soviet republics. This policy will allow U.S. subsidized agricultural commodity sales to third-country buyers that act as intermediaries involving imports from the new states. This means that U.S. exporters receive cash on their sales to these buyers, essentially being paid the sales proceeds of the goods the buyers import from the new states. In late FY92 and early FY93, the USDA also announced P.L. 480 Title I credit sales agreements with seven new states. These concessional loans will facilitate sales of wheat, feed grains, and soybean meal to meet immediate needs, carry low interest rates, and allow these countries to make repayments for up to 30 years.

MIX OF U.S. AGRICULTURAL ASSISTANCE TO THE FORMER U.S.S.R.

While USDA guarantees, long-term concessional credits, and various forms of food aid have enabled the newly independent states to acquire needed commodities, some observers contend that the United States, in its assistance strategy, must consider longer-run approaches. They point out that most U.S. agricultural assistance is offered as a short-term response, in part driven to benefit the U.S. agricultural sector, but that little attention is given to pursuing a broader strategy on how such and other related U.S. assistance might help the new states over the long term. To illustrate, while USDA credit guarantees and food aid have accounted for 99 percent of total U.S. agricultural assistance offered to date, U.S. Government technical assistance, training, and educational exchanges targeted toward addressing critical problems in the agricultural and food sectors of the former Soviet republics represent only about 1 percent (Table 3).

Some observers argue that the U.S. Government should increase resources available for activities in the new states to increase the capacity of their institutions (governmental entities, and emerging private businesses and organizations) to introduce broad market reforms in their agricultural and food sectors. These would include efforts to help them think through how to create market mechanisms appropriate to their social and political contexts, and to help them introduce these to better ensure the delivery of ample food supplies to the large cities and food deficit regions. Some Russians, while acknowledging the immediate benefits of food assistance, maintain that their need for technical assistance and appropriate agricultural equipment and technology is even more critical. [19] Some have further argued that if Russia is not expected to repay the credits that the USDA guarantees, then prudent U.S. policy would be to acknowledge this up front, and use some of resources

---

[19] Elizabeth Ross. *Christian Science Monitor.* "Former Soviets Critique US Aid Program." May 21, 1992. p. 7.

attributable to likely unrecoverable loan repayments to promote agricultural and food sector reforms in the new states.

Some recommended that U.S. technical assistance and related efforts to help make the transition to free markets be expanded and structured to facilitate U.S. agribusinesses' understanding of the market and investment potential that exists in these new states. Some U.S. agribusinesses have already realized that technical assistance targeted, for example, to develop the capacity of private farmers and emerging cooperatives to process and market food products can go far to boost available food supplies. They have come to understand that such involvement can help them comprehend the changes that are occurring in one of the world's largest untapped markets, and help them take advantage of the trade and business opportunities that will arise once economic growth resumes. Iowa and Maryland, among other states, are developing sister relationships between their agribusiness firms and agricultural academic institutions, and counterparts in the new states. These ties have facilitated reciprocal exchanges and offered training opportunities for agricultural specialists and students to come to the United States.

Some note that U.S. Government support of U.S. agribusiness (particularly small- and medium-sized firms) exploring trade and investment prospects in the new states has been minimal when compared to the priority that Administration statements have placed on helping them transform their agricultural and food sectors and when measured against the almost $6 billion in credit guarantees offered to meet Russian and Ukrainian requests for food import assistance. These observers frequently point out that agribusinesses based in other Western countries are far ahead in establishing a foothold in these new markets because their governments actively support their efforts. While the USDA has had no program to provide U.S. agribusiness with project assistance overseas, it is currently formulating a program to make credit guarantees available to help U.S. firms finance projects that improve food handling, marketing, processing, storage, and distribution capabilities in the new states and lend managerial skills to enterprises there. However, this "emerging democracies" provision in current law limits guarantee-backed financing, though, to projects that expand U.S. agricultural trade. [20] As a result, U.S. firms will likely face difficulties in ensuring that some proposed projects in the new states will primarily benefit U.S. agricultural exports and not those of our competitors.

Other alternatives may be more promising and flexible in helping U.S. firms explore business prospects in the new states. U.S. agribusiness could seek financial backing for exporting agricultural and food processing equipment and technology under the U.S. Export-Import Bank's credit guarantee and insurance programs. Those U.S. agribusiness firms exploring joint venture possibilities with business partners in the new states could seek investment protection against economic and political risk under the programs

---

[20] Section 1542(b) of the Food, Agriculture, Conservation and Trade Act of 1990 (P.L. 101–624), as amended and codified at 7 U.S.C. 5622 note.

offered by the Overseas Private Investment Corporation (OPIC). [21] The U.S. Trade and Development Program (TDP) is authorized to fund larger feasibility studies that could help U.S. firms make decisions on whether and how best to be involved in these new and changing markets. It is possible that some of the FY93 foreign aid funds Congress appropriated for AID humanitarian and technical assistance efforts in the new states might be made available to help small-to medium-sized agribusinesses cope with the risks associated with developing projects that help the new states restructure their agricultural and food sectors and that position these firms to take advantage of future opportunities.

COMPOSITION OF FUTURE AGRICULTURAL IMPORTS BY THE FORMER SOVIET UNION: IMPLICATIONS FOR THE UNITED STATES

Changes within the agricultural and food sectors of the former Soviet republics as economic reforms slowly are introduced can be expected to alter the composition of U.S. agricultural and other exports to these markets. Although the former Soviet Union has been a critical market for U.S. wheat, corn, and oilseeds since the early 1970s, changes in the import needs of the new states could: (1) affect the mix and proportions of commodities that benefit from USDA guarantees allocated for export sales to Russia, Ukraine, and other potential eligible countries, (2) influence the way the USDA exercises discretionary authority granted by farm legislation to operate its price support and supply control programs for these commodities, and (3) require U.S. exporters to look for other overseas markets to offset declining sales of some traditionally exported agricultural commodities to the new states.

The adjustments in the agricultural and food sectors that have started to take place in some of the new states of the former U.S.S.R. include the following: (1) collective and state farms are shifting toward producing more profitable crops in order to cover the much higher costs of purchasing needed agricultural equipment, machinery and other inputs; (2) more private farmers are trying to get established (though small in number and in total area farmed); (3) governments of the new states are offering relatively higher procurement prices for agricultural commodities (particularly grain) to encourage farms to sell more of their output to procurement organizations; (4) more commodities are moving through new nonstate marketing channels in response to higher free market prices, and (5) consumers' food consumption is shifting from meat and dairy products to relatively cheaper bread and other grain products in reaction to large price increases. Also, plans by the Russian and Ukrainian Governments to privatize food processing facilities and other components of the food sector could start to inject some competition into the food marketplace and improve operating efficiencies.

These adjustments in the agricultural and food sectors are expected to provide financial incentives for farms and food processors to reduce current losses as harvested output moves through the

---

[21] For additional information on the Export-Import Bank and OPIC, refer to the papers by William Cooper and Daniel Bond in volume 1 of this study.

food chain. As this occurs, various analyses [22] indicate that some of the new states by the late 1990s could very well be more self-sufficient in producing such commodities as wheat and feed grains. As a result, their agricultural import requirements are expected to decline, or the composition of what they import will likely shift from bulk commodities to higher value food products that, once economic growth resumes, would become affordable to consumers.

These analyses sketch out a scenario in which some of the new states over time reduce their wheat imports as farms improve their yields and quality of output by responding to price incentives to sell their wheat to flour mills rather than to feed it to their livestock. Imports of feed grains may also fall, since the potential exists to expand their production. Some even foresee Kazakhstan and Ukraine exporting grain on the world market when they have a surplus to earn hard currency rather than selling to Russia and other former republics. [23] Because the new states are not expected to fully produce their own protein requirements, imports of soybeans and soymeal will likely increase as efforts are undertaken to improve feeding efficiencies in the livestock sector. What is not clear in this scenario is over what time period these developments will occur, and to what extent the new states will look outward for market outlets for their agricultural surpluses rather than trade with each other as they did before the breakup of the U.S.S.R.

What this scenario suggests is that by the late 1990s the United States could, with respect to the former Soviet Union, lose a key market for wheat and see reduced levels of corn exports. Over time, though, exports of oilseeds and other agricultural products and services are likely to increase. For U.S. policymakers and agribusinesses, this would mean rethinking what future U.S. wheat and feed grain programs policy should be, or redirecting efforts toward developing other prospective markets overseas. Some of the new states also can be expected to turn to overseas suppliers of food products, inputs (e.g., farm equipment and machinery, food processing equipment and facilities), and improved agricultural technology. Those familiar with this region believe that what U.S. agribusinesses do now to explore these export opportunities (as foreign competitors are currently aggressively doing) will be vital to their long-term business prospects in the region.

Some observers urge that the USDA, in allocating credit guarantees among commodities and offering export subsidies on selected commodities and food products, take into account the change in the mix of commodities and food products that Russia, Ukraine, and other new states will want to import from the United States over the next few years. One criterion suggested to guide these decisions would be to ask whether or not they assist and/or complement the agricultural adjustments taking place. To illustrate, some suggest

[22] These include: (1) Alan Barkema. *Economic Review* [Federal Reserve Bank of Kansas City]. "How Will Reform of the Soviet Farm Economy Affect U.S. Agriculture." September/ October 1991. pp. 16–17; (2) *Financial Times.* "CIS grain trade switch forecast." June 4, 1992; (3) International Wheat Council. *Grain Market Report.* "Former USSR: Factors Affecting Grain Import Demand." PMR 204, July 30, 1992. pp. S.2, 1.1–1.5; (4) The WEFA Group. *US Agriculture and World Trade: Long-Term Forecast and Analysis.* "The Former Soviet Union: A Disappearing Market." No. 1, May 1992. pp. 1.9–1.10.

[23] International Wheat Council. *Ibid.* p. 1.5; *Agra Europe.* "Ukraine—An Importer or Exporter of Grain?" No. 1507, September 4, 1992. p. M/13.

that USDA programs should not be used in the short term to subsidize U.S. livestock products, such as pork, into these markets at a time that their livestock herds are being reduced and meat storage warehouses are full. Though officials in the large cities are seeking sources of meat for state store shelves to sell at affordable prices, increased meat imports could actually hurt the livestock adjustment process now taking place. These meat surpluses are accumulating because consumers are refusing to purchase meat, previously subsidized by the Russian government, at the current relatively high market prices.

Some Members of Congress, U.S. agribusinesses, and buyers in the new states seeking access to financing have urged that the USDA allow for an expansion of, or a change in, the mix of commodities sold under the guarantee program or subsidized under EEP and related export subsidy programs. Advocates expect that this would lead to the broader inclusion of processed and higher value food exports, primarily meat and dairy products, to the new states.

CONCLUSION

With uncertainty associated with future economic and political reform in Russia and the other new states, U.S. Government policy makers will face conflicting pressures on the course to chart for future U.S. agricultural export and assistance policy with respect to the former Soviet republics. Those that benefited from past U.S. export sales to the U.S.S.R. will continue to advocate policies that seek to maintain the status quo—essentially continuing traditional commodity export sales because of the obvious short-term economic benefits for the U.S. farm and agribusiness sectors. Also, Russian and Ukrainian bureaucracies will seek to maintain their key role in arranging for Western grain imports to meet procurement shortfalls. Others, though, will argue that overall long-term U.S. interests would best be served by aggressively formulating creative approaches that not only help the new states meet some of their immediate commodity import needs, but more important, help them improve the availability of their own food supplies by incorporating market mechanisms in their agricultural and food sectors. As these new states begin to produce a larger portion of their food needs, these proponents argue that U.S. policies should not thwart the trend toward reduced imports of certain traditional commodities, but rather seek to help the U.S. private sector identify those business opportunities that will arise as these economies change. For U.S. agriculture, this might mean increased U.S. Government support for expanded technical assistance initiatives and for exports of other than traditional agricultural products (e.g., agricultural technology, processed food products). Other U.S. economic sectors can be expected also to benefit from increased trade as resources formerly committed to purchase agricultural commodities overseas are freed to purchase other U.S. goods and services that these new states need to transform their economies.

Accordingly, the challenge for the U.S. Government will be to frame an agricultural trade and assistance strategy flexible enough to address the historically unique situation that Russia and the other new states face. This may include altering the forms and mix of current U.S. assistance in ways that help recipient governments and the fledgling private sectors introduce those reforms that demonstrate that these emerging democracies are able to better meet their peoples' food needs than before and that enhance the prospects for popularly accepted and stable democracies in this part of the world.

REFERENCES

Carol Brookins. *World Perspectives: Ag Review.* "A Proposal for Soviet Agricultural Assistance." July 1, 1991. pp. 15–17.

Geonomics Institute. *Geonomics.* "Geonomics to Implement Pilot Program to Privatize and Commercialize Dairy Industry in Estonia." July/August 1992. p. 1.

Interfax-U.S. Agricultural Report. 1992. Various issues.

Iowa State University. Center for Agricultural and Rural Development. Communication received on agribusiness centers project in Russia and Ukraine.

U.S. Agency for International Development (USAID). "Factual Update on USAID's Farmer-To-Farmer Program in the New Independent States of the Former Soviet Union." April 7, 1992; "Farmer-To-Farmer Special Initiative Program in the New Independent States of the Former Soviet Union." March 20, 1992, and September 15, 1992; "New USAID Farmer-To-Farmer Program Sends U.S. Experts to the Former Soviet Union." Office of External Affairs. Press release #92–26, April 6, 1992.

USAID. Bureau of Food and Humanitarian Assistance. Office of Private and Voluntary Cooperation. Phone conversations with staff administering the Farmer-to Farmer Program.

USAID. Bureau for Europe. Office of Development Resources. Food Systems Division. Communications received from and phone conversations with staff administering AID's agricultural and food sector assistance efforts in the Baltics.

USAID. NIS Task Force. "Project Memorandum: Food Systems Restructuring," May 5, 1992. "Amendment No. 1 to the Project Memorandum," May 22, 1992.

U.S. Department of Agriculture (USDA). Office of Public Affairs. News Division, Office of Press and Media Relations. "USDA Backgrounders," "Fact Sheets," and press releases (various dates).

USDA. Foreign Agricultural Service (FAS). Program announcements (various dates).

USDA. FAS. *AgExporter.* "Fact File: Status of U.S. Assistance to the Former Soviet Union." July 1992. pp. 17–19.

USDA. Phone conversations with staff in Agricultural Marketing Service, Extension Service, FAS, and Office of International Cooperation and Development, administering various technical assistance and training efforts in the former Soviet Union.

U.S. Trade and Development Program. Phone conversation with staff. News release announcing grant to develop agribusiness centers in Russia and Ukraine, March 6, 1992.

U.S. Library of Congress. Congressional Research Service (CRS). *AID Development Projects for the Former Soviet Union*, by Patrice Curtis. September 9, 1992.

——. *U.S. Agricultural Assistance to the Former Soviet Union: Policy Issues*, by Remy Jurenas.

——. *U.S. Agricultural Assistance Strategy for the Former Soviet Union: Summary of a CRS Seminar*, by Remy Jurenas. December 31, 1992.

The World Bank. Country Department III, Europe and Central Asia Region. *Food and Agricultural Policy Reforms in the Former USSR: An Agenda for the Transition*. September 1992.

C. Environment

THE ENVIRONMENTAL IMPLICATIONS OF THE DISSOLUTION OF THE U.S.S.R.

By Philip R. Pryde *

CONTENTS

SUMMARY

The 15 new countries of the former Soviet Union vary tremendously, both in size and in population characteristics (Table 1). Some, such as Russia, Ukraine, and Kazakhstan, are large and rich in natural resources. Others, such as Tadzhikistan, Armenia, Moldova, and Latvia have relatively few mineral resources. Some of the more interior republics are land-locked, and lack any direct access to the ocean. Almost all have severe environmental problems that have been well studied and reported upon in recent years. [1] In many areas the state of the environment is so deteriorated that other problems, such as public health, agriculture, and even the ability to site new industry are being severely affected by the ecological crisis. Some of the new states will devote a modest amount of financial resources to environmental enhancement, and

---

* Philip R. Pryde is a Professor with the Department of Geography at San Diego State University.

[1] Included among these works are DeBardeleben, J., *The Environment and Marxism-Leninism*, Boulder: Westview Press, 1985; Feshbach, M. and Friendly, A., *Ecocide in the USSR*, New York: Basic Books, 1992; Jancar, B., *Environmental Management in the Soviet Union and Yugoslavia*, Durham: Duke Univ. Press, 1987; Pryde, P., *Environmental Management in the Soviet Union*, Cambridge: Cambridge Univ. Press, 1991; Stewart, J.M., *The Soviet Environment: Problems, Policies, and Politics*, Cambridge: Cambridge Univ. Press, 1992; and Ziegler, C., *Environmental Policy in the USSR*, Amherst: Univ. of Massachusetts Press, 1987.

(567)

others will not, as the competition for scarce state funds will be fierce. Yet it must be understood that there is no such thing as a healthy economy built on top of a polluted environment, and that environmental degradation is merely the postponement of necessary costs of production, often at the cost of public health.

TABLE 1. Population Data.

Republic	1989 Population (Millions)	Area (Sq. Km.)	Pop'n per Sq. Km	Titular Group as % of population	Russians as a % of population
Russia	147.4	17,075,400	8.631	81.5	81.5
Ukraine	51.7	603,700	85.65	72.6	22.1
Uzbekistan	19.9	447,400	44.49	71.3	8.3
Kazakhstan	16.5	2,717,300	6.086	39.7	37.8
Belorus	10.2	207,600	49.13	77.8	13.2
Azerbaidzhan	7.0	86,600	81.17	82.6	5.6
Gruzia (Georgia)	5.4	69,700	78.18	70.2	6.3
Tadxhikistan	5.1	143,100	35.72	62.2	7.6
Moldova	4.3	33,700	128.8	64.4	12.9
Kyrgyzstan	4.3	198,500	21.62	52.3	21.5
Lithuania	3.7	65,200	56.6	79.6	9.4
Turkmenistan	3.5	488,100	7.24	71.9	9.5
Armenia	3.3	29,800	110.2	93.3	1.6
Latvia	2.7	63,700	42.09	52.1	34.1
Estonia	1.6	45,100	34.88	61.5	30.3

Source: Schwartz, L., "USSR Nationality Redistribution by Republic, 1979–1989," *Soviet Geography*, vol. 32, no. 4 (April 1991), pp. 209–248.

The process of national independence typically constitutes a period of great euphoria followed by a long period of increasing realization that severe economic hardships are frequently the price of independence. In the case of the former Soviet republics, a number of sobering implications of independence can quickly be inferred. This paper will examine some of those implications in the specific context of environmental management.

ECONOMIC IMPLICATIONS FOR THE ENVIRONMENT

The economic implications of independence for the former republics of the U.S.S.R. are daunting, and the redirection of economic resources will be a necessity in most of the newly independent countries [2] Each new country will now be largely responsible for funding its own environmental improvements. In many, economic development will clearly be given a priority over environmental enhancement, echoing a philosophy found in numerous developing nations. In such republics, environmental conditions may at best fail to improve, and in some might actually deteriorate further from 1991 levels. To achieve environmental improvements, in many cases outside economic help will need to be sought.

[2] McAuley, A., "The Economic Consequences of Soviet Disintegration," *Soviet Economy*, vol. 7, no. 3 (July–September 1991), pp. 189–214.

There will also be consideration of natural resource availability resulting from the inherently uneven distribution of such resources throughout the former Soviet Union. Many of the new nations may find themselves cut off from easy access to key natural resources that exist mainly in other republics, or at least find them to be more expensive. For example, many southern republics will now have to import much of their timber needs, their metallurgical resources, and perhaps petroleum products as well, from Russia or other foreign countries and pay market prices. Under the economic umbrella of the former Soviet Union, their access to such economic necessities was easier, and the terms of their acquisition much more favorable.

Energy resources are central to the economy of all nations, and will be a critical factor for many of the new republics. Russia, Kazakhstan, and Ukraine have them in abundance, but other republics will become net importers of energy products. Table 2 indicates the relative advantages or disadvantages of each republic with regard to internal fossil fuel resources. New agreements are needed regarding the movement of these fuels, but not all negotiations are starting smoothly. For example, it has been reported that Ukraine has concluded a deal with Iran to acquire a portion of Iranian oil and gas resources, rather than continuing to buy them from the Russian Federation. And Turkmenistan, rather than continuing to ship natural gas via existing pipelines through (and to) Russia, Ukraine, and the Transcaucasus republics, may sell this much sought-after resource to Turkey or Pakistan instead. [3]

TABLE 2. Fossil Fuel Production, by Republic, 1990.

Republic	1989 Population (millions)	1990 Oil Output (Mmt/yr)	Tons of Output per Capita	1990 Natural Gas Output (bill. m³/yr)	1000 Cubic Meters per Capita	1990 Coal Output (Mmt/yr)	Tons of Output per Capita
Russia	147.4	516.4	3.50	640.4	4.34	395	2.68
Ukraine	51.7	5.0	0.09	29.0	0.56	165	3.19
Belorus	10.2	2.0	0.19	0.2	0.02	0	0
Kazakhstan	16.5	25.1	1.52	7.1	0.43	131	7.94
Uzbekistan	19.9	2.8	0.14	40.8	2.05	6	0.30
Turkmenistan	3.5	5.6	1.60	87.8	25.08	0	0
Kyrgyzstan	4.3	0.2	0.05	0.1	0.02	4	0.93
Tadzhikistan	5.1	0.2	0.04	0.2	0.04	1	0.20
Azerbaidzhan	7.0	12.2	1.74	9.0	1.29	0	0
Gruziya (Georgia)	5.4	0.2	0.04	0	0	1	0.18
Armenia	3.3	0	0	0	0	0	0
Moldova	4.3	0	0	0	0	0	0
Lithuania	3.7	0	0	0	0	0	0
Latvia	2.7	0	0	0	0	0	0
Estonia	1.6	0	0	0	0	0	0
Former Soviet Union	286.7	569.7	1.99	814.7	2.84	703	2.45

Source: Sagers, M. J., "Review of Soviet Energy Industries in 1990," *Soviet Geography*, vol. 32, no. 4 (April 1991), pp. 251–280.

---

[3] *Izvestiya*, January 18, 1992, p. 2, and February 3, 1992, p. 1.

On the other hand, some republics will have valuable resources to export to improve their foreign trade balance. As noted, Turkmenistan has natural gas, and in addition Ukraine and Georgia have manganese, Azerbaidzhan has oil, and Kazakhstan possesses a wealth of mineral resources of many types. In some cases, however, access to world trade routes may be a problem. Also, some republics, in the interest of gaining foreign income, may have to mine deposits they might prefer to leave in the ground for environmental reasons. For example, Estonia may have to mine at least a small portion of its phosphate deposits in the interest of its international trade balance.

Among the environmental consequences of the former Soviet system with which the new countries will have to deal are those relating to public health, especially among workers. The generally adverse state of the natural environment in the former Soviet Union has been well known for over two decades. [4] More recently, detailed information has appeared on the disastrous effects on human health that has resulted from the Stalinist insistence on industrial development at any cost, most notably in the recent volume by Feshbach and Friendly. [5]

DECENTRALIZATION CONSIDERATIONS

Under the structure of the Union of Soviet Socialist Republics, decisions concerning natural resources conservation and environmental protection were made by what were termed all-Union, or Union-republic, ministries and state committees. With the dismemberment of the U.S.S.R., a new process will be needed to fulfill these functions. The new Commonwealth of Independent States, although a possible vehicle, seems an unlikely choice due to the 14 minority republics' distrust of any centralized authority. Independent control by agencies within each of the new nations seems a far more likely course of action.

This means that, in all probability, 15 different structures will emerge. Some republics may divide responsibilities among a number of regulatory agencies, others may opt for a "super-agency" concept. Given that no form of governmental structure is perfect, leadership priorities will become an important factor. Each republic will have to create its own mechanisms for ensuring a high level of environmental quality, and find the resources to carry them out in practice. Well-worded laws that have meaning only on paper, a long-standing Soviet stock-in-trade, will clearly not suffice.

One of the most critical of regulatory concerns will be nuclear energy. Most commercial nuclear reactors are located in Russia and Ukraine, and sufficient expertise may exist in these large and diverse nations to satisfactorily carry out their own nuclear control programs. But commercial nuclear facilities also exist in Lithuania, Armenia, and Kazakhstan (the latter including a breeder reactor). Both Lithuania and Armenia had earlier talked about creating a nuclear-free energy base, but economic realities will require both of these nuclear facilities to be either restarted (Armenia) or continue

---

[4] Goldman, M., *The Spoils of Progress*, Boston: MIT Press, 1972; Pryde, P., *Conservation in the Soviet Union*, Cambridge: Cambridge Univ. Press, 1972.
[5] Feshbach, M., and Friendly, A., *op. cit.*

producing (Lithuania) for some years to come. Thus, political decentralization engenders a host of questions. Will these reactors be operated by local nationals, or by Russians? Will the Russians conduct training programs? What arrangements will be made for disposing of radioactive wastes? Will waste repositories be needed in the republic containing the nuclear facility, or will Russia accept these wastes? Will the smaller states ask for Russian assistance in dismantling the reactors at the end of their active life? And at that time, what form of energy facility will replace them?

The example of nuclear energy outlined above can be transferred to a number of other industries that are inherently "dirty": iron and steel, petroleum refining, chemicals, fossil fuel power plants, etc. Each republic will need an effective mechanism to control emissions from every category of polluting industry. This has major funding implications. The problem will not be helped by the probable necessity of retaining in their jobs many of the middle-management personnel that were a part of the ineffective regulatory process under the previous Soviet governmental system.

GEOGRAPHIC AND POLITICAL IMPLICATIONS

Under the previous system, only one state was involved. Currently, 15 independent countries are involved in environmental decision-making processes. The geographic/political implications of this are immense. At a minimum, it is inevitable that a great many new bilateral and multilateral treaties will be required, both among the new states themselves, and with outside powers.

As one prime example, consider the water problems of Central Asia. Formerly, a decision, wise or unwise, would have been made in Moscow, and would have been binding on all republics concerned. Today, however, five separate countries are involved, and the experience in the American West suggests that self-interest will quickly divide these new nations into upstream (suppliers) and downstream (consumer) negotiating blocks. Some sort of multilateral basin compact seems essential. Further, it should be noted that parts of the upper basins lie in China and Afghanistan.

An important geographic consideration is that many of these new states are land-locked (Table 3). When they existed as merely a constituent republic of the U.S.S.R., this was not a particularly limiting constraint; a nationwide system of railroads and waterways existed to move goods in and out of these republics.

Today, with independence, the right to move goods over these transportation life-lines will probably have to be negotiated, and will also require maintaining good relations with one's neighbors. The current unfortunate situation in Armenia and Azerbaidzhan illustrates well what can happen when the latter process fails. A key portion of this transport system is the Volga River and associated canal systems, all of which lie in the Russian Republic. The Azerbaidzhan, Turkmenistan, and Kazakhstan republics all front on the Caspian Sea, and could benefit from the continued accessibility to this system. It is always at the least an inconvenience for a country to not have a port city accessible to the world ocean, as many key economic items are best shipped by bulk cargo vessels over water. Land-locked countries may also find fish products to be more ex-

TABLE 3. Geographic Situation of the Former U.S.S.R. Republics.

Republic	Area (sq. km.)	Access to Ocean		Neighboring Countries	
		Direct	River or Canal	Former U.S.S.R.	Other
Russia (Rus)	17,075,400	yes	yes	a	b
Kazakhstan (Kaz)	2,717,300	no	yes	Rus, Tur, Uzb, Kyr	China
Ukraine (Ukr)	603,700	yes	yes	Rus, Bel, Mol	c
Turkmenistan (Tur)	488,100	no	yes	Kaz, Uzb	Iran, Afghanistan
Uzbekistan (Uzb)	447,400	no	no	Kaz, Tur, Kyr, Tad	Afghanistan
Belorus (Bel)	207,600	no	yes	Rus, Ukr, Lit, Lat	Poland
Kyrgzstan (Kyr)	198,500	no	no	Kaz, Uzb, Tad	China
Tadzhikistan (Tad)	143,100	no	no	Uzb, Kyr	China, Afghanistan
Azerbaidzhan (Azr)	86,000	no	yes	Rus, Arm, Gru	Iran
Gruziya [Georgia] (Gru)	69,700	yes	yes	Rus, Azr, Arm	Turkey
Lithuania (Lit)	65,200	yes	yes	Bel, Lat Rus d	Poland
Latvia (Lat)	63,700	yes	yes	Rus, Est, Lit, Bel	(none)
Estonia (Est)	45,100	yes	yes	Rus, Lat	(none)
Moldova (Mol)	33,700	no	yes	Ukr	Romania
Armenia (Arm)	29,800	no	no	Gru, Azr	Iran, Turkey

Source: *Atlas SSSR,* 1983.
a Russia shares a border with Estonia, Latvia, Belorus, Ukraine, Gruziya (Georgia), Azerbaidzhan, and Kazakhstan.
b Russia borders on Norway, Finland, China, Mongolia, and North Korea.
c Ukraine borders on Poland, Czechoslovakia, Hungary, and Romania.
d Lithuania borders on Kaliningrad Oblast, an exclave of the Russian Republic.

pensive, as the former Soviet fishing fleet was largely in the Russian republic, and fish catches from the Caspian Sea have declined (and those from the Aral almost extirpated).

Another important environmental consideration having a strong spatial element is the movement of transboundary pollutants. This issue has at least four main components: (1) airborne pollutants, including not only smokestack and exhaust emissions but also windblown pesticides and other harmful particulates; (2) pollutants transmitted by international river systems or across international lakes; (3) pollution of seas (Baltic, Black, etc.) whose coastlines are shared by two or more nations; and (4) deliberately conveyed pollutants, that is, those that are legally moved, or in some cases illegally smuggled, across national borders. Because many of the countries in Eastern Europe are small, transboundary pollution has become a significant international issue. Attempts to control this situation are embodied in such accords as the Convention on Long-Range Transboundary Air Pollution of 1979.

MILITARY CONFLICT AND THE ENVIRONMENT

It has been frequently observed that the greatest of environmental disasters is war, a point that was vividly driven home during, and after, the 1991 Gulf War in Kuwait and Iraq. Unfortunately, at the time of this writing, at least four armed conflicts are raging in various parts of the former Soviet Union, specifically, in Nagorno-Karabakh and surrounding portions of Azerbaidzhan, in the South Ossetian region of Georgia (Gruziya), in Tadzhikistan, and in the

Transdniester region of Moldova. Not only is the environment in these areas directly harmed by the destructive activities of the conflict, but the economic cost of the military activities often hampers effective environmental clean-up once the hostilities cease. Substantial levels of foreign capital are often necessary for environmental restoration in such cases, which may not be readily available, especially if there are several claimants for this aid.

An even more critical example involves nuclear weapons. For decades, the United States and the U.S.S.R. were able to negotiate between themselves concerning the possibility of nuclear arms reduction. Suddenly, in 1991, the number of nations possessing strategic nuclear weapons and delivery systems increased by three, as Belorus, Ukraine, and Kazakhstan, all containing former Soviet missile sites, became independent nations. Thus, in 1992, the United States had to expand the scope of its START (Strategic Arms Reduction Treaty) negotiations to deal with four countries, rather than one. The fact that some of these new states may view the temporary retention of these weapons as a very important political bargaining chip does not help the cause of nuclear non-proliferation.

This leads immediately to another military-related environmental legacy of the cold war. Although the vast improvements in U.S.-U.S.S.R./Russian relations over the past few years have led to a significant level of mutual disarmament, even this comes at an environmental price. The frequently cited adage of ecologists that "everything has to go somewhere" takes on immutable significance here. How will both sides dispose of the chemical weapons, bomb-grade nuclear materials, rocket propellants, chemical explosives, etc., that will still exist even after their conveyance systems are dismantled? This may become one of the major environmental challenges of the 1990s.

INTER-REPUBLIC ENVIRONMENTAL COORDINATION

A high level of inter-republic cooperation will be essential if environmental concerns are to be adequately addressed in the post-Soviet period. This cooperation would need to occur at two levels, the official governmental level, and the NGO (non-governmental environmental organization) level. At the governmental level, coordination could be effected by umbrella organizations established under the Commonwealth of Independent States (CIS). However, in 1992 the CIS was not showing much evidence of being a strong coordinating body. Lacking a strong unifying body, this coordination could be accomplished by bilateral and multilateral agreements, the need for which has already been noted.

The most obviously needed compact would be one to manage the water resources of Central Asia. The Colorado River Compact among the southwestern states of the United States could in some ways serve as a model (although admittedly a less than perfect one). The most preferable form of such a compact would be a five-republic accord encompassing the entire Aral Sea basin, which ideally might be expanded to include also Afghanistan and its portion of the upper Amu-Darya (Pyandzh) basin. Less ideal would be separate compacts for the Amu-Darya and Syr-Darya basins. The latter approach might prove faster to achieve, but would respond poorly to the problem of resolving the Aral Sea desiccation crisis. A number of other bilateral or multilateral water compacts might be useful. Among them would be agreements among Russia, Belorus and Ukraine concerning the Dnieper and its tributaries, between Ukraine and Moldova concerning the Dniester, among Russia, Belorus, and Latvia concerning the Western Dvina (Daugava), between Russia and Ukraine concerning the Donets, between Russia and Kazakhstan concerning the Irtysh (and Tobol and Ishim), between Georgia and Azerbaidzhan concerning the Kura, and between Russia and Estonia concerning Lake Peipus and related drainages. In a more peaceful world, an agreement concerning the Araks River among Armenia, Azerbaidzhan, Turkey, and Iran might even be envisioned. Another area of discord exists between Ukraine and the Krasnoyarsk Territory of the Russian Federation. Because Ukraine has not supplied adequate amounts of food to the Krasnoyarsk region, the latter was threatening in 1992 not to receive any further radioactive wastes from Ukrainian nuclear power plants. [6]

Multilateral agreements include a number of economic accords already signed between former U.S.S.R. republics and outside nations. A notable example would be the 1992 Declaration on Black Sea Economic Cooperation, entered into by Russia, Ukraine, Moldova, Georgia (Gruziya), Armenia, and Azerbaidzhan, as well as by Turkey, Albania, Romania, Bulgaria, and Greece. This compact could easily be expanded into covering environmental protection for the Black Sea as well.

With regard to the nongovernmental organizations (NGOs), as of 1992 they might be even better organized than their official counterparts. The most impressive organization at present is the Socio-Ecological Union (SEU), headquartered in Moscow. It was founded before the breakup of the Soviet Union, and hence retains good ties to environmental groups in almost all of the former U.S.S.R. republics, and is perhaps the most reliable source of information about them. In the spring of 1991 the SEU and the Institute for Soviet-American Relations (ISAR) hosted the first U.S.S.R.-U.S. conference of nongovernmental environmental organizations in Moscow, at which dozens of such groups from both countries were represented by delegates. [7] Other similar organizations exist, such as "Ekologiya i mir," but none appear to be as well organized as the SEU.

OTHER CONSIDERATIONS

The 15 new countries will be facing other new problems and challenges related to environmental management. One group of such problems relates to demographic factors.

One of the most pressing of these concerns is high birth rates. Among the former Soviet republics, birth rates tend to be lowest in the Slavic and Baltic regions, and highest in the Islamic republics. Birth rates in Georgia and Armenia, formerly high, dropped off somewhat during the 1980s. In Central Asia and Azerbaidzhan, the

[6] *Izvestiya*, January 11, 1992, p. 2.
[7] Klose *et al.*, *Joint US-USSR NGO Conference on the Environment*, Washington: ISAR, 1991.

unfortunate combination of high birth rates and limited employment opportunities could lead to a philosophy of subordinating environmental concerns to an overriding effort to create jobs. This would be particularly unfortunate in a portion of the former Soviet Union already known to have severe problems of water pollution and toxic pesticide contamination. [8] On the other hand, in the Russian Federation the mortality rate exceeded the birth rate in early 1992 for the first time since World War II. [9]

The interests of minority populations also have environmental implications. This is particularly true in the Russian Federation, where the largest individual political sub-unit, the Yakut Autonomous Republic, has asked for greater local control over its vast wealth of natural resources. The Tatar Republic (Tatarstan) has voted for political sovereignty, implying that in the future much of the extensive oil deposits within the Russian Federation could be controlled locally, rather than from Moscow. If local ethnic regions attempt to control natural resources, there are three possible subsequent scenarios, two of which hold adverse environmental implications. First, the local area, feeling exploited, might opt to decrease or halt production from one or more mineral deposits, forcing increased production in other areas, at possibly higher environmental costs. Or, needing income, the local area might increase production, with potentially greater environmental damage. The more favorable outcome, that the local area might act to cause present production to take place in a more environmentally benign manner, while possible, is unlikely to be widely carried out.

Another consideration is the large number of ethnic Russians living in many of the minority regions (see table 1). Some republics wish to see these ethnic Russians relocated, but some of these Russians would be technicians knowledgeable in environmental management practices. Their premature departure could prove unfortunate.

The factor of money can hardly be overemphasized. Environmental cleanup requires capital, huge amounts of it, and none of the republics have such a luxury. In 1992, Russia and other new nations were eagerly seeking foreign financial aid to assist their struggling economies, and environmental clean-up was not at the top of the needs list. Perhaps the most optimistic scenario is that the new nations will simply shut down the worst polluting industries, and the foreign aid can help to build newer factories that use inherently cleaner technologies. In the short run, however, there is little question that much pollution will simply continue.

A final consideration is the environmental effect of foreign developmental investments. Will the new nations have sufficient wisdom and experience to insist on adequate environmental safeguards? The proposed development of the huge Tengiz oil field in Kazakhstan by Chevron comes quickly to mind. American companies are not required by U.S. law to carry out environmental impact analyses on projects in foreign countries; local laws must see that this procedure is performed.

---

[8] Pryde, P., *Environmental Management*; and Feshbach and Friendly, *op. cit.*
[9] *Izvestiya*, March 30, 1992, p. 2.

CONCLUSION

Within the territory of the former Soviet Union, these are both exciting and troublesome times. While it would be easy to argue that most of these new nations have more urgent problems than environmental improvement, this would be an unfortunate and misleading conclusion. In many areas the state of the environment is so deteriorated that other problems, such as public health, agriculture, and even the ability to find sites for new industry, are being severely affected by the ecological crisis itself. Thus, the proper way to view the situation is not that environmental improvement is in fourth or sixth place on a shopping list of national capital needs, but rather that it is an essential component of all items on that shopping list. It must be understood that there is no such thing as a healthy economy built on top of a polluted environment, and that environmental degradation is merely the postponement of necessary costs of production, often at the cost of public health. Future generations thus must pay twice, once to cover the (inflated) cost of the clean-up, and once to cure health problems. The most responsible approach to avoid this is to internalize the costs of a healthy environment into the production and pricing procedures of today. Only in this way can the countries of the former Soviet Union avoid repeating the environmental mistakes of the past and inflicting them upon their own future generations.

ENVIRONMENTAL CALAMITIES: WIDESPREAD AND COSTLY

by Murray Feshbach *

CONTENTS

SUMMARY

The lack of financial and other resources is well known. Less well known is the drawdown (demand) for these scarce monies for environmental clean-up and pollution abatement costs due to neglect, abuse, and destruction of the land, air, and water, due to radioactivity from military and civilian nuclear explosions and due to decisions made at the very beginning of the (former) Soviet state to have production regardless of cost. As the State Advisor on Environment and Health, Alexey Yablokov, succinctly put it: "The situation is not bad, but desperate." Highlights include overuse of pesticides, diversion of waters from the Aral Sea, air polluted by industrial facilities and by military use of radioactive devices and reactors, three-quarters of surface waters polluted, rise in birth defects and birth deformities, and new information about the depth of radioactivity present throughout the area. Land, air, water, and radioactivity are subjected to review and analysis of their level of environmental degradation. The range of locations and quantities of radioactivity, as far as is known and for the time available, is described as well. Based on official statistics, a tabular display by region and by cause of pollution, prepared by a Soviet environmentalist/geographer is included at the end of the paper as Figure 1. Using a weighing system and some brief analysis, regional differen-

---

* Murray Feshbach is Research Professor of Demography, Georgetown University.

tials emerge that highlight the relative degrees of degradation and implied priority regions for clean-up and abatement.

INTRODUCTION

An analysis of the current condition in the former Soviet Union would likely yield a conclusion of death by ecocide. [1]

"When historians finally conduct an autopsy on the Soviet Union and Soviet Communism, they may reach the verdict of death by ecocide. For the modern era, indeed for any event except the mysterious collapse of the Mayan empire, it would be a unique but not an implausible conclusion. No other great industrial civilization so systematically and so long poisoned its land, air, water and people. None so loudly proclaiming its efforts to improve public health and protect nature so degraded both. And no advanced society faced such a bleak political and economic reckoning with so few resources to invest toward recovery."

The early decision of the State and its rulers to have production at any cost was followed to a degree unparalleled in industrialized countries. Production was achieved without regard to costs in human lives, renewability of natural resources, or the condition of the air, land, and water. The legacy of the former government will be long-lasting not only in terms of economic costs but also in terms of human costs. In addition to "normal" pollution—the extent of which will be shown—radioactivity and the potential for more nuclear accidents is manifest. Potential disasters emanating from operating facilities that would be closed if viable alternatives were readily and immediately available, are reported in the former Soviet press as well as in Western sources. The German government has been among the most specific in reviewing the condition of all Soviet-designed and built nuclear reactors. According to their 1991 white paper, the problems with the Soviet nuclear reactors include: 1) no spatial separation between fresh steam and feedwater supply; 2) insufficient fire safety measures; 3) no measures taken to provide protection against external stress, such as from aircraft crashes or explosion blast waves; 4) poor quality and reliability of subsystems and components; 5) no safety containment vessel, as called for in Western safety requirements; and many others. [2]

New information, moreover, on other sources of radioactivity—their spread, level, and potential for negative consequences—exceeds any expectations from even previous levels of ecocidal-type behavior by the authorities, especially the military. A total disregard for human lives, both in terms of events and in the proliferation of residual toxic waste sites, has led to a legacy of ill populations (the labor force included), current and future birth defects

---

[1] This submission is based primarily on the book *Ecocide in the USSR: Health and Nature Under Siege*, by Murray Feshbach and Alfred Friendly Jr., New York: Basic Books, 1992, 376 pages. The quotation is from page 1 of the book.
[2] See the White Paper issued by the Federal German Government, entitled (in English translation) *Report of the Federal Minister for the Environment, Conservation and Nuclear Safety and Environmental Problems Associated with Energy Supply in Central and Eastern Europe.* Bonn, 6 November 1991, p. 17; also see pages 15, 18–20.

and deformities, and enormous clean-up costs, in addition to all the other economic, social, and political burdens that the current governments must face. Some former republics such as Russia, Ukraine, and Belarus, as well as the Baltic States, are actively concerned. Several others are moderately so, but the rest are too busy with internal (Georgia) or external (Armenia and Azerbaydzhan) conflicts to pay serious attention. The problems will not disappear and the costs may be even larger when finally addressed, than if they were dealt with now.

While information and revelations about the range of problems presented by former and present Soviet government advisors, members of the Supreme Soviet, and environmentalists provide the context for determining costs, the growing sense among the population of the value of protecting the environment may prove to be equally important. Largely latent during this period of transition, the potential for pressure on resource allocations, for stopping production at polluting facilities, and for protests against political authorities remains high.

Aleksey Yablokov, the Yel'tsin government's State Counsellor for Environment and Health and Deputy Chairman of the Ecology Committee of the Supreme Soviet, describes the problem as follows:

"The situation is not bad, but desperate. Sixteen percent of the territory of the former USSR, where something on the order of 45 million to 50 million people (of a total population of some 290 million) live, lies within ecological hazard or disaster zones. Most of these are major industrial regions, such as the southern Urals, Kemerovo Oblast, and so forth. We are breathing increasingly dirty air. We are drinking increasingly dirty water. We are eating increasingly dirty and unsafe foods. As a result, the incidence of disease is growing, the frequency of congenital defects is increasing, and life expectancy is declining. So ecology today is a state security problem." [3]

The last and perhaps still incompletely revealed reason for the current situation listed in the draft document prepared for the Rio de Janeiro Earth Summit of June 1992 is "the extreme scale of the military-industrial complex whose production [and polluting activities] was closed to public ecological scrutiny." [4]

Thus, if we look into Soviet history, decisions made at the very beginning of the State's formation led to threats to its survival, to potential delays in economic recovery, to the demand for resources that the country does not have to clean up radioactive waste sites, find energy, and to purify the air, the land, surface waters, and seas. Some highlights can be given here:

---

[3] L. Glazkova's interview with Yablokov in, "Ecology Today Is a State Security Problem, in the View of A.V. Yablokov, RSFSR State Advisor and USSR People's Deputy," *Torgovaya gazeta*, 22 October 1991, p.4, translated in *JPRS Report, Environmental Issues*, JPRS-TEN-91-019, 15 November 1991, pp. 66–67.

[4] Ministerstvo prirodopol'zovaniya i okhrany okruzhayushchey sredy SSSR, *Proyekt. Natsional'nyy doklad SSSR k konferentsii OON 1992 goda po okruzhayushchey srede i razvitiyu*, Moscow, 1991, p. 9.

1. Overuse of pesticides and toxic agricultural chemicals such as DDT have depleted the soil's viability and contaminated much of the nation's food;

2. Diversion of water from the Aral Sea led to its desiccation—the volume of water in the sea is now 40 percent less than it was 20 years ago—to changes in the climate of the region, to extraordinary sickness rates, and to increases in other costs to the economy and population;

3. Industrial growth, fostered without regard to costs, has led to a situation in which 70 million former Soviets live in 103 cities considered dangerous to the respiratory system and suffer life-shortening diseases from the ambient air in which just one pollutant exceeds the maximum permitted concentration by five or more times;

4. Perhaps three-quarters of the surface water of the ex-Soviet Union is polluted, many rivers threaten to become open sewers, and seas are losing their ability to provide clean water for fish to grow. The severe energy crisis due to the decline in oil, good quality coal, minimal increases in natural gas production, and problems in the nuclear power sector have led to strains in the energy sector of major dimensions and to a reduction in foreign hard currency earnings. The inheritance of nuclear disasters and pollution from 700 major breaks in oil and gas pipelines every year add to their problems;

5. A rise in birth defects and birth deformities due to general environmental conditions, especially the consequences of radioactivity, have led to the formation of a Russian Mutagenic Society worried about the gene pool of the country;

6. Disruptions in many republics/countries and a perceived threat of Islamic fundamentalism are leading to large outflows of trained Russian medical personnel. This could well exacerbate the already poor health situation in Central Asia, especially poor health derived from environmental causes.

7. Radioactivity throughout the country, actual and potential, from civilian and military programs, from nuclear accidents, from toxic waste sites near research reactors, and from dumping of reactors and containers that could yield immense amounts of radioactivity, is much more extensive than previously known or thought. The costs of clean-up and medical treatment are likely to be enormous once fully addressed. But the financial aspect may be less important than the threat to the gene pool of the population.

LAND, AIR, AND WATER POLLUTION—STANDARD POLLUTANTS

LAND

Problems are so extensive that the cost of correction may be much beyond the expectations or willingness of the West to pay for it. DDT continues to be used (directly by that name or as a euphemism such as hexochloropane, as in Lithuania at the beginning of 1990). By the end of the 1980s, nearly one-half of the 1.5 billion acres of cultivated land in the former U.S.S.R. was endangered. Erosion affects 279 million acres, salinization affects 388 million. Sixty-two million acres were waterlogged or swampy, and an additional 13 percent of the 1.5 billion, or 190 million acres, are marginal, rocky, overgrown, or hilly, and are thus less viable for full agricultural development. Excluding the latter, not quite 730 million of the 1.5 billion acres—or one-half of the cultivated land—is eroded, swamped, or saline. The use of DDT on 25 million acres compounds the problem, but more damage is done by the poor condition of the polluted water table when it sinks into the soil. One of the major consequences is the contamination of food. Overall, 30 percent of all food is contaminated by pesticides; or 42 percent of baby food is also contaminated.

Yablokov describes the situation as follows:

"Agricultural monitoring of food products is supplemented by monitoring [through a] network of sanitation and epidemiological stations . . . but not all of them have . . . good equipment and the capability to conduct highly skilled analyses. Nevertheless, they study each year nearly two percent to three percent of all basic food products.

The results are not only alarming, they make you shudder. Up to 40 percent of the output of children's milk kitchens contain pesticide levels hazardous to health. DDT is found in 70 percent of all dietetic butter. Half of all vegetables are dangerous because of contamination with pesticides and mineral fertilizers, mostly nitrogen fertilizer . . . . that is why they keep so poorly. On the whole, nearly 30 percent of all food products are contaminated." [5]

Other than direct use of these pesticides and herbicides, the accidental dissemination into the ground of mineral fertilizers left uncovered and uncontrolled and heavy metals and other pollutants from rivers penetrating the adjacent river banks contribute to the poor environment. The impact of radioactivity on the lands will be discussed below.

AIR

Industrial and other machine-made pollution is devastating the adjacent lands as well as the population's health. The energy sector contributed about one-quarter of all recorded airborne pollutants emitted (in 1988), excluding those from automotive transport. Ferrous and non-ferrous metallurgical industries, when combined, produced slightly more, for a combined total of almost half. [6] Evidence shows that the recorded emissions, however, not only omit emissions from air transport, river transport, and many other sources, but also the heavily polluting military sector. Automotive transport's share of pollution within the total is about one-third the national figure. In cities such as Moscow, the situation is reversed, with automotive pollution contributing about 70 percent of all air pollution recorded in the city. The lack of catalytic converters indicates that there would be a large market for them, if they could be imported and properly installed. In addition, a minimum of 20 to 30 or as high as 50 percent undercount results from monitoring procedures (the timing of the arrival of monitoring vans is known to the polluting factories). Of the 3,100,000 stationary sources of

---

[5] Glazkova interview of Yablokov, op.cit.
[6] See Feshbach and Friendly, Ecocide, 1992, p. 304, for table listing the emissions, by kind, of 15 administrative agencies.

pollution (smokestacks), about one-half have filters, and about 30 percent of these filters work. The remainder need repair, are bypassed, or, in many cases, reportedly capture only solids but not gases. The recent drop in pollution is less attributable to the successful environmental abatement than to the shutdown of much of Soviet industry because of political and economic disruptions and strikes.

Air pollution exists in all former Soviet cities, but it is worse in some than others. As noted above, 70 million persons (out of an urban population of 190 million in the former Soviet Union), live where the maximum pollution concentration (PDK) of at least one pollutant is 5 or more times the maximum. Fifty million urban residents live where the PDK is exceeded by 10 or more times, and 43 million where it is exceeded 15 or more times. With each additional "five" the morbidity rate per 100,000 population doubles. An alternative set of figures has recently been cited for Russia by the Minister of Ecology of Russia, Viktor Danilov-Danilyants. Referring to an interviewer's comment that the totality of environmental problems is "most gloomy," Danilov-Danilyants responded that the comment is "specifically correct." For Russia alone, 35 cities "have entirely unacceptable air pollution indicators" and 65 to 110 additional cities have "unacceptable air pollution indicators." [7] "In many places pollutants seem to be superimposed. Transport gives off nitric oxide; metallurgy yields sulfur dioxide and benzopyrene; chemistry yields formaldehyde, phenols, and aromatic hydrocarbons." The chemical "bouquet" menaces the health of the residents of Kemerovo, Nizhniy Tagil, Sverdlovsk, Perm, Chelyabinsk and Saratov. [8] The minister earnestly sought outside help, both technical and financial, knowing that the large investments needed are not forthcoming from his government. If the aid is not forthcoming, then Danilov-Danilyants is convinced from recent data that they "will not be able to" save the ecosphere of the country. If so, he continued, "irreversible changes in the natural systems and in the gene pool will occur faster than the economy developing without Western aid can gain enough strength to restore nature."

Several passing references have been made recently about problems with the ozone layer in the atmosphere. Yablokov is not oblique; he defines the problem as being the "biggest threat to us" and declares it "will give us a hard time." He continues:

"Over the past few years, until mid-1991, the amount of ozone in the middle latitudes of the Northern Hemisphere diminished by 3 percent, which, in my estimation, increased cancer incidence by 12,000 cases per year in the European part of the country; in 1991, the ozone layer dwindled another 40 percent." [9]

A Ukrainian newspaper cites a senior scientific associate of the Hydrometeorological Research Institute of Kiev to the effect that for Moscow, St. Petersburg, and other regions of the Common-

[7] Interview by Dmitriy Frolov, "Russia Has Found Itself in Ecological Time Trouble," *Nezavisimaya gazeta,* 6 May 1992, p. 6.
[8] *Ibid.*
[9] Interview with Aleksey Yablokov by Arkadiy Dubnov, "Aleksey Yablokov: 'The Threat of Ecological Disaster is No Secret to the President," *New Times,* no. 14, April 1992, p. 13.

wealth of Independent States (CIS), the ozone layer has been thinned by almost one-half. According to this individual, the institute has monitored the ozone level in Ukraine since 1973. Analysis of these data show that the layer has been thinning since 1980. A "marked rise" in the number of ozone anomalies has occurred. In Kiev and several other cities, a drop in overall ozone content by 43 percent was noted in January 1992. "That is the lowest level recorded in the past 20 years.... ultraviolet radiation has increased as well." [10]

WATER

If three-quarters of the surface water is polluted, and many seas are polluted, then to this must be added water reservoirs. Danilov-Danilyants notes that they are in "an unacceptable state." He reserves stronger words for the Volga. "The Volga is no longer a great Russian river, but by analogy with the Danube, which is called the cesspool of Europe, it fully deserves to be called 'the cesspool of Russia.'" Further, practically all rivers in the Urals are polluted. [11] This turns out to be an allusion to the radioactivity problem, as will be shown below, and not just water pollution per se.

Six hundred cities of the former Soviet Union have inadequate water treatment and thus impure water. Many major cities such as Moscow and Riga do not treat their water adequately. Both the Siberian and Volga Basins have recently become infested with helminths (worms). The reported number of parasitic disease patients was 4.5 million in 1987; the unofficial number estimated by the head of the Institute of Medical Parasitology and Tropical Medicine of the Medical Academy is 45 million or so. Reduced productivity of the affected labor force, as well as costs to obtain medicines and staff to treat this number of patients, has to add an unexpected large sum to the already considerable sum of monies that the authorities need to spend but do not have.

RADIOACTIVITY—THE NON-STANDARD POLLUTANT

On the one hand, we are probably at the beginning stage of important revelations about the extent of radioactivity throughout the former Soviet Union. On the other hand, enough is already known to be able to say that it is much worse than imagined or known, and may be calamitous. The information now available includes maps and data on illness, and is documented in books, articles, and personal conversations. The population affected by Chernobyl is now known to be not 5 oblasts—2 in Ukraine, 2 in Belarus, and 1 in Russia—as initially announced in April 1986, but 15 territories in Russia alone, where there is an average contamination density of cesium–137 of over 1.0 curie per square kilometer. These include Bryansk oblast (over 34 percent of the oblast territory); Kaluga oblast (17 percent); Belgorod oblast (8 percent); Voronezh oblast (1.5 percent); Kursk oblast (4.4 percent); Leningrad oblast (1

[10] Valentin Bludov, "Timely Interview: We do Not Have to Throw out our Refrigerators to Save the Ozone Layer," *Vecherniy Kiev*, 5 May 1992, p. 3, translated in FBIS, *JPRS Report. Environmental Issues*, JPRS-TEN-92-011, 23 June 1992, pp. 107–108.
[11] *Ibid.*

percent); Lipetsk oblast (ca. 8 percent); Orel oblast (40 percent); Penza oblast (3 percent); Ryazan oblast (15 percent); Smolensk oblast (0.5 percent); Tambov oblast (1.7 percent); Tula oblast (47 percent); Ulyanovsk oblast (0.6 percent); and Mordovia (2 percent). Regions with less than 1 curie per square kilometer affected include Tver, Novgorod, and Nizhengorod oblasts. Saratov oblast and Udmurtia had between 0.5 and 0.6 curies per square kilometer affected. Karelia had less than 0.3; and Astrakhan, Kaliningrad, Kostroma, and Rostov oblasts along with Chuvashia and Kalmykia, all had less than 0.2. Many other regions showed less than 0.1 curies per square kilometer affected; these included Archangel'sk, Vladimir, Vologda, Ivanovo, Kirov, Samara, Moscow, Murmansk, Orenburg, Perm, Pskov, and Yaroslavl districts, Stavropol Krai, Bashkiria, Mariy El, and Komi. The Siberian and Far East regions beyond the Urals also are known to have traces of radiation from Chernobyl. It has not yet been fully determined to what degree these regions are contaminated, but they will be added to the already lengthy list. And this list omits the impact of Chelyabinsk, Semipalatinsk, Novaya Zemlya, Shokhotka–22, secret cities such as Tomsk–7, and others not cited here. [12] This list can serve as a first-order list of where health and associated clean-up problems will likely occur, as they have already, especially in terms of birth defects.

This paper is not the place to go into all details regarding radioactive pollution, but several comments are needed to place the Chernobyl-associated list in context.

First, the Three Mile Island accident in Pennsylvania released "only" 15 curies of radionucleides.

Second, the Three Mile Island accident is in no way comparable to the Chernobyl accident, where 50 million curies of cesium–137, strontium–90, and plutonium–239 and –240 were released.

Third, in its turn, Chernobyl's 50 million curies is dwarfed by the release in the Chelyabinsk area of 1,200 million curies.

Fourth, Chelyabinsk is probably eclipsed by the estimated 1,000 to 3,500 million curies in the northern region around Novaya Zemlya, in the Barents, White, and Kara Seas.

The number of curies released by Semipalatinsk is not available, but it is estimated that perhaps 100,000 died and 800,000 were affected by the above- and underground testing. Nor is the number of curies from 115 civilian nuclear explosions—air, surface, and underground—in the Volga region (20), in Yakutiya (12), Chukhotka and other locales. Prof. V. Mikhaylov, the Russian Federation Minister for Atomic Energy, noted that between 1949 and 1962, some 124 air or surface nuclear weapons tests were conducted at the Semipalatinsk range, and 343 underground tests were conducted from 1963 to 1990. In comparison, at the Northern range (i.e., in Novaya Zemlya), beginning in 1955, 90 nuclear weapon tests were conducted in the air or on the surface, and 42 were conducted underground, for a total of 132 tests. [13] As noted above, there are radio-

---

[12] See especially, *Argumenty i fakty,* no. 16–17, May 1992, p. 7.
[13] V. Mikhaylov, "Nuclear Weapons," *Rossiyskaya gazeta,* 8 May 1992, p. 4, translated in FBIS, *JPRS Report. Environmental Issues,* JPRS-TEN-92-011, 23 June 1992, p. 78.

active waste sites in Moscow, St. Petersburg, Ulyanovsk, and many other localities. One Kazakh scientist estimated that the total release of radioactive substances into the atmosphere in the U.S.S.R. was 3 trillion curies, equal to one-half of the world's total discharge. [14]

THE IMPACT OF RADIOACTIVITY AND STANDARD POLLUTION ON HEALTH

Several examples should suffice to underline the health consequences aspect even more clearly, and to recall the economic implications of these events for medical services as well as containment vessel construction, clean-up of radioactive substances dumped uncontained into rivers and lakes, or purchase of clean food for sufferers of radioactivity.

The villages within the 30-kilometer zone around the testing range at Semipalatinsk suffer from the "Kaynar Syndrome," Kaynar being the name of one of these villages. The syndrome is

"transmitted genetically from generation to generation . . . One-third of the babies born here are either dead or are monsters. . . . the increase in infant mortality from congenital anomalies caused by genetic defects because of a worsening of the ecological balance . . . the proportion of congenital defects in the development of children less than a year old has grown by 50 up to 100 percent in the past 10–15 years." [15]

In Chukhotka, the Leningrad Radiation Health Research Institute found that the "total radiation exposure was twice as high as the average for the USSR, ... approximately equal to the average dose . . . in the monitored areas affected by the Chernobyl [accident]." [16] This was due to Chernobyl according to a member of a delegation assigned to study the region's condition. As a result of this exposure, the lead–210 content of the bone tissue of reindeer meat eaters is 10 to 20 times higher, and the cesium–137 content is 100 times higher than lead–210 content of the bone tissue of the population in the monitored areas referred to above. Life expectancy at birth among the indigenous populations is 45 to 46 years for both sexes on the average, or 25 years less than the national average. "Virtually 100 percent of the indigenous population suffer from tuberculosis." New data released for Belarus and Ukraine demonstrate the impact of the Chernobyl accident on the local populations. In late March 1992, Ukraine's Parliamentary Commission on Chernobyl affirmed that 37 Ukrainian and 51 Belorussian children were diagnosed with thyroid cancer in 1991 and 1992; before the accident in April 1986 only 1 or 2 cases per year were reported. In mid-April 1992, the Parliament of Belarus was informed that 1,700 cases of thyroid cancer were recorded in Belarus at the begin-

---

[14] I. Chasnikov, "Tears of the Test Site: An Eyewitness Account," *Kazakhstanskaya Pravda*, 28 August 1991, p. 3, translated in JPRS, *USSR. Political Affairs*, JPRS-UPA-91-046, 20 November 1991, p. 81.
[15] Viktor Dik, "The Kaynar Syndrome," *Kazakhstanskaya Pravda*, 23 February 1991, p. 1.
[16] Vladimir Lupandin and Ye. Gayer, "I Ask for the Floor: A Chernobyl on Chukhotka.—The Peoples of the North are Paying for Nuclear Test," *Moskovskiye novosti*, no. 324, August 20, 1989, p. 5.

ning of the year, with 55 children afflicted. Prior to the accident, for 20 years up to 1986, only 5 adults and no children were recorded as being diagnosed with thyroid cancer. Another 299 persons (in addition to the 1,700 cited for the beginning of the year) were "officially recorded," including 52 children, in the first few months of 1992.

At the Belorussian Congress on Chernobyl, held in April 1992, a speaker indicated that "Almost 200,000 Byelorusian children now have enlarged thyroids." In Ukraine, the rate of thyroid cancer increased by 17 times in the period 1986 to 1991. Perhaps 6,000 to 8,000 persons have died in Ukraine alone. [17]

These reports completely contradict the findings of the International Atomic Energy Agency's (IAEA) report on the health consequences of Chernobyl. The study was performed too early, the sample did not include all the persons involved, and the IAEA did not inquire about the secret data in the Ministry of Health's Third Administration. The situation will likely be exacerbated if insufficient attention is paid to Moscow's Radio Rossii report of a crack in the sarcophagus of the 4th reactor, from which radioactive particles reportedly can easily escape. [18] Previous estimates of the costs of "clean-up" may have been seriously underestimated.

OTHER ENVIRONMENTAL DISASTERS

In the space allotted for this paper it is impossible to array all the disasters, and past, current, and future burdens on the economies of the newly independent states of the former Soviet Union. A brief selection is made here. In addition, a chart prepared from official publications by Dr. Ruben A. Mnatsakanian of Moscow is incorporated, with values assigned by me to dissect the geographic priorities for environmental attention.

The divergence of the Amu-Darya and Syr-Darya river waters from the Aral Sea is both a cause and an effect of large expenditures, whose effect has virtually destroyed the Aral Sea and caused major environmental problems in the area, including problems of climate and health.

A new proposal to reduce the level of the Caspian Sea, which is climbing almost to flood stage and is already inundating industry and lives along its banks in Turkmenistan, calls for the construction of a canal to transfer its waters to the Aral Sea. Obviously, this would be very expensive, but perhaps less so than the other proposals made for the divergence of Siberian rivers to the Aral Sea. No price tag has been given, but it cannot be an idle expenditure for the countries involved. Caution is needed in drawing waters from the Caspian because these waters are polluted and would need much treatment to eliminate the discharges into the sea of treated and untreated materials. Azerbaydzhan alone discharges 300 million cubic meters of treated effluents as well as 500 million untreated heavily polluted effluents, in addition to "more

---

[17] See my Letter to the Editor, The Washington Post, 23 June 1992, based on various sources published or broadcast, including Rossiyskaya gazeta, 10 March 1992, p. 7; Radio Free Europe/Radio Liberty, Daily Report, 23 April 1992; and Izvestiya, 16 April 1992, p. 2.

[18] Moscow, Radio Rossii Network (in Russian), 1200 gmt, 10 June 1992, cited in FBIS, Daily Report. Central Eurasia, FBIS-SOV-92-113, 11 June 1992, pp. 58-59.

587

than 3,000 tons of petroleum products, 28,000 tons of suspended matter, 74,000 tons of sufanol, more than 300,000 tons of chlorides, tens of tons of phenols, and hundreds of tons of synthetic surfactants," per year into the Caspian Sea. [19] Together with the rise of the sea, it threatens, as noted earlier, Turkmenistan's industry and farmlands in the Lenkoran area of Azerbaydzhan. Another study of the Caspian Sea indicated that the rise will continue for up to 20 years and the sea level will increase by 2 to 3 more meters. A proposal to divert these waters to the Aral Sea is estimated to cost only 1/15 of what it would cost to divert the northern rivers of Siberia by reversing the direction of their flow. [20] Perhaps. By the time the project is agreed to, assigned, monies spent, and actual construction initiated and completed, both the Aral and Caspian Seas will be very different places.

Ust-Kamenogorsk in Kazakhstan is a disaster zone. A two-year study found that the population was seriously affected by the Semipalatinsk range (possibly by Chinese nuclear testing also). The local sports stadium posts the day's radiation count, along with the time and temperature. In addition, lead concentration in soil leads to weekly consumption of 2.5 to 11.5 times more lead than the UN's standard deems safe. The water (as well as the soil) contains lead, arsenic, vanadium, chrome, and copper. Practically no water meets drinking standards. High levels of some 25 chemical elements are found in children's blood leading to "mutagenesis, ... the number and nature of violated chromosomes is very high and is close to the [levels found in] inhabitants of the Chernobyl region..." [21] Strongly carcinogenic beryllium was released by a September 12, 1990, accident at the Ulba Metallurgical Combine, adding to the local environmental hazards of daily life in the city.

New information has been presented in the press and elsewhere on the spread of dioxin in the air and soils of the former U.S.S.R. *Komsomol'skaya Pravda* reported in February 1991 that "dioxins were found in horrifying amounts in all the water samples drawn for analysis," in Ufa, the capital of Bashkiriya. *Stolitsa*, a Moscow weekly publication, reported that, "The deadly poison dioxin has been discovered in Kiev tap water." "Moscow tap water," according to V. Goncharuk, Director of the Institute of Colloidal Chemistry and Chemistry of Water, of the Ukrainian Academy of Sciences, "is contaminated with dioxin concentrations exceeding 1,000-fold the maximum permissible concentration." [22] Phenol contaminates much of Ufa's water as well. The Chief Pediatrician of the city found phenol to be the cause of much illness; a follow-up review by a commission of the Russian Republic's Ministry of Health excused the phenol dischargers and said it was an already existing condition in the water. [23] Congenital anamolies among newborns in the

[19] Namik Azizov, "The Khazar Can Still be Saved," *Delovoy mir*, 9 July 1991, p. 4, translated in FBIS, *JPRS Report. Environmental Issues*, JPRS-TEN-91-019, 15 November 1991, p. 8.
[20] A. Bushev, "Why Does the Volga Still Flow Into the Caspian Sea?," *Komsomol'skaya Pravda*, 10 August 1991, p. 3.
[21] A. Akava, "Four Chernobyls: That is How Many Catastrophes Independent Experts Feel the People of Ust-Kamenogorsk Have Lived Through," *Kazakhstanskaya Pravda*, 28 January 1992, p. 2.
[22] G. Agisheva, "Ufa in Shock," *Komsomol'skaya Pravda*, 21 February 1991, p. 2, and A. Smagin, "Water—A Life Hazard," *Stolitsa*, no. 16, 1991, p. 17.
[23] M. Merzabekov, "To Have Children, or Wait," *Sovetskaya Rossiya*, 29 October 1991, p. 2.

city have increased by more than 7 times in the last 10 years, according to the city pediatrician. [24] Cancer has grown in the city as well.

This is only a very abbreviated selection from all the possible cities (e.g., Sverdlovsk and anthrax), territories (Karakalpakia), surface waters (Lake Baykal), seas (Kara, Barents and White), and air (Mariupol, Noril'sk). But it is illustrative of the types of problems facing the former Soviet republics.

Figure 1 at the end of this paper provides an overview of the variety and dimensions (in broad terms) of environmental problems. The basic table was prepared by Dr. Ruben Mnatskanian, an independent ecologist. He prepared it while he was at the University of Edinburgh. With only one amendment regarding upgrading the radioactivity problem in Kazakhstan from "very serious" to "catastrophic," and with a weighting scheme I devised, the table is as published (except for scoring). It is based on officially recorded statistics, and does not incorporate many elaborations from nongovernmental agencies, organizations, or individuals, that question many of the officially reported figures. [25]

Figure 1 can be analyzed by column or row. The columns highlight geographic units; the rows highlight the types of environmental problems. If we use the numerical assignments given to indicate the seriousness of the problems in the categories as determined from official sources, then clearly the Urals, with a score of 62 points, is far and away the most catastrophic place in the former Soviet Union. Kazakhstan follows (51) [26]. The East Siberian Region of Russia (47) is surprisingly ahead of the Donetsk-Dnepr Region of Ukraine (at 43 points). The high score for Uzbekistan (46) is also unexpected. Low cumulative scores are given for Latvia, Lithuania, and the Kaliningrad region of Russia.

From the viewpoint of the rows, a clear "winner" is the 74-total found for "high air pollution levels with toxic compounds." It is not surprising when one finds that benzopyrene is present in almost all of the cities with environmental problems. [27] Benzopyrene is a serious carcinogenic substance. This category is given according to the source of the pollution of flowing water, found in 27 of the 28 administrative-territorial units in Figure 1. The second highest cumulative figure is 65 for "point source pollution of flowing water." It is found in 25 of the 28 administrative-territorial units. Radioactivity is recorded at a level of 34 points; it is likely that the constraint of "wide territories" in its categorization reduces the point total. Average point scores for each category for all territories if recorded, are also shown. The highest average score is 3.6 for "problems from liquid wastes." Thus, while recorded in only 10 territories, if a location has this problem, it is very serious. Radioactivity is next,

---

[24] R. Batyrshin, "Perrmanentnaya katastrofa v Ufe," *Nezavisimaya gazeta*, 15 May 1992, p. 6.

[25] These other estimates are included in *Ecocide in the USSR.*

[26] Even without the adjustment indicated in the text of 2 additional points, Kazakhstan would still rank 2nd, at 49 points. The Kazakh Cabinet of Ministers designated as ecological disaster zones: 1. all of Semipalatinsk oblast; 2. the cities of Semipalatinsk and Kurchatov; 3. 6 rayons (districts) and the city of Kamenogorsk in East Kazakhstan oblast; 2 rayons in Karaganda oblast; and 3 rayons of Pavlodar oblast. (Alma-Ata, Kazakh Radio Network, 1400 gmt (in Russian) 23 June 1992, transcribed in FBIS, *Daily Report. Central Eurasia*, FBIS-SOV-92-123, 25 June 1992, pp. 5-6.) Other areas may be categorized as less than a "disaster."

[27] See, especially, Feshbach and Friendly, *Ecocide in the USSR*, 1992, table A.14.

with an average score of 3.4, spread over 10 locales as well. The lowest score is for "acidification" of soils, with an average score of 1.0 and only in 4 locales.

It will be interesting to contrast this figure with a similar one in the future. If in 5 years, as expected, the situation is much worse given the lack of domestic funding to improve it, then most scores should be affected negatively.

THE ECONOMICS OF THE ENVIRONMENT

If we could put aside such questions as: Where is the money to repair the environment to come from? Will the government survive? What will be given priority—economy or ecology? Will the population survive until the time when many, if not all, problems in health and associated environmental problems are corrected? and the like, what would be the cost of correcting environmental problems throughout the former U.S.S.R.? Probably these costs will be beyond the means of the people in the region in any foreseeable future. In an unpublished manuscript written several years ago, entitled *Economics of Health and Environment in the USSR*, I estimated that the costs (in current prices of 1989) would be some 6 or 7 times the Gross National Product of the time. That estimate was extremely conservative, was not based on information currently available, especially about the even more horrendous dispersion of radioactivity throughout the country, nor on new information about dioxin, on new details about environmental pollution in Russia, Ukraine, and Kazakhstan now available from sources that include unpublished data for Russia, as well as new environmental statistical handbooks for Ukraine and Kazakhstan, handbooks on the monitoring of pollution throughout the country (of those days) from Leningrad (St. Petersburg) that were previously for internal use only, and so forth.

However, inflation has been rampant since that time. All previous estimates could readily be multiplied by 10, 100, or a 1,000 times to obtain a ruble equivalent for 1989 in current 1992 prices—if the goods and services were to be available. During a conversation about this estimate with Minister Danilov-Danilyants in April 1992, he proposed a multiplier of 5 times. This would also be minimal—again excluding any estimate of reducing or cleaning up the radioactive pollution, as well as the dioxin that has only been discussed publicly since 1991.

Some Soviet estimates of the annual economic losses from environmental damage were in the range of 15 to 17 percent of GNP. Expenditures on environmental abatement measures and capital investment were on the order of 13 billion rubles in 1990 (in constant prices). This was 1.3 percent of the GNP for the year (1,000 billion rubles, in current prices). In contrast, the estimated costs of replacing the entire water pipeline system, described by the Soviet Minister of Housing and Municipal Services as 'completely worn out' in the Russian Republic even in 1987 were 800 billion rubles. And this was just for water pipelines providing water to households, industry and other consumers. It was not for sewage pipes, for cleaning rivers and seas, for providing water to the Aral Sea, nor did it include the other kinds of water pollution in aquifers, reservoirs, and so forth designated in Figure 1. Expenditures for air, land, radioactivity, forests, national parks, natural resources, fish, animals, etc., also need to be added. Expenditures for the environmental correction of air pollution were scheduled in the 15-year Goskompriroda draft plan for 1991–2005 to be 39 billion. Instead, the estimated expenditures for the capital investment needed to reduce sulfur dioxide emissions alone (excluding nitrous oxide, carbon dioxide, soot, heavy metals, benzopyrene, etc.) has been estimated to be 50 billion rubles! The overall costs are horrendous to contemplate, albeit necessary. The detrimental linkage of ecology and health in the former Soviet Union is clear and pervasive, and the threat, especially from other nuclear reactors, contained and uncontained nuclear wastes, as well as from new threats to the ecology and health of the population and work force, is more than abundantly spread throughout the country. Unless international agencies, multilateral organizations such as IAEA, the World Health Organization, the Organization for Economic Cooperation and Development, and the European Community, as well as individual countries and their citizens' organizations, provide both much needed short-term assistance and adequate long-term assistance, momentum and activity inside the former U.S.S.R. cannot be maintained. Nor will we be able to protect ourselves.

FIGURE 1. Seriousness of Environmental Problems by Former Soviet Republic and Region of Russia and Ukraine.*

Category of Pollution	Russian Regions:				
	Kaliningrad	North	Northwest	Central	Black Soil
Air Pollution:					
High emission levels (nitrous sulphur, carbon oxides and dust)		+ +	+	+ +	+
High air pollution levels with toxic compounds	+ +	+ +	+ +	+ +	+
Acid rain precipitation	+	+ +			
Water Pollution:					
Point source pollution of flowing water	+ +	+ +	*	*	+
Non-point source pollution of flowing water			+	+ +	+
Pollution and eutrophication of lakes		+ +	*	+	
Pollution of seas	+ +	+ +	*		
Aquifer contamination				+	+ +
Pollution and other problems of reservoirs			+	*	
Soil and Land Use Problems:					
Soil erosion				+	*
Wind erosion					+
Desertification					
Salinization					
Water-logged					
Acidification		+	+		
Pollution of soils with heavy metals		+ +		+ +	
Contamination of soils with pecticides				+	
Destruction of landscape due to mining		+ +		+	+ +
Radioactive pollution of vast territories		*	+	*	
Problems with solid waste disposal			+	*	
Problems from liquid wastes		+	*	*	
Deforestation:					
Overall forest cutting	+	*	+	+	
Forest fires		+			
Forest degradation from industrial pollution		*	+ +	+	
Total Score:	11	42	34	45	16

* See note at end of table for assigned weights.

FIGURE 1. Seriousness of Environmental Problems by Former Soviet Republic and Region of Russia and Ukraine.—Continued

Category of Pollution	Russian Regions:				
	Volga-Vyatka	Volga	North Caucasus	Urals	West Siberia
Air Pollution:					
High emission levels (nitrous sulphur, carbon oxides and dust)	+	*	+	++	*
High air pollution levels with toxic compounds	++	*	+	*	++
Acid rain precipitation				+	+
Water Pollution:					
Point source pollution of flowing water	++	*	++	*	*
Non-point source pollution of flowing water	+	++	*	+	
Pollution and eutrophication of lakes				*	+
Pollution of seas		++	*		++
Aquifer contamination				*	
Pollution and other problems of reservoirs	*	*	++		
Soil and Land Use Problems:					
Soil erosion	+	++	++	+	+
Wind erosion		+	++	++	++
Desertification		*	*		
Salinization		++	+		
Water-logged					
Acidification					
Pollution of soils with heavy metals				++	+
Contamination of soils with pecticides		+	+		
Destruction of landscape due to mining				*	*
Radioactive pollution of vast territories				*	
Problems with solid waste disposal			++	*	++
Problems from liquid wastes				*	
Deforestation:					
Overall forest cutting	++			*	++
Forest fires					
Forest degradation from industrial pollution				*	+
Total Score:	17	36	34	62	35

FIGURE 1. Seriousness of Environmental Problems by Former Soviet Republic and Region of Russia and Ukraine.—Continued

Category of Pollution	Russian Regions:		Ukrainian Regions:		
	East Siberia	Far East	West	South	Donetsk-Dnepr
Air Pollution:					
High emission levels (nitrous sulphur, carbon oxides and dust)	*	+			++
High air pollution levels with toxic compounds	*	++	+	+	*
Acid rain precipitation		+			
Water Pollution:					
Point source pollution of flowing water		++	+	+	++
Non-point source pollution of flowing water	+		++	++	
Pollution and eutrophication of lakes	*	+			
Pollution of seas	+	++		++	*
Aquifer contamination				++	*
Pollution and other problems of reservoirs	*	+	++		++
Soil and Land Use Problems:					
Soil erosion		+	+		+
Wind erosion	+				
Desertification					
Salinization				++	
Water-logged				*	
Acidification					
Pollution of soils with heavy metals	+	*			++
Contamination of soils with pecticides				+	
Destruction of landscape due to mining	+	+			*
Radioactive pollution of vast territories	+	*			
Problems with solid waste disposal					*
Problems from liquid wastes	++			++	*
Deforestation:					
Overall forest cutting	*	*			
Forest fires	++	*			
Forest degradation from industrial pollution	*	+			
Total Score:	47	30	15	23	43

594

FIGURE 1. Seriousness of Environmental Problems by Former Soviet Republic and Region of Russia and Ukraine.—Continued

Category of Pollution	Belorussia	Moldova	Estonia	Latvia	Lithuania
Air Pollution:					
High emission levels (nitrous sulphur, carbon oxides and dust)		+	+		
High air pollution levels with toxic compounds	+ +	+		+ +	+
Acid rain precipitation	+		+		+ +
Water Pollution:					
Point source pollution of flowing water	+		+	+	+
Non-point source pollution of flowing water		*			
Pollution and eutrophication of lakes	+		+ +		
Pollution of seas			+	+ +	+ +
Aquifer contamination		+ +		+	
Pollution and other problems of reservoirs			+	+	
Soil and Land Use Problems:					
Soil erosion	+	+ +			
Wind erosion	+ +	+			+
Desertification					
Salinization					
Water-logged					
Acidification	+		+		
Pollution of soils with heavy metals					
Contamination of soils with pecticides		*		+	
Destruction of landscape due to mining	+		*		
Radioactive pollution of vast territories	*				
Problems with solid waste disposal	+ +	+	+ +		
Problems from liquid wastes				+ +	
Deforestation:					
Overall forest cutting					
Forest fires					
Forest degradation from industrial pollution	+				+ +
Total Score:	21	20	17	13	12

FIGURE 1. Seriousness of Environmental Problems by Former Soviet Republic and Region of Russia and Ukraine.—Continued

Category of Pollution	Armenia	Azerbaydzhan	Georgia	Kazakhstan	Kyrgyzstan
Air Pollution:					
High emission levels (nitrous sulphur, carbon oxides and dust)	·	+		++	
High air pollution levels with toxic compounds	++	++	++	*	+
Acid rain precipitation					
Water Pollution:					
Point source pollution of flowing water	+		+	*	+
Non-point source pollution of flowing water	+	++	++	++	++
Pollution and eutrophication of lakes	++	*		*	+
Pollution of seas		++	++	++	
Aquifer contamination		++		*	
Pollution and other problems of reservoirs	+	+			++
Soil and Land Use Problems:					
Soil erosion	++		++		++
Wind erosion				+	
Desertification				+	
Salinization	+	++		++	++
Water-logged	+	++	+	+	
Acidification					
Pollution of soils with heavy metals	+	+		++	++
Contamination of soils with pecticides	+	++	+		++
Destruction of landscape due to mining	++			++	
Radioactive pollution of vast territories		+	+	*	
Problems with solid waste disposal		*	+	+	
Problems from liquid wastes		*		+	
Deforestation:					
Overall forest cutting				+	
Forest fires					
Forest degradation from industrial pollution	+				+
Total Score:	20	40	17	51	23

FIGURE 1. Seriousness of Environmental Problems by Former Soviet Republic and Region of Russia and Ukraine.—Continued

Category of Pollution	Tadzhikis-tan	Turkmenis-tan	Uzbekistan	Average Score	Frequency of Occurrence (n=28)	Total Score
Air Pollution:						
High emission levels (nitrous sulphur, carbon oxides and dust)			+	2.2	17	39
High air pollution levels with toxic compounds	+	+	++	2.7	27	74
Acid rain precipitation				1.4	9	13
Water Pollution:						
Point source pollution of flowing water		+	+	2.6	25	65
Non-point source pollution of flowing water	+	++	*	2.6	19	49
Pollution and eutrophication of lakes		*	*	3.3	15	49
Pollution of seas		++		3.2	17	53
Aquifer contamination		*	+	3.2	11	35
Pollution and other problems of reservoirs	++		++	2.8	16	44
Soil and Land Use Problems:						
Soil erosion	+	+	+	1.9	18	34
Wind erosion		+	++	1.9	13	25
Desertification	+	++	+	3.3	6	20
Salinization	++	*	*	3.0	10	30
Water-logged	+	*	*	2.8	8	22
Acidification				1.0	4	4
Pollution of soils with heavy metals				2.4	11	27
Contamination of soils with pecticides	++	++	*	2.2	13	29
Destruction of landscape due to mining				3.0	12	36
Radioactive pollution of vast territories				3.4	10	34
Problems with solid waste disposal		+	++	2.9	14	40
Problems from liquid wastes				3.6	10	36
Deforestation:						
Overall forest cutting	+			2.8	11	31
Forest fires				3.0	3	9
Forest degradation from industrial pollution				2.4	11	27
Total Score:	15	37	46	2.7	309	825

Source: Adapted from Ruben A. Mnatsakanian, *Environmental Legacy of the Former Soviet Republics (as collated from official statistics)*, Edinburgh, Scotland, Centre for Human Ecology, University of Edinburgh, 1992, pp. 3–4. One change was made to the original classificaiton. The level of radioactive pollution in Kazakhstan was upgraded from "++" (serious) to "*" (catastrophic), based on other information and official Kazakh classification of much of Kazakhstan as an "ecological disaster zone."
Note: The scores are based on an arbitrary assignment of points—"+" = 1 (problem); "++" = 3 (serious); "*" = 5 (catastrophic).

D. Science and Transportation

TRANSPORT IN THE COMMONWEALTH OF INDEPENDENT STATES: AN AGING CIRCULATORY SYSTEM

By Holland Hunter *

CONTENTS

SUMMARY

Since 1988 the transport sector in the Soviet Union has followed the surrounding economy downward as the command economy has disintegrated. Poor passenger service grew slowly while freight traffic declined. Transport plant has been deteriorating. Commonwealth of Independent States (CIS) republics vary widely in their transport endowments and activities, as shown in newly compiled evidence. Comparison with other countries demonstrates an inefficient excess of heavy freight traffic, along with passenger services far below the levels prevailing elsewhere. Arrangements for managing the railroad system are unsettled. Multimodal transport possibilities may help to revive the economy.

---

* Holland Hunter is Emeritus Professor of Economics, Haverford College.

TRANSPORT DEVELOPMENTS SINCE 1985

FREIGHT TRAFFIC—OVER THE HILL

Decades of freight transport growth came to an end as the CIS economy started downward at the close of the 1980s. The peak year for most carriers was 1988, though gas pipeline traffic is still growing and internal waterway traffic stopped growing in 1985, as shown in Table 1. The decline reflected primarily a falling off in the demand for freight movement, though for some commodity groups it occasionally arose from transport bottlenecks.

The principal transport mode remains the railroads, but their share of traffic measured in ton-kilometers fell from 50 percent to 46 percent because of gains by gas pipelines, whose share rose from 15 percent to 21 percent. Oil pipelines found their share falling from 18 percent to 16 percent, while the maritime share stayed slightly above 12 percent, the internal-waterway share fell from 3.5 percent to 2.9 percent, and the share of road traffic remained under 2 percent. Trucks in the CIS operate mainly in and around cities, and around collective and state farms; their average length of haul is only 21 kilometers (about 14 miles).

Overall, the average distances for freight movement continued to drift upward as the economy reached out for natural resources farther from old industrial and population centers. The average distance moved for natural gas rose from about 2350 kilometers to 2700 kilometers; for rail freight the increase was from 940 kilometers to over 960. As Table 1 shows, oil traffic moved on average around 2100 kilometers, maritime hauls rose from 3800 to 4100 kilometers, internal waterway hauls fell from around 400 to 330 kilometers, and average hauls for the modest amount of air freight handled by common carriers dropped from 1060 to 1030 kilometers.

PASSENGER TRAFFIC—INADEQUATE SERVICE

Trends in CIS passenger traffic are somewhat different. Looking first at mass transit for urban and suburban passengers, we see in Table 2 that long-term growth has continued during 1985–1991 at a slow but steady rate. In terms of quantity, urban mass transit has stayed ahead of population growth, but in qualitative terms the service leaves much to be desired. Autobuses handle 53 percent of the passenger-kilometers and trolley buses carry another 16 percent, leaving 13 percent each for trams and subways and about 5 percent for taxis. Average trips are for 6.3 kilometers, though subway rides average 10 kilometers and the average taxi ride is over 13 kilometers.

Suburban passenger traffic is mostly by autobus or railroad (bus share 56 percent, rail share 44 percent). Suburban bus trips are usually for 13–14 kilometers, while suburban rail trips average 43 to 44 kilometers. A few passengers use internal waterway and maritime carriers, mostly for holiday jaunts.

During 1985–1990 the number of passengers carried by long-distance carriers fluctuated a little below the 2.6 billion level, while the volume of passenger-kilometers rose from 535 to 630 billion (see Table 3). The rise reflected an increased share of air travel, where the average trip is between 1725 and 1750 kilometers, and a slight

TABLE 1. Total Freight Traffic, U.S.S.R., By Mode, 1985–1991.

Year	Rail	Gas Pipeline	Oil Pipeline	Maritime	Internal Water	Road	Air	All Modes
			Ton-Kilometers, in Billions					
1985	3,718.4	1,131.0	1,312.5	905.0	261.5	141.6	3.4	7,473
1986	3,834.5	1,231.0	1,401.3	970.0	256.6	141.3	3.4	7,838
1987	3,824.7	1,333.0	1,450.1	972.1	252.7	141.0	3.4	7,977
1988	3,924.8	1,431.0	1,466.4	1,011.4	251.2	143.3	3.4	8,232
1989	3,851.7	1,521.8	1,422.2	991.2	239.6	143.2	3.3	8,173
1990	3,718.3	1,653.3	1,306.7	997.0	230.0	139.4	3.3	8,048
			Tons Originated, in Millions of Metric Tons					
1985	3,951.0	482.0	630.8	240.0	633.0	6,320.0	3.2	12,260
1986	4,076.0	515.0	652.9	249.0	649.0	6,653.0	3.2	12,798
1987	4,067.0	548.0	663.6	252.0	673.0	6,853.0	3.2	13,060
1988	4,116.0	578.0	663.3	257.0	691.0	6,921.0	3.3	13,230
1989	4,017.0	599.0	650.1	245.0	694.0	6,776.0	3.2	12,984
1990	3,857.0	610.8	642.2	243.0	700.0	6,740.0	3.2	12,796
			Average Length of Haul, in Kilometers					
1985	941	2,346	2,081	3,771	413	22	1,063	610
1986	941	2,390	2,146	3,896	395	21	1,063	612
1987	940	2,432	2,185	3,858	375	21	1,063	611
1988	954	2,476	2,211	3,935	364	21	1,030	622
1989	959	2,541	2,188	4,046	345	21	1,031	629
1990	964	2,707	2,035	4,103	329	21	1,031	629
			Percent Shares of Ton-Kilometers					
1985	49.8	15.1	17.6	12.1	3.5	1.9	0.0	100.0
1986	48.9	15.7	17.9	12.4	3.3	1.8	0.0	100.0
1987	47.9	16.7	18.2	12.2	3.2	1.8	0.0	100.0
1988	47.7	17.4	17.8	12.3	3.1	1.7	0.0	100.0
1989	47.1	18.6	17.4	12.1	2.9	1.8	0.0	100.0
1990	46.2	20.5	16.2	12.4	2.9	1.7	0.0	100.0

Sources: USSR Ministry of Railways, Soviet Railways in 1990, Moscow, 1991; Goskomstat SSSR, Transport i sviaz': statisticheskii sbornik, 1990; Narkhoz SSSR v 1989 g.; Narkhoz SSSR v 1985 g.

decline in the rail and bus shares. The average long-distance rail trip is for 650 to 670 kilometers; for buses the average rose from 50 to 55 kilometers. Aeroflot handles over a third of the traffic, railroads around 47 percent, and buses about 17 percent. As in urban and suburban travel, internal waterway and maritime carriers play a minor role.

The quality of CIS public passenger transport is not impressive, largely because failure to increase capacity has led to chronic overcrowding. Equipment is often over-age and undermaintained. The carriers try to maintain schedules, but on-time performance is not up to European or Japanese standards. Foreign visitors and members of the *nomenklatura* are accorded special treatment, but ordinary citizens have little leverage for obtaining good service.

A July 1990 sample survey found that the average time spent at ticket offices to get an airline ticket was two hours and 25 minutes, varying from 67 minutes in Tallin to four hours in Ukraine. For rail tickets the time varied from 16 minutes in Erevan to two hours and 17 minutes in Belarus for a national average of 89 minutes. Even for bus tickets, ticket-office times averaged 25 minutes, going from 2 minutes in Moscow to two hours and 21 minutes in Vil'nius. Of those seeking an air ticket, 33.9 percent had to visit the ticket office at least twice; the fraction for rail travelers was 17.1 percent

TABLE 2. Urban and Suburban Passenger Transport,
U.S.S.R., By Mode, 1985–1990.

Year	Autobus	Trolley Bus	Trams	Subway	Taxi	Total
	Urban, Millions of Passengers Carried					
1985	32,821	9,964	8,512	4,434	1,455	57,186
1986	34,581	10,529	8,725	4,624	1,436	59,895
1987	36,120	11,187	9,006	4,694	1,440	62,447
1988	37,238	11,570	9,144	4,792	1,431	64,175
1989	37,177	11,718	9,071	5,024	1,341	64,331
1990	36,991	11,439	8,517	5,844	1,336	64,127
	Urban, Billions of Passenger-Kilometers					
1985	191.8	58.2	49.7	44.6	18.8	363.1
1986	201.7	61.4	50.9	45.9	18.7	378.6
1987	209.0	64.7	52.1	46.9	19.1	391.8
1988	214.9	66.8	52.8	47.8	19.2	401.5
1989	212.9	67.1	51.9	50.2	18.3	400.4
1990	212.9	65.8	49.0	58.9	17.5	404.1

Year	Autobus	Rail	Internal Water	Maritime	Total Public
	Suburban, Millions of Passengers Carried				
1985	12,146	3,768	46.0	46.8	16,007
1986	12,243	3,928	47.3	47.4	16,266
1987	11,891	3,932	42.6	46.4	15,912
1988	11,493	3,964	44.6	45.8	15,547
1989	11,363	3,895	44.0	41.9	15,344
1990	11,308	3,834	44.0	42.1	15,228
	Suburban, Billions of Passenger-Kilometers				
1985	158.2	116.0	0.6	0.7	275.5
1986	160.6	122.2	0.6	0.7	284.1
1987	158.7	122.7	0.6	0.7	282.7
1988	158.4	125.2	0.6	0.7	284.9
1989	159.4	123.7	0.6	0.7	284.4
1990	159.6	122.9	0.6	0.7	283.8

Sources: USSR Ministry of Railways, Soviet Railways in 1990, Moscow, 1991; Goskomstat SSSR, Transport i sviaz': statisticheskii sbornik, 1990; Narkhoz SSSR v 1989 g.; Narkhoz SSSR v 1985 g.

and for bus travelers, 6.3 percent.[1] Besides time spent at ticket offices, travelers spend additional time awaiting scheduled departures. Severe delays at airports have become frequent, especially during peak periods.

Individually owned passenger automobiles are only beginning to supplement these common-carrier passenger services. There were 12.4 million privately owned cars at the end of 1985; the stock rose to 16.0 million by the end of 1989 and 16.4 million at the end of 1990.[2] This limited population of private vehicles reflects a modest level of domestic production, as indicated by recent output and sales shown in Table 4. State policy has kept production at these levels since the mid-1970s, and with so modest a rate of production and sales, the stock of usable vehicles cannot grow rapidly.

[1] Goskomstat SSSR, Transport i sviaz': statisticheskii sbornik, Moscow, 1991, p. 50.
[2] Ibid., p. 21.

601

TABLE 3. Long-distance Passenger Transport, U.S.S.R., By Mode, 1985–1990.

Year	Auto-bus	Rail	Air	Internal water	Other	Total
Long-Distance, Millions of Passengers Carried						
1985	2,039.0	392.4	109.0	49.5	13.2	2,603.1
1986	1,986.4	414.0	112.7	50.9	12.9	2,576.9
1987	1,971.6	423.9	115.0	54.2	13.2	2,577.9
1988	1,992.0	426.2	120.8	54.4	13.1	2,606.5
1989	1,956.0	420.6	127.4	53.7	12.7	2,570.4
1990	1,960.1	431.6	132.7	53.0	12.6	2,590.0
Long-Distance, Billions of Passenger-Kilometers						
1985	96.2	258.0	175.1	5.2	0.9	535.4
1986	100.1	268.0	182.7	5.2	0.8	556.8
1987	102.5	279.5	189.0	5.0	0.6	576.6
1988	106.6	288.6	198.8	4.7	0.6	599.3
1989	107.8	287.0	211.1	4.7	0.5	611.1
1990	108.0	294.2	224.3	4.6	0.5	631.6
Percent Shares of Long-distance Passenger-Kilometers						
1985	18.0	48.2	32.7	1.0	0.2	100.0
1986	18.0	48.1	32.8	0.9	0.1	100.0
1987	17.8	48.5	32.8	0.9	0.1	100.0
1988	17.8	48.2	33.2	0.8	0.1	100.0
1989	17.6	47.0	34.5	0.8	0.1	100.0
1990	17.1	46.6	35.5	0.7	0.1	100.0

Sources: USSR Ministry of Railways, Soviet Railways in 1990, Moscow, 1991; Goskomstat SSSR, Transport i sviaz': statisticheskii sbornik, 1990; Narkhoz SSSR v 1989 g.; Narkhoz SSSR v 1985 g.

TABLE 4. Private Vehicle Production and Sales.

(thousands of units)

Year	1985	1986	1987	1988	1989
Production	1,332	1,326	1,332	1,262	1,217
Sales	1,171	1,352	1,300	1,288	1,204

Source: Goskomstat SSSR, Narkhoz SSSR v 1989 g., pp. 116 and 407.

CURRENT FORCES AT WORK

Why has transport output leveled off and declined? While general economic disorganization is clearly the underlying cause, chronic shortages of key inputs have been the proximate difficulty for all carriers, especially the railroads. Planned allocations of steel, fuel, and spare parts have not been received. These constraints on transport performance have prevailed for many years, but since 1988 they seem to have grown far more severe. When an input-constrained carrier is unable to meet a shipper's demand for freight movement, inbound or outbound, the shipper's capacity to produce and deliver is impaired. If the shipper's difficulties spread to his customers, the shortfall may in due course reach firms supplying transport with current inputs, thus causing reciprocal lowering of output levels. Causation becomes circular.

Rail transport bottlenecks on key routes used to reflect physical capacity limits reached under traditional operating methods. As traffic has receded, spare capacity has emerged at many points. Reserves of capacity are available but not being drawn on. Hard pressed railroad officials now stress, not the lack of line or yard or rolling stock or motive power capacity, but their difficulties in obtaining current supplies. Erosion of the command system and the rise of regional autonomy have undermined the long-standing expectation that key operating divisions would normally get fuel and other crucial inputs when absolutely necessary.

Recently it has appeared that the railroads and other carriers have themselves lost any incentive to raise the volume of freight traffic. Discipline imposed from the top down used to induce strenuous efforts to overcome input shortages; now this discipline has disappeared. With prices no longer held down by decree, transport agencies have been augmenting their revenue by raising freight tariffs instead of seeking ways to carry more freight.

DETERIORATING INFRASTRUCTURE

An unfortunate consequence of reduced input flows has been a pervasive tendency to defer maintenance and replacement of transport assets as they suffer wear and tear and obsolescence. Railroad track and ballast have deteriorated all over the country. Freight cars (goods wagons), passenger cars (coaches), and motive power are all badly undermaintained. The stock of usable trucks and tractors is declining as new vehicles fail to make up for those that have to be retired. The merchant fleet is over-age and increasingly unseaworthy; many ports are decrepit.

Traffic declines since 1988 have provided a breathing spell for hard pressed railroads and other transport providers in specific areas. Nevertheless the period of respite has not been used to catch up on deferred maintenance and raise transport assets to a high state of readiness for renewed growth. Instead, the plant is decaying. The traditional capital investment projects put on the docket in 1987 and 1988 are far behind schedule; many have in effect been abandoned. Eventually standby capacity itself will crumble.

Even if investment funds were available, the choice of where to apply them is now complicated by uncertainty over where bottlenecks might appear when revived production generates new traffic flows. Given the switch from coal to natural gas and oil, along with the decline of the steel industry, some of the old coal flows westbound across the Urals are never likely to regain their previous levels. New flows of exports to world markets may be impending, but how soon will they press against route capacities at particular points? Current congestion at border crossing points seems to reflect operational disorder rather than physical capacity limits. In the present period of basic economic reorganization, fresh thought is needed to determine optimal transport investment priorities.

MAJOR TRANSPORT ISSUES

THE ROLE OF INTRA- AND INTER-REPUBLIC TRANSPORT

The railroads and other carriers provide basic lifelines joining together the widely scattered cities, towns, and settled rural areas of the former U.S.S.R. Now that its numerous component territories are becoming independent, how will the transport sector's role change? Table 5 offers some basic geographic perspective, showing the size of major regions (in square kilometers of area), their 1990 population and estimated gross domestic product, and their basic transport facilities and activity. Some republics are here grouped together, creating eight parts of CIS territory to be examined.

In order to highlight major differences among the CIS regions and emphasize their contrasts with other parts of the world, Table 5 presents the same measures for eight diverse nations, ranging in size from the United Kingdom to Canada, in ascending order of area. The second column shows, for example, that the Russian Republic has about 70 percent more territory than Canada, though of course large portions of both countries' territory are almost unusable. The Ukrainian republic, however, is only about 9 percent larger than France, and 20 percent larger than Spain. The Kazakh republic is more than four times as large as Ukraine, and the four Central Asian republics together have twice Ukraine's territory. The republic of Belarus is about 15 percent smaller than Germany or the United Kingdom, and the republics of the Caucasus and the Baltic region are even smaller.

In terms of population density, the contrasts are strikingly different. None of these CIS regions approaches the population-per-square-kilometer levels of Germany or the UK. Moldova has the same overall population density as China, while Ukraine and the Caucasian republics show densities about 10 percent above that of Spain. The four Central Asian republics display the same population density as the United States. The sparsely settled Kazakh republic has three times the population density of Canada, and the Russian republic appears more densely settled, though if Russia is divided into its European part and Siberia, the respective densities are 27 and 3 persons per square kilometer, putting Siberia at Canada's level.

The rough estimates of regional per-capita outputs, measured in 1990 dollars at purchasing-power-parity rates, indicate further marked contrasts. Average output per capita in CIS regions varies from under $2500 in the Central Asian region to over $6100 in the Baltic republics. None approach the Spanish level of $8200, to say nothing of the $13,000–$14,600 range in Western Europe or the $14,000–$20,000 range exhibited by Australia, Canada, and the United States. The CIS levels are, however, two or three times the Chinese level, except for the Central Asian republics, where per capita output matches China's level exactly.

Table 5 shows two measures of transport endowment: kilometers of railroad line and kilometers of hard-surfaced road, together with two measures of transport activity: ton-kilometers of freight and passenger-kilometers of traffic carried. The unrounded data for CIS regions show that the Ukrainian republic is the best-endowed with railroad lines per square kilometer of area, while Russia, the Kazakh republic, and the Central Asian republic are least well supplied in this respect. Most CIS regions have about the same territorial density of railroad line as Spain, but far less than France or the United Kingdom. Germany's rail endowment is remarkably high. U.S. railroad mileage is 40 percent longer than all CIS common-carrier first main track, but in terms of line per square kilometer the United States is well below five of the eight CIS regions.

TABLE 5. Comparative Regional Transport Endowment and Activity, Eight CIS Regions and Eight Other Nations.

Republic or Nation	Area in Sq. Kms. (thousands)	Population (Millions)	GDP in PPP$ (Billions)	Kms. of RR Line (Thousands)	Kms. of Roads (Thousands)	Total Ton-Kms. (Billions)	Total Passenger-Kms. (Billions)
Russia	17,075	148	895	87.18	394.4	4,305.0	682.9
Ukraine	604	52	236	22.80	157.2	920.7	177.4
Kazakh	2,717	17	68	14.46	80.3	580.1	67.1
C. Asian	1,277	33	81	6.43	81.7	110.8	64.3
Belarus	208	10	64	5.57	46.3	100.5	41.4
Caucasus	186	16	55	4.50	53.4	71.6	38.9
Baltic	175	8	49	5.44	54.5	63.6	35.9
Moldova	34	4	19	1.15	9.7	21.4	8.9
United Kingdom	245	57	739	17	354	140	609
Germany	249	61	889	27	497	233	652
Spain	505	39	319	14	153	115	217
France	552	56	753	35	806	184	684
Australia	7,682	17	242	35	605	156	179
United States	9,373	246	4,847	205	5,617	3,997	4,695
China	9,561	1,105	2,708	53	811	1,565	573
Canada	9,976	26	461	94	806	436	265

Republic or Nation	Pop per Sq. Km.	GDP per Capita	RR Line/ Sq. Km.	Roads/ Sq. Km.	Ton-Kms/ $ of GDP	Passenger-Kms/ Person
Russia	9	6,046	5	23	4.81	4,613
Ukraine	86	4,564	38	260	3.90	3,431
Kazakh	6	4,112	5	30	8.53	4,058
C. Asian	26	2,455	5	64	1.37	1,948
Belarus	49	6,275	27	223	1.57	4,059
Caucasus	86	3,438	24	287	1.30	2,431
Baltic	46	6,125	31	311	1.30	4,488
Moldova	118	4,750	34	285	1.13	2,225
United Kingdom	233	12,965	69	1,445	0.19	10,684
Germany	245	14,574	108	1,996	0.26	10,689
Spain	77	8,179	28	303	0.36	5,564
France	101	13,446	63	1,460	0.24	12,214
Australia	2	14,235	5	79	0.64	10,529
United States	26	19,703	22	599	0.82	19,085
China	116	2,451	6	85	0.58	519
Canada	3	17,731	9	81	0.95	10,192

Sources: Derived from the analysis by Dr. Clell G. Harral in European Bank for Reconstruction & Development, *Transport Operations Policy*, March 1992, Tables 1–3; PlanEcon GNP estimates; Goskomstat SSSR, Transport i sviaz', 1991; several Narkhozy.

Compared with Germany, France, and the United Kingdom, the eight regions of the CIS are very badly endowed with all-weather, hard-surfaced roads and highways. The total length of paved roads in the Russian republic, for example, is 13 percent greater than in the United Kingdom, but only 80 percent of France's total and half that of Germany. The Ukrainian republic has about the same length of paved roads as Spain. In roads per square kilometer of territory, Russia, the Kazakh republic, and the Central Asian republics fall far below the level shown for China, Canada, and Australia, while the smaller CIS regions rank with Spain in relative road endowment.

The volume of freight traffic in CIS regions is enormous, both in absolute and relative terms. In absolute terms, only the United States and China generate more freight traffic than the Russian republic; the Ukrainian and Kazakh republics produce much more freight traffic than Canada. Relative to the size of each region's gross domestic product, the contrasts are even more striking.

The Russian republic generates six times as much freight per dollar of GDP as is required in the United States. The ratio of freight traffic to GDP in the Kazakh republic is 45 times the United Kingdom ratio. The Ukrainian ratio is 11 times that of Spain. Even the lowest ratios in CIS regions are more than twice that of China and well above those of Canada and Australia.

Clearly the heavy industrial heritage of CIS regions includes an excessive burden of freight traffic. Spokesmen for the railroads have long taken pride in breaking records for freight volume, but in terms of economic efficiency the ratios shown above bespeak failure rather than success. Other economies have found that it pays to wash and clean the coal, beneficiate the ores, convert roundwood to sawn timber, and clean and dry the grain before presenting these mass freights to the railroads for shipment. Other economies have found that it pays to raise the quality of iron and steel so as to reduce the bulk of iron and steel products and cut the volume of scrap generated at the manufacturing level. Soviet railroads, however, have borne unnecessary costs because similar measures have not been taken in the surrounding Soviet economy.[3]

An ideal economy, producing an optimal GDP, would display a combination of production and transport costs that would minimize their sum through efficient, judicious use of freight transport. Territorial dispersion may require some regions to move more freight than others, and in this respect most CIS regions suffer by comparison with more fortunate regions, but the contrasts shown in Table 5 expose a striking excess of rail freight traffic in the former U.S.S.R.

Again the picture for passenger traffic is a different one. The average person in CIS regions travels about 3900 kilometers a year (excluding a small amount of travel by private automobile, which I am unable to allocate to regions). In the Central Asian republics the figure is slightly below 2000 and in the Baltic republics it approaches 5000. This is only about 70 percent of the Spanish level though it is more than 7 times the Chinese level. In the United Kingdom, Germany, Australia, and Canada, people travel about 10,000 kilometers a year; in France the figure is 12,000 and in the United States, 19,000.

While CIS regions should look for ways to reduce the volume of freight traffic, the obvious goal for serving passengers is clearly to raise both the quantity and the quality of passenger traffic. In the short run, this will mean investment in upgrading urban mass transit and suburban public transport. Down the road a few years, it probably means a long period of extensive highway construction.

---

[3] For background see Holland Hunter and Janusz M. Szyrmer, *Faulty Foundations: Soviet Economic Policies, 1928-1940*, Princeton: Princeton University Press, 1992.

On a broader scale, considering both freight and passenger transport, how much will be needed for economic progress in CIS regions? The data briefly reviewed above are consistent with the view that the peoples distributed widely over this Eurasian land mass are unusually dependent on long-distance transport. In densely settled parts of the world, freight and passengers need not go far to carry out mutually beneficial exchanges, but in the vast territory between Eastern Europe and the Pacific Ocean, productive activity requires extensive transportation, primarily to link people with their neighbors.

Compared with most other large regions on other continents, however, the great majority of CIS territory is not well served by internal waterway or maritime transport. In other parts of the world, producers tend to have ready access to international markets via water and highway as well as rail routes to the outside world. The typical CIS community, by contrast, is relatively far from ports or border crossing points and thus isolated from the world economy. Shipping distances are so long that even if per-ton-kilometer costs are low, transport charges add prohibitively to the delivered price of inputs from and outputs going to the world market. Economic rationality therefore leads inexorably toward fostering exchange with nearby centers.

Thus even if CIS regions are able to lower the relative transport component of national output in the future, their geographic situation seems likely to require a large volume of intra-Republic freight movement linking each republic's factories and farms within the republic. Similarly, geographic logic suggests that each republic's neighbors are likely to be the least-cost suppliers of many of its inputs and the most natural customers for its output.

RAILROAD MANAGEMENT QUESTIONS

Can the railroads of the former U.S.S.R. continue to operate as a unified system, the largest in the world? For seven decades the Ministerstvo Putei Soobshcheniia (MPS, Ministry of Means of Communication) has managed a single giant railroad, divided into regional units for operating purposes. Though the ministry's name implies control of all carriers, pipelines have been operated by the oil and gas ministries, internal waterways have been managed by a separate ministry, maritime fleets have had their own ministry, and road transport has been managed under numerous local authorities. Thus other carriers have been somewhat decentralized, but the railroad network under the MPS served all parts of the former U.S.S.R. in a tightly coordinated way.

On January 20, 1992, however, President Yeltsin abolished the old MPS and replaced it with a Russian Federation Ministry of Railroads. Asked how it would relate to railroads in neighboring republics, the new Minister of Railroads said that his ministry would retain day-to-day management of the transport process during a transition period, until an inter-state, intergovernmental body is created. He expected that the railroads would continue to work as a single technical system but foresaw difficult problems ahead, especially concerning freight and passenger cars. "Right now they belong to all of us in common, but when the railroads are divided, each railroad car will be owned by a specific republic." [4] To complicate matters further, a new transport ministry has been set up to supervise all transport modes, but it has a very small staff; day-to-day control seems to remain with the separate ministries.

Already the republics are moving to take control of the railroad lines, yards, terminal facilities, and service installations on their territory. Management of the locomotive stock also seems to center fairly easily in the railroads of each republic. As noted, the most difficult problem concerns the freight car fleet, since inter-regional shipments can take cars from one end of the entire network to the other.

The handling of information and billing charges concerning freight cars owned by many individual railroads has been a perennial problem for railroads all over the world, but unified systems for keeping track of a diversified fleet have been greatly improved in recent years. The MPS has been in the enviable situation of managing a single, national fleet of cars; it could now benefit substantially from an advanced computer-aided system to provide instantaneous information about cars en route for shippers, receivers, and railroad managers. Though management of separately owned cars is obviously feasible, it would seem to be a retrogressive step if the MPS fleet were to be split up among the republics as Minister Fadeyev anticipates. Moreover, it is not easy to perceive a logical basis for assigning cars to republics or individual railroads. As yet the issue is unresolved.

The railroad system in recent years has been divided into 32 non-overlapping regional roads, as enumerated in Table 6, which classifies them roughly according to republic boundaries. Seventeen are in the Russian republic; they account for 58 percent of the line operated, 68 percent of the freight traffic, and 73 percent of the passenger traffic. The Ukrainian republic has six of the regional roads, making up 16 percent of the line, moving 13 percent of the freight traffic and handling 16 percent of the passenger movement. In the Kazakh republic there are three regional roads accounting for just under 10 percent of the line, carrying 11 percent of the freight, and handling 10 percent of the passengers. The remaining railroads serve their territories as indicated in Table 6.

MULTIMODAL TRANSPORT POSSIBILITIES

For 60 years Soviet writers called for a "unified transport system," but there has never been much coordination between the MPS and the other carriers. Meanwhile in market economies railroads have learned to work jointly with trucking firms, maritime carriers, and internal waterway carriers to provide shippers with timely and reliable multimodal freight services. Spurred by competitive pressures, traditional intermodal rivalry has increasingly given way to multimodal cooperation under which a shipper can negotiate a transport contract covering joint movement from origin

---

[4] *Izvestia*, Feb. 3, 1992, p. 2 (excerpted in *Current Digest of the ex-Soviet Press*, vol. 44, no. 5, p. 29).

TABLE 6. 1990 Line Operated, and Freight, and Passenger Traffic, 32 Former U.S.S.R. Railway Administrations.

CIS Transport Railway	Year-End Line Operated (Kms.)	Tons Originated (Millions)	Tons-Kms. (Billions)	Average Length of Haul (Kms.)	Suburban Passengers (Millions)	Long-Distance Passenger (Millions)
October	10,186	194.2	161.0	829	547.0	30.3
Moscow	9,360	187.6	178.3	950	1,336.8	54.3
Gorky	5,672	99.2	191.9	1,934	167.1	18.1
Northern	6,047	146.5	171.0	1,167	50.5	14.2
North Caucasus	6,504	173.9	142.9	822	91.4	18.7
South-Eastern	3,650	75.5	144.9	1,919	66.2	9.1
Volga	4,098	67.1	74.3	1,108	42.1	9.8
Kuibyshev	4,835	119.8	178.5	1,490	82.0	14.1
Sverdlovsk	7,147	218.7	183.6	840	115.5	18.4
South Ural	4,935	150.9	258.4	1,712	50.8	13.9
West-Siberian	4,181	58.2	233.0	4,001	99.5	15.9
Kemerovo	1,916	238.3	68.1	286	49.9	5.9
Krasnoiarsk	3,167	110.1	112.3	1,020	33.1	7.1
East-Siberian	2,665	113.0	132.4	1,172	36.3	6.8
Trans-Baikal	3,436	38.1	163.2	4,285	14.2	5.5
Far-Eastern	4,448	62.1	93.0	1,499	59.2	13.5
Baikal-Amur	3,834	26.0	36.2	1,393	2.1	2.4
Russian Rep.	86,081	2,079.2	2,522.9	1,213	2,843.9	258.0
South-Western	4,681	84.3	94.7	1,123	177.0	24.7
L'vov	4,521	107.1	50.3	470	88.8	18.9
Odessa	4,279	75.9	78.9	1,040	36.2	14.1
Southern	3,715	115.3	82.4	715	123.4	11.8
Dnepr	3,255	254.6	88.4	347	85.4	16.7
Donets	2,903	371.1	93.5	252	64.0	11.1
Ukraine Rep.	23,354	1,008.3	488.2	484	574.8	97.2
West-Kazakh	3,817	32.0	116.1	3,627	0.0	6.3
Virgin Lands	5,751	237.0	175.8	742	15.6	9.0
Alma Ata	4,591	76.1	115.1	1,512	1.8	8.3
Kazakh Rep.	14,159	345.2	407.0	1,179	17.4	23.5
Belarus	5,488	121.5	75.4	621	139.0	20.6
Central Asian	6,330	122.5	110.7	903	15.8	11.5
Trans-Caucasus	2,377	43.0	15.5	360	12.6	5.2
Azerbaidzhan	2,125	33.0	37.1	1,123	11.3	4.0
Baltic	6,280	84.3	45.5	540	205.6	15.8
Moldava	1,328	19.9	14.8	742	13.3	4.0
Total	147,522	3,857.0	3,717.1	964	3,833.6	439.7

Source: Derived from MPS U.S.S.R. statistical reports.

to destination of a specific commodity by two or three modes working together.

Rapidly growing traffic between Pacific Rim shippers and the East Coast of the United States, using ships carrying large containers across the Pacific and double-stack railcars moving the containers in unit trains across the United States, is a dramatic example of the possibilities. In the former U.S.S.R. a somewhat similar "land bridge" service between Japan and Western Europe via rail across the U.S.S.R. has been in operation for over a decade, but slow and unreliable performance has stymied the growth of traffic. Soviet railroad managers, concentrating on meeting ton-kilometer traffic targets, have never found it necessary to focus on meeting the needs of shippers and receivers for prompt, reliable service. Even in recent times, railroad clients have been ill served by managers responding to traditional incentives.[5] Facing fuel and other input shortages, railroad officials have paid little attention to organizing speedy door-to-door service for perishables and high-value consumer goods, or supplying clean empty cars on schedule to shippers of mass freight. While republic economies continue to deteriorate and traffic continues to decline, there are very few signs that tradition-minded transport managers for railroads and the other modes are beginning to take the initiative in seeking to revive traffic by improving its quality.

Market-minded producers, however, may soon be able to bring pressure on transport suppliers by pressing for service and offering to pay higher freight rates. Local transport agencies, hard up for revenue, may start to respond. Some alert shippers may be in a position to play off one trucking firm, or rail route, against another, and some alert transport firms may see possibilities for intermodal service yielding attractive revenue. If the transport sector in CIS economies develops along these lines, it can support and stimulate economic restructuring that will make the best possible use of the region's transport resources.

---

[5] See Holland Hunter, *Soviet Transportation Policy* (1957); Harvard Univ. Press, Holland Hunter, *Soviet Transport Experience* (1968), Brookings Inst.; and Holland Hunter and Vladimir Kontorovich, "Transport Pressures and Potentials," pp. 382–96 in U. S. Joint Economic Committee, *Gorbachev's Economic Plans*, vol. 2 (1987).

SCIENCE AND TECHNOLOGY IN THE FORMER SOVIET UNION: CAPABILITIES AND NEEDS

By William C. Boesman *

CONTENTS

SUMMARY

Science and technology (S&T) resources and capabilities in the former Soviet Union are heavily concentrated in Russia, particularly in Moscow and St. Petersburg. Russia has about two-thirds of the researchers and major research institutes, and almost 60 percent of all research organizations, of the former Soviet Union. The second major concentration, about 17 percent, is in the Ukraine, mainly in Kiev. Belarus is third with about 4 percent. The other 12 nations of the former Soviet Union account for approximately 12 percent of total researchers and 20 percent of total research organizations.

The Soviet Union historically had the largest number of scientists and engineers (about 1.5 million in 1988), scientists and engineers per million of population (5,387), and R&D expenditures per gross national product (6.2 percent) among the major nations of the world. Russia, by itself, not only retains first rank in these measures among the nations of the world, but, in terms of scientists and

---

* William C. Boesman is a Specialist in Science and Technology, with the Science Policy Research Division, Congressional Research Service.

engineers per million population (9,398 in 1989) is even more clearly the leader. But, probably because of the problems in Russia, the number of Russian scientists and engineers decreased from 1,385,300 in 1989 to 1,227,400 in 1991.

Numbers, however, do not tell the entire story. S&T in Russia and the rest of the former Soviet Union is strong and vital in some areas, but weak and deteriorating in many other areas. For example, some areas of fundamental science and much military and space research and development (R&D), especially in Russia, are world class. However, most areas of civilian R&D, especially in areas like computers and consumer electronics, are below world standards. Military influence and funding have played a major role in S&T. Historically, about one-half of the funding of the former Soviet Academy of Sciences came from the military. Overall, military R&D accounted for about 75 percent of the state budget allocations for R&D in the former Soviet Union. About 80 percent of military R&D was conducted in Russia.

A crisis in funding, caused by the broader economic crisis, is the most serious problem in S&T today in the former Soviet Union. Most of the limited funds currently available for S&T are being used for salaries. Consequently, scientific facilities are deteriorating and needed equipment and supplies cannot be purchased. This situation seems to be affecting all laboratories, even the best. A number of scientists (but, apparently, no nuclear weapons scientists) have left, and there is evidence that a significant number intend to remain abroad. Leaders of the Russian S&T establishment consider that preserving that establishment is now their first priority. The former Soviet Union, particularly Russia, also must deal with the conversion of its military establishment, including its large and numerous military laboratories. Related to this is the transformation of the governmental applied research and development capabilities to support the evolving civilian market economies.

Increased technology transfer between the United States and the former Soviet Union will benefit both regions. The U. S. Administration recently announced its policy to "actively seek opportunities to acquire goods, services, and technologies from the [former Soviet Union] that benefit our economy and other security interests, and to encourage private business to expand their search for new opportunities," and to further reduce U.S. COCOM [1] controls on U.S. exports of dual-use technologies to the former Soviet Union to only those most vital to U.S. security.

If the former Soviet Union can mobilize S&T effectively, science and technology will be able to contribute to a successful evolution of those societies and economies. But a report of the Russian Academy of Sciences suggests that a more likely scenario is Russian S&T falling even further behind the West. The S&T establishment in the former Soviet Union, particularly in Russia, has been reorganized in an attempt to cope with the current social and economic situation and to better prepare for the future. The Baltic nations

---

[1] The Coordinating Committee on Export Controls, the West's non-treaty, non-binding organization whose members are the nations of the European Community minus Ireland plus the United States, Australia, and Japan.

are even reorganizing their university research structure on the Western model and eliminating their Academy of Sciences structures, the most visible legacy of the former Soviet S&T structure.

A window of opportunity, possibly brief, exists for the former Soviet Union during which its S&T, along with capital, free social institutions, and other factors have the potential to transform those societies and contribute to their economic development. A number of these factors, including U.S. S&T assistance, are discussed in other papers of this volume.

GEOGRAPHIC DISTRIBUTION OF SCIENCE & TECHNOLOGY IN THE FORMER SOVIET UNION [2]

It has been said that our solar system consists of the planet Jupiter plus a lot of debris. During much of the history of the Soviet Union, and particularly from World War II until its dissolution, Russia seemed to be the Jupiter among the 15 republics of the Soviet Union and its Eastern European satellites, at least militarily and politically. While much has changed militarily and politically over the last two or three years, the S&T personnel and research organizations of the former Soviet Union still are concentrated heavily in Russia, particularly in Moscow and St. Petersburg. Other centers of science and technology in Russia include Niznij Novgovod, Sverdlovsk, Novosibirsk, Vladivostok, and several, until recently, closed cities devoted to nuclear weapons research and development.

The second major concentration of S&T capabilities is in the Ukraine, mainly in Kiev. The Ukrainian S&T capability, however, is only about 25 to 30 percent of the Russian in terms of the total number of scientific researchers and engineers and the total number of scientific research organizations. The Ukraine, moreover, has only about 10 to 17 percent as many major research institutes as does Russia. (See table 1.)

Belarus has the next largest number of researchers and engineers, but this number is only about 6 percent of the Russian and 22 percent of the Ukrainian researchers and engineers. The other republics of the former Soviet Union have even fewer researchers and engineers and research organizations. Figure 1 shows the areas of heavy R&D concentration in the former Soviet Union.

The Soviet Union historically has had the largest number of scientists and engineers, scientists and engineers per million of population, and R&D expenditures per gross national product among the major nations of the world. Russia itself not only retains first rank, but, in terms of scientists and engineers per million population, is even more clearly the leader (the Soviet Union and Japan had been comparable). (See table 2.) This result occurs statistically because Russia accounts for about two-thirds of the total number of researchers and engineers, but only about 50 percent of the population, of the former Soviet Union. [3] Russia also has about two-thirds

---

[2] See also Congressional Research Service. *Soviet Civilian Research and Development Facilities and Funding.* CRS Report No. 91–778 SPR, by William C. Boesman and Genevieve J. Knezo. Washington, October 30, 1991.

[3] Based on a 1989 population of 290,939,000 for the former Soviet Union and 147,400,000 for Russia, from *The World Almanac and Book of Facts: 1992.* New York, Newspaper Enterprises

Continued

TABLE 1. Scientific Researchers, Engineers, and Organizations in the Former Soviet Union.

Republic	Total Researchers and Engineers 1991 (thousands)	Total Number of Research Organizations 1991	Major Research Institutes	
			Identified by Berry	Identified by CIA
Russia	1,227.4	4,646	274	287
Moscow	—	—	(151)	(147)
St. Petersburg	—	—	(37)	(34)
Novosibirsk	—	—	(14)	(23)
Other	—	—	(72)	(83)
Armenia	24.8	158	10	11
Azerbaijan	17.9	152	10	10
Belarus	69.0	312	10	11
Estonia	7.0	73	5	10
Georgia	22.4	131	7	9
Kazakhstan	31.3	279	9	6
Kyrgyzstan	6.8	70	3	5
Latvia	19.0	189	8	6
Lithuania	22.3	NA [a]	5	7
Moldova	14.4	107	4	4
Tajikistan	5.5	73	2	6
Turkmenistan	5.8	69	0	5
Ukraine	313.1	1,400	47	28
Uzbekistan	36.5	314	6	8
Total	1,823.2	7,973 [b]	400	413

Sources: Total researchers and engineers—Russian Academy of Sciences. Analytical Center for Problems of Socio-Economy and Science-Technology Development. *Science in Russian Today and Tomorrow: Part II.* Moscow, March 1991. p. 21–22; Total number of research organizations—Ibid., p. 15. Major research institutes identified by Berry—Michael J. Berry. *Science and Technology in the U.S.S.R.* Harlow, Essex, United Kingdom. Longman Group U.K. Limited, 1988. 405 p.; major research institutes identified by CIA—*Directory of Soviet Officials: Science and Education.* LDA 91–13542. Fall 1991. 203 p.

[a] The number of research organizations in Lithuania is probably about the same as in Latvia, that is, about 190.

[b] If the number for Lithuania is about 190, the total number is about 8,163.

of the major research institutes and almost 60 percent of all research organizations of the former Soviet Union.

Such statistics indicate the dominance, using some quantitative measures, of Russian S&T among the nations of the former Soviet Union and its strong standing among the other leading nations of the world. (The quality of this S&T is discussed in the next section.) Because of this and because of the relative lack of information on science and technology in the other nations of the former Soviet Union, the following discussion deals mainly with Russian S&T. Two caveats about Soviet S&T statistics are in order. Reliable sta-

Association, Inc., 1991. p. 810.

[4] Russian Academy of Sciences. Analytical Center for Problems of Socio-Economy and Science-Technology Development. *Science in Russia Today and Tomorrow: Part II.* Moscow, March 1991. p. 21.

[5] This is discussed in more detail in U.S. Library of Congress. Congressional Research Service.

FIGURE 1. AREAS OF HEAVY R&D CONCENTRATION.

Source: Congressional Research Service.

tistics on military versus civilian R&D, for example, are not available, and estimates are used herein. Moreover, statistics do not tell the entire story. For example, officially there has been little or no unemployment among the work force of the Soviet Union, although it is known that, in general, the work force was notoriously underemployed. This probably extended to the S&T work force as well and thus the current official number of scientists and engineers may not represent the number that the former Soviet Union can support, or needs, in a free-market system. It is interesting to note in this regard that the Russian Academy of Sciences records a decrease in the number of Russian researchers and engineers from 1,385,300 in 1989 to 1,227,400 in 1991. [4] Moreover, S&T in Russia and the rest of the former Soviet Union is strong and vital in some areas, but is weak and deteriorating in other areas. The rest of this paper addresses this situation.

---

[4] Russian Academy of Sciences. Analytical Center for Problems of Socio-Economy and Science-Technology Development. *Science in Russia Today and Tomorrow: Part II*. Moscow, March 1991. p. 21.

TABLE 2. Selected R&D Indicators for Russia and Other Major Nations.

Nations	Scientists and Engineers	Scientists and Engineers Per Million of Population	R&D Expenditures Per Gross National Product (percent)
United States [a]	806,200	3,317	2.6
Japan [b]	614,854	5,029	2.8
United Kingdom	101,400 [c]	1,782 [d]	2.2 [e]
France (1987)	109,400	1,973	2.3
W. Germany (1987)	165,614	2,724	2.8
U.S.S.R. (1988)	1,522,200	5,387	6.2
Russia (1989)	1,385,300 [e]	9,398 [g]	NA

Sources: Unless otherwise noted, the data are for the years indicated are from UNESCO Statistical Yearbook 1990. France, UNESCO, 1990. p. 5-19, 5-20, 5-105, 5-106, 5-110.

[a] Dates for columns 1, 2, and 3 are 1987, 1987, and 1988, respectively.

[b] Dates for columns 1, 2, and 3 are 1988, 1988, and 1987, respectively.

[c] 1987, from U.S. National Science Foundation. *International Science and Technology Data Update: 1991.* Washington, NSF, 1991. p. 43.

[d] 1987, calculated from column 1 and a United Kingdom 1987 population of 56,890,000 from UNESCO Statistical Yearbook: 1989. France, UNESCO, 1989. p. 1-10.

[e] 1988, from *International Science and Technology Data Update: 1991,* op. cit., p. 3.

[f] From Russian Academy of Sciences. Analytical Center for Problems of Socio-Economy and Science-Technology Development. *Science in Russia Today and Tomorrow: Part II.* Moscow, Mar. 1991. p. 21.

[g] Calculated from column 1 and a Russian 1989 population of 147,400,000 from *The World Almanac and Book of Facts; 1992.* New York, Newspaper Enterprises Association, Inc., 1991. p. 810.

STATE OF SCIENCE AND TECHNOLOGY [5]

The Russian Academy of Sciences was created by Peter the Great in 1725. It was reestablished in November 1991. In between, it became the Soviet Academy of Sciences and, as such, was organized to be the central scientific organization of the Soviet Union, with a mission to serve the techno-economic and, later, military needs of the state. The scientific research institutes of the Soviet Academy of Sciences and the 14 associated republic Academies of Science (which were modeled on the Soviet Academy) have been responsible mainly for conducting the fundamental research of the nations of the former Soviet Union. The research institutes and other R&D organizations of the Government's industrial ministries have been responsible mainly for applied research and development related to the missions of those ministries. The institutes of higher education (IHEs) have been responsible mainly for educating future scientists, although they also conducted limited research.

---

[5] This is discussed in more detail in U.S. Library of Congress. Congressional Research Service. Eastern Europe and Soviet Science and Technology: Capabilities and Needs. CRS Report No. 91-114 SPR, by William C. Boesman. Washington, February 5, 1991.

The personnel and funding resources devoted to these three S&T sectors in the former Soviet Union typically have been approximately as follows: [6]

S&T Institution	No. of Research Organizations	Personnel (%)	Expenditures (%)
Research Institutes of Soviet and Republic Academies of Sciences.	1,193	13	12
Institutes of Higher Education (IHEs).	777	7	7
Research Institutes, Industries Enterprises, etc. of the Governmental Ministries.	5,741	80	81

Military influence and funding have played a major role in this structure. Historically, about one-half of the funding of the Soviet Academy of Sciences came from the military. Overall, military R&D accounted for about 75 percent of the state budget allocations for R&D in the former Soviet Union. [7] About 80 percent of the military R&D was conducted in Russia. [8]

The organizational structure of S&T in the Soviet and 14 republic Academies of Sciences, IHEs, and ministry research organizations, plus military dominance of that structure, contributed to excellence in some areas of fundamental science and in much military and space R&D, especially in Russia. It also led to unsatisfactory civilian R&D, especially in areas like computers and consumer electronics. In the other republics of the scientific research has been weaker than in Russia because it always was dominated by Moscow. On the other hand, the Academies of Sciences of the other republics were more heavily involved in applied research than has been the Soviet Academy. This has been particularly true of the Ukraine and Belarus, where perhaps as much as 60 percent of their funding has been for industrial R&D. This suggests that these republics may be more successful in adapting and contributing to the changed R&D needs of competitive, consumer-oriented, free-market economies than will be Russia. Moreover, the success of much Russian-dominated Soviet military R&D probably will not be transferable to the civilian economy because Soviet military R&D achieved its elite status by expropriating, from the rest of the Soviet economy, whatever it needed to be successful. An analysis of the views of Soviet expatriate scientists and engineers suggests: [9]

The only "secret" of military R&D management is priority; the technology is superior not because of a separate system but because of higher standards; and the higher

[6] The data are from Science in Russia Today and Tomorrow: Part II, op. cit., pp. 7, 14, 19.
[7] According to Boris Saltykov, head of Russia's new Ministry of Science, Higher Education, and Technology Policy. Funding for Basic Science Remains Doubtful Despite Changes. Foreign Broadcast Information Service JPRS Report (JPRS-UST-92-003), April 15, 1992. p. 28.
[8] The percentage estimates in this section, unless otherwise noted, are based upon conversations with experts on S&T in the former Soviet Union.
[9] Balzer, Harley D. Soviet Science on the Edge of Reform. Boulder, Westview Press, 1989. p. 135.

standards are achieved through a massive inspection system at enormous cost. No civilian consumer could afford the real costs of the products produced by and for the Soviet military.

The former Soviet Union, and particularly Russia, is comparable to the United States in some areas of science, especially in several areas of theoretical science (oceanography, high-energy physics, condensed-matter physics, laser physics, astrophysics), mathematics, and several areas of experimental science (materials science, fluid dynamics, molecular biology). It is weaker than the United States in many other scientific areas, especially in experimental sciences. [10] This is due in large part to the lack of adequate scientific equipment, but also to the prestige historically associated with theoretical scientific studies and mathematics in the former Soviet Union.

A number of studies have evaluated Soviet technology. Perhaps the most recent comprehensive and in-depth analysis was published in 1977. [11] That study concluded that, for most of the technologies examined, [12] which were those in which the Soviet Union generally was considered to be strong, "there is no evidence of a substantial diminution of the technological gap between the U.S.S.R. and the West in the past 15–20 years, either at the prototype/ commercial application stages or in the diffusion of advanced technology." [13] A later study found that the Soviet Union gave priority to, and was a leader in, high-voltage transmission of electricity, machine tools, and military technology, but, beyond such priority sectors, it "lags behind the West in the development and utilization of technology across the broad spectrum of economic activities." [14] More recent studies have found that the former Soviet Union also is several years behind the West in the very important areas of microelectronics and computers [15] and that it lags the United States in 16 of 20 selected militarily critical nonnuclear technologies. [16]

Part of the problem with Soviet S&T was organizational. Its basic research (largely conducted in the research institutes of the Academies of Sciences, particularly the Soviet Academy) was separated organizationally from those organizations that carried out applied research, mainly the research institutes and other research organizations of the Government's mission-oriented industrial ministries. Moreover, the ministerial research organizations had little

---

[10] [U.S. Intelligence Community] A Study of Soviet Science. December 1985. p. 18.

[11] Amann, Ronald, Julian Cooper, and R. W. Davies (eds.). The Technological Level of Soviet Industry. New Haven, Yale University Press, 1977.

[12] Iron and steel technologies, metalcutting and numerically controlled tools, high voltage electrical power transmission, the chemical industry, industrial process (including computer) control technology, computer technology in general, military technology, rocketry, and passenger cars.

[13] Amann, op. cit., p. 66.

[14] Brada, Josef C. "Soviet-Western Trade and Technology Transfer: An Economic Overview." In Parrott, Bruce. Trade, Technology, and Soviet-American Relations. Bloomington, Indiana University Press, 1985. p. 9.

[15] Bengston, J. et al. FASAC Integration Report II: Soviet Sciences as Viewed by Western Scientists. Science Applications International Corporation, McLean, VA, April 1989; and Bengston et al. FASAC Integration Report III: The Soviet Applied Information Sciences in a Time of Change. Science Applications International Corporation, McLean, Virginia, July 1991.

[16] U.S. Dept. of Defense. Critical Technologies Plan. March 15, 1990.

incentive to incorporate innovations from the research institutes into their production processes. They were more concerned with meeting the production quotas established by the central planning process. In addition in the Soviet system, the institutes of higher education performed little research and thus their students received little or no experience in experimental research.

Another, and perhaps the most important, reason for the lag of S&T in the former Soviet Union was attitudinal. The general malaise that existed in Soviet society for many years manifested itself as a "'universal apathy' pervading the entire R&D community." [17] That apathy, perhaps, has changed into fear, fear of losing scientific positions and the associated prestige. A prevalent attitude today in the scientific community of the former Soviet Union seems to be to preserve the R&D establishment at all costs.

A third set of factors that adversely affected Soviet S&T was restrictions on scientific communications, personnel exchanges, and technology transfer. The first two of these factors were alleviated politically during glasnost to a great extent, but now scientific communications and personnel exchanges are constrained by new and severe funding difficulties in the former Soviet Union. Restrictions on technology transfer, although often troublesome, continue to be eased, as discussed in a separate section below.

The crisis in S&T funding, caused by the broader economic crisis, is the most serious problem in the former U.S.S.R. S&T today. The current situation is summarized in a recent report of a U.S. National Academy of Sciences workshop: [18]

> The FSU [former Soviet Union] is in crisis. Dramatic changes in the region, although undoubtedly positive in a political sense, leave scientists in a precarious niche since there is very limited money for science. Salaries for scientists within and outside the academy structure are pitifully low, and FSU scientists are becoming increasingly isolated from their international colleagues owing to the virtual absence of hard currency necessary for western journals and for travel to meetings outside the FSU. Outstanding research groups are disintegrating, and some of the best scientists of all ages are leaving for temporary, and in some cases permanent, positions abroad. If the exodus of FSU scientists continues, and if FSU science and technology wither and flounder, it is difficult to see how the FSU nations can prosper. Science and technology, together with capital and free social institutions, propel a modern economy.

Most of the limited funds currently available for S&T are being used for salaries. Consequently, scientific facilities are deteriorating and needed equipment and supplies cannot be purchased. In addition, if such equipment and supplies need to be purchased abroad, scarce hard currency would be needed. This situation

---

[17] Balzer, op. cit., p. 88.
[18] U.S. National Academy of Sciences. *Reorientation of the Research Capability of the Former Soviet Union: A Report to the Assistant to the President for Science and Technology.* Washington, National Academy Press, 1992. p. 7.

seems to be affecting all laboratories, even the best. According to the director of a leading laboratory located in Moscow, "Leading laboratories and their heads bear such losses that they are in a worse situation than the weak and inefficient laboratories." [19] Even a temporary lack of funds may cause some irretrievable S&T losses. Russia, for example, has unique whaling, seismic, and plant genetics data that may be lost if the information systems are not maintained.

S&T BRAIN-DRAIN

Brain-drain is a potentially serious long-term S&T problem facing the former Soviet Union. It has several aspects, including the possible loss of nuclear weapon scientists and engineers; long-term, short-term, and reverse brain-drain; and internal and external brain-drain.

There are several estimates of the numbers of nuclear weapons scientists and engineers in the former U.S.S.R. The numbers most frequently range from about 1,000 to 2,000 key weapon design scientists and engineers [20] up to tens of thousands of scientists and engineers with various critical skills necessary for nuclear weapons research, development, and testing.

In early 1992, there was a flurry of reports warning of an exodus of former U.S.S.R. nuclear weapon scientists to third world countries. [21] However, a number of reports from the former Soviet Union contradicted these reports. Viktor Mikhailov, head of the new Ministry of Atomic Energy (Minatom), stated that there have been no instances of weapon scientists emigrating. [22] The mayor of one of Russia's formerly closed science cities, Arzamas-16, echoed that statement specifically for his city. [23] There are similar reports from the Ukraine [24] and Kazakhstan. [25] Part of the reason that there was not an exodus of nuclear weapons scientists from the former Soviet Union are the restrictions on foreign travel of persons having secret information. If such restrictions are eased or lifted and if the conditions facing scientists in the former Soviet Union get worse, a brain-drain of nuclear weapon scientists may occur.

Although such a brain-drain does not appear now to be a problem, there is an exodus of other scientists from the former Soviet Union. Any brain-drain, however, might be a partial and short-term benefit in that it temporarily relieves the S&T funding prob-

---

[19] Panel Discusses Future of FSU Science. "*Scientist to Scientist,*" v. 1, April 1992. p. 2.

[20] U.S. Congress. Senate. Committee on Governmental Affairs. Testimony of Robert M. Gates, Director of the Central Intelligence Agency. Hearing, 102d Congress, 2d session. February 15, 1992. (forthcoming)

[21] See, for example, "Pay Lures 50 Soviet Experts to Aid Iraq's Nuclear Effort." *Washington Times*, March 3, 1992.; and "[NATO Secretary General Manfred] Woerner Confirms Attempts to Recruit Experts." Foreign Broadcast Information Service (FBIS) *Daily Report* (FBIS-SOV-92-017), January 27, 1992. p. 2.

[22] "Russian Nuclear Energy Minister on 'Brain Drain.'" *FBIS Daily Report* (FBIS-SOV-92-45), March 17, 1992. Annex, p. 1; and "Minister: No Nuclear Scientists Working Abroad." *FBIS Daily Report* (FBIS-SOV-92-945), March 6, 1992. p. 1.

[23] "Arzamas-16 Mayor Views Nuclear Brain Drain." *FBIS Daily Report* (FBIS-SOV-92-052), March 17, 1992. p. 6.

[24] "Ukrainian Research Scientists Affected." *FBIS Daily Report* (FBIS-SOV-92-024), February 5, 1992. p. 6.

[25] "Kazakh Brain-Drain Issue Addressed." *FBIS Daily Report* (FBIS-SOV-92-024), February 5, 1992. p. 6.

lem. Probably most of the former U.S.S.R. scientists currently abroad intend to return to their own countries and would prefer to do so if jobs are available and living conditions are not unbearable. On the other hand, there is evidence that a significant number intend to remain abroad. Boris Saltykov, the director of the new Russian Ministry of Science, Higher Education, and Technology Policy, stated that, of about 500 scientists of the prestigious Soviet Academy of Sciences who left the Soviet Union in the last three years, only about 100 intend to return. [26] TASS reported that 51 percent of Moscow-based scientists "are ready to go abroad on a temporary contract, another six percent are ready to leave the country forever." [27] Many former Soviet Union scientists are finding scientific positions in the United States, particularly in universities. [28] In addition to this general brain-drain, there has been a specific brain-drain of Soviet Jewish scientists to Israel. In the last few years, entire laboratories were "trying to sell themselves as a group to Israel." [29] Israel, however, appears to be having difficulty absorbing these scientists, some of whom already may have returned to the former U.S.S.R.

A third aspect of the brain-drain is that, while some of it is external, that is, to other nations, some of it is internal, that is, a loss of scientific jobs by trained scientists and engineers who remain in their own country. There is much anecdotal information about former Russian scientists, for example, driving taxi cabs in Moscow. But, because of the historically large number of underemployed scientists, such an internal brain-drain, especially under current conditions, appears to be inevitable and might even strengthen S&T in the former U.S.S.R. in the long run.

Another type of internal brain-drain that may become significant if the economies of the former Soviet Union continue to evolve into market-oriented economies is that of scientists and engineers shifting careers and becoming commercial S&T entrepreneurs. Apparently, this has occurred already in a few cases. If it were to occur often enough, it might stimulate a version of the Route 128 (around Boston) and Silicon Valley (California) phenomena of U.S. scientists and engineers stimulating and profiting from commercial products developed from their S&T skills.

NEW S&T PRIORITIES

In the 1989–90 period, the Soviet Government established 15 priority S&T programs. Subsequently, it transferred about 5 billion of its 45 billion ruble R&D budget from military to civilian R&D, the majority for civilian space exploration. [30] According to Nikolai Laverov, head of the now defunct State Committee on Science and Technology (the principal science and technology policy organiza-

[26] "Minister Estimates 500 Scientists Have Left." *FBIS Daily Report* (FBIS-SOV-92-019), January 29, 1992. p. 3.
[27] "51 Percent 'Ready to Go.'" *FBIS Daily Report* ((FBIS-S0V-92-033), February 19, 1992. p. 1.
[28] McDonald, Kim A. "U.S. Universities Lure Many Renowned Physicists and Mathematicians from Former Soviet Union." *The Chronicle of Higher Education*, v. 38, June 3, 1992. p. A1, A33-A34.
[29] Holden, Constance. "Soviet Emigres Swamp Israeli Science." *Science*, v. 248, June 1, 1990. p. 1070.
[30] Seltzer, Richard J. "State Committee Head Laverov Talks on Soviet Science, Technology." *Chemical and Engineering News*, v. 68, June 4, 1990. p. 19–20.

tion of the Soviet Union), the priority areas were high-energy physics; high-temperature superconductivity; Mars-related research; human genome research; new information technologies; technology, machines, and processes of the future; new materials; advanced biological engineering methods; high-speed, ecologically clean transport; ecologically clean power engineering; resource-saving and ecologically clean metallurgical and chemical processes; high-efficiency food production processes; combating widespread diseases, construction in the year 2000; and nuclear fusion. [31]

These S&T priorities were established in anticipation of a stable period of transition to a more civilian-oriented market economy in the Soviet Union. They reflect plans for continued support of fundamental science, such as high-energy physics and materials science, areas in which the former Soviet Union, especially Russia, excels. They also reflect an enhanced commitment to several scientific and technological areas in which the former U.S.S.R. lags the West, but in which it has significant S&T needs, such as in public health and medicine, energy, environment, transportation, and telecommunications and computers.

These "Soviet" S&T priorities, however, have been overtaken to some extent by the events of the last couple of years. Lack of adequate funding for S&T, including the 15 priority programs, now is a serious problem among the nations of the former Soviet Union. In addition, given the other governmental problems facing these nations, S&T itself has become a relatively low priority among other governmental priorities. Leaders of the Russian S&T establishment consider that preserving that establishment, especially its world-class science facilities and personnel, is now their main priority. [32]

Another critical S&T priority now is the conversion of much of the military R&D establishment of the former Soviet Union to civilian ends. The Russian military may be cut to about 10 to 20 percent of its former size. [33] This would have an unknown, but significant, impact on both military and civilian R&D in the former U.S.S.R. especially in Russia, which has most of the military R&D capacity. Converting the large military R&D laboratories of the former Soviet Union, according to Soviet professor Sergei Kapitza,

will not be a simple matter. Built and manned for a very special purpose, such laboratories are both powerful and vulnerable. In some, a long-term effort has been made to develop activities in other fields, as Livermore and [Los Alamos National Laboratory, two U.S. nuclear weapons laboratories] have done. Unfortunately most [former Soviet Union] laboratories have only recently begun to take similar steps. However noble and good these adjustments may be, I do not think that they can resolve all problems on a

---

[31] Ibid., p. 21.
[32] Private conversations with U.S. experts in S&T from the former U.S.S.R., May 7 and 8, 1992.
[33] Kapitza, Sergei. "Soviet Scientists: Low Pay, No Pay, Now Insults." *The Bulletin of the Atomic Scientists*, v. 48, May 1992. p. 8. The author is a professor at the P. L. Kapitza Institute for Physical Problems of the Russian Academy of Sciences and president of the (formerly Soviet) Physical Society.

long-term basis. The laboratories were built for a specific purpose. [34]

The chief engineer of a submarine plant in one of Russia's former closed R&D cities (Severodvinsk) is reported as stating that the number one priority for such defense plants is obtaining "the technology and technical know-how to convert to a civilian economy." [35]

In addition to the conversion of some facilities from military to civilian R&D, a third new former Soviet Union S&T priority is to rapidly transform and improve applied and commercial R&D capabilities in support of the transition to market economies. This involves, however, not only technically successful applied research and development, but the creation of a legal and financial infrastructure to support commercial R&D ventures. An infrastructure to support Western-style commercial technological development requires, for example, the formulation and legal institution of the concept of private property rights, including private intellectual property rights, and private company ownership and control of property. Among other things, former Soviet Union R&D facilities may have to be split off from the government and be treated as individual companies. Commercial R&D ventures also would benefit significantly from a convertible currency so that scientific and technological equipment and supplies not available in the former U.S.S.R. could be purchased from abroad. It has been reported that the Russian ruble will become fully convertible on July 1, 1992. [36] In any case, successful commercial R&D ventures might require partnerships with foreign companies, which could provide needed hard currencies, equipment, and supplies as part of their contributions to the partnerships.

TECHNOLOGY TRANSFER

Technology transfer includes the transfer of technological information and know-how through public and proprietary writing, exchanges of technical personnel, patent licensing arrangements, and sales of technological products and processes. The former Soviet Union needs technology from the other nations of the world, particularly from the West and Japan, and needs to transfer, and especially sell, its technology to these nations. The United States stands to benefit both from its sales of technology to the former U.S.S.R. and from purchases of technology from that region that it otherwise would not obtain or would not obtain at an acceptable price.

Technology transfer in both directions has been restricted for about 45 years by the U.S. Government (as well as other nations) for national security reasons, but over the last several years, these restrictions have been eased considerably. Another step in that direction was taken by the President on March 3, 1992. As announced then, the Administration's policy is to "actively seek opportunities to acquire goods, services, and technologies from the

---

[34] Ibid., p. 9.
[35] Ibid., p. 6.
[36] Hiatt, Fred. "Russian Ruble to Become Fully Convertible July 1," *Washington Post*, May 6, 1992.

new republics [of the former U.S.S.R.] that benefit our economy and other security interests, and to encourage private business to expand their search for new opportunities." [37] The Administration's policy also is to further reduce U.S. COCOM controls on U.S. exports of dual-use (applicable to both military and civilian use) technologies to the former Soviet Union to only those required to protect the most vital U.S. security interests.

In regard to easing restrictions on U.S. imports from the former U.S.S.R., the Administration authorized [38] an $8 million Department of Defense (DOD) purchase of a Russian Topaz II space power unit and a $300,000 DOD purchase of four Hall thrusters, devices used for moving objects in space. The Administration also approved a license application for a private U.S. company to purchase thrusters. In addition, the Department of Energy (DOE) was authorized to enter into discussions with Russia for the purchase of $6 million worth of plutonium–238, a fuel for radioisotope thermonuclear generators used for space missions. Such a sale would be subject to a commitment by Russia not to use the $6 million to support its nuclear weapon production complex.

In regard to further easing of COCOM export restrictions, the Administration stated that it will

> review license applications promptly; consider with a presumption of approval all export licenses for dual-use items to civilian end-users in the republics of the former Soviet Union; and deny such applications *only* if the export would jeopardize the security interests of the U.S. and its allies. [39]

In a separate action, the Administration also proposed to the members of COCOM that it "increase the access of the former Soviet republics and Eastern European countries to controlled technology and create close cooperation between them and Western nations" through the formation of a COCOM Cooperation Council. [40]

Another aspect of technology transfer is joint ventures. A recent example is a joint venture [41] between DOE's Argonne National Laboratory, several U.S. industrial companies, and Russia' Kurchatov Institute of Atomic Energy to further develop a Russian process for recovering hydrogen from hydrogen sulfide extracted during petroleum production. It has been reported that such a technological development could save U.S. oil refiners up to $1 billion per year. [42]

---

[37] White House press release, March 27, 1992. p. 1.

[38] White House press release, March 27, 1992. p. 1; and Seltzer, Richard J., "U.S. Buys Russian Technology, Eyes Expanded Science Cooperation." *Chemical and Engineering News*, v. 70, April 6, 1992. pp. 24–25.

[39] White House press release, Fact Sheet, March 27, 1992. p. 2. (Underlining in original.)

[40] Inside the White House, v. 11, May 28, 1992. p. 16.

[41] The joint venture would take the form of two Cooperative Research and Development Agreements (CRADAs) between the DOE laboratory and the other parties.

[42] "Russians Agree to Two CRADAs." *R&D Magazine*, v. 34, April 1992. p. 5.

SOME POSSIBLE S&T FUTURES

The Russian Academy of Sciences analyzed the future of Russian S&T in 1991. In its report, it suggested three possible scenarios, [43] although it acknowledged that, because of the major changes now taking place in Russian society, S&T may evolve according to yet another scenario.

1. "Gradual transformation into an advanced country of the 'first world' to become eventually a leader in world science."

The Academy report suggested that this would occur only if there is a "successful political and economic reform" in Russia, a "powerful integrating ideology" to replace the one operating since 1917, and "breakthroughs in emerging and cutting-edge fields" of S&T. The report claims that this scenario is unlikely to occur although, if progress occurs in certain fields of S&T (for example, space technology, new materials, or microbiology), Russia might become either a competitor to, or a partner with, the United States, Western Europe, and Japan in certain areas of S&T.

2. "Establishing of a new, 'second world.'"

This scenario, in which the report associates Russia with such nations as Greece, Portugal, and Turkey, is based on Russia's importation of modern, needed technologies and the further upgrading of Russia's "scientific, technological and economic levels to the world standards." It contemplates that the Russian S&T system probably will require the help of, and often will be controlled by, foreign research centers. A danger identified with this scenario is that it is likely to cause Russia's technological lag with the West to increase rather than to decrease, even in those areas of S&T in which Russia is now a world leader or co-leader.

3. "Transformation into a 'third world' country, not devoid of the opportunity of transition to the 'second world.'"

The dangers identified in this scenario are that Russia becomes a nation of environmentally harmful industries and a raw materials supplier to advanced countries, with its S&T so limited that it cannot make a real contribution to Russian life and culture as it has in the past.

These three scenarios are not optimistic. The Academy report states that the most favorable scenario (the first) is unlikely. Additionally, all three scenarios have one thing in common, the "inevitable curtailment of [the] R&D sphere," which must decrease in "scale and undergo a structural reform." The report continues that

Today's sphere of R&D, based on big research institutes, is not viable, either on the whole, or in parts. Additional resources granted to science, taking into account their amount and structure, can not secure its survival.

Whatever the validity of these possible scenarios, they suggest the reality of negative attitudes within the Russian S&T establishment today concerning Russia's S&T prospects. The report suggests that the main S&T priority today, as mentioned above, is preserving the Russian S&T establishment. This will involve eliminating some un-

---

[43] Russian Academy of Sciences. Analytical Center for Problems of Socio-Economy and Science-Technology Development. *Science in Russia Today and Tomorrow: Part I.* Moscow, December 1991. The quotations in this section are taken from pp. 56–60.

necessary and unproductive parts of it, including personnel, reorganizing the rest, and creating new "organization, legal and material guarantees for [the] survival of [the new S&T system]."

S&T REORGANIZATION

Soviet organization for S&T was complex. [44] The organization for S&T is shaken and evolving. Basically the Soviet S&T structure involved three parallel systems (Academy, governmental ministries, and Ministry of Higher Education) with interconnecting lines of coordination under the overall direction of the Soviet Council of Ministers.

The principal Soviet S&T policy organization, which is now defunct, was the State Committee for Science and Technology, last headed by Nikolai Laverov. In conjunction with that organization, the Soviet Academy of Sciences had principal responsibility for formulating policy for fundamental science, as well as for conducting much of the Soviet Union's fundamental research in its research institutes. The Soviet Academy of Sciences, last headed by Guriy Marchuk, has been disestablished. The newly established, nongovernmental Russian Academy of Sciences has taken over the assets of the former Soviet Academy that are located in Russia. The Academies of Sciences of the other 14 republics continue to exist, although there are movements in the three Baltic republics (Latvia, Estonia, and Lithuania) to abolish their Academies, which are perceived to be legacies of both the Soviet and Tsarist regimes. These Baltic nations also are reorganizing their science toward the Western model of conducting significant amounts of research in universities, unlike the Soviet system. [45] In the Soviet Union, the Ministry of Higher and Specialized Secondary Education, now defunct, was responsible for the Institutes of Higher Education, which principally were teaching, not research, institutes.

In the Soviet Union, the various governmental ministries had their own research organizations, mainly devoted to applied research and development related to the individual missions of those ministries. It is not clear at this time what is going to replace this ministerial structure and their research institutes in the former Soviet Union. Even in Russia, there appears to be little or no development of a structure or mechanism for connecting the applied research and development capabilities of these ministerial institutes to the evolving market structure.

In Russia the Ministry of Science, Higher Education, and Technology Policy, under Boris Saltykov, has been established as the principal S&T organization, responsible for policy direction and funding of much R&D and science education. Saltykov, thus, has become the principal spokesman for Russian S&T policy. In addition, Yuriy Osipov, head of the Russian Academy of Sciences, Anatolii Rakitov, President Yeltsin's S&T policy adviser, and Yevgeniy

---

[44] See, for example, Cocks, Paul M. *Science Policy: USA/USSR, Volume II: Science Policy in the Soviet Union.* Washington, U.S. Govt. Print. Off., 1980, and Kruse-Vaucienne, Ursula M. and John M. Logsdon. *Science and Technology in the Soviet Union. A Profile.* Washington, The George Washington University, 1979.

[45] Bollag, Burton. "Baltics Dismantle Soviet-Style Science Academies in an Effort to Return Research to Universities." *The Chronicle of Higher Education,* v. 38, October 30, 1991. pp. A41, A43.

Velikhov, vice president of the Russian Academy of Science and responsible for the conversion of Russia's defense industry, have important responsibilities. Other new organizations are the Russian Space Agency, headed by Yuri Kopeteb, and the Ministry of Atomic Energy (Minatom), headed by Viktor Mikhailov, which is now responsible for Russia's military and civilian nuclear complex. These latter two organizations and the Russian Academy of Sciences receive their R&D funding through Saltykov's Ministry of Science, Higher Education, and Technology Policy.

Although there have been a few important changes at the top of the Russian S&T structure, most notably the appointments of Saltykov and Osipov, and although that structure itself has changed considerably, former Soviet S&T leaders are still mainly in charge of Russian S&T. Thus, the new Russian S&T policy structure may have some stability as it continues to evolve. This would seem to be important for the health of Russian S&T in the face of the broad social, economic, and S&T funding problems facing the nation.

In the other nations of the former Soviet Union, there is now an S&T policy vacuum because most S&T issues formerly were addressed in Moscow. This is particularly true of basic research. The Ukraine, however, has initiated a new organization for S&T policy. In the other republics, the dominant S&T policy organizations continue to be their republic Academies of Science, although, as mentioned above, this appears to being changing in the Baltics.

Other S&T changes are occurring in the former Soviet Union. In Russia, efforts are under way to establish a Russian Science Foundation, roughly on the model of the U.S. National Science Foundation, which would fund basic research projects selected on the basis of scientific merit through a process of peer review. There was no precedent for this in the Soviet Union.

Russia also is moving toward a legislated S&T policy, based upon model legislation developed in the late 1980s before the dissolution of the Soviet Union. A draft of the new S&T policy, sent to President Yeltsin in December 1991, proposes that effective institutional and economic links be established between the hitherto largely separate parts of the Soviet S&T system (Academy, institutes of higher education, and ministries). It also proposes: [46]

> abolishing all legal distinctions between these branches and creating a unified legal, financial, and managerial "operational space" for Russian science. The state would surrender its traditional role of sole supervisor of Russian research and would adopt a more modest position as one of its patrons. The document recommends laws that would create a stable legal environment for scientific activity in Russia; and it introduces the concept of "domestic technology transfer," whose realization could open up channels between military and civil research and development. Finally, it proposes that solid financial support be given only to the most internationally recognized, renowned areas of Russian science and to those areas of applied and develop-

---

[46] Levin, Aleksei E. "Change in Russian Science Administration and Policy." RFE/RL (Radio Free Europe/Radio Liberty) Research Report, v. 1, February 14, 1992. p. 56.

mental science that within two or three years might come up with innovative production techniques and products.

It is possible that some of the S&T policy issues addressed generally in this section and specifically in the Russian draft S&T policy legislation could be dealt with on a Commonwealth of Independent States (CIS) basis, since the other nations of the former Soviet Union probably would benefit from Russian leadership in the area of S&T policy.

CONCLUSION

Former President Nixon believes that the former Soviet Union is at a potential turning point in world history and could turn to "a new despotism," which would be more dangerous than the old one, if the West does not assist it. Senator Nunn, upon his return from a visit to the CIS, stated that there now exists a "window of opportunity," which may remain open for only a short time, during which assistance will be effective. [47] These views would apply not only in general, but also in regard to S&T. Soviet S&T is facing several short-term crises as well as major long-term problems. There also are opportunities for S&T to make major contributions to the peaceful transformation of the former Soviet Union.

The short-term crises may or may not turn into long-term problems. The short-term brain-drain, for example, apparently now does not involve nuclear weapons scientists, although it may in the future. Moreover, if R&D funding increases and stabilizes, the existing general scientific brain-drain could reverse itself to some extent. The former U.S.S.R. needs immediate S&T assistance to weather these current S&T funding and personnel crises. The U.S. Government is continuing its existing S&T programs with these nations and is developing new programs, as discussed elsewhere in this study.

Most of the research institutes of the Academies and ministries and the institutes of higher education of the former Soviet Union probably will survive the current brain-drain and funding crises. There remains, however, the potential for serious long-term problems in maintaining their S&T capabilities at levels adequate to contribute fully to national needs, especially conversion to civilian market economies. Chronic funding and brain-drain problems may occur and the ongoing overall S&T deterioration is likely to continue. Some S&T personnel capabilities represented by the current generation of scientists and engineers may be irretrievably lost to the former Soviet Union in the future. The next generation of scientists and engineers may be considerably smaller and represent fewer S&T capabilities than the current one because of more limited educational and work opportunities. Existing research and educational facilities may be abandoned and not replaced for lack of funds and, in the case of military R&D facilities, the great cost of conversion to civilian uses.

The major long-term S&T opportunity in the former U.S.S.R. is that these R&D capabilities, particularly if they are upgraded,

---

[47] Oberdorfer, Don. "Nixon Warns Bush to Aid Russia, Shun 'New Isolationism.'" *The Washington Post*, March 12, 1992. pp. A1, A22.

could contribute significantly to the transformation to more civilian oriented societies and market economies in those nations. As in the past, both the United States and the former Soviet Union would benefit from scientific exchanges and these are likely to increase, and because U.S. import and export restrictions are easing, both trading partners are likely to benefit from significantly increased technology transfer between them.

In short, the former Soviet Union and its Western supporters need to look beyond the current S&T crises, some real and some imaginary, to the serious R&D, educational, and personnel problems and opportunities likely to be facing it over the next decade or two. Soviet scientists and engineers historically have been part of the leadership elite of their societies. The outcome of the transition in the former Soviet Union will be important to the West— whether most its scientists and engineers are involved in conversion to civilian market economies, or whether they revert to the principally military R&D of the past, and whether science and technology there is strong or weak.

THE POST-SOVIET SPACE PROGRAM

By Marcia S. Smith *

CONTENTS

SUMMARY

On December 30, 1991, nine of the eleven members of the Commonwealth of Independent States (CIS) signed an agreement providing for the continuation of what had been the Soviet space program. The future of this "post-Soviet" or CIS space program remains impossible to forecast, however, since issues such as organization and funding remain unresolved. Even before the dissolution of the Soviet Union, space officials increasingly were forced to justify expenditures on space activities in light of the dismal economic situation in the country. Economic woes and political uncertainty in the former Soviet republics may undermine their commitment to continue the space program.

Nevertheless, more than 150 CIS satellites are currently operating, and although the launch rate is down noticeably from earlier years, it is far too early to dismiss the significance of the CIS space program. Rather it is the nature of its potential impact on U.S. space activities that has changed. While the military implications

---

* Marcia S. Smith is a Specialist in Science and Technology Policy, Science Policy Research Division, with the Congressional Research Service.

(629)

of former Soviet space activities have diminished, a new era of economic trade and competition has begun.

Russia is by far the most important player in the CIS space program, with approximately 80 percent of the scientific and manufacturing personnel and infrastructure for space, including one of the two CIS launch sites (Plesetsk). Kazakhstan is important because the other launch site (Tyuratam, or the Baikonur Cosmodrome) is located there, as well as facilities for research into space nuclear power and propulsion (at Semipalatinsk), and a major military research and development center (Sary Shagan). Ukraine (which has not joined the CIS space program) is the site of a major launch vehicle factory (Yuzhnoye, in Dnepropetrovsk) and an important tracking site (Yevpatoriya).

Today, CIS governments and companies (mostly Russian) are selling space products, services and technologies. This activity poses issues for U.S. policymakers who are interested in purchasing some of these items for use in U.S. space activities, are worried about potential economic competition, or are concerned that sales of Russian rocket technology to other countries might contribute to ballistic missile proliferation.

Bush Administration policy is evolving on these issues, and the subject is quite dynamic. Information in this chapter is current through June 1992, at which time President Bush was taking cautious steps toward increasing U.S.-Russian space interaction, both economic and scientific. Among the potential users of CIS space technology are the National Aeronautics and Space Administration (NASA) and the Department of Defense (DOD).

THE COMMONWEALTH OF INDEPENDENT STATES (CIS) SPACE PROGRAM

In the wake of the August 1991 coup attempt and the resulting dissolution of the Soviet Union, the former Soviet space program entered an uncertain era. Following decades of stability and support from the country's leadership, cracks already had opened in its foundation of popular support during Gorbachev's years of glasnost and perestroika and the program was beset by public disaffection, bureaucratic disarray, and budget cutbacks. Those challenges now are compounded many-fold.

Amidst the chaos, however, satellites and crews continue to be launched into space. Two cosmonauts are aboard the *Mir* (Peace) space station and there are plans for routine crew rotations (including the flight of a Frenchman) at least through 1992. A variety of satellites continue to be launched for communications, navigation, ecological, and military missions. The launch rate in 1991 was lower than 1990 (59 compared to 75), but it had been declining since 1988, so the decrease cannot be entirely attributed to the current turmoil. How the space program will fare during the rest of 1992 and beyond is the question. For example, for the first five months of 1992, only 16 launches were conducted, compared to 27 during the same period in 1991.

THE MINSK AGREEMENT

Nine of the eleven CIS member states—Armenia, Azerbaijan, Belarus, Kazakhstan, Kyrgyzstan, Russia, Tajikistan, Turkmenistan, and Uzbekistan—signed an Agreement on Joint Activities in the Exploration and Use of Space at a meeting in Minsk on December 30, 1991. [1] The other two CIS members, Ukraine and Moldova, did not sign.

In one sense, the CIS appears to be following the model of the European Space Agency (ESA) [2] in that the space program will be funded by a multitude of countries, though the critical issue of funding levels has yet to be resolved. The agreement says only that funding will be "proportional" and each state pledges to "make provision for the allocation of the necessary funds . . . when compiling the state budgets," but what proportions and how much funding are not specified.

Whether there will be other parallels between ESA and the CIS space program is an open question. For example, will all the member countries have a voice in deciding what space projects to pursue or will Russia, as the largest financial contributor, make those decisions unilaterally or with only cursory discussion? The head of the Russian Space Agency, Yuriy Koptev, has indicated that he feels that the interstate space council created by the Minsk agreement will be no more than a conduit for financial contributions from the member states, not a policymaking organization. Whether the other members concur with that position remains to be seen.

Also, ESA conducts only civilian space activities, but so far the CIS is responsible for both military and civilian space activities. Former Soviet strategic assets, including the space program, are under the control of the CIS commander in chief (Marshall Shaposhnikov). A multinational military space program creates complexities that a national program does not have (who has access to intelligence data, who "tasks" satellites to look at particular targets, etc.), but they are not insurmountable. As with the civilian space program, however, Russia is by far the dominant nation. What course ultimately is chosen—a CIS military space program operating for and at the direction of the entire CIS, or one controlled exclusively by Russia—will be interesting to watch.

The preamble to the 12-article CIS space agreement identifies the importance of space science and technology to the development of Commonwealth member states, the need to combine efforts for effective research and utilization in the interests of the national economy and science, as well as defense capability and ensuring the collective security of Commonwealth members. Thus, it recognizes as important the broad range of space activities conducted by the former Soviet Union. This is good news for the diversity of scientists and engineers engaged in space activities, though it is still unclear as to what emphasis will be placed on various aspects of

---

[1] The text of the agreement is printed in Foreign Broadcast Information Service, *Soviet Union Daily Report*, FBIS-SOV-91-251, 31 December 1991, p. 21-22.

[2] ESA has 13 members—Austria, Belgium, Denmark, France, Germany, Ireland, Italy, the Netherlands, Norway, Spain, Sweden, Switzerland, and the United Kingdom.

the program (activities involving crews versus those conducted by automated spacecraft, space science versus space applications, etc.). Fulfillment of the interstate program is "ensured by the joint strategic armed forces." The Soviet Strategic Rocket Forces used to operate the launch complexes, a practice that is continuing under the CIS strategic forces, as noted earlier. Existing facilities (such as the launch sites and control centers) are specifically mentioned as part of the implementation of the interstate agreement. The signatories also agree to "retain and develop the existing scientific and technological and industrial potential" for designing, constructing, testing and developing space rocket technology.

Despite all the language in the Minsk agreement about operation of the space infrastructure, especially the launch sites, difficulties developed between Russia and Kazakhstan in the first half of 1992 concerning the operation of the Tyuratam launch site in Kazakhstan. The Kazakh government has stated that it owns Tyuratam, although Russians actually operate the site. Kazakh nationals work there only in support roles. A riot by Kazakh military construction workers at the site in February 1992 highlighted the poor living conditions and morale there. As the months progressed, the Kazakh government began charging Russia for certain phases of launch and landing operations.[3] In May, just before the CIS summit in Tashkent, launch of a military reconnaissance satellite from Tyuratam was delayed by the Kazakh government, ostensibly to underscore its ownership of the site. At the Tashkent meeting, another document concerning operation of Plesetsk and Tyuratam was signed by ten of the CIS countries. Two weeks later a further document on the same subject was signed on a bilateral basis between Russia and Kazakhstan, apparently resolving outstanding issues between the two countries. These events point to problems that could recur however.

LOCATION OF MAJOR SPACE FACILITIES

Space facilities for launching and tracking satellites, and factories for building them, are scattered across the various former Soviet republics, but primarily are located in Russia, Kazakhstan and Ukraine (see Figure 1). As shown in the accompanying map, the two primary space launch sites, Plesetsk and Tyuratam, are located in Russia and Kazakhstan respectively.[4] The launch sites are not redundant—each supports different types of space missions depending on the launch vehicle used and orbit required. Both are needed to conduct the diverse array of space activities pursued by the former Soviet Union.

Tyuratam (also called the Baikonur Cosmodrome) is used for launches of geostationary communications satellites, planetary probes, human spaceflight missions (including space stations, their crews and cargo resupply missions), navigation satellites, and a variety of other civilian and military missions. Plesetsk is the pri-

---

[3] The Soyuz spacecraft that take crews to and from the space station *Mir* not only are launched in Kazakhstan (at Tyuratam), but land in sparsely populated areas of the country east of the launch site.

[4] A third launch site, Kapustin Yar (in Russia, near Volgograd) is no longer used for orbital launches.

mary launch site for satellites that must be placed in polar orbits (such as reconnaissance and weather satellites).

Russia has not only the Plesetsk launch site, but about 80 percent of the enterprises associated with the space industry. [5] In and around Moscow are the Russian Academy of Sciences, whose Institutes are chiefly responsible for the space science program (such as planetary exploration, astrophysics, and space life sciences); Star City, where the cosmonauts live and train; the Flight Control Center, similar to NASA's Mission Control in Houston and NASA and DOD satellite command and control facilities; the Energiya Scientific Production Association (NPO) and the Lavochkin NPO, the two major enterprises for designing and building launch vehicles and spacecraft; and the Khrunichev factory, which builds modules for the *Mir* space station and the Proton launch vehicle. Other space-related enterprises are located in other Russian cities including St. Petersburg, Krasnoyarsk, and Samara.

FIGURE 1

MAJOR CIS SPACE FACILITIES

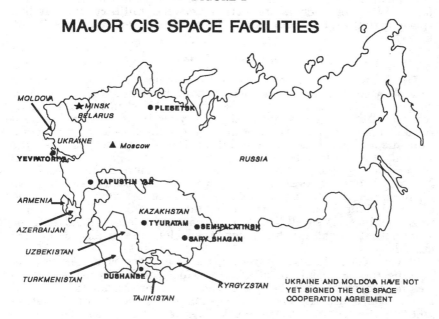

Source: Congressional Research Service.

The Ukrainian Academy of Sciences produces equipment and sensors for spacecraft. The Yuzhnoye factory in Dnepropetrovsk, builds, among other things, the Zenit and Cyclone launch vehicles. A major satellite tracking station is at Yevpatoriya in the Crimea.

Kazakhstan is the home of Tyuratam, as well as Sary Shagan, a major military testing center which, according to the DOD, is the location of a laser that could be used to attack satellites. (Some

---

[5] According to Yuriy Koptev, Director of the Russian Space Agency, June 1992.

DOD officials have asserted in the past that a second ASAT laser is located at Nurek, near Dushanbe in Tajikistan.) Semipalatinsk, also in Kazakhstan, is known in the West primarily as the former site of Soviet nuclear weapons testing. Although the Kazakh government terminated nuclear testing at the site, it also is home to facilities used by the Kurchatov Nuclear Power Institute for space nuclear power and propulsion research, including hardware for the Topaz space nuclear reactor (see below). [6] Use of the facilities has been offered to Western scientists.

Though a formal structure for the CIS space program has yet to emerge, four former republics have created their own space agencies: Russia, Kazakhstan, Ukraine, and Azerbaijan. Clearly the most important is the Russian Space Agency, headed by Yuri Koptev. According to Koptev, as of June 1992 Russia was the only country paying for the CIS space program, and it seems likely that Russia will be the predominant force in space. The Russian Space Agency is responsible only for the civilian space program; Russia's role in military space activities is overseen by the Ministry of Defense. Whether such a distinction between military and civilian space activities has been made in other former republics is unknown.

EVOLVING U.S. POLICY

The focus of this report is on the economies of the former Soviet republics, so this chapter is correspondingly focused on space issues as they relate to economic topics. However, it would be misleading to suggest that the only interest the United States has in the post-Soviet space program is economically oriented. Scientific cooperation in space continues to be a hallmark of interaction between the United States and Russia, and a new five-year agreement on such cooperation was signed at the Bush-Yeltsin summit in June 1992. Military space cooperation is also a possibility today, and the two countries are discussing creation of a joint center for early warning of missile launches, which would include use of data from U.S. (and presumably CIS) satellites. A proposal for a joint global defense system that might involve space-based elements is also being discussed.

In the economic area, however, much activity is under way regarding the potential use of space products, technologies, and services developed for and by the Soviet space program. As discussed below, there are at least two economic angles to this debate—whether the cost of U.S. space activities can be reduced by purchasing products from the CIS, and whether purchasing such products could bolster the economies of the former republics in a manner that does not require direct financial aid.

Initial interest in buying Soviet space hardware came in 1990–1991 from the DOD's Strategic Defense Initiative Office (SDIO), which expressed a desire to purchase Topaz II space nuclear reactors. The next formal expression of interest came from the House and Senate appropriations subcommittees that fund NASA (VA-

---

[6] For a discussion of other former Soviet R&D facilities, see Boesman, William C. and Genevieve J. Knezo. *Soviet Civilian Research and Development Facilities and Funding.* CRS Report 91-778 SPR. October 30, 1991.

HUD-Independent Agencies) which directed NASA at the end of 1991 to investigate the possibility of using Soyuz TM spacecraft as Assured Crew Return Vehicles for the U.S./International Space Station *Freedom* program. [7] Also during 1991, a U.S. company (Space Systems/Loral) indicated interest in purchasing Hall thrusters.

Hearings were held in early 1992 both by the Senate Appropriations VA-HUD-Independent Agencies Subcommittee, and the House Science, Space and Technology Committee (which has jurisdiction over NASA authorizations) on the overall issue of buying CIS space products. At the hearings, Members complained that the State Department was taking too long to approve applications for licenses to import space products from the former Soviet Union. (Import, as well as export, of items on the Munitions List—which includes virtually all space-related hardware—is prohibited by the Arms Export Control Act.) Finally, in March 1992, President Bush approved the import of three space-related items (Topaz II reactors, Hall thrusters, and a quantity of plutonium–238 for nuclear devices that provide electricity on certain spacecraft). NASA experts made initial visits to Russia shortly thereafter to look at the Soyuz TM spacecraft. At the Bush-Yeltsin summit in June 1992, a contract was signed for further technical investigations of the Soyuz TM spacecraft and other space products by NASA. Also during the summit, President Bush agreed that Russia could compete to launch a satellite being built by an American company for an international organization (INMARSAT), reversing previous U.S. policy of prohibiting export of satellites containing U.S. components to the Soviet Union (or its former republics). The Bush Administration asserted that this was a one-time exception for the INMARSAT launch, but some observers view it as the beginning of a general thaw in U.S. restrictions.

Throughout all these discussions, emphasis has been placed on industry's role in these efforts. NASA officials have made clear that NASA itself will not purchase CIS space hardware, but rather will contract with U.S. industries that would then purchase the hardware for integration into elements of the U.S. space program. The Bush Administration is encouraging industry representatives to travel to the CIS (primarily Russia) to see what is available. A Department of Commerce-sponsored delegation of industry representatives is expected to make a trip in July 1992, though several companies have sent their own experts already.

In general, Administration policy is evolving slowly, though the trend is toward increasing opportunities for Russian space products to be used in the U.S. space program and for allowing the CIS to compete in international space markets. One concern that already has arisen, however, is whether sales of certain CIS space products to other countries might create ballistic missile proliferation concerns. The Russian company Glavkosmos plans to sell a rocket engine to the Indian Space Research Organization (ISRO). The United States claims that the engine could be used for ballistic

---

[7] Space Station *Freedom* is a cooperative effort among the United States, Canada, Japan, and 9 of the 13 nations that belong to the European Space Agency. See CRS Issue Brief 85209, *Space Stations*, by Marcia S. Smith. (Regularly updated).

missile purposes, in violation of the Missile Technology Control Regime (MTCR) to which Russia has agreed to abide. India asserts that the engine will be used only for peaceful purposes, and Indian and Russian officials have complained that the United States is simply attempting to prevent Russia from entering the market for rocket engine technology. The State Department imposed sanctions against Glavkosmos and ISRO in May 1992 because of the announced sale, and the Senate Foreign Relations Committee added language to the proposed Freedom Support Act (S. 2532), which would provide aid to the former Soviet republics, stating that the aid would not be provided if the MTCR is violated.

Not only does this issue demonstrate the relationship between space activities and other national concerns such as proliferation, but it also shows how abruptly U.S. policy can be affected by a single action by a Russian company. This uncertainty contributes to the aura of caution that surrounds talk of deals with Russian enterprises.

SPACE FOR SALE: "BUYING RUSSIAN" [8]

Issues abound over whether "buying Russian" is good—because it supports their economy, keeps their scientists employed, and might lower the costs for U.S. space activities, or bad—because it could take jobs away from Americans and help maintain the scientific and manufacturing infrastructure that until so recently posed such a threat to the United States.

Soviet space officials had begun marketing space products and services in the 1980s, an activity that intensified as space budgets waned in 1990 and 1991. The Soviet government bureaucracy that spearheaded those space commercialization efforts no longer exists, but the new bureaucracies (primarily in Russia and Ukraine), as well as individual institutes, scientific-production associations (NPOs), and other entities are actively marketing space wares.

The list of items of potential interest to the U.S. Government and industry grows daily, though today that interest is primarily only at the stage of window shopping. Few details are known about most of the space products and technologies available. The first step is to assess them before making decisions about their potential application to U.S. needs. In fact, exactly what the United States needs is an open issue itself. Congress is now debating the future of NASA space activities, the Strategic Defense Initiative, and military space programs. Determining what CIS space products and technologies would fit in with the U.S. space program is difficult to assess without first deciding the near-term and long-term fate of that program.

Another complicating factor is the disarray in the post-Soviet space program. On top of the fundamental uncertainties about the political and economic future of the CIS and its member states, there are specific questions about, for example, who owns and has the authority to sell what, the validity of contracts, and what reme-

---

[8] While "Buying CIS" might be more precise, in fact most of the products, services, and technologies being offered are Russian. The only major exception is launch services, which might also involve Ukraine—where some of the launch vehicles are built, and Kazakhstan—where launches to geostationary orbit take place.

dies Western companies or the U.S. Government would have if a contract was not fulfilled. Export laws and other legislation are still pending before the Russian legislature, leaving open questions as to whether some items might be denied for export because of broader national concerns. Thus, caution may be warranted before actually attempting to purchase CIS space products, though these concerns should not impede browsing to see what is available. In fact, some observers express concern that the United States may miss opportunities if it delays action while other countries move ahead.

Some of the items already identified as of potential interest are discussed below. Each has specialized issues associated with it, but there are several common questions. Should the United States reverse its policy (contained in the Arms Export Control Act) of not importing items on the Munitions List from the former Soviet Union? Would buying these products from a foreign supplier hurt the U.S. aerospace industry, already suffering from cutbacks in defense spending? Would buying these products provide economic assistance to the former republics as an alternative to giving them direct foreign aid? Would buying these products help keep CIS scientists from leaving the CIS and possibly working for unfriendly countries? As discussed earlier, U.S. policy is evolving slowly on these issues.

THE MIR SPACE STATION

Shortly after the attempted coup in August 1991, press reports that the Soviet space station *Mir* was "for sale" prompted interest in whether NASA might purchase the existing station, or a new version of it, instead of or in addition to building the U.S./International Space Station *Freedom*. As the discussion progressed, it became clear that there would be no advantage in buying *Mir* itself (if for no reason other than its age) and the dialogue shifted to the possibility of *using Mir*, rather than buying it.

The Soviet Union began launching space stations in 1971. *Mir* is the seventh successful space station it developed, and the first designed to be "permanently occupied" (staffed year-round with crews rotating on a regular basis). A modular space station, the *Mir* complex currently consists of *Mir* itself (the core module where the cosmonauts live and operate the space station) plus three other modules: *Kvant-1*, for astrophysics (which also contains some of the space complex's main systems); *Kvant-2*, primarily a logistics module that has a large airlock for egress into space and has additional systems for operating the complex; and *Kristall*, specially designed for materials processing experiments. [9] The core module was launched in 1986; the Russians stated in 1991 that it would have to be replaced by 1994, though recently they have provided more optimistic assessments that it may continue to operate until 1997. Crews are expected to make repairs to the station to extend its lifetime.

---

[9] Materials processing in space (microgravity materials processing) studies how the near-absence of gravitational forces enables, for example, growing purer crystals that might ultimately become the computer chips of the future, or manufacturing purer vaccines.

Crews are transported to the complex two or three times a year on Soyuz TM spacecraft. Usually two cosmonauts remain aboard the station for 5–6 month tours of duty and then are replaced by a new crew. Cargo (food, water, air, experiments, personal items, repair parts, etc.) is taken to the space station on Progress M spacecraft four to five times a year.

The Soviet Union started marketing services aboard *Mir* years ago, with modest success. For example, customers can pay to have representatives visit the space station. A Japanese journalist was the first of these commercial customers. His company (not the Japanese government) paid $12 million for his 8-day flight in December 1990. Three more paying customers (from Britain, Austria and Germany) since have flown, and a Frenchman is scheduled for July 1992. [10] The United States and Russia have agreed to fly an American to *Mir* and a Russian on a U.S. shuttle mission (details have not been worked out yet), though this presumably would be a cooperative rather than a commercial flight, with no exchange of funds.

Alternatively, experiments can be placed aboard the station and operated by the cosmonauts, if necessary. An American company, Payload Systems Inc., flew commercial protein crystal growth experiments to *Mir* in 1989 and 1992 and has options for additional flights.

As the only existing space station, *Mir* offers unique capabilities. Studies of long-duration human reaction to weightlessness, needed before committing crews to make trips to Mars, for example, only can be done aboard a space station. The Soviet Union kept crews aboard *Mir* for as long as one year and shared their biomedical data with U.S. scientists, but NASA wants to conduct its own studies and plans to do so on *Freedom*. Use of *Mir* could give NASA scientists a head start in conducting this type of research. The main question is how much Russia would charge for such experiments, and whether NASA could afford it, considering its increasingly constrained budget. During the June 1992 Bush-Yeltsin summit, NASA agreed to study prospects for utilizing *Mir*.

LAUNCH VEHICLES

The CIS has a wide variety of expendable launch vehicles (ELVs). [11] From smallest to largest they are Cosmos, Vostok, Soyuz, Molniya, Cyclone, Zenit, Proton, and Energiya. [12] The three most often discussed for potential use by the West are Proton, first flown in 1965, Zenit (1985), and Energiya (1987). All three currently can be launched only from the Tyuratam launch site in Kazakhstan, and are manufactured either in Russia (Proton), or jointly in Russia and Ukraine (Zenit and Energiya), meaning that customers wanting to use them might have to reach agreement with more than one former republic.

---

[10] Prior to initiation of this "commercial cosmonaut" arrangement representatives of 13 nations, including France and (then) East Germany, visited Soviet space stations over the years as part of cooperative (no exchange of funds) rather than commercial missions.
[11] "Expendable" launch vehicles can only be used once, compared to "reusable" space vehicles (like the space shuttle) that can be flown many times.
[12] The conversion of military missiles to space launch purposes is being actively pursued by the CIS as well, especially the SS-18, SS-19, SS-20 and SS-25.

U.S. policy sharply limited the success of the Soviet Union in offering commercial launch services by prohibiting the export of satellites containing U.S. components to the Soviet Union for launch; virtually all satellites in need of launch services contain U.S. components. Some Members of Congress now want that policy reversed, while others fear that competition from the CIS may hurt U.S. companies that offer similar services. Interest also has developed in using the heavy lift launch vehicle Energiya in the U.S. space program and in buying some of the RD-170 engines that power it.

Proton, Zenit, Energiya and the RD-170 Engine

Proton is used to launch space stations (like *Mir* and its modules), communications satellites destined for geostationary orbit (GEO), [13] and planetary missions, for example. Proton can place 20,000 kilograms (kg) of payload into low Earth orbit (LEO), or 2.2 tons into GEO. Before the coup, 10-12 Protons were successfully launched annually. [14] Protons are built entirely in Russia.

Zenit is both a launch vehicle itself, and part of the larger Energiya launch vehicle. As a launch vehicle, it has two stages and can place 15,000 kg into LEO. Although there have been discussions about developing a three-stage version capable of placing satellites in GEO, one does not now exist. Zenits are manufactured in Ukraine, while its engines are built in Russia. There have been conflicting reports as to whether the Yuzhnoye production facility in Ukraine will continue to produce Zenits. The only launch site for Zenit is at Tyuratam; plans to build launch pads for it at Plesetsk apparently have been abandoned.

Four one-stage Zenits are used as the first stage of the Energiya launch vehicle. The one-stage Zenits are attached to the central Energiya core, and are called "strap-ons." Zenit's first stage is powered by an RD-170 kerosene/liquid oxygen engine. [15] Some U.S. engineers believe that the RD-170 contains design improvements over similar Western rocket engines. Considerable discussion has ensued about getting access to one or more RD-170 engines so U.S. engineers can study it and possibly use the knowledge in designing new engines for U.S. launch vehicles, actually buying RD-170 engines and incorporating them into a new U.S. launch vehicle, or creating a Russian-American joint venture company to develop and build engines based on the RD-170.

Eight one-stage Zenits have successfully flown as strap-ons for Energiya. Twelve successful two-stage Zenit launches were made from 1985-1990. However, the next three launch attempts ended in failure (October 1990, August 1991, and February 1992). [16] In the

---

[13] Geostationary orbit (GEO) exists 35,800 kilometers above the equator. A satellite placed there will retain a fixed position relative to a point on Earth. Most satellites for which commercial launch services are sought require placement in GEO.

[14] Success rates for CIS rockets cannot be determined since for most of the last 34 years the Soviets did not publicly admit failures. Although they have since released some statistics, there is no independent, unclassified method to verify them.

[15] The RD-170 is often referred to as an Energiya engine since the one-stage Zenit is used as part of Energiya.

[16] The first Zenit launch attempt in June 1985 also was a failure. It is not clear if it was a one- or two-stage version of the rocket.

first case, it was the RD–170 that failed, causing the rocket to explode 5 seconds after launch. The vehicle, its payload (reportedly a military electronic intelligence satellite), and its launch pad were all destroyed. In the second failure, it was the second stage engine (called the RD–120, also fueled by kerosene and liquid oxygen) that failed. The third failure also apparently involved the RD–120.

Energiya is a heavy lift booster that can place 100,000 kg in LEO, similar to the capability of the U.S. Saturn V that was used to send Apollo crews to the Moon (but is no longer produced). Energiya consists of a large central core powered by liquid hydrogen/liquid oxygen engines (called RDO–120), surrounded by four one-stage Zenits. The four Zenits are referred to as Energiya's first stage, while the central core is the second stage. Whatever payload is being taken into orbit is mounted on the side of the Energiya core, and it has engines for providing the final thrust to attain orbit. One payload that Energiya can launch is the space shuttle *Buran*. Other payloads can be placed in a canister and affixed to the booster. Since Zenit is an integral part of Energiya, the launch vehicle depends on production facilities in both Russia and Ukraine.

Energiya has made only two flights. The first, on May 15, 1987, ended in failure when the engine on the canister did not work properly; the payload landed in the Pacific Ocean. The second flight, November 15, 1988, successfully placed *Buran* in orbit (this was a test flight and no crew was aboard; there have been no other flights of *Buran*).

Commercial Space Launch Services

Competition in the launch services market is intense because the market for such services is small and the suppliers many. [17] Three U.S. companies (McDonnell Douglas, General Dynamics, and Martin Marietta) offer launch services for communications satellites that must be placed in GEO, the largest segment of the market at this time. Competing with them are Europe's Arianespace with the Ariane, and China's Great Wall Industry Corp. with the Long March series. Japan may enter the market once its new H–2 vehicle is operational. The Soviets were unsuccessful in attracting Western customers for commercial launch services primarily because U.S. policy did not permit the export of satellites containing American components to the former Soviet Union. [18] The often cited reason for the policy was avoidance of technology transfer, though economic competition was undoubtedly also a major concern since the Soviet Union, with its nonmarket economy, could have offered very low prices that might have undercut Western suppliers.

---

[17] For more information on launch services, see U.S. Congress. House. Committee on Science, Space and Technology. *Commercial Space Launch Services: The U.S. Competitive Position.* Committee Print. Prepared by the Congressional Research Service. Washington, U.S. Govt. Print. Off., 1991 and *Space Launch Options.* CRS Issue Brief 86121, by David P. Radzanowski and Marcia S. Smith. (Regularly updated).

[18] A proposal to build a launch site at Cape York, Australia, from which Zenit rockets would be launched on a commercial basis has encountered many obstacles, both financial and technical (with the successive failures of the Zenit). The concept would have circumvented the U.S. restrictions since the satellites would be exported to Australia, rather than the Soviet Union.

Some Members of Congress question whether U.S. policy should be changed to permit the CIS to offer commercial launch services. [19] Not only are technology transfer questions less pressing, but permitting the CIS to earn hard currency in this manner could lessen requirements for direct financial aid. Other Members are concerned about the impact on U.S. companies offering similar launch services. Although the CIS is attempting to develop a market economy, their costs undoubtedly are much lower than those in Europe or America for building launch vehicles and hence they could offer services for much lower prices and still abide by international norms for how to determine a fair price.

President Bush modified U.S. policy slightly during the June 1992 summit with Russian President Yeltsin by agreeing to allow the Russians to compete for the launch of an International Maritime Communications Satellite (INMARSAT) satellite using the Proton launch vehicle. Both the United States and Russia are members of INMARSAT. Whether this is a one-time exception because of INMARSAT's international nature, or the beginning of a broader thaw in U.S. restrictions, is a controversial issue.

Using Energiya in the U.S. Space Program

The potential use of Energiya is a special case because the United States currently does not have a launch vehicle with this lift capability (nor does any other country). Thus it does not pose an economic competitive threat to U.S. launch services companies. Also, there are no commercial spacecraft that require the capability of Energiya, so potential interest on the part of the United States is likely to be limited to Government programs.

The question has been raised, for example, as to whether NASA should use Energiya instead of the U.S. space shuttle to launch *Freedom*, and whether NASA and DOD should use Energiya in the post–2000 time frame instead of building their own heavy lift launch vehicle. Today, the two agencies are developing a new family of launch vehicles called the National Launch System (NLS) for missions such as resupplying *Freedom* after the turn of the century, launching elements of the Strategic Defense Initiative (SDI) ballistic missile defense system, and sending humans back to the Moon and on to Mars (President Bush's Space Exploration Initiative). [20]

Using Energiya for *Freedom* would enable the space station to be placed in orbit with fewer flights. Currently, NASA estimates that 17–18 space shuttle flights will be required for assembly. Suggestions have been made that only three to five Energiya flights could replace a significant number of the shuttle missions. If *Freedom* was launched on Energiya (or any launch vehicle other than the shuttle), the space station would have to be repackaged, and segments outfitted with propulsion systems to enable them to remain in proper orbits until space shuttle crews arrive to assemble them

---

[19] The only commercial launch contracts the Soviets signed were with India for several satellites that contained no U.S. components. One was launched in 1988, another in 1991; two more are planned.

[20] See also CRS Issue Brief 85209, op. cit.; *The Strategic Defense Initiative: Issues for Congress*, CRS Issue Brief 85170, by Steven C. Hildreth; and *The Moon/Mars Proposal: President Bush's Space Exploration Initiative*, CRS Issue Brief 85209, by Marcia S. Smith.

or until they could be attached to another device that could maneuver them in orbit. Energiya can be launched only from the Tyuratam launch site in Kazakhstan; the space station segments would have to be transported there. [21] Costs associated with these activities have not been formally estimated.

The future of the SDI program is difficult to forecast. Proposals are now being made for a joint U.S.-Russian global space defense system, but what elements of such a system would be based in space, and whether they would require the lift capability of Energiya, is not clear. The current U.S. SDI plan does not require a large launch vehicle. President Bush's Moon/Mars program, however, is expected to require this class of launch vehicle. As noted, NASA and DOD are now developing the NLS for such future projects. The largest version of NLS now planned is smaller than Energiya, however (150,000 pounds, or 67,500 kilograms). An even larger version thus would have to be built, and therefore some suggest that the United States simply buy Energiyas instead.

The difficulty is that the United States probably will not be ready to launch major elements of the Moon/Mars program until well after the turn of the century. Whether the Energiya production lines will still be operating then is unlikely unless other customers for Energiya come forward. The Soviet Union had planned to use it for futuristic projects such as huge communications satellites in geostationary orbit, solar power satellites that would generate electricity for transmission to Earth, and for sending humans to Mars. Such projects are not likely to be pursued by the CIS (or anyone else) for quite some time.

If the United States chose to use Energiya for the Moon/Mars program instead of building a larger version of NLS, it would raise issues of U.S. dependency on a foreign supplier of launch services (a supplier enmeshed in economic and political turmoil) and the loss of U.S. aerospace jobs, versus potential savings from buying an existing vehicle rather than developing a new one. [22]

SOYUZ TM

Soyuz spacecraft have been used to take crews into space since 1967. [23] The spacecraft has undergone many modifications; twice the changes were significant enough to warrant redesignation of the vehicle. Soyuz TM, the current version, was first launched in 1986. Soyuz TM-14 is now docked with the *Mir* space station where two cosmonauts are conducting experiments. Soyuz TM can carry a crew of three (though the Russians reportedly are developing a larger capacity version) and could fit inside the U.S. space shuttle's cargo bay for launch.

---

[21] Building a launch pad for Energiya in the United States would be extremely expensive. NLS would also require a new launch pad, though one of the two space shuttle launch pads might be able to be modified for this purpose.

[22] The joint DOD-NASA NLS program is designed to create a new family of launch vehicles, from small to large, using new technology (see CRS Issue Brief 86121). It has become controversial because it is viewed primarily as a "heavy lift" launch vehicle for very large payloads, and opponents argue that there are no U.S. payloads requiring such a capability for at least the next decade. Congress significantly cut funding for NLS in the FY1992 budget.

[23] The Soyuz spacecraft itself is also used in an automated mode for the military reconnaissance spacecraft program.

The Soyuz spacecraft has had its share of problems. One cosmonaut died on the maiden flight of Soyuz in April 1967 when the parachute lines tangled during descent. Three more died in 1971 when the crew improperly closed a vent in the spacecraft during descent and the cabin's atmosphere escaped into space. The men were not wearing spacesuits and asphyxiated; subsequently cosmonauts have been required to wear spacesuits during launch and re-entry. In 1988, two cosmonauts (a Soviet and an Afghani) were stranded in Earth orbit for one day when the Soyuz computers malfunctioned. Throughout the history of the Soviet/CIS space station program [24] docking problems have occurred between the Soyuz and space stations. Using the Soyuz TM series, these problems can be surmounted by the crew taking manual control of the spacecraft.

Interest has developed in the possibility of using Soyuz TM as an Assured Crew Return Vehicle (ACRV) for *Freedom*. A Soyuz is always docked with Soviet/CIS space stations as an emergency escape vehicle whenever they are occupied. NASA has decided that it will not allow crews to occupy *Freedom* permanently without an ACRV that could be used in a medical emergency or if the space shuttle is grounded for a long period of time. Under the strong urging of the House and Senate appropriations subcommittees that fund NASA (VA-HUD-Independent Agencies), NASA began assessing the possibility of using Soyuz. During the June 1992 Bush-Yeltsin summit, a contract for more detailed technical studies was signed between NASA and a Russian enterprise, NPO Energiya. (Russian Space Agency director Yuri Koptev signed on behalf of NPO Energiya.)

Specific issues concerning the use of Soyuz TM as an ACRV involve technical compatibility with *Freedom*, how often they would have to be replaced (the longest a Soyuz TM has remained in orbit is 179 days), and how much it would cost to buy the requisite number and modify them to meet U.S. safety standards (the computer would probably have to be replaced, for example) versus the cost of developing a new ACRV. NASA is also looking at the potential of using Soyuz spacecraft for materials processing experiments, and the Progress cargo spacecraft, a derivative of the Soyuz, for potential space station resupply missions.

DOCKING SYSTEMS

NASA is assessing the *Mir* docking system to see if it has applicability to space station *Freedom*. NASA has not yet designed the docking system for joining the U.S. shuttle to *Freedom*. One item of interest is a docking adapter currently attached to *Mir* for docking the space shuttle *Buran*. Based on the design of the androgynous docking adapter developed for the 1975 Apollo-Soyuz Test Project (ASTP), [25] it has not been used yet. [26]

---

[24] See Smith, Marcia S., *Space Activities of the United States and Other Launching Countries/Organizations: 1957-1991*. CRS Report 92-427 SPR. May 11, 1992.

[25] ASTP involved docking a U.S. Apollo with a Soviet Soyuz for two days of joint experiments by the three astronauts and two cosmonauts involved.

[26] The expected date of the next launch of the *Buran* space shuttle has slipped repeatedly, but Soviet space officials had announced that on its next flight it would be launched without a crew and then dock with *Mir*.

Separate from the docking adapter, NASA apparently also is interested in the rendezvous and docking system used for linking *Mir* and Soyuz TM, called Kurs (Course). As noted above, problems are not uncommon with this system, requiring crews to manually complete the docking. Kurs is also used for docking modules to *Mir* as well as the cargo ships that resupply the crews. Three modules have been added so far, and each experienced docking problems. Since no crews were aboard these modules, ground controllers had to resolve the problems, and ultimately did so successfully. The cargo ships (called Progress M) have not encountered similar problems. [27]

The primary issues regarding purchase of the docking adapter and/or Kurs docking system involve reliability and technical compatibility with the U.S. space shuttle and *Freedom*. A corollary issue concerns an often expressed desire that space-faring countries design a standard docking system so one country's astronauts could rescue another's. If the United States chose to use the CIS docking adapter, it clearly would be a step in that direction.

HALL THRUSTERS

A U.S. company, Space Systems/Loral (SS/L), has contracted with the Russians for purchasing a special type of rocket engine called a Hall thruster. This type of small engine can be used for placing a satellite into its final orbital location and keeping it there. SS/L asserts that using the Russian Hall thrusters, as modified by SS/L, can reduce the total weight of a spacecraft by 20 percent, potentially a significant savings in terms of launch costs. SS/L and two Russian aerospace organizations, Fakel and RIAME, are in the process of forming a joint venture, International Space Technology Inc., to build, test, and market the devices. Separately, DOD's Strategic Defense Initiative Organization (SDIO) is planning to buy four of the Russian thrusters, a purchase approved by President Bush in March 1992.

SPACE NUCLEAR REACTORS: TOPAZ II

One way of generating electricity for spacecraft is nuclear reactors, [28] which are useful for missions that require large amounts of power and/or must be compact. The United States has launched only one nuclear reactor (in 1965). By contrast, the Soviets focused on the development of space nuclear reactors for a type of military satellite called a RORSAT (radar ocean reconnaissance satellite) that carried a radar for tracking ships at sea.

RORSATs were launched from 1967 to 1988. In a typical mission profile, after the RORSAT's mission was complete (the longest was 135 days), the portion of the spacecraft containing the reactor core and reactor vessel would be boosted into a high orbit (approximately 1,000 kilometers) from which it would not reenter the atmos-

---

[27] Only 1 of the 12 Progress M (a new version) cargo craft has experienced docking problems, and that was because part of the antenna on *Mir* had been dislodged by one of the crews during a spacewalk. (The earlier type of Progress cargo ships did not use the Kurs system.)

[28] Nuclear power sources for spacecraft can be either radioisotope thermal generators (RTGs), or nuclear reactors. The United States does use RTGs for several types of spacecraft, particularly those travelling far from the Sun.

phere for hundreds of years. The reactor used for these spacecraft, called Topaz, contained approximately 50 kilograms of enriched uranium-235.

In 1978 and 1983, RORSATs accidentally reentered Earth's atmosphere. In the first case (Cosmos 954), radioactive debris was spread over northern Canada. In the second (Cosmos 1402), the satellite reentered in two pieces over the Indian Ocean and the South Atlantic. In 1988, another of these satellites, Cosmos 1900, almost reentered, though ultimately a fail-safe system worked and boosted the reactor to the higher orbit. No more have been launched since.

In 1987, however, the Soviets tested a new, higher-powered version of the reactor, called Topaz II, a thermionic reactor that can generate 6-7 kilowatts of electricity. Two satellites (Cosmos 1818 and 1867) carried Topaz II reactors; one operated for approximately 6 months, the other for a year. In 1989, the Soviets announced that the Topaz II was for sale.

The United States began developing a space nuclear reactor called the SP-100 in 1983 to generate up to 100 kilowatts of power. The SP-100 design is thermoelectric (the electricity is generated outside of the reactor core, instead of inside as with a thermionic reactor). SP-100 was a joint program among the Department of Energy (DOE), DOD and NASA. DOD's most recent interest in space nuclear power sources has been for potential use in the Strategic Defense Initiative (SDI) ballistic missile defense program; NASA's primary interest today is for powering bases on the Moon and Mars.

According to Strategic Defense Initiative Organization (SDIO) officials, in the past two years they concluded that the SP-100 thermoelectric design is not optimum for their purposes and that a thermionic design would be better. Hence, when the Soviet Union offered to sell Topaz II, SDIO became interested in buying one to see what they could learn that could be applied to U.S. development of such reactors. At the end of 1991, SDIO terminated its participation in the SP-100 program, prompting some to argue that SDIO was choosing Topaz II over SP-100. SDIO insists that its decision was based on mission requirements, specifically that its missions do not require the power levels generated by a thermoelectric reactor so a thermionic system is preferable, and that in any case SP-100 is too expensive and will not be ready in time. [29]

NASA and DOE want to continue the SP-100 program; NASA's mission requirements (such as a lunar base) are for large amounts of power, for which the thermoelectric system is better suited. The debate became centered less on the differing requirements for DOD and NASA (and therefore the possibility that both designs may be needed), however, and more on Topaz II versus SP-100 and whether the Government should buy Topaz II and give work to Russian scientists, or continue with SP-100 and keep the jobs at home. Also, use of nuclear power in space inevitably evokes health and safety concerns. The specter of a "Chernobyl in Space" already has been raised in the press regarding the potential use of a CIS space reactor.

---

[29] Testimony by Dwight Duston, SDIO, to the House Science, Space and Technology Committee, Subcommittee on Energy, Jan. 28, 1992 (unpublished).

As noted above, in March 1992 President Bush approved the purchase of two Topaz reactors from Russia, and they have been delivered to the Department of Energy's Los Alamos National Laboratory in New Mexico for study. To date, the SP-100 program is also continuing to be funded.

SPACE NUCLEAR PROPULSION

Propulsion systems are used to launch satellites from Earth into space and to place them in their proper orbit around the Earth or enroute to other destinations. Today, chemical propulsion is primarily used for these purposes, but there has been long-standing interest in developing nuclear propulsion. NASA's nuclear propulsion program, NERVA, was terminated in 1972 because of a lack of mission requirements. Nuclear propulsion would be useful for sending humans to Mars because it could significantly shorten the trip time. The Air Force is now engaged in nuclear propulsion research aimed at using it for a second or third stage of a rocket for placing satellites in Earth orbit (the Air Force asserts it would not be operated within Earth's atmosphere).

The CIS also has developed nuclear propulsion technology, and in January 1992, CIS scientists announced that they wanted to establish a cooperative program with the United States to build, test, and use nuclear propulsion for human trips to Mars. Areas of special interest to U.S. scientists are the alloys developed by the CIS and the facilities and personnel at Semipalatinsk.

Like nuclear reactors for electrical power generation, the use of nuclear propulsion is certain to evoke environmental, health, and safety concerns. If the United States does want to pursue nuclear propulsion, however, access to CIS facilities, personnel, and technology could accelerate these efforts. The strong interest on the part of the United States in ensuring gainful employment for former Soviet nuclear experts might also be a factor in the decision. However, budget constraints, coupled with the lack of need for nuclear propulsion in the near future, argue against such agreements.

CONCLUSIONS

Unquestionably, issues about the Russian space program and the prospect of purchasing space goods and services for use in the U.S. space program pale in comparison to questions about the political and economic future of the CIS and its member states. Still, because it employed so many people (800,000 according to the head of the Russian Space Agency), the space program's future plays a part in the overall health of Russia, at least.

A multitude of complex technical, political, and economic questions must be answered about whether the United States should purchase space products from the CIS. The key point is that for most of the products and technologies that have been mentioned, too little is known today to make a valid assessment of their applicability to the U.S. space program. "Window shopping" visits to the former Soviet Union by U.S. Government and industry delegations, already under way, should answer many of these questions and enable a better informed debate on the broader issues outlined earlier.

NASA has stressed that it does not intend to directly purchase items from the CIS, but rather to contract with U.S. industry to make such arrangements. This may temper concerns about U.S. industry losing jobs to Russian scientists and engineers. For its part, some industry executives seem interested in establishing joint ventures with Russian enterprises rather than simply buying products off the shelf. Such deals are fraught with hazards today, from determining who has the authority to sell what, to ensuring that terms like "exclusivity" do not lose anything in translation to Russian. Despite concerns about missing opportunities if action is not taken quickly, companies may well exercise caution in moving forward on this front.

From a congressional standpoint, perhaps the most contentious issue will be the question of whether to loosen U.S. policy to enable the CIS to enter the launch services market. President Bush's June 1992 decision not to oppose Russian competition for an INMARSAT launch was clearly stated as a one-time exception, but the same White House statement announced initiation of negotiations with the Russians over guidelines that will allow them to compete for other launches. The debate pits those who want to protect U.S. commercial launch services companies from potentially unfair competition against those who want to support the democratization of the former Soviet Union by providing them a method of earning hard currency.

At its roots, however, the question of whether integrating Russian technology into the U.S. space program will succeed depends primarily upon deciding the future course of the U.S. space program, such as whether or not NASA should build space station *Freedom*. Until those decisions are made, government and industry executives will have a difficult time making wise choices about developing or buying any space technologies, regardless of their national origin.

SCIENTIFIC AND TECHNICAL COLLABORATION WITH FORMER SOVIET COUNTRIES

Genevieve J. Knezo *

CONTENTS

SUMMARY

This report [1] surveys the disarray in former Soviet Union science and technology; discusses U.S. Government, professional, and private sector activities to assist former Soviet Union scientists, and examines dilemmas confronting U.S. policymakers, who appear to be cautious about augmenting S&T cooperative programs with the former Soviet Union.

New U.S. Government programs for expanded cooperation in science and technology with the republics of the former Soviet Union consist primarily of support for an international center to "retrain" former weapons scientists, small programs to include scientists in activities supplementary to existing extramural research awards made by Federal agencies, and educational exchange programs oriented to aiding former defense scientists. It is not clear that these are, or should be, large enough or designed to stem the brain drain of former Soviet Union (FSU), scientists or to strengthen the infrastructure of science.

Some say it is in the U.S. national interest to augment science and technology capacity in the former Soviet Union states in order to promote the conversion to democracy and flourishing market economies and to eliminate the potential for Soviet scientists be-

---

* Genevieve J. Knezo is a Specialist in Science and Technology Policy, Science Policy Research Division.

[1] This report is based, in part, on interviews with John O'Neill (OSTP), Gerson Sher (NSF), Cathy Campbell and Jacqueline Shire (Department of State), Grey Handley (NIH) and a CRS seminar that heard presentations from Mr. Sher as well as Robert Gallucci, Department of State and Harley Balzer, Georgetown University.

coming a source of high technology weapons proliferation to other nations. Recommendations have been made, by the National Academy of Sciences, and others to devote more resources to such activities, to better design and coordinate programs, and to liberalize export control regulations that hamper commercial activity and governmental purchases of Soviet advanced technology. U.S. professional societies and the private sector have initiated some active cooperation with their counterparts in the former Soviet Union. Private foundation-funded support for FSU science exceeds the amount pledged by the U.S. Government. U.S. Government policies to deal with the science and technology capabilities in the FSU states probably would benefit if they were coordinated better with these activities.

Some policymakers believe that it may not necessarily be in the best interests of the United States to strengthen S&T in the successor republics to the former Soviet Union. It is suspected that some Soviet scientists may be industrial spies or intelligence agents who seek to "expropriate" Western technology illegally. There is also the view that strengthening Soviet capabilities poses a potential long-term security threat to the United States.

DISARRAY IN SCIENCE OF THE FORMER SOVIET UNION

Science in the Soviet Union was a vast, multi-centered and formidable enterprise funded and directed by the State. Much of the work was directed to serve military and space functions or, because of tradition and lack of laboratory resources, stressed theoretical explanations, as opposed to experimentation. With the dissolution of the nation and the radical changes and reduction of governmental support in the successor nations, research and development funding has been cut and many programs have lost momentum and personnel. Science budgets in states which comprise the former Soviet Union have been cut drastically due, in part, to the fact that the rapidly shrinking defense sector was the Soviet Union's largest supporter of basic research and provided employment for more than "70% of the . . . Soviet Union's scientists." [2]

Laboratories and other research facilities, which had been closed to foreigners on the grounds of national security and military secrecy, have been opened and former Soviet Union scientists who have become entrepreneurs are even offering to sell militarily-relevant technology to international businessmen. There is considerable instability because "Science policy makers in the new republics are seeking a middle passage between the Soviet model of science-by-command and more laissez-faire, self-supporting scientific enterprises." [3] As a result, the scientists are experiencing massive underemployment, unemployment, and cuts in salaries, research budgets, and subscriptions to scientific journals. Also, according to

---

[2] U.S. Congress. House. Committee on Science, Space and Technology and Committee on Foreign Affairs. Science, Technology, and American Diplomacy, 1992. *Thirteenth Annual Report Submitted to the Congress by the President* Pursuant to Section 503(b) of Title V of Public Law 95–426. Washington, D.C., May 1992, Joint Committee Print. p. 182

[3] Title V report, 1992, op.cit., p. 182.

many of these scientists, increasingly virulent anti-Semitism has emerged, potentially affecting large numbers of scientists. [4]

Taken together, these developments have undermined the conduct of research in even the finest laboratories and are forcing many of the young and the best and the brightest of former Soviet Union scientists to emigrate permanently or temporarily to other nations that can pay higher salaries or offer better research opportunities. (The former Soviet Union reportedly has about one-fourth of the world's scientific workers and about half of the world's engineers.) [5] For example, during the February 1992 meeting of the American Association for the Advancement of Science, the Director of the Institute of Molecular Genetics in Moscow reported that as of December 1991, 30 leading scientists, including 7 out of 9 senior researchers, had left the institute to go abroad. Former Soviet Union scientists have gone, often after deliberate recruitment campaigns, to the United States and Brazil (in physics, chemistry, space research, aerodynamics, and propulsion systems), [6] and to Israel (in theoretical physics and mathematics). [7] Russian scientists also reportedly are swamping Japanese universities, scientific research institutes, and other basic research organizations with resumes and job applications. [8] China is actively recruiting scientists and technology from former Soviet Union for the first time since 1960 when the U.S.S.R. withdrew all its experts in a dispute over ideological differences and rivalry over leadership of the world Communist movement. Many suspect that the Chinese are seeking to upgrade their nuclear weapons capability. [9]

In addition, Russia has signed agreements for scientific and technological cooperation wherever it can get needed resources and capital. Such cooperation may have unforseen strategic implications. For instance, in June 1992 South Korea and Russia signed an agreement on technological cooperation, and Chinese and Russian scientists signed an agreement to collaborate on a fusion research project, an area in which Russian scientists are highly regarded. (The United States is also collaborating with Russian scientists on fusion research.)

Assessments of the implications of the brain drain are mixed. Many postulate that the massive exodus of scientists, scholars, and technicians from the former Soviet Union is threatening the future of regional science and reforms in general, so that it could set scientific research back for decades and rob the successor nations of the talent needed to develop economically. [10] There also is the fear that former Soviet Union science will be weakened by the "inter-

---

[4] Birman, Joseph L. "The Fate of Scientists From the Soviet Union." *The Chronicle of Higher Education,* Feb. 12, 1992, pp. B1, B2; Tolz, Vera. " 'Brain Drain' The Main Problem of Soviet Science?" *Report on the USSR,* v. 3, June 28, 1991, p. 23.

[5] Data attributed to Georgetown University in Seib, Gerald F. and John J. Fialka. "Scientists of Former Soviet Union Find the U.S. Slow in Putting Out the Welcome Mat for Them." *Wall Street Journal,* Feb., 3, 1992, p. A14.

[6] *S&T Perspectives.* v. 7, Mar. 31, 1992, pp. 11–12 and May 29, 1992, p. 13.

[7] Specter, Michael. "An Unusable Windfall: Israel's Soviet Scientists." *New York Times,* February 4, 1992.

[8] Report on Russian Scientists Seeking Work in Japan, JPRS-UST-92-004, May 6, 1991, p. 40.

[9] "China To Seek To Import Soviet Scientists," *Technology,* March 12, 1992, AP.

[10] Tolz, op. cit., pp. 21–25.

nal brain drain," the migration of scientists from science to better-paying careers in the nascent private sector. [11]

Some believe that the brain drain will benefit Western science, just as the World War II exodus of scientists from Nazi Germany advanced American science. But some observers predict resentment and job displacement among Western scientists, who will be forced to share already scarce research dollars and postdoctoral faculty positions with, some say, unwelcome and untrustworthy foreigners. (In the United States, for example, several renown Soviet physicists have been hired by the Theoretical Physics Institute of the University of Minnesota, thereby strengthening the academic department, but taking jobs that, it is argued, could have gone to U.S. researchers.) Some fear that large numbers of the former Soviet Union's 2,000 nuclear weapons designers and 100,000 ballistic missile engineers [12] will "defect," emigrate, or sell their technology to countries seeking to evade the nuclear nonproliferation regime such as Iran, Iraq, Libya, Pakistan, and South Africa, thereby escalating world tensions. (On this point, the Russians say their weapons scientists are prohibited from working in other countries due to travel and security restrictions.)

OFFICIAL U.S. GOVERNMENT COOPERATIVE PROGRAMS

The U.S. Government initiated cooperative science and technology (S&T) activities with the Soviet Union during the 1972-74 period, with the signing of 11 agreements for Federal agency cooperation in a variety of basic and applied fields. Typically, no separate funding is appropriated for these activities and Federal agencies determine their own priorities. Programs generally require reciprocity in joint research and visits, meaning that the sending side pays airfare and the receiving country pays all in-country expenses. During the early 1980s, exchange activities lapsed to 20 percent of the 1979 level in reaction to Soviet military intervention in Afghanistan in 1979 and repression in Poland in 1981, and in response to accusations that Communist party spies were exchanged, rather than leading scientists whose collaboration with Americans might have enhanced world science. Following the Soviet attack on a Korean airliner in 1983 and increasing complaints that the Soviets were unfairly benefitting from U.S. technology transfer from permitted activities, agreements in science and technology, space, energy, and transportation were allowed to expire. Some basic science-oriented activities continued, and the framework of cooperation was maintained. These difficulties generally were overcome by 1989, when the two governments signed a new agreement for Cooperation in the Field of Basic Scientific Research, which was expanded by amendment in May 1991 to include cooperation specifically in social sciences and experimental/theoretical physics. As of October 1991, the U.S. Government and Federal agencies had 22 major S&T cooperative programs with the Soviet Union.

---

[11] McDonald, Kim A. "U.S. Universities Lure Many Renowned Physicists and Mathematicians from Former Soviet Union." *The Chronicle of Higher Education.* June 3, 1992, pp. A1, A33, A34.
[12] Data attributed to Robert Gates, director of the CIA, in Seib, op.cit., p. A14.

Reportedly U.S.-Soviet collaborative activities during 1991, especially in agriculture and natural resources, have been hampered by the lack of funds on the Soviet side and difficulties in determining with whom Americans should communicate to arrange travel and exchanges. But according to the 1992 State Department Title V report (for 1991), since the dissolution of the USSR, cooperative activities continued in basic sciences, health and life sciences, energy, environment and economics, and emerging technologies. Some activities are geared specifically to enhance the government/science interface in a noncommand system. For example, the National Science Foundation organized a workshop for the Russians on how the agency operates and awards grants in a competitive peer-reviewed process. Cooperation in space increased as U.S. scientists were granted access to formerly closed facilities.

During the June 1992 Summit, U.S. President Bush and Russian President Yeltsin signed two new agreements: (1) the Agreement for Cooperation in the Exploration and Use of Outer Space for Peaceful Purposes, (and accompanying statements that describe plans for crew exchanges, joint projects to study space technology, and for planned U.S. purchases of Russian technology for docking and for launch of an INMARST 3 satellite); and (2) the Agreement for Scientific and Technical Cooperation in the Field of Fuels and Energy. The two nations also issued a Joint Statement on S&T Cooperation and related statements focusing on conversion of defense research industries; support for the newly established International Science and Technology Center for Soviet weapons scientists; the importance of the private sector in S&T; cooperation in the Superconducting Super Collider, the international thermonuclear experimental reactor; research, conservation of the Bering Sea ecosystem; and conservation of Lake Baikal.

Because Presidents Gorbachev and Yeltsin agreed to cede to the Russian republic most of the apparatus and property of the U.S.S.R. Academy of Sciences and the State Committee on Science and Technology that belonged to the Soviet party, the terms of the U.S.-U.S.S.R. bilateral agreements will apply to the Russian republic. According to the State Department, some joint activities have begun between the United States and successor states, authorized by the interpretation that the terms of the U.S.-Soviet bilateral agreements extend to the former Soviet Union successor republics, exclusive of the Baltic states. But it is likely that the United States will eventually have to conclude new agreements with the eleven other republics if there is to be collaboration on a full range of S&T activities. The State Department reported in early 1992 that "There were signs that the newly independent republics were disposed to forge inter-state cooperative links and mechanisms in areas such as space and the environment." [13]

POLICY DILEMMAS UNDERMINING NEW COOPERATIVE PROGRAMS

Both governmental and nongovernmental officials recognize that the West needs to deal with the capabilities and dilemmas of science and technology of the former Soviet Union. But policy makers

---

[13] Title V report, p. 182.

have been challenged to design programs which meet the range of conflicting needs in this complex policy arena.

Former Soviet Union scientists say that new programs should consist not of technical assistance or welfare, but should be cooperative programs that recognize their strengths and need to develop infrastructure and entrepreneurship. Ideally U.S. programs would meet these needs, but at the same time focus on the most productive areas of the former Soviet Union S&T, stem the brain drain, forge relationships with Soviet scientists before they are monopolized by other countries, and weed out the military and industrial spies well known to be part of the Soviet scientific establishment and exchange activities. Also, programs, especially for converting military scientists to civilian work, need to be implemented quickly to allow action in the "window of opportunity" during which it can be demonstrated that science and technology can contribute to economic growth and democracy in the former Soviet Union.

Policymakers, however, are confronted by a bewildering set of problems. There are numerous research institutes in the former Soviet Union, some of dubious quality. Another obstacle is to develop creative ways to assist without directly transferring dollars, since it is widely acknowledged that 90 percent of currency that flows into former Soviet Union goes to taxes, middlemen, and so called "overhead," [14] rather than to the conduct of science or the creation of productive market capabilities. Direct purchases of services and goods produced by the Soviet military-space-industrial complex have also been discouraged by those who believe such programs aid and abet the former Soviet Union military sector, thereby strengthening a potential enemy, even though the United States might save millions of development dollars. [15]

Facing such competing policy elements, the U.S. Government has taken some steps to examine and design new programs for S&T cooperation with the former Soviet Union, but has not yet instituted a fully formulated program that targets the pressing scientific and technical needs and capabilities of the republics. Some critics say that U.S. S&T policy for the former Soviet Union is dominated inappropriately by the highest political echelons of the State Department and by the European Bureau of the Agency for International Development, and not by science and technology agencies, such as Office of Science and Technology Policy, the Bureau of Oceans and International Environmental and Scientific Affairs in the State Department, or by the technical agencies, which have long experience in cooperating with the former Soviet Union. U.S. policy has been cautious in regard to cooperative programs that might harm the United States in the long run. The Departments of State, Defense, and Commerce, pursuant to export control regulations, review joint venture agreements with, imports from, and exports to the former Soviet Union. Liberalization of export controls has been proceeding

---

[14] "A Russian tax of as much as 60 per cent on foreign donations of funds and equipment and an official exchange rate that can significantly reduce the value of financial contribution," according to Loren Graham, a professor of the history of science at MIT. In McDonald. Kim A., "Plight of Russian Scholars in Weak Economy Prompts New U.S. Efforts to Support Them." *Chronicle of Higher Education.* Jan. 22, 1992, p. 43.

[15] Broad, William J., "Panel Calls for Wider Help for Ex-Soviet Arms Experts." *New York Times,* March 14, 1992.

but somewhat slowly and, therefore, is widely criticized outside government. The Interagency Group on Soviet S&T, chaired by the State Department, is looking at all collaborative government programs with Russia and the Commonwealth of Independent States and developed some initiatives for the Yeltsin-Bush Summit in June 1992. Reportedly, it is interested in removing impediments to cooperation. The International Committee of the Federal Coordinating Council for Science, Engineering, and Technology in the White House initiated a study over a year ago to look at science and technology cooperation with Eastern Europe. It does not have a similar study of the former Soviet Union.

During January 1992 the State Department held a conference to assess U.S.-Soviet cooperation. Shortly thereafter the President's science advisor asked the National Academy of Sciences, to hold a meeting in March 1992 to discuss reorienting U.S. S&T programs for the former Soviet Union. This resulted in a report, *Reorientation of the Research Capability of the Former Soviet Union*. Also, there have been congressional fact finding trips to some of the republics and a video conference between senior Russian science administrators and members of the House Committee on Science, Space, and Technology. [16] Hearings on S&T cooperation were held by the House Committee on Science, Space, and Technology (on May 19, 1992) and by the Senate Foreign Relations Committee (on March 17, 1992).

GOVERNMENT INITIATIVES

Among the new initiatives for cooperation discussed in this section are the International Science and Technology centers, small supplemental grant programs in the National Science Foundation (NSF) and the National Institutes of Health (NIH), immigration, and other proposed programs.

THE INTERNATIONAL SCIENCE AND TECHNOLOGY CENTERS

The cornerstone of the U.S. program to aid S&T in the former Soviet Union has been promotion of the International Science and Technology Centers, designed specifically to redirect weapons scientists (chemical, biological, ballistic missile, and nuclear) to peaceful civilian research. Attributed largely to German Foreign Minister Hans-Dietrich Genscher, [17] the Centers (one was proposed first for Moscow and, subsequently, one is being designed for Kiev, Ukraine) would serve as a clearinghouse for former weapons scientists by developing, selecting, financing, and monitoring civilian oriented science and technology projects to be conducted at facilities in Russia, Georgia, and other countries. According to a State Department press release, "Projects approved by the [Russian] center could be in virtually any area of applied or basic research, including environmental protection, health, energy production, nuclear reactor safety and nuclear waste management." Funding, to-

[16] U.S. Congress. House. Committee on Science, Space, and Technology. Science and Technology Cooperation With the Russian Federation—Videoconference with Moscow. Hearing, March 25, 1992, 102d Congress, second session. Washington, U.S. Govt. Print. Off., 1992, 35 p.

[17] Nisbet, Stephen. West Rushes Plan to Prevent a Nuclear Brain Drain From Russia. Reuters, March 11, 1992.

taling $25 million for the Russian Center and $10 million for the Ukraine Center, will come from the $400 million appropriated by the Congress for denuclearization activities through Title II of P.L. 102–228, passed in fall of 1991. (Subsequently in P.L. 102–484 this was increased to $800 million.) The Center's initial contributions total about $75 million. In addition to the United States, the other founding members of the Russian Center are Japan, contributing about $10 million; the European Community, about $25 million; Canada, about $1 million; and Russia, which has contributed the site, "a small city 32 kilometers southeast of Moscow....," according to the CIA. [18] The United States is also encouraging other entities, such as private corporations and universities, to join the centers and to sponsor research projects. All funds will be used for expenses and awards. The center has a two-year life, after which continuation will be re-evaluated.

U.S. Ambassador Richard L. Armitage testified in May 6, 1992 that the agreement establishing the Russian Center would be signed in May 1992, and that members of the governing Board would meet to approve a site and adopt project proposal format and guidelines. However, the agreement was not signed until Nov. 27, 1992. The delay in signing, according to State, occurred because of the need to translate the document into languages of all signatory nations. The State Department has officially committed $25 million to the Center. [19] No monies will be pledged formally until the document is ratified by the EC and the Russian Parliament. Negotiations have not been completed on operating procedures, as of December 1992.

Some attribute the delay in signing the documents creating the Russian Center to criticisms that have been made about it. Critics of its purposes and "clientele" say that Soviet weapons scientists will be funded to continue working as teams in their own laboratories on weapons-related projects and American scientists will not participate in collaborative projects or oversee former Soviet Union work. A report, attributed to an aide of Senator Jeff Bingaman who visited Russia and Ukraine, says that since most of the research that the Center will fund will be conducted by scientists affiliated with the institutes of the Russian Academy of Sciences, the Center is not targeting the right group, that is, weapons technicians and fabricators who work in laboratories of the defense and atomic power and industry ministries [20] whose services could be bought by other countries. [21]

Criticism also has been directed at the Center's planned awards approval process. A three-step process is proposed: review for scientific merit by the Center's technical staff, review by the contributing nations on the governing board to determine if proposals meet the country's and the Center's criteria, and then review by each individual country partner or private partner to determine which sponsor will fund the project. Some argue that a one-step review

---

[18] S&T Perspectives, v. 7, May 29, 1992, p. 14.
[19] Tutwiler, Margaret, State Dept. Briefing, July 14, 1992, Reuter transcript.
[20] Charles, Dan. "Western Funds for Russia May Miss Their Target." *New Scientist*, Mar. 21, 1992, p. 13.
[21] "Soviet 'Brain Drain' Fears Ignore Technicians, Senate Panel Is Told." *New York Times*, March 18, 1991.

process directly by the funding countries would suffice. It is not required that Western scientists collaborate on projects with their Russian counterparts. The National Academy of Sciences criticized the Center for lacking authority to fund projects "without the explicit approval of its member nations' representatives." To avoid rendering the center a " 'needless and powerless middleman,' " the Academy continued, "its members should allow it to distribute as much as one quarter of its funding unilaterally." [22]

There was some initial disagreement between the United States and the European Community about who would manage the Center, with Europeans suggesting as head Carlo Rubbia, a Nobel Prize winner and president of the European Center for Nuclear Research in Geneva. [23] The U.S. candidate, Glenn E. Schweitzer, Director of the U.S. National Academy of Sciences Committee on the U.S.S.R. and Eastern Europe, was selected. A Governing Board with one representative from each of the four founding countries will be named after the agreement is ratified. The United States has nominated Victor Alessi of the Department of Energy to be a member of the governing Board, according to a State Department official. [24] Apparently close to 200 unsolicited proposals have been received. [25]

According to a State Department official, the technical details have not yet been finalized on the agreement creating the Ukraine Center; U.S. support totaling $10 million has not yet been committed. [26]

ADDITIONAL PROGRAMS AND PROPOSALS

Some critics of the International Science and Technology centers programs say the centers will serve only nuclear weapons scientists, but that scientists in other fields and disciplines also require support. As a result, other kinds of foundations and centers have been proposed. The European Commission (EC) has endorsed an idea, spearheaded by French President François Mitterand, to establish an international foundation that would offer grants and contracts directly to individuals and groups of the former Soviet Union to work on precisely determined research projects, but in cooperation with teams of Western scientists. Contributing country approval would not be required. Ninety percent of funds with the foundation would be spent in Russia. [27] The EC approved an initial budget of ECU 4 million ($US 5.2 million) in October 1992 for startup.

Rep. George E. Brown, Jr., chairman of the House Committee on Science, Space and Technology, introduced H.R. 4550 to create a

---

[22] Hamilton, David P. "A Plea for Aid to Ex-Soviet Science." *Science,* v. 255, Mar. 20, 1992, pp. 1503–1504.
[23] Wolberg-Stok, Andrews. "West Sets Out to Keep CIS Nuclear Scientists Busy." Reuters, March 11, 1991.
[24] Some information from Statement of Ambassador Richard L. Armitage, May 6, 1992, In Aid to the Former Soviet Union. Remarks by Mr. Kerrey. *Congressional Record,* May 6, 1992, p. 6068–9. Also based on interviews.
[25] Lippman, Thomas W. "Russian Scientist Aid is Developing." *Washington Post,* Apr. 24, 1992, p. A10.
[26] Tutwiler, Margaret, State Dept. Briefing, July 14, 1992, Reuter transcript.
[27] Dufour, Jean-Paul. "Home Help for Russian Scientists Planned." *Manchester Guardian Weekly,* May 17, 1992.

657

partially governmental-endowed, but eventual nongovernmental, operating "AmeRus" Foundation. (The Senate companion bill is S. 2401, introduced by Senator Albert Gore.) As originally proposed, the Foundation's endowment would be funded initially by the U.S. Government over four years for a total of $200 million. The proceeds of the endowment and any returns to it would be used: (1) to give scientists and engineers of the former Soviet Union opportunities to conduct joint research and development with U.S. counterparts, and (2) to enable scientists, engineers and entrepreneurs to conduct joint research and development with U.S. industries (along the lines of the existing U.S.-Israeli binational foundations). The Administration opposed the Brown proposal on the grounds that the Government already has sufficient authority to fund programs of this nature. This legislation has not yet been reported.

However, parts of it were incorporated into Section 504 of H.R.4547, the Freedom Support Act of 1992, as reported by the Foreign Affairs Committee. (H. Rept. 102-569, June 16, 1992.) The bill was referred sequentially to the House Committees on Science, Space, and Technology; Agriculture; Armed Services; and Banking. It authorizes the Director of the National Science Foundation, in consultation with the director of the National Institute of Standards and Technology, to create an endowed nongovernmental, nonprofit foundation between the United States and the independent states of the former Soviet Union in order to promote joint research and development and private sector linkages between U.S. scientists and their counterparts in the former Soviet Union. The foundation's objectives would be to focus on subjects of mutual interest to halt the deterioration of S&T infrastructure in the former Soviet Union, to advance defense conversion by funding collaborative civilian R&D between U.S. and FSU scientists, to develop relationships between high technology entrepreneurs in the new states and U.S. industrial research and development scientists and technicians in order to develop entrepreneurial skills and a market economy, and to provide access for U.S. businesses to FSU technologies.

S. 2532, amended, the Freedom for Russian and Emerging Eurasian Democracies and Open Markets Support Act, contains language similar to H.R. 4547 with respect to the foundation. It was signed as P.L. 102-511 on October 24, 1992.

Funding to create the foundation and endow it may be transferred from DOD as authorized by the National Defense Authorization Act for FY 1993, P.L. 102-484 (H.R. 5006). P.L. 102-511 also requires minimum contributions to the endowment by the participating FSU states, and permits funding from debt conversions, use of local currencies, and contributions by other governmental or nongovernmental entities. After FY 1993, no more than 50 percent of funds for the foundation may be appropriated from national defense funds.

In P.L. 102-484, the Secretary of Defense was given permissive authority, that is he "may spend" up to $25 million for the cooperative R&D projects with the FSU, as spelled out in P.L. 102-511, but the projects must be designed to offer scientists R&D employment alternatives to emigration and to help prevent proliferation of weapons and "dissolution of technology infrastructure." (Secs. 1421 and 1441.) The thrust of this language is different from the basically civilian research orientation of P.L. 102–511. Funds are appropriated via P.L. 102–229.

Because other cooperative projects are to be supported with these funds (under provisions of the Soviet Nuclear Threat Reduction Act of 1991, called the "Nunn-Lugar" amendment), the National Security Council, as of December 1992, is examining which of the several projects authorized will be funded and for how much. Current expectations at NSF are that the AmeRus Foundation will be awarded about $10 million, primarily for start-up activities especially in communications, because the amount is too small to constitute part of the planned endowment.

FEDERAL AGENCY PROGRAMS

Most Federal R&D agencies engage in joint research and exchange activities with the former Soviet Union. These activities are being conducted even in the absence of signed agreements with the CIS states because most republics, eager for collaboration with the United States, assume that the agreements between the Untied States and the Soviet Union can serve to guide cooperative activities. (The NSF seeks to avoid having to conclude separate basic science cooperative agreements with each republic of the former Soviet Union and, therefore, has issued joint statements with the academies of science of Estonia and Ukraine which refer to the basic agreement signed between the United States and the U.S.S.R. on June 8, 1989, and the subsequent NSF-Academy of Science memorandum on Understanding on Cooperation in the Fields of Basic Scientific Research. The NSF hopes that these will be prototypes for arrangements with other countries.) Some agencies that had cooperative programs with the U.S.S.R. are enlarging them to include cooperative science and technology with the other new republics, but at a slow rate due to the general lack of funds.

Most is known about the programs of the NSF and the NIH. Besides their regular cooperative programs, [28] both these agencies have initiated supplemental cooperative programs that do not transfer research funds directly (in order to avoid taxes on foreign hard currency imports and skimming by corrupt officials). Instead, the programs provide small competitively awarded supplements to the funding of existing U.S. grantees, allowing them to identify former Soviet Union research collaborators, and to assist them by sending subscriptions, supplies and equipment, and plane tickets (and preferably bringing these items themselves into the former Soviet Union countries). With respect to NSF, in March 1992, the National Science Board, a governing body of NSF, authorized a specific program, called infrastructural supplements of no more than $10,000 to currently funded NSF principal investigators to support an expansion of their research and the funding of research expenses of former Soviet Union scientists. The program totals about

---

[28] The NSF will spend $1.2 million for FY1992, primarily for U.S. researcher costs, for core collaborative programs with former Soviet Union, authorized by cooperative agreements. The foundation programs also will provide about $692,000 for the core program of cooperative research with Russia for about 40 projects involving former Soviet Union and U.S. researchers, and just over $800,000 for National Academics of Science interacademy exchanges, about one-third of which will be for former Soviet Union.

$1 million, shifted from other NSF programs, and an additional contribution of $100,000 from the Department of State.

Also, in February 1992 the National Science Board authorized temporary, emergency waivers of financial reciprocity requirements governing cooperative programs. Program agreements generally had required former Soviet Union scientists to pay for activities of U.S. researchers in the former Soviet Union and for the sending country to pay travel costs. This requirement has been dropped, [29] permitting American principal investigators to pay airfare for their colleagues to come to the United States for short-term, agreed-upon scientific work. [30]

The NIH has initiated a low-level supplemental program through the Fogarty Center, called Fogarty International Research Collaboration Awards. Like the NSF program, it provides supplements to current awardees for collaborative research with scientists of the former Spoviet Union. Piggy-backing on a program originally designed for Eastern Europe and Latin America, the expanded program for the former Soviet Union permits supplements of no more than $20,000 of additional funds to an NIH grantee to collaborate with a former Soviet Union scientist. Money must be used exclusively for supplies, equipment, or travel expenses for both the U.S. principal investigator and the foreign collaborator. No awards are made to institutes. Apparently the demand is so great that only 20 percent of the proposals have been funded. NIH received a small award of $1 million from Congress for the original program for each of two years, and, subsequently, NIH expanded it to include the former Soviet Union. The NIH also has started programs of small training awards for former Soviet Union scientists and research collaboration by intramural NIH scientists with these researchers from the former Soviet Union. There is no new money for these programs, and NIH has shifted some research dollars from other support programs (such as for Western European collaboration) to support supplemental cooperative programs.

Other agencies could design similar programs, targeting the unique strengths of former Soviet Union science, a suggestion made by a staff member of the White House Office of Science and Technology Policy. These, according to the Department of State, include space, high-energy physics, nuclear and particle physics, genetics and biotechnology, including mapping of the human genome in Russia; [31] cybernetics and new materials in Ukraine and Belarus; astrophysics in Armenia; theoretical mathematics in Georgia; geology and space in Kazakhstan; and seismology in Tadzhikistan. [32]

In its report to the President's science advisor, the National Academy of Sciences urged the Federal Government to expand financial support for nonmilitary research to $25 million to be car-

[29] "Falling Budgets, Rising Travel Costs Threaten U.S.-Russian Exchange Agreements." NTIS Alert. Foreign Technology. March 3, 1992, pp. i, v.
[30] Testimony of Dr. Frederick M. Berenthal, Deputy Director, National Science Foundation., May 29, 1992, before the Subcommittee on Science of the Committee on Science, Space, and Technology, on H.R. 4550, The Amerus Foundation for Research and Development Act of 1992, pp. 4-5.
[31] "Breakup of Soviet Union to have Significant Effect on International S&T Programs." NTIS Alert. February 18, 1992, pp. i, vii.
[32] Title V report, op.cit., p. 179.

ried out by current grantees of extramural programs of the Department of Energy, NIH, and NSF with funds allocated from those appropriated for nuclear dismantlement. Such funding could go far since it is generally agreed that now it costs about $1,200 a year to support a scientist or engineer from the former Soviet Union. The NAS also recommended that the U.S. Government establish an equipment and information fund of $50 million to $100 million with support from appropriate bilateral and multilateral assistance agencies to halt deterioration of former Soviet Union labs, data, and libraries. It urged the Government to create an administrative mechanism to transfer to former Soviet Union scientists the equipment from U.S. laboratories that has been displaced by more recent acquisitions and that remains capable of producing valuable research results.

The NAS recommended that a bilateral advisory committee should be established to assist the former Soviet Union and U.S. governments in designing and implementing future programs of cooperation and to assist in defining a framework for intellectual property rights. In this connection the OECD science ministers in March approved a $750,000 study of the state of science in Russia and a proposal to host a conference on the brain drain from the former Soviet Union.

The U.S. Government has launched educational exchange programs, largely for defense scientists. Defense conversion advisers will be sent to Nizhniy Novgorod and there are plans to send additional advisers to Yekterinburgae later in 1992.[33] The Special American Business Internship Training Program, is being administered by the Department of Commerce. This program, which will cost $1 million, will bring 150 former Soviet defense managers and scientists to the United States for three- to six-month internships at R&D companies. Another program under development by the State Department will bring 150 scientists, primarily from the former Soviet defense sector, to the United States for research and lecturing at U.S. universities for one to two years. This is estimated to cost about $1.5 million.[34]

IMMIGRATION

The Congress approved P.L. 102–509 (S. 2201) to expedite the immigration of 750 former Soviet scientists in nuclear, chemical, biological, or other high technology fields or who are working on high-technology defense projects for each of the next four years, by making it easier for them to obtain permanent residency status. The objective is to attract qualified scientists to the United States rather than to other advanced countries.

---

[33] Remarks of the Hon. Lee H. Hamilton. Extensions of Remarks, June 1, 1992. *Congressional Record*, June 1, 1992. P. E1599.
[34] Seltzer, Richard J. "U.S. Buys Russian Technology, Eyes Expanded Science Cooperation." *Chemical and Engineering News*, April 6, 1992, p. 24. McDonald, Kim. "U.S. Plan for Aid to Scientists in Former Soviet Union could Strengthen Deteriorating Research Enterprise." *Chronicle of Higher Education*. April 8, 1992, pp A41, A42.

U.S. GOVERNMENT CONTRACTS

Many scientists of the former Soviet Union, arguing that labor costs there are at least 10 times lower than U.S. labor costs, are seeking direct grants or contracts from U.S. agencies. They argue that U.S. industry and Government would get more for their money in research activities conducted in the former Soviet Union, especially in fields where their scientists excel, such as plasma physics, high-energy physics, spectroscopy, and electronics research. [35]

The U.S. Government has been moving very slowly toward expanding purchases of research services and technology from the former Soviet Union, since all purchases need to be approved for security and technology transfer on a case-by-case basis. Some allege that such purchases are sometimes rejected on the grounds that an infusion of hard currency into an area of military-industrial research ultimately could compromise U.S. national security. The National Academy of Sciences and others have criticized U.S. export control laws and have urged liberalization of them. Some argue that the purchase or licensing of advanced technology of the former Soviet Union, especially Russia, will save the West millions of dollars in development costs and that purchases of this nature are crucial to demonstrating the advantages of capitalism.

In addition to the space technology purchases agreed to in June 1992 following the Summit, other contracts and agreements have been publicly announced. The Department of Energy, through a company called General Atomics, agreed to a one-year $90,000 contract for the services of Russian scientists for fusion reactor research at the world-renown Kurchatov Institute of Atomic Energy in Moscow. [36] Presidential science advisor Bromley testified before the Senate Foreign Relations Committee on March 17, 1992 that this work would cost $10 million to $15 million if done by U.S. researchers. It was reported in September 1992 that in order to conduct the research the Institute would need to purchase eight high-power gyrotrons, whose cost exceeds the proceeds of the DOE contract, whose terms permitted support only for salaries. [37] There are also reports that the Department of Energy is discussing a contract with scientists at a laboratory at Novosibirsk to manufacture non-super conducting magnets for the Superconducting Super Collider's low-energy booster. [38] The White House has also authorized three additional high-tech purchases from Russia totaling $14.3 million, including Department of Defense's purchase of a Topaz II thermionic nuclear space power system, four Hall thrusters for the DOD SDI program, and the Department of Energy's purchase of about $6 million worth of plutonium. [39] It was reported that, during March 1992, the directors of two U.S. nuclear weapons labs, Los Alamos National Laboratory and Lawrence Livermore National Laborato-

---

[35] Beardsley, Tim. "Brain Drain." *Scientific American*, April 1992, pp. 17, 20.
[36] William J. Broad. "U.S. Plans to Hire Russian Scientists in Fusion Research." *New York Times*, March 6, 1992.
[37] Charles, Don. "Marriage of Convenience for Russian Research." *New Scientist*, Sept. 15, 1992, pp. 12–13.
[38] "Unified Team to Aid SSC." *Science*, Feb. 28, 1992, p. 1059.
[39] Seltzer, op. cit, p. 24–25.

ry, visited two similar former top secret Russian labs, Arzamas-16, and Chelyabinsk-70, presumably to discuss research contracts. [40]

PRIVATE AND PROFESSIONAL SECTOR COOPERATION

Most of the professional association activities announced so far are stopgap measures to assist in maintaining a core of former Soviet Union scientific research in specific disciplines. For instance, the American Association for the Advancement of Science has started publishing a newsletter, *Scientist to Scientist*, which reports actions being taken by U.S. scientific and engineering societies to assist colleagues in the former Soviet Union. The AAAS plans to reinstate, at its own expense, subscriptions for individuals and libraries in the former Soviet Union to *Science* magazine. The American Astronomical Society has raised $45,000 in personal contributions from members to provide research grants of $100 each to 300 astronomers in the former Soviet republics, and it will use the balance of funds for subscriptions to eight U.S. astronomy journals. The American Institute of Physics will provide close to 200 journals free to researchers in the former Soviet Union. The American Chemical Society has a similar program. The American Physical Society is seeking to raise $100,000 for the same purposes, to be matched by $100,000 from the Alfred P. Sloan Foundation. [41] Reportedly, the Federation of American Scientists is working on a plan to bring the directors of Russian research institutes to the United States to discuss subcontracts for specific research projects. [42] The American Society for Engineering Education has sponsored teams of U.S. engineering specialist to visit Russian counterparts in an attempt to raise levels of Russian technical education more in line with Western equivalents.

It has been estimated that 8,000 Soviet refugee scientists arrived in the United States within the last two years. Several scientific or ethnic groups located in the New York area act to acculturate immigrant scientists and introduce them to networks that will assist in locating jobs or technical schools for retraining. This includes the Association of Engineers and Scientists for New Americans, the Program for Refugee Scientists, and the Scientific Career Transitions seminar series. [43]

Some believe that U.S.-Soviet commercial R&D relationships are the key to the stabilization of major former Soviet Union R&D facilities and to the creation of a market for technology in the former Soviet Union, since they provide hard currency and commercial experience. There have always been a few U.S. companies, such as Kiser Research Inc., which sought to transfer technology from the Soviet side to the West and to develop joint ventures to assist in marketing technology in the West. Such activities have expanded in the last two years, for instance with the creation of firms such as Science Solutions and VentureWest Technologies. [44] The Rus-

---

[40] Broad, William J. "Scientists Press East-West Accord." *New York Times*, March 19, 1992.
[41] "Dispatch Case." *Chronicle of Higher Education*. June 127, 1992, p. A36.
[42] McDonald, op. cit., Jan. 22, 1992, p. A41.
[43] Stone, Richard. "Hard Times in the Promised Land." *Science*, v. 256, May 8, 1992, pp. 728–9.
[44] "Scientist to Scientist." AAAS. April 1992, pp. 3–4.

sian Academy of Sciences formed an American corporation, Russian-American Science, Inc., to solicit commercial contracts for research involving Russian scientists at the institutes that are affiliated with the academy. The company has facilitated agreements made with Science Applications International Corporation of San Diego to develop environmental technologies, including the use of electron beams for sterilizing municipal and industrial waste and the use of accelerators to convert nuclear waste to nonradioactive substances. In another agreement with the Federal Computer Corporation of Falls Church, Virginia, Russian scientists will develop computer software for U.S. firms. [45] AT&T Bell Laboratories has formed a contract with the Russian Academy of Sciences' General Physics Institute, a world leader in Moscow, for fiber-optics research; Corning reportedly has signed agreements for basic research on glass by 115 scientists at two research institutes in St. Petersburg. Salaries average about $60 per month for each former Soviet Union scientist. [46] The American firms say they will own the international patents that might result, while the Russian workers will own the Russian patents. [47] Monsanto has awarded a contract to the Shemyakin Institute in Moscow, where for about $500,000, ten scientists are conducting research on drugs and plant and animal growth. Monsanto also has another contract with former Soviet Union researchers to "exploit technology to put a diamond-hard coating on plastics." [48] U.S.-Soviet cooperation among oceanographers is being facilitated through "Intermarine," the Western partner in a licensed joint venture with the research arm of the former Soviet Ministry of Fisheries and Oceanography. [49] Other approved agreements include Sun Microsystems, a computer company in Silicon Valley supporting the research of Boris Babayan and his team of about 50 computer scientists from the Institute of Precision Mechanics and Computer Technology of the Russian Academy of Sciences, a leading computer designer. [50]

One disadvantage reported so far to private cooperation is the possibility that some former Soviet Union scientists who might visit the United States in conjunction with these arrangements could be industrial spies, could work for the KGB, or could have total disregard for U.S. intellectual property rights and patents. As a result, U.S. firms, reportedly, have been cautioned by the Federal Bureau of Investigation and the Central Intelligence Agency to curtail the access of these scientists to U.S. industrial research and trade secrets. This was discussed in hearings held in the spring of 1992 by the House Commercial Law Subcommittee. [51]

[45] McDonald, Kim A. "Russia's Science Academy Forms U.S. Firm to Solicit Commercial Research Contracts." *The Chronicle of Higher Education.* June 10, 1991, pp. A32-A33.
[46] Seltzer, Richard. "Bell Labs, Corning Fund Work at Russian Labs." *Chemical and Engineering News,* June 1, 1992, p. 6.
[47] Burgess, John. AT&T, "Corning Set Research Deals With 200 Russian Scientists." *Washington Post,* May 27, 1992.
[48] Seib and Fialka, op. cit., p. A14.
[49] "Scientist to Scientist." AAAS. June 1992, p. 3.
[50] Charles, Dan. "Bargain Hunters Snap Up Russian Brainpower." *New Scientist,* March 14, 1991, p. 13; Burgess, John. "The Search for Soviet Science is Well on Its Way." *Washington Post,* February 23, 1992.
[51] "AT&T's Bell Labs Teams Up with Russian Fiber Lab." *Communications Daily,* May 27, 1992, p. 3, and "Spies Posing as Scientists said to Pose Commercial Espionage Threat." *Communications Daily,* June 15, 1992, p. 2.

In December 1992, a Hungarian-born U.S. financier, George
Soros, announced creation of an International Science Foundation
in Moscow. It will be capitalized at $100 million, to prove direct
support to FSU scientists for research, equipment and salaries.
This amount exceeds the funds pledged by the U.S. Government for
new science center and foundation activities, and is estimated, at
current exchange rates, to equal one-fifth of the entire science
budget of Russia. [52]

CONCLUDING OBSERVATIONS

U.S. policies for Eastern Europe and the successor states to the
former Soviet Union have incorporated programs designed to
hasten conversion of military resources to civilian purposes, to promote economic growth, and to develop market economies and technological advance. It can be argued that strengthening of scientific
and technological infrastructure, including retention of scientific
personnel, should be essential elements of these policies.

Others, however, could argue that augmentation of the former
Soviet Union republics' S&T capabilities poses a potential long-
term security and competitive threat to the United States. Some
policymakers believe that some former Soviet Union scientists are
industrial spies or intelligence agents who will "expropriate" Western technology without paying for it or without honoring U.S. intellectual property rights or laws. Others stress that the successor
states, especially Russia, pose a significant potential national security threat, that their R&D infrastructure is formidable as is and
should not be strengthened by special U.S. programs. Some say
that the quality of the science of the former Soviet Union is low
and does not deserve much attention.

Official U.S. programs for expanded cooperation with the republics of the former Soviet Union do not appear to be adequate to
stem the brain drain of scientists from the republics and to
strengthen the infrastructure of science there. This may be a reasonable policy, from the perspective of some security analysts. On
the other hand, some might conclude that policies which do not
adequately support the large science and technology community of
the former Soviet Union could be destabilizing and costly in the
long run. Recommendations have been made by the National Aca-
demyof Sciences and others to devote more resources to S&T activities and to design improved programs. U.S. Government policies
that are intended to promote science and technology in the former
Soviet Union probably would benefit if they were coordinated with
private sector activities.

---

[52] Southerland, Dan and David Brown. "Former Soviet Union to Get Science Aid." *Washington Post*, Dec. 10, 1992, B11 and Bohlen, Celestine. "American Vows Millions To Ex-Soviet Science." *New York Times*, Dec. 10, 1992, A17.

TOWARD A CIS PROTECTION SYSTEM FOR INVENTIONS

By Katlijn Malfliet *

CONTENTS

INTRODUCTION AND SUMMARY

The U.S.S.R. law on inventions of May 31, 1991, introduced a commodity approach in scientific technical activities before the collapse of the Soviet Union. This paper will not discuss the content of industrial property protection (e.g., patents), but will focus on the relations between the legislative levels of the former republics-independent states and the Commonwealth of Independent States (CIS). The evolution of industrial property protection can be seen as a test of the assumption that the disintegration of the Soviet federation was well prepared and that the disintegration of the post-Stalinist central organizations was a *conditio sine qua non* for the building of new, market-based relations.

The main summary points of the paper are as follows.

* The recognition of intellectual scientific work as a good was fully accepted before the disintegration of the Soviet Union.
* The establishment of independent national protection systems may appear legitimate, but the dictates of reason must be to safeguard common interests shared by all former republics in the granting and administration of intellectual property rights, turning to good use appropriate institutions that still exist and have stood the test of time.
* Until the creation of a working interstate protective system the Russian federation will temporarily take over the role of the Union: Gospatent becomes Rospatent.
* The ultimate aim is to bring the former Soviet patent system as soon as possible to the level of West European patent protection.

---

* Katlijn Malfliet is with The Leuven Institute for Central and East European Studies.

MODERNIZING INTELLECTUAL PROPERTY PROTECTION

An international exchange of intellectual property, *"Dom uchen-nykh,"* has recently been set up in Moscow. [1] At this "market-place" scientists can offer their enormous potential of innovation capacity to the economic world. The interest shown by Russian scientists in the market is perfectly understandable in this period of systemic transformation: they are trying to overcome bankruptcy of their scientific institutes, while at the same time, provide valuable information for enterprises in their attempts to innovate. [2]

This exchange, however, started in a legislative vacuum because in February 1992 the U.S.S.R. patent law had not yet been replaced by a Russian legislation. Although such exchanges do not exist anywhere else in the world, and moreover, the scientists are commercializing industrial property, with an uncertain ownership title, the organizers of the exchange assert that "the enormous need of scientific-technical projects will take away any contradictions."

Industrial property rights are essential instruments for an appropriate economic and technical competition. [3] This is true for both domestic and foreign relations. In this era of technological societies, an effective system of protection of intellectual property is a condition for the progress in society and for its socio-economic development.

With foreign sales and investments increasing throughout the region, better intellectual property rights are needed and enforcement needs to be significantly upgraded. Intellectual property rights can provide protection from antitrust enforcement to allow firms to engage in cooperative research and development. [4] Russia's intention to actively commercialize technologies and to control the export of sensitive technology from Russia has become very clear in recent months. Russia wants to introduce its own COCOM committee (Coordinating Committee on Export Controls) and stresses that this is only possible with the help of the other CIS-countries and Georgia. [5]

The process of modernizing intellectual property protection was complicated by the breakdown of the Union. One business report described the disruption in this way: "The breakup of the former USSR has negated existing laws ... each new republic now has to draft its own laws." [6] This paper argues that there is some continuity behind that disintegration process. The new concept of intellectual property rights was carefully prepared before the collapse of the Soviet Union. The paper does not go into the discussion on the

---

[1] Leskov, S. *"U uchennykh tozhe est' svoia birzha"* (Scientists Also Have Their Exchange), *Izvestiia*, February 1992, p. 4.

[2] Gal'perin, L.B. and L.A. Mikhailova, *"Intellektual'naia Sobstvennos' i pravovaia priroda"* (Intellectual Property: Its Essence and Legal Nature), *Sovetskoe Gosudarstvo i Pravo*, no. 12, 1991, p. 37.

[3] According to the Paris Convention for the Protection of Industrial Property of March 20, 1883, industrial property includes inventions, utility models, industrial designs, trade marks and service marks, trading names, appellations of origin and unfair competition. In the Soviet Union the concept also includes rationalization proposals. The law on enterprises in the U.S.S.R. (art. 33) included know-how in the concept of industrial property.

[4] J.R. Gilbert, "Legal and Economic issues in the Commercialisation of New Technologies," *Journal of Institutional and Theoretical Economics*, vol. 147, no. 1, March 1991.

[5] *"Rossiiski Kokom. Tozhe ne mozhet sushchestvovat' v otdel'no vziatoi strane"* (The Russian COCOM cannot exist in one isolated country), *Kommersant*, no. 29, 1992, p. 12.

[6] *Business Eastern Europe*, vol. 21, no. 18, May 4, 1992, p. 209.

content of industrial property protection, but it focuses on the relations between the legislative levels of the former republics and the CIS. One can see the evolution in industrial property law as testing the assumption that the disintegration of the Soviet federation was well prepared and that the disintegration of post-Stalinist central organizations was a *conditio sine qua non* for the building of new, market-based relations.

THE INTRODUCTION OF A COMMODITY CONCEPT FOR INDUSTRIAL PROPERTY

At the beginning of the nineteenth century pre-revolutionary law introduced the ownership concept of intellectual property in Russia as an exclusive subjective right to execute all activities not forbidden by law related to the protected goods, while at the same time excluding all others to act without the consent of the rightholders. [7]

This "property" system to protect inventions was relinquished with the introduction of a Soviet system for protection of inventions. A decree of 1919 introduced a protection of inventions through certificates of invention. In 1924, as part of the New Economic Policy (NEP) a patent decree reintroduced exclusive patents for a short period. The decree became inoperative at the end of the New Economic Policy in 1931. [8] From that year on, the former Soviet system offered Soviet inventors two ways to protect their inventions: patents and certificates of invention. Patents enabled the rightholder to exclude others, certificates of invention did not contain this right. Until recently, however, the concept of industrial property was only used in the Soviet doctrine and in some normative acts in cases that related to the participation of the U.S.S.R. in international bilateral and multilateral agreements. [9] In practice the government only issued patents to foreigners who decided to protect their inventions in the U.S.S.R. An invention, protected by a certificate, could be used by any state-owned enterprise without the consent of the inventor.

The Soviet system for protection of inventions was consistent within Marxist-Leninist ideology. An invention could not be attributed to an individual inventor because it was considered to be a social good. The inventor worked at a state enterprise and used social assets and the knowledge of former generations to create an invention. The whole system relied on central planning as opposed to competition and patent monopoly. Rather than serving as an incentive for research, Soviet patent law functioned primarily as a formal channel for the distribution of information about inventions. [10] The salary was the principal reward for this achievement.

---

[7] G.F. Shershenevich, *Uchebnik Russkogo grazhdanskogo prava* (Handbook of Russian Civil Law), Moskva, 1912, p. 407.

[8] Dietz, *"Die Patentgesetzgebung der Osteuropaischen Lander,"* Gerwerbliche Rechtsschutz und Urheberrecht, Internationaler teil (*GRUR* International), 1976, p. 311.

[9] For example, addendum II to art. VIII of the agreement between the governments of the U.S.S.R. and the United States of January 8, 1989, on cooperation in the field of basic scientific research, SP SSSR (Sobranie Postanovleniiakh), (otdel vtoroi), no. 2, 1990, p. 4.

[10] P.B. Maggs, "The Restructuring of the Soviet Law on Inventions," *Columbia Journal of Transnational Law*, vol. 28, no. 1, 1990, p. 277.

This system found its full expression in the 1973 decree on discoveries, inventions, and rationalization proposals. [11] After publication of this decree, state enterprise managers and inventors began to criticise the whole system, as not encouraging innovation because inventors were not rewarded adequately for their creativity. Moreover, managers of pioneering firms complained that the law forced them to share too many of their inventions. [12]

In December 1988 *Pravda* published a draft statute on inventive activity. [13] In terminology, the draft law resembled the legislation of market economies, but in substance inventions remained subordinate to the principle of social distribution. The draft patent law represented a precarious compromise (a "half measure") between the traditional Soviet patent law principles and the capitalist patent system. "The ultimate fate of the draft must await a political decision on whether plan or market should prevail in the new technology of the USSR," Peter Maggs commented. [14] The draft law abolished the certificate of invention. The patent became the only way to protect inventions. Moreover, the patent guaranteed an exclusive right, and the concept of the patent as a commodity (*tovar*) was introduced. [15]

But, although recognizing these principles, the law also said that patents could only be used if they did not harm the interests of the state or society. [16] If a state firm required the use of an invention to fulfill a task assigned by the plan, the Committee of Science and Technology might award the firm a compulsory licence. A compulsory licence was also possible, according to the draft, when the invention was of special significance to the state. The planned sector of the economy would operate under an obligatory licensing system, while freely negotiated patent licensing would exist only in the market sector of the economy. Moreover, the U.S.S.R. patent law introduced two new legal institutions, which made inventions available to the public: the "open licence" (according to which the patent owner sets the price at which any enterprise may obtain a licence to the invention) and patents made available to all, royalty-free through the State Patent Fund. Afterward, the 1988 draft was modified in several aspects. The changes concerned mainly the State Patent Fund. [17]

The U.S.S.R. accepted the obligation to renew its legislation on intellectual property as part of the 1990 Soviet economic commercial agreement, which stated that the statute of most-favored-nation status could only be introduced if the U.S.S.R. guaranteed

---

[11] *Polozhenie ob otkrytiiakh, izobreteniiakh i ratsionalizatorskikh predlozheniiakh* (Statute on Discoveries, Inventions and Rationalization Proposals), SP SSSR, no. 19, 1973, p. 109.

[12] R. Malakhimova, *"Kliuchevoi vopros: sobstvennost' na izobretenii"* (The Crucial Question: Property on Inventions), *Ekonomicheskaia Gazeta*, no. 10, March 1989, p. 20.

[13] *Pravda*, December 27, 1988, pp. 2–3.

[14] P. B. Maggs, see note 9, p. 277.

[15] A commodity distinguishes itself from other forms of value precisely by the protection which the legal system confers upon them and by the autonomy of the owner to negotiate the terms to their exchange: G. Armstrong, "From the Fetishism of Commodities to the Regulated Market: the Rise and Decline of Property," *Nortwestern University Law Review*, no. 682, 1987, p. 79.

[16] *"Obsuzhdaem proekt zakona ob izobretatel'skoi deiatel'nosti"* (We Discuss the Draft on Inventory Activity), *Ekonomicheskaia Gazeta*, no. 7, February 1989, p. 14.

[17] EIPR (European Intellectual Property Report), 1991, p. D–76.

effective legal protection to objects of intellectual and industrial property. [18]
The first mention of a property right on products of creative activity was the union legislation "On Property in the USSR" of 6 March 1990. In that law, the first concern did not seem to be the content of this ownership, but the levels of legislation affected (union, union republics, autonomous republics). According to art. 2 pt. 4 the protection of objects of intellectual property concerns both the union and the republican legislator. At the time of the discussion of this law, F. Burlatskii and A. Sobchak claimed that intellectual property should be the subject of separate legislation. This proposal was much criticized. [19]

In the U.S.S.R. law on enterprises there is a short article on commercial secrets. The R.S.F.S.R. law on enterprises and entrepreneurial activity stated that enterprises have the right not to provide information that contains a commercial secret which can be defined by the enterprise management. [20]

The Principles of Civil Legislation, approved by the U.S.S.R. Supreme Soviet on 31 May 1991, were scheduled to come into force on January 1, 1992. [21] They consolidated a Western concept of industrial property law. The regulation of patent law was kept outside the constituent republics, only the U.S.S.R. patent office was entitled to issue patents. [22] A U.S.S.R. Patent Court was also announced.

Art. 1 of the Principles on Investment Activity of the U.S.S.R. allows for the possibility to introduce products of intellectual activity as a contribution in the authorized capital of enterprises, joint ventures, joint stock companies, and other economic entities.

The U.S.S.R. Law on Inventions of May 31, 1991, confirmed the "commodity-approach" in scientific-technical activities. [23] Perestroika proceeded as promised: the proportion of economic activity covered by central planning steadily diminished. [24] Already fully accepted before the disintegration of the Soviet Union were the recognition of intellectual scientific work as a good, the idea of free appropriation of the fruits of intellectual production, and as a logical consequence of this, of ownership to scientific-intellectual work. [25] Two other laws were accepted by the Supreme Soviet of the Union at the beginning of July 1991: the law on trademarks and service marks and the law on industrial designs. [26] The Su-

---

[18] L. Pitta, "Strenghtening the Legal Basis of Perestroika: The U.S.S.R. Draft Law on Inventive Activity," *Santa Clara Computer and High Technology Law Journal*, vol. 7, no. 2, December 1991, p. 321.
[19] S. Leskov, *S ideiami ne rasstavaites. Otsutstvie v SSSR zashchity intellektual'noi sobstvennosti uvelichivaet otstavanie nauki ot mirovogo urovnia* ("The Omission in the USSR of Protection of Intellectual Property Enlarges the Distance of Science from the World Level"), *Izvestia*, 29 August 1990).
[20] IU. Vinokurov, *"Vprave li prokuror istrebovat' dlia proverki pravovye akty, soderzhashchie kommercheskuiu tainu"* (Does the Public Prosecutor have the Right to Examine Legal Acts, Containing Commercial Secrets?), *Zakonnost'*, no. 1, 1992, p. 18.
[21] VVS SSSR, no. 26, 1991 p. 733.
[22] C. Prins, "The New Civil Code of the Soviet Union: Major Changes in the Field of Intellectual Property Rights," EIPR, 1991, p. 10.
[23] VVS SSSR, no. 25, 1991, p. 979.
[24] W. Seiffert, *"Das letzte Patentgesetz der UdSSR und das private Eigentum,"* GRUR International, no. 3, 1991, p. 161.
[25] I.A. Zenin, *"Rynok i pravo intellektual'noi sobstvennosti v SSSR"* (The Market and Intellectual Property Rights in the USSR), *Voprosy Izobretatel'stva*, no. 3, 1991, p. 21.
[26] VVS SSR, no. 30, 1991, 864, p. 1258; VVS SSSR, no. 32, 1991, 908, p. 1344.

preme Soviet of the U.S.S.R. failed to enact a draft law on the new
Patent Court, promised by art. 43 of the U.S.S.R. Patent Law. The
U.S.S.R. law foresaw a Patent Court that could consider appeals
against decisions of the appeal council concerning the refusal to
issue a patent and on forced licences and royalties. These were all
topics on which courts previously had no right to decide. [27] This
U.S.S.R. patent court was never established. On the other hand,
both the U.S.S.R. and the R.S.F.S.R. managed to enact a competition law before the collapse of the U.S.S.R. [28]

The new patent law of the Union reflected the ideology of the
market economy in several ways: inventor's certificates were replaced by patents, and pending certificates could be exchanged for
patents on request for a period of one year from the effective date
of the law. [29] The privatization law of the Russian federation stipu-
lates that patents, licences, and other nonmaterial assets can be
transferred to the property of private (natural or legal) persons. [30]

At the same time, however, administrative command methods
were not abolished. The inventor had the option of assigning his
invention to the state in which case a patent would be issued to the
State Fund of Inventions. [31] The law continued to provide for compulsory licences, although these would gradually be eliminated in
favor of negotiated ones. [32] However, in general the law reflected
much of what is contained in the Draft Patent Harmonization
Treaty, prepared by World Intellectual Property Organization
(WIPO). The law did not refer to the Patent Cooperation Treaty
(PCT) to which the Soviet Union belongs. Evgenyi Buryak of the
Soviet Patent Office agreed that the absence of any reference to
the PCT might be considered as a shortcoming, but said that this
would not prevent full use of the PCT in the Soviet Union, because
art. 50 of the U.S.S.R. patent law established the priority of international treaties. He noted that this might even be an advantage
for foreign applicants:

> Under PCT Article 29(1) provisional legal protection of an
> invention (...) shall be effected by international publica-
> tion of the PCT application having the designation of the
> USSR. Under PCT article 29(2) the national law may pro-
> vide that this effect shall be conditioned by a translation;
> as a result of the law's silence on this matter such provi-
> sional protection shall be effected irrespective of the lan-
> guage of the international publication. [33]

The U.S.S.R. patent law was the only legislation on industrial
property dating from 1991 which actually came into force in the
former U.S.S.R. Other new legislation on industrial Design (10 July
1991), Trademarks and Service Marks (3 July 1991) and the sec-

---

[27] F. Aisina, K. H. Aisin, *"Sudebnoe rassmotrenie sporov izobretatelei"* (The Judicial Review of
Inventor's Cases), *Sovetskaia Iustitsiia*, no. 4, 1991, p. 21.
[28] VVS SSSR, no. 31, 885, 1991, p. 1300; VVS RSFSR, no. 16, 499, 1991, p. 410.
[29] M. Iurtaeva, *"Prava i obiazannosti avtora izobreteniia"* (Rights and Duties of an Author of
an Invention), *Zakonnost'*, no. 1, 1992, p. 25.
[30] "Law of the RSFSR on Privatization of State and Municipal Enterprises in the RSFSR of 3
July 1991," *Sovetskaia Rossiia*, 17 July 1991, pp. 3–4.
[31] "Law of the Union of Soviet Socialist Republics on Inventive Activities in the USSR," dated
May 31, 1991 and effective July 1, 1991, World Intellectual Property Report, 1991, vol. 5, 216evv.
[32] W. Dementjev, "Über das letzte Patentgesetz der UdSSR, *GRUR*, no. 3, 1992, p. 169.
[33] E. M. Buryak in: World Intellectual Property Report, no. 5, vol. 5, 1991, p. 208.

tions of the Principles of Civil Legislation of the U.S.S.R. and Union Republics (31 May 1991) concerning copy right and industrial property rights were to come into force in early 1992, but were lost when the U.S.S.R. ceased to exist in December 1991. [34]

In practice, this union law on patents that formally came into force from July 1, 1991, has not been applied on the territory of the former republics. The law foresaw the issuing of patents but did not take measures to make these rights enforceable. Neither the Ministry of Finance nor the courts wanted to consider claims related to the infringements of patent holders' rights. [35] It seems only to have had an impact on Gospatent, that in its turn, ended activity at the end of January 1992.

Good legislation that satisfies modern standards is relatively easy to draft, but almost insuperable difficulties are involved in setting up institutions necessary to implement these laws. The new patent system apparently posed problems of patent information, and of effective organization and execution of the protection in the domestic field. [36]

THE DEBATE ON NATIONAL PATENT SYSTEMS

There was a time when the Soviet patent system was decentralized: in 1936–1955 the Narkomaty were entrusted with filing patents and drawing up documents. This experience, when compared with the centralized systems of 1924–1935 and from 1956 on, did not seem to be very productive.

From 1957 on the patent system became highly centralized, and the central patent institutions worked to the satisfaction of domestic and foreign experts. According to art. 1 of the U.S.S.R. law "on basic economic relations between the union, the union and autonomous republics," a patent service for the whole union would be organized. [37]

However, from 1990 on, steps were undertaken to break up the central agencies at the union level. For example, in a "prikaz" of the president of Goskomizobretenii of 30 July 1990 "On the Temporary Procedure for Filing Patents in Foreign Countries," the authorization procedure of Goskomizobretenii was kept intact, but the authorization of the ministry or department as an higher organ for the patenting economic actor (the enterprise), was omitted. [38] Under the new Union law "On Inventive Activities in the USSR of May 31, 1991" and effective since July 1 1991, the monopoly of Soiuzpatent (on the representation of foreign applicants) was broken and independent patent agents and patent firms could be set up. [39]

---

[34] W. A. Vab Caeneghem and M. Elst, "Russia goes Public with Patent Law," *Patent World*, July-August 1992, p. 2.

[35] V. Rassokhin, *"Information émanant du Comité pour les Brevets et les Marques de la Fédération de Russie," Propriété Industrielle*, no. 520, 15 April 1992, p. 2.

[36] I. V. Bestuzhev-Lada, *"Izobretatel'stvo: Kontury budushchego"* (Inventorship: a Framework for the Future) *Voprosy Izobretatel'stva*, 1–2, 1992, p. 13.

[37] N. V. Lynnik, *"Sostoianie i perspektivy patentnoi sluzhby strany"* (Situation and Perspectives for a Patent Office of the Country), Voprosy Izobretatel'stva, no. 1, 1991 p. 43.

[38] Prikaz of the President of Goskomizobretenii, no. 112; and *Voprosy Izobretatel'stava*, no. 11, 1990.

[39] Y. A. Bespalov, "Industrial Property in the USSR Status Report and Outlook," *Industrial Property*, September 1991, p. 320.

672

The 1991 patent law of the Union added a few new institutions: the State Patent Fund *(Gosudarstvenyi patentnyi fond)*, the Appeal Board, the Patent Court, and an Institute for private patent agents. Also the authority for industrial property matters in the U.S.S.R. was reorganized. The State Committee for Inventions and Discoveries attached to the U.S.S.R. State Committee for Science and Technology was changed into the U.S.S.R. State Patent Agency (Gospatent), which came under the direct supervision of the U.S.S.R. Cabinet of Ministers. For purposes of coordination of industrial property activities of the republics, a council of representatives of each republic was set up in the office.

In the framework of the discussion on two projects of new patent law of the union, Mamiofa pleads for republic patent laws, [40] not only for political reasons, because the tendency toward autonomy was already becoming clear, but also for patent-related reasons. A republic patent law can be relatively simple, with a fast and cheap procedure for the filing of patents. The republic system could, if the legislator so decides, issue patents without a preliminary examination. Such a procedure gives less certainty to the patent holder and his competitors, but those who want to have a secure patent have to file for a union patent. Mamiofa referred to the systems of France, Belgium, Italy, Spain, Portugal, and Greece to show the merits of this system. Industrial producers in a republic would not be hampered by patents that only have their applications in other republics. Competition between legislators would be healthy: republic legislators could improve union legislation and help the furthering of market relations. The filing of patents at the republic level could be done in the language of the republic. At the level of the republic, a republic and a union patent would have the same force on the territory of the republic. The republic law must foresee the resolving of conflicts between the republic legislation. It is true that the states in the United States, the provinces in Canada, the Länder in Germany, and the cantons in Switzerland have no patent laws. But these states either never were sovereign states, or relinquished their sovereignty long ago. But above all, they have no economic reason for enacting a local patent law because the producers of patent-abled products work at the level of the unified market, with local markets only playing a minor role. Industrialists do not need a monopoly at the local market.

But in the U.S.S.R., local markets were being organized at that moment. The problem of legislative levels was foreseeable: the sovereign states claimed their own legislation. The fragmentation of the previously uniform system of protective rights by newly independent republics will entail serious dangers for the producers of economic goods.

In most foreign countries the state has a monopoly on patent protection, which it delegates to a patent administration. Integration processes were activated in recent years. The European patent administration issues one protective document for members of the European Patent Convention. This inspiration was taken up by

---

[40] I. E. Mamiofa, (Boston, USA), *"Patentnyi zakon respubliki, byt' ili ne byt'"* (A Patent Law of the Republics, To Be or Not To Be), *Voprosy Izobretatel'stva*, no. 3, 1991, p. 26.

patent specialists in the former Soviet Union already some time ago. [41] The question is what the CIS attitude should be toward this. Mamiofa explicitly refers to the European Community (EC) example, where each national state has its own national patent law which has proved its usefulness for the furthering of market economic relations within states. But at the "European level" an EC patent law is based on supranational patent legislation. [42]

The ultimate aim of the CIS representatives seems to be to bring the Soviet patent system to the level of West European patent protection as soon as possible.

TOWARD AN INTERSTATE PATENT SYSTEM

As early as the autumn of 1991, representatives of the former republics began to elaborate an interstate patent system that could replace the former patent system of the U.S.S.R. In October 1991 a joint protocol was signed by the authorized representatives of the former republics on their intention to conclude a Convention (*Konventsiia*) on the protection of industrial property. In the meantime, they decided to prepare a provisional agreement on the protection of industrial property, for the term of one year, with a possibility of renewal. [43]

This "pre-collapse" agreement on protection of industrial property did not appear out of nowhere. M. Boguslavskii stresses that eight republics, together with President Gorbachev, signed an Agreement for the Building of an Economic Commonwealth on October, 18 1991, according to which the former republics (except Azerbaidjan, Georgia, Moldova, the Ukraine and the three Baltic republics) promised to coordinate their economic policy in several fields, among which, explicitly, patent affairs. [44]

After the disintegration of the Soviet Union, prompt action was taken in the field of industrial property. In a one-sided declaration, the Minister of Foreign Affairs of the Russian Federation communicated in a letter of December 26, 1991, that the Russian Federation would succeed the U.S.S.R. as a member of the World Intellectual property Organization, in all its bodies, to participate in all international conventions and other legal agreements, signed in the framework of WIPO or under its auspices. [45] Russia was also prepared to take over all rights and obligations of the U.S.S.R. within WIPO, including financial obligations. All persons in charge of representation of the U.S.S.R. at that moment would be author-

---

[41] N. V. Lynnik, *"Antimonopol'naia politika i promyshlennaia Sobstvennost'"* (Antimonopoly Policy and Industrial Property), *Voprosy Izobretatel'stva,* no. 3, 1991, p. 5.

[42] In equatorial Africa (the former French colonies), only a regional patent exists.

[43] *Vremennoe soglashenie ob okhrane promyshlennoi sobstvennosti* (Temporary Agreement on the Protection of Industrial Property), *Voprosy Izobretatel'stva,* no. 1-2, 1992, p. 6.

[44] M. Boguslavskij, "Die Bildung der Gemeinschaft Unabhngiger Staaten (GUS) und der gegenwrtige Stand des gewerblichzen Rechtsschutzes und Urhebersrechts in der ehemaligen Sowetunion," *GRUR,* no. 5, 1992, p. 342.

[45] These conventions include the Paris Convention on Protection of Industrial Property, the Madrid Arrangement on International Registration of Brands, the Nice Arrangement on the International Classification of Products and Services for the Registration of Marks, the Locarno-Arrangement for the International Classification of Industrial Designs and Models, the Patent Cooperation Treaty, the Strasbourg Arrangement on the International Classification of Patents, the Treaty on the Registration of Brands, the Convention on the Distribution of programme-carrying signals, transmitted by satellite, the Budapest Treaty concerning the Deposit of Microorganisms, the Nairobi Treaty concerning the Protection of Olympic Symbols. Notification of this letter has been made to all these treaties, La Propriété Industrielle, February 1992, p. 52.

ized to represent the Russian Federation in the WIPO-agencies. This is another manifestation of Russia's determination to consider itself the legal successor to the Soviet Union.

Simultaneously, however, a Preliminary Agreement of Minsk was signed during a meeting of December 25–27 in Minsk by Armenia, Belarus, Moldova, the Russian Federation, Tadjikistan, and Ukraine. [46] This preliminary agreement is a temporary measure, until the Convention comes into force. The preliminary agreement is an intergovernmental agreement in the sense of art. 19 of the Paris Convention for protection of industrial property of 1883: it underlines the autonomy of the states in the formation and execution of their own policies in the field of industrial property. But at the same time the co-signers recognize long-term interests in economic and scientific mutual collaboration. They want to eliminate barriers to the development of entrepreneurship, to free movement of goods, services, and technology.

Parties to the Minsk Agreement took the obligation to fulfill the international duties of the U.S.S.R. on this territory in the field of protection of industrial property (art. 18). Some authors raised a certain doubt about the willingness of independent states, other than Russia, to assume all obligations under the Paris Convention and other international agreements. [47] But the Minsk Agreement does not hinder the independent states to participate autonomously in international agreements. [48] As members of the United Nations, for example, the former republics can seek membership individually to the WIPO-agreement, as well as to the Paris, Bern, and other international collaboration agreements. [49]

The agreement provides for an interstate system of patent filing and protection. The interstate protective document will be the patent (for inventions and industrial models) or the certificate (for trade and service marks). Such documents have a binding force for the whole territory of the state-members, but each state can enact its national protective documents. After a long discussion it was decided that author's certificates on inventions and industrial models will not be exchanged for interstate patents. One impediment to the exchange of author's certificates into interstate patents is the difficult legal situation, related to the division of all-union property. Enterprises that had declared inventions, or in which inventions were integrated on the basis of the inventor's certificates, are now situated on the territory of different states. The "transformation problem" will be resolved in a definitive manner when a convention on interstate patent collaboration is concluded. In this perspective Rospatent will not admit the transformation of certificates of invention against patents if the demand is deposed after December 27, 1991 (the Minsk Agreement). [50]

It is not clear, however, whether the agreement will lead to one universal patent system for the CIS or preservation of a system of

---

[46] Kazakhstan did not sign, but only initialed this agreement. For a translation into German see *GRUR*, no. 5, 1992, p. 382.
[47] P. H. Kort, "Intellectual Property in the Ukraine," *Patent World*, July-August 1992, p. 12.
[48] M. Boguslavskij, op. cit., note 44, p. 346.
[49] Art. 5 of the WIPO-agreement allows members of the United Nations to become members of the World Intellectual Property Organization.
[50] Rassokhin, see note 26, 53.

industrial protective rights going beyond the borders of the independent states.

The Minsk agreement provides provisional protection among member republics until a more permanent system is established. [51] The "Common Patent Territory" does not have to coincide with the CIS territory. The agreement is self-sufficient and autonomously defines the rights and duties of member states. The normative bases on which this temporary agreement will work are the U.S.S.R. laws on inventions, industrial models, and trademarks and service marks. It is most significant (1) that the legislation of the former Soviet Union, which was previously applicable, continues to be established law after this agreement has come into force and until new national legislation is enacted; (2) that protective rights already granted in application of Soviet legislation will be recognized in all member states on their territory (i.e. to recognize the validity on their territory of existing patents) and (3) that it will be possible to file applications for protective rights that are valid in these republics. The continuity is to be preserved by guaranteeing the further existence of the Patent Office, at first through the Russian Federation and by recognizing Russian as an official language. Those who filed patents before Gospatent for the protection of their invention, trademarks or service marks, or models can wait until the provisional agreement comes into force, and until an interstate patent office is set up and a procedure for the delivery of interstate protection titles has been introduced, without losing priority rights. [52]

The aim of the agreement is to provide a supranational institutional framework for the protection of industrial property until a final agreement on the territory has been reached: the provision of an Interstate Organization for the Protection of Industrial Property (*Mezhgosudarstvennaia organizatsiia po okhrane promyshlennoi sobstvennosti* (MOOPS), composed of an administrative council, a patent department, and a patent court. This organization is yet to be established. It will be involved in examination of claims, computerization of data banks, research on the protection of industrial property rights and training specialists. The European Patent Organization is mentioned as being "analogical" to this organization. However, the financial and budgetary affairs are regulated differently (art. 15). In the case of the European Organization, duties are paid directly to the European organization; the CIS organization will be financed by payments of the state-partners. The taxes for the patent claims and the maintenance of patents will be collected by the state-members. The payment to the organization will depend on the number of claims, coming from each independent state. Special financial contributions can be asked for the financing of project programs, for example computerization. The contribution of each state will be decided on by the administrative council.

---

[51] The Minsk Agreement of December 8, 1991, on the Establishment of the CIS provided that no legal rules of other states, including the former U.S.S.R., may be applied in the signatory states. However, the ratification by Russia of the Minsk Agreement stated that until new legislation was passed by the Supreme Soviet of the Russian Federation, old U.S.S.R. legislation concerning subject areas for which no Russian (as opposed to Soviet) legislation yet existed would remain in force in the Russian Federation itself: Van Caeneghem and Elst, see note 25, 2.

[52] Rassokhin, ibid., p. 54.

The administrative council is composed of representatives from all participant states and is the collegial leadership of the organization: it coordinates joint activity in the field of legal protection of industrial property and control of the activity of the patent department. The administrative council chooses a president and vice president from its members. It meets not less than once in six months. Extraordinary meetings are possible at the initiative of the president or at least three state members. The patent department receives and studies filed patents for inventions, industrial models, and marks of goods and services, organizes examination; enacts interstate protective documents; organizes the education of specialists in the field of protection of industrial property; attests and registers authorized agents and organizes scientific research. The interstate Patent Court will judge conflicts on the handing over and working of interstate protective documents. Its statute (*polozhenie*) will be worked out by the administrative council.

There is also the transitory problem of property. Gospatent was based on all-union property. Because the property base is not clear, the Russian Federation will for the time being provide the material-technical base for the activity of the organization (art. 2, in fine). In practice this means that the organization can use data bases and technical services of the former VNIIGPE (*Vsesoiuznyi nauchno-issledovatel'skii Institut gosudarstvennoi patentnoi ekspertizy*).

Once the preliminary Agreement of Minsk has been ratified by at least three of the independent states, it will come into force (art. 17). These adherents will have to fulfill certain requirements: (1) to recognize on their territory the normative basis of the agreement, in this case the former U.S.S.R.-legislation; (2) to recognize on their territory the protective documents of the U.S.S.R. on objects of industrial property, handed over before the U.S.S.R. disintegrated; (3) to nominate their representative and his deputy to the Administrative Council of the Organization. This would decisively stimulate the willingness of other countries to cooperate in technical and economic fields, and it would certainly meet with the approval of the international community: "It would be according the dictates of economic reason that the other republics too, make use of the possibility to join the preliminary agreement and to contribute to organising the new forms of intellectual property protection." [53]

In the international field the state member co-signers recognize the legal succession of Russia, related to international obligations of the U.S.S.R. in the field of industrial property. At the same time, however, the state members have the right to participate autonomously in international organizations and to organize international cooperation in the field of industrial property. The agreement (*soglashenie*) is open to adherence by all states on the territory of which protective documents existed according to the U.S.S.R. laws on intellectual property (art. 16). The agreement relates to inventions, industrial models, and trademarks and service marks as objects of industrial property. But the state members can also introduce "in a coordinated manner (*v soglasovannom poriadke*) the pro-

---

[53] E. Haeusser, "Industrial Property Protection in the Commonwealth of Independent States," World Intellectual Property Report, vol. 6, 1992, p. 103.

tection of appellations of origin, firm names, manufacturing secrets, semiconductors, useful models" (art. 14).

The Agreement of Minsk foresees a two-level protection: the interstate and the national (individual state) level.

The division of rights between the center and the states, however, has not yet clearly been defined: the patent administration has the right to delegate rights to the related organs of the state members. The relations between the patent department and the authorized organ in the independent states are defined by agreement: the authorized organ of the state-partners can organize their own expertise, beforehand and in the way they wish it.

Legal and economic relations related to the application of the patent in each of the state members is regulated in accordance with the legislation of the state members, on the territory of which these relations originated (art. 3). This will obviously create a problem of conflict of laws. The problem of secret inventions will be considered in the framework of national legislations of the independent states.

The Situation in the Former Republics

None of the former republics, not even the Russian Federation, possessed their own laws on the protection of industrial property. Nor did they have their own departments for the protection of industrial property. This made the end of Soviet statehood and the collapse of union structures such as Gospatent even more painful. [54]

Article 5 of the Preliminary Agreement of Minsk clearly confirms that in the individual member states, common protective documents can co-exist with national patents.

The establishment of independent national systems and the performance by national patent offices may appear legitimate but, as foreign experts would be the first to say: "The dictates of reason must be to safeguard the common interests shared by all republics in the granting and administration of intellectual property rights, turning to good use appropriate institutions which still exist and have stood the test of time." [55]

Although the trend among the various republics has been to establish their own intellectual property laws and offices (national patent offices have been created in Russia, Belarus and Ukraine), the best solution would be an interstate intellectual property system, with an interstate patent office.

To assume that foreigners will file a significant number of applications for protective rights in the smaller and less developed republics seems to be an unrealistic approach. It would be difficult to find foreign investors willing to appoint a national representative and to file a translation in the respective national languages of 15 independent states. They would only invest in applications for protective rights where sufficient chances are discernible and in particular where serious domestic competition is found. Furthermore,

---

[54] Gospatent: U.S.S.R. State Committee for Inventions and Discoveries, later U.S.S.R. State Patent Office). Gospatent discontinued its activities by January 1992, yet this well organized authority is carrying on its work as the Russian Patent Office (Rospatent).

[55] E. Haeusser, p. 102.

the institutional requirements are enormous. It does not suffice to entrust a state agency with the task of operating a patent office; also needed are representation structures (patent experts in enterprises, patent agents, attorneys-at-law) and establishment of expert courts (including boards of arbitration indispensable to enforcing these rights. A modern patent office also needs the necessary document holdings and the necessary experts in both technological and scientific disciplines. These prerequisites seem to be met only by some independent states, particularly the Russian Federation and perhaps the Ukraine. [56]

In January 1992 the Latvian Council of Ministers adopted a resolution providing for the protection of intellectual property on Latvian territory. It is now possible to file patent and design applications. This resolution only serves for securing priority. There is no examination or patent grant, and there is no final patent law. First filings and filings of priority applications in English or Russian have to be translated into Latvian within two months of filing of the patent application. This makes the system expensive: "The cost of translating chemical applications of 300 pages in Latvian for this tiny market will discourage many applicants, especially as this protection will apply only to Latvia and not to the other Baltic states. However, there are serious problems of transition: "Owners of trade marks will have to reregister their marks in Latvia by December 31, 1992. Famous marks that are not reregistered by that time could face the possibility of being registered by local agents and 'sold back' to their real proprietors." [57]

THE SPECIAL ROLE OF RUSSIA

Because of the size of its territory, population, and industrial diversity, Russia has a special place in the field of industrial property. The lion's share of CIS-inventions is done in the Russian Federation.

The recent amendments to the Russian Constitution underline that intellectual property is protected by law (art. 60). The legal regulation of intellectual property is a joint competence of the federation and the republics. Practice will show how this provision is to conciliate with the regulation that the federal organs enact in this matter Principles of Legislation, in the framework of which the organs of the republics can enact their own regulations (chap. 8, art. 81, 1). [58]

Four separate intellectual property bills were moving toward enactment in Russia in March 1992. These laws are aimed at substituting four earlier laws of the former U.S.S.R. [59]

---

[56] E. Haeusser, (President of the German Patent Office) "Industrial Property Protection in the Commonwealth of Independent States," World Intellectual Property Report, vol. 6 , 103.

[57] Only those former Soviet patents or patent applications filed prior to 1992 may be extended to Latvia upon request, thus leaving out applications with Gospatent in January, prior to its January 31 closing see A. Von Funer, "Latvia, Council of Ministers adopts intellectual Property Rules, World Intellectual Property Report, vol. 6, 1992, p. 97.

[58] *Vedomosti S'ezda Narodnykh Deputatov Rossiiskoi Federatsii i Verkhovnogo Soveta Rossiiskoi Federatsii*, no. 20, 1992, p. 1084.

[59] The draft patent law was subject to a second reading and further revision in mid-March. In addition, legislation to protect trade and servicemarks, integrated circuits, computer programs, data bases and appellations of origin was also pending. These three bills also passed their first reading in February. But they too were still subject to revision. See World Intellectual Property Report, vol. 6, 1992, p. 97.

The Russian bill on patents was drafted and introduced in the Russian Supreme Soviet before the August events in Moscow, which have accelerated the disintegration of the U.S.S.R. The bill provided that its rules were not applicable to industrial property protected by U.S.S.R. patents and U.S.S.R. laws were in force on the Russian Federation territory. The R.S.F.S.R. patent was deemed an alternative to the U.S.S.R. patent. [60]

The new patent law of the Russian Federation was finally accepted by the Supreme Soviet on June 18, 1992. This new law, which not only covers patents for inventions, but also utility models (petty patents) and industrial designs, is set to replace the old U.S.S.R. law on inventions, which came into force on May 1991. [61]

In accordance with the Provisional Agreement, the Russian Federation, as the other parties thereto, recognizes the validity on the territory of the Russian federation of the protection, issued earlier on the basis of U.S.S.R. legislation. [62] The development of Russian (and other national) laws on industrial property protection and the work on creating interstate legislation in the field, which will be applied by the former republics of the Soviet Union, are continuing in parallel. It is not yet clear what exactly the relation will be between the soon-to-be established body of Russian law and the Minsk agreement, signed by six former Soviet republics in December.

The edict of the President of the Russian Federation of January 24, 1992, no. 50 created a committee on patents and trademarks of the Ministry of Sciences, Higher Education and Technical Policy of the Russian Federation (Rospatent), the successor of Gospatent. [63] Until the conclusion of the Provisional Agreement Rospatent will, on a temporary basis, receive claims and fulfill some international functions necessary for the protection of foreign claimants' industrial property on the territory of the state members. It appears logical to ask the state that is closest to solving the problem of protection of industrial property (elaboration of a national protection system, specialists and specialized literature are in Moscow) to create a patent department and to take the lead. Afterward, the interstate organization for the protection of industrial property could take over this function of study of claims. A Russian Patent Department will temporarily look after the patent system of the CIS until the creation of an interstate Organization for the Protection of Industrial Property is created. [64]

---

[60] EIPR, 1992, p. D-9.

[61] It will be possible to obtain a patent for an industrial design as well as for an invention or an utility model. This is perhaps unusual in Western legislation, but it is quite understandable in the Soviet tradition: the Statute on Industrial Designs of 8 June 1981 already provided a system of patent protection as well as author's certificates. See Van Caeneghem and Elst, note 25, 2.

[62] On the basis of their applications with Gospatent, applicants who consider it inexpedient to wait until the procedure of interstate patents of the CIS becomes effective will be given titles of protection, valid on the territory of the Russian Federation, after the Russian Laws come into force. In such a case, a Russian patent will be issued, only after the applicant sends a letter of consent to such transformation, and pays the prescribed fee. See World Intellectual Property Report, vol.6, 1992, p. 97.

[63] Chairman of Rospatent is Vitalii Petrovich Rassokhin, a former member of the Institute of State and Law at the Academy of Sciences who also worked at VNIIGPE.

[64] V. P. Rassokhin, V. V. Belov, E. I. Pekin, M. M. Tsimbalov, "Pervyi shag k edinoi patentnoi sisteme sodruzhestva" (The first step in the direction of a unified patent system of the Commonwealth), Vorposy Izobretatel'stva, 1–2, 1992, p. 2.

Conclusion

A reliable legal machinery for the protection of industrial property rights is a precondition for the development of a market for scientific and technological achievements. The former Soviet state has drastically changed its function in this field and the CIS has adopted to a commodity approach toward intellectual property. It is now up to economic agents to capture market shares and to protect them by means of healthy competition. One cannot imagine that the Minsk Agreement of December 27 will not come into force and that no CIS-wide patent structure is established. In Russia, Ukraine and Belarus preparations for ratification are ongoing. The national protective systems will need interstate collaboration and institutions. Meanwhile, it is important for potential and actual patentees that there should be continuity and certainty. The Russian Federation is the only candidate to guarantee that continuity. For that purpose, it can use the old buildings and the qualified personnel. Once an inter-state patent cooperation has been set up, (part of) these offices and personnel can be handed over to that interstate structure. Will Gospatent then take on a new shape?

IV. DEFENSE AND CONVERSION

OVERVIEW

By Richard F Kaufman *

Among the more serious problems inherited by Russia and the other successor states are those surrounding the defense sector. This section contains papers on the possible emergence of a new military doctrine in Russia, defense downsizing and dissolution, and the conversion of defense industries from military to civilian production. Because of the heavy influence defense exerts on the economies of the successor states, some experts believe that the pace, if not the success, of the transformation process will be determined by developments in this sector.

MILITARY DOCTRINE

Military doctrine, properly interpreted, can shed light on a nation's strategic intentions and its material capabilities. It embodies, among other things, the principles that guide peacetime preparations for military contingencies, and judgments about the types of wars to prepare for and the conditions under which they may occur. An understanding of Soviet military doctrine was important for the reason that the Soviets placed great weight on doctrine and theoretical justification for actions in the military sphere. Presumably, the Russians, and perhaps others in the former Soviet Union, hold similar views.

Mary C. Fitzgerald traces the origins of Russia's new military doctrine. She reasons that it is based on a logical elaboration of Soviet views about the significance of advanced technologies and current views about the nature and requirements of future war. In the 1980s Soviet military theorists understood that the U.S.S.R. was lagging behind the West in the qualitative arms race. They argued that the United States was developing a new type of warfare characterized by massive use of advance technologies such as long-range cruise missiles, Stealth technology, and directed energy weapons. The objectives of future wars would be achieved through destruction of the opponents' military capabilities and infrastructure, rather than by seizing and occupying territory. From the Soviet perspective, the United Nations coalition won the Persian Gulf War by employing the new concepts while Iraq fought with

* Richard F Kaufman is General Counsel of the Joint Economic Committee, United States Congress.

(681)

the older ones. The Gulf War was the prototype of "technological war."

Russian military theorists carry the analysis several steps further. They believe Iraq lost because it fought with Soviet doctrine and Soviet weapons. According to one Russian source, the war ended the era of massive ground forces and began the era of high-tech warfare comprised of remote battles and electronic fire operations. Military leaders now agree that large armored forces have become obsolete. The Armed Forces must be smaller, more professional, more mobile, and equipped with cutting-edge technologies. This increases the importance of research and development.

The new doctrine, Fitzgerald concludes, reflects the end of Gorbachev's defensive doctrine and a shift to large-scale offensive operations. It also implies that strikes with conventional weapons against Russia's strategic targets may elicit a nuclear response. If the latter implication is, indeed, part of the new doctrine, it represents a change from the Soviet doctrine of no first-use of nuclear weapons.

DEFENSE DOWNSIZING

Richard F Kaufman examines the decline in defense spending from Gorbachev to Yeltsin and the consequences of it, the political breakup, and the economic difficulties for the Russian military. Although the rate of growth of defense expenditures had been slowing for a number of years, the downsizing of the military began with Mikhail Gorbachev's 1988 announcement of prospective cutbacks and redeployments from the Warsaw Pact area and the Far East. Driven by the need to reduce the military burden on the economy, defense expenditures were reduced by an estimated 6 percent in each of the years 1989 and 1990. There was a greater contraction in 1991 when defense declined by an estimated 15 percent. Although there is much uncertainty surrounding the figures, due to the incompleteness of official reporting and inflation, there were many indications of more dramatic cutbacks in 1992.

Reductions have been across-the-board, affecting conventional and strategic forces. The cuts in the procurement of arms and equipment and in R&D have been deeper than the overall rate. Manpower has been greatly reduced since 1988. The breakup of the Soviet Union complicated the problem of financing the military program as the independent republics have withheld or sharply reduced contributions to Moscow for the forces of the Commonwealth of Independent States. Arms spending by the republics has been primarily to maintain their own military forces. Kaufman goes on to discuss the issues of arms exports, collective security within the Commonwealth of Independent States (CIS), attempts at peacekeeping by Russian forces, and the problems of conflict within and among the former Soviet republics.

The arms industries have suffered perhaps the most serious domestic consequences of the defense cuts. The remaining papers address the post-Soviet industrial sector and varying aspects of the efforts to convert defense plants and other defense resources to civilian uses.

Donald Creacey describes the defense industries of the newly independent states. The defense industrial base of the former Soviet Union contained 3,000 to 5,000 production facilities and a work force of 7 million to 10 million people. About 70 percent of the defense industry enterprises were located in Russia, where all major categories of equipment were produced. About 74 percent of military research, development, and test facilities were also located in Russia. The second largest portion of the industrial base was in Ukraine, which, among other facilities, has the only shipyard capable of producing aircraft carriers, and the major base facilities for the Black Sea Fleet. The other states have smaller but significant shares of the industrial base, as well as important test facilities. The author also explains the interdependency of military production under the Soviet regime and the current situation.

DEFENSE INDUSTRY CONVERSION

Martin C. Spechler reviews the origins of conversion strategy and the results to date in Russia and Ukraine. In the 1970s and early 1980s the defense industries produced a substantial amount of consumer goods. Conversion was conceived under Gorbachev as a way to expand civilian production without permanent loss of the capacity to produce military goods or involuntary unemployment. The early results of this strategy of direct, controlled diversification were disappointing. There was some expansion of civilian production but little improvement in industrial efficiency or competitiveness.

Yeltsin has moved tentatively toward a market-based conversion strategy. He supports separation of military and civilian production and the closing of some military plants. Some officials favor privatization of unneeded enterprises. But there is opposition within the Russian government to this approach to reform and the future direction of change is still in doubt.

There has been less progress toward market-based reform generally in Ukraine. The conversion program still follows the state-planned approach initiated by Gorbachev, although President Kravchuk supports selling military enterprises for hard currency. Spechler comments on appropriate U.S. policies toward former Soviet military enterprises in light of Western experience with defense conversion and recent developments in Russia and Ukraine. Among his recommendations is the observation that, unless a market-based conversion strategy is put into effect, the West should allow Russian and Ukrainian military capacity to atrophy.

Steven W. Popper views defense conversion in both the narrow sense of what to do about arms factories now in excess of defense needs and in the broader context of the transformations of economic institutions taking place throughout the former Soviet Union. He discusses how important it is that the approach used to convert defense industries not run counter to the strategies intended to bring about the transition to an economic system based on market principles.

Industrial managers are interested in preserving the existing enterprise structures. They prefer plant-by-plant conversion by which factories are retooled or provided with parallel lines for the shifting of production resources from military to civilian goods. The localities and regions where defense production facilities are located share this preference. But these interests may conflict with the economy-wide goals that might require shutting down enterprises and reallocating the assets for other uses. Popper maintains that Western business interests can help reconcile the divergence in conversion objectives through foreign direct investment and related activities.

Two papers discuss problems related to the management of defense conversion. John Thomas argues that Russia's economic progress and its political development will be heavily influenced by the outcome of the struggle between the competing approaches to conversion. On the one hand, reformers advocate placing defense production and research and development facilities under civilian management and control, further scaling down of arms production capabilities, and privatization of facilities in excess of military needs. On the other hand, the groups that comprised the Soviet military industrial complex want to retain control of R&D and production facilities and to extend their activities into consumer areas by way of diversification rather than actual conversion.

Thomas finds that the Yeltsin government has not been able to remove the defense managers and associated bureaucrats in the Russian government. The defense managers have enlarged their influence in the government and joined others to form a new political party. In alliance with the military and the ultra-nationalists, they continue to oppose economic and political reform.

In the second paper on conversion management Shelley Deutch and Nicholas Forte focus on the challenges facing plant managers who want to convert to civil production in the budding market economy. Some problems are beyond the control of the managers. They must adapt to market conditions while lacking many of the tools required for successful market operations such as legal protection of private property, a well developed financial system, a wholesale industry and a retail distribution network, and currency convertibility.

Other difficulties demand changes in behavior and thinking. Plant managers will have to acquire new managerial skills and a new orientation to productivity, quality and cost controls, and marketing requirements. Excess capacity and nonproductive assets will have to be curtailed or eliminated. The walls of secrecy that existed for defense production will have to be dismantled. Information technologies and the techniques for attracting foreign investment will have to be mastered. Factories must become environmentally sound. An efficient work force must be created and managers will need to learn a new design philosophy and understand the requirements for capital investment and modernization.

The paper by Ronald L. Davis provides a useful basis for comparing defense conversion in the former Soviet Union and China. Beijing has been following a state-directed defense conversion program since the late 1970s. The objective has been to integrate the defense industry into the civilian economy. The strategy is one of diversification. Consumer production is enlarged or introduced in defense factories, while military capacity is retained. The central government, and in some cases the military, retains control over production enterprises which continue to receive resources and financing on a priority basis.

Some defense plants have had difficulty in meeting conversion objectives, especially those in remote locations with poor access to transportation and foreign capital. The government's response has been to continue financial support, and to encourage foreign arms sales, in order to maintain employment. But many enterprises have been successful. They produce a wide variety of capital equipment and consumer goods for domestic use and export. Civilian goods now comprise about 70 percent of the defense industry's total production.

Davis points to several factors that differentiate China's situation from the former Soviet Union's. For example, China's defense industry never assumed the relative size or dominance over the economy as was the case in the Soviet Union. Second, Beijing put into place programs, such as a network of high-technology zones, intended to promote commercialization of research in the defense industry. Third, the government has adopted measures that have enabled enterprises to import foreign technology and attract foreign capital. The political stability in China since conversion has also contributed to the successes of the conversion program.

Another factor that could be mentioned is the rapid economic growth that has taken place in China over the past decade, in contrast to the stagnation and deterioration in the former Soviet Union. The adjustments required by restructuring are obviously facilitated by economic expansion.

RUSSIAN MILITARY DOCTRINE: PROGRAM FOR THE 1990s AND BEYOND

by Mary C. FitzGerald *

CONTENTS

SUMMARY

In May 1992, a draft of Russia's new military doctrine was published in *Military Thought*, the main theoretical journal of the Russian Armed Forces. Despite much discussion about the ascendance of civilians, the military has reasserted its dominance over the development of this doctrine.

The essence of the new doctrine lies in current Russian views on the nature and requirements of future war. An examination of Russian military writings reveals both the visionary nature of these views and their unbroken continuity with Soviet military art. As in the Soviet period, the new political leadership has not sought to impede the development of those technologies perceived to be at the heart of future military capabilities: advanced conventional munitions (ACMs), directed-energy weapons, and space-based systems.

This paper will analyze the military-technical aspects of Russia's new military doctrine by documenting Russian views on the technologies, operational concepts, and R&D requirements for future war. Because Russian doctrine constitutes a logical elaboration of Soviet views, the paper will first trace its roots in the Soviet period. For both periods, Operation "Desert Storm" serves as the paradigm of future war in strategy, operational art, and tactics.

THE MILITARY-TECHNICAL "REVOLUTION"

In the early 1980s, Marshal Ogarkov and others began to stress that the emergence of advanced non-nuclear technologies was en-

---

* Mary C. FitzGerald is a Research Fellow at the Hudson Institute.

gendering a new "revolution" in military affairs. [1] Ogarkov thus argued that, in the matter of modernizing military theory and practice, "stagnation and a delayed 'perestroika' of views . . . are fraught with the most severe consequences." [2] Throughout the 1970s and 1980s, he lobbied persistently for a timely incorporation of the new non-nuclear technologies into Soviet military art and force structure, contending that the principal weapons systems are now being replaced every 10–12 years. [3] A review of Soviet writings since 1977 moreover reveals no evidence of a dispute between Ogarkov and the rest of the military leadership on this issue.

During the 1980s, Soviet military theorists focused on technologies associated with automated decision-support systems, microelectronics, telecommunications, lasers, and enhanced munitions lethality. In general, these technologies include "high-precision weapons" (advanced conventional munitions) and "weapons based on new physical principles." More specifically, Soviet officials focused on the combat potential of: 1) kinetic energy weapons (e.g., magnetic rail guns and hypervelocity projectiles); 2) particle-beam weapons; 3) laser weapons; 4) electromagnetic pulse (microwave) weapons; and 5) third-generation nuclear weapons, which include separate weapon systems as well as means for supplying power to other systems (e.g., the nuclear-pumped x-ray laser).

Soviet theorists were more visionary than those in the West when assessing the potential application of these technologies to military science. They argued that under current conditions, wherein the interval between new generations of weapons systems is sharply reduced, military art must be based not only on existing military technology, but especially on a "forecasting" of its possible development. [4] While these theorists rarely described a specific time horizon for implementing the new revolution, they were convinced that a future war *will* be waged in a high-tech environment. The basic scientific research had been completed, and the mass deployment of these systems was viewed as an eventuality.

Owing to these technological trends, the Soviet military stressed the elevation of "quality" over "quantity" in future military development. Military scientists argued that while the arms race was formerly "qualitative-quantitative," today it is a rivalry in "the qualitative improvement of military-technical systems and the creation of weapons with fundamentally new physical, chemical, biological, and geographic qualities." [5] If success used to mean equipping troops with weapons, it now means the tempo of developing new design concepts and prototypes. Soviet military economists thus described the current military-technological competition as follows:

---

[1] MSU N.V. Ogarkov, *Vsegda v gotovnosti k zashchite Otechestva* (Moscow: Voenizdat, 1982), p. 31.; MSU N.V. Ogarkov, *Istoriya uchit bditel'nosti* (Moscow: Voenizdat, 1985), p.41; Colonel-General M.A. Gareyev, "The Creative Nature of Soviet Military Science in the Great Patriotic War," *Voenno-istoricheskiy zhurnal* (hereafter cited as *VIZh*) 7 (1985): 29.

[2] Ogarkov, *Istoriya*, p. 47.

[3] Mary C. FitzGerald, "Marshal Ogarkov on the Modern Theater Operation," *Naval War College Review* 4 (Autumn 1986): 8.

[4] General-Lieutenant Ye. D. Grebish, "On the Dialectical Interconnections in the Development of Military Affairs," *Voennaya mysl'* (hereafter cited as *VM*) 1 (1988): 63.

[5] N.A. Chaldymov, et al., (eds.), *Novoe myshlenie i voennaya politika* (Moscow: Filosofskoe Obshchestvo, 1989).

In contemporary conditions, as a result of the military-technical revolution, advantage in the area of technical equipping of the armed forces accrues not only to the side that has a larger store of military materiel, but first of all to the side that is the leader in the development and introduction into the forces of qualitatively new systems. [6]

The Soviet military further believed that conventional weaponry will be the chief beneficiary of contemporary technological advancements. As Colonel Bondarenko wrote in 1986:

If, in the recent past, strategic nuclear-missile weapons were the main area in which the newest scientific ideas were used, then at the present time these ideas are being actively used in the development and creation of conventional types of armament, increasing to a significant degree the combat effectiveness, reliability, and other characteristics of these weapons. [7]

Another recurrent theme associated with the military-technical "revolution" was the Soviet charge that the United States and NATO seek to deprive the Soviet Union of its superpower status with the so-called "competitive strategy." Such luminaries as then Defense Minister Yazov and then Chief of the General Staff Moiseyev thus warned that the West was striving to exhaust the Soviets economically with a qualitative arms race in emerging technologies. [8] According to military scientists, the West was developing over 150 types of new military technologies (not counting radioelectronic means), 80 percent of which will have entered the inventory by the year 2000. [9] Western military planners, they charged, believe that microelectronics and computer technology are becoming the key factors in the qualitative development of weaponry, and hence in the achievement of decisive superiority over the Soviet Union. [10] The United States plans to achieve such superiority with "non-nuclear strategic (global)" weapon systems. Superiority in airborne systems, for example, will be achieved by increasing the combat potential of strike aircraft, remotely piloted vehicles, and long-range, conventionally armed, "high-precision" missiles. [11]

Finally, the Soviet military argued that the military-technical revolution is occurring in the most developed countries, and that the technologies involved are universal rather than country-specific. According to a 1991 article by Colonel Yu. Alekseyev, military-technological modernization—just like scientific thought itself—cannot be stopped. [12] Moiseyev and others thus stressed that mili-

[6] Colonel S. Bartenev, *Ekonomicheskoe protivoborstvo v voine* (Moscow: Voenizdat, 1986), p. 122.
[7] Colonel V. Bondarenko, "Scientific-Technical Progress and Military Affairs," *Kommunist vooruzhennykh sil* (hereafter cited as *KVS*) 21 (1986): 14.
[8] For example, see General of the Army M. Moiseyev, "Soviet Military Doctrine: Realization of Its Defensive Thrust," *Pravda* (hereafter cited as *PR*), 13 March 1989.
[9] Colonel Ya. V. Safonov and Lt. Colonel S.K. Kolpakov, "Military-Technical Policy in the Pentagon's Plans," *VM* 6 (1989): 79–80.
[10] General-Lieutenant I. Bobrov, "The U.S. Military-Political Course and Direction of Development of the Armed Forces," *Zarubezhnoe voennoe obozrenie* (hereafter cited as *ZVO*) 12 (1989).
[11] Ibid.
[12] Colonel Yu. Alekseyev, "Air-Launched Cruise Missiles: The Search for Options Goes On," *Krasnaya zvezda* (hereafter cited as *KZ*), 8 January 1991.

tary science must be focused on solving problems of the *long-term* future. [13]

THE SOVIET IMAGE OF FUTURE WAR

It is important to note that long before "Desert Storm," the Soviet military had already developed a comprehensive and revolutionary vision of future war. With the development of the Air-Land Battle/FOFA concepts that incorporated the combat deployment of advanced conventional munitions (ACMs), Moscow perceived that the West was gaining an edge in the qualitative arms race. In late 1990, *Military Thought* explained that the "Air-Land Battle/Future" concept is based on: 1) highly effective ground-, air-, and space-based reconnaissance, surveillance, and target acquisition systems; 2) powerful fire with great precision, range, and destructiveness; and 3) automated C³ (Command, Control, and Communications) systems that ensure the delivery of strikes in real time. Especially on maritime axes, the concept is said to be closely entwined with the Maritime Strategy. [14] A special role is assigned to naval operations in sea and ocean TVDs, which will be conducted according to the concept of the "Air-Naval Operation." Soviet theorists stressed that since 1987, the United States has been developing the unified concept of an "Air-Land-Naval Operation." [15] Since a future war was expected to be global, the Soviets argued that control of space will be decisive for operations aimed at controlling large sections of the earth.

Space-based reconnaissance, surveillance, and target acquisition systems linked in real time to long-range strike means would make the Soviet vision of global, non-nuclear war a reality. These so-called "reconnaissance-strike complexes" were thus viewed as the nucleus of warfare in the twenty-first century. [16]

Prominent Soviet military scientists argued that the ongoing development of nuclear and non-nuclear strategic offensive forces provides a basis for predicting a near-term shift toward the waging of an "essentially new type of war—the aero-space war." [17] Such a war is characterized by a massive employment of cutting-edge technologies: ballistic missiles with maneuvering warheads, long-range cruise missiles, advanced conventional munitions, reconnaissance-strike complexes, orbital aircraft, wide-scale application of Stealth technology, directed-energy weapons, space-based strike weapons, and third-generation nuclear weapons. According to General-Major Slipchenko, head of the Scientific Research Department of the General Staff Academy, by the year 2000 the space-based layer alone will be capable of destroying 30–50 percent of the opponent's retaliatory strike means. [18]

---

[13] Colonel-General M.A. Moiseyev, "From Positions of a Defensive Doctrine," *KZ*, 10 February 1989.

[14] Colonel A.A. Zhuravlev, "On the Air-Land Operation," *VM* 6 (1990): 79.

[15] Yur'yev, "U.S. Military Doctrine."

[16] Colonel V.V. Krysanov, "On Certain Trends in the Development of Ground Forces," *VM* 10 (1990): 23–30.

[17] General-Major V.G. Slipchenko, "Impending Changes from Reform Plans for Employing the Soviet Armed Forces," Presentation at National Defense University, Washington, D.C., 15 and 20 March, 1991.

[18] Ibid.

Proceeding from such analyses, Soviet military scientists envisioned a future war whose politico-military objectives are achieved not by seizing and occupying territory, but by destroying the opponent's military capabilities and military infrastructure. According to these experts, the three criteria for achieving victory are 1) destruction of the opponent's armed forces, 2) destruction of the opponent's military-economic potential, and 3) overthrow of the opponent's political system. In the past, achieving these objectives was said to be impossible without capturing and occupying the opponent's territory. Today, however, the capture and occupation of territory are unnecessary. With the help of ACMs alone, it is possible to deliver powerful strikes against important strategic targets and to destroy the opponent's military infrastructure. As a result, the political system will not survive. [19]

According to the Soviets, past warfare had two dimensions—the longitudinal and latitudinal. But air- and space-based systems are now giving war a new, third dimension. The Soviets asserted that while they lack sufficient quantities, they have already developed the technologies required to wage such a war: air- and sea-launched cruise missiles, remotely piloted vehicles, and space-based means of supporting ground actions. They predicted that by the year 2000, both sides will have accumulated these systems in sufficient numbers to conduct the aero-space war. During the ongoing transition period, warfare will resemble that conducted in the Persian Gulf, with a declining role for piloted aircraft and a growing role for air-, sea-, and space-based directed-energy weapons. [20]

SOVIET VIEWS ON DESERT STORM

According to the Soviets, the operations in the Persian Gulf represent the first concrete example of "intellectualized" warfare. General-Major Slipchenko explained that the Persian Gulf War was a clash between two concepts of war: the past (Iraq) and the future (the U.S.-led coalition). The coalition forces won because they were fighting in the future, and Iraq lost because it was fighting in the past. The war was thus viewed by the Soviets as a "transition between old and new," a stage that has now arrived because the basis of victory was the action of air attack weapons. Marshal Ogarkov's prescient demands for a rapid incorporation of emerging technologies into Soviet military theory and praxis were vindicated.

Prominent military scientists characterized the Gulf War as prototypical of an "air war." Colonel M. Ponomarev, for example, has described the allied air operation as a contemporary version of Douhet's strategy of command of the air, but applied in this case to create an "aerial blitzkrieg." [21] According to General-Lieutenant A. Malyukov, the Gulf War was conceived from the outset as an air war to wear out the opponent by means of air strikes, disorganize his C^2 systems, destroy his air defenses, and weaken the strike

---

[19] Ibid.
[20] Ibid.
[21] Colonel M. Ponomarev, "The Picture Begins to Clear," *KZ*, 25 January 1991.

power of the ground forces. In terms of choice of objectives, it was therefore more a classical air offensive than an air-land battle. [22]

According to these experts, the Gulf War was also the prototype of a "technological war." Such a war will be conducted with massive employment of advanced technologies. Remotely piloted vehicles, robotics, and means of electronic warfare, reconnaissance, and deception will be widely employed. Long-range guided weapons systems with "artificial intelligence" are appearing. Space-based weapons that employ various means of destruction are being developed to a significant degree, and they will always pose a great threat to the opponent.

Soviet experts argued that all of this is radically changing the nature of future war. Large groupings of ground troops will not be employed in it. Massive strikes will be delivered by remotely piloted precision-guided weapons and reconnaissance-strike systems capable of automatically finding and destroying the target to any depth of the opponent's territory. The entire country being subjected to precision strikes will become the battlefield, and the war will proceed without borders or flanks. The terms "front" and "rear" will be replaced by the concepts of "subject to strikes" and "not subject to strikes" (targets and non-targets). First-priority targets will be state and military command-and-control points, energy sources, and military targets—especially retaliatory strike means.

By concentrating the enormous might of strikes on the farthest depth of the opponent's territory, it is now possible to achieve not only operational-strategic but also strategic objectives. In fact in such a war, the Soviets argued, the lines between tactics, operational art, and strategy disappear. The war can begin and end with a powerful strike by precision-guided weapons—painstakingly planned and precisely executed within a designated period of time.

According to Slipchenko, large groupings of ground forces will not be employed in such a war if the protagonists are the United States and the Soviet Union. The war will begin and end with the conduct of "global strategic offensive air operations" without aviation. Aircraft will simply release the cruise missiles and return for more. And the same role will be played by naval forces. Strikes will be delivered by strategic, intercontinental cruise missiles armed with conventional warheads.

By August 1991, the Soviets argued that "Desert Storm" had already generated a critical revision of Soviet military art: the identification of a new type of combat action. The experience of military operations in the Persian Gulf zone showed that in the very near future, *"the delivery of a surprise first strike and numerous subsequent massive missile, aero-space, and electronic strikes in combination with strikes by naval forces may decide the outcome of war without the invasion of enemy territory by ground force groupings."* [23] The legitimacy of that conclusion can be confirmed by the very high effectiveness of fire and electronic strikes as well as operations by assault-landing forces that has been manifested in local

---

[22] General-Lieutenant A. Malyukov, "Gulf War: Initial Conclusions; Air Power Predetermined Outcome," *KZ*, 14 March 1991.

[23] Korotchenko, "Military Art."

wars of recent years. Therefore, the beginning of initial operations most likely will assume the nature of fierce fire engagements.

The combination of fire engagements as well as massed or single fire and electronic strikes conducted for a certain time and under a common concept and plan will represent a new type of military operation: the "strike operation." The experience of the war against Iraq confirms that it can be conducted for several days or weeks. Its goals may be to disrupt state and military command and control; destroy nuclear forces' installations; defeat air defense and air force groupings and force groupings of the first operational echelon; disrupt mobilization deployment and forward movement of follow-on forces; destroy supplies; and demolish the most important economic areas (installations), transportation hubs, and ecologically dangerous installations (atomic electric power stations, hydroelectric stations, dams, water reservoirs, and so on). It was noted that the opponent will make special efforts to demoralize the country's population in the course of such an operation. [24]

Writing in late 1991, Colonel A.N. Zakharov examined the major trends governing the development of warfare from the end of the twentieth to the beginning of the twenty-first centuries. After singling out such general features as "the increase in types of weapons in all spatial spheres as a result of the growing role of 'weapons, air, seas, and space'," he enumerated seven specific trends:

1. A higher degree of mutual influence among combat actions in various spheres, and a shift from primarily ground actions to warfare on land, sea, and in the air—with a growing emphasis on the latter.
2. A capability to strike the depth of the operational zone with simultaneous combat actions.
3. A striving for simultaneous destruction of targets and groupings.
4. A shift on all levels and in all spheres to combat actions of a combined-arms nature, based on massed, group, and concentrated strikes by various types of troops.
5. A rising level of simultaneous influence by troops and weapons in each sphere in the course of any operational task.
6. A shift in the brunt of influence from military equipment and arms to support and information systems.
7. A reduction of time and expansion of methods for unleashing military (combat) actions. [25]

According to Zakharov, the first trend reflects the ceaseless growth in quantity of aviation and naval forces for destroying ground groupings—since the capabilities of ground troops have become clearly inadequate. This trend is confirmed by the Gulf War, wherein coalition ground troops commenced active operations only after multi-day aviation and naval strikes on Iraq's ground targets (even with total command of the air and sea by aviation and naval forces). Success in operations, especially at the outset of war, will therefore depend directly on gaining and maintaining superiority in the air and at sea. This trend presupposes a successive

---

[24] Ibid.
[25] Colonel A.N. Zakharov, "Trends in the Development of Warfare," *VM* 11–12 (1991): 9–15.

concentration of efforts to seize the initiative first in the air, then at sea, and only later on land. [26]

The seventh trend, writes Zakharov, proceeds from the constant growth in the number of forces and means capable of inflicting destruction with conventional means (B–2s, SLCMs, reconnaissance-strike complexes, and others), as well as the higher degree of their constant readiness to deliver strikes. With each year, he continues, that side which articulated a "non-aggressive" doctrine will have fewer and fewer capabilities (with respect to both time and combat means) to rebuff successfully a carefully planned attack if it begins the first defensive operation only after detecting the fact of aggression.

And even with the highest level of readiness to deliver a strike, Zakharov notes, there can be a scenario wherein the opponent's preparation for and unleashing of aggression becomes "*irreversible.*" In theory it is therefore possible "to begin a defensive operation *with preemptive strikes* to thwart aggression—without betraying the obligations of military doctrine." Zakharov argues further that preemptive strikes can soon become "*the only means of thwarting aggression and successfully beginning the first defensive operation.*" Today it is therefore necessary to plan operational-strategic defensive actions with preemptive strikes on those means of the opponent whose combat use at a certain moment assumes "*an aggressively irreversible character.*" [27]

SOVIET MILITARY R&D

The new Soviet vision of future war—with its focus on the growing role of ACMs, directed-energy weapons, and space-based systems—was clearly reflected in military programs and R&D. Despite galloping domestic economic difficulties, the Soviets continued to produce technologically advanced weapons systems and to fund expensive military R&D activities. A review of Soviet writings reveals that a significant degree of civil-military convergence proceeds from the interdependence of the military-technical and scientific-technical "revolutions." In early 1985, for example, the Politburo approved a state-wide program to develop the production and effective utilization of computer technology and automated systems up to the year 2000. Not long after his accession to power in March 1985, Gorbachev stressed that:

> Machine-building plays the dominant, key role in implementing the scientific and technological revolution. ... Microelectronics, computer technology, instrument-making, and the entire informatics industry are the catalysts of progress. They require accelerated development. [28]

Here it should be stressed that the foregoing civilian requirements for implementing the scientific-technical "revolution" are *identical* to the military's requirements for implementing the new military-technical "revolution." [29] As Colonel N. Goryachev noted:

---

[26] Ibid.
[27] Ibid., p. 15.
[28] M.S. Gorbachev, Speech, *PR*, 12 June 1985.
[29] General-Major M. Yasyukov, "The Military Policy of the CPSU: Essence, Content," *KVS* 20 (1989): 20.

In the struggle for improving the technical equipping of the military, it is difficult to over-estimate the basic trends of scientific-technical progress: the further priority development of machine-building—especially machine-tool manufacturing, robotics, computer technology, instrument-making, and microelectronics. It is precisely these trends which are today the basic catalysts of military-technical progress. [30]

More recently, Colonel-General K. Kobets has stressed that in the field of technology and software for automated systems, development should proceed along the lines of military robotics, artificial intelligence systems, distributed and multi-function processing, personal computers, and multi-purpose networks." [31]

Inspired by the new military-technical revolution and galvanized by Gorbachev's defense cuts, the Soviet military's vision of military restructuring was quality enhancement across the board. The stated objective was to "upgrade not only the material and technical foundation of the Army and Navy, but also the system of manning and training, as well as military art and science in general," in order to "boost performance *by an order of magnitude.*" [32] Military experts thus stressed a more intensive exploitation of such existing technologies as microprocessors and other computers, lasers, fiber optics, robotics, radioelectronics, expert systems based on artificial intelligence technologies, and advanced sensors, imagers, and munitions. [33] They also stressed the ability to "develop, exploit, and weaponize such cutting-edge technologies as electron-beam, plasma, pulse, membrane, biochemistry, and radiology." [34] Soviet science had to discover and apply "as yet unknown properties of matter, natural laws, and phenomena that would generate a qualitative leap in developing new types of weapons." [35] The stated objective of "preventing the imperialists from achieving a so-called 'technological breakthrough' in weapons development" was said to justify "the continued diversion of the required scientific resources toward fortifying the nation's defense might." [36]

According to authoritative Soviet analyses, the application of existing and cutting-edge technologies will result not only in modernization of current systems but especially in the development of "principally new weapons systems." Indeed the main task consists in shifting from the "evolutionary path" of modernization to "a path characterized by qualitative leaps, whereby weapons acquire

---

[30] Colonel N. Goryachev, "Know and Capably Apply Entrusted Weapons and Military Equipment," *KVS* 2 (1987): 76.

[31] Interview with Moiseyev and Kobets, pp. 3–7.

[32] General of the Army V.M. Shabanov, "Adequate Armaments are Vital," *Soviet Military Review* 3 (1987).

[33] For example, see Colonel V. Bondarenko, "Scientific-Technical Progress and Military Affairs," *KVS* 21 (1986); Colonel-General V.N. Lobov, "High Quality—An Important Criterion of Combat Readiness," *KVS* 1 (1989): 12–18; Colonel-General I. Golushko, "The Rear: Yesterday, Today, Tomorrow," *Tyl vooruzhennykh sil* 2 (1988): 6–10; Colonel Yu. Molostov and Major A. Novikov, "High-Precision Weapons Against Tanks," *Soviet Military Review* 1 (1988): 12–13; General-Lieutenant F. Gredasov, "Reconnaissance—The Most Important Type of Combat Support," *VV* 3 (1987): 2–6.

[34] "The CPSU 27th Congress on Further Strengthening the Country's Combat Capability and Improving the Combat Readiness of the Armed Forces," *VIZh* 4 (1986): 1–12.

[35] Ibid., p. 8.

[36] Ibid. See also Shabanov, "Adequate Armaments;" and interview with Fleet Admiral N. Smirnov, *KZ*, 26 July 1987.

principally new combat characteristics."[37] The Soviets thus predicted that fewer but higher-quality systems manned by smaller but better-trained crews will enhance combat effectiveness despite quantitative reductions.[38]

THE RUSSIAN IMAGE OF FUTURE WAR

In late 1991, the then Soviet General Staff began to focus primarily on the need for a revised military doctrine and force structure in order to cope with such stark realities as: 1) the dissolution of the Warsaw Pact and withdrawal of Soviet Armed Forces from Eastern Europe; 2) the ongoing economic crisis; 3) mounting problems with conscription; 4) uncertainty regarding the maintenance of a unified Armed Forces and military policy; 5) the ominous lessons of the Persian Gulf War; and 6) Western superiority in conventional forces and "emerging technologies." A review of pre-Russian military writings thus reflected such recommendations as the following:

- A reevaluation of the nuclear no-first-use pledge
- Replacement of "reasonable sufficiency" by "sufficient reasonableness"
- Replacement of the defensive doctrine by "preemptive strikes"
- U.S.-Soviet "condominiums" in advanced conventional munitions (ACMs), third-generation nuclear weapons, and ABM technologies
- Cost-effective counters to reconnaissance-strike complexes
- A new strategy, operational art, and tactics based on the lessons of the Gulf War

A review of Russian military writings reveals such strong continuities with their predecessors as the following:

- A reevaluation of the nuclear no-first-use pledge
- A Yazov-like re-definition of the defensive doctrine that encompasses only the socio-political (not military-technical) side of doctrine; i.e., Russia has no intention of attacking anyone
- A call for a new military art and tactics based on the "long-distance" (remote) warfare exemplified in the Persian Gulf War[39]

In addition, the new Russian military leaders continue to articulate a spectrum of threats that varies little from that of their Soviet predecessors. First, the United States is said to be modernizing its nuclear arsenal in order to implement a counter-force strategy. Second, Russian military scientists argue that only two changes have occurred in NATO strategy: 1) a CFE-imposed shift in focus away from the central front and toward the northern and southern TVDs, and 2) a revitalization of the "flexible-response" strategy in order to counter the growing probability of low-intensity conflicts. Third, the military continues to charge the West with

---

[37] Interview with General of the Army A.D. Lizichev, *Kommunist* 3 (February 1989): 14–43. See also Colonel B. Makarenko, "The Material Basis of Combat Readiness," *VV* 8 (1987): 6–9.
[38] Moiseyev, "Defensive Doctrine."
[39] "Several Problems of Preparing the Army and Navy in Modern Times," Ibid., No. 1, 1992, pp. 3–10; and Colonel A.F. Klimenko, "On the Role and Place of Military Doctrine in the Security System of the CIS," Ibid., No. 2, 1992, pp. 11–21.

superiority in conventional forces and an ongoing lead in emerging
technologies (E.T.). Finally, these experts warn of the territorial
ambitions of Islamic states and the nuclear potential of Asian
states.

As a result, Russian military scientists continue to develop a new
doctrine and force structure to counter these perceived threats. For
example, *Military Thought* offers a dramatic proposal by Colonel-
General A.A. Danilevich, reputed to be Marshal Ogarkov's long-
time collaborator if not ghost-writer. [40] His arguments can be summarized as follows:

1. In contrast to nuclear war, the aggressor in conventional war
   can count even now on a temporary if not final victory.
2. Owing to its current difficulties and weakness, the CIS offers a
   vulnerable target to not only nuclear but also conventional
   strikes by highly developed states. This disparity must be
   eliminated if political stability and deterrence are to be maintained.
3. As the Gulf War demonstrated, modern warfare is based on
   the delivery of prolonged ACM strikes throughout the opponent's entire territory without the deployment of ground
   forces.
4. It is therefore necessary to create "a new class of weaponry"
   that can destroy (or at least threaten to destroy) the opponent's
   important political, economic, and strategic targets at any
   range with only conventional warheads.
5. At the present time, such "strategic non-nuclear deterrence
   forces" (SNNF) can be developed most realistically on the basis
   of corresponding elements of the strategic nuclear forces. It is
   now expedient to "unilaterally convert a certain portion of the
   strategic nuclear forces to conduct non-nuclear actions."
6. The resulting disruption of parity in strategic nuclear means is
   unimportant, because the potential for deterring conventional
   war—the most probable form of warfare today—will be improved.

Danilevich then describes several stages in the development of
the SNNF: 1) strategic aviation, whose entirety (or at least bulk) is
easily converted to conventional use; 2) a strategic triad armed
with conventional warheads and consisting of intercontinental ballistic missiles, strategic bombers with long-range cruise missiles,
and submarines and surface ships with cruise and possibly ballistic
missiles; and 3) intercontinental information (intelligence) strike
systems for use in a conventional war. Since the basic delivery vehicles of conventional warheads will be long-range cruise missiles,
the main problem in developing the SNNF will be modernizing
Soviet cruise missiles.

According to Danilevich, the SNNF can have four basic target
sets. The first group consists of the opponent's nuclear means and
related targets, whose destruction would prompt escalation and involve technical complexities. The second group consists of the opponent's nuclear power and chemical plants, whose destruction would

[40] Colonel-General A.A. Danilevich and Colonel O.P. Shunin, "On the Strategic Non-Nuclear
Deterrence Forces," Ibid., pp. 46–54.

be simpler technically but still escalatory. The third group consists of such general-purpose military targets as air and naval bases. But Danilevich argues that with a limited number of SNNF, it would be extremely difficult to inflict substantial damage on the opponent by destroying a relatively small number of even important military targets.

Finally, the fourth group consists of those targets that constitute the opponent's "military-economic potential." Danilevich argues that this target set is the most advantageous for the SNNF in the near future, considering the limited number and currently feasible accuracy of the new weapons. In comparison with the effect of destroying targets of the other groups, disabling key targets of the military economy would ensure a prolonged reduction of industrial potential and substantially hinder any waging of war.

According to Danilevich, the SNNF can be used to deliver selective strikes on a certain category of targets as well as simultaneous strikes on all types of targets. Under certain conditions, the actions of the SNNF will assume the form of a "special strategic operation." Of all future programs, he concludes, the development of the SNNF could be the "most economical and technically feasible."

It should be noted that throughout the 1980s, Marshal Ogarkov and other Soviet military experts alluded to the ultimate development of the SNNF, but usually referred to ongoing U.S. technological developments. While Russian military experts clearly acknowledge the crippling effects of recent events on the future of their Armed Forces, they continue to prepare for Ogarkov's vision of future war. In the meantime, the Russian political leadership must likewise be seeking the "most economical, technically feasible" means of both deterring and fighting such a war, if war should come.

RUSSIAN VIEWS ON DESERT STORM

Like their Soviet predecessors, Russian military scientists view "Desert Storm" as the paradigm of future war in strategy, operational art, and tactics. For example, General-Major I.N. Vorob'yev has recently summarized the central lessons of "Desert Storm."[41] He begins with a statement unprecedented for both the Soviet and Russian press: the Iraqis lost the Gulf War because they fought with Soviet doctrine and Soviet weaponry. Indeed the thrust of his article consists in a call for a "new military thinking" on the part of "our generals and officers" who are still locked into the "inertial thinking" of the World War II generation.

According to Vorob'yev, "Desert Storm" represents one of those rare "turning points" in military affairs—akin to the Franco-Prussian War—that stands at the juncture of two epochs in military art. It has ended the era of multi-million-man armies and begun the era of high-tech wars fought in the air, space, and "ether." While new systems were employed only singly in past wars, a multitude of new systems was employed on a mass scale in "Desert Storm."

---

[41] General-Major I.N. Vorob'yev, "Lessons of the Persian Gulf War," *VM* 4/5 (1992): 67–74.

Vorob'yev argues that because it constitutes the first victory achieved without massive ground forces, "Desert Storm" has prompted a radical re-examination of the structure of armed forces and the roles of particular branches. The emphasis has shifted from quantity to quality because technological superiority nullified quantitative superiority in divisions and conventional arms. As a result, the technological indices of new weapons—which are capable on the whole of predetermining the outcome of military actions—now constitute the basis for analyzing the combat potential of the sides.

Vorob'yev argues further that "Desert Storm" has demonstrated a shift in the balance of the spheres of military art. While tactics were dominant in all past wars, strategy and operational art are decisive now. As a result, the "battle" has ceased to be the sole means of achieving victory in war. Indeed the revolutionary nature of "Desert Storm" lies specifically in its having generated such new forms of operational/tactical actions as the "long-distance" (remote) battle and the "electronic-fire operation." According to Vorob'yev, the "electronic-fire operation" consisted of massed and prolonged missile, aerospace, and electronic strikes in conjunction with naval strikes. This operation predetermined the successful outcome of "Desert Storm."

Vorob'yev notes that the novelty of this operation lies in the emergence of EW as a weapon equal to "fire strikes" in combat effectiveness. The essence of this new phenomenon lies in 1) the duration of the electronic-fire phase, 2) the large quantity of new EW means employed, 3) a simultaneous effect on Iraqi C^2 (Command and Control systems) at all levels, and 4) the *synergism* created by precise coordination of EW and fire strikes.

According to Vorob'yev, "Desert Storm" has also generated a shift from positional to maneuver warfare. While both types of actions were conducted equally in past wars, maneuver is now the dominant form. "Desert Storm" has generated a new method of penetrating the defense: prolonged, continuous, and massed electronic-fire strikes in conjunction with a double envelopment of troops—by land and air, and by the creation of an active front in the opponent's rear with air, air-mobile, and naval landing forces. This operation signals the eventual demise of linear actions, close-in combat, stable fronts, and long operational pauses. The author notes, however, that some positional combat can still be conducted between technological equals.

Finally, Vorob'yev describes six changes in the principles of military art that have been generated by "Desert Storm": 1) a shift from concentration to mobility of troops; 2) a shift from the massing of troops to the massing of ACMs; 3) a shift from uni-dimensional to multi-dimensional warfare, whose essence consists in decisive superiority not only on land but also in the air and ether; 4) a shift from selecting axes for the main strike to selecting "areas for concentrating efforts," since the epicenter of the opponent's defense consists not in positions and lines but in a fire grouping—means of nuclear attack, air defense systems, anti-tank systems, EW systems, reconnaissance-strike complexes, and reconnaissance-fire complexes that are widely dispersed; 5) the achievement of surprise by the mass employment of technologically new systems; and

6) precise coordination of land, air, and space-based systems with regard to objective, place, and time during the conduct of the air offensive.

Similarly, Rear-Admiral V.S. Pirumov argues that the effectiveness of information systems has led "developed countries" to acknowledge the dominant role of the "electronic-fire" concept of waging war. [42] In force structure and equipment, this concept manifests itself not in competing for numerical superiority in motorized rifle (tank) formations for conducting ground battles, but in using industrial and technological advantages to create high-precision sea- and aerospace-based weapons and global C^2 systems that facilitate "surprise first and subsequent massed radioelectronic and fire strikes that decide the outcome of the war without the invasion of ground forces."

Pirumov argues further that a war's main objective is shifting away from seizure of the opponent's territory and toward 1) "the suppression of his political or military-economic potential," and 2) "ensuring the victor's supremacy in the political arena or economic markets." The primacy of this concept has generated a new form of utilizing armed forces: the "electronic-fire operation."

This operation will typically begin with a surprise air attack rather than an invasion by deployed ground forces, which permits not only seizure of the strategic initiative but also disruption of the opponent's strategic deployment by striking a series of his most important targets with a first strike. In addition, losses of personnel are significantly lowered since ground troops are used only after achieving space and air superiority—which guarantees their success. Pirumov concludes by arguing that parity and defense sufficiency thus require calculations of not only the fire component of combat but especially the "information component"—which must govern the allocation of scarce defense resources.

According to Colonel V.V. Krysanov, the next stage in the development of military actions is connected with weapons based on new physical principles and cutting-edge technologies. Here preference is given to "revolutionary" directions in developing the means of warfare: 1) the robotization of military technology and 2) directed-energy weapons. Both of these developments will generate new types of military action, which will reduce the participation and hence the losses of personnel. In the first stage, the use of combat robots will merely supplement existing weapons, but later it could lead to two-sided independent battles on particular axes. The advantages of remotely piloted vehicles are obvious, Krysanov continues: they can be used in radioactive areas and areas saturated with air defense weapons, as well as under various conditions of visibility. In time, he concludes, they could become "the basic means of air attack." [43]

Krysanov argues further that the "electronization" of military actions is also a prospective direction in their development. Numerous foreign specialists view "electronic weapons"—which have a

---

[42] Rear-Admiral V.S. Pirumov, "Two Aspects of Parity and Defense Sufficiency," Ibid., pp. 26–34.

[43] Colonel V.V. Krysanov, "Special Features in the Development of the Forms of Military Action," Ibid., No. 2, 1992, pp. 42–45.

direct destructive effect—as "absolute" weapons. U.S. experts in particular discuss another new type of warfare: "electronic-beam," which will be characterized by speed, high accuracy, instantaneous destructive effect, and the impossibility of maneuvering to escape the strikes of beam weapons. The development of such super-high-frequency, infra-sonic weapons designed to affect specifically the opponent's personnel is generating a special type of warfare with a "psychogenic" effect. Krysanov concludes that these and other essentially new systems urgently require the development of systems capable of defending against them.

RUSSIAN MILITARY R&D

It is noteworthy that a strong civil-military consensus exists regarding the R&D priorities for the Russian Armed Forces. First, such leaders as Defense Minister Grachev and Deputy Defense Minister Kokoshin agree that large armored forces have become "dinosaurs" in modern warfare. [44] Second, all parties agree that the Russian Armed Forces must be smaller, more professional, more mobile, and equipped with emerging technologies.

Third, civilian and military leaders agree that "there is no alternative" to the development of ACMs—despite the current "time of troubles." For example, both the military leadership and the leaders of the Russian Supreme Soviet view ACMs as the "basic deterrence factor" of future war. Other experts argue that 1) ACMs are cheaper than both nuclear weapons and large armored forces, and 2) ACMs will permit a Russian Armed Forces of even less than 1.5 million men.

As a result, civilian and military leaders agree that R&D must be maintained at the expense of procurement as the defense budget declines. According to Marshal Shaposhnikov, for example, the current Russian lag (e.g., in Stealth and ACMs) prohibits any cuts in the R&D budget. "Here we cannot be second best," he has argued, "where our partners are concerned." [45] Other experts note the current Russian lag of 7–10 years in ACMs, and warn that the United States can double or treble its arsenal by the year 2000.

On the other hand, such spokesmen as Deputy Defense Minister Kokoshin have announced that Russia remains "quite competitive" in at least 6 areas: 1) several trends in shipbuilding, 2) aircraft construction, 3) rocketry construction, 4) heavy power machine-building, 5) composite materials, and 6) laser and space weaponry. [46] Russian military experts have even gone so far as to assert that despite the current technological lag, Russia enjoys superiority in "intellectual developments." [47]

This striking civil-military consensus is reflected in the new list of seven priorities for the Russian Armed Forces that was recently announced by both Vice-President Rutskoi and Defense Minister Grachev: highly mobile troops, army aviation, long-range ACMs,

---

[44] For example, see "Kokoshin Outlines Future Military Needs," in FBIS-SOV-92-053, 18 March 1992, p. 27.
[45] "Shaposhnikov Comments on Defense Ministry Tasks," in FBIS-SOV-91-183, 20 September 1991, p. 35.
[46] "Kokoshin on Potential of Defense Enterprises," in FBIS-SOV-92-069, 9 April 1992, p. 33.
[47] "Smart Weapons Potential Versus U.S. Viewed," in FBIS-SOV-92-103, 28 May 1992, p. 4.

C³I (Command, Control, Communications, and Intelligence) systems, military space systems, air defense systems, and strategic arms. [48]

The consensus is also reflected in the 1992 Russian defense budget, which is stated to be about 400 billion rubles. Both civilian and military spokesmen assert that current allocations represent a 71 percent cut in procurement as opposed to a 16 percent cut in R&D. According to Deputy Prime Minister Gaydar, the R&D budget is being maintained "to preserve the main most important projects at the 1991 level, as far as Russia's share ... regarding Russian science." [49]

RUSSIA'S NEW MILITARY DOCTRINE

The Russian leadership is currently focusing not only on creating the Russian Armed Forces, but also on developing a new military doctrine for the 1990s and beyond. In May 1992, a draft of Russia's new military doctrine was published in *Military Thought*. This doctrine is based on "defense documents adopted by the Russian president and Supreme Soviet, as well as by the CIS Council of Heads of State." [50]

The new doctrine describes two "direct" military threats to Russia: 1) the introduction of foreign troops in contiguous states, and 2) the buildup of forces near Russian borders. In addition, a violation of the rights of Russian citizens and of persons "ethnically and culturally" identified with Russia in the former Soviet republics is viewed as "a serious source of conflicts." Finally, it is extremely interesting that Russia now views *conventional* strikes on its nuclear and other "dangerous" targets as an escalation to weapons of mass destruction—which implies that such strikes will elicit a nuclear response.

According to Russian doctrine, local wars are becoming the most probable type of warfare. But large-scale conventional wars may arise when local wars aimed against Russia or the CIS escalate, or after a "prolonged threat period" that involves general mobilization. The doctrine assigns priority to wars fought with existing and emerging conventional weapons.

The new doctrine describes three distinct components of the Russian Armed Forces: 1) a limited number of forces in permanent readiness in the theaters to repel local aggression, 2) mobile reserves or rapid-response forces capable of quickly maneuvering (deploying) to any region to repel mid-level aggression together with the permanent readiness forces, and 3) strategic reserves formed during the threat period and during war to conduct large-scale combat actions.

The new doctrine also describes the two priorities of Russian military-technical policy: 1) "emerging high-precision, mobile, highly survivable, long-range, stand-off weapons," and 2) arms,

---

[48] See A. Rutskoi, "We Must Build an Army Worthy of Great Russia," *KZ*, 22 May 1992, and Colonel G. Miranovich, "Russia's Armed Forces Today and Tomorrow," *KZ*, 2 June 1992.

[49] "Gaydar Delivers Budget Message to Parliament," in FBIS-SOV-92-062, 31 March 1992, p. 36.

[50] "The Fundamentals of Russia's Military Doctrine (Draft)," *VM*, Special Edition, May 1992, pp. 3–9.

equipment, and C³I systems whose *quality* will permit a reduced *quantity* of arms. The doctrine stresses that Russia must have a military-technical policy and weapons programs on a par with world standards. In order to achieve this objective, the doctrine calls for 1) reducing procurement of arms and equipment in serial production, and 2) maintaining R&D and production capacities to ensure the development *and rapid surge production* of emerging combat technologies.

A comparison of Russia's new doctrine with the 1990 Soviet military doctrine reveals at least five key changes. [51] First, in 1990 the main "wartime objective" was to "repel aggression." In 1992, the main "wartime objective" is to "repel aggression and defeat the opponent." Second, in 1990 the main "development goal" was to "repel aggression." In 1992, the main "development goal" is to "optimize the TO&E" (Tables of Organization and Equipment) for all possible wars and combat missions.

Third, the 1990 doctrine held that nuclear war "will" be catastrophic for all mankind, while the 1992 doctrine holds that it "might" be catastrophic for all mankind. In addition, the 1990 doctrine stated that nuclear war "will assume a global character," and that calculations on limiting it to a single region are untenable. In 1992, however, both of these provisions have been deleted—which implies that limited nuclear war-fighting is now a possibility.

Fourth, the 1990 doctrine held that conventional "sufficiency" meant that no large-scale offensive operations could be conducted. In 1992, however, conventional "sufficiency" means that no large-scale offensive operations can be conducted "without additional deployments."

Finally, the 1990 doctrine stressed that Soviet military art was based on a "defensive strategy," and that the U.S.S.R. excluded the delivery of a preemptive strike. Defense was said to be the main type of military action at the outset of war. In 1992, however, these provisions are deleted. Instead, the Russian Armed Forces will conduct "all forms of military action," will conduct defense and offense equally, and will seize the strategic initiative to destroy the opponent.

One explanation for these striking divergences from the 1990 Soviet doctrine lies in the dramatic changes that have since occurred in the former Soviet Union. Nevertheless, the new doctrine clearly rejects the long-time civilian call for forces structured solely to conduct *defensive* operations.

The new Russian doctrine also reflects the pervasive impact of Operation "Desert Storm" on Russian military thought. Since the early 1980s, such prominent military thinkers as Marshal Ogarkov have argued that emerging technologies are generating a new "revolution" in military affairs. Russian military scientists now argue that "Desert Storm" confirmed these predictions and serves as the paradigm of future war in strategy, operational art, and tactics.

First, Russia's new doctrine assigns priority to the new systems employed during "Desert Storm": advanced conventional munitions (ACMs), EW, and C³I. Russian military scientists have argued, for

---

[51] "On the Military Doctrine of the USSR (Draft)," *VM*, Special Edition, November 1990, pp. 24–28.

example, that ACMs accomplished nuclear missions during the war. Electronic warfare is said to be a weapon equal to "fire strikes" in its combat effectiveness. Advanced C^3I systems are said to be just as important as the entire "correlation of forces and means." In fact, superiority in EW and C^3I is said to ensure victory in future war.

Second, the doctrine lists a new strategic mission for the Russian Armed Forces: to repel a surprise "aviation-missile attack." Military scientists now argue that the Gulf War generated a new type of combat action—the "electronic-fire operation"—which consists of surprise, massed, and prolonged missile, aerospace, electronic, and naval strikes conducted for several days or weeks. The objectives of the new operation will be achieved without the seizure and occupation of enemy territory. Instead, the new objectives consist in: 1) "suppressing the opponent's political or military-economic potential" and 2) "ensuring the victor's supremacy in political or economic arenas."

Third, the new doctrine stresses the decisive importance of the war's initial period, which is said to consist of air and naval strikes aimed at disrupting strategic deployments, disorganizing civilian and military C^2, and removing CIS states from the war. The destruction of economic and military targets by ACMs will be accompanied by simultaneous or preemptive EW. In *subsequent* periods, the opponent *may* deploy ground troops under strong air cover.

What can we conclude about the military-technical aspects of Russia's new doctrine? First, the doctrine assigns priority to wars fought with existing and emerging conventional weapons. Second, the doctrine views the Gulf War as the paradigm of future conventional wars. Third, the doctrine calls for the maintenance of R&D at the expense of procurement as the defense budget declines. Fourth, the doctrine reflects changing views on nuclear war, implying that 1) a limited nuclear scenario is possible, and 2) *conventional* strikes on Russia's nuclear and other dangerous targets will elicit a nuclear response. Finally, the doctrine reflects the demise of Gorbachev's "defensive doctrine" and a shift to the conduct of all forms of military action—including "large-scale offensive operations."

Russian military doctrine thus remains highly dynamic and visionary even in the current "time of troubles." Despite much discussion about the ascendance of civilians, the military has reasserted its dominance over the development of this doctrine.

For the near term, the new doctrine calls for rapid-response forces in order to prepare for local conflicts. For the long term, it calls for the development of emerging combat technologies in order to prepare for the new "technological war." But the future of Russia's economy and defense industries, as well as the nature of its political leadership, will serve as the final determinants of whether and when Russia will implement the future-oriented aspects of its new military doctrine.

PROBLEMS OF DOWNSIZING AND DISSOLUTION: RUSSIAN DEFENSE POLICY AFTER THE BREAKUP

By Richard F Kaufman *

CONTENTS

SUMMARY

Defense spending and the size of military forces in Russia and the other newly independent states of the former Soviet Union declined at an accelerating pace in 1992. Political, social, and economic developments added to the disarray. Cutbacks, shortages of funds, and the lack of housing facilities contributed to low morale within the services, while draft evasion and desertions rose to alarming proportions. The breakup of the former Soviet Union and the economic downturn fractured much of what was left of defense production, deprived the military of substantial portions of its infrastructure, and forced a reduction in operations and maintenance activities. The downward trends in defense extended to arms exports, although there were reported sales of sophisticated items to Iran, China, and other countries. Actual and threatened conflicts among and within several of the states, disputes over how to divide up military assets located in the non-Russian states, and the presence of large numbers of Russians in those states left unresolved many issues about the role of the Russian military in the former Soviet republics.

DEFENSE SPENDING UNDER GORBACHEV

Mikhail Gorbachev followed his predecessors' policy of modest growth in defense spending for several years after assuming power in 1985. During this period, he repeatedly called for a shift in economic priorities from defense to the civilian sector and seemed to downgrade the importance of the military. He advocated two new military doctrines: "reasonable sufficiency" for strategic forces and

---

* Richard F Kaufman is General Counsel for the Joint Economic Committee, United States Congress.

a "non-offensive defense" posture. Both suggested a shift in policy toward a smaller and less threatening force. [1] In his speech at the United Nations in December 1988, Gorbachev announced unilateral troop and conventional arms cuts. Forces and budgets were reduced in each of the next three years.

The Central Intelligence Agency (CIA) estimated that real defense spending for the three-year period, 1989–1991, declined by more than 25 percent, with the largest reduction (about 15 percent) occurring in 1991. Reductions were across-the-board, affecting all major resource categories and mission areas. The decline in procurement outpaced the rest of the defense budget. At the end of 1991 they were one-third lower than in 1988. Again, the largest reduction (about 20 percent) was in 1991. By the end of 1991, total defense spending and procurement were about as low as, and perhaps lower than, the early 1970s. [2]

There were deep procurement cuts in most categories. In 1991 alone the numbers of tanks, armored vehicles, and artillery pieces procured fell by 40–45 percent or more. Over the three-year period procurement was reduced by about 40 percent for ground forces, 30 percent for naval forces, and one-third for strategic offensive forces. The smallest decline was in strategic defense forces, estimated at less than 10 percent. Procurement for the space program was reduced by about 50 percent.

In the same period, military manpower declined by about 1 million and spending for operations and maintenance fell by about 10 percent. A high degree of uncertainty surrounds U.S. intelligence estimates for research, development, testing, and evaluation. According to the CIA, its own assessments, together with official Soviet statements and other reports, suggest spending in this area fell by about 10 percent in 1990 and 25 percent in 1991.

DEFENSE SPENDING UNDER YELTSIN

The first phase of the Soviet defense build-down, in 1989–90, was a more or less orderly process that followed Gorbachev's plan for redeployments and restructuring. The decline accelerated in 1991 and came close to getting out of control in 1992, after the break up of the Soviet Union. By then rising inflation, budget deficits, and the demands of the newly independent republics for further cuts placed severe downward pressures on the defense program.

A draft defense budget submitted to the Russian cabinet in March 1992 suggested a cut of 50 percent from the 1991 budget. [3] In June the official budget message proposed a substantial reduction of arms purchases, a reduced volume of scientific research, and cuts in the size of the armed forces. As the year progressed, the non-Russian republics became reluctant to make financial contributions for defense of the Commonwealth of Independent States

---

[1] Richard F Kaufman, "Changing Patterns of Soviet Defense Expenditures," prepared for the First Bedford Colloquium on Soviet Military-Political Affairs, Dalhousie University, Nova Scotia, August 28, 1989, reprinted in George Mellinger, editor, Soviet Armed Forces Review Annual, Academic International Press, Gulf Breeze, Florida, 1993 (in press).

[2] CIA, Moscow's Defense Spending Cuts Accelerate, Directorate of Intelligence, May, 1992, pp. 4–5, reprinted in Global Economic and Technological Change, Hearings before the Joint Economic Committee, 102d Cong. 2d sess., (GPO, June 8, 1992), pt. 2.

[3] CIA, Ibid.

(CIS), some reserving whatever resources they could afford for their own newly established defense forces.

In October 1992 a military advisor to the Russian Defense Ministry said spending constraints caused deep cuts in arms purchases and that only 10 tanks had been ordered for the entire year.[4] In November a Russian commentator claimed that military expenditures had been slashed by 70 percent.[5] While the accuracy of such statements could not be determined, it was clear that defense spending declined substantially in 1992.

Political, social, and economic developments added to the disarray in the defense sector. The U.S. intelligence community concluded mid-way through the year, "The economic resources of the former Soviet Union no longer can be mobilized as an aggregate to develop and sustain military forces."[6] The full dimensions of the military decline could not be satisfactorily quantified.

As if to assure the military-industrial complex that there would be no further shrinkage, Yeltsin announced that the defense budget would be at the same level in 1993 as it was in 1992, and that the budget for military equipment would increase by 10 percent.[7] This decision, if implemented, would represent a change in government policy regarding the composition of spending. The 1992 budget message emphasized that military pay, pensions, and social services were being increased, in contrast to cuts in procurement. But it was unclear how much of total defense spending would be reflected in the official budget. Generally speaking, with inflation approaching the near hyperinflation level, the value of the ruble falling precipitously, and continuing shortcomings in public accounting for military activities, monetary estimates of defense spending became problematic.

Much the same could be said for the new non-Russian states. For them, the dissolution of the Soviet Union required the establishment of national military programs under conditions of extreme austerity. This meant fielding relatively modest forces intended to both maintain domestic order and defend against separatist movements and neighboring states. In many cases governments simply laid claim to the former Soviet forces located in their lands and reconstituted them as their own. Ukraine planned a military manpower force of 200,000–450,000. The other non-Russian states planned much smaller manpower levels, in the tens rather than the hundreds of thousands. The force structures would be sized accordingly.

MILITARY MANPOWER

In January 1992 a military spokesman for the Russian General Staff said that the CIS armed forces would total 2.5 million men

---

[4] Alla Glebova and David Silverberg, "Ex-Soviet Gear Awaits New Life," *Defense News*, 7–13 December 1992.

[5] Vladislav Kozyakov, Moscow Radio Moscow World Service in English, 13 November 1992, in FBIS-Sov-92-221, 16 November 1992, p. 7.

[6] Testimony of Kathleen Horste, Defense Intelligence Agency, in *Global Economic and Technological Change*.

[7] Moscow *Interfax*, 23 November 1992, in FBIS-SOV-92-22, "Stresses Need for Control Over Nuclear Weapons," 24 November 1992, p. 18.

when President Yeltsin's planned personnel cuts were made. [8] A few months later, U.S. intelligence estimated that personnel expenditures in the former Soviet Union had dropped by about 20 percent and the number of military personnel had declined by about 1 million since 1988 when the number of uniformed military was about 5 million. [9] By the end of 1992, there had been further declines in military manpower, and Russia, the largest of the parts of what used to be the U.S.S.R., had dramatically fewer forces than the whole. Russian forces, viewed separately from the newly independent states, were less than 50 percent of the size of the former Soviet forces.

The Russian Defense Minister, Pavel Grachev, announced in May 1992 that the Russian Armed Forces would be reduced to 1.5 million men by 1995. Some military officials wanted that target to be stretched out to the year 2000. But the issue may have become moot. In October Grachev said the number had already fallen to 2.2 million. [10] It is possible that actual manpower levels may have fallen to 1.5 million at the end of 1992 or in early 1993.

Draft evasion and military desertion rose to alarming proportions as a result of the popular resentment against the armed forces and the low morale within the military. These problems were exacerbated by the shrinking defense budget, the deterioration in living standards, and the increasingly violent ethnic conflicts. In addition, large numbers of draft-age persons were exempt or had deferments from the draft, or were unfit for service because of poor health. In some areas conscription was nonexistent.

There were widespread reports of manning shortages. According to a November 1992 report in *Krasnaya Zvezda*, the Russian Defense Ministry was worried that even with the planned reduction to 1.5 million men, it would not be possible to bring the Army and Navy completely up to strength. [11] A high Russian military official said in January 1993 that the draft was providing only 22 percent of troop requirements and warned that the situation "could lead to a self-reduction of the armed forces to a level that is lower than planned, and a sharp reduction in combat readiness." [12]

Russian leaders cited the lack of housing on several occasions as the reason for suspending or slowing troop withdrawals. Defense Minister Grachev said in mid-March 1993 that 120,000 servicemen's families were not being provided with housing, that about 60,000 servicemen discharged into the reserve were on the housing waiting list, and that the number of those in need of apartments will increase by another 400,000 with the withdrawal of troops to

[8] "Diplomatic Panorama," Moscow INTERFAX, 30 January 1992, in FBIS-SOV-92-021, 31 January 1992, p. 8.
[9] CIA, Ibid., p. 6.
[10] Stephen Foye, "Rebuilding the Russian Military: Some Problems and Prospects," *RFE/RL Research Report*, 6 November 1992, p. 54.
[11] Aleksandr Zotov, "Problems With Conscripts," Moscow *Krasnaya Zvezda*, 12 November 1992, p. 1, in FBIS-SOV-92-220, 13 November 1992, p. 56. See also Moscow *Interfax* (untitled), 15 October 1992, in FBIS-SOV-92-200, 15 October 1992, p. 19.
[12] Interview with Colonel General Vitaliy Bologov, "The Draft Has Ended. The Dispatch of New Recruits to the Troops Continues," Moscow, *Izvestiya*, 6 January 1993, p. 2, in FBIS-SOV-93-005, 8 January 1993; Aleksandr Ivanor, "Commander in Chief Prudnikov on Problems of Russia's Air Defense," Moscow *Krasnaya Zvezda*, 26 January 1993, in FBIS-SOV-93-016, 27 January 1993, p. 36; Lt. Colonel Yuriy Mamchur and Major Aleksandr Dolinin, "Russia Will Keep Its Nuclear Shield," Moscow *Krasnaya Zvezda*, 14 November 1992, in FBIS-SOV-92-221, 16 November 1992, p. 2.

Russia from other countries. At the end of the month Grachev announced a halt to troop withdrawals from the Baltic countries because of the housing problem. [13]

DEFENSE INDUSTRY AND THE ARMED FORCES

The troubles for the military were not limited to budget constraints, planned force reductions, and morale problems. The political breakup and the economic downturn caused further "shocks" to reverberate throughout the military establishment. The combined effects fractured much of what was left of defense production, deprived the military of substantial portions of its infrastructure of bases and research and test facilities, and forced a reduction in operations and maintenance activities.

About 70 percent of the production plants and about 75 percent of the research, development, test and evaluation (RDT&E) facilities of the Soviet defense sector were located in Russia. That left a portion of the defense sector in the non-Russian republics. Russia was substantially self-sufficient because of its size and the vertical integration of its defense industries. But it relied on the republics for various strategic materials and other supplies, as well as for important bases, port facilities, and testing sites. In addition, under the Soviet system of central planning there was a tendency to establish sole source suppliers of parts, and many were located in the non-Russian republics. The non-Russian republics, in turn, were highly dependent on Russia and one another for materials, components, and subassemblies. [14]

The dynamics of the breakup and the downturn, superimposed on the decision to reduce the size of the forces, are illustrated by what happened to the Russian navy. First, substantial reductions began to be made in the size of the navy. More than 100 nuclear powered submarines and about 300 other combatant ships were due to be scrapped in the 1990s. In January 1993 the navy announced that about 80 nuclear submarines had been decommissioned, and the nuclear reactors removed from about one-third of them. [15] Given what is known about replacement rates, the Russian Navy could be less than half its 1992 size by the turn of the century.

Second, the navy was deprived of much of the former Soviet coastal areas and of important segments of its industrial infrastructure and other assets. Russia inherited 60–64 percent of the former Soviet Union's shipbuilding potential. [16] It lost access to a number of ports and facilities along the southern and eastern portions of the Baltic Sea, including ports at Tallinn in Estonia and Riga in Latvia. Its access to ports along the Black Sea was curtailed and it became embroiled with Ukraine over ownership and control of the Black Sea Fleet. Ukraine took possession of the only shipyard in

[13] Aleksandr Pelts and Vladimir Gundarov, "Russian Defense Minister at the Northern Fleet," Moscow, *Krasnaya Zvezda*, 20 March 1993, in FBIS-SOV–93–053, 22 March 1993; "Grachev Announces Halt to Baltic Troop Withdrawals," *RFE/RL Daily Report*, 30 March 1993, p. 3.
[14] Donald Creacy, "The Defense Industries of the Newly Independent States of Eurasia," in this volume.
[15] Roman Zadunayiskiy, "Navy Commander Admiral Gromov Comments on the Problem of the Russian Navy Shipbuilding Program," Moscow *Krasnaya Zvezda*, 23 January 193, in FBIS-SOV–93–015, 26 January 1993, p.30.
[16] Roman Zadunayskiy, Ibid.

the former Soviet Union that could build aircraft carriers. About one-third of the production of engines, weapons, and equipment for ships was produced outside of Russia. [17]

The Northern and Pacific fleets were especially hard hit. Seriously undermanned because of recruitment problems, they suffered from inadequate support, repair delays, and shortages of fuel and spare parts. Many of the same facilities used for scrapping ships were also used for repairs and maintenance. As a consequence, the extensive scrapping of ships, under way since about 1987, crowded out the capacity for repairs. The high costs of scrapping depleted scarce budget resources, and "cannibalization" of ships for parts for others became common. [18] In December 1992, the Pacific Fleet's commander told a group of U.S. Senators that the fleet's ships had ceased military duty in the ocean, including submarine patrols of the United States. [19]

The effects of the shortages and inflation were far reaching. The manpower and supply deficiencies drastically reduced naval activities such as exercises and training, while price increases made it difficult for commands to purchase food and other basic items. The reduced priority for naval forces added further difficulties. The shortfall of funds delayed the withdrawal of ships from the fleet and caused suppliers to seek out non-military customers who could pay in hard currency.

The former Soviet goal of developing a "blue-water" navy that could compete with the United States appears to have been postponed indefinitely. There were no new ships started by the Russian Navy in 1992. Meanwhile, the older Kiev-class carriers were being scrapped and the two newer ones in the Pacific fleet, the Minsk and the Novorossisyk, were laid up awaiting repairs. Some Russian Navy leaders envisioned future construction of larger carriers, and the maintenance of at least three carriers for each of the four fleets. But the Ministry of Defense recognized in early 1993 that the economic crisis would make it difficult to implement such a plan. [20]

The other military forces experienced similar difficulties. For example, the air force and air defense forces were also hampered by shortages of supplies and manpower, and inadequate logistics support. There were spillover effects from navy cutbacks, such as reduced carrier aircraft, and the shutdown of radar facilities as Krasnoyarsk and elsewhere. The Air Force cut flying time because of lack of fuel. Strategic bomber production was reportedly halted as aircraft plants shifted to commercial airliners.

The Russian Army was perhaps the most impaired. Its problems went beyond the manpower difficulties mentioned earlier, the cutbacks ordered by the government, and the loss of purchasing power. At the time of the political breakup some of the best

[17] George F. Krause, Jr., "Morskoy Flot, The Once and Future Russian Navy," *FSRC Analytical Note,* 13 November 1992.

[18] George F. Kraus, Jr., Ibid.

[19] Moscow *Interfax,* 2 December 1992, in FBIS-S0V-92-233, 3 December 1992, p. 1.

[20] Robert Holzer, "Russia Guns for More Carriers," *Defense News,* 21–27 December 1992; Moscow *Interfax,* 19 March 1993, in FBIS-SOV-93-053, 23 March 1993, "Navy Chief Comments on Cuts," p.68; George F. Krause, Jr., "Some Notes On Russian Ship Dismantlement," *FSRC Analytical Note,* 20 November 1992.

equipped combat-ready portions of the former Soviet army were deployed in the western non-Russian republics, the Baltics, Germany, Hungary, and Czechoslovakia. According to Defense Minister Grachev, the troops deployed in Europe were disbanded, and the Baltic Military District was being phased out. Ukraine and Belarus inherited the former Soviet forces within their borders. What remained within Russia were understaffed noncombat units that lacked the most advanced equipment and a reliable command system. Russia, Grachev said, had to create its own army "from scratch." [21]

ARMS EXPORTS

The downward trends in defense extended to arms exports. There is considerable uncertainty about the specific figures. Those who cite them often do not differentiate between the value of agreements to sell arms and the value of actual deliveries. Many reports of agreements are unverified media accounts which are sometimes reported canceled. As in other areas of economic activities, there are difficulties in converting prices and the values of products into U.S. dollars. Before the Soviet breakup, Western estimates generally discounted official statistics about arms exports. Nevertheless, all agree that arms exports from the former Soviet Union have plummeted in recent years and that a recovery is not in sight.

The U.S. government estimates that Soviet arms exports averaged about $20 billion annually during 1984–89, using selling prices in 1991 dollars. The figure for 1990, in the U.S. estimate, declined to $13.3 billion in 1990 and then fell by half in 1991 to $6.5 billion. [22] The Russian figures for arms exports are $7.8 billion in 1991 and $3 billion or $4 billion in 1992, depending upon the official source. [23] A U.S. government estimate for 1992 was not available at the time of this writing.

There were several reasons for the collapse of the Soviet arms market. First, past exports were heavily subsidized and recipient third world nations willing to accept Soviet arms paid little, if anything, for them. The decision to end grant aid and drastically reduce subsidies and the shift to a hard currency basis for sales on commercial terms would inevitably narrow the market. The decline in demand for Soviet arms from the former communist states in East and Central Europe; adherence to UN sanctions against arms transfers to countries such as Iraq, Libya and Yugoslavia, once important Soviet arms customers; and the lack of competitiveness with sources of arms in the West further limited opportunities for the former Soviet Union. Finally, the global arms market itself became saturated with supplies from countries in the West, as well as in the former Soviet Union, where defense purchases were cut back at a time when economies were stagnating or in decline.

[21] Moscow Interfax, 26 November 1992, in FBIS-SOV-92-230, 30 November 1992, p. 36; Interview with Defense Minister Pavel Grachev, Moscow Russian Television Network, 22 February 1993, in FBIS-SOV-93-035, 24 February 1993, p. 31.
[22] Richard F. Grimmett, "Conventional Arms Transfers to the Third World, 1984–1991," Congressional Research Service. Library of Congress, July 20, 1992, p. 62.
[23] Moscow Interfax, 19 November 1992, in "Hard Currency Payments Cause Decrease in Weapons Exports," FBIS-SOV-92-226, 19 November 1992, p. 4; Moscow Interfax, 1 December 1992, in "Government Seeks New Markets for Arms Sales," FBIS-SOV-92-231, 1 December 1992, p. 1; "Hello, Weapons," Moscow Rossiyskaya Gazeta, 26 January 1993, in FBIS-SOV-93-016, 27 January 1993, p. 22.

It was hoped in Russia, at the beginning of 1992, that hard currency earned from the export of arms would partially offset budget constraints and help maintain some defense firms and their workers. Initially, the government viewed arms sales as a way to absorb the shock of procurement cuts. Hardliners and military officials attached other significance to this activity, and it became something of a litmus test of one's commitment to a resurgence of Russian power and influence. In late 1992 acting Prime Minister Yegor Gaidar, in an action widely interpreted as an attempt to win favor with military-industrial forces, announced a series of major arms agreements and reaffirmed the government's commitment to promote arms sales. [24]

Gaidar's announcement mentioned sales valued at $2.25 billion to China, India, and Iran. There were disclosures by others of sales or talks about sales to countries such as Pakistan, Turkey, Syria, the United Arab Emirates, Malaysia, and South Korea. Typically, the announcements did not provide full details about the types and numbers of weapons and equipment or the time within which they were to be delivered. They did indicate that Russia was willing to sell some of its most advanced conventional weapons at very attractive prices, and that it placed special importance on cultivating the arms markets on the Central Asian and Far Eastern borders of the CIS.

Among the more sophisticated items sold to Iran were 3 diesel powered submarines, one of which was delivered in 1992, Mig-29 fighter aircraft, and reportedly there were negotiations to sell 12 Backfire bombers. Early in 1993, President Yeltsin said during a trip to India that Russia was prepared to continue supplying it with spare parts for Soviet arms previously purchased and to give assurance that factories building arms to be shipped to India would continue operating. In the same period, Defense Minister Grachev was reported visiting the United Arab Emirates, Kuwait, and Bahrain to promote arms exports. [25]

COLLECTIVE SECURITY, PEACEKEEPING, AND CONFLICT

The existence of conflicts among and within several of the states, disputes over how to divide up military assets located in the non-Russian states, and the presence of large numbers of Russians (estimated at 25–28 million) in those states left unresolved many issues about the role of the Russian military in the former Soviet republics. The approach to these issues has already influenced Russian military policy within the CIS and is likely to affect the future size and structure of forces.

There was an expectation in some quarters that the former Soviet republics would sign a collective security agreement and achieve a degree of military unification within the CIS framework. In May 1992 a collective security treaty was signed by Russia, Ar-

---

[24] Margert Shapiro, "Russian Reformer Pledges Arms Sales," *Washington Post*, 3 December 1992; Umit Enginsoy, *Defense News*, 7–13 December 1992.

[25] Bill Sweetman, " 'Backfire' bomber for export soon," *Jane's Defence Weekly*, 17 October 1992; Glen E.Howard and Robert T.Kramer, "Iran's Quest For Greater Air Power", *FSRC Analytical Note*, 28 October 1992; Umit Enginsoy and Vivek Raghuvanshi, "Russia Vows to Bolster Arms Supplies to India," *Defense News*, 1–7 February 1993; and Philip Finnegan, "Russia Boosts Sales Drive To Middle East Nations," *Defense News*, 22–28 February 1993.

menia, and four Central Asian states, Kazakhstan, Uzbekistan, Kyrgyzstan, and Tajikistan. The other states, most notably Ukraine, declined to become signatories. Belarus stayed out on the grounds of its policy of neutrality but later began to reconsider its position, in part because of the difficulties in securing arms and material for its forces. [26] Still, despite numerous attempts by Yevgeniy Shaposhnikov, the CIS Joint Armed Forces Commander in Chief, to promote the idea of a unified defense program, he had only limited success even among the six who signed the agreement. In January 1993 Shaposhnikov conceded, "The Commonwealth is currently an amorphous entity." [27]

Some of the underlying reasons for the lack of headway in this area were revealed in the reports of the first meeting of the defense ministers of the signatories to the collective security treaty, which took place in Moscow on February 27, 1993. When questions were raised about the structure of the CIS armed forces, two models emerged. Russia and Uzbekistan favored a structure similar to that of the Warsaw Treaty. The others voted for a NATO-type body.

The differences in the two models say much about Russian and non-Russian attitudes toward mutual security. The Warsaw Treaty Organization was a hierarchical entity under Moscow's control. NATO is a coordinating body in which decisions are taken more by consensus than by the decision of the strongest member. Those that support the NATO approach are obviously concerned about becoming too dependent upon Russia and being subject to its dictates. [28]

The use of Russian "peacekeeping" forces in the newly independent states was an increasingly nettlesome issue. Many Russian leaders advocated the use of existing forces to maintain the peace within the CIS. Some drew a parallel between Russia's sphere of vital interests in the CIS and the U.S. Monroe Doctrine for Latin America. Non-Russians harbored the kind of suspicions about Moscow's intentions that contributed to the breakup. A Ukrainian official said flatly that Ukraine would never agree that any single CIS member, including Russia, had "special peacekeeping rights" within the CIS. The government of Moldova also denounced Russia's wishes to assume that role. [29]

The former Soviet Union had become a region of "flash points," in which there were numerous imminent or actual conflicts between ethnic and religious groups and forces in opposition to established governments. The Russian military leadership's position with regard to ethnic conflict was clear. In a radio interview, De-

26 "Presidential Bulletin," *Interfax*, 18 March 1993, in FBIS-SOV-93-052, 19 March 1993, p. 48; "Will the Republic Remain Neutral?" *Nezavisimaya Gazeta*, 17 March 1993, p. 3, in FBIS-SOV-93-052, p. 49; Igor Sinyakevich, "Vyacheslav Kebich Argues for Participation in Collective Security System ...," *Nezavisimaya Gazeta*, 24 March 1993, in FBIS-SOV y-93-056, 25 March 1993, p. 53.

27 Remarks by Shaposhnikov at a news conference, Moscow Mayak Radio Network, 19 January 1993, in FBIS-SOV-93-012, 21 January 1993, p. 9.

28 Moscow Russian Television Network, 27 February 1993, in FBIS-SOV-03-038, 1 March 1993; Leg Falischev, "Collective Security in the CIS: The NATO or Warsaw Pact Model?" *Krasnaya Zvezda*, 2 March 1993, in FBIS-SOV-930040, 3 March 1993.

29 Suzanne Crow, "Russian Peacekeeping: Defense, Diplomacy, or Imperialism?" *RFE/RL Research Report*, 18 September 1992; Moscow INTERFAX, 2 March 1993, in FBIS-SOV-93-040, "Official Disagrees With Russia's 'Special' Peacekeeping Role," 3 March 1993, p. 53; Bucharest Radio Romania Network, 5 March 1993, in FBIS-SOV-93-042, "Ministry Condemns Yeltsin's Statement on 'Peacemaker' Role," 5 March 1993, p. 49.

fense Minister Grachev gave two reasons why the Russian Armed Forces would continue to involve itself in these conflicts: First, because the Russian Army is "the only manageable unit in the former USSR" that can perform the task of stopping bloodbaths. Second, "In all states where interethnic conflicts take place, there is a large community of Russian speakers ... whom we have the right and the duty to defend." [30]

There was hardly a country of the former Soviet Union in which Grachev's doctrine could not apply. Ukraine, with more than 11 million Russians, was a special case. Russians were a majority in the Crimea area, and there was talk in that area of independence and in the Donbas-Odessa region of a separatist movement. The more immediate problems concerned the Black Sea Fleet and nuclear weapons. Early in 1992 Russia asserted that all military strategic assets should be under the control of the CIS armed forces. It claimed that the Black Sea Fleet performs a strategic mission in the Mediterranean. Ukraine responded that each state has a right to the property on its territory and as its coastline is the location of the Fleet's operating base and shipyards, the Fleet, except for the ships carrying nuclear weapons, belonged to it.

The controversy over the nuclear weapons was similar. Ukraine argued that its ownership of the property of the former Soviet Union located in Ukraine extended to all the property of the Strategic Nuclear Forces. It conceded that the CIS forces had the right of usage of the weapons, but maintained it owned the physical components, including the material in the nuclear warheads, which happened to be quite valuable. Ukraine reportedly transferred all tactical nuclear weapons to Russia, after some hesitation. But in early 1993 the disputes over the Black Sea Fleet and the strategic nuclear weapons were still unresolved.

There were nuclear arms in two other states, Belarus and Kazakhstan. Belarus was the more accommodating with Russia's wishes. It quickly transferred all tactical nuclear weapons to Russia and at the end of 1992 agreed to remove the remaining weapons by the end of 1994. Kazakhstan transferred all tactical nuclear weapons to Russia but wavered as to the strategic weapons. As Ukraine had done, it first agreed to transfer the weapons to Russia, then hesitated. At the beginning of 1993, it seemed to have rejected Russia's claims of ownership but to have acceded to Russian administrative control. [31]

In the Baltic states the presence of Russian troops was a source of continuing friction and the large Russian minorities a matter of concern to Moscow. Moscow went beyond expressions of concern about Russian minorities in several other countries where there were demands by Russian and other minorities for independence and struggles over territory.

There was escalating violence in two of the European states and the Caucuses. In Moldova the Russian minority formed a separatist

[30] Moscow Radio Rossi Network, 23 February 1993, in FBIS-SOV-93-035, 24 February 1993, p. 24.

[31] Thomas O'Keefe, "Republic Views Of Nuclear Weapon Dismantlement And Destruction," *FSRC Analytical Note,* 4 May 1992; John W.R. Lepingwell, "Ukraine, Russia, and the Control of Nuclear Weapons," *RFE/RL Research Report,* 19 February 1993, pp. 4-20; John W.R. Lepingwell, "Kazakhstan and Nuclear Weapons," Ibid, pp. 59-61.

movement and created an armed force to achieve its goals. Former Soviet forces stationed in Moldova, the 14th Army, came under ostensible CIS control and declared themselves neutral. The Moldovan government accused them of supporting the separatists, and at one point there was a possibility of fighting between Moldova and Russia. In early 1993 Moldovan officials formally protested Russian army exercises in Moldova and called them a ploy intended to destabilize the situation. Discussions with Russia about the removal of the 14th Army from Moldova continued into 1983. [32]

Separatist movements of different minority groups in two areas of Georgia led to violent confrontations and the involvement of Russian forces. In the spring of 1992 Russian Vice President Alexander Rutskoi (who had previously made a statement in support of the Russian minority seeking independence in Moldova) expressed support for the South Ossetian separatists seeking unification with the North Ossetians in Russia. Two months later President Yeltsin and Georgian leader Eduard Shevardnadze agreed to the introduction of a peacekeeping force, but there was soon disagreement about its composition and mission and the timetable for its withdrawal. [33]

Russia and Georgia agreed in September to the introduction of a Russian peacekeeping contingent in the Abkhazia region where another separatist movement was under way. The violence there reached a new peak in early 1993 when there was a three-day intensive bombing attack of Sukhumi by what appeared to be Russian aircraft. Shevardnadze, who earlier had warned that "Russia has not fully shaken off the imperial disease," denounced the act. Russian Defense Minister Grachev countercharged that the aircraft involved in the attack were Georgia's, painted to look like they were Russian. Shervardnadze replied, "I think that the Russian special services impose their crazy ideas on Grachev and use him as their mouthpiece all over the world." [34]

Russian peacekeeping forces were not sent to Armenia or Azerbaijan when renewed fighting occurred in the spring of 1992. Indeed, observers point out that Armenia launched a major offensive after Russian troops were withdrawn from the Karabakh region of Azerbaijan. Russian forces, under CIS control, were present in both countries. The renewed fighting in 1992 threatened to involve all the bordering nations—Russia, Turkey and Iran.

---

[32] Moscow *Interfax*, 17 February 1993, in FBIS-SOV–93–031, "Russian Military Exercises Continue Despite Protest," 18 February 1993, p. 57; Bucharest *Rompres*, 20 November 1992, in FBIS-SOV–92–225, "Russia Proposes Withdrawal of 14th Army Within Two Years," p. 52; and "Moldovan-Russian Troop Talks," *RFE/RFL Daily Report*, 5 February 1993, p. 5.

[33] Suzanne Crow, "The Theory and Practice of Peacekeeping in the Former USSR," *RFE/RFL Research Report*, 18 September 1992, pp.31–36; Bernard Gold, "Georgia: Basic Facts," Congressional Research Service, The Library of Congress, CRS Report for Congress, 10 June 1992; Moscow *Itar-Tass*, 17 September 1992, in FBIS-SOV–92–182, "Peacekeepers Report Situation Calm in S.Ossetia", 18 September 1992, p. 39; Interview with Oleg Teziyev, Moscow *Nezavisimaya Gazeta*, 25 November 1992, in FBIS-SOV–92–229, "South Ossetian Government Aide on Russian Membership, Unification," 27 November 1992, p. 61.

[34] Interview with Eduard Shevardnadze, Moscow, *Moskovskiye Novosti*, 21 February 1993, in FBIS-SOV–93–031, "Shevardnadze Says Russia Key to Abkhaz Conflict," 18 February 1993, p. 70; Moscow *Itar-Tass*, 18 March 1993, in FBIS-SOV–93–052, "Russia's Grachev Denies Bombing; Alleges Smear Campaign," 19 March 1993, p. 54; Moscow *Interfax*, 18 March 1993, in FBIS-SOV–93–052, "Russian Military Command Warns Georgia," 19 March 1993, p. 54; Moscow *Interfax*, 19 March 1993, in FBIS-SOV–93–052, "Shevardnadze on 'Cynicism' of Grachev Statement," 19 March 1992, p. 54.

Both Armenia and Azerbaijan made accusations that Russian troops were aiding the other side. Moscow issued denials and condemned the fighting. At the same time, both sides were equipped largely with arms of the former Soviet military purchased or otherwise acquired after the break up.[35]

Conditions in Central Asia and the Far East were also unstable or potentially so. Concerns about Islamic fundamentalists and other opposition groups, and sensitivity to the Russian minorities, contributed to the decision by four of the Central Asian countries to move towards a collective security arrangement with Russia and their willingness to rely on Russian troops and support for indigenous forces. A number of understandings with Russia were achieved about bilateral and collective military activities.

Tajikistan was the scene of an all-out civil war in the second half of 1992. In that period about 20,000 people were reported killed, and 200,000 people became refugees. Russian forces guarded the border with Afghanistan, a nation that was said to be aiding the rebels. Despite assertions that it would not take sides, the Russian 201st motorized rifle division, based in Tajikistan, appeared to have played an active role in the fighting in support of the government.[36]

Kyrgyzstan agreed to allow its defense industry to keep meeting Russian orders so long as they were financed and materially backed by Russia, and to let Russia pay 80 percent of the cost of guarding its border with China.[37] Uzbekistan announced in late 1992 that the 15th Air Defense Division was passing to its jurisdiction but that operationally it would remain in the Russian air defense system. In early 1993 the President of Uzbekistan and the Russian Defense Minister held talks in Tashkent to discuss joint use of air defense and other facilities and joint military exercises.[38] The president of Kazakhstan stated in December 1992 that he envisioned joint defense actions with other states in the framework of the CIS Collective Security Treaty. It was also disclosed that Kazakhstan would ask Russia to help replenish Kazakh troops and provide them with weapons and uniforms, and that a treaty

[35] Carol Migdalovitz, "Armenia-Azerbaijan Conflict", *CRS Issue Brief,* Congressional Research Service, The Library of Congress, 22 March 1993; Yerevan *Radio Yerevan International Service,* 9 September 1992, in FBIS-SOV-92-176, "Ministry on Russian Transfer of Aircraft," 10 September 1992, p. 52; Moscow, *Programma Radio Odin Network,* 2 August 1992, in FBIS-SOV-92-150, "Veteran Appeal Russian Mercenary Involvement," 4 August 1992, p. 78; Moscow *Radio Rossii Network,* 10 May 1992, in FBIS-SOV-92-091, "7th Army Spokesman Denies Role in Attacks," 11 May 1992, p. 73; Interview with Tofik Gasymov, Baku *Turan,* 10 March 1993, in FBIS-SOV-93-046, "Russian Role in Conflict Cited," 11 March 1993, p. 77; and Baku *Azertac,* 25 February 1993, in FBIS-SOV-93-037, "Foreign Ministry: Russian Army Participation 'Inadmissible,' " 26 February 1993, p. 51;

[36] "Official Casualty Figures Cited For Tajik Civil War," *RFE/RL Daily Report,* 5 February 1993; Anatoliy Ivlev, "Tajikistan: Russian Motorized Rifle Division Remains the Nucleus of the Peacekeeping Forces," Moscow *Krasnaya Zvezda,* 11 Nov 1992, in FBIS-SOV-92-221, 16 November 1992, p. 81; Moscow *Interfax,* 6 December 1992, in FBIS-SOVA-92-235, "Russian Troops Rebuff Rebel Advance," 7 December 1992, p. 20; and Moscow *Itar-Tass,* 4 December 1992, in FBIS-SOV-92-235, "Russian Commander Committed To Defend Dushanbe," 7 December 1992, p. 23.

[37] Moscow *Interfax,* 10 September 1992, in FBIS-SOV-92-177, "Armed Neutrality Linchpin of Defense Doctrine," 11 September 1992, p. 41; Moscow Radio Rossii Network, 8 November 1992, in FBIS-SOV-92-218, "Russia Agrees to Underwrite Cost of Guarding Border," 10 November 1992, p. 64.

[38] Aleksandr Ivanov, "15th Air Defense Division Transferred to Uzbek Jurisdiction," Moscow *Krasnaya Zvezda,* 25 November 1992, in FBIS-SOV-92-229, 27 November 1992, p. 56; and Moscow *Itar-Tass,* 3 February 1993, in FBIS-SOV-93-022, 4 February 1993, p. 53.

would be concluded on military cooperation. Subsequently Russia and Kazakhstan agreed to coordinate military policy and defense activities. [39]

Finally, independence movements in various areas of Russia, especially the Russian Far East and in Sakhalin, and the dispute with Japan over the Kurile Islands, could conceivably lead to greater Russian military involvement in those areas.

[39] Moscow *Itar-Tass*, 8 December 1992, in FBIS-SOV-92-236, "Nazarbayev Discusses Defensive Military Doctrine," 8 December 1992, p. 36; Moscow *Interfax*, 8 December 1992, in FBIS-SOV-92-236, "Government to Ask Russia for Aid Equipping Troops," 8 December 1992, p. 36; Vladimir Urban and Anatoliy Ladin, "Russia and Kazakhstan Need Each Other . . .," Moscow *Krasnaya Zvezda*, 2 March 1993, in FBIS-SOV-93-040, p. 21; and Umit Enginsoy, "6 CIS States Discuss Combined Force Plan," *Defense News*, 8–14 March 1993.

CONVERSION OF MILITARY INDUSTRIES IN THE SUCCESSOR STATES OF THE FORMER SOVIET UNION

By Martin C. Spechler *

CONTENTS

SUMMARY

Conversion from defense production to civilian purposes offers real hope for the successor states of the former Soviet Union, but only over several years. Like market reforms generally, conversion is being resisted by powerful interests. At present, a compromise policy of partial, subsidized conversions of plants and research institutes *within* the defense complex is still being pursued, together with bottom-up initiatives by plants deprived of defense orders. Nonetheless, severe budget cuts and supply breakdowns have left much defense complex capacity idle. Ultimately the success of conversion depends on taking resources out of the control of conservative bureaucrats and making whole plants subject to competition in civilian markets. Only such irreversible conversion and reform should attract Western support.

INTRODUCTION

As first developed as part of perestroika in 1988, Soviet military conversion strategy was a cautious half-measure born of compromise with the bureaucracy, especially the military-industrial complex. Though much has changed in the successor states of the former Soviet Union, the proclaimed strategy of conversion re-

* Martin C. Spechler is Professor of Economics at Indiana University-Purdue University at Indianapolis. This research has been supported by the Indiana Center for Global Change and World Peace and the U.S.-Soviet Project of the Council on Economic Priorities. Vyacheslav Malygin, Maya Shukhgal'ter, and other Russian and Ukrainian colleagues suggested useful material for this paper.

mains essentially unchanged. Even in independent Ukraine, important defense producers have not yet departed from that model. The conversion strategy was designed to conserve arms production capacity and the power of the military-industrial complex itself, in addition to its declared objective of increasing supplies of sophisticated civilian machinery and instruments. The military-industrial complex or VPK (*voenno-promyshlennyi kompleks* in Russian) has not been disassembled in any of the successor states, and many of its supporters remain in high posts. Consequently, the strategy has not been abandoned, despite the disappointing results so far. To this observer, at least, it would be unlikely to have major positive effects even if fully funded. [1]

The present paper reviews the basic conversion strategy, updates its results, particularly for Russia and Ukraine, and presents some reasons from Western experience to believe that diversification within the former Soviet military-industrial complex will not contribute to structural change within the successor states.

BASIC CONVERSION STRATEGY

In Russian parlance, *konversiia* (conversion) can mean the physical transformation or dedication of existing items to civilian purposes. Here, though, we will limit discussion to the far more impressive potential of using capital equipment and primary inputs previously devoted to the military for civilian production. In the comprehensive conversion plan finally approved in December, 1990, the seven ministries of the VPK were assigned twelve priority tasks, such as creating new medical instruments, civilian aircraft, and food processing equipment. Besides producing new types of equipment as direct state orders, these defense ministries were supposed to spread the technological knowledge developed in military facilities to civilian ones.

Comprising perhaps 2,000 to 5,000 separate plants and employing as many as 7 to 16 million workers, according to various estimates, the defense complex produced about 17 percent of Soviet industrial production in 1990. [2] The VPK ministries always enjoyed priority access to the best specialists and to crucial materials, such as aluminum, stainless steel, transistors, computers, and optical devices. These advantages would be exploited by conversion of part of its existing production capacity to consumer goods. Direct conversion would use scarce high-quality materials that might otherwise be wasted, since it was often illegal or at least imprudent to dispose of unused resources in the sellers' markets of the former U.S.S.R. For example, the aviation industry used spare aluminum to produce baby carriages. Indeed, the defense-industry ministries of the former U.S.S.R. produced the vast majority of household appli-

---

[1] The present author analyzed the Soviet strategy and explained the reasons for its likely failure in "Conversion of Military Enterprises: the Choice of Strategy" [Russian], *Voprosy ekonomiki*, no. 2 (1991), pp. 10–20 [with A. Ozhegov and V. Malygin]

[2] According to A.V. Yablokov, State Counselor on Ecology and Public Health, *Izvestia*, April 13, 1992, p. 2; Julian Cooper, "Military Cuts and Conversion in the Defence Industry," *Soviet Economy*, vol. 7, no. 2 (April, 1991), p. 131.

ances, cameras, and electronic equipment that became widely available to the Soviet public during the 1970s and 1980s. [3] Originally, the conversion strategy was largely a matter of diversifying existing enterprises. To allow reversibility in case of need, civilian lines would be added without permanently shutting down military ones. Of the more than 528 Soviet plants to be affected by conversion in the first plan, nearly half were to shift less than 20 percent of their volume, another 180 were to shift from 20 to 30 percent, and only 40 (34 of them previously classified as "civilian" anyway!) would be completely converted. [4] That is, only six of the thousands of VPK plants would be transformed. In addition, the VPK took over plants formerly housed within civilian ministries. It swallowed the Ministry of Light and Food Machinery (transferred to the Ministry of Atomic Energy in 1987), the ministries of communications and civil aviation in 1989, and the State Committee on computers and information technology. As a result of this and previous reorganizations, there were reportedly 400 purely civilian plants within the VPK empire. [5]

While the Soviet military-industry bosses went along the regime's plan to increase the civilian share of output in defense plants to 60 or 65 percent, as proposed by Gosplan, academic critics charged that this widely publicized target was intended to be met mostly by price increases without significant quality improvement. [6] Even three years ago Western visitors to defense plants met obviously capable VPK managers eager to diversify as an offset to declining military orders, preferably with Western investors. Meanwhile, the fruits of conversion actually on display were the familiar simple consumer goods produced on the side by using scrap materials. The price tags suggested fairly high costs.

The original conversion strategy—direct, controlled diversification—left authority with the same State Commission on Military Industry, which had often been able to refuse civilian orders. Many large Soviet enterprises were (and remain) sole sellers. The chronic seller's market compounded their monopolistic advantages. Early results of the conversion plan were disappointing. [7] Articles in the press complained about the strange demands ("macaroni lines!") made by local organs upon sophisticated defense plants previously immune to such pressures.

The Gosplan department head for the defense complex, Yu. A. Glibin, tried to defend this privileged preserve. Any losses caused

[3] For a full list of defense industry production of civilian goods as of 1990, see Julian Cooper, *The Soviet Defense Industry* (New York, Council of Foreign Relations Press, 1991), Table 4.1. As of 1987–88, about 23 percent of all consumer durables were produced within the VPK. Table 8.6 in Julian Cooper, "The Soviet Defense Industry and Conversion: The Regional Dimension," in Liba Pauker and Peter Richards (eds.), *Defence Expenditures, Industrial Conversion, and Local Employment* (Geneva, ILO, 1991), pp. 157–78.

[4] *Kommunist*, no. 32 (1990).

[5] Julian Cooper, "Military Cuts," p. 132.

[6] Y. Yaremenko, E. Rogovski, and A. Ozhegov, "Conversion of the Defense Industry and the Restructuring of the Defense Industry," mimeo, 1990; *Problemy prognozirovaniia*, no. 2 (1990), p. 24.

[7] Not one plant was converted. In 1989 planned deliveries for agricultural processing equipment were underfulfilled, though of course blame was cast on non-delivery of parts."Konversiia: nadezhdi i real'nost'," *Trud*, February 20, 1990. Of 120 new types of goods planned for introduction by defense branches, only 23 began production. Of these, only five were reported to meet international standards. *Kommersant*, no. 32 (1990), August 13–20, 1990.

by conversion would be made good "ruble for ruble," he wrote. [8]
No involuntary unemployment would be permitted. In 1989 the defense ministries were granted 350 million rubles to reprofile 100 defense plants and shift a half million workers. Spokesmen of the military-industrial complex were particularly concerned that skilled workers would be induced to leave the military sphere for the growing private and cooperative sector. Rather than disperse precious research and development teams, it would be better to export weapons and use the proceeds to modernize the economy.

Pride in the VPK's unique capabilities did not prevent its supporters from pleading poverty when asked to contribute to the civilian economy. Glibin asserted to me that, unlike the Pentagon, the Soviet defense ministry has never funded the cost of weapons cutbacks or provided money for conversion. [9]

Even before the attempted coup in 1991, bureaucratic resistance had already subverted part of the original conversion design. Leasing to collectives, a form of privatization in Gorbachev's economic reform, [10] would not be permitted in this sector. [11] (But one VPK manager told me that "moonlighting" on enterprise premises was common. Indeed, according to Cooper, there are hundreds of cooperatives attached to defense enterprises. [12]) In the defense industry, unlike most of the rest of the economy, state orders—meaning supply regardless of profitability—were to predominate. [13] Instead of self-financing, the defense complex asked for 63 billion rubles for construction of new plants.

RUSSIAN UPDATE

Although the early achievements of conversion were disappointing, relative to plans, some expansion of civilian production can be identified. Between 1988 and 1990, production of food equipment within the defense complex did increase from 1.0 to 1.7 billion rubles, while medical equipment jumped six times from a modest base. With some other small increases in volumes of appliances, consumer goods production in the VPK grew 11.7 billion rubles in nominal value. The VPK share of all consumer goods grew from 12 percent to 15 percent of total Soviet production of such goods. [14] What is more, the share of civilian goods in total VPK production grew from 42.6 percent in 1988 to 50.2 percent in 1989 and 54 percent by October of 1991. These rapidly increasing shares, of course, also reflect declining military production. The common view that "nothing has happened" [15] may be a partisan exaggeration, at least judged by volume of civilian production in military plants. But the cost, quality, and exportability of these goods is another matter.

---

[8] Glibin promised three years of subsides, credits and retraining for defense complex workers. *EKO*, 5 (191), p. 159.
[9] Meeting with V.I. Smyslov, Yu. A. Glibin, V.G. Kotov, and others at Gosplan headquarters, Moscow, October 11, 1990.
[10] A.S. Isaev, "Reform and the Defense Fields," *Kommunist*, April 1989.
[11] P. Bunich in *Izvestia*, May 26, 1990, pp. 1–2. This idea had first been raised by economists within the aviation industry, but the minister nixed it.
[12] Cooper, *Soviet Defence Industry*, p. 56.
[13] *Izvestia*, May 18, 1990.
[14] Cooper, *Defense Industry*, p. 38.
[15] *Izvestia*, December 27, 1991; *Trud*, January 11, 1992.

While defense cutbacks in real terms had occurred in 1990 and (over Gorbachev's objections) in 1991, the regimes that came to power late in 1991 deepened the budget cuts. Acute budgetary shortages in 1991–92 have pressured VPK enterprises to adjust more rapidly than they had originally intended. In his speech of October, 1991, Russian President Boris Yeltsin supported a global cut of 10 percent in the republic's defense spending overall, on top of the 20 percent cut for 1991. Defense spending by the Commonwealth of Independent States would fall another 12 percent in 1992, though the actual cuts might be greater if Russia's partners fail to make their expected contributions or if inflation is greater than what was foreseen. [16] Indeed, acute budgetary shortages in 1991–92 have pressured enterprises of the military-industrial complex to adjust more rapidly than they had originally intended. By the end of 1991, 12 had been forced to close. Within the defense budget, procurements have fallen more than other items: 68 percent in Russia as a whole this year, or as much as 85 to 90 percent for some enterprises.

Of the 82 billion rubles, apparently in 1992 prices, to be spent on conversion, according to First Deputy Minister of Economics Andrei Nechaev, about half is for definite reinvestment projects and half for social support to prevent disruptions in the most heavily impacted districts. [17] In a speech to the Congress on April 7, Yeltsin said 10 billion had been spent, about the rate to be maintained through the balance of the year. In addition to this central funding, conversion will be aided by tax abatements and a three percent charge on output in VPK enterprises.

Yeltsin did not address conversion as an important economic policy priority in his first speeches, but from the first he has supported the separation of military and civilian production, shutting down some military plants and reconfiguring others. First Deputy Defense Minister Andrei Kokoshin urged that support be given to civilian industries with real hope for success, not necessarily defense industries. [18] Whether this amounts to a shift in conversion strategy is still doubtful.

Yeltsin's appointee as chairman of the State Conversion Committee, Mikhail Bazhanov, has elaborated this strategy of "temporarily" shutting down military capacity and privatizing up to 90 percent of VPK enterprises. After national and regional plans are drawn up, Bazhanov says, specific conversion projects will be funded. A new law on the "legal and social basis for conversion" was signed in April, but the text is not yet available. Bazhanov gave a spending figure of 150 billion rubles (in 1989 prices) over 5 or 6 years, a lower figure than mentioned before, but complained that funding was not forthcoming for conversion. Most recently, he has called for slowing down the conversion process to 3 percent yearly. To avoid dismemberment of facilities and research teams, conversion authorities might have to resort to sale of surplus equipment, contract production, and especially foreign partners.

---

[16] RFE/RL Report, vol. 1, no. 22 (May 29, 1992), p. 52.
[17] Wall Street Journal, April 20, 1992.
[18] ITAR-TASS, April 8, 1992, as cited in RFE/RL Research Report, vol. 1, no. 18 (May 1, 1992).

Things are not going well: "it's convulsion, rather than conversion." [19]

Because of the budgetary austerity, foreign ties are more important than ever to the Russian conversion strategy. In the first place, arms sales have been and will continue to be a source of foreign currency. The Soviet Union exported more than $10 billion in arms each year during the late 1980s, though this fell by more than half in 1991. [20] Not only VPK chiefs, but also President Yeltsin and Foreign Minister Andrei Kozyrev have supported such sales in principle, excluding only those to "unstable regions." A newly created Russian Federal Export Control Commission, under Gaidar and other senior ministers, will monitor sales of arms and military technology. According to Mikhail Malei, state counselor for conversion, exports of reactor-grade plutonium, Nikonov attack rifles, anti-missile systems, and other advanced weaponry could finance as much as 40 percent of the conversion effort. [21] Of course, the limited ability of erstwhile Third World customers like Libya, Vietnam, India, and Syria to pay in hard currency will curtail this source of revenue to the budget. In addition, the VPK welcomes joint ventures or even takeovers of superfluous facilities in exchange for financing and technology, particularly if the foreign currency comes directly to the industry. High hopes, I discovered, are placed on the Batterymarch financial group from Boston in this connection.

Press accounts do reveal some of the conflict apparently taking place over budgetary allocations between the VPK and the reform leadership, presently Deputy Prime Minister Yegor Gaidar. Leading the critics of reform is Vice President Aleksandr Rutskoi, who was put in overall charge of conversion. Rutskoi, a former general, has been outspoken since late 1991 in opposing defense cuts and reportedly wishes to preserve the old system of direct state orders coordinated by the Military-Industrial Commission. [22] In this he is seconded by the new parliamentary opposition associated with the Russian Christian Democrats, led by Viktor Aksyuchits.

As a response to the withering of the central planning mechanism in Russia, some of the military enterprises have united regionally to press their interests. This does not necessarily mean they support privatization and market competition. [23] The opposite is more likely.

With the weakness of the administration in Moscow and rising unemployment, it is hard to predict what will happen in this conflict between the liberal pro-Western faction around Yeltsin and the conservative nationalists now also included in the decision

---

[19] *Rossiiskaia Gazeta*, February 24, 1992, p. 2; FBIS, January 23, 1992, pp. 53–56, as quoted in Kenneth L. Adelman and Norman Augustine, "Defense Conversion: Bulldozing the Management," *Foreign Affairs*, 1992, pp. 26–47. On May 22, 1992, Vitaly Shlykov, Deputy Chairman of the Russian State Committee on Defense Matters, was quoted as saying that Russia has no coherent conversion policy. RFE/RL *Report*, 1:23 (June 5, 1992).

[20] Statement by the president of the League of Defense Enterprises, created in early 1992. FBIS-USR, 92–057, May 13, 1992.

[21] Statement by the president of the League of Defense Enterprises, created in early 1992. FBIS-USR, 92–057, May 13, 1992.

[22] *Ekonomika i zhizn*, no. 52 (December 1991), p. 9. While supporting a state-planned strategy to major conversion projects, Rutskoi would allow the VPK to use spare capacity as it sees fit.

[23] Cf. Cooper, *Soviet Defense Industry*, chapter 5, who cites the VPK support for arms exchanges and joint stock companies.

making at the national security council. As indicated above, authority to deal with conversion is confused. One possibility is a kind of industrial feudalism, in which VPK enterprises and allied local officials take over regional economies and attempt to trade with all outsiders for foreign currency or needed consumer goods.

CASE OF UKRAINE: DESPERATE BUT NOT IMPOSSIBLE

In some ways the situation of Ukraine, viewed less than a year after its independence, is more difficult than that of Russia. Though reliable statistics are still scant, my impression from a trip in May 1992 is that leading Ukrainian economists have a sense of vulnerability to events in Russia. Ukrainian production is falling and unemployment rising even faster than in Russia, I was told. Because of the inability to raise taxes from a declining tax base and sharp disagreements about spending cuts, approval of a draft budget was been long delayed in parliament. The eventual agreement reportedly allowed 16 percent for defense. [24]

A further impending cut in oil and gas deliveries from the Russian republic is creating much unease. [25] Computed in Western currency, according to one Ukrainian study, the southern republic has a massive deficit with its larger and richer neighbor. Energy self-sufficiency is a mere hope, given geological conditions in the Donets coal fields and resistance to nuclear power. Other vital raw materials are available only in barter. Distrust of monetary manipulation by the Russian central bank, moreover, has led the Ukrainian government to call a halt to the use of the Russian ruble for domestic purchases, though money and credit emissions, whether in coupons or grivna, are hardly under control.

Up to late 1991 the Union VPK ministries in Moscow had been responsible for the sales and budgets of the some 330 large defense plants located on the territory of Ukraine. Design requirements were also dictated from Moscow. Official sources say the defense sector accounted for over one-third of industrial production there, but this may be an exaggeration of its net role. It employed about 18 percent of the Ukrainian industrial labor force, according to Julian Cooper. Of his partial list of 510 military enterprises in the former Soviet Union, 78 (13.7 percent) were located in Ukraine. But only a few in Kiev and the Black Sea coast produced end-products—notably missiles and warships. Most of Ukraine's defense plants have been in the optical and electronics areas, where the republic's ample female work force offered a necessary input, as well as railway rolling stock and metal products. Provided commercial customers can be found, these specialties could yet prove assets to Ukrainian civilian development. [26]

Economic policy in Ukraine has so far been fairly conservative, and criticism from liberal intellectuals has been less forceful than in Russia. The economics profession remains somewhat provincial, its leadership remaining in the hands of ex-Soviet nominees. West-

---

[24] RFE/RL *Reports*, vol. 1, no. 19 (May 8, 1992), p. 47.
[25] Reuters reported that national income fell 20% in 1991 and industrial output 15%. RFE/RL *Reports*, vol. 1:18 (May 1, 1992), p. 50.
[26] V.V. Moroz, "Problemy konversii i prakticheskie puti ikh resheniia," *Ekonomika ukraini: minule, suchasne i maibutne (tezi i materiali)*. (Donetsk: mimeo., 1992), p. 177.

ern advisors to the government of President Leonid Kravchuk—and Western influence generally—has been less evident than in Moscow. So far, reforms have dealt mainly with loosening restrictions on foreign trade and investment, not releasing prices. Viktor Antonov, Minister of Machine Building, the Military-Industrial Complex, and Conversion since 1990, remains in office. His conversion program reflects the state-planned approach of pre-independence times. According to President Kravchuk's top economic advisors, state enterprises and state orders will continue a long time in military industries. When it comes to granting subsidies and investment funds for conversion, priority will be given food and farm machinery production, medical instruments, environmental equipment, and then consumer goods. But progress has been slow in the conversion field, as in several others, because the 1992 budget was not approved until mid-June.

As in Russia, steep cuts in Ukrainian military procurements—30 percent to 75 percent or more—are forcing the pace of demilitarization, if not conversion. Displacements of workers are expected every day, and scarcity of essential materials (e.g., nonferrous metals) has shut down production. There is little money in the republic for new investments. Only a paltry 450,000 rubles have been made available for conversion this year, according to one report. [27] Little wonder Ukrainian officials put most hope on developing foreign links, previously coordinated from Moscow. President Kravchuk has supported selling military-industrial facilities for hard currency. When former Arms Control and Disarmament Agency chief Kenneth Adelman visited Ukraine recently, someone asked him the urgent question, how could they sell AK–47 semi-automatic rifles. [28] (Minister Antonov was heard to threaten selling weapons abroad if $200 million were not granted for conversion.) [29] The most likely customers would be Ukraine's nearest sources of energy—Iran and other countries the Middle East. Ukraine has already agreed to sell spare parts or replacements for Soviet-made combat equipment to Hungary in exchange for food or help in conversion. [30] A very similar situation has arisen in Slovakia, likewise under severe economic pressure.

WESTERN EXPERIENCE AND PROSPECTS IN THE FORMER SOVIET UNION

Western experience after World War II confirms that the cost and time required for conversion of defense plants is often underrated and the benefits exaggerated. [31] The Truman Administration's policy of selling off wartime synthetic rubber, aluminum, and magnesium facilities was costly and could not be completed until the late 1950s under Eisenhower. When combined with privatization, conversion problems are all the more complicated when the government prefers to avoid reinforcing monopoly positions. New, properly financed competitors are always hard to find, as we now

27 Radio Kiev, January 28, 1992, as reported in RFE/RL Reports, vol. 1, no. 5 (February 7, 1992), p. 45.
28 Adelman and Augustine, p. 40.
29 National Public Radio interview, February 3, 1992.
30 Izvestia, March 4, 1992, p. 2.
31 Ethan B. Kapstein, "From Guns to Butter in the USSR," Challenge September-October, 1989, pp. 11–15.

see in reunited Germany. Finance will be even scarcer in Russia, despite the larger monetary overhang, and new foreign entrants more reluctant because contract enforcement is more difficult to obtain internationally than it is within a (re)united country.

At the microeconomic level, the direct approach of converting plant and equipment to civilian production did not work well when tried in the United States and Western Europe. There was a tendency to overestimate the commercial value of equipment formerly used for arms and aircraft. Sale of this equipment took longer than expected and the eventual price was lower than expected. Conversion of large, specialized aircraft and shipbuilding facilities was particularly problematic. [32] Steel and rubber plants changed customers most readily, and auto plants returned to essentially prewar models. Russian planners I have met tend to exaggerate the value of physical capital controlled by the VPK for civilian purposes, while they tend to minimize the flexibility of the specialists employed there.

When defense workers are released into a prosperous civilian economy, by contrast, the results have been better. After all, most workers in military industries have job classifications identical or similar to those in civilian industry—e.g., forklift driver or electronics assembler. When the British TSR–2 fighter aircraft program was terminated in 1965, the released workers were fairly easily reabsorbed in civil aviation or other fields without major problems because of the generally low unemployment rates of the time. The same was true in the mid-1950s in the United States and France, while the higher rates of unemployment around 1973 made conversion more challenging for those not prepared to accept jobs far away at lower rates of pay.

Defense production organizations are not well adapted to the managerial and behavioral culture characteristic of the best civilian plants. The differences may be summarized in a table of schematic, ideal-typical characteristics (see Table 1). To the extent that these characteristics mark organization behavior and culture, they affect the relative size and standing of departments within the enterprise and the values shared by employers, specialists, and managers. One's promotions and status are normally determined according to one's adherence to these values. Most important for our purpose, these organizational characteristics usually determine the production methods chosen—flexibility of equipment, supervisory methods, flow vs. batch production, and the relative size of overhead costs to the variable. It seems to typify military plants to have high fixed, overhead costs per unit with sharply declining average variable cost as the cumulative volume of production increases. "Learning by doing" was first discovered in military plants. [33] Obvious excess capacity is frequently observed in defense plants, leading to export sales efforts and government funding at slack times. Civilian production of final goods and equipment has lower overheads, lower per worker wage costs, and flatter average variable cost curves.

---

[32] Arthur J. Alexander, "Defense Industry Conversion in China, the Soviet Union, and the United States," RAND mimeo, May 1990.

[33] Ely Devons, *Planning in Practice* (Cambridge, 1950).

TABLE 1. Behavioral and Organizational Characteristics of Military and Civilian Production in Advanced Industrial Societies.

Military Production	Civilian Production
One customer with unlimited resources	Many customers, with limited resources
Customer has few or no alternatives	Customer has several alternatives
Customer defines need or performance specifications	Producer must define need
Designers try for highest possible technical performance, safety, and reliability	Designers, in cooperation with marketing, seek optimal quality at reasonable cost and vendibility
Zero-defects quality control or on-site supervision by customer	Quality control statistical—some percentage defects acceptable—with guaranteed replacement to customer
Production runs predictable,* homogeneous output	Uncertain production runs, modification common
Secrecy mandatory	Technology may be divulged to customers, partners, or licensees

* In practice, of course, unexpected defense cutbacks make defense runs less predictable than they should be; complaints by defense contractors make this quite apparent.

In consequence of these generalizations, direct conversion of firms and enterprises would be costly in any economic system. A partial shift from military to civilian production within the same organization would raise costs at commercially saleable quantities, delay the introduction of simple product modifications, and bias design of major improvements toward excessive quality for demand conditions. Civilian production by military-oriented organizations will be marked by behavior typical of the military-industrial complex, particularly in monopolistic sellers' markets such as those of the former Soviet Union. Because of specialization, relatively little physical capital could be efficiently switched to production of civilian machinery. [34]

Several kinds of empirical evidence testify to the validity of this reasoning. In the West many firms and corporations contain both military and civilian divisions, for the sake of financial diversification and risk reduction, for exploitation of proprietary skills and technologies, and for spreading the overhead expenses of headquarters. "Conversion" of effort is frequent as the corporation tries to increase (usually) its civilian production.

But such diversification is not tantamount to direct conversion. Switching equipment between divisions of the same firm is infrequent, except perhaps in electronics and some raw materials. When the Swedish Bofors concern switches to civilian production, equipment often has to be "thrown out." [35] British telecommunications and aerospace found that separate accounting systems were necessary to keep costs under control. When a French aerospace company tried to produce laboratory instruments for blood tests, again overhead costs were unsustainable. Attempts to have mixed production in a Saab plant producing both jet engines and automobile

---

[34] Only 3–4% according to V. Protasov, "Ne znaia brodu?" *Literaturnaia gazeta*, May 9, 1990. I am indebted to Vladimir Kontorovich and Boris Rumer for this reference.
[35] Bernard Udis, *From Guns to Butter* (New York: Ballinger, 1978), p. 202.

gears proved unsuccessful, as the cost of the latter proved too high. Perhaps, then, it is not surprising that few instances of mixed plants can be found in diversified (military and civilian) corporations in the West. One exception to this rule was the nationalized FFV's plant at Eskilstuna, Sweden, where a largely military plant produced kingpin housings for Saab automobiles, steering columns for Volvos, and parts for the Tetra Pak beverage boxes. (Whether it does so at a profit could not be determined.) [36]

Usually in FFV and elsewhere in Western Europe companies' separate divisions are created for military work, as is true in America at Chrysler, General Motors, General Electric, and so on. Chrysler, Honeywell, and Goodyear have recently sold or are divesting themselves of their military divisions, apparently in the belief that they did nothing for the civilian side of their business.

There are legions of examples of failed commercial projects by large military contractors. Norman Augustine, chairman of Martin Marietta, the missile maker, said, "When it comes to diversification, the defense industry's record is unblemished by success." [37] (Nonetheless, his corporation is developing an automation program for the Postal Service, a single customer like the Defense Department.) Boeing failed when its Vertol division tried to produce subway cars, instead of military helicopters. Rohr Corporation's subway systems built for the San Francisco Bay Area and the Washington, D.C., area—while technically progressive—suffered from cost overruns traceable to technical excesses and poor management of spending. According to Murray Weidenbaum, a pro-market critic of direct conversion, diversification of military-industrial companies into sport boats, prosthetic devices, stainless steel caskets, heavy land vehicles, adhesives, wall panels, welding equipment, gas turbines, and cargo-handling have all been half-hearted and usually abandoned. [38] These were mostly efforts of airframe prime contractors, however.

On the other hand, there are a few instructive exceptions to the rule. Kaman Aerospace succeeded in making guitars and bearings, albeit not with the same work force. Survival Technologies went from producing nerve gas antidote to bee sting antidote, but it had apparently always produced commercial products. [39] The Varel plant near Bremen, Germany, quickly converted to making precision measuring instruments and test benches, thus avoiding unemployment. [40] Raytheon successfully adapted its microwave technology for home use.

So it can be done, particularly in military electronics and communications. This would seem to lend some hope to conversion efforts in Ukraine, where electronics industries are common. The key challenges would be paring down the research and development

---

[36] Svante Iger, "Possibilities for Conversion Within the Swedish Defense Industry, Two Case Studies," in Inga Thorsson, *In Pursuit of Disarmament. Conversion from Military to Civil Production in Sweden,* 2 vols. (Stockholm, 1984), section 13.3.7.

[37] *The New York Times,* August 4, 1991, p. A18.

[38] "The Transferability of Defense Industry Resources to Civilian Uses," in *Convertibility of Space and Defense Resources to Civilian Needs: A Search for New Employment Potentials* (Subcommittee on Employment and Manpower, 89th Congress, 1964.

[39] *The New York Times,* August 8, 1991, p. C1ff.

[40] Klaus Engelhardt, "Conversion of Military Research and Development: Realism or Wishful Thinking?" *International Labour Review* 124:2 (March-April, 1985).

overhead costs to a commercially acceptable level and increasing sensitivity to the needs of the market.

POLICY CONCLUSION

Conversion of military industries is a desirable change in the successor states of the U.S.S.R. To the extent that Russian (or Ukrainian) conversion is thoroughgoing and irreversible, the threat of war is reduced, whatever the complexion of future governments there. Conversion and market reforms reinforce one another, and market reforms are likewise in the interest of the American people, because prosperous successor states with thicker links with the developed world are likely to be less aggressive than desperate and deprived regimes. Reducing the risks of nuclear war, environmental catastrophes, terrorism, worldwide· epidemics, and famine should enlist the efforts of the former Soviet peoples if they are to succeed. Though the area is hardly the neediest case in the world today, it has a political importance that cannot be denied. Effective conversion, therefore, should be supported by Western governments, including our own.

At the same time, American aid and encouragement should be deliberate and well-directed. It should not reinforce the power of the military-industrial complex, which has been unwilling or unable to help the civilian sector. Aid should not assist the defense sector renovate its military production capacity, as is envisioned. Nor should our aid favor central executive authorities, however attractive in person, against democratic aspirations as expressed in parliament or regional bodies. That was a mistake of the Gorbachev era. Though our own national experience indicates the usefulness of economic union, this cannot be imposed by Moscow on non-Russian areas suspicious of Great Russian hegemony.

For the time being, until a consensus on economic policy is achieved that includes irreversible demilitarization, Western assistance should probably be confined to expertise, humanitarian supplies such as food and medicines, and support for individual and small group projects likely to benefit a free and open society. Humanitarian assistance includes a welcome for those individuals who exercise their right to emigrate. Expertise should include objective monitoring of progress on conversion, economic reform, and human rights.

During the period of transition to lower defense spending and a market system, the best strategy of conversion for Western experts to recommend would be complete conversion of a definite number of plants each year to the civilian market with full cost-accounting and control over productive assets. Some enterprises or even whole branches—for example, electronics—should be removed from their subordination to the VPK ministries. For a few years the former ministry, or a quasi-public association, could assist firms in obtaining current inputs but would have no obligatory authority over its activities. Eventually, the converted firm would operate independently, seeking technological advice from research institutes as it thinks proper and paying for development assistance out of revenues, paid in capital or specially targeted government grants.

Instead of subsidizing former military-industrial complex producers directly, it would be more effective to subsidize user enterprises (or local-regional entities in the case of environmental amelioration). Subsidized contracts provide a strong incentive to producer enterprises to design efficient and user-friendly devices and to spread information.

As we have seen in this paper, Yeltsin is only groping toward such a market-based conversion strategy, and there is powerful opposition to that change from within the Russian government. In Ukraine there is little or no sign of change from the state-planned strategy. Unless such a market-based conversion strategy is adopted and implemented, it would be better for Western democracies to allow Russian and Ukrainian military capacity to atrophy on its own. Privatization of subsidized, secret, and probably superfluous enterprises does not seem feasible, at least to this observer. Military enterprises should be allowed to close, their valuable personnel to find better uses for their skills and their capital to be sold.

Despite the often-expressed requests for financial assistance by liberal and democratic economists within the former Soviet Union and despite clear needs for infrastructure repair and environmental cleanup, no convincing strategy has been advanced yet to achieve conversion or economic revival generally by means of foreign assistance on any practical scale. To promise more aid than we in the West can and should deliver and thus to engender false hopes is not the act of real friends, but of naive opportunists.

DEFENSE CONVERSION IN THE FORMER U.S.S.R.: THE CHALLENGE FACING PLANT MANAGERS

By Nicholas Forte and Shelley Deutch *

CONTENTS

SUMMARY

Managers of defense industry plants in the former Soviet republics that are seeking to convert to civil production in the nascent market economy will find that most of the management practices developed under the planned economy of the former U.S.S.R. will be of little use. The ultimate success of the conversion process will depend on the ability of the managers to break with the past and to adopt approaches to planning, personnel, design, production, and marketing that make efficient operation possible in a market economy.

CHALLENGES

Plant managers whose industries operated for some 70 years under a centralized command economy face monumental difficulties as they attempt to shift from military to civil production. Some of the difficulties are caused by the broader economic environment and are beyond the plant manager's control. Plant managers, at least for the near term, must try to operate in an economy lacking

---

* Nicholas Forte and Shelley Deutch are with the Office of Slavic and Eurasian Analysis, Central Intelligence Agency.

in many of the tools required for successful market operations, including the lack of legal structures necessary for a market system—such as protection of private property, foreign investment, contract law, and patent rights; an undeveloped financial system that cannot provide sufficient funds for needed capital improvements; a poorly developed retail distribution network and the lack of wholesale industry, which will hamper efforts at converting enterprises to find outlets for their goods; and ruble inconvertibility (at least for the time being), that provides yet another disincentive to foreign investment. Many of the problems, however, the plant managers must resolve on their own.

MANAGING A SUCCESSFUL CIVIL ENTERPRISE

New managerial skills and new thinking by enterprise managers will help to determine the success of defense conversion. Many of the skills and practices that factory managers acquired under the Soviet centrally planned economy—including some common to all Soviet industrial managers and others specifically in the defense industry sector—are almost inimical to the skills needed to run a successful business in a market economy.

ADAPTING TO NEW SUCCESS CRITERIA

Under the conditions of a market economy, the manager of a converted factory will have to change his criteria for decision making. In the past, the enterprise manager's world was centered on the production target assigned by the central planning authorities. Standard indicators, such as percentage of plan fulfillment or actual output levels, were used to judge performance. Such simplistic criteria caused distortions and inefficiencies as managers sought to maintain output—and thus protect their incentives—at the expense of quality, investment in new technology, and labor efficiency. Managers regularly inflated man-hour, material, and overhead costs to deceive central planners and qualify for larger allocations to build reserves to be secretly retained for use in the event of unforeseen circumstances.

When it proved impossible to meet production targets, enterprise managers would often "simulate" meeting their goals. Such practices included shifting production to overfulfill one part of the plan to compensate for the underfulfillment of another part. Managers also would deliberately lower the quality of produced goods to increase the levels of output. This could reach a point, in the absence of adequate outside quality control, at which the delivered product was completely unusable to the customer.

Under a market economy, the manager will be forced to reorient his primary focus from meeting quarterly production goals to maximizing the profits of his firm. Such a reorientation will require a new emphasis on productivity, quality control, reduction of wasted resources, and new marketing techniques. Factory managers will need to show greater flexibility than they have needed in the past. For example, the typical Soviet plant manager was trained in an environment of steady orders that increased at a predictable rate. The new market environment will confront a plant manager with fluctuating demand and will strain his ability to properly target his production levels.

LEARNING NEW MODES OF ACCOUNTING

Because of the inadequate traditional financial accounting systems used in Soviet industry, plant managers will have difficulty making sound business decisions. The elimination of the central planning apparatus and the introduction of the market will require the plant manager to strike a balance between financial risk and profitability—two concepts that are alien to most former Soviet enterprise directors. As an added complication, enterprise managers under the former Soviet system had little knowledge of or concern about the actual costs of making their products. Without making the effort to develop a realistic understanding of these costs, managers can only guess the proper price to set for their goods.

In the past, the Soviet enterprise manager also had very little incentive to maximize the profit of his plant. Although enterprises were given targets for profits that they could retain, profits above this level were routinely confiscated by the state. Shortfalls in profits would also be made up by the ministry. Such practices—within limited bounds—led the enterprise manager to virtually disregard the costs of production. In a market economy, however, an accurate system of cost accounting and an understanding of the role of profit become essential for survival.

CREATING AND MANAGING SUPPLY NETWORKS

The key to the success of the Soviet military-industrial base was the high and almost blind priority given to national defense. The defense industries received the highest quality raw materials and were given preferential access to the transportation and distribution networks for delivering materials. A massive bureaucracy in the government, the military, and the Communist Party monitored the operation of the defense industry to ensure that it received the supplies it needed.

Loss of priority access to materials has come as a serious shock to many defense plant managers. The elimination of the central planning apparatus has ended the ability of defense plants to appeal to higher authorities for the priority diversion of material. The changed supply needs of converting enterprises will magnify the supply problems for plant managers, moreover, particularly if the traditional insulation of the defense industries from the civilian sector precluded familiarity with new sources of material. Until new supply chains are created, commodity exchanges—where the price and availability of raw materials are set by competitive bid—will help alleviate this problem to some extent but, according to the Soviet press, commodity exchanges only account for a small percentage of total trade.

LEARNING TO "THINK CIVIL"

Managers of converting defense plants must reorient their thinking toward the civilian market. In the past, defense plants needed an organization that was geared toward dealing with a single customer—and therefore could be highly centralized. Enterprises producing for the civilian sector, on the other hand, need a more flexible and decentralized organization to compete in the ever-shifting open market.

This change will be particularly difficult for enterprises that only partially convert when there are conflicting management requirements for civilian and military production. As in the West, firms in the former U.S.S.R. will find it difficult to structure a company that can operate well in both environments, and most will probably have to separate these activities entirely.

DOWNSIZING FOR INCREASED EFFICIENCY

The sheer size of many defense plants will make them uneconomical to run. Production in the former Soviet Union is usually concentrated in large plants, some of which are parts of multipurpose facilities. Production facilities are generally much larger than those producing similar items in the United States, in part due to the Soviet practice of constructing new buildings when they wanted to introduce a new product line rather than retooling old facilities, and also in part because the Soviets frequently collocated plants producing components for the same system. This development, similar to the vertical integration of component and final-assembly plants, has been employed over the decades as a hedge against the inefficiency of the Soviet transportation and supply network and the vagaries of central planning.

There are high—perhaps excessive—overhead costs in simply maintaining these large plants, without even considering the expense of conversion. In a market economy, a company typically expands into a new field by building only enough capacity to meet its initial demand and expanding its production capacity as demand increases. Large converted factories, however, are too big to use this strategy. Many will begin with excess capacity whose upkeep will be a drain on profits from the start.

Former Soviet defense firms will also find it necessary to reduce the number of nonproductive assets they maintain. Under the Soviet system, the workplace was not only a source of wages, but also a key provider of many of other needs, such as food, shelter, education, and recreation. The larger of the defense plants frequently were the center of entire communities, for which plant funding subsidized cafeterias, day care centers, apartments, and sports facilities. Most plants also owned vacation homes and rest facilities located in the countryside or in resort areas such as the Black Sea. Workers have come to rely on these benefits, and both workers and management see it as part of a plant's responsibility to provide them. Nevertheless, these assets are frequently a serious drain on plant financial resources, and under a market economy will need to be separated and privatized.

DISMANTLING THE "INTERNAL COCOM"

The history of extreme secrecy in the defense industries poses a further obstacle to converting defense plants. A barrier has traditionally existed between plant shops and design elements performing military work—even when collocated with their civilian counterparts—that has effectively prevented the transfer of technology and processes between the two. This secrecy has been described as an "internal COCOM," inhibiting the free flow of ideas between the defense and civilian sectors and keeping the civil sector from sharing the fruits of the large investments enjoyed by military producers.

Some defense plant managers have begun to show a new openness regarding the activities of their plants. The more enterprising managers are giving potential business partners—particularly foreigners with hard currency to invest—free access to their plants. Nonetheless, many plant managers are still operating under the old constraints and are not allowing visitors past the director's office.

EXPLOITING INFORMATION TECHNOLOGY

Although over the past decade computers have found their way into more and more Soviet enterprises, few plants have yet to fully tap into the assistance that could be provided by management information systems. Much remains to be done to computerize payrolls, plant operations and product throughput, inventory, accounting, and historical or technical recordkeeping. Such computer systems could prove a great aid in helping plants adjust to the new market by allowing them to better calculate the value of products produced or stocks on hand. Unfortunately for most defense plants that do not already have these systems in place, however, the expense of such systems will limit their ability to install them in the near future. Only those plants that manage to find generous foreign partners are likely to be able to afford to expand their computer capabilities soon.

ATTRACTING BUSINESS PARTNERS

Most defense plants are highly motivated to find foreign partners. Indeed, they see Western investors as offering salvation on a number of fronts. First and foremost, Western partners offer the prospect of sufficient funding during the conversion of an enterprise to allow that enterprise to remain solvent. Western partners offer technical expertise and business experience, and the hard currency they bring can persuade central and regional authorities to look favorably on an enterprise's need to bend tax rules and other regulations during the conversion process.

To date, however, many defense plant managers have little understanding of what is required to attract a foreign partner. They turn up at trade fairs or business meetings with a photograph of a new civil product (frequently in prototype stage), a photograph of their plant, and a contract in hand, and expect Western investors to sign a deal on the spot. When confronted with a long list of questions, many refuse to answer: after all, only a few years ago even their plant's existence, let alone data regarding work force and assets, was a state secret, and providing such information to a foreigner an act of treason. More and more, financial desperation and pressure from reformers are changing the attitudes of such managers, and an increasing number are throwing open their doors to anyone who might have cash. Nevertheless, the combination of residual secrecy and lack of understanding about how to attract foreign partners remains a problem.

BECOMING ENVIRONMENTALLY SOUND

Many former Soviet defense plants are heavy polluters. Heavy industrial facilities belch smoke in the air, pour hazardous fluids into lakes and rivers, and store toxic materials unsafely. This problem has been recognized in the past few years, but given financial constraints and until very recently, leadership disinterest, little has been done to correct it. Given the other priorities of the governments of the former Soviet republics at present, it is unclear whether, despite pronouncements, much attention will be paid this issue in the next few years, but if it is, the expense of converting from high-polluting to more environmentally friendly processes and equipment could prove a serious challenge to defense plant managers.

CREATING AN EFFICIENT WORK FORCE

The labor practices of the defense sector are ill-adapted to the efficient operation of a profit-driven factory. Labor has traditionally been treated in the Soviet economy as an inexhaustible commodity, particularly in the extremely labor-intensive machine-building sector. Large numbers of relatively unskilled or semiskilled workers historically have been employed to operate such tools as lathes, milling machines, and boring and broaching equipment. This approach was, at least in the past, the result of the Soviet policy of full employment, which had the added purpose of ensuring a large pool of workers readily available to expand production in case of war. As a result, however, the development of an efficient work force has been hampered by the absence of incentives to economize on labor and by the toleration of indifferent labor discipline—poor attendance, high rates of alcoholism, and theft from the shop floor. To function efficiently in a market economy, factory managers will need to reduce the numbers of unskilled and semiskilled workers that they employ, placing greater emphasis on increasing labor productivity.

Conversely, during the past few years, many Soviet factory managers found themselves operating in an increasingly unstable and tight market for skilled workers. While the decrease in defense production will lessen the demand for skilled workers, the loss of a few critical, highly skilled workers can cripple production at a plant. Defense industries have reported losing many of their best and most highly skilled workers—dissatisfied by the loss of prestige and bonuses associated with the shift from military to civilian production—to higher paying jobs in cooperatives. To cope with this problem, some factories have tried to increase incentives—such as bonuses for critical specializations—to convince skilled workers to stay, spending scarce resources that could otherwise be used for new equipment.

APPLYING NEW DESIGN AND PRODUCTION CRITERIA

A heritage of low-risk, gradualist approaches toward improvements in design and capital modernization will hamper the development and production of new civilian goods.

NEED FOR NEW DESIGN PHILOSOPHY

The Soviet emphasis on strict adherence to design and development schedules encouraged technological conservatism on the part of designers once a decision had been made to proceed with the development of a weapon, thus ensuring a high probability of development success. Although the Soviets produced highly capable weapons, changes in design were made mostly by a series of gradual improvements that often took extended periods of time to fully develop. Factories producing for the civilian market, however, will need to become adept at developing designs more quickly to respond to the changing needs of that market.

Converting enterprises will have the additional handicap of not having a secure source of designs for new products. Traditionally, Soviet defense plants, rather than having in-house design capabilities, have relied on a number of separate design bureaus—whose work was usually integrated by one central design bureau—for designs of new products, especially in the case of advanced designs. In-house engineering departments often were used only to assist in integrating the final design with the plant's production facilities and will not be able to design sophisticated new products without outside help. Traditional design bureaus in the military-industrial complex are very specialized and have little expertise in designing civilian goods that could be produced by converting plants.

Moreover, Soviet military design and production practices, as in the West, have been more concerned with meeting performance criteria than with cost-effectiveness. This practice has led to the production of civilian goods by defense plants that, while meeting design specifications, cost many times that of similar products manufactured in civilian facilities. Despite these shortcomings, Soviet designers were capable of making reliable systems from unreliable parts, and this talent will be useful in the chaotic supply environment that will exist at least in the immediate future.

NEED FOR NEW CAPITAL INVESTMENT

Despite the massive capital stocks of the defense industries, converting plants will need large inputs of additional funds to retool their production. Many of the current production lines will prove to be inappropriate for the production of civilian goods. Of those lines that would be compatible with civil applications, a large number are in need of replacement.

Soviet managers typically did not replace equipment until it became obsolete—long after such equipment would be replaced in the West—and on occasion they sequestered and stockpiled replacement equipment without putting it into use. Even when new equipment was installed, plant managers tended to keep the older equipment as a backup. These practices diluted the effectiveness of capital investment, especially reducing its impact on productivity. Managers resisted installing the new equipment because of the resulting downtime, and central planners frequently discouraged such modernization by failing to lower the plant's production target for the period involved. Moreover, enterprise managers reportedly did not trust new equipment to work well and were loath to replace old, but operating, equipment. A new production process made them dependent on outside experts and on new suppliers of components and services. Managers will need to change their basic attitude toward modernization and recognize it as a means to increase the efficiency of their plants.

However, even with such a change of attitude, the past system of retooling would fail to meet the needs for conversion of defense plants. In the past, Soviet planners charged central retooling institutes with the development of new machine tools and production processes. This practice led to the development of general-purpose machine tools that were relatively easy to produce in large quantities rather than special-purpose, complex machinery optimized for a specific product. While this practice yielded economies of scale that lowered machine tool production costs, it sacrificed diversity in machine tools and failed to lower the labor requirements of the retooled factory. To increase profitability, plant managers will need to develop new production processes and the in-house capability to plan their own retooling requirements that are geared more to their own particular needs.

LEARNING TO MARKET PRODUCTS

The collapse of the planning apparatus has also left the enterprise manager adrift as to where and how to sell his products. These decisions—central to any attempt to successfully run a factory in a market—are totally beyond the managerial experience of converting enterprises. In the past, the central planners told the enterprise manager what to produce, and where and when to deliver it. Now authority for these decisions has been passed down to the level of individual factories, whose managers have no training and experience in marketing their products.

Managers in a market system analyze the market to assess what products are in demand. However, the market in the Commonwealth of Independent States (CIS) is still too underdeveloped to act as a reliable gauge of demand, and market research in the CIS is virtually unknown. In the absence of proper indicators of market demand, enterprise managers are drawing up production plans based primarily on intuition and guesswork.

Factories in the CIS also lack proper marketing and sales departments. The breakdown of the command economy system means that factories now will have to find their own customers—a new phenomenon to a sector accustomed to a guaranteed market. Comments by the managers of currently converting plants, however, show that they are still devoting most of their energies to organizing production and very little to marketing. This lack of attention given by plant managers to identifying market demands and determining how to sell their products will lead many plants to build up excessive inventories of unsold—and in many cases unwanted—goods.

PROSPECTS AND IMPLICATIONS

The plant-level challenges that face defense enterprise managers seeking to convert in the emerging market are perhaps the most fundamental of the obstacles to their successful conversion. Those enterprises that hope to convert successfully will have to undergo both internal reorganization and attitudinal shifts. They will also have to develop market research, product design, and sales departments.

The inability of enterprises to meet these challenges will contribute to the failure of many of them, adding to the unemployment rolls and increasing the threat of civil unrest. The recent introduction of bankruptcy laws in Russia suggests many enterprises could be disbanded before they have a chance to address these issues. There will be a strong temptation for the governments of the other newly independent states to continue to subsidize many of these plants to alleviate this threat to stability. The propping up of loss-making enterprises, however, would retard the growth of new companies that are the only real long-term solution to the unemployment problem.

Some of the governments and enterprises of the former Soviet republics are looking abroad for help in retraining managers to operate in a market environment. Some options being explored include the Western sponsorship of business seminars in Russia and the other former republics, training of plant managers at Western business schools, and Western loans or grants of seed money for entrepreneurs starting new companies that would create alternative jobs for unemployed workers.

CHINA'S UNHERALDED DEFENSE CONVERSION

By Ronald L. Davis *

CONTENTS

SUMMARY

China is in the midst of an extensive, state-directed defense conversion program that, despite numerous obstacles, can claim a number of successes. The program is an integral part of the country's massive, state directed, industrial modernization program launched in the late 1970s, under which hundreds of defense industrial plants have turned to civilian production. After a decade of restructuring, civilian output has moved from barely 20 percent to at least 70 percent of defense industry's total output. This sector is now producing an impressive array of capital equipment and large quantities of consumer goods for both domestic consumption and export. There are many parallels between China and the former U.S.S.R. as both regions struggle to switch their militarized economies to more market-based, consumer-oriented systems.

---

* Ronald L. Davis is a Senior Economist with the Department of State, Intelligence and Research Division, where he specializes in defense economics of the former U.S.S.R.

The Decision to Convert

The Chinese decision to reallocate defense industrial resources to civilian purposes was laid down at the 11th Party Congress in 1978. As was the case with its Soviet mentor, Communist economic failures—abetted by huge defense outlays—and the judgement that the threat of war had diminished, underlie this major policy shift. The leadership directed China's defense industries to begin expanding their production of goods for the civilian economy in the late 1970s. The effort accelerated in 1985, when the armed forces began a one million man reduction, and weapon cuts meant excess capacity and potentially millions of idled workers in defense industries.

Beijing's solution was to make integration of defense industry into the civilian economy a key part of its larger political-economic reform program.

The Chinese started with a defense-industrial base that over the previous three decades had grown to dominate the country's modern industrial sector, including electronics, precision instrumentation, optics, aviation, motor vehicles, and shipbuilding. The military also controlled virtually all advanced technical research. In addition, many of the plants for processing minerals and chemicals and related mines were under this complex. In total, by the early 1970s it is estimated that about 40 percent of China's key industrial enterprises were part of the old military-industrial complex.

China's "conversion" program—largely unheralded in the West—is better described as "diversification." Under this approach, military production capacity is, in U.S. terminology, "laid away" on site, where it is used far below capacity, or not at all. Simultaneously, a plant's civilian production is either greatly expanded or, if nonexistent, established anew. The exact extent to which this "warm" capacity has been retained is unknown, but this approach is costly—and recognized as such in market economies. It runs directly counter to the advice offered by most U.S. and West European industrial specialists who usually recommend "mothballing" or scrapping excess or obsolete weapons tooling. Lack of Chinese confidence in mobilizing industry for a military emergency partially accounts for this approach. In addition, the ability to respond quickly to export orders is retained.

The Defense Conversion Policy Apparatus

Conversion in China has been a top-down, state directed program under the direction of the Party elders, the Politburo, the State Council, and the Central Military Commission. (See Figure 1.) The key organizations responsible for coordinating and implementing conversion policies are:

- The State Commission for Science, Technology, and Industry for National Defense (COSTIND).
- The State Planning Commission (SPC).
- The State Science and Technology Commission (SSTC).
- The High-Technology Plan Coordination Group.

FIGURE 1

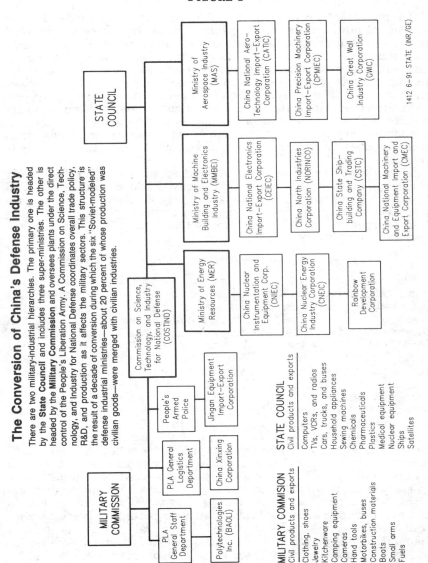

The Conversion of China's Defense Industry

There are two military-industrial hierarchies. The primary one is headed by the **State Council** and includes three super-ministries. The other is headed by the **Military Commission** and oversees plants under the direct control of the People's Liberation Army. A Commission on Science, Technology, and Industry for National Defense coordinates overall trade policy, R&D, and production as it affects the military sectors. This structure is the result of a decade of conversion during which the six "Soviet-modeled" defense industrial ministries—about 20 percent of whose production was civilian goods—were merged with civilian industries.

MILITARY COMMISSION

STATE COUNCIL

Commission on Science, Technology, and Industry for National Defense (COSTIND)

PLA General Staff Department

PLA General Logistics Department

People's Armed Police

Ministry of Energy Resources (MER)

Ministry of Machine Building and Electronics Industry (MMBEI)

Ministry of Aerospace Industry (MAS)

Polytechnologies Inc. (BAOLI)

China Xinxing Corporation

Jingan Equipment Import-Export Corporation

China Nuclear Instrumentation and Equipment Corp. (CNIEC)

China National Electronics Import-Export Corporation (CEIEC)

China National Aero-Technology Import-Export Corporation (CATIC)

China Nuclear Energy Industry Corporation (CNEIC)

China North Industries Corporation (NORINCO)

China Precision Machinery Import-Export Corporation (CPMIEC)

Rainbow Development Corporation

China State Ship-building and Trading Company (CSTC)

China Great Wall Industry Corporation (GWIC)

China National Machinery and Equipment Import and Export Corporation (CMEC)

MILITARY COMMISION
Civil products and exports

Clothing, shoes
Jewelry
Kitchenware
Camping equipment
Cameras
Hand tools
Motorbikes, buses
Construction materials
Boats
Small arms
Fuels

STATE COUNCIL
Civil products and exports

Computers
TVs, VCRs, and radios
Cars, trucks, and buses
Household appliances
Sewing machines
Chemicals
Pharmaceuticals
Plastics
Medical equipment
Nuclear equipment
Ships
Satellites

1412 6-91 STATE (INR/GE)

A Defense Conversion Strategy

To implement conversion, the seven narrow Soviet-model defense industrial ministries were consolidated, and three new streamlined ministries subordinate to the State Council were formed. These new ministries retain broad policy-enforcement and monitoring responsibilities over their affiliated civil and military plants. Day-to-day operational control varies by ministry, but is relatively limited in most cases. The primary role of these ministries has been to provide direction, financing, and the domestic and foreign contacts needed to bring hundreds of defense enterprises into the civilian economy. They also direct the numerous "trade corporations" that were created to support the import and export needs of their plants.

In addition, there are several hundred plants under the direct control of the People's Liberation Army (PLA) subordinate to the Military Commission. They also are deeply involved in civilian production and have their own "trade corporations." Overall coordination of trade policy, R&D, and production as it affects the military sectors is handled by COSTIND.

The Merging of Defense and Civilian Industry

The role of the three new ministries and COSTIND is to break down defense industry's wall of secrecy by promoting cross-sectoral information exchanges, the publication of journals devoted exclusively to conversion, and exhibitions both at home and abroad. An important player in this process is the China Association for Peaceful Use of Military Industrial Technologies (CAPUMIT). According to its General Director, Jin Zhude, CAPUMIT is a "nongovernmental" organization that helps coordinate conversion policies among various organizations in the Chinese government. Its advisory council, however, is composed of the vice-ministers of the key state organizations responsible for economic and defense policy, including Huai Guomo, Deputy Director of COSTIND.

According to Jin Zhude, conversion efforts have been complicated by the strategically remote location of China's so-called "third tier" defense industries, which long isolated the country's best science and technology (S&T) and manufacturing assets from the technology-starved civilian industrial base. (See figure 2.) A major development is the ongoing relocation of personnel and equipment to coastal regions where—coupled with imported technology and equipment—new "totally civilian" industrial plants have been spun-off. These plants are still considered to fall under defense industry auspices. In many cases these spin-off plants are owned by provincial or city governments because they put up the land and capital for their development. However, stock in these companies cannot be sold and individuals hold no equity in the vast majority of these companies.

Priorities and Subsidies

Weapons plants are still state-owned and the government continues to guarantee them priority access to raw materials, electricity, and transportation. Moreover, a number of these plants are cur-

FIGURE 2. CHINA'S INDUSTRIAL BASE, 1991.

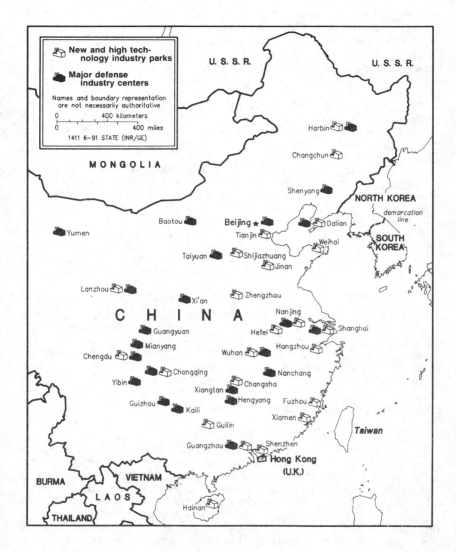

rently receiving national and provincial budgetary subsidies and loans to bridge their move to civilian production. Officials maintain it would be impossible to abandon these defense "company towns" because of the state's obligation to provide jobs, housing, and other social needs.

IMPORTED MODERNIZATION SETS THE PACE

Though often cited by Chinese officials for its superior engineering skills and manufacturing capabilities, the defense sector during the 1980s has often been a follower, not an innovator, in modernization. China's entry into new civilian products has been heavily based on imported technology and equipment, and only partly on defense industry's own resources. From 1978 to 1987, China imported over 2,500 pieces of high technology equipment for the machine-building sector that significantly enhanced its capabilities in micro-electronics, pharmaceuticals, motor vehicles, and machine tools, according to Chinese press reports. Many of these imports were instrumental in giving defense plants the ability to diversify into civilian production.

Whether using its own or imported equipment, Chinese defense managers have been given much authority to select their own civilian product lines, albeit a veto power is retained at ministerial level. Where possible, plants have moved into product areas having an affinity for the particular labor skills, processes, and tooling that were gained from making weapons and equipment. They have, for example, moved from military communications gear to consumer electronics, from naval ships to rail cars, from uniforms to blue jeans, and from tanks to motor vehicles and spare parts.

DEFENSE INDUSTRY "EYES" CIVILIAN PROFITS

Faced with sharp cuts in military orders, many defense industrial managers saw expansion into the successful civilian manufacturing sector as an increasingly attractive alternative. The lure of big profits, higher wages, hard currency, and the prospect of moving from the remote interior to economically active coastal regions become important factors driving conversion. Like their counterparts in the former USSR, they wanted to retain as many of their perks and special privileges as possible.

A CONVERSION SUCCESS STORY

China's largest TV plant, the Changhong State Machinery Factory, began in 1958 as a manufacturer of airborne radar and other military communications equipment. Despite its location in the country's interior, the existing facilities were utilized and expanded. The plant manager attributes successful conversion to the plant's prowess as a defense electronics producer and its access to imported Japanese equipment and components. These factors, plus the plants low paid, highly skilled work force enable it to turn out 1 million TVs a year—mostly color—with military electronics accounting for only 14 percent of production. Moreover, the plant is highly profitable and has won numerous awards for quality.

CONVERSION CAN ALSO MEAN LOSSES

Many defense managers, however, find switching to civilian products is an arduous undertaking. Plants in remote locations face special difficulties establishing contact with domestic or foreign sources of capital and technology needed to develop new products. Moreover, the lack of access to road and rail transport pushes up their production costs. As with most large state-run industrial enterprises, the central government averts layoffs by providing loans and tax relief. Some who have made the transition, particularly electronics plants, are finding it very difficult to remain competitive and profitable in a field where technological change is so rapid and the marketplace is constantly changing.

These problems and rigid socialist habits, combined with a lack of experience in tailoring production decisions to market demand, have hampered efforts to convert defense industry. Beijing has opted to keep otherwise idle military production lines in operation by expanding weapons exports. Hard currency earnings from foreign arms sales, in turn, have helped fund technical modernization of military plants, although it is unclear to what extent such earnings have been used to aid conversion to civilian production.

HIGH-TECH ZONES

China has two programs, "Torch" and "863," that are designed to promote the commercialization of research work and the improvement of Chinese technology. According to CAPUMIT's director, military plants interested in conversion are participating in these economic development programs as much as possible because the programs help facilitate transition to civilian production.

Under the SSTC's "Torch" program, announced in 1988, over 20 national-level zones have been created—many in commercially accessible coastal areas—to develop and manufacture new products for domestic and international markets. (See figure 2.) Moreover, the SPC favors high-tech zone industries with favorable bank loans, export-promoting regulations, and tax incentives. Zones in the northeast are well placed to take advantage of the large concentration of defense industry there, while zones in south-central China will take advantage of that area's aviation and space industries.

THE "863" PROGRAM

In addition to the manufacturing-oriented "Torch" program, a parallel, "863" program has existed since March 1986—hence the 86/3 designation—through which Beijing seeks to narrow the S&T gap with advanced countries by the year 2000. This program, which involves many military S&T facilities, centrally coordinates priority technologies in an effort to accelerate their development and application for both commercialization and new weapons development. The priority technologies—all dual use—are space, lasers, biotechnology, information systems, automation, high-energy sources, and advanced materials.

According to Chinese conversion officials, defense industry managers are eager to participate in both "Torch" and "863" because these programs provide improved access to funds for research, retooling, marketing assistance, and help with exports.

RESULTS PAYING OFF

China's progress is reflected in an impressive publication, "Monograph of Ten Years' Integration of Military and Civilian Production of China National Defense Industries," which portrays the results of a decade of conversion at 150 defense plants. (See photographs, pp. 748–753.) According to Chinese officials, defense industry's output is now at least 70 percent civilian and only 30 percent military. Civilian output is said to be increasing each year. These goods—including TVs, radios, electronic components, toys, hand tools, electric appliances, kitchen ware, and textiles—have played an important part in the dramatic rise in China's export of consumer goods. Clearly, the distinction that existed a decade ago between China's military and civilian sectors is now very blurred.

OBSTACLES REMAIN

CAPUMIT Chairman Jin Zhude sees the lack of investment for retooling as a continuing stumbling block in China's conversion program. He indicates that even though the state makes loans to military plants eager to switch production, such financing is insufficient. He hopes that the large supply of highly trained defense industry personnel, at low wages, will attract foreign investors who will gear their products for export, especially in electronics and household appliances.

The focus is on exports because civilian industry can now meet domestic demand for most consumer products. In addition, exports generate hard currency that can be reinvested to further modernization. Another motivation, according to Jin Zhude, is resistance from managers of purely civilian plants who bitterly oppose new competition from military factories, particularly those that have a strong capability in machine building and electronics. Clearly, as conversion progresses, China's consumers stand to benefit from the competition and lower prices.

BITTER SOVIET RESISTANCE TO CONVERSION

Defense managers in the former Soviet Union had been strongly resisting market-based reforms and conversion that would dismantle much of their weapons production capacity and personal privileges. Moreover, the scope of defense industry in the former U.S.S.R., particularly in Russia and Ukraine, and its enormous bureaucracy and 10–12 million strong labor force is much larger than was China's, and resistance to change is proportionately stronger. Until the August 1991 coup attempt—in which defense industrial leaders were implicated—and the subsequent turmoil after which the U.S.S.R. was dissolved, Soviet defense industrial leaders saw few reasons to undertake conversion.

POST COUP TURMOIL

The post coup situation has, of course, shaken defense industry to its roots. The 75 percent of Soviet weapons plants and military R&D institutes that were located in Russian territory are now under the new Russian Ministry of Industry, but the tight operational control once exercised by the Military Industrial Commission (VPK) is gone. In this confusion, most defense enterprises instantly renamed themselves "Corporations" with most of the same directors in charge. In the absence of control from Moscow, many of these managers have assumed authority over their enterprises and are now acting independently.

FACING THE INEVITABLE

The second blow from which this sector is reeling is the Yeltsin government's decision to cut military procurement at least 75 percent in 1992. The termination of military orders provided the "shock therapy" that most defense industry managers needed for them to take conversion seriously. Now—not unlike their Chinese counterparts—the only way most of these enterprises can survive is by relying on and expanding the civilian output that many already had. Those without existing civilian capacity are now frantic to transfer whatever military technology and skilled labor they can to turning out civilian products. In the meantime, plants are temporarily surviving by obtaining uncollateralized bank loans and by extending each other billions of rubles in inter-enterprise loans.

LOCAL INITIATIVE GROWING

Russian regional and local governments are now beginning to realize that they must move into the vacuum left by Soviet central planners. It is now very likely that under various proposals "ownership" of some defense enterprises might well pass to local control as has occurred in China. The Chinese undertook this process in a far more orderly process thanks to their relatively stable political environment. In China's case, while such locally "owned" firms generally operate in market conditions, they are not stock companies with individual shareholders and "privatization" has not yet been a factor. The possibility for genuine privatization of some large Russian defense enterprises exists, however, if a proposed East European type "voucher" system is enacted. However, this issue is far from resolved and Russia is likely to retain a large nationalized—albeit converted—defense industrial sector for many years.

A SOVIET ADVANTAGE?

If Yeltsin's reforms result in a high degree of local autonomy and large-scale foreign investment becomes a reality, Soviet conversion might actually face fewer obstacles than did China. For example, Russia's defense plants, its technological level, and the country's overall economic infrastructure are superior to China's of a decade ago. Although many plants are located beyond the Urals in defense "company towns," they are not nearly as isolated as China's "third tier." Moreover, there are hundreds of major plants in Moscow, Leningrad, and other industrial cities far closer to potential domestic and international markets than in China's case. Even in the current unsettled environment, some Russian defense managers have been pursuing Western technology, capital investment, loans, and joint ventures because they see access to international markets as the key to successful conversion.

国营华龙机械厂
STATE-RUN HUALONG
MACHINERY FACTORY

AK民用枪

26吋轻便自行车

厂长金石根同志

国营华龙机械厂是福建省大中型骨干企业之一，拥有职工3200余人，工程技术人员350余人。贯彻军民结合方针以来，该厂大力开发民品，目前已建成具备数万支民用枪械和30万辆轻便自行车的生产规模。并引进开发了双人牌家用自动给水泵、健身车、民用出口的W30栓动式步枪等新产品。由于重视产品质量，该厂生产的四大系列五十多种型号的产品赢得了国内外用户的信誉。1988年，工厂实现总产值3100万元，创汇707万美元，成为福建省机械行业创汇大户。

新开发的健身车之一

Add: Longyan, Fujian P.R.C　Tel: 23261　Cable: 7364
地址: 福建省龙岩市　电话: 23261　电挂: 7364

地方军工企业荟萃

沈阳飞机制造公司
SHENYANG AEROPLANE MANUFACTURING COMPANY

Add: Lingbei St., Huanggu District, Shenyang P.R.C. Tel: 62680 Cable: 3058

沈阳飞机制造公司研制生产的高空高速歼击机

沈飞牌 SL650 中型空调客车

沈飞牌 SF665 豪华型旅游客车

地址: 沈阳市皇姑区陵北街   电话: 62680   电挂: 3058

航空航天工业部企业荟萃

国营长安机器总厂
（国营第〇八七一总厂）
STATE-OWNED CHANGAN MACHINE GENERAL WORKS

国营长安机器总厂（国营第〇八七一总厂）是安徽省大型军工企业。现有职工3037人，专业技术人员934人。该厂1985年起贯彻"军民结合"方针组建了10条吊扇专业生产线；先后开发出天柱峰牌系列豪华吊扇、3M（6M）卫星电视地面接收站、QHR型汽车后视防撞雷达等10多种民用产品。354、405雷达先后获全国科学大会奖、安徽省科学大会奖；589雷达1985年获电子工业部科技进步二等奖。FC-15型1050mm豪华吊扇获安徽省优质产品奖、轻工业部优质产品奖。

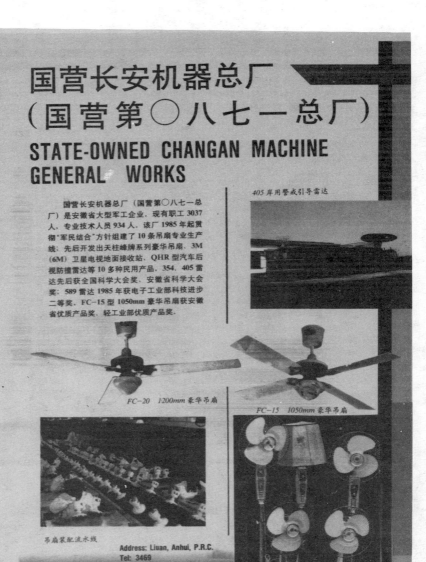

405岸用警戒引导雷达

FC-20 1200mm 豪华吊扇

FC-15 1050mm 豪华吊扇

吊扇装配流水线

Address: Liuan, Anhui, P.R.C.
Tel: 3469
CAble: 8402

北京北方车辆制造厂
BEIJING NORTH VEHICLE MANUFACTORY

Crawler forest fire engine   履带式森林消防车

Beifang brand BN 208 Coach   北方牌BN208中型旅游客车

Address: Zhujiafen, Changxindian, Fengtai District, Beijing, P.R.C.

Tel: 818231 - 542 or 965   Cable: 9937

RUSSIAN DEFENSE CONVERSION UNDER OLD MANAGEMENT

By John R. Thomas *

CONTENTS

SUMMARY

Large-scale conversion of the former Soviet military-industrial complex to meet civilian needs is the most important economic measure needed to assure a democratic Russia's future. This is because U.S.S.R.'s defense R&D and industry were such a dominant part of its economy, and remain so in Russia, as a result of the priority they enjoyed in the Soviet era.

In turn, Russia's economic progress will determine its political development. Yeltsin himself has said that by the fall of 1992 his own political future will hinge on the state of Russia's economy. The latter will be affected greatly by the contribution of its defense industry, since, directly or indirectly, it is responsible for most of Russia's output. [1] Russia's defense industry currently remains under the control of the nomenklatura management which tends to oppose reform and conversion.

INTRODUCTION

To date, little progress has been made in converting defense facilities to full civilian production; instead, a far less effective policy of diversification, under which military facilities are used to produce some civilian products, has prevailed. This approach has preserved the military-industrial base while, ironically, extending its activities into the consumer areas, with the long-term implications of remaining a large, if not dominant, part of the nation's

---

* John R. Thomas is Senior Assistant for Russian and CIS Science and Technology, Office of the Secretary of Defense, Department of Defense. (This assessment represents the views of the author alone. It does not reflect the views of the Department of Defense or the U.S. Government. It is based largely on the author's discussions, observations, and site visits in the U.S.S.R./Russia in 1990–1992, complemented by review of relevant literature.

[1] The defense and associated heavy industry enterprises, which are members of the influential Union of Entrepreneurs, are responsible for two-thirds of Russia's industrial output. (*The Economist*, London, June 27-July 3, 1992, page 60.)

total economy. At the same time, defense laboratory directors, industrial managers, and associated bureaucrats in the new Russian government (who formed a significant part of the former Soviet nomenklatura) remain entrenched and still in command of the military-industrial complex.

Thus far the Yeltsin reform leadership has been unable to carry out the major reform of removing the defense managers or minimizing their political influence. On the contrary, many internal and external developments have opened a significant possibility that the former Soviet military-industrial complex will remain in place for some time to come and that the critically needed massive defense conversion (as part of significant de-militarization of the former U.S.S.R.) will not occur soon. This has major economic and political implications for a democratic Russia.

This situation has developed because of: 1) a flawed conversion policy under Gorbachev that left the defense industry virtually intact under old nomenklatura managers; 2) Yeltsin's stated goals and actions, which have given continued life to that industry and provided rationale for its survival, e.g., arms sales abroad and the establishment of a Russian Ministry of Defense and Army; 3) conditions beyond Yeltsin's control, e.g., ethnic strife on Russia's borders, perceived maltreatment of Russian minorities in former Soviet Republics and alarming claims on what is regarded as Russia's territory and property (Ukraine regarding Crimea and the Black Sea Fleet), and resurfacing of traditional strategic concern over the loss of forward areas (East Europe, Baltic states)—all of which have provided a basis for the former Soviet military-industrial complex to claim it must remain intact to meet legitimate needs of Russia's national security and national interest; and, 4) Yeltsin's political weakness that prevents him from fundamentally restructuring the defense industry and reducing its influence and that of its allies, namely, the KGB and the military.

In the face of a bleak economic situation, large-scale relief for the Russian people can come through large-scale conversion that includes wholesale removal of former Soviet managers, directors, and associated bureaucracies; massive transfer of defense research and production capabilities to civilian-oriented management and operation; and ultimately genuine privatization of those capabilities. Such an outcome may eventually be aided by successful devolution of power and ownership from the Central Russian government to local authorities and people. Russia's reform leaders have already asserted their intent to downsize the defense production base, to accord with plans to limit the size and role of the newly established Russian Army. Moreover, the reform leaders intend to privatize industry and invite foreign investment that could lead to current defense plants being put into local and foreign private hands. To defeat these plans, the defense managers have gone on the political offensive, forcing the appointment of their colleagues to the Yeltsin Government and forming parties and coalitions for a political struggle after the 1991 coup failure frustrated their own plans.

These defense managers are motivated by the belief that they should remain in place to carry out the conversion of Russia's defense industry and R&D, since only they have the managerial and organizational capabilities to do so. They also believe they should remain in control because they have a better sense of, and more devotion to, Russia's national interests and security. Indeed they have much different values from the reformers: they are more nationalist and patriotic. The reformers believe that Russia needs to be more integrated into the world community and to that end it will have to give up what the defense managers believe are vital aspects of Russia's dignity and sovereignty, including control over Russia's capabilities and resources, starting with defense industry. In the defense managers' view, such control would be lost if that industry was privatized to include foreign ownership in joint ventures, as advocated by the reformers.

Because of the foregoing mindset, defense managers are potentially dangerous to the reformers' drive toward a democratic and free-market Russia. Their opposition can range (and already has) from political action and bureaucratic sabotage to supporting a coup. As long as the old defense managers remain in place, they will—in alliance with the KGB, the military and ultra-nationalists—continue to be a potent force against much-needed political and economic reform in Russia. Therefore, the future course of genuine defense conversion and related democratization will depend on whether the reformers can remove the defense managers and reduce their political influence, as well as persuade Russian workers that such conversion will be good for them.

CONVERSION UNDER GORBACHEV

The defense conversion effort and achievements in the former U.S.S.R. to date have been small in absolute terms and very marginal relative to the civilian economy. This is due primarily to a flawed and failed policy under Gorbachev. That led to today's bleak economic situation with negative implications for the current reformist government of Russia and its future.

Under Gorbachev, few defense plants totally ceased production. Moreover, instead of genuine conversion, diversification was carried out so as to preserve the former Soviet military production base with only modest changes. Some military plants began to produce some civilian output (estimated in overall terms at 10 percent of the total industrial output, even though in selected items the defense-produced share was somewhat greater); but few identifiable large-scale military production facilities lost their former management or were replaced with reform-minded entrepreneurs. Even in their last months of power, the Soviet officials admitted that less than 10 defense plants (out of several thousand) had been fully converted—this was in the third year after Gorbachev announced a major Soviet policy to drastically downsize the U.S.S.R.'s huge military machine and its supporting research and production infrastructure.

This lack of progress explains the refusal of former Soviet defense enterprise officials, when pressed, to show the author the civilian production lines on which they claimed the consumer goods on display in the Plant Directors' offices were produced (bicycles, tents and poles, gym equipment, tricycles and baby carriages, pots and pans, etc.). Requests were often met with polite but evasive replies ("the line is undergoing repair or maintenance," "the workers and researchers are tied up in other work," etc.) reminiscent of distant past excuses. To be fair, those excuses concerned far less sensitive facilities than military-related ones. Indeed, the Soviet authorities under Gorbachev get credit for Westerners visiting any military-related facilities, considering the secrecy in which these were cloaked earlier. [2]

The foregoing experience indicates at this time that existing, dual-run military (and not new, fully dedicated civilian) production lines are turning out consumer output. In fact and contrary to logic, numerous *civilian* facilities in the Gorbachev era were placed under central defense production ministries, on the Soviet leadership's assumption that military administrators and managers are more efficient and skillful than their civilian counterparts. [3] The assumption was accepted even though it should have been challenged for several reasons. Soviet defense research and production facilities in the past received policy priority. Consequently, they got first call on: the best trained and brightest scientists and engineers; raw materials and supplies; and, equipment and instrumentation. It remains to be seen whether these military laboratories and plants can operate as efficiently without such priorities, and conversely, whether their civilian counterpart facilities might not do as well if given the same priority enjoyed by the defense facilities under Soviet rule.

Then, too, the notion that the former Soviet military-industrial complex is best able to meet Russia's current and future civilian needs arises from the long-held view that it was (and still is) the most advanced part of the Soviet economy. Yet, the complex contains much in the way of dated processes, machinery, and equipment. For example, just like civilian plants, many former Soviet military plants use obsolete equipment, symbolized by very dated U.S.-made machinery. Thus, the Volgograd (ex-Stalingrad) Tractor Plant, built with U.S. engineers' help in late 1920s, had equipment (e.g., heavy press) made in Detroit in 1930. Similarly, the Ural-Transmash plant (turning out self-propelled, tracked artillery) also has a heavy press, built in Cleveland and brought to former Sverdlovsk in the early 1940s under U.S. lend-lease aid to the then-embattled U.S.S.R. This press was still in use as recently as late 1991, and probably continues even now, given the shortage of hard currency to obtain the latest equipment.

Why did conversion policy fail under Gorbachev? First and foremost because it was left in the hands of the Soviet military-industrial complex itself to formulate and implement. This "conversion" effort was directed by the Military-Industrial Commission (VPK)

---

[2] In some cases, Americans were setting foot behind the Ural Mountains for the first time in decades, e.g., at plants producing 152mm self-propelled howitzers, tanks, and armored personnel carriers, and in cities that were closed to all foreigners until last year. Whether such freedom of movement and access will continue unabated may now be in question. The Russian Supreme Soviet recently passed new legislation that closes military facilities and renews closed areas, requiring government permission for visits. (*Washington Post*, July 15, 1992, p. 12). If enforced, this legislation will begin to restore the highly restrictive, xenophobic situation of the Soviet era.

[3] This assumption was validated seemingly in the Yeltsin era by the recent (May 1992) appointment of ex-defense managers to Russian Government posts, e.g., Shumeiko and Khizha as First Deputy Prime Minister and Deputy Prime Minister, respectively.

that had been responsible for building up the Soviet defense R&D and industry in the first instance, and was implemented by the central defense production ministries in Moscow.

Then, instead of *genuine conversion*, the VPK conducted a policy of *diversification:* the big military production complex was left intact as defense plants were allowed to turn out a mix of civilian and military goods on their existing production lines; many were, in some instances, even allowed to add separate civilian production lines. As a result, the diversification policy served to enhance the defense production's role in the nation's economy and increase the policy influence of its managers. This was reinforced by the abolition of the Ministry of Light Industry in the perestroika era instead of working through that ministry to facilitate a policy of taking plants out of military production ministries and putting them under civilian administration.

CONVERSION UNDER YELTSIN

Since conversion under Gorbachev left the military-industrial complex entrenched more than ever, the Yeltsin reform government had been left to face an even more daunting task of obtaining genuine conversion. This has been compounded by: 1) Yeltsin's own actions, perhaps unintentionally validating the defense industry's role in the new Russia; 2) objective conditions related to legitimate national security concerns and perceived threats to Russia's national interest; 3) the further entrenchment of defense managers at various political and administrative levels, particularly in their home bases; and, 4) the defense complex going on a political offensive to preserve and protect its interests since the dissolution of the U.S.S.R. and installation of a reformist government in Russia.

Many of Yeltsin's actions, since he became Russia's undisputed leader, have provided the rationale and selling points for the military-industrial complex. For example, however reluctant he was to do so, Yeltsin's establishment of Russia's own Ministry of Defense and active Armed Forces in the Spring of 1992 has created a need and customer for Russia's defense industry. Then, too, his support of Russian arms sales abroad, however well-intentioned to obtain much needed hard currency for conversion, has added another reason to continue the defense industry's mission.

In fact, going beyond support of arms exports, Yeltsin has even noted the possibility of Russian defense industry supplying U.S. needs: "Russia is currently going through a crisis right now. But we have a sufficient potential to propose cooperation in other areas. We can supply many types of production for heavy industries and defense, and we can do this by providing prices which are very advantageous." [4] Such sentiments cannot help but provide encouragement to defense managers to persevere in their struggle against conversion.

These developments favorable to the defense industry have been enhanced by external and internal developments beyond Yeltsin's control. For example, ethnic strife on Russia's southern borders;

---

[4] From his remarks to the U.S.-Russian Business Summit in Washington, (see p. 5 of text released by White House Press Secretary's Office on June 17, 1992.)

actual and potential disputes involving what Russia considers its own territory and property, e.g., with Ukraine over Crimea and the Black Sea Fleet [5]; a perceived loss of former Soviet strategic territorial depth necessary to defend its borders against any future threat, e.g., the Baltic states and East Europe; and the perceived need to defend the 25-million Russian minority from alleged oppression in former Soviet territories, e.g., Moldova and the Baltic states—all create arguably (from Russia's viewpoint) a need for retaining a vigorous and modernized defense industry to support its army and provide for Russia's national security and interests in the face of current and potential challenges and threats. This situation impinges heavily on Yeltsin's freedom to drastically cut the size and political influence of the defense managers.

Understanding the resulting advantage, they have gone on the offensive in the political arena to insure that Yeltsin reformers do not succeed with genuine conversion. Whereas the defense managers were content to exercise their influence behind the scene in the Gorbachev era, they have openly entered the political process at all levels: national government (legislature and executive), oblast (regional), and local. Thus, they have formed parties and joined coalitions, e.g., Arkadii Volsky and his Union of Scientific-Production Entrepreneurs, which includes most of the defense industry managers, have joined other groupings to form a new political party that will undoubtedly field candidates to Russia's Parliament and, if necessary, to the Presidency. [6]

Added to this has been the consolidation and expansion of political power of the former Soviet military-industrial complex at its home base. A primary reason for this is, ironically, a carryover from the Soviet era when the defense managers were part of a powerful nomenklatura that ran the Soviet system. In that era, they occupied unchallenged dominant positions in their communities as directors of defense laboratories and plant managers. Many of these communities were and still are "company towns," i.e., the defense research facility or industrial plant is the only enterprise in the town or area; this is most particularly true of the major defense industry network behind the Urals. As a result, thousands of staff and workers in these towns are dependent on the enterprise not only for employment but, with their families, also for housing, food delivery and distribution, and social amenities (movie houses, recreation and rest facilities, "clubs of culture," etc.).

The total dependence of the defense employees is reinforced by the virtual labor immobility that still persists in today's Russia. Therefore, when Russia's defense lab directors and plant managers fight to keep their facilities in business by opposing conversion and retrenchment, they receive virtually unanimous backing of their staffs, workers and families. In fact, the local nomenklatura now enjoys greater genuine popularity than the distant Yeltsin govern-

---

[5] Reportedly tensions between Russia and Ukraine over this issue have spilled over into use of force at Fleet Headquarters in Sevastopol. (See *Washington Post*, July 15, 1992, p. 16). Comparable future incidents are likely, given strong feelings on both sides.

[6] Volsky is to head Civic Union, a coalition of his own group, Vice President Aleksandr Rutskoy's People's Party of Free Russia and Nikolai Travkin's Russian Democratic Party. This new group describes itself as a "moderate conservative" party in "constructive opposition" to the Yeltsin/Gaidar regime. (*RFE/RL Research Report*, Vol. 1, no. 27, 3 July 1992.)

ment ministers in Moscow. Even though some of these are reformers who are promoting policies for the benefit of the people, they are viewed in the Urals and elsewhere as unfeeling bureaucrats who want to shut down the plants and create unemployment.

Ironically, the local people now view their defense managers and lab directors as more genuinely representing their interests than was the case in the Soviet system when they were seen as puppets of the Central Ministries. As a result the managers have enjoyed sizable political success against the reformers, e.g., they have won local elections and forced Yeltsin in the Spring of 1992 to appoint former defense industry managers to his reformist government.

In addition to getting involved in politics, the defense managers have done other things to ensure their survival. They have managed to keep their enterprises going and to retain the support of their workers by subsidizing each other's facility (by not collecting the money they owe each other) and by pressuring the local, and even central, banks to make new, or not collect old, loans.

The defense managers have also reorganized their enterprises under the guise of "private associations" and, in some cases, they have manipulated the sale of ownership stocks to leave them in control. These "privately-owned" facilities are now beyond the reach of the Yeltsin reform government, with the defense managers ironically taking advantage of that Government's dedication to privatization and appearing to be in tune with reform.

Finally, the staying power of the defense industry has been strengthened by the fact that its close allies, the KGB and the military, have not been restructured or fully reoriented toward democratic values. Thus, regarding the KGB, it is ironic that Bakatin, appointed after the August 1991 coup as the only genuine reformer head of the KGB under Gorbachev, lost his job with the dissolution of the U.S.S.R. that December. His replacement, Baranikov, appointed by Yeltsin, is a typical apparatchik who rose to the top through the KGB ranks. It remains a mystery as to why Yeltsin appointed Baranikov since Baranikov stopped Bakatin's first steps to reform the KGB. The mystery is compounded by Yeltsin's appointment of Nikolai Golushko—another KGB apparatchik who rose to head the Ukrainian KGB in the former U.S.S.R.—as the first deputy to Baranikov. [7] In any case, the very much intact KGB, which was transferred wholesale to the new Russian Ministry of Security, remains a close ally of the defense industry, with all this implies for promoting their common cause of survival at the expense of the Russian people's welfare if necessary.

At the same time, the newly emerging Russian military has become a close ally of the defense industry, as the military was in the Soviet era. While Russia's military establishment has undergone downsizing and reorganization since the demise of the U.S.S.R., it is a great force for resistance to a democratic Russia integrated into the world community and economy. The army is now in the hands of younger and tough-minded nationalist generals who are more capable than the octogenarian, flabby military apparatchiki who headed the former Soviet army. The new breed

---

[7] *RFE/RL Research Report*, Vol. 1, no. 27, 3 July 1992, p. 77. Yeltsin signed the appointment decree *after* he returned from the Summit meeting in Washington.

starts with the Defense Minister appointed by Yeltsin, General Pavel Grachev, a forty-four-year-old veteran of the Afghan War. A no-nonsense officer, he has asserted sharp nationalist views, including that of the Russian army's duty to protect Russian minorities in the new, independent states of the former U.S.S.R. from oppression by those states.

The influence of the new Russian military over Yeltsin can be inferred from his recent (July 1992) appointment of General Boris Gromov as Deputy Defense Minister, also an Afghan war veteran and hero. It should be recalled that Gromov was Deputy to Boris Pugo, the hard-line Soviet Interior Minister who was one of the leaders of the August 1991 coup.

These military appointments parallel those of the defense industry managers and seem to demonstrate the power of the military-industrial complex in the reform government. The new generals indicate they want to reorganize the bloated, overaged, former Soviet army into "a lean and mean military machine." Consequently, they believe they will need a modernized, efficient defense industry and R&D to provide the necessary technological innovations and arms for such a military force. This brings the new Russian military back into alliance with the old defense managers, as was the case in the Soviet era.

Some of this reconverging military-industrial complex now links up with or shares the views of ultra-nationalists who believe Russia is being disarmed and deprived of its nuclear shield; these groups believe that this capability is needed more than ever in a developing situation in which, with the dissolution of the U.S.S.R., Russia has been stripped of its in-depth border areas and left to face hostile ethnic forces with a reduced army and production capabilities, (moreover, to the strategic advantage of the United States) [8]

All the above developments indicate that Yeltsin will not have easy or early success in any genuine and significant defense conversion. Of all people, he is familiar with the attitude of the defense managers since he came out of their ranks from behind the Ural mountains heartland of the former Soviet military-industrial complex.

Indeed, he shares some of their views. Thus, while many defense managers want a return of the priorities and privileges they enjoyed in the former Soviet system, their yearning is not necessarily for the system itself. Many recognize its shortcomings, but they are at the same time Russian nationalists and patriots who, in addition to their own bureaucratic interests, also believe that Russia is still a *Velikaya Derzhava* (a great power); as such it has an historic tradition of greatness that was not erased by the Soviet period. (Yeltsin has expressed similar sentiments.)

From this it follows that Russia is entitled to have appropriate military capabilities, both as befits its international status and to defend its rightful, legitimate national interests. (At a meeting with Russian Army commanders in early June 1992, Yeltsin indicated that the United States was trying to obtain advantage in the-

---

[8] For an example of these views in detail, see the roundtable discussion in *Nash Sovremennik* (Our Contemporary), Moscow, no. 10, 1991, p. 143-62. This organ of the former R.S.F.S.R. Union of Writers provides the arena for Russian super-nationalist expression.

then ongoing bilateral strategic talks and that he would not allow this to happen.) And, of course, to have the necessary military capabilities, Russia needs a defense research establishment and industry that are capable of developing and supplying modern military technology and arms. (Influential Academician Genady Mesyats, the new Russian Academy Vice President and leader of the Urals military industrial complex, typifies and has openly expressed the above attitude.) Feeling as they do about Russia's place in the sun, many defense managers and laboratory directors voted for General Makashov, the hardline former Volga/Ural Military District Commander who ran against Yeltsin in the June 1990 free elections that resulted in Yeltsin's elections as President of Russia. [9]

Their negative attitude extends to subsequent events in post-coup Russia. For example, the reform-minded new first Deputy Minister of Defense Andrey Kokoshin (the only civilian in the top ranks of the Russian MOD) has expressed his views on the future of the Russian defense industry. According to him, Russian political leaders and military specialists will soon reach an agreement on the basics of Russia's national interests and formulate a military doctrine that will define the course of Russian defense industry. [10] Presumably, the defense managers will obediently accept this planned action by reformers. This is unlikely if the active resistance of the defense managers to date is any indication. Aside from substantive differences, the defense managers and many professional military have thinly veiled contempt for both "the politicians" (in general and reformers in particular) and "the military specialists" who, like Kokoshin, are primarily from "think tank" research institutes. The military-industrial complex considers the defense reformers as academics without practical managerial and operational experience relevant to running industry and meeting Russia's real national defense and economic needs.

POSSIBLE ROUTE TO GENUINE CONVERSION

Does the bleak situation noted above preclude genuine conversion? Since the conversion plan and its implementation under Gorbachev were not designed to produce genuine change—namely, to remove defense plants from central jurisdiction and from military-linked authorities and transfer them to local civilian control and management, and ultimately to private hands—such conversion could in principle emerge from the disappearance of the Soviet Central Government and the rise of the reform-minded Russian Republic leadership in 1992.

Many defense plants could be shifted to civilian production, instead of being maintained as part of stand-by military production base, as was the case in the perestroika era. Such an outcome would arise logically from the intended limited mission for, and the

---

[9] In recent months, Makashov has been involved in Moldova's internal conflict between the local Russian minority and non-Russian majority. He made trips there, undoubtedly to provide political support and military advice. This conflict has already led Russian leaders, such as Vice-President Rutskoy, to threaten armed Russian help to their co-patriots in Moldova.

[10] See Lt. Col. A. Dolgikh and Captain 3rd Rank Yu. Gladkevich, "Status and Future of Russian Defense Industry," *Krasnaya Zvezda*, June 17, 1992, p. 2.

greatly reduced size of, the Russian armed forces. (Yeltsin, among others, has signalled his views on this point.) These forces are to be only for the defense of Russian borders against any external attack. Some Russian reform officials and advisers have stated that their army would no longer have the Soviet army's global mission of promoting "Proletarian Internationalism," or of defending "socialist gains abroad," as was asserted by the Brezhnev Doctrine. Moreover, the reform leaders indicate that the new Russian Forces would not be used as internal policemen or against other Republics, as were Soviet Army units as late as 1991 under Gorbachev.

Beyond this, the rise of the Russian Republic has led to defense plants being removed from control of the former central military production ministries. This has created the basis for placing the defense facilities under civilian management and control. And, potentially, Russia's scaling down of the still vast Soviet defense production capabilities could ultimately lead to the turnover and sale of excess facilities to private hands in Russia and abroad. During his "informal" trip to the United States in June 1991 (reinforced a year later by his summit trip to United States, as the unchallenged Russian leader), Boris Yeltsin indicated he wants to create an investment climate in Russia that will attract foreigners to joint or private ventures. This would include the current defense industry, given its importance and scale in Russia's economic activities. Such a conversion and disposal of defense enterprises would result in a genuine large-scale contribution to civilian production, and not the marginal additions made to date.

In addition to genuine privatization, Russia's economic well-being requires not only removal of old defense managers, but also installation of new managers who will know how and be willing to compete in a free market without the state priorities and subsidies that the old managers are used to and do not want to give up.

Similarly, the devolution of power from the central Soviet government to the Russian Republic and removal of old nomenklatura directors could lead to genuine conversion in the research and development (R&D) area where innovation could lead to much needed modernization to enable the new Russia to compete in the world. Until now, former Soviet scientists and technologists were heavily involved, directly or indirectly, in military and military-related work since their laboratories made up a significant part of the defense industry complex. Even the former U.S.S.R. Academy of Sciences' own laboratories were heavily involved in military work under contract to the then-Soviet Ministry of Defense and to the numerous Defense production ministries. [11] As a result, Russian scientists voice strong views that only genuine conversion could "liberate" them from their dependence on the military and defense industry budgets and orders, and from the many restrictions, e.g., on publication and travel abroad, that applied even in the perestroika era. (Clearly, progress was made after that era began in 1985: the Soviet labs and scientists could at least have contacts and

---

[11] Contrary to the long-held view in the West of little or no Academy involvement with the military, its research institutes worked on a wide range of weaponry, from nuclear-missiles to conventional weapons. They became heavily dependent essentially on military funding. (See John R. Thomas, "Militarization of the Soviet Academy of Sciences," *Survey*, (London), Spring 1985, vol. 29, no. 1, pp. 29–58.)

discussions with foreigners in the U.S.S.R., even if not abroad. In the more distant past, such contacts were few and visits to military labs and other facilities were totally out of the question because their very existence was concealed by the former Soviet authorities.)

Devolution and genuine conversion would allow Russian scientists not only to earn funds in the civilian area and benefit Russian consumers, but also to rejoin the international science community that would ultimately enable them to reach Western levels of scientific achievement. Since they are intrinsically as talented as any in the West, many former Soviet scientists are vocal about having fallen behind in many S&T areas under the stifling Soviet procedures. Even more, they are embarrassed and even bitter about having been forced in the past to publicly claim exaggerated achievements by the Soviet system.

Now they face a different problem. Instead of bureaucratic procedures, ideological straightjackets and security regulations, the lack of hard currency prevents them from traveling abroad for cooperative projects or international meetings. But they hope that the reform government and genuine conversion will remove the directors with old nomenklatura ties and lead to productive work that will provide the incentives for many gifted and well-trained former Soviet scientists to put their talent to work for Russia in the type of open and profitable environment that is taken for granted in the West. Otherwise they fear an internal and external "brain drain": a flow of talented scientists out of science at home or to scientific work abroad.

The United States can play a role in this context, even though regretfully the relevance of U.S. conversion experience to the current Russian scene is negligible or minor, given the political, economic, and societal differences between the United States and the former U.S.S.R. For example, all Soviet military production facilities were State-owned (unlike U.S. defense production facilities, which are primarily private.) Therefore, unlike U.S. defense companies, which are largely driven by the market and can opt out of military production (as many have done or are doing), former Soviet military producers at this time have no comparable options, and will not, until a market economy takes hold, genuinely and massively.

But to this end, U.S. assistance in how to operate in a market economy (focused on marketing, banking, accounting, legal, and other practices designed to meet civilian consumer needs) would be in order. Such aid is particularly needed since the Soviets were, and the Russians now are, pressing the United States for joint ventures and have little, if any, understanding of the need for relevant infrastructure and processes for successful operation of such ventures. This is reflected by their naive notion that U.S. company representatives will simply show up in places like the former Sverdlovsk (and elsewhere in Russia) to sign profitable contracts. This does not consider how the still primitive Russian communication system (internally and externally) and the lack of an appropriate legal, credit, and banking framework would prevent such U.S. company representatives from negotiating any agreements that would be approved by their home offices.

Relevant to U.S. help in Russian defense conversion is the assistance the United States is providing in the field of science out of the overall $400 million appropriated by Congress this year for conversion aid. The newly formed International Science and Technology Center in Moscow, set up with $25 million funding by the United States and another $50 million by other Western countries and Japan, will help to provide civilian-oriented work for members of former Soviet weapon laboratories.

If properly administered, this aid could help reduce the dependence of Russian scientists on their military-industrial complex. For example, the funding must be given to individual Russian scientists on specific civilian-oriented projects and not turned over as grants to the management of the Russian research institutes for their disposition. Since much of that management is in the hands of the former military-industrial complex, there can be little doubt that many of such grants would be allocated to projects and people unintended by either the Russian reform government or the U.S.

CONCLUSIONS, POSSIBLE OUTCOME AND IMPLICATIONS

The developments noted above lead to the following conclusions. First, the old defense industry managers believe that they should remain in place to carry out the conversion of Russia's defense industry and R&D, since only they have the organizational and managerial capabilities to do so. (Of course, they disregard the fact that they have no knowledge or experience of how to produce civilian goods in free market conditions.)

Second, the defense managers also believe they should continue to run the industry because they have a better sense of and more devotion to Russia's national interests and security. (They do, indeed, have much different values from the reformers. The latter believe that Russia needs to be more integrated into the world community and to that end it will have to give up what the defense managers believe are vital aspects of Russia's dignity and sovereignty, including control over Russia's capabilities and resources, starting with defense industry. Such control would be lost, in the managers' view, if that industry was privatized to include foreign ownership in joint ventures, as advocated by the reformers.)

Next, because of their current mindset, defense managers are potentially dangerous to the reform government's drive toward a democratic and free-market Russia; their opposition can range (and already has) from political action and bureaucratic sabotage to supporting a coup. Consequently, as long as the old defense managers remain in place, they will—in alliance with the KGB, the military and ultra-nationalists—continue to be a potent force against much needed political and economic reform in Russia.

Considering the bleak developments to date but also the ideal course spelled out above, what are the prospects for genuine defense conversion sought by Yeltsin's reformers? Primarily it depends on their political capability (which they do not now have) to remove the defense managers from their posts and limit their political influence in resisting such conversion. (To date, few of these managers have been displaced.)

Of course, over time these managers could fall of their own weight, e.g., from not having customers because of lack of state orders for arms or from a failure to sell these abroad. Some might even change their mind on their own: take the long view and reorient their enterprises to contribute to meeting civilian needs even if they feel it is below their dignity, as some have said contemptuously, "to produce pots and pans" instead of turning out advanced systems such as space and defense.

Alternatively, of course, if Russia's current political and economic reforms are reversed—either by political means (in elections) or otherwise (by another coup)—then defense conversion will be significantly set back, if not strangled, early after its birth. In sum, in the current struggle of the Yeltsin reformers for a democratic and free market Russia will both affect and be affected by the success or failure of genuine conversion.

Whatever the outcome, it has vital implications for Russia and the West:

- Unless the former Gorbachev policy of diversification is radically reversed, the vast former Soviet military production base will be preserved. It may even be strengthened, if it acquires greater capability and flexibility in producing a mix of civilian and military output.
- The former Soviet defense production bureaucracy (still in control even in reformist Yeltsin's Russia) is already using such diversification potential to lobby for greater investment in defense production capabilities.
- But any strengthening of the defense industries by new investment will make genuine conversion to civilian production even more difficult because most of the former Soviet military-industrial complex is solidly anti-market and anti-reform.
- Since Russia is now actively seeking advanced technology abroad in order to modernize its industries and laboratories, such acquisition will also strengthen the former military production base—again, unless large components of that base are transferred to civilian jurisdiction and production, and, ultimately, are genuinely privatized.
- Only such a radical change can lead to an irreversible outcome that would allow the West to lower significantly its concern over transfer of sensitive advanced technology to the former U.S.S.R. and to drastically downsize its own defense production base.

CONVERSION, REGIONAL ECONOMIES, AND DIRECT FOREIGN INVESTMENT IN RUSSIA

By Steven W. Popper *

CONTENTS

SUMMARY

Conversion of the defense sector is only a specific instance—albeit a particularly crucial one—of a process of "conversion" that needs to take place in many sectors of Russia's economy. Conversion has most often been treated as an enterprise-specific task. Yet, the record of success in the West using this approach to conversion is spotty at best. Excessive reliance on plant-level, project-by-project conversion in the majority of defense enterprises may be a disservice not only to the larger national purpose behind the conversion effort but to former arms producers themselves. A broader application of the term "conversion" would be to consider it as an economy-wide phenomenon. The type of conversion most typically found in the West is for alternative employers to bid away underutilized resources. This is not now a realistic option in many areas of Russia, yet the less that plant-level conversion proves practical, the more that regional economic development becomes an issue. There is a potential conflict of economic and political interests between current enterprise management and local government authorities; the degree of actual conflict will depend upon how quickly the already existing enterprises operating within the current industrial structure can help bring about the larger purpose sought by central policymakers. There are several areas where the activities of private Western business interests, in looking after their own interests, may also contribute in a profound way to easing the course of conversion. It is possible that in several ways Western business interests could help to reconcile the divergence in conversion objec-

---

* Steven W. Popper is an analyst specializing in international policy with RAND, Santa Monica.

tives between enterprises and governments. The enhancements direct investment may bring to the conversion process will not stem from charitable instincts. Western businessmen will remain true to their own self interest. But in doing so, they are likely to magnify their contribution to the conversion process at both the level of the enterprise and of the larger economy, particularly at the regional level.

INTRODUCTION

Even before the demise of the Soviet Union as a political entity, the policy of converting assets of the defense sector to meet the needs of the civilian economy had already been widely accepted. [1] Since that time, the need to boost non-defense production has become even more pressing, brought about by the collapse of former economic institutions. At the same time, the change in the domestic and international political environment has been so profound as to reduce even more the demand for the traditional outputs of the arms-producing sectors of industry. Conversion has come even more to be seen as a pressing economic—and political—issue.

The pressure for conversion ensuing from political change has also affected the former Soviet Union's erstwhile rivals in the West. Yet, unlike them, Russian defense contractors are being forced to undergo conversion in the context of an even more sweeping, fundamental transformation of economic institutions while at the same time experiencing conditions of severe economic crisis. The problem in Russia, therefore, goes beyond being an exercise in down-sizing and reallocation of resources. It becomes part of the larger question of how to go about establishing a new economic structure designed to support decisions on how best to allocate resources and improve the efficiency of their utilization.

At the same time as conversion is being implemented, means of production are being prepared for privatization, trade is being liberalized, and the active participation of foreign direct investment is being encouraged. There are several areas where the activities of private Western business interests, in seeking out opportunity and looking after their own interests, may also contribute in a profound way to easing the course of conversion of the defense industries of the Russian Federation.

DEFINING THE GOALS OF CONVERSION

To consider the various possibilities for Western business to assist the conversion process, a better understanding of the nature of the endeavor is required.

"Conversion" is a term much bandied about but which lacks a clear definition. Moreover, it is used to refer to a wide range of phenomena. Not all of these activities are consistent with each other. In the most restricted sense of the term, conversion refers to

---

[1] This paper is based on an earlier version prepared for the OECD Seminar on Military/Industrial Conversion held in Krasnoyarsk, Russian Federation, 24–25 March 1992. The views expressed in this paper are the author's own and do not necessarily represent those of the OECD and its member states or of RAND and its clients.

placing the resources of the defense industrial sector at the disposal of the civilian economy. The precise strategy for doing so may vary considerably, depending on the purposes the process is intended to serve.

Conversion has at different times been used to refer to retooling so as to produce civilian goods on lines previously reserved for military production (the popular conception of the word), to setting up parallel lines to run alongside dedicated military production lines, to shifting production resources from military to civilian producers, and to amalgamating defense plants with civilian production plants to share expertise, among other things. The common thread in all of these is to conceive of conversion as being put into effect without greatly modifying the existing structure of industry. The existing arms-producing enterprises become both the instruments and principal focus of conversion in this strategic design. Conversion in this light is viewed as a process implemented on a plant-by-plant basis.

As an aside, it should also be noted that conversion in this context does not necessarily imply the complete cessation of military production. Such conversion may well be accompanied by investments to increase the efficiency of production or by joint ventures with foreign partners to co-develop or co-produce new generations of military output. This aspect will be explored below.

A broader application of the term "conversion" would be to consider it as an economy-wide phenomenon. Conversion, in this sense, would refer to employing labor, skills, and capital, previously bound into the production process for defense goods, to produce a different assortment of goods corresponding better to the society's changes in demand. If the object is to guarantee useful and efficient employment of the economy's productive assets, conversion in this sense might well require a repackaging of those assets into new economic and technological units better suited to meet those ends than are the existing enterprises.

The distinction between this approach and the first is two-fold. First, preservation of the existing industrial structure is not explicitly one of the goals of the conversion process. Second, an economy-wide focus means that a wider range of policy instruments may be chosen to achieve these ends. If the goals the political authorities hope to achieve are those indicated by the broader approach to conversion, then the interests of the central government and those of the managers of arms-producing enterprises may not necessarily be similar. The primary purpose of the latter will be to preserve the existing structure of the enterprise and its existence as a functioning entity. The goals sought by the former may well be best achieved by having the current enterprise pass out of existence and bring something new in its stead.

Clearly, the extent to which the interests of these two groups conflict will depend upon how quickly the already existing enterprises operating within the current industrial structure can help bring about the larger purpose sought by central policymakers. This balance may be profoundly affected by the actions of foreign business partners. Nevertheless, the ultimate purpose of the conversion effort must be made clear before it is possible to consider how the participation of Western business may help the process achieve its ends.

APPROACHES TO CONVERSION

Conversion of the defense sector is only a specific instance—albeit a particularly crucial one—of a process of "conversion" that needs to take place in many sectors of the economy. The stated purpose of almost every successor government in Eastern Europe and the former Soviet Union is to bring about a transition to an economy operating along market principles and not directed by the preferences and microeconomic decision making of central authorities. Yet, in several instances the mechanisms used to implement conversion resemble precisely the type of decision making that characterized the old regime. This raises a concern that the instruments and programs chosen to further the process will run counter to the broader economic strategies of the respective governments of the economies undergoing transition. Conversion could take on the aspect of a "campaign" not much different from those of the past.

There are several reasons why successor governments may find themselves drawn toward specific actions that are antithetical to the larger purpose they hope to achieve through economic transformation. In many cases the decisions are practical ones; there has not yet been time to institute a new decision making apparatus for the central government. There is a need to use what is already available. Therefore, it is not surprising that the policy-making process, operating through the same bureaucracy that has existed in the past, will lead to similar policy outcomes. In addition, there do not yet exist in most cases institutions outside of government to permit politicians to feel confident that a less centrally directed approach to conversion will succeed. Here is another instance where the Western nations undergoing conversion are at an advantage because of their ability to rely upon functioning capital markets, an existing system of market-clearing relative prices, specialists providing various intermediary and background services, and so forth.

Beyond the problem of alternative governmental means for policy formulation and a lack of economic institutions outside of government bureaucracies, there is a profound shortage of available information. Both governments and defense contractors are attempting to chart a course in an environment where there do not exist adequate means for assessing costs, determining trade-offs, and therefore considering the full range of opportunities and alternatives.

There are additional reasons for taking the narrow approach to conversion—concentrating on conversion as a plant-by-plant, often a project-by-project phenomenon (one, if not actually directed by central authorities, then certainly actively and intimately supported by them.) Under the prevailing atmosphere of crisis, there is a quite natural desire to preserve as much as possible of what might be of value. So much of what has been built up through decades of investment seems imperiled and there appears to be little to take the place of what currently exists. In many locales, given the priorities and past patterns of centrally planned development, there are no alternative employers of labor and productive resources other than the local arms producer. The large defense plant is the only industrial employer for kilometers around.

This problem is exacerbated by the fact that the socialist enterprise has traditionally also been the major purveyor of services which form the social safety net. Not only employment, but training and retraining, child care, health, recreation, education and cultural benefits, supplementary income for pensioners, etc., all were obtained from the enterprise. In many locales the enterprise was the sole dispenser of such social amenities. The desire to save these entities when the local authorities seem unlikely to be able to pick up the slack is, again, understandable. But, there is danger if these concerns become the primary factor directing conversion policy.

There may be other related reasons why conversion of particular arms-producing enterprises is made a government priority. There may be an implicit conception that concentrating on converting defense plants might be the quickest way to provide employment and produce high value-added exports because of the technological level of such plants. Under the regime of central planning, the argument runs, defense was the most productive and efficient sector because it received a disproportionate share of investment resources and, in particular, of high technology investment. Therefore, it is reasonable to expect these enterprises to provide the motive force that will, especially in the earliest days of wide-scale transformation, be able to carry along industry and the economy as a whole.

This view may be in error for several reasons. The current government officials may be misunderstanding the source of the perceived efficiency of this sector under the old regime. To be sure, the defense sector did receive the favored portion of investment capital, but a good share of their superior performance relative to the non-defense sectors of industry was owing to the priority they achieved in many other categories of allocation under conditions of chronic supply shortages. By virtue of the letter of the annual plan for material supply, but most important, through the *de facto* actions of bureaucrats when the plan began to manifest inconsistency and infeasibility in application, the defense sector was the recipient of resources for which the civilian sectors were starved. This was an important source of the superior performance of the sector as a whole.

There might also be misunderstanding about the nature of the technology the arms plants deploy. True, there is a good deal of leading-edge technology in place in the arms sector, but a good portion of that technology is dedicated, single-purpose technology not readily suitable to civilian production. To make this sector a priority for investment in hopes of building upon its technological base may be to underestimate the effort and resources required to actually render this technology usable.

Finally, governments interested in conversion of arms producers for the purpose of having them jump-start the wider range of industry into more profitable activity may seriously overestimate the flexibility of the management structures in these plants. Although there can be no doubt about the genuine interest and incentives of arms producers to convert their activities to civilian production, there may be less willingness to change their fundamental approaches for planning and managing production activities. Because of the distinctive character of the defense sector's management

methods in the past, and the pride still attached to the separate-
ness that distinguished it from the way the rest of industry operated, this sector might actually prove more intractable and impervi-
ous to new methods of doing things than would the civilian sectors
whose managers can harbor no illusions about the efficacy of retaining old methods of management.

Enunciating reasons why the hopes based on the inherent competitiveness and flexibility of former arms producers, and so in the
ability of defense conversion to be a catalyst for general change,
may be misplaced, should in no way be interpreted as a defamation
of Russian defense sector managers. This is only to say that there
is no reason to believe the experience with plant-level conversion
schemes in the economies in transition should be any different
from that of the West. The record of success in the West using this
approach to conversion is spotty at best. In Russia, as in the West,
specific schemes will work in specific plants for good and understandable reasons. By the same token, these same reasons suggest
why in a large share of cases conversion *in situ* will prove to be a
drawn out, expensive, and possibly frustrating endeavor. Neither
should this discussion be taken as an aspersion of the new governments of the countries in transition. They are being forced to operate in an environment where they possess less information and less
experience than their Western counterparts—and where the stakes
of success or failure in conversion are much greater.

The point being raised in this discussion is that excessive reliance on plant-level, project-by-project conversion in the majority of
arms producing enterprises may be a disservice not only to the
larger national purpose behind the conversion effort but to former
arms producers themselves. The defense plants *do* possess resources, both material and human, that their nations desperately
require. The trick will be to gain as objective as possible an ap-
praisal of true possibilities within individual plants and within the
economy as a whole, pursuing those possibilities in tandem with a
more general reallocation of resources through emerging market
means, flexibly shifting specific strategies, and exploiting and
learning from successes as they appear.

REGIONAL ECONOMIC DEVELOPMENT

The issue of conversion in Russia is intimately bound with the
problem of regional economic development. Unlike the pattern of
development usually observed in market economies, in many parts
of Russia regional economies are narrowly based upon a small assortment of sectors—perhaps as few as only one or two giant plants
in one industry. Production resources, labor in particular, is much
less mobile than is the case in Western Europe, to say nothing of
the United States. A large incentive for keeping plants in production, even if the chance for successful transition is small, is to preserve local employment. The type of conversion most typically
found in the West, having alternative employers bid away underutilized resources, is not now a practical option in many areas. Yet,
this might be the only realistic option in many instances over the
long run. This looms as the most serious specter confronting the
Russian economy today.

There is also a political dimension. The hallmark of the revolution leading to the dissolution of the Soviet Union has been the increase in the responsibilities of local governments. The changes in the political environment have also led to an increase in their authority, but these limits are still being explored. Local officials must now think seriously about developing local revenue bases and balancing them against present and prospective requirements. They must be intimately concerned with the fate of local industrial enterprises and the management decisions that will determine that fate. At the same time, the changes of the past few years have led to a decrease in the authority of local industry managers. The conversion effort, in part, must be read as an attempt by managers to retain their authority against the ebb and to ensure their positions—a matter of increasing importance as privatization looms larger. Thus both local governments and enterprise managers will have a similarity of interest—and different views of the goals of the conversion effort.

Many of the potential conflicts lying at the intersection of the underdeveloped economic institutions of Russia and her new and still-forming political system will be played out at the local level in the years to come. The issues of the conversion and future direction of local industries will be at the heart of these conflicts. Anything that will assist the development of local economies will reduce the acrimony and the strain on individuals and institutions. The less that plant-level conversion proves practical, the more that regional economic development becomes an issue.

A Role for Western Business

In an arena beset by difficulties, but also by many potential opportunities, the intrusion of Western business interests into the process could prove a useful, perhaps even crucial asset. Western business interests could by their own actions help to bridge a number of gaps, overcoming obstacles both to large-scale conversion, (shifts in resource allocation through the economy as a whole,) and conversion at a lower level, (salvaging as much as possible of the structure of existing arms manufacturers.)

One can go further. It is possible that in several ways Western business interests could help to reconcile the divergence in conversion objectives between enterprises and governments noted above.

The balance of this paper will briefly sketch the ways in which the involvement of Western business may ease the course of conversion at both levels. Before proceeding, several assumptions should be made explicit. First, the discussion will concentrate on indicating several beneficial outcomes resulting from Western involvement. Discussion of the avenues for that involvement will be limited, but are presumed to include joint ventures with existing Russian arms enterprises, investment in new start-ups, and foreign purchase of existing plants. That is, the emphasis is on foreign direct investment (FDI). It is also possible for business to assist in specific areas on a strict fee-for-service basis, but it is assumed this prospect will be limited by economic realities in the near term.

The second point is crucial: The enhancements FDI may bring to the conversion process in Russia will not stem from charitable instincts. Western businessmen will remain true to their own self interest. But in doing so, they are likely to contribute more assistance to the conversion process than otherwise. This is so for two major reasons.

The governments in transition must decide which conversion efforts to back and where to allocate scarce resources to assist individual efforts and initiatives. This presents a considerable problem given their unfamiliarity with the task, lack of experience and background information, and the previously noted lack of supporting market institutions to assist decision making. External lenders of assistance, whether international agencies or sovereign governments, face similar difficulties. In addition, in both cases it is clear that governmental decision makers, whether foreign or domestic, will have long political agendas. To introduce much more than a minimum of political considerations into an already complex economic decision making environment may appear expedient in the short run, but runs the long-term risk of delaying or derailing the transition to new economic institutions. Long-term stability will be based on swift transition.

Businessmen, however, are specialists in precisely this form of decision making. It has been suggested that Western governments might help to smooth the conversion process by providing the means to hire "experts" to evaluate conversion prospects in Russia and elsewhere. But it is in the business community that a good deal of this expertise lies. With sufficient confidence in conditions for FDI, Western businesses will make these assessments using their own resources and then, out of self-interest, will place their own money at hazard to try bringing worthy projects they have identified into being. They will not always be right. In particular, they will not be fully familiar with inherent possibilities in what will appear a turbulent investment environment and will need to make more than cursory assessments; dialogue with local experts will be crucial. Neither is this to suggest there will then be no further role for governments. In many cases government action may be required because the interests of the private sector won't be directed to addressing all possible needs. Yet, FDI on a sufficient scale will contribute a great deal of expertise and insight into sifting and assessing available information.

In this respect, FDI will serve as a probe for testing the value of specific projects. It will also provide a valuable indicator of the actual course of change in the economic system itself. Clearly, a prerequisite for FDI will be the existence of a conducive environment for investment. To the extent foreign business feels comfortable with the course of reform and the prospects for the economy, FDI may increase to sizable proportions. Similarly, in a milieu of severe information shortage, the level of FDI activity may be a useful indicator to the governments in transition as to how the long-term success of their efforts is being judged and appraised by informed outsiders. Victory must not merely be proclaimed; it needs to be achieved in actuality for FDI to begin to assume significant weight. Having a reform effort judged by Western business as serious, and the involved government seen as being committed, is the best way to avoid what might best be termed the "carpet bagging" problem—when foreign business invests little, becoming involved only to take advantage of various short-term disequilibria in the economy. The net contribution to an economy from this type of activity could well be negative. Again, the more that foreign investors feel it is in their own long-term best interest to be a participant in the economy, the less likely this is to be a serious concern.

What follows is an elaboration of how FDI might assist conversion. In truth, we don't really know definitively how these possibilities will play out. Much will depend on the particularities of specific business endeavors. The discussion below might be best viewed as a catalogue of suggestions as to how collateral benefits might ensue from the involvement of Western business investment. This type of assessment is only a first step. It is then the job of the Russian government to tailor specific policies to increase the likelihood of achieving such outcomes.

ASSISTING LARGE-SCALE CONVERSION

The activities of Western business could prove an asset to governments seeking to achieve the objectives of economy-wide conversion: the shifting of productive resources from meeting defense procurement needs to non-defense alternatives. [2]

A principal benefit would be to help bring alternative employment to areas hard hit by downturns in defense procurement. Specific FDI efforts would provide such alternatives, whether by erecting new plant or making use of existing plant that might otherwise lie idle. In either case, they would contribute a much needed infusion of capital. This is the most obvious instance of the assistance FDI would provide to the transition processes associated with conversion. In many discussions, this becomes the exclusive focus of possible benefits to be expected from direct investment by foreign business. It is certainly crucial. The industrial structure throughout Eastern Europe and the former Soviet Union labors under various forms of debt, not all of them visible. Besides the more open forms of debt, there are also the debts owed to the environment and the debt to the capital stock, which in many industrial sectors has become technically obsolete and poorly maintained. [3] These debts must be cleared. In view of the domestic shortage of investment capital, FDI might be a source of funding to clear these debts in return for equity participations under various joint venture arrangements or outright sales.

Along with, or as part of the capital infusion would come transfer of technologies. [4] This, along with several of the benefits listed here, would operate at the enterprise level on a deal-by-deal basis, but would contribute powerfully to economy-wide conversion. Technology transfer would enable more efficient employment of the economy's productive assets. Western business might be unwilling to transfer leading edge technologies under joint venture arrangements. The merits of this point may be debated; there exist

---

[2] In some respects, the division of possible effects into those affecting the economy as a whole, and those affecting the ability of individual enterprises to survive, is arbitrary. Several actions listed below will clearly have benefits in both spheres. This magnifies their value.

[3] Even in the technologically developed defense sector, some activities not traditionally seen as contributing to production, such as material transport, are poorly developed.

[4] And what is likely to prove of greater importance in Russia, transfer of the techniques of technology management and application.

counter-examples. But even in the Russian defense sector, despite its clear technological prowess, there is considerable need for the types of technologies, both products and processes, that would enable enterprises to produce world-class goods. This is especially true of production technologies that will allow plants to convert to the production of civilian commodities.

It should be noted that especially when the high-technology-oriented Russian defense sector is considered, technology transfer may work in two directions. A great deal of the R&D muscle of Russia is bound up in the defense industry structure whether at the ministerial or enterprise level. There is considerable anxiety over the short-term prospects for employment of the technical intelligentsia who previously worked in the arms sector. This is fruitful ground for mutually beneficial FDI. Western multinationals could fund entire laboratories of researchers to work on industrial R&D projects. This is already starting to occur in several areas.

The benefit to the Western side is clear, being able to utilize the talents of highly skilled technical personnel and obtain the right to profit from their development work. On the Russian side, the benefit lies in preserving and sustaining the technical cadre of Russia at a time when domestic resources are likely to prove insufficient. As domestic demand picks up with a revitalization of the economy, the R&D personnel will be there to meet it. Further, R&D workers in multinational corporations are automatically tied into a global network for the transfer of information and expertise. In the case of former employees of the Soviet defense sector who have characteristically been cloistered and shut out from foreign contact, the benefit of exposure to this type of information is likely to be great. A good deal of learning by example will occur.

But in addition to capital infusion and technology transfer, FDI could contribute to economy-wide conversion by providing the expertise to identify production possibilities with existing assets that now run the risk of being unemployed. The economic and political system operating in Russia during the Soviet period did not permit enterprises and localities to gain adequate information on production or market opportunities within Russia itself, to say nothing of the international prospects. Businesses engaging in FDI will be precisely pitched to finding and developing such intrinsic capacities. That is the nature of their principal activity. This will be crucial especially in those localities where there are few alternative employers. Western business people, looking for opportunities for profit, may do a better job of identifying inherent capacities in existing industrial areas than any government body or commission.

So far, the discussion has centered on benefits stemming from specific deals and joint venture FDI. Such individual efforts that do occur, however, also carry the possibility of conveying considerable collateral benefit to the localities in which they operate and to the all-Russian conversion process. Studies of industrial location in market-type economies stress the importance of developing a pioneer firm in a given locality. Once the pioneer has demonstrated feasibility—and is seen to be earning a profit or is likely to do so in the future—other entrants seek to build upon success. They do so not only because of the demonstration effect, but because the pioneer has passed along skills through worker training and has begun to develop the infrastructure necessary to support that particular manufacturing activity. The pioneer's own actions will have lowered the cost threshold for competitors to follow into the region. At the same time, another class of new firms may now come into being. Industrial organization in the West is rarely based on the vertical integration common in Russian industry, but often seeks to develop regional networks of supply. This tendency is most highly developed in Japan but is characteristic of high-growth regions around the world. Establishing pioneer joint ventures in a region may be a necessary, if not sufficient, condition for a network of local suppliers of goods and services to come into being. At first, the locals would depend crucially on the stability of orders from the FDI pioneer, but as the region began to develop, this would be less the case.

The fact that the pioneer firm will most likely be foreign is also a potential benefit. The FDI venture could serve as a link, tying the nascent local network into a global network. This could provide stability to the local economy but is not likely to be a practicable development in most parts of Russia without the presence of an initial foreign investor. It is even conceivable that such linkage can be made through the Western business venture even if local start-up firms are not producing goods and services directly for the joint venture. In either case the link would occur through having the Western business concern providing the type of service infrastructure that is so notably lacking in every sector of the Russian economy. Western businesses that commit to investing in a region may also be willing to undertake various brokerage services to strengthen the local economy by increasing the chances of local efforts to restructure production and steer it toward the national or global markets.

All of these points are speculative. They need not occur in every instance nor are they likely to alleviate all suffering caused by procurement cutbacks and plant closures. These benefits may not necessarily reduce pain over the short run. But they may help to ensure that the short run is of limited duration, that its ills do not become chronic, and that the pain that is endured in Russia as a whole and in its localities will turn out to not have been suffered in vain.

Nevertheless, some plants will be shut down. This is unavoidable; not every existing enterprise can be saved with its present managerial structure intact. In fact, such enterprises might well prove to be the exception. In many instances the local government may turn out to be the principle equity holder in an idle plant, a ghost industrial park. The question is whether some use can still be made of the capital assets and skill base that the enterprise once possessed. Is it possible to recombine some of the labor, capital, and knowledge once held by defunct plants into new technological and economic packages more suited to evolving circumstances? The answer is almost certainly, yes.

One of the inherent advantages the market principle of economic organization has over central planning is that economies operating under market institutions possess considerable capacity for self-assembly of complex structure. That is, groups or individuals will come together in the presence of some perceived need and autonomously find avenues for cooperation. This is how new firms start. Cooperation then leads to an increase in the total output of goods and services and so benefits the economy as a whole—in the process of generating a large profit for the partnership. The natural tendency is toward equilibrium. One of the few advantages the present disequilibrium conditions in the Russian economy might hold is that as market interactions come more to be the norm, the possibility for this type of self-assembly increases.

Self-organized groups of workers, managers, technicians, and engineers could well find ways of profitably utilizing the same capital stock that the enterprise itself is unable to use successfully in conversion to new output lines. [5] They would need to be given access to this capital. They would also need considerable help. If existing enterprises, unable to make the conversion transition successfully, were treated as large industrial parks with parts of the former capital stock allocated to groups with ideas for putting it to work, something may yet be salvaged.

These working groups and proto-firms would require considerable financial, managerial, marketing, and other infrastructure help. A far-sighted Western entrepreneur could be of considerable assistance in meeting some of these needs and at the same time stand in good stead to benefit considerably from the native ingenuity and determination to succeed of the Russian people and the defense industry skill base. The Western business partner would, in essence, be transferring the information and skills necessary to make a profit under conditions of disequilibrium, to achieve business stability and viability, and to pick potential winners. On the aggregate level, national income would be increased.

In return, the Western partner would obtain a presence in this emerging market and be given the opportunity to gather useful information at little cost. It should also be noted there is an additional benefit to this small scale involvement of Western business people in conversion of the productive resources of Russia, if not of the existing enterprises per se. This type of involvement is likely to be of such a scale that Western business would be more inclined to enter into ventures early—less would be at hazard so there would be more inclination to take a risk. The course of marketization in Eastern Europe, as well as economic development experience elsewhere, suggests the cumulative weight of such initially small-scale operations can have a decisive effect on the growth possibilities of the economy at large.

ASSISTING CONVERSION AT THE LEVEL OF THE ENTERPRISE

The previous section examined the role of Western business in the large-scale conversion process; that is, how FDI activity might help reallocate defense production resources to alternative uses.

---

[5] The automaticity of this phenomenon has already been seen to work in practice in the still-socialist economies that introduced some measure of market interaction and personal incentive. Cases include the agricultural sector in Hungary in the 1970s, the industrial sector in the same country in the 1980s with the introduction of the Enterprise Economic Working Group (VGMK) concept, and the reforms in China. Again, in the West, it is common for some firms to be able to make good use of capital that other firms are not able to retain in productive use. The problem in Russia is that these alternative firms do not yet exist. The conversion process could be the occasion for them to come into being.

The same activity might also help small-scale conversion—helping existing arms plants survive. More important since these initiatives would be driven by the same incentives that drive those discussed above, this help would not be antithetical to the goals and mechanisms intended to foster a fundamental transformation of the Russian economic system. Thus a potential source of conflict between the interests of existing enterprises and those of the economy at large would be alleviated.

The survival prospects of many Russian arms plants are not good. This appears counter to the intuition of those raised in the belief that the defense sector is the major repository of high technology in Russia. The problem is not that this view is necessarily false. Rather it is that there are many other deficiencies in the structure of production and the organization of industry sufficient to trump the technology card. These deficiencies are present in the enterprises themselves and in the external service infrastructure that in the West would help management move in new directions. Again, this should not be interpreted as a criticism of Russian defense industry or its management. Rather, this is an *a fortiori* argument, stemming from consideration of the limited success Western defense plants have had in translating their technological prowess into market success in civilian commercial ventures. Possession of high technology has even proven to be a detriment if it leads to an unwillingness to change practices that were successful in the past under different conditions. The successful cases have been based on radical internal restructuring and heavy reliance on a wide range of market institutions and services.

It is almost certain that Western businesses, either as equity holders or as joint venture partners, can help overcome many of these obstacles. Once more, an obvious source of assistance would be to provide working capital, on the basis of negotiated business agreements, to enterprises going through conversion. It is also conceivable that even if a Western firm enters into some sort of arrangement with a Russian producer that does not involve FDI in the classic sense, the Western business partner may still be able to provide assistance in lending financial brokerage services, trying to put together a package of financing using its good offices and contacts not otherwise open to the Russian partner.

But perhaps even more important, Western business can provide assistance on the types of "software" changes that will be required for the average Russian defense plant to survive through successful conversion. It will be difficult to resolve many of these deficiencies without such help because domestic and internal resources to do so are lacking. A few illustrative examples will be briefly listed below.

It is already clear to the management of almost all Russian defense enterprises that they are woefully deficient in marketing. Marketing departments that do exist often have been recently created and consist of a handful of young engineers who speak foreign languages. They are determined to succeed but often lack formal training in marketing and the information necessary to skillfully market the enterprise's output abroad. Western business partners could provide not only marketing services for their Russian counterparts, but could be an important source of information on how to develop the marketing skill base required for enterprises to improve the efficacy of their own efforts.

But "marketing" usually has a limited meaning in the enterprises of Eastern Europe and the former Soviet Union. It refers to selling the existing or similar array of enterprise products to foreign and domestic purchasers. There is another aspect of marketing, less supply-oriented, that might best be termed market assessment. This is a demand-oriented activity that seeks to uncover market niches that might be filled by products the firm is capable of making, but which are not necessarily congruent with the traditional product line. It is a crucially important activity especially in the context of conversion when there needs to be a radical reassessment of the enterprise's output profile and, in Russia and elsewhere, a shift in the orientation of producers to meeting the demands of the market. This skill is largely lacking in the countries undergoing transition but is one that potential foreign investors and multinationals have developed into a high art. The room for collaboration and learning is, again, great.

Closely allied with market assessment is technology assessment. It is not sufficient for a converting arms producer to possess an adequate technology base. A company must have a sense of the use to which its technology might be put. This requires an objective assessment combined with a large amount of experience. It is another service vital to any enterprise seeking to convert its output to a new profile and one likely to be difficult to perform in Russia using local resources. The FDI partner of Russian arms producers will view this function as one of its first orders of business, indeed will be a precursor to any formal business arrangement. If the management of a former defense enterprise is willing to be objective during the "courting" period when it is holding discussions with a number of Western suitors, it may be able to gather a considerable store of information on external assessment of the enterprise's technological base by inference, even if no deal is actually consummated.

There is a major problem with conversion in all formerly socialist economies that deserves considerable attention. It will only be possible to give a cursory overview in the present context.

Virtually all proposals that have emerged for reform of the system of central planning stop at the enterprise front door. The implicit assumption is that if the external environment is radically altered and the context of relations between the enterprise and the central economic authorities on the one hand, and between enterprises on the other, is changed, the enterprise will come to be more truly entrepreneurial and will behave more like a Western firm. This assumption may be invalid.

The socialist-type enterprise was specifically designed for one purpose: to function as a part of a system of production that no longer possesses relevance. This legacy remains enshrined in prevailing methods of production management and in the structure of the enterprise itself. Though quite large in comparison with the average Western firm, the enterprise is more simply organized. The organization is hierarchic and based on functional departments rather than product groups or task-type orientation. As a result, there are many levels of responsibility, staffed with what might only be termed quasi-managers because true decision authority rests almost solely at the top of the pyramid. Horizontal communication between departments is awkward so it is difficult to move swiftly on problems that do not receive the attention of senior management. This meant the easiest production course to follow in any given time period was to implement the same set of plans and decisions worked out in the previous period. This course will not be adequate to meet the challenges of conversion.

Association with Western business partners under almost any form of business agreement might be of profound help in addressing several of these deficiencies and so improve the prospects both for conversion and enterprise survival. Active involvement by a Western business partner could help by illuminating at an early stage areas where change is needed and also provide some guidance in choosing more appropriate models for management. Several areas come to mind, beyond the production management aspect noted above. Accounting practices in Russian enterprises are almost universally inadequate to the needs of a market-oriented firm. Current practices are not intended to provide managers with the information they need to assess production; rather, they are intended to provide the central authorities with the means to control the enterprise and guarantee plan compliance. It is not easy using these means to assign appropriate costs to individual work stations or aspects of the production process. Help will be required to devise and institute accounting practices more in tune with the present needs of enterprise management.

Closely allied with accounting, Western joint venture partners of East European defense contractors undergoing conversion have found personnel management practices to be inadequate to the task of operating viable, competitive production facilities. Labor within the plant is a severely underutilized resource, one requiring more attention and maintenance than has been given heretofore. The same is likely to be true in many of the Russian defense works undertaking conversion. The Western partners have discovered they are able to give insight into management practices which turn out to be to the advantage of all concerned—including the workers.

Finally, it must be remembered that the situation facing the defense industry of Russia is qualitatively different from that facing the arms sectors of other countries in transition. Russia is, and will remain, a major military power if only because it is a gigantic state with a number of legitimate security needs. Although the defense sector has traditionally taken a far greater share of national resources than was healthy for the economy as a whole, there is still a need for a pared-down domestic defense industry. This industry will satisfy domestic needs and will also export for the same reasons almost all national arms industries do. Given the radical change in the international political environment, there is the possibility for Russian arms producers to enter into several forms of collaborative arrangements with Western, including U.S., defense contractors. These collaborations could lower the production, and hence presumably the procurement costs of defense goods. At the same time, contact with Western partners and transfer of various forms of production and managerial technologies could work to improve the viability of current defense production in Russia, thereby enhancing its competitive stature.

CONCLUSION

Western business, in following its own best interests by taking advantage of the remarkable business opportunities presented by the transformation of the Russian economy, and in particular the conversion of large parts of the former Soviet arms industry, will provide several crucial benefits. These could have decisive weight in determining the successful outcome of the conversion effort. Besides filling several of the gaps that now exist in the service infrastructure and knowledge base of Russian industry, foreign direct investment could provide an essential link between the converting enterprises and world business, and most important, between the goals and interests of enterprise managers and those of the reformist Russian and local governments. Western business partners will lend an otherwise missing expertise to their Russian opposite numbers and will be able to point out deficiencies the converting enterprises might not otherwise become aware of until it was too late and led to failure in the conversion process.

Foreign direct investment will be of value to the Western business community for obvious reasons. But it will also provide a channel of activity and a new focus for those who will come to manage and own the enterprises of the former Soviet defense sector. This should help ease what would otherwise be a painful transition from their former positions of priority and prestige.

THE DEFENSE INDUSTRIES OF THE NEWLY INDEPENDENT STATES OF EURASIA

By Donald Creacey *

CONTENTS

SUMMARY

Through years of intensive investment, the former Soviet Union developed the world's largest defense-industrial base with 3,000 to 5,000 production facilities and a work force of 7–10 million people. The sector included about 150 major final assembly plants, thousands of component and material production facilities, and more than 1,500 research, development, and test facilities. In addition to producing weapons and other military equipment, the former Soviet defense industry also produced a significant quantity of producer durables, such as computers, machine tools, tractors, and consumer goods, including washing machines, televisions, radios, VCRs, and other products. Defense-industrial production was heavily concentrated in Russia and Ukraine, with the rest scattered among the remaining states.

The breakup of the Soviet Union has severely disrupted the defense industry; each of the former republics is faced with determining what weapon production infrastructure it requires and how best to utilize the rest. Production and final assembly of major weapon systems and military equipment takes place in five of the newly independent states: Russia, Ukraine, Georgia, Uzbekistan, and Kazakhstan. The Baltic countries and four other states—Be-

---

* Donald Creacey is an analyst with the Office of Slavic and Eurasian Analysis, Central Intelligence Agency.

(783)

larus, Moldova, Tajikistan, and Kyrgyzstan—are suppliers of military electronics and key weapon system components. Two states—Armenia and Azerbaijan—produce only minor components, and one state—Turkmenistan—has no identified defense production. Almost all of the newly independent states have announced their intention to downsize their defense industries and convert a large part of the present capacity to civil production. Most have yet to resolve the size and scope of the defense industries they wish to maintain and how to compensate for the loss or potential loss of access to input from other—now independent—states.

INTERDEPENDENCY OF MILITARY PRODUCTION: THE SOVIET INHERITANCE

With the exception of Russia, the new states are highly dependent on one another for armaments production. In the former Soviet Union, military production relied on a considerable amount of cooperation between facilities that are widely dispersed over several republics. Final assembly plants and specialized plants that supply major subsystems—such as chassis, engines, and computers—or small components and parts were constructed in different locations with little regard to transportation costs:

- Some of the plants were geographically dispersed for strategic reasons, an outgrowth of World War II experience, to reduce their vulnerability to invading armies of concentrated strategic attack.
- Other plants were developed (and types of military products were chosen) to take advantage of local resources of materials, skilled labor, or complementary industry.
- Some plants were set up to provide high-tech industry for local labor or colonizing Russians. The Tashkent aircraft factory in Uzbekistan, for example, formerly was staffed with a large percentage of Russian managers, engineers, and technicians.
- For some facilities the choice of locations was simply a result of strong-willed personalities.

Under the Soviet regime, plants and the military product mix were allocated in an atmosphere devoid of political or economic restrictions on the internal flow of trade within Union borders. A plant's output of military products, and generally also its input of supplies of materials and component parts, were based on state orders to meet the needs of national forces. Consequently, there was no requirement nor apparent attempt to develop diversified independent defense industries within the individual republics.

Defense industry in the Soviet Union—unlike its Western counterparts—was highly integrated vertically through both formal organizational subordination and a well-established line of supply. The development of "pyramid" structures facilitated weapon programs by ensuring reliable supplies from the mine to the final assembly plant. But reliance on formal ties and structures also resulted in both inefficiency and inflexibility in supply systems, making them more vulnerable to disruption than their Western counterparts. Russia alone, because of its size and diversity, currently has the industrial base to operate autonomously in many areas. Even it, however, requires imports of some strategic materials—such as ilmenite and rutile for titanium and alumina and bauxite for aluminum—and in the short term will have to purchase some components and subsystems that are only produced elsewhere. None of the other states approaches Russia's degree of autonomy. Even Ukraine's military sector is at present tooled to manufacture only a limited range of products whose primary market is in Russia. The end result of this dispersed-yet-integrated military production is that it makes the states highly dependent on one another, not only as sources of supply, but also as markets for their output.

CURRENT STATUS

RUSSIA

Russia contains some 70 percent of the former Soviet defense industry enterprises with an estimated 2,000 to 4,000 plants and 5–8 million employees. It produces all major categories of military equipment: land arms, aircraft, missiles, spacecraft, naval ships, and radars. Because of its size and diversity, it is the only state that produces nearly all types of components that make up weapon systems. Nearly all of the key chemical warfare, biological warfare, and nuclear weapons-related production facilities are in Russia. Roughly three-fourths of the former Soviet Union's military research, development, and test facilities are also located there.

Russia is a major producer of many key commodities and strategic materials, accounting for nine-tenths of the former Soviet output of oil, three fourths of the natural gas, half of the crude steel, and most of the aluminum and cobalt. It produces titanium, but imports the ore from Ukraine and other countries.

UKRAINE

Ukraine contains roughly 15 percent of the former Soviet defense plants and military R&D facilities—some 700 plants with 500,000 employees directly employed in the defense industry and perhaps another 1 million people contributing to defense output, according to Ukrainian estimates. It is the second-largest producer of military weapons and equipment after Russia. It is capable of assembling all major categories of military equipment—naval ships, missiles, transport aircraft, land arms, and radars—although not as diverse in types and models as those produced in Russia. Component and subsystem plants within Ukraine supply aircraft engines, avionics, and other electronic systems, and missile parts for domestic use and for plants in Russia and other newly independent states. Ukrainian defense industry, however is not self-sufficient, despite its variety of defense output. It depends heavily on Russia for many components and subassemblies. Ukraine has up to 15 percent of the known former Soviet military R&D facilities, including the sole popup test range for submarine-launched ballistic and cruise missiles.

Some Ukrainian facilities have unique capabilities, and others have been sole producers of key systems. Ukraine has the only shipyard in the former Soviet republics currently capable of building aircraft carriers. For missiles and space, Dnepropetrovsk Southern Machine-Building Plant has been the sole producer of the SS-18 ICBM and the SL-16 space launch vehicle, and a plant in Pavlograd was the sole final assembly facility for the SS-24 ICBM.

Ukraine is also an important supplier of strategic materials for plants throughout the former Soviet Union. In 1991 it produced about half of the Union's iron ore, 40 percent of its metallurgical coking coal, and one-third of its manganese ore and crude steel. Plants in Zaporozh'ye are important producers of aluminum, titanium, magnesium, and also specialty steels for military equipment. Ukraine, however, depends heavily on Russian petroleum and natural gas for fuel and chemical industry inputs.

BELARUS

Belarus has about 5 percent of the former Soviet defense industrial base. Leaders of Belarus have claimed that their defense industry contains 120 plants employing some 370,000 people. Belarus' major military contribution has been in vehicles and electronics. Minsk is the industrial center, providing military trucks and heavy-duty chassis for ballistic missile and air defense missile support equipment, including those for the Russian-produced SS-25 ICBM and at least one system Russia is currently trying to export—the SA-10 surface-to-air missile system. Minsk is also a center for design and production of computers and computer-based command and control systems. A plant in Gomel' has been the primary producer of radars for strategic ballistic missile defense. Other plants in Belarus produce various components, such as avionics for military and civil aircraft. The Defense Minister of Belarus has claimed that the republic cannot produce everything that its armed forces need and that it would participate in cooperative ventures to produce equipment and weapons. Belarus has less than 2 percent of the identified former Soviet RDT&E facilities.

Belarus is largely dependent on the other republics for most of its strategic materials. Foreign Minister Petr Kravchenko said in a press interview that to achieve economic independence from Russia, Belarus would have to restructure its industry with advanced technology to make production less energy-demanding and not so completely dependent on supplies of oil, gas, and iron ore; he cited in particular the need to transform the military and electrotechnical industry, the engineering industry, and the production of specialized instruments.

MOLDOVA

Moldova has less than 1 percent of the former Soviet Union's defense industry; it has specialized in electronics, mostly subsystems and components used in military equipment produced elsewhere, primarily Russia. Plants in Chisinau (Kishinev) produce military communications equipment and military computers. Moldova has less than 1 percent of the identified former Soviet military RDT&E facilities and no significant strategic mineral resources.

KAZAKHSTAN

Kazakhstan has about 3 percent of the identified former Soviet defense industry facilities, the largest military-industrial sector outside the Slavic republics. According to the Kazakh minister of industry, the Kazakh defense industry comprises over 50 enterprises. A plant in Petropavlovsk produces the SS-21 SRBM. Other Petropavlovsk plants produce ballistic missile support equipment, torpedoes, and naval communications equipment. Another major torpedo producer is located in Alma-Ata. All these plants rely on inputs of components from other states, primarily Russia. A plant in Ust Kamenogorsk produces nuclear power reactor fuel and beryllium products, and a plant at Aktau (Shevchenko) processes uranium ore. In addition, Kazakhstan has the only known plants outside Russia designed for production of chemical and biological warfare materials.

Kazakhstan's roughly 1 percent of the known former Soviet military RDT&E facilities are much more significant than the count indicates. Kazakh test ranges have played a vital role in the development and production of aerospace systems. The range at Vladimirovka is used for integration of aircraft with airborne weapons, the center at Saryshagan is used for development and flight testing of strategic air defense missile and ballistic missile defense systems, and the center at Emba performs similar functions for tactical air defense missile systems. The facility at Tyuratam is used to launch spacecraft (including all manned missions) and to test liquid-propellant ICBMs. The Semipalatinsk Nuclear Weapons Proving Ground is one of two facilities in the former Soviet Union where nuclear weapons were tested; in 1991 Kazakhstan banned further nuclear testing and announced plans to convert the installation to civil uses.

Kazakh plants are key suppliers of such strategic materials as titanium, magnesium, tantalum, niobium, gold, silver, and alumina. Up to 1984 at least, the Soviets imported ore—probably from Australia—for the Ust Kamenogorsk titanium-magnesium plant, apparently in part because of delays in developing the nearby Karaotkel' ilmenite deposit. A plant in Pavlodar is one of the three largest producers of alumina in the newly independent states, and is a major supplier to Russia's aluminum plants in Siberia.

UZBEKISTAN

Uzbekistan has less than 1 percent of the identified former Soviet defense industry. The state's major defense-industrial facility is the Tashkent Chkalov aircraft plant, which produces the Il-76 Candid transport and its Midas tanker and Mainstay AWACS variants, as well as components for air-to-surface missiles. The plant is now preparing for production of the Il-114, a new short-haul twin turboprop transport designed for civil and military uses. An associated aircraft components plant in Fergana manufactures assemblies for aircraft produced at Tashkent. The Fergana plant also modifies military transports for specialized missions. Tashkent-built aircraft are heavily reliant on engines and avionics supplied by plants in Russia. Tashkent electronics plants produce computers, integrated circuits, and other electronics components. Less than 1 percent of the known former Soviet RDT&E facilities were in Uzbekistan. Among these, however, were the principal Soviet open-air biological warfare test range on Vozrozhdeniya Island in the Aral Sea and a chemical warfare test range on the Ustyurt plateau; both test facilities were closed in 1992.

Uzbekistan's strategic materials production includes gold and tungsten. The largest gold plant in the former Soviet Union is at a mining complex in Muruntau; other gold plants are at Altynkan and Samarkand. Tungsten ore is mined at Ingichka and processed at a concentration plant nearby.

TAJIKISTAN

Tajikistan's defense industry constitutes less than 1 percent of the former Soviet Union's military-industrial base. A plant in Taboshar has produced solid-propellant rocket motors for strategic missiles. Tajikistan has no other identified defense industry facilities of significance and no identified military RDT&E facilities.

Tajikistan produces some strategic materials. The aluminum plant at Tursunzade is the third largest in the CIS and the world, and is the industrial pillar of the Tajik economy. Sixty percent of the plant's output is exported to other former Soviet states, and it in turn relies on them for raw materials. Tajikistan mines gold ore and is expanding its own gold-processing capabilities: it operates one ore concentration plant at Taror and is building another concentration plant at Kansay and a gold refinery at Khudzhand (Leninabad). Tajikistan also operates a uranium ore concentration plant in Khudzhand.

KYRGYZSTAN

Kyrgyzstan has less than 1 percent of the former Soviet production plants; it manufactures torpedo components, small arms, and specialized vehicles on armored personnel carrier chassis, but produces little else of defense significance. Most of the facilities are located in the capital, Bishkek. Less than 1 percent of the identified former Soviet RDT&E facilities are located in Kyrgyzstan; among these is an underwater ordnance test area at Lake Issyk Kul used for testing of torpedoes produced in Kazakhstan.

Kyrgyzstan produces few identified strategic materials. It processes uranium ore at a plant at Kara-Balta and is developing a gold mine and building a gold ore concentration plant near Kazarman.

GEORGIA

Georgia has less than 1 percent of the identified former Soviet defense industry. Its most significant military production facility—the Tbilisi aircraft plant—produces the Su-25 Frogfoot ground attack aircraft, but is dependent on Russia for engines and some avionics and other components. Georgia assembles no other major weapon systems. Electronics plants in Tbilisi, Akhmeti, Telavi, and Tsalki produce microcircuits, sensors, and other microelectronics for military systems, including missiles, produced in Commonwealth states. Georgia has less than 2 percent of the known former Soviet military RDT&E facilities. There are two nuclear R&D institutes—in Tbilisi and Sukhumi—but no nuclear production plants.

Georgia produces about a fifth of the former U.S.S.R.'s output of manganese ore—a key input in steel production—but no other significant strategic materials.

ARMENIA

Armenian plants probably constituted less than 2 percent of the former Soviet defense industrial base. Products from Armenian plants reportedly included instruments for Soviet submarines and ships, aircraft computer systems, other aviation electronics, telescope lenses, and other electronic equipment. Armenia has roughly 3 percent of the estimated former Soviet Union's military R&D facilities.

Armenia's strategic materials output includes gold, copper, aluminum, zinc, and molybdenum. The state is heavily dependent on imported fuel and ferrous metals.

AZERBAIJAN

Azerbaijan has less than 1 percent of the former Soviet defense industry and produces only minor components. Plants in the capital, Baku, produce computer components and display devices, printed circuit boards and other electronic subcomponents, and associated electronic equipment. Less than 1 percent of the known former Soviet military R&D facilities are in Azerbaijan. The state's strategic materials production includes aluminum from a small plant in Sumgait and oil from both onshore complexes (principally at Baku and elsewhere on the Apsheron Peninsula) and from offshore fields in the South Caspian Sea.

BALTIC STATES

The Baltic states have only a small number of defense industry enterprises, mostly electronic component plants that supplied plants in the other former republics with small parts and components such as integrated circuits and semiconductors; only a minor part of that output went to the military sector. The Baltic states produce no major weapon systems. Baltic leaders have announced their intention to convert virtually all of their defense enterprises to civil production and to privatize them along with the rest of the economy:

- In Latvia, several plants in Riga produce integrated circuits and semiconductors. Latvia has less than 2 percent of the identified former Soviet military RDT&E facilities, primarily electronics.
- Officials in Lithuania have said that only about 10 electronics and radio instrument enterprises—which provided only a small portion of their output for the military—could be considered defense industrial enterprises. Plants headquartered in Vilnius produce minicomputers, and a plant in Alytus makes tape recorders. About 1 percent of the identified former Soviet military RDT&E facilities, mostly electronics, are in Lithuania.
- Defense industry enterprises in Estonia produced avionics, mechanical components for rocket motors, nuclear reactors for satellites and submarines, and electronic components for the shipbuilding industry, relying primarily on Russia for inputs of

raw materials. Less than 1 percent of the identified former Soviet military RDT&E facilities, mostly electronics, are located in Estonia.

V. HUMAN RESOURCES AFFECTING THE ECONOMY

OVERVIEW

By James Voorhees *

For most of the 70 years between the founding of the Soviet Union and its collapse, the needs of the population were neglected for the sake of achieving other goals of the state. The birth of the Soviet Union required sacrifices from virtually everyone within the former Russian Empire. Its survival through civil war and total war required great heroism and terrible hardship. The communist ideology, with its promise of a utopian future, provided justification for these sacrifices and more on the part of the Soviet people.

The sacrifice of human needs came to be an intrinsic part of an economic system that was devoted largely to the production—for production's sake—of large quantities of high priority goods, principally weapons and machines that make machines. Not only were consumer goods and housing neglected, but so were services essential to the quality of people's lives, such as health, the environment, and some aspects of education. The growing sclerosis of the system doomed efforts to reform it. Even as it became clear that the Soviet Union could not catch up with the West without giving greater priority to the well-being of its population, the system successfully resisted efforts to introduce change.

Moreover, the population at the beginning of the Soviet era in the 1920s was largely poor. Life became easier for each generation, at least through most of the Brezhnev period (1964-1982), as the Soviet economy grew. And the standard for comparing the quality of one's life was the life of one's forebears, not life in the wealthier West. Life there was largely hidden by official propaganda and barriers to information about the outside world. These barriers also long hid the true quality of Soviet life and the growing paralysis of the system from most Soviet citizens and from many of those officials who could have improved the lives of the Soviet people.

The leaders of the states now being formed from the wreck of the Soviet Union are facing the consequences of decades of neglect of the people they govern. Democratization in many of these states requires that the citizenry be provided with adequate health care, housing, and education. It may be threatened if these needs are not satisfied. But the legacy of the Soviet Union will not easily be overcome, as the contributors to this section make clear. (The related

---

* James Voorhees is a Technical Information Specialist at the Congressional Research Service and editor of the newsletter *Parliamentary Development*.

(791)

792

legacy of environmental degradation is causing problems that may
be even more intractable. See the chapters in this volume by
Murray Feshbach, "Environmental Calamities: Widespread and
Costly," and Philip R. Pryde, "The Environmental Implications of
the Dissolution of the U.S.S.R.")

HEALTH

As the title of his chapter implies, Murray Feshbach found little
that was encouraging in the demographic data he examined. In the
past year, deaths exceeded births in Russia and Ukraine. The reported number of cases of dysentery, whooping cough, syphilis,
diphtheria, bacterial dysentery, salmonella, and tuberculosis increased in 1991 or early 1992 over the number in the same period
in the previous year.

The incidence of disease can be reduced through vaccination, but
vaccines are not available in sufficient quantities. In the Soviet
Union as a whole in 1989, only 80 percent of the population was
vaccinated against diphtheria and polio. In Uzbekistan and Kyrgyzstan less than two-thirds of the population received those vaccinations, too small a proportion to prevent the incidence of those diseases from becoming widespread. Feshbach suggests that such diseases are becoming woefully common.

Feshbach and Christopher Mark Davis both describe the inadequacy of the medical infrastructure in the former Soviet Union.
Hospitals lack basic equipment and medicines. Rural hospitals in
particular too often lack even hot water and sewage treatment facilities. Many medical staffs are inadequately trained. According to
Davis, decreasing proportions of the amount of medicine required
were supplied by either domestic industry or imports between 1985
and 1991. That proportion fell to 60 percent in 1991.

The ability of the Russian medical system to respond to the increasing challenges it faces is being severely challenged as the
economy continues to decline. Inflation and budgetary constraints
have left the health care system underfunded. Consequently, only a
little more than half as many new hospital beds were provided in
1992 as in the first six months of 1991, and only minor repairs can
be made to health care facilities and equipment though major repairs are often needed.

Despite these problems, Davis sees no sign that the health of the
Russian population has yet been markedly affected by the post-
Soviet deterioration of the medical system. But he concludes with
an echo of Feshbach's pessimism: the deterioration of health conditions and medical care is severe, and the health of the Russian population can be expected to reflect that deterioration later in this
decade.

HOUSING

The sad state of housing under the Soviet system is well known.
Living quarters were crowded; the quality of construction was
dismal. Michael Alexeev found that since 1990, the housing situation has become worse, despite the efforts made under perestroika
to reform it. The amount of construction has fallen off, while the
demand for housing has increased as the number of refugees has

grown and as large numbers of military personnel have been brought home from abroad. Moreover, as in the health sector, needed repairs are not being made. As poor-quality Soviet housing deteriorates, the costs of providing adequate housing for the people of the post-Soviet republics can only rise.

Alexeev argues that a comprehensive privatization plan for the private sector should include four elements. Housing itself should be privatized. So should the construction industry and the construction materials industry. A market for land should be established. Lastly, the legal constraints on the ability of people to live where they please should be removed. Alexeev focuses his attention on the problems of privatization of housing and industry.

Only a small proportion of housing has been privatized in the former Soviet Union, although efforts at privatization have been under way since 1989. Households have little incentive to buy the apartments that have become available to them, partly because apartment rents and utility costs are still subsidized, as they were under the old system.

Similarly, genuine privatization of the construction and construction materials industries has not yet taken place. The construction industry, long accustomed to building the high rise apartment complexes that ring Russian cities, needs a major overhaul to enable it to provide the smaller-scale housing now in demand. Alexeev finds encouragement, however, in the rise of construction cooperatives despite many obstacles and in the emergence of a system of commodity exchanges.

SCIENCE AND EDUCATION

Science and education are widely regarded as major achievements of the Soviet Union. Harley Balzer concurs with that assessment, but argues that while significant achievements were made in science and education, the limited resources available meant that achievement in one area was often matched with the neglect of another. Moreover, Balzer finds that the achievements were often merely formal, disassociated from practical problems.

The collapse of the economy has created a crisis in science and education. New organizations created as a result of the 1987 economic reforms have collapsed along with the old organizations. Those that remain are being pressed by the discrepancy between the three-fold rise in their budgets and the ten-fold rise in prices. Specialists are finding it impossible to continue their work. Balzer says that two-thirds of the people employed in science are likely to be working in some other field by the end of 1993. This is one form of "brain drain" that promises to have lasting consequences.

Another consequence is the emigration of scientific personnel to other countries. In contrast to the problems addressed in the other chapters in this section, Steven Popper argues that this problem may not be serious. It may be simply a sign of the normalization of the closed Soviet system. Moreover, Popper argues that the emigration of a large part of the scientific community can bring benefits to a society as well as impose costs. For example, it could enable the emigrants to become more proficient at their professions through exposure to the work of others. It could also allow scientists and engineers to work at their professions until their societies can once again afford to support their work. Popper concludes that rather than adopt policies that restrict the emigration of scientists and engineers, it would be better to encourage the emigrants to return by addressing the problems that make emigration attractive in the first place.

DEMOGRAPHY

W. Ward Kingkade addresses the demographic trends of the former Soviet Union over the last few decades and projects them well into the twenty-first century. He finds that the significant differences in the fertility rates of the European parts of the former Soviet Union, Central Asia, and the Transcaucasus are diminishing. Fertility in the European republics has long been lower than elsewhere in the former Soviet Union. But fertility has declined in the Transcaucasus since 1958–59. In Central Asia fertility rates are now much lower than they were in the mid-1970s.

The differences in fertility rates will have their effects on the size of the populations of these new countries in the next century. The populations of all the countries are projected to increase for at least 30 years. A comparison of the projected age structures of Russia and Uzbekistan suggests that the European republics will face vastly different problems than Central Asia. Russia, and probably the European republics as a whole, will have an aging population; the old will slightly outnumber the young. This will mean fewer workers and more beneficiaries of social security programs. The productivity of the former will have to be higher so that their societies can supply the goods and services going to the latter. If it is not, either those benefits will have to be smaller than they might otherwise be, or the standard of living of workers will have to be reduced. This problem awaits these countries after they have adjusted to the shocks that are now jolting them.

Uzbekistan and Central Asia as a whole are expected to face less onerous choices in the longer term, though they now face the problems associated with managing a rapidly increasing population. If actual trends follow the projections, their populations will double by 2050. But the young will greatly outnumber the old, as in Third World countries. Because of the decline in fertility, there will be fewer dependents of working age adults: they will have fewer children to take care of and fewer old people to support.

Even if these potential problems stemming from demography are similar to those that are being faced elsewhere, the problems of health care, housing, and education examined in the other papers in this section are legacies of the Soviet system. Through them, the Soviet Union is exacting its last sacrifices from those over whom it ruled.

DEMOGRAPHIC PROSPECTS IN THE REPUBLICS OF THE FORMER SOVIET UNION

By W. Ward Kingkade *

CONTENTS

---

* W. Ward Kingkade is a statistician with the Center for International Research, U.S. Bureau of the Census.

Introduction

The radical political and economic transformations in the former Soviet Union are occasioning fundamental reassessments of social and economic prospects of this region. To the extent that these changes involve people, they influence and are influenced by the composition and distribution of the population of the region. Demographic characteristics and trends thus represent an important element of the setting in which the current societal changes are taking place in the Soviet Union's emerging successors. This paper discusses the principal demographic trends over the recent past in the 15 republics of the former Soviet Union and presents projections of the future populations of these newly independent states.

Population Growth

The basic trends in the distribution of the total populations of the union republics over successive postwar censuses are presented in Table 1. The lopsidedness of the distribution is its most salient feature. Russia's predominance in population size reflects an importance in terms of human resources that promises to endure well beyond the breakup of the former Union. Ukraine's population, while totalling only about one third of Russia's, is large by European standards: comparable to those of France, Italy, or the United Kingdom. The next largest former Soviet republics, Uzbekistan and Kazakhstan, are similar in population size to Australia and the Netherlands, respectively. The majority of the former Soviet republics resemble smaller European countries in terms of population size.

TABLE 1. Total Populations of the Union Republics in Postwar Soviet Censuses.

Republic	Total Population (thous.)				Growth (thous.)			Growth Rate (per 1000)		
	1959	1970	1979	1989	1959–70	1970–79	1979–89	1959–70	1970–79	1979–89
U.S.S.R.	208,827	241,720	262,436	286,717	32,893	20,716	24,281	13.30	9.14	8.85
RSFSR	117,534	130,079	137,551	147,386	12,545	7,472	9,835	9.22	6.21	6.91
Ukraine	41,869	47,126	49,755	51,704	5,257	2,629	1,949	10.75	6.03	3.84
Belorussia	8,056	9,002	9,560	10,200	946	558	640	10.09	6.68	6.48
Lithuania	2,711	3,128	3,398	3,690	417	270	292	13.01	9.20	8.24
Latvia	2,093	2,364	2,521	2,681	271	157	160	11.07	7.14	6.15
Estonia	1,197	1,356	1,466	1,573	159	110	107	11.34	8.67	7.04
Moldavia	2,885	3,569	3,947	4,341	684	378	394	19.34	11.19	9.51
Georgia	4,044	4,686	5,015	5,449	642	329	434	13.40	7.54	8.30
Armenia	1,763	2,492	3,031	3,283	729	539	252	31.46	21.76	7.99
Azerbaydzhan	3,698	5,117	6,028	7,029	1,419	911	1001	29.53	18.21	15.36
Uzbekistan	8,119	11,799	15,391	19,906	3,680	3,592	4,515	33.98	29.53	25.72
Kazakhstan	9,295	13,009	14,684	16,538	3,714	1,675	1,854	30.56	13.46	11.89
Kirgizia	2,066	2,934	3,529	4,291	868	595	762	31.89	20.52	19.55
Turkmenia	1,516	2,159	2,759	3,534	643	600	775	32.14	27.25	24.76
Tadzhikistan	1,981	2,900	3,801	5,112	919	901	1311	34.65	30.06	29.63
European U.S.S.R.	176,345	196,624	208,198	221,575	20,279	11,574	13,377	9.90	6.36	6.23
Transcaucasus	9,505	12,295	14,074	15,761	2,790	1,779	1,687	23.40	15.02	11.32
Central Asia	22,977	32,801	40,164	49,381	9,824	7,363	9,217	32.36	22.50	20.66

Source and Methodology: The population figures are those given in Goskomstat, 1989, pp. 8–9. Exponential growth has been assumed in calculating rates.
Note: The subtotal for Central Asia includes Kazakhstan.

Although the total population of every union republic increased between each census in Table 1, sizable regional variations in rates of growth prevailed. Between successive censuses the Central Asian population grew on average, about three times faster than the population of European union republics, including the R.S.F.S.R., while the population of Transcaucasia grew about twice as fast as the population of the European republics. The populations of the Central Asian republics (more or less) doubled over the period covered in Table 1, while much smaller relative gains were experienced in the European republics.

With few exceptions, republic growth rates have declined with the passage of time in keeping with long-term trends in fertility. In all republics the rates of population growth between the two most recent censuses (1979 and 1989) were lower than those between the earliest two postwar censuses (1959 and 1970). However, recent increases in fertility may account for the increases in growth rates observed between the two latest intercensal periods in the R.S.F.S.R. and Georgia, while they may have slowed the pace of decline in the growth rates elsewhere.

One important consequence of the differences in growth rates between the European union republics on one hand and the rest of the former U.S.S.R. on the other, has been the rising share of the non-European share of the U.S.S.R.'s total population. Since 1959 the proportion of the total Soviet population residing in Central Asia and Kazakhstan rose from 11 to 17 percent, while the Transcaucasian population share also increased. Among the European republics, in contrast, Moldavia alone registered an increasing proportion of the U.S.S.R.'s population. Although as of the 1989 Census the R.S.F.S.R. still contained the majority of the U.S.S.R.'s population, its share had fallen to 51 percent by that time. Nevertheless, the European republics taken as a whole continue to account for the overwhelming majority of the population of both the CIS and the former U.S.S.R.—more than three quarters as of 1989.

Trends in the distribution of the U.S.S.R.'s urban population among union republics are examined in Table 2. At each postwar census, European republics contained greater shares of the U.S.S.R.'s urban population than of its total population, reflecting the greater urbanization in the European area. While the urban population of the non-European union republics has on average grown faster than that of European republics, the differential in urban growth rates is smaller than that observed for total population growth. Moreover, the urban populations of some European union republics have grown more rapidly than those of certain Central Asian and Transcaucasian republics. In particular, Moldavia's urban growth rate since 1979 surpasses that of all other republics, thanks partly to the major drop in the corresponding rate for Uzbekistan.

The distribution of the U.S.S.R.'s rural population is examined the Table 3. Unlike the total population and urban population, the rural population of the U.S.S.R. has been shrinking. As the table indicates, the rural population decline is confined largely to the European union republics. Outmigration from rural areas is primarily responsible for the observed declines in the rural populations of the European republics. Opposite tendencies are exhibited

TABLE 2. Urban Populations of the Union Republics in Postwar Soviet Censuses.

Republic	Total Population (thous.)				Growth (thous.)			Growth Rate (per 1000)		
	1959	1970	1979	1989	1959–70	1970–79	1979–89	1959–70	1970–79	1979–89
U.S.S.R.	99,978	135,991	163,586	188,791	36,013	27,595	25,205	27.97	20.53	14.33
RSFSR	61,611	80,981	95,374	108,419	19,370	14,393	13,045	24.85	18.18	12.82
Ukraine	19,147	25,688	30,512	34,591	6,541	4,824	4,079	26.72	19.12	12.55
Belorussia	2,481	3,908	5,263	6,676	1,427	1,355	1,413	41.31	33.08	23.78
Lithuania	1,046	1,571	2,062	2,509	525	491	447	36.98	30.22	19.62
Latvia	1,174	1,477	1,726	1,907	303	249	181	20.87	17.31	9.97
Estonia	676	881	1,022	1,127	205	141	105	24.08	16.50	9.78
Moldavia	643	1,130	1,551	2,037	487	421	486	51.26	35.19	27.26
Georgia	1,713	2,240	2,601	3,033	527	361	432	24.38	16.60	15.37
Armenia	882	1,482	1,993	2,225	600	511	232	47.18	32.92	11.01
Azerbaydzhan	1,767	2,564	3,200	3,785	797	636	585	33.84	24.62	16.79
Uzbekistan	2,729	4,322	6,348	8,106	1,593	2,026	1,758	41.80	42.71	24.45
Kazakhstan	4,067	6,538	7,920	9,465	2,471	1,382	1,545	43.16	21.31	17.82
Kirgizia	696	1,098	1,366	1,641	402	268	275	41.45	24.27	18.34
Turkmenia	700	1,034	1,323	1,603	334	289	280	35.46	27.39	19.20
Tadzhikistan	646	1,077	1,325	1,667	431	248	342	46.47	23.03	22.96
European U.S.S.R.	86,778	115,636	137,510	157,266	28,858	21,874	19,756	26.10	19.25	13.42
Transcaucasus	4,362	6,286	7,794	9,043	1,924	1,508	1,249	33.22	23.89	14.86
Central Asia	8,838	14,069	18,282	22,482	5,231	4,213	4,200	42.26	29.10	20.68

Source and Methodology: The population figures are those given in Goskomstat, 1989, pp. 8–9. Exponential growth has been assumed in calculating rates.
Note: The subtotal for Central Asia includes Kazakhstan.

in Central Asian republics, whose rural populations are growing at appreciable rates. In several of these republics, the pace of rural population growth appears to be increasing.

TABLE 3. Rural Populations of the Union Republics in Postwar Soviet Censuses.

Republic	Total Population (thous.)				Growth (thous.)			Growth Rate (per 1000)		
	1959	1970	1979	1989	1959–70	1970–79	1979–89	1959–70	1970–79	1979–89
U.S.S.R.	108,849	105,729	98,850	97,926	−3,120	−6,879	−924	−2.64	−7.48	−0.94
RSFSR	55,923	49,098	42,177	38,967	−6,825	−6,921	−3,210	−11.83	−16.88	−7.92
Ukraine	22,722	21,438	19,243	17,113	−1,284	−2,195	−2,130	−5.29	−12.00	−11.73
Belorussia	5,575	5,094	4,297	3,524	−481	−797	−773	−8.20	−18.91	−19.83
Lithuania	1,665	1,557	1,336	1,181	−108	−221	−155	−6.10	−17.01	−12.33
Latvia	919	887	795	774	−32	−92	−21	−3.22	−12.17	−2.68
Estonia	521	475	444	446	−46	−31	2	−8.40	−7.50	0.45
Moldavia	2,242	2,439	2,396	2,304	197	−43	−92	7.66	−1.98	−3.92
Georgia	2,331	2,446	2,414	2,416	115	−32	2	4.38	−1.46	0.08
Armenia	881	1,010	1,038	1,058	129	28	20	12.42	3.04	1.91
Azerbaydzhan	1,931	2,553	2,828	3,244	622	275	416	25.38	11.37	13.72
Uzbekistan	5,390	7,477	9,043	11,800	2,087	1,566	2,757	29.75	21.13	26.61
Kazakhstan	5,228	6,471	6,764	7,073	1,243	293	309	19.39	4.92	4.47
Kirgizia	1,370	1,836	2,163	2,650	466	327	487	26.62	18.21	20.31
Turkmenia	816	1,125	1,436	1,931	309	311	495	29.19	27.12	29.62
Tadzhikistan	1,335	1,823	2,476	3,445	488	653	969	28.32	34.02	33.03
European U.S.S.R.	89,567	80,988	70,688	64,309	−8,579	−10,300	−6,379	−9.15	−15.11	−9.46
Transcaucasus	5,143	6,009	6,280	6,718	866	271	438	14.15	4.90	6.74
Central Asia	14,139	18,732	21,882	26,899	4,593	3,150	5,017	25.57	17.27	20.64

Source and Methodology: The population figures are those given in Goskomstat, 1989, pp. 8–9. Exponential growth has been assumed in calculating rates.
Note: The subtotal for Central Asia includes Kazakhstan.

Tendencies in the redistribution of the Soviet population between rural and urban areas are reflected in the figures for the urbanization of union republics given in Table 4. Major regional differences in urbanization trends are evident. Urbanization is proceeding at the swiftest pace in the European republics, particularly those that were least urbanized earlier in the postwar period (Belorussia, Lithuania, Moldavia). In Central Asia, on the other hand, urbanization has not only proceeded at a substantially lower pace during the postwar period; it practically came to a halt in recent years. The cessation, however temporary, of Central Asian urbanization results from the major rural-urban differences in fertility levels in this region. In spite of the growth of the urban population of Central Asia, whose rate of growth is above the all-union average, Central Asia's rural population is growing much more rapidly, so that the urban share of the population has failed to grow, or has even declined.

TABLE 4. Urbanization of the Union Republics in Soviet Postwar Censuses.

Republic	Percent Urban 1959	Percent Urban 1970	Percent Urban 1979	Percent Urban 1989
U.S.S.R.	47.88	56.26	62.33	65.85
RSFSR	52.42	62.26	69.34	73.56
Ukraine	45.73	54.51	61.32	66.90
Belorussia	30.80	43.41	55.05	65.45
Lithuania	38.58	50.22	60.68	67.99
Latvia	56.09	62.48	68.46	71.13
Estonia	56.47	64.97	69.71	71.65
Moldavia	22.29	31.66	39.30	46.92
Georgia	42.36	47.80	51.86	55.66
Armenia	50.03	59.47	65.75	67.77
Azerbaydzhan	47.78	50.11	53.09	53.85
Uzbekistan	33.61	36.63	41.24	40.72
Kazakhstan	43.75	50.26	53.94	57.23
Kirgizia	33.69	37.42	38.71	38.24
Turkmenia	46.17	47.89	47.95	45.36
Tadzhikistan	32.61	37.14	34.86	32.61
European U.S.S.R.	49.21	58.81	66.05	70.98
Transcaucasus	45.89	51.13	55.38	57.38
Central Asia	38.46	42.89	45.52	45.53

Sources and Methodology: The population figures are those given in Goskomstat, 1989, pp. 8–9. Exponential growth has been assumed in calculating rates.
Note: The subtotal for Central Asia includes Kazakhstan.

Assessing the relative roles of migration and natural increase is of considerable interest, since these two processes respond to different stimuli and are distinct from one another in their social and economic effects. The recent publication of time series of annual births and deaths for the union republics make it possible to estimate the intercensal natural increase precisely, allowing net migration to be estimated as the residual left over after the amount of natural increase has been deducted from total population growth (the "vital statistics" method).

Table 5 presents the decomposition of total population growth in the 15 union republics for the two most recent intercensal periods. Natural increase accounted for the predominant share of population growth in most republics. The exceptions were Baltic republics (Latvia and Estonia) in which the contribution of net migration somewhat exceeded the sizable proportion of growth due to natural increase.

TABLE 5. Components of Total Population Growth in the Union Republics, 1970–1989.

Republic	Population Growth (thous.)		Natural Increase (thous.)		Net Migration (thous.)		Natural Increase Share of Growth (percent)		Net Migration Share of Growth (percent)	
	1970–79	1979–89	1970–78	1979–88	1970–78	1979–88	1970–78	1979–88	1970–78	1979–88
U.S.S.R.	20,716	24,281	20,419	24,423	297	−142	98.56	100.59	1.44	−.59
RSFSR	7,472	9,835	7,195	8,060	277	1775	96.29	81.96	3.71	18.04
Ukraine	2,629	1,949	2,373	1,795	256	154	90.25	92.09	9.75	7.91
Belorussia	558	640	640	648	−82	−8	114.68	101.18	−14.68	−1.18
Lithuania	270	292	205	192	65	100	75.89	65.92	24.11	34.08
Latvia	157	160	53	67	104	93	33.45	41.61	66.55	58.39
Estonia	110	107	50	52	60	55	45.06	49.05	54.94	50.95
Moldavia	378	394	399	450	−21	−56	105.54	114.09	−5.54	−14.09
Georgia	329	434	466	487	−137	−53	141.59	112.22	−41.59	−12.22
Armenia	539	252	423	559	116	−307	78.43	221.76	21.57	−121.76
Azerbaydzhan	911	1,001	966	1,266	−55	−265	106.01	126.52	−6.01	−26.52
Uzbekistan	3,592	4,515	3,349	5,021	243	−506	93.23	111.21	6.77	−11.21
Kazakhstan	1,675	1,854	2,155	2,639	−480	−785	128.66	142.32	−28.66	−42.32
Kirgizia	595	762	671	919	−76	−157	112.82	120.57	−12.82	−20.57
Turkmenia	600	775	601	857	−1	−82	100.17	110.57	−0.17	−10.57
Tadzhikistan	901	1,311	875	1,412	26	−101	97.07	107.69	2.93	−7.69
European U.S.S.R.	11,574	13,377	10,913	11,264	661	2,113	94.29	84.20	5.71	15.80
Transcaucasus	1,779	1,687	1,854	2,312	−75	−625	104.24	137.07	−4.24	−37.07
Central Asia	7,363	9,217	7,651	10,847	−288	−1630	103.91	117.69	−3.91	−17.69

Source and Methodology: Population growth has been computed from table 1. Figures for natural increase have been obtained from Goskomstat, 1989, pp. 38–54. Net migration has been estimated as the difference between population growth and natural increase.

The overall direction of net migration in the former U.S.S.R. during the 1980s is apparent from the results in Table 5. In general, the European union republics gained population through net migration while Transcaucasia and Central Asia experienced net outmigration. This regional orientation of migration flows existed prior to 1979, but it gained momentum in the past decade.

Urban population growth in the Soviet republics is decomposed into migration and natural increase in Table 6. In the U.S.S.R. as a whole and in most republics, the balance shifted in favor of natural increase over the two preceding intercensal periods. Natural increase accounted for the larger portion of the U.S.S.R.'s urban growth between the last two censuses. In the European republics, which contain the majority of the U.S.S.R.'s urban population, the contribution of migration slightly exceeded that of natural increase in urban areas during the period 1979–1988. However, natural increase in Central Asia and Transcaucasia, which accounted for most of the growth of urban areas in these regions, was sufficient to swing the all-U.S.S.R. balance in favor of natural increase.

TABLE 6. Components of Urban Population Growth in the Union Republics, 1970–1989.

Republic	Urban Population Growth (thous.)		Urban Natural Increase (thous.)		Urban Net Migration (thous.)		Natural Increase Share of Urban Growth (percent)		Net Migration Share of Urban Growth (percent)	
	1970–79	1979–89	1970–78	1979–88	1970–78	1979–88	1970–78	1979–88	1970–78	1979–88
U.S.S.R.	27,595	25,205	11,947	14,500	15,648	10,705	43.29	57.53	56.71	42.47
RSFSR	14,393	13,045	5,612	6,360	8,781	6,685	38.99	48.76	61.01	51.24
Ukraine	4,824	4,079	1,943	1,940	2,881	2,139	40.28	47.56	59.72	52.44
Belorussia	1,355	1,413	551	721	804	692	40.63	51.05	59.37	48.95
Lithuania	491	447	173	193	318	254	35.24	43.18	64.76	56.82
Latvia	249	181	61	69	188	112	24.55	37.91	75.45	62.09
Estonia	141	105	56	56	85	49	39.99	53.77	60.01	46.23
Moldavia	421	486	150	226	271	260	35.71	46.53	64.29	53.47
Georgia	361	432	234	263	127	169	64.84	60.98	35.16	39.02
Armenia	511	232	263	341	248	−109	51.41	147.17	48.59	−47.17
Azerbaydzhan	636	585	425	604	211	−19	66.87	103.23	33.13	−3.23
Uzbekistan	2,026	1,758	892	1,504	1,134	254	44.05	85.57	55.95	14.43
Kazakhstan	1,382	1,545	898	1,273	484	272	65.01	82.39	34.99	17.61
Kirgizia	268	275	197	270	71	5	73.41	98.19	26.59	1.81
Turkmenia	289	280	241	338	48	−58	83.34	120.75	16.66	−20.75
Tadzhikistan	248	342	249	340	−1	2	100.30	99.47	−0.30	0.53
European U.S.S.R.	21,874	19,756	8,547	9,566	13,327	10,190	39.07	48.42	60.93	51.58
Transcaucasus	1,508	1,249	922	1,209	586	40	61.15	96.78	38.85	3.22
Central Asia	4,213	4,200	2,477	3,726	1,736	474	58.80	88.70	41.20	11.30

Source and Methodology: Population growth has been computed from table 2. Figures for natural increase have been obtained from Goskomstat, 1989, pp. 38–54. Net migration has been estimated as the difference between population growth and natural increase.

The decomposition of rural population growth in the union republics is presented in Table 7. As the figures demonstrate, the rural population of the U.S.S.R. declined over the two preceding intercensal periods, particularly the first. This was largely due to outmigration from rural areas in the European republics. In Central Asia and Transcaucasia, the natural increase of the rural population exceeded the volume of rural outmigration in both intercensal periods. The negative natural increase registered in the majority of European union republics between the last two censuses was itself a consequence of outmigration, which has depleted the countryside of its population in the reproductive ages, resulting in fewer births than deaths. Some reduction in the volume of net rural outmigration between the two intercensal periods is evident in European republics, excluding Moldavia. While the reduction observed in the RSFSR might not be unrelated to policy measures undertaken to attract population to rural areas of the Nonchernozem Zone, similar reductions appear elsewhere.

FERTILITY

The range of variation in fertility among the republics of the former Soviet Union spans most of the range observed around the world. Central Asian fertility levels are comparable to those of Third World countries. In contrast, fertility in many of the European union republics has, for a significant portion of the postwar

TABLE 7. Components of Rural Population Growth in the Union Republics, 1970-1989.

Republic	Rural Population Growth (thous.)		Rural Natural Increase (thous.)		Rural Net Migration (thous.)		Natural Increase Share of Rural Growth (percent)		Net Migration Share of Rural Growth (percent)	
	1970-79	1979-89	1970-78	1979-88	1970-78	1979-88	1970-78	1979-88	1970-78	1978-88
U.S.S.R.	-6,879	-924	8,472	9,923	-15,351	-10,847	-123.16	-1,073.97	223.16	1,173.97
RSFSR	-6,921	-3,210	1,582	1,700	-8,503	-4,910	-22.86	-52.97	122.86	152.97
Ukraine	-2,195	-2,130	429	-145	-2,624	-1,985	-19.56	6.80	119.56	93.20
Belorussia	-797	-773	89	-74	-886	-699	-11.22	9.55	111.22	90.45
Lithuania	-221	-155	32	-1	-253	-154	-14.43	0.34	114.43	99.66
Latvia	-92	-21	-9	-2	-83	-19	9.37	9.70	90.63	90.30
Estonia	-31	2	-7	-4	-24	6	21.98	-198.75	78.02	298.75
Moldavia	-43	-92	249	223	-292	-315	-578.08	-242.82	678.08	342.82
Georgia	-32	2	232	224	-264	-222	-724.21	11,179.85	824.21	-11,079.85
Armenia	28	20	160	217	-132	-197	571.48	1,087.08	-471.48	-987.08
Azerbaydzhan	275	416	540	663	-265	-247	196.54	159.26	-96.54	-59.26
Uzbekistan	1,566	2,757	2,456	3,517	-890	-760	156.86	127.56	-56.86	-27.56
Kazakhstan	293	309	1,257	1,366	-964	-1,057	428.86	441.95	-328.86	-341.95
Kirgizia	327	487	475	649	-148	-162	145.11	133.21	-45.11	-33.21
Turkmenia	311	495	360	519	-49	-24	115.81	104.82	-15.81	-4.82
Tadzhikistan	653	969	626	1,072	27	-103	95.84	110.60	4.16	-10.60
European U.S.S.R.	-10,300	-6,379	2,366	1,698	-12,666	-8,077	-22.97	-26.62	122.97	126.62
Transcaucasus	271	438	932	1,104	-661	-666	344.00	251.95	-244.00	-151.95
Central Asia	3,150	5,017	5,174	7,122	-2,024	-2,105	164.24	141.95	-64.24	-41.95

Source and Methodology: Population growth has been computed from table 3. Figures for natural increase have been obtained from Goskomstat, 1989, pp. 38-54. Net migration has been estimated as the difference between population growth and natural increase.

period, [1] been below the replacement rate which is consistent with a stationary population in the long run. [2] As a result, rapid population growth is taxing local resources in the least developed regions of the former U.S.S.R., while the European republics are concerned about diminishing supplies of indigenous entrants to the labor force.

An official and typically Soviet response to these pressures was the development of a regionally differentiated fertility policy aimed at stimulating the fertility of the European population while promoting fertility decline in regions of higher fertility. [3] In 1981 the 26th Congress of the Communist Party adopted a set of measures for the benefit of mothers and children that included such incentives as partly paid maternity leave for a year for working women (extended later to 1.5 years), whose effects were probably greatest in the European population with its low fertility and high rate of female employment. There were concurrent low-profile efforts to encourage family limitation in Central Asia through the medical professions, public education, and the introduction of family planning clinics.

---

[1] The replacement fertility rate is the rate that would maintain equal sizes of generations if maintained indefinitely. A total fertility rate of 2.1 is typically taken to be the replacement value; the value is slightly greater than 2 because not all children survive to childbearing age.
[2] Empirically, a population whose fertility is at the replacement rate in a given year can register growth or decline at that time and for a substantial period thereafter, depending on its previous history. Zero growth occurs only when replacement fertility has been maintained in the population for generations.
[3] Weber and Goodman, 1981; Kingkade, 1987

The fertility rates of the various union republics at selected dates is summarized in Table 8 in terms of total fertility rates, which indicate the number of children a woman would bear if she survived to the end of her reproductive life under the current fertility schedule for the given year. According to the data, the overall fertility rate of the U.S.S.R. as a whole declined over most of the period since 1960, except for a brief reversal around the early 1970s and a more sustained turnaround in the 1980s. The increase in fertility after 1981 recovered a decade's worth of decline, returning the U.S.S.R.'s fertility rate as of 1987 to the neighborhood of its value in the early 1970s. However, an appreciable drop has been registered in the period since 1987, so that by 1990 fertility was once again about as low as at the beginning of the 1980s.

There are major differences in fertility trends as well as rates between republics of the Soviet Union. Most European republics ended the 1950s with total fertility rates above the replacement rate of 2.1; by the late 1960s a majority had fertility rates below replacement. All of the European republics shared in the upturn in fertility of the early 1970s, which brought most of these republics again above replacement by 1971–72. Thereafter, each European republic experienced sustained declines in fertility for the remainder of the decade, so that by 1980–81, all except Moldavia had below-replacement fertility rates. All European republics participated in the rise in fertility in the 1980s, and all except Moldavia converged to the neighborhood of replacement by 1984–85.

Subsequently the fertility levels of the European republics have diverged, and in most cases fertility is dropping once more. Intriguingly, these changes have left the Baltic republics with higher fertility rates than the three Slavic republics, whose fertility rates have fallen sharply since 1988.

The developments in fertility in the European union republics in the 1980s are consistent with the experience of East European countries under pronatalist policies; in most of these countries, annual fertility indicators rose for a few years after the policies were adopted, then fell. However, the recent movements in the fertility levels of the European republics of the Soviet Union could well be influenced by other factors, such as popular morale under perestroika or the anti-alcoholism campaign.

Demographers in the former Soviet Union typically consider the European population of the U.S.S.R. to have completed the "demographic transition" from natural to controlled reproduction, while regarding the indigenous Central Asian population as being in the initial stage of the transition and classifying Transcaucasia as transitional. [4] The data in Table 8 corroborate these assignments. In two of the Transcaucasian republics, Armenia and Azerbaijan, fertility declined over the period covered by the figures from rates typical of Central Asia to rates comparable with several European republics at the end of the 1950s or to present-day Moldavia. Georgian fertility was already at such a point at the beginning of the period of observation.

---

[4] Belova et al., 1983; Tatimov, 1987; Vishnevskiy and Volkov, 1983.

TABLE 8. Total Fertility Rates for the Union Republics, 1958–1988.

	1958–59	1965–66	1969–70	1975–76	1980–81	1982–83	1984–85	1985–86	1987	1988	1989	1990
U.S.S.R.	2.810	2.461	2.389	2.389	2.253	2.367	2.405	2.462	2.532	2.451	2.334	2.263
RSFSR	2.626	2.125	1.971	1.969	1.895	2.050	2.058	2.111	2.218	2.124	2.007	1.888
Ukraine	2.296	1.986	2.044	2.023	1.935	2.037	2.055	2.069	2.035	2.039	2.019	1.902
Belorussia	2.795	2.282	2.298	2.139	2.023	2.092	2.078	2.096	2.051	2.021	1.924	1.844
Lithuania	2.627	2.228	2.354	2.185	1.976	2.026	2.096	2.138	2.166	2.090	1.986	2.044
Latvia	1.938	1.735	1.926	1.946	1.887	2.028	2.071	2.091	2.151	2.112	2.049	2.020
Estonia	1.946	1.920	2.143	2.078	2.029	2.094	2.110	2.102	2.223	2.237	2.211	2.054
Moldavia	3.573	2.683	2.563	2.518	2.403	2.569	2.676	2.770	2.733	2.629	2.464	2.362
Georgia	2.587	2.596	2.616	2.516	2.250	2.245	2.329	2.359	2.295	2.247	2.129	2.203
Azerbaijan	5.005	5.271	4.633	3.916	3.227	3.009	2.928	2.936	2.885	2.824	2.791	2.767
Armenia	4.730	3.908	3.195	2.786	2.339	2.352	2.488	2.553	2.544	2.492	2.604	2.827
Uzbekistan	5.044	5.564	5.636	5.660	4.805	4.650	4.653	4.699	4.610	4.309	4.039	4.089
Tajikistan	3.926	5.489	5.903	6.313	5.627	5.473	5.492	5.601	5.683	5.376	5.103	5.077
Turkmenistan	5.123	6.039	5.930	5.713	4.920	4.755	4.666	4.725	4.787	4.599	4.300	4.188
Kirgizstan	4.320	4.709	4.846	4.850	4.089	4.090	4.140	4.183	4.210	4.005	3.808	3.695
Kazakhstan	4.462	3.503	3.307	3.258	2.911	2.927	3.034	3.081	3.192	3.122	2.804	2.704

Sources: B. Ts. Urlanis, *Narodonaseleniye stran mira*, 1983 & 1978; *Vestnik statistiki* 1985 #11, 1984 #11, 1983 #11; Goskomstat SSSR 1989, pp. 328–343; 1988 pp. 209–214.

Note: The total fertility rate represents the number of children a woman would bear in her life if she spent it under the regime of age-specific fertility rates prevailing in the given republic and time period. The total fertility rates in this table were computed from published age-specific fertility rates for five-year age groups, and may differ from official figures computed from single-year age data.

Fertility decline in Central Asia is a comparatively recent phenomenon. Except in Turkmenia, the fertility rates of these republics appear to have increased up to some time in the 1970s. In addition to improvements in completeness of birth registration, changes in marriage patterns and increases in fecundity associated with developments in nutrition and control over diseases may underlie the observed fertility gains. In any case, each Central Asian republic entered a period of sustained fertility reduction around the early to mid-1970s. The evidence suggests that the onset of the fertility transition has in all likelihood arrived. Although every Central Asian republic took part in the rise in fertility in the early 1980s, this did not appreciably lessen the impact of fertility decline except in Kazakhstan. In the latter republic, fertility was relatively low to begin with, largely because European nationalities comprise a majority of the population. The fertility rates of the remaining Central Asian republics in 1990 are substantially lower than those observed in the mid-1970s. This is particularly true of the three Central Asian republics whose indigenous nationalities predominate (Uzbekistan, Tadzhikistan, and Turkmenia), and whose target fertility rates have dropped by one child or more.

The final year's data appear to suggest the slackening or abatement of the fertility decline in each of the Central Asian republics, influenced perhaps by the outmigration of the European population and changes in national morale. Although the duration of this interruption remains to be determined, a reversal of the secular decline would seem highly unlikely, except possibly with the growth of extreme variants of Islamic fundamentalism.

Fertility is typically higher in rural than urban areas, partly as a result of the lower educational level and greater traditionalism of rural populations and because they have less access to modern contraceptives than do urban populations. Official figures on the fertility rates of the urban and rural populations of union republics at selected dates are presented in Table 9. According to the data, the fertility of the urban population of the U.S.S.R. has been below the replacement rate for the better part of the period since the late 1950s. Such is the case for all European republics. Urban fertility in the Transcaucasian republics appears to be approaching the replacement rate. Although fertility in the urban areas of Central Asian is well above the replacement rate, it is considerably lower than the fertility rate of the rural populations of the region. In general, there is considerably less variation between republics in urban fertility than in rural fertility, so that one might anticipate further convergence in union republic fertility rates as the urbanization process progresses.

TABLE 9. Official Total Fertility Rates for the Union Republics, Urban and Rural Areas, 1969-88, Selected Years.

Republic	Total					Urban					Rural				
	1969-70	1975-76	1980-81	1986-87	1988	1969-70	1975-76	1980-81	1986-87	1988	1969-70	1975-76	1980-81	1986-87	1988
U.S.S.R.	2.416	2.396	2.239	2.521	2.452	1.952	1.914	1.827	2.076	2.031	3.252	3.546	3.271	3.696	3.556
RSFSR	1.992	1.973	1.875	2.194	2.130	1.736	1.723	1.667	1.947	1.896	2.609	2.838	2.636	3.162	3.057
Ukraine	2.059	2.029	1.927	2.089	2.026	1.839	1.831	1.728	1.916	1.892	2.439	2.479	2.471	2.597	2.436
Belorussia	2.331	2.146	2.014	2.075	2.031	2.027	1.852	1.804	1.895	1.889	2.736	2.868	2.633	2.675	2.523
Lithuania	2.362	2.194	1.970	2.163	2.095	2.004	1.912	1.762	1.879	1.764	2.926	2.914	2.532	3.095	3.273
Latvia	1.934	1.948	1.873	2.151	2.114	1.701	1.727	1.695	2.005	1.977	2.496	2.637	2.412	2.589	2.528
Estonia	2.155	2.085	2.022	2.185	2.247	1.965	1.853	1.867	2.073	2.113	2.682	2.864	2.503	2.534	2.677
Moldavia	2.576	2.517	2.390	2.777	2.635	2.003	1.844	1.792	2.043	1.984	2.899	3.106	3.054	3.868	3.667
Georgia	2.654	2.538	2.248	2.332	2.261	2.324	2.244	2.015	2.175	2.112	3.044	3.044	2.558	2.533	2.448
Armenia	3.241	2.786	2.314	2.559	2.512	2.659	2.457	2.050	2.247	2.271	4.437	3.747	2.976	3.254	3.074
Azerbaydzhan	4.661	3.922	3.221	2.893	2.796	3.407	3.136	2.612	2.642	2.595	6.330	5.040	4.175	3.289	3.104
Uzbek	5.674	5.674	4.807	4.631	4.283	3.716	3.575	3.086	3.197	3.027	7.203	7.543	6.426	5.946	5.410
Kazakh	3.351	3.273	2.903	3.159	3.126	2.431	2.327	2.261	2.419	2.384	4.580	4.850	3.991	4.707	4.745
Kirgizia	4.891	4.867	4.072	4.201	4.000	3.141	2.930	2.616	2.738	2.657	6.372	6.635	5.391	5.544	5.242
Tadzhikistan	5.926	6.322	5.642	5.680	5.348	4.104	3.967	3.563	4.006	3.608	7.362	8.367	7.183	6.759	6.417
Turkmenia	5.972	5.738	4.930	4.752	4.570	4.498	4.085	3.653	3.765	3.667	7.758	7.881	6.503	5.866	5.574

Source: Goskomstat SSSR, 1989, pp. 113-116.

Note: The total fertility rate represents the number of children a woman would bear in her life if she spent it under the regime of age-specific fertility rates prevailing in the given area and time period.

Rural fertility is above the replacement rate at every date in Table 9, both for the U.S.S.R. as a whole and in every union republic. Major regional differences in fertility trends as well as rates are evident. In three of the seven European republics, fertility is currently higher than in the mid-1970s as a result of the increases in the 1980s. In Transcaucasia, particularly Armenia and Azerbaijan, impressive declines have been registered since the end of the 1950s. In fact, rural fertility in Armenia and Azerbaijan is now approximately equal to that in the RSFSR. Moreover, as of 1988, rural fertility in Georgia is lower than in any European republic except Ukraine, while two European republics (Lithuania and Moldavia) exhibit higher rural fertility than any Transcaucasian republic.

Current fertility rates among the rural populations of the Central Asian republics vastly exceed those of their counterparts elsewhere in the former U.S.S.R. However, there can be little confusion as to whether the Central Asian population has entered the demographic transition. The rural populations of Central Asian republics exhibit fertility declines of greater magnitude than do the urban populations, except in Kazakhstan where the presence of sizable rural contingents of European nationalities may obscure developments among the indigenous population. Moreover, in the three Central Asian republics where the titular nationality predominates (Uzbekistan, Tadzhikistan and Turkmenia) there is no evidence of any rise in rural fertility in the 1980s. This is entirely consistent with the official fertility policy and what is understood about the labor force participation of indigenous Central Asian women.

MORTALITY

Variations in mortality between regions in the former Soviet Union are less pronounced than are the variations in fertility. A summary measure of overall mortality in a given population is life expectancy at birth, which indicates the amount of time a newborn infant would live if it spent its life under the given regime of age-specific mortality rates. Because official life expectancies at birth for the U.S.S.R. and union republics are deceptive due to the unconventional Soviet definition of infant mortality, the Bureau of the Census employs an adjusted series of life expectancies. Table 10 presents adjusted life expectancies for the republics of the former Soviet union in the recent past.

According to the data in Table 10, improvements in life expectancy were registered in the 1980s in most of the former Soviet republics. The spectacular drop in Armenia's 1988 life expectancy undoubtedly reflects the consequences of the December earthquake; these and the stresses of the conflict with Azerbaijan probably account for the overall decline in Armenian male and female life expectancies since 1981. In general, the greatest increases in life expectancy were registered in the mid-1980s, concurrent with the advent of Gorbachev's anti-alcoholism campaign. The mid-decade gains are particularly visible among males.

In terms of regional patterns, the data in Table 10 indicate that overall life expectancy is generally highest in Transcaucasia and

TABLE 10. Adjusted Life Expectancies at Birth in the Union Republics, 1978–1990.

Republic	Male								
	1978–79	1980–81	1982–83	1984–85	1986–87	1987	1988	1989	1990
RSFSR	60.47	60.40	61.18	61.14	63.85	63.70	63.79	63.25	62.82
Ukraine	63.85	63.63	63.87	63.92	65.76	65.68	65.64	65.39	64.91
Belorussia	65.33	64.93	65.14	64.74	66.55	66.50	66.18	66.07	65.55
Moldavia	60.86	60.67	60.65	60.37	63.17	63.56	63.32	64.46	64.00
Lithuania	64.80	64.58	64.93	64.69	67.11	67.08	66.98	66.29	65.95
Latvia	62.82	62.69	63.24	63.72	66.21	65.69	65.55	64.77	63.47
Estonia	63.30	63.18	63.50	63.85	65.42	65.52	65.96	64.92	64.07
Georgia	65.85	65.42	66.20	66.16	66.51	66.73	66.67	67.03	68.03
Armenia	68.07	68.61	68.76	68.69	69.61	69.75	60.38	67.93	67.44
Azerbaijan	62.61	62.82	64.10	63.93	64.50	64.59	64.13	64.99	65.80
Kazakhstan	60.48	59.87	60.65	60.95	63.34	63.43	63.33	62.51	62.48
Kirgizstan	59.31	59.30	60.86	60.27	62.87	62.60	62.28	62.49	62.79
Uzbekistan	62.21	61.41	61.53	61.75	63.01	63.20	63.27	63.95	64.37
Turkmenistan	58.50	57.29	57.92	58.23	58.71	59.32	59.46	58.84	60.73
Tajikistan	59.87	60.68	61.96	63.54	64.84	64.88	64.21	64.33	64.97

Republic	Female								
	1978–79	1980–81	1982–83	1984–85	1986–87	1987	1988	1989	1990
RSFSR	72.11	72.10	72.82	72.31	73.74	73.74	73.79	73.72	73.57
Ukraine	73.29	73.30	73.66	73.21	74.16	74.12	74.00	74.58	74.32
Belorussia	75.35	74.90	75.03	74.35	75.29	75.22	75.17	75.70	75.24
Moldavia	67.48	67.62	67.75	67.34	69.57	69.56	70.00	71.29	71.12
Lithuania	74.54	74.68	74.97	74.72	75.98	75.88	75.91	75.78	75.74
Latvia	73.04	73.49	73.82	73.50	74.49	74.53	74.60	74.62	73.93
Estonia	73.67	73.25	73.78	73.60	74.14	74.18	74.33	74.22	74.37
Georgia	73.94	73.37	74.39	74.06	74.31	74.47	74.70	74.74	75.70
Armenia	74.27	75.16	74.97	74.64	75.37	75.48	61.30	73.87	74.42
Azerbaijan	70.59	70.73	72.19	71.80	72.07	72.29	72.21	72.72	74.09
Kazakhstan	71.30	70.50	71.23	71.33	73.04	73.15	73.09	71.95	72.11
Kirgizstan	68.39	68.50	69.58	68.60	70.76	70.64	70.21	70.77	71.54
Uzbekistan	69.21	68.68	68.60	68.90	69.20	69.21	69.57	70.27	71.23
Turkmenistan	65.34	64.84	65.29	65.61	65.45	66.11	66.43	65.68	68.01
Tajikistan	65.44	66.14	67.32	68.71	70.39	70.15	69.94	69.51	70.52

Sources: Goskomstat SSSR 1989; Goskomstat Press Release #336, Nov. 4, 1991.
Note: In calcalculating life expectancies, the official infant mortality rates have been adjusted for an understatement on the order of 58 percent of the actual value.

lowest in Central Asia. Although the highest overall life expectancy is exhibited by Lithuania, the life expectancies of the remaining European union republics are lower than those of Georgia and (in ordinary years) Armenia.[5] The sex detail reveals that the Transcaucasian advantage in mortality rates and the comparative European disadvantage is principally a male phenomenon. The male life expectancy in the RSFSR is actually lower than the male life expectancy in some Central Asian republics; among females no comparable disadvantage is observed.

---

[5] Serious concerns have been raised about the quality of the Soviet regional mortality data, particularly in infancy and old age (Anderson and Silver, 1990; Bennett and Garson, 1983; Myers, 1964). The Census Bureau's adjustment applies exclusively to infant mortality, and makes no provision for inaccuracies at the older ages. These ages account for much (if not all) of the Transcaucasian lead in life expectancy.

Prospective Population Trends

Our projections of the future populations of the former Soviet republics begin with the distributions of population by age and sex from the 1989 Census, [6] advancing them into the future by application of both observed and assumed future trends in fertility, mortality, and migration in the respective countries. In this process, various scenarios depicting possible alternative developments in the components of population growth have been considered. The projections presented in this paper correspond to the median scenario, which represents the most reasonable prognosis in our judgement.

FERTILITY ASSUMPTIONS

In projecting fertility we have grouped republics into three regions for which distinct assumptions are made: the European republics, the Transcaucasian republics, and the Central Asian republics including Kazakhstan. Separate short-run and long-run assumptions are distinguished. Over the short-run, fertility in each republic has been extrapolated from the last year of reported data (1990) to 1993 at the 1987–1990 pace. Thereafter the fertility rates in the republic are assumed to decline more gradually at the average regional rates observed in the 1970s, eventually reaching long-run limits of less than two children per couple. The limits have been selected in relation to the U.S. Census Bureau's guidelines for world population projections. The European republics have been assigned the limiting value of 1.7 assumed for European countries. The Transcaucasian republics, along with Kazakhstan, have been given asymptotic target fertility rates of 1.8. For the high-fertility Central Asian republics the asymptotic target fertility rate of 2.0 employed in the Bureau's projections of high-fertility countries has been adopted.

MORTALITY ASSUMPTIONS

As with fertility, in projecting mortality we distinguish assumptions about the near future from those for the long-run. Our assumptions have been devised to preserve the rank order of republic life expectancies at birth observed in the last year of reported data (1990). For the remainder of the present century the life expectancies of most republics are assumed to increase at the pace observed over the 1980s. In certain European and Transcaucasian republics where life expectancies have grown atypically slowly (e.g., Latvia, Belorussia) or have declined (Armenia), improvements are projected at the average pace for republics in their respective regions or that for the U.S.S.R. as a whole. The average relative improvement in life expectancy at birth for the Central Asian republics including Kazakhstan has been employed to project the life expectancies of these five republics to the year 2000. The improvements in life expectancy over the 1990s are assumed to follow logistic trends rather than to proceed in uniform annual increments.

---

[6] Prior to projection, the census age distributions reported by Goskomstat are adjusted at the U.S. Bureau of the Census for underenumeration of young children.

810

In the long-run, target life expectancies for the year 2050 have been chosen in relation to those assumed for countries of Europe in the U.S. Census Bureau's current world population projections. By the year 2050 the European and Transcaucasian republics of the former Soviet Union are assumed to attain the Census Bureau's European target values of 80 years for males and 86 years for females. For the Central Asian republics and Kazakhstan lower target values of 78 years for males and 85 years for females have been adopted. The long-term improvements in life expectancy are assumed to follow logistic trends in each republic.

FIGURE 1. FERTILITY IN THE EUROPEAN REPUBLICS, 1970–1990.

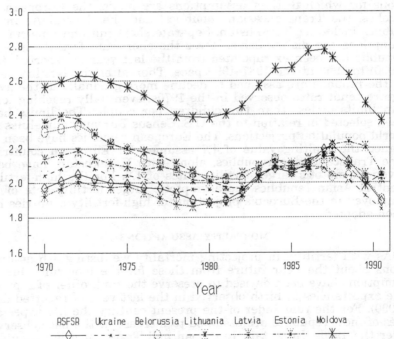

MIGRATION

Migration is the most difficult of the three components of population growth to model, but is often of great interest. The present economic instability and social unrest throughout the former Soviet bloc raise concerns about the possibility of large-scale population movements, and has led the Census Bureau to formulate several scenarios involving the repatriation of national subpopulations in the former Soviet Union. The results of this analysis are not

811

available at the time of writing this paper, but will be issued in a forthcoming Census Bureau report.

FIGURE 2. FERTILITY IN THE CENTRAL ASIAN REPUBLICS WITH PREDOMINANTLY INDIGENOUS POPULATIONS, 1970–1990.

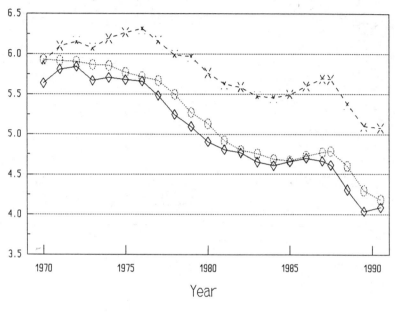

Total Fertility Rate

Year

Uzbekistan Tajikistan Turkmenistan

A rough effort to incorporate migration is attempted in the present analysis. Two projection series are compared. One series applies constant schedules of net internal migration between union republics for the period 1979–89 throughout the projection period. The second projection series assumes zero migration.

PROJECTED POPULATION TRENDS

Projected population totals for each of the former Soviet union republics are presented in Table 11. In each republic the population is currently growing, and several will experience substantial population increases in the near future. Uzbekistan's population will grow by 6.1 million persons from 1992 to 2000 under the scenario with no migration and by 5.4 million with net migration at the 1979–89 observed rates. Only Russia in the constant migration series exhibits a roughly comparable gain, thanks to its preeminence as a destination for internal migration in the former

FIGURE 3. FERTILITY IN THE TRANSCAUCASIAN REPUBLICS, 1970–1990.

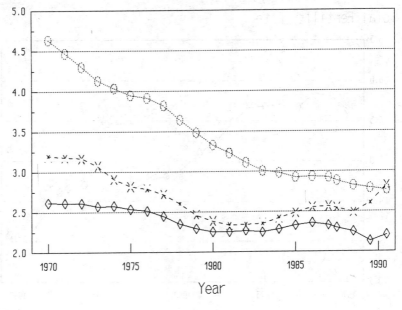

Total Fertility Rate

Year

Georgia Armenia Azerbaijan

U.S.S.R. and the immense size of its population. In the absence of migration, all of the ethnically Moslem republics (Azerbaijan and the Central Asian republics) will grow by more than one million persons during the remainder of this century, and some will do so even in the presence of substantial net outmigration.

According to the results in Table 11, each republic will undergo continued population growth for at least 30 years, and the majority will experience net gains in population over the projection period. This growth will occur even with below-replacement fertility and no migration due to the natural momentum of population growth. As a result of their previous history of above-replacement fertility, the former union republics possess age distributions that ensure increases in the population of childbearing age for at least a generation (25–30 years). Consequently, their populations will continue to grow for some time after fertility has fallen below the replacement rate.

Over the long-term horizon of the projection period (1989–2050), the regional differentials in population growth will probably exer-

TABLE 11. Projected Total Population in the Republics of the former Soviet Union, 1989–2050.

(Absolute figures in thousands)

Republic	With 1979–89 Net Migration Rates								
	1989	1992	1993	1994	1995	2000	2010	2025	2050
RSFSR	147,510	148,965	149,300	149,609	149,909	151,460	155,933	160,338	158,214
Ukraine	51,566	51,787	51,821	51,847	51,868	51,931	52,280	52,210	49,326
Belorussia	10,192	10,333	10,370	10,405	10,437	10,576	10,864	11,087	10,702
Moldova	4,357	4,436	4,456	4,473	4,490	4,565	4,738	4,913	4,743
Estonia	1,572	1,600	1,608	1,617	1,625	1,670	1,776	1,927	2,097
Latvia	2,677	2,722	2,736	2,749	2,763	2,833	3,009	3,280	3,645
Lithuania	3,695	3,790	3,820	3,848	3,876	4,007	4,263	4,609	4,926
Georgia	5,432	5,586	5,634	5,681	5,726	5,925	6,253	6,597	6,647
Armenia	3,328	3,440	3,481	3,522	3,557	3,685	3,854	3,969	3,685
Azerbaijan	7,093	7,458	7,573	7,684	7,790	8,243	8,995	9,950	10,426
Kazakhstan	16,577	17,037	17,156	17,268	17,377	17,886	18,794	19,529	18,790
Kirgizstan	4,307	4,552	4,626	4,698	4,770	5,119	5,810	6,784	7,797
Tajikistan	5,182	5,676	5,836	5,995	6,155	6,956	8,619	11,305	15,125
Turkmenistan	3,572	3,833	3,915	3,995	4,075	4,474	5,277	6,501	8,007
Uzbekistan	20,099	21,639	22,128	22,609	23,089	25,467	30,380	37,714	46,969
Former U.S.S.R.	287,160	292,853	294,462	296,000	297,508	304,796	320,844	340,713	351,098
CIS	273,783	279,155	280,664	282,105	283,518	290,361	305,543	324,300	333,784

Republic	No Migration								
	1989	1992	1993	1994	1995	2000	2010	2025	2050
RSFSR	147,510	148,634	148,846	149,025	149,188	149,947	152,557	153,970	146,424
Ukraine	51,566	51,686	51,688	51,681	51,670	51,588	51,714	51,430	48,614
Belorussia	10,192	10,298	10,324	10,348	10,370	10,467	10,690	10,832	10,407
Moldova	4,357	4,464	4,493	4,520	4,547	4,680	4,981	5,349	5,519
Estonia	1,572	1,584	1,586	1,589	1,591	1,602	1,632	1,660	1,608
Latvia	2,677	2,691	2,693	2,696	2,698	2,705	2,734	2,763	2,664
Lithuania	3,695	3,749	3,765	3,780	3,794	3,854	3,962	4,069	3,968
Georgia	5,432	5,577	5,622	5,666	5,708	5,898	6,221	6,565	6,683
Armenia	3,328	3,514	3,582	3,650	3,714	3,992	4,500	5,201	5,851
Azerbaijan	7,093	7,522	7,661	7,796	7,926	8,514	9,574	11,040	12,299
Kazakhstan	16,577	17,296	17,506	17,711	17,916	18,946	21,044	23,721	26,155
Kirgizstan	4,307	4,602	4,695	4,787	4,880	5,349	6,345	7,888	10,062
Tajikistan	5,182	5,702	5,873	6,045	6,217	7,096	8,968	12,092	16,890
Turkmenistan	3,572	3,865	3,959	4,051	4,144	4,612	5,592	7,170	9,414
Uzbekistan	20,099	21,792	22,340	22,884	23,432	26,200	32,091	41,389	54,739
Former U.S.S.R.	287,160	292,975	294,633	296,227	297,795	305,449	322,606	345,137	361,298
CIS	273,783	279,375	280,967	282,497	284,004	291,391	308,057	330,081	346,375

Source: author's calculations.

cise greater influence. The three Central Asian republics whose titular nationalities predominate in their populations (Tajikistan, Turkmenistan, Uzbekistan) are projected to more than double in size by 2050. In contrast, the projected population of the three Slavic republics in 2050 are comparable to their populations in 1989. By 2050 Uzbekistan's population will be similar in size to Ukraine's, while the population of Tajikistan will substantially outnumber that of Belorussia.

The importance of migration as a component of population growth is clearly illustrated by the projection results. In the 1980s the prevailing orientation of net internal migration out of Central Asia into European republics in the U.S.S.R. partly offset the effects of regional fertility differences, and would continue to do so if projected into the future. Russia's population, for instance, is projected to grow by 10 million in the series with 1979–89 net migration rates, but it is projected to decline over the projection period in the zero migration series. Migration at the rates observed in 1979–89 would represent a major source of population growth in the Baltic republics as well. Armenia provides the clearest illustration of migration's effect as a suppressor of population growth, a role exercised in lesser measure in Central Asia, the other Transcaucasian republics, and Moldavia.

Another fundamental aspect of the demographic future is the dynamics of the population's age-sex composition. Demographic aging, defined as an increase in the share of the elderly in population and the corresponding decline in the proportion of the young, is an inevitable consequence of sustained fertility decline. Prolonged below-replacement fertility rates, in particular, lead ultimately to a population in which the old outnumber the young. The implications of such scenarios for social security financing and labor force development have been a source of unease to economic policymakers in most advanced industrialized countries, including the former U.S.S.R. In the Third World, on the other hand, the economic strains imposed by rapidly mounting numbers of young children are a principal concern.

The projected development of Russia's age-sex composition is illustrated in Figure 4. At the beginning of the projection period, the Russian population is in rough conformity with the pyramid shape typical of growing populations. Various catastrophes of Russian history are reflected by irregularities in the Russian age-sex pyramid. The small sizes of the cohorts born during the Second World War, who were of ages 45–49 in 1989, are especially noteworthy. Closer to the base of the pyramid, the children of these cohorts correspond to the dip at ages 20–24. A further echo effect of World War II is in progress at the present time, when these small cohorts occupy the prime reproductive ages and are producing markedly fewer births than did their immediate seniors in the preceding five years. This leads to narrowing at the base of the projected Russian age pyramid in the year 2000 and to a perceptible dent in the age distribution in subsequent years as the small cohorts born in the 1990s move up the age ladder.

Over the projection period a shift in the form of the Russian age-sex distribution is clearly evident in Figure 4. Whereas Russia's 1989 age pyramid is wider at the base than at its top, with the passage of time the pyramid narrows at the base as a result of projected below-replacement fertility. By 2050 the Russian age-sex distribution has assumed the form of a rather topheavy barrel. Among the implications of such an age structure is a steady reduction for many decades in the pool of potential young entrants to the labor force. [7]

A further tendency in the development of Russia's age-sex structure, namely the progressive smoothing out of the Russian age pyramid, is apparent in Figure 4. This is a consequence of the projection assumptions, which postulate gradual, unspectacular changes

---

[7] Figures 4 and 5 illustrate a scenario with constant 1979–89 net migration rates, which involves a steady flow of migrants into Russia and out of Uzbekistan. The age-sex structures corresponding to the zero migration scenario do not differ enough from the present scenario in their major features to warrant separate illustration or to enter into this discussion.

815

FIGURE 4. THE AGE-SEX COMPOSITION OF RUSSIA IN 1989, 2000, 2025, AND 2050.

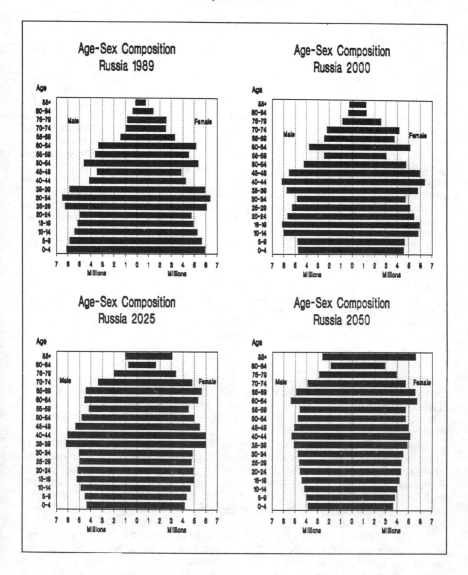

in fertility and mortality typical of normal demographic evolution. The jaggedness of Russia's 1989 age-sex composition reflects the particulars of her 20th century experience. Barring unforeseen events such as future civil and world wars, a substantial evening out of Russia's age-sex structure is to be expected.

Figure 5 depicts the evolving age-sex structure of the population of Uzbekistan, the largest Central Asian republic. Uzbekistan's 1989 age pyramid follows the pattern typical of Third World countries, in which young people greatly outnumber their elders. The steep gradient in the size of successive age cohorts dampens the fluctuations associated with historical swings in fertility and mortality. In striking contrast to Russia's age-sex pyramid, the effect of World War II is barely visible in Uzbekistan's.

The transformation of Uzbekistan's age-sex composition over the projection period reveals the impact of observed and projected reductions in fertility rates. The major fertility decline experienced since the mid-1970s underlies the abrupt flattening of the base of Uzbekistan's projected age pyramid in the year 2000. In the twenty-first century the base of the Uzbek age pyramid is projected to widen much more gradually. By 2050 Uzbekistan's projected age-sex pyramid takes on a more rectangular appearance, and actually begins to narrow at its base.

The rectangularization of Uzbekistan's age-sex structure has favorable economic implications for the dependency burden on the adult population. In 1989 the adult population of Uzbekistan was small in relation to the number of children depending for their sustenance on adult workers. Uzbekistan's projected 2050 age-sex structure implies a much lower ratio of dependents to adults.

CONCLUSIONS

Demography is an essential ingredient of the setting in which economic and social change will occur in the former Soviet Union. The trends and projections discussed above provide several insights about the future human resource pools of the newly independent states and their welfare needs.

One basic conclusion that can be drawn from the projections is that all of the newly independent republics can look forward to continued population growth for many years to come. Even though fertility is currently below the replacement rate in most of the republics of the former Soviet Union, their heritage of previous growth carries its own momentum. What level of growth is perceived as adequate for societal needs is, of course, another matter.

In the long-run, the effect of below-replacement fertility on age structure may have serious consequences. In countries with social security systems, demographic aging implies an increase in the ratio of beneficiaries to the workers who produce the goods and services they consume. The greater the share of the elderly in the population, the greater will be the rise in labor or productivity required to avert a deterioration in real benefits or in the standard of living of workers. Unless their fertility rises substantially, the European republics of the former Soviet Union can expect to confront this long-run scenario after they emerge from the radical shocks of the economic present and near future.

817

FIGURE 5. THE AGE-SEX COMPOSITION OF UZBEKISTAN IN 1989, 2000, 2025, AND 2050.

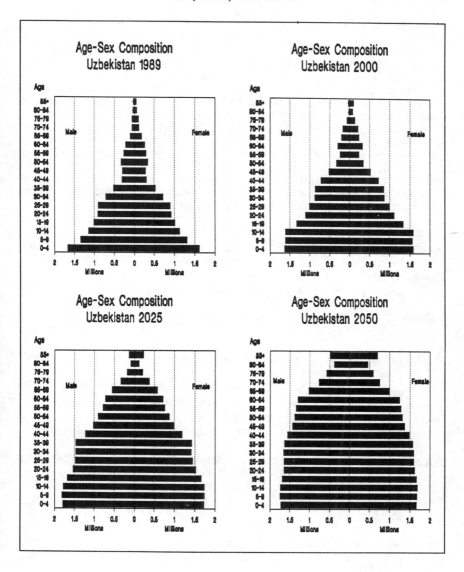

An entirely different set of demographic problems and prospects characterizes the Central Asian population, whose explosive growth entails major demands on limited local resources. In these countries, the need to feed, clothe, and house rapidly growing new generations drains away resources that could otherwise be used for industrial investment. Unfortunately, further massive population increases appear inevitable in every Central Asian republic: assuming major reductions in fertility, we project a doubling of the Central Asian population in the next 60 years. However, the beneficial shift in age composition associated with fertility decline may help cushion the impact of population growth in this region.

Migration is one short-term outlet for Central Asian population surpluses as well as a potential source of labor for European regions of the former Soviet Union. This was the prevailing direction of net migration flows in the 1980s. [8] The breakup of the U.S.S.R. may not mean the end of this phenomenon. If Western experience is any guide, migration from Central Asia to the newly independent European republics may even increase.

BIBLIOGRAPHY

Anderson, B.A. and B.D. Silver, "Trends in Mortality of the Soviet Population," *Soviet Economy*, vol. 6, no. 3, 1990, pp. 191–251.

Bennett, N.G. and L.K. Garson, "The Centenarian Question and Old Age Mortality in the Soviet Union," *Demography*, vol. 20, no. 4, 1983, pp. 587–606.

Belova, V., G. Bondarskaya and L. Darskiy, "Dinamika i differentsiatsiya rozhdayemosti v SSSR," *Vestnik statistiki*, no. 12, 1983, pp. 13–24.

Goskomstat SSSR, *Demograficheskiy yezhegodnik SSSR 1990*. Moscow: Finansy i statistka. 1991.

———, *Naseleniye SSSR 1988*. Moscow: Finansy i statistika. 1989.

———, *Naseleniye SSSR 1987*. Moscow: Finansy i statistika. 1988.

Karakhanov, M.K., *Nekapitalisticheskiy put' razvitiya i problemy narodonaseleniya*. Tashkent: Izdatel'stvo "FAN" Uzbekskoy SSR. 1983.

Kingkade, W.W., "Demographic Trends in the Soviet Union", in J.P. Hardt (ed.), *Gorbachev's Economic Plans*. Washington: US Government Printing Office. 1987.

Myers, R.J., "Analysis of Mortality in the Soviet Union according to 1958–59 Life Tables," *Transactions of the Society of Actuaries*, vol. 16, pp. 309–317.

Rowland, R.H., "Economic Region Net Migration Patterns in the USSR: 1979–89," *Soviet Geography*, vol. 31, no. 9, 1990, pp. 657–678.

Tatimov, M.B., *Razvitiye narodonaseleniya i demograficheskaya politika*. Alma-Ata. Izdatel'stvo "Nauka" Kazakhskoy SSR. 1987.

Vishnevskiy, A.G. and A.G. Volkov, *Vosproizvodstvo naseleniya SSSR*. Moscow: Finansy i statistika. 1983.

---

[8] Rowland, 1990.

Weber, C. and A. Goodman, "The Demographic Policy Debate in the USSR," *Population and Development Review*, vol. 7, no. 2, 1981, pp. 279-295.

A NOTE ON THE EMIGRATION OF RUSSIA'S TECHNICAL INTELLIGENTSIA

By Steven W. Popper *

CONTENTS

SUMMARY

Nothing in recent experience has prepared the states of the former Soviet Union for seeing scientists, trained at public expense, exercise the freedom to work abroad. But when viewed in a wider context, the typical presentation of the problem faced by Russia in particular appears to be distorted. Emigration of highly skilled personnel is by no means solely a Third World phenomenon. For Russia to now be confronted with the problem might be viewed as an instance of normalization in an era when scientific interactions have come increasingly internationalized.

Policymakers will be faced with the problem of determining whether the initial surge of emigration among skilled professionals is a harbinger of a permanent tendency or merely the necessary outflow for the technical cadre to come into equilibrium. Further, it is possible that emigration of certain types may afford many benefits over the short and long term. Employing policies directed only

* Steven W. Popper is a senior researcher with the International Policy Department, RAND, Santa Monica. This paper is based on an earlier version prepared for the Conference on Emigration from the Former Soviet Union held at RAND, 5 November 1991 and sponsored, in part, by the Ford Foundation. The views expressed in this paper are the author's own and do not necessarily represent those of the Ford Foundation or of RAND and its clients.

to deal with the apparent "problem" by restricting outflows by administrative means would prove to be the most likely to precipitate precisely the disaster such measures are intended to avoid.

INTRODUCTION

Among the specters haunting Europe today is the possibility of emigration on a massive scale from the territory of the former Soviet Union. The prospect is most daunting for the states immediately bordering former Soviet territory and for the attractively wealthy countries of Western Europe. For one aspect of this prospective movement, however, the balance of concern shifts. Policymakers in the Soviet successor states share a deep fear of a possible mass emigration of the cadre constituting the technically trained intelligentsia: a "brain drain." Emigration of scientists, engineers, technologists, and academics on a large scale could, it is feared, seriously enfeeble the shaky new economies of the region and rob them of the cadre most needed to effect transition to a new order.[1] The fears are heightened by a perception that this is one class of migrants the potential recipient countries would not be loathe to receive and might, indeed, actively woo.

The term, "brain drain" has been used in the Soviet context to refer to three distinctly different phenomena. The first is the classic usage: emigration of technically trained personnel, or promising students, to other countries where they then ply their craft or pursue their studies either on a temporary basis, eventually returning home, or taking up permanent residency. This is the sole concern of this paper.

A second instance loosely cited as brain drain by Soviet commentators is when trained technical personnel leave the state sector for alternative employment to perform roughly similar tasks in the cooperative sector.[2] The cry of "brain drain" is raised by those concerned with large-scale abandonment of the state sector by its most productive workers. Clearly, this is a more parochial and questionable use of the term. It is entirely likely that such a move, when viewed in the perspective of the larger society, would actually lead to an increase in the productivity and contribution to the economy of those who are "lost" in this way to the state sector. Certainly, in an era when the clear tendency of post-socialist economic policy is to increase the size of the private sphere and to sensitize individuals to market-type economic signals, to lump this with actual emigration betrays an orientation toward the old order having little to do with true policy concerns.

Finally, "brain drain" has been used on occasion to refer to the phenomenon of technically skilled personnel who remain in the country but leave their former careers to follow different paths. One peculiar instance has been to use the term to describe the entry of scientists and engineers into the formal political process as legislators.[3] Again, this is clearly distinguishable from the instance

---

[1] In some instances, these fears might better be classified as hysteria: "It is a truism to say that the loss of scientific potential [through emigration and domestic underemployment] is irreversible. The future is crossed out for decades to come," (from "Grey Gold for Sale," in *RADIKAL*, as cited in FBIS-SOV-91-088, 7 May 1991, p. 32).

[2] See, e.g., "Kontrakt dlya studenta?," *Delovoi Mir*, 26 September 1991.

[3] See, e.g., Kapitsa (1990).

of actual emigration. It is not at all certain that the decision by these individuals to cease their former activities and move into new areas is harmful to general economic welfare. One defining characteristic of an actual transition to a new system of economic interaction must be the change to a new equilibrium mix of skills within the economy. Retraining and retooling through individuals moving into new fields and new sectors will be precisely the means by which transition will occur. This cannot be included in the discussion in this paper.

This paper suggests ways for both Russian and Western policy-makers to begin to frame the range of issues raised by the prospective phenomenon of emigration. While focussed on Russia, many aspects of this analysis will find application in the situations of the other newly independent republics.

THE EMIGRATION PHENOMENON

RUSSIA IN THE WORLD SETTING

Emigration of technical elites, a prospect the Soviet Union had not faced since the late 1920s, is a startling departure from past experience. It is seen as a serious problem by most post-Soviet commentators and policymakers. Nothing in recent experience has prepared the institutions, the leadership, or the lay populations of the Soviet successor states for the prospect of seeing scientists and technologists, trained in Soviet institutions at public expense, exercising their new freedom to work abroad. The possibility of a mass hemorrhaging of the nation's technical cadre was one of the factors specifically cited as slowing the move to passing a liberalized Law on Emigration.[4] Almost as much as the practical problems such emigration might cause, it would be seen as yet another blow to Russia's claim of being a developed industrial nation. The best of the technical elite, it is feared, will be drawn to work elsewhere, a problem typically associated in the popular imagination with developing countries like India and Egypt.

When viewed in a wider context, this typical presentation of the problem appears to be distorted in at least two respects. In the first instance, emigration of highly skilled personnel is by no means solely a Third World phenomenon. The term "brain drain" initially was coined to describe the migration of British scientists to the United States in the 1950s and 1960s. It is still viewed as a problem in many countries of Western Europe. Even officials of nations such as Canada and Australia, considered to be traditional magnets for immigrants, address the problem of emigration of their technical elites in terms of alarm that would be familiar to their Russian counterparts. For Russia to now be confronted with the problem might justly, and perhaps more accurately, be viewed as much an instance of coming of age—of normalization—as it could as an indictment of Russian society.

This consideration leads to the second point. It is a characteristic of contemporary scientific and technological interactions for re-

---

[4] Indeed, this appears to have been Mikhail Gorbachev's principal cause for concern. He is reported to have openly worried that no one would be left to help build perestroika ("Soviets Enact Law Freeing Migration and Trips Abroad," *New York Times*, 21 May 1991.)

search and development efforts to be internationalized. This necessarily means far greater movement of personnel than was previously the case. What may be viewed as emigration by one country might also be seen as the necessary requirement for its technical elites to participate in these activities. Indeed, this movement would come as a natural consequence of many of the reforms Russia is trying to establish. For example, if the Russians are successful in significantly increasing the number of joint ventures and multinational corporations operating on their soil, this necessarily means that a significant share of skilled workers will become active participants in the internal labor markets these entities represent. These organizations are necessarily cross-national in character and often operate through the movement of personnel to expatriate postings. This would be an important mechanism for imparting knowledge and transferring skills, one of the main reasons for desiring an increase in foreign participation in the Russian economy.[5]

In the initial stages, Russian policymakers will be faced with an identification problem. There will be an initial surge of emigration among skilled professionals. It will remain to be seen if this is a harbinger of a permanent tendency or merely the necessary outflow for the technical cadre to come into an equilibrium of movement consonant with contemporary international practice. It is crucial to understand that the inevitable initial outward movement might not actually mark the beginning of a new crisis but rather the end of an old aberration. In other words, this necessary movement might only appear as a drain when viewed against the background of former Soviet practice. Whether, in fact, this alternative reading is accurate is a legitimate object for future research.

Much will depend on gaining a better understanding of who is leaving and why they are leaving. There have been many studies outside Russia of the international movement of skilled personnel. These include undergraduate students going to universities abroad, advanced students working toward graduate degrees, newly graduated professionals looking for initial employment, and older, more skilled workers whose services are eagerly sought by institutions around the world. A great deal of emigration is short term rather than permanent. Various studies have asked emigrants what motivated their action. Among the most commonly cited reasons for emigration were the desire to travel, to gain experience otherwise unobtainable at home, to take advantage of environments offering greater apparent opportunity (both general and specific), to make more money, and dissatisfaction with their professional lives in their home countries.

A good deal of emigration is ephemeral. Studies of scientists and engineers in OECD countries show a high degree of mobility, especially among scientists, with a large share of emigrants returning to the country of origin after a few years abroad. The reasons most

---

[5] Fears had been expressed in the Soviet press that in fulfilling this function, joint ventures will play the role of the Pied Piper, leading technicians and scientists into emigration. It has even been alleged that this is their primary purpose (Kasatonov, 1990). On the other hand, it could also be argued that joint ventures represent the best chance for providing technical workers with the types of opportunities they would seek abroad without having to leave the country or ceasing participation in the economy.

often cited in studies of why people return are family concerns (by far the most frequent), the job they returned to, issues related to way of life (not to be confused with quality of life), dissatisfaction with their situations abroad, and patriotism. There is much in this listing of general factors stimulating cross-national movement, both emigration and return, that would seem to strike a familiar chord when viewing the specific instance of Russia.

RUSSIA SUI GENERIS

And yet, Russia may be a special case. Even if all goes well over the course of the next few years, the economy will be in a serious state of decline and true transformation, if and when it comes, will be a wrenching experience. A complete change in institutions and former methods of operation are in the offing in every sector. The sectors of fundamental research and applied RDI will not be spared.[6]

Certainly, if internal political conditions drastically deteriorate, the evaluations made by members of the technical intelligentsia will be qualitatively different from those done by their counterparts in other developed countries. In such cases, it would be more appropriate to speak of refugees than of emigrants. People with salable skills will seek opportunities elsewhere, but the issue will no longer be one of career as much as survival. Under such conditions something approaching the mass exodus of skilled professionals sometimes feared by Russian commentators could develop. In this instance, however, the ill effect on science and technology would not be primarily a result of such emigration. Rather, the emigration would be a natural reaction to the same deleterious conditions which would have already rendered scientific and technological work difficult.

Barring a catastrophic political collapse, there are other reasons to believe that Russia, if not quite sui generis, might at least represent an extreme example of trends observable elsewhere. Ethnic tensions, particularly an upswing in overt anti-Semitic rhetoric and activity, would also give an additional dimension often missing from calculations of factors affecting the net migration balance in other countries.

The serious economic storms that surely lie ahead for the economy, whether or not the transition to a market economy ultimately proves successful, will also affect the decisions of individuals, tipping the scales in favor of emigration.[7] The behavior of the technical intelligentsia would differ from the Russian mass only in as much as they would have more opportunity to emigrate and in that their leaving might have a greater effect on the domestic economy.

Russia also differs from other developed industrial countries in the severe restrictions it formerly placed upon travel abroad. This might lead to strong forces pulling in opposite directions. In the first instance, the desire for travel, just to get abroad for a while, must be strong indeed. People will want to avail themselves of op-

---

[6] RDI stands for the integrated processes of research, development, and innovation.

[7] This might be even more the case with younger researchers, already intrinsically more mobile, who may find themselves "cut out" from their slice of the ever-shrinking research support pie by older researchers who are better connected.

portunities that never before existed. At the same time, this very restrictiveness may have also bred an unfamiliarity with and insecurity about things foreign. At its extreme, years of propaganda about crime, unemployment, and racial tensions in the West might give pause to those considering more than tourist travel. Less virulent, but probably more important, the former insularity in itself might be sufficient to cause fewer members of the technical elite to consider the foreign employment option than would others in countries at a similar level of development. This unfamiliarity could work in both directions. In several fields, the Russian research scene is terra incognita for outside researchers. The demand for and invitations to Russian technicians to come abroad may initially be lower than might be expected. This period will not last long, however.

There is another former Soviet institution causing scientists and engineers to view emigration in a different light. The requirement in law of registering the place of residence and obtaining what amounts to a residence permit [propiska] makes it difficult to change jobs or move to another city. If anything, economic deterioration and uncertainty over future political arrangements will make the former Soviet territory even less of a common economic space. Emigration might, in certain respects, be easier than internal movement for professionals seeking other employment and opportunities for career advancement.

Finally, a factor difficult to gauge is the degree to which émigré skilled workers would feel comfortable outside Russia. The sense of bond with the native soil is said to be particularly strong for Russian intellectuals, who often feel ill at ease when deprived of familiar strong cultural elements. The tendency of Soviet émigré populations, particularly Russians, to recreate as much as possible the conditions and cultural institutions they left behind has been noted in the course of several emigrations during this century. This patriotic factor might mark this emigration as qualitatively different from other brain drains.

THE DIMENSIONS OF EMIGRATION

Whether the inevitable outflow of technically proficient individuals actually becomes a serious enough problem to warrant the attention and concern of policymakers depends largely on the scale of this flow. The quantity will also partly determine the qualitative assessment: whether the phenomenon may be characterized as normalized movement of professionals, more or less permanent emigration at acceptable levels, or a true hemorrhaging of the most vital element of the work force. At present, it is difficult to determine which of these characterizations will come closest to the mark.

SUPPLY AND DEMAND

Any movement other than a panicked exodus of refugees fleeing a desperately deteriorating economic and political situation will be affected by fundamental factors of supply and demand for former Soviet technical specialists. These factors may be categorized, if not satisfactorily quantified given the poor present state of available information.

In terms of gross numbers, there is no question that Russia is a major source of scientific and technical manpower. Even accounting for differences in definition, the stock of technical practitioners theoretically available for emigration is quite large.[8] This, however, represents a notional stock, by no means an indication of the supply available to participate in overseas labor markets.

The foremost determinant of the supply of technical personnel available for immigration in the short-term will be domestic demand for their services. In part, this will depend on the overall health of the economy and the degree to which various successor political regimes will make opportunities available to all former Soviet citizens on a wide basis. Discrete policy choices will also determine supply. Much of the technical intelligentsia has been associated with military R&D and industry. Wide-scale conversion, depending on the precise nature of the strategies employed, will affect a good number of scientists and engineers and so the effective supply of potential emigrants. Furthermore, changes in the nature of scientific/technical institutions will also have an effect. Matters of organization, management, assessment, and funding under the present drastically altered circumstances have yet to be resolved and these, in turn, will profoundly determine the nature of individual career paths.

It should also be noted that the former Soviet Union is not the sole possible source for personnel desired by employers in the developed world. Aspirants will have to compete with those coming from other traditional sources of technically trained labor. This will reduce the potential demands that Russian migrants might be able to place on their employers. This will, in turn, reduce the potential attraction of the emigration option. The reality of employment opportunities abroad may be far from the tantalizing vision imagined by those most frightened by the prospect of a mass evacuation by the intelligentsia. This will affect the number choosing emigration.

Given the many factors already discussed above demand may be the single most important factor in determining the actual numbers for emigration by the technical intelligentsia. Here, again, hard information has been spotty to date and we are left to speculate by "bounding the region." Two questions come to the fore: How attractive are Russian technologists and scientists for potential employers abroad, and where would these technical personnel likely be the most welcome?

There are certainly many reasons to believe Soviet research and development workers would seem attractive. According to the U.S.S.R. Academy of Sciences, relying as well on evaluations by foreign experts, Soviet science was either leading the world or sharing the lead in 40 percent of research "priority directions."[9] For some specialties, the developing world might be the most likely employer of former Soviet talent, although for many obvious rea-

---

[8] Many Soviet workers characterized as "engineers," for example, would not warrant that rating in the West and would instead be labelled as mechanics.

[9] A. Karavayev, 1990.

sons such employment might have a lesser attraction for trained specialists. Employment opportunities in the developed world are inherently more attractive, but, again, the demand will not be boundless nor the obstacles necessarily minimal. For example, engineers in many traditional fields are unlikely to find their services as much in demand as they might have been in earlier years. Immigration and work laws, and domestic professional groups not eager to see an influx of potential rivals willing and eager to "bust the rate" will also serve as means of limitation. Clearly, these barriers will not present obstacles against the immigration of holders of key skills or highly regarded individuals. But these are likely to prove exceptions to the rule.

Israel represents a case unto itself as a potential destination. The Law of Return means that any Jewish specialist, as well as accompanying non-Jewish immediate family members, will be able to obtain residency automatically. Given the disproportionate share of Jews in the Russian intelligentsia, this has been viewed as an especially serious source of leakage.[10] Yet while this option is likely to remain legally available in the foreseeable future, neither demand on the Israeli end nor supply on the Russian one will remain unaffected by the massive wave of migration that has already occurred. Problems of housing and physical absorption are notorious, resentment by already resident Israeli professional groups is growing, and prospects for plying one's present profession after emigration to Israel are far from assured.[11] Barring catastrophic breakdown or virulent ethnic violence, problems of this kind must surely affect the decisions of specialists contemplating emigration. This might prove all the more so if such individuals become convinced that Russia has now truly entered onto a radically different development path and political course.

The emigration of specialists in the production of nuclear, biological, and chemical weapons warrants special attention, not because of the likely size of such an emigration but because of the deleterious effect their skills might have on the world as a whole if used to accelerate the proliferation of unconventional weaponry. This looms as a potential danger inasmuch as both supply, fed by a sharp downturn in Russian defense procurement, and demand, in the form of governments of developing states eager for regional dominance, appear to be waxing. Of course, one must ask what might have previously prevented such states from hiring all the French, German, American, British, or Italian experts they wished. Iraq and Libya—even Iran and Pakistan—already had sufficient means for hiring expertise at several times the civil service scale the experts would have been receiving in their home country.

---

[10] Indeed, some on the right have identified Zionist activities within Soviet borders as deliberately "inflicting serious political, economic and moral harm on the country ... weakening [the] state, holding back its economic development, and lowering the intellectual potential," through brain drain (*Krasnaya Zvezda*, 19 December 1990, p. 3). The paradoxical and even counter-productive nature of this type of argument is too obvious to require further discussion.

[11] Less than 5 percent of Soviet doctors taking the required Israeli medical examination are able to pass without special instruction. This compares with 65 percent for physicians arriving from Argentina and even higher levels for those from Western Europe. (The test is waived for immigrant doctors from North America.) Immigrant mathematicians who have already arrived in Israel would be sufficient to staff all of the country's mathematics departments several times over. Furthermore, the evidence seems to be, at least in this specialty, that the best mathematicians have remained in Russia (Margalit, 1991).

What may have been lacking was desperation in the individuals making up the supply side. At any rate, though related to the problem of Soviet brain drain, the solution to the problem of proliferation in these several fields clearly must encompass more than just an embargo of former Soviet weapons experts. Special measures, perhaps some form of monitoring, might be indicated. But here, as in other aspects of the emigration problem, the solution does not lie in administrative restrictions on emigration, if for no other reason than that they would be unlikely to work.[12] Rather, policy should be directed to developing domestic institutions offering attractive alternative employment within a growing economy. Furthermore, the opportunity to emigrate to developed countries and to ply skills in new areas would be one factor stanching the flow in the direction of the ambitious military regimes of the developing world.

EARLY EVIDENCE

At present,[13] most data available on the scale and course of emigration are from preliminary figures on numbers of exit visas granted and on public opinion polling. Neither have proven satisfactory in giving a real definition of the likely scope of the problem. The phenomenon of emigration is too new to provide any means for reasonable extrapolation of equilibrium rates, and opinion surveys are not well suited to measuring anything more than notional intent.

Polls

Not surprisingly, results from polls are widely conflicting. They depend on the way questions are framed and what point the organizations using the polls are trying to prove. For example, a preliminary report of a poll of 2,500 Moscow university students conducted by the social-analytic group of the Moscow Student Foundation was released in late 1990. The poll reportedly found that 80-90 percent of respondents want to go abroad for varying durations. Students in the third year and above are almost unanimous in their position.[14]

When the full data were released, the results appeared less startling and redolent of crisis.[15] Among those replying that they would like to leave the Soviet Union, 9 percent answered they would like to leave permanently and another 18 percent replied, "for a long time." When asked why they would wish to leave the Soviet Union, the replies were:

45%—To see the world and how people live abroad and then return;

29%—To work and earn some money and then return;

21%—To get a good education;

---

[12] If, for example, efforts were made to monitor and govern the movements of a list of identified experts in these fields, almost certainly lower level laboratory workers and researchers who previously had not had opportunities to establish their own eminence would take the positions that might otherwise have been offered to their senior colleagues. A good deal of the relevant technology would be transferred in this manner.

[13] As of autumn 1991.

[14] *Komsomol'skaya Pravda*, 26 December 1990.

[15] *Komsomol'skaya Pravda* 4 July 1991.

13%—To open a business;
21%—To live and work in a country that suits me better than
the U.S.S.R.[16]

While these figures are startling when measured against past practice, they do not appear to be remarkably different than from those
to be expected through a similar poll of 18–21 year-olds in other
countries.

Another poll was published on the specific question of working
abroad. Conducted by the All-Union Center for the Study of Public
Opinion, it indicated that 8 percent of those asked would like to
work abroad.[17] Among those, only 27 percent had begun or completed or had higher education; 39 percent of those interested in
employment abroad worked in science, culture, education, or medicine. Ten percent of the members of the intelligentsia responding
to the poll indicated an interest in emigration, while only 5 percent
of the skilled workers did so. Vladimir Kosmarsky, the sociologist
who presented the poll's results, noted that "the desire to go
abroad among the significant part of the population is of an abstract character. That is, only 11 percent of those who expressed
the desire to work abroad were prepared to leave their present job
shortly, 40 percent are merely 'thinking that step over.' "

Finally, a poll conducted solely in Russia and sponsored by the
USIA showed that while 60 percent expressed an interest in some
form of travel or work abroad, only 2 percent wanted to emigrate
and 8 percent wanted to live overseas for more than two years.[18]
While these views would, of course, be subject to change once such
individuals were actually overseas, the actual direction of change is
not necessarily a forgone conclusion. Among those 18–29 years old,
23 percent wanted to emigrate or reside abroad for more than two
years while for 30–39 year-olds the share was 12 percent. Among
those with higher education, 3 percent wanted to emigrate, 12 percent wanted to stay abroad for an extended period, while 71 percent wanted only to travel, engage in short visits, or stay for periods of less than two years. It should be noted that this poll was
taken in late February of the harsh winter of 1991 during the
period of Mikhail Gorbachev's "turn to the right" and before the
aftermath of the August coup completely changed the Soviet
Union's political and economic prospects.

Exit Data

According to official data, 452,000 people "emigrated"[19] from
the Soviet Union in 1990. Of these, one-third were unemployed or
retired, one-third were laborers, and one-third were professionals of
various sorts. Apparently extrapolating from these figures, the
U.S.S.R. Minister for Labor reported that 1.5 million citizens have
"already decided to seek work abroad" and at least 8 million would
seek work abroad in the next three years.[20]

---

[16] Responses add up to more than 100 percent presumably because the respondents were
asked to indicate all that applied.
[17] *Izvestiya*, 10 August 1990.
[18] "A Russian Exodus?" USIA Research Memorandum M–75–91, 17 May 1991.
[19] Presumably this represents the number of exit visas issued.
[20] As reported in *RFE/RL Daily Report*, 25 April 1991.

It has been reported that 2,653 employees of the Soviet Academy of Sciences left the country in 1989. This is five times the number who left in any previous year. No data are reported for length of stay abroad or the percentage who have returned. Many left on personal invitations to work abroad for 3 months to a year with a provision to extend the stays further. The number of scientists going to work in the United States has increased five-fold (Karavayev, 1990). Some sociologists forecast that 1.5 million "specialists with higher education" will leave in the next ten years if conditions do not improve.[21] The bases for such projections are not made explicit.

A closer look at the exit figures suggest that the emigration occurring in 1990 was of a fairly specific kind. Sixty percent of those who left went to Israel. Another 30 percent left for Germany.[22] In both instances the decision to emigrate involved factors not readily applicable to the mass of Soviet technical elites. Similarly, both of these nations are by law unconditionally willing to receive as migrants only those meeting specific criteria.[23] These rates of exit might not be sustained. According to the same source, the number of applicants for permanent exit visas declined 8.9 percent in the first five months of 1991 relative to the same period of 1990. No reason was offered for this decline.

These data in themselves do not adequately define the nature of the emigration that has occurred nor do they give any outlines about the likely future course. Yet, several projections have been offered, usually without explicit discussion of the underlying reasoning.

Prior to passing the Emigration Law, the U.S.S.R. Supreme Soviet asked the Ministry of Economics' (formerly *Gosplan*) Research Institute to prepare a forecast of the likely size of emigration. The research suggested that every fifth skilled worker (*spetsialist*) and every other person with higher education would leave the former Soviet Union if offered a job abroad. According to the forecast, the realistic annual net migration in the "nearest term" is likely to be 500,000–700,000 people, including 260,000–330,000 scientists and engineers. The forecast for skilled workers was 100,000–150,000 annually.[24]

Another forecast, given by the General Director of the Center of Socio-Strategic Research, Anatoly Antonov, attempted to introduce concepts of external demand into the equation. If the present immigration policies of the West remain unchanged, then 2.5 million would leave the former Soviet Union in the next 10 years. If South Africa opens its gates, then the size of Soviet emigration could grow to 4 million.[25]

It would be inappropriate to evaluate these data and projections based upon reports in the popular press. None give the impression of having captured all the subtleties inherent in the phenomenon

---

[21] "Soviet Scientists Flocking to the West, Lured by Better Pay and Political Stability," *RFE/RL Soviet/East European Report*, vol. 8, no. 37, 10 July 1991, pp. 1–2.

[22] *Novoye Vremya*, no. 28, 1991.

[23] Note, however, that the country appearing on the Soviet exit visa and the country in which the emigrant will eventually reside are not necessarily the same.

[24] *Argumenty i Fakty*, no. 29, 1991.

[25] *Poisk*, no. 6, 1991.

of emigration. Basic, and somewhat simplistic, assumptions—exit equals loss, emigration means cost without benefit—appear unchallenged. This is not necessarily the fault of the research. Data are too sparse and many institutional and legal details remain to be elaborated. If any strong result may be inferred from these reports of polls and various forecasts, it is that further research is clearly warranted. The next section explores what the net cost of emigration might be.

NET EFFECT OF EMIGRATION

The very term "brain drain" carries a strongly negative connotation. At first glance, it would seem superfluous to explore in detail exactly how (and whether) this phenomenon might affect the country of origin adversely.[26] Yet, in order to frame effective policies both for dealing with the results and for stanching the flow of technically trained citizens, it is useful to elaborate on the specific traumas brain drain may entail. Perhaps even more important in helping obtain an appropriate policy perspective would be to explore whether there might not also be hidden *benefits* to Russia from this flow.

COSTS

The costs might be divided according to when they exert their primary effects, in the short or long term.

Short Term

A major effect in the early days of the democratic transformation of Russia might be the political one from the disproportionate loss from one of the most progressive and democratically oriented segments of the society. Many academics, scientists, and technologists, if not visible in the forefront of politically active dissent, are likely, because of a broader contact with the West, to be more familiar than the average population with the prospects for and obligations of participatory democracy. To effectively remove a large share of the most politically advanced part of the population might actually have some influence over the course of events and the types of new institutions that will evolve out of the current ferment. There needs to be a leavening of individuals willing to conduct themselves, and to insist on the conduct of others, in accord with the newly legitimized democratic course for these ideas to permeate society as a whole. Their absence would be sorely felt by those building the new political structure.

The remaining costs are largely economic in character. It is possible that a large-scale brain drain would mean a dilution of quality in the domestic RDI and educational cadre if the best and the brightest are the most likely to heed the siren call. This, however, is by no means certain and is indeed in itself an important and researchable question. Nevertheless, if this proves to be the case it will have several secondary effects.

---

[26] This is so much the case that it appears rare in the voluminous literature on "brain drain" for the precise nature of its ills to be specified. Further, it must be noted that the "costs" are those assumed to be borne by the society and economy of origin of the emigrant. These costs are rarely weighed against the benefit gained by the individual migrant.

The first of these would be harm to the ability to absorb technology from abroad. Imported technology usually requires a good amount of reworking and adaptation to a new setting in order to work properly.[27] Therefore, it requires ability and creativity on the part of the recipient of the transferred technology to elicit from it the full measure of its inherent capability. It is conceivable that the loss of personnel in certain critical sectors could adversely affect the speed with which Russia might be able to absorb foreign technology, particularly of the disembodied variety (that is, "software" as opposed to "hardware").[28]

A further consequence of losing the most valuable segment of the technical intelligentsia might be a loss of direct revenues from foreign sources. Precisely those scientific and technical workers who would be of greatest interest to employers in the West would be those most likely to possess knowledge and techniques that could generate contract work and salable licenses over the short term.

A final adverse consequence would be a pervasive cult of pessimism and inferiority. If emigration is taken as a signal of worth or quality, this will not only lead to an acceleration of the propensity to emigrate but also malaise among those who remain. This carries an air of self-fulfilling prophesy about it. It is the more chilling in the Russian case because the country has long suffered from a paucity of internal objective measures of quality and achievement and has so long been isolated from the mainstream of scientific and technical development which would assist in the evaluation of individuals. In the absence of other ills this is unlikely to be a long-term phenomenon but it is not impossible.

Long Term

Over the long term, the costs to the economy will depend upon the scale, duration, and typology of emigration. If we assume an emigrant flow that draws off an appreciable portion of the available technical and scientific talent with a high degree of permanence, the costs could be quite tangible.

The major specter haunting Russian perceptions of emigration is loss of an ability to generate technology. If the most gifted technologists take their skills and experience elsewhere, many assume that the ability of the economy to be a primary engine for innovation on the world market would be seriously compromised. A further assumption, implicit in this vision, is that the technological cadre, heretofore underrepresented by achievement in this competitive field, would be benefited and assisted by changes in the overall structure of the economy. With the shackles of the command economy's institutions struck off, more useful inventions and applications would issue from the nation's laboratories and design bureaus. If so, however, this might have an even greater effect on the less stellar members of the RDI cadre who are less likely to be known, and so lured, abroad. That being the case, the loss of personnel might actually prove to have a smaller net effect than is

---

[27] This is true even of transfers that do not cross national frontiers.

[28] Note that this is listed as a short term cost because even if this phenomenon is seen to occur, it is unreasonable to expect in the context of a liberalized Soviet economy that in the long run these critical slots would not be filled by new graduates or retrainees.

currently feared. When balanced by changes enhancing the productivity of the remainder, the net change in the nation's technology strength might prove less than some notional, optimal amount, but positive nonetheless.

Another fear for the long term stems not from fears of diminishing the size of the RDI cadre, but that of the scientific personnel engaged in less directly applied, more fundamental research. It is even more difficult to measure the potential cost to the economy in this respect than in the applied dimension for the simple reason that the relationship between science and technology on the one hand, and economic performance on the other, is not well understood.[29] It is, nevertheless, an important point because fears for national competitiveness and loss of market share in many countries frequently are expressed as concern for preserving a domestic capability for scientific research and result in important policy choices. It is not at all certain that such choices are well advised.

A scientific research community almost certainly does contribute to RDI—not so much through the actual fruits of its research but through the coincident skill-building that occurs during the course of the research. If the teachers of the next generation, the present cadre of scientists, are lost, the skills, traditions, and experiential knowledge they embody will not be passed along. If the loss is of sufficient magnitude, this carries the potential of establishing a vicious, downward spiral. Similarly, if a sufficient share of gifted advanced studies students are lost to emigration, going abroad for training and then not returning, the results could be similar.

The preceding discussion strongly suggests that the true potential costs of massive emigration among technical elites can only be properly assessed by far more detailed analysis than is usually brought to the question by governments and policymakers faced by the actual prospect of this type of loss. The question is one of degree, although it is understandable why officials frequently see it in starker terms. The need for balanced assessment becomes even more clear if we examine some potential sources of *benefit* to be accrued by the emigrants' country of origin.

BENEFITS

To speak of the benefits to a nation from the emigration of some of its technical intelligentsia would seem oxymoronic. Yet, the apparent contradiction might be as much because of an overly simplistic, almost mercantilist, view of the process than because of an accurate assessment of the actual consequences. What follows below should be regarded only as suggestions for thinking about the emigration of technical elites that are not usually factored in when assessing the net costs of "brain drain." These should be contemplated, along with the costs outlined above, to arrive at some more accurate assessment of how seriously concerned policymakers should be.

---

[29] See Popper (1991) for a partial discussion of this question in the context of former centrally planned economies.

Short Term

The first potential short term benefit is more social or political than economic. There could be no more stark indication of how sharp the break has been with the past than to allow the free passage of former Soviet citizens across the borders. This has not been possible for more than 60 years. It would signal an unprecedented level of confidence and a degree of commitment to real change. Paradoxically, it is entirely possible that a visibly porous frontier will actually reduce pressures for emigration: as long as people can feel confident that they could, in principle, leave for abroad at any time they chose, there would be less need for each individual to test the reality. And to the extent that they will it test and so relieve long pent-up desires to see the outside world, the more likely it is that they will return in short order if there is reason to believe that the initial trip might merely be the first of many. Such feelings might be expected to be strongest precisely among the technical intelligentsia and the potential psychological release all the greater.

Emigration might relieve several domestic pressures over the short term. The transition from the state-directive system to a new economic order based on the market and private ownership will be a rough one. It is entirely likely that the economy will not be in a position to sustain the present cadre of technical personnel as well as it did in the past—nor as well as it is likely to do after the initial turbulence. Emigration might be seen as a way to keep scientists and technologists actively engaged in the pursuits they were trained for until such time as the domestic economy can once more support their work—in much the same way as the soon-to-be-occupied countries of Europe shipped their gold reserves off to Britain for safekeeping during the Second World War. This potential outlet for talent to express itself and retain its keen edge would counteract the short term signals to seek other types of training and occupations better suited to current conditions. Otherwise, there is a prospect that in heeding the signals of a newly marketized economy at a time of considerable disequilibrium, people would make career decisions seriously affecting the future composition of the work force.

The prospect of emigration could serve to sustain and increase incentives for individual excellence during a hard transition accompanied by a temporarily depressed national economy. If émigrés subsequently return to help with the rebuilding, the benefit might be considerable. But what if they do not return? Here, in assessing potential costs, one has to be careful to state explicitly to whom these costs accrue. There may be a net cost to society and the population who remain. But this must be weighed against the personal benefit to the individual émigré who is thus better able to realize his or her full economic and personal potential. Again, with the passing of the old order a new calculus of social welfare must be applied. It is no longer solely the interests of the "state" which determine the balance of net benefit. Indeed, if social welfare is now to be measured as the aggregate of individual welfare then the balance of cost and benefit is not straightforward. To complicate things further, we must also consider the benefits to those staying at home who will now have been given a chance by the departure of the émigrés to move into the (presumably more desirable) places that will have been vacated.

One reason why emigration often benefits the individual is that it permits a technical professional to gain an increased awareness of current practice and the range of technique available in his or her field. There are considerable externalities attached to this personal benefit that would accrue to society as a whole if the emigrant returns. This might lead to a long term social benefit.

Finally, in an era when national resources are likely to be stretched to meet the many needs of the moment, emigrants abroad are a possible source of hard currency remittances. While workers' remittances are an important source of foreign earnings for several countries, this is unlikely to loom as large in the case of Russia. The technical elites are more likely to take their immediate families with them than are traditional migrant workers. Furthermore, the sheer size of the post-Soviet Russian economy is likely to dwarf the earning power of even fairly substantial emigration. Yet, some extended family members will be left behind. And a portion of the emigration is likely to divert a considerable share of its earnings to assure an improved standard of living when they do return home. They will do so by taking advantage of changes in the economy to purchase assets and amenities they deem necessary for that purpose. Any source of hard currency remittances and external sources of investment, even if not sufficient to solve all problems, is likely to be welcome.

Long Term

The potential long term benefits of emigration of technical elites fall into two groups depending upon the type of emigration. If the emigration proves merely to be an initial surge, a transitory phenomenon necessary for technical workers to merge into a steady-state system of international movement, then after coming to some equilibrium many of the initial émigrés can be expected to return. Others would then take their place as temporary expatriates. Benefits would accrue to the economy as a whole when these emigrants return home.

The most obvious benefit would be transfer of disembodied technology, that is, technology not embodied in capital assets—"software" as opposed to hardware. Scientists, technologists, and academics who go abroad will learn things. They will bring new knowledge back with them when they return. One of the great difficulties of the transition facing Russia is the legacy of its past insularity. In research labs and design bureaus, but much more so in enterprises, knowledge of world techniques and practice is often woefully deficient. One of the best ways to address this deficiency is to have personnel go abroad to work and gain experience and to then return to their old jobs.

Embodied technology transfers could also be improved by having on hand a substantial cadre of returned émigrés. Even when technology is transferred in the form of machinery, it is frequently quite difficult to actually elicit its full potential in a foreign setting. This is so for several reasons. One is a lack of appreciation for how much "tacit," unrecorded knowledge, is required to operate complex machinery or apply techniques appropriately. Another is an inherent resistance to "foreign" equipment, especially that requiring a redrafting of current practices and job flows within the plant. The "Not Invented Here" syndrome is familiar to students of technological change. Having on hand a cadre who have experience in operating machinery in its original setting, who are familiar with the "work-arounds" necessary to operate such equipment efficiently, and who are less threatened by the intrusion of the new, in part because of their experience as emigrants would be vital for easing technical transitions. This could even increase the flow of technology and the speed of diffusion of new technology by helping reduce teething problems and so increase the receptivity of the recipients of new technology.

Another benefit returnees would confer on the science-technology system as a whole would be to provide alternative voices. The social-psychological aspects of reform are often the most troubling. Old habits die hard. People are familiar with the old system and find it to be natural. New approaches seem forced and are difficult to comprehend. When confronted by challenges, individuals often resort to previously learned responses and the system as a whole reverts. The structure for organizing scientific and technological endeavors in the former Soviet Union still reflects the legacy of the directive management style characteristic of the old regime. This rigid hierarchy and strictly linear approach to process is not conducive to the needs of the present and the future. Yet change will be difficult if the system is staffed solely by those schooled in the old system. On the other hand, if sufficient numbers of returned émigrés who possess something more than just a theoretical awareness of other approaches come to inhabit the various levels of the hierarchy, they might provide a leavening sufficient to profoundly change on the domestic system for organizing RDI efforts.

Finally, a steady state movement of technical elites traveling abroad and then returning could be viewed as effectively expanding the capacity for training beyond what domestic resources can support. "Brain drain" is frequently cited as a dispersion of society's resources. Those schooled and trained at home then go abroad, thereby depriving the economy of the fruits of its investment in the education of the individual. If this is so, then the reverse process must be viewed as a gain. Even those emigrants who have already achieved considerable professional standing will learn from their experience abroad. This learning would then constitute an unlooked-for boon to domestic resources if the migrants return.

Clearly, all of the potential benefits cited above depend crucially on the opportunity and willingness of emigrants to return. This suggests an important point for policy consideration. Rather than consider means to stem the outflow of technical elites, the efforts of Russian policymakers might be better rewarded by finding what it might take to ensure that an eventual return of those who go abroad can be made more attractive, and likely prospect.

Some members of the technical intelligentsia will leave never to return. Depending on their domestic prospects and the demand for their services abroad, the number in this category might be large. Yet it is still possible to see some aspects of a permanent emigration, a true brain drain, that might still confer some benefits upon

Russia. These are almost of necessity quite difficult to quantify. Given the peculiarities of Soviet history and institutions, however, they are worth noting.

Soviet science and technology had split off from the global research community by the 1930s. Excessive fear of foreign contact has meant that Soviet research had lower efficiency and lost opportunities for development. Individuals with high technical training who emigrate and do not return can become human bridgeheads to the institutions that receive them overseas. They may not return. Students who will follow them, because the émigrés will have provided them with a previously non-existent entree to the recipient institutions, and many of these students will return. These returning students and colleagues of the permanent émigrés will come back enriched by the experience and will contribute to the general store of domestic technical knowledge. Furthermore, in their positions in their new institutions the permanent émigrés may become, purposely or serendipitously, agents for making the larger world aware of the existence and efforts of their former colleagues who remain at home. This may be a tremendous boon for Russia, more so than for other countries suffering from brain drain, because of the difficulty experienced by former Soviet technical workers in trying to break free of the habits and orientations of the past.

A final possible benefit from permanent emigration may seem like cold comfort indeed, but deserves serious consideration nonetheless. If, after an initial spurt, it becomes apparent that there is a continuous flow out of the country of highly skilled individuals, few of whom return, it will be an important signal that something is seriously wrong with the institutional structure of Russian science and technology. On the other hand, if emigration settles into a steady state balanced by returns, it will be a useful indication that Russian science and technology is on the right track. One of the characteristics of Soviet institutions as they existed in the past was their inability to develop measures providing early warning when something was going wrong. A lack of market signals, insularity in developing and assessing research designs, and a lack of resource and human mobility often hampered Soviet efforts to determine what was being done right—and more important, what was being done wrong. Net migration will provide such an indicator. Again, the appropriate policy course for utilizing the knowledge that net emigration would suggest is not necessarily to stanch the flow. Rather, it would permit early consideration of what course might be necessary to make return seem more attractive.

CONCLUSIONS

As an initial attempt to come to grip with the policy issues surrounding emigration by technical elites, and in the absence of sufficient information about the particulars of the Russian case, this paper has raised a number of hypotheses for consideration. Among these, three stand out.

The first is that emigration may actually be but part of a larger process. Russia's scientists, technicians, and academics are now, for the first time, in a legal position to take part in the major movement of personnel across national frontiers. This is one of the most

838

significant characteristics of the current state of global intellectual activity. As such, it leads to the suggestion that as the Russian economy rebuilds and the internal institutions come to some new equilibrium there will be less cause for individuals to consider participation in such movement as the occasion for permanent emigration.

A second point is closely related to the first. Especially in the earliest days after the lifting of legal barriers to emigration and travel, policymakers will be confronted with an identification problem: Will the initial great outpouring of technically skilled personnel prove to be ephemeral, the necessary initial deposit of Russia's share in the larger global movement of technical elites in which it will now become a fully participating member, or are the rates of outflow likely to continue, unmatched by a significant number of returnees, leading to the nightmare situation many now fear? At first, it will be difficult to determine, based on superficial evidence of numbers of exit visas, what the appropriate assessment should be. This will cause anxiety among some policymakers. It is imperative that policy not be crafted solely to react to fears of the worst case but rather to address the actual situation confronting the nation. To do otherwise runs the serious risk of making the extreme prophesies of doom self-fulfilling.

This is the third hypothesis. Barring a general crisis leading to near total economic and political breakdown, policies directed only to dealing with the apparent "problem" by restricting outflows by administrative means would prove to be the policies most likely to precipitate precisely the disaster they would be intended to avoid. Nothing is more likely to start a rush for the exits than the sense that the door might be swinging shut. Policymakers must accept the paradox that whereas in the early days many will wish to test the liberality of the new exit laws, the best way to keep larger numbers from running the experiment is to allow the first experimenters to be eminently and visibly successful. The only effective way to ensure that such exits are part of a healthy movement rather than an emigration indicative of serious internal problems is to address those problems in order to make return home an attractive prospect. There would be a collateral benefit from such policies. These would also be the best way of ensuring the most productive utilization of those specialists who remain.

BIBLIOGRAPHY

Kapitsa, S. P. (1990). "Lyudi mogut est' odno i to zhe, no dumayut oni, k schast'yu, po-raznomu . . ., *Leninigradskaya Pravda*, 17 June.

Karavayev, A. (1990). " 'Utechka umov' mozhet obeskrovit' sovetskuyu nauku," *Pravitel'stvennyi Vestnik*, no. 5, May.

Kasatonov, V. (1990). "Kulibiny na Eksport," *Dialog*, no. 5, pp. 90–98, as in JPRS-UST90-005-L, July 30, 1990, pp. 26–32.

Lien, Da-Hsiang Donald (1987). "Economic Analysis of Brain Drain," *Journal of Development Economics*, vol. 25, pp. 33–43.

Margalit, Avishai (1991). "The Great White Hope," *The New York Review of Books*, 27 June, pp. 19–25.

Popper, Steven W. (1991). "Science and Technology in Eastern Europe after the Flood," RAND P-7698, August.

CONTINUING NEGATIVE HEALTH TRENDS IN THE FORMER U.S.S.R.

by Murray Feshbach *

CONTENTS

SUMMARY

After a brief comment on the rare positive moments in the "Soviet" medical scene, the dimensions of the medical crisis in the former Soviet Union are addressed in terms of overall trends in mortality and morbidity. Mortality is climbing in Russia and Ukraine sufficiently to exceed fertility in the last several years, and morbidity in many cases is exploding as difficulties continue in quality of health services, living conditions, lack of medications, poor facilities, and so forth. Details on the explosion of diphtheria cases in Moscow as well as the former U.S.S.R. as a whole are given as a (hopefully worst-case) scenario of the relative dimensions of the overall problem. Vaccination coverage is worsening and the potential for increases in this and other diseases are increasing. Infant mortality figures are adjusted to account for various difficulties in determining their actual level. Both Soviet and my own adjusted figures are shown. Poor facilities, poor supplies, and poor medical staff finish the basic review. Additionally a very brief description of some of the outside assistance is given, but the demand for drugs and other supplies is so great that major problems contin-

---

* Murray Feshbach is Research Professor of Demography, Georgetown University.

ue. A table on infectious diseases (incidence and rate per 100,000 population) during the years 1960 to 1990 is appended.

INTRODUCTION

When a government's policy allows the health of its people to deteriorate as the Soviet regime did over the last several decades through the choices it made to maximize production regardless of human, natural resource, and environmental costs, [1] then the price to be paid has to be enormous. It is no surprise that conditions have deteriorated. The cost was compounded even further when the military was given priority over all production preferences, especially since the late 1930s when Stalin began to gear up for the coming war. Military excesses in nuclear, chemical, and industrial research and production led to major medical as well as environmental hazards.

POSITIVE ASPECTS

Searching for positive aspects of the current health scene, perhaps two items can be adduced—the low number of AIDS cases and the development of fee-for-service medical care. Both may radically change, however, especially regarding AIDS. First, the number of persons who have contracted AIDS appears to be much smaller than most Soviet researchers, myself included, expected by this time. On the one hand, the number is much lower than projected for this point in time, but not as low as the Soviet official estimate of something less than 100 with full-blown AIDS, nor as low as the projections made by the U.S.S.R. Ministry of Health in April of 1990 of 7,000 in 1991 or about 1.5 million by the year 2000. My estimate of some 4,000–5,000 cases of full-blown AIDS in the former U.S.S.R. in 1989–90 is derived from a model prepared for the United States pattern of risk takers; none of these figures, however, is equivalent to the tragic figure for the United States of 200,000 with full-blown AIDS, of whom 140,000 or more have died. However, the dramatic and major increase in the former Soviet Union in 1991 and 1992 in the spread of drug abuse, the chronic shortage of single-use syringes, prostitution, and the overt practice of homosexuality may add to the number of risk-takers significantly. This increase, as well as contacts with Western individuals in and out of their former U.S.S.R., may lead to a revival of the expected growth patterns. This would, in the future at least, lead to a contradiction of Russian Minister of Health Vorobyev's statement that Russia is "probably the only country in the world where the number of AIDS patients is not increasing." [2] This boast may prove to be premature. Perhaps because such a low number of AIDS patients is recorded, the expenditures planned will be less than needed. To have a double standard in regard to AIDS patients by failing to give them appropriate special care and treatment, and

[1] Most of the material for this submission is drawn from the book, Murray Feshbach and Alfred Friendly, Jr., *Ecocide in the USSR: Health and Nature Under Siege*, New York, Basic Books, 1992, 376 pp.
[2] BBC, *Summary of World Broadcasts, Part I, Former USSR*, 13 June 1992, p. SU/1406 C2/2.

not spend the appropriate amount of money, would be unconscionable even with major economic constraints.

The second major positive change, if applied properly, is the opening of widespread fee-for-service medical facilities and care. With the introduction of private services derived from medical insurance payments based on payments by employers, it is hoped that there will ensue a marked improvement in health delivery and the health status of the population. The original plan to implement the program no later than 1 January 1993 appeared to have been accelerated to 1 July 1992. This appears to have been too hasty but is driven by the shortage of state budgetary funds available for the health sector. If the health sector was to have received 60 odd billion rubles, it has been allocated something over 20 billion rubles instead. Thus the monies derived from a 9 to 10 percent transfer payment from the wage bill of each organization and institution will provide the underpinning for new salary payments, supplies, equipment, buildings, and other infrastructure of new medical facilities. This is a positive step, but it is also another tax-like burden on the individual enterprise. It also means an inevitable delay in full implementation—even delaying the purchase of bandages, syringes, fetal monitoring devices and the point in time until their delivery, distribution, installation, clean-up, etc. can be undertaken. It also raises the question—What is to happen to treatment procedures necessary during the interval?

DETERIORATING HEALTH

As the country undergoes a transition from a command to a market economy, and as nationalistic preferences and competing demands for very scarce resources become more evident, it would appear that the medical situation may well deteriorate. Resources are devoted principally to production for the consumer market or even for the military, to defend Armenia, Azerbayzhan, Moldova, the Baltics, Checheniya, Georgia, Abkhaziyaa, Ossetia (South and North), Crimea perhaps, Tuva and possibly other regions. The medical establishment before and after the breakup of the Soviet Union frequently referred to the shortage of medication as the primary reason for 1 million or so excess deaths. And this was before many of the recent nationality conflicts which engender a larger number of deaths than anyone could have expected. Local military actions also have blocked shipments of medicinal production from local factories to other republics/states.

But even without military action in both Russia and Ukraine in the past year, the number of deaths exceeded the number of births. In Russia it did so for the second year in a row. This pattern emerged in part from the disarray of the medical system, the lack of production of medical and pharmaceutical products, disarray among medical staffs galvanized into conducting strikes during the past year, and major increases in life-threatening illnesses such as diphtheria and polio, as well as plague and tuberculosis. The year 1991 was reported to have witnessed more cases in Russia of dysentery, whooping-cough, syphilis, and diphtheria. By the end of the first quarter of 1992, more cases of bacterial dysentery, salmonella, diphtheria, and tuberculosis, were reported than for the same period in the previous year. The Russian Federation showed a quadrupling in the number of cases of diphtheria recorded over the decade 1981 to 1991, increasing from 474 in 1981 up to 1869 in 1991 (45 of whom died in 1991). [3] According to a deputy minister of health, diphtheria is "epidemic in character" in large cities such as Moscow, St. Petersburg, Khabarovsk, and Kaliningrad. Diphtheria-specific data are not available for St. Petersburg. Chief Pediatrician of the City, Professor Igor Vorontsov, wrote in April of 1992 that 144 children died in child-care institutions run by the government from diphtheria as well as botulism, tuberculosis, and whooping cough. This was due not only to air pollution, he noted, but also to the fact that many children suffer from varying degrees of hunger (golodaniya). If a survey of 300 children that showed "only 3 percent of pre-school and school-age children receive full-value food for consumption" is typical, then Vorontsov's separate evaluation can be deemed correct—that "practically healthy children—according to expert evaluation for the city of St. Petersburg—are no more than 2.5 percent [of the total], and this is the best that could be cited." [4]

Data are available for Moscow that closely fit this perilous description regarding diphtheria. Diphtheria cases in Moscow alone have skyrocketed in the recent period. Climbing from 46 cases in Moscow (with 9 million population) in 1988, to 94 in 1989, to 688 in 1990, they reached 1,100 in 1991. For the first few months of 1992, the reported number of cases in Moscow totalled 346; for Russia as a whole, 904 persons had contracted diphtheria by June 1992, with 16 deaths, of whom 6 were children. Two of these children are reported to not have been vaccinated for medical causes, and 4 had not been vaccinated because of parental refusal to permit it. [5] These figures should not be surprising, once it is known that some 60,000 children in Moscow were not vaccinated as required by the immunization schedule, [6] and were thus vulnerable to the various diseases that could have been prevented. Thus while the number and proportion of deaths is shocking, it should not be unexpected. In 1989, for instance, of a national total of 840 cases of diphtheria (see Table 1), 65 persons died—20 of whom were between 15 and 19 years of age, that is, many were of the military ages of 18 and 19. (In the United States, with a population only 15 percent smaller than that of the former Soviet Union—250 compared with 290 million persons—the total number of cases of diphtheria was 2, with no deaths.) In 1989 the mean age at death from diphtheria in the former Soviet Union was 24.7 years, in Russia it was 42.0, in Turk-

---

[3] A. Monisov, "Vaktsinoprofilaktika: shto v osadke?," *Meditsinskaya gazeta,* 5 June 1992. Monisov is a Deputy Chairman of the State Committee on Sanitary Epidemiological Oversight (*nadzor*). Monisov asserts that their DPT, polio, and measles vaccines meet the "leading indicators" of safety requirements set by the World Health Organization. What are the non-leading indicators, how safe are they, has their proportion changed over time in terms of safety, etc.?
[4] Igor Vorontsov, "O zdorov'ye, i ne tol'ko ... Ne prinosite ikh v zhertvu," *Nevskoye vremya,* 22 April 1992, p. 2. Vorob'yev also mentions, critically, that even more telling about the failure of the health delivery system is the number and share of children dying outside of medical facilities. This "sad number" demonstrates that they died "without adequate medical aid." And this is St. Petersburg/Leningrad. And elsewhere?
[5] Radio Mayak, Moscow, 0845 gmt, 6 June 1992, cited in BBC, *SWB, Part 1, Former USSR,* 19 June 1992, p. SU/W0235 A/18.
[6] *Ibid.*

TABLE 1. Major Illnesses in the U.S.S.R.: Morbidity and New Cases per 100,000 Population, 1980–90.

Year	Total Population (100,000s) (mid-year)	Acute Poliomyelitis		Diphtheria		Measles		Pertussis (Whooping Cough)		Scarlet Fever	
		Morbidity	Per 100,000	Morbidity	Per 100,000	Morbidity	Per 100,000	Morbidity	Per 100,000	Morbidity	Per 100,000
1960	2,123.72	7,167	3.30	53,185	24.80	2,083,333	972.0	554,087	258.5	671,186	313.2
1961	2,162.88	3,752	1.72	31,426	14.40	1,969,975	903.1	437,981	200.6	599,277	274.7
1962	2,200.03	1,692	0.76	15,365	6.90	2,148,599	968.1	471,124	212.5	527,169	237.8
1963	2,234.57	959	0.43	8,980	4.00	1,647,104	731.8	364,722	162.1	492,911	219.0
1964	2,266.69	475	0.21	8,722	2.90	2,034,066	891.6	287,970	126.2	507,570	222.5
1965	2,296.28	303	0.13	4,691	2.00	2,128,666	921.8	190,045	82.3	530,836	229.9
1966	2,322.43	287	0.12	3,102	1.30	1,747,219	748.3	145,729	62.4	691,588	296.1
1967	2,348.23	135	0.06	2,595	1.10	1,798,116	761.9	114,709	48.6	597,280	253.1
1968	2,371.85	120	0.05	2,235	0.93	1,579,829	662.9	119,383	50.1	502,015	210.7
1969	2,394.68	194	0.08	1,710	0.71	510,440	212.2	52,709	21.9	434,887	180.8
1970	2,417.20	270	0.11	1,101	0.45	471,500	194.2	39,510	16.3	469,903	193.6
1971	2,438.91	188	0.08	765	0.31	588,445	240.1	42,561	17.4	510,220	208.2
1972	2,463.28	183	0.07	516	0.20	291,435	117.8	34,534	14.0	319,468	129.1
1973	2,486.74	183	0.07	319	0.13	286,245	114.2	30,237	12.1	318,665	127.6
1974	2,509.31	139	0.06	285	0.11	374,247	148.4	30,895	12.3	367,097	145.6
1975	2,533.32	133	0.05	199	0.07	363,784	143.0	14,885	5.9	361,139	142.0
1976	2,556.05	106	0.04	198	0.07	320,844	125.0	33,022	12.9	383,564	149.4
1977	2,579.16	264	0.14	238	0.09	315,304	121.8	22,610	8.7	308,367	119.1
1978	2,601.42	152	0.06	270	0.10	545,392	208.9	17,180	6.6	287,242	11.0
1979	2,624.36	214	0.08	270	0.10	382,647	145.3	25,153	9.5	246,822	93.3
1980	2,644.86	165	0.06	345	0.13	255,654	133.9	13,908	5.2	230,142	86.7
1981	2,665.99	307	0.11	560	0.21	342,819	128.2	25,637	9.6	226,757	84.8
1982	2,688.44	257	0.09	917	0.34	466,210	172.8	27,481	10.0	324,686	120.4
1983	2,712.39	181	0.06	1,411	0.51	233,812	85.9	19,321	7.1	293,081	107.7
1984	2,738.41	115	0.04	1,609	0.58	252,510	91.9	25,985	9.4	261,682	95.2
1985	2,762.90	138	0.05	1,511	0.54	272,807	98.4	53,781	19.4	277,943	100.3
1986	2,787.84	170	0.06	1,160	0.41	165,000	59.0	17,700	6.3	354,000	128.0
1987	2,816.89	174	0.06	1,076	0.39	190,552	67.4	20,217	7.2	329,893	116.7
1988	2,860.60	157	0.06	870	0.30	164,509	57.6	45,405	15.9	214,724	75.2
1989	2,876.78	90	0.03	840	0.29	52,000	18.0	37,000	12.9	225,000	78.0
1990	2,893.50	340	0.12	1,440	0.50	47,000	16.0	33,600	12.0	180,000	62.0

TABLE 1. Major Illnesses in the U.S.S.R.: Morbidity and New Cases per 100,000 Population, 1980–90.—Continued

Year	Total Population (100,000s) (mid-year)	Tetanus Morbidity	Tetanus Per 100,000	Typhoid/Paratyphoid Morbidity	Typhoid/Paratyphoid Per 100,000	Typhoid Morbidity	Typhoid Per 100,000	Paratyphoid, ABC Morbidity	Paratyphoid, ABC Per 100,000	Infectious Hepatitis Morbidity	Infectious Hepatitis Per 100,000	Influenza and Upper Respiratory Infections Morbidity	Influenza and Upper Respiratory Infections Per 100,000
1960	2,123.72	2,319	1.09	47,291	22.3	40,834	19.1	6,457	3.0	513,052	239.4	19,831,029	9,337.9
1961	2,162.86	2,258	1.04	46,989	21.7	39,258	18.0	7,731	3.5	579,410	265.6	24,063,443	11,125.8
1962	2,200.03	2,172	0.99	40,763	18.5	34,391	15.5	6,372	2.9	462,054	208.4	44,451,912	20,205.1
1963	2,234.57	2,043	0.91	41,215	18.4	33,458	14.9	7,757	3.4	433,744	192.7	29,511,467	13,206.8
1964	2,266.69	1,641	0.72	31,541	13.9	25,512	11.2	6,029	2.6	517,883	227.0	23,834,272	10,515.0
1965	2,296.28	1,362	0.59	25,487	11.1	19,919	8.6	5,568	2.4	470,129	203.6	42,137,941	18,350.5
1966	2,322.43	1,305	0.56	27,489	11.8	21,925	9.4	5,564	2.4	465,222	199.2	29,771,456	12,819.1
1967	2,348.23	1,100	0.47	23,900	10.2	19,064	8.1	4,884	2.1	372,857	158.8	NA	NA
1968	2,371.65	900	0.38	23,300	9.8	17,842	7.5	5,430	2.3	371,309	155.8	NA	NA
1969	2,394.68	700	0.29	22,800	9.5	17,324	7.2	5,507	2.3	339,139	141.0	NA	NA
1970	2,417.20	652	0.27	22,462	9.3	17,808	7.3	4,654	1.9	404,224	166.5	55,841,700	23,101.8
1971	2,438.91	668	0.27	18,881	7.7	14,612	6.0	4,269	1.7	442,388	180.5	42,211,500	17,307.5
1972	2,463.28	617	0.25	19,558	7.9	14,346	5.8	5,212	2.1	480,437	194.1	41,692,100	16,925.4
1973	2,486.74	495	0.20	19,842	8.0	14,644	5.9	5,198	2.1	541,621	216.8	55,366,900	22,264.9
1974	2,509.31	539	0.21	23,332	9.3	16,658	6.6	6,674	2.7	527,038	209.0	46,747,200	18,629.5
1975	2,533.32	490	0.19	25,969	10.3	18,613	7.3	7,356	2.9	663,794	260.9	54,942,100	21,687.8
1976	2,556.05	430	0.17	21,000	8.2	14,653	5.7	6,320	2.5	606,812	236.4	NA	NA
1977	2,579.16	420	0.16	22,900	8.9	16,378	6.3	6,569	2.5	602,653	232.1	NA	NA
1978	2,601.42	360	0.14	18,100	7.0	13,049	5.0	5,073	1.9	589,204	225.5	NA	NA
1979	2,624.36	400	0.15	18,400	7.0	14,038	5.3	4,339	1.6	750,623	284.9	60,369,000	22,761
1980	2,644.86	300	0.11	16,900	6.4	12,836	4.8	4,024	1.5	801,545	301.9	NA	NA
1981	2,665.99	350	0.13	17,100	6.4	13,195	4.9	3,914	1.5	842,379	315.3	NA	NA
1982	2,688.44	350	0.13	18,600	6.9	13,179	4.9	3,980	1.5	951,617	352.8	NA	NA
1983	2,712.39	360	0.13	18,900	6.9	13,621	5.0	4,953	1.8	1,171,337	430.3	NA	NA
1984	2,738.41	330	0.12	17,600	6.0	13,342	4.8	5,543	2.0	885,762	322.4	NA	NA
1985	2,762.90	280	0.10	13,200	5.0	13,106	4.7	4,463	1.6	934,085	337.0	71,869,000	25,928
1986	2,787.84	260	0.09	12,596	4.0	NA	NA	NA	NA	842,000	301.0	76,641,000	27,383
1987	2,816.89	194	0.06	11,516	4.0	8,968	3.2	3,328	1.3	861,175	304.7	59,447,000	21,025
1988	2,860.60	201	0.07	9,500	4.0	8,076	2.8	3,440	1.2	716,426	251.0	79,905,541	27,999
1989	2,876.78	210	0.07	9,500	3.3	6,127	2.1	3,317	1.2	910,000	317.0	68,108,000	23,761
1990	2,893.50	240	0.12	8,600	3.0	5,890	2.0	2,736	1.0	914,000	317.0	64,635,000	22,414

Source: Murray Feshbach, *A Compendium of Soviet Health Statistics*, Washington, D.C. 1985, pp. 78–81, official Soviet statistical publications, and Feshbach and Friendly, *Ecocide*, 1992, pp. 275–278.
NA—Not Available.

menistan it was 6.0, and there were no deaths in Estonia. [7] The contrast in average age at death is an important indication of the quality of medical services. It appears that those who succumbed to diphtheria in 1989 were mostly adults—possibly because they were not vaccinated in the early postwar period, or because the vaccine was not long-lasting, or because they ignored the signs of illness with its rapid onset and did not investigate it until too late. In Turkmenistan, such young deaths were probably due to the lack of vaccinations combined with ignorance on the part of medical personnel. Estonia and the remainder of the Baltic region had a different level of medical care—albeit one still constrained by Soviet practice and shortages.

VACCINATION AND THE POSSIBILITY OF EPIDEMICS

One of the largest questions that needs to be addressed is the lack of vaccinations among the population. This leads to the possibility of epidemics among the work force and the general population not only of diphtheria but also of whooping cough, polio, and birth defects due to the lack of vaccination of young females for rubella. In the last case, the former Soviet Union and apparently its successor states do not include rubella shots in their immunization calendar. Pressures by UNICEF, the World Health Organization, the World Bank, and other intergovernmental, governmental, and private organizations and businesses may well push them into including this vaccine as a major step toward reducing the potential for birth defects in newborn children. The increase in birth deformities—more likely due to environmental pollution from radioactivity, as well as chemical, aluminum, and other industrial pollution, has grown to a very serious level and rate. However, domestic production of high-quality vaccines is not assured in the short run; donations of medicines from abroad, purchases, or both are necessary, even for psychological reasons, since many people do not trust domestic medications. Simultaneously, of course, the availability and distribution of single-use syringes and needles among the medical institutions of these countries is crucial.

In order to prevent widespread or epidemic levels of diphtheria and polio, it is necessary that 95 percent of the appropriate population (especially children in their first year of age) be given the appropriate vaccines. In 1989 the coverage in the former Soviet Union did not even reach 80 percent for both polio and diphtheria (74.6 percent of all children for polio and 78.9 percent for diphtheria coverage). It was much lower in several of the Central Asian states: 57.5 percent in Uzbekistan, 61.6 percent in Kyrgyzstan, and (surprisingly) only 67.7 percent in Georgia. The rates of incidence of these diseases can be expected to increase significantly because of past undercoverage. It was reported that in 1991, some 40 percent of all children under 1 year of age did not receive a DPT shot, and 20 to 40 percent of 1-to-2-year-olds did not get vaccinated against measles and mumps. [8] In Moscow city, due to fear that was

---

[7] New information provided by a former Soviet national medical agency.
[8] Monasov, loc.cit.

generated, a media report claimed that polio vaccines required biological material from monkeys, and that the hard currency shortage prevented purchase of more so that the vaccine could not be effective or appropriate. As a consequence, only 1 in 3 children were properly immunized against polio in 1991. [9]

For a period of 5 months between late 1988 and early 1989, there was no production of measles vaccines in the country, not for environmental reasons *per se*, but because the immune-inducing products were affected by "poor quality of ampules, of the raw materials, and the medium (*sred*)". [10] This could lead to another cycle of increased incidence of measles if foreign supplies are not forthcoming.

INFANT MORTALITY

It is particularly difficult to ascertain the trends in infant mortality from official statistics. Given all that we know about the reproductive health of women, poor health care facilities, lack of good nutrition, lack of vaccinations, and the multitude of other problems related to the environment, particularly radioactivity, nationality conflicts, and internal refugee problems causing disruptions in living conditions (perhaps 1 to 1.5 million persons are displaced within the country, some 600,000 to 700,000 who have come to the Russian Federation alone), and so forth, the officially reported decline in infant mortality is not logical. Moreover, the problem is compounded by recent information about errors of commission— neither errors purely of methodology, nor errors purely of omissions, but deliberate lying about infant mortality.

Among the last and perhaps among the best activities of the former Goskomstat U.S.S.R. was to invalidate (indirectly, but clearly) the official infant mortality statistics, based on a special survey pointing to errors of commission. Many medical facilities deliberately had children survive "on the books," i.e., the hospital admission register, as still alive beyond the point of 12 months since birth. These errors of commission led to an undercount of 19 percent in Russia and an undercount of up to 86 percent in Central Asia. If one applies the set of undercount rates to rural infant mortality rates alone for the year 1987, then instead of the reported rate of 25.4 deaths per 1,000 live-born children, approximately 35 to 37 deaths can be estimated depending on whether all adjustments for methodology and estimates of omissions are included.

Alternatively, newly available unpublished estimates by the Russian Medical Socio-Economic Information organization (Rosmedsotsekoninform), based on world definitions, experience, and statistical practice, come close to my estimates for 1987. Estimates made by Rosmedsotsekoninform for 1980 and 1987, for the former U.S.S.R. as a whole and by republic are given in Table 2.

The ratios between official and adjusted figures vary by time and area. In 1980, the adjustment was at a minimum 30 percent (in Estonia) and at a maximum 78 percent (in Ukraine and Azerbaydzhan). In 1987, the min/max range was minus 11 percent in Estonia

---

[9] *Rossiyskaya gazeta,* 8 February 1992, p. 8.
[10] *Ibid.*

TABLE 2. Infant Mortality Rates, 1980 and 1987.

Area	Infant Mortality Rate: 1980			Infant Mortality Rate: 1987		
	Official	Adjusted	Ratio	Official	Adjusted	Ratio
U.S.S.R.	27.3	43.47	1.59	25.4	37.35	1.47
R.S.F.S.R.	22.1	37.71	1.71	19.4	23.40	1.21
Ukraine	16.6	29.53	1.78	14.5	19.90	1.37
Belorussia	16.3	24.86	1.53	13.4	16.68	1.25
Moldavia	35.0	52.00	1.49	25.9	35.90	1.39
Estonia	17.1	22.23	1.30	16.1	14.35	0.89
Latvia	15.4	23.69	1.54	11.3	13.47	1.19
Lithuania	14.7	24.86	1.69	12.3	15.22	1.24
Armenia	26.2	43.31	1.65	22.6	39.17	1.73
Azerbaydzhan	30.4	54.09	1.78	28.6	50.07	1.75
Georgia	25.4	41.70	1.64	24.3	36.25	1.49
Kazakhstan	32.7	52.81	1.61	29.4	41.21	1.40
Kirgiziya	43.3	70.35	1.62	37.8	58.92	1.56
Tadzhikistan	58.1	90.96	1.57	48.9	77.12	1.58
Turkmenistan	53.6	87.74	1.64	56.4	81.46	1.44
Uzbekistan	46.8	71.64	1.53	45.9	68.26	1.49

Source: Rosmedsotsekoninform.

(perhaps too many stillbirths or miscarriages were included) and 75 percent in Azerbaydzhan. Regardless of which approach is taken, the difference overall is some 50 percent in these estimates—roughly the same as the ratio between the official estimates and the estimates made using my (different) approach. How these trends play out over time, especially now with all disruptions in the economy and society, and how statistical information is collected in various areas of disturbance, is indeterminate. Certainly the poor health conditions described here and elsewhere will contribute to an increase in infant mortality. Particularly important in this will be the effects of radioactivity and other pollution. [11]

RESOURCES AVAILABLE FOR HEALTH

In the discussion of social issues included in the rejected Shatalin 500-day economic reform plan it was revealed that every fourth adult and every sixth child in the (now former) U.S.S.R. was chronically ill. That was in 1990, and perhaps the ratio is higher now for adults and children given the lesser amounts of medications available and competing demands for resources. External assistance from international agencies, various governments, private voluntary organizations, and undoubtedly individuals have helped specific cities and regions, but not enough since current data show a worsening of morbidity and mortality figures.

INFRASTRUCTURE

Very likely, in addition, little has been done to improve the material infrastructure of medical facilities in order to reduce the share of rural hospitals that do not have hot water (65 percent),

---

[11] Feshbach and Friendly, *Ecocide in the U.S.S.R.*; Murray Feshbach, "Environmental Calamities: Widespread and Costly," in this volume.

sewage (27 percent) or that have no water at all (17 percent). It is likely that some improvement in the supply of electrocardiogram machines probably has taken place (because of external suppliers) so that the 35 percent of hospitals and 37 percent of polyclinics that did not have one earlier now have a machine available. Whether they have paper for these machines, whether they are under repair, and whether the attending physician can read the print-out is another matter. (The former U.S.S.R. Minister of Health confirmed to me in October 1991 his estimate that 40 percent of new medical school graduates could not read a cardiogram.) A lack of sanitation in maternity homes in Moscow, for example, led to a spread of illness beyond just those crowded facilities. In early 1987, Chazov noted that 12 of 33 maternity homes in the capital city "met modern requirements and public health standards." The remaining 21 did not. Adding to this problem of health standards is the failure to meet their own standard for space between beds. Wards are overcrowded and illnesses can spread within medical facilities as the space around beds is only 42 square feet rather than the 70 square feet that is the standard norm. Maternity homes in some locations have only 20 to 30 square feet of space around beds.

STAFF

The quality of medical staffs is highly varied. With individual exceptions, however, many practicing physicians should not be doing so. For example, in Turkmenistan's Tashauz Oblast—perhaps a worst-case location—70 percent of the obstetrician-gynecologists lack surgical skills. In a 1989 report, it was found that half of their patients died as a result of surgery, and that two of every three deaths of pregnant women, recently confined women, and gynecology patients, "could have been prevented." One-quarter of Turkmenistan's rural midwives and one-third of its rural pediatricians could not meet rudimentary professional requirements. No wonder the official infant mortality rate in the republic/country was officially about double that of the average for the former U.S.S.R., and in my adjusted estimates was closer to triple the national rate, which was already high. The inadequate skills of the medical staff, even outside Central Asia, in the Ukraine, for example, led to extensive amounts of asphyxia, pneumonia, respiratory-disorder syndrome, and very premature births, according to a September 1988 disclosure about the inadequate skills of attending medical personnel.

Successes in some areas such as orthopedics, opthamology, and surgical stapling must be acknowledged. But the lack of capabilities in other areas can be astonishing—partly due to a lack of quality but perhaps even more to a lack of instrumentation, sterile room facilities, CAT scans, basic diagnostic equipment, single-use syringes, bandages, disposable needles, wheelchairs, and other simple equipment, in addition to hot water, aspirins, sheets, and complex antibiotics. One of the results of this is an inability to match blood accurately. Thus, it is not surprising that the success rate in treating children with leukemia in the former Soviet Union is only 10 percent, whereas in the Federal Republic of Germany (before its consolidation with East Germany) the success rate for treatment of such patients was 75 percent, and in the United States, 70 percent. As one former Soviet commentator noted, military dependent children who became ill with leukemia, and were sent home from Germany because the parents could not pay for medical treatment, received what was tantamount to a death sentence.

FOREIGN ASSISTANCE

Thus the effort of many foreign organizations to provide emergency help as well as equipment to the former Soviet Union is crucial. In the case of one organization, the Gorbachev Foundation, there is an effort under way to collect over $2,000,000 to pay for a sterile room and equipment for the treatment of children by a Dr. Rumyantsev (of Moscow), whose record for successful treatment is close to that of the Western countries noted. Whether the Foundation will be able to collect such monies is not known at this time. But it is part of a pattern of outside funding that is assisting the former republics of the former U.S.S.R. to overcome the health crisis they face in the short term. The lack of money for state budgetary allocations witnessed in the Russian Federation, for example, has led to an acceleration of the time for introduction of medical insurance in order to obviate the non-availability of some 40 billion rubles for the health sector. Of a planned budget of over 60 billion rubles, only projects costing some 25 billion rubles were funded. Correspondingly, the shortage of funds can be demonstrated from the inability to meet plans for the purchase of pharmaceuticals. Russian medical plans called for an expenditure of 650 million foreign currency rubles in the first 6 months of 1992; in actuality, only 12 million were available. [12] In the spring of 1991, *Kommunist Tadzhistana* reported that "there are no drugs in the pharmacies," but at the same time, many drugs and medical supplies were being retained in local warehouses—perhaps to ensure that enough would be available for an emergency until the last minute before their expiration date, perhaps to be distributed to favored pharmacies in the capital city, or just as likely, to be stolen by the warehouse staff for sale on the black market or to patients. [13] Moreover, 558 drugs were not produced by the domestic drug industry. The Deputy General Director of the Moscow's Pharmacy Association decried the state of supply in mid-1991 in Moscow (as in Tadzhikistan) and concluded that "if the government does not urgently find the funds and take resolute action, the lives of millions (sic) of our people will be in jeopardy." [14] She claimed "our so-called production capacities, because of their unique antiquity, are incapable of resolving a single problem. Output has been declining year after year even at leading enterprises of the country." Funds have certainly not been available from domestic sources and outside help in supplying medications may help only up to a point, perhaps not

[12] Itar-TASS (in English) World Service, 1640 gmt, 9 June 199 cited in BBC, *Summary of World Broadcasts, Part 1, The Former USSR*, 13 June 1992, p. SU/1406 C2/2.
[13] Z. Pulatova, "Where Do the Drugs Go?," *Kommunist Tadzhikistana*, 3 April 1991, p. 3, translated in JPRS, *USSR. Behavioral and Life Sciences, ULS-91-017, 7 October 1991, p. 43.*
[14] N. Ragimov, "Publication Follow-up: Save Yourselves, Whoever Can! But What If You Can't?," *Moskovskaya Pravda*, 26 June 1991, p. 2, translated in JPRS, *Soviet Union: Political Affairs*, JPRS-UPA-91-038, 26 August 1991, p. 61.

sufficiently to reduce the hazard to many among the millions of persons referred to above.

HEALTH DATA

Under conditions of uncertainty, with priority given to economic growth, and with breakdowns in cooperation among statistical agencies, it is likely that much health data will be either incomplete or undercounted. For example, a number of statistical sources stipulate that their tables "exclude Lithuania." Perhaps Armenia and Azerbaydzhan, too occupied with their internecine struggles, will not bother to submit mundane statistical tables to a Moscow organization. At the same time, many people will not go to a medical facility given their knowledge about the lack of medications, or because of the stress of everyday life. The allegation that there has been a major increase in suicide among the elderly could be a signal for others who have trouble coping with current conditions. I would hazard that mortality figures will be more accurate than morbidity figures given the necessity for a death certificate. Mortality figures, therefore, will be more complete than morbidity figures. What might look like an improvement could, in reality, be quite different. Analysis of health and the demand for resources will therefore be more complicated because of "poorer" medical statistics.

THE HEALTH SECTOR IN THE SOVIET AND RUSSIAN ECONOMIES: FROM REFORM TO FRAGMENTATION TO TRANSITION

By Christopher Mark Davis *

CONTENTS

SUMMARY

In the traditional Soviet command economy, there were pervasive, chronic shortages and the health sector had a low priority. As a consequence, the medical system operated subject to tight budget constraints, received inadequate supplies from medical industry and import agencies, and developed on an extensive basis. On the output side, it provided the population with insufficient quantities of medical services and distributed medical care inequitably

* Christopher Mark Davis is Lecturer in Russian and East European Political Economy, Oxford University and Fellow, Wolfson College. Research for this paper was supported by grants from the Economic and Social Research Council through a project at Oxford University on "Central Control, Disequilibrium and Private Activity in Socialist Economies" and the British Government through a project at the University of Birmingham, "The Soviet Biotechnological, Pharmaceutical and Chemical Industries." This paper is dedicated to my father, Professor Russell Davis.

through a variety of rationing devices. During the period of *perestroika*, numerous reforms were introduced in medical institutions and attempts were made to raise the priority of the health sector. These remedial efforts were undermined, however, by the slackening of central control of economic processes after 1988 and the eventual collapse of production and exchange. Following the demise of the U.S.S.R. as a nation, the previously unified health sector was fragmented into 15 separate ones located in the successor states. They introduced a variety of medical reforms. At roughly the same time, the new governments launched radical programs of transition from command to market systems. To date, developments in the transitional economy of Russia have not been more conducive to the promotion of the health of the population than were those in the Soviet economic system. It remains to be seen whether the situation will improve in the future. [1]

THE SOVIET HEALTH SECTOR IN A COMMAND ECONOMY DURING PERESTROIKA

THE HEALTH SECTOR IN THE TRADITIONAL COMMAND ECONOMY

Developments in the health sector of the Soviet command economy were determined by the dynamics and interactions of health conditions, illness patterns and demand, six medically related economic institutions, and final health outputs (such as mortality rates). [2] In the period 1965–85 health conditions in the U.S.S.R. deteriorated, illness increased, and the demand for curative medical services grew substantially. [3] The institutions in the health sector that produced and distributed medical services and products were constrained in their responses because the government forced them to operate with a low priority status in a shortage economy. [4] The Soviet medical system adopted an extensive development strategy that placed greatest emphasis on expanding output in quantitative terms and neglected improvements in the quality of services. The excess demand for medical services caused chronic shortages of medical equipment, medicines, and instruments. Medical care was rationed through differentiations in subsystems, queuing, and waiting lists. Technological innovation in health institutions was inhibited and patients were increasingly forced to rely on the second economy. Finally, the malfunctioning medical system was unable to prevent the deterioration of health output indicators; age-specific death rates rose and life expectancy declined.

---

[1] This article presents an abbreviated version of the author's analysis and limited documentation. Assessments of the health sector in the traditional, reforming, and transitional economies can be found in Davis (1983, 1987, 1989, 1992).

[2] At the start of the *perestroika* period these institutions were: the central health bureaucracy (e.g., *Gosplan*), medical system (the Ministry of Health USSR), medical supply network (the *Glavnoe Aptecheskoe Upravlenie* (*GAPU*), or Main Pharmaceutical Administration, and *Soyuzmedtekhnika* for medical equipment), medical industry (the Ministry of Medical Industry USSR), biomedical R&D (the Academy of Medical Sciences USSR), and medical foreign trade (the foreign trade organization *Medexport*).

[3] Feshbach (1987) and Davis (1988).

[4] Davis (1989).

GORBACHEV'S HEALTH PROMOTION STRATEGY AND PLAN

The Gorbachev regime acknowledged the deficiencies in the health sector and criticized the past work of all institutions. A new health promotion strategy was adopted that called for health-maximizing behavior by the population (e.g., a reduction in alcohol consumption), shifting health-sector institutions onto an intensive development path, and more effective coordination of their activities. In the medical system, a major experiment was carried out in three regions of the U.S.S.R. that introduced quasi-market relations between medical establishments in an attempt to improve both the quality and efficiency of their work. [5] However, the conservative 12th Five-Year Plan did not significantly increase the resources of health institutions. In 1987 a more radical health reform program was adopted and additional funds were allocated to the medical system. [6]

DEVELOPMENTS IN THE HEALTH SECTOR DURING 1985–88

During the early phase of *perestroika* there were some improvements in demographic conditions, food supply, and housing. On the negative side, industrial pollution worsened and the April 1986 accident at the Chernobyl nuclear reactor released large amounts of radioactive material into the atmosphere. The inputs, finance, and output of the medical system increased as shown in Tables 1–3. There was modest growth in the facilities, personnel, and output of the medical supply network (Table 4). The output of pharmaceutical, vitamins, and medical equipment by the medical industry increased at close to the planned rate of 7 percent per annum, from 4.7 to 5.7 billion rubles (Table 5). Despite this, the satisfaction of the country's requirements for medicines by the domestic industry's output worsened from 52.1 to 48.1 percent. The supply deficit was reduced by imports of medicaments worth about one billion foreign trade rubles (Table 6). Over 90 percent of these goods came from socialist countries.

The prevalence of most infectious diseases (e.g., typhus, diphtheria, tetanus) and the accident rate decreased. Infant mortality declined to 24.7 deaths per 1,000 live births and life expectancy increased to a peak of 69.8 in 1987 (Table 7). In sum, health sector institutions were moderately effective at this time in enhancing the health of the population.

---

[5] In this experiment regional polyclinics were given the whole budget allocation for the region and then had to purchase services from other medical facilities.

[6] These new measures were outlined in the document "Basic Guidelines for the Development of Protection of the Population's Health and for the Restructuring of the USSR's Health-Care System During the 12th Five Year Plan and the Period Up to 2000."

TABLE 1. Soviet Medical Facilities and Personnel, 1985-91.

Indicator	1985	1986	1987	1988	1989	1990	1991
Hospitals (thousands)..............................	23.3	23.5	23.6	23.5	23.7	24.1	24.3
Outpatient Clinics (thousands)	39.1	40.1	40.8	41.3	42.8	43.9	44.4
Hospital Beds (thousands)	3,607.7	3,659.8	3,711.8	3,762.6	3,822.3	3,832.1	3,837.0
Hospital Beds (per 10,000 population) ..	129.9	130.1	130.6	131.3	132.9	132.6	132.3
Doctors (thousands)...............................	1,170.4	1,201.7	1,231.2	1,255.7	1,278.3	1,279.2	1,279.7
Doctors (per 10,000 population)...........	42.0	42.7	43.3	43.8	44.4	44.2	44.1
Middle Medical Personnel (thousands) ...	3,158.9	3,226.9	3,288.6	3,351.7	3,386.0	3,420.2	3,437.3
Scientific Workers in Medical Science and Pharmacology (thousands).........	77.3	78.6	80.2	81.4	84.5	86.0	86.8

Sources: Hospitals: 1985, 1988-90—*Narodnoe 1990*, p. 257; 1986-87—*Okhrana* (1990), p. 113; 1991—Estimate. Outpatient Clinics: 1985-90—*Narodnoe 1990*, p. 242; 1991—Estimate. Hospital Beds: 1985, 1990—*Narodnoe 1990*, p. 258; 1986-89—*Okhrana* (1990), p. 114; 1991—Estimate. Hospital Beds Per 10,000: 1985, 1990—*Narodnoe 1990*, p. 258; 1986-89—*Okhrana* (1990), p. 114; 1991—Estimate. Doctors: 1985, 1990—*Narodnoe 1990*, p. 254; 1986-89—*Okhrana* (1990), p. 81; 1991—Estimate. Doctors Per 10,000: 1985-89—*Okhrana* (1990), p. 81; 1990—*Narodnoe 1990*, p. 254; 1991—Estimate. Middle Medical Personnel: 1985, 1990—*Narodnoe 1990*, p. 255; 1986-89—*Okhrana* (1990), p. 81; 1991—Estimate. Scientific Workers: 1985-88—*Okhrana* (1990), p. 107; 1989-91—Estimates.

TABLE 2. Soviet Medical System Finance, 1985-91.

Indicator	1985	1986	1987	1988	1989	1990	1991
State Health Budget (billion rubles)	17.5	17.9	19.3	21.7	24.4	28.3	36.6
Health Share of Total State Budget (percent)	4.6	4.3	4.5	4.8	5.1	5.6	5.4
Total Health Expenditure (billion rubles)...............	22.5	23.5	25.3	28.9	33.6	36.0	46.3
Annual Rate of Growth of Health Expenditures (percent)	NA	4.4	7.7	14.2	16.3	7.1	28.6
Real Total Health Expenditures (billion 1985 rubles)..	22.5	22.8	23.7	26.0	28.7	28.1	24.1
Health Expenditure Per Capita (rubles)	81.4	84.3	89.8	101.6	117.2	124.7	159.6
Health Expenditure Share of National Income Utilized (percent)..	4.0	4.1	4.3	4.7	5.1	5.1	5.0
Health Expenditure Share of Gross National Product (percent)	2.9	2.9	3.1	3.3	3.6	3.6	3.5
Medical Wage as a Percent of Whole Economy Wage...	0.70	0.69	0.71	0.69	0.68	0.68	0.66

Sources: State Health Budget: 1985—*Gos. Byud. SSSR 1981-85, p. 32*; *1986, 1987—Gos. Byud. 1988*, p. 14; 1988, 1989—*Gos. Byud. 1990*, p. 16; 1990—*Narodnoe 1990*, p. 16 but deduct 0.2 billion rubles for physical education; 1991—Pavlyutkin et al. (1991), p. 6. Health Share of Budget: 1985-1990—Divide row 1 by the total expenditure in *Narodnoe 1989*, p. 612 and *Narodnoe 1990*, p. 16; 1991—Estimate. Total Expenditure: Row 1 plus non-budget spending given in Davis (1992). Annual Rate of Growth: Calculate with usual methodology. Real Total Expenditure: Current series deflated in accordance with the methodology in Davis (1966). Medical system inflation rates for 1985-90 estimated to be one-half national one given in Stepanov (1991), p. 64. 1991 rate estimated to be 50 percent. Expenditure Per Capita: Divide row 3 by the Soviet population. Share of NIU: Divide row 3 by national income utilized given for 1985-89 in *Narodnoe 1989*, p. 15 and for 1990 in *Narodnoe 1990*. 1991 estimated to be 15 percent less than 1990. Share of GNP: Divide row 3 by gross national product for 1985-90 given in *Narodnoe 1990*, p. 5. 1991 estimated to be 17 percent less than 1990. Medical Wage Percent: 1985-90—Divide average wage of health service by average wage of whole economy given in *Narodnoe 1990*. NA—Not available.

TABLE 3. Outputs of Medical Services in the U.S.S.R., 1985-91.

Indicator	1985	1986	1987	1988	1989	1990	1991
Outpatient Visits plus Doctor Home Visits (million)	3,168.4	3,200.1	3,231.8	3,063.9	2,896.0	2,867.0	2,838.4
Preventive Screenings (million)	123.2	125.0	127.9	124.7	121.9	118.9	116.0
Hospital Bed Days (million)	1,172.5	1,164.9	1,156.2	1,146.8	1,139.0	1,116.3	1,106.6
Hospitalizations (million)	69.6	71.9	73.4	73.5	70.3	70.3	69.6
First Aid Delivered on Outpatient Basis or by Emergency Services (million cases)	94.9	95.4	95.9	100.5	98.3	98.4	97.4
Hospital Bed Utilization Per Year (days)	325.0	318.3	311.5	304.8	298.0	291.3	288.4
Operations Carried Out in Hospitals (million)	11.0	11.4	11.6	11.6	11.6	11.8	11.6

Sources: Outpatient Visits: 1985, 1989—*Okhrana* (1990), p. 126; 1986-88, 1990-91—Estimates. Screenings: 1985, 1989—*Narodnoe 1989*, p. 227; 1987—*Narodnoe 1987*, p. 550; 1988—*Narodnoe 1988*, p. 230; 1986, 1990-91—Estimates. Bed Days: 1985—Davis (1987); 1986-91—Estimates (hospital beds x bed utilization). Hospitalizations: 1985-89—*Okhrana* (1990), p. 123; 1990-91—Estimates. First Aid: 1985, 1990— *Narodnoe 1990*, p. 259; 1987—*Narodnoe 1987*, p. 553; 1988—*Narodnoe 1988*, p. 227; 1989—*Okhrana* (1990), p. 132; 1986, 1991—Estimates. Bed Utilization: 1985, 1989—*Okhrana*. Operations: 1988, 1989— *Okhrana* (1990), p. 136; 1985-87, 1990-91—Estimates.

TABLE 4. The Soviet Medical Supply System, 1985-91.

Indicator	1985	1986	1987	1988	1989	1990	1991
Pharmacies (thousands)	29.5	29.7	30.2	30.2	30.3	30.5	30.6
Pharmacists (thousands)	271.3	280.0	285.5	291.0	307.6	318.0	323.7
Total Sales Turnover (million rubles)	4,385.3	4,547.2	4,811.0	5,203.4	5,666.8	6,228.8	6,757.9
Retail Sales (million rubles)	2,411.9	2,513.2	2,618.8	2,728.7	2,887.0	3,008.3	3,832.6
Wholesale Sales (million rubles)	1,973.4	2,034.0	2,192.2	2,474.7	2,779.8	3,220.5	2,925.3
Total Sales Turnover (million 1985 rubles)	4,385.3	4,410.8	4,504.5	4,677.4	4,841.9	4,868.5	4,397.9
Medicine Sales per Capita (rubles)	12.5	12.9	13.5	14.4	15.6	17.0	15.4
Satisfaction of Requirements for Medicines by Domestic Production and Imports (percent)	86.0	83.0	81.5	78.0	86.0	72.0	60.0

Sources: Pharmacies: 1985, 1989—*Okhrana* (1990), p. 145; 1986—Kluyev (1987), p. 2; 1987—Shmakov (1987), p. 3; 1988, 1990-91—Estimates. Pharmacists: 1985-90—*Narodnoe 1990*, p. 242; 1991—Estimate. Total Sales: Row 6 plus row 7. Retail Sales: 1985—Davis (1987); 1989—Apazov (1991), p. 7 states that retail sales rose by 80.1 percent from 1979 to 1989. The 1979 value was 1,603 million rubles. This implies a 1989 value of 2,887.0 million rubles; 1986-1988, 1990-91—Estimates. Wholesale Sales: 1985—Davis (1987); 1986-91—Estimates based on the magnitude of the medicaments article in the health budget. Medicine per Capita: Estimates of medicine sales (about 80 percent of turnover) are divided by the Soviet population. Satisfaction of Requirements: 1985—Davis (1987); 1986—Estimate; 1987—Apazov and Belikov (1987), p. 1 states that satisfaction was in the range 80-83 percent; 1988, 1989—"Analiticheskie" (1991), p. 3; 1990, 1991—Pavlyutkin (1991), p. 6.

TABLE 5. The Soviet Medical Industry, 1985–91.

Indicator	1985	1986	1987	1988	1989	1990	1991
Output of Total Medical Industry (million rubles)	4,698.0	5,071.3	5,386.3	5,710.8	6,105.9	6,559.7	9,977.3
Index of Medical Industry Output (1985 = 100)	100.0	108.0	114.7	121.6	130.0	139.6	212.4
Annual Rate of Growth of Medical Industry Output (percent)	NA	8.0	6.2	6.0	6.9	7.4	52.1
Output of the Pharmaceutical Industry (million rubles)	2,878.0	3,118.0	3,321.0	3,482.0	3,687.0	3,911.0	5,948.6
Index of Output of the Pharmaceutical Industry (1985 = 100)	100.0	108.0	115.0	121.0	130.0	138.0	206.7
Annual Rate of Growth of Pharmaceutical Industry Output (percent)	7.6	8.3	6.5	4.9	5.9	6.1	52.1
Output of the Vitamin Industry (million rubles)	923.0	996.8	1,061.5	1,116.8	1,199.9	1,273.7	1,937.3
Output of the Medical Equipment Industry (million rubles)	897.0	956.5	1,003.8	1,112.0	1,219.0	1,375.0	2,091.4
Output of Total Medical Industry (million 1985 rubles)	4,698.0	4,921.3	5,044.8	5,131.9	5,214.9	5,124.2	4,611.8
Satisfaction of Requirements for Medicines by Domestic Industry (percent)	52.1	50.8	49.4	48.1	46.7	39.1	36.0

Sources: Total Industry Output: Includes Synthetic Medicinal Substances, Antibiotics, Prepared Medicines, Vitamins, Medical Equipment, and Medical Products of Glass and Plastic. X_{4j}, X_{7j}, X_{8j}, j = 1 ... 7. Total Output Index: $X_{1j}/(4,623.0$ million rubles) x 100, j = 1 ... 7. Total Rate of Growth: $(X_{1j} - X_{1,j-1})/X_{1,j-1}$ x 100. Pharmaceutical Output: Includes Synthetic Medicinal Substances, Antibiotics, and Prepared Medicines. 1985, 1988–90—*Narodnoe 1990*, p. 411; 1986–87—*Narodnoe 1989*, p. 394; 1991—Estimate. Pharmaceutical Output Index: 1985–90—*Narodnoe 1990*, p. 409; 1991—Calculated from data in row 4. Pharmaceutical Rate of Growth: $(X_{4j} - X_{4,j-1})/X_{4,j-1}$ x 100. Vitamin Output: 1985—Davis (1987); 1986–91—Estimated to grow at the same rates as pharmaceutical output given in row 6. Medical Equipment Output: Includes Medical Equipment and Medical Products of Glass and Plastic. 1985, 1988–89—*Okhrana (1990)*, p. 147; 1990—According to Orlov et al. "Resursnoe" (1991), p. 107 output in 2000 will be 2,000 billion rubles or 8 times the 1990 level. This implies that the value of output in 1990 was 1,375 billion rubles; 1986–87, 1991—Estimates. Satisfaction of Requirements: 1985, 1989–91—Apazov (1991), p. 1; 1986–88—Estimates.
NA—Not available.

CHANGES IN HEALTH STRATEGY AND REFORMS IN LATE PERESTROIKA

During 1989–91, the Gorbachev regime attempted to implement the remedial measures announced earlier and introduced a number of supplemental reforms. Changes in organization included the transfer of the medical equipment industry from *Minpribor* to the Ministry of Medium Machine Building U.S.S.R. [7] The Ministry of the Medical and Microbiological Industry U.S.S.R. was disestablished in the spring of 1991 and replaced by the State Corporation for the Production of Medicines and Medical Products (*Farmindustriya*). [8] By July it had submitted a proposal to President Gorbachev for a remedial program entitled "Medicine for the People," but this was never officially adopted. [9] There was additional turnover of health sector leaders: E. Chazov was replaced by B. Denisov as Minister of Health U.S.S.R., the Minister of the Medical Indus-

[7] Orlov, Soloshenko, and Panchenko (1991).
[8] Markar'yants (1991).
[9] Efimova (1991).

try (V. Bykov) was retired, and V. Markar'yants became the President of *Farmindustriya*.

TABLE 6. Soviet Foreign Trade in Medical Products, 1985–91.

Indicator	1985	1986	1987	1988	1989	1990	1991
Imports of Pharmaceuticals (million foreign trade rubles)	1,165.5	1,232.0	1,249.4	1,316.9	1,847.4	2,273.2	1,295.7
Exports of Pharmaceuticals (million foreign trade rubles)	104.8	102.6	107.6	107.8	100.2	89.2	44.6
Pharmaceuticals Share of Total Imports (percent)	1.7	2.0	2.1	2.0	2.6	3.2	3.2
Annual Rate of Growth of Pharmaceutical Imports (percent)	5.0	6.1	1.4	5.4	40.3	23.1	−43.0
Pharmaceutical Exports as a Share of Pharmaceutical Imports (percent)	9.0	8.3	8.6	8.2	5.4	3.9	3.4
Share of Pharmaceutical Imports from Socialist Countries (percent)	89.6	92.5	93.6	92.7	83.8	78.1	68.5
Import of Medical Equipment and Instruments (million foreign trade rubles)	362.3	349.1	343.2	396.6	462.8	904.1	515.3

Sources: Imports of Pharmaceuticals: 1985–86—*Vneshnyaya 1986*, p. 44; 1987–88—*Vneshnyaya 1988*; 1989–90—*Vneshnyaya 1990*, p. 47; 1991—Estimated from *Vneshnyaya 1991* (1992). Exports of Pharmaceuticals: 1985–86—*Vneshnyaya 1986*, p. 30; 1987–88—*Vneshnyaya 1988*; 1989–90—*Vneshnyaya 1990*, p. 33; 1991—Estimate. Pharmaceutical Share: Row 1 value divided by the value of total Soviet imports. Growth of Pharmaceutical Imports: 1985—Davis (1987); 1986–91—Calculated using the formula $(X_{1j} - X_{1,j-1})/X_{1,j-1}$ x 100, $j = 2 \ldots 7$. Pharmaceutical Exports as Share of Imports: Calculated using the formula (X_{2j}/X_{1j}) x 100, $j = 1 \ldots 7$. Socialist Share of Imports: 1985—Davis (1987); 1986–90—Add up imports from Bulgaria, Czechoslovakia, Romania, East Germany, Poland, Hungary, and Yugoslavia found in the annual volumes of *Vneshnyaya* . . . Divide sum by total of imports of pharmaceuticals. Import of Medical Equipment: 1985–86—*Vneshnyaya 1986*, p. 37; 1987–88—*Vneshnyaya 1988*; 1989–90—*Vneshnyaya 1990*, p. 40; 1991—Estimate.

TABLE 7. Health Output Indicators in the U.S.S.R., 1985–91.

Indicator	1985	1986	1987	1988	1989	1990	1991
First Diagnoses of Cancer, Age Adjusted (Cases per 100,000 population)	263.0	270.0	273.0	274.0	268.0	266.0	264.0
Salmonellosis Morbidity (cases per 100,000 population)	27.5	27.3	34.0	46.8	54.6	56.0	57.6
Temporary Work Incapacity (cases per 100 workers)	101.0	103.0	94.5	106.3	102.3	101.7	104.0
Infant Mortality Rate (deaths per 1,000 live births)	26.0	25.4	25.4	24.7	22.7	21.8	21.4
Crude Death Rate (deaths per 1,000 population)	10.6	9.8	9.9	10.1	10.0	10.3	10.6
Life Expectancy at Birth (years)	68.4	69.6	69.8	69.5	69.5	69.5	69.0
First Diagnoses of Tuberculosis (per 100,000 population)	45.7	44.8	43.7	42.0	40.0	36.9	35.9
Accidents in Production (per 10,000 workers)	56.0	56.0	55.0	54.0	55.0	57.0	59.0

Sources: 1985–88—*Okhrana* (1990) p. 37; 1989–90—*Narodnoe 1990*, p. 249; 1991—Estimate. Cancer: 1985–90—*Narodnoe 1990*, p. 246; 1991—Estimate. Salmonellosis: 1985–89—*Okhrana* (1990), p. 55; 1990—*Narodnoe 1990*, p. 245; 1991—Estimate. Accidents: 1985–90—*Narodnoe 1990*, p. 251; 1991—Estimate. Work Incapacity: 1985, 1990—*Narodnoe 1990*, p. 243; 1989—*Narodnoe 1989*, p. 223. Infant Mortality: 1985–90—*Narodnoe 1990*, p. 92; 1991—Estimate. Crude Death Rate: 1985–89—*Okhrana* (1990), p. 8; 1990—*Narodnoe 1990*; 1991—"Ekonomike stran" (1992), p. 15. Life Expectancy: 1989–90—*Okhrana* (1990), p. 20; 1991—Estimate.

Other reforms affected the functioning of health sector institutions. The economic experiment in financing the network of medical facilities in regions was continued and plans were elaborated to introduce this mechanism nationwide. By 1991 the union authorities were discussing the establishment of medical insurance to finance to provision of certain medical services. [10] Measures were taken to transform pharmacies from cost-accounting (*khozraschet*) to self-financing (*samofinansirovanie*) entities. [11] Medical industry establishments operated more independently of ministerial authorities and with greater market-orientations. In the foreign trade area, responsibility for transactions continued to be devolved and joint venture legislation was liberalized.

DEVELOPMENTS IN THE HEALTH SECTOR DURING 1989–91

In this period the conditions in the Soviet economy and its performance worsened. Shortages of food intensified while the consumption of alcohol and tobacco rose. The construction of housing fell substantially in 1991 and sanitary conditions in public establishments deteriorated. There was some reduction in pollution, but the contraction of capital investment meant that there was little progress made in altering technologies or cleaning up the environment. The incidence of a number of illnesses from infectious and degenerative diseases went up. As Table 7 indicates, the incidence of salmonellosis rose from 46.8 cases per 100,000 in 1988 to 56.0 in 1990.

The reorientation of economic plans in favor of welfare resulted in a significant increase in health expenditure in current rubles and in the health share of the budget (Table 2). But health spending in constant 1985 rubles dropped slightly in 1990 and substantially in 1991. Wages in the health sector grew more slowly than the inflation rate and were below the all-economy average.

The size of the medical system continued to expand due to the inertia of higher education and capital construction programs, the higher priority of health, and the real growth of resources (Table 1). It was unable to respond effectively to the rising demand for its services, however, because of intensifying problems with its capital stock, labor, and supplies. For example, a survey of hospitals revealed that 9 percent were in dangerous condition, 14 percent needed major reconstruction, 15 percent had no water supply, 49 percent had no hot water, and 24 percent had no sewage system. [12] The output of most medical services and their quality worsened in this period (Table 3). A substantial amount of the demand of the population for medical care remained unsatisfied.

The medical supply network continued to grow and its turnover increased (Table 4). However, the strained financial situation of pharmacies deteriorated further because controls were kept on the prices of the commodities they sold whereas the costs of domestically produced and imported goods went up 3–10 times. Their operating losses in 1991 amounted to 15 billion rubles. [13] There were growing difficulties in obtaining domestic supplies:

---

[10] Pavlyutkin, Boiko, Kravets, and Lukashov (1991).
[11] Apazov (1991)
[12] *Okhrana* (1990), p. 150.
[13] Chernyavskii (1991).

For this reason the satisfaction of the requirements of the health service for medicaments by domestic industry decreases every year: in 1985—52.1 percent, in 1989—46.7 percent, while in 1990 it is expected to be 39.1 percent, and the prognosis for 1991 is even worse. In the face of orders of 7.5 billion rubles, it is anticipated that domestic industry will provide resources worth 2.7 billion rubles, that is 36 percent of requirements . . . [14]

In 1991 the enterprises of the medical industry were located in old buildings requiring substantial repairs and "80 percent of the equipment being used in the branch was completely worn out." [15] Many plants had hazardous working conditions and generated substantial air and water pollution. These poor conditions reflected the low priority the state attached to the medical industry and a development strategy that placed great emphasis on imports of medicines from East European countries. [16] The current price output of the industry rose to 10.0 billion rubles in 1991, but was only 4.6 billion constant 1985 rubles in 1991 (Table 5). Its satisfaction of domestic requirements for medicines fell to 36 percent in 1991.

In accordance with new priorities, the government increased imports of medicaments by 40 percent in 1989 and 23 percent in 1990, causing the pharmaceutical share of total imports to rise from 2.0 to 3.2 percent (Table 6). The OECD share of imports grew substantially, whereas that of the socialist countries fell from 93 to 78 percent. In 1991 purchases of medicaments from the ex-CMEA area declined by 43 percent after trade with that region was shifted onto a convertible currency basis. [17] Severe cut-backs were also made in imports for the medical industry. [18]

The combined deterioration of health conditions and of medical services generated a worsening of many health output indicators (Table 7). Rates of degenerative and infectious diseases rose, as did accidents in production, temporary work incapacity, and invalidity. Infant mortality continued to decline, but age-specific death rates for all adult age groups increased. [19] There were growing numbers of deaths from murder, suicide and war. The crude mortality rate went up to 10.6 in 1991, its 1985 magnitude. Life expectancy at birth fell to 69.0 years in 1991.

THE FRAGMENTATION OF THE SOVIET HEALTH SECTOR IN 1991

THE FIGHT TO MAINTAIN CENTRAL CONTROL OF THE HEALTH SECTOR

In 1990, the final full year of existence of the U.S.S.R., health conditions and illness patterns varied considerably across republics. The distribution of health institutions is shown in Table 8. Only Russia and Ukraine possessed the medical facilities, distribution

---

[14] Apazov (1991), p. 1.
[15] Markar'yants (1991), p. 3.
[16] According to Bykov (1991, p. 4) the industry was so neglected in the 1980s that no new factories were put into operation during the decade.
[17] Vneshnaya 1992, p. 14; Ekonomika stran (1992), p. 16.
[18] Markar'yants (1991) stated that "the deliveries of imported raw materials and pharmaceutical substances used in the production of medicines and medical products have practically stopped."
[19] Narodnoe 1990 (1991), p. 90.

networks, industrial enterprises, and R&D establishments necessary for reasonably self-sufficient health sectors.

TABLE 8. Soviet Health Indicators by Republic in 1990.

Republic	Tuberculosis Incidence [a]	Hospital Beds Per 10,000	Outpatient Treatment Capacity [b]	Pharmacies [c]	Doctors Per 10,000	Middle Medical Personnel Per 10,000	Infant Mortality [d]
All U.S.S.R.	36.9	132.6	193.2	30,304	44.2	118.3	21.8
RSFSR	34.2	137.5	217.4	14,851	46.9	122.6	17.4
Ukraine	31.9	135.5	173.1	6,126	44.0	117.5	12.9
Byelorussia	29.8	132.3	185.1	1,129	40.5	115.6	11.9
Uzbekistan	46.1	123.7	133.7	2,073	35.8	110.7	34.6
Kazakhstan	65.8	136.2	182.8	1,899	41.2	123.9	26.4
Georgia	28.9	110.7	239.2	665	59.2	118.3	15.9
Azerbaijan	36.2	102.2	146.9	734	39.3	98.9	23.0
Lithuania	NA	124.4	233.4	383	46.1	127.4	10.3
Moldova	39.6	131.4	195.4	455	40.0	118.6	19.0
Latvia	27.4	148.1	216.9	374	49.6	117.4	13.7
Kirghizia	53.3	119.8	131.8	359	36.7	NA	30.0
Tadzhikistan	44.4	105.8	97.4	412	27.1	81.3	40.7
Armenia	17.6	89.8	137.8	297	42.8	103.0	18.6
Turkmenia	63.6	113.3	118.6	326	35.7	105.0	45.2
Estonia	20.6	121.0	215.7	221	45.7	96.2	12.3

Sources: Tuberculosis: *Narodnoe 1990*, p. 249. Hospital Beds: *Narodnoe 1990*, p. 258. Outpatient: *Narodnoe 1990*, p. 256. Pharmacies: *Okhrana* (1990), p. 145. Doctors: *Narodnoe 1990*, p. 254. Middle Medical: *Narodnoe 1990*, p. 255. Infant Mortality: *Narodnoe 1990*, p. 92.
[a] Tuberculosis incidence is measured by number of first diagnoses per 100,000 population.
[b] Outpatient treatment capacity is measured by thousands of visits per shift per 10,000 population.
[c] The number of pharmacies is for the year 1989.
[d] Infant mortality is measured by deaths per 1,000 live births during the first year of life.

During the two years following the Supreme Soviet elections in the spring of 1989, pressure mounted on the union health authorities to devolve their power. There was some progress in this direction. By 1991 the Ministry of Health U.S.S.R. had agreed to reduce its size, narrow its functions to those of a strategic nature, and pass on most responsibilities for operational planning and management of medical care to the republic ministries. One official even raised the possibility that the union ministry could be abolished after a transition period of several years.

But in this period the Moscow authorities believed that it was essential to keep under central control the organizations concerned with the distribution, production, research, and foreign trade of medical products. This cautious approach conflicted with the aspirations of several republics, notably Russia and Ukraine, to gain complete control of their health sectors. The RSFSR government elaborated a market-oriented health reform program and in 1991 introduced legislation to transform the medical system into one based on insurance financing. [20] The Ukrainian *NPO Ukrmedbioprom*, which was set up in 1989 to oversee the development of the medical industry in the republic, came into increasing conflict with

---

[20] See "Zakon" (1991) for the law on medical insurance.

the center. In January 1991 it received notice from *Minmedbio-prom SSSR* of the suspension of all transfers to Ukraine of capital investment, budget support of biomedical R&D, hard-currency, and medical products.[21]

Following the failure of the August 1991 coup attempt, demands for a radical change in the Soviet health sector intensified. On 7 September 1991 the Ministry of Health U.S.S.R. hosted a meeting of republic health officials to discuss the future of central leadership.[22] Union officials argued for the transformation of the ministry into an inter-republic coordinating body with limited responsibilities for issues of common concern, such as production and distribution of medical products. The Russian representative disagreed and stated that his ministry did not consider that the continued existence of a central body was necessary. Most other republic officials spoke in favor of some type of all-union body.

THE BREAK-UP OF THE SOVIET HEALTH SECTOR

Debates about the future of the Soviet health sector continued through the early autumn as the economic situation deteriorated, negotiations continued on a revised union treaty, central power crumbled, and the republics asserted control over state property on their territory. Working conditions in all health establishments worsened and anxiety increased among staff. For example, an article in November 1991 argued that medical industry enterprises could continue to function on an all-union basis or could adapt to their transformation into republican units, but the existing uncertainty made planning for the future impossible.[23] In the end, developments in the health sector were determined by higher-level political decisions. In November the ministries of the union government were disestablished and their staff, resources, and subordinate units were transferred to the independent states evolving from the republics. The next month the commonwealth treaty was signed and the U.S.S.R. was dissolved.

At the end of 1991 the Baltic and commonwealth states were experiencing worsening health conditions and rising illness rates. Each had an almost random assortment of health institutions, many of which were highly specialized, monopolistic, and designed to operate under central control in a unified Soviet economy. Their medical facilities had demoralized staff with falling real wages and acute shortages of all supplies. The commonwealth treaty provided no mechanism for meaningful inter-state coordination in the health field. To cope with these challenges, each country had to develop emergency health programs that were consistent with their efforts to shift from command to market economies. For example, in November 1991 Estonia began to lay the foundation for the national system of medical insurance that was introduced in January 1992.[24] Due to space constraints only developments in Russia can be examined in this paper.

[21] Kalita (1991).
[22] "Ministry" (1991).
[23] Efimova (1991).
[24] Grave (1992).

THE RUSSIAN HEALTH SECTOR IN A TRANSITIONAL ECONOMY: 1992

ECONOMIC TRANSITION AND HEALTH REFORM IN RUSSIA

In January 1992 the Russian government implemented a "shock therapy" program to promote the rapid transition from a command to a market economy. The economic results this generated were not especially positive during the first half of 1992. [25] Industrial production fell by 13 percent, investment by 46 percent, and foreign trade turnover by 30 percent from depressed first-half 1991 levels. Wholesale and retail prices rose 8–10 times their December 1991 levels. The state budget remained in severe deficit and social welfare programs were underfunded. Little progress was made in privatization or in promoting competition.

During 1991–92 the Russian government developed a health reform strategy to complement the economic transition program. [26] It made the usual calls for a greater emphasis on preventive medicine and for participation by the population and enterprises in health promotion. More originally, it proposed a decisive reduction of the role of the state in health care, the introduction of national medical insurance, the shift of virtually all health institutions onto a commercial basis, and the involvement of foreign firms in the development of the health sector. The legal basis for these reforms was to be provided by a law "On Safeguarding the Health of Citizens." In July, the Russian government unveiled proposals to augment the medical insurance program with a social protection voucher system. [27] This would give all citizens set amounts of quasi-money that they could spend on health, education, social security, and housing.

Since Russia became independent in autumn 1991, the names of most organizations in the health sector have changed, but their functions, and often their staff, have remained largely unaltered. The old Ministry of Health has been divided into preventive and curative branches, respectively the State Committee for Sanitary and Epidemiological Inspection and the Ministry of Health of the Russian Federation. Medical workers are represented by the Trade Union of Health Service Workers of the Russian Federation. The medical supply system is managed by the production associations *Rosfarmatsiya* (the old *Soyuzfarmatsiya RSFSR*) and *Medtekhnika* (the former *Soyuzmedtekhnika SSSR*). The medical industry in Russia is still organized into the corporation *Farmindustriya*. Medical foreign trade is run by a state firm *Farmimpex*, incorporating components of the former *Medexport* and *Soyuzfarmatsiya SSSR*.

At lower levels, all medical facilities are being encouraged to offer "supplemental" services (which often are quite basic) for fees to individual patients and on a contract basis to economic organizations. Restrictions on the provision of medical care by private practitioners and cooperatives have been lifted and regulations have been altered to make it easier for them to rent state medical equipment. Polyclinics are being reorganized so that comprehensive first-contact care can be provided by family doctors who can be se-

---

[25] "Sotsial'no ... kvartale" (1992), "Sotsial'no ... polugodii" (1992).
[26] "Rossiiskoe" (1991), "Kakoi" (1991)
[27] Kaser (1992b).

lected by patients. Pharmacies and medical industry enterprises have become self-financing and steps are being taken, in the midst of controversy, to privatize them in 1993. [28] Finally, medical foreign trade has been put on a hard-currency, commercial basis, although it is dominated by *Farmimpex.*

DEVELOPMENTS IN THE HEALTH SECTOR DURING 1992

The continuing collapse of the economy and Russian government policies caused a worsening of health conditions in the initial six months of 1992. Real per capita income and the consumption of food sharply declined. By the middle of 1992, 90 percent of families in Russia were living in poverty. [29] The birth rate (11.5 per 1,000 in 1992) fell and the number of refugees in Russia rose to 320 thousand in July. [30] The integrated index of the quality of life fell from 1.07 in 1988 to 0.95 in 1991 to 0.87 in the first half of 1992. [31] Drastic cuts in social investment (30–40 percent) accelerated the physical deterioration in public facilities, residential neighborhoods, and water and sewage systems. Increments to the housing stock dropped by 34 percent in 1992. Although inadequate funds were provided to promote environmental protection, pollution probably declined due to falling industrial production. The rapid growth of the unregulated private market in food products and the breakdown in public hygiene caused a worsening of the bacterial environment. Sanitary inspectors were routinely intimidated by criminals with links to firms in industry and trade that were violating safety or hygiene norms. [32] Dietary deficiencies weakened the population and made them more susceptible to illness. The incidence of food poisoning grew and acute intestinal infections more than doubled in Moscow. Cancer and heart disease rates went up, as did that of tuberculosis.

The ability of the Russian medical system to respond to these health challenges and to implement its reform program was severely constrained by the effects of tight budget constraints, price rises, and the decline of the economy. The health service needed 35 billion rubles during the first quarter but only 17.9 was allocated initially. Actual spending apparently was increased to 24 billion rubles by a wage settlement in January. A March version of the annual state budget called for expenditure of 153.2 billion rubles on health over the whole of 1992, which was 7.4 times more than in 1991 and 7.3 percent of the total budget (Table 9). Of this, 31 billion rubles were to be spent by the republic ministry of health and 122.0 billion by the local health departments. A revised budget in June allocated an additional 93 billion rubles to health, raising the total to 246.3 billion rubles. But the lower health share of the revised budget, 5.6 percent, was the same as that of the U.S.S.R. budget of 1990.

---

[28] See Vakatov (1992) on the privatization of pharmacies. Article 2.3.8 of "Gosudarstvennaya" (1992) in principle authorizes the private ownership of medical industry enterprises.
[29] "Nam vsegda" (1992).
[30] Tishuk (1992), "Sotsial'no ... palugodii" (1992), p. 5.
[31] According to Sagradov (1992) this index takes into account health, education, qualifications, birthrate, and marriage.
[32] Prokin (1992).

TABLE 9. Projected Russian Government Health Expenditure in 1992.

| Budget Component | Budget Message of 10/3/92 | | | Supplements | | | Total for 1992 | | |
| | Consolidated Budget | Budget Breakdown | | Consolidated Budget | Budget Breakdown | | Consolidated Budget | Budget Breakdown | |
		Republic	Territory		Republic	Territory		Republic	Territory
Health Expenditure (billion rubles)	153.2	31.1	122.0	93.1	18.4	74.7	246.3	49.6	196.7
Total Budget Expenditure (billion rubles)	2,107.1	1,485.4	621.8	2,267.1	1,563.6	703.5	4,374.2	3,049.0	1,325.2
Health Share of Budget (percent)	7.3	2.1	19.6	4.1	1.2	10.6	5.6	1.6	14.8

Source: Verkhovnyy (1992), p. 130, 145.

Reports from localities and institutions corroborate the charge of insufficient funding. In Moscow, medical establishments received only 45 percent of the necessary amount during the first quarter. Sufficiency varied by budget article, from 10 percent of the necessary sum for capital repairs to 67 percent for acquisition of medicaments. [33] In June the Minister of Health stated that medical science was receiving 4.5 times less than it requested and the Chairman of the State Committee for Sanitary-Epidemiological Inspection complained that his organization had received 42 percent of necessary funds in the first quarter and not much more in the second. [34] Throughout Russia resource-starved facilities were forced by circumstances to market their services for extra revenue. For example, the Cardiological Scientific Center obtained only 30–40 percent of its finances from the state and had to earn the rest by cutting back on research and selling basic medical services. [35] The Erevan republican maternity hospital began to offer "birth in comfortable circumstances" for 1,000 rubles. Prices of medical services rose on average by a factor of seven over the year from May 1991 and by 21 percent during May 1992 alone. [36]

During 1992 the functioning of Russian medical facilities was severely disrupted by problems with their inputs of labor, capital, and supplies. The falling real wages of medical staff prompted the medical trade union to call for nationwide strikes in January and April. [37] But these were cancelled after pay settlements in January, April, and June ensured that average medical wages would increase 2.7 times during 1992. [38]

---

[33] Smirnov (1992a).
[34] Smirnov (1992c).
[35] Chazov (1992).
[36] Tseny (1992).
[37] Zolotova (1992a, b)
[38] Vasil'eva (1992a, b).

During the first half of the year the budgets of medical establishments for capital construction, repair, and acquisitions were cut disproportionately severely, while the prices of capital inputs soared to about 17 times their December levels. [39] Real investment in all types of "nonproductive" construction dropped by 42 percent from the 1991 level. As a result, the number of hospital beds introduced (1,900) was 57 percent that of the first half of 1991. Only minor repairs were made to facilities or machinery that was in miserable shape before the transition commenced.

In December 1991 the Russian Ministry of Health identified 600–700 vital drugs, vaccines, and sera and allocated extra resources to support their production or import. [40] Over the next six months, though, medicine acquisition budgets were held below minimum requirement levels, drug prices rose substantially (by a factor of 16 for medicines used by the Botkin hospital), domestic output fell, and imports were cut back. [41] As a consequence, only about 50 percent of health service demand was satisfied. Hospitals and polyclinics were forced to function with severe deficits of medicines, anesthetics, instruments (scalpels and needles), bandages, linen, x-ray film, and food.

There has been much discussion of the transition to medical insurance and debate of its merits. [42] But only the most modest progress has been made in establishing the administrative guidelines, legislation, and infrastructure of the program. Doubts have been raised about the availability of non-state resources to support an insurance system. [43] One article made the point that European countries had developed their insurance systems over 100 years, whereas Russia wanted to make an transition to insurance in the course of several months without adequate preparation. [44]

There is some continuity in medical care organization. The network of well-endowed medical facilities serving the political and economic elite, criticized by President Yeltsin while in opposition, remain in existence. In an interview in April, the director of the Botkin Hospital stated: "To us it is known that 25 percent of the doctors in Moscow work in elite hospitals of the former Fourth Main Administration, atomic industry, MVD, of the KGB. There all has remained the same: better conditions, much higher pay." [45]

The former head of the elite service, E. Chazov, said he was not involved in treating the current leaders in Russia: "And I even do not know which doctors are involved in this. I suspect, of course, that they are specialists from the same Fourth Main Administration. It is true that now it is called something different . . . ." [46]

In the evolving, somewhat chaotic, market conditions, medical cooperatives continue to function. But there has been greater interest among enterpreneurial staff in developing private facilities and

[39] "Sotsial'no . . . polugodii" (1992), p. 5.

[40] Essential (1992).

[41] In Kuzin (1992) the director of the Botkin hospital said that its annual budgetary requirement in 1992 would be 100 million rubles instead of 14.5 million rubles as in 1991.

[42] An excellent recent article by Helmstadter (1992) examines the official medical insurance program in Russia and progress in implementing it.

[43] Korepanov (1992).

[44] Smirnov (1992a).

[45] Kuzin (1992).

[46] Chazov (1992).

in positioning themselves to take advantage of the state program of privatization. In one case, health officials apparently were bribed into illegally transferring ownership of polyclinic serving pensioners to a private company, which planned to fire the staff and rent out the building to a foreign firm for conversion into a hard currency hotel. [47]

The performance of medical facilities in Russia has clearly worsened during 1992. The quantity of services provided has fallen either because of production bottlenecks caused by shortages or because potential patients have avoided the queues, waiting lists, and increasingly ineffectual medical care. In the Botkin hospital gynecological operations have had to be postponed because of the shortage of anesthetics. There have been numerous reports of doctors performing surgery with razors, re-using disposable equipment, and being unable to provide necessary drugs.

The medical supply system entered 1992 in a bankrupt condition. The Russian government maintained tight controls on the prices of about 250 critical drugs and continued to guarantee certain vulnerable groups their supplies of free or subsidized medicines. It authorized increases in the retail prices of other medicaments, but the acquisition prices of the commodities that pharmacies distributed increased to a greater extent over subsequent months. [48] Their position was undermined as well by rent increases, which made the typical pharmacy with its large production area financially unviable. Other obstacles to their self-financing were the poor state of their capital stock and restrictions on their product lines that prohibited them from selling profitable goods like perfume, cosmetics, and female sanitary products. [49] There was considerable concern among staff about the prospects for and consequences of privatization. [50]

The medical industry in Russia has experienced serious difficulties in obtaining supplies due to chain-reaction declines in production throughout the industrial and agricultural sectors and the drop in trade with traditional partners in other former Soviet republics. Virtually no hard currency has been made available to import equipment, raw materials, or active substances from OECD countries. Investment in the branch was cut by an estimated 60-70 percent percent, with the usual consequences. [51] The industry's labor situation has worsened because employees have become progressively more dissatisfied by poor work conditions, falling real wages, and the grim prospects for their enterprises and for employment. Managers have been reluctant to fire staff, so workers in idle factories usually have been given extended vacations.

The financial circumstances of the industry have remained strained because the prices of its inputs went up 8-10 times but those of most medicines have been allowed to increase only 4-fold. Furthermore, the falling real incomes of the population and budgets of medical establishments have meant that it has become increasingly difficult to sell finished goods, despite the severe deficits

---

[47] Smirnov (1992b).
[48] Vakatov (1992).
[49] Tokarenko (1992).
[50] Tokarenko (1992); Ivchenko (1992).
[51] "Investitsii" (1992).

in medical facilities. One article in June stated that: "In the four months of this year the turnover of production has sharply fallen, the arrears in payments have risen from 40 million rubles to 2 billion 557 million. In sum, factories are insolvent and in hospitals and pharmacies there are no medicines." [52]

The depressed demand and input constraints resulted in a fall in medical industry production during the first half of 1992. [53] Its composition became difficult to plan because of the unpredictability of supplies and sudden governmental demands for the production of vital drugs on an urgent basis (formerly known as "storming"). The output of the domestic pharmaceutical industry met only 15–25 percent of requirements in this period. But there evidently were some success stories. [54]

In 1992 all foreign trade in medical products of Russia is on a hard currency basis, compared with 5 percent of Soviet trade in 1988. Purchases from Western companies are hampered by the fact that they were owed 219.5 million rubles by successor states to the U.S.S.R. for deliveries in 1990 and 1991. [55] The devaluation of the ruble from 0.6 to the dollar in 1990 to 100 in 1992 has made most medical goods from OECD countries prohibitively expensive. [56] Finally, the break-up of the Soviet Union resulted in an externalization of and fall in trade between Russia and other CIS countries.

In December 1991 the Yeltsin government established a new program to improve the drug supply in Russia during 1992–95 and allocated $1,350 million to purchase essential medicaments abroad. [57] This had a beneficial effect during the first quarter of 1992, when imports of medicaments were 3.4 times greater than in the same period in 1991. [58] Despite this, micro-level reports indicated that there were acute shortages of imported medicines. By the end of the half year, total Russian imports were down 30 percent from the previous year. It is likely that the volume and value of pharmaceutical imports were lower as well.

During 1992 most of the previous joint ventures, cooperation, and licensing agreements in the health field have continued to function, and some important new business deals have been concluded. An important innovation in the foreign economic sphere was the decision of the international community Western countries in January 1992 to provide substantial quantities of medical aid to Russia, other CIS states, and the Baltic nations. The program is being coordinated by WHO and UNICEF, which sent investigative missions to the region in February and March. They recommended aid amounting to $418 million over 1992–93 to assist the former Soviet republics in meeting acute challenges in the areas of health, nutrition, family planning, and the environment. [59] About two-

---

[52] Efimova (1992).

[53] "Sotsial'no . . . polugodii" (1992), p. 6.

[54] According to "Prognozy" (1992), the output of a number of medicines will be higher in 1992 than in the previous year: metapyrin by 11 percent; papaverine by 36 percent; euphyline by 9 percent; and nitroglycerin by 1 percent.

[55] Ivchenko (1992).

[56] Kaser (1992a).

[57] "Essential" (1992), p. 8.

[58] "Sotsial'no . . . kvartale" (1992), p. 15.

[59] UNICEF/WHO (1992).

thirds of these funds would be used to purchase vaccines and drugs. The first deliveries emanating from this program were made by NATO flights in March 1992. The impact of all these developments on the health of the Russian population has been negative, but to date output indicators do not show a marked deterioration. The prevalence of a number of illnesses has increased, but the Minister of Health of Russia does not believe that there is an immmediate danger of epidemics. He also stated that infant mortality has not risen. Adult age-specific death rates probably are continuing to increase and the crude death rate has risen from 11.4 deaths per 1,000 in 1991 to 12.1 in the first quarter of 1992. [60] This is the first time that this mortality rate has been higher than the birth rate since World War II. Life expectancy in Russia fell by 0.9 years from its level in 1987 to 69.2 years in early 1992. These minimal changes in health output indicators should not be interpreted optimistically. Given the severity of the worsening of health conditions and medical care in Russia and the long time-lags between cause and effect, it is likely that the adverse consequences of economic collapse and transition on the health of the population will manifest themselves later in the 1990s.

BIBLIOGRAPHY

"Analiticheskie materialy: Ob obespechennosti lekarstvennymi sredstvami i meditsinskoi tekhnikoi," *Statisticheskii Press-Byulleten'*, 1991, no. 3, pp. 3–6.

Apazov, A.D. and Belikov, V.G. (1987) "Puti perestroika kadrovoi politiki aptechnykh upravlenii v svete reshenii yanvarskogo (1987 g.) plenuma TsK KPSS," *Farmatsiya*, no. 4, pp. 1–5.

Apazov, A.D. (1991). "Problemy lekarstvennogo obsepecheniya naseleniya strany," *Farmatsiya*, no. 2, pp. 1–11.

Bykov, V.A. (1991) "Lekarstva i politika," *Radikal*, no. 15, p. 4.

Chazov, E. (1992) "Ya zdorov, potomu chto zanyat lyubimym delom," *Meditsinskaya Gazeta*, 17 April 1992.

Chernyavskii, S. (1991) "Komu eto vygodno?" *Meditsinskaya Gazeta*, 7 November 1991.

Davis, C. (1983) "The economics of the Soviet health system," in U.S. Congress, Joint Economic Committee *Soviet Economy in the 1980s: Problems and Prospects*, Washington D.C.: USGPO.

Davis, C. (1987) "Developments in the health sector of the Soviet economy: 1970–90" in U.S. Congress, Joint Economic Committee *Gorbachev's Economic Plans*, Washington D.C.: USGPO

Davis, C. (1988) "The organization and performance of the contemporary Soviet health system," in Lapidus, G. and Swanson, G.E. (eds.) (1988) *State and Welfare, USA/USSR*, Berkeley, Institute of International Studies.

Davis, C. (1989) "Priority and the shortage model: The medical system in the socialist economy," in Davis, C. and Charemza,

---

[60] Sagradov (1992).

W. (eds.) (1989) *Models of Disequilibrium and Shortage in Centrally Planned Economies*, London: Chapman and Hall.

Davis (1992) *The Pharmaceutical Market in the Soviet Union and Its Successor States: From Economic Reform to Transition*, London: Scrip Country Report.

Davis, R. (1966) *Planning Human Resource Development*, Chicago, Rand McNally.

Efimova, N. (1991) "Tabletki ot . . . putcha," *Meditsinskaya Gazeta*, 15 November 1991, p. 12.

Efimova, N. (1992) "Tupikovaya situatsiya farmatsii," *Meditsinskaya Gazeta*, 5 June 1992, p. 2.

"Ekonomika SSSR v 1990 godu," *Ekonomika i Zhizn'*, 1991, no. 5, pp. 9–13.

"Ekonomika stran—chlenov sodruzhestva nezavisimykh gosudarstv v 1991 godu," *Ekonomicheskaya Gazeta*, 1992, no. 6, pp. 13–16.

"Essential drug list for Russia," *Scrip*, 1 July 1992.

Feshbach, M. (1987) "Issues in Soviet health problems," in U.S. Congress, Joint Economic Committee *Gorbachev's Economic Plans*, Washington D.C.: USGPO.

"Gosudarstvennaya programma privatizatsii gosudarstvennykh i munitsipal'nykh predpriyatii v Rossiiskoi Federatsii na 1992 god," *Ekonomicheskaya Gazeta*, 1992, no. 29, pp. 15–18.

Gosudarstvennyy Byudzhet v 1981–1985 gg., ..v 1988 g., ..v 1990 g., Moscow: Ministerstvo Finansy, 1986, 1989, 1991.

Grave, E. (1992) "Minzdrav preduprezhdaet: strakhuites," *Meditsinskaya Gazeta*, 3 July 1992.

Helmstadter, S. (1992) "Medical insurance in Russia," *RFE/RL Research Report*, vol. 1, no. 31, pp. 65–69.

"Investitsii i promyshlennoe proizvodstvo: spad prodolzhaetsya," *Ekonomicheskaya Gazeta*, 1992, no. 26, p. 1.

Ivchenko, L. (1992) "Lekarstva: situatsiya ne beznadezhna," *Izvestiya*, 22 February 1992, p. 2.

"Kakoi byt' reforme zdravookhraneniya Rossii?" *Meditsinskaya Gazeta*, 20 December 1991.

Kalita, V. (1991) "Ne do zhiru—byl by kontsern," *Pravda Ukrainy*, 1 March 1991, pg. 12.

Kaser, M. (1992a) "CIS: Healthcare crisis," *Oxford Analytica Healthcare Brief*, 29 April 1992.

Kaser, M. (1992b) "Russia: Healthcare reforms," *Oxford Analytica Healthcare Brief*, 22 July 1992.

Klyuev, M.A. (1987) "Lekarstvennaya pomoshch naseleniyu v odinnadtsatoi pyatiletke i zadachi na perspektivu," *Farmatsiya*, no. 1, pp. 1–7.

Korepanov, V. (1992) "Bol'noi ne dolzhen platit' dvazhdy," *Meditsinskaya Gazeta*, 21 February 1992.

Kuzin, I. (1992) "Mozhno li kupit' Botkinskuyu?" *Meditsinskaya Gazeta*, 17 April 1992.

Manucharova, E. (1992) "Poka my perekhodim k platnoi meditsine," *Izvestiya*, 5 February 1992.

Markar'yants, V. (1991) "Pochemu nyet lekarstv?" *Pravda*, 22 August 1991, p. 3.

"Ministry ishchut soglasiya," *Meditsinskaya Gazeta*, 11 September 1991, pp. 1, 3.

"Nam vsegda ne khvatolo deneg na zdorov'e ... ," *Meditsinskaya Gazeta*, 24 April 1992, p. 8.

Narodnoe Khozyaistvo SSSR v 1986 g. ... v. 1990 g., Moscow, Finansy i Statistika, 1987 ... 1991.

Okhrana Zdorov'ya v SSSR, 1990, Moscow: Finansy i Statistika.

Orlov, G., Soloshenko, I., Popov, N. and Panchenko, B. (1991) "Resursnoe obespechenie zdravookhraneniya," *Planovoe Khozyaistvo*, no. 1, pp. 104–110.

Orlov, G., Soloshenko, and Panchenko, B. (1991) "Minmedprom, Minpribor, Minobshchemash ... Kto sleduyushchii?" *Meditsinskaya Gazeta*, 8 May 1991.

Pavlyutkin, A., Boiko, E., Kravets, T. and Pukashov, N. (1991) "Strakhovoi polis zdrov'ya," *Pravitel'stvennyy Vestnik*, No. 16 (94), pp. 6–7.

"Prognozy: Khimiko-lesnoi promyshlennost," *Ekonomicheskaya Gazeta*, 1992, no. 25, p. 16.

Prokin, A. (1992) "Mafiya protiv sanitarnoi sluzhby," *Meditsinskaya Gazeta*, 3 April 1992.

"Rossiiskoe zdravookhranenie: podstupy k novoi kontseptsii," *Meditsinskaya Gazeta*, 13 September 1991.

Sagradov, A. (1992) "Luchshe byt' zdorovym i bogatym ... ," *Ekonomicheskaya Gazeta*, no. 27, p. 14.

Shmakov, N.M. (1987). "Farmatsiya za 70 let sovetskoi vlasti," *Farmatsiya*, no. 5, pp. 1–6.

Smirnov, F. (1992a) "Na grani finansogo krakha," *Meditsinskaya Gazeta*, 21 February 1992.

Smirnov, F. (1992b) "Lovushka dlya prostakov," *Meditsinskaya Gazeta*, 24 April 1992.

Smirnov, F. (1992c) "Vroz' iz krizisa ne vyiti," *Meditsinskaya Gazeta*, 19 June 1992.

"Sotsial'no-ekonomicheskoe polozhenie Rossiiskoi Federatsii v pervom kvartale 1992 goda," *Ekonomicheskaya Gazeta*, 1992, no. 17 (April), pp. 14–15.

"Sotsial'no-ekonomicheskoe polozhenie Rossiiskoi Federatsii v pervom polugodii 1992 goda," *Ekonomicheskaya Gazeta*, 1992, no. 30 (July), pp. 5–7.

"Strakhovaya meditsina: Mesto pod solntsem," *Meditsinskaya Gazeta*, 24 April 1992.

Tishuk, E. (1992) "Nas stanovitsya vse men'she ... ," *Meditsinskaya Gazeta*, 3 April 1992, p. 6.

Tokarenko, E. (1992) "Apteki v dolgovoi yame," *Meditsinskaya Gazeta*, 3 July 1992.

"Tseny na platnye uslugi" *Ekonomicheskaya Gazeta*, 1992, no. 27.

872

UNICEF/WHO (1992) *The Looming Crisis in Health the Need for International Support: Overview of the Reports on the Commonwealth of Independent States and the Baltic Countries,* New York, 17 March 1992.

Vakatov, S. (1992) "Aptechnyy disbalans," *Meditsinskaya Gazeta,* 5 June 1992.

Vasil'eva, L. (1992a) "Trud i zarplata," *Meditsinskaya Gazeta,* 1 July 1992, p. 8.

Vasil'eva, L. (1992b) "Trud i zarplata," *Meditsinskaya Gazeta,* 5 August 1992, p. 8.

Verkhovnyy Sovet Rossiiskoi Federatsii (1992) *Byudzhetnoe Poslanie na 1992 god,* Moscow.

Vneshnyaya Torgovlya SSSR v 1986 god . . . 1990 god (After 1989 the title is *Vneshnye Ekonomicheskie Svyazy SSSR v . . .*), Moscow, 1987 . . . 1991.

"Vneshnyaya torgovlya v 1991 godu," *Ekonomicheskaya Gazeta,* 1992, no. 13, pp. 14–15.

"Zakon Rossiiskoi Sovetskoi Federativnoi Sotsialisticheskoi Respubliki O Meditsinskom Strakhovanii Grazhdan," *Meditsinskaya Gazeta,* 1 February 1991.

Zolotova, L. (1992a) "Aktsiya protesta," *Meditsinskaya Gazeta,* 17 April 1992, p. 2.

Zolotova, L. (1992b) "Zabastovka nachalas," *Meditsinskaya Gazeta,* 24 April 1992, p. 2.

THE CURRENT CONDITIONS AND REFORM IN THE HOUSING SECTOR OF THE FORMER SOVIET UNION

By Michael Alexeev *

CONTENTS

SUMMARY

The traditional Soviet system failed to solve the problem of providing its population with adequate housing. The need for radical reform of the housing sector in the former Soviet Union is clear. This paper reviews the housing situation inherited by the newly independent states and considers the main issues in the transition of the housing sector to a market system. These issues include privatization of the existing housing stock, development of private enterprise in the housing sector, and reform of the land-use management system.

INTRODUCTION

In the traditional Soviet system the housing sector used to be one of the most rigidly managed and highly subsidized areas of consumption. At least on the surface of it, construction and allocation

---

* Michael Alexeev is an Associate Professor, Department of Economics, at Indiana University. Part of the research for this paper was conducted while the author was working under contract with the Office of Housing and Urban Development of the Agency for International Development. The support of AID is gratefully acknowledged.

(873)

of most housing was accomplished through purely administrative methods. [1] Unlike many other consumer goods, state-owned housing was not supposed to be allocated according to "the ability to pay." In part for this reason, the transition to a market-oriented economy that is now being attempted in the republics of the former Soviet Union promises to be particularly long and difficult in the housing sector. At the same time, housing serves as a vivid example of the inability of the traditional Soviet system to solve even the most pressing problems in the area of consumption. Despite the potential difficulties, the transition to a market-oriented system in the provision of housing will have to be accomplished if the newly independent countries are to solve their housing problems.

The paper consists of two main parts. The first part reviews the housing situation in the Soviet Union immediately prior to its breakup. Since the institutional arrangements prevailing in the Soviet housing sector are well known and have been described elsewhere, the emphasis here is on the physical state of the housing stock. [2] The second part addresses the most important issues in the market transition of the housing sector, namely privatization of the existing housing stock, development of private and crypto-private enterprise in the construction sector, and reform requirements in urban land use management. Due to the poor availability of data on the smaller republics, most of the information on recent reforms in this paper pertains to Russia, Ukraine, and Kazakhstan.

OVERVIEW OF THE HOUSING SECTOR

Despite the proclaimed determination of the Soviet leaders to resolve the housing problem in the former Soviet Union, the newly independent republics inherited a difficult situation in regard to residential housing. As of the beginning of 1991 the Soviet housing stock amounted to almost 4.6 billion square meters of useful housing space or about 16.0 square meters per person (see Table 1). [3]

The breakdown of the per capita housing space endowment by republic (Table 2) reveals significant regional variations with the population of the Baltic republics (Estonia, Lithuania, Latvia) enjoying about 50 percent more housing space per capita than the residents of Armenia, Azerbaijan, Tadjikistan, Turkmenia, Kazakhstan, and Kyrgyzstan. Notice, however, that the per capita figures probably overstate the true disparities due to the economies of scale in consumption of housing by the relatively large families in

---

[1] Of course, rather well-developed second economy mechanisms were operating under the surface. The informal activities resulted in housing allocation, which was significantly different from the one prescribed by the official rules. Nonetheless, the influence of administrative rationing on production and allocation of housing was probably more important than it was for most other consumer goods, at least in urban areas. For a more detailed discussion of the role of the second economy in Soviet housing allocation, see M. Alexeev, "The Effect of Housing Allocation on Social Inequality: A Soviet Perspective," *Journal of Comparative Economics*, 12, 2: 228–234, 1988 and M. Alexeev, "Market vs. Rationing: The Case of Soviet Housing," *Review of Economics and Statistics*, 70, 3:414–420, 1988.

[2] For the most recent surveys see M. Alexeev, "Soviet Residential Housing: Will the 'Acute Problem' be Solved?" in U.S. Congress, Joint Economic Committee, *Gorbachev's Economic Plans*, Washington, D.C.: U.S. Government Printing Office, 1987; G. Andrusz, "Housing Policy in the Soviet Union," in J.A. Sillince, ed., *Housing Policies in Eastern Europe and the Soviet Union*, (Routledge, 1990); and L. Baker, M. Alexeev, and M. Westfall, *Overview of the Soviet Housing Sector*, a report prepared for the Office of Housing and Urban Programs, AID, December 1990.

[3] *Narodnoe khoziaistvo SSSR v 1990 godu* (Moscow: Finansy i Statistika, 1991), p. 194 (hereafter referred to as *Narkhoz 1990*).

TABLE 1. Residential Housing Stock, 1980–90.

(Millions of square meters of housing space)

Stock Characteristics	1980	1985	1986	1987	1988	1989	1990 [a]
Total Stock	3,573	4,072	4,191	4,316	4,431	4,540	4,568
State-Owned	1,866	2,278	2,508	2,596	2,524	2,604	2,792
Cooperative	103	136	159	167	NA	NA	NA
Private	1,604	1,658	1,683	1,720	1,748	1,769	1,776
Per capita, sq. m.	13.4	14.7	14.9	15.2	15.5	15.8	16.0
Urban Housing Stock	2,205	2,567	2,646	2,725	2,801	2,890	2,925
State-Owned	1,553	1,850	2,056	2,126	2,037	2,108	2,298
Cooperative	102	133	NA	NA	156	164	NA
Private	548	584	590	599	608	618	627
Per capita, sq. m.	13.2	14.3	14.5	14.7	14.9	15.3	15.5
Rural Housing Stock	1,368	1,505	1,545	1,591	1,624	1,650	1,643
State-Owned	311	428	452	470	481	488	494
Cooperative	1	3	NA	NA	3	11	NA
Private	1,056	1,074	1,093	1,121	1,140	1,151	1,149
Per capita, sq. m.	13.8	15.3	15.7	16.2	16.6	16.8	16.9

Source: *Narodnoe khoziaistvo SSSR v 1990 godu* (Moscow: Finansy i Statistika, 1991), p. 188; Goslsomstat, *Zhilishchnye, usloviia naseleniia SSSR* (Moscow, 1990), pp. 15–17. There were minor discrepancies in the data in these two sources. Whenever such discrepancy occurred, the *Narkhoz 1990* data were given priority.
[a] Without the data for Lithuania.
NA—Not available.

the second set of republics.

TABLE 2. Per Capita Housing Space by Republic, 1990.

(Square meters of living space)

Republic	All Housing	Urban Areas	Rural Areas
U.S.S.R.	16.0	15.5	16.9
Russia	16.4	15.7	18.2
Ukraine	17.8	16.5	20.6
Belarus	17.9	15.5	22.6
Uzbekistan	12.1	12.7	11.8
Kazakhstan	14.2	14.8	13.4
Georgia	18.8	16.5	21.6
Azerbaijan	12.5	12.8	12.0
Lithuania [a]	18.0	16.8	24.0
Moldova	17.9	14.3	21.0
Latvia	19.8	17.9	24.5
Kyrgyzstan	12.1	12.4	12.0
Tajikistan	9.3	12.1	8.0
Armenia	15.0	14.0	17.1
Turkmenia	11.1	11.5	10.8
Estonia	21.6	19.9	26.1

Source: *Narodnoe khoziaistvo SSSR v 1990 godu* (Moscow: Finansy i Statistika, 1991); Lithuania *Zhilishchnye, usloviia naseleniia SSSR* (Moscow, 1990), pp. 69, 79.
[a] 1989 data.

The "Housing 2000" program adopted in 1985 set a commendable goal to improve radically the housing situation in the U.S.S.R. and to provide each Soviet household with a self-contained separate dwelling. Nonetheless, in 1989 almost 15 percent of all households in the U.S.S.R. lived in communal apartments or dormitories, or they shared individual houses (Table 3). In fact, the number of urban households on the waiting lists for improved housing reached 14.5 million (24 percent of all urban households) at the beginning of 1991, an increase of 2.2 million since 1986. About 12 percent of these households lived in communal apartments and 14 percent lived in dormitories. Almost 2 million households had been waiting for over 10 years (Table 4). [4] Even prior to the collapse of the Soviet Union the fulfillment of the "Housing 2000" program was widely considered "unrealistic." The political and economic events after 1990 caused a drastic reduction of housing construction, the appearance of numerous refugees, and the retirement and return from abroad of a significant number of military personnel, thus worsening the overall housing situation. [5]

The "square meter per person" indicator together with the number of dwellings and the number of rooms in them have served as the main criteria in evaluating the performance of the housing sector, but these indicators may often be misleading in evaluating such a heterogeneous commodity as housing. Other factors (e.g. age, wall materials, quality of workmanship, availability of amenities, and location) play an important role in determining the volume of housing services received by a household. The emphasis on square meters as well as on the number of apartments and rooms, naturally led to the disregard of many of the other characteristics of housing by the designers and builders.

The notoriously poor quality of materials and workmanship is characteristic of much of residential housing in the former Soviet Union, particularly that built since the late 1950s. Approximately half of all urban housing built after 1971 was made out of concrete, large panels, or blocks (Table 5). The panels were often of inferior quality and were put together poorly.

The poor quality of Soviet-built housing results in large repair and maintenance (R&M) expenditures, and a growing quantity of dilapidated and condemned housing. In 1989 the R&M expenditures amounted to R4.3 billion (R2.3 billion in 1980). This growth is largely due to inflation of repair costs per square meter. These

---

[4] *Narkhoz 1990*, p. 191, and Goskomstat SSSR quoted in *Chestnoe slovo*, no. 38, September–October 1991, p. 5. The republic breakdown of the waiting lists for 1990 is shown in Table 4. Note that, with some exceptions, the rules currently in effect in most republics required a household to have less than 7 square meters of housing per person to become eligible to join a waiting list.

[5] Only 37.4 million square meters of housing were constructed during the first half of 1991. This constitutes only 85 percent of the corresponding number for 1990, and 80 percent of that for 1989 (*Pravitel'stvennyi vestnik*, no. 35, August 1991). The situation apparently has worsened in 1992. During January-May in the Russian Federation the rate of completion of residential construction reached only 73 percent of the corresponding rate in 1991 (*Ekonomicheskoe polozhenie Rossiiskoi Federatsii, dopolnitel'nye dannye, v ianvare-mae 1992 goda*, (Moscow: Goskomstat RF, 1992). By the fall of 1991 the number of officially registered refugees has risen to 700,000. At about the same time there were 185,400 military personnel without apartments of their own. The last two numbers appeared in *Pravitel'stvennyi vestnik*, no. 37, September 1991, p. 10, and *Krasnyia zvezda*, September 26, 1991, p. 2, respectively (quoted from A. Trehub, "Soviet Housing Policy: Perestroika and Beyond," mimeo, November 1991).

TABLE 3. Distribution of Families and Singles According to the Type of Dwelling and Size of Living Space Occupied, 1989.

(Millions of Families)

Type of Family and Dwelling	Total	Size of Living Space per Person, Square Meters						
		<5	5–6	7–8	9–12	13–14	15–19	over 20
All Areas								
All families	71.1	4.4	9.4	12.3	22.4	7.1	9.7	5.8
Apartments	38.6	1.4	4.4	7.5	14.6	4.3	5.0	1.4
Private houses	24.3	1.4	2.6	3.3	6.1	2.5	4.3	4.1
Communal apartments	3.5	0.6	1.0	0.7	0.8	0.1	0.2	0.05
Sharing a private house	2.4	0.3	0.5	0.4	0.6	0.2	0.2	0.2
Dormitories	2.3	0.7	0.9	0.4	0.3	0.02	0.01	0.0
Singles	15.1	0.6	1.1	0.5	1.6	0.6	4.0	6.7
Apartments	5.4	0.0	0.01	0.03	0.4	0.2	2.5	2.3
Private houses	5.1	0.0	0.02	0.05	0.3	0.1	0.7	3.9
Communal apartments	1.3	0.0	0.03	0.05	0.4	0.2	0.4	0.2
Sharing a private house	0.6	0.0	0.01	0.02	0.1	0.04	0.2	0.3
Dormitories	2.7	0.6	1.1	0.3	0.4	0.08	0.2	0.04
Urban Areas								
All families	48.2	3.1	6.7	8.6	16.2	4.9	6.2	2.5
Apartments	33.1	1.1	3.6	6.2	12.8	3.8	4.4	1.2
Private houses	8.3	0.5	1.0	1.1	2.1	0.9	1.5	1.2
Communal apartments	3.2	0.6	0.9	0.7	0.7	0.1	0.2	0.04
Sharing a private house	1.5	0.2	0.3	0.3	0.4	0.1	0.1	0.09
Dormitories	2.1	0.7	0.9	0.3	0.2	0.01	0.01	0.0
Singles	10.3	0.5	1.0	0.4	1.2	0.5	3.2	3.5
Apartments	4.7	0.0	0.0	0.02	0.2	0.2	2.3	2.0
Private houses	1.6	0.0	0.0	0.02	0.1	0.04	0.3	1.1
Communal apartments	1.2	0.0	0.02	0.04	0.4	0.1	0.4	0.2
Sharing a private house	0.4	0.0	0.0	0.01	0.07	0.03	0.1	0.2
Dormitories	2.4	0.5	1.0	0.3	0.4	0.08	0.1	0.03
Rural Areas								
All families	22.9	1.3	2.7	3.7	6.2	2.2	3.5	3.3
Apartments	5.5	0.3	0.8	1.3	1.8	0.5	0.6	0.2
Private houses	16.0	0.9	1.6	2.2	4.0	1.6	2.8	2.9
Communal apartments	0.3	0.05	0.1	0.07	0.1	0.0	0.0	0.01
Sharing a private house	0.9	0.1	0.2	0.1	0.2	0.1	0.1	0.1
Dormitories	0.2	0.0	0.0	0.1	0.1	0.01	0.0	0.0
Singles	4.8	0.1	0.1	0.08	0.4	0.1	0.8	3.2
Apartments	0.7	0.0	0.0	0.01	0.1	0.04	0.2	0.3
Private houses	3.5	0.0	0.01	0.03	0.2	0.06	0.47	2.8
Communal apartments	0.1	0.0	0.01	0.01	0.03	0.01	0.02	0.02
Sharing a private house	0.2	0.0	0.0	0.0	0.04	0.01	0.05	0.1
Dormitories	0.3	0.1	0.08	0.03	0.04	0.01	0.02	0.01

Source: *Zhilishchnye, usloviia naseleniia SSSR* (Moscow, 1990), pp. 56–58.

grew by about 350 percent between 1980 and 1989. [6] At the end of 1989 approximately 50 million square meters of space, housing about 4 million people, were classified as dilapidated and in need of emergency repair (see Table 6). Moreover, these numbers do not in-

---

[6] See Goskomstat SSSR, *Zhilishchnye usloviia naseleniia SSSR*, (Moscow, 1990), p. 4 (hereafter *Zhilishchnye*, 1990).

TABLE 4. Changes in Housing Conditions and Waiting Lists in Urban Areas,
by Republic, 1990.

Republic	Number of Households whose housing was improved, thousands	Same Households on Waiting List		Number of Households on Waiting List as of January 1, 1991	
		Thou-sands	% of those on waiting list	Thou-sands	% of all families & singles
U.S.S.R.	1,728	1,629	11.5	14,524	24.2
Russia	1,158	1,102	12.0	9,456	25.6
Ukraine	227	206	8.2	2,593	22.9
Belarus	80	76	12.3	635	28.8
Uzbekistan	46	45	20.6	204	11.5
Kazakhstan	98	91	16.6	520	18.8
Georgia	9	9	6.9	128	16.1
Azerbaijan	19	17	12.5	138	15.6
Lithuania [a]	22	20	14.1	142	16.7
Moldova	20	16	7.4	218	33.3
Latvia	15	12	8.1	156	22.6
Kyrgyzstan	9	9	10.2	85	18.6
Tajikistan	10	10	11.8	90	24.6
Armenia	12	12	10.6	142	34.6
Turkmenia	12	12	10.6	108	30.9
Estonia	13	12	29.3	51	12.1

Source: *Narodnoe khoziaistvo SSSR v 1990 godu* (Moscow: Finansy i Statistika, 1991), p. 191.
[a] 1989 data.

clude privately owned rural housing the quality of which is low
even by Soviet standards. The large quantities of poorly built housing will present an even more severe problem in the near future
when the cheap housing constructed under Khrushchev will have
to be retired *en masse*. Normally, 20–25 percent of all retired housing is retired due to old age and disrepair, another 25–30 percent in
order to free up space for new construction, and the rest for other
reasons. [7] Soon, however, these proportions may change significantly. According to a Soviet researcher, most of the five-story walk-ups
built from 1956 to 1970 are not worth maintaining for more than
50 years. [8]

While the availability of amenities in the former Soviet Union
has been increasing steadily over the years, even in urban areas
the situation leaves much to be desired (Table 7). In rural areas
only 20 percent of the population enjoys running water, 7 percent
have hot water, and only 13 percent have access to sewage facilities. [9] The availability of amenities is the worst in the Central
Asian republics. The poor quality of existing amenities exacerbates
the situation. In many places hot water service is interrupted for
several weeks in the summer for maintenance. Every several years
running water is turned off completely for repairs of the pipes and

[7] L. Ia. Gertsberg, "Problemy rekonstruktsii zhiloi zastroiki," in *Zhilishchnyi kompleks SSSR: problemy i resheniia*, (Moscow: U.S.S.R. Academy of Sciences, 1989).
[8] Ibid. While data on the share of these buildings in the total housing stock are not readily available, in 1970 they made up close to 60 percent of all housing space constructed by the state (see *Kapital'noe stroitel'stvo SSSR* (Moscow, 1988), p. 161.
[9] *Zhilishchnye*, 1990, p. 5.

TABLE 5. Distribution of Housing by Age and the Outside Wall Material,
1951–60 to 1981–88.

(Percent)

Outside Wall Material	All Houses	Year of Construction			
		1951–60	1961–70	1971–80	1981–88
Urban and Rural Areas					
All Houses	100	100	100	100	100
Brick	37.5	36.8	41.8	39.2	34.3
Concrete, Large Panels, Blocks	27.1	7.5	23.5	39.7	47.6
Wood	18.6	30.3	16.4	9.2	7.6
Mixed Material	4.4	7.0	4.7	3.2	2.7
Clay	10.5	15.5	11.5	7.2	6.3
Other Materials	1.9	2.9	2.1	1.5	1.5
Urban Areas					
All Houses	100	100	100	100	100
Brick	42.1	49.2	48.9	38.9	32.0
Concrete, Large Panels, Blocks	38.6	11.2	35.9	53.3	61.4
Wood	11.2	22.3	7.7	4.1	3.8
Mixed Material	3.1	6.8	2.8	1.5	1.1
Clay	3.8	7.8	3.6	1.6	1.1
Other Materials	1.2	2.7	1.1	0.6	0.6
Rural Areas					
All Houses	100	100	100	100	100
Brick	29.7	18.7	31.0	39.6	38.9
Concrete, Large Panels, Blocks	7.5	2.1	4.7	10.9	19.0
Wood	31.3	42.1	29.9	20.1	15.7
Mixed Material	6.6	7.3	7.4	6.8	6.0
Clay	21.8	26.7	23.4	19.1	17.0
Other Materials	3.1	3.1	3.6	3.5	3.4

Source: *Zhilishchnye, usloviia naseleniia SSSR* (Moscow, 1990).

other elements of the system. According to Goskomstat, "in a
number of settlements (*naselennye punkty*) water is supplied with
interruptions, rationing of water is being introduced." [10] Moreover,
the quality of recently built utility lines appears to be worse than
the quality of the older lines. A city official in Dnipropetrovsk,
Ukraine, complained that the utility lines built after 1980 had to
be repaired almost twice as often as those built prior to 1980. [11]
The poor quality of the utility plant leads to waste and environmental damage. According to *Ekonomika i zhizn'*, 7 percent of
water and 3 percent of heat are lost solely because of unsatisfactory conditions of the utility lines, and the lack of capacity of the
treatment facilities results in a quarter of all sewage being dumped
into the lakes and rivers untreated. [12]

Most of residential housing in the former Soviet Union is owned
by the state, either directly (municipal housing) or through state-
owned enterprises. State ownership is dominant in urban areas (73
percent of all housing space), but it plays a much less important
role in the countryside, where it accounts for only 30 percent of

[10] Ibid.
[11] Personal interview.
[12] *Ekonomika i zhizn'*, no. 41, October 1991, p. 6.

TABLE 6. Dilapidated and Condemned Housing Stock, 1987 and 1989.

(End of year)

Republic	State and Public Housing Stock				Privately Owned Housing Stock in Urban Areas, 1989	
	1987		1989			
	Total Space 1,000 sq. m.	% of Total	Total Space 1,000 sq. m.	% of Total	Total Space 1,000 sq. m.	% of Total
U.S.S.R.	59,313	2.8	49,733	1.8	9,622	0.5
Russia	35,171	2.2	29,758	1.7	5,137	0.8
Moscow	1,242	0.8	1,118	0.7	70.8	13.5
Leningrad	523.3	0.6	572	0.7	30.7	2.6
Far East	3,662	4.1	2,901	3.0	396.4	2.7
Ukraine	4,219	1.1	4,421	1.0	390	0.1
Lithuania	1,822	4.6	1,517	3.5	1,202	4.3
Latvia	4,320.4	11.6	3,890	10.0	65.6	0.7
Estonia	1,179	5.1	1,078	4.5	14.2	0.1
Georgia	965.3	3.3	394.1	2.9	71.5	0.1
Azerbaijan	389.1	1.3	368.3	1.2	NA	NA
Armenia	534.0	2.2	756.2	3.2	742.3	3.0
Uzbekistan	1,096.8	1.5	1,066	1.4	1,482.6	0.9
Kyrgyzstan	340.3	2.1	284.7	1.7	4.1	0.01
Tajikistan	316.1	1.9	254.9	1.4	82.7	2.7
Turkmenia	738.9	5.0	664.9	4.4	NA	NA
Kazakhstan	6,892.1	4.7	4,097.5	2.6	249.5	0.3
Belarus	893.1	1.0	355.9	0.4	168.7	0.2
Moldova	442.5	2.0	373.4	1.6	11.4	0.02

Source: *Zhilishchnye, usloviia naseleniia SSSR* (Moscow, 1990), p. 26–32.
Note: In 1989 3,052,000 people lived in dilapidated and condemned housing.
NA—Not available.

housing space (Table 8). Through 1990 the role of state ownership of housing had been perpetuated by the fact that most new housing space was built and financed by the state. However, the share of the state in housing construction declined steadily from about 71 percent in the mid-1980s to 66.4 percent in 1990. [13] Presumably, the state share has declined even further since then. Moreover, the role of central budget allocations in housing construction, formerly a major source of housing financing, has been reduced virtually to zero over the last two years. [14] The financing of state-owned housing nowadays comes from state-owned enterprise budgets.

City planners in the former Soviet Union often cite a lack of available land, particularly developed land, as one of the main bottlenecks in improving the urban housing situation. The Master Plans of many cities suggest increases in construction density to solve this problem. This view appears to be grounded in the fundamental lack of understanding of the value of land and its role in the allocation of land to various uses. According to a Russian researcher, 40 percent of all developed urban land is zoned for indus-

---

[13] *Narkhoz 1990*, p. 175.
[14] Obviously, the central Soviet budget itself no longer exists. Some republics, however, continue to make small occasional allocations for housing construction from the republican budgets.

TABLE 7. Percentage Available Utilities and Other Amenities, by Republic, 1989.

Republic	Housing Space Amenities					
	Running water	Sewer lines	Central heating	Hot water	Bathtubs	Gas
Urban State-owned and Public Housing, and Housing Cooperatives						
U.S.S.R.	93.2	91.4	90.3	76.3	86.0	77.3
Russia	93.2	91.4	91.4	77.6	86.1	71.9
Ukraine	94.0	92.6	89.3	77.5	87.8	87.1
Belarus	95.1	94.4	94.0	88.4	91.4	86.2
Uzbekistan	88.5	83.8	84.7	70.6	80.0	93.1
Kazakhstan	91.5	88.3	88.5	72.0	83.8	81.9
Georgia	96.7	95.9	90.4	59.4	84.2	83.7
Azerbaijan	92.4	90.8	77.7	24.4	76.8	97.4
Lithuania	95.7	95.3	91.9	88.6	91.1	85.2
Moldova	96.5	94.9	91.4	78.2	85.9	90.4
Latvia	93.5	93.0	80.5	76.6	80.0	89.9
Kyrgyzstan	91.3	85.6	86.9	70.0	78.6	92.4
Tajikistan	87.6	85.1	87.9	68.0	80.4	82.7
Armenia	99.0	98.5	97.4	84.3	95.0	80.4
Turkmenia	77.3	71.7	75.2	23.8	68.2	93.1
Estonia	95.8	95.3	81.7	67.9	81.6	62.2
Privately Owned Urban Housing						
U.S.S.R.	25.1	17.1	28.3	8.4	10.5	65.9
Russia	20.1	12.4	35.5	7.3	7.4	53.5
Ukraine	19.3	16.9	21.1	4.6	12.1	63.4
Belarus	24.5	22.0	40.9	9.0	8.4	89.4
Uzbekistan	31.9	11.3	21.1	1.5	8.4	79.0
Kazakhstan	23.3	13.6	23.3	0.9	7.5	87.9
Georgia	64.0	47.9	18.1	14.4	24.5	94.5
Azerbaijan	31.5	6.7	NA	NA	5.7	96.8
Lithuania	61.7	61.0	68.9	13.7	37.6	84.6
Moldova	18.2	15.8	16.0	NA	9.4	91.3
Latvia	52.2	50.1	42.8	21.9	31.0	81.1
Kyrgyzstan	42.7	32.4	14.0	1.4	3.3	77.2
Tajikistan	13.8	1.6	2.5	NA	0.4	82.5
Armenia	94.0	79.8	50.7	42.5	61.7	96.9
Turkmenia	46.5	3.1	5.0	NA	1.1	92.8
Estonia	60.2	60.1	16.7	15.0	24.6	46.0
Rural State-owned and Public Housing, and Housing Cooperatives						
U.S.S.R.	45.0	34.2	34.9	16.8	29.4	77.6
Russia	46.7	35.2	36.3	17.2	30.7	75.5
Ukraine	43.8	33.2	30.4	14.5	28.9	77.5
Belarus	59.8	51.8	41.1	26.4	46.0	92.0
Uzbekistan	49.8	32.4	27.8	11.1	25.0	75.3
Kazakhstan	20.1	10.6	21.0	4.0	8.0	86.2
Georgia	50.4	45.2	36.0	8.8	34.4	49.2
Azerbaijan	13.9	9.7	6.3	1.5	6.4	60.8
Lithuania	73.5	68.4	79.6	51.2	61.9	87.7
Moldova	69.6	74.8	58.4	31.7	45.1	84.4
Latvia	67.1	64.6	53.6	44.9	58.0	77.6
Kyrgyzstan	40.1	31.5	30.3	10.0	22.4	88.6
Tajikistan	28.7	16.4	14.5	4.9	13.2	74.6
Armenia	70.7	58.7	44.4	9.6	44.4	77.7
Turkmenia	27.3	7.2	16.0	1.0	4.7	68.7
Estonia	77.3	76.2	56.0	54.8	63.8	61.9

Source: *Zhilishchnye, usloviia naseleniia SSSR* (Moscow, 1990), pp. 41–42.
NA—Not available.

TABLE 8. Breakdown of Housing Stock, by Forms of Ownership and by Republic, 1989.

(Million square meters of living space)

Republic	Total Urban	Urban			Total Rural	Rural		
		State	Co-ops	Private		State	Co-ops	Private
U.S.S.R.	2,890	2,108	164	618	1,650	496	3	1,151
Russia	1,679	1,333.5	89.3	256.4	700.3	318.9	0.4	381
Ukraine	562	351.8	34.2	176	346.2	41	0	305.2
Belarus	102.3	70.6	11	20.7	76.2	19.3	0	56.9
Uzbekistan	99.4	53.3	4.2	41.9	139.8	18.9	2	118.9
Kazakhstan	137.4	101.3	3.5	32.7	95	53.8	0.1	41.1
Georgia	48.9	25	4	19.9	50.9	1.4	0	49.5
Azerbaijan	46.6	27.8	1.5	17.3	36.3	1.4	0	34.9
Lithuania	42.2	27.8	5.7	8.9	28.4	9.2	0.4	18.8
Moldova	28.7	18.5	2.6	7.6	47.6	2.4	0	45.2
Latvia	33.3	25.8	2.3	5.1	19.1	10.7	0	8.4
Kyrgyzstan	19.8	11.2	1	7.6	31.4	4.7	0	26.7
Tajikistan	19.6	12.6	0.9	6.2	28.4	4.2	0.1	24.1
Armenia	30.3	19.4	1.8	9	18	2.1	0	15.9
Turkmenia	18.1	13	0.2	4.9	20.7	1.9	0	18.8
Estonia	22.2	16.6	1.7	3.9	11.6	5.6	0.1	5.9

Source: *Zhilishchnye, usloviia naseleniia SSSR* (Moscow, 1990), pp. 15–17.

trial and warehousing use. [15] A large portion of this land could undoubtedly be used more efficiently if it were zoned for housing and housing related projects. To improve the efficiency of land allocation, however, the newly independent countries must create a land market.

The traditional Soviet system of land allocation essentially treated land as a free good. The Soviets did not have an explicit process of differentiation between centrally located and peripheral plots of land. This treatment of land resulted in enormous waste ranging from flooding prime agricultural land in order to build hydroelectric stations to building warehouses in the center of large cities. Moreover, since the ministries controlling land zoned for industrial use in the cities did not have to pay for its use, they had no incentive to relocate. The difficulties of improving the efficiency of land use are exacerbated by the lack of clarity about the present allocation of land and the responsibilities for land maintenance.

REFORMING THE HOUSING SECTOR

As the previous section made clear, the traditional Soviet system of housing delivery failed to provide adequate housing conditions for the majority of the population. The main source of improvement in the housing situation in the former Soviet Union would have to be new construction. This would require a major commitment of resources to the housing sector. Even without a massive increase in new construction, however, the efficiency of the existing housing allocation could be raised significantly by establishing

---

[15] G. S. Ronkin, "Problemy sbalansirovannosti razvitiia zhilishchnogo kompleksa," in *Zhilishchnyi kompleks SSSR: problemy i resheniia* (Moscow: U.S.S.R. Academy of Sciences, 1989).

a legal, well-functioning market in residential housing. Since most housing in the former Soviet Union is state-owned, the prerequisite for this is privatization of a large part of the state-owned housing stock.

While privatization of housing has received a great deal of attention in the media in the former Soviet Union, its effectiveness will be limited even in the short run unless it is conducted as a part of a comprehensive reform of the entire housing sector in the newly independent republics. In addition to privatization of existing housing, such a reform should contain the following major elements: a) privatization of the construction industry and the construction materials industry; b) establishment of a market for land (this may or may not include privatization of land); c) elimination of legal restrictions on people's mobility, i.e. elimination of the *propiska* system in its existing form. Other important components of the reform include development of a privately funded system of housing financing, improvements in record keeping and titling of housing and land, and streamlining the bureaucratic procedures for land allocation and housing permits. Due to space limitations, only privatization of housing, privatization of construction industry, and land reform will be discussed below.

PRIVATIZATION OF THE EXISTING HOUSING STOCK

From the point of view of economic efficiency, it may not matter that much how privatization is conducted, as long as in the end an overwhelming share of residential housing is privately owned. Some important qualifications, however, must be added to this statement to incorporate the economic, political, and social realities of the current situation in the former Soviet Union. To begin with, this assertion disregards the transaction costs that accompany the process of privatization itself, including the costs of households moving from one dwelling to another. These transaction costs may be significant. Given the high degree of inefficiency of the existing allocation, however, at least the costs of moving are probably unavoidable under any reasonable privatization scheme. [16]

Second, as was pointed out by Shleifer and Vishny among others, any potentially successful privatization process has to take into account the already existing implicit property rights to the privatized assets. [17] In the case of residential housing these property rights are quite clear. The tenants of state-owned apartments consider these apartments essentially their own. One way or another a politically feasible privatization scheme must allow the majority of the tenants to become legal owners of their current residences.

The third, and perhaps the most intractable issue, is the issue of fairness. Giving state housing to its current residents free of charge or for a nominal fee may be considered grossly unfair by those who

---

[16] Even though housing in the U.S.S.R. was supposed to be allocated without regard to the ability to pay, it has been shown that income and housing endowments even in the state-owned sector were positively correlated (see Alexeev, 1988). One has to keep in mind, however, that the recent reforms resulted in a significant redistribution of income, almost surely creating a much more serious disparity between households' ability to pay and their current endowments of housing.

[17] A. Shleifer, and R. Vishny, "Privatization in Russia: First Steps," NBER Conference on Transition in Eastern Europe, February 1992.

do not live in state-owned housing or who occupy inadequate quarters in it. The Soviet people were certainly aware of great inequities in housing allocation. Even prior to perestroika the newspapers often carried reports about the illegalities and irregularities in allocation of state-owned housing. Clearly, the nomenclatura enjoyed much better than average housing conditions. Not everybody who resided in good state-owned housing, however, acquired it in an objectionable manner. After all, housing in the U.S.S.R. did serve as a work incentive and could in many cases be considered as part of the remuneration for good work. [18]

This last consideration pertains to another aspect of the fairness issue, namely the fact that there exists a large minority of the population who owned (and directly paid for) their housing prior to privatization. These people feel they have the right to compensation if housing is privatized at below market prices. Moreover, it can be argued that state-owned housing tenants have already received substantial subsidies by paying only nominal rent, and that they should not be further subsidized during privatization. [19] Even though some privatization paths may appear more fair than other ones, the issue of fairness is too complicated to hope for a clearly fair solution.

Finally, the designers of privatization schemes should take into account the opportunities for corruption and abuse that are opened by their versions of privatization. As long as the bureaucracies have a say in determining the prices charged for privatized apartments or the length of process of privatization, there will be opportunities for extortion and bribery.

The above discussion will help us to evaluate the existing or proposed privatization schemes. These schemes can be classified into four broad categories. [20]

1) Transfer of housing to tenants free of charge. In a modification of this version of privatization the tenants have to pay more or less symbolic amounts of money for housing space above a specified quota. This basic scheme appears to be quite popular. It has been adopted (or is close to adoption) in the Russian Federation, Ukraine, Kazakhstan, and Lithuania. For example, in the Russian Federation the "Law on Privatization of Housing Stock" specified that at least 18 square meters of housing per person plus 9 square meters per household must be transferred to the tenants free of charge. In the Ukrainian draft of the privatization law the corresponding figures are 21 square meters per person plus 10 square

---

[18] One cannot carry this argument too far, however. The role of housing as remuneration appears to have been rather limited.

[19] Alexeev notes, however, that it may be difficult to ascertain who was the actual recipient of the housing subsidy in any given case. Many state-owned apartments (or at least their parts) were actually "purchased" by their tenants through side-payments or bribes. Thus in many cases the housing subsidy could have been capitalized, and the current tenants should really be considered its recipients. (Alexeev, "The Effect of Housing Allocation").

[20] Similar classification appears in N. Kosareva, "The Housing Market and Social Guarantees," *Studies on Soviet Economic Development* (translation of *Problemy rognozirovaniia*), 3, 1:38–46, February 1992. For other discussions of housing privatization see, for example, O. Bessonova, "Zhilishchnaia strategiia: kak uiti of gorodov-'khrushcheb'," *EKO*, no. 5, 1991; T. Boiko, "Posmotrim v zuby 'darenomu' zhl'iu," *EKO*, no. 5, 1991; B. Renaud, "Housing Reform for Socialist Countries," World Bank Discussion Paper 125, World Bank, Washington, DC, 1991; A. Trehub, "Soviet housing Policy: Perestroika and Beyond," mimeo, 1991.

meters per family. [21] Even though these laws are somewhat vague about the prices to be charged for the extra housing space (they leave local authorities some discretion in this respect) those prices usually end up being much lower than those in the open market. The advantages of this type of a scheme are that it is relatively simple to implement, it recognizes the implicit property rights, and it opens few opportunities for corruption. Its disadvantages include concerns about fairness (this scheme essentially preserves the current distribution of housing) [22] and does little to raise revenues for the local budgets.

2) Sale of housing to tenants at or close to the prevailing market prices. This scheme would probably be advisable in a well-functioning market economy with a relatively small public housing sector where housing subsidies did not exist or were relatively small. Under these circumstances it would produce little redistribution of wealth and would result in the least amount of distortions. In addition, this scheme would generate large revenues for the government. In the former Soviet Union, however, such an approach does not appear to be feasible. First of all, the prevailing market prices for housing in the former Soviet Union may not reflect relative scarcities well. The housing markets are rather thin and housing prices are quite volatile. Also, this approach would probably result in relatively high transactions costs; it does not recognize implicit property rights; and it opens great opportunities for corruption in setting prices. It does have advantages, however, over other approaches in terms of fairness. While a modification of this approach was proposed for St. Petersburg, [23] it is unlikely that it can be implemented anywhere in the former Soviet Union.

3) Transfer of a fixed amount of housing space to tenants free of charge, while charging market or above-market prices for the excess floor space. This scheme is a combination of the previous two. Naturally, it combines the effects of both. This method limits the negative features of the second approach to the households with high housing endowments. Even that may be enough of an obstacle, however, since it may be precisely these households who have the biggest political clout in many localities.

Under all existing approaches privatization is viewed as a voluntary process. Therefore, successful privatization requires raising rental payments for state-owned housing in order to make housing ownership more attractive than renting. Increases in rental payments appear to be politically unpopular. Thus far state rents have remained at the old highly subsidized levels, despite the more than ten-fold increase in most other prices in the state retail trade network and in the open market prices of housing over the last 2 years. While utility rates have gone up considerably, they continue to be subsidized in Russia, Ukraine, Belarus, and presumably in the other republics of the former Soviet Union. The subsidies are scheduled to continue in the near future even after privatization in

---

[21] The Russian law can be found in the supplement to *Ekonomika i zhizn'* (no. 33, August 1991). The Ukrainian draft was discussed in *Zakon i biznes* (no. 7, February 1992).

[22] Note that even though most of the housing privatization laws of this type envisage some compensation to those who do not reside in state-owned housing or have too little housing, this compensation appears to be too small to make much of a difference.

[23] Kosareva, "The Housing Market and Social Guarantees," p. 43.

Russia and Ukraine. In Belarus, however, subsidies will discontinue after privatization.

Other relatively minor considerations to be addressed during privatization include elaboration of the status of partially privatized multi-family buildings, setting standards for exterior maintenance of privatized housing, developing the system of individual (i.e., by apartment) metering of utilities, and so on.

Both the Russian law and the Ukrainian draft preserve the eligibility for improvement in housing conditions of the households currently on the waiting list. Even the citizens who privatized their currently occupied housing may be eligible for state housing in the future. However, each citizen can privatize free of charge only once.

It has to be noted that privatization of housing has been taking place in the former Soviet Union since 1989. Citizens have been allowed to purchase their apartments at their book value, which was based essentially on the original nominal construction costs. In the inflationary environment of the former Soviet Union these costs quickly became negligible for most households. Nonetheless, until recently only a small share of housing has been privatized. The households often do not want to spend even a small amount of money for something they may soon be able to receive free of charge. More important, since housing rents and utility services in state-owned housing remain highly subsidized by the state in all republics of the former Soviet Union, residents do have the incentive to privatize. [24] Also, households are afraid that privatized dwellings would soon be assessed high property taxes based on their current market value. So far, apartments have been privatized mostly by those who plan to emigrate in the near future or those who wish to bequeath housing to their heirs.

PRIVATIZATION OF THE CONSTRUCTION INDUSTRY

Traditionally, the Soviet construction industry was dominated by very large construction enterprises using mostly large panel construction technology. In the late 1980s there were approximately 550 technically obsolete and inefficient housing construction enterprises (*kombinats*) with an annual production capacity of 60–70 million square meters of housing. These enterprises accounted for almost 60% of state housing construction. They mass-produced a limited number of multistory residential buildings. [25] Clearly, the transition to a market-driven housing sector requires a major overhaul if not the closing of these enterprises. The major technological change dictated by market demand is to switch from the large panel construction techniques to production of single family units and low-rise multifamily buildings. [26]

---

[24] In the beginning of this year housing officials in Ukraine estimated that the cost to a household of maintaining and operating a typical two room apartment would increase more than six-fold due to the loss of state subsidies after privatization (personal information).

[25] Ronkin, "Problemy sbalansirovannosti."

[26] According to the forecast in "Osnovnye napravleniia zhilishchnogo stroitel'stva v RSFSR," (*Pazvitie*, no. 36, November 1991, p. 9), the share of individually financed construction should reach 25 percent by 1995, and 40 percent by the year 2000. The same forecast predicts that single family units will be favored by individual households.

Even if such technological change proves to be possible, the newly created market environment requires small and flexible privately owned construction enterprises. Most private enterprise in the construction sector in the former Soviet Union takes the form of cooperatives—private partnerships that initially served as a compromise between the "socialist" and the "capitalist" modes of ownership. [27] At the end of 1990 there were 75,522 active construction cooperatives in the U.S.S.R. employing 2.5 million people including part-timers. In terms of the volume of business the construction cooperatives were the most numerous and fastest growing type of cooperative in the country, leaving all other types of cooperatives far behind. [28] It has to be noted, however, that these private construction organizations sold their output primarily to state-owned enterprises and public organizations. At least until recently, this tendency was due to the ability of state-owned enterprises to help the cooperatives to procure construction materials and transport. Construction cooperatives, especially those involved in the production of construction materials, often begin their existence by taking over poorly performing state enterprises.

The fast growth of construction cooperatives has been taking place despite significant obstacles that they face in their development. These include the political instability in the country, the unpredictability of the future legal environment and taxation rules, the large discretion of local authorities in the implementation of legislation and in licensing construction activities, the instability of the financial system, the undeveloped capital markets, the lack of a business culture and the essential business skills such as accounting, the poor state of the transportation and communication infrastructure, and the rise in crime directed at private enterprises. While most of these problems affect all private businesses in the former Soviet Union, housing construction enterprises suffer more than others due to the relatively lengthy and capital-intensive nature of their production process.

Genuine privatization of most state housing construction enterprises has not yet taken place in the former Soviet Union. Many of them, however, have been leased by their work force. Leaseholds represent an intermediate form of enterprise re-organization combining the features of both state enterprises and cooperatives. The assets of leased enterprises continue to belong to the state, but these enterprises acquire a significant degree of independence from the state management structure. Lately, of course, even bona fide state enterprises have become essentially independent of the central government. Even though state ownership does not impose nearly as many constraints on construction enterprises as it used to, their privatization remains important for revitalization of the construction industry. Privatization will raise the efficiency of asset utilization at these enterprises. It would also make it easier to break them up and to downsize them, for example, by selling their assets piecemeal to smaller enterprises.

---

[27] Construction cooperatives should not be confused with housing cooperatives, the organizations of citizens for collective ownership of housing.

[28] See V. Barbashov, and I. Chebatkov, "Kooperativnyi sektor: problemy i perspectivy," *Ekonomika i zhizn'*, no. 20, May 1991, p. 12, for more information on construction cooperatives.

The emerging system of commodity exchanges constitutes a vital element of the market infrastructure in the construction industry in the former Soviet Union. Their importance has been enhanced by the breakdown of the state supply system. While the transactions on these exchanges often represent a thinly veiled form of barter and are subject to various irregularities, they provide the beginnings of the genuine market supply system.

REFORM OF URBAN LAND USE MANAGEMENT

The major republics of the former Soviet Union have begun to recognize the importance of charging positive prices for land. Both Russia and Ukraine have passed laws regulating payments for land. Implementation of these laws is in question, however, since none of these countries has a well-functioning system for valuation of land. Moreover, all countries of the former Soviet Union impose serious restrictions on the forms of ownership of land and on the ability to trade it. While significant improvements in the efficiency of land use do not require transfer of all land in private ownership, successful land reform should probably include the following provisions: a) protection from termination of the rights to use land, except through well-defined legal process; b) the ability to trade these rights more or less freely; c) taking into account significant externalities arising from use of land, e.g. payments for damaging the surrounding lands; d) procedures for financing trunk infrastructure. [29]

---

[29] This classification is based on N. Tideman, "Efficiency and Justice for a Reformed Russian Economy," mimeo, 1992.

SCIENCE, TECHNOLOGY, AND EDUCATION IN THE FORMER U.S.S.R.

by Harley Balzer *

CONTENTS

SUMMARY

The Soviet Union created an impressive but also contradictory system of education and science. Tremendous resources were devoted to priority programs, but the achievements were often formal. The result after 70 years was a system reflecting the economy and society: an extensive network of educational and scientific institutions, only a limited number of which were of high quality or generated substantial returns. Since the late 1950s, reform of the education and science systems has been a constant topic of discussion.

Following the initiation of perestroika, reform efforts became more sweeping and more serious. But the changes continued to be based on the premise that the state could plan personnel needs and research programs. Despite some local successes, education and science reforms in 1987–1989 were fragile and limited. In the face of economic crisis since 1990, the situation has become chaotic and, in 1992, tragic. It is likely that a significant portion of the educational and scientific institutions created in the U.S.S.R. will cease to exist, and that a large percentage of the personnel will move to other activities.

* Harley Balzer is Associate Professor of Government and Director of the Russian Area Studies Program at Georgetown University. This chapter draws on research supported by the National Council for Soviet and East European Research; the National Science Foundation; and the Carnegie Corporation of New York.

INTRODUCTION

The network of scientific and educational institutions represented both one of the greatest achievements and one of the most expensive failures of the Soviet regime. The Bolsheviks were able to concentrate impressive resources on path-breaking scientific research, and brought the formal educational level of their population to one of the highest standards in the world. But in education and in science and technology (S&T), formal achievements were not translated into material rewards. Successes in the space and weapons programs produced little economic payoff. In the past three decades, revolutionary energy was replaced by careerism and stultification, leaving only a few exceptional points of excellence on a dreary landscape. As in so many aspects of Soviet life, it is difficult to convey simultaneously both how far the people came from the pre-Revolutionary situation, and how far short they fell of their own stated goals.

CHARACTERISTICS OF RUSSIAN/SOVIET SCIENCE AND EDUCATION

There are many ways to present the legacy of tsarist and Soviet attributes in the science and education systems. The following dozen characteristics cover most of the important features. [1]
1. Education and science have always had a high profile, closely identified with the prestige of the state. In Russia, the Academy was the *Imperial* Academy of Sciences, and many of the major institutions of higher education were named for rulers. In the Soviet period, the regime devoted tremendous resources to scientific projects that promised high returns in political prestige if not in economic development, most notably the space race with America in the 1960s and 1970s. [2]
2. Partly due to priorities of prestige and defense, and partly as a result of gross inefficiency, science and education were allocated large budgets despite relatively low returns. This was particularly true of the enormous network of scientific research institutions that developed after the Second World War. But throughout the system, even in tsarist times, large expenditures for showcase facilities were not accompanied by calculations of the returns on these investments. Perhaps the most glaring example of failure to contemplate the costs of behavior is visible in the ecological disaster zone that has been created throughout the former Soviet empire. [3]
3. Cultural and institutional behavior has favored continuity, stability, and risk-aversion. Most large bureaucratic systems tend toward conservatism, and neither the Russian nor the Soviet system was an exception. The ability to continue research on a specific topic for decades without being pressured for results is a scien-

---

[1] For analyses focusing mainly on S&T, see Thane Gustafson, "Why Doesn't Soviet Science Do Better Than it Does?" in *The Social Context of Soviet Science*, Linda L. Lubrano and Susan Gross Solomon, eds., (Boulder, CO: Westview Press, 1980), pp. 31–67; and Harley Balzer, *Soviet Science on the Edge of Reform* (Boulder, CO: Westview Press, 1989), Chapter 5.

[2] On the political uses of space activities in particular see Walter McDougall, *The Heavens and the Earth: A Political History of the Space Age* (New York: Basic Books, 1985); and David Potts, "The Soviet Man in Space," Ph.D. Dissertation, Georgetown University, 1992.

[3] Murray Feshbach and Alfred Friendly, Jr., *Ecocide in the USSR: Health and Nature Under Siege* (New York: Basic Books, 1992).

tist's dream and sometimes produces important results. But more often R&D activities have swallowed resources without generating returns. Where all science is bureaucratic, there are few incentives for risk-taking or innovation.

4. The major strength of Russian and Soviet scientific activity has been in theoretical fields, while applied work, innovation, and diffusion have been relatively weak. It is, as they say, no accident that the two best-known pre-Revolutionary scientists, Mendeleev and Lobachevskii, are famous for their theoretical paradigms. Mendeleev's extensive writings on industrial planning are virtually unknown today. This pattern continued in the Soviet period, reinforced by the education system, the character of leading scientific schools, a lack of equipment for experimentation, and the political difficulties involved in large projects.

5. Russian and Soviet science and education evolved a distinct style, a somewhat extreme variant of Continental European patterns, that differs in some marked respects from the way Americans approach similar disciplines. Few Russians would think of beginning work on a topic without first formulating a "general conception." Educational programs tend to be detailed and encyclopedic, even in the early grades of elementary school. New educational institutions that have opened in the past year or two in most cases are continuing these traditions. The benefits of excellent secondary school programs in math and science were frequently dissipated by stultifying higher education experiences. And successes in math and science were accompanied by abysmal levels of skills in the social sciences, psychology, economics, and business. When scientists present their work in print, it is often in a form that is fully understandable to their Russian colleagues but less accessible to scholars outside the system.

A crucial aspect of Russian style is the system of scientific schools that was developed. As they attempt to fend off pressures for change, members of the Russian Academy in particular are emphasizing the unique nature of these groups of researchers, centered around the personality of a leading scholar who often is their social and moral leader as well as scientific and administrative chief. At its best, the system produced scholar-teachers like Lev Landau, whose demanding standards and concern for his disciples were legendary. [4] But just as often the system has engendered abuses, with administrators putting their names on hundreds of articles written by subordinates. The practice of "organizing" rather than writing doctoral theses continues to this day.

6. In Russian and Soviet administrative practice, rampant departmentalism has been dominant. Before the Revolution, every Ministry of the tsarist government operated its own network of educational institutions to train cadres for its purposes. In the 1920s higher education continued to be a point of contention between the educational and financial/industrial bureaucracies, and after 1930 a ministerial approach again prevailed. A similar divi-

---

[4] For a good description of the Landau school, see Mark Ya. Azbel, *Refusenik: Trapped in the Soviet Union* (Boston: Houghton Mifflin, 1981), pp. 119–127 and *passim*. Also see Kendall E. Bailes, *Science and Russian Culture in an Age of Revolution: V.I. Vernadsky and His Scientific School, 1863–1945* (Bloomington, IN; Indiana U. Press, 1990).

sion prevails in scientific research, with three separate systems—
the Academy, higher education, and branch industrial research—
having their own approaches, sources of funding, and priorities.

7. One of the highest priorities, particularly in the Soviet period,
has been the military. We now know that perhaps as much as
three-quarters of R&D expenditures went to finance projects that
were in some way military-related. The statistics are problematic,
since there are no good measures of how effective or even necessary this vast R&D empire was, and there were obviously strong
incentives to get even dubious research projects stamped "secret"
to enhance their prestige and improve chances for regular appropriations.

The tsarist tradition of military education was revived in the
Soviet period, with a large network of military schools producing
the professional officer corps that played such a prominent role in
military affairs. A lesser-known but equally important aspect of
the military emphasis is seen in the "Soviet" language, including
discussions of changes in science and education. Even current reformers tend to speak in terms of activity at the "front" of S&T, of
mobilizing "reserves," and of "taking key positions." The militarization of language by the Bolsheviks during the civil war has been
so thoroughly assimilated that it will take a long time to dimin-
ish. [5]

8. Emphasis on the military was only the most salient result of
broad political involvement in education and science. These areas
were hardly immune to political influences before the Revolution,
though for a century the Education Ministry had been grudgingly
conceding the lower levels of the education system to greater
public involvement, seeking to preserve total control only over the
classical gymnazia and the universities whose graduates could
become members of the nobility. In the Soviet era, political control
became a crucial aspect of the life of all institutions, and science
and education were closely monitored. Successes in priority areas
were achieved not so much by creating separate systems as by committing resources, including political capital, to overcome obstacles.

It should be stressed that the consequences of politicization were
not one-sided. Political motives led to lavish funding and tremendous prestige for many specialists in the weapons and space programs, while cases of extreme degradation like the Lysenko episode
were exceptions. It was the day-to-day grind of political accountability, the stifling of initiative, and especially the growing pressure to fill administrative positions with party people in the past
few decades that may have been the most debilitating consequence
of politicization. [6]

9. Departmentalism, militarism and politicization inevitably accentuated problems of inhibited information flow. In the tsarist
period, underdeveloped communications infrastructure and the

---

[5] Sheila Fitzpatrick, "The Civil War as a Formative Experience" in *Bolshevik Culture: Experiment and Order in the Russian Revolution*, Abbott Gleason, Peter Kenez and Richard Stites, eds.
(Bloomington, IN; Indiana U. Press, 1985), p. 58.

[6] My analysis differs from that of some other commentators, who see the detrimental effects
of political influence as more pervasive and more damaging. For example, see Mark Povovsky,
Manipulated Science: The Crisis of Science and Scientists in the Soviet Union Today, translated
by Paul S. Falla (Garden City, NY: Doubleday, 1979).

lack of commercial demand held back rapid dissemination of information. In the Soviet period, particularly after Stalin's rise to power, withholding information became much safer than sharing it. It will take a long time for these habits to change. [7]

10. Despite the priority accorded to some disciplines and projects, science and education have generally been starved for resources and characterized by weak infrastructure. The waste of resources on showcase projects during the past century may not have been any more egregious than in other industrial nations, but it has been more striking due to the overall stringency. Western visitors to Soviet facilities were almost always struck by the difficulty in obtaining even the most basic supplies and equipment. This has now become a serious crisis.

11. One aspect of the infrastructure and information problems has been so serious that it deserves special mention—computing. The micro-computer revolution has changed virtually every branch of science in the past decade, including the theoretical fields once thought to be "exempt" from the need for technology. A lack of computing capacity threatens to leave many Russian scientists behind in their ability to carry out research, their ability to keep up with developments in their fields using data banks and electronic pre-prints, and their ability to communicate with colleagues via electronic-mail. In education, grand plans for universal computer literacy have come up against harsh economic realities.

12. Finally, most of these difficulties have not been a secret. In both Russia and the U.S.S.R., education and science have been subjects of virtually perpetual superficial reform. [8] The tsarist government had committees at work on reform of the education system almost incessantly. In the Soviet period, both education and science were subject to the well-known "experiments work" syndrome, whereby demonstration projects were accorded special resources and priority attention. With these extras, the experiments often succeeded, but they were hardly ever replicable on a broad scale.

THE SOVIET ACHIEVEMENT

The U.S.S.R. was the first nation to undertake the peacetime planning of R&D, and even in the 1920s devoted substantial resources to scientific activity that did not necessarily promise immediate returns. Both Vladimir Vernadsky, the "father of the biosphere," and the physiologist Ivan Pavlov chose to continue their path-breaking work in Russia because the Bolsheviks were willing to support their research at a level well beyond what any European or American institution would provide. [9] During rapid industri-

---

[7] For a perceptive analysis of information issues in Russian and Soviet society see S. Frederick Starr, "New Communications Technologies and Civil Society," in *Science and the Soviet Social Order*, Loren Graham, ed., (Cambridge, MA: Harvard U. Press, 1990), pp. 19–50.

[8] On the "reform syndrome" and earlier reform efforts see Harley D. Balzer, "Is Less More? Soviet Science in he Gorbachev Era," *Issues in Science and Technology*, Summer 1985, pp. 29–46; E. Zaleski et. al., *Science Policy in the USSR* (Paris: OECD, 1961). The phenomenon is not unlike the Hawthorne experiments in American experience.

[9] For data on government support for science in the 1920s, see Robert Lewis, *Science and Industrialization in the USSR* (New York: Holmes & Meier, 1979), pp. 7–11. On Vernadsky, see Kendall E. Bailes, *Science and Russian Culture in an Age of Revolution: V.I. Vernadsky and His Scientific School* (Bloomington, IN: Indiana U. Press, 1990). On Pavlov see the as-yet unpublished conference papers by Daniel Todes.

alization in the 1930s, as part of post-war reconstruction after 1945, and again in the Khrushchev era, there was exponential growth in the number of specialists and institutions.

In education, the Soviet achievement was particularly impressive, as the nation achieved levels of literacy and formal education that are among the highest in the world. In every case, however, the approaches taken to attain these goals carried with them serious costs. In the 1920s, the literacy campaign focused on adults for political reasons, leaving many children outside the education system. In the 1930s, secondary and particularly higher technical education were expanded with an emphasis on narrow specialties and on large numbers of politically selected students rather than on content and quality. [10]

Perhaps most striking to a Western observer is the formal character of so many of the accomplishments. Students attended school and learned things, but most did not develop the ability to put that knowledge to use in ways that helped them to deal with everyday problems. Scientists conducted research, but all too often they did so in a vacuum, divorced from efforts to use that research for purposes other than having it completed. This was particularly the case in the technical sciences, where it was not unknown for individuals to write dissertations about improvements in obsolete technical processes, and where much contract R&D was done "for the shelf." The gulf between the formal/theoretical and the practical may be one of the most difficult vestiges of the old system to overcome.

SHORTCOMINGS AND STAGNATION

Even before Mikhail Gorbachev encouraged efforts to lift the veil concealing problems in Soviet life, some critics and reformers had sought to confront the difficulties. In the Khrushchev era a broad public discussion of education reform involved the public in unprecedented if still limited ways. [11] As a result of the discussions, debates, and policy changes, education became a constant focus of reform. The Khrushchev-era changes were revised and in important instances rescinded by a reform in 1966, and this program was subjected to sharp criticism leading to another major reform in 1984. [12] Similar cycles of reform in other countries raise the question of whether any society ever gets a truly satisfactory education system. [13]

Comparable developments in reforming the S&T system were embodied in debates accompanying the economic reforms associated with Evsei Liberman. "Libermanism" both framed the problem

---

[10] Harley D. Balzer, "Engineers: The Rise and Decline of a Social Myth" in *Science and the Soviet Social Order*, Loren Graham, ed., pp. 141–167. For a somewhat different perspective, see Sheila Fitzpatrick, *Education and Social Mobility in the Soviet Union, 1921–1934* (Cambridge: Cambridge U. Press, 1979).

[11] James B. Bruce, *The Politics of Soviet Policy Formation: Khrushchev's Innovative Policies in Education and Agriculture* (Denver: University of Denver, 1976); Mervyn Matthews, *Education in the Soviet Union: Policies and Institutions Since Stalin* (London: Allen & Unwin, 1982).

[12] Matthews, *Education in the Soviet Union*; and Robert Campbell, et al., *Soviet Science and Technology (S&T) Education* (McLean, VA: Science Applications, 1985).

[13] For discussion of the cycles of education reform in New York City, see Diane Ravitch, *The Great School Wars: New York City, 1805–1973* (New York: Basic Books, 1974).

and set the limits of discussion for more than two decades. [14] While many proposals to introduce market elements and competition were aired, an opposition based on ideological rigidity and entrenched bureaucratic interests blocked serious change. [15] It became clear that discussion of "local" abuses and limited experiments would be acceptable, but that more fundamental criticisms of a systemic nature would not be allowed. This balance underlay the "era of stagnation" that was so harshly criticized after 1985.

PERESTROIKA

It is not at all apparent that Mikhail Gorbachev came to office intending anything beyond a more efficient and purposeful version of earlier reforms. In its initial incarnation, perestroika focused on the same search for a technological quick fix and the same emphasis on increased efficiency and productivity that underlay virtually all Soviet reform proposals beginning in the late 1930s. (It is worth recalling that the Second Five-Year Plan, 1932–37, was hailed as the "Plan of Quality," but it quickly succumbed to pressures for short-term production.)

During 1985–87 the Gorbachev team prepared a series of reforms that sought to extract maximum efficiency from the old centralized system while only tinkering with its basic character. [16] But after two or three years of shocking disclosures and ineffectual reform efforts, Gorbachev himself and many of his key associates articulated what could well be the epitaph for perestroika: "We did not know the country in which we lived." [17] By 1988 they had come to understand that the system had to be changed rather than merely repaired or fine tuned, and the main focus shifted to political reforms.

The 1987 economic reforms included a full-scale effort to address S&T. [18] Like standard Central Committee decrees, it began by noting the most serious problems. This discussion was notable not for the novelty of the difficulties mentioned, which had become part of a regular litany, but for the degree of frankness in describing those difficulties. The authors asserted that technical progress had slowed to the point that often even the most advanced Soviet technology was not able to compete on world markets. Ministries, departments, and individual enterprises had no incentive to concern themselves with improving S&T. There was no solid system for the collection, analysis, dissemination, and use of information

---

[14] For a discussion of Liberman and his impact in economics see Richard W. Judy, "The Economists" in *Interest Groups in Soviet Politics*, H. Gordon Skilling and Franklyn Griffiths, eds. (Princeton, NJ: Princeton U. Press, 1971), pp. 209–251, particularly 233–245. On the reform proposals in S&T, see Zaleski et al.

[15] In a discussion at the Library of Congress in 1992, Mikhail Gorbachev spoke of having been a member of the Central Committee when that body voted to curtail the Liberman reforms.

[16] *O korennoi perestroike upravleniia ekonomikoi. Sbornik dokumentov* (Moscow: Politizdat, 1987).

[17] On the political history of perestroika see Stephen White, *Gorbachev and After* (Cambridge: Cambridge U. Press, 1991); and Harley Balzer, "Politics as Process" in Balzer, ed., *Five Years That Shook the World: Gorbachev's Unfinished Revolution* (Boulder, CO: Westview Press, 1991) pp. 61–90. For repetition of the phrase by the President of the Soviet Academy of Sciences, see Gurii Marchuk, "Kakoi byt' nauke?" *Poisk*, No. 12, July 1989, pp. 1–3.

[18] The Postanovlenie TsK KPSS i SovMin SSSR of July 17, 1987 No. 817, "O povyshenii roli gosudarstevennogo komiteta SSSR po nauke i tekhnike v upravlenii nauchno-tekhnicheskim progressom v trane," appeared in *O korennoi perestroike upravleniia ekonomikoi*, pp. 91–108.

about developments in Russia or abroad. International scientific and technical cooperation was poorly organized. This applied particularly to the East European allies. And there were serious shortcomings in training and management of personnel.

To address these needs, the government offered a typically Soviet document emphasizing planning and coordination. One of the characteristic features of the Soviet mentality was a belief that any difficulty could be addressed by planning. If the results were not satisfactory, it was taken as reflecting the need for more and better planning, rather than as a reason to question planning itself.

The most important feature of the reform was broad adoption of the principle of self-financing and cost accounting (khozraschet). Improved planning of S&T at all levels would permit a privileged position for programs of "general state significance." This would be particularly true in the case of Interbranch Science-Technology Complexes (MNTKs) and priority State Programs. Special rights were also accorded to temporary scientific collectives and other "progressive" forms of integrating Academy, VUZ (vysshoe uchebnoe zavedenie, higher education institution), and branch science with production.

The system of khozraschet included a review of the financing of all R&D work, initiating a switch from financing organizations to financing projects under contracts with interested parties. Work on the most important theoretical research in social, natural, and technical sciences continued to receive support from the state budget, as did important interbranch S&T programs, with particular emphasis on creating new technology to "revolutionize production."

These economic changes were the true heart of the 1987 reform measures concerning S&T. Other proposals, including improvements in the system of scientific-technical information, more emphasis on international cooperation, and attention to the training and quality of personnel, were couched in language that was prescriptive and general.

The new financial arrangements did have a serious impact. Over the next four years, important changes took place in the way enterprises and ministries structured their support for R&D. These actions were not always carried out in the spirit intended by reformers, but what took place was a rational response to the new situation. The self-financing and cost accounting reforms had only a limited impact on production, most of which continued to be regulated by state orders under de facto monopolies. But the legislation encouraged new types of R&D organizations, spurring rapid increases in financing and salaries. Thousands of new cooperatives and other small organizations were established.

During the Brezhnev era, government policies had levelled wages to the point where scientists, engineers, and bus drivers earned about the same base pay, while Stalin-era laws continued to prohibit working more than one job. After 1987, the self-financing and contract arrangements generated a "boom" in financing science. Funds from all sources—state budget, contracts, and special projects—were increased. Enterprises found R&D an attractive use for excess cash in their development funds. Under new laws, many researchers were able to moonlight as consultants or members of cooperatives, while still drawing their full salaries at institutes or enterprises and utilizing the resources of these institutions.

In some ways, the 1987 reforms set up the scientific community for a hard fall. Despite growth of thousands of new R&D organizations, few of the existing institutions ceased to exist. Rather than seeking new areas of activity, leaders of most large institutions devoted their energy to arguing that their establishments were so important to the nation that they deserved to remain in the state-financed sector. As much of the burden of financing shifted to enterprises, science and education became dependent on their economic health. It was a precarious situation—many of the new scientific organizations relied on existing institutions for space, staff, and equipment. The state sector was in effect subsidizing the new private sector, so that the collapse of the state sector is destroying both. By 1991 the situation became critical, and in 1992 it became desperate. Salaries are not keeping pace with inflation; people are working more hours and many are working at two or more jobs; and hundreds of thousands of people are leaving work in R&D. [19]

The impact of perestroika on education was even more contradictory. Mikhail Gorbachev inherited from his predecessors a program for reforming secondary education that was driven by economic and labor force considerations. His team added a restructuring of higher education that began from the same premises, but that also reflected some of the humanistic considerations of "new thinking." In 1988 they sought to give all of education a more Gorbachevian character by "deepening" both reforms. [20] The semantic difference is important. The secondary school *reform* was in many ways a Brezhnev-era program: The result of years of preparation and experimentation, it emphasized gradual change over an extended period of time, and implementation was slow. By contrast, the *restructuring* of higher education reflected Mr. Gorbachev's approach. It was more radical, featuring an announcement of sweeping generalizations with details to be supplied later, and was characterized by a willingness to try bolder experiments and take risks. Both programs were complex and at times contradictory. Increasingly, the locus of initiative shifted from the center to republican and local authorities, a process markedly accentuated by the breakup of the U.S.S.R.

---

[19] A valuable treatment of developments in the period 1987–1991 is found in Russian Academy of Sciences, Analytical Center for Problems of Socio-Economy and Science-Technology Development, *Science in Russia Today and Tomorrow* (Moscow, December 1991).

[20] Draft guidelines for the reform of general education were published in the central press January 4, 1984. Following three months of public discussion, a revised version was published April 14, 1984. "Basic Directions" for the restructuring of higher and specialized and secondary education appeared in the central press June 1, 1986. There was again a public discussion, but the issues proved difficult to resolve. The Politburo approved the Basic Directions "in principle" August 28, 1986, but instructed MinVuz to continue working on the legislation. On January 6, 1987 the Politburo again referred the project back to their specialists for additional work. In February Mr. Gorbachev acknowledged that there were sharp differences of opinion about the reform. On March 21, 1987 the central press published a revised version of the "Basic Directions," followed by five major decrees implementing portions of the reform (March 25–29, 1987). Despite, or more likely because of the prolonged deliberations, these documents were less specific than the general education reform materials.

The combining of the two reforms and their extension was first articulated at the Central Committee Plenum February 17–19, 1988. See Egor Ligachev's speech at the Plenum, *Komsomol'skaia pravda, February 18, 1988; and the Decree of the Central Committee "O khode perestroiki srednei i vysshei shkoly i zadachakh partii po ee osushchestvleniiu," Sovetskaia Rossiia, February 20, 1988.*

Major provisions of the general education reform included adding an additional year by having children begin school at age six; overhauling the curriculum to make it less complex and more intensive, while adding new courses in social and political topics; increasing the vocational component of education by requiring vocational training at all levels, increasing the proportion of students attending vocational schools and establishing a program of vocational guidance; achieving universal computer literacy; and increasing the resources for the education system, particularly for teacher salaries. All of this was to be carried out over two to three five-year plans. [21]

The basic principles of higher education reform articulated in 1986–1987 included improving quality, in large measure by raising standards and eliminating weak students and institutions; new, more carefully targeted admissions policies, including special arrangements for veterans and workers; more accountability in the system of planning admissions and placing graduates; revised and individualized curricula, with increased emphasis on student participation in scientific research; "continuous" education, with retraining and recertification every five years; and increased resources for education, mainly from the ministries and enterprises employing the graduates. The thrust of the reform was greater independence and diversity within a context of more rational use of scarce human and material resources. [22]

Underlying both reforms was an emphasis on creativity and a more individualized approach stressing development of a student's personality and abilities. The other side of this coin was increased emphasis on the responsibility of students, their families, and their collectives for a "mature attitude" toward education. The state would provide new educational opportunities and a better system of gauging an individual's aptitudes and inclinations; in return, those studying should work harder during their education and subsequently in the jobs for which they were trained.

At all levels of education the goal was to make better use of the time devoted to education and to increase quality. Education was to be not only more intensive, but also more *appropriate*: The amount of education an individual received was to be more carefully monitored, and training was to be integrated with subsequent employment. The extra year of primary education was introduced at the

---

[21] For details on the primary, secondary and vocational education reforms, see Harley Balzer, "From Hypercentralization to Diversity: Continuing Efforts to Restructure Soviet Education" in *Technology In Society* No. 3, 1990, pp. 123–149; Balzer, "Secondary Technical Education in Russia/USSR: The Muddled Middle Level," in *Education and Economic Development Since the Industrial Revolution* Gabriel Tortella, ed., (Valencia: Generalitat Valenciana, 1990) pp. 289–305; Balzer, "Soviet Education in 1988," *Journal of Comparative Education Annual Survey of Events* May 1989; Jeanne Sutherland, "Perestroika in the Soviet General School: From Innovation to Independence," in *Soviet Education Under Perestroika*, John Dunstan, ed. (London: Routledge, 1992) pp. 14–29; Dunstan, "Soviet Education Beyond 1984: A Commentary on the Reform Guidelines," *Compare* Vol. 15, No. 2, 1985, pp. 161–187; and B. B. Szekely, "The New Soviet Educational Reform," *Comparative Education Review* Vol. 30 No. 3, 1986, pp. 321–343.

[22] Details on higher education reform are available in Harley Balzer, "The Soviet Scientific-Technical evolution: Education of Cadres," in *The Status of Soviet Civil Science*, ed. Craig Sinclair, (Dordrecht: Martinus Nijhoff, 1987) pp. 3–18; Balzer, "Educating Scientific-Technical Revolutionaries?: Continuing Efforts to Restructure Soviet Higher Education," in Dunstan, ed., *Soviet Education Under Perestroika* pp. 164–195; Stephen T. Kerr, "Debate and Controversy in Soviet Higher Education Reform: Reinventing A System," in Dunstan, ed., *Soviet Education Under Perestroika* pp. 146–163; and Kerr, "The Soviet Reform of Higher Education" *Review of Higher Education*, vol. 11, No. 3, 1988, pp. 215–246.

"front end," so that no time would be lost from productive labor. War was declared on "wasted" time by raising standards at all levels, tracking more students to vocational schools, reducing VUZ admissions and threatening to close poor quality programs.

In addition to the punitive steps of limiting access to higher education and clearing out "dead wood," positive steps were taken in curriculum and resource allocation. Funds were made available to increase teachers' salaries, purchase computers, raise VUZ student stipends, improve vocational training, and increase the remuneration of productive R&D workers. The curriculum at all levels provided opportunities for productive activity: vocational labor for secondary school students; scientific research for higher education students; and advanced research for those pursuing post-graduate degrees. Along with improving quality, a major effort was made to tap the R&D potential of VUZ.

The attempts at centrally directed reform are now widely acknowledged to have been unsuccessful. The reform programs of 1984, 1986–87 and 1988 represented the last gasp all-Union initiatives in education. Discussion of these reforms produced a wealth of unprecedented commentary, criticism and documentation, giving observers their fullest picture ever of conditions in Soviet schools. But, like so much of perestroika, diagnosing the symptoms did not lead to a cure. More sophisticated planning was still planning, and administrators remained highly skilled in techniques of resistance.

Despite the greater involvement of Gorbachev reformers in preparing the VUZ reform program, raising the hope that it might surpass achievements in general education, change was painfully slow. Although a few leading VUZ, led by innovative administrators, implemented interesting experimental programs, most institutions of higher education remained under the control of conservative rectors, while the higher education administration was slow to act in encouraging meaningful change. [23]

Since 1988, centrifugal tendencies have been the dominant feature of Soviet political life, and this has been particularly evident in education. Authority over the schools is increasingly passing into the hands of regional and local governments. The result could eventually be an impressive and healthy diversity, with far more varieties of education available to students. But someone has to pay the bills.

DIVERSITY

In 1990 and 1991, perestroika gave way to a much more diverse and less centralized approach to reform. Whatever possibility still existed for changes directed from the center was destroyed by the August 1991 coup attempt. In its wake, the U.S.S.R. ceased to exist, and the ability of Russia to maintain a strong centralized authority came into serious question. In this situation, it has become impossible to speak of policies and conditions in the nation as a whole. Rather, it is and will continue to be necessary to examine regional

---

[23] For one of the most recent critiques of "talk rather than action," see Iu. Kimov, A. Kushel', and V. Meshalkin, "Attestatsiia i akkreditatsiia vuzov" *Alma mater* [formerly *Vestnik vysshei shkoly*] No. 4, April 1991, pp. 11–14.

and local situations. In what follows, the emphasis will be on the Russian Federation.

A full program for reform of general education was developed in the Russian Republic even before the disintegration of the U.S.S.R. Based on work conducted for a number of years under the direction of E.D. Dneprov, now Minister of Education of Russia, it emphasizes humanistic principles and recognition of diversity. [24] Comparable documents for higher education were prepared by the Russian State Committee for Science and Higher Education. [25] Reflecting the emphasis on linking science and higher education, this program is also the most comprehensive treatment of intended changes in Russian science—there is not and is not likely to be another separate centrally designed S&T reform program.

Characteristically, both programs begin with harsh critiques of defects in the existing system, and it is worth noting which problems receive emphasis. Unlike previous critiques, including the oft-cited one by Ligachev in 1988, which emphasized a utilitarian (economic) rationale for reform, these documents stress humanism and personality. They represent a "human capital" approach in the best sense of that term—that investing in people will ultimately pay off. But the goal of maximizing each individual's potential is tempered by a serious dose of economic reality.

The consequences predicted if the prevailing "ineffective" system of education continues include losing the possibility of democratic development because of inadequate legal, economic, and political education; a crisis among youth resulting from their defenselessness in a market system; Russia's inability to compete in the world economy; and severance from Russia's humanitarian culture.

The basic principles underlying Russia's education programs are to be: decentralization and democracy (*samorazvitie*); quality; diversity; a unified system of uninterrupted education; [26] attention to the needs of various regions and republics (effectiveness); and equality of opportunity. Administration is to be decentralized, with authority vested in local, regional, and republican bodies. Regional development strategies and labor resources, along with the determination of regional priority directions in science, will be the responsibility of regional centers of science and higher education.

In higher education, the number one social issue mentioned is unsatisfied demand. [27] The higher education system will consist of four levels or stages, with broad access to the first level and competitive procedures for those wishing to study at more advanced

---

[24] The fullest statement of the school reform program is in *Rossiiskoe obrazovanie v perekhodnyi period: Programma stabilizatsii i razvitiia* (Moscow: Ministerstvo obrazovaniia RSFSR, 1991).
[25] *Gosudarstvennaia programma razvitiia vysshego obrazovaniia v RSFSR (Proekt)* (GKNVS RSFSR, 1991); and *Vremennoe polozhenie o mnogourovennevoi sisteme vysshego obrazovaniia v RSFSR (Proekt)* (GKNVS RSFSR, 1991).
[26] The use of the words "diversity" and "unified" here do not represent a contradiction. In the Russian context unified does not mean standardized, but rather refers to a system in which each level of education may lead to the next higher level—a system where no type of school represents a "dead end" precluding further study. The issue is particularly sensitive in the history of Russian pedagogy, due to the tsarist government's effort to maintain two separate systems of education, one for the nobility and one for the lower classes. "Liberal" Russian educators consistently fought for a "unified" school system that would allow all qualified students to attain a higher education.
[27] "Every year the need for continued education is not met for some 400,000 citizens of Russia who present their documents at VUZ on the territory of the RSFSR, including almost 100,000 who successfully pass the entrance examinations." *Gosudarstvennaia programma*, p. 3.

levels. Reflecting the emphasis on broad, humanistic education, universities are to be accorded a special role in the system, and are to receive priority financing. [28]

The higher education reform plan includes very specific provisions regarding scientific research, designed to make VUZ the key institutions not only in training but also in the conduct of R&D. The Russian Republic is to shift to a competitive contract system of financing scientific work. Before 1993 Russia is to complete the combining of academic, branch, and VUZ scientific structures on the basis of universities and leading VUZ. VUZ are to become the major centers of scientific research, housing new centers of science-intensive industry and small-scale production of new technologies, and unifying the scientific and educational processes to involve teachers and students in the research process. But thus far the budgetary support promised for these changes has not been forthcoming.

The government has promised to provide legal and tax stimuli for innovation activity, as well as gearing the education system to enhance the climate for innovation. Increasingly, financing of science should be on the basis of program and competitive contract funding, credit, and venture capital. Scientific organizations will be self-governing. Fundamental research will be supported by a system of grants administered by the Russian Science Fund. [29] Efforts will be supported to finance parallel (competing) lines of research. Advantageous conditions are to be created for alternative small innovation firms, Centers of Scientific-Technical Creativity for Youth (TsNTTMs), cooperatives, and other small, flexible initiatives.

Five concrete measures are proposed to foster innovation. 1) immediately reallocate funds for financing research, putting up to 80 percent of the resources at the disposal of "group" programs; 2) a commercial bank to finance scientific-technical development; 3) a fund for financing fundamental and exploratory scientific research under the GKNVSh RSFSR; 4) technology parks and technopolises (by 1995 no fewer than 12 technology parks and technopolises should be in operation); 5) a system for forecasting and evaluating the main directions of science and a system for concrete and competitive financing of R&D.

There are two possible variants of VUZ funding proposed. One envisions bringing all 495 RSFSR VUZ "up to the Western level" by somewhere between 1995 and 2000. The second variant would provide major support for the 100 strongest VUZ, insuring a nucleus of high quality institutions. Given resource stringency, the more modest proposal will likely be more than enough of a challenge. (In June 1992, top officials of the GKNVSh stated that resolution of this issue is currently "in a fog.")

---

[28] Priority in financing universities may help explain the current rush among VUZ to redefine themselves as universities. Iurii Afanas'ev's Historical-Archives Institute has become the "Humanities University;" the Bauman Moscow Higher Technical School is now a "Technical University;" the Nikolaev Shipbuilding Institute is a "Maritime University"; and several pedagogical institutes have dubbed themselves "Pedagogical Universities."
[29] The Russian Science Fund was finally established in August 1992, but it controls only a small portion of the funding for basic science.

This latest higher education reform program retains a number of the principles articulated during perestroika, while departing significantly from others. The most important departure underlying all the new Russian Republic education proposals is a humanistic and pedagogical motivation, in place of the previous emphasis on demographic and labor force priorities. For the first time since the First Five-Year Plan, the major emphasis in Russian education is on maximizing human potential rather than meeting specific economic and personnel needs.

The linkage of science and higher education is a priority, but will not be carried out in the manner of an old-style campaign. Minister of Science Boris G. Saltykov has stressed that artificial ties will not be of much value. Rather, the government should encourage development of organic links between education and industry. In education, the state can never surrender its role completely. In science, pressure for continued state involvement—particularly state financing—is coming from many quarters. But now the state lacks the resources to maintain existing structures.

THE CURRENT CRISIS

By mid-1992, conditions in the economy, S&T and the education system could be encapsulated in a single word: crisis. The August 1991 coup resulted in a stampede to independence with disastrous consequences for the economy. In the belief that independence would allow them to retain "their" wealth, politicians at all levels demanded new arrangements, severing the complex linkages in the Soviet economic system. Many of these links were indeed irrational, but destroying them without replacements has been even worse. The economies of the Commonwealth of Independent States (CIS) are suffering more from these disruptions than from the effects of Russia's shock therapy reforms.

S&T leaders have been in the forefront of those endeavoring to preserve some sort of linkages. In science, as in industry, interdependencies are being smashed for political reasons, without adequate calculation of the costs. It is not a transition, but an obliteration of old structures.

The U.S.S.R., to its credit, built up a massive edifice of science and education. But no nation could possibly afford to support that infrastructure at world prices. It will require a generation or several before the private sector is in a position to take up the slack. In these circumstances, reductions are unavoidable. The only question is whether the cuts will be on the basis of a rational plan or the law of the academic jungle. Given that no politician could possibly want to put his or her name to a program abolishing scientific and educational institutions, smart money would bet on unplanned reductions, with the inevitable accompanying outcries.

It is a crisis that will almost certainly leave much of the scientific and educational infrastructure created in the U.S.S.R. in ruins. Barring a deus ex machina (outside assistance) of unimaginable proportions, it is doubtful that more than one-third of the individuals employed in science will still be working in their fields by the end of 1993. A sizable number of educational institutions will have to be closed or amalgamated.

The parameters of the crisis are already apparent. For example:

—Financial disaster: Prices have increased 10 to 15 times, while budgets have gone up perhaps 3 times. Institutions now must pay for heating, lighting, repairs, and other infrastructure costs at rapidly inflating rates, with the prospect of major increases in energy costs in the coming two years. Scientific institutions in the former U.S.S.R. are now on quarterly or even monthly budgets, a situation providing no job security and no ability to conduct serious research. Even when promised, funds, including salaries, are not being delivered. [30]

The consequences of inflation and budgetary uncertainty are exacerbated by the virtually complete collapse of other sources of funding. The ministries and enterprises are themselves broke, and no longer in a position to support either institutional or contract research. There has been a massive reduction of previously generous funding by the military—encompassing everything from direct research to support for philology departments because the foreign language specialists could work as military translators. [31]

—Lack of scientific equipment and journals: The total cutoff of hard currency at most institutions has made it impossible to obtain crucial supplies and equipment, or to maintain subscriptions to scientific journals. Scientists are increasingly unable either to conduct their own work or to keep up with the work of their colleagues. In a world where scientists exchange preprints of cutting edge articles, falling behind by a year or two is tantamount to professional obsolescence. [32]

—A growing brain drain: The financial crisis, questionable food supply, and general uncertainty are making it virtually impossible for most specialists to continue their work. The combination of economic stringency and professional frustration is causing a serious "brain drain." There are multiple processes at work here. The aspect that has received extensive media attention is the movement of scientists to jobs in other countries. [33] But emigration abroad *thus far* has been the least serious disruption. The departure of Russian specialists is limited by legislation prohibiting those who held security clearances

---

[30] There is a continuing battle between the Ministry of Finance and the Ministry of Science, with the Financial department dismissing practically everything the Science Ministry proposes. See Marina Lapina, "There is no money for science. And it is unknown ..." *Radikal*, No. 10, March 1992, p. 10. For a discussion of the chaos far milder budgetary uncertainty is causing at American universities see *The New York Times*, July 19, 1992, p. A12.

[31] For a discussion of the extent of military involvement in the R&D sphere see Balzer, *Soviet Science on the Edge of Reform*, pp. 133-134.

[32] The Russian government appropriated $12 million in hard currency for the Russian Academy of Sciences to purchase foreign scientific literature in 1992. But no money was actually provided. Instead, the Academy has inherited a hard currency debt of $175 million from the Soviet Academy. These data were provided by Russian Academy of Sciences President Yurii Osipov in remarks at Georgetown University, April 27, 1992.

[33] Compare *Moskovskaia pravda*, March 11, 1992 pp. 1, 2 where in an interview with S. Kh. Khakimov, S. V Antipov, Assistant Director of the Russian Kurchatov Institute Scientific Center dismisses most talk about a brain drain of physicists to the East as propaganda, with Valerii Zadko, "Are they Waiting for us in South America?" *Krasnaia zvezda*, March 14, 1992, p. 5, where the author asserts that South American nations are recruiting Russian specialists.

from going abroad without special permission. These Soviet-era laws are still in force. [34]

The more extensive and thus far more damaging aspect of the brain drain involves the movement of individuals out of their fields of specialization into activities that promise greater short-term material rewards or greater physical safety. In some instances this entails geographic relocation either within the former U.S.S.R. or, in a more limited number of cases, abroad. Changing employers is particularly problematical in the former U.S.S.R., where many families' housing, day care, vacations, and other aspects of life have been tied to their workplaces. [35]

The costs of this multi-faceted movement of personnel are not always fully appreciated. A partial list of the consequences includes:

—Reversion of some former republics to third world levels of S&T staffing: In at least six of the former Soviet republics, a sizable majority of technical and managerial personnel were Russians or other Slavs (see Table 1). Incomplete data suggest that perhaps half of these individuals have sought to move "back" to Russia and the other "central" republics due to concerns about ethnic animosities and potential discrimination. [36]

—Enterprises denuded of personnel: In many instances, talented specialists reacted to impending reforms by leaving the "targeted" sectors. This included but was hardly limited to enterprises in the defense sector faced with conversion. The result has been that many top "teams" have been gutted, and many facilities are attempting to operate with staffs stripped of their best workers.

—Employment in other sectors: Talented individuals have increasingly sought employment in other sectors, often removed from their previous specialties. There has been an influx of people into various sorts of software development cooperatives and consulting firms. Unfortunately, this is symptomatic of a general preference for employment in the service sector of an economy that still produces far too little. [37]

—Unemployment: A growing number of individuals with specialized education in S&T are unable to find work. The problem is

[34] One recent Moscow survey found that only 6 percent of those who wish to go abroad to work would like to migrate permanently. Aleksandra Mukhina, "A New Odyssey?" *Poisk,* No. 11 (149), March 1992, p. 3. This author also makes the absurd claim that Russia loses about $300,000 on the departure of one specialist.

[35] The pervasive role of workplace in individuals' lives has been described as "Communist neo-traditionalism." the best discussion of the situation is Andrew G. Walder, *Communist Neo-Traditionalism: Work and Authority in Chinese Industry* (Berkeley, CA: U. of California Press, 1986).

[36] Mukhina, "A New Odyssey?"; Timur Pylatov, "Dogoniim i peregonim angolu!", *Moskovskie novosti,* October 14, 1990, p. 7. The situation is exacerbated by so many of the "native" specialists in non-Slavic regions having opted for specialties in culture and the humanities, rather than for scientific, technical, or managerial careers. See *Sotsial'no-kul'turnyi oblik sovetskikh natsii* (Moscow: Nauka, 1986), pp. 60–68.

[37] Scientists and other professionals are leaving their jobs and even their careers in significant numbers. One estimate suggests a figure of 600,000 since the beginning of 1991, with most of these coming since the autumn of 1991 and during 1992. They are working in new places, and even organizing agricultural and craft ooperatives. Sergei Ustinov, "Oni emigrirovali bez OVIRa," *Chas pik* January 27, 1992, p. 3.

particularly acute among recent graduates. As the economic reforms bite, the number is likely to increase markedly. [38]
—Shutoff of the professional "pipeline": Having once been regarded as a highly desirable and prestigious career, science is now considered to be an activity with little promise, causing talented young people to choose other careers. For this to take place in a nation with outstanding secondary school math and science education is a particularly serious loss.
—Emigration: No one knows how many specialists have emigrated. The impact, however, is not measured just by numbers alone. The people who are departing are in many cases key individuals: those with international reputations, with marketable skills, and in a position to land on their feet. For example, at one Academy of Sciences biology lab this year seven of the nine laboratory directors were working abroad. [39]

The following table provides a rough picture of the ethnic distribution of S&T specialists in the former Soviet Union. By comparing data on the number of specialists of a particular nationality in the U.S.S.R. with the number in individual republics, it is possible to see which groups were under-represented and which "exported" specialists. It is clear that the Central Asian region relied on Slavic and other groups for a large portion of the scientific, technical and managerial personnel.

TABLE 1. Scientific Workers of the Former U.S.S.R. by Republic and by Nationality, 1987.

Republic and Nationality	Number in Republic	Number by Nationality in U.S.S.R.
Russia/Russians	1,033,300	1,023,369
Ukraine/Ukrainians	215,000	170,888
Belarus/Belorussians	44,500	38,486
Latvia/Latvians	13,800	7,391
Lithuania/Lithuanians	15,200	13,356
Estonia/Estonians	7,200	6,264
Armenia/Armenians	22,000	32,374
Georgia/Georgians	28,500	26,601
Azerbaidzhan/Azeris	22,800	19,814
Uzbekistan/Uzbeks	39,100	23,026
Kazakhstan/Kazakhs	41,300	18,716
Kirgizstan/Kirghiz	10,100	4,526
Tadzhikistan/Tadzhiks	9,000	4,858
Turkmenistan/Turkmen	5,600	3,593
Moldova/Moldovans	10,500	5,504

Source: *Nauchno-tekhnicheskii progress v SSSR* (Moscow: Finansy i statistika, 1990), pp. 23, 25.

Over the past few years, this writer was one of those who argued that a "small" brain drain was not a bad thing—that increasing

---

[38] For a good recent discussion of the unemployment problems and their context see A. N. Kochetov, Skrytaia bezrabotitsa sredi spetsialistov," *Sotsiologicheskie issledovaniia* No. 5, 1992, pp. 14–23.
[39] Personal communication.

the contact and communication between Soviet and Western specialists would benefit everyone, and that the saturation of the market for Soviet talent in Europe and the United States would provide natural limits to the phenomenon. However, this was before the economy collapsed. Now that former laboratory directors are happy to drive taxicabs in Warsaw, the problem has taken on an entirely different dimension. It is no longer a "brain drain," but rather a large-scale abandonment of the R&D and education sectors.

In education, VUZ administrators do not know if they will be able to pay students' stipends from month to month. There are no funds for publishing textbooks, purchasing equipment or materials, or even for journals. Some speak of a "new iron curtain" where access to information is concerned. As in basic science, Yeltsin's promise of additional funds has remained only on paper. [40] Even the democratization of academic life has had its "down side," as elections for rectors and department heads often turn into messy political conflicts and sometimes scandals. [41]

Complaints about cost of living and inadequate stipends were voiced from the beginning of the year and have grown despite increases in the stipends. [42] The system of job assignments has broken down almost completely. The commissions that previously assigned graduates to three years of obligatory work now function as advisory bodies and clearing houses, but most employers are not in a position to hire new workers. Students are finding that employment in the private sector, and especially in commercial ventures, pays far better than jobs in which their education plays a direct role. For example, it is generally more lucrative to give private lessons than to teach in a state educational institution. [43]

The portrait is not universally bleak, though it is mostly dark. The inability of government to finance education is accelerating local and private initiatives, encouraging an exciting and often healthy diversity of schools. There are now private, religious, and community schools. Expensive private day-care programs are appearing. [44] The diversity is a promising development, but it will not be for everyone. Virtually all the private education initiatives are dependent on donors, often foreign partners or social organizations. For many, the search for solutions involves simply asking authorities for money they do not have. [45]

---

[40] "I tri korochki khleba dlia vysshei shkoly," *Rossiiskaia gazeta* interview with Genndaii Rassokhin, Rektor of the Ukhtinsk Industrial Institute by Iana Iurova, April 17, 1992, p. 2.

[41] Vadim Nesvizhskii, "Kto vozglavit nash iurfak, znaet tol'ko mer Sobchak," *Smena*, March 19, 1992, p. 2.

[42] Vladimir Sobol', "Studenty-narod veselyi, no est' vse ravno khochetsia," *Nevskoe vremia*, January 29, 1992, p. 1. In June 1992 I met with Minister of Science, Higher Education and Technology Policy Boris Saltykov on the same day that he spoke with leaders of student organizations in an effort to persuade them not to call a student strike protesting the amount of their stipends.

[43] One of the major attractions of work in the state sector, government pensions, has little meaning when the country is experiencing hyper-inflation.

[44] Discussions of the new varieties of education are only just beginning to appear in the Western scholarly literature. For a foretaste see the contributions to Dunstan, ed., *Soviet Education Under Perestroika*; and I. Bogachev, "Help the New School? It is Open!" *Uchitel'skaia gazeta*, No. 42, October 1991, p. 4; and the unpublished manuscript by Marie W. Bream, Lev Lurie and Mikhail Ivanov, "Soviet Schools in Transition: The New Schools of St. Petersburg."

[45] In Petersburg, the university rektor, after outlining the disastrous economic situation in which the University finds itself, ended an interview by noting that the Mayor understands how

Continued

Faced with seemingly insurmountable crises, the most typical response has been to look to someone for salvation. The Academy looks to Yeltsin to sign yet another decree promising increased state financing. Specialists make the argument that science is so defenseless and so important that the government—Russian and local—must recognize this fact and act accordingly. [46] There is much thrashing about among administrators.

The cruelest irony is that the financial catastrophe has come just when the Russian government had produced programs reorienting the approach to science and education at all levels. For the first time in more than six decades, there is an emphasis on human values and individual needs rather than training cadres to match state-mandated slots. But by 1992, discussions of reform in the press gave way to bitter laments regarding effects of the economic crisis.

The successes and achievements of the Soviet regime will continue to have an impact on the inevitable changes, both conditioning their character and determining some of the choices. For example, it is difficult to think of a measure that will be as unpopular as closing educational institutions, especially VUZ. One has only to remember that in the years of the Civil War and famine in 1918–1921, the number of higher schools more than doubled—a reflection of both the government's concern for education and the popular desire for upward social mobility. Even though the wages to be made in business are now far higher than those for credentialed specialists, it will still be difficult to adjust to reduced educational opportunity. On the other hand, for the first time in 60 years, social mobility has to some extent been separated from access to higher education.

There is still massive resistance to real change. Sociological surveys indicate that most of the scientific community is not ready for major changes, but would prefer gradual evolution. This is a normal human response, but it is no longer realistic. Some Academy officials have already complained that the government is preparing "repressive measures" against institutes. [47] But the choice is to eliminate some of the institutions or watch them all die.

In science and education, as in the economy, Russia is now at a crossroads. It is probably impossible to rebuild the old centralized state system. But this does not mean people will refrain from trying. The desire to preserve familiar structures remains strong, and will continue to slow the transition to a new system. Every retrenchment aimed at catching the chimera of stability prolongs the process of transition. The alternative, moving rapidly to a highly uncertain, more diverse and more dynamic new system, involves

---

important it is to have a university known in Europe. "Kto khochet dom i 'mercedes'—ni poidet v nauku ..." Anton Gubankov interview with Petersburg University Rektor Stanislav Merkur'ev, *Nevskoe vremia*, April 9, 1992, p. 4.

[46] Sergei Zelinskii, "I molcha gibnut' ia dolzhna? ..." *Nevskoe vremia*, April 10, 1992, p. 3. For recent discussions of arrangements for financing basic science, compare the reform proposals by Natalia I. Ivanova, "Organizatsiia i finansirovanie issledovanii v usloviiakh razvitoi rynochnoi ekonomiki" *Vestnik Akademii Nauk SSSR*, No. 9, 1991, pp. 28–39, and by Spartak T. Beliaev, "Finansirovanie fundamental'noi nauki" *Vestnik Rossiiskoi Akademii Nauk*, No. 4, 1992, pp. 28–33, with the harsh attack on grant funding by Iurii I. Aleksandrov, "Samoubiistvennaia zhazhda grantov" *Vestnik Rossiiskoi Akademii Nauk*, No. 5, 1992, pp. 41–50

[47] See Vladimir Pokrovskii's report on the February 5, 1992 Academy of Sciences conference in *Radikal*, No. 5, Feb. 1992, pp. 9, 10.

sharp pain and massive dislocation. But it is unavoidable. The only question is whether the pain will be concentrated in a few years, or spread out over decades. It seems the Stalinist experiment to avoid the consequences of building capitalism was a failure. That effort, with the costs involved, remains ahead.

VI. POLITICAL-ECONOMIC PROFILES

OVERVIEW

By Jim Nichol *

The contributors to this section examine several issues of importance in assessing whether the newly independent states of the former Soviet Union will be successful in forging stable, democratic, peaceful, and economically viable systems. These include their economic, social, and demographic conditions prior to independence, the political and economic reform policies being formulated and implemented, and the trends in economic performance in various sectors just before and during the first few months after the breakup of the Soviet Union at the end of 1991.

ECONOMIC, SOCIAL, AND DEMOGRAPHIC CONDITIONS IN THE SUCCESSOR STATES

The success of economic reform efforts at least partly depends on the economic legacies of the successor states, such as valuable natural resources, agricultural capabilities, and, to a lesser degree in the short term, industrial capabilities. Many industries are obsolete or produce unneeded defense items, necessitating investment in new equipment, conversion to civilian production, or closure. In the short term, these disruptions mean that the industrial component of national income will decline. Agricultural production and natural resource exports and exploitation may provide an economic cushion to several successor states as they work to revamp their industrial sectors.

John Dunlop, Marc Rubin, Lee Schwartz, and David Zaslow have compiled data that highlight in many cases the relative underdevelopment of the former Soviet republics on the eve of their independence compared to Western standards. They rely heavily on official Soviet data, supplemented in some cases by their own or those of the World Bank and CIA estimates. The data show alarming rates of infant mortality, especially in Central Asia. Their survey of housing conditions reveals that in the Central Asian states, only around 55 percent or less of the housing units had indoor plumbing. Among the more alarming data are those dealing with air pollution. In many major cities of Russia and other former republics, air pollution levels exceed World Health Organization standards by at least ten times. The authors generally conclude

---

* Jim Nichol is a Senior Technical Information Specialist, Foreign Affairs and National Defense Division, Congressional Research Service.

that the former Baltic republics enjoyed the highest standard of living, while the former Central Asian republics had the lowest.

The authors also highlight the over-representation of ethnic Russians in most of the former republics in high-paying sectors of employment such as industry, construction, and science. Titular nationalities, on the other hand, were over-represented in low-paying sectors such as state agriculture. This disparity was particularly glaring in Central Asia where the titular nationalities are traditionally pastoral or nomadic. In terms of language use, a table emphasizes the "imperial" insularity of ethnic Russians residing outside of Russia who mostly refused to learn local languages. Last, a map and table depict 168 actual or potential sources of inter-ethnic conflict in the early 1990s, many of which pose serious threats to economic and political development in the successor states.

In examining macro-economic indicators, the authors show that republic growth in productivity during the 1980s declined, meaning that it took more resources to produce a given unit of output at the end of the 1980s. To rectify the deterioration in the standard of living, substantial labor force and capital stock restructuring are necessary. Foreign trade earnings have also declined. When valued in terms of world market prices, in 1989 only Russia had a positive trade balance, while all other republics had negative trade balances. On the other hand, a note of optimism is provided by tables showing a considerable increase in the percentage of the labor force employed in cooperative or private enterprises and the burgeoning sales of these enterprises in several republics prior to independence. Likewise, the authors show that some of the former Soviet republics are richly endowed with valuable resources, such as oil and gas in Kazakhstan and Turkmenistan. Others, such as Belarus and Moldova, are not so well endowed with exploitable resources.

POLITICAL AND ECONOMIC REFORM POLICIES

Several authors focus on the internal political climate within which economic reforms have been considered and carried out in the successor states during 1992. As Keith Bush points out, Russia was the first to implement a comprehensive radical economic reform program early in the year. He notes that although reform targets for deficit reduction, privatization, and lowering inflation have continually been revised during the year, some progress has occurred and most economic reformers have retained their positions and influence in government. Steven Woehrel juxtaposes the Russian program to Ukraine's halting reform efforts throughout the year until the appointment of former industrial leader Leonid Kuchma as prime minister in late 1992. Ukrainian President Kravchuk and other ex-Communist Party functionaries dominant in the government had little real enthusiasm for or understanding of free markets. Kuchma in late 1992 appointed several economic reformers and launched an urgent reform program, convincing the legislature that the gravity of the economic situation called for granting him the power to enact economic decrees. The Belarussian leadership, Kathleen Mihalisko points out, has also been resistant to Russian-style "shock therapy." Sergiu Verona stresses the ongoing conflict and tensions in Moldova between ethnic Russians and Moldovans that gravely affect Moldova's chances for economic recovery. Similarly, Elizabeth Fuller notes that the economies of the Transcaucasus states have been decimated by war and internal strife. Economic recovery and development in each of the states have been assessed by indigenous experts as taking a decade or longer. Bess Brown similarly notes the challenging economic situation faced by the Central Asian states caused by the ending of Soviet subsidies, the disruption of trade patterns with Russia and other former republics, and the pressures caused by burgeoning populations and unemployment. The mostly conservative ex-communist leaders of these states have embraced a cautious attitude toward privatization and marketization.

ECONOMIC DEVELOPMENTS IN THE SUCCESSOR STATES

PlanEcon authors David Johnson, Gail Albergo, Donald Green, *et al.*, examine economic trends and prospects for development in the successor states. They provide a bleak picture of large negative growth rates for all the republics in 1991 and 1992 (estimated), with the largest declines in 1992 occurring in Armenia, Latvia, Lithuania, and Tajikistan. As also mentioned by Bush, Johnson *et al.* underline the preeminent economic status of Russia among the former Soviet republics and the significant "spillover" effects of its reform efforts on other former republics. Its population was just over half of that for the Soviet Union, produced 61 percent of the GNP in 1991, a similar share of industrial output, and about 50 percent of agricultural output. Russia's economy limped along in the 1980s, then sharply declined in the 1990s, with GNP estimated as contracting by more than 25 percent in 1991–1992. Russia's trade surplus also was largely eroded in 1991–1992. Earnings from the export of Russian heavy machinery plummeted as the Eastern European states have looked to the West for such machinery. This decline in Russian exports may be partly a function of underreporting by the Russians, as the figures do not reflect smuggling or transshipments through other republics. Most Russian exports and imports in 1992 were with the developed West. Oil and gas continued to be the most critical Russian export, and sharp price increases for energy have had a serious impact on all the successor states.

In regard to other successor states, the authors remind the reader that whereas Ukraine in terms of population is about the size of Italy, Britain, or France, its economy is considerably smaller. Heavy industry plays a significant role in the economy compared to other former republics, but the industries are old and investments are needed. Loose credit policies have allowed most of these industries to continue to produce, although their products are unneeded or sold to other republics on credit. Considered the third-ranking economic power in terms of GNP of the former Soviet Union, Belarus did not suffer greatly economically in 1989–1990, but its NMP slumped badly in early 1992. According to the authors, the output of heavy industries in Belarus has been seriously affected because the new state is dependent on raw materials or components that are difficult to obtain from other former Soviet republics. In Moldova, antagonistic relations with Russia caused by tensions over ethnic Russians residing in Moldova have led to large reductions in Russian exports needed by Moldovan industries. The growth of agricultural production and related industries may cushion the decline in the Moldovan economy in coming years, however. During 1992, industrial production seriously declined in Estonia and Lithuania, less so in Latvia. These states are heavily reliant on oil shipments from Russia, which continues to be their major trade partner.

In Central Asia, the Kazakh economy lagged during most of the 1980s and slumped in the 1990s, though less so than that of Tajikistan or the Transcaucasus states. Oil production increased in both 1991 and 1992 (partial year figures), and grain production increased in 1992. Kazakh trade patterns have significantly changed during 1991–1992, with Kazakhstan exporting more raw materials to developed Western countries, and China emerging as the major source of Kazakh imports. The authors describe Uzbekistan, Kyrgyzstan, Turkmenistan, and Tajikistan as mainly raw material exporters to the other republics, describing their economies as "colonial." They predict that living standards in these states will certainly deteriorate significantly, since the states were dependent on health, education, and other subsidies from Moscow that have ended. Only in Turkmenistan may the relatively small population benefit from oil exports. Gold exports by Uzbekistan may partly cushion its decline in living standards. Kyrgyzstan's high share of industry compared to the other Central Asian states (except Kazakhstan) contributed to its more severe economic downturn in 1990 and 1991 (although in per capita terms, the slump in Tajikistan is far greater). Concurring with Fuller, the authors report that the economies of the Transcaucasus states (Armenia, Azerbaijan, and Georgia) are in "free fall." Of the three, only Azerbaijan may be able to establish a positive balance of trade through oil exports at world market prices.

RECENT ECONOMIC DEVELOPMENTS IN THE 15 FORMER SOVIET REPUBLICS

By David C. Johnson, Gail Albergo, Dr. Donald Green, Jay K. Mitchell, Dr. Vadim Myachin, Dr. Matthew Sagers, Elizabeth M. Sellers, and Dr. Jan Vanous *

CONTENTS

SUMMARY

The formal resignation of Soviet President Mikhail Gorbachev on December 26, 1991, and the dissolution of the central Soviet government has led to the creation of a host of new successor states. Incorporating a huge expanse, the former Soviet republics differ greatly in the structure of their economies ranging from Latvia's concentration in light industry to the monoculture of cotton production in the Central Asian republics. Performance has also varied over the past decade. The purpose of this paper is to review recent economic developments in each of the former Soviet republics. The focus on the economic performance of the republics is on developments in national income, industry, agriculture, consumer welfare, and foreign trade.

INTRODUCTION

The demise of the U.S.S.R. in December 1991 and its fragmentation into 15 independent states was the climax of the nearly three years of progressive decentralization of political power unleashed

---

* The authors are all members of PlanEcon staff. This paper is extensively adapted from the *PlanEcon Review and Outlook*, November 1992.

(913)

by Gorbachev's political reforms. Critical issues such as economic reform, fiscal and monetary policy, price control, and privatization no longer have major significance at the aggregate level of the former Soviet Union, despite the formation of a "Commonwealth of Independent States" (the CIS) which presently includes 11 of the 15 former Soviet republics. Whereas much of the past study of the Soviet economy centered upon the all-Union economy, study of economic developments in the individual former Soviet republics is now of paramount importance as each fledgling republic struggles to become a viable, stable economy. As better information about the evolving successor states becomes available, both domestic policymakers and investors (foreign and domestic) will be better able to react to the changing environment.

While there is a great need to explore the economies of the successor states, securing reliable, consistent data has presented problems. [1] For instance, in the *1990 Narodnoye khozyastvo*, the growth in Kyrgyzstan's NMP produced in 1990 was negative 0.9 percent. However, according to unpublished revised Goskomstat figures, Kyrgyzstan's NMP (net material product or national income) produced in 1990 actually grew by 3.9 percent. Below we provide our best estimate of economic performance in each of the republics. When inconsistencies arise, we have generally opted for IMF data or provided PlanEcon estimates. Most inconsistencies occur in the 1990 data, so we feel fairly comfortable about pre–1990 data. Statistics for 1991 were taken from the CIS end-year report. Data for non-CIS successor states (i.e., the Baltics and Georgia) for 1991 are generally PlanEcon estimates based on a variety of published sources. The IMF has recently published an *Economic Review* for each of the former Soviet republics. These have been valuable sources of information.

Before reviewing economic developments in each former Soviet republic, we present an index of per capita NMP produced since 1980. In view of the wide differences in population growth in individual republics, per capita data best illustrate where each republic actually stands. Thus, while Uzbekistan registered an impressive average annual growth of 2.5 percent in NMP produced during 1980–91, population growth of about the same magnitude implies economic stagnation over this time period on a per capita basis. Notably, five republics show significant positive changes in per capita NMP produced between 1980 and 1991: Belarus—34 percent, Latvia—23 percent, Ukraine—11 percent, and Lithuania and Kyrgyzstan—8 percent each. The Russian economy, which dominates the former Soviet economy, stood at a level already achieved in 1980. By our estimates, in five republics—Uzbekistan, Azerbaijan, Kazakhstan, Georgia, and Turkmenistan—the real level of per capita NMP produced in 1991 fell 10–15 percent below the 1980 level. Tiny Tajikistan fared worst of all. By 1991, Tajikistan's per capita NMP produced was over 25 percent below its level in 1980 (See Table 1).

---

[1] For further discussion on how PlanEcon has reconciled conflicting national income statistics, please see *PlanEcon Report*, Nos. 11–13, Vol. VIII, March 27, 1992.

TABLE 1. Developments in Per Capita Indices of National Income (NMP Produced) in the Former Soviet Republics, 1980–92.

Index 1985 = 100

	1985	1986	1987	1988	1989	1990	1991	1992 ᵃ
Former U.S.S.R.	100.0	101.4	101.9	106.4	106.6	102.1	91.1	72.3
Russia	100.0	101.7	101.6	106.2	106.7	102.0	90.4	70.4
Ukraine	100.0	101.3	106.3	108.9	112.2	107.9	95.6	81.1
Belarus	100.0	103.7	106.6	109.1	116.3	110.1	106.8	90.4
Uzbekistan	100.0	97.0	94.4	103.4	101.4	104.7	101.8	83.8
Kazakhstan	100.0	101.0	98.9	104.7	95.1	96.2	84.6	72.5
Georgia	100.0	98.2	95.8	102.4	95.7	83.6	62.6	51.1
Azerbaijan	100.0	100.2	102.6	103.2	93.8	82.0	81.6	64.0
Lithuania	100.0	105.3	109.2	120.9	121.2	112.9	95.8	67.8
Moldova	100.0	106.2	107.2	109.3	114.5	112.4	98.8	74.0
Latvia	100.0	103.9	104.4	110.9	117.7	115.6	111.5	79.9
Kyrgyzstan	100.0	98.8	98.0	110.4	112.4	113.3	107.0	79.6
Tajikistan	100.0	100.1	95.5	107.2	92.9	93.1	83.3	60.3
Armenia	100.0	100.3	98.4	95.8	113.5	103.7	89.2	57.9
Turkmenistan	100.0	101.7	102.8	113.3	100.5	100.4	97.3	77.4
Estonia	100.0	102.2	103.4	108.5	113.8	100.9	88.9	66.2
Annual Growth in Percent								
Former U.S.S.R.	NA	1.4	0.5	4.4	0.2	−4.2	−10.8	−20.7
Russia	NA	1.7	−0.1	4.5	0.5	−4.4	−11.3	−22.2
Ukraine	NA	1.3	4.9	2.5	3.1	−3.9	−11.3	−15.2
Belarus	NA	3.7	2.8	2.4	6.7	−5.3	−3.1	−15.3
Uzbekistan	NA	−3.0	−2.7	9.5	−1.9	3.2	−2.7	−17.7
Kazakhstan	NA	1.0	−2.1	5.8	−9.1	1.1	−12.1	−14.2
Georgia	NA	−1.8	−2.4	6.9	−6.6	−12.6	−25.1	−18.4
Azerbaijan	NA	0.2	2.4	0.6	−9.1	−12.7	−0.5	−21.5
Lithuania	NA	5.3	3.7	10.7	0.3	−6.8	−15.2	−29.2
Moldova	NA	6.2	0.9	1.9	4.8	−1.8	−12.1	−25.1
Latvia	NA	3.9	0.5	6.2	6.1	−1.7	−3.6	−28.4
Kyrgyzstan	NA	−1.2	−0.9	12.7	1.8	0.8	−5.6	−25.6
Tajikistan	NA	0.1	−4.6	12.2	−13.3	0.2	−10.6	−27.6
Armenia	NA	0.3	−2.0	−2.6	18.5	−8.6	−14.0	−35.1
Turkmenistan	NA	1.7	1.1	10.2	−11.3	−0.1	−3.1	−20.4
Estonia	NA	2.2	1.2	4.9	4.9	−11.3	−12.0	−25.5

Source: Goskomstat (published and unpublished sources) and IMF (*Economic Review*).
ᵃ PlanEcon forecasts.
NA—Not applicable.

RUSSIA

The Russian Federation was the largest of the "Union" republics that comprised the U.S.S.R. Spanning over 6,000 kilometers (and 11 time zones) from the Kaliningrad exclave on the Baltic Sea to the Pacific Ocean, it encompassed 76.2 percent of the territory of the former U.S.S.R. Now an independent state, it is the world's largest nation in area, with a size about 2.5 times the second largest nation (Canada).

The Russian Federation's population of more than 148 million represented 51.3 percent of the Soviet total. Covering such a large expanse, the Russian Federation's territory included not only Russians (who comprised 81.5 percent of the republic's population at the time of the last census in 1989), but over 150 other ethnic groups.

The giant Russian Federation dominated the former Soviet economy. It accounted for 61 percent of the total 1991 GNP of the former Soviet Union, and a similar share of industrial output. Its share of agricultural output was much less, but still nearly 50 percent, and accounted for an even larger share of foreign exports (around 80 percent in 1991) as well as foreign imports (60 percent in 1991). Russia was one of the "rich" republics with a higher than average per capita GNP. Whereas the average for the former U.S.S.R. in 1991 was less than 6,100 rubles, Russia's per capita GNP was around 7,200 rubles, which put it in fourth place behind Estonia, Latvia, and Belarus.

Because of its large size, the Russian Federation is in fact a collection of highly disparate regions, each of which has an economy larger than nearly all of the other former Soviet republics. Considered in terms of the 11 official "economic regions" within Russia, the Center (which includes Moscow) is the largest. In the mid-1980s, the Center accounted for approximately 12.5 percent of total Soviet NMP or about 21.2 percent of Russia's NMP. As a highly industrialized region the Center produced about 13.5 percent of the former U.S.S.R.'s industrial output but only 6.8 percent of Soviet agricultural output. The Central region is followed in economic importance by the Urals (9.4 percent of Soviet NMP, 10.0 percent of industrial output, 6.1 percent of agricultural output), the Volga region (7.0 percent of Soviet NMP, 6.9 percent of industrial output, and 6.4 percent of agricultural output), and then West Siberia (6.4 percent of Soviet NMP, 6.5 percent of industrial output, and 5.3 percent of agricultural output). The smallest of the economic regions in Russia is the North (2.4 percent of Soviet NMP, 2.7 percent of industrial output, and 1.1 percent of agricultural output), but even the North's limited economic punch is greater than all the former Soviet republics except Ukraine, Kazakhstan, Belarus, and Uzbekistan.

Like the overall Soviet economy of which it was the major part, Russia's economy had been limping along in the 1980s before entering a severe downturn in 1990. During 1980–89, Russian NMP produced grew at an average annual rate of 2.7 percent. There is still some uncertainty as to what happened to Russia's NMP produced in 1990 which likely dropped in the 3.7 percent to 5.0 percent range. The drop in NMP domestically used in 1990 was 4.0 percent, with consumption increasing a healthy 3.6 percent, but net investment and other expenditures were down 29.3 percent in comparable price terms. For 1991, Russian NMP produced declined about 11 percent, and NMP domestically used, about 12 percent. Based on retail trade statistics, PlanEcon estimates the drop in consumption at around 6 percent while net investment and other uses may have fallen more than 40 percent.

Russia's economic results for 1992 are particularly discouraging and do not bode well for other former Soviet republics. During the first half of 1992, Russian NMP (net material product, a measure of national income excluding depreciation and most services) fell 18 percent compared to January-June 1991. The rate at which NMP is declining has worsened over the course of the year. Based on sharp declines in gross industrial output, we estimate that the drop in NMP during the third quarter of 1992 may have reached some 30 percent. For 1992 as a whole, we project a 22 percent decline in NMP produced. The drop in GNP is likely to be only slightly smaller, perhaps 20 percent. After a 9 percent drop in Russian GNP in 1991 and a 20 percent decline this year, Russian GNP would be only 72.5 percent of that achieved in 1990. Further economic declines through 1994 will make the plight of Russia even worse.

INDUSTRY

The Russian Federation on average is one of the more heavily industrialized republics of the former U.S.S.R. It is well above the Soviet average in terms of industrial output per capita. Russia's industrial structure is fairly similar to that of the former U.S.S.R. as a whole, although it tends toward more heavy industry (about 70 percent of Russia's output is concentrated in heavy industry branches), with somewhat smaller shares for the light and food industries. Machine building and metalworking is the largest industrial branch, accounting for about 30 percent of total Russian industrial output, followed by the food industry (14.5 percent), light industry (13 percent) fuels (9 percent), chemicals and petrochemicals (8 percent), ferrous metallurgy (6 percent), wood, paper, and woodworking (over 5 percent), and then nonferrous metallurgy (5 percent).

The importance of heavy industry in the Russian Federation is reflected in the list of its 25 largest industrial enterprises ranked by value of output in 1989 (See Table 2). Energy producers, metallurgical plants, and automobile and agricultural equipment manufacturers dominate the list of the largest Russian enterprises. The list contains six iron and steel mills, four oil production associations, four automobile plants, and three petroleum refineries.

TABLE 2. The 25 Largest Enterprises in Russia.

(Ranked by value of output in 1989)

Name of Enterprise	Primary Activity	Employ. (ths.)	Output (mil.R)	Assets (mil.R)	% Profit
1. Nizhnevartovsk PA 'NizhnevartovskNefteGas'	13111 Crude petroleum	12.2	2,706.4	6,568.2	29.4
2. Magnitogorsk Metallurgical Combine	33120 Blast furnaces & steel mills	45.9	2,690.7	2,819.8	30.0
3. Naberezhnye Chelny Automobile Assembly Works	37110 Motor vehicles	100.0	2,586.6	4,566.6	17.8
4. Togliatti Volga Automobile Works n.a.50-ann of USSR	37110 Motor vehicles	89.0	2,584.3	2,930.8	22.9
5. Novy Urenboy PA 'UrengoyGasProm'	13115 Natural gas	2.7	2,440.3	4,705.1	46.7
6. Norisk Mining and Metallurgical Combine n.a.Zavenyagin	10610 Crude ferroalloys ores	41.0	2,337.9	7,234.9	35.2
7. Cherepovets Metallurgical Combine	33120 Blast furnaces & steel mills	37.4	2,247.5	2,923.8	22.8
8. Lipetsk Novolipetskiy Metallurgical Combine	33120 Blast furnaces & steel mills	33.2	2,108.5	3,498.3	29.5
9. Nizhniy Novgorod Motor Vehicle Works	37110 Motor vehicles	100.6	1,856.8	1,678.3	9.8
10. Chelyabinsk Metallurgical Combine	33120 Blast furnaces & steel mills	29.5	1,619.3	1,961.1	12.8
11. Nefteyugansk PA 'YuganskNefteGas'	13111 Crude petroleum	6.6	1,540.9	4,946.5	30.2
12. Moscow Works n.a. Likhachev	37110 Motor vehicles	58.4	1,450.7	1,104.3	0.0
13. Angarsk PA 'AngarskNefteOrgSintez'	29110 Petroleum refining	17.0	1,396.5	1,385.8	14.3
14. Nizhniy Tagil Metallurgical Combine n.a.Lenin	33120 Blast furnaces & steel mills	35.5	1,281.1	1,587.8	0.0
15. Surgut PA 'SurgutNefteGas'	13111 Crude petroleum	6.5	1,278.1	5,221.5	14.4
16. Omsk PA 'OmskNefteOrgSynthez'	29110 Petroleum refining	7.6	1,260.8	900.8	15.5
17. Petropavlovsk-Kamchatskiy PA 'KamchatRybProm'	20920 Fresh or frozen fish & other seafood	18.3	1,219.9	938.2	14.1
18. Nizhnekamsk PA	28690 Industrial organic chemicals, n.e.c.	16.2	1,215.3	1,864.0	23.7
19. Novokuznetsk West Siberian Metallurgical Combine	33120 Blast furnaces & steel mills	25.3	1,202.7	1,873.2	27.0
20. Verkhnyaya Pyshma Combine 'UralElectroMed'	33310 Primary copper	4.5	1,196.1	180.4	0.0
21. Novy Urengoy PA 'YamburgGasDobycha'	13115 Natural gas	0.7	1,037.1	1,159.7	53.0
22. Monchegorsk PA of Nickel Industry 'Nikel'	10610 Crude ferroalloys ores	9.9	1,030.2	601.6	4.6
23. Rostov-na-Donu PA 'RostSelMash'	35230 Farm machinery and equipment	46.4	1,013.5	1,261.0	11.1
24. Almetyevsk Units of Association 'TatNeft'	13111 Crude petroleum	18.2	973.4	5,057.0	17.6
25. Kstovo PA 'GorkNefteOrgSyntez'	29110 Petroleum refining	5.9	960.4	515.2	14.1

Source: *PlanEcon.*

919

Russia's industrial sector has suffered from declining growth rates in recent years similar to those experienced elsewhere in the former U.S.S.R., with a slight absolute decline in output (-0.1 percent) registered in 1990. This was followed by a plunge of 8.0 percent in 1991.
During the first half of 1992, industrial output declined 13 percent compared to the corresponding period of 1991. Industrial output in July was down 22 percent; August—27 percent; and September—an estimated 30 percent. Since 1987, the composition of industrial output has shifted from producer goods toward consumer goods. However, during the first eight months of 1992, output of consumer goods fell 17 percent, slightly more than the decline for total industrial output, 16.4 percent. This implies that output of producer goods outpaced that of consumer goods. If firms were responding to market forces (i.e., pent-up consumer demand for goods and services), production of consumer goods should have performed better than producer goods.
On the positive side, within the industrial sector, energy producers have fared better than average (see energy section below). As orders for investment goods have plummeted and supply links have been broken, the machine-building and metal working sector has been hit the hardest. Still, even this sector is feeling some positive effects of the restructuring taking place. Consumer demand has helped mitigate declines in automobile production, which was down 4 percent for the first eight months of 1992. In August 1992, car production actually rose 3 percent compared to July. Output of medical instruments, watches, and clocks has increased 9 percent in constant ruble value terms during the first eight months of 1992. The chemicals and petrochemicals industry has performed about average, though general production in August outpaced that of July. Production of construction materials has fallen substantially, caused by the sharp contraction of gross investment this year.
Gross industrial output during the first eight months of 1992 varied considerably by region. The Central region, which includes Moscow and is the largest of Russia's eleven economic regions, fared the worst with industrial output declining 21.9 percent. Industrial output in Moscow alone declined 27.1 percent. The Northwest region (which contains Saint Petersburg) and the Far East region performed about average. Output in the West Siberian region surpassed the Russian average by 2.4 percent. Within this region, the tiny Altay republic, with less than 0.01 percent of total Russian gross industrial output, recorded the only increase in industrial output, 1.6 percent. In the Tyumen region, a major producer of crude oil and natural gas, industrial output declined only 11.7 percent. The East Siberian region managed to limit its gross industrial output decline to 13 percent. In regions where ethnic strife is apparent, industrial output declines were correspondingly sharper. In Chechenya-Ingush gross industrial output was down 27.2 percent, and in North Ossetia, 33.3 percent.
The rise of inter-enterprise credit by extension is a growing cause for concern in the Russian industrial sector. As orders for industrial goods have fallen, enterprises have not responded by cutting costs. Enterprises have been buying and selling goods on credit, using any cash receipts to pay wages and purchase vital

goods (either inputs or consumer goods for employees) on commodity exchanges. By June 1992, the stock of inter-enterprise credits had exploded to 3.5 trillion rubles. While accumulating profits on paper, a growing number of enterprises became basically insolvent. Faced with this credit crisis, Russian officials relied upon old means of dealing with such a crisis. Newly appointed Chairman of the Russian Central Bank, Viktor Gerashchenko (former head of Gosbank), indicated that 1.5 trillion rubles worth of inter-enterprise credits accumulated during the first half of 1992 would be taken over by the Bank. Industry called the government's bluff and has continued to resist long-term restructuring—what real incentives does industry have to restructure if it can successfully lobby the government to bail it out?

The vast Russian Federation is the largest energy producer among the former Soviet republics—in 1991, it accounted for 89.5 percent of Soviet crude oil, 79.3 percent of Soviet natural gas, and 56.1 percent of Soviet coal production; this represented about 80 percent of the total fossil fuel output of the former U.S.S.R. Total output of primary energy in the republic declined slightly in 1989, dipped even further in 1990, and slumped badly in 1991.

Energy consumption and production are very unevenly distributed over the huge space of the Russian Federation. Most energy production occurs in the eastern portion (Siberia), while the more densely settled and industrialized "European" portion accounts for the bulk of consumption. European Russia contains 75–80 percent of the republic's population, industry, and social infrastructure, while Siberia contains over 90 percent of the republic's energy resources.

As the dominant producer of most of the former U.S.S.R.'s fuel, the Russian Federation supplied most of the country's foreign energy exports as well as much of the energy needs of the other former Soviet republics. On a net basis, the Russian Federation has exported (either abroad or to the other republics) over 30 percent of its energy production. This includes over 40 percent of its crude oil production for the past decade and around 25 percent of its natural gas production. At the same time, the Russian republic is a net importer of coal, typically representing some 12–15 percent of its coal use.

The decline in Russia's output of crude oil has been the most significant development in Soviet energy production in recent years. This is because the Russian Federation, the source of the bulk of Soviet crude, provides not only all the other former Soviet republics with oil, but also accounts for virtually all of the former U.S.S.R.'s oil exports, the single most important source of foreign exchange. For the Russian Federation, crude oil output peaked in 1987 at 569.5 mmt (million metric tons) (while for the former Soviet Union as a whole peak output came a year later), then declined by 0.1 percent in 1988, 2.9 percent in 1989, and then 6.5 percent in 1990. In 1991, crude output for the Russian Federation slid by 10.7 percent. During the first eight months of 1992, Russian production of crude oil (including condensate) stood at 271 mmt, or 14 percent below that of the corresponding period of 1991. Should the magnitude of decline remain the same through the remainder of the year, Russian crude oil production for the year will likely be about 397 mmt, a decline of 14 percent (64 mmt).

AGRICULTURE

Russia's agricultural sector has performed quite poorly in the last two decades. While the general overall trend has been a slow expansion of output, there has been considerable fluctuation and variability in performance from year to year, reflecting not only the vagaries of weather conditions, but also much deeper problems in the agricultural system. During the recent economic slide, gross agricultural output in Russia fell 3.6 percent in 1990 and then 6.7 percent in 1991. Agriculture should not be as adversely affected as industry in the next few years, particularly if there is movement on land reform.

Russia produces a variety of agricultural products, both crops and animal products. Because of differing climate, soil, and other conditions among the regions, different parts of the republic specialize in different types of agricultural activities—some produce mostly wheat, others potatoes, rye, sugar beets, or even rice (although most rice output in the former U.S.S.R. is from other, more southerly republics), while other regions specialize in meat production or dairying (such as the North region); at the same time, several of the better endowed regions in European Russia tend to be highly diversified in terms of their agricultural output.

INVESTMENT

The general economic crisis in the former U.S.S.R. contributed to a severe downturn in the volume of construction activity on investment projects in Russia. Gross investment, after posting a slight expansion in 1990 (up 0.1 percent), slid by 11 percent in 1991, while construction activity, which had already dropped by 7.6 percent in 1990, fell by about 10 percent in 1991. For the first half of 1992, gross investment collapsed by 46 percent. New capital actually put into operation fell by about a third during the first half of the year. New housing, measured in square meters, was down 27 percent during the first eight months of the year compared to the same period in 1991. In Moscow, additional housing space amounted to 751 square meters, 23 percent less than that introduced during January-August 1991. Performance was much worse in Saint Petersburg, where new housing space was off 42 percent. For 1992, we expect gross investment to decline about 50 percent, though on a net basis investment will likely decline about 30 percent. Such sharp declines in investment should not be too worrisome, since a great deal of past investment was misguided toward defense and economically irrational projects that produced little additional welfare for the Russian population.

CONSUMER WELFARE

Compared with the other former Soviet republics, most indicators of personal consumption placed the Russian Federation slightly above average. It was thus one of the more "prosperous" republics. In terms of ranking, it was just ahead of Belarus and Ukraine, but well behind the living standards enjoyed by the three Baltic republics of Estonia, Latvia, and Lithuania.

Living standards have been taking a beating as part of the overall economic deterioration in recent years, although Russian consumers apparently fared somewhat better in 1991 than their counterparts in the other republics. Total retail sales of goods and services experienced a 7.7 percent drop in 1991 compared with an 8.9 percent drop for the twelve republics comprising the CIS as a whole. The year 1992 does not promise to be a good year for retail sales. Retail sales in state and cooperative stores have fallen 42 percent in comparable prices during the first eight months of 1992. In January, retail sales fell 63 percent when the consumer price index rose 245 percent as people consumed goods hoarded in anticipation of this price rise. Since then, retail sales have gradually recovered. During May-August 1992, retail sales (in comparable prices) have consistently been one-third lower than those of the same period a year before. Production of consumer goods indicates that consumption is not likely falling as much as indicated by state retail sales levels. During January-August, consumer goods output fell 17 percent, with production of non-food consumer goods falling 14 percent, and processed food down 22 percent.

INFLATION

In Russia, inflation has been rampant, accelerating in 1990 and especially in 1991 into an inflationary spiral as the former Soviet government continued to print money to cover deficit spending. The overall price level increased by about 8.5 percent in 1990 and about doubled in 1991 with the big change coming in wholesale prices in January of 1991, followed by the retail adjustment in April by the former Soviet government. In January 1992, the Yeltsin government liberalized the overwhelming majority of consumer and wholesale prices. The retail price index rose 245 percent in January alone. Monthly inflation in February was 38 percent, and only by April had the monthly inflation rate fallen into the twenties. During the second quarter, monthly inflation averaged 18 percent. Slower increases in food prices (8 percent in July and 6 percent in August) helped reduce monthly inflation to 11 and 10 percent for July and August, respectively. Unfortunately, there is not much grounds for optimism that the Russians are really reducing inflation; in September, inflation shot back up to 20 percent. By the end of September, the retail price index was about 14.6 times that of December 1991. If monthly inflation subsides to between 10–12 percent during the last quarter of 1992, the inflation rate for the whole of 1992 should be about 1,400 percent.

FOREIGN TRADE

During the 1980s, Russia generated significant surpluses in foreign trade while other republics recorded deficits. The trade surpluses gained by the U.S.S.R. from Russian energy and gold exports were generally used to cover the trade deficits of other republics or to finance Soviet credits extended to developing countries and client states.

The Russian government reported a substantial contraction in foreign trade for 1991. However, the meaning of reported value changes remains unclear because of the integration for the first time of ruble and dollar trade. In 1991, Russian exports were valued at $36.8 million and imports totalled $25.6 million. The trade surplus amounted to $11.2 billion.

The figures released do provide a sense of the composition of Russian trade. Russia exported $13.4 billion worth of fuels last year, accounting for 36.3 percent of total exports. The share of machinery and equipment in Russian exports was less than 13 percent. This share is far less than in past years. Clearly, foreign demand for low-quality Russian machinery has plummeted; former CMEA (Council for Mutual Economic Assistance) countries have switched to Western suppliers. The next largest reported category of exports was precious metals and diamonds, amounting to $3.1 billion (8.3 percent of exports). Shipments of non-ferrous metal products were not far behind.

During January–August 1992, Russia's trade surplus fell to less than one-tenth the level achieved in the same period of 1991— down to $0.5 billion, from $6.0 billion. Exports fell by one-third in dollar value terms to $21.6 billion. The share of fuels in Russian exports increased dramatically, to 52 percent, while that of machinery fell further, to less than 10 percent. The fall in Russian exports is due, in part, to sharp declines in domestic production, export quotas and evasion (some goods exported likely leaked through Russian customs, or were routed through other former Soviet republics). Imports held up better, falling 20 percent to $21.1 billion. Trade prospects for the remainder of the year are far from clear. In September, the government increased the main import duty rate to 15 percent, up from 5 percent. This move was taken to increase government revenues and limit imports. On the export side, quotas will reportedly soon be abolished, replaced by a variety of export taxes. The government is currently considering a proposal to force enterprises to immediately relinquish all hard currency revenues to the Central Bank at the prevailing inter-bank auction rate. Such action will encourage evasion, particularly if the Central Bank "taxes" enterprises by moving to an unrealistically low exchange rate.

As expected, the relative importance of former CMEA countries in Russian trade is falling. Former CMEA members (including former Soviet republics) have sought higher quality products for their hard currency and more stable export markets. During the first seven months of 1992, the share of the former CMEA in Russian trade turnover fell to 19 percent, down from 26 percent last year. Russia exported 56 percent of its goods to the developed West while 63 percent of imports came from this region.

Turning to the commodity composition of imports, purchases of machinery dominated the picture, accounting for about 35 percent of purchases from abroad. Imports of food remain substantial. In 1991, Russia imported about $4.5 billion worth of food, 17.5 percent of total imports.

With the collapse of the Soviet Union, trade between former Soviet republics has taken on increased importance. Central planners can no longer dictate flows of goods across republican borders.

As relative prices for traded goods adjust (or do not adjust for that matter) to emerging conditions in the former Soviet Union, inter-republic trade patterns will be altered as well. [2] Because Russia exported energy to other republics at low prices relative to imports of machinery and consumer goods, for instance, Russia will undoubtedly receive a terms of trade gain to the extent it liberalizes energy prices.

One estimate prepared by the former U.S.S.R. government concluded that Russia's trade surplus with the rest of the republics would have been $50 billion in 1989 had such trade been conducted at world market prices. It is reasonably certain that this surplus was falling in volume terms in 1990–91, although the value of the surplus may have risen again in 1991 with higher oil prices.

DEBT

According to the Debt Allocation Treaty of December 1991, Russia is officially responsible for 61 percent of the former Soviet Union's debt at January 1, 1991. This 61 percent figure is roughly in line with Russia's share of Soviet national income. Since convertible-currency debt stood at about $60 billion at the end of 1990, Russia's share amounts to about $37 billion in old Soviet debt. Debt incurred during 1991 and 1992 becomes the responsibility of the republic to which loans were actually disbursed. By mid-1992, Russia may have owed about $42–45 billion, plus about $4–5 billion in arrears and a similar amount for domestic obligations in convertible currency. About three-quarters of Russian debt is owed to official creditors.

Throughout 1992 Russia has made overtures to other former Soviet republics that it would assume all former Soviet debt in return for uncontested claim to former Soviet assets. These assets consist of convertible currency and gold held abroad as well as embassies, land, and other assets held abroad. Virtually all of the former Soviet republics have already signed on to the "zero option." Stressing its independence as a sovereign nation, Ukraine refused to negotiate a deal with Russia (though Ukraine has yet to service its share of former Soviet debt). However, recently warming relations will undoubtedly pave the way for a settlement between these big neighbors over former Soviet debt.

Russia has not had great success in negotiating a debt rescheduling deal with either official or commercial creditors. Thus far, Germany, to which Russia owes the most money, has not succumbed to pressure from other G–7 countries (notably the United States) to forgive or reschedule much debt. The uncertain political environment and talk of decelerating or abandoning economic reforms certainly does not help the Russian negotiations. An agreement with commercial creditors is very unlikely without an IMF-approved economic reform package, which now seems doubtful anytime soon.

---

[2] For detailed analysis of inter-republic trade, see the paper by Stuart Brown and Misha Belkindas in this JEC report, volume I.

UKRAINE

Ukraine is the third-largest former Soviet republic in terms of area and the most populous after Russia, with a population of more than 50 million, which is about as large as that of Britain, France, or Italy. However, while the size of its economy is also larger than that of any other former Soviet republic except for Russia, it is considerably smaller than the economies of those Western countries. This is true in both absolute and per capita terms. PlanEcon estimates that per capita GNP in 1989 was $4,700, only the seventh highest level among the 15 republics of the former U.S.S.R.

Ukraine's economy has been suffering from sharp deceleration in the rate of growth of aggregate output in recent years. Whereas gross national product (GNP) measured in terms of dollars at purchasing power parity (PPP) grew at a 3.4 percent average annual rate during 1981–85, between 1985 and 1990 this growth rate slowed to 2.4 percent. In 1990, the Ukrainian economy experienced its first decline in GNP since 1985, posting a 1.5 percent drop. This rate of decline accelerated to 10.0 percent in 1991 as the recession that hit Eastern Europe two years ago moved east. Recent developments show further intensification, with Ukrainian GNP falling 12 percent during the first nine months of 1992 (relative to the first nine months of 1991). For all of 1992 we anticipate a 13 percent decline in Ukrainian GNP, by far the worse economic performance in recent years. This year's decline in GNP in Ukraine will be smaller than for several other former Soviet republics, including Russia. The reason for this is slower progress on economic restructuring in Ukraine, however, rather than superior condition of the republic's economy.

INDUSTRY

Ukraine is one of the more heavily industrialized republics of the former U.S.S.R. However, much of Ukraine's industry is old (even relative to other Soviet republics) and badly in need of investment. More than two-thirds of Ukraine's industry (69 percent in 1990) is concentrated in branches of heavy industry, with light industry and food processing accounting for only 11 and 18 percent, respectively, of total industrial output in 1990. The leading branches of heavy industry in Ukraine in 1990 (in share of total industrial output) were: machine-building (about one-third—33 percent), metallurgy (12.5 percent), wood and chemicals (9 percent), and fuel and energy (8 percent). These four branches taken together account for the lion's share of Ukrainian industrial output (90 percent of heavy industry and 62 percent of total industry in 1990).

Ukrainian industry has suffered from declining growth rates in recent years similar to those experienced for other regions of the former U.S.S.R. In 1990 there was a 0.1 percent drop in Ukrainian industrial output, the first such drop experienced in many years. This was followed by a decline of 4.5 percent in 1991. During the first half of 1992, gross industrial output contracted by 12.3 percent, and for 1992 as a whole, the decline is expected to be 14–15 percent. These figures make it clear that industry has not suffered as serious output declines as other sectors of the Ukrainian economy in recent years. Loose credit policies by the Ukrainian government have allowed many enterprises to continue producing goods even though many of these products end up in warehouses or are sold to other former Soviet republics on credit.

Despite the fairly mild 12.3 percent drop in overall industrial output for the first six months of 1992, certain branches of industry suffered large output losses. Output of the food processing branch was cut 23.1 percent during the first half of 1992 (relative to the first half of 1991), a disturbing trend for a country whose livelihood is so dependent on agriculture and food processing. Non-ferrous metallurgy suffered a 21.0 percent decline in output during the same period as energy shortages and other problems hit production hard. Ferrous metallurgy fared little better, registering a 14.0 percent output decline for January-June 1992. Several other major industrial branches registered output declines in the range of 10–12 percent for this period: fuels (down 10.4 percent), petrochemicals (down 10.5 percent), machine building (down 11.1 percent, clearly wide-scale closures of military equipment manufacturers have yet to hit Ukraine's industry), and construction materials (down 12.2 percent).

ENERGY

Ukraine ranks second after the Russian Federation in terms of overall fuel production of former Soviet republics. However, its share of total Soviet energy production has been declining, due both to rising output elsewhere (mainly in Russia) and declines in indigenous production. This share fell to only 8.1 percent in 1990 from 20.4 percent in 1970.

A major factor in Ukraine's lower share has been the decline in coal output, particularly from the Donets Basin (Donbas), which has a favorable location with respect to markets, but with unfavorable mining geology. In 1991, coal output fell 18 percent to 136 mmt, although this still maintained Ukraine as the second-largest coal producer in the former U.S.S.R. (just ahead of Kazakhstan with 130 mmt and well behind Russia with 353 mmt). Ukraine's oil and gas reserves have been extensively depleted. The small amounts of oil and gas extracted are only of minor local significance. Thus, Ukraine must import most of its oil and gas supplies.

During the first half of 1992, Ukrainian coal put in a surprisingly good performance given recent declines. Total coal output was close to stagnant, with a slight 0.5 percent decline reported. Moreover, there was actually an increase in coal output in Ukraine during the second quarter of 1992 (relative to the second quarter of 1991). The Ukrainian government is emphasizing coal output in an attempt to minimize dependence on imported crude oil and natural gas from Russia and Kazakhstan. While in the short term this might appear to make some sense, as a long-term policy it could hurt Ukraine's economy by slowing the transition to consumption of cheaper and less polluting forms of energy, particularly natural gas. The coal sector also presents other problems in Ukraine, such as the frequency of accidents.

AGRICULTURE

Agriculture is generally considered a strong point of the Ukrainian economy. However, here too there have been serious problems in recent years. Gross agricultural output fell 3.5 percent in 1990 despite a near-record grain harvest. In 1991, crops brought down agricultural performance the most. The grain harvest was only 38.6 mmt, down 24 percent from 1990 and the lowest result since the early 1980s.

The outlook for the 1992 harvest is considerably better despite late sowing, a reduced park of farm equipment, and problems with various inputs. Estimates of this year's grain harvest are in the 41–42 mmt range, which would be 6–9 percent higher than last year's result, but still nearly one-fifth lower than the level in 1990. However, continued low prices paid by the state to farmers have kept official government purchases low. Farmers are seeking to sell grain on commodity markets (where it fetches much higher prices) or feed it to their own livestock instead.

CONSUMER WELFARE

Given its favorable geographical location, considerable agricultural output, and highly developed industry, one might expect Ukraine to be one of the more prosperous republics of the former U.S.S.R. in terms of living standards. Most indicators of personal income and consumption suggest this is not the case. Ukraine has traditionally lagged behind the U.S.S.R. average in terms of both wages and personal consumption. The average monthly wage for Ukrainian workers in the state sector in 1990 was 248.4 rubles. This was 10 percent lower than the average for the U.S.S.R. as a whole. Average annual per capita retail expenditures of Ukrainians on goods and services in 1990 totalled 1538 rubles, which was 5 percent lower than the average for the entire U.S.S.R. (1619 rubles) and less than the average for neighboring republics such as Russia and Belarus.

In 1991, consumers in Ukraine were harder hit by declining economic conditions than in most other republics. Total retail sales of goods and services fell 10.1 percent in 1991 (in constant prices), compared with a 7.7 percent drop for Russia and an 8.9 percent drop for the twelve republics making up the CIS. As was the case for most other republics, Ukrainian retail sales of services dipped more than sales of goods in 1991 (18.9 vs. an 8.6 percent decline).

In 1992, declining real wages have cut even more sharply into the living standards of Ukrainian citizens. For all of 1992, Ukrainians are expected to suffer a one-fifth drop in their total personal income (in constant price terms) as nominal salaries and wages did not grow as fast as inflation. The decline in real income, along with general pessimism about the economic future of their republic, have forced Ukrainians to cut their retail expenditures drastically (even from last year's already depressed levels). For this year as a whole, we expect retail sales to fall by more than one-quarter, with sales of goods down 27 percent and sales of services slashed by 32 percent (both figures are computed in constant price terms). The very large declines in retail sales during 1991 and 1992 will mean that over just a two-year period, retail sales of goods and services will have been slashed by well over one-third.

In 1991, inflation accelerated considerably. Retail prices for goods and services rose 82.5 percent for the year overall. Nonetheless, Ukraine had one of the lowest inflation rates among CIS republics—the retail price rise for the CIS as a whole was 86.0 percent. The fact that Ukrainian price rises lagged behind other CIS republics last year, however, is not necessarily a good sign. Rather, it suggests that this republic may have taken longer to introduce much-needed price liberalization aimed at bringing domestic prices more in line with world market levels.

Ukrainian authorities introduced a liberalization in pricing policy in January 1992. While the result was a large-scale rise in the wholesale and retail price index, this move did not represent a total freeing of prices. Limits were set for rises in the prices of many goods and services. In general, Ukraine's government sought to limit price increases on certain basic food items and consumer goods as well as on selected industrial inputs. Since January, however, inflation has accelerated rather than slowed in Ukraine. Ukrainian statistical sources announced that for the first eight months of this year, retail prices rose more than seven-fold. By October 1992, monthly inflation rates in Ukraine reached 30 percent. Clearly, Ukraine has already approached hyperinflation and this could have disastrous impact in the next year or so as this becomes just one more problem that the government must address.

FOREIGN TRADE

The Ukrainian economy is dependent on foreign trade. In 1989, 16 percent of Ukrainian domestic output was exported from the republic and about 18 percent of internal consumption came from outside the republic. Most of this trade was with the former Soviet republics rather than foreign countries; 84 percent of Ukrainian exports and 73 percent of imports in 1989 were within the former U.S.S.R., although these figures are subject to the distortions of the domestic Soviet pricing system. Thus, the actual impact of foreign trade with countries outside the former U.S.S.R. is of lesser importance. During the first ten months of 1991, for example, Ukraine accounted for less than 10 percent of total Soviet (foreign) exports and barely 15 percent of total (foreign) imports. Moreover, Ukrainian foreign trade with countries outside the former U.S.S.R. has registered large deficits in recent years—nearly 3.3 billion valuta (or foreign trade) rubles in 1991, compared with 3.4 billion rubles in 1990 and 7.0 billion rubles in 1989. If we revalue Ukraine's trade at world market prices, we find that in 1989, this republic's trade deficit was an incredible $8.1 billion.

Ukrainian foreign trade contracted sharply along with most other former Soviet republics in 1991, with exports down 46 percent in valuta ruble terms and imports down 39 percent. Looking at the commodity composition of Ukrainian exports, one is struck by the fact that three commodity groups accounted for more than three-fourths of all foreign exports in 1991—machinery (including transport equipment, with a 28 percent share), metal products (18 percent), and hard coal (32 percent). This demonstrates the overwhelming importance of heavy industry in Ukrainian exports. The commodity composition of Ukrainian imports from foreign countries in 1991 was somewhat different from that of exports. Machinery and transport equipment is again a leading category, accounting for a very high 50 percent of imports in 1991. The second-largest category was textiles and apparel, with a 14 percent share. Chemicals were another leading import category in 1991, with a 10 percent share. Reliable information on Ukrainian foreign trade in 1992 has not been made available.

BELARUS

Despite its small size compared to the former U.S.S.R. (accounting for less than 1 percent of its territory), Belarus is considered the third-ranking economic power among the Commonwealth members (the republic accounted for 4.4 percent of the GNP of the former U.S.S.R.).

In some sense Belarus, despite its dearth of natural resources, has been a star performer among the 15 former Soviet republics. In 1991, its per capita NMP produced was still 39 percent above its 1980 level in real terms—no other republic shows similar performance.

But even though it fared so well during the 1980s, Belarus fell into recession in 1990. The degree of decline in NMP produced in 1990 was likely in the range of 1.4–4.8 percent. However, NMP domestically used reportedly still slightly increased in 1990 (0.2 percent), with consumption up (8 percent) while net investment and other expenditures fell by one-quarter. The increase in Belarus's trade deficit with foreign countries and other former Soviet republics in 1990 helps explain how consumption could have risen in the face of declining NMP produced. The reported decline in NMP produced in 1991 was only 3 percent, a figure consistent with the rather modest drop in Belarus's industrial production. NMP utilized in 1991 appears to have fallen only about 4 percent in 1991, with consumption of material goods declining about 1 percent and net investment and other expenditures about 20 percent. As expected, NMP dropped precipitously during the first quarter of 1992 (14 percent, compared to January–March 1991) with no recovery anticipated in the short-run. [3]

INDUSTRY

Having long been a poor agricultural backwater, Belarus experienced rapid industrialization during the post-war period, with industrial growth remaining strong even in the 1970s and 1980s. Until 1990, when the Soviet economy began its downturn, Belorussian manufacturing had experienced rather steady annual growth in the 5–7 percent range. For example, in the last decade, the output of metallurgy has more than tripled in the republic (albeit from a small initial base) with the expansion of the Mogilev rolling mill and the opening of the new mini-mill at Zlobin in 1984. The machine-building sector, which forms the backbone of Belorussian industry, grew at rates of up to 10 percent per year. In 1991, Be-

---

[3] SWB, May 15, 1992, p. A/1.

larus escaped with one of the smallest declines in industrial output registered in the former Soviet republics. Though falling only 2 percent in 1991, Belorussian industrial output is likely to suffer heavy losses this year. Belorussian industrial output in the first half of 1992 fell 12 percent below the level achieved in the first half of 1991. However, some of the leading industries had contracted even further: Belorussian enterprises produced 65 percent fewer electric motors, 33 percent fewer refined oil products, 34 percent less sulfuric acid, 30 percent less fertilizer, 21 percent less paper, 20 percent less farm machinery, 18 percent fewer trucks, and 17.5 percent fewer tires than in the first six months of 1991.

Specialization in the intermediate and final stages of metal- and energy-consuming industrial processes has made the Belorussian economy extremely dependent on the smooth functioning of the whole Soviet economic system, a condition that even in former days could not be assured. Virtually every enterprise of the two leading branches of Belorussian industry (chemicals and machine-building) depends entirely on raw material deliveries from outside the republic—oil and gas from Russia, iron and steel from Ukraine, nonferrous metals from Kazakhstan, and various parts and components from all over the former U.S.S.R. The lack of these supplies due to the general shortages that now plague the former Soviet system, as well as abrogation of existing agreements, republic-level trade restrictions, and monopolistic "free" prices has led to a complete halt of production at several major plants, including the truck plant in Minsk, the chemical fibers plant in Mogilev, and many electronic enterprises and machinery producers. Easily seen, Belorussian industry suffering over the next few years will correspond directly to declines registered in inter-republic trade. And, with limited ability to generate hard currency revenue in the near term, Belorussian industry will not likely be able to buy necessary inputs from abroad.

ENERGY

Belarus does produce a small amount of crude petroleum and associated gas, but these cover only a fraction of the republic's consumption. Other than its peat deposits, which are exploited commercially as well, Belarus must rely heavily on imported oil and gas from Russia. The republic would have to import nearly 40 mmt of crude oil annually to meet the capacities of its two refineries. Still, with Russian oil production declining sharply, it is unlikely to receive this amount in the future. For 1992, inter-governmental and direct agreements between enterprises will promise at most 35 mmt of petroleum, and actual deliveries may be far less. During the first quarter of 1992, Belarus already felt the impact of lower fuel deliveries from Russia—oil refinery output in Belarus was down 40 percent and 35 percent compared to the first quarters of 1990 and 1991, respectively. However, since 25 and 30 percent of refined product output has historically been shipped out of the republic, Belarus could supply domestic demand (particularly with the expected declines in industrial output) with significantly less crude oil imports.

Though the Belorussian economy relies on Russia for energy inputs, Russia depends on Belarus, in particular, as a transit route for gas pipelines ("Northern Lights") that bring gas from West Siberia and the Komi ASSR to Eastern Europe and Lithuania. The "Druzhba" (Friendship) oil pipeline to Eastern Europe also crosses Belarus; it forks at Mozyr, with the northern branch supplying Poland and eastern Germany, while the southern branch supplies Hungary and Czechoslovakia. Given this transport structure, Belarus should be able to earn significant hard currency for transporting Russian oil and gas.

AGRICULTURE

The southern, swampy region of Belarus is the least favorable area for agriculture in the entire western part of the former Soviet Union. In spite of this, Belarus has a substantial agricultural output, exceeding that of the Baltic states taken together or the Transcaucasus. The distribution of agricultural output in Belarus is fairly typical of the overall Soviet pattern; animal husbandry contributes 58 percent to the total output of the sector, and crops, 42 percent.

Among the individual crops, potatoes are the most important due to the cool, moist conditions and an acidic soil; potato output exceeds that of grains, a situation not found in any of the other former Soviet republics. Belarus ranks fourth among former Soviet republics in grain production (7–9 mmt a year), but still must import wheat, mainly from Kazakhstan.

CONSUMER WELFARE

Belarus, which produces more consumer goods per capita than most other republics, nevertheless lags behind in terms of wages and personal income. The average monthly wage for Belorussian workers and employees in the state sector in 1990 was 264.5 rubles, notably smaller than the Soviet average of 274.6 rubles per month. While inflation has taken a large bite out of nominal wage increases, the retail price index in Belarus did not increase as much as the Soviet average. In 1991, the Belorussian retail price index (including paid services) increased only 81.3 percent, compared to an 86 percent increase in the retail price level for the CIS.

Since 1985, retail sales (in constant prices) grew an estimated 41 percent. In 1991, Belarus was the only republic where officially reported retail turnover (in constant prices) did not decline. This was likely accomplished by a sharp reduction in shipments of consumer goods to other republics, thereby compensating for the sharp drop in imports, particularly those from Eastern Europe.

FOREIGN TRADE

Thanks to central planning, Belarus has been allowed to run large trade deficits. In 1990, the value of Belarus imports (external trade only) exceeded exports by an estimated $840 million. In 1991, Belarus experienced a large contraction of its external trade, with exports down 42 percent and imports down 47 percent in valuta ruble terms. The larger decline in imports drove down the estimated trade deficit to less than $300 million. In the first half of 1992,

Belarus has achieved an astonishingly strong positive balance with $384.5 million worth of exports and $185.6 million worth of imports. However, the volume of trade has contracted immensely.

Exports by Belarus are overwhelmingly dominated by machinery products—transport equipment (36 percent), and other machinery and equipment (17 percent), followed by chemicals (13 percent). This structure of exports means that Belarus is likely to be hit very hard when it starts trading independently and inter-republic trade of the CIS adjusts to world market prices. Not surprisingly, as a large exporter of machinery, Belarus's imports are also dominated by machinery and equipment (44 percent of total imports), followed by chemicals (12 percent), and textiles and apparel (9 percent).

In addition to running trade deficits in external trade, Belarus imports far more from other republics than it exports to the Commonwealth. Valued at world market prices, Belarus's inter-republic trade deficit may have reached almost $2 billion in 1991. The main trading partner of Belarus is Russia, which accounts for 64 percent of all Belorussian imports. Imports of relatively underpriced energy and raw materials from Russia are exchanged for overpriced machinery and equipment. To the extent that Russia liberalizes energy prices for inter-republic trade, Belarus is in for a terms-of-trade shock.

MOLDOVA

Moldova remains a tiny, politically unstable state bordering Romania. Without energy or mineral sources, and lacking a highly developed industrial sector, but with an inflammable ethnic mix, the republic's future economic prospects are dismal.

Following 1–7 percent drop in NMP produced in 1990, Moldovan NMP produced fell by 12 percent in 1991. PlanEcon estimates that NMP domestically used declined about 13 percent, with consumption down 15 percent and net investment and other expenditures down 3 percent or so. Perhaps surprisingly, Moldova, in per capita terms, fared better than the Soviet average during the 1980s. In 1990, Moldova's per capita NMP was 18–25 percent higher than the level of 1980 (for the U.S.S.R., about 15 percent higher). In 1992, Moldova's antagonistic relations with Russia have caused aggregate economic output to drop precipitously.

INDUSTRY

Moldova is one of the least industrialized states of the former Soviet Union, particularly in relation to the European republics. Industry contributes just over one-third of Moldova's NMP produced. Due to the predominance of agriculture in Moldova, processed food and light industry dominated its industrial structure. Reflecting this industrial structure, most of Moldova's industrial enterprises are small, not necessarily a handicap in the present environment. Only a few goods produced by Moldovan industry were clearly distinguished in the former Soviet "market": canned food, wines, and household appliances.

Industrial output was still growing in 1990, increasing by 3.2 percent, which was the highest rate registered among all the former

Soviet republics. This trend was reversed sharply in 1991; industrial output declined by at least 7 percent. The Dniestr region produces about half of total Moldovan industrial output and contains the region's only hydroelectric power station. Because of the turmoil in this region, the sharp downturns in industrial output here affect the entire republic. In 1991, output of such products as electricity, cement, plastics, and silk fabrics fell by 13–16 percent, while food processing output declined by 17 percent.

ENERGY

Moldova is practically devoid of fuel resources and nearly all the primary energy produced in the republic comes from the small 40 MW hydroelectric power station located in Dubossary. This station provides only a fraction of energy consumption in the republic (around 13 million tons of standard fuel annually), and so Moldova depends heavily on outside supplies. With a five-fold increase in Russian oil, coal, and gas prices (and Ukrainian coal prices as well) in January 1992, and further price increases for Russian energy imminent, Moldova faces a hike in energy costs that will seriously affect its electricity generation, agriculture, and industry.

AGRICULTURE

Even under Soviet rule, Moldova remained a predominantly agricultural country—over 40 percent of NMP produced came from the agricultural sector. Crop production dominates the agricultural sector of Moldova, contributing almost 60 percent of gross agricultural output. Moldova's grain output is among the highest grain yields in the former U.S.S.R., twice the Soviet average, and it is the third-largest producer of sugar beets, fruit, and sunflower seed, behind only Ukraine and Russia.

After modest growth in 1988 and 1989 (averaging 2.9 percent), Moldovan agricultural output suffered severe declines in 1990 and 1991. Gross agricultural output declined 12.9 percent in 1990 and an estimated 11 percent in 1991. Meat and milk output dropped by 17 and 14 percent, respectively, in 1991, though grain and potato output increased by 26 and 20 percent, respectively, compared to 1990. Delayed land reform and political turmoil in Moldova do not bode well for quick recovery in this sector.

The 1992 harvest is expected to be a good one despite a severe drought. Production of grains, sunflower oil, and sugar beets will be much higher than last year. However, many state and collective farms refuse to sell the grain to the state in anticipation of further price increases. Neither threats nor promises have brought results so far, and an estimated 0.2 million tons of grain have to be imported.

CONSUMER WELFARE

Moldovan income levels were not high by Soviet standards. In 1990, the average monthly wage in Moldova was 233 rubles, about 15 percent less than the Soviet average. Inflation in Moldova accelerated to the same rates as in the wealthier republics, bringing about a steep decline in real incomes. In 1991, the retail price level (including paid services) rose 97.4 percent. Retail trade turnover dropped by 15 percent (in comparable prices) in 1991, and services contracted even more, by 24 percent. This places Moldova among the most seriously affected regions in the present crisis.

FOREIGN TRADE

The export structure of Moldova mirrors its industrial structure. The bulk of exports is comprised of food and agricultural products, accounting for about half of total exports. The republic imports a wide range of products, including most types of machinery and equipment, light industrial materials, and chemicals. Despite its strong agricultural base, Moldova imports significant quantities of food not grown in the republic.

Moldova's foreign and inter-republic trade turnover is very high. Unfortunately, after adjusting to new market mechanisms (i.e., real relative prices) Moldova may find it has few products with prospects for reaching the world market. Both inter-republic and foreign trade balances show large deficits if calculated in world market prices. The foreign trade deficit fluctuated in the range of $1-2 billion in 1989-91, being determined mostly by import volumes. In 1991, Moldovan foreign trade collapsed with a 50 percent reduction in imports. Exports also fell by 41 percent, plunging below the $500 million level.

BALTIC STATES

Together, the Baltic states of Estonia, Latvia, and Lithuania contribute only 3 percent of former Soviet GNP. Yet, they enjoy the highest levels of per capita GNP in 1991. While the average for the 15 republics was less than 6,100 rubles, per capita GNP in Estonia amounted to almost 8,500 rubles, followed by Latvia—8,200; and Lithuania—6,200 (the latter actually placed fifth, after Belarus and Russia).

In 1991 the Baltic republics could not avoid a drop in national income. However, the declines were less steep than in most other former Soviet republics. According to the Latvian statistical office, Latvian GNP fell 5.6 percent; other sources register an 8 percent drop. Net material product reportedly contracted by only 5 percent. PlanEcon estimates that Estonian GNP fell 6.5 percent in 1991. Lithuanian GNP is estimated to have fallen 6.1 percent in 1990 because of Gorbachev's economic blockade of the republic. In 1991 Lithuania likely suffered an additional 4.3 percent decline in GNP. However, it did not suffer as severely as in 1990 when the cutoff in energy supplies by the Soviet government stymied domestic producers.

Most of the declines in the three republics were the result of cuts in supplies of fuels and raw materials and the disintegration of horizontal economic links among enterprises. Agriculture was hurt by shortages of feedstocks that led to a sharp reduction in output of animal products.

INDUSTRY

Before World War II, when they were independent, Estonia and Latvia had achieved a relatively high level of industrial development. Lithuania developed most of its industry under Soviet rule.

The industrial structure in each of the three countries is quite diversified, but the small size of the economies and the lack of natural resources make the Baltics highly dependent on outside suppliers.

The Baltic States are one of the few areas of the former U.S.S.R. that specialized in the production of consumer goods. The strongest sectors of industry are those producing fabrics, apparel, shoes, processed food and fish, furniture, electronics, electrical appliances and other consumer durables, jewelry, cosmetics, musical instruments, and sporting goods. However, there are several enterprises in machine building that were virtual monopolists on the former Soviet market, for example, the enterprises that supplied compressors for automobiles (Panevezis Autocompressor Works), vans (Jelgava RAF), computer chips (Riga VEF), and milking equipment.

Last year the results for industry in the Baltics were fair relative to the sharp downturns experienced by most other former Soviet republics. In Lithuania, industrial output fell by only 1.5 percent, less than the 3.3 percent drop in 1990 caused by Gorbachev's economic blockade. However, the food processing sector recorded a 9 percent decline. Latvian industrial output remained at the 1990 level, as a 2 percent decrease in the state sector output was offset by a substantial rise in the non-state sector. Growth varied significantly by sector, from a 23 percent increase in the glass and porcelain industry to a 25 percent decrease in the microbiological industry. Estonian industry suffered the steepest decline; in 1991, gross industrial output fell by an estimated 7.5 percent compared to 1990.

The first half of 1992 was a difficult time for the economies of all three republics. Many industrial enterprises could not operate fulltime or at full capacity because of frequent cuts in supplies of input materials. Liberalized but unsettled prices, broken ties among long-existing partners, ill-grounded political decisions—all contributed to the collapse of the centrally planned industrial mechanism.

As a result, in Latvia the drop in industrial output reached 29.5 percent in January-July 1992, the Lithuanian statistical agency reported even steeper drop of 47.5 percent in January-September compared to the same period of 1991 (while petrochemical output collapsed by 60 percent), and the output of Estonian industry decreased by 35 percent in the first eight months of 1992. Thus, 1992 will be a very difficult year for the industrial sector in the Baltic republics.

ENERGY

All three Baltic republics are heavily dependent on imports of primary energy. Their own sources are limited to oil shale mines in Estonia, small oil deposits in Lithuania, peat, and some very small hydroelectric stations. A Chernobyl-type nuclear power station at Snieckus, Lithuania uses reactor fuel imported from Russia.

The oil refinery at Mazeikiai, Lithuania, is able to satisfy the need for selected refined petroleum products of the whole region, including Kaliningrad oblast, a non-contiguous part of Russia. The plant, however, has operated at only 40–60 percent of its full capacity since 1990 because of cuts in crude oil supplies from Russia. All the coal and natural gas consumed in the region is imported. Despite their reliance on imports for primary fuels, Lithuania and Estonia are net exporters of electricity. The major power stations in these two republics are the Ignalina Nuclear Power Station in Lithuania and the two shale-based thermal power stations at Narva in Estonia.

AGRICULTURE

Despite their cool climates and poor soils, the Baltics have developed highly productive agricultural sectors due in part to their millennium-long traditions of soil cultivation. Crop and livestock yields are the highest in the moderate climatic zone of the former U.S.S.R., though less than in similar European areas. The Baltics tend to specialize in animal husbandry. They were net exporters of many agricultural products, supplying Leningrad and the whole Northwestern region of Russia. Lithuania is the largest producer of agricultural goods in the region. The agricultural sector contributes 33 percent to Lithuanian NMP and provides 19 percent of total employment.

In 1991, agricultural output dropped in all three republics. The decline was most pronounced in Latvia, where the grain harvest dropped by 21 percent. There, production of potatoes fell by 15 percent, and output of major livestock products decreased by 9–10 percent. In both Latvia and Lithuania gross agricultural output contracted only 4 percent. In Lithuania, output of animal husbandry products fared poorly, declining 11–12 percent in 1991.

CONSUMER WELFARE

Price liberalization began in the Baltic states before it did in the Commonwealth states. Unlike the Commonwealth states, the Baltic states already purchase energy and fuels at world market prices; in early 1992, gasoline in the Baltics was about 10 times more expensive than at Russian filling stations. The Estonian Statistical Agency reported that consumer prices rose nine-fold in 1991. During the first two months of 1992 prices of foodstuffs have risen 72 percent, industrial goods, 64 percent, and services, 137 percent. In Lithuania and Latvia, price increases were less dramatic (about four-fold in 1991), but prices for food products were up more 1,000 percent. Such high rates of inflation have forced Lithuania to reconsider its allowance of free prices. Indeed, under intense public pressure, Lithuania has returned to setting price ceilings for several critical goods.

Increases in retail trade turnover in the Baltic states fared only average over the latter half of the decade. Compared to retail trade turnover in 1985, the volume of Soviet retail trade turnover was 18 percent higher in 1989 and 30 percent higher in 1990 (in comparable prices). While Latvian retail trade turnover increased a remarkable 27 percent through 1989, a small increase in 1990 put it on par with the Soviet average. Lithuania outpaced the Soviet average increase in retail sales by 2 percent during 1985–90, while Estonia fell behind the Soviet average by 4 percent. Retail trade turn-

over fell sharply in 1991. In Latvia, for instance, retail trade turnover dropped 23 percent (in comparable prices).

Still, in per capita terms, the Baltics have relatively high retail
trade turnover. In 1990, Estonia had per capita retail sales of 1,439
rubles, the highest of any former Soviet republic. Latvia followed
closely behind with 1,407 rubles. Lithuania took third place of all
Soviet republics, with per capita retail trade turnover of 1,162
rubles. The average per capita retail sales in the former Soviet republics amounted to only 907 rubles in 1990.

FOREIGN TRADE AND BALANCE OF PAYMENTS

All three Baltic states have traditionally had a negative overall
trade balance, running around one billion rubles each. This trade
deficit was covered by the transfers from the All-Union budget.
However, the sum also includes transfers to cover the costs of sta-
tioning the Red Army in this region, so the actual figure is higher
than the real transfer of resources to local residents. Machinery
and equipment constituted more than 30 percent of imported goods;
petroleum and chemicals constituted another 20–25 percent. All
three republics were net exporters of products within the food and
light industrial sectors, and also in wood and paper.

The main trading partner among the former Soviet republics for
all the Baltic states is Russia, which provided more than half of
their trade turnover. Mutual trade within the Baltic region has
been surprisingly low. The other Baltic states contribute less than
10 percent to each republic's exports or imports, even less than
Ukraine or Belarus. Aside from these republics, only Kazakhstan
contributes more than 2 percent to the Baltics trade.

Lithuania may have closed its trade deficit with the former
Soviet republics in 1991, which it has had since 1989, primarily by
importing less fuel and equipment. In the first nine months of
1991, it had a trade surplus of 3 billion rubles, but this achievement cannot likely be repeated in 1992 as prices continue to adjust
to world market levels.

Since regaining independence, none of the Baltic republics has
accumulated a foreign debt, and, basically, they do not accept responsibility for any part of the Soviet external debt. However, each
of the republics will receive IMF credits (starting this year)
amounting to between $50 and 150 million.

KAZAKHSTAN

Kazakhstan is a very large and very diverse republic. Often
grouped with its Central Asian neighbors, Kazakhstan has important characteristics that set this republic apart. In particular, the
northern half of this republic is industrialized, (extractive industries mainly) and dominated by Russians. Alone, Kazakhstan is the
second largest republic of the former Soviet Union in terms of territory, the third in terms of NMP produced, and the fourth in both
population and industrial output. The republic lags in terms of per
capita NMP, ranking ninth out of the 15 former Soviet republics,
at 3,445 rubles in 1991.

The Kazakh economy turned in a lackluster performance
throughout most of the 1980s, as evidenced by NMP produced,

which grew at an average annual rate of less than 1 percent during 1980–87. Following a growth spurt in 1988—NMP grew 5.9 percent—the Kazakh economy entered a recession as NMP produced dropped 0.4 percent in 1989. Once again, 1990 growth of national income produced is in doubt—one source puts it at 2.1 percent, another source implies a 1.7 percent drop. With NMP domestically used up 3.5 percent in 1990, the former growth figure for NMP produced is more plausible. The officially reported 1991 decline for NMP produced was 10 percent and PlanEcon estimates that NMP domestically used declined by 11 percent.

While the Kazakh economy has not fared well in NMP produced during the 1980s, growth rates in NMP domestically used grew twice as fast as NMP produced. By 1991, PlanEcon estimates that Kazakh NMP domestically used was still 14.9 percent higher than the level achieved in 1980, while NMP produced was 1.3 percent lower than that of 1980. This implies that Kazakhstan ran increasingly large net imports in trade with other former Soviet republics and foreign countries.

The first half of 1992 has brought no relief to the Kazakh economy: GDP and NMP fell 19 and 20 percent, respectively (compared to the first half of 1991), though there were no serious political troubles in the region.

INDUSTRY

Like the other former Soviet republics, Kazakhstan's industrial output fell in 1991, although the drop was less severe than in many of the other republics. Much of the blame for the loss in industrial production goes to energy and shortages of raw materials.

Kazakhstan's main industries include fuels (coal and oil), iron, steel, non-ferrous metals, cement, and mineral fertilizer. Its largest industrial enterprise, by value of output, is the Temirtau Karaganda Metallurgical Combine, a complex of blast furnaces and steel mills, whose combined output was valued at 1,176 million rubles in 1989. The second largest is the Ust-Kamenogorsk Lead-Zinc Combine, with an annual output of 776 million rubles. Other important enterprises produce crude petroleum, hard coal, copper, textiles, and farm machinery.

ENERGY

In terms of overall primary energy production, Kazakhstan accounted for only 5–6 percent of total Soviet production during the 1980s, which ranks it third among the republics, well behind the Russian Federation and Ukraine. Kazakhstan is also the third largest energy consumer among the former Soviet republics. For the past two decades, it typically accounted for about 5–5.5 percent of total Soviet consumption.

On a net basis, Kazakhstan is self-sufficient in energy; aggregate production has typically exceeded primary energy consumption by about 15 percent. However, Kazakhstan is heavily involved in inter-republic energy exchanges, typically exporting about 65 percent of its production while importing about 56 percent of its own consumption. This is mainly due to the republic's large area. For example, fuel produced on one side of the republic is exported to neighboring republics, while on the opposite side, energy is imported from neighboring republics. There is also a mismatch between the specific types of fuels produced and consumed in the republic. Another factor in the significant inter-republic energy shipments is that Kazakhstan serves as a transit zone for the large flow of natural gas from the Central Asian republics to Russia.

Kazakhstan produces coal from two large basins, the Karaganda and the Ekibastuz, as well as several smaller basins. The Karaganda Basin yields a high-quality hard coal suitable for coking. Most of its production is from underground mines, but in recent years a series of outlying strip-mined deposits have been developed. These yield a lower rank brown coal suitable for use in local electric power stations. The Ekibastuz Basin (located in northern Kazakhstan) produces a sub-bituminous coal from several huge strip-mining operations. Coal output at Ekibastuz reached a peak of 89.9 mmt in 1988, making it the third largest producing basin in the former U.S.S.R.

Kazakhstan is a large coal exporter. Most of the exports are to Russia (Karaganda coal for the Urals iron and steel industry and Ekibastuz coal for the Urals power plants), but some Karaganda coal is also used in Ukraine, Tajikistan, Kyrgyzstan, and Turkmenistan.

In the oil sector, Kazakhstan is the only republic (besides Russia) which produces more crude oil than its refineries process; its crude oil output of 24–26 mmt considerably exceeds its refinery throughput of around 18–19 mmt. Despite this, the bulk of its refinery throughput actually consists of Russian crude oil from West Siberia.

The energy sector was able to avoid a drop in production in both 1991 and 1992. Oil and gas extraction were up 4.6 and 11.1 percent, respectively, during the first half of 1992, but coal output was down by 5.7 percent (including a drop in coking coal by 18 percent). Electric energy output also declined by 1.8 percent.

AGRICULTURE

Agriculture's share in Kazakhstan's NMP produced in 1990 reached 40 percent, twice that of industry. Unfortunately, many areas in this sector have suffered from deep declines in the past year, especially the crop harvests. The overall decline in agricultural output was about 8 percent in 1990.

Shortfalls in specific crops are particularly serious on top of the declines in recent years. For example, grain output, at 11.9 million tons in 1991, was down 58 percent from 1990 harvest levels. The grape harvest fell by 58 percent from 139 tmt to 60 tmt. The 1991 potato harvest performed relatively well, falling only 7 percent to 2.2 million tons.

The non-crop agricultural sector did not fare as poorly as the crop sector. Meat production in 1991 only fell a fraction of a percentage point from 1990 levels, to 1.55 million tons. Milk production, at 5.5 million tons in 1991, was down only 2 percent from 1990.

These reports of agricultural output in Kazakhstan, given the republic's climate and land type, are not necessarily a result of recent economic difficulties. Output of the republic's dry "virgin lands" area fluctuates widely, depending on the particular weather conditions of the year. Therefore, the value of agricultural output in the republic is extremely volatile from year to year.

As such, in 1992 Kazakhstan gathered an exceptionally good grain harvest (preliminary estimates indicate a 150 percent increase to some 30 million tons, which allowed this republic to export significant amounts of grain to Russia (up to 8 million tons), to the drought-affected Western republics, and to Kazakhstan's southern neighbors. Belarus, for example, sent two battalions of troops to help gather a portion of the grain harvest in Kazakhstan which will be imported by the former. Help with manpower, equipment, and fuels will somewhat reduce the cost of the grain, which is set at $130 per ton by Kazakhstan.

INVESTMENT

Between 1985 and 1990, investment in fixed capital in Kazakhstan rose an average of 3.9 percent per year. The only year in which it fell was 1990, when investment declined 2.9 percent. In 1991, however, investment slipped a dramatic 11 percent, and the outlook for the near future is even bleaker.

Centralized investment (which is about one half of total investment) into Kazakhstan can be broken down into several categories. Some interesting investment trends have appeared over the past decade. In 1990, the largest category of investment was technological improvements in existing enterprises, which took 40.0 percent of disbursements. This category's share of total investment has grown steadily since 1980, when it accounted for 23.9 percent of central investment. The next largest investment category in 1990 was for new construction (34.7 percent), followed by expansion of existing enterprises (16 percent).

CONSUMER WELFARE

Kazakhstan's residents have found themselves worse off after price liberalization. The Kazakh statistical agency reported a 14.5 percent decline in real income of the population for the first half of 1992 (compared to the same period of 1991). Average per capita income is believed to be below the subsistence level, and 71 percent of the population is, in fact, below that level according to official statistics. However, since March, salaries have risen faster than prices, and real incomes are moving closer to their 1991 level.

Reflecting weakening purchasing power of the population, retail commodity trade turnover in Kazakhstan is falling at a steep rate of 43 percent this year, following a 12 percent cut in 1991 (in comparable prices). Most of the population's expenditures go to food purchases, and the demand for non-food consumer goods has fallen even more.

Retail prices in 1992 have risen substantially following price liberalization. To offset the price increases somewhat, local governments subsidize a longer list of the "necessities" than in Russia, but the amounts of subsidies and commodity lists vary among oblasts, which leads to great regional differences in retail prices in Kazakhstan.

FOREIGN TRADE

Kazakh foreign trade was adversely affected in 1991. In ruble value terms, imports dropped 39.4 percent to 1.35 billion valuta rubles while exports declined 38.4 percent to 2.88 billion rubles. Kazakhstan's trade deficit improved considerably (by 1 billion rubles) to 1.5 billion rubles in 1991.

The overwhelming majority of exports (97 percent) are comprised of raw materials. Raw material exports can be broken into exports of metal products (38 percent of total exports), fuels and minerals (24 percent of total) and chemicals (21 percent of total exports). Kazakhstan's imports consisted mostly of machinery and equipment (33 percent), textiles (19 percent), and fuels and minerals (9 percent).

Trade patterns have significantly changed during the last year and a half. Data for the first half of 1992 show that Kazakhstan tends to export more to the developed West (50 percent of total exports), for hard currency, while export-import operations with other countries are conducted on a barter basis. China has become the major partner of Kazakhstan, supplying an amazing 56 percent of all foreign imports to Kazakhstan (compared to only 10 percent a year ago).

CENTRAL ASIA

The four Central Asian republics of Kyrgyzstan, Tajikistan, Turkmenistan, and Uzbekistan enjoyed growth in NMP produced averaging between 3 and 5 percent for the 1985–89 period better than the average experience among all former Soviet republics in this period. These averages mask the high degree of volatility in growth rates of these republics, however, engendered by the agricultural economic base of the region. While the performance of Soviet agriculture as a whole has been highly variable over the years, harvest results for irrigated lands in the extremely dry conditions of Central Asia have shown even wider swings, and, given the dominant role of the agricultural sector in aggregate output there, national income has closely followed agricultural cycles. While a negative impact of agriculture's failures has been more typical for the longer historical perspective, the harvest in one exceptionally good year (in 1988, when a jump in total NMP produced by republic was Tajikistan—13.9 percent, Kyrgyzstan—11.0 percent, Turkmenistan—10.6 percent, and Uzbekistan—9.7 percent) gave the Central Asian republics their overall high average rate of growth in the late 1980s.

The four Central Asian republics did not fare very well in 1991. However, official statistics on economic performance in this region seemed skewed. For instance, officially NMP produced in Uzbekistan was down only 0.9 percent in 1991. With the estimate of consumption down around 8 percent, net investment and other expenditures would have had to rise significantly (an implausible development given the general state of the Soviet economy last year) to explain how this level of aggregate output could have been distributed domestically. PlanEcon's revised estimate puts the fall in Uzbekistan's NMP produced in 1991 in excess of 10 percent, forcing net investment and other expenditures to fall by nearly one-quarter (a pattern consistent with most other republics). PlanEcon estimates that Kyrgyzstan's NMP produced in 1991 declined 14.5 percent in 1991, and Turkmenistan's NMP produced by 10.6 percent. Only Tajikistan's reported 9 percent decline in NMP produced was plausible.

In 1991 these republics had per capita GNP levels of less than one-half of the average for the former U.S.S.R.: Tajikistan—2,500 rubles, Uzbekistan—2,700 rubles, Kyrgyzstan—3,100 rubles, and Turkmenistan—3,400 rubles. If we compare these per capita income levels with that of Estonia, the former Soviet republic estimated to have had the highest standard of living in 1991 according to this indicator, we note that the Central Asian republics range from just over 40 percent of the Estonian figure for Turkmenistan, which is a major gas producer with a small population, down to less than 30 percent of that level for Tajikistan, where cotton production is the major activity. Thus, all four of these republics rank at the very bottom of the heap among the former Soviet republics in terms of this measure.

The economy of Uzbekistan is driven by three commodities in the following order of importance: cotton, natural gas, and gold. Uzbekistan's total raw cotton production accounted for about 60 percent of the former U.S.S.R. total in 1991. Uzbekistan currently produces more than 40 billion cubic meters (bcm) of natural gas annually, but less than 10 percent of the natural gas was exported on a net basis in 1990. It also produces one-third of the former U.S.S.R.'s gold output while Russia produces the remaining two-thirds. While the availability of natural gas and gold improve Uzbekistan's economic outlook in the 1990s, the extreme dependence of its agriculture on cotton is not healthy. The Uzbeks, like the Ukrainians with regard to grain, believe that higher cotton prices will lead to an overall improvement in their terms of trade with Russia. However, cotton was already relatively overpriced in the past in an effort to encourage production.

Despite the importance of its natural gas industry, Turkmenistan is overwhelmingly agricultural; again, the single most significant crop is cotton. The contribution of agriculture to national income produced (albeit with very distorted official Soviet price weights) in 1990 was more than three times the NMP produced in the industrial sector. Natural gas production holds much promise for Turkmenistan. PlanEcon estimates that the value of Turkmenistan's net energy exports in 1991 amounted to $1,711 when valued at world market prices.

Kyrgyzstan has the highest share of industry in the aggregate economy among the four Central Asian republics. The agricultural sector is dominated by the livestock sector. With a considerably different economic character than its neighbors, Kyrgyzstan suffered a considerably sharper downturn in national income produced in 1990 and 1991.

On a per capita basis, the poorest of the Central Asian republics, Tajikistan, is largely unindustrialized. Despite its overwhelmingly mountainous topography, its fertile valleys support the highest yields of cotton per hectare in the region.

INDUSTRY

Central Asia is predominantly unindustrialized, with most of its industry concentrated in the light and food processing sectors. The economies of all four Central Asian republics can best be described as "colonial"—having relied on the other 11 republics, and Russia especially, to be the sole market for its primary exports—raw materials.

During 1985–90 Uzbekistan's gross industrial output grew at an average annual rate of 3.3 percent. Since the Soviet Union as a whole grew at an annual average rate of 2.5 percent during the same time period, Uzbek performance was quite good. Industry's share in Uzbek NMP produced in 1991 was only 24.2 percent, compared to 42.7 percent for the Russian republic. Uzbekistan is a Central Asian leader in the production of investment goods. In 1989 it was the primary or sole producer in the region of asbestos sheets and cement (9.2 percent of U.S.S.R. total), roofing materials and insulation (6.6 percent), mineral fertilizer (5.6 percent), chemical fibers (5.3 percent), and electric bridge cranes (a whopping 25.2 percent of total U.S.S.R. production).

During the latter half of the 1980s, Turkmenistan's average annual growth in gross industrial output (3.7 percent) outpaced that of Uzbekistan. Turkmenistan is the major hydrocarbon-producing republic of Central Asia, a supplier of chemical raw materials (sulfur, iodine and bromine) and cotton. Natural gas deposits were discovered in eastern Turkmenistan in the early–1960s, and now gas is the most important sector. Nevertheless, industry contributed only a tiny 15.3 percent share of total NMP produced in Turkmenistan in 1991.

No less than 11 of Turkmenistan's 25 largest enterprises by value of output are cotton-ginning plants, a vivid example of the republic's lack of industrial diversification. The remaining enterprises in the top 25 are for primary wool processing, fertilizer production, chemical fiber and silk processing, sulfur mining, and flour and grain processing.

Kyrgyzstan's gross industrial output expanded at the same average rate as that of Uzbekistan during 1985–90, but annual growth was much more volatile (ranging from –0.8 percent to 6.6 percent). Kyrgyzstan is a producer of metal ores. It produces over 90 percent of the former U.S.S.R.'s mercury, uranium, and some coal. However, the republic's industrial capacity is mostly in light industry and food. Industry made up exactly one-third of total NMP produced in 1991. Gross industrial output fell an estimated 7.8 percent in 1991.

Tajikistan registered the smallest average annual gain in gross industrial output in the region. However, even its 3.0 percent average annual growth outpaced that of the U.S.S.R. as a whole. Tajikistan's industrial development is centered around cheap hydroenergy, with some mining—uranium, mercury, and gold. Industry's contribution to total NMP produced in 1991 was 27.2 percent, growing steadily from 24.2 percent in 1980. Tajikistan's largest enterprise is the Tursunzade Aluminum Works, which produced 393 million rubles worth of output in 1989 and employed 7,400 people. Like Kyrgyzstan, Tajikistan is also oriented toward light industry.

ENERGY

When discussing energy production in Central Asia, Turkmenistan shines. In terms of population, Turkmenistan is the fourth smallest former Soviet republic but it is a major energy producer. In 1991, it produced nearly 6 mmt of crude oil and 88 bcm of natural gas. Turkmen natural gas accounted for 10.8 percent of Soviet gas output in 1990. This makes it the second-largest gas producing republic after the Russian Federation.

Turkmenistan has a huge energy surplus, exporting more than 80 percent of its primary energy production (on a net basis). It does import some energy from the other republics. In the mid-1980s, energy equivalent to about 30 percent of its consumption was imported into the republic, while an amount of energy equivalent to almost 90 percent of production was exported.

AGRICULTURE

Vast irrigation networks helped Central Asia become the major production area for cotton, rice, grapes and some other fruits in the former U.S.S.R. About three-fifths of irrigated fields are devoted to cotton. The whole region accounted for just under 90 percent of total former Soviet raw cotton fiber production (half of which came from Uzbekistan alone), but only around 11 percent of cotton cloth production.

The Uzbek contribution to the national economy has been primarily in the agricultural field—cotton, cottonseed oil, and fruits, much of this made possible by the vast areas of irrigated land in the republic—accounting for 20 percent of total irrigated land in the former U.S.S.R.—4,155,000 hectares in 1990. Uzbekistan's share in total raw cotton production on the former territory of the U.S.S.R. fell slightly from 65.0 percent in 1990 to 59.7 percent (or 4,643 tmt) in 1991. Most of this was exported to Russia, other republics, and abroad. Gross agricultural output in Uzbekistan fell 6.5 percent in 1991 over 1990, stemming from an 8 percent drop in crop output (cotton production was down 8.2 percent) and a smaller 4 percent decline in animal products.

Since virtually all of Turkmenistan is covered by the Kara Kum Desert, its agricultural sector depends totally on irrigation. Despite its limited arable acreage, Turkmenistan is a sizable cotton producer, with 18.3 percent (1,428 thousand metric tons, tmt) of total CIS production in 1991.

Kyrgyzstan's gross agricultural output plunged 14.5 percent in 1991. Animal husbandry, which forms most of Kyrgyzstan's agricultural sector, registered steep declines. Output of animal products dropped by 15.7 percent in 1991.

Cotton is king in Tajikistan. In 1991, Tajik raw cotton production fell only 2 percent (compared to production in 1990) to 818 tmt and still accounted for 10.5 percent of total CIS production. Agriculture contributed about 37 percent of total NMP produced in Tajikistan in 1991. Most of the republic's agro-industrial enterprises are loss-makers. Since subsidies from Moscow have dwindled to nothing, there has been some discussion about privatizing them.

CONSUMER WELFARE

While always lagging behind the other republics, consumer welfare in Central Asia has taken a considerable beating in the past year. Declines registered in this region's retail sales in comparable prices are among the highest drops in the CIS: Tajikistan, 22 percent; Kyrgyzstan, 16 percent; Turkmenistan, 12 percent; and Uzbekistan, 8 percent.

In terms of public consumption of goods and services, the region was heavily subsidized by other republics, primarily Russia, by means of allocations from the all-Union budget. In the absence of these large subsidies, it is certain that in the medium-term the already low standard of living in the region will deteriorate significantly. The overall standard of living across all the Central Asian republics will most certainly decline even further as their share of subsidization from Moscow for various public services (health, education, etc.) is cut back.

The notable exception to this dismal forecast may be Turkmenistan. As a major gas producer with a small population, the liberalization of energy prices and the substantial export of natural gas may provide a significant boost in the future to the value of the republic's aggregate product on a per capita basis, and hence room for improvement in living standards as well as investment. Uzbekistan, which is a significant gold producer, may also reap considerable benefit from marketing its own production at world market prices rather than delivering gold to Moscow authorities at an arbitrary low ruble price. On the other hand, Uzbekistan is a relatively densely populated republic and the loss of the transfers from the Soviet state budget to provide public goods and services will harm it considerably.

FOREIGN TRADE

With 30 percent declines in the volume of foreign trade typical in Central Asia, external trade took a real beating in 1991 as the U.S.S.R. became enmeshed in a liquidity crisis. As the Central Asian republics benefitted from import subsidies from the Soviet central government, these states had become accustomed to substantial external trade deficits. Unfortunately for the Central Asian population, these subsidies dried up with the collapse of the Soviet government at the end of 1991. The strong trade deficits have "improved" to small deficits or even surpluses. Of course, this "improvement" stems from slashing imports, resulting in a correspondingly lower level of consumption for the population.

Most exports from the republics of Central Asia (primarily agricultural or mineral raw or semi-processed materials and some light manufactures) were destined for other Soviet republics, while most Central Asian imports (primarily industrial producers and consumer goods and food) originated from the more industrialized republics of the former Soviet Union. This trade took place at artificially set prices, significantly different from relative world market prices. Past imbalances were generously covered through budgetary transfers. Even at internal Soviet prices, which severely undervalued energy and other raw materials vis-a-vis manufactured goods, these four republics have run chronic trade deficits with the rest of the former Soviet Union.

Uzbek foreign exports are dominated by cotton (64 percent of the total), followed by chemicals (14 percent, mostly urea) and metals (4.5 percent, excluding gold, mostly aluminum). In 1992, cotton deliveries abroad increased sharply, and may exceed the previous year's level by 2–3 times. The fact that Uzbekistan produced roughly one-third of all Soviet gold, and thus should be a major gold exporter, is not yet reflected in the republic's trade statistics. On the import side, foodstuffs accounted for 47 percent and consumer goods for 44 percent of foreign imports.

Turkmenistan's exports and imports fell by 38 percent and 37 percent, respectively, with the trade deficit declining from 0.8 billion rubles in 1990 to 0.5 billion rubles in 1991. Turkmenistan's exports in 1991 involved mostly textile products (36 percent), followed by metal products (18 percent), food raw materials (15 percent), and chemicals (14 percent). Imports were fairly evenly divided between machinery and equipment (30 percent), textile products (25 percent), plastics and rubber products (17 percent), and other (28 percent). As indicated above, however, the price paid to Turkmenistan for its exports of natural gas has been ridiculously low (and in the reporting of trade that was furnished for 1990–91 exports of gas, which might rightfully be attributed to Turkmenia, were probably claimed by Russia or Ukraine). As the price the republic receives approaches that on the world market, Turkmenistan should be able to generate more than adequate export earnings, especially in light of its small population.

Kyrgyzstan's exports fell 39 percent in 1991 (but they have traditionally been almost negligible—the lowest of all 15 republics of the former U.S.S.R.) while imports fell 43 percent. Kyrgyzstan's aggregate trade deficit declined from 1.6 billion rubles in 1990 to 0.9 billion rubles in 1991. Its exports in 1991 involved mostly chemicals (35 percent) and metal products and machinery (27 percent). On the import side, products of machine-building (73 percent of the total) and textiles and shoes (another 16 percent) accounted for most of this republic's imports.

Tajikistan also experienced very sharp declines in its foreign trade last year, with exports down 40 percent and imports down 45 percent. Its trade deficit was cut by about one-half from 0.6 billion rubles in 1990 to 0.3 billion rubles in 1991. Tajikistan's exports in 1991 were mostly metal products (61 percent) and textiles (24 percent), while on the import side chemicals (32 percent) were the most important item, followed by machinery and equipment (20 percent), textiles (16 percent), and transport equipment (15 percent). Tajikistan's ability to import will likely be difficult in the future, much like Kyrgyzstan, because it has few resources that might command high relative prices on external markets.

TRANSCAUCASUS

The economies of all three Transcaucasian republics (Georgia, Armenia, and Azerbaijan) are in a free fall. Violent ethnic conflicts, unstable political situations, and even natural disasters have reinforced the overall economic downturn common to all the former Soviet republics in 1991. Economic chaos and, in particular, the disintegration of economic links among republics and territories affected to a greater degree the smaller, less diversified economies of this region that are dependent on supplies of various critical manufactures and raw materials from Russia and other former Soviet republics.

National income had begun to decline in the Transcaucasus as early as 1989, a full year before a drop was registered in this indicator for the U.S.S.R. as a whole. Already in 1990, the region's NMP produced fell to 4 to 8 percent below its pre-perestroika 1985 level, more drastically than in any other region of the country with the exception of Tajikistan (where a state of emergency lasted the whole year). The sequence of the periods of sharpest decline in NMP, however, was different for each of the three republics and reflected the tragic political events in this region.

Georgia, though not involved in the Armenian-Azerbaijani conflict, could not avoid its own serious economic and political difficulties. Although in 1990 NMP produced fell only by 4 percent, last year's results are estimated to be 20 percent below the already depressed 1990 level. Notably, PlanEcon estimates that in 1991 Georgian consumption fell by 25 percent and net investment and other expenditures fell by one-fifth.

Engaged in conflict with one another, Armenia and Azerbaijan both performed poorly in terms of economic output. Following a 10 percent drop in NMP produced in 1990, Armenian NMP produced declined by another 11 percent in 1991 (based on official reporting). After falling 6.1 percent in 1989 and a further 7.9 percent in 1990, Azerbaijani NMP produced officially declined only 0.4 percent in 1991—hardly a plausible result. A drop in Azerbaijani NMP produced in 1991 was more likely about 10 percent.

INDUSTRY

Of the three republics, only Georgia has a more or less diversified industrial structure, but it is far from self-sufficient and depends on imported fuels and raw materials. Armenia is the most industrialized republic, but has less mineral resources and specializes in a narrow range of manufacturing, namely electrical engineering, light, and food industries. Azerbaijan has focused its industrial development around oil extraction and refining. Thus, almost all industrial activities are concentrated around Baku, while the rest of the country is agricultural.

During the latter half of the 1980s, gross industrial output in the Transcaucasus performed horribly. Georgia had the highest average annual growth in gross industrial output from 1985–90 in the region at a paltry 0.5 percent. Both Armenian and Azerbaijani gross industrial output in 1990 were below levels achieved in 1985. In the case of Azerbaijan, the 1990 level was only 0.9 percent lower, for Armenia, a whopping 8 percent lower. During the first three quarters of 1992, Armenian industrial output declined by half. Armenia's deteriorating relationship with Azerbaijan is the main culprit.

ENERGY

Only Azerbaijan is self-sufficient in primary energy requirements, but there are still structural problems in its energy balance.
Azerbaijani energy consumption is based entirely on oil and associated gas, which have long been extracted on the Apsheron peninsula and offshore. At the beginning of this century, Baku was the
world's largest oil-producing center, but the deposits have been depleted and abandoned wells in the "Black City" are the only souve-
nirs of the boom era. Most of the oil from the Baku region is now
extracted offshore, and regional output totals have gradually decreased (from 20 million metric tons (mmt) in 1970 to 13.1 mmt in
1990). The Baku region now accounts for only about 2 percent of
the total output of crude oil in the former Soviet Union.

Georgia, produces only small amounts of crude oil and coal. The
only reliable local source of energy is hydroelectricity, produced by
a number of small electric power stations. To support about three-
quarters of its energy demand, Georgia needs about 5 mmt of refined oil products, half from direct imports, half from local refining
of imported oil; and about 5 billion cubic meters of natural gas as
well.

Armenia produces no fossil fuels whatsoever, and faces the most
serious energy problems in the region. The only border it has with
a friendly neighbor is with its longtime rival, Georgia, but all
energy supply and transport routes were constructed through a
valley, part of which is in Azerbaijani territory. Naturally, all of
them are now cut off. A complete energy and supply blockade can
be breached only by new construction across the Georgian border,
but Georgia itself is very unstable politically, and supplies from
Russia are often disrupted even before they can reach Georgian
territory.

AGRICULTURE

Located in a subtropical zone, the Transcaucasus has produced
exotic and relatively expensive agricultural products for the Soviet
market. The Caucasian republics supply wines, tea, and cotton
(Azerbaijan). The region's natives often make substantial profits
from treks to Russian farmers' markets to sell tangerines, spices,
and flowers.

Agricultural performance has been poor in all three republics
during the last three years and in the 1980s as a whole. Production
output remained at the 1980 level in Georgia and Azerbaijan, and
shrank by 20 percent in Armenia. Volume and yield of almost
every crop was significantly lower in 1990 than it was in 1985. The
production of grapes in Armenia, for example, was halved in a
period of five years. A similar trend can be observed in animal husbandry; both livestock and livestock products were down sharply.

CONSUMER WELFARE

Unfortunately, official statistics do not capture a large portion of
consumption in the Transcaucasus. The black market absorbs an
estimated 40 percent of consumer spending in this region. Still,
with no other consistent source of domestic consumption available,
a discussion of official retail sales figures follows.

Retail trade turnover in the region has jumped quite dramatically during 1988–90. Over this three-year period, retail sales (in comparable prices) rose 25 percent in Georgia and Armenia, and 22 percent in Azerbaijan. However, the turmoil that gripped the region took its toll on retail trade in 1991. Georgian retail trade turnover likely fell below its level achieved in 1985. By official statistics, retail trade turnover in Armenia plunged 25.8 percent in 1991, while in Azerbaijan it dropped 11.8 percent.

FOREIGN TRADE

On external accounts in Transcaucasia, only Azerbaijan may be in a good position. Exports by Azerbaijan fell 38 percent in 1991 and imports declined by 44 percent. The republic's foreign trade deficit was cut by nearly one-half from 1.6 billion rubles in 1990 to 0.85 billion rubles in 1991. Azerbaijan's exports are dominated by crude oil (57 percent), textile products (16 percent), and chemicals (10 percent)—a rather desirable export structure in the present economic environment of the CIS. On the import side, machinery and equipment (40 percent) is the most important category, followed by textile products (29 percent), and animal husbandry products (11 percent).

Armenia has typically run huge deficits, obviously financed by transfers from Moscow. In 1991 Armenian imports declined 19 percent in valuta rubles to 1,380 million rubles. Exports declined precipitously (40 percent) in 1991 to only 120 million rubles. The value of the Armenian trade deficit was ten times that of its exports! Obviously, without financial help from Russia, Armenian imports will plummet in 1992 in order to achieve a more manageable trade deficit. Armenian exports mostly involve machinery and equipment including transport machinery (45 percent) while on the import side consumer goods accounted for most imports (80 percent of the total).

The 1991 trade results of Georgia were also quite disappointing. Exports declined 37 percent in valuta ruble terms and imports fell 42 percent. Georgia customarily runs one of the largest foreign trade deficits of all republics (3.8 billion rubles in 1990), but was able to cut the deficit to 2.2 billion rubles in 1991. Under the old economic system, it made a great deal of sense to try to maximize one's per capita foreign trade deficit and the Georgians excelled at that. In terms of commodity structure of trade, Georgian exports are dominated by metal products (56 percent) and raw food materials (24 percent), while on the import side the leading commodity category is machinery and equipment (40 percent), followed by processed food (9 percent), and textiles and apparel (8 percent).

In the short-term, only Azerbaijan can expect to maintain a positive trade balance in a trading environment using world market prices, with most of its revenues from oil and oil product sales. If the most recent trade flows were repriced at world market prices, Georgia would have incurred a deficit of about 2 billion hard rubles, and Armenia only slightly less (about 1.4 billion rubles).

POLITICAL-ECONOMIC ASSESSMENTS:

RUSSIA

By Keith Bush *

CONTENTS

SUMMARY

By mid-1992, the Russian economy was well into a major depression, after a gradual decline in economic growth extending over four decades. The GNP was expected to decrease by over 40 percent during the period 1990–93. Some of the contributory factors are discussed, as are the prospects for recovery.

RUSSIA'S POSITION IN THE U.S.S.R. AND THE COMMONWEALTH

In 1991, the last year of the U.S.S.R.'s existence, Russia accounted for 51 percent of the country's population, 76 percent of its territory, and 61 percent of its GNP. It contained about 90 percent of the U.S.S.R.'s oil and 75 percent of its natural gas, and it mined 55 percent of its coal. [1] Russia was the only republic with a healthy foreign trade position, registering an aggregate trade surplus of 19.6 billion rubles; all other republics had substantial trade deficits. It ran an overall current-account surplus (including gold sales) of

---

* Keith Bush is a senior economist with Radio Free Liberty/Radio Liberty Research Institute.
[1] *Narkhoz 90* and other U.S.S.R. Goskomstat data.

$7.1 billion, of which $3.4 billion was in convertible currency. [2] When valued at world market prices, Russia enjoyed an estimated overall trade surplus of some $40 billion in 1989; and, despite the subsequent fall in economic activity and the sharp drop in foreign trade, a Western adviser to the Russian government put its 1991 trade surplus at around $20 billion. [3] Furthermore, a respected Western consultancy reckons that Russia would still generate a trade surplus of $20-$30 billion in 1992 if world prices were used, whereas all other members of the Commonwealth of Independent States (CIS) would face substantial deficits. [4]

REFORM PROGRAM

By mid-1992 of all members of the CIS only Russia had produced and started to implement a comprehensive radical economic reform program that had obtained the—albeit conditional—blessing of the International Monetary Fund (IMF) and the Group of Seven (G-7) industrialized nations. Its latest manifestation was *The Memorandum on the Economic Policy of the Russian Federation*, adopted by the Yeltsin government on 27 February and published on 4 March 1992. [5] This provided, among other things, for the lifting of price controls on most of the 10 percent of retail prices and 20 percent of wholesale prices that had not been liberalized on 2 January 1992, plus a gradual raising of fuel and energy prices to approximately two-thirds of the world level by the end of 1992. It restated the very ambitious 1992-1995 targets for privatization that were set out in the presidential decree of 29 December 1991. Since the memorandum's publication, these already high targets have been raised again. The stated intention of the Russian government's latest economic program was to reduce the budget deficit, which was equivalent to some 26 percent of the GDP in 1991 (using the IMF measures) to 1 percent of the GDP during the first quarter of 1992; it aimed at a balanced budget by the end of 1992. The program also provided for a punitive tax on excessive wage growth. It projected a drop in inflation by the end of the first quarter of 1992 to a monthly average of 1-3 percent. Finally, the program reaffirmed the Russian government's commitment to move rapidly toward a single exchange rate and full convertibility for the ruble.

REFORM PROGRESS

When the memorandum was published, many of its main provisions were judged to be unrealistic and unviable. [6] Indeed, by mid-1992 the further raising of fuel prices had been postponed once again; the budget-deficit reduction targets had been greatly eased; inflation during the first five months had exceeded 740 percent; interenterprise debt was approaching the 2-trillion ruble mark; and several features of the reform program had been modified. Yet the

---

[2] PlanEcon, "The Emerging Picture of Foreign Economic Relations of CIS Member Republics," 13 March 1992.
[3] Anders Aslund, "Ruble-Shooters," *The New Republic*, 4 May 1992.
[4] PlanEcon, "The Emerging Picture." This was written before a first-quarter trade deficit of $2.3 billion was announced.
[5] TASS, 4 March 1992.
[6] See Keith Bush, "Russia: Gaidar's Guidelines," *RFE/RL Research Report*, no. 15, 10 April 1992.

government team, headed by Egor Gaidar, had survived massive criticism by the Congress of People's Deputies in April and the reform program had been conditionally accepted by the International Monetary Fund and by the potential Western donor nations.

THE RUBLE

As of mid-June, the Russian ruble was still the currency of all former Soviet republics other than Estonia, although parallel or substitute currencies were in use or pending in several states of the commonwealth, and it was Russia that printed the notes and that, in effect, controlled the cash supply throughout most of the CIS. With the bold pledge made on May 5 of establishing a single exchange rate by July 1992 and full convertibility by August 1992, Russia gave notice that it intended to continue to try to set the budgetary, financial, and credit-policy rules for all states within the ruble zone. [7]

POSTWAR ECONOMIC GROWTH

Russia was in the midst of the deepest peacetime depression that it had ever experienced. The slump followed a secular, gradual decline in average growth rates after the roaring 1950s—when the Soviet growth rates were often roughly twice as high as those of the member countries of the Organization for Economic Cooperation and Development (with the exception of Japan)—through the end of the 1980s. The causes of this decline were many, albeit subject to debate. Perhaps five could be considered preeminent.

First, the Stalin growth model, whereby ever-greater shares of the GNP had to be devoted to new investment in order for the capital stock to grow, was unsustainable over the long run. Second, although socialist spokesmen boasted about their long-term plans, in reality it was only the current year's plan that really mattered. Its fulfillment or over-fulfillment brought bonuses, promotion, and glory, while under-fulfillment could lead to penalties, demotion, disgrace, and, indeed, to imprisonment or worse. With such a short effective time horizon, the cheapest and most accessible deposits were exploited first and rapid gains were emphasized at the expense of conservation, the environment, and rational development. Demography provided the third cause: a high labor participation ratio was reached shortly after the war; the massive transfer of labor from the countryside to the cities was also completed early on; and the population and work force growth rates slowed. Fourth, the joint factor productivity of capital and labor grew only slowly: the system did not encourage innovation; competition was lacking; the degree of monopolization was astonishingly high by world standards; and the U.S.S.R.'s foreign trade participation remained low. The final contributing factor was a monstrous defense burden, the size of which has still not been fully estimated, documented, or comprehended.

---

[7] *The Financial Times*, 7 May 1992.

THE GREAT DEPRESSION OF 1990-1993

The depression got under way in 1990, when the command economy had started to be dismantled but had still not been replaced by market mechanisms or institutions. The last statistical yearbook for the U.S.S.R. put the drop in national income for the RSFSR in 1990 at around 5 percent. [8] It declined even more in 1991, with a reported drop in the GDP of 9 percent. [9] As of mid- June the GNP was expected to decline by a further 15-20 percent in 1992, and most observers predicted recovery and renewed growth not before 1994 at the earliest. In sum, the GNP of Russia could well fall by over 40 percent during 1990-93.

To be sure, some of this reduction is overstated, attributable to a switch from traditional over-reporting to under-reporting of total output. Whereas managers of industrial enterprises and farms had formerly been motivated, for the reasons given above, to exaggerate the output and delivery figures in order to be able to report targets either fulfilled or over-fulfilled, under prevailing conditions, when few people want to accept rubles in payment for goods or services, those same managers will often understate production and sales totals in order to retain a greater share for bartering and for transactions through unofficial channels.

There are other mitigating aspects of the Great Depression cloud. The command economy was notorious for turning out machine tools to make more machine tools, and so on *ad infinitum*. Ever so slowly, factories were switching to products that someone actually wanted and for which buyers were waiting. With the severance of vertical and horizontal links, the traditional statistical systems had also broken down and might not be reporting economic activity accurately. They also proved unable to capture fully and to record the growing activity of the private and cooperative sectors. And, of course, part of the drop in output reflected the decline in the massive overproduction of the defense industry, for which all—apart from the millions of defense workers and their families—should be grateful.

FACTORS CONTRIBUTING TO THE DEPRESSION

THE BUDGET DEFICIT

Prominent among these was the collapse of the ruble as a viable medium for economic transactions. This collapse has been strikingly manifest in the scale of budget deficits recorded—equivalent to about 26 percent of the GDP in 1991 and anticipated to exceed 10 percent of the GDP in 1992. [10] (It might, however, be noted that the term "deficit" was loosely defined and even more loosely used for politically partisan purposes. Thus it was not always clear whether government spokesmen or their critics were referring to the federal budget deficit, federal plus local budget deficits, or to a global concept embracing federal, local, and off-budget funds.)

---

[8] *Narkhoz* 90, p. 12.
[9] *Ekonomika i zhizn'*, No. 4, 1992.
[10] See Philip Hanson, "The Russian Budget Crisis," *RFE/RL Research Report*, no. 14, 3 April 1992.

The budget deficit took off under Gorbachev. Modest deficits occurred in the early 1980s, although these were not revealed until *glasnost* corrected the hitherto immaculate budgetary balances published by the U.S.S.R. Ministry of Finance and the U.S.S.R. Goskomstat. But the deficit really burgeoned with the ill-conceived anti-alcohol campaign of 1985–1986, when official production and sales of vodka and other alcoholic beverages were curtailed and, with them, the highly remunerative excise duties. The production of home brew, or *samogon*, quickly grew to fill the gap. It tasted much the same and had similar aftereffects, but it did not generate any revenues for the treasury.

Apart from a drop in revenues from the sale of alcohol, shortfalls in budgetary income in recent years might be ascribed to a variety of factors. The decline in economic activity meant a shrinking of the tax base. The substantial reduction in imports and exports, especially in 1991, led to a drastic drop in taxes on "foreign economic activities." Populist pressures forced through cuts in the value-added taxes on such items as basic foodstuffs and on school meals. The inadequacy of tax-collection facilities was acknowledged when it was announced, in April 1992, that an additional 100,000 tax inspectors were to be hired by the end of the year. [11] The imposition of excessive rates of taxation inevitably led to tax evasion. And, ironically for Russian President Boris Yeltsin, who had led the "tax revolt" against the Gorbachev center, his own treasury was subsequently denuded by massive withholding on the part of Russian regional and local authorities. Finally, Russia's privatization program got off to a slow start and did not yield the anticipated revenues.

On the expenditures side, overruns were incurred when the levels of minimum wages for budget enterprises and of minimum retirement pensions were raised far beyond initial projections. [12] The government came under intense pressure, notably during the lead-up to the Congress of People's Deputies in April 1992, to maintain and even increase the subsidies payable to the agricultural sector and to loss-making industrial enterprises. Although the numbers of workers and employees formally registered as unemployed remained relatively low during the first half of 1992, the totals were expected to climb dramatically during the second half of the year and, with them, the sums payable in benefits. Yet there were indications that funding for these benefits had not been provided. [13] The drawdown of Russia's armed forces proceeded much more slowly than most observers had hoped or predicted. And the realization dawned, albeit belatedly, that the conversion of defense plants was going to require enormous capital inputs before they could contribute significantly to the output of consumer goods. (Mikhail Malei, the Russian government's conversion *supremo*, recently gave an estimate of $150 billion over 15 years. [14])

---

[11] Radio Mayak, 12 April 1992.
[12] Ibid., 3 April 1992.
[13] ITAR-TASS, 2 April 1992.
[14] Ibid., 3 June 1992

THE MONEY SUPPLY

To paraphrase a famous saying about the weather: everyone complained about the loss of control over the money supply, but nobody seemed to be doing anything about it. Much lip service was paid to the need to cut down on the issuing of money: both potential benefactors and beneficiaries acknowledged that any ruble-stabilization fund was likely to fail unless inflation was checked and budgets balanced. Yet the government printing presses—all of them in Russia—continued to operate flat out, seven days a week, twenty-four hours a day, with the only solution proffered being to issue bank notes of ever-higher denominations.

HYPERINFLATION?

There appeared to be no general agreement on the definition of hyperinflation, [15] but Russia was experiencing a phenomenon that met most criteria. Consumer prices were reported to have risen by 740 percent during the first five months of 1992. [16] The regulated price of oil was scheduled to rise from roughly 3 percent of the world level (at an exchange rate of 50 rubles to the dollar) to about 18 percent in mid-1992; this alone was expected to raise the overall price level by a further 50–70 percent. [17] The planned additional credit emission of some 200 billion rubles, announced in April 1992, was expected to raise prices by 30–40 percent. [18] Another 120 billion rubles' worth of credit was promised by President Yeltsin to the oil and gas industries in June, and First Deputy Prime Minister Vladimir Shumeiko that month announced what appeared to be additional credits amounting to some 500 billion rubles. [19] It looked as if the inflation rate for the year would amount to several thousand percent.

INTERREPUBLIC TRADE

The economic organism of the RSFSR/Russia had been established and maintained for decades on the basis of centrally ordained and enforced interrepublic ties. The disintegration of the former Soviet Union brought with it the collapse of these links. The rupture may prove to have an even more adverse impact on the economy of Russia and the other CIS members than the demise of the Council for Mutual Economic Assistance had (at least in the short run) on its East European members, as well as on the former U.S.S.R.

FOREIGN TRADE

Russian exports dropped by 29 percent and imports by 46 percent in 1991. [20] A detailed analysis of the composition of imports was

---

[15] Konstantin Kagalovsky, the Russian government's economic adviser for liaison with international institutions, defined hyperinflation as "more than 50 percent per month" (*Moskovskiye novosti*, no. 1, 1992, p. 14).
[16] Russian television, 18 March 1992.
[17] *Izvestiya*, 7 April 1992.
[18] Interfax, 27 April 1992.
[19] ITAR-TASS, 19 June 1992
[20] *Ekonomika i zhizn'*, no. 4, 1992.

not available but, as requirements for foodstuffs and medical supplies remained high, it would appear that purchases of technology and equipment must have declined disproportionately. Anecdotal evidence also suggests that convertible-currency imports of spare parts were curtailed. All these factors could have a deleterious effect on investment plans and long-term growth prospects.

PROSPECTS FOR PRINCIPAL EXPORTS

Even more ominous for the short and medium term were the immediate prospects for Russia's principal convertible-currency earners. These were oil, natural gas, arms, machinery, and gold. Oil output fell again in 1991 but domestic oil consumption did not decline commensurately with the drop in economic activity. Thus the net export surplus of oil dropped by nearly half, and a further decline was expected in 1992 and 1993. The output of gas declined only marginally, but exports could be expanded only slowly. Gas was being substituted, wherever possible, for oil. More important, any rapid expansion of gas exports was limited to the existing networks of pipelines. New grids take many years to lay, and so far little progress had been recorded in gas liquefaction for shipment by tanker.

Military hardware has long been virtually the only Russian fabricate that can compete on world markets, and Russia (and the former U.S.S.R.) was for many years among the world's leading suppliers of arms. Estimates of the income derived from these sales vary considerably, but in a recent statement Russian state counsellor for conversion Malei said arms sales had reached a peak of $14 billion in 1990. Only $4 billion of this was "in cash," while the balance went to "our ideological friends at that time." [21] The Russian government had made clear that it intended to push arms sales for the foreseeable future, albeit with pious assurances that weapons and equipment would not be peddled in areas of instability. An arms export control commission, headed by Acting Prime Minister Egor Gaidar, was set up to oversee this export drive. [22] But the defense industry did not remain unscathed by the disruption and the breakdown in the availability of supplies that affected the rest of the Russian economy. And the image of Soviet-made hardware was believed to have suffered from its performance during the Gulf War.

Most Russian machinery exports went to soft-currency purchasers in Eastern Europe, other socialist countries, and to the Third World. Now that Russia was increasingly demanding payment in hard currency, its traditional customers were likely to favor the higher-quality products from the more advanced industrial nations.

After more than half a century of secrecy, the veil over Soviet gold output, reserves, and sales was finally lifted in 1991, revealing that all three were far lower than had been estimated in the West. [23] With gold reserves at an uncomfortably low level and with output expected to decline further (at least in the short run [24]), sales were unlikely to boost Russia's earnings greatly.

---

[21] *Izvestiya*, 1 April 1992.
[22] *Rossiiskaya gazeta*, 16 April 1992.
[23] *Moscow News*, 17–24 November 1991, pp. 6–9.
[24] *Izvestiya*, 6 June 1992

FOREIGN INDEBTEDNESS

At the end of 1991 the net convertible-currency debt of the former U.S.S.R. was believed to have totalled around $65 billion, [25] although no authoritative figure seemed to have been published and the IMF was apparently sworn to discretion. Roughly 61 percent of this debt was assumed by Russia, which, as of mid-1992, was reported to be the only former Soviet republic repaying some capital and interest. [26] Almost all the debt comes due before the end of 1995, which suggests that Russia will need considerably more help from the IMF, the World Bank, and the G-7 nations over and above the $24-billion package that has already (conditionally) been offered.

WESTERN INVESTMENT

With a few notable exceptions, Western capital and expertise had stayed away or were waiting in the wings. There were several good reasons other than political uncertainty for this discretion. Until the ruble became convertible, the repatriation of profits was difficult and complicated, and there was a limit to barter or countertrade. Property rights were still a clouded issue. Laws applying to Western investors and traders were frequently changed and subject to varying interpretations. Taxation legislation was also fluid and the rates excessive—for instance, a marginal rate of 60 percent on worldwide personal incomes of over 420,000 rubles a year (about $4,200 a year at the exchange rate prevailing in mid-June) on expatriates residing in Russia for more than 183 days a year. [27] Basic services were poor or nonexistent, while the infrastructure was often like that found in developing countries. Above all, Western businessmen had complained about uncertainty and unpredictability in the whole environment of legislation, jurisdiction, regulations, and contracts.

CONVERSION

The conversion of the former U.S.S.R.'s huge defense industry from making military hardware to producing civilian goods was long seen as the simple and rapid panacea for most of the woes of the Soviet economy. Here was the most efficient sector of Soviet industry, into which had been channelled an estimated 10 percent of the national income for more than half a century [28] and which employed the cream of managerial and technical personnel. What could be simpler than switching its production lines from high-grade and competitive machine guns to high-grade and competitive meat grinders? Only comparatively recently did it become clear that the process would be long, arduous, painful for the work force, and enormously expensive. As has been mentioned, the projected convertible-currency cost of conversion was huge, and the only

---

[25] This figure excludes commercial arrears (about $4 billion at the end of 1991) and the roughly $17 billion owed to former socialist countries—a dollar value variously interpreted depending on which rate of exchange is used.

[26] Egor Gaidar, cited by Interfax, 16 May 1992.

[27] See *The Wall Street Journal*, 24–25 April 1992.

[28] Mikhail Bazhanov, the chairman of the State Committee for Conversion Matters, Radio Mayak, 6 February 1992.

likely source of funding seemed to be from the intensified sales of arms on the world market. This could mean that ever more investment in armaments factories will be needed if they are to remain competitive.

In early 1992, encouraging claims were made about the progress made so far in conversion. Representatives of the defense industry told President Yeltsin in May that only 20 percent of the capacity of their industry (employing 6.5 million people) was involved in producing weapons, with the rest going to civilian production. [29] It was also claimed that the defense industry was the only sector of the former Soviet economy that fulfilled and over-fulfilled its production plans in 1991, including those for civilian goods. [30] Yet these claims ran counter to the overwhelming majority of reports from officials in the industry and managers of individual plants. It appeared that conversion had not yet provided the hoped-for increase in civilian output or checked the downturn in industrial activity.

CONCLUSION

At mid-1992 Russia was well into a great depression, with the GNP expected to decline by over 40 percent during 1990–1993. A massive retrenchment of economic activity was to be expected, as the command economy was virtually abandoned before market institutions and mechanisms were in place. The severity of the downturn was likely to be more pronounced than in many other former socialist economies, because the system was entrenched in the U.S.S.R. for a longer period and the defense burden was proportionately heavier. The impact of such a depression upon the social fabric of any nation would be profound, and especially upon a society that had undergone the political and economic upheavals that had beset Russia during the past few years.

When he unveiled his reform proposals in October 1991, President Yeltsin warned of "some decline in living standards" but promised that "we shall see real results by the fall of 1992." [31] However, consumption levels by mid-1992 had reportedly fallen to the levels registered in the late 1950s, [32] and were expected to drop further. The first signs of stabilization were promised for the end of 1992, although monthly data in mid-1992 at best indicated a marginal easing in the rate of decline of output.

The long-term prospects for the Russian economy were good. The country possesses some of the largest deposits of fuel, timber, and minerals in the world. It has a highly educated work force. At the kind of exchange rates envisaged, its labor costs would be highly competitive on the world market. Moreover, two sea changes of commitment were apparent in mid-1992. After years of hesitation, the industrialized West and the international financial community seemed firmly committed to underwriting Russia's blueprint for stabilizing its economy and making its currency convertible. Within Russia, few really wanted to return to the command econo-

---

[29] ITAR-TASS, 13 May 1992.
[30] Bazhanov on Radio Mayak.
[31] Central Television, 28 October 1991.
[32] *Argumenty i fakty*, no. 22–23, 1992.

my, and the bulk of the population appeared at last committed to the long, arduous, and perilous road to the market. What was at issue was the pace at which stabilization and transition should be pursued.

President Yeltsin had assembled an impressive government team of young, market-oriented economists who had also developed considerable political acumen. Egor Gaidar survived a massive battering from the Russian Congress of People's Deputies in April, with his reform program still recognizable. A non-event had strengthened Yeltsin's hand: there were none of the major uprisings and street demonstrations protesting shortages and hardships that had been predicted by many Russian and Western observers for the winter of 1991-92. And despite widespread threats of strike action, the number of industrial man-days lost to walkouts during the first four months of 1992 was considerably lower than during the same period of 1991.

After months of bare shelves, goods appeared again, albeit at often breathtaking prices. Market forces made a spontaneous, disorganized, and often chaotic debut in the cities in the shape of citizens trading in just about everything that could be sold or resold for rubles. Stock exchanges and rudimentary commodities exchanges sprang up, although their activity had fallen into decline by mid-1992.

And yet the short- and medium-term prospects at mid-1992 were opaque at best and alarming for concerned Russia-watchers. No meaningful and comprehensive reform of the agro-industrial sector had been initiated. Parliament was effectively blocking many of the government's proposed moves toward the market. Privatization was well behind schedule. De-monopolization legislation was still under discussion. The money supply seemed to be out of control. Hyperinflation was looming. The budget deficit—insofar as it could be quantified—was probably well in excess of 10 percent of the GDP. It looked unlikely that full external convertibility of the ruble could be attained by August 1992, as envisaged. No hard budgetary constraint had been introduced, and inter-enterprise debts were approaching a total of 2 trillion rubles. A packet of new reform measures was announced on the eve of President Yeltsin's departure for Washington, but it was not immediately clear how viable these decrees were.

The Yeltsin government and the IMF were in open disagreement over the parameters and contents of Russia's reform program and over the degree of its implementation, and it was by no means certain that the $24 billion rescue package agreed to by the Western industrialized nations would be forthcoming before the G-7 summit in July—with all of the concomitant political risks for Yeltsin. Yet this aid package represented relatively little in the way of new money and hardly anything tangible for the leadership to show to the expectant population. It was also merely a down payment on the far larger sums that will eventually be needed to buttress Russia's transition to the market.

Perhaps most fundamentally, despite protestations to the contrary and despite the promotion of Egor Gaidar to the post of Acting Prime Minister in June, the earlier appointment of Messrs. Shumeiko, Khizha, and Chernomyrdin to the government and other like-minded officials to important posts was widely seen as signalling the "Abalkinization" of Gaidar and his colleagues and the turning away from the straight and narrow path of rigorous reform. The immediate picture was clouded and the course of events unpredictable.

POLITICAL-ECONOMIC ASSESSMENTS:
UKRAINE

By Steven J. Woehrel *

CONTENTS

SUMMARY

Unlike in Russia, where a radical free-market reform program is already in place, reform efforts in Ukraine have been hampered by the country's focus on securing its independence and by the predominant position of ex-Communist Party functionaries, who have little enthusiasm for or understanding of the free market. While Russia moved forward with a "shock therapy" economic reform package in January 1992, contending factions in Ukraine engaged in a struggle over control of the reform process. The result was that a series of economic reform plans were drafted, adopted, and abandoned over the course of the year, and no substantial economic reform occurred.

The largest role in making economic policy was played by former Communist Party and government *apparatchiks* in both President Kravchuk's entourage and in the government. They stressed increased state control of the economy in order to strengthen Ukraine's independence from Russia and to halt a rapid decline in production. They pursued lax fiscal and monetary policies, in part to prop up state-owned firms, that caused explosive inflation by the end of the year. Yet their desire to control these enterprises and increase revenue to state coffers led them to impose high taxes, triggering complaints from the industrialists.

Kravchuk and then Prime Minister Fokin's emphasis on safeguarding Ukraine's independence won them support from part of the former nationalist opposition. A free market reformer from the opposition was included in the government but was soon dismissed when he refused to acquiesce in what he called a "simulation of

* Steven J. Woehrel is an Analyst in European Affairs with the Foreign Affairs and National Defense Division, Congressional Research Service.

reform." In November 1992, a new government composed of leaders of Ukrainian industry, led by new Prime Minister Leonid Kuchma, and several economic reformers close to the opposition offered hope that economic reform might get underway in 1993.

STRUCTURE OF UKRAINE'S ECONOMY

Aside from Russia, Ukraine has the largest economy of any Commonwealth of Independent States (CIS) country. In 1990, it accounted for almost 17 percent of Soviet industrial output. Unlike many of the newly independent states, it is rich in natural resources, with deposits of coal, iron ore, manganese, sulfur, and a significant amount of natural gas. Heavy industry plays a critical role in the Ukrainian economy, making up 69 percent of industrial production. Key heavy industries include machine-building (33 percent of industrial output in 1990), metallurgy (12.5 percent), wood and chemicals (9 percent) and fuel and energy (8 percent). Ferrous metallurgy and mining alone accounted for 40 percent of industrial assets in 1990. Coal mining is concentrated in the Donets Basin (Donbas), forming an integrated complex with heavy industry, also located in the Donbas and along the Dnieper River bend. In contrast, light industry and food processing accounted for only 11 percent and 18 percent respectively of Ukrainian industrial production in 1990. Ukraine's defense industries play an important part in the economy, employing 1–1.2 million employees (15–17 percent of industrial workers) in over 700 plants.

Ukraine's industry poses many problems for economic reformers. It is dominated by monopoly producers that will be difficult to break up into smaller, more efficient competing firms. Because Soviet planners have concentrated investment in Siberia and other regions of Russia in recent decades, Ukrainian industrial equipment is old, even by ex-Soviet standards. Ukraine's heavy industries pose serious environmental problems and are voracious consumers of increasingly expensive energy. Ukraine's own key natural resources, coal and iron ore, are expensive to extract, are polluting, and are less easily sold on world markets than oil and other natural resources.

Agriculture is another critical sector of Ukraine's economy. Ukraine was often called the "breadbasket" of the Soviet Union because of its rich, black soil, which provided about 20 percent of Soviet agricultural production and about 30 percent of Ukraine's Net Material Product in 1990. [1] However, Ukrainian agriculture faces difficulties in obtaining fuel and labor supplies and in creating adequate storage and distribution systems. Perhaps most importantly, production has been hampered by low state procurement prices, which give farms little incentive to produce more. Competition and protectionism from the EC and other producers will make it difficult for Ukraine to export its farm production.

The collapse of central planning and the desire to keep more local production at home caused the interruption of trading links

---

[1] Myaschin, Vadim and Matthew J. Sagers. The Ukraine: An Economic Profile through the First Nine Months of 1991. Plan Econ Report, November 27, 1991, Volume VII, no. 42, 7 and Jay K. Mitchell, "Outlook for Ukraine," Plan Econ Review and Outlook for the Former Soviet Union, 1992. p. 71–75.

among CIS states. In recent years, Russo-Ukrainian trade made up more than two-thirds of all interrepublic trade in the Soviet Union. In recent years, Ukraine has run a trade deficit with the republics of the former Soviet Union. In 1991, Ukraine had a $7.6 billion trade deficit with Russia and the other former Soviet republics, if one uses world market prices for the commodities traded. Based on 1991 ruble trade data not converted to world market prices, 75 percent of Ukraine exports were in just three areas: machinery, metal products, and coal. These products are largely uncompetitive on world markets. Light industry and food composed less than 10 percent of exports. Leading imports in 1991 were machinery (50 percent), textiles and apparel (14 percent) and chemicals (10 percent). [2]

Interruption of these trade ties has been especially damaging to Ukraine's economy. Former Prime Minister Fokin claimed that 70 percent of Ukraine's products require parts or raw materials supplied by other CIS states. Ukraine has run increasingly large trade deficits in the past few years. The most critical current problem is fuel. While Ukraine produces 95 percent of the coal it needs, it only produces 22 percent of the natural gas and 8 percent of the oil it requires. [3] Eastern Ukraine's heavy industry and agriculture have been hard hit by a lack of energy supplies. Russia, Kazakhstan and Turkmenistan, the sources of most of Ukraine's oil and natural gas, have increased fuel prices substantially and are planning to bring them eventually to world market levels, which will greatly intensify this problem. Ukraine does have some leverage against these states, however; the major oil and natural gas pipelines that carry the exports of these states to Western Europe pass through Ukrainian territory.

POLITICAL SITUATION IN UKRAINE

Part of the blame for Ukraine's failure to move forward with economic reform lies with President Leonid Kravchuk. Kravchuk won a strong mandate to rule Ukraine during December 1, 1991, elections which overwhelmingly approved Ukraine's declaration of independence and elected him President with over 61 percent of the vote, 38 percent more than his closest rival Vyacheslav Chornovil, a former political prisoner and the candidate of the main opposition movement Rukh. Instead of using this mandate to push forward with economic reform like Yeltsin did in Russia, however, Kravchuk concentrated on consolidating and expanding his power base by trying to hold on to the support of old-style apparatchiks, while splitting the opposition. Kravchuk continued to support Prime Minister Vitold Fokin and his conservatively oriented Cabinet of Ministers until October 1992, despite strong opposition pressure to dismiss Fokin and radically restructure the Cabinet.

Kravchuk also moved to assert his authority on the local level. Taking a lesson from Boris Yeltsin in Russia, Kravchuk asked the Supreme Rada, in February 1992, for the right to appoint his personal representatives to each region, who would be charged with making sure Kiev's orders are carried out. However, Kravchuk's

---

[2] Mitchell, p. 79–80.
[3] Sekarev, Alexei. Die Ukrainische Aussenwirtshaft zwischen GUS und Weltwirtschaft, Bundesinstituts fur ostwissenschaftliche und internationale Studien, no. 20, 1992. p. 8.

representatives are more powerful than Yeltsin's. While Yeltsin's representatives can only monitor implementation of presidential decisions, Kravchuk's men are the leading administrative officials of their regions and are responsible only to him. Observers characterize the political views of the representatives as centrist, ranging from rather conservative former Communist Party officials to moderate reformers with few ties with the opposition. Opposition leaders complain that their nominees for the posts have been ignored.

Kravchuk moved skillfully to divide the opposition. As in Russia, the opposition is fragmenting now that the Communist Party has been repudiated, if not the Communists themselves. The opposition is split over what attitude to take toward Kravchuk. Moderate intellectuals, like Ivan Drach, Mykhaylo Horyn and Dmytro Pavlychko, want to offer support to Kravchuk in his efforts to build up Ukrainian statehood and are willing to soft-pedal his hesitancy to move forward on economic reform. Chornovil, on the other hand, wants Rukh to remain firmly in opposition to Kravchuk, challenging him to move further and faster on economic reform.

A further split within the opposition is between the groupings like Rukh that are mainly nationalist in orientation and those that put less emphasis on national issues and stress the need for rapid economic reform. While some nationally oriented intellectuals may be willing to downplay Kravchuk's slowness to commit to radical economic reform in order to support his strong stand on building an independent Ukrainian state, these groups fear that Kravchuk's new nationalism draws attention away from his economic failures and damages critical trading ties with Russia. In early 1992, these latter groups and political parties formed a loose grouping called "New Ukraine." A wide variety of opinion exists within the nascent movement, which includes ex-Communist Party reformers, entrepreneurs, and ecological groups. Prominent figures in "New Ukraine" include former Deputy Prime Minister Lanovyi and Supreme Rada Deputy Chairman Vladimir Grinev.

The difference in focus between Rukh and New Ukraine partly mirrors regional differences. The most significant difference is between western Ukraine (especially the regions of Lviv, Ivano-Frankivsk, and Ternopil) and the eastern and southern regions of the country. In general, western Ukrainians are more nationally conscious than those in other regions and have led the drive for Ukrainian independence. They form the leadership and much of the rank-and-file of the Rukh movement, as well as other, more radical, nationalist groups. In contrast, eastern Ukrainians, subjected to centuries of Russification, tend to look more skeptically on Ukrainian nationalism. In addition, ethnic Russians, who make up 22 percent of Ukraine's population, are concentrated in the east and south. Like eastern Ukrainians, ethnic Russians have by and large supported Ukrainian independence for pragmatic, economic reasons. There appears to be no widespread support for secession of regions and their union with Russia. They are more interested in the economic benefits independence provides or does not provide. Many of the leaders of the "New Ukraine" bloc are from eastern Ukraine. And while former Communist Party functionaries have been swept out of leading positions in western Ukraine, they are still deeply entrenched elsewhere.

In one case, Ukraine's territorial integrity remains fragile. Russians make up 67 percent of Crimea's population, Ukrainians, only 26 percent. In December 1991, a bare majority of Crimeans voted for Ukraine's independence. But this attitude could well change if economic conditions deteriorate. A group called Republican Movement of Crimea collected over 257,000 signatures for a referendum to be held on Crimean independence, far more than the 180,000 required. On May 5, 1992, the Crimean Supreme Soviet, in a surprise move, declared Crimea's independence from Ukraine. However, the Crimean Supreme Soviet suspended the resolution on May 21, after Kravchuk warned Crimea that bloodshed could occur if Crimea tries to assert its independence from Ukraine. Crimea and Ukraine seemingly stepped back from confrontation in June, when negotiators for the two sides agreed that Crimea was an "integral part of Ukraine" but would have economic autonomy and the right to "independently enter into social, economic and cultural relations with other states." On July 9, the Crimean parliament voted to cancel plans for a referendum on Crimean independence.

Crimea is a potentially dangerous issue in the Russo-Ukrainian relationship. Crimea was part of Russia until 1954, when Khrushchev transferred the peninsula to Ukraine to commemorate the 300th anniversary of the union of Ukraine with Russia. Many Russians feel that Crimea rightfully belongs to Russia. Yeltsin has thus far ruled out a territorial claim to Crimea, but influential forces (including Vice President Alexandr Rutskoi and the current Russian Ambassador to the United States Vladimir Lukin) have advocated raising such a claim in order to pressure Kiev into giving up its claim to the Black Sea Fleet. On May 21, 1992, the Russian parliament overwhelmingly voted to nullify the 1954 transfer. While denying that Russia had any territorial claims on Ukraine, the parliament also asserted that Russia must be involved in any future talks on the status of Crimea. Ukraine condemned the Russian move and says it considers Crimea a purely internal matter.

Linked to the Crimea question is the issue of the Black Sea Fleet. The Black Sea Fleet possesses over 350 ships, including 55 major surface combat vessels (about 26 percent of the Soviet total) and 20 attack submarines (roughly 7 percent of the Soviet total). The fleet's major base is at Sevastopol on the Crimean peninsula, although there are other important bases in Novorossiysk in Russia and Poti in Georgia. Ukrainian military leaders say that Ukraine wants all of the Black Sea Fleet ships based on Ukrainian territory. For its part, the CIS high command seemed willing to cede to Ukraine a small part of the fleet for coastal defense, but wanted major combatant ships to remain part of the CIS Navy. In August 1992, Yeltsin and Kravchuk agreed that the Black Sea Fleet would be jointly administered by Russia and Ukraine (removing it from the CIS command structure) for a three-year transitional period, in order to allow tensions over the issue to subside. However, there seems to be some differences in interpretation of the accord: Russian military leaders say that the fleet should remain united until 1995, while Ukrainian leaders say the process of division should take place gradually within the three-year transition period.

People in eastern and southern Ukraine are disturbed by the confrontational relations between Russia and Ukraine. They strongly support efforts to restore critical trading ties with Russia. In September 1992, miners from the eastern Ukrainian region of Donetsk, who had played an important role in the struggle against Soviet rule, called for greater autonomy from Kiev in response to Kiev's economic policy and the alleged domination of the government by western Ukrainians. A possible area of future friction with Kiev could be over unemployment caused by government economic austerity measures and attempts to restructure the many highly inefficient and unprofitable industrial firms and mines in the region.

In addition to playing the "nationalist card," Kravchuk weakened the opposition by appointing some of his supporters in the former opposition as advisors in his administration and as ambassadors to foreign countries. Kravchuk also appointed several opposition figures to the government, coopting them without giving them real power to impose change on the ex-Communist bureaucracy. Most prominent of these was leading reformer Volodymyr Lanovyi to the post of Economics Minister and Deputy Prime Minister in charge of economic reform in early March 1992. Ukrainian spokesmen touted Lanovyi as "our Gaidar," referring to the architect of Russian economic reform.

Kravchuk's exclusion of the opposition from important decision-making roles and the slow pace of reform has led part of the opposition to consolidate its forces and take a stronger line against Kravchuk. Both New Ukraine and Rukh have called for the establishment of an effective coalition to pressure Kravchuk and have demanded the dissolution of the Ukrainian Supreme Rada, the holding of parliamentary elections in 1993 and the convening of a constitutional assembly to write a new Ukrainian Constitution. On the other hand, Mykhaylo Horyn, Pavlychko and others who favor supporting Kravchuk organized a rival Congress of National-Democratic Forces in August 1992 that is aimed at providing a counterweight to the Chornovil-led Rukh. New Ukraine leader Filenko has stated that only 40–50 members of the parliament are in real opposition to Kravchuk, as compared to 120 members when the parliament was elected in 1990.

STRUGGLE OVER ECONOMIC REFORM

In late March 1992, the Ukrainian Supreme Rada approved in principle an economic reform package called "Fundamentals of National Economic Policy." The package drawn up under the leadership of Oleksandr Yemelyanov, a former senior official in the republic's State Planning Committee who became a member of a new advisory body to Kravchuk called the State Council. The plan was less an economic reform package than an attempt to establish economic independence from Russia in the wake of Russian plans to increase prices for major commodities supplied to other former Soviet republics. Yemelyanov's plan called for Ukraine to introduce its own currency immediately and to leave the ruble zone rapidly. The blueprint also called for restricting imports from Russia and other ruble zone states and reorientation of Ukrainian exports toward new markets. Lanovyi attacked the plan, saying that introducing a new currency and cutting trade ties with Russia so quickly could only lead to the collapse of Ukraine's economy. Lanovyi in turn put forth another economic reform program entitled the "Plan for Economic Policy and Market Reforms." In late April, Lanovyi submitted the plan to the International Monetary Fund when the body was considering Ukraine's application for membership. The plan called for tight monetary and fiscal policies and sweeping privatization.

In July 1992, Kravchuk fired Lanovyi, ostensibly for belonging to the New Ukraine opposition movement while being part of the government. He replaced him with Valentin Symonenko, who had earlier served as Communist Party boss in the Odessa region and was for nine years mayor of the city. In an interview shortly after taking office, Simonenko said he was "categorically against any help from the West," but added he favored "equal, mutually beneficial cooperation." The government developed another reform plan. Viktor Pynzenyk, a prominent reform economist from Lviv and member of the Supreme Rada, attacked a draft of the plan as a "full-scale restoration" of the command economy, pointing to reported proposals such as permitting the government to set or control wages most prices and interest rates, and giving the government powers to manage enterprises directly instead of merely administer laws.[4] The plan came under heavy attack in the Supreme Rada. Particularly important was the attitude of parliament chairman Ivan Plyushch. A former Kravchuk loyalist, Plyushch attacked the Fokin/Symonenko plan for calling for a further expansion of the executive branch's already preponderant power at the expense of the already weakened parliament.[5]

Hoping to decrease the pressure on Kravchuk and the government, Fokin resigned on October 1, 1992. The next day, however, the government as a whole collapsed when the Ukrainian parliament voted a motion of no confidence. Observers speculate that the Ukrainian parliament's vote of no-confidence in his predecessor Vitold Fokin was due to the disgust of the economic elite (industrial managers and collective farm chairmen) at Fokin's mismanagement of the economy.

FAILURES OF THE FOKIN GOVERNMENT

A key failure of Fokin's economic policy so far has been lax fiscal and monetary policies that have fueled inflation. Official statistics show a state budget deficit of 324 billion rubles for the first nine months of 1992, as compared to total expenditures of 645 billion.[6] In addition, the Ukrainian central bank also gave huge low-interest loans to Ukrainian enterprises; current Economy Minister Viktor Pynzenyk has stated that the government issued 800 billion rubles

---

[4] Buhenbay, Ibrayev. The Professor's Gloomy Forecasts. Robitnychna Hazeta, October 23, 1992. p. 2; in Foreign Broadcast Information Service (FBIS), Central Eurasia, November 15, 1992, FBIS-USR-92-147. p. 75.

[5] Solychanyk, Roman. Ukraine: The Politics of Economic Reform. Radio Free Europe/Radio Liberty Weekly Report, November 20, 1992. p. 4.

[6] The Economy of Ukraine in the Nine Months of 1992. Uryadovyy Kurier, October 16, 1992, 9 as translated in FBIS-USR-92-146. p. 86–89.

in these loans in May and June alone. [7] Consumer prices jumped 1,014 percent in the first eight months of 1992. [8]

In order to compensate for the Russian Central Bank's unwillingness or inability to supply Ukraine with enough rubles to pay wages and to move toward the introduction of its own currency, Ukraine established a coupon system that in effect operates as a parallel currency to the ruble. The system was introduced in January 1992 in order to protect the local consumer market from buyers from other republics and to compensate for a shortage of rubles provided by the Russian Central Bank. Ukraine gradually took steps to eliminate the use of the ruble for most purposes in Ukraine; by August 1992 the coupon accounted for 97 percent of official cash transactions in Ukraine. On November 12, Ukraine took the final step in leaving the ruble zone. Kravchuk issued a decree that eliminated the use of the ruble for non-cash as well as cash transactions. The future of this provisional currency, the karbovanets, is not bright. The government's lax monetary and credit policies caused a sharp drop in the value of the coupon/karbovanets relative to the dollar, and has even caused the coupon to depreciate relative to the ruble.

The introduction of a new, "permanent" currency, the hryvnia, originally scheduled for late 1992, has been delayed indefinitely by the Kuchma government until hard currency reserves are built up and an economic stabilization plan is drawn up and partially implemented.

Fokin's government also failed to make much headway on privatization. In March 1992, the Supreme Rada passed several laws on privatization and approved a government privatization program in July 1992. According to the plan, Ukrainian citizens will receive a privatization voucher with a face value of 30,000 rubles (inflation and the switch to the karbovanets will likely change this figure), deposited in a privatization account. The voucher cannot be sold for cash or transferred to another person. They will be able to use the non-transferable voucher, along with cash and hard currency, to buy privatized firms.

Perhaps the most problematic feature of the plan are provisions on leasing. During its deliberations on the plan, the Supreme Rada amended the government's draft in a way that seems to allow a firm's assets to be leased without competitive bidding. Moreover, another law passed by the Rada on leasing, makes it nearly impossible for the state to refuse to lease an enterprise if the enterprise's workers approve of the deal. This could allow the managers of the firm, in conjunction with the workers, to evade the voucher privatization process. [9]

THE KUCHMA GOVERNMENT: A NEW BEGINNING?

After the fall of the Fokin government, Kravchuk appointed Symonenko as acting Prime Minister, and some analysts believe that Kravchuk wanted to name him permanently to the post. Instead,

---

[7] Freeland, Chrystia. A Very Ukrainian Reformist. Financial Times, November 27, 1992.
[8] Economy of Ukraine in the Nine Months of 1992. p. 87.
[9] Johnson, Simon and Santiago Eder. Prospects for Privatization in Ukraine, Fuqua School of Business, Duke University, 1992.

perhaps as a compromise with radical reformers and the "industrialists," Kravchuk appointed as Prime Minister Leonid Kuchma, the former director of Yuzhmash, the largest missile factory in Ukraine. Kuchma was approved by the Supreme Rada by an overwhelming margin on October 12, 1992. Kuchma at first pledged to move forward cautiously with economic reform, and displayed great skepticism about rapid privatization. Kuchma named Ihor Yukhonovsky, former leader of the opposition faction in the parliament, as first Deputy Prime Minister and Viktor Pynzenyk as Deputy Prime Minister in charge of economic reforms and Economics Minister. Several other key positions went to "industrialists," who like Kuchma have had experience running large enterprises. Vasily Yevtushkov, deputy Prime Minister for industry and construction, was President of the Ukranian Union of Entrepreneurs, which unites Ukraine's large, state-owned enterprises. Yuli Ioffe, deputy Prime Minister for fuel and power, was head of the Stakhanov Coal Production Association.

In his first speeches to the parliament, Kuchma launched blistering attacks on Fokin's economic policy (without mentioning Fokin by name), saying that Ukraine so far has not had economic reform but only "economic crime." Kuchma said Ukraine had to "build everything from scratch, as we did after the Second World War." Kuchma said that in the first nine months of 1992, gross national product fell 18 percent, industrial production dropped by 19.7 percent, and prices increased 22.5 times.

Kuchma's economic program, unveiled on November 18, calls for a sounder monetary and fiscal policy. One priority is to curb Ukraine's huge budget deficit (which Kuchma estimated at over 44 percent of GNP) by sharply cutting subsidies to unprofitable state enterprises, which Fokin's government had bailed out by issuing 400 billion rubles in credits. Upon taking office, the new government raised the central bank's lending rate to 80 percent. Kuchma also said that he wants legislation that would forbid the government to finance its deficit by printing money. Kuchma's program also calls for "forced" privatization of both small and large enterprises and stimulating the growth of the private sector. Kuchma stressed the need to cut taxes on enterprises. However, Kuchma also called for tighter government regulation of state enterprises in the transition period, including controls on wages. Another focus of Kuchma's economic efforts, in line with his "industrialist" background, will be restoring critical economic links with Russia.

The parliament, shocked by Kuchma's report on the economy, granted the government the authority to enact decrees on economic reform and restricted its own right to pass legislation on this issue for six months. [10] On December 26, the government issued a decree removing price controls on some basic foodstuffs. But the decree tightened price controls in the metallurgical and chemical industries, machine-building and for such products as oil, cement, salt, sugar, vegetable oil, meat and eggs. Prices for goods produced by monopolies would also be controlled to prevent enterprises exploiting their market position. The government has drafted or is

---

[10] Freeland, Chrystia. Deepening Crisis Pushes Ukraine into Urgent Reform. Financial Times, November 19, 1992. p. 3.

drafting decrees on privatization, trade, social benefits and other issues.

The first moves of the Kuchma government provide hope that economic reform in Ukraine may now be underway, after over a year of marking time since Ukraine's declaration of independence. However, the new government faces daunting tasks ahead, including the reining in of hyperinflation, the introduction of a new Ukrainian currency, and the restructuring of an economy that is uncompetitive in many areas, even by ex-Soviet standards.

POLITICAL-ECONOMIC ASSESSMENTS:

THE CENTRAL ASIAN STATES

By Bess Brown *

CONTENTS

SUMMARY

The five Central Asian states began to receive foreign recognition as distinct entities only at the beginning of 1992. None has created a Western-style democracy, but all hope for acceptance by the world community, from which, rather than from the other Commonwealth of Independent States (CIS), they hope for investment and development assistance.

INTRODUCTION

Four of the Central Asian republics of the Soviet Union declared their independence in the period between the Moscow coup in August 1991 and the formal dissolution of the U.S.S.R. in December, but the rest of the world began to take cognizance of their status as independent states only at the beginning of 1992. During debates in 1990 and 1991 over the future structure of the U.S.S.R., the leaders of the Central Asian republics had argued for a type of confederation that would allow its constituent states maximum control over their own economies, natural resources, and cultural and social development while retaining a central power that would coordinate relations among the partners. Because the economies of the Central Asian republics were so closely intertwined with those of the rest of the U.S.S.R. and dependent on subsidies from Moscow, the leaders of these states were convinced that their republics could not exist on their own.

With the rise in Russian national consciousness in the wake of the failed hard-line coup, the leaders of the Central Asian republics, with the exception of Kazakhstan, concluded that formal inde-

---

* Bess Brown is with the Radio Free Europe/Radio Liberty Research Institute.

pendence would keep them from being overwhelmed by the Russian Federation, which might seek a restoration of the strictly centralized empire. Some of the more conservative Central Asian leaders, in particular the presidents of Tajikistan and Turkmenistan, admitted that they feared the influx of democratic ideas from Russia, and hoped that the independence of their countries would enable them to limit the influence of Western liberal ideas.

When the presidents of Russia, Ukraine, and Belarus established a Commonwealth in December 1991, the question for their Central Asian counterparts was whether to join the Slavic states or to create a separate association of Central Asian states. The first steps toward the creation of a Central Asian confederation had already been taken at meetings of the presidents of Kazakhstan, Uzbekistan, Kyrgyzstan, Tajikistan, and Turkmenistan in June 1990 and August 1991, but little substantive results had emerged. When the five Central Asian presidents gathered in Ashkhabad, Turkmenistan, in December 1991 to decide whether to join the Slavic Commonwealth, they agreed to activate the Consultative Council that had been set up the previous August to coordinate economic policy among the five states, but nearly a year later there was little sign of coordination. In February 1992 all the Central Asian states except Kazakhstan joined the Economic Cooperation Organization, which already included Turkey, Iran, and Pakistan. This group has shown no greater ability to coordinate economic policy among its members than has the Consultative Council set up by the Central Asians themselves. In the economic as well as the political sphere, the five states are independently determining their own paths of development.

Uzbekistan views itself as the natural leader of any consortium of Central Asian countries on grounds of population, and regards itself as the direct heir of the prerevolutionary states of the Turkestan region. Uzbek President Islam Karimov commented in February 1992 that if the Central Asian states would pool their rich resources they could make the region a power in its own right. The other Central Asian countries are not willing, however, to submit to the dictates of Tashkent. Significantly, there has been no sign of intent on the part of the independent Central Asian states to coordinate their foreign policies.

Since the appearance of the Central Asian countries on the global scene, there has been widespread concern, particularly in the West, that the new states would either fall under the influence of Iranian-style revolutionary Muslim fundamentalism or would be driven by poverty to sell nuclear weapons or weapons components to anti-Western regimes such as those in Tehran, Bagdad, or Tripoli. A stream of Western visitors to Central Asia since independence has urged them to follow the Turkish model of a secular, Western-oriented society with functioning democratic institutions. All Central Asian leaders and most intellectuals believe that the Turkish model would be the most appropriate; the leadership prefers a secular society, fearing the potential challenge of Muslim political groups, and the intelligentsia is mostly Western-oriented. For Turkic- speaking states, there is a strong linguistic and ethnic affinity with Turkey, but even the highest-ranking Tajik Muslim clergyman, the influential Akbar Turadzhonzoda, has said that for

Iranian-speaking Tajikistan, which is actively developing cultural and economic ties to Iran, Turkey is the best model for his country's social and political development. The ending of subsidies from Moscow has brought serious dislocations for the economies of all the Central Asian states. Not only are the Central Asians no longer receiving direct financial contributions to their budgets, but they must also find alterative buyers for their raw materials. Uzbekistan announced in late 1991 that it would no longer sell cotton to the Russian Federation—the Uzbeks insisted on payment in hard currency—but it was immediately faced with the problem of where to sell its cotton. After long negotiations, an agreement was finally reached in May 1992 between Russia, the textile mills of Ivanovo having gone nearly bankrupt without Uzbek cotton, and Uzbekistan. Before the agreement was reached, however, both sides had turned to the United States: the Russian Federation investigating an alternate source of cotton, and Uzbekistan seeking a market for its cotton fabric.

It was only in 1991 that the Central Asian states obtained control over their own industries, most of which had formerly been directly subordinate to ministries in Moscow. The ability of the Central Asian countries to maintain former levels of industrial output is being affected by the problems of obtaining supplies from other Commonwealth states—although each of the Central Asian states has made numerous agreements with the new countries that were its former suppliers, interruptions have become the rule, as is the case elsewhere in the former U.S.S.R.

The mass departure of the Russian population from every Central Asian country except Kazakhstan was under way well before these countries gained their independence. Many Russians were uncomfortable with the increasing assertiveness of Central Asians seeking to advance their national interests, but when violence broke out in the region, particularly that in Uzbekistan in 1989 and Tajikistan and Kyrgyzstan in 1990, the Russian outmigration became a flood. At the same time, Central Asian officials have sought to encourage Russian professionals and administrators to stay, fearing that their departure will have a serious negative effect on education and health care, and on industry as well, because most skilled workers are Russians.

For more than ten years before independence, Moscow had been reducing its rate of investment in Central Asia, presumably because economic officials in the Soviet government saw that the mounting social problems in the region, especially its exploding population and increasing unemployment, would prevent a reasonable return on funds invested.

To rescue themselves from the crisis precipitated by the decline of the Soviet economy and exacerbated by the loss of subsidies and collapse of interrepublic economic ties, all Central Asian leaders have declared their intent to introduce a market economy, although the rates at which this is to occur vary from country to country. Kazakhstan and Kyrgyzstan have launched what are intended to be rapid privatization and marketization programs. Tajikistan had begun laying the legislative basis for a rapid market reform when virtual civil war broke out in the country in late May

1992 and not only paralyzed the country's economy but put on hold all reform plans.

The leaderships of both Uzbekistan and Turkmenistan have committed themselves to a slower pace of marketization on the grounds that this will prevent popular upheaval that would occur if living standards declined precipitately. The student riots that accompanied the freeing of prices in Uzbekistan at the beginning of 1992 indicated that the potential for social disruptions is very real.

KAZAKHSTAN

The disintegration of the U.S.S.R. forced independence on Kazakhstan, the only one of the Central Asian states not to have declared itself independent in the wake of the August 1991 coup. Only a handful of extremist Kazakh nationalists had believed earlier that independence was a possibility for the largest of the Central Asian states because of the ethnic makeup of its population. As a result of Russian settlement, particularly in connection with the Virgin Lands project of the 1950s, which brought thousands of Russians and other non-indigenous nationalities into Kazakhstan to cultivate large areas of the Kazakh steppes and make the republic a major grain-growing region of the U.S.S.R., the Kazakhs were a minority in the land that bore their name. The census of 1989 showed that the Kazakh share of the population had finally grown equal to the Russian share (both were approximately 40 percent, with representatives of nearly every other ethnic group in the U.S.S.R. making up the rest). But the Kazakhs still contribute less than half of the population of Kazakhstan.

The ethnic structure of the country has ensured that tensions between Kazakhs and Russians are kept simmering: many of the Russian inhabitants of Kazakhstan, particularly in the northern oblasts with their overwhelmingly Slavic populations, are resentful of Kazakh national assertiveness. Kazakhs, unhappy over decades of Russification at the expense of their own national identity, react angrily to any proposal that the northern oblasts be transferred to the Russian Federation. Interethnic frictions remain the greatest threat to stability in Kazakhstan, and also threaten the country's territorial integrity. Months after Kazakhstan achieved its unexpected independence, however, the non-Kazakh inhabitants seem to have accepted the country's new status with equanimity.

The potential for interethnic violence has been cited by Kazakh President Nursultan Nazarbaev as a major reason for the political conservatism that accompanies his policy of a rapid introduction of market mechanisms and rapid privatization of housing, retail trade, and eventually major industries. Like Uzbek President Karimov, Nazarbaev has warned that the social stresses that will inevitably accompany the transition to a market economy make political instability a dangerous possibility. Nazarbaev has, however, permitted the development of a number of opposition political groups and parties. Kazakhstan was the first Central Asian state to have an influential opposition press.

Leaders of the Kazakh non-Communist parties have criticized Nazarbaev for not severing his ties with Kazakhstan's Communist Party—he did not resign as its leader until after the August 1991 coup—and for entrusting former Communist officials with the implementation of the economic reform program. Although the Communist Party was banned after the coup, it was allowed to reemerge as the Socialist Party of Kazakhstan, and remains almost the only political grouping with a multinational membership. Other parties are based largely on a single ethnic group, thereby complicating the development of a truly pluralistic political life.

KYRGYZSTAN

Kyrgyzstan has come closest of any Central Asian state to developing a Western-style democracy, thanks largely to the efforts of its president, the physicist Askar Akaev, who won an unexpected upset victory over the conservative Communist establishment in 1990. Like Kazakhstan, Kyrgyzstan has an ethnically mixed population, one-third of which is Russian and approximately two-thirds of which is Kyrgyz. The influence of the Western- oriented democrats, among whom are both Kyrgyz and Russians, is largely confined to the cities. Akaev sought to ensure that his administration reflected the ethnic mix of the country, but he has been accused by Kyrgyz intellectuals of neglecting Kyrgyz national interests. Although various parties are represented in the Kyrgyz parliament, Akaev belongs to none, and political power is effectively concentrated in the president's hands. Because he has taken a number of arbitrary measures to try to stop the collapse of the country's economy, Akaev has been criticized in early 1992 for having adopted a dictatorial method of ruling. Probably the greatest danger to Akaev's vision of Kyrgyzstan as the Switzerland of Central Asia is the weakness of the country's economy and the danger that deepening poverty will lead to social instability. In June 1992 the International Monetary Fund prescribed a strict regimen of financial reorganization to put a stop to the economic decline, but the plan required outside assistance of at least $400 million, and it was not clear where potential donors would be found.

Although Kyrgyzstan's democratic leadership and its supporters among the intelligentsia would like to develop close ties with Europe, geographical reality dictates that the country seek trade partners and investment sources in East Asia. Prior to independence, Kyrgyzstan was attempting to develop ties with South Korea. In May 1992, Akaev paid a highly publicized visit to China, returning with a number of agreements that could represent the beginning of important trade opportunities for Kyrgyzstan.

UZBEKISTAN

The most populous state of Central Asia, Uzbekistan remains under the control of its former Communist Party power structure. Uzbek President Islam Karimov has argued on many occasions that only the Communist Party, which took the name National-Democratic Party in October 1991, has the administrative experience necessary to run the country and guarantee political stability. Karimov has shown far less tolerance for political opposition than has Kazakhstan's Nazarbaev. The Uzbek president has often reacted with great bitterness to Western and Russian liberal political observers who accuse him of being unwilling to tolerate political liberalization in Uzbekistan. One of the few points of agreement between Karimov and the democratic-minded Uzbek intelligentsia has been anger at the superiority complex adopted by many Russian liberals when describing Uzbekistan. This "imperial" mentality, as well as Moscow's exploitation of Uzbekistan's resources, particularly the enforcement of the cotton monoculture, contributed significantly to Uzbekistan's decision to declare independence immediately after the August 1991 coup. Unlike Tajikistan and Kyrgyzstan, which declared independence at almost the same time but hoped to use the move to gain maximum freedom of action under any future federation, Uzbekistan took its independence seriously from the start, even if the outside world did not recognize it until the collapse of the U.S.S.R. Although the Uzbek Communists' hold on power remains firm, Uzbekistan has developed a sizable opposition Popular Front organization, Birlik (Unity), which claims a membership in the millions. The group espouses Western-style democracy and the restoration of the Uzbek national heritage, including Islam. It does not suppose the creation of an Islamic state and agrees with Karimov on the value of the Turkish model for Uzbekistan. The president has viewed Birlik with suspicion since its creation, and it has been the target of continuous harassment by the authorities. It has never been allowed to register as a political party, which would give it the right to nominate a presidential candidate, and its Tashkent headquarters were closed down in early 1992. It remains, however, Uzbekistan's most influential opposition group. The resurgence of popular interest in Uzbekistan's Islamic heritage has been tolerated, if not actively approved, by the former Communist officialdom, but this tolerance does not extend to Muslim political parties. The Uzbek branch of the Islamic Renaissance Party was banned almost as soon as it was founded in 1990, and small Muslim groupings in various parts of the country, especially in the Fergana Valley, have not been allowed to register as parties on the grounds that the law on freedom of conscience prohibits political parties based on religious affiliation. The real reason that such parties are not permitted recognition as such is almost certainly the fear of Uzbek Communists that an Islamic party would be a serious rival for power.

TAJIKISTAN

Tajikistan is the Central Asian country that is closest linguistically and culturally to Iran. The Muslims of Tajikistan have traditionally been Sunni, however, and have had little sympathy for Iranian-style revolutionary Shiite fundamentalism. Since its independence, Tajikistan has established diplomatic, economic, and cultural ties with Iran, but the Turkish secular state remains the most attractive foreign model.

According to Soviet statistics, Tajikistan was the poorest republic of the U.S.S.R. in per capita income. The rural population was growing faster than the urban, and unemployment was officially acknowledged to be a serious problem even before the advent of glasnost. The desperate economic situation in Tajikistan led to outbreaks of violence in Dushanbe, the capital, in February 1990 and on the Tajik-Kyrgyz border in the summer of the same year. Social tensions caused by widespread poverty are a constant threat to economic reform plans. A series of laws adopted in the spring of 1992 is intended to lay the basis for introduction of a market economy, but first priority seems to have been the creation of conditions favorable to foreign investment.

Tajikistan's hopes for foreign investment have been endangered by the outside world's perception of political instability in the new country. Tajikistan was, until May 1992, the only successor state to the U.S.S.R. that still had a ruling Communist Party. It also has an influential opposition coalition of three more or less Western-oriented political groups, which staged a demonstration in Dushanbe in March and April 1992 seeking to force the resignation of President Rakhmon Nabiev, a former Communist Party chief who defeated the candidate of the democratic coalition in November 1991. Nabiev became the first directly elected president of the country, and the Communist-dominated legislature. When he tried to crack down on the demonstrators at the end of April, violence broke out in the capital and the president was frightened into agreeing to a power-sharing arrangement under which the representatives of the opposition coalition were given a third of the seats in a new Government of National Reconciliation.

Because one of the three parties in the opposition coalition is the Tajik Islamic Renaissance Party and its vice-chairman was appointed a deputy premier in the new government, the outside world concluded prematurely that Tajikistan had become an Islamic state. The Islamic party has set the creation of an Islamic social order as a long-term goal, but for the present it remains committed to a secular and democratic state. Soon after the agreement was signed between Nabiev and the opposition, the two sides found themselves having to make common cause to prevent the disintegration of Tajikistan, as two of the three oblasts making up the country refused to recognize the new government, and fighting between supporters and opponents of the old order broke out everywhere except Gorno-Badakhshan. At the end of June, Nabiev created a National Guard, and the State Defense Committee was empowered to create special units to restore order, as the economy slid further into decline and foreign investors hesitated before the real possibility of chaos and civil war.

TURKMENISTAN

Turkmenistan was the only country of Central Asia to put the question of independence to a popular referendum before the legislature adopted an independence declaration (Uzbekistan held a referendum several months after its declaration had been adopted). The vote was overwhelmingly in favor of independence, as it had been strongly in favor of retaining the union the previous March. Turkmenistan has adopted some of the trappings of democracy, in particular the holding of frequent elections and referendums, but the Communist power structure remains intact, although the party's name has been changed to Democratic, and there is no effective opposition.

Turkmenistan's president, the former Communist Party chief Saparmurad Niyazov, is the least tolerant of opposition of any Central Asian leader. He boasts, with justification, that Turkmenistan is the most stable politically of the Central Asian states. Two tiny democratic-minded groups of intellectuals have been constantly harassed by the authorities since their creation in 1989 and 1990; the leaders of one, Agzybirlik (Unity), were put under house arrest during the visit of U.S. Secretary of State James Baker in February 1992.

Since the country achieved independence, its leadership has shown considerable skill in extracting agreements from other CIS states to pay world market prices for its products, particularly petroleum and gas. It was able to obtain a commitment from Iran, with which Turkmenistan has actively cultivated relations since independence, to help build a gas pipeline to Turkey so that Turkmenistan can sell its natural gas directly to Western Europe. It has eagerly accepted offers of membership in Western institutions such as the CSCE and the North Atlantic Council, and its foreign minister has become a familiar sight at international gatherings. Although Turkmenistan's economy remains weak, it has considerable cause for optimism about its chances for development: with a relatively small population and readily salable resources, it is widely considered to be the Central Asian state that is most attractive to foreign investors.

POLITICAL-ECONOMIC ASSESSMENTS:

THE TRANSCAUCASUS

By Elizabeth Fuller *

CONTENTS

SUMMARY

In all the former Transcaucasus republics—Armenia, Azerbaijan, and Georgia—the implementation of economic reform is being hampered by internal political turmoil, interethnic conflict, or both. Adverse political conditions may in turn deter foreign investment, thus exacerbating economic decline and social hardship. All three post-Communist governments are vulnerable to opposition pressure.

INTRODUCTION

Georgia, Armenia, and Azerbaijan can without doubt be characterized as among the politically least stable of the Soviet successor states. Both the Georgian and the Azerbaijani leaderships have at best a dubious claim to legitimacy, having come to power via the overthrow of a democratically elected president, while the Armenian government is under increasing pressure from a militant opposition to resign. Internal conflicts with ethnic minorities or over territorial questions remain seemingly insoluble and contribute to both political destabilization and economic stagnation.

Of the three former Transcaucasian republics, Georgia never joined the Commonwealth of Independent States; Azerbaijan argues that its membership is invalid because it was never ratified by the republic's parliament; and as of mid-June 1992, Armenia was threatening to withdraw from membership. While Armenia and Azerbaijan were swiftly accorded international recognition after the disintegration of the U.S.S.R. and duly applied for and were accepted into membership of various international organizations (the United Nations, Conference on Security and Cooperation

---

* Elizabeth Fuller is with the Radio Free Europe/Radio Liberty Research Institute.

in Europe (CSCE), and the International Monetary Fund). Georgia remained an international pariah for two months following the overthrow of President Zviad Gamsakhurdia in January 1992. Only after the return of former Soviet Foreign Minister Eduard Shevardnadze to Tbilisi in March 1992 bestowed some degree of respectability on the Military Council that had seized power did the international community belatedly recognize Georgia's independence. The ongoing conflict in South Ossetia may, however, prove an obstacle to Georgia's acceptance to membership of some international organizations.

All three Transcaucasus states likewise face tremendous problems in the economic sphere. All lagged behind key All-Union economic indicators during the 1980s; and in the past few years the economies of the three states have been seriously damaged either by civil war (in Georgia) or by the ramifications of the four-year struggle over Nagorno-Karabakh (in the case of Armenia and Azerbaijan). The respective leaderships advocate transition to a market (or mixed) economy, despite the inevitable short-term repercussions (unemployment, inflation, social unrest).

While seeking to renegotiate economic agreements with Russia as traditionally their most important trading partner, all three states are simultaneously hoping both to attract investment from the West and to expand economic relations with Turkey and Iran. All signed the June 1992 Istanbul agreement on creation of the Black Sea Economic Cooperation Zone. With the exception of Azerbaijan, however, which has significant oil reserves, none of the three Transcaucasus states could expect to register an aggregate trade surplus when world prices are used. Ongoing political instability may further deter potential Western investors.

ARMENIA

Political life in Armenia since early 1988 has been dominated by the campaign launched by the Armenian population of Azerbaijan's Nagorno-Karabakh Autonomous Oblast for the region's transfer to Armenian jurisdiction, and the ongoing response to this demand by Moscow and Baku. It was the Karabakh Committee, founded in Erevan in February 1988, that formed the basis for the creation of the opposition Armenian Pan-National Movement (APNM) which emerged as the strongest party in the Supreme Soviet elected in the summer of 1990. Armenia thus became one of the first republics of the then-Soviet Union to make the transition from a Communist-dominated to a non-Communist government. The oriental scholar and APNM chairman Levon Ter-Petrossyan was elected parliament chairman.

The policies adopted by the new Armenian leadership were outlined in a Declaration of Independence adopted in late August 1990. They included the establishment of armed forces, the creation of a national currency and national bank, and the introduction of a multi-party system. The Declaration of Independence also affirmed Armenia's right to pursue an independent foreign policy, one of the cornerstones of which was a rapprochement with Turkey. This latter policy, in conjunction with the abjuring of any territorial claims on Turkey, has been condemned as a betrayal of Armenian national interests by virtually all the other political parties represented in the new parliament.

In March 1991 the Armenian parliament voted to boycott the upcoming All-Union referendum on the preservation of the U.S.S.R., and instead hold a referendum in September 1991, under the terms of the U.S.S.R. Law on Secession. The failed coup of August 1991 and the subsequent declarations of independence by virtually all the constituent republics deprived the Armenian referendum of its relevance; nonetheless, 94 percent of the Armenian electorate still participated, voting overwhelmingly for independence from the U.S.S.R. One month later Ter-Petrossyan was elected president.

Since the demise of the U.S.S.R. made Armenian independence a reality, Armenia's primary diplomatic objective has been to try to negotiate a settlement of the Karabakh conflict that would guarantee autonomy for the Armenian population, provide for unimpeded transport links between Armenia and Karabakh, and exclude the possibility of future Azerbaijani aggression. Efforts to achieve this have, however, been undermined by the refusal of independent Armenian guerrilla units fighting in Karabakh to observe the various ceasefire agreements brokered by Iran, and by the insistence of the Dashnak-dominated parliament of the self-proclaimed Nagorno-Karabakh Republic that it will never acknowledge Azerbaijani sovereignty. To date, all mediation efforts by Iran and the CSCE have proved fruitless.

Ter-Petrossyan's pragmatic and conciliatory approach to resolving the Karabakh conflict has fueled dissatisfaction among the Armenian opposition parties, which have sought to use the Armenian government's refusal to recognize the Nagorno-Karabakh Republic as an independent state as a pretext for forcing a vote of no confidence. On June 16 the Dashnak Party and the radical Organization for National Self-Determination called on the Armenian government to resign, charging that it was betraying the interests of the Armenian people. An ongoing diplomatic stalemate or military reoccupation by Azerbaijani forces of those areas of Karabakh from which Azerbaijanis have been expelled in recent months could further undermine public support for Ter-Petrossyan's government.

In addition to the obstacles that all the former Soviet republics must contend with in making the transition to a market economy, Armenia is faced with four specifically local problems:

1) Rebuilding. The aftermath of the earthquake of December 1988 was destruction of over 10 percent of the republic's industrial potential and 17 percent of housing. The rebuilding program was predicated on funds from the central budget that will not now be forthcoming.

2) Energy problems. Armenia produces no oil, coal, or gas. It is dependent on imports for approximately 80 percent of its fuel supplies. Until now, the lion's share of oil and gas has come via Azerbaijan, which has been imposing an energy blockade for the past three years in retaliation for the Armenian campaign for control of Nagorno-Karabakh. The gas pipeline from Russia via Georgia has been blocked by the North Ossetian government in protest at Georgia's policy over South Ossetia. In order to reduce its vulnerability,

Armenia has signed an agreement to buy the greater part of its natural gas, and 500,000 metric tons of fuel oil per year from Iran.[1]

3) Transportation difficulties. Armenia has no outlet to the sea, and has in the past been almost entirely dependent on rail links to Azerbaijan and Georgia, both of which have been interrupted for long periods by deliberate blockade or internal unrest. The absence of alternative transport arteries contributed to industrial paralysis over the past two years, inasmuch as 84 percent of the raw materials for industry were imported. A planned Turkish-Armenian project was initiated to develop the Turkish Black Sea port of Trabzon in order to provide Armenia with a road and sea link to the West and in turn facilitate the transport of Turkish goods via Armenia to Azerbaijan and the states of Central Asia. This plan was abandoned because of rising Turkish hostility toward Armenia over Nagorno-Karabakh.[2]

4) Ecological challenges affecting electricity and chemical industry. Armenia is suffering from the consequences of concessions to the 'ecological lobby,' specifically the electricity deficit that resulted from the decision following the 1988 earthquake to shut down the Medzamor nuclear power station (which provided up to 36 percent of the republic's electricity), and the closure of the Nairit chemical plant in Erevan, upon which the entire Armenian chemical industry (which accounts for 6.5 percent of total industrial output), is dependent. After a lengthy and acrimonious public debate, Nairit was reopened in April 1991; a government committee is expected to come to a decision in the summer of 1992 on reactivating the Medzamor power station. Armenia hopes to borrow 100m ecus ($130m) from the European Bank for Reconstruction and Development (EBRD) to complete alternative energy generating projects.[3]

These four factors (together with conversion in the defense industry) have combined virtually to paralyze Armenia's industrial sector. In 1991 national income produced fell by 11 percent and industrial output dropped to 15 percent of the level for the preceding year. During the winter of 1991–92 Erevan was totally without gas for domestic purposes; industry ground to a halt for several months, but by April was functioning at 70 percent of capacity. Electricity and water supplies are still rationed. Produced national income for the period January-March 1992 was marginally over half that for the corresponding period in 1991; labor productivity fell by 50 percent.[4] In April 1992 Armenian Finance Minister Dzhanik Dzhanoyan told the republic's parliament that Armenia was "on the verge of bankruptcy," and that the budget deficit for the first six months of 1992 was over 1,600 million rubles.[5] Speaking on the eve of an EBRD conference in Budapest a few days later, Dzhanoyan said that Armenia needs $1.4 billion in loans from the West to dismantle the legacy of Communist central planning.

[1] *The Washington Post,* June 5, 1992.
[2] *The Washington Post,* March 30, 1992.
[3] *The Economist,* May 23, 1992.
[4] Radio Rossii, May 2, 1992.
[5] Intertax, April 8, 1992.

Such loans are, however, largely dependent on the existence of a comprehensive program of economic reform underpinned by legislation, and to date the Armenian parliament has failed on at least two occasions to endorse the program proposed by President Levon Ter-Petrossyan.

Despite such apparently insurmountable problems, Armenian government officials continue to express cautious optimism over the prospects for successful economic reform. Armenia was one of the first republics to proceed with the privatization of land, and to date some 70 percent of land has been distributed to peasant farmers under the terms of a law that two U.S. scholars have termed "a model for the region." [6] The sale by auction of retail stores and small businesses was scheduled to begin in the spring of 1992. In addition, Armenia has a centuries-old tradition of entrepreneurship, and can call upon the skills of an extensive, well-connected and educated diaspora, many of whom have relocated to Erevan in order to play a first-hand role in building an independent Armenian state.

Nor is Armenia totally devoid of natural resources. It ranked fourth among the former Soviet republics in mineral production, supplying 40 percent of Soviet molybdenum and large quantities of gold, copper, and salt, as well as iron, zinc, and other minerals. In 1990 mineral production was worth approximately $600m per year, accounting for approximately 18 percent of Armenia's total economic output.[7] (Armenia also produces geranium and other essential oils used in the cosmetics industry.) A draft program for economic independence drawn up by the Armenian Academy of Sciences in 1991 highlighted the need for more effective exploitation of both precious metals and deposits of limestone and marble.[8]

AZERBAIJAN

In Azerbaijan, as in Armenia, a political opposition emerged primarily as a response to the Nagorno-Karabakh issue. Unlike the Karabakh Committee and its successor organization, the APNM, however, the Azerbaijan Popular Front could count on only limited support from the republic's intelligentsia, and found during the course of 1989 that it could rally public opinion only by adopting an increasingly militant anti-Armenian stance. It was radical elements within the Azerbaijan Popular Front that were held responsible for the anti-Armenian program and mass rallies in Baku in January 1990 in which some 150 people, mostly innocent bystanders, were killed. This incident, which prompted intervention by the Soviet military, engendered intense antagonism toward Moscow, but also deep shock and political apathy. The Azerbaijan Communist Party (CP) under technocrat Ayaz Mutalibov took advantage of the situation to strengthen its position. In the multiparty Supreme Soviet elections in September 1990, the Azerbaijan CP won an overwhelming majority.

---

[6] See Ben Slay and John Tedstrom, "Privatization in the Post Communist Economies," in RFEIRL Research Report, vol. 1, no. 17, 24 April 1992, p. 6.
[7] *The Financial Times*, October 3, 1991.
[8] Golos Armenii, July 31, 1991.

The opposition nonetheless launched a campaign of attrition within the new parliament, resorting to boycott threats, walkouts, and endless arguments over procedural questions. Following Mutalibov's ill-advised and hastily retracted expression of support and approval for the abortive Moscow coup in August 1991, the Azerbaijan Popular Front resolved to topple him and replace him with a candidate of their own choosing.

In early March 1992 the Azerbaijani parliament met in an emergency session to debate the killing of several hundred Azerbaijani civilians by Armenian forces in Nagorno-Karabakh. Blame for the incident was laid squarely on Mutalibov: it was argued that it was his administration's failure to expedite the creation of an effective national army that had precipitated the massacre. Mutalibov was forced to resign; Baku Medical Institute rector Yagub Mamedov was elected interim president in his place pending new presidential elections in June.

A comeback attempt by Mutalibov in mid-May precipitated a virtually bloodless coup in which the Azerbaijani Popular Front seized power. Three weeks later, the Popular Front candidate, Abulfaz Elchibey, was elected president and announced his intention of creating a secular parliamentary democracy with strong political, economic, and cultural ties with Turkey. Elchibey also made it clear that Azerbaijan was not interested in membership of the (Commonwealth of Independent States), although he advocated bilateral political and economic agreements with Russia. Insofar as popular support for the new leadership in Baku appears to be founded primarily on expectations that it will fulfill its promises to reestablish Azerbaijani control over Nagorno-Karabakh and defend Azerbaijan's territorial integrity, Elchibey's political future depends to a considerable degree on the success of the military assault begun immediately after his election (in violation of a preelection commitment to seek a diplomatic solution to the conflict).

The Azerbaijani economy was for decades primarily weighted toward production of raw materials—oil, gas, cotton (of which it was the second largest producer after Uzbekistan) and, at least until the ill-fated anti-alcohol campaign of 1985, grapes. It could be argued that, by virtue of its oil reserves, Azerbaijan has the best chances of any of the Transcaucasian states of achieving some degree of economic self-sufficiency.

Azerbaijan currently produces 11–12 million tons of oil annually (as compared with 15.5 million in 1979.) Successive leaderships have pinned their hopes for successful economic reform on attracting foreign investment both in oil extraction and refining and in modernization of the obsolete Glavnetemash factory in Baku that produced up to 65 percent of the machinery and spare parts for the entire Soviet oil industry.

In 1991 AMOCO and five other Western oil companies concluded an agreement with the Azerbaijani government on evaluation and development of an offshore Caspian field some 600 km southeast of Baku that is believed to contain reserves of up to 200 million tons. The project is, however, jeopardized by logistical problems. First, the field is at a depth of 300 meters and cannot be exploited using locally manufactured technology; pipes, cooling and repair systems, compressors, and extraction equipment would all have to be imported.[9] Second, the project will entail construction of a new oil pipeline from Baku to a port on the Black Sea—possibly through Georgia. This would greatly increase the cost of the entire project above the estimated initial $3-5 billion.[10] Moreover, ongoing political instability in Georgia may prove a deterrent.

It was presumably in anticipation of attracting foreign investment that, in the summer of 1991, the Azerbaijani parliament set about creating the necessary legislative basis, enacting laws on property, taxation, and the protection of foreign investments. The Law on the Fundamentals of Economic Sovereignty, however, advocated transition to a mixed, rather than a market economy, with the state retaining a considerable degree of control.[11] Specifically, land was to be exempt from privatization, and the oil and petrochemical sectors were to remain in state ownership, because oil income was envisaged as a tool to mitigate both existing social problems and the additional hardships engendered during the transition to a market economy. It was further envisaged that the state would retain control over "the rational use of labor resources."

This latter point is of significance insofar as in 1990 Azerbaijan had the highest unemployment—27.6 percent—of any republic; this figure is expected to rise during the transition to the market. (In Sumgait, Azerbaijan's second largest industrial center, which has a population of 250,000, unemployment currently stands at 30 percent.[12] In addition, 69 percent of the population lives on less than the minimum subsistence wage. Speaking at the 32nd Congress of the Azerbaijani Communist Party in June 1990, Mutalibov vowed that price liberalization would not extend to removing the state subsidy on bread, as it formed the staple diet of a large sector of the population.[13] When bread prices were raised on January 1, 1992, in violation of this commitment, popular dissatisfaction reached such a pitch that Mutalibov was constrained to reduce the new price by 30 percent. In the spring of this year, strikes were reported in Baku by such varied professional groups as police and university teachers, to demand massive wage increases to compensate for inflation. (Consumer prices increased seven-fold during the first five months of the year, whereas average salaries only doubled.[14]

The Law on Economic Sovereignty did, however, abolish centralized planning and decision-making, devolving responsibility for decision-making on plant managers, who are reportedly increasingly turning to barter deals with foreign partners, the majority of which involve bartering raw materials (iron, aluminum) for food.[15]

As far as can be ascertained from Elchibey's preelection pronouncements, he too favors transition to a mixed economy, with income from the oil sector being used to finance social programs for the disadvantaged.[16] Privatization of land and small enter-

[9] The Financial Times, August 31, 1990.
[10] Forbes Magazine, October 14, 1991.
[11] Bakinsky Rabochii, June 12, 1991.
[12] The Wall Street Journal (European edition), February 14, 1992.
[13] Bakinsky Rabochii, June 8, 1990.
[14] Bakinsky Rabochii, June 3, 1992.
[15] The Wall Street Journal (European edition), February 14, 1992.
[16] Nezavisimaya gazeta, 9 June, 1992; Izvestia, 10 June, 1992.

prises is to begin by the late summer of 1992. As in the case of Armenia, however, the success of economic reform is predicated on an end to the undeclared war over Nagorno-Karabakh. A leading Azerbaijani economist was recently quoted as estimating that war-related losses over the last four years totaled more than 11. 5 billion rubles.[17] Former Azerbaijani Prime Minister Hassan Hassanov has intimated that "the Armenian lobby" had succeeded in dissuading numerous foreign companies that had expressed an interest in investing in Azerbaijan.[18]

GEORGIA

Georgia is currently struggling to overcome the legacy of the Gamsakhurdia era and the civil war that ended it—political instability, profound social divisions, economic ruin, secession movements in two of its three autonomous formations (Abkhazia and South Ossetia), and an almost total breakdown of law and order.

The landslide victory of former dissident Zviad Gamsakhurdia's Round Table/Free Georgia coalition in the parliamentary elections of October 1990, and Gamsakhurdia's election to the post of president in May 1991, are to be explained primarily In terms of the Georgians' collective aspiration for independence at any cost, and of Gamsakhurdia's personal status as the symbol of resistance to Russian imperialism.

Paradoxically, Gamsakhurdia's fervent nationalism ultimately precipitated his downfall because it mutated into aggressive chauvinism and isolationism. Georgia boycotted both the March 1991 referendum on the future of the U.S.S.R. and the negotiations on a new Union Treaty; instead, the Georgian parliament proclaimed independence on April 9, 1991. Gamsakhurdia himself grew increasingly dictatorial and paranoid, arresting political opponents, imposing censorship of the media, and blaming Moscow for any manifestations of dissent. Plans for privatization of land and economic reform were abandoned. (Legislation was passed during the autumn of 1991 on the privatization of state enterprises and of housing, but remained unimplemented.)

In early September 1991 moderate and radical opposition parties combined forces and organized daily demonstrations in Tbilisi to call for Gamsakhurdia's resignation. After Gamsakhurdia responded by ordering the National Guard to open fire on peaceful demonstrators, a part of the National Guard together with its commander Tengiz Kitovani, and Gamsakhurdia's former prime minister Tengiz Sigua, aligned themselves with the opposition, accusing the Georgian President of sabotaging the country's economy and of "wanting to create a closed dictatorial state like Albania in which he would reign supreme." For a period of six weeks Tbilisi was the scene of mass pro- and anti-Gamsakhurdia demonstrations that petered out only when the rebel faction of the National Guard withdrew from the capital.

On December 20 the opposition issued a new call for Gamsakhurdia's resignation. The rebel faction of the National Guard launched

---

[17] Reuters, March 29, 1992.
[18] Bakinsky Rabochii, September 18, 1990.

an all-out attack on the parliament building where Gamsakhurdia was under siege. On January 6 Gamsakhurdia fled with his family and bodyguards and, after an abortive comeback attempt, settled in Grozny; armed clashes between his supporters in Western Georgia and National Guardists continued for several weeks. A military council headed by rival militia leaders Tengiz Kitovani and Dzhaba Ioseliani assumed power in Tbilisi and formed a provisional government, reinstating Sigua as Prime Minister, but was unable to win over the moderate opposition which called for its resignation. In early March former Georgian CP first secretary and Soviet Foreign Minister Eduard Shevardnadze returned to Tbilisi and was elected chairman of a new State Council, which represented 37 registered political parties and various ethnic minorities.

As noted above, it was Shevardnadze's return that bestowed much-needed respectability on the new government and provided the impetus for diplomatic recognition and for the dispatch of urgently needed Western food and medicine. It did not, however, lead to the desired internal political stabilization. Although four weeks after Shevardnadze's return opinion polls indicated that he enjoyed the support of 75 percent of the population, large areas of the countryside, particularly in Western Georgia where support for Gamsakhurdia is strongest, are still prey to roaming armed bands. There is an almost total breakdown of law and order. The curfew imposed on Tbilisi in January was to be suspended at the end of June, but at the same time the State Council granted itself emergency powers to deal with crime. The car bomb attacks directed against Mkhedrioni leader Dzhaba Ioseliani and his deputy in mid-June, and the abortive attempt by Gamsakhurdia supporters one week later to reinstate the ousted president, serve to underscore Shevardnadze's political vulnerability.

Within the State Council there are serious differences of opinion between Shevardnadze and Ioseliani on the one hand, and Sigua and Kitovani on the other, primarily over the Ossetian conflict and over the future course of Georgian-Ossetian relations. (On both issues Shevardnadze is considered by his rivals to be too conciliatory.) The various moderate political parties have not succeeded to date in forming a coalition to contest the parliamentary elections scheduled for October 11, in which the ultra-nationalist, anti-Russian National Democratic Party headed by Giorgi Chanturia is expected to win 40 percent of the vote, if not a clear majority.

The fundamental weakness of the Georgian economy lies in the fact that, of the country's more important products (citrus fruit, tea, wine, coal, manganese) only the latter is viable on the world market. Georgia's undisputed potential as a tourist paradise cannot be exploited while the region is still plagued by violence.

Economic reform as a prerequisite for political stabilization was one of the State Council's top priorities. The devastation inflicted during the civil war on property, agriculture, industry, the transport infrastructure, and tourism has been compounded by severe shortages resulting from the rupture of economic ties with other former Soviet republics and by the effect of price liberalization in Russia. It has been estimated that the volume of production in 1991 was 30 percent lower than in 1990, and that the 1992 figures will be worse. The budget deficit for 1991 was six billion rubles ($60m at the Russian central Bank fixed 'market' rate), which is approximately 8 percent of GNP.[19] Inflation in May of 1992 had reached 340 percent.[20]

Within weeks of Shevardnadze's return a basic program for economic reform was drawn up by a team of young Georgian economists headed by vice-premier Roman Gotsiridze. As conveyed in outline to Izvestia's Georgian correspondent, the program entailed the immediate abolition of state economic oversight bodies and complete liberalization of trade and business activity, followed by privatization of land as a necessary precondition for agricultural reform. (The Gamsakhurdia administration had delayed privatizing land pending the adoption of a law on citizenship which, it was anticipated, would be extended only to ethnic Georgians, with representatives of other nationalities being denied citizenship. Lack of citizenship would, in turn, preclude the right to own land. This restriction was prompted by a mood of paranoia among many ethnic Georgians, including some members of the moderate intelligentsia, who were profoundly alarmed at the incidence of misappropriation of state land by non-Georgians in the late 1980s.) The land privatization scheme drawn up by the provisional government increased the size of the plot to which each peasant household would be entitled from 0.75 to 1.25 hectares and abolished the restriction imposed by the previous administration on the sale of land. Gotsiridze explained this decision in terms of the pressing need to allow for the sale of land in order to reduce the percentage of the population engaged in agriculture from its current level of just under 50 percent to 20–25 percent, and to forestall a situation in which the state would have to intervene to bail out bankrupt peasant farmers.[21]

The course proposed by the Georgian interim government was set out in greater detail in the "Basic Principles of Economic Reform in the Republic of Georgia" (Stage 1) adopted in early May, the proclaimed aims of which were to minimize the social impact of adverse economic processes, create favorable conditions for stimulating private economic activity, protect property rights, and create a legislative basis for more sweeping economic reform.[22] Foreign trade is to be expanded, if necessary, on the basis of barter deals. An agreement has been concluded with the Russian government on bartering Georgian tea and wine for oil.[23]

A further lynchpin of the economic reform process is the envisaged $5 billion project for the development by an international consortium of the Black Sea port of Poti, which would expand its cargo-handling capacity from 5 million tons to about 40 million tons per year and provide access to Central Asia and the Middle East.[24]

[19] Reuters, April 15, 1992.
[20] *Newsweek*, May 25, 1992.
[21] *Izvestia*, March 29, 1992.
[22] Svobodnaya Gruziya, May 12, 1992.
[23] Reuters, February 12, 1992.
[24] Reuters, April 5, 1992.

Tentative Conclusion

The three newly emerged states of the Transcaucasus are, it would seem, trapped in a vicious circle. All desperately need to maintain political stability as a prerequisite for successful economic reform; conversely, continued economic decline may fuel popular discontent and undermine the existing governments. In each case, the hopes of the population are pinned on one individual (Ter-Petrossyan in Armenia, Elchibey in Azerbaijan, and Shevardnadze in Georgia), whose position thus becomes even more vulnerable. Even the most optimistic prognoses rule out a significant economic upswing in the short term. The director of the Azerbaijani Gosplan Institute of Economics has estimated that economic stabilization will take a minimum of 5–10 years and only if the Karabakh conflict is defused, and in conditions of "exceptional economic pragmatism." [25] Similarly, an unidentified Georgian economist has predicted that it will take 30 years for Georgia to attain the present standard of living of Turkey. [26] The short-term prospects for peace and prosperity thus seem bleak indeed.

---

[25] *Izvestia,* June 10, 1992.
[26] Der Standard, April 10, 1992.

POLITICAL-ECONOMIC ASSESSMENTS: MOLDOVA

By Dr. Sergiu Verona *

CONTENTS

SUMMARY

For an orderly political and economic transition throughout the former Soviet Union, the question of identity must be resolved. Moldova may be a case study in this regard. With its ethnic mix including large numbers of Russians supported by the Russian 14th Army, and Moldova's close ties to neighboring Romania, the future may hold continued economic deterioration and military confrontation, possibly drawing in other states, if the issues are not resolved.

INTRODUCTION

Since Moldova declared its independence it has been rift by ethnic unrest and confrontation. In this context, we have to admit that "geopolitics is back," and Moldova may be one of the major case-studies of a European trouble spot. Many analysts think that after the changes in Eastern Europe in 1989, the dissolution of the Soviet Empire, and the appearance of new states on the map of Europe and Asia, geopolitics remains an important analytical instrument explaining contemporary evolution.

Less than one year after proclaiming independence, the Republic of Moldova became a stage of armed confrontation and remains so today. Many observers believe that the former Soviet republic is threatening to become another Nagorno-Karabakh, an area of continuing ethnic violence in Azerbaijan. The Moldovan conflict involves the Moldovan population and ethnic Russians living in the mostly non-Slavic republic. The situation represents an outgrowth of contemporary historical development under Russian and Soviet expansionism. Moldova can be correctly perceived to lie at the

---

* Sergiu Verona is an analyst with the Foreign Affairs and National Defense Division, CRS.

junction of the cultural and geopolitical interests of various states. Specifically, as a Russian publication stated: "A redistribution of zones of influence is under way in Europe. ... The interests of Russia, Ukraine, and Romania are in fact openly interwoven here." [1]

ECONOMIC CONDITIONS

Moldova's economy has declined in the last two years. The estimated national income (January to May 1991) was 13 percent lower than the same period in 1990. According to information published in January 1992, Moldova's 1991 national income corresponded to the level of 1985. Industrial production in 1991 declined to 1988 levels. Twenty percent of all economic enterprises operated unprofitably, and inflation grew. The government supports the introduction of economic reform, particularly the rapid privatization of land and enterprises.

Several circumstances of Moldova's economic and political heritage must be considered in order to perceive and evaluate its development accurately. Included are: (a) Stalin's emphasis on building an industrial base in the Trans-Dniestr region as an "appealing long-range factor" in his plans to include all of Moldova in the Soviet empire; (b) the heavy economic dependence of Moldova on the Soviet economy; and (c) the dependence of Moldova primarily on agriculture.

As a result of the former U.S.S.R.'s centralized economic policies which integrated Moldova deeply into the Soviet economy, export and import with the Soviet Union accounted for over 50% of the country's GDP. [2] This factor is thought to be the real motivation for Moldova's recent attempts to cooperate with the CIS, and reflects the reason for the ambivalence to reintegration with Romania.

Moldova has a moderate continental climate and very fertile soil. The current economy is based on agriculture as it was, according to *PlanEcon* throughout the Soviet period. [3] Moldova was a large-scale exporter of fruits, vegetables, grapes (and wine), sunflower and other vegetable oils as well as tobacco. Of the former Soviet republics, Moldova had the highest agricultural output, contributing more than 2 percent of the total Soviet agricultural production. Moldova also enjoys among the highest grain yields in the former U.S.S.R., twice the Soviet average. [4] Moldova's agricultural production grew until 1990. However during the following years it declined by 13 and 11 percent, [5] lowering the agricultural output to 1970 levels. Data for the first ten months of 1992 show that the harvest of main agricultural crops was 15–25 percent below that of 1991. [6] The United States has already granted $10 million in credits for Moldovan purchases of American grain.

---

[1] *Literaturnaia Gazeta*, 23 December 1992, quoted by FBIS-USR-92-167, p. 112.
[2] The Economist Intelligence Unit, *Ukraine, Belarus, Moldova, Country Profile*, 1992–93, p.44.
[3] *PlanEcon*, Review and Outlook for the Former Soviet Union, December 1992, p. 102–3.
[4] Ibid.
[5] The assessment varies. According to another publication, *The Economist Intelligence Unit* (for 1992) the decline was bigger: –19.8 in 1990 and –14.1 in 1991. (p. 46)
[6] Ibid., p. 45.

Economic publications note that Moldova is the least industrialized of the republics in the European part of the former U.S.S.R., and industry here is dominated by light and food branches, which are clearly related to agriculture. One half of the republic's industrial capacity and all of the region's electricity generation capacity is located on the left bank of the Dniestr river with a large manufacturing sector in Tiraspol and Bendery. Industrial output was still growing in 1990, increasing, according to *PlanEcon* by 3.6 percent, but this reversed sharply in 1991, with a decline of 7.6%. The same process has taken place in construction, which declined 18% in 1991.

Economic forecasts remain extremely pessimistic. According to *PlanEcon*, a rapid recovery of Moldova's economy is not anticipated. GNP is expected to decline in 1992 by 24 percent followed by a further decline of 12 percent in 1993. A slow recovery can possibly begin in the second half of the decade only after the political conditions are redefined. A general assumption is that Moldova's economic recovery is likely to begin in the agricultural sector. [7]

HISTORICAL BACKGROUND

The area known as Bessarabia is somewhat vaguely defined on historical and geographical grounds. As a region, Bessarabia is delimited physically by the Prut River on the west, the Dniestr on the north and east, the Black Sea on the southeast, and the Kiliya (Chilia) arm of the Danube delta on the south. Bessarabia borders Bukovina (an area considered to be the northern part of the principality of Moldova, annexed in part in 1940 by the U.S.S.R.), Moldova (in Romania), the Ukraine, and Dobrudja (an area on the Black Sea divided in 1940 between Romania and Bulgaria).

This entire area—Bessarabia—was an integral part of the Romanian principality of Moldova until 1812 when it was ceded to Russia by the Ottoman Empire, and was incorporated into the Russian empire. Russia retained control of the region until World War I, with the exception of a strip of southern Bessarabia, which was in Moldova's possession from 1856 to 1878.

In 1918, Bessarabia declared its independence from Russia and united with Romania. The Treaty of Paris (October 1920) confirmed this union. In June 1940, as a consequence of the Nazi-Soviet pact, Soviet troops occupied Bessarabia and the northern part of Bukovina. The Soviet Government split Bessarabia into several parts. The Moldavian Soviet Socialist Republic was created (August 1940), out of the central districts of Bessarabia and a strip of Ukrainian territory on the other side of the Dniestr River, the "trans-Dniestr" area. It has an area of 33,700 sq. km. and a population of 4,341,000 (1989 census). The northern region of Bessarabia, as well as the coastal plain (formerly two southern Bessarabian counties) and northern Bukovina were attached to Ukraine. During Stalin's period, nearly 1 million Russians and Ukrainians were brought to Moldavia to dilute the ethnic Romanian majority. After 1944, this territorial rearrangement was reestablished.

---

[7] *PlanEcon*, Ibid.

On August 27, 1991, Moldavia declared its independence and became the Republic of Moldova. However, Moldovan independence represented, to some extent, the beginning of a significant political crisis, reflected by a secession movement. In response to Moldova's independence, the Dniestr area and the Gagauz region formed a "Dniestr Soviet Socialist Republic," and a "Gagauz Soviet Socialist Republic," with the support of the Russian-speaking local population and, according to some media, Moscow hardliners and local military officers.

The area that today constitutes the Trans-Dniestr region was neither a part of former Bessarabia nor Romania, but rather part of Ukraine before 1940. It represents the only highly industrialized area of Moldova, and it supplies most of the rest of the country with gas and electricity. In the past year, this region was one of few in the former Soviet Union whose economy has grown.

CONFLICT IN MOLDOVA

The conflict in Moldova began in early March 1992 after Moldovan nationalists stepped up a campaign to unite with neighboring Romania. The Russian population—according to official explanations from their leaders—feared that such a merger would make them second-class citizens in Romania. After several unsuccessful cease-fires, the clashes between Moldovan police and Dniestr guardsmen took on a new dimension when a number of Cossack mercenaries were involved in the armed clashes on the side of the Russian separatists.

As the fighting intensified, Ukraine and Romania began to express their concerns regarding the events in Moldova. On March 24, in Helsinki, the foreign ministers of Moldova, Russia, Romania, and Ukraine called upon the parties involved in the conflict to show restraint and to refrain from employing force as a means of settling disputes. Throughout April, the diplomatic activity was overshadowed by constant fighting and violations of cease-fires. Furthermore, Aleksander Rutskoi, Vice President of Russia, after returning from a visit to the Dniestr area, urged the Russian parliament to order former Soviet soldiers to protect ethnic Russians in the self-proclaimed Dniestr Republic.

On April 6, 1992, a declaration of the foreign ministers of Moldova, Romania, Russia, and Ukraine called for an immediate and comprehensive cease-fire to go into effect on April 7. The United States welcomed the cease-fire agreement and urged all parties to respect it, announcing that, "The United States supports the appeal for a peaceful, political settlement of the conflict which will ensure the territorial integrity of Moldova while enhancing the responsibility of local government authorities."

After a brief interruption, clashes between the Moldovan police and the Dniestr guardsmen resumed on May 18, 1992. On May 27, 1992, President Boris Yeltsin announced Russia's intention to withdraw the 14th Army from Moldova. However, the fighting resumed just hours after Yeltsin's statement, and continued to expand.

On June 25, 1992, in Istanbul, an agreement was concluded between the Presidents of Russia, Ukraine, Moldova, and Romania, concerning the conflict in Moldova. The provisions of the Communique on the Four-Power Summit on the Dniestr conflict included the request for an immediate and unconditional cease-fire along the whole line of confrontation; the separation of both sides' armed formations; the setting up of security zones and corridors for the movement of civilian populations, medical personnel, and the delivery of humanitarian aid; the implementation of these measures through a bilateral parliamentary commission; neutrality of the Russian 14th Army, and the status, schedule, and procedure for its withdrawal to be determined at talks between the Russian Federation and the Republic of Moldova; the proposition by presidents attending the Istanbul Conference that Moldova's parliament consider and resolve the status of the Moldovan republic's left bank regions.

However, the impact of the Istanbul Conference was limited. The cease-fire was not implemented. Heavy fighting erupted again during the last week of June and continued during the beginning of July 1992. During the first week of July Russian President Yeltsin met in Moscow with Moldovan President Snegur and agreed "to work out a mechanism for a cease-fire."

On July 6, 1992, the conference of the leaders of the Commonwealth of Independent States (CIS) decided to create a joint peacekeeping (later named peacemaking) force to help end ethnic conflicts. In its first deployment, the force was supposed to be sent into Moldova. During the Helsinki summit, Russia failed to obtain a mandate from the Conference for Security and Cooperation in Europe (CSCE) for the dispatch of CIS "peacemaking" forces to Moldova, due to the objection of several Western delegations. Media reports emphasized that the CIS plan would have provided a multilateral framework for an operation which was likely to be Russian dominated. [8]

Two weeks later, on July 21, Presidents Snegur and Yeltsin met in Moscow and signed an agreement for a peaceful settlement of the conflict in the Trans-Dniestr region. The military provisions specified the end of hostilities and the phased withdrawal of heavy equipment and troops from the region within seven days of the signing of the agreement. In addition, the sides were to create a peacekeeping force including units from Russia, Moldova, and Trans-Dniestr, and a force of observers. There was also a provision that the 14th Army remain neutral.

The political provisions of the agreement were the most important. The settlement was founded on the observation of Moldova's territorial integrity, on human rights, including the rights of the national minorities, and on a politically recognized special status for Trans-Dniestr. The document also guaranteed the inhabitants of the left Bank of the Dniestr River the right to self-determination should Moldova change its status, a reference to unification with Romania [9]. The document included a number of economic measures which would make it possible to remove the blockade, resume the free movement of goods, ensure the return of refugees, and to provide refugee assistance.

---

[8] *RFE/RL Daily Report*, No. 131, 132, July 13 and 14, 1992.
[9] *Interfax*, July 22, 1992.

The agreement seemed sound. Many analysts concluded that Moldovan interests had been respected and that it had achieved an important diplomatic victory. Apparently they were wrong. Tudor Panzaru, Permanent Representative of the Republic of Moldova to the United Nations, said in a recent Washington interview that the agreement concluded in Moscow on July 21, 1992, "was a tragic defeat for Moldova." He explained that in fact, the negotiations had been held under tremendous political pressure from Russia, including some indirect military constraints. "To sign the Treaty was the only possible choice for Moldova's security." [10] Twenty-four hours after Russia and Moldova agreed to send a peacekeeping force to the Dniestr region (Russian military forces were the most important contingent of this peacekeeping force) the Moldovan defense ministry representative and a Dniestr spokesman stated that new clashes had erupted in the city of Bendery and in another location.

THE STATUS OF TRANS-DNIESTR

Moldova's official policy toward the Trans-Dniestr area remains unchanged. According to the Moldovan president, various ministers, and the parliament, the Dniestr region is an integral part of the Republic of Moldova, with the status of a local government. All other countries granting diplomatic recognition to Moldova, feel the same.

To solve the crisis, Moldovan authorities proposed to amend this status by establishing a free economic zone on the left bank of the Dniestr, and to change the republic's status so that if Moldova should reunite with Romania, "the population of the left bank regions will be entitled to decide independently with whom they want to live in the future." [11] This position was reiterated in a document adopted by the Moldovan parliament as evidence of concessions. [12] The document continued to refer to "local administrative bodies in the eastern rayons (regions) of the Republic."

The chronology of political developments in the Trans-Dniestr region emphasized that the separatist actions started immediately after Moldova's proclamation of independence. On September 2, 1990 it was proclaimed the Transnistrian Moldavian Soviet Socialist Republic, a unique political entity preserving the former U.S.S.R. transcription. Igor Smirnov, a Russian Communist, and resident of Moldova since 1987 was named as president. On August 19, 1991, the leaders of Trans-Dniestr expressed their support for the coup in Moscow. On September 6, 1991, Trans-Dniestr decided to create its own army. The armaments were offered by the 14th Army of the U.S.S.R. [13]

Finally, on May 30, 1992, the Dniestr region proclaimed its independence as the Dniestr Socialist Republic and called on Russia and Ukraine to recognize the new republic. On June 26, 1992, the spokeswoman of the Trans-Dniestr government rejected the Istan-

---

[10] Interview with Ambassador Pantaru, CRS, Washington, D.C., February 3, 1993.
[11] Statement made by Moldovan Prime Minister, Valreiu Muravschi, Mar. 18, 1992.
[12] Accord on the Basic Principles of Peaceful Settlement of the Armed Conflict, voted on June 16, 1992.
[13] *The Republic of Moldova*, Chisinau, June 1992, pp. 21–2.

bul agreement as unacceptable, emphasizing that the four-powers decision "failed to take into account the interests of the Trans-Dniestr residents." Furthermore, she said the local residents no longer accepted the idea of federation or confederation with Moldova, nor the status of a free economic zone. Describing the Trans-Dniestr, a Russian publication made the following remarks: "The Dniestr people already in fact created their own state with all the requisite state institutions. It has a parliament, president, and government. It has the first professional army on the territory of the former Soviet Union. There are border guards and customs houses. There are banks. There is finally, economic recognition: Economic cooperation agreements have been concluded between the Dniestr region and several oblasts of Russia and Ukraine, not to mention the direct contacts of enterprises not only in countries of the CIS but in Europe also." [14]

By signing the May 8 agreement with Moldova's government, the Trans-Dniestr regime had seemed willing to accept a negotiated solution of the conflict. However, shortly thereafter, the Dniestr position hardened radically. The sudden change coincided with Russia's decision to create its own army, and assume control over all the military structures of the former Soviet armed forces, including troops and naval forces outside the borders of the Russian Federation, among them the former 14th Army.

Some observers saw a connection between the Dniestr and Russian actions. The first indication of this was a formal appeal for help from Russia. In a news conference, Dniestr parliamentary speaker Grigory Marakutsa asked that Russia and Ukraine take a tougher position on Moldovan leadership. He called for self-rule, and advocated pressure for full independence. He also referred to the possibility of imposing economic sanctions on the rest of Moldova. A few weeks later, Trans-Dniestr turned off a gas pipeline to neighboring Moldovan areas.

These developments indicated a change in the Dniestr strategy toward a stronger commitment to use force by putting more military pressure on Moldova. In a surprise development, the Dniestr side agreed on May 27 to a cease-fire. This occurred simultaneously with President Yeltsin's declaration to pull Russian troops from Moldova. However, a few hours later, fighting resumed around the Dniestr region and shooting broke out north of Bendery.

There were major differences between Trans-Dniestr's position and what could be considered areas of agreement at Istanbul. Trans-Dniestr objected to the peacemaking activities of the four-power foreign ministers, which, according to Trans-Dniestr officials, had "lost their significance." Furthermore, Igor Smirnov, the Trans-Dniestr president, felt it necessary that the 14th Army remain in the region: "I am confident that the 14th Army, as well as the Ukrainian forces, could become a stabilizing factor." [15] Finally, Smirnov denied autonomy to Trans-Dniestr, as proposed by Ukrainian President Kravchuk.

A relatively new change in the Trans-Dniestr official position occurred after Rutskoi's visit and his negotiations with the Trans-

---

[14] *Literaturnaia Gazeta*, 23 Dec. 1992.
[15] *Interfax*, June 26, 1992.

Dniestr leaders and the command of the 14th Army on July 14, 1992. The same day, in an interview with the German news agency DPA, Igor Smirnov said that he did not insist "on complete sovereignty from Moldova. Even if a federative state were suggested to us, that would be an excellent step." However, he reiterated that Trans-Dniestr had applied for full membership in the CIS. Trans-Dniestr also applied to Russia and Ukraine to assume the functions of protectors and guarantors of human rights, freedom, and interests of the region.

The agreement concluded in Moscow on July 21, was accepted by Trans-Dniestr. Thus, said Smirnov, the agreement signed by Russian President Yeltsin and Moldovan President Snegur is "an effective document," since Russia stands as guarantor of peace in this region.

THE RUSSIAN 14TH ARMY

Russia's contradictory course of action on the conflict in Moldova may reflect an ongoing dispute between the Russian conservatives and the moderates in Yeltsin's cabinet. This could explain the frequent changes in Russian policy, from one extreme to another, in approaching the issue. Currently, it seems that the prevailing concept is to "protect the Russians" outside Russia's borders, including in the Dniestr area. This policy is supported by various groups in the Russian leadership: some members of the Yeltsin cabinet, top military commanders, and representatives of the Foreign Office. [16]

In fact these Russian concerns were related to the 14th Russian Army's presence and activity in Moldova. For a long time, Moldova's officials accused the 14th Army of direct involvement in the conflict. Moldova's accusations received various—and to some extent contradictory—responses from Russian military officials. The CIS-commander-in-chief, Yevgeny Shaposhnikov, insisted that the 14th Army had remained neutral in the fighting. Nevertheless, at a news conference, he declared that one could not rule out the possibility that "a number of military officials have assisted local armed forces in removing military equipment."

Izvestia reported that, according to the 14th Army military council, local groups in the Dniestr area wanted to transfer the army to the jurisdiction of the Dniestr republic and Dniestr fighters were trying to seize their weapons. The number of Russian troops which were involved in the fighting was also in question. According to a spokesman for the 14th Army, some of the 5,000 Russian soldiers stationed in Moldova had joined the Trans-Dniestr forces on their own initiative. *The Financial Times*, quoting a Trans-Dniestr offi-

---

[16] Russian Vice-President Rutskoy, suggested "the transfer" of Soviet experience in fighting in Afghanistan to Russia's relations with its neighbors, in order to protect ethnic Russians. General Grachev, the new Russian Minister of Defense, was one of the first to declare that Russia would never abandon Russians in the Dniestr region. (ITAR-TASS news agency, June 3, 1992). Finally, Foreign Minister Kozyrev advised in an interview with the French daily *Le Monde* (June 5, 1992) that the conflict in Moldova could be solved by dismembering the republic or creating a federation: "It is important that Moldova give up its unrealistic views. I do not understand why Moldova must at all cost be a unitary state when it includes regions, like the left bank of the Dniestr and Gagauzia, which have a very special history and demographic make-up." He also suggested that the Dniestr region could potentially be included in Russia, even though the area now has no border with Russia.

cial, put the level of the 14th Army in Moldova between 10,000–20,000 well-trained troops. [17]

When President Yeltsin announced initially, on May 27 his decision to pull Russian troops out of their Dniestr deployments in Moldova, there were several objections raised by top Russian military officers. First, the military would have to be relocated: "The withdrawal is unrealistic and impossible for the simple reason that there is no place for the Army to withdraw to today. There are 200,000 officers and warrant officers without apartments in Russia, and it is simply unwise to increase that number." [18] Secondly, some officials asserted that most of the 14th Army officers came from the Dniestr area: "I doubt that the withdrawal would be easy to accomplish [because] more than half of the unit's personnel consists of local inhabitants." [19] Third, "legalistic" motivations prevented the move: "The withdrawal could only take place if a special accord among the two states is signed, and that could only be done after the conflict in that zone is settled." [20]

An important change concerning the 14th Army occurred on June 20, 1992. According to a Russian government resolution issued on that day, the servicemen were instructed "to take adequate measures, exerting the right to self-defense." Apparently, this decision had a direct impact on the 14th Army's actions in the Trans-Dniestr area. Russian media comments stressed that the decision "has marked the beginning of an important stage in the development of events in the Dniestr region and South Osetia." [21] After this date major daily papers such as the *Financial Times*, the *Guardian*, and the *Independent* quoted an increasing number of statements by Russian military commanders admitting involvement in the fighting. Moreover, the *Independent* (June 24, 1992) referring to a Russian government source, mentioned that "the order for the 14th Army to engage was given by the high command in Moscow, though the aim was to make a show of force rather than to wage war."

Shortly after the Istanbul summit, Russia appointed two new high military officials—a new Deputy Defence Minister of Russia, Colonel-General Boris Gromov, and a new head of the 14th Army in Moldova, Major-General Aleksander Lebed. The media emphasized that "Russia has appointed two hardliners to key military positions in a move which could give the army more muscle to react to ethnic conflicts along the fringes of the former Soviet Union." [22] The first statement, made by General Lebed, offered some insight concerning his position: "The (Russian) army will continue to preserve its neutrality. But the quality of this neutrality will change. It will become armed neutrality."

---

[17] *Financial Times*, June 22, 1992.
[18] General Stolyarov, chairman of the committee for work with personnel of CIS Unified Armed Forces.
[19] General Netkachev, until June 27 the 14th Army commander.
[20] General Pavel Grachev, Russian Defense Minister.
[21] ITAR-TASS, June 21, 1992. Quoted by FBIS-SOV-92-121, 23 June 1992, p. 12.
[22] *Reuters*, June 29, 1992.

RELATIONS WITH ROMANIA

Under the Communist regime in Romania, the issue of Bessarabia was an entirely prohibited subject until the last years of Ceausescu's reign. Then, it became an issue in Romanian politics, when Ceausescu's critics charged him with relinquishing national territory to the Soviet Union. There was no single Romanian position on the Bessarabia issue after the 1989 Revolution. Silviu Brucan, then a leading member of the National Salvation Front (NSF), said during a press-conference on January 4, 1990, that the Front would make no claim to Bessarabia. "The Bessarabian question does not exist for the National Salvation Front." He also noted on that occasion, underlining the Front's indifference to Bessarabia, that "the territory bears the name of the Moldavian Soviet Socialist Republic." [23] Echoing this statement, the new Romanian Ambassador to Moscow, Vasile Sandru, was more specific, saying on Soviet television that Romania would respect the existing border with the Soviet Union. "Romania is fully committed to the existing borders of Europe." [24] This "legalist" approach, according to which there was no alternative to the existing borders in Europe, remained for a long period the fundamental official position of the Romanian NSF regime. In fact, it coincided with a common Romanian and Soviet attitude, [25] and Moscow acceded to these Romanian interests, in announcing that plans were being made to ease border restrictions between Romania and then Soviet Moldavia. In May 1990, President Iliescu stated that the Soviet annexation of Romanian territories was an "historical injustice," but added that it would not be in Romanian interests to raise the question of redrawing borders. This continued to be Romanian official attitude for more than a year, until the coup failed in Moscow in August 1991.

The process of "rethinking" on Moldova took quite a while. Immediately after the failed coup and following Moldova's declaration of independence, an attitude of immobility prevailed on the part of the Romanian regime. Official statements made on the proclamation of Moldova's independence did not mention any new Romanian position on its relationship with Moldova. [26] Instead the existing ideas on extensive cooperation between the two countries were reiterated. No word suggesting the desire for a possible reunification between Moldova and Romania could be found. Perhaps there was a hint of a policy change, however, in Iliescu's statement that "We should not force the hand of processes that follow their own course," [27] evidently suggesting that reunification must ultimately occur.

---

[23] *Reuters/TASS,* January 4, 1990.

[24] *Radio Free Europe,* January 25, 1990.

[25] During his first visit to Romania (January, 7, 1990), the Soviet Foreign Minister E. Shevarnadze, according to media reports, appeared to dismiss the possibility of reunification, saying existing European treaties guaranteed the territorial integrity of all the nations of Europe and their existing borders. Radio Free Europe, January, 7, 1990.

[26] President Iliescu statement (August 27, 1991); Prime Minister Roman's message (August 27, 1991); Prime Minister Roman Interview with French TV (August 27, 1991); the Declaration of the Romanian Government (August 27, 1991); National Salvation Front Statement (August 27, 1991); Romanian Parliament Declaration (August 28, 1991); and President Iliescu Interview with Chisinau Radio Station (August 28, 1991).

[27] FBIS-EEU-91-168, 29 August 1991, p. 17.

Continued

The first move suggesting a shift in the Romanian position toward Moldova was made by the Romanian foreign minister, Adrian Nastase, during his visit to Washington shortly after the September 1991 miners' riots in Romania. He elaborated on a previously "taboo" subject, namely the reunification between Romania and Moldova. Nastase said that the eventual unification of Romania and Moldova would represent the normal course of history and added a vague timetable to Iliescu's earlier statement: "I don't know if this will occur in 20 years or five years or 50 years. Very much will depend on the processes taking place in Moldova and Romania, in the Soviet Union . . . and in Europe in general." [28] However, the Romanian foreign minister confirmed that the old "legal" position was still in force in Bucharest, when he mentioned that "any change had to take account of the Helsinki Final Act of 1975 which laid down permanent international borders within Europe." [29] On some occasions, Romania's relationship with Moldova began to be compared with Germany's division into East and West Germany. Some Romanian officials suggested that the German unification, which was sanctioned by an international process involving interested external powers, could serve as an example for the two states. [30]

During this period it was easy to distinguish between official position and public opinion. Moldova's declaration of independence was seen by a large part of the population as a move toward reunification with Romania. According to a private opinion poll, 44 percent of the Romanian population favored union with Moldova as soon as possible, while 45 percent did not favor reunification in the near future. [31]

Many times, the issue of Bessarabia was also used to warn Romania against pressing its claim. For example, the Moscow newspaper *Izvestiya* considered that Romania's official policy of returning the territories that Romania lost in 1940, "would set a very dangerous precedent." And the newspaper added: "Who can guarantee that in the future, citing this precedent, all the states whose borders were changed in one way or another as a consequence of World War II will not start making claims against one another." [32]

Moldova's official position concerning its relationship with Romania can be seen as retreating from a highly emotional stand in

---

It still prevailed the same high level of ambiguity which could be, for example seen in the following between Prime Minister Roman and his interviewer from the Austrian daily Die Presse:

[Die Presse] The Soviet Republic of Moldova has been independent for some time. Do you personally want its reunification with Romania?

[Roman] At the moment, the Republic of Moldova is a reality as an independent and sovereign state. They are our brothers, the historical background is well known: it is clear that this was one of the oldest Romanian areas. However, the people of Moldova themselves decide on their future.

[Die Presse] What does Romania want?

[Roman] We must accept something that is in the spirit of history. Of course we do that. (FBIS-EEU-91-184, 23 September 1991. p. 21)

[28] *Reuters,* October 3, 1991.

[29] Ibid.

[30] The Romanian Foreign Ministry spokesman referring to the relations between Romania and Moldova, stated that "the existence of two neighboring Romanian states was not incompatible since that was only a partial correction of the consequences of the Soviet-Nazi Pact." (FBIS-EEU-91-234, December 5, 1991, p. 26).

[31] *The New York Times,* January 2, 1992.

[32] *Izvestiya,* November 29, 1991.

favor of reunification to a more cautious and balanced position. One of the most vocal supporters of Moldova's reunification with Romania, the former Prime Minister Mircea Druc, [33] was removed from office following an overwhelming vote of no confidence on May 22, 1991. [34]

It is still difficult to assess the relative power of groups that support or oppose reunification with Romania. According to some media reports and various experts, reunification with Romania is backed only by a small part of Moldova's population, a few leading personalities, and such organizations as the Moldovan People's Front, and "16th of December." Some maintain that the deputies who support reunification with Romania are mostly poets, journalists, artists, and for these people such a move could signify new opportunities, expansion of scientific and literary contacts, and closer European ties. The Popular Front intensified its activity at the beginning of 1992. In February, the Front elected Mircea Druc as its new leader and adopted a new program stating that "the main goal of the Popular Front is to contribute to the liberation of the occupied Romanian territories and their reunification (with Romania)." Moreover, the Front decided that it would try to take part in Romania's general election, in May 1992.

Different media reports emphasized that the proportion of those who rejected reunification with Romania and wanted to maintain independence seemed stronger. Its main representative is Moldovan President Mircea Snegur, who obtained an impressive victory in the first democratic election, on December 8, 1991. In an official statement after his election, Snegur stated: "My year as president has clearly convinced people that I have kept my promise to be the guarantor of Moldova's independence. Yes, Moldova and Romania are states whose citizens speak the same language. But there can be no question of joining Romania or any other country. I am in favor of Moldova's territorial integrity." [35] Snegur's position emphasizes the desire to proceed toward more tangible cooperation in areas of cultural and economic integration areas, but stopping well short of unification of Moldova and Romania. [36] During his visit to Washington (February 18, 1992), Snegur informed President Bush on Moldova's stand on the issue of relations with Romania, which he described as "good relations of integration and brotherhood." [37]

RECENT DEVELOPMENTS

The end of 1992 and the beginning of 1993, brought new developments in the political evolution of Moldova. Most of them question previous political moves. Possibly one of the most important developments refers to the status of the 14th Army and implicitly to the

---

[33] The international media reported, still in February 1991, on President Mircea Snegur "inability to work" with Premier Mircea Druc. (Keesing's Record of World Events, 1991. p. 38015)

[34] After Moldova's declaration of independence (August 27, 1991), Mircea Druc asserted that "Moldova's independence will mean nothing unless a solemn oath is taken for union [with Romania]".

[35] FBIS-SOV-92-005, January 8, 1992. p. 67.

[36] FBIS-SOV-92-003, January 6, 1992. p. 57. On another occasion, Snegur elaborated more on this issue: "I think Romania also has an interest in our two sovereign countries having close scientific and cultural contacts, creating joint enterprises, and exchanging students and specialists." (FBIS-SOV-92-004, January 7, 1992. p. 68.)

[37] Bucharest Radio Romania Network.

projected terms of its withdrawal. On the February 3, 1992, in Chisinau consultations took place between the military departments of Moldova and the Russian Federation about the status and timing of the 14th Army's withdrawal. Colonel General Eduard Vorobyov, head of the Russian delegation, said after the consultation that both sides had come to an understanding on most of the questions involved. According to Vorobyov "it is impossible to withdraw all of the army's equipment, armaments, and staff before the end of 1994, as insisted upon by the Moldovans." [38]

Several days later, the communique published in Moscow after the meeting between Presidents Yeltsin and Snegur, offered a different version of the same issue. It is said that Russia and Moldova agreed to keep Russian troops deployed in Moldova's eastern province "until the situation returns to normal." [39] In a special statement to the media, President Yeltsin said: "The troops will leave when President Mircea Snegur and I are sure the flame of conflict will not rise ever again." [40] This statement doesn't reflect any kind of deadline for the withdrawal of the 14th Army. Even the end of 1994 was not confirmed by Moscow. In addition, two other conditions were restated by Moscow: (a) Withdrawal of the 14th Army would be conditional upon a settlement left bank status, acceptable to the Trans-Dniestr authorities; (b) and the problem of relocating the military. Yeltsin mentioned the "sad experience" of the Baltic countries and "the need of an attentive attitude for the rights of the military."

Another meeting between Snegur and Yeltsin took place in the middle of May, on the occasion of the extraordinary summit of the 10-member Commonwealth of Independent States, and the signing of an economic union between the former Soviet republics. The document emphasized that nine of the former republics, including Moldova, joined the new economic union. Was this a new Moldovan concession? Apparently yes, at least because official statements in Chisinau supported the new move and explained—as did the Prime Minister Andrey Sangely—that Moldova's economy is in a critical state, mostly because of a collapse in economic links between former Soviet republics.[41] In addition, Yeltsin's statement, after meeting Snegur (the day after the CIS meeting) refers to some new agreements between Russia and Moldova "based on the main idea of preserving the integrity and indivisibility of Moldova." [42]

---

[38] *Interfax*, Feb. 3, 1993.
[39] *Reuters*, Feb. 9, 1993 and *Interfax*, Feb. 9, 1993 and Information Bulletin provided by the Permanent Mission of the Republic of Moldova to the U.N., 10 Feb. 1993.
[40] *Reuters*, Feb. 9, 1993.
[41] *Reuters*, May 13, 1993.
[42] *Reuters*, May 15, 1993.

POLITICAL-ECONOMIC ASSESSMENTS:

BELARUS

By Kathleen Mihalisko *

CONTENTS

SUMMARY

The reform process in post-Soviet Belarus is severely hampered by polarity between totalitarian and democratic forces in the Supreme Soviet and by a lack of middle ground. To a large extent the impetus for change has come from external rather than internal Belarusian factors. Yet Belarus, unlike a number of other republics of the former Soviet Union, is attractive to potential Western investors because of its absence of economic and social turmoil. Although the goal of integration with the rest of Europe is a paramount ideal for Belarus, basic questions about the character and priorities of the new Belarusian state remain, for decision makers and the public alike, without answers.

INTRODUCTION

The death sentence for the Soviet Union was pronounced on December 8, 1991, in the Belarusian [1] capital of Minsk, following a

---

* Kathleen Mihalisko is a Senior Research Analyst with Radio Free Europe/Radio Liberty in Munich, Germany.

[1] For the sake of consistency, the forms "Belarus" and "Belarusian" are used throughout this paper in reference to events both before and after September, 1991, when the republic officially changed its name. An exception is made in the case of citations where English-language titles employ "Belorussia," "Belorussian," and so forth. *Belarus* is simply the Belarusian-language equivalent of Belorussia.

weekend of secluded negotiations between Leonid Kravchuk, Stanislau Shushkevich, and Boris Yeltsin, that led to the signing of an agreement to establish a Commonwealth of Independent States. The participation of each of the three Slavic republics of Belarus, Russia, and Ukraine in the founding of the CIS was essential; no combination of two out of three would have had the same result. As Shushkevich, the chairman of the Belarusian Supreme Soviet, admitted in an interview in January 1992, he and Yeltsin had to work to convince newly elected President Kravchuk to go along with the idea for a new kind of association despite Ukraine's overwhelming vote for national independence in its December 1 referendum.[2] Yet it is equally important to realize that Shushkevich's own agreement to dissolve the U.S.S.R. and create in its place a Commonwealth—with an administrative seat in Minsk—constituted perhaps the most abrupt and unexpected betrayal of Soviet president Mikhail Gorbachev and the proposed Union treaty that any republic ever presented. Until the eve of the so-called Slavic summit, support in Belarus at the official level for the renewed political and economic union envisaged by Gorbachev had been firm and virtually unquestioned.

Some Belarusians attributed Shushkevich's about face to Belarus's habit of bending to Russia's will; another body of opinion gave credit to Shushkevich for wisely concluding that without Ukraine, the U.S.S.R. would be doomed to a more protracted and painful death. In any event, the end result was that in abandoning previous intentions to preserve the U.S.S.R. in some form, Belarus cleared the way for its own entry into the ranks of modern European nations. Throughout the Gorbachev era nationally minded elements of the population, above all, the cultural intelligentsia, drew attention to the paradoxical fact that despite its location in the geographic center of Europe, Belarus, with a population of 10.2 million, existed on the margins of European civilization. Nowadays many Belarusians are determined to right that wrong and, indeed, the collapse of the U.S.S.R. has presented the country with an historically unprecedented opportunity to determine its own national agenda in the fullest sense of the term.

Making the best of that challenge, however, will require a complex and all-encompassing effort to transform the foundations of political, economic, and social life in Belarus. Though the goal of integration with the rest of Europe is a paramount ideal, basic questions about the character and priorities of the new Belarusian state remain, for decision-makers and the public alike, without answers. Since the time of the ill-fated August coup attempt in Moscow, Belarus has undergone the least amount of personnel turnover at the highest level of legislative and executive power of any European successor state to the U.S.S.R. Despite the suspension of the Belarusian Communist Party, much of the pre-coup policy-making apparatus is still intact. Old faces are attempting to come to terms with wholly new conditions; the question whether it is easier for people to change themselves, or to change the people, is open to debate.

---

[2] *Kosomol'skaya pravda,* January 9, 1992.

For those reasons, early in 1992 a coalition of democratic parties and political movements organized a petition drive to collect signatures in support of holding a nationwide referendum on confidence in the current Supreme Soviet, arguing that the incumbent body is too much a relic of the old regime. The initiative was successful: in April, the legally required minimum of 350,000 signatures was surpassed and, by law, a date for the referendum must be set. In addition, there is mounting frustration with Shushkevich, the only leader of a CIS state who has not stood for election as president. Characteristically, the man who connived with the presidents of Russia and Ukraine to dissolve the U.S.S.R. was unable, after that historic event, to gain parliament's approval for his preferred candidate for the vacant post of deputy Supreme Soviet chairman. Instead, he had to content himself with a deputy chosen by former Party apparatchiks from among their own ranks.[3] Many Belarusians seem to consider Shushkevich not a relic of the past but a hostage to it.

Needless to say, the relics, legacies, and products of Soviet Communism pose ubiquitous dilemmas throughout the former U.S.S.R. But in the words with which Leo Tolstoy began his novel *Anna Karenina*: "All happy families are alike; unhappy families are unhappy each in their own way." The material presented here will examine some of the trends and developments at work over the past several years that have made for a particularly Belarusian complex of issues. The paper is less concerned with descriptions of current policies, which, at any rate, are at an early stage of evolution (and subject to change, if indeed a new parliament is elected in the near future) than with providing some framework for understanding the influences on political and economic life in Belarus.

THE IDEA OF THE NATION

Belarus in the last few years of the Soviet Union's existence did not give birth to a mass movement for independence and national aspirations. Those ideals were championed by a relatively small group of activists and intellectuals. Therefore, when Belarus found itself an independent state at the end of 1991, many Belarusians were perplexed by the implications. Even now, six months after the creation of the CIS, mainstream Belarusian newspapers continue to prefer the less emotion-ridden *suverenna Belarus*. The entrenchment of a sense of Belarusian nationhood and statehood is, however, most likely a matter of time. A common mistaken assumption among observers of the U.S.S.R. in the pre-Gorbachev era was that the resounding success of linguistic Russification had wiped away the Belarusian ethnos—if ever there had been one to begin with, some argued. But subsequent events brought forth abundant evidence for both the survival of a Belarusian national identity and the resilience of the national idea in the most adverse of circumstances.

---

[3] Vvacheslav Kuznetsov, an ethnic Russian, who became deputy chairman of the Belarusian Supreme Soviet in April, 1992.

BELARUSIAN REVIVAL

National assertiveness rose to the surface in Belarus as early in Gorbachev's tenure as 1986 and 1987, when prominent cultural figures addressed open letters to the Kremlin to draw the new general secretary's attention to the parlous state of the Belarusian language.[4] In what was to become a common plea throughout the non-Russian areas in the early years of glasnost, the signatories called for a return to Leninist nationality policies. A fact-finding team that Gorbachev dispatched to Minsk to investigate the matter reported back, after speaking solely to local Party authorities, that the intellectuals had Belarusian as the language of instruction.[5] The assessment, however, ignored the fact that enrollment in the Russian-language schools accounted for no less than 80 percent of all schoolchildren and that not a single Belarusian-language school existed in any urban area of the republic.[6]

With the raising of the language issue, relations between intellectuals and the Russian-speaking apparatus of the Belarusian Communist Party (CP) went from bad to worse.[7] In the Brezhnev era, precisely one high Communist Party official, namely, former Central Committee secretary Alyaksandr Kuzmin, had enjoyed a good reputation among Belarusian intellectuals for efforts on behalf of the native language and culture. With that single exception, the intellectual elite had faced a Communist leadership that had striven determinedly for the linguistic and cultural Russification and "Sovietization" of the Belarusian population. (After all, on a trip to Belarus in the early 1960s where he was able to witness the inroads already made by Russification, Nikita Khrushchev had gleefully predicted that Belarusians would be "first to reach communism."[8]) Given the sorry plight of the indigenous tongue by the 1980s, it is not difficult to understand why intellectuals seized an opportunity to air grievances when the reformist Gorbachev took over the reins of power in the Kremlin.

After a long campaign, legislation was passed in February 1990, making Belarusian the state language of the republic.[9] By that time, however, the national revival movement was in full swing and affecting, crucially, the field of historical studies, where a younger generation of scholars began to discard such recurrent themes in Soviet historiography as Belarus's centuries-old struggle for "reunification with Russia" and the myths associated with the Bolshevik Revolution. Eventually, articles in *Litaratura i mastatstva* (Literature and Art), the liberal organ of the Writers' Union and a flagship of glasnost in Belarus, sought to rehabilitate the government of the short-lived independent Belarusian National

---

[4] *Letters of Gorbachev: New Documents from Soviet Byelorussia* London: The Association of Byelorussians in Great Britain, 1987.

[5] The incident with Gorbachev's team of investigators was described in a recent interview with the writer Vasil' Bykau in *Narodnaya hazeta* (Minsk), May 13, 1992.

[6] See, *inter alia*, "Na matchynai move . . . bez aksentu?" *Zvyazda*, June 13, 1989.

[7] See Roman Solchanyk, "Party Leader Rejects Criticism About Status of Byelorussian Language," *Radio Liberty (RL)* 180/87, May 7, 1987.

[8] Quoted in A. Kudravets, "Zalozhniki Chernobylya," *Nëman*, no. 1, 1990, pp. 3–8.

[9] The "Law on Languages of the Belorussian SSR" was published on February 13, 1990, in all major newspapers of the republic. It took effect on September 1, of that year. Russian was accorded the status of "language of inter-nationality communication." The Belarusian language is closely related to Russian but is more intelligible to a speaker of Ukrainian.

Republic (1918–1919). The application of glasnost to history held immediately tragic revelations, too. In June 1988, tangible physical evidence of the crimes committed against the Belarusian people saw the light of day when a little-known historian and archaeologist named Zyanon Paznyak published the findings of his unofficial excavation of the Kurapaty woods, near the Minsk beltway.[10] Paznyak's initiative, which earned Soviet-wide and international publicity, had unearthed the remains of some of the tens of thousands of people believed to have been executed and buried *en masse* there in the years 1937–41 by Stalin's NKVD.

The Belarusian revival movement served the important function of creating a mirror in which Belarusians could view their national experience outside the Soviet context. The erasure of historical memory had reached an acute level in Belarus: by 1990, for instance, the number of specialists working in the field of history with the title of doctor or candidate of science amounted to 680 individuals. No less than 90 percent of their dissertations had been devoted to the Soviet period and close to 60 percent were on aspects of Communist Party history.[11] The buoyant spirit of rediscovery perhaps was best exemplified in the return to the stage of Yanka Kupala's play *Tuteishyya* (The Locals) after a 64-year ban. The play explored Belarus' peculiar position between two powerful neighbors, Poland and Russia, and both the individual and collective compromises that position engendered. In its revived edition beginning in October, 1990, *Tuteishyya* ended in a Bolshevik orgy of murder; out of the grave, though, rose an enormous red-on-white Belarusian national flag. All this played to packed audiences in the Yanka Kupala Theater, located directly across the street from what was, until recently, the headquarters of the Central Committee of the Belarusian Communist Party.

THE CHERNOBYL DISASTER

As important as the above developments were, none had as widespread and shattering an impact on the public at large as the revelations concerning the 1986 disaster at the Chernobyl nuclear plant, located a few miles to the south of Belarus's border with Ukraine. Some observers have dated the advent of the policy of glasnost to the profoundly embarrassing events that accompanied the accident; nonetheless, glasnost on Chernobyl did not reach the Belarusian population until 1988, when the press at last began to examine the affair in all its aspects. It is impossible in a short space to do justice to the human dimension and political ramifications of the Chernobyl disaster. The consequences, in terms of the impact on human health and the environment, will be felt until well into the twenty-first century. It was not until 1990, three years after the accident at the nuclear power plant, that Belaru-

---

[10] For literature in English on Kurapaty, see Kathleen Mihalisko, "Mass Grave of Stalin's Victims Discovered in Minsk," *RL 288/88*, June 26, 1988, and "The Archeology of Stalinist Genocide in Belorussia,"*RL 452/88*, October 3, 1988. Paznyak's reports on the finds in Kurapaty were published under the titles "Kurapaty—Daroha smertisi," *Litaratura i mastatstva* [hereafter: *LiM*], June 3, 1988 and "Shumvats' nad mahilai sosnv.," *LiM*. September 16, 1988. Due to the inaccessibility of Belarusian sources for most readers of this paper, the author gives preference in footnote citations to material more readily available in Radio Free Europe/Radio Liberty publications. These publications cite original source material for interested readers.
[11] *LiM*, April 12, 1991.

sians learned from official sources that radioactive contamination to one or another degree had affected territory inhabited by 2.2 million residents of Belarus, of whom 800,000 were children.[12] Exposes of the official coverup of Chernobyl's consequences, together with examples of gross negligence on the part of local and central authorities, appeared in local and central newspapers virtually on a daily basis. Physicist Stanislau Shushkevich was one of a number of scientists who strove to draw the nation's attention to the extent of the catastrophe; in 1990, in the Soviet Union's first multicandidate elections to republican-level and local soviets, he was elected people's deputy of the Belarusian SSR on the strength of his Chernobyl platform.[13]

A number of commentators held up Chernobyl and Kurapaty as the twin symbols of evil, and many posed the question whether "survival" rather than "revival" was really at stake. Both calamities, but especially the former, with its sinister and invisible threat to present and future generations, forced Belarusians to confront the precariousness of their own existence as a distinct historical people. Chernobyl also served to underscore the injustices brought on by Belarus's subservience to the central powers, particularly when, in 1990, Moscow agreed to pay only three billion of a 17-billion ruble aid request from Minsk (a figure representing twice the republic's annual budget) for further decontamination and evacuations. It has proven difficult in Belarus, however, to translate popular emotions and outrage into a national agenda with concrete goals. History has taught Belarusians not to change their conditions but to adapt to the terms imposed on them by others, as the play *Tuteishyya* taught.

CLASH OF OLD AND NEW POLITICAL FORCES

The Gorbachev era witnessed the emergence of the first organized opposition to the communist regime in Belarus, a republic which previously had contributed relatively little to the Soviet dissident movement of the Brezhnev years. The political arena in the past several years was dominated by the sharp confrontation between the opposition as spearheaded by the Belarusian Popular Front and forces belonging—and fiercely loyal—to a Communist Party organization that refused to give way to reform and reformists. Given the lasting influence of these factors, any understanding of today's developments must take into account the political environment bequeathed to post-Soviet Belarus.

RISE OF THE NATIONAL DEMOCRATIC OPPOSITION

Launched in October 1988, the "Adradzhen'ne" (Rebirth) Belarusian Popular Front (BPF) borrowed heavily from the ideas and programmatic goals of the new movements in Estonia, Latvia, and

---

[12] A map showing radiation levels in Belarus was first published on February 9, 1989, i.e., nearly three years after the Chernobyl' accident in *Sovetskaya Belorussiya* and other newspapers. One year later, in an appeal to governments and organizations throughout the world to render assistance to Belarus that was printed in the Belarusian press on February 21, 1990, official sources revealed that one-fifth of the arable land in the republic had been contaminated.

[13] Shushkevich's candidacy was backed by the Belarusian Popular Front. After his election, however, he broke ties with the organization, possibly to clear the way for his selection as deputy Supreme Soviet chairman in May, 1990.

Lithuania and adapted them to Belarusian conditions. The BPF's initial organizing committee consisted of the cream of the cultural intelligentsia, activists from well-known independent youth groups like "Talaka," [14] Paznyak and several other vocal regime opponents. Soon, however, organizers who were also members of the Communist Party, such as poet and chairman of the Writers' Union, Nil Hilevich, came under intense pressure to abandon their popular front activities [15] (an exception to the list of drop-outs was the renowned writer Vasil' Bykau, who had managed, despite his standing as a Soviet author of international stature, not to join the Party).

That left the organization in the hands of staunch anticommunists like Paznyak, who became chairman of the BPF in 1989 at its founding congress in Vilnius, Lithuania. The situation stood in interesting contrast to Ukraine, for example, where "Rukh" leaders such as the poets Ivan Drach and Volodymyr Yavorivsky retained their Communist Party memberships until well into 1990. The Belarusian CP could not maintain—indeed, it displayed little interest in the argument—that the push for change came from within the Party, as reformed communists in Kiev or Moscow at one time were anxious to prove, and it produced no one in the mold of a Leonid Kravchuk, much less a Boris Yeltsin. Belarus presented quite a different picture in which it proved impossible to reconcile the aims of the national democrats with the priorities of the Party's conservative and Russocentric inner circle. What is more, the Central Committee as headed by the then first secretary Efrem Sakalau, a 1987 Gorbachev appointee,[16] was entirely successful in nipping in the bud attempts within Party ranks to launch a reformist wing along the lines of the Communist Party of the Soviet Union Democratic Platform.

With an electoral platform resting "on the ideals of political and economic pluralism, cultural revival, democracy, freedom and sovereignty for Belarus," [17] candidates representing the BPF took 30 seats in the 360-member republican Supreme Soviet in the spring elections of 1990, in addition to gains in the city soviet of Minsk and other urban centers.[18] Two BPF leaders who gained entry into parliament were Paznyak and his close associate, the economist Uladzimir Zablatsky. Toward the closure of the first session of the newly elected parliament, the BPF deputies established a caucus

---

[14] On Talaka's early activities, see "Profile of Patriotic Youth Groups in Belorussia," *RL* 318/88, July 4, 1988 and "Talaka Takes up Latest Cause: Restoration of Belorussian National Flag," *RL* 409/88, September 7, 1988.

[15] See Vasil' Yakavenka, *Sovetskaya kul'tura*, June 24, 1989.

[16] Interesting details on the appointments of Sakalau and his counterpart in Kazakhstan, Gennadii Kolbin, are provided in Alexander Rahr, "Efrem Sokolov Elected New Party Chief of Belorussia," *RL* 71/87, February 19, 1987. Sakalau, whom Gorbachev elevated over the heads of more senior comrades, was lauded at the time in the central press as a dynamic and open-minded leader. Whatever his qualities, he rapidly succumbed to the antireformist direction of the Belarusian Central Committee.

[17] Walter Stankievich, "Belorussian Popular Front Announces Its Electoral Platform," *Report on the USSR*, No. 2, January 12, 1990, pp. 20–23.

[18] At present 20 seats in the parliament of the Republic of Belarus remain vacant, the result of an election law requirement stipulating that at least 50 percent of voters in a given district must cast ballots in order for the results of an election to be valid. Repeat elections have failed to fill the empty seats. The BPF holds 60 of 203 seats in the Minsk City soviet. See Berhard Schneider, "The New Political Forces in Russia, Ukraine and Belorussia," *Report on the USSR*, no. 50 December 13, 1991, pp. 10–18.

and announced that they were formally in opposition to the Communist majority in the Supreme Soviet. Indeed, due to electoral legislation containing built-in advantages to the ruling party-plus a generous fixed quota of 50 (of 360) seats that were reserved for the representatives of official veterans' and handicapped persons' organizations—no less than 75 percent of the Supreme Soviet consisted of representatives of the Party and state apparatus.[19] That, in a nutshell, remains the profile of the incumbent parliament.

AN ANTIREFORMIST PARTY

The Central Committee (CC) long was dominated by a rather shadowy group of right-wing ideologues under the apparent helmsmanship of Savelii Pavlov, chief of the Propaganda and Agitation Department of the CC from 1972 to 1989, and as of 1990, rector of the Higher Party School in Minsk (renamed in 1991 to the Institute for Political Science and Social Administration). The patron of a rather notorious collection of neo-Stalinist academics and publicists—chief among them, the well-known anti-Semite Vladimir Begun [20]—Pavlov and his associates in the CC conducted a ceaseless struggle against reformists of all stripes, radical and moderate. This campaign perhaps was without parallel in any other republic of the western U.S.S.R. in the Gorbachev period, and earned Belarus the epithet of "the Vendée of perestroika," in reference to the regional counterrevolutionary uprisings in France.[21] The BPF and liberal Belarusian intellectuals were regularly attacked in the CC monthly organ *Politicheskii sobesednik* (Political Collocutor), on the pages of the Minsk evening paper *Vechernii Minsk* and in the Russian chauvinist publications, printed at Belarusian CC facilities, called *Slavyankskie vedomosti* (Slavic News) and *My i vremya* (We and Time). Several hate-mongering organizations from Russia were invited to set up shop in Belarus.

Far from being a problem contained in Belarus, the situation carried the potential for regional destabilization, as suggested by evidence that the Party was providing not only publicity but concrete aid to the militant Russian-speaking "interfront" movements in the three Baltic states.[22] It also posed a direct challenge to Gorbachev's position. In increasingly open fashion, Sakalau's team, which enjoyed warm relations with archconservative Politburo member Yegor Ligachev, threw support behind calls to replace

[19] On the Belarusian electoral law, see Kathleen Mihalisko, "Reaching for Parliamentary Democracy in Belorussia and Ukraine," *Report on the USSR*, no. 50, December 15, 1989, pp. 27–21.
[20] Vladimir Begun of the Institute of Philosophy in Minsk, whose name became practically synonymous with official anti-Semitism, was the author of numerous openly anti-Jewish books and articles in the Brezhnev era. He died in 1989. The first anniversary of his death was solemnly commemorated in issue No. 7, 1990, of *Politicheskii sobesednik (PS)*. One or two liberal newspapers in Belarus began to draw the public's attention to the base level of *PS* publishers in the Central Committee. See, for instance, Semen Bukchin, "Opasnaya igra," *Znamy yunosti*, February 23, 1990, for a critique of an anti-Semitic piece by Eduard Skabaleu, a Central Committee employee, in *PS*, No. 2, 1990.
[21] Ales' Adamovich, "Oglyanis' okrest!" *Ogonek*, no. 39, 1988, pp. 28–30.
[22] Details on the "Ligachev connection" and on the anti-Baltic campaign in Belarus are provided in Kathleen Mihalisko, "Belorussia in 1989," *Report on the USSR*, no. 52, December 29, 1989, pp. 21–22; "Official and Independent Labor Unions Compete for Allegiance of Belorussian Workers," *Report on the USSR*, no. 43, October 27, 1989, pp. 16–19; and "For Our Freedom and Yours: Support among Slavs for Baltic Independence," *Report on the USSR*, no. 21, May 25, 1990, pp. 17–19. On the United Front, see Vera Tolz, "The United Front of Workers of Russia: Further Consolidation of Antireform Forces," *Report on the USSR*, no. 39, 1989, pp. 11–13.

Gorbachev as general secretary of the CPSU.[23] Finally, at the Thirty-First Congress of the Belarusian CP in December, 1990, Sakalau was quietly invited by delegates to step down as first secretary because a more outspoken Gorbachev opponent, former Soviet ambassador to Poland Vladimir Brovikov, had expressed interest in the job. It reportedly took an eleventh-hour telephone call from Gorbachev to thwart the selection of his fierce critic, and Minsk Oblast party chief Anatoly Malafeyeu defeated Brovikov for the post by only a few votes.[24] The incident took place in the midst of a brewing storm in the Kremlin that ended in the resignation of Eduard Shevardnadze and the gathering of forces for the bloody crackdown in Vilnius and Riga in January 1991.

FROM SOVEREIGNTY TO INDEPENDENCE

The reform process in Belarus was—and, emphatically, still is— severely hampered by the absence of a political middle ground in the Supreme Soviet. If, to take Ukraine again as a point of comparison, leading Communists in Kiev found it in their interests to coopt the ideals of "Rukh" in order to maintain their grip on power, oppositionist pressure on their counterparts in Minsk was more easily resistible. Mikalai Dzemyantsei, who served as chairman of the Supreme Soviet from May 1990 until the unravelling of the August 1991 coup, was an unreformed CP functionary. With frustrating frequency, proposed bills and other initiatives put forth by the parliamentary opposition never made it to a session's agenda or else were voted down by the majority bloc of communist loyalists. For its part, the Belarusian government as headed by Prime Minister Vyacheslau Kebich was regarded as only somewhat more attuned to changing realities, with emphasis placed on economic rationalization rather than a comprehensive reform of the system. Hence, on January 1, 1990, Belarus became the first republic outside the Baltic states to switch to regional economic autonomy and self-financing methods.[25] Capturing the official Belarusian approach to perestroika, trade official Viktar Andrushyn said at the time that "we've gone about this in a better way than the Balts. Our neighbors thought and talked more about politics, we've been more concerned with the economic side of life." [26]

COMING TO TERMS WITH SOVEREIGNTY

To a large extent the impetus for change came from external rather than internal Belarusian factors. There is no better example than the circumstances behind Belarus's Declaration of State Sovereignty, which was approved by virtually unanimous vote in the republican Supreme Soviet on June 27, 1990. The third republic of the U.S.S.R. after Russia and Ukraine to declare its sovereignty, Belarus adopted a declaration which was slightly less triumphant in spirit than its Ukrainian equivalent but which incorporated all the essential points of the latter, including the assertion of the re-

---

[23] See the interview with Sakalau in *Pravada*, July 31, 1990.
[24] Information relayed to the author by Minsk journalist Yurii Drakohrust.
[25] See Kathleen Mihalisko and John Tedstrom, "Belarus Moves to Self-Financing," *RL* 458/88, October 5, 1988.
[26] *Belarus*, No. 2, 1990, pp 2–3.

public's right to establish its own army and national bank and to conduct an independent foreign policy. Following in Ukraine's footsteps, Belarus also proclaimed its intention to become a neutral, nonaligned, and nonnuclear state and to claim exclusive jurisdiction over its land, mineral wealth, and natural resources.

On the surface, it appeared that Belarus had moved to the forefront of the drive for sovereignty. However, the truth was that *Moscow had ordered Dzemyantsei and the Communist-dominated Belarusian parliament to draw up and approve a state sovereignty declaration.* Convening for its first session in May 1990, the newly elected body decisively rejected the opposition's proposal to place the issue of state sovereignty on the agenda.[27] Remarkably, when Dzemyantsei came back from Moscow on June 19 after attending a meeting of the U.S.S.R. Council of the Federation, he presented a draft declaration of Belarusian sovereignty to the Supreme Soviet and called on deputies to approve it. The curious turn of events was prompted by tactical maneuvering on the part of the Kremlin, which was anxious to bring republican sovereignty causes under its control by tying them to a proposed new Union treaty. Therefore, so far as Moscow was concerned, of overriding importance in the Belarusian and analogous declarations was the provision for "urgently entering into negotiations for a new treaty of union of sovereign Socialist states."

Until the creation of the CIS, official policy in Belarus remained faithful to the Union treaty provision enshrined in the sovereignty declaration, even if other articles of the same document were more or less forgotten. The opposition's subsequent and repeated failures to obtain majority approval for legislation aimed at strengthening Belarusian sovereignty led to numerous accusations that the ruling party was far more active in the conservative struggle to oust Gorbachev than in the business of elaborating policies for a self-governing state. Indeed, many Belarusians remain sensitive to reminders that first sovereignty, then independence, were thrust upon them by the force of events. Such reminders serve as further confirmation that Belarusians have far to go before they can claim to be masters of their own destiny.

THE WORKERS' MOVEMENT

It was not until the republic was shaken to the core by mass labor unrest in April 1991 that the authorities realized the potential advantages of Belarus's sovereign status, both as a means to reduce the impact on their territory of the general crisis situation in the Soviet Union and, as a corollary, to keep the Belarusian Communist Party in power. The strikes were sparked by the across-the-board price hikes ordered by then U.S.S.R. Prime Minister Valentin Pavlov that went into effect on April 2 across the Soviet Union, only four weeks after Gorbachev had assured Belarusian workers during a tour of the republic that they would not feel the effects of price reform too much. On April 10–11, at the height of the general walkout, hundreds of thousands of workers at enter-

[27] The events surrounding the sovereignty declaration are described in "Belorussia as a Sovereign State: An Interview with Henadz' Hrushavv." *Report on the USSR*, No. 35, August 31, 1990, pp. 11–16.

prises in Minsk, Homel, the potassium mining center of Salihorsk, Zhadina—home to the famous Belaz truck plant—and Orsha demonstrated in the streets and backed demands for an end to Communist rule, the nationalization of CPSU property, and the resignation of the Soviet and Belarusian leaderships. In Minsk, which witnessed the largest antiregime demonstrations in Belarusian history, participants raised a call for the convening of an emergency session of the Supreme Soviet to take action on these and other key demands. Factory-level and regional strike committees were created, pushing aside the notoriously ineffectual official trade unions.[28]

The authorities successfully deflated the workers' movement with a swift, twofold response; sweeping concessions to wage and other economic demands; and flat refusal to give in to demands of a political nature, accompanied by threats to deal harshly with independent labor organizers. The main strategist was Prime Minister Kebich.[29] On May 8, two weeks before the suspended strikes were scheduled to begin anew, Kebich and Uladzimir Hancharyk, chairman of the Communist Party-controlled Council of the Federation of Professional Unions, signed a major agreement providing for salary increases of up to 200 percent for workers and employees at cost-accounting enterprises, to be paid out of net profits, and a promise to reexamine wage scales for employees in other sectors.[30] Kebich also invited the economist Nikolai Shmelev to Minsk to look over a Belarusian "anticrisis plan." At the same time, Belarusian state prosecutor Heorii Tarnausky announced the institution of criminal proceedings against the leaders of the Minsk Strike Committee and organizers of a railroad blockade in Orsha.[31]

It is worth taking account of two concurrent developments at the all-Union level. April 23 marked the signing of the so-called Novo-Ogarevo (or Nine-plus-One) agreement between President Gorbachev and the leaders of nine republics. The agreement, which granted concessions to the sovereign states of the U.S.S.R., also called for an end to the wave of strikes throughout the country and strong measures to stabilize the situation in industry and in the economy. Immediately after his return from the meeting outside Moscow, Kebich took steps behind the scenes to tighten up internal security in the republic, raising suspicions among some observers that the principle of sovereignty in Belarus might be put to the service not of greater freedom but of home-grown dictatorship.[32] In addition, Belarusian Party chief Anatoly Malafeyeu was particularly vocal in calling for the imposition of a U.S.S.R.-wide state of emergency at the CPSU plenum in April. Malafeyeu, of course, was not alone, and Gorbachev's unwillingness to heed such calls from the archconservative camp was an important factor weeks later in the decision to stage a coup d'etat. But as an observer recently

---

[28] A description and chronology of the April strikes is contained in Kathleen Mihalisko. "The Workers' Rebellion in Belorussia." *Report on the USSR*, No. 17, April 26, 1991, pp.–21-25.

[29] See Kathleen Mihalisko, "Workers and Soviet Power: Notes from Minsk," *Report on the USSR*, No. 27, July 5, 1991, pp. 15–21.

[30] The text of the agreement was published in, among other sources, *Sovetskaya Belorussiya* and *Zvyazda*, May 14, 1991.

[31] BELTA news agency, May 14, 1991.

[32] "Workers and Soviet Power . . .," op. cit.

argued, the alarmed reaction of Belarusian leaders to the labor unrest in their normally placid republic fed directly into the larger events in Moscow to an extent that has generally been overlooked.[33]

THE COUP AND ITS AFTERMATH

In light of the foregoing discussion it should come as no surprise that the Belarusian Central Committee stood out during the events of August 19–21 for its barely concealed support for the aims of the State of Emergency Committee: it appealed to the republic's communists to understand the Committee's just concerns and published the decrees of the outlaw group until as late as August 22.[34] For their part, the Presidium of the Supreme Soviet and the government maintained a strict silence throughout the coup,[35] as if signalling a preparedness to adjust in the event of its success. Indeed, information that came to light after the coup collapsed demonstrated that the Ministry of Justice, the Ministry of Internal Security, and the State Committee for Radio and Television, among others, carried out the orders of the putsch leaders, while several other officials, notably Foreign Minister Petr Krauchenka, came within inches of compromising themselves.[36]

One of a very small handful of leading Belarusian officials who did not manage to survive the events of August was Dzemyantsei, who was forced to resign as Supreme Soviet chairman at the insistence of the opposition during an emergency session of parliament.[37] That cleared the way for Shushkevich to take over the post (a precedent-breaking event, insofar as he was not a product of the Central Committee apparatus and he made good on his promise to quit the Party), but the aftershocks of the coup scarcely stopped there. When news came of Gorbachev's resignation as general secretary and the suspension of the CPSU, Malafeyeu, though not a people's deputy, insisted that he be allowed to address parliament. On August 25, the Belarusian Party chief, heeding the instinct for self-preservation, called for Belarus to declare its political and economic independence and for the republican CP to sever its ties to the CPSU. The parliament speedily approved the first proposal, though not without voting—again, at the insistence of the BPF opposition—to temporarily suspend the activities of the Belarusian CP.

It was ironic, to say the least, that following an independence proclamation that was proposed by the Belarusian Party leader as

---

[33] See the commentary by Yurii Drakohrust in *Znamya yunosti*, May 12, 1992.

[34] *Sovetskaya Belorussiya*, August 22, 1991.

[35] The Presidium issued a belated and cautiously worded statement on August 21, by which time it was fairly clear that the State of Emergency Committee was losing its nerve and that Yeltsin would prevail.

[36] According to an open letter dated September 27 and signed by V. Yanovsky, an editor at *Belarus* magazine, it emerged that Krauchenka had intervened during the coup to halt the publication of an issue that was to feature an interview with the foreign minister on the development of Belarus's sovereignty policies. With the collapse of the coup, Krauchenka renewed interest in its publication—provided the interview was accompanied by a photograph of himself in conversation with Eduard Shevardnadze. Krauchenka had spent the eve of the coup in the company of Soviet Foreign Minister Aleksandr Bessmertnykh, then vacationing at a dacha in Belarus, though he subsequently denied that the two had discussed the events about to unfold. See *Zvyazda*, September 5, 1991.

[37] See Walter Stankievich. "The Events behind Belorussia's Independence Declaration," *Report on the USSR*, No. 38, September 20, 1991, pp. 24–26.

a ploy to try to escape the fate of the CPSU, Belarus acquired some of the attributes of a nation-state that had long been anathema to the communist regime. In September and October, all references to Soviet and socialist were struck from the republic's name and constitution; the long-banned flag and historical emblem of Belarus were elevated to official status; and a progressive new law on Belarusian citizenship was put in place. None of this meant, however, that the majority bloc in parliament had converted to the side of the national democratic faction. To the contrary, the political situation in Belarus at the end of 1991 had reached an impossible impasse, as Shushkevich no doubt was profoundly aware. That realization may well have factored into his decision to join forces with Yeltsin and Kravchuk, despite his assurances, as late as November 25, that Belarus was ready to sign a Union treaty without further ado.[38]

But to list all the ironies and contradictions present in Belarus during the final months of the Soviet Union would be a time-consuming task. Many are of continuing relevance today. As noted earlier, Kebich's government underwent no significant personnel changes after the coup, apart from a limited shakeup in the justice ministry. Not a few commentators in the liberal press have pointed out the irony of retaining a Council of Ministers staffed exclusively by members of the former Central Committee—the very same that had expressed approval for the aims of the coup. What is more, the findings of an official investigation into the conduct of Belarusian leaders and institutions in August, which constituted a damning indictment of the Communist regime overall, found their way only into a few relatively obscure newspapers; in effect the report was squelched.

CURRENT IMPERATIVES AND ISSUES

It is hoped that the above discussion has conveyed a sense of the political traditions inherited by post-Soviet Belarus. Yet another irony is that if there is a middle ground between the two polarities represented in the Supreme Soviet, it is largely occupied by the Belarusian public—but it is precisely the public that has few means to exercise power or influence. Approximately eight political parties exist,[39] but the largest of these, claiming some 14,000 members, is the recently registered Party of Communist Belarus, the successor to the outlawed Belarusian Communist Party;[40] it is led by a virulent reactionary, Viktor Chikin, formerly in charge of ideological affairs for the city of Minsk and editor of the newspaper *My i vremya*. The only noncommunist political party represented in the Supreme Soviet—the BPF being a movement, not a party—is the Social Democratic Society, with ten deputies drawn primarily from the cultural intelligentsia.

The BPF and a number of nascent political parties formed a committee in January, 1992, to collect the 350,000 signatures required by law to force the Supreme Soviet to call a nationwide referen-

---

[38] BELTA-TASS, November 25, 1991.
[39] The better known parties include the United Democratic Party, the Peasant Party, the Social Democrats, Christian Democrats, and the National Democratic Party.
[40] The statute of the PCB was published in *My i vremya*, No. 13, 1992.

dum. As noted earlier, the drive was successful, despite the rather complicated wording of the proposed referendum which would ask voters if they favored holding early, multiparty elections to parliament in the fall of 1992 and on the basis of a new electoral law drafted by the BPF faction. The Supreme Soviet abruptly terminated its session at the end of April, apparently in order to avoid putting the relevant draft law to a vote and setting a date for the referendum. But no matter the outcome, the issue of confidence in the country's elected representatives and government will not fade any time soon.

THE ECONOMIC CRISIS

In presenting their case for early elections to the public, referendum supporters frequently point to the deteriorating economic situation in Belarus—the result, they maintain, of "Minsk's dithering between Scylla and Charybdis on market-oriented reform." [41] What is certain is that the ongoing crisis stands in sharp contrast to the economic picture in Belarus before Moscow embarked on its course of reform. Indeed, as measured against Soviet standards, Belarus entered the Gorbachev era with an efficient economy, productive labor force, and a reputable capacity to meet production targets.[42] By the time the Soviet leader ushered in perestroika, Belarusian industrial and agricultural workers enjoyed incomes that were higher than the U.S.S.R. average.[43] Such rosy indicators have become a thing of the past: production was off by 14 percent at the start of 1992 and was heading, according to some calculations, for a catastrophic 25 percent decline.[44] National income also registered a drop of 12 percent in the first months of 1992, and there were dire predictions in the press of 500,000 unemployed by year's end.[45]

Few place the entire blame at Kebich's door, but there is growing impatience with what some believe to be a toe-in-the-water approach to market reform and privatization. In May 1992, for instance, a group of prominent Belarusian entrepreneurs, politicians, and journalists launched an independent East-West National Center for Strategic Initiatives, the aim of which is to devise an economic reform agenda and "prepare society for Belarus's integration with the world economy." [46] Officials defend their record by pointing out that several cornerstone pieces of legislation already are in place, including laws on enterprises, property ownership, investment activity and bankruptcy, in addition to a program for privatization. Belarus did not hesitate to apply for membership in the International Monetary Fund and seek credits from foreign governments, with Italy becoming the first—in April, 1992—to extend credit directly to Minsk.

In general, the government's case rests on the notion that Belarus should not leap too fast into the unknown, lest it reach an intolerable level of economic dislocation: it is a question of better safe than sorry. The privatization program for 1992 is a good exam-

[41] *Znamya yunosti,* April 8, 1992.
[42] See Mihalisko and Tedstrom, op. cit.
[43] SSSR v tsifrakh v 1987, Moscow, 1987.
[44] *Znamya yunosti,* March 11, 1992.
[45] *Ibid.*
[46] *Znamya yunosti,* May 15, 1992.

ple of the government's instincts to serve up economic liberalization in carefully measured doses. At stake are 147 state-owned plants worth a total 4.7 billion rubles. Enterprises comprising about half that total value were slated to become joint stock companies, while most of the remainder was to be sold to private concerns.[47] (For the sake of comparison, only 19 enterprises under the republic's jurisdiction were privatized in 1991, one year after Minsk proclaimed its intention to move to a market economy.) Economic officials also say that they are carefully studying the relative merits of the Hungarian, Polish, eastern German, and Czechoslovak approaches to privatization, and are experimenting with mixed private/communal arrangements.

STABILITY AS LEITMOTIF

It is somewhat unfortunate that the sharp debate under way in Belarus over the pace and nature of economic (and political) reform does not draw much attention from the West; certainly, Belarusians are constantly drawing the West, or, rather, what they perceive to be the interests of the West, into the arsenal of polemics. Hence, critics of Shuchkevich and Kebich charge that the West will not take more than a passing glance at Belarus if it does not pursue change more aggressively. They further maintain—and it is difficult to disagree—that neither leader has articulated a vision for the country's direction over the crucial next few years.

For their part, the heads of the Belarusian state and government have taken the concept of stability as their leitmotif. Both have repeatedly argued before domestic and international audiences that what makes Belarus attractive to potential Western partners and investors is its moderation, "reasonable behavior," and absence of economic and social turmoil. On those grounds, Shushkevich and Kebich have opposed the referendum and all other calls for the resignation of the government and the voluntary disbanding of the Supreme Soviet, which is not up for reelection until 1995. Though not against early elections as such, Shushkevich has stated they should wait until after the adoption of a new Belarusian constitution and be concurrent with the election of a president. That, in turn, raises the question of what kind of constitution can be expected from a parliament with a majority of communist loyalists. The issue, like so many others for Belarus, has become a vicious circle.

WHO ELSE CAN RUN THE COUNTRY?

Another issue falling into the category of vicious circle is the question touched on in the introduction to this paper: is it better to make do with "holdovers," who at least have accumulated experience in running the affairs of state and government, or does Belarus stand more in need of fresh ideas and faces? As the foregoing discussion has dwelt at length on the far from ideal backgrounds of the incumbents, a problem of a different nature should be underlined here. There is a great shortage of experienced specialists in fields where input and ideas free of ideological fetters are most

---

[47] The government's privatization program and concepts were described in *Sovetskaya Belorussiya*, March 17, 1992.

needed—economics, the social sciences, law and state administration, and security issues, to name a few. The Soviet Belarusian education system was not fashioned to produce theorists and thinkers on the grand scale: there is, for instance, an institute of economic administration in Minsk, once primarily concerned with the mechanisms of the planned economy, but students who wanted to study economic theory and comparative economics had to go to Moscow—where many if not most remained. The level of scholarship in the social and political sciences was deplorable and constrained, as suggested by the change in name last year of the Higher Party School to the Institute for Political Science and Social Administration.

It would not be just, however, to end the present survey of Belarus on such a pessimistic note. As Belarusians see it, the primary advantage of serving as the "coordinating center" of the Commonwealth of Independent States is that it draws the international community closer to Belarus—and vice versa. In short, the CIS is viewed not as an end in itself but as a useful mechanism to boost Belarus's standing among the leading nations of Europe and the rest of the world.[48] In the meantime, individuals and organizations, mainly from the younger generation, already have started to claim positions in which they hope to play a role in speeding up the transition from totalitarianism to democracy, from production targets to the free market. Much is dependent on the passing of the old guard into history and a sustained interest on the part of the West in encouraging this peaceable country to achieve its long-term aims.

---

[48] More information on Belarus and the CIS is provided in Kathleen Mihalisko, "The CIS and the Republics: Belarus," *RFE/FL Research Report,* No. 7, February 14, 1992, pp. 6–10; and "The Outlook for Independent Belarus," *RFE/RL Research Report,* No. 24, June 12, 1992, pp. 7–13.

PROFILES OF THE NEWLY INDEPENDENT STATES: ECONOMIC, SOCIAL, AND DEMOGRAPHIC CONDITIONS

by John Dunlop, Marc Rubin, Lee Schwartz, and David Zaslow [*]

CONTENTS

---

[*] John Dunlop, Marc Rubin, and David Zaslow are with the Center for International Research, U.S. Bureau of the Census. Lee Schwartz is with the Office of the Geographer, U.S. Department of State.

FIGURES

MAPS

SUMMARY AND INTRODUCTION

This report provides background information on economic, social and demographic conditions in the newly independent states of the former Soviet Union. In the interest of covering the widest possible array of topics,[1] we have gathered most data from as far back as the late Gorbachev period and updated, where appropriate and practicable, through August 1992. We also have tried to describe some of the historical forces producing trends in the data. Thus, this document serves as something of a current situation fact book and primer, but it makes no pretense to being an up-to- the-minute intelligence briefing.

The five major sections covered in this report are geography, population, quality of life, nationality and the economy. Given the general lack of knowledge about this area of the world, we decided to publish data in a detailed format, often down to the "oblast"

---

[1] We have not treated "agriculture" as a separate sector. This sector is dealt with by William Liefert, Allan Mustard, Christopher Goldthwaite, Barbara Severin, and Remy Jurenas in this volume.

(province) level. At the same time, we have tried to avoid overwhelming the reader with minutiae, so summaries are also provided at the republic level of aggregation. To orient the reader further to these topics, the former Soviet Union, as a whole, is generally retained as a reference point throughout the text and tables. In this context, comparative statements about the republics become meaningful because definitions of variables and methodologies for gathering and processing data are common and fairly well understood. Unfortunately, this orientation has limitations for users who wish to draw international comparisons. We caution the reader not to assume that Soviet statistics conform to Western practice, and, accordingly, we have placed caveats where the problems tend to be the most severe.

Most of the data found in this report come from official sources. We relied heavily on the statistical abstracts and other publications of the various republican Goskomstats: the official statistical agencies responsible for collecting and disseminating data. However, there are numerous clearly marked instances where we made estimates or reconstructions of official data.

Regions of the Former Soviet Union (as of January 1, 1992)

Russian Federation

Northern region
- Arkhangel'sk
- Nenets ASR
- Other Arkhangel'sk
- Vologda
- Murmansk
- Rep. of Karelia
- Komi SSR

Northwestern region
- 1–2 Leningrad
- 1 St.Petersburg city
- 2 Leningrad oblast
- 3 Novgorod
- 4 Pskov

Central region
- 5 Bryansk
- 6 Vladimir
- 7 Ivanovo
- 8 Kaluga
- 9 Kostroma
- 10–11 Moscow
- 10 Moscow city
- 11 Moscow oblast
- 12 Orel
- 13 Ryazan'
- 14 Smolensk
- 15 Tver'
- 16 Tula
- 17 Yaroslavl'

Volgo-Vyatsk region
- Kirov
- Nizhegorodsk
- 18 Rep. of Mariy El
- 19 Mordov SSR
- 20 Chuvash Rep.

Central Chernozem region
- 21 Belgorod
- 22 Voronezh
- 23 Kursk
- 24 Lipetsk
- 25 Tambov

Povolzhkiy region
- 26 Astrakhan'
- 27 Volgograd
- 28 Penza
- 29 Samara
- 30 Saratov
- 31 Ulyanovsk (Simbirsk)
- 32 Rep. of Kalmykia
- 33 Rep. of Tatarstan

North-Caucasus region
- 34–35 Krasnodar Kray
- 34 Rep. of Adygeya
- 35 Other Krasnodar Kray
- 36 Stavropol' Kray
- 37 Rostov
- 38 Rep. of Dagestan
- 39 Kabardino-Balkar Rep.
- 40 Karachayevo-Cherkess SSR
- 41 North-Ossetian SSR
- 42 Chechen-Ingush Rep.

Urals region
- 43 Kurgan
- 44 Orenburg
- 45–46 Perm'
- 45 Komi-Permyat AO
- 46 Other Perm'
- 47 Sverdlovsk (Yekaterinburg)
- 48 Chelyabinsk
- 49 Rep. of Bashkortostan
- 50 Udmurt Rep.

West Siberian region
- 51 Altay Kray
- 52 Kemerovo
- 53 Novosibirsk
- 54 Omsk
- 55 Tyumen'
- Khanti-Mansiysk AOkr
- Yamalo-Nenetsk Rep.
- 56 Other Tyumen'

East Siberian region
- 57 Rep. of Gorniy Altay
- Krasnoyarsk region
- Krasnoyarsk Kray
- Taymyr AOkr
- Evenki AO
- Other Krasnoyarsk Kray
- Irkutsk
- Ust-Ordynsk Buryat AOkr
- Other Irkutsk
- 58 Chita
- Aga Buryat AOkr
- Other Chita
- Rep. of Buryat
- Rep. of Tuva
- 59 Rep. of Khakasia

Far Eastern region
- 60 Primor Kray
- 61–62 Khabarovsk Kray
- 61 Yevreysk AO
- 62 Other Khabarovsk Kray
- 63–64 Amur
- 63 Kamchatka
- Koryak ASR
- Other Kamchatka
- 64 Magadan
- Chukotka ASR
- Other Magadan
- 65 Sakhalin
- Rep. of Sakha (Yakutia)
- 66 Kaliningrad

Ukraine

Donets-Dnieper region
- 67 Dnepropetrovsk
- 68 Donetsk
- 69 Zaporozh'ye
- 70 Kirovograd
- 71 Lugansk
- 72 Poltava
- 73 Sumy
- 74 Khar'kov

Southwestern region
- 75 Vinnitsa
- 76 Volyn'
- 77 Zhitomir
- 78 Zakarpat'ye
- 79 Ivano-Frankovsk
- 80 Kiev
- Kiev city
- Kiev oblast
- 81 L'vov
- 82 Rovno
- 83 Ternopol'
- 84 Khmel'nitskiy
- 85 Cherkassy
- 86 Chernigov
- 87 Chernovtsy

Southern region
- 88 Krym ASSR
- 89 Nikolayev
- 90 Odessa
- 91 Kherson

Belarus
- 92 Brest
- 93 Vitebsk
- 94 Gomel'
- 95 Grodno
- 96 Minsk
- Minsk city
- Minsk oblast
- 97 Mogilev

Moldova
- 98 Chisinau city
- 99

Lithuania
- 100 Vil'nyus city
- 101

Latvia
- 102 Riga city
- 103

Estonia
- 104 Tallinn city
- 105

Georgia
- 106 Tbilisi city
- 107 Abkhaz ASSR
- 108 Adzhar ASSR
- 109 South Ossetian AO
- 110 Republic territories

Azerbaijan
- 111 Baku city
- 112 Nakhichevan ASSR
- 113 Nagorno-Karabakh AO
- 114 Republic territories

Armenia
- 115 Yerevan city
- 116 Republic territories

Kazakhstan
- 117–118 Aktyubinsk
- 117 Alma-Ata city
- 118 Alma-Ata oblast
- 119 East Kazakhstan
- 120 Gur'yev
- 121 Dzhambul
- 122 Dzhezkazgan
- Gur. Karaganda Kzyl-Orda
- 123 Kokchetav
- 124 Kustanay
- 125 Mangistausk
- 126 Pavlodar
- North Kazakhstan
- Semipalatinsk
- 127 Taldy-Kurgan
- Turgay
- Ural'sk
- Tselinograd
- Chimkent

Uzbekistan
- 128 Andizhan
- 129 Bukhara
- 130 Dzhizak
- 131 Kashkadar'ya
- 132 Namangan
- 133 Samarkand
- 134 Surkhandar'ya
- 130 Syrdar'ya
- 135–136 Tashkent
- 135 Tashkent city
- 136 Tashkent oblast
- 137 Fergana
- 138 Khorezm
- 139 Karakalpak ASSR

Kyrgyzstan
- 140 Bishkek city
- 141 Issyk-Kul'
- 141 Naryn
- 142 Dzhalal-Abad
- 142 Osh
- 143 Talas
- 143 Republic territories

Tajikistan
- 144 Gorno-Badakhstan AO
- 145 Dushanbe city
- 146–147 Khatlon
- 146 Kulyab
- 147 Kurgan-Tyube
- 148 Khudzhand
- 149 Republic territories

Turkmenistan
- 150 Ashkhabad city
- 151 Mary
- 152 Tashauz
- 153 Chardzhou
- 154 Balkan
- 154 Republic territories

Other
- 155 Aral Sea
- 156 Caspian Sea
- 157 Lake Baikal
- 158 Lake Balkash

Notes: Gur.—This oblast is shown as part of the Gur'yev oblast on the map; ASR—Autonomous Soviet Socialist Republic; ASSR—Autonomous Soviet Socialist Republic; SSR—Soviet Socialist Republic; AO—Autonomous Oblast; AOkr—Autonomous Okrug.

MAP 1: REGIONS OF THE FORMER SOVIET UNION

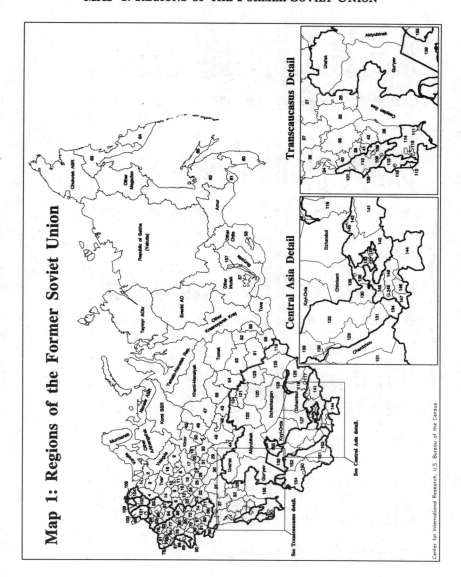

Map 1: Regions of the Former Soviet Union

Transcaucasus Detail

Central Asia Detail

Center for International Research, U.S. Bureau of the Census

I. GEOGRAPHY AND ADMINISTRATIVE STRUCTURE [2]

RUSSIAN FEDERATION

The Russian Federation (or Russia) is the largest of the 15 former Soviet republics stretching from the eastern borders of Europe all the way to the Pacific. It has an area of about 17,075,400 square kilometers, comprising over three quarters of the entire land mass of the former U.S.S.R.; Russia alone is still larger than any country in the world. Finland and the Estonian, Latvian, Belorussian, and Ukrainian republics are its western neighbors; the Georgian and Azerbaijani republics are located along its southern, Transcaucasus border; Kazakhstan shares a common frontier with European Russia and western Siberia to the south; and finally, Mongolia and China border parts of Siberia in the south and southeast.

Russia has the most administrative divisions of any of the former Soviet republics. It is divided into 74 separate regions (49 oblasts, 6 krays, and 19 autonomous republics). [3] Moreover, 10 of these oblasts and krays have one or two autonomous sub-regions (autonomous republics, autonomous oblasts, and/or autonomous okrugs).

UKRAINE

Ukraine is 603,700 square kilometers, nearly the size of Texas and larger than any other European state outside of the former Soviet Union. The territory of Ukraine extends westward from the shores of the Black Sea and the Sea of Azov to the Carpathian Mountains and beyond where it borders Poland, Slovakia, and Hungary. Romania and the republic of Moldova lie to the south and Belarus is Ukraine's northern neighbor; Russia shares over 1,000 kilometers of the border to the east. Ukraine ranked second in the former Soviet Union in population, and third in area, behind Russia and Kazakhstan. Ukraine is divided into 24 oblasts and one autonomous region (the Crimean ASSR); these are further broken down, administratively, into 481 rayons (1991) in which there are 436 cities.

BELARUS

The Republic of Belarus (formerly Byelorussia) is 207,600 square kilometers, about the size of Kansas, making it the sixth largest republic of the former Soviet Union. Belarus has five neighbors: Poland to the west, Russia to the east, Lithuania and Latvia to the north, and Ukraine to the south. It is a compact, landlocked territory, centered on the capital and largest city of Minsk. Along with the Russians and Ukrainians, the Belorussians ("White" Russians)

---

[2] The country and republic names for the former Soviet Union and new states may be confusing. In this report, we use the following designations: the whole former Soviet Union may be referred to as the Newly Independent States (NIS), depending on the time frame and context. The former republics/new states are referred to by their current names and spellings. The more significant changes in the names are noted in Section I. The Commonwealth of Independent States is a less inclusive term than former Soviet Union or Newly Independent States. The Commonwealth excludes the Baltics and Georgia. References to the Commonwealth (CIS) is occasionally referred to in this report because some of the data presented here are from the statistical office of the Commonwealth.

[3] The major administrative divisions of the former Soviet Union are oblasts, generally analogous to provinces or counties, krays, rayons, and autonomous regions.

were the Soviet Union's third major eastern Slavic group, which together comprised 70 percent of the U.S.S.R.'s total population in 1989. Belarus was one of 19 Soviet economic regions formed in 1963, and administratively is divided into 6 oblasts, 118 rayons, 99 cities, and the capital city of Minsk.

MOLDOVA

Of all the former Soviet republics, Moldova (formerly Moldavia) is only larger than Armenia. At 33,700 square kilometers, it is about twice the size of New Jersey. Moldova is a landlocked strip of territory lying in the southwest portion of an ancient structural block known as the Russian Platform. The Prut River forms its western (Romanian) border and the Dniester River roughly delimits its Ukrainian frontier. Lying just to the east of the great arc of the Carpathian Mountains, Moldova is in the hinterland of the Ukrainian port of Odessa. Despite this proximity, most of the republic's economic and political activity is centered around its own capital city, Chisinau. The territory of Moldova contains no oblast divisions, but consists of 40 rayons and 21 cities.

LITHUANIA

Lithuania is the largest, southernmost, and most populous of the three Baltic states. With a land area of 65,200 thousand square kilometers (about the size of West Virginia), it is just slightly larger than Latvia, and ranked eleventh of the 15 Soviet republics in both size and population. It is a coastal state wedged between the Baltic Sea in the west, Latvia in the north, Belarus in the south and east, and Poland in the south and west. As of January 1, 1990, Lithuania was divided administratively into 44 rural districts and 11 cities, all of which came under direct jurisdiction of the republic.

LATVIA

Latvia is the "middle" Baltic state in terms of size, population, and geographic location. It is situated between Estonia and the Gulf of Riga to the north and Lithuania to the south. Russia and Belarus border Latvia to the east and the Baltic Sea lies to its west. At 64,500 square kilometers (about the size of West Virginia), Latvia ranked twelfth in area of the 15 Soviet republics, larger than only Estonia, Armenia, and Moldova. Latvia is organized into 8 broad administrative regions.

ESTONIA

Estonia is the northernmost and smallest of the three Baltic states, which are located along the northwestern border of the former Soviet Union. With an area of about 45,100 square kilometers (about the size of New Hampshire and Vermont combined), it is one of the smaller states in Europe, and ranked thirteenth in size and last in population of the 15 former Soviet republics. Estonia is bounded on the north by the Gulf of Finland and on the west by the Baltic Sea and the Gulf of Riga; Latvia is Estonia's southern neighbor while Russia borders it to the east. Administratively, Estonia is organized into 6 cities and 15 other districts.

GEORGIA

Lying at the eastern end of the Black Sea and occupying the western portion of Transcaucasus, Georgia is a country of high mountains, fertile valleys, and a complicated political geography. Its area of 69,700 square kilometers (about the size of South Carolina) placed it tenth in size of all the republics of the former Soviet Union. It is located approximately at the same latitude as the city of Rome (41° 52' N). The republic is bounded on the north by Russia, on the east and southeast by Azerbaijan and Armenia, and on the southwest by Turkey. In the north, Georgia is bounded by the barrier formed by the Greater Caucasus Mountains and in the south, by the Lesser Caucasus system.

In terms of its current territorial-administrative structure, Georgia consists of 65 rayons and 61 cities, including those of the Abkhaz Autonomous Republic (5 rayons and 6 cities, with its capital at Sukhumi), the Adzhar Autonomous Republic (5 rayons and 2 cities, with its capital at Batumi), and the South Ossetian Autonomous Oblast (4 rayons and its capital of Tskhinvali).

AZERBAIJAN

With an area of 86,600 square kilometers (a little larger than Maine and about the same size as Portugal), Azerbaijan placed ninth in size of the republics of the former Soviet Union. It occupies the eastern corner of the Transcaucasus, making Russia its northern and Armenia its western neighbors. It is bounded in the east by the Central Asian Muslim republics and the waters of the Caspian Sea. To the south lies the Azerbaijan region of Iran.

The complex political geography of Azerbaijan includes the Nagorno-Karabakh Autonomous Oblast (population 175,000, three-quarters of which was Armenian in 1989) and the Nakhichevan Autonomous Republic, an Azeri exclave created by a corridor of Armenian territory. The republic is divided, administratively, into 61 rayons and 63 cities. This overall structure embraces the Nagorno-Karabakh Autonomous Oblast (5 rayons and 4 cities, including its capital of Stepanakert), the Nakhichevan Autonomous Republic (5 rayons and 4 cities, including its capital of Nakhichevan), the remaining rayons and the coastal capital city of Baku.

ARMENIA

At only 29,800 square kilometers (about the size of Maryland), Armenia was the smallest of all the republics of the former Soviet Union, occupying only 0.13 percent of its territory. Armenia lies in the south central portion of the Transcaucasus region; to the north and east it is bounded by Georgia and Azerbaijan and to the west and south by Turkey and Iran. Armenia's shape effectively fragments its eastern neighbor, Azerbaijan, into two parts, with Armenian territory cutting off the Nakhichevan Autonomous Republic from the rest of Azerbaijan proper. Armenia occupies some of the most rugged and earthquake-prone territory of the Transcaucasus region. Its capital, Yerevan, is located on the banks of the Razdan River within site of the Turkish border. Across this western border lies the ethnically Armenian portion of Turkey (147,630 square kilometers), which is the site of Mount Ararat, a landmark symbolically important for the Armenian nation and the highest point in the region. In terms of its territorial-administrative units, Armenia is divided into 37 rayons and 27 cities.

KAZAKHSTAN

Kazakhstan was the second largest republic in the U.S.S.R., at 2,717,000 square kilometers larger than all of Western Europe, over twice the size of Alaska, and about four times the size of Texas. Its total area is more than that of all the other republics combined, with the exception of Russia. Although it ranked fourth in total population (16.8 million—January 1, 1991 estimate), its tremendous extent made Kazakhstan the least densely settled (6.2 persons per square kilometer) republic of the former Soviet Union. Kazakhstan is located deep in the Eurasian continent, nearly equidistant from the Atlantic and Pacific Oceans. At its greatest expanse, the territory of Kazakhstan stretches over 1,000 miles from north to south and nearly 2,000 miles from west to east. It is bounded on the north by the Volga, Urals, and West Siberian regions of Russia, and on the south by the Central Asian republics of Turkmenistan, Uzbekistan, Tajikistan, and Kyrgyzstan. Kazakhstan stretches from the Caspian Sea in the west to the Xinjiang Province of China in the east. As of January 1, 1991, Kazakhstan was divided administratively into 19 oblasts which contained 211 rayons, 84 cities, and the capital at Alma-Ata.

UZBEKISTAN

Uzbekistan is a land of desert landscapes interspersed with fertile oases. It is located in the heart of Central Asia between the region's two major rivers: the Amu Dar'ya to the southwest and the Syr Dar'ya to the northeast. Uzbekistan's area of 447,400 square kilometers (about the size of California) made it the fifth largest Soviet republic. Uzbekistan is bounded on the north and northwest by Kazakhstan, on the east and southeast by Kyrgyzstan and Tajikistan, on the west and southwest by Turkmenistan, and, for a short distance in the south, by Afghanistan. Administratively, Uzbekistan is broken down into one autonomous republic, (Karakalpak Autonomous Republic), 11 oblasts, 149 rayons, 124 cities, and the capital city of Tashkent.

KYRGYZSTAN

Kyrgyzstan is located in the mountainous southeastern corner of Central Asia, bounded by Kazakhstan to the north and northwest, Uzbekistan to the west, Tajikistan to the southwest and south, and the Xinjiang Province of the People's Republic of China to the east and southeast. At 198,500 square kilometers (about the size of Nebraska), Kyrgyzstan ranked seventh in area of all the Soviet republics, but was the second smallest (behind Tajikistan) east of the Urals. Most of its borders run along the crests of mountains, except where they extend to encompass the only lowland areas of the region, the Chu Valley in the north, the Talas Valley in the northwest, and the Fergana Valley in the west. Lowland regions occupy only 15 percent of Kyrgyz territory, but have tremendous significance in terms of settlement and agriculture.

In December of 1990 a new territorial-administrative structure was established on Kyrgyz territory. Two oblasts (Naryn and Talas) that had been abolished in 1988 were reestablished; the two oblasts which were existing at that time (Issyk-Kul' and Osh) had their areas reduced; an oblast that had been abolished in 1959 (Dzhalal-Abad) was recreated; and an entirely new oblast (Chu) was formed, largely out of 13 rayons that had previously been under the direct subordination of the republic. Altogether, the 6 oblasts of Kyrgyzstan contain 27 rayons and 21 cities. Thus, in less than 4 years Kyrgyzstan's internal territorial structure has shifted from a set of four oblasts (Naryn, Talas, Osh, and Issyk-Kul', as well as the capital, Bishkek, and several rayons administered directly by the republic), to two oblasts (Issyk-Kul' and Osh, plus Bishkek and an expanded number of "rayons of republic subordination"), to the 6 oblasts (plus Bishkek) in existence by January, 1991.

TAJIKISTAN

Tajikistan lies in the mountainous heart of Central Asia, bounded by China on the east, Afghanistan on the south, and Uzbekistan and Kyrgyzstan on the west and north. Its area of 143,000 square kilometers is about the same as Wisconsin. Of the 15 republics of the former Soviet Union, Tajikistan ranked eighth in size (as it also did in population), and is the smallest of the Central Asian republics. Tajikistan (as of January 1, 1991) was administratively divided into 4 oblasts containing 37 rayons and 14 cities, in addition to 8 rayons (containing 4 cities) and the capital city of Dushanbe, which come under the direct subordination of the republic.

TURKMENISTAN

Turkmenistan is a landlocked desert country slightly larger than California in area (488,100 square kilometers). It extends from the shores of the Caspian Sea in the west to the Amu Dar'ya along the border of Uzbekistan in the east, and occupies the southwest corner of what formerly was Soviet Central Asia. Turkmenistan is bounded in the north by Kazakhstan and by the Karakalpak Republic of Uzbekistan; to the south, high mountains (including the Kopet Dag range) separate it from Iran and Afghanistan. The capital, Ashkhabad (Ashgabat), and Kushka were respectively the former Soviet Union's southernmost capital and southernmost metropolis. Turkmenistan ranked fourth in area and twelfth in population of the republics of the former Soviet Union. The combination of these two features produced an average density of 7.4 persons per square kilometer (January 1, 1990) making Turkmenistan the second least densely populated (after Kazakhstan) of the former Soviet republics.

Prior to becoming a Soviet republic at the end of 1924, Turkmenistan occupied part of the region of what was known as Turkestan. The division of Turkmenistan into modern oblasts took place in 1939, with the creation of Ashkhabad, Chardzhou, Krasnovodsk, Mary, and Tashauz Oblasts. Since that time there have been several administrative reorganizations; the most recent abolished Ashkhabad and Krasnovodsk Oblasts and placed their rayons under the direct subordination of the republic. As of January 1, 1990, Turkmenistan consisted of 3 oblasts (which contained 28 rayons and 8 cities), and an additional 13 rayons (with 8 cities including the capital) which were administered by Ashkhabad.

II. POPULATION

A. BASIC POPULATION CHARACTERISTICS

With a population of over 290 million people at the beginning of 1991, the U.S.S.R. was the third largest country in the world. Between 1979 and 1989 (the two most recent census years), the U.S.S.R.'s population grew an average nine-tenths of a percent annually. Between 1989 and January 1, 1991 (the date of the most recent official population estimate for the entire country), the population grew an average of six-tenths of a percent per year. By the year 2010, the population of all 15 states that made up the former Soviet Union is projected to grow to 321 million people.

Significant regional differences in population trends and characteristics exist within the former Soviet Union (Tables 1 and 2). Population growth was higher in the Central Asian republics than in other regions of the country. This region grew an average of 2.1 percent per year between 1979 and 1989, with Tajikistan having grown the fastest at 3 percent per year. The northwest regions (Ukraine, Belarus, and the Baltic republics) grew at the slowest rate. Additional regional differences exist as well.

The majority of the population of the former Soviet Union is concentrated in the lower growth areas—the European (except in Russia, east of the Ural mountains) and Transcaucasus regions. The Central Asian republics, on the other hand, are the least densely populated republics.

The overall ratio of males to females is less than one, as is the case in many developed countries. However, the Siberian regions of Russia (areas east of the Ural mountains) generally have a significantly higher ratio of males to females than the rest of the former U.S.S.R. This is due in large part to the fact that economic activity in Siberia is heavily oriented toward extractive industries with physical demands on a predominantly male labor force.

Despite its limited population, Siberia is generally more urbanized than the rest of the country because the industrial and natural resource extraction operations there tend to be site specific and require large numbers of workers. Finally, the Central Asian region is the least urbanized due to the central importance of agriculture and the nomadic traditions of its people.

Relative to the U.S.S.R., many areas in Siberia have below-average dependency ratios [4] and all have low percentages of elderly persons, many less than 10 percent (Table 2). The highest proportion of elderly along with above-average dependency ratios are found in the western regions near Moscow. As would be expected, the areas with the largest family sizes, such as Central Asia, also have the highest proportion of young people.

---

[4] See the notes in Table 2 for a definition of dependency, as well as for definitions for young and old.

TABLE 1. Population, 1979–91.

Geographical Unit	1979 Total Population (1000)	1989 Total Population (1000)	1979–89 Average Annual Growth	1989 Population Density (persons per square km.)	1989 Urban Population (percent)	1991 Total Population (1000)
	(1)	(2)	(3)	(4)	(5)	(6)
U.S.S.R. [1]	262,085	286,731	0.9	12.8	65.9	290,076
EUROPEAN USSR [2]	207,860	221,589	0.6	12.2	70.8	223,104
TRANSCAUCASUS [2]	14,057	15,761	1.2	84.7	57.5	15,977
CENTRAL ASIA [2]	40,167	49,381	2.1	12.4	45.5	50,995
RUSSIAN FEDERATION	137,410	147,400	0.7	8.6	73.6	148,543
Northern economic region	5,596	6,123	0.9	4.2	76.5	6,161
Arkhangel'sk	1,466	1,570	0.7	2.7	73.4	1,577
Nenets ASR	47	55	1.5	0.3	61.8	55
Other Arkhangel'sk	1,419	1,515	0.7	3.7	73.8	1,522
Vologda	1,309	1,354	0.3	9.3	65.1	1,361
Murmansk	978	1,147	1.6	7.9	92.1	1,159
Republic of Karelia	732	791	0.8	4.6	81.7	799
Komi SSR	1,110	1,261	1.3	3.0	75.5	1,265
Northwestern economic region	7,654	8,284	0.8	42.2	86.6	8,305
Leningrad	6,081	6,685	1.0	77.8	91.5	6,705
St.Petersburg city	4,569	5,024	1.0	NA	100.0	5,035
Leningrad oblast	1,513	1,661	0.9	19.3	65.9	1,670
Novgorod	722	753	0.4	13.6	69.6	755
Pskov	851	846	−0.1	15.3	63.1	845
Central economic region	28,871	30,386	0.5	62.6	82.5	30,478
Bryansk	1,509	1,475	−0.2	42.3	67.3	1,464
Vladimir	1,586	1,654	0.4	57.0	79.2	1,660
Ivanovo	1,324	1,317	−0.1	55.1	81.6	1,316
Kaluga	1,008	1,067	0.6	35.7	68.9	1,080
Kostroma	802	810	0.1	13.5	68.5	813
Moscow	14,266	15,661	0.9	333.2	91.2	15,722
Moscow city	7,932	8,967	1.2	NA	100.0	9,003
Moscow oblast	6,334	6,694	0.6	142.4	79.3	6,718
Orel	895	891	0.0	36.1	62.3	901
Ryazan'	1,366	1,346	−0.1	34.0	65.8	1,349
Smolensk	1,116	1,158	0.4	23.3	68.0	1,166
Tver' [3]	1,659	1,670	0.1	19.9	100.0	1,676
Tula	1,908	1,867	−0.2	72.6	81.0	1,855
Yaroslavl'	1,433	1,470	0.3	40.4	81.6	1,476
Volgo-Vyatsk economic region	8,371	8,457	0.1	32.1	68.9	8,481
Kirov	1,667	1,693	0.2	14.0	69.9	1,700
Nizhegorodsk [4]	3,712	3,714	0.0	49.7	77.2	3,712
Republic of Mariy El	704	749	0.6	32.3	61.1	758
Mordov SSR	990	965	−0.3	36.8	56.6	964
Chuvash Republic	1,299	1,336	0.3	73.0	57.9	1,346
Central Chernozem economic region	7,807	7,741	−0.1	46.2	60.3	7,761
Belgorod	1,308	1,381	0.5	51.0	63.1	1,401
Voronezh	2,483	2,470	−0.1	47.1	60.9	2,474
Kursk	1,395	1,339	−0.4	44.9	57.9	1,336
Lipetsk	1,227	1,230	0.0	51.0	62.6	1,234
Tambov	1,393	1,321	−0.5	38.5	56.3	1,315
Povolzhkiy economic region	15,568	16,409	0.5	30.6	73.3	16,586
Astrakhan'	915	998	0.9	22.6	68.1	1,007
Volgograd	2,478	2,593	0.5	22.8	75.9	2,633
Penza	1,510	1,504	0.0	34.8	62.0	1,512
Samara [5]	3,094	3,266	0.5	60.9	80.8	3,290
Saratov	2,563	2,686	0.5	26.8	74.3	2,708
Ulyanovsk (Simbirsk)	1,268	1,401	1.0	37.6	71.4	1,430
Republic of Kalmykia (Khalmg Tangch)	295	323	0.9	4.2	45.8	329
Republic of Tatarstan	3,445	3,638	0.5	53.5	73.0	3,679
North-Caucasus economic region	15,362	16,751	0.9	47.2	57.3	17,030
Krasnodar Kray	4,744	5,113	0.8	61.2	54.3	5,175
Adygeya SSR	404	432	0.7	56.8	52.1	437
Other Krasnodar Kray	4,339	4,681	0.8	60.8	54.5	4,737

TABLE 1. Population, 1979-91.—Continued

Geographical Unit	1979 Total Population (1000)	1989 Total Population (1000)	1979-89 Average Annual Growth	1989 Population Density (persons per square km.)	1989 Urban Population (percent)	1991 Total Population (1000)
	(1)	(2)	(3)	(4)	(5)	(6)
Stavropol' Kray [6]	2,130	2,440	1.4	36.2	54.5	2,499
Rostov	4,079	4,308	0.5	42.7	71.3	4,348
Republic of Dagestan	1,628	1,803	1.0	35.8	43.6	1,854
Kabardino-Balkar Republic	667	760	1.3	60.8	61.2	778
Karachayevo-Cherkess SSR [6]	367	417	1.3	29.4	48.7	427
North-Ossetian SSR	592	634	0.7	79.3	68.8	643
Chechen-Ingush Republic	1,156	1,276	1.0	66.1	41.5	1,307
Urals economic region	19,399	20,279	0.4	24.6	74.7	20,397
Kurgan	1,080	1,105	0.2	15.6	54.8	1,111
Orenburg	2,088	2,174	0.4	17.5	65.0	2,194
Perm'	3,008	3,100	0.3	19.3	77.3	3,109
Komi-Permyat AO	172	160	-0.7	1.7	30.0	160
Other Perm'	2,836	2,940	0.4	43.1	79.9	2,949
Sverdlovsk (Yekaterinburg)	4,455	4,717	0.6	24.2	87.1	4,730
Chelyabinsk	3,431	3,624	0.5	41.2	82.5	3,641
Republic of Bashkortostan [7]	3,844	3,950	0.3	27.5	63.8	3,984
Udmurt Republic	1,492	1,609	0.8	38.2	69.7	1,628
West Siberian economic region	12,973	15,003	1.5	6.2	72.8	15,158
Altay Kray [8]	2,514	2,630	0.5	15.6	58.2	2,655
Kemerovo	2,958	3,176	0.7	33.3	87.4	3,180
Novosibirsk	2,620	2,782	0.6	15.6	74.7	2,796
Omsk	1,957	2,141	0.9	15.3	67.8	2,163
Tomsk	867	1,002	1.5	3.2	69.0	1,012
Tyumen'	1,885	3,080	5.0	2.1	76.0	3,156
Khanti-Mansiysk AOkr	571	1,268	8.3	2.5	90.9	1,314
Yamalo-Nenetsk Republic	159	486	11.8	0.7	78.0	493
Other Tyumen'	1,156	1,326	1.4	8.2	61.1	1,349
Republic of Gornyy Altay [8]	172	192	1.1	2.1	27.1	197
East Siberian economic region	8,156	9,155	1.2	2.2	71.9	9,243
Krasnoyarsk Kray [9]	2,700	3,027	1.1	1.3	72.9	3,048
Taymyr AOkr	45	55	2.0	0.1	67.3	54
Evenki AO	16	24	4.2	0.0	29.2	25
Other Krasnoyarsk Kray	2,639	2,948	1.1	4.2	73.4	2,969
Irkutsk	2,558	2,831	1.0	3.7	80.5	2,863
Ust-Ordynsk Buryat AOkr	132	136	0.3	6.1	18.4	138
Other Irkutsk	2,426	2,695	1.1	3.6	83.6	2,725
Chita	1,232	1,378	1.1	3.2	65.2	1,392
Aga Buryat AOkr	69	77	1.1	4.1	32.5	78
Other Chita	1,163	1,301	1.1	3.1	67.2	1,315
Buryat SSR	899	1,041	1.5	3.0	61.5	1,056
Republic of Tuva	268	309	1.4	1.8	46.9	307
Republic of Khakasia [9]	498	569	1.3	9.2	72.4	577
Far Eastern economic region	6,845	7,941	1.5	1.3	75.8	8,057
Primor Kray	1,977	2,259	1.3	13.6	77.5	2,300
Khabarovsk Kray	1,558	1,824	1.6	2.2	78.4	1,851
Yevreysk AO	189	216	1.4	5.9	66.2	220
Other Khabarovsk Kray	1,369	1,608	1.6	2.0	80.0	1,631
Amur	936	1,058	1.2	2.9	67.7	1,074
Kamchatka	384	466	2.0	1.0	81.3	473
Koryak ASR	35	39	1.1	0.1	38.5	40
Other Kamchatka	349	427	2.0	2.5	85.2	433
Magadan	477	543	1.3	0.5	81.0	534
Chukotsk ASR	140	157	1.2	0.2	72.6	154
Other Magadan	337	386	1.4	0.8	84.5	380
Sakhalin	662	710	0.7	8.2	82.4	718
Republic of Sakha (Yakutia) [10]	852	1,081	2.4	0.3	66.7	1,109
Kaliningrad	808	871	0.8	57.7	79.1	887
UKRAINE	49,609	51,704	0.4	85.2	66.9	51,944
Donets-Dnieper economic region	21,014	21,778	0.4	98.1	79.1	21,853

TABLE 1. Population, 1979–91.—Continued

Geographical Unit	1979 Total Population (1000)	1989 Total Population (1000)	1979–89 Average Annual Growth	1989 Population Density (persons per square km.)	1989 Urban Population (percent)	1991 Total Population (1000)
	(1)	(2)	(3)	(4)	(5)	(6)
Dnepropetrovsk	3,639	3,883	0.7	121.3	83.3	3,909
Donetsk	5,150	5,328	0.3	197.3	90.3	5,347
Zaporozh'ye	1,950	2,081	0.7	77.1	75.8	2,100
Kirovograd	1,241	1,240	0.0	49.6	59.9	1,245
Lugansk [11]	2,788	2,864	0.3	106.1	86.4	2,871
Poltava	1,741	1,753	0.1	60.4	56.5	1,757
Sumy	1,465	1,433	-0.2	59.7	61.8	1,430
Khar'kov	3,040	3,196	0.5	103.1	78.6	3,195
Southwestern economic region	21,522	22,257	0.3	82.1	55.1	22,305
Vinnitsa	2,039	1,932	-0.5	71.6	44.4	1,914
Volyn	1,016	1,062	0.4	53.1	48.9	1,069
Zhitomir	1,594	1,545	-0.3	51.5	52.9	1,511
Zakarpat'ye	1,156	1,252	0.8	96.3	41.1	1,266
Ivano-Frankovsk	1,327	1,424	0.7	101.7	42.0	1,443
Kiev	4,045	4,084	0.1	140.8	78.0	4,590
Kiev city	2,120	2,144	0.1	NA	100.0	2,643
Kiev oblast	1,925	1,940	0.1	66.9	53.7	1,946
L'vov	2,569	2,748	0.7	124.9	59.3	2,764
Rovno	1,118	1,170	0.5	58.5	45.3	1,177
Ternopol'	1,162	1,169	0.1	83.5	40.8	1,175
Khmel'nitskiy	1,556	1,527	-0.2	72.7	47.3	1,521
Cherkassy	1,545	1,532	-0.1	73.0	52.9	1,531
Chernigov	1,499	1,416	-0.6	44.3	53.4	1,406
Chernovtsy	897	938	0.5	117.3	42.1	939
Southern economic region	7,074	7,669	0.8	67.3	66.4	7,786
Krym ASSR	2,136	2,456	1.4	91.0	69.8	2,550
Nikolayev	1,243	1,331	0.7	53.2	65.7	1,342
Odessa	2,528	2,642	0.4	80.1	66.0	2,635
Kherson	1,166	1,240	0.6	42.8	61.2	1,259
BELARUS	9,533	10,200	0.7	49.0	65.5	10,260
Brest	1,360	1,458	0.7	45.6	56.5	1,484
Vitebsk	1,385	1,413	0.2	35.3	64.5	1,434
Gomel'	1,595	1,674	0.5	41.9	63.9	1,628
Grodno	1,127	1,171	0.4	46.8	57.2	1,189
Minsk	2,818	3,199	1.3	78.0	73.6	3,256
Minsk city	1,273	1,612	2.4	NA	100.0	1,658
Minsk oblast	1,545	1,587	0.3	38.7	46.9	1,598
Mogilev	1,247	1,285	0.3	44.3	65.8	1,269
MOLDOVA	3,950	4,341	0.9	127.7	46.9	4,366
Chisinau city [12]	506	720	3.6	NA	98.8	754
LITHUANIA	3,391	3,690	0.8	58.6	68.0	3,728
Vil'nyus city	476	582	2.0	NA	100.0	NA
LATVIA	2,503	2,681	0.7	41.9	71.1	2,681
Riga city	828	915	1.0	NA	100.0	910
ESTONIA	1,464	1,573	0.7	35.0	71.6	1,582
Tallinn city	442	503	1.3	NA	100.0	502
GEORGIA	4,993	5,449	0.9	75.7	55.7	5,464
Tbilisi city	1,056	1,264	1.8	NA	100.0	1,283
Abkhaz ASSR	486	537	1.0	59.7	47.7	534
Adzhar ASSR	354	393	1.0	131.0	46.1	381
South Ossetian AO	98	99	0.1	24.8	50.5	NA
Republic territories	2,999	3,156	0.5	56.4	40.6	NA
AZERBAIJAN	6,027	7,029	1.6	80.8	53.8	7,137
Baku city	1,533	1,757	1.4	NA	100.0	1,713
Nakhichevan ASSR	240	295	2.1	49.2	30.2	306
Nagorno-Karabakh AO	162	188	1.5	47.0	51.6	194
Republic territories	4,091	4,789	1.6	62.2	38.5	4,924
ARMENIA	3,037	3,283	0.8	109.4	67.8	3,376
Yerevan city	1,031	1,215	1.7	NA	99.3	NA

TABLE 1. Population, 1979–91.—Continued

Geographical Unit	1979 Total Population (1000)	1989 Total Population (1000)	1979–89 Average Annual Growth	1989 Population Density (persons per square km.)	1989 Urban Population (percent)	1991 Total Population (1000)
	(1)	(2)	(3)	(4)	(5)	(6)
KAZAKHSTAN [13]	14,684	16,538	1.2	6.1	57.2	16,793
Aktyubinsk	630	738	1.6	2.5	54.1	753
Alma-Ata	1,750	2,110	1.9	20.1	63.9	2,154
Alma-Ata city	900	1,132	2.3	NA	100.0	1,160
Alma-Ata oblast	850	978	1.4	9.3	22.1	993
East Kazakhstan	879	934	0.6	9.6	65.0	949
Gur'yev [14]	370	755	—	2.7	72.6	447
Dzhambul	931	1,050	1.2	7.3	47.4	1,056
Dzhezkazgan	449	496	1.0	1.6	78.2	496
Karaganda [15]	1,255	1,352	—	11.5	84.8	1,340
Kzyl-Orda	562	651	1.5	2.9	64.8	665
Kokchetav	616	664	0.8	8.5	39.2	669
Kustanay [15]	943	1,221	—	10.6	50.5	1,074
Mangistausk [14]	253	—	—	—	—	332
Pavlodar	807	944	1.6	7.4	64.1	957
North Kazakhstan	573	600	0.5	13.6	47.8	610
Semipalatinsk	773	838	0.8	4.7	51.2	842
Taldy-Kurgan	663	721	0.8	6.1	45.1	731
Turgay [15]	270	—	—	—	—	305
Ural'sk	586	631	0.8	4.2	42.6	648
Tselinograd [15]	809	1,002	—	10.9	57.1	794
Chimkent	1,565	1,831	1.6	15.8	40.7	1,879
UZBEKISTAN	15,389	19,906	2.6	44.5	40.7	20,708
Andizhan	1,355	1,728	2.5	411.4	32.3	1,795
Bukhara	1,267	1,141	–1.0	8.0	34.8	1,708
Dzhizak [16]	512	—	—	—	—	780
Kashkadar'ya	1,124	1,594	3.6	56.1	26.0	1,698
Namangan	1,101	1,475	3.0	186.7	37.3	1,558
Samarkand	1,782	2,778	4.5	113.4	33.3	2,386
Surkhandar'ya	897	1,255	3.4	60.3	19.5	1,336
Syrdar'ya [16]	448	1,316	—	51.4	30.9	580
Tashkent	3,552	4,236	1.8	271.5	71.7	4,299
Tashkent city	1,759	2,079	1.7	NA	100.0	2,120
Tashkent oblast	1,793	2,157	1.9	138.3	44.4	2,179
Fergana	1,698	2,153	2.4	303.2	32.7	2,226
Khorezm	747	1,016	3.1	161.3	27.9	1,069
Karakalpak ASSR	906	1,214	3.0	7.4	48.1	1,274
KYRGYZSTAN [17]	3,523	4,291	2.0	21.6	38.2	4,422
Bishkek city [18]	526	626	1.8	NA	99.5	641
Dzhalal-Abad	—	—	—	—	—	782
Issyk-Kul'	351	665	—	7.3	27.5	426
Naryn	229	—	—	—	—	260
Osh	1,545	2,010	—	25.9	28.7	1,323
Talas	—	—	—	—	—	199
Chuysk	—	—	—	—	—	791
Republic territories	872	990	—	32.9	26.2	—
TAJIKISTAN	3,806	5,112	3.0	35.7	32.6	5,358
Gorno-Badakhshan AO	128	161	2.3	2.5	12.4	167
Dushanbe city	500	604	1.9	NA	98.7	592
Khatlon [19]	—	1,703	—	69.2	21.3	—
Kulyab [19]	492	—	—	—	—	668
Kurgan-Tyube [19]	703	—	—	—	—	1,114
Khudzhand [20]	1,195	1,559	2.7	60.0	33.8	1,636
Republic territories	789	1,085	3.2	13.7	14.8	1,182
TURKMENISTAN	2,765	3,534	2.5	7.2	45.4	3,714
Ashkhabad city	312	402	2.6	NA	99.8	416
Mary	632	815	2.6	9.4	27.2	860
Tashauz	532	699	2.8	9.4	31.5	738
Chardzhou	579	735	2.4	7.8	43.8	775

TABLE 1. Population, 1979–91.—Continued

Geographical Unit	1979 Total Population (1000)	1989 Total Population (1000)	1979– 89 Average Annual Growth	1989 Population Density (persons per square km.)	1989 Urban Population (percent)	1991 Total Population (1000)
	(1)	(2)	(3)	(4)	(5)	(6)
Balkan [21]	312	—	—	—	—	—
Republic territories [22]	398	883	—	3.8	49.6	926

SOURCES: Column 1: *Itogi Vsesoyuznoy Perepis' Naseleniya 1979 goda, Tom I.* 1989, pp. 45–55. Column 2: *Naseleniya SSSR, Perepis' Naseleniya 1989.* 1990, pp. 10–19. Column 3: Calculation based on columns 1 and 2. Column 4: Calculation based on column 2 and the size of the territory. Column 5: *Naseleniya SSSR, Perepis' Naseleniya 1989.* 1990, pp. 10–19. Column 6: *Chislennost' Naseleniya Soyuznykh Respublik po Gorodskim Poseleniyam i Rayonam, na 1 Yanvarya 1991g.* 1991, pp. 3–443.

NOTES:
Components may not sum to totals due to rounding.
NA Data not available.
—Data not applicable.
The following notes apply to all tables in this document:
[1] Data are for the entire former Soviet Union.
[2] The former Soviet Union can be divided into three distinct areas: the European U.S.S.R. region, the Transcaucasus region, and the Central Asia region. The European U.S.S.R. includes Russia (consisting of both the European part and the Asian part), Ukraine, Belarus, Latvia, Lithuania, Estonia, and Moldova; the Transcaucasus region includes Georgia, Azerbaijan, and Armenia; the Central Asia region includes Kazakhstan, Uzbekistan, Kyrgyzstan, Tajikistan, and Turkmenistan.
[3] Tver' oblast was formerly known as Kalinin oblast.
[4] Nizhegorodsk oblast was formerly known as Gorkiy oblast; it is sometimes referred to as Nizhne Novgorod oblast.
[5] Samara oblast was formerly known as Kuybyshev oblast.
[6] Karachayevo-Cherkess SSR was part of Stavropol' Kray before 1992.
[7] Republic of Bashkortostan was formerly known as Bashkir oblast.
[8] Republic of Gornyy Altay was part of Altay Kray before 1992.
[9] Republic of Khakasia was part of Krasnoyarsk Kray before 1992.
[10] Republic of Sakha (Yakutia) was formerly know as Yakut ASSR.
[11] Lugansk oblast was formerly called Voroshilovgrad oblast.
[12] Chisinau city was formerly known as Kishinev city.
[13] The January 1, 1991 total population for Kazakhstan is 91.5 thousand people greater than the sum of the reported population figures for each of the oblasts.
[14] During the 1989 census, Mangistausk oblast was part of Gur'yev oblast, but in 1979 and after 1989 the two were separated.
[15] Khatlon oblast did not exist in 1979 or after the 1989 census—it was split into the Kulyab and Kurgan-Tyube oblasts.
[16] During the 1989 census, Dzhizak oblast was part of Syrdar'ya oblast, but in 1979 and after 1989 the two were separated.
[16] Kyrgyzstan underwent a complete reorganization after 1989. None of the oblasts currently have the same boundaries as they did in 1989. Two oblasts, Issyk-Kul' and Osh, have the same names as in 1989, but their borders have been changed since then. Naryn existed in 1979 and after 1989 but not during the 1989 census. The republic territories are no longer in existence—the new oblasts were drawn from this and the old oblasts. The data shown here are for the oblasts and territories as they were in the year shown, hence apparent population changes, particularly between 1989 and 1991, are potentially misleading.
[18] Bishkek city was formerly called Frunze city.
[19] During the 1989 census, Turgay oblast was a part of Kustanay and Tselinograd oblasts, but in 1979 and after 1989 the three were separated. In addition, Tselinograd oblast had part of Karaganda oblast's 1989 territory in 1979 and after 1989.
[20] Khudzhand oblast was formerly known as Leninabad oblast.
[21] Balkan oblast was part of republic territories during 1989, but was known as Krasnovodsk oblast before and immediately after the 1989 census.
[22] Before the 1989 census, the republic territories were known as the Ashkhabad oblast.

TABLE 2. Age and Sex Structure, 1989. [1]

Geographical Unit	Total Population (1000)	Population distribution [2] Young (1000)	Working Age (1000)	Old (1000)	Percent Distribution Young	Working Age	Old	Dependency [3]	Males (1000)	Females (1000)
	(1)	(2)	(3)	(4)	(5)	(6)	(7)	(8)	(9)	(10)
U.S.S.R.	285,743	77,905	158,911	48,818	27.3	55.6	17.1	797	134,687	151,056
EUROPE	220,868	53,451	125,108	42,302	24.2	56.6	19.2	765	102,981	117,887
TRANSCAUCASUS	15,727	4,915	8,785	2,026	31.3	55.9	12.9	790	7,605	8,122
CENTRAL ASIA	49,148	19,539	25,103	4,490	39.8	51.1	9.1	957	24,101	25,046
RUSSIAN FEDERATION	147,022	35,995	83,831	27,196	24.5	57.0	18.5	754	68,714	78,308
Northern economic region	6,124	1,618	3,638	868	26.4	59.4	14.2	683	2,983	3,141
Arkhangel'sk	1,570	418	910	241	26.6	58.0	15.4	724	764	806
Nenets ASR	54	17	33	4	30.9	61.4	7.7	628	28	26
Other Arkhangel'sk	1,516	401	877	237	26.5	57.9	15.6	728	736	780
Vologda	1,349	329	744	276	24.4	55.2	20.4	813	631	718
Murmansk	1,165	318	746	100	27.3	64.1	8.6	561	580	585
Republic of Karelia	790	202	461	126	25.6	58.4	16.0	713	376	414
Komi SSR	1,251	351	776	124	28.0	62.1	9.9	611	633	618
Northwestern economic region	8,241	1,720	4,788	1,734	20.9	58.1	21.0	721	3,739	4,503
Leningrad	6,644	1,374	3,917	1,353	20.7	59.0	20.4	696	3,010	3,635
St.Petersburg city	4,991	986	2,982	1,023	19.8	59.7	20.5	674	2,247	2,744
Leningrad oblast	1,654	388	936	331	23.4	56.6	20.0	768	763	891
Novgorod	752	168	412	171	22.3	54.9	22.8	822	343	408
Pskov	845	178	458	209	21.1	54.2	24.8	846	386	459
Central economic region	30,207	6,304	17,189	6,714	20.9	56.9	22.2	757	13,688	16,519
Bryansk	1,470	336	792	342	22.9	53.8	23.3	857	671	799
Vladimir	1,649	367	930	352	22.3	56.4	21.3	773	749	900
Ivanovo	1,314	278	726	309	21.2	55.3	23.6	809	589	725
Kaluga	1,064	236	603	225	22.2	56.6	21.2	766	490	574
Kostroma	804	182	440	182	22.6	54.7	22.7	828	369	435
Moscow	15,522	3,155	9,070	3,297	20.3	58.4	21.2	711	7,006	8,516
Moscow city	8,876	1,764	5,188	1,924	19.9	58.5	21.7	711	3,982	4,894
Moscow oblast	6,646	1,391	3,882	1,373	20.9	58.4	20.7	712	3,024	3,622
Orel	889	188	497	205	21.1	55.9	23.0	790	407	482
Ryazan'	1,348	274	749	325	20.3	55.6	24.1	800	615	733
Smolensk	1,154	257	631	265	22.3	54.7	23.0	827	529	625
Tver'	1,663	348	898	417	20.9	54.0	25.1	853	749	914
Tula	1,861	369	1,028	464	19.8	55.2	25.0	810	845	1,016

Yaroslavl'	1,469	313	826	330	21.3	56.2	22.5	779	668	801
Volgo-Vyatsk economic region	8,464	1,999	4,713	1,752	23.6	55.7	20.7	796	3,886	4,578
Kirov	1,694	408	935	351	24.1	55.2	20.7	813	791	903
Nizhegorodsk.	3,720	801	2,081	837	21.5	55.8	22.5	787	1,691	2,029
Republic of Mariy El	749	203	418	128	27.0	55.7	17.1	791	349	401
Mordov SSR	964	227	537	200	23.5	55.5	20.8	796	440	524
Chuvash Republic.	1,338	360	743	236	26.9	54.6	17.6	802	616	722
Central Chernozem economic region	7,733	1,654	4,219	1,860	21.4	54.2	24.1	833	3,525	4,208
Belgorod.	1,378	313	747	318	22.7	54.2	23.1	846	626	752
Voronezh	2,467	509	1,344	613	20.7	54.5	24.9	835	1,122	1,344
Kursk	1,335	287	722	326	21.5	54.1	24.4	849	609	726
Lipetsk	1,230	265	690	275	21.6	56.1	22.3	782	565	665
Tambov	1,322	279	715	328	21.1	54.1	24.8	849	602	720
Povolzhskiy economic region.	16,397	3,956	9,347	3,094	24.1	57.0	18.9	754	7,636	8,761
Astrakhan	992	259	561	172	26.1	56.6	17.3	768	472	520
Volgograd	2,593	606	1,461	526	23.4	56.4	20.3	774	1,209	1,384
Penza.	1,505	338	842	325	22.5	56.0	21.6	787	692	813
Samara	3,263	767	1,894	603	23.5	58.0	18.5	723	1,513	1,750
Saratov	2,684	624	1,542	519	23.2	57.4	19.3	741	1,253	1,431
Ulyanovsk (Simbirsk)	1,396	334	796	266	24.0	57.0	19.1	755	651	745
Republic of Kalmykia (Khalmg Tangch)	323	104	184	35	32.2	57.0	10.9	756	158	165
Republic of Tatarstan	3,642	925	2,068	649	25.4	56.8	17.8	761	1,689	1,953
North-Caucasus economic region	16,629	4,385	9,145	3,100	26.4	55.0	18.6	818	7,739	8,891
Krasnodar Kray	5,053	1,196	2,767	1,090	23.7	54.8	21.6	826	2,336	2,717
Adygeya SSR	432	107	234	91	24.8	54.2	21.0	847	198	234
Other Krasnodar Kray	4,621	1,089	2,533	999	23.6	54.8	21.6	824	2,137	2,484
Stavropol' Kray	2,410	610	1,335	465	25.3	55.4	19.3	805	1,123	1,287
Rostov	4,292	983	2,440	870	22.9	56.8	20.3	759	1,992	2,301
Republic of Dagestan	1,802	654	932	217	36.3	51.7	12.0	935	850	952
Kabardino-Balkar Republic.	754	223	421	109	29.6	55.9	14.5	789	353	400
Karachayevo-Cherkess SSR.	415	120	229	66	28.9	55.1	16.0	815	195	220
North-Ossetian SSR.	632	169	351	113	26.7	55.4	17.9	804	293	340
Chechen-Ingush Republic.	1,270	430	671	169	33.8	52.8	13.3	893	597	674
Urals economic region	20,239	5,206	11,446	3,587	25.7	56.6	17.7	768	9,483	10,756
Kurgan	1,104	283	610	210	25.7	55.3	19.1	810	514	589
Orenburg	2,171	580	1,217	374	26.7	56.1	17.2	783	1,022	1,149
Perm'	3,091	787	1,766	539	25.4	57.1	17.4	751	1,459	1,632
Komi-Permyat AO.	159	46	81	31	29.1	51.3	19.6	950	74	85
Other Perm'	2,933	740	1,684	508	25.2	57.4	17.3	741	1,385	1,548
Sverdlovsk (Yekaterinburg)	4,707	1,159	2,680	868	24.6	56.9	18.4	756	2,196	2,511
Chelyabinsk	3,618	906	2,056	656	25.0	56.8	18.1	760	1,694	1,924
Republic of Bashkortostan.	3,943	1,053	2,208	682	26.7	56.0	17.3	786	1,851	2,092
Udmurt Republic.	1,606	439	909	257	27.3	56.6	16.0	766	747	859
West Siberian economic region	15,013	4,061	8,650	2,302	27.0	57.6	15.3	736	7,179	7,834
Altay Kray	2,631	686	1,464	482	26.1	55.6	18.3	797	1,239	1,392
Kemerovo	3,171	808	1,809	554	25.5	57.0	17.5	753	1,507	1,664

TABLE 2. Age and Sex Structure, 1989. ¹—Continued

Geographical Unit	Total Population (1000)	Population distribution ²			Percent Distribution			Dependency ³	Males (1000)	Females (1000)
		Young (1000)	Working Age (1000)	Old (1000)	Young	Working Age	Old			
	(1)	(2)	(3)	(4)	(5)	(6)	(7)	(8)	(9)	(10)
Novosibirsk	2,779	693	1,592	493	25.0	57.3	17.8	745	1,297	1,481
Omsk	2,142	590	1,208	344	27.6	56.4	16.0	773	1,008	1,134
Tomsk	1,002	271	588	143	27.0	58.7	14.3	704	488	514
Tyumen	3,098	951	1,889	258	30.7	61.0	8.3	640	1,549	1,549
Khanti-Mansiysk AOkr	1,282	426	812	45	33.2	63.3	3.5	580	657	625
Yamalo-Nenetsk Republic	495	162	322	10	32.8	65.2	2.1	534	259	236
Other Tyumen'	1,320	363	755	203	27.5	57.1	15.4	750	632	689
Republic of Gornyy Altay	191	62	101	28	32.5	53.0	14.6	888	91	100
East Siberian economic region	9,153	2,654	5,286	1,213	29.0	57.8	13.3	731	4,453	4,700
Krasnoyarsk Kray	3,039	822	1,798	419	27.0	59.2	13.8	690	1,752	1,853
Taymyr AOkr	56	17	36	2	30.8	64.8	4.4	543	29	27
Evenki AO	25	8	15	1	32.7	62.4	4.9	602	13	12
Other Krasnoyarsk Kray	2,958	796	1,747	415	26.9	59.1	14.0	693	1,434	1,524
Irkutsk	2,825	802	1,642	381	28.4	58.1	13.5	721	1,368	1,457
Ust-Ordynsk Buryat AOkr	136	48	69	19	35.2	51.0	13.8	961	67	69
Other Irkutsk	2,689	754	1,572	363	28.0	58.5	13.5	710	1,301	1,389
Chita	1,375	425	777	173	30.9	56.5	12.6	770	677	698
Aga Buryat AOkr	77	30	39	8	38.7	51.0	10.3	962	38	39
Other Chita	1,298	395	738	165	30.5	56.8	12.7	760	639	659
Buryat SSR	1,038	329	579	130	31.7	55.8	12.5	793	504	534
Republic of Tuva	309	115	169	24	37.3	54.9	7.8	822	151	157
Republic of Khakasia	567	161	320	86	28.3	56.5	15.2	770	276	291
Far Eastern economic region	7,950	2,236	4,889	826	28.1	61.5	10.4	626	3,984	3,966
Primor Kray	2,256	593	1,374	289	26.3	60.9	12.8	642	1,119	1,138
Khabarovsk Kray	1,812	494	1,095	223	27.3	60.4	12.3	655	899	913
Yevreysk AO	214	66	121	27	30.9	56.3	12.7	775	105	110
Other Khabarovsk Kray	1,598	428	974	196	26.8	61.0	12.2	640	794	804
Amur	1,050	303	621	126	28.9	59.1	12.0	692	525	526
Kamchatka	472	133	314	25	28.2	66.5	5.3	504	246	226
Koryak ASR	40	13	25	2	31.4	63.5	5.1	575	21	19
Other Kamchatka	432	120	288	23	27.9	66.8	5.3	497	225	207
Magadan	556	163	372	21	29.3	66.9	3.8	494	288	267
Chukotsk ASR	164	50	111	3	30.6	67.4	1.9	483	86	78

	1	2	3	4	5	6	7	8	9	10
Other Magadan	392	113	261	18	28.8	66.7	4.5	499	202	190
Sakhalin	710	193	446	71	27.2	62.7	10.1	594	357	354
Republic of Sakha (Yakutia)	1,094	356	668	70	32.6	61.0	6.4	639	552	542
Kaliningrad	871	204	521	146	23.4	59.8	16.8	672	418	453
UKRAINE	51,452	11,828	28,722	10,895	23.0	55.8	21.2	791	23,745	27,707
BELARUS	10,152	2,483	5,685	1,984	24.5	56.0	19.5	786	4,749	5,402
MOLDOVA	4,335	1,282	2,390	663	29.6	55.1	15.3	814	2,063	2,272
LITHUANIA	3,675	886	2,093	696	24.1	57.0	18.9	756	1,739	1,936
LATVIA	2,667	606	1,508	553	22.7	56.5	20.7	769	1,239	1,428
ESTONIA	1,565	371	879	315	23.7	56.2	20.1	780	731	834
GEORGIA	5,401	1,423	3,039	939	26.3	56.3	17.4	777	2,562	2,839
AZERBAIJAN	7,021	2,433	3,888	700	34.7	55.4	10.0	806	3,424	3,597
ARMENIA	3,305	1,059	1,858	387	32.0	56.2	11.7	778	1,619	1,685
KAZAKHSTAN	16,464	5,551	9,079	1,823	33.7	55.1	11.1	812	7,974	8,490
UZBEKISTAN	19,810	8,507	9,720	1,583	42.9	49.1	8.0	1,038	9,784	10,026
KYRGYZSTAN	4,258	1,680	2,143	432	39.5	50.3	10.1	986	2,078	2,180
TAJIKISTAN	5,093	2,296	2,410	385	45.1	47.3	7.6	1,112	2,530	2,562
TURKMENISTAN	3,523	1,505	1,751	267	42.7	49.7	7.6	1,012	1,735	1,788

SOURCES: Column 1: *Naseleniya SSSR, Perepis' Naseleniya 1989.* 1990, pp. 10–19. Columns 2–4: *Vozrast i Sostoyaniye v Brake Naseleniya SSSR, Perepis' Naseleniya 1989.* 1990, pp. 24–41. Columns 5–7: Calculation based on columns 1–4. Column 8: Calculation based on columns 2–4 (see Dependency note 3 below). Columns 9–10: RUSSIA: *Chislennost' Naseleniya RSFSR, 1989.* 1990. pp. 97–374. OTHER REPUBLICS: *Demograficheskiy Yezhegodnik SSSR 1990.* 1990, pp. 33–72.

NOTES:

Data may not sum to total due to rounding.

[1] The population totals for Tables 1 and 2 differ because Table 1 shows defacto population, while Table 2 shows dejure population.

[2] The various age categories are defined as follows: young are people age 15 and under, old are people at or older than the retirement age (60 for males and 55 for females), and working-age are people not included in the other two categories. Data do not sum to total in original source because there is a residual (unspecified age) category for several republics.

[3] Dependency shows the number of dependents (young and old) for every 1000 working-age persons.

Figure 1. Age Structure, 1989

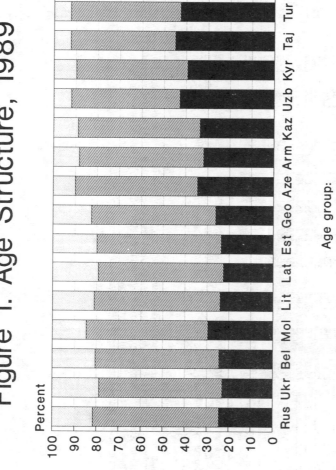

Percent

Rus Ukr Bel Mol Lit Lat Est Geo Aze Arm Kaz Uzb Kyr Taj Tur

Age group:

■ Young   ▨ Working age   ☐ Old

Young are people age 15 and under. Old ages reflect Soviet retirement definition: men age 60 and older, women age 55 and older.

Center for International Research

B. DEMOGRAPHIC CHARACTERISTICS

Population trends in the former U.S.S.R. shown in Table 1 can be explained by three basic factors: births, deaths, and migration (Table 3). Birth and death rates come from official Soviet sources; migration data are estimated. For the inter-censal period (1979–1989), the former U.S.S.R. experienced slight out migration, although its European portion gained 2 million inhabitants from population movement. Roughly 16 percent of the population increase for the European U.S.S.R. during that period can be attributed to migration. The majority of these people came from other Soviet republics, especially the Central Asian ones.

In the years after 1989, these trends have apparently continued. When the former Soviet republics gained their independence, each experienced an upsurge in nationalist feelings. Non-titular nationalities are often perceived as foreigners—and Russians, in particular, as occupiers—in the new states. This, combined with the fact that many non-titular nationalities did not speak the national language of the republic in which they resided (see Section IV, Table 24), may have induced many to move back to their native country. In 1990 alone, half a million Russians from various regions of the U.S.S.R. migrated back to Russia.

TABLE 3. Birth and Death Rates, Natural Increase, Net Migration, 1979–89.

Geographical Unit	Births (per 1000)	Deaths (per 1000)	Population Growth (1000) 1979–89	Natural Increase (1000) 1979–89	Net Migration (1000) 1979–89
U.S.S.R.	18.8	10.1	24,281	24,423	-142
Russian Federation	16.0	10.7	9,835	8,060	1,775
Ukraine	14.5	11.7	1,949	1,795	154
Belarus	16.0	10.1	640	648	-8
Moldova	20.9	9.7	394	450	-56
Lithuania	15.3	10.2	292	192	100
Latvia	15.4	12.1	160	67	93
Estonia	15.9	11.8	107	52	55
Georgia	17.3	9.0	434	487	-53
Azerbaijan	26.5	6.8	1,001	1,266	-265
Armenia	21.6	10.3	252	559	-307
Kazakhstan	24.6	7.7	1,854	2,639	-785
Uzbekistan	35.1	6.8	4,515	5,021	-506
Kyrgyzstan	31.2	7.4	762	919	-157
Tajikistan	40.0	7.0	1,311	1,412	-101
Turkmenistan	36.0	7.8	775	857	-82

SOURCES: Population growth has been computed from Table 1. Figures for birth and death rates and natural increase have been obtained from Naseleniye SSSR, 1988. 1989, pp. 38–72.
NOTES: Data may not sum to total due to rounding. Net migration has been estimated as the difference between the natural increase and the actual population growth.

Because of deficiencies in the official Soviet statistics on fertility, infant mortality, and life expectancy, the Center for International Research has produced separate estimates for these variables (Table 4). Although the corrections tended to be small, in at least one instance (infant mortality), the change was nearly 75 percent. Official Soviet infant mortality data understated the true level of infant mortality because the definition excluded infants that the World Health Organization (the definition used in the west) would have included. [5] In addition, it is believed that not all infant deaths were registered; infants not born in hospitals were often not counted. The following adjustments try to compensate for these and other problems. The adjusted infant mortality rates for all republics were significantly higher than the officially reported rates; consequently, the adjusted life expectancy was slightly lower. All regions of the European U.S.S.R., except Moldova, had fertility and infant mortality rates that were lower than corresponding rates for the U.S.S.R. as a whole. The Central Asian republics had the highest fertility and infant mortality rates in the country.

TABLE 4. Selected Demographic Measures, 1990.

	Official Statistics					CIR Estimates				
		Infant		Life			Infant		Life	
Geographical Unit	Total Fertility Rate [1]	Mortality Rate [2]		Expectancy [3]		Total Fertility Rate	Mortality Rate		Expectancy	
		Males	Females	Males	Females		Males	Females	Males	Females
U.S.S.R.	2.3	24.0	18.6	64.3	73.9	2.3	41.6	31.7	63.1	72.9
Russian Federation	1.9	19.6	14.5	63.8	74.3	2.0	34.0	24.8	62.8	73.6
Ukraine	1.8	14.5	10.8	65.6	74.9	1.9	25.0	18.5	64.9	74.3
Belarus	1.9	13.7	9.6	66.2	75.8	2.0	23.6	16.5	65.6	75.2
Moldova	2.4	21.1	16.3	65.0	72.0	2.5	36.5	27.9	64.0	71.1
Lithuania	2.0	10.7	9.7	66.5	76.3	2.1	18.6	16.6	66.0	75.7
Latvia	2.0	15.6	11.5	64.2	74.6	2.1	27.0	19.7	63.5	73.9
Estonia	2.1	14.0	10.0	64.7	74.9	2.1	24.3	17.2	64.1	74.4
Georgia	2.2	17.4	13.8	68.9	76.5	2.3	30.2	23.5	68.0	75.7
Azerbaijan	2.8	24.6	20.2	67.0	75.2	2.9	42.6	34.6	65.8	74.1
Armenia	2.8	20.4	16.4	68.5	75.3	2.9	35.3	28.0	67.4	74.4
Kazakhstan	2.7	28.8	23.0	63.9	73.3	2.8	49.9	39.3	62.5	72.1
Uzbekistan	4.1	37.8	29.4	66.3	72.8	4.2	65.4	50.3	64.4	71.2
Kyrgyzstan	3.7	32.9	26.1	64.4	72.9	3.8	57.0	44.7	62.8	71.5
Tajikistan	5.1	43.1	36.3	67.2	72.5	5.3	74.6	62.2	65.0	70.5
Turkmenistan	4.2	48.3	38.8	63.1	70.0	4.3	83.6	66.4	60.7	68.0

SOURCE: Center for International Research, U.S. Bureau of the Census.
[1] Total fertility rate represents the number of children a woman would bear in her life if she survived to the end of the reproductive ages and was subject over this period to the regime of age-specific fertility rates observed in the given republic and year.
[2] Infant mortality rate shows the number of infant deaths under one year of age in the given year per 1,000 live births in that year. See text footnote number 5 (below) for the definition of a live birth.
[3] Life expectancy shows the average number of additional years a person born in the given year would live if the current mortality schedule continued (also known as life expectancy at birth).

Table 5 shows a more detailed geographic comparison of infant mortality within the former Soviet Union based on the official, unadjusted infant mortality figures. The adjustments used to recalculate infant mortality rates for the U.S.S.R. and republics cannot be applied to each oblast within the republics because of a lack of necessary information. Regional comparisons can still be useful, particularly if one compares the rate to the U.S.S.R. average. Most of

---

[5] According to official Soviet statistics, live births excluded infants who were born before the 29th week of gestation, with a weight under 1000 grams, or with a length under 35 centimeters if they subsequently died in the first week of life. The World Health Organization's definition is broader. It defines a live birth as any infant who shows any sign of life (such as breathing or having a pulse) no matter its weight, length, or period of gestation. Source for the infant mortality definitions: Anderson and Silver, "Infant Mortality in the Soviet Union; Regional Differences and Measurement Issues," *Population and Development Review*, vol.12, no.4, 1986, pp. 705–738.

the infant mortality rates in the European U.S.S.R., Georgia, and Armenia were below the U.S.S.R. average, while Azerbaijan and Central Asia had significantly above average rates.

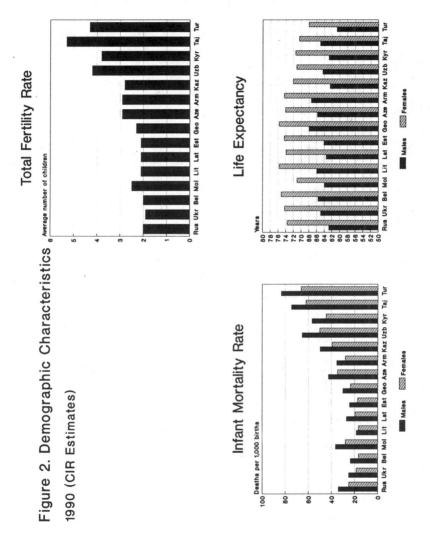

Figure 2. Demographic Characteristics 1990 (CIR Estimates)

Infant mortality rates have been generally declining since the 1950s, though there was an apparent increase during the 1970s. Some experts have attributed this to improved reporting rather than to real increases in the level of infant mortality.

TABLE 5. Infant Mortality Rate, 1989.

Geographical Unit	Infant Mortality (deaths per 1000 births)	Relative to USSR (USSR = 100)
U.S.S.R.	22.7	100
RUSSIAN FEDERATION	17.8	78
Northern economic region	15.5	68
Arkhangel'sk	15.1	67
Nenets ASR	NA	NA
Other Arkhangel'sk	NA	NA
Vologda	15.1	67
Murmansk	14.7	65
Republic of Karelia	12.8	56
Komi SSR	18.9	83
Northwestern economic region	16.6	73
Leningrad	16.6	73
St.Petersburg city	17.3	76
Leningrad oblast	14.6	64
Novgorod	19.3	85
Pskov	13.6	60
Central economic region	16.8	74
Bryansk	14.5	64
Vladimir	16.0	70
Ivanovo	15.4	68
Kaluga	16.0	70
Kostroma	19.2	85
Moscow	17.6	77
Moscow city	19.2	85
Moscow oblast	15.3	67
Orel	16.9	74
Ryazan'	15.5	68
Smolensk	16.0	70
Tver'	18.2	80
Tula	15.5	68
Yaroslavl'	14.0	62
Volgo-Vyatsk economic region	15.7	69
Kirov	16.2	71
Nizhegorodsk	15.5	68
Republic of Mariy El	15.8	70
Mordov SSR	18.2	80
Chuvash Republic	13.8	61
Central Chernozem economic region	16.3	72
Belgorod	15.2	67
Voronezh	15.7	69
Kursk	18.1	80
Lipetsk	14.6	64
Tambov	18.2	80
Povolzhkiy economic region	17.3	76
Astrakhan'	15.9	70
Volgograd	17.5	77
Penza	17.1	75
Samara	17.7	78
Saratov	18.3	81
Ulyanovsk (Simbirsk)	18.0	79

TABLE 5. Infant Mortality Rate, 1989.—Continued

Geographical Unit	Infant Mortality (deaths per 1000 births)	Relative to USSR (USSR=100)
Republic of Kalmykia (Khalmg Tangch)	23.5	104
Republic of Tatarstan	15.8	70
North-Caucasus economic region	20.2	89
Krasnodar Kray	17.3	76
Adygeya SSR	NA	NA
Other Krasnodar Kray	NA	NA
Stavropol' Kray	18.2	80
Rostov	18.6	82
Republic of Dagestan	22.8	100
Kabardino-Balkar Republic	19.5	86
Karachayevo-Cherkess SSR	NA	NA
North-Ossetian SSR	14.1	62
Chechen-Ingush Republic	31.1	137
Urals economic region	17.5	77
Kurgan	18.3	81
Orenburg	18.2	80
Perm'	17.6	78
Komi-Permyat AO	NA	NA
Other Perm'	NA	NA
Sverdlovsk (Yekaterinburg)	18.0	79
Chelyabinsk	16.5	73
Republic of Bashkortostan	17.3	76
Udmurt Republic	17.4	77
West Siberian economic region	19.0	84
Altay Kray	18.4	81
Kemerovo	20.4	90
Novosibirsk	19.1	84
Omsk	18.0	79
Tomsk	19.6	86
Tyumen'	18.8	83
Khanti-Mansiysk AOkr	NA	NA
Yamalo-Nenetsk Republic	NA	NA
Other Tyumen'	NA	NA
Republic of Gornyy Altay	NA	NA
East Siberian economic region	20.8	92
Krasnoyarsk Kray	20.5	90
Taymyr AOkr	NA	NA
Evenki AO	NA	NA
Other Krasnoyarsk Kray	NA	NA
Irkutsk	20.1	89
Ust-Ordynsk Buryat AOkr	NA	NA
Other Irkutsk	NA	NA
Chita	20.1	89
Aga Buryat AOkr	NA	NA
Other Chita	NA	NA
Republic of Buryat	19.1	84
Republic of Tuva	33.1	146
Republic of Khakasia	NA	NA
Far Eastern economic region	17.5	77
Primor Kray	16.7	74
Khabarovsk Kray	19.0	84
Yevreysk AO	NA	NA
Other Khabarovsk Kray	NA	NA
Amur	17.2	76
Kamchatka	15.4	68
Koryak ASR	NA	NA

TABLE 5. Infant Mortality Rate, 1989.—Continued

Geographical Unit	Infant Mortality (deaths per 1000 births)	Relative to USSR (USSR=100)
Other Kamchatka	NA	NA
Magadan	15.6	69
Chukotsk ASR	NA	NA
Other Magadan	NA	NA
Sakhalin	16.7	74
Republic of Sakha (Yakutia)	18.6	82
Kaliningrad	14.3	63
UKRAINE	13.0	57
Donets-Dnieper economic region	13.6	60
Dnepropetrovsk	13.8	61
Donetsk	12.9	57
Zaporozh'ye	15.0	66
Kirovograd	10.1	44
Lugansk	13.9	61
Poltava	11.9	52
Sumy	11.4	50
Khar'kov	14.5	64
Southwestern economic region	12.0	53
Vinnitsa	10.5	46
Volyn'	11.1	49
Zhitomir	11.2	49
Zakarpat'ye	13.2	58
Ivano-Frankovsk	13.9	61
Kiev	11.6	51
Kiev city	13.4	59
Kiev oblast	9.7	43
L'vov	12.8	56
Rovno	12.0	53
Ternopol'	11.3	50
Khmel'nitskiy	12.6	56
Cherkassy	10.5	46
Chernigov	12.3	54
Chernovtsy	13.5	59
Southern economic region	14.0	62
Krym ASSR	12.9	57
Nikolayev	12.4	55
Odessa	15.0	66
Kherson	16.0	70
BELARUS	11.8	52
Brest	11.2	49
Vitebsk	12.5	55
Gomel'	12.2	54
Grodno	10.8	48
Minsk	12.7	56
Minsk city	13.3	59
Minsk oblast	12.0	53
Mogilev	10.2	45
MOLDOVA	20.4	90
Chisinau city	18.1	80
LITHUANIA	10.7	47
Vil'nyus city	12.2	54
LATVIA	11.1	49
Riga city	10.9	48
ESTONIA	14.7	65
Tallinn city	16.0	70
GEORGIA	19.6	86
Tbilisi city	24.2	107

TABLE 5. Infant Mortality Rate, 1989.—Continued

Geographical Unit	Infant Mortality (deaths per 1000 births)	Relative to USSR (USSR=100)
Abkhaz ASSR	17.3	76
Adzhar ASSR	22.4	99
South Ossetian AO	22.5	99
Republic territories	17.9	79
AZERBAIJAN	26.2	115
Baku city	28.0	123
Nakhichevan ASSR	18.5	81
Nagorno-Karabakh AO	NA	NA
Republic territories	26.3	116
ARMENIA	20.4	90
Yerevan city	21.3	94
KAZAKHSTAN	25.9	114
Aktyubinsk	25.2	111
Alma-Ata	22.1	97
Alma-Ata city	19.5	86
Alma-Ata oblast	24.1	106
East Kazakhstan	25.7	113
Gur'yev	30.6	135
Dzhambul	29.8	131
Dzhezkazgan	25.1	111
Karaganda	20.8	92
Kzyl-Orda	30.1	133
Kokchetav	22.3	98
Kustanay	23.5	104
Mangistausk	NA	NA
Pavlodar	23.3	103
North Kazakhstan	17.3	76
Semipalatinsk	28.2	124
Taldy-Kurgan	23.4	103
Turgay	NA	NA
Ural'sk	25.3	111
Tselinograd	21.2	93
Chimkent	30.6	135
UZBEKISTAN	37.7	166
Andizhan	35.3	156
Bukhara	33.6	148
Dzhizak	NA	NA
Kashkadar'ya	34.0	150
Namangan	34.7	153
Samarkand	39.3	173
Surkhandar'ya	47.4	209
Syrdar'ya	43.0	189
Tashkent	28.6	126
Tashkent city	25.0	110
Tashkent oblast	31.0	137
Fergana	40.2	177
Khorezm	37.4	165
Karakalpak ASSR	52.0	229
KYRGYZSTAN	32.2	142
Bishkek city	30.8	136
Dzhalal-Abad	NA	NA
Issyk-Kul'	31.0	137
Naryn	NA	NA
Osh	33.9	149
Talas	NA	NA
Chuysk	NA	NA
Republic territories	29.3	129

TABLE 5. Infant Mortality Rate, 1989.—Continued

Geographical Unit	Infant Mortality (deaths per 1000 births)	Relative to USSR (USSR=100)
TAJIKISTAN	43.2	190
Gorno-Badakhshan AO	32.9	145
Dushanbe city....................................	31.9	141
Khatlon...	47.2	208
Kulyab..	NA	NA
Kurgan-Tyube....................................	NA	NA
Khudzhand...	44.1	194
Republic territories............................	40.0	176
TURKMENISTAN	54.7	241
Ashkhabad city..................................	44.8	197
Mary..	58.2	256
Tashauz	66.1	291
Chardzhou..	47.6	210
Balkan	NA	NA
Republic territories............................	50.7	223

SOURCE: *Statisticheskiy Press-byulleten' No. 21, 1990.* 1990, pp. 41–48.
NA—Data not available.

III. QUALITY OF LIFE

A. HEALTH

In general, health conditions have steadily improved in the Soviet Union since World War II. Despite overall progress, the republics of the former U.S.S.R. still lag behind western countries in several categories, and in certain categories, namely infant mortality rates, the international comparisons have worsened since the 1970s.

On the plus side, average maternal mortality rates declined in 9 of 15 republics between 1980 and 1989 (Table 6). A few notable rate increases occurred in Latvia, Estonia, and Georgia, but the actual number of maternal deaths was rather small (22 in Latvia in 1989). The rates in the Central Asian republics were slightly higher than the average for the U.S.S.R. as a whole, with 45.9 deaths per 100,000 births for Central Asia in 1989 as compared to 43.8 deaths per 100,000 births for the U.S.S.R.

Another positive sign is that deaths from all causes for both males and females have also declined during the 1980s (Table 7). [6] One of the trends shown in Table 7 is a steady increase in the rate of cancer deaths during the 1980s, particularly for males. [7] This trend is common in many countries, including the United States in the 1980s, because as fewer people die from infectious diseases they

---

[6] The standardized mortality rates shown in Table 7 use the European Standard age/sex distribution for calculation. This allows meaningful comparisons between sexes, among other former Soviet republics, as well as among countries using the same standard. Unfortunately, the data are somewhat dated.

[7] The Central Asian republics were exceptions to this trend: their rates either increased only moderately or actually decreased.

TABLE 6. Maternal Mortality, 1980, 1985, and
1987.

Deaths per 100,000 births

Geographical Unit	1980	1985	1989
U.S.S.R.	56.4	47.7	43.8
European U.S.S.R.	NA	48.3	43.6
Transcaucasus	NA	31.8	36.8
Central Asia	NA	49.8	45.9
Russian Federation	68.0	54.0	49.0
Ukraine	44.8	40.4	32.7
Belarus	29.1	17.0	24.8
Moldova	64.1	49.8	34.1
Lithuania	27.0	22.2	28.7
Latvia	25.3	30.2	56.5
Estonia	27.0	46.6	41.2
Georgia	25.7	22.5	54.9
Azerbaijan	38.7	41.1	28.6
Armenia	27.0	22.4	34.6
Kazakhstan	55.6	47.9	53.1
Uzbekistan	46.3	48.6	42.8
Kyrgyzstan	49.4	42.8	42.6
Tajikistan	94.2	59.1	38.9
Turkmenistan	40.8	56.8	55.2

SOURCE: *Okhrana Zdorov'ya v SSSR.* 1990, pp. 10–16.
NA Data not available.

have a greater chance of dying from cancer. In addition, other factors, such as increased smoking, have also influenced the cancer death rates.

Gorbachev's anti-alcohol campaign, begun in the mid 1980s, coincided with a decrease in the number of deaths associated with injuries. It is believed that the decrease in the availability of alcohol directly resulted in a reduction in the number of accidents (automobile, work, etc.). The anti-alcohol campaign may have also had an effect by contributing to the improvement of the general health of the population.

One of the most striking points in Table 7 is the very high Armenian death rate in 1988 compared to previous years. This high death rate is attributable to the devastating earthquake that occurred there that year. The deaths immediately caused by this disaster are reflected in the injuries category. The urban population obviously suffered a much higher death rate than the rural population because of the greater number of large buildings and other structures in cities that collapsed during the earthquake. In addition, the urban infrastructure was heavily damaged, thus making access to basic needs, such as potable water, very difficult; these problems caused health conditions to suffer. The particularly high death rate for women is most likely attributable to the fact that the earthquake took place in the middle of the day when women were at home in relatively insecure structures.

With a few exceptions, respiratory and circulatory illnesses generally decreased. This is in line with the long-term trend that displays reductions in these causes of deaths as the standard of living improves. Additionally, during the 1980s, the Soviet Union made attempts to expand the coverage of its health services, which may have improved the well-being of the people.

In the "deaths from all causes" category, rates declined between 1980 and 1987, but they increased slightly in 1988. As would be expected, male death rates for all causes were above female death rates. Urban populations generally suffered from circulatory and cancer problems more than rural populations, while respiratory illnesses and injuries plagued rural populations more than urban.

TABLE 7. Standardized Mortality Rates by Cause, 1980, 1987, and 1988.

Deaths per 100,000 persons

Geographical Unit	Males			Females		
	1980	1987	1988	1980	1987	1988
U.S.S.R.						
Total Population						
Deaths from all causes including:	1,729.1	1,527.4	1,539.9	950.8	874.4	879.2
circulatory illnesses	879.6	816.3	808.8	594.4	556.5	552.4
neoplasms	250.2	276.8	280.5	126.7	131.7	131.9
respiratory illnesses	192.9	134.8	134.7	89.4	58.5	58.1
accidents and injuries	243.0	150.6	168.4	58.4	43.1	51.3
Urban Population						
Deaths from all causes including:	1,742.6	1,546.8	1,554.2	962.3	892.9	898.6
circulatory illnesses	899.8	846.0	833.6	611.7	578.9	573.3
neoplasms	292.7	310.2	310.7	153.0	153.3	152.3
respiratory illnesses	152.0	101.8	102.1	59.7	36.7	37.6
accidents and injuries	232.9	140.5	161.2	57.4	41.8	52.7
Rural Population						
Deaths from all causes including:	1,739.2	1,534.4	1,556.6	949.7	864.5	866.4
circulatory illnesses	858.9	784.9	784.3	578.7	534.0	532.1
neoplasms	199.4	231.9	239.6	93.7	101.0	102.4
respiratory illnesses	245.9	183.3	183.7	127.8	89.6	87.9
accidents and injuries	269.4	178.5	193.9	62.4	47.3	50.6
RUSSIAN FEDERATION						
Total Population						
Deaths from all causes including:	1,868.2	1,587.0	1,589.5	955.4	859.8	854.6
circulatory illnesses	943.3	852.9	837.1	607.6	560.7	551.8
neoplasms	283.9	305.3	307.9	135.3	137.7	137.7
respiratory illnesses	183.6	116.6	117.4	70.3	40.3	41.0
accidents and injuries	294.9	170.4	188.6	67.8	46.0	48.8
Urban Population						
Deaths from all causes including:	1,843.3	1,607.3	1,604.9	973.4	896.4	891.7
circulatory illnesses	939.3	877.9	859.8	620.1	586.5	577.8
neoplasms	316.0	330.4	330.6	158.5	156.5	155.5
respiratory illnesses	154.6	99.6	100.3	54.7	31.9	32.9
accidents and injuries	269.5	154.0	172.2	63.3	43.8	47.0
Rural Population						
Deaths from all causes including:	1,952.9	1,601.6	1,622.8	944.0	814.7	810.0
circulatory illnesses	952.5	818.9	809.5	593.6	525.7	517.0
neoplasms	231.6	259.9	267.9	98.6	104.4	105.9
respiratory illnesses	237.3	154.6	156.1	96.9	56.6	56.9
accidents and injuries	367.0	227.4	251.3	82.3	55.5	57.6
UKRAINE						
Total Population						
Deaths from all causes including:	1,636.1	1,520.3	1,524.4	923.6	882.1	891.3
circulatory illnesses	913.0	848.3	834.3	628.7	598.5	601.5
neoplasms	222.8	268.1	276.2	117.1	128.4	130.7
respiratory illnesses	168.5	132.7	132.2	72.1	51.0	49.3
accidents and injuries	196.0	142.8	150.6	43.8	38.1	39.3
Urban Population						
Deaths from all causes including:	1,632.4	1,521.0	1,517.1	952.8	909.9	915.2
circulatory illnesses	907.0	866.8	848.0	645.1	618.2	617.9
neoplasms	265.6	296.3	299.3	145.8	151.7	152.9
respiratory illnesses	131.1	94.7	95.4	47.4	30.5	31.1
accidents and injuries	184.1	128.5	138.5	45.2	37.6	39.1

TABLE 7. Standardized Mortality Rates by Cause, 1980, 1987, and 1988.—Continued

Deaths per 100,000 persons

Geographical Unit	Males			Females		
	1980	1987	1988	1980	1987	1988
Rural Population						
Deaths from all causes including:	1,666.7	1,572.0	1,588.9	904.5	866.5	879.2
circulatory illnesses	922.1	839.1	829.9	617.6	584.5	590.5
neoplasms	181.2	240.6	255.1	89.6	103.5	105.8
respiratory illnesses	209.0	180.6	180.3	96.1	73.2	70.0
accidents and injuries	224.0	183.0	190.9	45.0	42.6	43.6
BELARUS						
Total Population						
Deaths from all causes including:	1,476.3	1,436.2	1,466.9	819.5	811.5	815.5
circulatory illnesses	746.8	796.4	793.3	507.6	535.5	533.2
neoplasms	204.9	253.1	267.3	105.8	119.8	121.3
respiratory illnesses	230.6	154.6	148.6	112.3	63.5	62.0
accidents and injuries	178.9	130.8	143.6	36.8	34.0	36.6
Urban Population						
Deaths from all causes including:	1,433.2	1,405.3	1,414.5	818.1	808.1	817.3
circulatory illnesses	750.5	795.5	767.6	516.0	525.3	521.8
neoplasms	261.4	287.5	304.8	136.8	149.1	148.1
respiratory illnesses	148.2	101.3	96.8	64.6	36.6	39.4
accidents and injuries	152.6	111.6	123.3	36.5	30.6	35.1
Rural Population						
Deaths from all causes including:	1,565.6	1,543.0	1,596.3	839.3	836.9	838.9
circulatory illnesses	758.2	812.5	829.4	508.6	551.3	551.9
neoplasms	178.1	240.4	251.2	90.5	98.7	103.1
respiratory illnesses	278.5	198.1	192.5	140.9	82.6	80.4
accidents and injuries	230.2	186.1	203.8	42.9	45.3	44.6
MOLDOVA						
Total Population						
Deaths from all causes including:	1,711.6	1,725.9	1,811.6	1,201.7	1,164.9	1,179.9
circulatory illnesses	925.6	983.9	1,022.9	744.1	747.3	761.1
neoplasms	167.8	216.3	226.3	108.8	121.8	122.2
respiratory illnesses	180.5	147.8	157.4	96.0	64.7	68.0
accidents and injuries	202.0	153.4	177.9	74.7	61.9	65.1
Urban Population						
Deaths from all causes including:	1,723.8	1,556.3	1,555.5	1,131.9	1,038.5	1,019.1
circulatory illnesses	908.6	838.2	827.3	704.8	671.9	652.3
neoplasms	259.8	271.5	280.3	158.7	149.0	148.2
respiratory illnesses	143.1	108.9	102.1	60.0	33.9	45.9
accidents and injuries	187.7	123.6	146.4	69.1	50.7	53.4
Rural Population						
Deaths from all causes including:	1,723.6	1,849.7	2,012.1	1,248.9	1,258.1	1,299.5
circulatory illnesses	932.8	1,067.4	1,150.5	765.4	794.8	832.2
neoplasms	127.4	186.3	196.6	85.8	107.7	107.5
respiratory illnesses	201.4	173.7	196.3	115.6	85.1	83.6
accidents and injuries	215.6	183.1	215.7	81.0	72.7	76.2
LITHUANIA						
Total Population						
Deaths from all causes including:	1,453.3	1,352.7	1,355.7	824.0	762.3	755.2
circulatory illnesses	689.6	720.4	705.7	505.6	492.9	479.6
neoplasms	233.3	261.9	268.2	134.6	129.1	132.1
respiratory illnesses	147.6	91.7	92.4	59.4	28.6	29.8
accidents and injuries	250.8	164.0	180.0	53.5	45.2	47.1
Urban Population						
Deaths from all causes including:	1,399.8	1,271.4	1,294.9	797.0	732.6	743.5
circulatory illnesses	675.8	678.8	687.3	474.4	458.1	452.0
neoplasms	257.5	278.9	279.6	152.6	144.9	152.0
respiratory illnesses	109.5	62.4	64.2	40.7	20.2	22.2
accidents and injuries	213.4	133.2	151.1	49.2	41.0	43.7
Rural Population						
Deaths from all causes including:	1,541.5	1,490.5	1,473.4	853.9	815.8	784.5
circulatory illnesses	696.3	760.1	723.6	530.9	535.4	514.0
neoplasms	218.1	250.3	263.2	117.6	112.8	110.4
respiratory illnesses	179.4	126.0	124.7	77.2	40.2	39.7
accidents and injuries	321.7	237.2	251.3	64.0	57.4	58.2

TABLE 7. Standardized Mortality Rates by Cause, 1980, 1987, and 1988.—Continued

Deaths per 100,000 persons

Geographical Unit	Males			Females		
	1980	1987	1988	1980	1987	1988
LATVIA						
Total Population						
Deaths from all causes including:	1,669.5	1,541.2	1,548.7	911.9	878.1	863.3
circulatory illnesses	941.2	896.5	891.9	609.0	587.2	575.7
neoplasms	247.9	294.3	290.6	135.7	144.2	137.8
respiratory illnesses	95.7	68.4	68.2	33.8	23.4	21.0
accidents and injuries	249.4	158.4	170.0	63.7	48.6	54.9
Urban Population						
Deaths from all causes including:	1,589.1	1,468.3	1,475.6	884.5	857.5	839.9
circulatory illnesses	873.9	851.8	840.2	566.4	555.4	543.1
neoplasms	281.2	309.2	302.9	156.8	160.9	152.8
respiratory illnesses	86.1	55.6	59.5	31.3	19.6	17.8
accidents and injuries	208.7	134.1	147.8	60.4	44.5	52.0
Rural Population						
Deaths from all causes including:	1,826.0	1,701.1	1,713.9	963.1	930.1	914.4
circulatory illnesses	1,020.6	973.7	985.7	672.7	649.5	637.0
neoplasms	209.7	278.6	273.4	102.5	115.4	110.0
respiratory illnesses	110.1	90.9	88.8	39.1	31.3	27.5
accidents and injuries	348.6	218.9	226.0	75.6	61.2	64.1
ESTONIA						
Total Population						
Deaths from all causes including:	1,688.6	1,529.0	1,521.1	916.2	878.1	882.5
circulatory illnesses	968.6	912.2	897.5	619.8	599.0	596.2
neoplasms	262.5	278.4	291.9	137.8	141.9	141.7
respiratory illnesses	87.0	50.8	45.8	23.6	18.3	15.8
accidents and injuries	233.0	164.3	160.7	64.0	46.7	51.8
Urban Population						
Deaths from all causes including:	1,627.7	1,488.6	1,504.3	863.5	854.0	848.6
circulatory illnesses	894.4	875.0	882.0	557.1	561.6	551.1
neoplasms	284.7	297.9	300.8	150.7	157.1	155.4
respiratory illnesses	90.9	48.1	38.6	22.0	17.3	17.4
accidents and injuries	210.8	147.1	147.9	62.5	45.4	46.7
Rural Population						
Deaths from all causes including:	1,803.7	1,634.5	1,582.7	1,005.8	930.7	953.3
circulatory illnesses	1,060.0	979.1	932.0	713.7	667.1	677.4
neoplasms	235.5	249.0	282.2	118.4	114.1	116.5
respiratory illnesses	84.8	60.4	59.2	29.4	21.8	13.6
accidents and injuries	289.5	208.4	197.0	68.4	52.0	68.2
GEORGIA						
Total Population						
Deaths from all causes including:	1,361.2	1,311.4	1,304.6	812.1	773.6	773.4
circulatory illnesses	855.1	836.8	826.0	560.5	540.4	535.0
neoplasms	143.2	155.5	148.8	92.0	91.1	94.3
respiratory illnesses	105.2	80.3	81.3	64.6	45.5	47.2
accidents and injuries	104.6	86.0	94.7	26.7	24.7	25.4
Urban Population						
Deaths from all causes including:	1,449.4	1,358.2	1,347.5	888.3	808.4	808.8
circulatory illnesses	900.8	854.4	832.6	615.1	555.0	568.9
neoplasms	178.0	184.0	180.5	120.4	115.5	117.9
respiratory illnesses	84.8	67.4	67.1	49.2	33.1	34.7
accidents and injuries	109.5	83.0	93.8	29.7	24.5	26.7
Rural Population						
Deaths from all causes including:	1,274.1	1,262.2	1,264.3	754.1	741.2	740.3
circulatory illnesses	805.2	814.4	817.4	521.9	528.7	525.8
neoplasms	114.4	128.7	121.6	67.8	67.7	71.4
respiratory illnesses	120.0	91.9	94.3	76.3	56.2	58.5
accidents and injuries	100.4	90.7	97.1	24.5	25.5	24.2
AZERBAIJAN						
Total Population						
Deaths from all causes including:	1,439.3	1,420.7	1,448.3	870.8	811.3	825.5
circulatory illnesses	746.2	835.3	866.9	491.6	501.7	520.8
neoplasms	205.7	218.3	214.9	112.8	106.3	100.5
respiratory illnesses	176.1	118.0	124.1	112.2	75.5	80.4
accidents and injuries	94.5	75.4	78.2	34.9	28.3	27.3

TABLE 7. Standardized Mortality Rates by Cause, 1980, 1987, and 1988.—Continued

Deaths per 100,000 persons

Geographical Unit	Males			Females		
	1980	1987	1988	1980	1987	1988
Urban Population						
Deaths from all causes including:	1,567.5	1,486.1	1,488.8	926.5	840.1	840.6
circulatory illnesses	902.4	929.2	946.7	592.9	557.7	573.3
neoplasms	237.4	251.6	240.7	138.1	131.5	119.8
respiratory illnesses	112.8	70.7	73.6	61.2	35.8	41.0
accidents and injuries	106.1	84.5	84.4	37.7	33.1	30.1
Rural Population						
Deaths from all causes including:	1,307.7	1,333.8	1,388.2	800.9	756.4	789.0
circulatory illnesses	600.4	728.0	772.0	390.4	430.7	452.1
neoplasms	166.0	175.2	181.5	78.6	71.3	73.5
respiratory illnesses	236.3	167.0	178.0	159.6	115.6	121.5
accidents and injuries	80.9	65.8	70.3	31.2	22.1	23.2
ARMENIA						
Total Population						
Deaths from all causes including:	1,113.3	1,056.8	1,468.2	720.5	692.4	1,214.7
circulatory illnesses	536.7	552.6	583.4	412.6	402.7	383.3
neoplasms	171.7	180.6	185.1	93.3	103.2	99.5
respiratory illnesses	166.5	110.4	117.7	98.5	63.1	56.7
accidents and injuries	83.1	65.5	437.8	24.3	29.6	577.7
Urban Population						
Deaths from all causes including:	1,123.9	1,062.7	1,588.0	735.5	687.0	1,400.2
circulatory illnesses	562.1	548.3	590.0	439.0	399.5	394.3
neoplasms	193.0	201.0	207.5	113.5	120.5	117.4
respiratory illnesses	132.1	95.2	97.4	72.8	43.7	40.7
accidents and injuries	80.0	63.4	545.9	24.4	29.3	745.7
Rural Population						
Deaths from all causes including:	1,093.6	1,037.3	1,222.9	691.9	700.9	823.7
circulatory illnesses	493.6	548.6	568.5	371.1	409.3	364.6
neoplasms	137.5	143.8	146.3	59.1	72.5	67.0
respiratory illnesses	219.1	136.8	153.1	138.4	94.8	83.3
accidents and injuries	91.2	71.3	216.4	24.6	30.8	220.3
KAZAKHSTAN						
Total Population						
Deaths from all causes including:	1,673.0	1,431.4	1,435.3	904.4	789.9	792.0
circulatory illnesses	706.5	664.0	660.7	467.1	426.5	428.1
neoplasms	291.1	290.4	290.5	142.8	142.5	141.3
respiratory illnesses	233.7	159.8	158.1	118.5	74.8	74.2
accidents and injuries	225.5	145.8	152.9	62.3	44.1	43.9
Urban Population						
Deaths from all causes including:	1,817.7	1,592.8	1,606.5	973.4	881.8	884.7
circulatory illnesses	799.3	775.9	780.4	532.4	509.0	516.8
neoplasms	323.6	338.0	337.7	162.0	165.6	163.0
respiratory illnesses	224.7	145.4	145.6	98.4	57.5	57.4
accidents and injuries	255.2	152.1	163.0	70.2	47.4	46.0
Rural Population						
Deaths from all causes including:	1,544.5	1,306.8	1,300.7	829.6	708.7	716.7
circulatory illnesses	626.6	576.5	566.6	399.2	353.1	351.6
neoplasms	260.3	244.1	241.4	120.0	115.2	117.0
respiratory illnesses	247.0	179.7	176.5	139.6	95.2	94.2
accidents and injuries	191.8	142.3	146.8	51.7	40.4	42.2
UZBEKISTAN						
Total Population						
Deaths from all causes including:	1,390.1	1,274.8	1,300.3	934.2	896.8	895.4
circulatory illnesses	705.6	651.1	694.8	524.7	497.8	510.2
neoplasms	156.7	172.8	161.1	94.3	105.7	102.4
respiratory illnesses	193.8	162.0	156.1	141.3	116.8	107.9
accidents and injuries	133.3	90.6	97.4	40.6	34.1	35.0
Urban Population						
Deaths from all causes including:	1,555.2	1,316.2	1,343.2	949.7	853.9	852.3
circulatory illnesses	786.3	666.2	706.6	552.9	485.0	492.0
neoplasms	213.8	222.8	206.5	125.9	129.7	125.4
respiratory illnesses	175.4	131.8	131.0	104.7	78.5	74.5
accidents and injuries	160.0	101.6	111.3	48.6	38.3	38.1
Rural Population						
Deaths from all causes including:	1,244.8	1,215.6	1,244.8	908.6	917.0	920.2

TABLE 7. Standardized Mortality Rates by Cause, 1980, 1987, and 1988.—Continued

Deaths per 100,000 persons

Geographical Unit	Males			Females		
	1980	1987	1988	1980	1987	1988
circulatory illnesses	638.6	629.4	678.9	501.3	506.1	525.9
neoplasms	111.4	128.0	118.9	64.7	79.9	76.6
respiratory illnesses	199.8	177.9	170.6	163.2	144.2	133.1
accidents and injuries	109.4	79.3	83.9	31.2	27.9	29.6
KYRGYZSTAN						
Total Population						
Deaths from all causes including:	1,589.3	1,405.3	1,463.7	934.5	853.6	891.3
circulatory illnesses	665.4	671.1	687.2	463.4	449.6	466.9
neoplasms	187.5	200.2	192.5	100.9	104.2	112.1
respiratory illnesses	342.9	240.0	263.2	203.0	137.2	149.5
accidents and injuries	196.9	124.3	136.5	49.3	44.0	45.9
Urban Population						
Deaths from all causes including:	1,672.0	1,390.8	1,364.9	899.3	811.7	826.3
circulatory illnesses	760.8	697.4	655.1	497.2	474.1	459.8
neoplasms	254.2	252.5	245.3	131.3	124.8	138.8
respiratory illnesses	249.7	157.4	154.8	112.7	64.5	75.3
accidents and injuries	215.1	126.9	138.3	55.7	48.5	49.8
Rural Population						
Deaths from all causes including:	1,528.7	1,405.4	1,519.0	948.9	876.4	933.0
circulatory illnesses	616.2	655.8	707.7	445.9	434.5	476.5
neoplasms	145.8	161.7	153.7	79.5	88.3	89.5
respiratory illnesses	383.8	284.6	327.7	251.8	181.0	197.2
accidents and injuries	186.4	124.3	136.8	44.3	39.6	40.0
TAJIKISTAN						
Total Population						
Deaths from all causes including:	1,303.3	1,087.4	1,136.6	953.7	801.5	810.3
circulatory illnesses	560.3	478.2	521.8	440.3	366.8	389.4
neoplasms	152.2	145.8	151.6	84.7	90.1	84.2
respiratory illnesses	250.5	174.1	166.3	198.8	140.5	132.9
accidents and injuries	112.7	69.6	82.5	36.7	29.1	31.0
Urban Population						
Deaths from all causes including:	1,606.4	1,339.5	1,403.5	951.8	825.4	811.4
circulatory illnesses	718.0	630.7	681.8	474.5	421.8	440.1
neoplasms	241.7	231.4	239.3	124.9	129.1	114.1
respiratory illnesses	206.4	148.3	126.5	119.6	83.1	61.8
accidents and injuries	174.8	97.3	119.3	57.3	38.3	46.0
Rural Population						
Deaths from all causes including:	1,139.3	963.1	1,004.3	945.3	776.6	798.8
circulatory illnesses	482.3	410.7	450.8	419.9	334.9	360.0
neoplasms	104.5	101.6	108.1	56.0	62.0	62.7
respiratory illnesses	265.7	182.8	179.0	241.8	170.7	170.1
accidents and injuries	74.1	53.8	62.5	21.5	22.3	20.9
TURKMENISTAN						
Total Population						
Deaths from all causes including:	1,664.2	1,491.8	1,520.9	1,112.6	1,023.7	1,018.2
circulatory illnesses	848.3	796.2	799.2	597.2	558.2	563.0
neoplasms	221.8	191.4	205.6	143.1	130.4	122.1
respiratory illnesses	252.2	193.5	187.1	193.2	142.5	130.9
accidents and injuries	121.1	98.2	103.6	36.1	35.9	36.4
Urban Population						
Deaths from all causes including:	1,798.8	1,531.3	1,555.8	1,056.1	965.0	938.6
circulatory illnesses	912.6	799.0	807.5	595.2	535.2	531.9
neoplasms	267.2	234.4	244.0	159.7	147.9	126.9
respiratory illnesses	196.9	140.2	129.8	112.5	85.1	80.2
accidents and injuries	173.1	122.1	125.6	51.0	42.2	41.0
Rural Population						
Deaths from all causes including:	1,518.5	1,438.6	1,477.1	1,159.6	1,075.0	1,096.6
circulatory illnesses	790.9	786.0	789.4	601.8	581.1	597.4
neoplasms	178.9	152.1	170.0	125.4	110.8	116.8
respiratory illnesses	289.3	230.7	230.8	260.2	194.5	177.3
accidents and injuries	67.9	75.3	82.4	19.7	27.5	30.4

SOURCE: *Naseleniye SSSR, 1988.* 1989, pp. 664–678.

Figure 3. Mortality Rates, 1988
Males

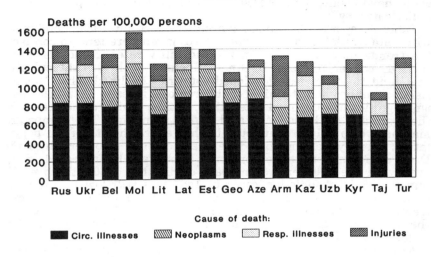

Females

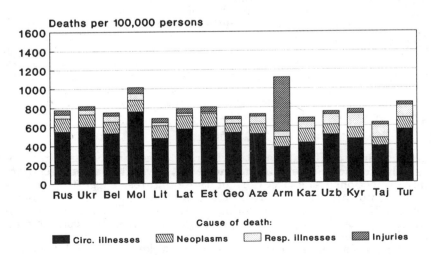

Source: *Naseleniye SSSR, 1988.*

Currently available morbidity rates for the former U.S.S.R. are potentially misleading. Official published data show only those people who went to hospitals or who otherwise came into contact with the health service infrastructure. The data do not count the sick who did not see a doctor or other medical personnel. In addition, people with illnesses that were not treated by a specialist could have been misdiagnosed or not classified in the proper morbidity category.

Table 8 reports the official morbidity rates for 1989. Combined with data available for 1985, the figures given here tend to confirm the trends that are shown in the mortality rates. Some diseases, such as cancer, increased. Other illnesses, such as tuberculosis, that tend to afflict less developed countries declined. The Central Asian republics had the highest tuberculosis rates in 1989. Alcoholism significantly declined after 1985, a time which coincides with the beginning of Gorbachev's anti-alcohol campaign. This campaign may have also helped contribute to the general health of the population, thereby helping to reduce the incidence of other illnesses. Drug addiction, on the other hand, has steadily increased. But, even with the 400 percent increase during the 1980s, the overall number of drug addiction cases in 1989 was still low by international standards. The number of cases of HIV infection is also extremely low, though one must seriously question the accuracy of these statistics given the limited amount of testing done in the former Soviet Union.

All republics of the former U.S.S.R. have historically followed the centralized Soviet model health care system, where there was little role for family doctors and private health services. Although private medical practice is now legal, the state still provides the majority of health care. Caution should be used when comparing statistics for Soviet health facilities with other countries. The same holds true for comparisons among the former Soviet republics because health standards may not be uniform (Table 9).

In 1990, Russia and the Baltic republics generally reported higher inputs of medical resources than other regions of the former U.S.S.R. The level of these reported inputs steadily increased throughout the 1980s. For example, in Russia, doctors increased from 40.3 per 10,000 persons in 1980 to a high of 47.3 in 1989, followed by a slight drop in 1990 to 46.9. On the other hand, coverage in Central Asia was less extensive, with only 27.1 doctors per 10,000 people in Tajikistan (1990).

B. EDUCATION

According to official statistics, literacy is near universal throughout the former Soviet Union. However, several Western scholars have questioned the accuracy of these figures, suggesting a substantial upward bias. To avoid this controversy, we feel it is more informative to examine educational attainment. Table 10 shows the percentage of the population age 15 and over that has completed a specified level of education.

When referring to Table 10, one must keep in mind that the older population (those aged 60 and above) have generally not attained the average level of education for the former U.S.S.R. as a whole. Thus, regions with a higher proportion of old people tend to have lower education levels. This partially explains why historical-

TABLE 8. Morbidity Rates, 1989.

(Per 100,000 persons, except as noted)

Cause of Death	U.S.S.R.	Russian Federation	Ukraine	Lithuania	Latvia	Estonia	Georgia	Azerbaijan
Malignant neoplasm	267.8	278.0	282.0	271.0	259.0	323.0	145.0	228.0
Psychological disorders	119.8	124.1	161.2	92.1	134.6	107.3	55.9	66.6
Tuberculosis	40.0	37.6	34.5	32.5	26.8	25.8	27.9	42.2
Alcoholism	149.0	191.0	152.0	129.0	165.0	85.0	16.0	15.0
Drug addiction	5.4	5.5	7.0	3.1	6.5	3.3	2.3	4.9
Syphilis	4.1	4.3	4.1	2.2	2.2	3.6	16.2	3.1
Gonorrhoea	105.7	137.5	81.9	93.7	103.7	128.4	60.3	22.7
Typhoid and paratyphoid	3.3	0.8	0.4	0.8	0.2	0.3	1.4	3.0
Other salmonellosis infections	54.6	70.8	25.4	31.7	125.8	85.5	19.7	25.5
Acute intestinal diseases	510.7	658.0	223.4	170.8	141.0	295.2	259.4	228.7
including: bacterial dysentery	136.7	201.0	54.7	66.1	45.0	70.6	36.6	28.8
Brucellosis	1.9	0.4	0.0	0.0	0.0	0.0	4.0	1.9
Meningococcic infections	4.3	5.0	3.5	2.9	3.0	2.4	1.3	0.8
Tetanus	0.1	0.1	0.2	1.3	1.7	1.0	0.2	0.1
Hepatitis	317.4	192.9	213.9	206.6	295.3	86.7	226.3	310.5
including: hepatitis B	43.3	25.1	31.6	35.9	24.8	8.7	41.0	23.3
Parotitis epidemic	57.7	49.2	102.2	17.6	8.0	33.2	18.0	10.7
Rickettsiosis	0.6	0.9	0.2	0.1	0.0	0.0	0.1	0.0
Malaria	0.5	0.4	0.4	0.3	0.2	0.9	0.1	1.1
Flu and acute infections of the respiratory track	23,761	28,619	24,550	12,403	15,725	20,220	12,037	11,538
Registered HIV cases (number) [1]	584	453	68	3	14	12	4	0

Cause of Death	Armenia	Uzbekistan	Kyrgyzstan	Tajikistan	Turkmenistan	Kazakhstan	Belarus	Moldova
Malignant neoplasm	235.0	172.0	220.0	170.0	200.0	286.0	260.0	219.0
Psychological disorders	47.3	93.4	98.1	56.5	59.2	88.9	106.0	140.5
Tuberculosis	20.1	50.4	49.6	47.0	59.2	72.8	31.0	46.1
Alcoholism	11.0	44.0	68.0	34.0	42.0	120.0	132.0	149.0
Drug addiction	0.9	5.0	6.4	3.2	10.6	5.3	1.7	1.6
Syphilis	3.4	3.1	2.6	1.7	6.7	1.8	2.1	10.0
Gonorrhoea	40.7	24.9	60.3	23.0	30.0	107.0	107.7	118.4
Typhoid and paratyphoid	1.9	15.5	7.9	47.1	39.3	2.9	0.2	0.4
Other salmonellosis infections	32.1	43.1	38.5	40.1	37.5	41.0	38.8	115.3
Acute intestinal diseases	249.5	635.4	580.7	920.3	579.3	410.0	131.1	571.4
including: bacterial dysentery	59.7	69.5	98.7	131.9	46.4	108.7	47.3	168.2
Brucellosis	4.4	5.9	14.3	6.4	11.6	10.6	0.0	0.1
Meningococcic infections	1.3	2.5	5.8	4.2	5.2	4.3	5.3	7.0
Tetanus	0.0	0.1	0.1	0.0	0.0	0.1	0.1	3.7
Hepatitis	279.0	1,074.5	710.8	918.3	735.1	465.6	431.7	351.7
including: hepatitis B	23.4	217.0	50.3	94.2	100.8	30.8	21.2	65.3
Parotitis epidemic	36.8	33.8	41.5	70.3	51.6	90.5	54.9	32.5
Rickettsiosis	0.0	0.7	1.1	0.1	0.1	0.9	0.3	1.0
Malaria	0.1	0.4	0.1	3.9	0.5	0.1	0.7	0.6
Flu and acute infections of the respiratory track	15,941	10,232	13,274	14,119	10,276	18,428	26,501	14,986
Registered HIV cases (number) [1]	1	3	0	0	1	6	14	5

Sources: *Okhrana Zdorov'ya v SSSR.* 1990, pp. 34–56. *Narodnoye Khozyaystvo SSSR v 1990g.* 1991, pp. 244–250.
[1] Data are as of the end of 1990. Registered HIV cases show the number of citizens of the former U.S.S.R. who have tested positive for HIV infection. According to official statistics, the total number of cases of HIV infection in the territory of the former U.S.S.R., including both citizens and foreigners, is about double the number of infected citizens. As of the end of 1990, 30 people were officially reported as having died because of the AIDS virus.

ly more developed areas, such as the Baltic republics, appear to have had lower educational levels than less developed areas, such as Central Asia. Populations in Central Asian republics did not necessarily have access to more education, they just had a much higher proportion of young people. [8]

---

[8] Despite having a below average proportion of the elderly, Moldova had the lowest level of complete secondary education in the former U.S.S.R.

TABLE 9. Health Facilities, 1990.

(Per 10,000 persons)

Geographical Unit	Doctors	Mid-Level Medical Personnel	Hospital Beds
U.S.S.R.	44.2	118.3	132.6
European U.S.S.R.	45.8	120.8	136.5
Transcaucasus	46.8	106.2	102.4
Central Asia	36.7	110.9	124.8
Russian Federation	46.9	122.6	137.5
Ukraine	44.0	117.5	135.5
Belarus	40.5	115.6	132.3
Moldova	40.0	118.6	131.4
Lithuania	46.1	127.4	124.4
Latvia	49.6	117.4	148.1
Estonia	45.7	96.2	121.0
Georgia	59.2	118.3	110.7
Azerbaijan	39.3	98.6	102.2
Armenia	42.8	103.0	89.8
Kazakhstan	41.2	123.9	136.2
Uzbekistan	35.8	110.7	123.7
Kyrgyzstan	36.7	104.9	119.8
Tajikistan	27.1	80.3	105.8
Turkmenistan	35.7	105.0	113.3

Source: *Narodnoye Khozyaystvo SSSR 1990.* 1991, pp. 254–258.
[1] Mid-level medical personnel covers a wide variety of medical professions including nurses, doctors' assistants, and midwives.

Georgia and Armenia had the highest proportion of the population with complete higher education in 1989. They also had the highest level of secondary education for any republic of the former Soviet Union. Given the impact of age structure, it is understandable why all of the Central Asian republics and Azerbaijan had above average shares of the population with complete secondary education.

TABLE 10. Education, 1989.

Geographical Unit	Complete Higher [1] (percent)	Complete Secondary and Above [2] (percent)	Complete Higher (USSR=100)	Secondary and Above (USSR=100)
U.S.S.R.	10.8	61.2	100	100
RUSSIAN FEDERATION	11.3	59.6	105	97
Northern economic region	9.7	60.7	90	99
Arkhangel'sk	8.8	56.4	81	92
Nenets ASR	8.9	60.3	82	99
Other Arkhangel'sk	8.8	56.3	81	92
Vologda	8.2	53.9	76	88
Murmansk	13.9	72.4	129	118
Republic of Karelia	9.6	58.1	89	95
Komi SSR	8.9	64.8	82	106
Northwestern economic region	16.5	66.9	153	109
Leningrad	18.3	70.2	170	115
St.Petersburg city	21.3	74.2	197	121
Leningrad oblast	9.4	58.1	87	95
Novgorod	8.8	52.5	81	86
Pskov	8.1	52.0	75	85
Central economic region	15.5	62.2	144	102
Bryansk	7.7	52.4	71	86
Vladimir	9.2	56.0	85	92
Ivanovo	8.9	54.3	82	89
Kaluga	11.1	58.7	103	96
Kostroma	8.3	52.0	77	85
Moscow	21.4	69.5	198	114
Moscow city	26.4	74.6	244	122
Moscow oblast	14.8	62.8	137	103
Orel	8.8	53.5	81	87
Ryazan'	8.7	53.2	81	87
Smolensk	8.7	53.0	81	87
Tver'	8.8	53.6	81	88
Tula	9.3	52.6	86	86
Yaroslavl'	9.5	55.9	88	91
Volgo-Vyatsk economic region	8.9	55.6	82	91
Kirov	7.9	52.7	73	86
Nizhegorodsk	9.6	55.1	89	90
Republic of Mariy El	9.7	58.2	90	95
Mordov SSR	8.8	59.0	81	96
Chuvash Republic	7.9	56.6	73	92
Central Chernozem economic region	8.9	54.1	82	88
Belgorod	8.3	55.1	77	90
Voronezh	10.4	56.3	96	92
Kursk	7.9	52.1	73	85
Lipetsk	8.4	54.1	78	88
Tambov	8.0	51.1	74	83
Povolzhkiy economic region	10.0	58.7	93	96
Astrakhan'	9.7	59.9	90	98
Volgograd	9.7	59.6	90	97
Penza	8.8	52.9	81	86
Samara	11.2	61.4	104	100
Saratov	11.0	57.6	102	94
Ulyanovsk (Simbirsk)	8.9	56.3	82	92
Republic of Kalmykia (Khalmg Tangch)	9.2	60.0	85	98
Republic of Tatarstan	9.5	59.4	88	97
North-Caucasus economic region	9.7	56.9	90	93
Krasnodar Kray	9.2	55.8	85	91
Adygeya SSR	9.1	57.2	84	93
Other Krasnodar Kray	9.2	55.7	85	91
Stavropol' Kray	9.6	56.6	89	93
Rostov	10.6	58.2	98	95
Republic of Dagestan	8.3	54.1	77	88
Kabardino-Balkar Republic	10.1	61.3	94	100
Karachayevo-Cherkess SSR	9.6	58.5	89	96
North-Ossetian SSR	13.3	64.1	123	105
Chechen-Ingush Republic	7.6	53.5	70	87
Urals economic region	8.4	56.6	78	92
Kurgan	7.2	51.1	67	83
Orenburg	7.9	55.6	73	91

TABLE 10. Education, 1989.—Continued

Geographical Unit	Complete Higher [1] (percent)	Complete Secondary and Above [2] (percent)	Complete Higher (USSR = 100)	Secondary and Above (USSR = 100)
Perm'	8.0	53.9	74	88
Komi-Permyat AO	4.3	38.3	40	63
Other Perm'	8.2	54.7	76	89
Sverdlovsk (Yekaterinburg)	9.1	58.0	84	95
Chelyabinsk	9.0	58.7	83	96
Republic of Bashkortostan	7.6	56.5	70	92
Udmurt Republic	9.2	58.8	85	96
West Siberian economic region	9.6	59.2	89	97
Altay Kray	8.2	53.7	76	88
Kemerovo	8.0	56.2	74	92
Novosibirsk	11.7	57.3	108	94
Omsk	9.7	58.7	90	96
Tomsk	11.6	62.1	107	101
Tyumen'	10.2	69.5	94	114
Khanti-Mansiysk AOkr	10.4	78.9	96	129
Yamalo-Nenetsk Republic	12.5	81.5	116	133
Other Tyumen'	9.1	55.9	85	91
Republic of Gornyy Altay	8.0	53.1	74	87
East Siberian economic region	10.0	59.0	93	96
Krasnoyarsk Kray	9.8	59.8	91	98
Taymyr AOkr	11.0	76.3	102	125
Evenki AO	11.6	72.3	107	118
Other Krasnoyarsk Kray	9.7	59.4	90	97
Irkutsk	10.1	58.9	94	96
Ust-Ordynsk Buryat AOkr	7.1	48.3	66	79
Other Irkutsk	10.3	59.4	95	97
Chita	10.3	57.3	95	94
Aga Buryat AOkr	9.9	57.5	92	94
Other Chita	10.3	57.3	96	94
Republic of Buryat	11.8	61.1	109	100
Republic of Tuva	7.9	57.3	73	94
Republic of Khakasia	8.0	56.1	74	92
Far Eastern economic region	12.5	66.7	116	109
Primor Kray	12.8	64.0	119	105
Khabarovsk Kray	12.7	62.8	118	103
Yevreysk AO	7.7	51.8	71	85
Other Khabarovsk Kray	13.4	64.3	124	105
Amur	11.2	60.5	104	99
Kamchatka	15.5	77.3	144	126
Koryak ASR	10.7	72.2	99	118
Other Kamchatka	15.9	77.8	148	127
Magadan	13.9	78.1	129	128
Chukotsk ASR	14.9	81.5	138	133
Other Magadan	13.5	76.7	125	125
Sakhalin	11.2	68.3	104	112
Republic of Sakha (Yakutia)	11.3	73.7	105	120
Kaliningrad	12.4	64.5	115	105
UKRAINE	10.4	61.0	96	100
Donets-Dnieper economic region	10.3	61.9	95	101
Dnepropetrovsk	11.5	65.4	106	107
Donetsk	9.6	62.4	89	102
Zaporozh'ye	10.6	63.1	98	103
Kirovograd	7.9	58.8	73	96
Lugansk	9.0	59.7	83	98
Poltava	8.4	58.3	78	95
Sumy	8.0	56.5	74	92
Khar'kov	14.4	64.5	133	105
Southwestern economic region	9.9	59.1	92	97
Vinnitsa	7.0	52.0	65	85
Volyn	7.4	56.2	69	92
Zhitomir	6.9	56.2	64	92
Zakarpat'ye	7.2	59.3	67	97
Ivano-Frankovsk	8.3	55.4	77	91
Kiev	NA	NA	NA	NA
Kiev city	24.4	82.2	226	134
Kiev oblast	8.3	57.9	77	95

TABLE 10. Education, 1989.—Continued

Geographical Unit	Complete Higher [1] (percent)	Complete Secondary and Above [2] (percent)	Complete Higher (USSR=100)	Secondary and Above (USSR=100)
L'vov	11.1	61.7	103	101
Rovno	7.5	55.9	69	91
Ternopol'	7.4	52.5	69	86
Khmel'nitskiy	7.1	54.5	66	89
Cherkassy	8.1	56.2	75	92
Chernigov	7.4	51.2	69	84
Chernovtsy	7.6	54.3	70	89
Southern economic region	11.8	63.5	109	104
Krym ASSR	12.7	65.7	118	107
Nikolayev	10.0	62.3	93	102
Odessa	13.3	63.7	123	104
Kherson	9.1	60.5	84	99
BELARUS	10.8	60.2	100	98
Brest	8.5	55.9	79	91
Vitebsk	8.7	56.0	81	92
Gomel'	9.0	59.0	83	96
Grodno	8.6	54.7	80	89
Minsk	NA	NA	NA	NA
Minsk city	22.9	80.6	212	132
Minsk oblast	7.9	54.3	73	89
Mogilev	8.6	58.4	80	95
MOLDOVA	8.7	55.1	81	90
Chisinau city	20.5	78.1	190	128
LITHUANIA	10.6	57.2	98	93
Vil'nyus city	20.3	73.8	188	121
LATVIA	11.5	60.4	106	99
Riga city	18.1	73.1	168	119
ESTONIA	11.7	59.1	108	97
Tallinn city	17.9	72.2	166	118
GEORGIA	15.1	72.5	140	118
Tbilisi city	29.3	84.0	271	137
Abkhaz ASSR	12.3	68.2	114	111
Adzhar ASSR	11.4	71.2	106	116
South Ossetian AO	15.0	66.6	139	109
Republic territories	10.2	68.9	94	113
AZERBAIJAN	10.5	68.6	97	112
Baku city	19.1	75.7	177	124
Nakhichevan ASSR	9.0	70.6	83	115
Nagorno-Karabakh AO	8.6	62.1	80	101
Republic territories	7.0	65.8	65	108
ARMENIA	13.8	71.5	128	117
Yerevan city	23.9	80.9	221	132
KAZAKHSTAN	9.9	64.0	92	105
Aktyubinsk	8.5	62.5	79	102
Alma-Ata	NA	NA	NA	NA
Alma-Ata city	22.9	76.6	212	125
Alma-Ata oblast	7.4	62.0	69	101
East Kazakhstan	8.8	59.1	81	97
Gur'yev	9.7	71.5	90	117
Dzhambul	9.5	63.7	88	104
Dzhezkazgan	10.7	67.3	99	110
Karaganda	10.5	65.8	97	108
Kzyl-Orda	12.6	71.4	117	117
Kokchetav	6.9	57.0	64	93
Kustanay	7.6	60.6	70	99
Mangistausk	NA	NA	NA	NA
Pavlodar	7.8	62.1	72	101
North Kazakhstan	7.2	55.3	67	90
Semipalatinsk	10.0	63.1	93	103
Taldy-Kurgan	7.6	61.4	70	100
Turgay	NA	NA	NA	NA
Ural'sk	8.3	59.9	77	98

TABLE 10. Education, 1989.—Continued

Geographical Unit	Complete Higher [1] (percent)	Complete Secondary and Above [2] (percent)	Complete Higher (USSR=100)	Secondary and Above (USSR=100)
Tselinograd	8.4	62.3	78	102
Chimkent	9.1	64.6	84	106
UZBEKISTAN	9.2	66.9	85	109
Andizhan	6.4	66.8	59	109
Bukhara	8.5	68.5	79	112
Dzhizak	NA	NA	NA	NA
Kashkadar'ya	7.2	67.6	67	110
Namangan	5.9	69.0	55	113
Samarkand	8.5	66.6	79	109
Surkhandar'ya	6.4	63.1	59	103
Syrdar'ya	8.1	64.4	75	105
Tashkent	NA	NA	NA	NA
Tashkent city	21.1	74.9	195	122
Tashkent oblast	8.1	62.0	75	101
Fergana	7.0	65.6	65	107
Khorezm	7.2	66.3	67	108
Karakalpak ASSR	7.8	63.3	72	103
KYRGYZSTAN	9.4	65.8	87	108
Bishkek city	19.7	75.3	182	123
Dzhalal-Abad	NA	NA	NA	NA
Issyk-Kul'	9.2	64.3	85	105
Naryn	NA	NA	NA	NA
Osh	6.6	66.9	61	109
Talas	NA	NA	NA	NA
Chuysk	NA	NA	NA	NA
Republic territories	7.1	58.0	66	95
TAJIKISTAN	7.5	62.6	69	102
Gorno-Badakhshan AO	8.9	70.3	82	115
Dushanbe city	17.2	69.8	159	114
Khatlon	5.4	60.5	50	99
Kulyab	NA	NA	NA	NA
Kurgan-Tyube	NA	NA	NA	NA
Khudzhand	6.8	63.6	63	104
Republic territories	4.9	57.7	45	94
TURKMENISTAN	8.3	65.1	77	106
Ashkhabad city	18.0	71.0	167	116
Mary	6.7	65.3	62	107
Tashauz	5.5	60.7	51	99
Chardzhou	8.3	64.7	77	106
Balkan	NA	NA	NA	NA
Republic territories	6.5	65.2	60	107

Source: *Uroven' Obrazovaniya Naseleniya SSSR, Perepis' Naseleniya, 1989.* 1990, pp. 14–58.
NA Data not available.
[1] Complete higher education shows the percent of the population age 15 and older who have completed higher education.
[2] The complete secondary and above education embraces the data in the first column (complete higher education), but is more inclusive. Coverage extends to those who finished general high school, "technicums" (secondary specialized education), and those who entered higher education (baccalaureate programs) but failed to graduate; those who did not complete general high school are excluded.

Table 10 shows educational levels which have already been attained by the population. But, if one wants to find out what access the population currently has to education, the number of schools and students presently in the system must be examined (Table 11). As with Table 10, the age distribution of a particular region may distort the picture. Regions with a higher proportion of young people will have a comparatively higher number of secondary students per 1000 people. One way to examine the data more effectively is to show secondary students per 1000 persons age 15 and under. Though certain regions have slightly different education systems, and the age 15 cutoff may exclude a small percentage of the population that is still in school, this method of presentation does reduce the age distribution effect. Finally, there is the potential that regional differences in the definition of a school may also distort inter-republic comparisons.

With this correction, the Russian Federation no longer appears to have proportionally fewer students than the Central Asian republics and it nearly equals the U.S.S.R. average. This upgrading is consistent with the fact that during the 1990–1991 school year, Russia had the highest number of higher educational institutions, accounting for over half of all those in the former U.S.S.R. Nevertheless, it was Armenia that ranked first in terms of the number of students per 10,000 persons in higher education institutions.

TABLE 11. Schools and Students During the 1990/91 School Year.

Geographical Unit	Second- ary Schools (1000)	Second- ary School Students (mil.)	Second- ary School Students (per 1000 persons)	Second- ary School Students (per 1000 persons age 15 and under)	Higher Educa- tion Schools	Higher Educa- tion Students (1000)	Higher Educa- tion Students (per 10,000 persons)
U.S.S.R.	135.9	45.3	156.2	581.5	911	5,161.6	177.9
European U.S.S.R.	102.4	31.3	140.3	585.6	732	4,086.5	183.2
Transcaucasus	9.4	2.9	181.5	590.0	50	277.4	173.6
Central Asia	24.1	11.1	217.7	568.1	129	797.7	156.4
Russian Federation	69.6	20.9	140.7	580.6	514	2,824.5	190.1
Ukraine	21.8	7.1	136.7	600.3	149	881.2	169.6
Belarus	5.4	1.5	146.2	604.1	33	188.6	183.8
Moldova	1.7	0.7	160.3	546.0	9	54.7	125.3
Lithuania	2.2	0.5	134.1	592.6	11	65.6	176.0
Latvia	1.0	0.4	149.2	660.1	10	46.0	171.6
Estonia	0.7	0.2	126.4	606.5	6	25.9	163.7
Georgia	3.7	0.9	164.7	632.5	19	103.9	190.2
Azerbaijan	4.3	1.4	196.2	575.4	17	105.1	147.3
Armenia	1.4	0.6	177.7	566.6	14	68.4	202.6
Kazakhstan	8.8	3.2	190.6	576.5	55	287.4	171.1
Uzbekistan	8.5	4.7	227.0	552.5	46	340.9	164.6
Kyrgyzstan	1.8	1.0	226.1	580.4	9	58.8	133.0
Tajikistan	3.2	1.3	242.6	566.2	10	68.8	128.4
Turkmenistan	1.8	0.9	242.3	581.4	9	41.8	112.5

Source: *Narodnoye Khozyaystvo SSSR 1990.* 1991, pp. 214 and 222.
Higher education includes universities, technical, and other higher education schools and students.

C. PERSONAL STANDARD OF LIVING

The standard of living of the population is an important, but very difficult, subject to address for the former U.S.S.R. Comparisons between present day incomes (for which data are sketchy) and incomes for 1990 (the year of the most recent comprehensive set of data) are extremely tenuous. Until the value of the ruble is established and inflation measured properly, current assessments should be avoided. Nevertheless, several tables are presented that show how the 15 republics have historically compared to each other.

Table 12 presents CIR (Center for International Research, U.S. Bureau of the Census) estimates of the average levels and sources of income for the republics. In 1990, the Baltic republics had the highest levels of total income in the former Soviet Union, while the Central Asian republics and Azerbaijan had the lowest. Of total income, Armenia had the highest share (22 percent) coming from sources other than earned income (i.e., transfer receipts). This high share derives from the great number of state loans for new housing that Armenians are still receiving as a result of the 1988 earthquake.

TABLE 12. Levels and Sources of Income, 1990.

Rubles per capita

Geographical Unit	Total Income	Total Income Currently Earned	Including:		Transfer Receipts	Including:		
			State Wages and Salaries			Pensions and Allowances	Sti-pends	Other Trans-fers
U.S.S.R.	2,275.5	1,883.9	1,449.0		391.6	292.4	10.8	88.3
Russian Federation	2,546.7	2,129.6	1,741.8		417.1	325.1	11.4	80.6
Ukraine	2,235.7	1,800.2	1,255.2		435.6	322.4	10.7	102.5
Belarus	2,480.3	2,025.1	1,475.3		455.2	339.4	11.4	104.4
Moldova	2,130.7	1,767.6	1,001.9		363.1	238.8	7.9	116.4
Lithuania	2,624.9	2,111.8	1,507.0		513.1	324.5	10.5	178.1
Latvia	2,988.1	2,445.1	1,604.5		543.0	344.6	11.0	187.5
Estonia	3,288.5	2,617.2	1,988.1		671.3	390.5	13.8	267.0
Georgia	2,208.2	1,832.2	1,198.7		376.0	236.5	8.2	131.3
Azerbaijan	1,476.8	1,197.2	763.7		279.6	172.0	8.4	99.1
Armenia	2,149.7	1,677.2	1,338.8		472.6	255.5	10.7	206.5
Kazakhstan	1,882.0	1,622.6	1,337.1		259.4	204.9	11.0	43.5
Uzbekistan	1,342.1	1,093.7	722.9		248.4	166.5	9.4	72.5
Kyrgyzstan	1,502.8	1,251.8	810.9		251.0	186.2	10.0	54.8
Tajikistan	1,181.1	965.1	593.7		215.9	151.0	8.2	56.8
Turkmenistan	1,453.1	1,220.7	782.4		232.4	153.3	7.7	71.3

Source: Tretyakova and Kostinsky, *Gross National Product Accounts of the Newly Independent States of the Former Soviet Union, 1987–90*. Center for International Research, U.S. Bureau of the Census, 1992, p. 14.
Data may not sum to total due to rounding.
[1] Includes state farms.

Looking at the distribution of expenditures from income on different categories of goods and services provides further insight into the personal standard of living. Unfortunately, the most recently available family budget expenditure data come from a survey of over 300,000 people taken in 1988: Table 13 presents these data.

All of the Central Asian republics except Kazakhstan, and all three of the Transcaucasus republics had above average levels of expenditure on food. At the same time, the Baltic republics, particularly Estonia, had the lowest levels of food expenditures. The republics with large historically Muslim populations (the Central Asian republics and Azerbaijan) all had significantly below-average expenditures on alcoholic beverages.

The average amount spent on food for all of the republics of the former Soviet Union amounted to slightly more than one-third of a family's total income. Table 14 shows the amount and types of foods that people of the various republics eat. In 1990, Ukraine, Belarus, and Moldova had the highest average daily caloric intakes, while the Armenia, Azerbaijan, and most of the Central Asian republics (which also spent the highest share of their incomes on food) had the lowest average daily caloric intakes. At the same time, each one of the Transcaucasus and Central Asian republics had above average starchy-staple ratios. [9] Every republic, except Georgia, saw a decrease in this ratio between 1980 and 1990 which could indicate a more varied diet.

Additional insight into living standards is found in the data on possession of consumer durables per 100 families (Table 15). Generally, collective farm families are not as well provisioned as families of workers and employees.

TABLE 13. Family Budget Expenditures, 1988.

(Percent of income)

Geographical Unit	Food [1]	Soft and Durable Goods	Alcoholic Beverages	Personal Services	Taxes and Miscellaneous	Other Expenditures	Savings
A. Worker and Employee Families							
U.S.S.R.	32.2	31.3	2.8	10.1	9.7	5.1	8.8
Russian Federation	31.3	31.8	3.0	10.5	10.0	4.6	8.8
Ukraine	32.5	31.9	2.2	9.9	9.6	5.6	8.3
Belarus	30.3	30.0	3.7	10.3	9.5	5.8	10.4
Moldova	30.1	33.3	3.4	9.5	8.9	6.5	8.3
Lithuania	30.7	31.8	3.8	9.8	9.6	4.9	9.4
Latvia	30.5	31.0	2.8	9.8	10.0	5.7	10.2
Estonia	29.3	34.7	3.1	9.4	10.0	3.8	9.7
Georgia	38.3	26.2	2.1	9.2	7.9	7.8	8.5
Azerbaijan	43.7	26.8	1.4	8.5	7.3	7.1	5.2
Armenia	43.3	23.8	3.2	7.4	8.7	5.6	8.0
Kazakhstan	30.8	29.9	2.9	9.3	9.7	5.8	11.6
Uzbekistan	39.2	29.7	1.6	9.5	8.3	5.3	6.4
Kyrgyzstan	33.0	30.8	1.8	9.3	8.0	7.7	9.4
Tajikistan	38.3	31.3	1.2	9.3	8.0	5.2	6.7
Turkmenistan	37.4	31.2	2.1	9.8	8.9	7.1	3.5
B. Collective Farm Families							
U.S.S.R.	35.4	29.9	3.5	5.5	1.8	9.6	14.3
Russian Federation	31.7	30.0	3.8	5.9	1.9	9.0	17.7
Ukraine	35.2	29.4	3.2	5.0	1.8	10.6	14.8
Belarus	34.5	23.2	6.6	4.7	1.4	16.1	13.5
Moldova	32.9	32.5	6.8	6.6	1.5	12.3	7.4
Lithuania	25.3	24.0	5.3	5.3	1.1	12.5	26.5
Latvia	30.8	30.4	3.5	7.1	1.6	6.0	20.6
Estonia	24.3	37.9	4.4	6.9	1.7	6.9	17.9
Georgia	32.1	25.5	6.5	5.2	2.0	12.5	16.2
Azerbaijan	45.1	30.5	0.8	4.0	1.0	10.5	8.1
Armenia	38.7	31.0	3.5	6.1	2.2	10.2	8.3
Kazakhstan	32.5	30.6	3.3	5.8	2.0	7.6	18.2
Uzbekistan	47.1	31.9	1.6	6.2	2.9	7.4	3.8
Kyrgyzstan	35.8	32.2	1.9	6.4	1.7	11.0	11.0
Tajikistan	48.7	32.3	0.3	4.8	2.6	5.5	5.8
Turkmenistan	40.0	35.3	1.9	5.4	2.2	7.0	8.2

Source: *Byudzhety Rabochikh, Sluzhashchikh, i Kolkhoznikov v 1975–1988*, pp. 49–64, 277–292.

[1] It is not clear whether or not this includes a ruble evaluation of income-in-kind from self-produced goods.

---

[9] The starchy-staple ratio shows the percent of a person's diet that comes from food items such as potatoes, bread, and other grain products.

TABLE 14. Food Consumption, 1980 and 1990.

(Average daily caloric intake per capita)

Geographical Unit	Meat (with Sub-products)	Milk and Milk Products	Eggs	Potatoes	Vegeta-bles	Bread and Grain Products	Fish and Fish Products	Sugar	Vegetable Oil	Total Consumed	Starchy-Staple Ratio (percent)
1980											
U.S.S.R.	407	516	64	209	56	1,248	24	424	213	3,161	46.1
European U.S.S.R.	436	547	72	240	56	1,191	28	455	223	3,247	44.1
Transcaucasus	275	532	37	75	48	1,504	7	378	81	2,937	53.8
Central Asia	292	352	36	102	57	1,473	9	281	218	2,818	55.9
Russian Federation	435	539	75	226	54	1,139	31	446	220	3,165	43.1
Ukraine	428	544	64	255	66	1,320	23	494	242	3,436	45.8
Belarus	428	607	79	384	44	1,266	22	413	179	3,422	48.2
Moldova	344	436	49	144	66	1,600	19	448	242	3,348	52.1
Lithuania	569	682	68	288	45	1,004	23	393	153	3,225	40.1
Latvia	533	662	69	280	41	967	32	442	213	3,239	38.5
Estonia	576	745	82	234	48	868	34	439	218	3,244	34.0
Georgia	302	508	36	88	45	1,718	11	428	114	3,250	55.6
Azerbaijan	225	462	36	48	41	1,447	5	379	61	2,704	55.3
Armenia	330	710	39	105	68	1,266	6	296	65	2,885	47.5
Kazakhstan	393	452	55	165	48	1,329	14	366	189	3,011	49.6
Uzbekistan	218	304	24	56	67	1,600	6	208	252	2,735	60.5
Kyrgyzstan	267	291	29	107	43	1,347	8	313	179	2,584	56.3
Tajikistan	225	270	21	67	55	1,600	4	230	242	2,714	61.4
Turkmenistan	288	276	25	59	64	1,519	6	262	194	2,693	58.6

TABLE 14. Food Consumption, 1980 and 1990.—Continued.

(Average daily caloric intake per capita)

Geographical Unit	Meat (with sub-products)	Milk and Milk Products	Eggs	Potatoes	Vegeta-bles	Bread and Grain Products	Fish and Fish Products	Sugar	Vegetable Oil	Total Consumed	Starchy-Staple Ratio (percent)
1990											
U.S.S.R.	470	588	69	192	53	1,202	23	429	247	3,273	42.6
European U.S.S.R.	515	635	79	221	53	1,129	27	462	253	3,373	40.0
Transcaucasus	267	531	39	74	49	1,424	9	360	93	2,845	52.6
Central Asia	331	399	41	99	54	1,434	9	301	279	2,947	52.0
Russian Federation	526	635	80	203	51	1,076	28	448	247	3,294	38.8
Ukraine	477	613	73	251	59	1,275	24	506	281	3,559	42.9
Belarus	526	699	87	326	45	1,139	27	468	206	3,523	41.6
Moldova	407	498	82	132	64	1,546	16	468	341	3,554	47.2
Lithuania	632	789	82	301	47	1,004	25	382	162	3,424	38.1
Latvia	583	746	69	240	40	967	31	458	257	3,391	35.6
Estonia	590	801	77	198	37	696	33	420	170	3,022	29.6
Georgia	295	475	38	79	47	1,655	11	372	145	3,117	55.6
Azerbaijan	225	480	38	52	39	1,365	6	344	61	2,610	54.3
Armenia	309	733	44	111	76	1,166	10	372	75	2,896	44.1
Kazakhstan	498	505	59	163	43	1,320	14	372	264	3,238	45.8
Uzbekistan	225	345	32	56	62	1,537	7	239	305	2,808	56.7
Kyrgyzstan	379	437	41	132	45	1,257	9	353	257	2,910	47.7
Tajikistan	182	265	30	67	55	1,510	5	267	293	2,674	59.0
Turkmenistan	302	348	27	50	71	1,492	6	305	203	2,804	55.0

Source: Diamond and Kisunko, *Slavic and Eurasian Republics: Food Consumption in Recent Years in the Former Republics of the USSR.* Center for International Research, U.S. Bureau of the Census, 1992, pp. 22–24.

Data may not sum to total due to rounding.

[1] Share of total caloric consumption per capita from potatoes, bread, and grain products.

TABLE 15. Supply of Consumer Durables in 1989.

(Per 100 families)

Type of Consumer and Geographical Unit	Televisions (all types)	Tape Recorders	Camera Equipment	Refrigerators and Freezers	Washing Machines	Vacuum Cleaners	Sewing Machines	Automobiles	Motorcycles
U.S.S.R.									
Workers and employees	104	50	16	96	79	61	59	19	12
Collective farmers	97	26	2	80	68	21	49	16	25
Russian Federation									
Workers and employees	106	53	19	98	82	66	61	17	14
Collective farmers	100	33	3	87	81	31	51	15	32
Ukraine									
Workers and employees	101	49	15	95	77	63	53	19	10
Collective farmers	96	18	2	78	67	18	40	13	25
Belarus									
Workers and employees	97	44	13	91	66	53	47	17	12
Collective farmers	96	21	3	79	67	17	39	11	20
Moldova									
Workers and employees	95	33	11	90	73	51	41	16	9
Collective farmers	93	12	1	83	64	17	24	10	20
Lithuania									
Workers and employees	108	45	12	94	75	71	47	39	6
Collective farmers	105	34	2	91	81	46	43	32	16
Latvia									
Workers and employees	108	56	31	95	82	77	62	29	12
Collective farmers	105	49	17	93	84	51	52	33	19
Estonia									
Workers and employees	114	59	45	97	80	84	74	35	7
Collective farmers	116	56	36	95	91	75	70	54	13
Georgia									
Workers and employees	101	33	5	97	76	38	62	27	2
Collective farmers	97	16	0	92	74	8	60	25	2
Azerbaijan									
Workers and employees	101	34	4	91	45	31	51	13	2
Collective farmers	94	20	1	81	23	8	50	13	9
Armenia									
Workers and employees	101	38	5	99	92	58	72	26	1
Collective farmers	95	23	1	97	90	41	74	34	2
Kazakhstan									
Workers and employees	101	42	10	96	86	51	62	22	14
Collective farmers	99	25	2	81	81	21	61	21	17

Uzbekistan									
Workers and employees.............	103	44	6	86	66	34	66	22	12
Collective farmers......................	98	26	1	57	36	3	64	21	26
Kyrgyzstan									
Workers and employees.............	99	38	7	85	83	38	70	21	10
Collective farmers......................	99	27	2	65	72	18	78	22	12
Tajikistan									
Workers and employees.............	100	39	5	73	57	25	70	21	9
Collective farmers......................	93	26	1	42	32	3	71	24	19
Turkmenistan									
Workers and employees.............	105	55	7	100	71	40	74	23	18
Collective farmers......................	98	47	1	90	51	14	80	25	43

Source: *Torgovlya, 1990.* 1991, pp. 36–42.
Data are results from a survey of 310,000 families conducted in March, 1989.

To complete our portrait of living standards, Table 16 shows the average amount of living space available to people living in the various regions within the republics as well as the availability of selected household amenities therein. The three Baltic republics had the largest amount of living space available per person, while the Central Asian republics, which generally had larger family sizes, had significantly below-average amounts of living space.

The Baltic republics were generally better supplied with household amenities, such as indoor plumbing, than other republics, while the Central Asian republics were the most poorly equipped. Less than half of all households in Tajikistan had running water or indoor plumbing. The urban areas of Moscow and St. Petersburg were among the most highly provided for areas in the former Soviet Union.

TABLE 16. Housing Conditions, 1989.

Geographical Unit	Total Housing Space per Capita (square meters)	Living Space Equipped with the Following Amenities (percent):						
		Running Water	Indoor Plumbing	Central Heating	Baths	Gas	Hot Water	Electric Stoves
	(1)	(2)	(3)	(4)	(5)	(6)	(7)	(8)
USSR..	15.8	76.7	71.9	71.4	66.7	77.4	56.0	11.3
RUSSIAN FEDERATION	16.1	80.3	75.9	76.2	70.9	73.3	60.9	15.5
Northern economic region....................	16.3	72.9	70.5	73.9	65.4	63.3	62.7	18.8
Arkhangel'sk.................................	16.6	62.3	60.3	64.7	54.4	67.4	51.8	7.5
Vologda......................................	18.6	67.1	63.7	64.4	59.8	90.0	58.1	2.8
Murmansk.....................................	13.5	96.2	96.1	96.3	92.1	39.5	92.9	47.7
Republic of Karelia..........................	17.0	67.8	66.6	66.3	59.7	61.9	48.4	28.5
Komi SSR.....................................	15.7	75.3	71.3	80.0	64.8	50.8	63.6	17.6
Northwestern economic region...............	18.0	91.8	90.5	90.5	83.9	86.9	74.9	9.7
Leningrad....................................	17.7	96.5	96.2	96.2	88.6	87.2	79.3	10.9
St.Petersburg city........................	17.4	99.5	99.5	99.3	91.0	86.0	82.0	13.0
Leningrad oblast...........................	18.5	87.5	86.2	86.9	81.5	90.7	71.2	4.5
Novgorod.....................................	18.8	70.9	68.4	68.7	62.3	94.0	55.6	2.3
Pskov..	19.6	63.5	61.4	57.6	55.5	91.4	44.1	3.4
Central economic region......................	17.4	90.4	88.0	86.5	83.0	83.6	74.4	13.4
Bryansk......................................	17.5	75.6	67.7	69.4	62.0	89.4	44.0	1.9
Vladimir.....................................	17.0	88.8	84.7	81.4	75.8	95.2	57.0	2.5
Ivanovo......................................	17.3	81.6	79.7	80.8	70.6	95.6	67.3	2.6
Kaluga.......................................	15.9	77.6	74.4	73.5	68.6	93.1	46.7	2.2
Kostroma.....................................	17.9	65.4	57.7	57.0	50.6	90.3	46.3	4.5
Moscow.......................................	17.2	98.7	98.5	98.4	96.5	73.3	91.3	25.2
Moscow city...............................	18.0	99.7	99.7	99.5	99.0	67.0	96.0	32.0
Moscow oblast.............................	16.1	95.6	95.1	95.3	89.1	92.2	77.3	4.6
Orel...	17.5	77.4	72.0	68.1	67.3	92.5	47.1	1.3
Ryazan'......................................	17.6	84.4	77.7	72.9	72.7	94.7	47.6	1.4
Smolensk.....................................	17.6	69.7	65.7	66.7	60.1	87.9	50.8	6.2
Tver'..	18.6	71.3	68.9	67.0	62.7	92.9	52.3	4.5
Tula...	18.1	93.0	84.9	81.1	80.7	91.0	72.9	0.9
Yaroslavl'...................................	17.8	86.1	83.4	83.9	76.1	93.8	70.9	3.4
Volgo-Vyatsk economic region	16.2	81.1	72.2	71.8	66.1	88.1	49.5	3.0
Kirov..	15.5	72.8	54.0	54.0	49.2	83.8	41.5	5.8
Nizhegorodsk.................................	16.9	89.5	85.6	83.5	78.3	90.7	57.0	1.7
Republic of Mariy El.........................	14.8	72.7	68.5	69.9	62.7	85.1	46.2	4.4
Mordov SSR...................................	16.9	75.5	66.5	67.0	58.5	84.3	42.5	2.8
Chuvash Republic	15.2	75.0	71.9	79.4	64.8	86.9	47.4	3.0
Central Chernozem economic region	18.0	79.7	73.3	67.6	68.3	84.8	54.0	5.2
Belgorod.....................................	18.4	80.6	75.3	67.5	72.3	79.9	53.6	8.9
Voronezh	18.2	75.3	70.4	63.5	66.4	83.3	50.1	4.5
Kursk..	18.7	78.4	73.0	62.0	67.6	81.9	48.3	7.6
Lipetsk......................................	17.7	87.4	81.7	87.5	76.9	91.3	76.9	NA
Tambov.......................................	16.9	77.8	67.2	54.9	60.6	87.1	41.1	2.3
Povolzhkiy economic region..................	16.3	79.6	74.4	77.3	68.4	87.0	55.2	6.7

TABLE 16. Housing Conditions, 1989.—Continued

Geographical Unit	Total Housing Space per Capita (square meters)	Living Space Equipped with the Following Amenities (percent):						
		Running Water	Indoor Plumbing	Central Heating	Baths	Gas	Hot Water	Electric Stoves
	(1)	(2)	(3)	(4)	(5)	(6)	(7)	(8)
Astrakhan'	14.6	70.7	62.6	67.0	56.8	79.5	41.4	2.9
Volgograd	17.0	76.6	74.2	76.9	71.7	94.3	68.0	2.3
Penza	16.7	80.0	71.6	64.0	65.4	93.1	42.4	1.3
Samara	16.4	91.1	87.2	93.2	80.7	77.9	70.1	18.7
Saratov	16.6	75.2	68.6	69.6	61.6	89.2	48.4	0.8
Ulyanovsk (Simbirsk)	16.2	80.4	73.1	77.4	66.1	80.0	44.9	17.9
Republic of Kalmykia (Khalmg Tangch)	15.0	32.4	29.9	37.4	28.6	88.9	24.3	2.9
Republic of Tatarstan	15.8	83.1	78.1	80.8	70.3	89.0	51.1	3.1
North-Caucasus economic region	15.8	73.8	66.6	60.5	61.5	83.0	46.6	3.3
Krasnodar Kray	16.2	78.6	70.6	63.7	65.5	86.7	50.7	2.9
Stavropol' Kray	15.6	79.6	71.5	61.0	66.1	89.1	53.0	5.1
Rostov	17.0	73.8	68.6	62.7	63.5	77.3	44.5	2.3
Republic of Dagestan	15.3	53.5	45.7	43.7	39.7	57.7	30.5	2.1
Kabardino-Balkar Republic	14.5	84.0	81.4	82.7	78.6	89.3	71.5	5.0
Karachayevo-Cherkess SSR	NA	NA	NA	NA	NA	NA	NA	NA
North-Ossetian SSR	16.1	84.6	81.7	74.6	72.9	87.7	42.8	8.5
Chechen-Ingush Republic	12.6	65.4	52.1	54.8	47.7	79.5	38.6	0.6
Urals economic region	15.3	79.9	75.3	78.6	70.3	82.3	61.1	7.0
Kurgan	15.6	56.5	51.7	59.9	47.0	91.9	36.9	2.1
Orenburg	15.7	76.5	68.5	75.1	62.2	92.3	52.2	2.0
Perm'	15.0	78.5	73.3	73.8	68.6	82.0	60.2	3.3
Sverdlovsk (Yekaterinburg)	16.0	86.3	84.3	85.7	79.3	73.8	71.1	10.0
Chelyabinsk	15.3	88.1	84.9	87.8	80.7	77.3	70.6	15.2
Republic of Bashkortostan	15.0	74.9	67.1	75.7	62.1	89.4	52.6	2.9
Udmurt Republic	13.3	79.6	70.8	72.1	64.7	85.6	56.1	2.9
West Siberian economic region	15.0	78.3	71.3	73.6	66.3	44.2	60.7	39.5
Altay Kray	15.8	71.9	60.1	59.4	54.1	56.7	45.7	27.1
Kemerovo	15.7	90.8	81.0	80.7	76.8	13.7	70.8	49.5
Novosibirsk	14.4	80.1	76.0	75.0	71.0	29.7	66.8	58.0
Omsk	15.7	69.1	65.8	65.2	62.8	94.6	57.9	2.1
Tomsk	14.4	71.5	65.7	68.0	57.3	34.6	56.8	43.7
Tyumen'	14.1	78.7	75.0	80.2	69.2	42.2	60.2	49.1
Republic of Gornyy Altay	NA	NA	NA	NA	NA	NA	NA	NA
East Siberian economic region	14.2	65.2	63.3	65.9	59.9	27.9	55.9	46.2
Krasnoyarsk Kray	15.3	71.6	68.3	71.1	65.3	34.2	61.7	47.3
Irkutsk	14.7	71.0	69.6	72.4	65.2	18.2	63.0	55.0
Chita	11.5	46.8	45.1	49.4	42.8	49.3	35.0	24.7
Republic of Buryat	13.0	53.9	51.9	53.7	48.1	NA	42.3	44.5
Republic of Tuva	11.6	33.0	32.0	35.9	29.2	55.1	30.6	21.6
Republic of Khakasia	NA	NA	NA	NA	NA	NA	NA	NA
Far Eastern economic region	14.0	76.2	72.9	75.4	67.4	39.1	54.5	29.0
Primor Kray	14.0	76.8	75.6	76.8	71.1	18.0	59.6	45.2
Khabarovsk Kray	14.5	77.3	76.3	80.0	73.5	68.1	67.3	13.4
Amur	13.6	58.9	56.9	61.5	53.5	47.8	40.8	22.9
Kamchatka	12.7	90.0	86.6	90.5	82.4	NA	46.3	57.1
Magadan	14.1	87.7	83.0	96.3	72.9	NA	72.3	47.6
Sakhalin	15.2	82.5	76.1	74.8	68.9	9.9	24.0	29.4
Republic of Sakha (Yakutia)	12.9	57.4	51.0	77.0	46.0	21.7	44.0	27.7
Kaliningrad	16.0	86.6	83.3	65.2	67.9	94.0	59.4	3.2
UKRAINE	17.6	77.4	72.9	69.8	68.3	83.9	56.6	4.6
Donets-Dnieper economic region	17.7	NA	NA	NA	NA	NA	NA	NA
Dnepropetrovsk	17.5	NA	NA	NA	NA	NA	NA	NA
Donetsk	17.8	NA	NA	NA	NA	NA	NA	NA
Zaporozh'ye	17.4	NA	NA	NA	NA	NA	NA	NA
Kirovograd	18.7	NA	NA	NA	NA	NA	NA	NA
Lugansk	18.2	NA	NA	NA	NA	NA	NA	NA
Poltava	18.4	NA	NA	NA	NA	NA	NA	NA
Sumy	17.9	NA	NA	NA	NA	NA	NA	NA
Khar'kov	16.7	NA	NA	NA	NA	NA	NA	NA
Southwestern economic region	17.9	NA	NA	NA	NA	NA	NA	NA
Vinnitsa	20.6	NA	NA	NA	NA	NA	NA	NA
Volyn'	17.0	NA	NA	NA	NA	NA	NA	NA

TABLE 16. Housing Conditions, 1989.—Continued

Geographical Unit	Total Housing Space per Capita (square meters)	Living Space Equipped with the Following Amenities (percent):						
		Running Water	Indoor Plumbing	Central Heating	Baths	Gas	Hot Water	Electric Stoves
	(1)	(2)	(3)	(4)	(5)	(6)	(7)	(8)
Zhitomir	18.2	NA	NA	NA	NA	NA	NA	NA
Zakarpat'ye	16.8	NA	NA	NA	NA	NA	NA	NA
Ivano-Frankovsk	17.3	NA	NA	NA	NA	NA	NA	NA
Kiev	18.0	NA	NA	NA	NA	NA	NA	NA
Kiev city	16.4	NA	NA	NA	NA	NA	NA	NA
Kiev oblast	20.1	NA	NA	NA	NA	NA	NA	NA
L'vov	15.8	NA	NA	NA	NA	NA	NA	NA
Rovno	17.4	NA	NA	NA	NA	NA	NA	NA
Ternopol'	17.6	NA	NA	NA	NA	NA	NA	NA
Khmel'nitskiy	18.8	NA	NA	NA	NA	NA	NA	NA
Cherkassy	19.9	NA	NA	NA	NA	NA	NA	NA
Chernigov	18.3	NA	NA	NA	NA	NA	NA	NA
Chernovtsy	17.2	NA	NA	NA	NA	NA	NA	NA
Southern economic region	16.4	NA	NA	NA	NA	NA	NA	NA
Krym ASSR	14.7	NA	NA	NA	NA	NA	NA	NA
Nikolayev	17.3	NA	NA	NA	NA	NA	NA	NA
Odessa	17.0	NA	NA	NA	NA	NA	NA	NA
Kherson	17.3	NA	NA	NA	NA	NA	NA	NA
BELARUS	17.5	82.9	79.7	75.7	75.7	88.2	67.0	8.5
Brest	17.4	NA	NA	NA	NA	NA	NA	NA
Vitebsk	18.2	NA	NA	NA	NA	NA	NA	NA
Gomel'	17.6	NA	NA	NA	NA	NA	NA	NA
Grodno	18.4	NA	NA	NA	NA	NA	NA	NA
Minsk	16.7	NA	NA	NA	NA	NA	NA	NA
Minsk city	15.0	NA	NA	NA	NA	NA	NA	NA
Minsk oblast	18.5	NA	NA	NA	NA	NA	NA	NA
Mogilev	17.9	NA	NA	NA	NA	NA	NA	NA
MOLDOVA	17.5	82.2	84.2	73.9	64.2	87.2	53.5	5.4
Chisinau city	14.1	NA	NA	NA	NA	NA	NA	NA
LITHUANIA	19.1	88.6	86.7	88.0	81.8	86.0	76.6	8.3
Vil'nyus city	15.8	NA	NA	NA	NA	NA	NA	NA
LATVIA	19.6	85.9	84.8	72.7	73.6	86.3	67.4	2.5
Riga city	17.5	NA	NA	NA	NA	NA	NA	NA
ESTONIA	21.5	90.6	89.9	74.4	76.6	62.1	64.2	28.0
Tallinn city	19.1	NA	NA	NA	NA	NA	NA	NA
GEORGIA	18.4	76.2	73.4	66.3	62.1	68.4	37.0	7.8
Tbilisi city	14.4	NA	NA	NA	NA	NA	NA	NA
Abkhaz ASSR	16.9	NA	NA	NA	NA	NA	NA	NA
Adzhar ASSR	17.0	NA	NA	NA	NA	NA	NA	NA
South Ossetian AO	21.2	NA	NA	NA	NA	NA	NA	NA
Republic territories	NA	NA	NA	NA	NA	NA	NA	NA
AZERBAIJAN	11.7	56.2	53.4	44.7	44.3	80.5	13.8	0.6
Baku city	12.0	NA	NA	NA	NA	NA	NA	NA
Nakhichevan ASSR	10.6	NA	NA	NA	NA	NA	NA	NA
Nagorno-Karabakh AO	NA	NA	NA	NA	NA	NA	NA	NA
Republic territories	NA	NA	NA	NA	NA	NA	NA	NA
ARMENIA	14.6	89.9	85.7	80.3	78.7	79.5	60.2	13.3
Yerevan city	12.6	NA	NA	NA	NA	NA	NA	NA
KAZAKHSTAN	14.0	61.0	55.1	59.6	51.4	83.7	42.9	7.2
Aktyubinsk	13.9	NA	NA	NA	NA	NA	NA	NA
Alma-Ata	13.9	NA	NA	NA	NA	NA	NA	NA
Alma-Ata city	14.8	NA	NA	NA	NA	NA	NA	NA
Alma-Ata oblast	12.8	NA	NA	NA	NA	NA	NA	NA
East Kazakhstan	14.1	NA	NA	NA	NA	NA	NA	NA
Gur'yev	12.9	NA	NA	NA	NA	NA	NA	NA
Dzhambul	13.5	NA	NA	NA	NA	NA	NA	NA
Dzhezkazgan	15.4	NA	NA	NA	NA	NA	NA	NA
Karaganda	15.3	NA	NA	NA	NA	NA	NA	NA
Kzyl-Orda	13.2	NA	NA	NA	NA	NA	NA	NA
Kokchetav	14.7	NA	NA	NA	NA	NA	NA	NA
Kustanay	15.0	NA	NA	NA	NA	NA	NA	NA
Mangistausk	NA	NA	NA	NA	NA	NA	NA	NA
Pavlodar	15.1	NA	NA	NA	NA	NA	NA	NA

TABLE 16. Housing Conditions, 1989.—Continued

Geographical Unit	Total Housing Space per Capita (square meters)	Living Space Equipped with the Following Amenities (percent):						
		Run-ning Water	Indoor Plumb-ing	Cen-tral Heat-ing	Baths	Gas	Hot Water	Electric Stoves
	(1)	(2)	(3)	(4)	(5)	(6)	(7)	(8)
North Kazakhstan	15.1	NA	NA	NA	NA	NA	NA	NA
Semipalatinsk	13.1	NA	NA	NA	NA	NA	NA	NA
Taldy-Kurgan	12.9	NA	NA	NA	NA	NA	NA	NA
Turgay	NA	NA	NA	NA	NA	NA	NA	NA
Ural'sk	13.9	NA	NA	NA	NA	NA	NA	NA
Tselinograd	14.7	NA	NA	NA	NA	NA	NA	NA
Chimkent	12.4	NA	NA	NA	NA	NA	NA	NA
UZBEKISTAN	11.8	65.6	53.3	51.0	47.4	82.5	35.3	0.9
Andizhan	10.0	NA	NA	NA	NA	NA	NA	NA
Bukhara	10.5	NA	NA	NA	NA	NA	NA	NA
Dzhizak	NA	NA	NA	NA	NA	NA	NA	NA
Kashkadar'ya	10.4	NA	NA	NA	NA	NA	NA	NA
Namangan	10.3	NA	NA	NA	NA	NA	NA	NA
Samarkand	11.6	NA	NA	NA	NA	NA	NA	NA
Surkhandar'ya	10.7	NA	NA	NA	NA	NA	NA	NA
Syrdar'ya	10.5	NA	NA	NA	NA	NA	NA	NA
Tashkent	13.4	NA	NA	NA	NA	NA	NA	NA
Tashkent city	14.8	NA	NA	NA	NA	NA	NA	NA
Tashkent oblast	12.1	NA	NA	NA	NA	NA	NA	NA
Fergana	12.1	NA	NA	NA	NA	NA	NA	NA
Khorezm	14.5	NA	NA	NA	NA	NA	NA	NA
Karakalpak ASSR	14.3	NA	NA	NA	NA	NA	NA	NA
KYRGYZSTAN	11.8	59.7	52.2	51.9	43.9	90.1	32.9	1.8
Bishkek city	13.3	NA	NA	NA	NA	NA	NA	NA
Dzhalal-Abad	NA	NA	NA	NA	NA	NA	NA	NA
Issyk-Kul'	10.5	NA	NA	NA	NA	NA	NA	NA
Naryn	NA	NA	NA	NA	NA	NA	NA	NA
Osh	11.4	NA	NA	NA	NA	NA	NA	NA
Talas	NA	NA	NA	NA	NA	NA	NA	NA
Chuysk	NA	NA	NA	NA	NA	NA	NA	NA
Republic territories	NA	NA	NA	NA	NA	NA	NA	NA
TAJIKISTAN	9.2	47.9	38.8	38.4	35.1	77.2	25.5	8.4
Gorno-Badakhshan AO	10.5	NA	NA	NA	NA	NA	NA	NA
Dushanbe city	11.9	NA	NA	NA	NA	NA	NA	NA
Khatlon	7.5	NA	NA	NA	NA	NA	NA	NA
Kulyab	NA	NA	NA	NA	NA	NA	NA	NA
Kurgan-Tyube	NA	NA	NA	NA	NA	NA	NA	NA
Khudzhand	8.5	NA	NA	NA	NA	NA	NA	NA
Republic territories	9.6	NA	NA	NA	NA	NA	NA	NA
TURKMENISTAN	10.8	50.0	36.5	42.9	33.5	79.8	11.3	0.7
Ashkhabad city	9.4	NA	NA	NA	NA	NA	NA	NA
Mary	10.9	NA	NA	NA	NA	NA	NA	NA
Tashauz	10.5	NA	NA	NA	NA	NA	NA	NA
Chardzhou	11.3	NA	NA	NA	NA	NA	NA	NA
Balkan	NA	NA	NA	NA	NA	NA	NA	NA
Republic territories	NA	NA	NA	NA	NA	NA	NA	NA

NA Data not available.
Sources: Column 1: *Zhilishchnyye Usloviya Naseleniya SSSR.* 1990, pp. 46–52. Columns 2–8: RUSSIAN FEDERATION: *Pokazatali Sotsial'nogo Razvitiya Avtonomnykh Respublik Krayev i Oblastey RSFSR.* 1990, pp. 389–416. OTHER REPUBLICS: *Zhilishchnyye Usloviya Naseleniya SSSR.* 1990, pp. 41–42.

D. ENVIRONMENTAL QUALITY

The natural environment of the former Soviet Union has been severely damaged by long-standing industrial policies that ignored pollution prevention, clean-up, or in general encouraged excessive waste of natural raw materials. Despite recent remedial efforts, progress is at best uneven. The handling of water resources is a case in point. Although efforts to improve water quality consumed 70 percent of the Soviet Union's pollution control budget in 1990 (Table 17), the amount was not up to the task. Large quantities of untreated sewage were still dumped into waterways. Reports indicate that over 60 percent of all sewage is insufficiently treated in Ukraine, Moldova, and Central Asia. As of 1988, cities such as Yerevan and Zaporozh'ye did not process any sewage water. Not surprisingly, 65 percent of water samples taken in 1990 in the former union did not meet health standards.

TABLE 17. Pollution Control Expenditures by Republic, 1990.

(Million rubles)

Geographical Unit	Total	Water	Air	Land
U.S.S.R.	2,932	2,056	409	467
Russian Federation	1,811	1,275	285	251
Ukraine	405	278	36	91
Belarus	87	65	14	8
Moldova	29	14	4	11
Lithuania	59	56	2	1
Latvia	40	39	1	—
Estonia	26	25	1	—
Georgia	53	31	2	20
Azerbaijan	29	19	4	6
Armenia	21	17	0	4
Kazakhstan	211	144	43	24
Uzbekistan	113	66	15	32
Kyrgyzstan	14	9	1	4
Tajikistan	19	8	—	11
Turkmenistan	15	10	1	4

Source: *Okhrana Zdorov'ya v SSSR.* 1991, pp. 224–225.
Data may not sum to total due to rounding.
— Zero or negligible.

In the case of air, quality suffers because of an insufficient number of operational smokestack filters and because Soviet vehicles are highly polluting (emitting up to eight times as much pollutants as Western or Japanese counterparts). Particulate filters, by far the most widely used devices, rarely perform up to standard. Approximately 81 percent of the 61,300 particulate filters examined in 1987 operated below their rated efficiency. This same survey showed that advanced age was a problem: most air pollution control equipment was kept in use well beyond its rated service life of 12 years. At the same time, many water pollution control devices were found to be over 20 years old.

Obviously, a considerable portion of the former Soviet population lives in heavily polluted areas. Data on concentrations of particulates, sulfur dioxide, carbon monoxide, and nitrogen dioxide are reported for 104 cities which include approximately one-fourth (24.7 percent) of the former all-union population, or 70.3 million people (Table 18). [10] In these cities, pollution levels exceed World Health

---

[10] By comparison, in 1987, 8.8 percent of the U.S. population lived in areas with excessive particulate concentrations.

Organization standards by at least ten times. These problems are well known, and much of the populace is concerned about the implications for physical health. Although direct linkages between pollution and the instance of disease in specific medical cases cannot be demonstrated, the pollutants reported in Soviet data (such as particulates, carbon monoxide, nitrogen oxide, and benzpyrene) have been linked to specific health effects. [11]

TABLE 18. Pollution Concentrations and Emissions, 1989. [1]

(Concentrations in milligrams per cubic meter, emissions in thousand tons)

Republic/City	Particulates	Sulfur Anhydride	Carbon Monoxide	Nitrous Dioxide	Autos	Emissions Stacks
RUSSIAN FEDERATION						
Angarsk	0.167	0.0170	1.580	0.035	NA	389.6
Arkhangel'sk	0.073	0.0070	0.810	0.019	30.7	79.2
Astrakhan'	0.214	0.0100	0.990	0.047	60.7	38.8
Balakovo	0.220	0.0420	0.790	0.019	9.3	70.6
Barnaul	0.213	0.0050	1.460	0.026	85.0	176.2
Berezniki	0.130	0.0370	1.600	0.060	11.9	43.5
Bratsk	0.108	0.0030	0.860	0.070	NA	132.6
Chelyabinsk	0.135	0.0100	1.860	0.046	81.6	390.8
Cherepovets	0.166	0.0100	2.000	0.070	NA	617.8
Groznyy	0.180	0.0300	1.730	0.057	77.4	266.9
Irkutsk	0.170	0.0110	1.078	0.041	NA	83.0
Kaliningrad	0.138	0.0200	3.860	0.060	36.3	48.5
Kamensk-Ural'skiy	0.130	0.0160	1.120	0.030	17.7	92.2
Kemerovo	0.080	0.0070	0.930	0.020	NA	110.5
Khabarovsk	0.313	0.0030	0.480	0.037	51.8	159.8
Kirov	0.100	0.0800	1.050	0.030	43.1	87.0
Komsomol'sk-na-Amure	0.540	0.1100	1.180	0.040	25.8	67.1
Krasnoyarsk	0.240	0.0070	0.570	0.040	106.6	263.3
Kurgan	0.210	0.0249	1.000	0.019	60.3	77.9
Leninogorsk	0.230	0.0200	2.300	0.038	NA	34.7
Lipetsk	0.340	0.1000	3.200	0.060	59.9	659.5
Magnitogorsk	0.280	0.1300	1.870	0.075	23.7	825.4
Moscow	0.100	0.0010	2.000	0.080	801.3	290.9
Murmansk	0.040	0.0270	0.730	0.030	32.1	31.6
Nizhnekamsk	0.346	0.0190	0.800	0.070	25.8	109.9
Nizhniy Novgorod	0.200	0.0060	1.000	0.040	130.9	155.4
Nizhniy Tagil	0.160	0.0130	0.860	0.020	24.7	606.6
Noril'sk	0.050	0.0260	0.780	0.040	24.3	2,300.2
Novokuznetsk	0.300	0.0270	1.600	0.030	NA	581.9
Novorossiysk	0.200	0.0080	1.190	0.050	51.5	66.1
Novosibirsk	0.190	0.1200	1.710	0.035	96.3	235.6
Omsk	0.100	0.0100	2.000	0.030	150.6	447.3
Orenburg	0.210	0.0520	0.385	0.040	NA	120.0
Perm'	0.157	0.0180	0.906	0.053	72.0	175.9
Prokop'yevsk	0.237	0.0230	NA	0.040	NA	39.6
Ryazan'	0.100	0.1000	2.000	0.030	62.8	121.0
Samara	0.280	0.0600	1.460	0.040	111.9	137.3
Saratov	0.117	0.0050	2.100	0.050	47.1	113.2
Shelekhov	0.146	0.2340	1.280	0.059	NA	46.4
St. Petersburg	0.100	0.0100	1.342	0.049	280.6	195.9
Stavropol'	0.131	0.0100	0.862	0.028	33.0	29.7
Sterlitamak	0.232	0.0100	0.600	0.020	31.4	141.2
Tol'yatti	0.174	0.0810	1.290	0.045	62.3	115.8
Tula	0.156	0.0020	0.624	0.037	81.3	NA
Tver'	0.200	0.0100	1.000	0.020	NA	31.0
Tyumen'	0.200	0.0140	1.973	0.086	90.5	34.1
Ufa	0.117	0.0140	0.889	0.036	143.7	291.9
Usol'ye-Sibirskoye	0.188	0.0210	2.725	0.052	NA	85.5

[11] Particulates and carbon monoxide impair the respiratory system by inhibiting the transfer of oxygen in blood (reducing manual dexterity and learning ability). Benzpyrene, a hydrocarbon derived from coal tar, is a strong carcinogen. Since all of these pollutants are produced in abundant quantities in the former U.S.S.R., significant portions of the populace are at risk.

TABLE 18. Pollution Concentrations and Emissions, 1989.[1]—Continued

(Concentrations in milligrams per cubic meter, emissions in thousand tons)

Republic/City	Particulates	Sulfur Anhydride	Carbon Monoxide	Nitrous Dioxide	Autos	Emissions Stacks
Volgograd	0.210	0.1620	0.454	0.038	NA	212.5
Volzhskiy	0.100	0.0100	1.132	0.040	22.6	60.2
Yaroslavl'	0.100	0.0020	3.311	0.038	NA	209.5
Yekaterinburg	0.112	0.0100	2.000	0.050	121.0	62.2
Yuzhno-Sakhalinsk	0.200	0.0060	1.000	0.020	17.9	26.0
UKRAINE						
Cherkassy	0.148	0.0310	1.523	0.056	40.9	39.9
Dneprodzerzhinsk	0.360	0.0100	1.550	0.050	19.7	286.2
Dnepropetrovsk	0.230	0.0130	1.690	0.040	90.5	277.5
Donetsk	0.547	0.0360	1.830	0.110	92.6	173.2
Kiev	0.100	0.0100	1.000	0.050	248.2	62.5
Kommunarsk	0.310	0.0600	3.700	0.080	10.5	234.6
Kremenchug	0.170	0.0100	1.890	0.040	18.5	157.0
Krivoy Rog	0.420	0.0370	2.260	0.084	67.8	1,167.3
Lisichansk	0.100	0.0280	1.480	0.060	13.9	123.1
Makeyevka	0.650	0.0260	1.640	0.100	NA	304.9
Mariupol'	0.200	0.0200	1.700	0.037	27.7	753.0
Odessa	0.345	0.0480	2.576	0.081	121.3	83.1
Severodonetsk	0.098	0.0270	1.675	0.049	12.6	19.8
Zaporozh'ye	0.210	0.0440	0.710	0.100	112.2	253.0
BELARUS						
Dzerzhinsk	0.200	0.0100	1.000	0.030	18.8	106.9
Gomel'	0.150	0.0550	0.210	0.030	65.3	33.9
Grodno	0.104	0.0960	0.740	0.040	24.8	37.7
Minsk	0.146	0.0300	1.470	0.030	149.6	110.1
Mogilev	0.110	0.0400	1.390	0.060	43.1	102.6
MOLDOVA						
Chisinau	0.300	0.0100	1.000	0.020	90.5	30.5
LITHUANIA						
Vil'nyus	0.087	0.0030	1.390	0.042	48.6	31.8
LATVIA						
Riga	0.100	0.0060	1.000	0.060	98.3	32.0
ESTONIA						
Tallinn	0.100	0.0690	1.220	0.019	85.2	37.8
GEORGIA						
Rustavi	0.790	0.0600	3.406	0.060	27.3	115.5
Tbilisi	0.490	0.1130	4.322	0.066	292.0	38.5
Zestafoni	0.540	0.0400	4.900	0.050	14.6	13.9
AZERBAIJAN						
Baku	0.152	0.0480	1.210	0.050	252.2	1,545.2
Gyandzha	0.290	0.0700	1.800	0.040	29.6	60.5
Sumgait	0.228	0.0750	3.369	0.066	18.1	101.8
ARMENIA						
Yerevan	0.610	0.0300	6.190	0.150	167.4	45.2
KAZAKHSTAN						
Alma-Ata	0.240	0.0080	2.760	0.048	NA	41.7
Chimkent	0.425	0.0190	1.358	0.047	NA	94.2
Dzhambul	0.240	0.0340	1.360	0.046	NA	99.9
Ekibastuz	0.128	0.0050	0.990	0.039	NA	715.3
Gur'yev	0.200	0.0002	1.500	0.015	NA	35.8
Karaganda	0.120	0.0100	1.240	0.030	NA	146.9
Pavlodar	0.104	0.0060	0.310	0.029	NA	259.3
Temirtau	0.222	0.0100	0.950	0.048	NA	942.5
Tselinograd	0.085	0.0020	1.178	0.021	NA	94.6
Ust'-Kamenogorsk	0.189	0.0820	1.020	0.090	NA	129.7
Zyryanovsk	0.290	0.0650	NA	0.140	NA	11.9
UZBEKISTAN						
Almalyk	0.290	0.0800	2.070	0.059	11.7	162.6
Fergana	0.312	0.0230	2.740	0.085	113.0	137.1
Tashkent	0.214	0.0260	1.110	0.089	354.7	48.2
KYRGYZSTAN						
Bishkek	0.487	0.0150	2.015	0.070	71.3	71.7
Novotroitsk	0.260	0.1200	1.340	0.050	7.8	223.9
Osh	0.714	0.0180	2.980	0.076	NA	8.3
TAJIKISTAN						
Dushanbe	0.400	0.0200	3.000	0.070	NA	25.2

TABLE 18. Pollution Concentrations and Emissions, 1989.[1]—Continued

(Concentrations in milligrams per cubic meter, emissions in thousand tons)

Republic/City	Particu-lates	Sulfur Anhy-dride	Carbon Monox-ide	Ni-trous Diox-ide	Autos	Emis-sions Stacks
TURKMENISTAN						
Ashkhabad	0.420	0.0100	1.800	0.024	59.1	7.3
Chardzhou	0.335	0.0660	1.359	0.019	35.8	9.0

Source: *Okhrana Zdorov'ya v SSR.* 1991, pp. 43–45, 52–54. 58–63.
NA Not Available.
The risk levels (in milligrams per cubic meter) for air pollutants are above .15 for particulates, .05 for sulfur anhydride, 3 for carbon monoxide, and .04 for nitrous dioxide.

E. SOCIAL INDICATORS

Table 19 presents a collection of social indicators that round out the Quality of Life section. Though some have already been featured and others may be discussed later, this summary table provides a useful, concise overview. It is not meant to be an exhaustive summary of social conditions, but rather a sample that is representative of the overall situation.

According to official data for various social indicators (consumption, savings, alcoholism, crime, family structure, and education), the highest standard of living exists in the Baltic States, while Central Asia is at the bottom. The Baltic States, as a group, have the highest per-capita consumption, the most extensive housing stock, the most doctors, the largest amounts of personal savings, some of the lowest rates of drug-related crime (on a per-capita basis), as well as some of the lowest infant mortality rates in the former union. However, the Baltic republics, in general, also have the highest rates of theft among the former Soviet republics, while Latvia has the highest divorce rate. By contrast, Central Asian republics have the lowest per-capita consumption spending, the least living space, the fewest doctors, the largest families, the shortest life expectancies, and the highest levels of infant mortality.

Caveats regarding official data are necessary before drawing overly favorable conclusions or making comparisons with other countries outside of the former U.S.S.R. For example, the former Soviet Union has a large number of physicians, but many are engaged in public health and administrative activities that are normally carried out by non-physicians in other countries. According to CIR estimates, infant mortality rates would have to by raised by nearly 75 percent to remove known sources of bias.

TABLE 19. Social Indicators.

(1989 data unless otherwise stated)

Measures	U.S.S.R.	Russian Federation	Ukraine	Belarus	Moldova	Lithuania	Latvia	Estonia
CONSUMPTION								
Consumption spending per capita (rubles)	1,833	2,039	1,759	1,970	1,720	2,276	2,493	2,670
Per capita living space (sq. m. per capita)	15.8	16.1	17.6	17.5	17.6	19.2	19.6	21.5
Centralized heat (pct. of urban living space)	90.3	91.4	89.3	94.0	91.4	91.9	80.5	81.7
Running water (pct. of urban living space)	93.2	93.2	94.0	95.1	96.5	95.7	93.5	95.8
OPTION INDICATORS								
Savings (average ruble deposit per person (1/1/90))	1,616	1,615	1,613	1,476	1,465	2,503	1,782	1,992
ALCOHOLISM								
Alcohol-related deaths (per 100,000 persons)	8.0	9.9	10.2	9.4	7.3	11.0	6.8	9.7
CRIME RATES (per 100,000 persons—1988)								
Premeditated murder	3.3	4.0	2.4	2.2	2.8	2.0	2.5	1.9
Theft of personal property	39.7	49.0	29.2	35.4	39.2	42.7	64.4	46.5
Theft of state/social property	31.2	35.3	26.5	37.4	41.7	37.1	41.5	40.6
Drug-related crimes	5.0	4.4	5.2	1.2	1.8	1.1	3.5	0.9
FAMILY STRUCTURE AND DIVORCE								
Average family size (members)	3.5	3.2	3.2	3.2	3.4	3.2	3.1	3.1
Divorces (per 1,000 women)	8.5	9.5	8.7	8.1	7.4	8.1	9.8	8.9
HEALTH INDICATORS								
Life expectancy (years at birth)								
Males (1990, CIR estimate)	63.1	62.8	64.9	65.6	64.0	66.0	63.5	64.1
Females (1990, CIR estimate)	72.9	73.6	74.3	75.2	71.1	75.7	73.9	74.4
Infant mortality (per 1,000 births)								
Males (1990, CIR estimate)	41.6	34.0	25.0	23.6	36.5	18.6	27.0	24.3
Females (1990, CIR estimate)	31.7	24.8	18.5	16.5	27.9	16.6	19.7	17.2
Doctors (per 10,000 persons)	44.4	47.3	43.9	40.6	40.1	45.7	50.0	48.3
OTHER								
Education (per 1000 persons, aged 15+, with higher or middle school education)	812	806	794	770	755	753	838	801

TABLE 19. Social Indicators.—Continued

(1989 data unless otherwise stated)

Measures	Georgia	Azerbaijan	Armenia	Kazakhstan	Uzbekistan	Kyrgyzstan	Tajikistan	Turkmenistan
CONSUMPTION								
Consumption spending per capita (rubles)	1,606	1,209	1,648	1,680	1,097	1,303	981	1,220
Per capita living space (sq. m. per capita)	18.3	11.8	14.7	14.1	12.0	11.9	9.4	11.0
Centralized heat (pct. of urban living space)	90.4	77.7	97.4	88.5	84.7	86.9	87.9	75.2
Running water (pct. of urban living space)	96.7	92.4	99.0	91.5	88.5	91.3	87.6	77.3
OPTION INDICATORS								
Savings (average ruble deposit per person (1/1/90))	2,145.0	1,259.0	2,701.0	1,352.0	1,443.0	1,375.0	1,294.0	1,655.0
ALCOHOLISM								
Alcohol-related deaths (per 100,000 persons)	1.6	0.3	0.6	3.1	0.7	4.1	0.8	1.4
CRIME RATES (per 100,000 persons-1988)								
Premeditated murder	2.7	1.7	1.8	4.4	2.2	3.5	1.5	4.1
Theft of personal property	17.9	8.8	11.5	47.5	22.1	25.6	19.1	26.7
Theft of state/social property	21.4	13.1	18.9	39.0	17.2	23.3	15.4	18.6
Drug-related crimes	6.7	4.6	0.8	11.4	7.2	11.8	2.8	6.8
FAMILY STRUCTURE AND DIVORCE								
Average family size (members)	4.1	4.8	4.7	4.0	5.5	4.7	6.1	5.6
Divorces (per 1,000 women)	3.4	4.6	3.5	7.8	5.0	5.9	5.1	4.6
HEALTH INDICATORS								
Life expectancy (years at birth)								
Males (1990, CIR estimate)	68.0	65.8	67.4	62.5	64.4	62.8	65.0	60.7
Females (1990, CIR estimate)	75.7	74.1	74.4	72.1	71.2	71.5	70.5	68.0
Infant mortality (per 1,000 births)								
Males (1990, CIR estimate)	30.2	42.6	35.3	49.9	65.4	57.0	74.6	83.6
Females (1990, CIR estimate)	23.5	34.6	28.0	39.3	50.3	44.7	62.2	66.4
Doctors (per 10,000 persons)	58.5	38.4	42.7	40.9	35.8	36.6	28.5	35.5
OTHER								
Education (per 1000 persons, aged 15+, with higher or middle school education)	877.0	878.0	901.0	838.0	867.0	842.0	837.0	864.0

Sources: *Narodnoye Khozyaystvo, 1989.* 1990, p. 17; *Narodnoye Khozyaystvo, 1990.* 1991, p. 67; Tretyakova and Kostinsky, *Gross National Product Accounts of the Newly Independent States of the Former Soviet Union, 1987–90.* Center for International Research, U.S. Bureau of the Census, 1992, p. 13; *Zhilishchnyye Usloviya Naseleniya SSSR.* 1990, pp. 11, 41; *Statisticheskiy Yezhegodnik Kazakhstana.* 1991, pp. 49–50, 97, 149–152, 201, 214; Goskomstat Press-Releases: (1990) #16, p. 5; #33, p. 1; #251, pp. 1–2; #358, p. 14; #440, p. 1; (1991) #154, p. 1; #230, p. 1; #356, p. 1; *World Development Report, 1989,* pp. 164, 165, 226, 227; *Sotsial'noye Razvitiye SSSR.* 1990, p. 216, 328–329.

IV. NATIONALITY

A. ETHNIC COMPOSITION—AN OVERVIEW

The Soviet Union was a vast multidimensional country. Because of its size and location (encompassing territory in both Europe and Asia), it had many distinct ethnic groups residing within it. These ethnic groups have a wide variety of diverse histories, cultures, and religious backgrounds with their respective roots in Europe, the Middle East, or the Far East. In preliminary reports of the 1989 census, 128 separate ethnic groups (or nationalities as they are called in the census report) are listed. Additional nationalities exist, but are grouped in the "other nationalities" category because of their relatively small numbers.

For ease of presentation in this overview, the nationalities have been divided into five broad categories: Russians, Other Slavic nationalities, Other European nationalities, Non-European and Non-Muslim nationalities, and Muslim nationalities.[12] An additional residual category is also shown. Although these categories provide a basis for comparison, the ethnic composition of each category can vary greatly (Table 20). The Russian and Other Slavic nationalities category is very homogeneous, consisting mostly of people of East European descent with similar historical and cultural backgrounds. The Non-European and Non-Muslim category, on the other hand, includes both well-educated Georgians and nomadic Eskimos from Siberia. The Muslim category also includes diverse groups, ranging from the Tatars who were assimilated into Russia at a fairly early date, to the Kurds who maintained their distance and ties to ethnic bretheren outside the former U.S.S.R.

The largest nationality group, Russians, accounted for about half of the total population of the former U.S.S.R. in 1989, and about four-fifths of the total population of the Russian Federation (Table 21). However, their proportion in the former Soviet Union, as well as in Russia, has declined since 1959. In the latter, the fall was two percentage points between 1959 and 1989. "Other Slavs" and "Muslims" were the second and third largest groups in the former Soviet Union, each accounting for nearly one-fifth of the total population. The groups account for a much larger share of population outside the Russian Federation. Muslims were the only group to have significantly increased their population share since World War II, especially in the Central Asian republics, Azerbaijan, and Russia.

Significant population shifts have occurred since 1989 (the date of the most recent census). Muslim nationalities have increased at a faster rate than other nationalities (largely due to higher fertility rates among their women). Because of their higher growth rate, Muslims are now likely to be the second largest group in the former Soviet Union. Specific regional situations have caused significant changes in some populations. For instance, the conflict between Armenia and Azerbaijan over Nagorno-Karabakh has caused many Azeris (part of the Muslim category) to emigrate from Arme-

---

[12] Here, the term Muslim does not refer to any currently expressed religious belief, but merely indicates a group held to have traditionally followed Islam. Reliable data on religion are not available for the former U.S.S.R.

TABLE 20. Ethnic Composition of Broad Nationality Categories, 1989.

Russian	Slavic	European	Non-Muslim	Muslim	Other
Russian	Ukrainian	Moldovan	Armenian	Uzbek	Other
	Belorussian	Lithuanian	Georgian	Tatar	Non-Response
	Polish	Jewish	Chuvash	Kazakh	
	Bulgarian	German	Korean	Azeri	
	Czech/Slovak	Latvian	Buryat	Tajik	
		Mordvin	Yakut	Turkmen	
		Estonian	Gypsy	Kyrgyz	
		Udmurt	Gagauz	Avar	
		Mari	Nents	Lesgi	
		Komi	Evenk	Dargin	
		Permyak	Khant	Kumyk	
		Greek	Chukchi	Lak	
		Hungarian	Even	Tabasaran	
		Saami	Nanay	Nogay	
		Karelian	Mans	Rutul	
		Rumanian	Koryak	Tsakhur	
		Finn	Dolgan	Agul	
		Veps	Nivkh	Bashkir	
		Albanian	Ostyak	Chechen	
		French	Ol'ch	Osset	
		Izhor	Udekh	Kabardin	
			Kamchadal	Karakalpak	
			Ket	Uygur	
			Orochon	Ingush	
			Yukagir	Karachay	
			Negidal'	Kurd	
			Tuvan	Abkhazian	
			Kalmyk	Khakas	
			Altay	Balkar	
			Assyrian	Circassian	
			Shor	Dungan	
			Udin	Iranian	
			Mongol	Abazin	
			Karaim	Tat	
			Indian	Beludzh	
			Eskimo	Afghan	
			Tofalar		
			Aleut		

Source: Kingkade, "The Demographic Development of the Soviet Nationalities: Post Mortem," *Migration, Population Structure, and Redistribution Policies.* 1992, p. 276.

nia and many Armenians to leave Azerbaijan (except from Na-gorno-Karabakh).

The Russian population share has also experienced declines in most of the Central Asian republics and all of the Transcaucasus republics between 1979 and 1989. Higher birth rates for women of the titular nationality and Russian out-migration are the principal reasons for the shift.

Kazakhstan is unique among the former Soviet republics in that it is the only one not to have a majority nationality. The Muslim category (mostly Kazakh) was the largest in Kazakhstan, though it accounted for less than half of the population in 1989. The effects of Soviet rule can be seen in the population change in the Muslim category between 1926, when Muslims, including Kazakhs, account-ed for more than half of the population, and 1959, when their shares had been reduced to only one-third of the population. [13]

---

[13] Soviet rule was not firmly set up in Kazakhstan and Central Asia until the 1930s, after which many people died due to famine or were killed resisting Stalin's collectivization. In addi-tion, other ethnic groups were relocated to Kazakhstan's territory either willingly or unwill-

Since then, the Muslim and Kazakh population shares have been increasing steadily. Russians were the second largest group, but their share has been declining since 1959. In the years since the last census, the Russian population share has declined even further. These same trends can be seen in the other Central Asian republics as well. Table 21 summarizes the ethnic composition of each republic from 1926 to 1989.

TABLE 21. Population by Nationality Group, 1926–1989.

Nationality Group	1926	1959	1970	1979	Specified Republic 1989	U.S.S.R. 1989
RUSSIAN FEDERATION						
Thousand persons						
Total	93,133	117,534	130,079	137,410	147,022	285,743
Russian	72,676	97,864	107,748	113,522	119,866	145,155
Other Slavic	7,778	4,377	4,441	4,854	5,702	55,747
Other European	4,769	5,029	5,041	4,885	4,935	16,356
Non European	2,269	2,805	3,313	3,591	4,152	12,837
Muslim	5,508	7,334	9,376	10,409	12,194	55,221
Other	132	124	161	149	173	426
Percent						
Total	100.0	100.0	100.0	100.0	100.0	100.0
Russian	78.0	83.3	82.8	82.6	81.5	50.8
Other Slavic	8.4	3.7	3.4	3.5	3.9	19.5
Other European	5.1	4.3	3.9	3.6	3.4	5.7
Non European	2.4	2.4	2.5	2.6	2.8	4.5
Muslim	5.9	6.2	7.2	7.6	8.3	19.3
Other	0.1	0.1	0.1	0.1	0.1	0.1
UKRAINE						
Thousand persons						
Total	28,995	41,869	47,127	49,609	51,452	285,743
Russian	2,677	7,091	9,126	10,472	11,356	145,155
Other Slavic	23,879	33,034	36,221	37,393	38,329	55,747
Ukrainian	23,219	32,158	35,284	36,488	37,419	44,186
Other European	2,357	1,510	1,502	1,416	1,317	16,356
Non European	30	93	127	138	195	12,837
Muslim	23	136	137	182	245	55,221
Other	29	5	13	7	10	426
Percent						
Total	100.0	100.0	100.0	100.0	100.0	100.0
Russian	9.2	16.9	19.4	21.1	22.1	50.8
Other Slavic	82.4	78.9	76.9	75.4	74.5	19.5
Ukrainian	80.1	76.8	74.9	73.6	72.7	15.5
Other European	8.1	3.6	3.2	2.9	2.6	5.7
Non European	0.1	0.2	0.3	0.3	0.4	4.5
Muslim	0.1	0.3	0.3	0.4	0.5	19.3
Other	0.1	0.0	0.0	0.0	0.0	0.1
BELARUS						
Thousand persons						
Total	4,983	8,055	9,002	9,532	10,152	285,743
Russian	384	659	938	1,134	1,342	145,155
Other Slavic	4,150	7,205	7,864	8,203	8,614	55,747
Belorussian	4,017	6,532	7,290	7,568	7,905	10,036
Other European	438	165	169	154	140	16,356
Non European	3	5	13	12	24	12,837
Muslim	4	20	17	27	31	55,221
Other	4	1	1	1	1	426
Percent						
Total	100.0	100.0	100.0	100.0	100.0	100.0
Russian	7.7	8.2	10.4	11.9	13.2	50.8
Other Slavic	83.3	89.4	87.4	86.1	84.9	19.5

ingly (Russians, Ukrainians, and Germans among others). A German autonomous region existed in Russia until the beginning of World War II when it was abolished; the inhabitants were exiled primarily to Kazakhstan (as well as to Kyrgyzstan and Siberia) to prevent any possible collaboration with the invading German armies.

1083

TABLE 21. Population by Nationality Group, 1926–1989.—Continued

Nationality Group	1926	1959	1970	1979	Specified Republic 1989	U.S.S.R. 1989
Belorussian	80.6	81.1	81.0	79.4	77.9	3.5
Other European	8.8	2.0	1.9	1.6	1.4	5.7
Non European	0.1	0.1	0.1	0.1	0.2	4.5
Muslim	0.1	0.3	0.2	0.3	0.3	19.3
Other	0.1	0.0	0.0	0.0	0.0	0.1
MOLDOVA						
Thousand persons						
Total	NA	2,884	3,569	3,950	4,335	285,743
Russian	NA	293	414	506	562	145,155
Other Slavic	NA	494	596	661	714	55,747
Other European	NA	1,988	2,412	2,622	2,876	16,356
Moldovan	NA	1,887	2,304	2,526	2,795	3,352
Non European	NA	104	138	152	171	12,837
Muslim	NA	5	6	9	12	55,221
Other	NA	0	2	0	1	426
Percent						
Total	NA	100.0	100.0	100.0	100.0	100.0
Russian	NA	10.2	11.6	12.8	13.0	50.8
Other Slavic	NA	17.1	16.7	16.7	16.5	19.5
Other European	NA	68.9	67.6	66.4	66.3	5.7
Moldovan	NA	65.4	64.6	63.9	64.5	1.2
Non European	NA	3.6	3.9	3.9	3.9	4.5
Muslim	NA	0.2	0.2	0.2	0.3	19.3
Other	NA	0.0	0.1	0.0	0.0	0.1
LITHUANIA						
Thousand persons						
Total	NA	2,711	3,128	3,392	3,675	285,743
Russian	NA	231	268	303	344	145,155
Other Slavic	NA	278	311	337	366	55,747
Other European	NA	2,189	2,539	2,736	2,947	16,356
Lithuanian	NA	2,151	2,507	2,712	2,924	3,067
Non European	NA	3	4	5	6	12,837
Muslim	NA	9	6	9	11	55,221
Other	NA	0	1	0	0	426
Percent						
Total	NA	100.0	100.0	100.0	100.0	100.0
Russian	NA	8.5	8.6	8.9	9.4	50.8
Other Slavic	NA	10.3	9.9	9.9	10.0	19.5
Other European	NA	80.7	81.2	80.7	80.2	5.7
Lithuanian	NA	79.3	80.1	80.0	79.6	1.1
Non European	NA	0.1	0.1	0.2	0.2	4.5
Muslim	NA	0.3	0.2	0.3	0.3	19.3
Other	NA	0.0	0.0	0.0	0.0	0.1
LATVIA						
Thousand persons						
Total	NA	2,093	2,364	2,503	2,667	285,743
Russian	NA	556	705	821	906	145,155
Other Slavic	NA	151	212	242	273	55,747
Other European	NA	1,375	1,431	1,421	1,461	16,356
Latvian	NA	1,298	1,342	1,344	1,388	1,459
Non European	NA	5	9	9	14	12,837
Muslim	NA	5	7	9	13	55,221
Other	NA	0	1	1	1	426
Percent						
Total	NA	100.0	100.0	100.0	100.0	100.0
Russian	NA	26.6	29.8	32.8	34.0	50.8
Other Slavic	NA	7.2	9.0	9.7	10.2	19.5
Other European	NA	65.7	60.5	56.8	54.8	5.7
Latvian	NA	62.0	56.8	53.7	52.0	0.5
Non European	NA	0.3	0.4	0.4	0.5	4.5
Muslim	NA	0.2	0.3	0.4	0.5	19.3
Other	NA	0.0	0.1	0.0	0.0	0.1
ESTONIA						
Thousand persons						
Total	NA	1,197	1,356	1,465	1,566	285,743
Russian	NA	240	335	409	475	145,155
Other Slavic	NA	28	50	60	79	55,747
Other European	NA	922	962	983	999	16,356

TABLE 21. Population by Nationality Group, 1926–1989.—Continued

Nationality Group	1926	1959	1970	1979	Specified Republic 1989	U.S.S.R. 1989
Estonian	NA	893	925	948	963	1,027
Non European	NA	2	3	4	5	12,837
Muslim	NA	6	5	9	8	55,221
Other	NA	0	1	0	0	426
Percent						
Total	NA	100.0	100.0	100.0	100.0	100.0
Russian	NA	20.1	24.7	27.9	30.3	50.8
Other Slavic	NA	2.3	3.7	4.1	5.1	19.5
Other European	NA	77.0	70.9	67.1	63.8	5.7
Estonian	NA	74.6	68.2	64.7	61.5	0.4
Non European	NA	0.2	0.2	0.3	0.3	4.5
Muslim	NA	0.5	0.4	0.6	0.5	19.3
Other	NA	0.0	0.1	0.0	0.0	0.1
GEORGIA						
Thousand persons						
Total	2,644	4,044	4,686	4,993	5,401	285,743
Russian	96	408	397	372	341	145,155
Other Slavic	18	59	59	53	64	55,747
Other European	99	137	156	135	135	16,356
Non European	2,099	3,052	3,591	3,891	4,234	12,837
Georgian	1,788	2,601	3,131	3,433	3,787	3,981
Muslim	324	388	482	541	620	55,221
Other	8	1	2	1	7	426
Percent Total	100.0	100.0	100.0	100.0	100.0	100.0
Russian	3.6	10.1	8.5	7.5	6.3	50.8
Other Slavic	0.7	1.5	1.3	1.1	1.2	19.5
Other European	3.7	3.4	3.3	2.7	2.5	5.7
Non European	79.4	75.5	76.6	77.9	78.4	4.5
Georgian	67.6	64.3	66.8	68.8	70.1	1.4
Muslim	12.3	9.6	10.3	10.8	11.5	19.3
Other	0.3	0.0	0.0	0.0	0.1	0.1
AZERBAIJAN						
Thousand persons						
Total	2,270	3,698	5,117	6,027	7,021	285,743
Russian	221	501	510	475	392	145,155
Other Slavic	24	31	36	33	41	55,747
Other European	48	48	55	49	37	16,356
Non European	295	455	507	492	413	12,837
Muslim	1,591	2,661	4,006	4,968	6,098	55,221
Azeri	1,438	2,494	3,777	4,709	5,805	6,770
Other	92	1	2	10	40	426
Percent						
Total	100.0	100.0	100.0	100.0	100.0	100.0
Russian	9.7	13.5	10.0	7.9	5.6	50.8
Other Slavic	1.0	0.8	0.7	0.5	0.6	19.5
Other European	2.1	1.3	1.1	0.8	0.5	5.7
Non European	13.0	12.3	9.9	8.2	5.9	4.5
Muslim	70.1	72.0	78.3	82.4	86.9	19.3
Azeri	63.3	67.4	73.8	78.1	82.7	2.4
Other	4.0	0.0	0.0	0.2	0.6	0.1
ARMENIA						
Thousand persons						
Total	879	1,763	2,492	3,037	3,305	285,743
Russian	20	56	66	70	52	145,155
Other Slavic	4	6	10	10	10	55,747
Other European	4	7	10	9	7	16,356
Non European	746	1,557	2,216	2,732	3,091	12,837
Armenian	744	1,552	2,208	2,725	3,084	4,623
Muslim	99	137	190	215	144	55,221
Other	7	0	0	0	0	426
Percent						
Total	100.0	100.0	100.0	100.0	100.0	100.0
Russian	2.2	3.2	2.7	2.3	1.6	50.8
Other Slavic	0.4	0.4	0.4	0.3	0.3	19.5
Other European	0.4	0.4	0.4	0.3	0.2	5.7
Non European	84.9	88.3	88.9	90.0	93.5	4.5
Armenian	84.6	88.0	88.6	89.7	93.3	1.6
Muslim	11.2	7.7	7.6	7.1	4.4	19.3

TABLE 21. Population by Nationality Group, 1926-1989.—Continued

Nationality Group	1926	1959	1970	1979	Specified Republic 1989	U.S.S.R. 1989
Other	0.8	0.0	0.0	0.0	0.0	0.1
KAZAKHSTAN						
Thousand persons						
Total	6,501	9,310	13,009	14,684	16,464	285,743
Russian	1,280	3,974	5,522	5,991	6,228	145,155
Other Slavic	894	934	1,209	1,148	1,151	55,747
Other European	89	858	1,047	1,103	1,139	16,356
Non European	5	123	143	161	168	12,837
Muslim	4,175	3,403	5,048	6,248	7,724	55,221
Kazakh	3,713	2,795	4,234	5,289	6,535	8,136
Other	58	19	41	33	55	426
Percent						
Total	100.0	100.0	100.0	100.0	100.0	100.0
Russian	19.7	42.7	42.4	40.8	37.8	50.8
Other Slavic	13.7	10.0	9.3	7.8	7.0	19.5
Other European	1.4	9.2	8.0	7.5	6.9	5.7
Non European	0.1	1.3	1.1	1.1	1.0	4.5
Muslim	64.2	36.5	38.8	42.5	46.9	19.3
Kazakh	57.1	30.0	32.5	36.0	39.7	2.8
Other	0.9	0.2	0.3	0.2	0.3	0.1
UZBEKISTAN						
Thousand persons						
Total	4,441	8,106	11,799	15,389	19,810	285,743
Russian	241	1,091	1,473	1,666	1,653	145,155
Other Slavic	32	109	140	146	188	55,747
Other European	46	143	192	177	173	16,356
Non European	20	182	212	236	269	12,837
Muslim	4,025	6,557	9,763	13,110	17,414	55,221
Uzbek	3,350	5,038	7,725	10,569	14,142	16,698
Other	77	24	19	54	113	426
Percent						
Total	100.0	100.0	100.0	100.0	100.0	100.0
Russian	5.4	13.5	12.5	10.8	8.3	50.8
Other Slavic	0.7	1.3	1.2	0.9	0.9	19.5
Other European	1.0	1.8	1.6	1.2	0.9	5.7
Non European	0.4	2.2	1.8	1.5	1.4	4.5
Muslim	90.6	80.9	82.7	85.2	87.9	19.3
Uzbek	75.4	62.2	65.5	68.7	71.4	5.8
Other	1.7	0.3	0.2	0.3	0.6	0.1
KYRGYZSTAN						
Thousand persons						
Total	990	2,066	2,933	3,523	4,258	285,743
Russian	116	624	856	912	917	145,155
Other Slavic	65	146	130	121	119	55,747
Other European	6	73	113	129	118	16,356
Non European	3	15	18	29	32	12,837
Muslim	790	1,206	1,811	2,331	3,049	55,221
Kyrgyz	661	837	1,285	1,687	2,230	2,529
Other	10	2	5	2	22	426
Percent						
Total	100.0	100.0	100.0	100.0	100.0	100.0
Russian	11.8	30.2	29.2	25.9	21.5	50.8
Other Slavic	6.6	7.1	4.4	3.4	2.8	19.5
Other European	0.6	3.5	3.9	3.7	2.8	5.7
Non European	0.3	0.7	0.6	0.8	0.8	4.5
Muslim	79.8	58.4	61.7	66.2	71.6	19.3
Kyrgyz	66.8	40.5	43.8	47.9	52.4	0.9
Other	1.0	0.1	0.2	0.1	0.5	0.1
TAJIKISTAN						
Thousand persons						
Total	827	1,980	2,900	3,806	5,093	285,743
Russian	6	263	344	395	388	145,155
Other Slavic	1	31	37	43	50	55,747
Other European	1	57	64	66	57	16,356
Non European	0	7	16	21	25	12,837
Muslim	815	1,621	2,436	3,280	4,570	55,221
Tajik	619	1,051	1,630	2,237	3,172	4,215
Other	5	0	2	1	1	426

TABLE 21. Population by Nationality Group, 1926-1989.—Continued

Nationality Group	1926	1959	1970	1979	Specified Republic 1989	U.S.S.R. 1989
Percent						
Total	100.0	100.0	100.0	100.0	100.0	100.0
Russian	0.7	13.3	11.9	10.4	7.6	50.8
Other Slavic	0.1	1.6	1.3	1.1	1.0	19.5
Other European	0.1	2.9	2.2	1.7	1.1	5.7
Non European	0.1	0.4	0.6	0.5	0.5	4.5
Muslim	98.5	81.9	84.0	86.2	89.7	19.3
Tajik	74.8	53.1	56.2	58.8	62.3	1.5
Other	0.6	0.0	0.1	0.0	0.0	0.1
TURKMENISTAN						
Thousand persons						
Total	976	1,516	2,159	2,765	3,523	285,743
Russian	75	263	313	349	334	145,155
Other Slavic	9	26	41	45	46	55,747
Other European	4	17	17	21	15	16,356
Non European	15	23	30	34	39	12,837
Muslim	862	1,186	1,756	2,315	3,088	55,221
Turkmen	720	924	1,417	1,892	2,537	2,729
Other	10	1	2	1	1	426
Percent						
Total	100.0	100.0	100.0	100.0	100.0	100.0
Russian	7.7	17.3	14.5	12.6	9.5	50.8
Other Slavic	0.9	1.7	1.9	1.6	1.3	19.5
Other European	0.4	1.1	0.8	0.8	0.4	5.7
Non European	1.5	1.5	1.4	1.2	1.1	4.5
Muslim	88.4	78.3	81.4	83.7	87.7	19.3
Turkmen	73.8	60.9	65.6	68.4	72.0	1.0
Other	1.0	0.0	0.1	0.0	0.0	0.1

Sources: *Natsional'nyy Sostav Naseleniya SSSR, Perepis' Naseleniya, 1989.* 1991, pp. 5–19. Kingkade, "The Demographic Development of the Soviet Nationalities: Post Mortem," *Migration, Population Structure, and Redistribution Policies.* 1992, p. 276. The years shown above correspond to years that a census was taken. Two other censuses were taken in 1937 and 1939, but their results are not shown here. Moldova, Lithuania, Latvia, and Estonia were not part of the Soviet Union in 1926. NA Data not available.

B. ETHNIC GROUPS BY REGION

For the majority of areas within the republics of the former Soviet Union, the titular nationality accounted for over half of the population (Table 22a–o). There are several notable exceptions, however. In 1989, Kazakhs held a majority in only 7 of the 20 regions of the country, the greatest being in the Kzyl-Orda oblast which was 79 percent Kazakh. Kazakhs were most heavily concentrated in the southern areas of Kazakhstan, while Russians, other Slavs, and Germans were most heavily concentrated in the northern oblasts. While Kazakhstan's titular nationality (Kazakhs) had the lowest share of the total population, Armenia's titular nationality (Armenians) had the largest share, with more than 93 percent of the population being Armenian.

Other exceptions to titular domination include: the Crimea in Ukraine (inhabited primarily by Russians), several republic capitals (i.e., Latvia's capital, Riga, inhabited mostly by Russians and other Slavs), the North-Caucasus oblasts in Russia (inhabited by a variety of distinct nationalities, many of culturally Muslim descent), certain areas along the Volga in Russia (with large Tatar populations), and others. Although it is not shown in the following table for Moldova, the majority of the Russian and Ukrainian populations that do not live in Chisinau (the capital), live in the eastern most regions of Moldova—east of the Dniester river.

Jews have traditionally been most heavily concentrated in urban areas, particularly in the capitals of the European republics. Russians have also tended to be most highly concentrated in the republic capitals, though in Belarus they have been spread more evenly.

With the recent changes in the political and economic situations in the republics, other important population shifts have also been occurring. In 1989, about half of the total Crimean Tatar population lived in Uzbekistan, but since then reports indicate that many of them have returned to the Crimea. [14] In that same year, about 180,000 Armenians lived in Baku, but after attacks by Azeris later in the year, no more than 10 percent remained by 1990. Many Germans (from both Russia and Kazakhstan, among other republics) have left for Germany since 1989.

---

[14] There were at least 218,000 Tatars in the Crimea before World War II, but 170,000 Tatars were deported from the Crimea to Central Asia in 1944. In 1989, all Tatars represented only about 1 percent of the total Crimean population. Reports now suggest that nearly 170,000 Tatars (7 percent of the population) now live in the Crimea. Although the 1989 census listed the Crimean Tatar population as 272,000 people, it is suspected that this is an understatement because many may have listed their nationality as simply Tatar.

TABLE 22a. The Ten Largest Nationalities in the Russian Federation, 1989. (Part 1).

(Thousand persons, except percent)

Geographical Unit	Total Population	Russian No.	Russian %	Tatar No.	Tatar %	Ukrainian No.	Ukrainian %	Chuvash No.	Chuvash %	People of Dagestan [1] No.	People of Dagestan [1] %
U.S.S.R.	285,742.5	145,155.5	50.8	6,648.8	2.3	44,186.0	15.5	1,842.3	0.6	2,063.9	0.7
RUSSIAN FEDERATION	147,021.9	119,865.9	81.5	5,522.1	3.8	4,362.9	3.0	1,773.6	1.2	1,749.1	1.2
Northern economic region	6,124.3	5,016.8	81.9	47.7	0.8	310.1	5.1	21.0	0.3	2.4	0.0
Arkhangel'sk	1,569.7	1,446.2	92.1	5.4	0.3	53.4	3.4	2.9	0.2	—	—
Nenets ASR	53.9	35.5	65.8	0.5	1.0	3.7	6.9	0.2	0.3	—	—
Other Arkhangel'sk	1,515.8	1,410.7	93.1	4.9	0.3	49.7	3.3	2.8	0.2	—	—
Vologda	1,349.0	1,301.5	96.5	1.8	0.1	19.1	1.4	1.2	0.1	—	—
Murmansk	1,164.6	965.7	82.9	11.5	1.0	105.1	9.0	3.9	0.3	0.1	0.0
Republic of Karelia	790.2	581.6	73.6	3.0	0.4	28.2	3.6	1.8	0.2	2.3	0.2
Komi SSR	1,250.8	721.8	57.7	26.0	2.1	104.2	8.3	11.3	0.9	—	—
Northwestern economic region	8,241.3	7,461.0	90.5	54.7	0.7	230.0	2.8	11.3	0.1	—	—
Leningrad	6,644.5	5,951.8	89.6	51.8	0.8	200.2	3.0	12.2	0.2	—	—
St.Petersburg city	4,990.7	4,448.9	89.1	44.0	0.9	151.0	3.0	12.2	0.2	—	—
Leningrad oblast	1,653.7	1,502.9	90.9	7.8	0.5	49.2	3.0	9.0	0.1	—	—
Novgorod	751.6	711.8	94.7	2.0	0.3	14.4	1.9	3.2	0.2	—	—
Pskov	845.3	797.4	94.3	1.0	0.1	15.4	1.8	—	—	—	—
Central economic region	30,206.9	28,185.6	93.3	263.5	0.9	674.8	2.2	47.9	0.2	3.3	0.0
Bryansk	1,470.1	1,411.0	96.0	—	—	27.1	1.8	—	—	—	—
Vladimir	1,648.8	1,578.8	95.8	9.2	0.6	21.8	1.3	3.1	0.2	—	—
Ivanovo	1,313.6	1,258.0	95.8	9.9	0.8	15.3	1.2	2.5	0.2	—	—
Kaluga	1,064.2	998.4	93.8	3.0	0.3	30.2	2.8	—	—	—	—
Kostroma	804.3	774.6	96.3	3.0	0.4	9.7	1.2	1.2	0.1	—	—
Moscow	15,521.9	14,175.7	91.3	208.4	1.3	438.0	2.8	31.7	0.2	3.3	0.0
Moscow city	8,875.6	7,963.2	89.7	157.4	1.8	252.7	2.8	18.4	0.2	3.3	0.0
Moscow oblast	6,646.4	6,212.5	93.5	51.1	0.8	185.4	2.8	13.4	0.2	—	—
Orel	889.1	861.9	96.9	—	—	11.5	1.3	—	—	—	—
Ryazan'	1,347.8	1,295.3	96.1	4.9	0.4	15.5	1.2	1.4	0.1	—	—
Smolensk	1,153.6	1,085.2	94.1	2.2	0.2	21.8	1.9	1.2	0.1	—	—
Tver'	1,663.1	1,555.1	93.5	6.3	0.4	28.9	1.7	4.2	0.3	—	—
Tula	1,861.4	1,774.9	95.4	9.6	0.5	36.3	1.9	1.3	0.1	—	—
Yaroslavl'	1,469.0	1,416.6	96.4	7.2	0.5	18.5	1.3	1.3	0.1	—	—
Volgo-Vyatsk economic region	8,464.5	6,353.1	75.1	231.1	2.7	71.3	0.8	932.1	11.0	0.5	0.0
Kirov	1,694.0	1,531.7	90.4	45.7	2.7	18.9	1.1	2.7	0.2	—	—
Nizhegorodsk	3,719.6	3,522.1	94.7	58.6	1.6	33.3	0.9	12.2	0.3	—	—
Republic of Mariy El	749.3	356.0	47.5	43.9	5.9	5.3	0.7	9.0	1.2	0.2	0.0

Mordov SSR	963.5	586.1	60.8	47.3	4.9	6.5	0.7	1.3	0.1	0.2		0.0
Chuvash Republic	1,338.0	357.1	26.7	35.7	2.7	7.3	0.5	906.9	67.8	0.1		0.0
Central Chernozem economic region	7,732.9	7,362.7	95.2	7.8	0.1	249.2	3.2	1.9	0.0			
Belgorod	1,378.3	1,280.5	92.9	1.5	0.1	75.1	5.5					
Voronezh	2,466.7	2,304.6	93.4	1.9	0.1	122.6	5.0	1.9	0.1			
Kursk	1,335.4	1,293.7	96.9	1.1	0.1	22.7	1.7					
Lipetsk	1,230.2	1,198.1	97.4	1.0	0.1	15.0	1.2					
Tambov	1,322.4	1,285.9	97.2	2.3	0.2	13.7	1.0					
Povolzhkiy economic region	16,396.9	12,052.1	73.5	2,272.9	13.9	350.7	2.1	407.4	2.5	27.4	0.2	0.2
Astrakhan'	991.5	713.6	72.0	71.7	7.2	18.7	1.9	10.8	0.4	6.7	0.7	0.7
Volgograd	2,592.9	2,309.5	89.1	26.0	1.0	78.9	3.0	7.1	0.5			
Penza	1,504.6	1,296.1	86.1	81.3	5.4	14.9	1.0	117.9	3.6			
Samara	3,262.9	2,720.2	83.4	115.3	3.5	81.7	2.5	20.6	0.8			
Saratov	2,684.5	2,299.0	85.6	52.9	2.0	101.8	3.8	116.5	8.3			
Ulyanovsk (Simbirsk)	1,396.2	1,016.8	72.8	159.1	11.4	17.7	1.3	0.2	0.1	20.6	6.4	
Republic of Kalmykia (Khalmg Tangch)	322.6	121.5	37.7	4.1	1.3	32.8	1.3	134.2	3.7	1.2	0.0	0.0
Republic of Tatarstan	3,641.7	1,575.4	43.3	1,765.4	48.5	487.5	0.9	5.7	0.2	1,542.8	9.3	9.3
North-Caucasus economic region	16,629.1	11,234.4	67.6	62.8	0.4	195.9	2.9	0.4	0.0	1.5	0.0	0.0
Krasnodar Kray	5,052.9	4,300.5	85.1	17.2	0.3	13.8	3.9	0.4	0.0	0.8	0.2	0.2
Adygeya SSR	432.0	293.6	68.0	2.7	0.6	182.1	3.2			0.7		
Other Krasnodar Kray	4,620.9	4,006.8	86.7	14.5	0.3	62.9	3.9	4.0	0.1	56.8	2.4	2.4
Stavropol Kray	2,410.4	2,024.1	84.0	10.5	0.4	178.8	2.6	0.3	0.0	15.6	0.4	0.4
Rostov	4,292.3	3,844.3	89.6	17.1	0.4	8.1	4.2	0.3	0.0	1,444.8	80.2	80.2
Republic of Dagestan	1,802.2	165.9	9.2	5.5	0.3	12.8	0.4	0.2	0.0	4.7	0.6	0.6
Kabardino-Balkar Republic	753.5	240.8	31.9	3.0	0.4	6.3	1.7	0.2	0.0	14.9	3.6	3.6
Karachayevo-Cherkess SSR	415.0	175.9	42.4	2.5	0.6	10.1	1.5	0.3	0.0	12.6	2.0	2.0
North-Ossetian SSR	632.4	189.2	29.9	2.0	0.3	12.6	1.6	0.3	0.0	26.7	2.1	2.1
Chechen-Ingush Republic	1,270.4	293.8	23.1	5.1	0.4	442.8	1.0	185.4	0.9	0.9	0.0	0.0
Urals economic region	20,239.1	14,769.0	73.0	1,971.2	9.7	14.0	2.2	2.6	0.2			
Kurgan	1,103.7	1,008.4	91.4	22.6	2.0	102.0	1.3	21.5	1.0			
Orenburg	2,170.7	1,568.4	72.3	158.6	7.3	45.7	4.7	10.8	0.3			
Perm	3,091.5	2,592.2	83.9	150.5	4.9	1.2	1.5	0.1	0.1			
Komi-Permyat AO	158.5	57.3	36.1	1.5	0.9	44.5	0.7	10.6	0.4			
Other Perm'	2,933.0	2,535.0	86.4	149.0	5.1	82.2	1.5	16.3	0.3			
Sverdlovsk (Yekaterinburg)	4,706.8	4,176.9	88.7	183.8	3.9	109.6	1.7	12.7	0.3			
Chelyabinsk	3,617.8	2,929.5	81.0	224.6	6.2	75.0	3.0	118.5	3.0			
Republic of Bashkortostan	3,943.1	1,548.3	39.3	1,120.7	28.4	14.2	1.9	3.2	0.2	0.6	0.0	0.0
Udmurt Republic	1,605.7	945.2	58.9	110.5	6.9	583.8	0.9	79.9	0.5	0.3	0.0	0.0
West Siberian economic region	15,013.2	12,749.1	84.9	398.6	2.7	75.0	3.9	4.6	0.8	11.7	0.1	0.1
Altay Kray	2,631.3	2,354.5	89.5	7.7	0.3	65.2	2.9	24.4	0.2			
Kemerovo	3,171.1	2,870.1	90.5	63.1	2.0	51.0	2.1	6.1	0.3			
Novosibirsk	2,778.7	2,556.9	92.0	29.4	1.1	104.8	1.8	5.7	0.8			
Omsk	2,141.9	1,720.4	80.3	49.8	2.3	25.8	4.9	7.8	0.2			
Tomsk	1,001.7	883.8	88.2	20.8	2.1	260.2	2.6	31.2	0.3	11.7		0.4
Tyumen'	3,097.7	2,248.3	72.6	227.4	7.3	148.3	8.4	14.0	1.0	9.0		0.7
Khanti-Mansiysk AOkr	1,282.4	850.3	66.3	97.7	7.6		11.6		1.1			

TABLE 22a. The Ten Largest Nationalities in the Russian Federation, 1989. (Part 1).—Continued

(Thousand persons, except percent)

Geographical Unit	Total Population	Russian No.	Russian %	Tatar No.	Tatar %	Ukrainian No.	Ukrainian %	Chuvash No.	Chuvash %	People of Dagestan [1] No.	People of Dagestan [1] %
Yamalo-Nenetsk Republic	494.8	292.8	59.2	26.4	5.3	85.0	17.2	3.7	0.7	2.7	0.5
Other Tyumen'	1,320.4	1,105.1	83.7	103.3	7.8	26.9	2.0	13.6	1.0	—	—
Republic of Gornyy Altay	190.8	115.2	60.4	0.4	0.2	1.7	0.9	0.1	0.1	—	—
East Siberian economic region	9,152.5	7,651.8	83.6	117.6	1.3	279.5	3.1	42.3	0.5	1.0	0.0
Krasnoyarsk Kray	3,605.5	2,660.5	73.8	49.3	1.4	105.5	2.9	23.4	0.6	0.1	0.0
Taymyr AOkr	55.8	37.4	67.1	0.8	1.4	4.8	8.6	0.3	0.5	0.1	0.1
Evenki AO	24.8	16.7	67.5	0.3	1.3	1.3	5.3	0.1	0.6	—	—
Other Krasnoyarsk Kray	3,524.9	2,606.4	73.9	48.2	1.4	99.4	2.8	23.0	0.7	—	—
Irkutsk	2,824.9	2,499.5	88.5	39.6	1.4	97.4	3.4	11.4	0.4	—	—
Ust-Ordynsk Buryat AOkr	135.9	76.8	56.5	4.4	3.2	2.3	1.7	0.3	0.2	—	—
Other Irkutsk	2,689.1	2,422.6	90.1	35.2	1.3	95.2	3.5	11.1	0.4	0.1	0.0
Chita	1,375.3	1,216.3	88.4	12.3	0.9	38.2	2.8	2.3	0.2	0.1	0.1
Aga Buryat AOkr	77.2	31.5	40.8	0.6	0.8	—	—	0.1	0.2	—	—
Other Chita	1,298.2	1,184.9	91.3	11.7	0.9	38.2	2.9	2.2	0.2	0.8	0.1
Buryat SSR	1,038.3	726.2	69.9	10.5	1.0	22.9	2.2	1.3	0.1	—	—
Republic of Tuva	308.6	98.8	32.0	1.1	0.3	2.2	0.7	0.4	0.1	—	—
Republic of Khakasia	566.9	450.4	79.5	4.7	0.8	13.2	2.3	3.4	0.6	—	—
Far Eastern economic region	7,950.0	6,346.9	79.8	88.9	1.1	620.6	7.8	21.4	0.3	0.2	0.0
Primor Kray	2,256.1	1,960.6	86.9	20.2	0.9	185.1	8.2	5.1	0.2	1.4	0.0
Khabarovsk Kray	1,811.8	1,559.0	86.0	17.6	1.0	112.6	6.2	4.4	0.2	—	—
Yevreysk AO	214.1	178.1	83.2	1.5	0.7	15.9	7.4	0.5	0.2	—	—
Other Khabarovsk Kray	1,597.7	1,380.9	86.4	16.1	1.0	96.7	6.1	3.9	0.2	—	—
Amur	1,050.2	912.0	86.8	9.1	0.9	70.8	6.7	2.2	0.2	—	—
Kamchatka	471.9	382.4	81.0	5.8	1.2	43.0	9.1	2.3	0.5	—	—
Koryak ASR	39.9	24.8	62.0	0.5	1.2	2.9	7.3	0.1	0.3	—	—
Other Kamchatka	432.0	357.7	82.8	5.4	1.2	40.1	9.3	2.2	0.5	—	—
Magadan	555.6	402.8	72.5	8.0	1.4	85.8	15.4	1.7	0.3	0.1	0.0
Chukotsk ASR	163.9	108.3	66.1	2.3	1.4	27.6	16.8	0.5	0.3	0.1	0.0
Other Magadan	391.7	294.5	75.2	5.8	1.5	58.2	14.9	1.3	0.3	—	—
Sakhalin	710.2	579.9	81.6	10.7	1.5	46.2	6.5	2.5	0.3	1.3	0.1
Republic of Sakha (Yakutia)	1,094.1	550.3	50.3	17.5	1.6	77.1	7.0	3.1	0.3	—	—
Kaliningrad	871.2	683.6	78.5	3.6	0.4	62.8	7.2	2.7	0.3	—	—

TABLE 22a. The Ten Largest Nationalities in the Russian Federation, 1989. (Part 2).

(Thousand persons, except percent)

Geographical Unit	Bashkir No.	Bashkir %	Belorussian No.	Belorussian %	Mordvin No.	Mordvin %	Chechen No.	Chechen %	German No.	German %	Other No.	Other %
U.S.S.R.	1,449.2	0.5	10,036.3	3.5	1,154.0	0.4	956.9	0.3	2,038.6	0.7	70,211.2	24.6
RUSSIAN FEDERATION	1,345.3	0.9	1,206.2	0.8	1,072.9	0.7	899.0	0.6	842.3	0.6	8,382.5	5.7
Northern economic region	5.7	0.1	148.4	2.4	9.4	0.2	0.6	0.0	15.1	0.2	547.2	8.9
Arkhangel'sk	0.1	0.0	19.9	1.3	0.1	0.0	—	—	2.2	0.1	39.4	2.5
Nenets ASR	0.1	0.2	1.1	1.9	0.1	0.1	—	—	—	—	12.8	23.7
Other Arkhangel'sk	—	—	18.9	1.2	—	—	—	—	2.2	0.1	26.6	1.8
Vologda	—	—	7.4	0.5	—	—	—	—	—	—	18.0	1.3
Murmansk	0.3	—	38.8	3.3	4.2	0.4	—	—	—	—	35.4	3.0
Republic of Karelia	5.3	—	55.5	7.0	1.2	0.1	0.1	—	12.9	1.0	118.4	15.0
Komi SSR	3.0	0.4	26.7	2.1	3.9	0.3	0.5	—	3.6	0.0	336.0	26.9
Northwestern economic region	3.0	0.0	146.5	1.8	5.2	0.1	—	—	3.6	0.1	325.3	3.9
Leningrad	3.0	0.0	127.3	1.9	5.2	0.1	—	—	3.6	—	289.6	4.4
St.Petersburg city	—	0.1	93.6	1.9	5.2	0.1	—	—	—	—	232.6	4.7
Leningrad oblast	—	—	33.7	2.0	—	—	—	—	—	—	57.0	4.7
Novgorod	—	—	6.7	0.9	—	—	—	—	—	—	16.7	3.4
Pskov	—	—	12.5	1.5	—	—	—	—	—	—	19.0	2.2
Central economic region	5.4	0.0	220.8	0.7	79.8	0.3	1.0	0.0	12.8	0.0	711.9	2.4
Bryansk	—	—	11.3	0.8	—	—	—	—	—	—	20.7	1.4
Vladimir	—	—	7.3	0.4	5.1	0.3	—	—	—	—	23.4	1.4
Ivanovo	—	—	4.9	0.4	3.4	0.3	—	—	—	—	19.6	1.5
Kaluga	—	—	8.6	0.8	1.7	0.2	—	—	—	—	22.3	2.1
Kostroma	—	—	2.9	0.4	—	—	—	—	—	—	12.9	1.6
Moscow	5.4	0.0	129.5	0.8	59.2	0.4	—	—	4.7	0.0	465.8	3.0
Moscow city	5.4	0.1	73.0	0.8	30.9	0.3	—	—	4.7	0.1	366.6	4.1
Moscow oblast	—	—	56.5	0.9	28.3	0.4	—	—	—	—	99.3	1.5
Orel	—	—	3.0	0.3	—	—	—	—	—	—	11.7	1.3
Ryazan'	—	—	4.6	0.3	8.5	0.6	1.0	0.1	1.1	0.1	16.4	1.2
Smolensk	—	—	22.4	1.9	—	—	—	—	—	—	20.9	1.8
Tver'	—	—	10.9	0.7	1.8	0.1	—	—	7.0	0.4	57.7	3.5
Tula	—	—	9.9	0.5	—	—	—	—	—	—	20.6	1.1
Yaroslavl'	—	—	5.6	0.4	—	—	0.3	—	—	—	19.8	1.4
Volgo-Vyatsk economic region	0.8	0.0	19.3	0.2	370.6	4.4	—	—	—	—	485.4	5.7
Kirov	—	—	4.8	0.3	—	—	—	—	—	—	90.3	5.3
Nizhegorodsk	0.3	—	9.3	0.2	36.7	1.0	—	—	—	—	47.3	1.3
Republic of Mariy El	0.3	0.0	1.4	0.2	1.7	0.2	0.1	—	—	—	331.5	44.2
Mordov SSR	0.2	0.0	1.6	0.2	313.4	32.5	—	0.0	—	—	6.6	0.7

TABLE 22a. The Ten Largest Nationalities in the Russian Federation, 1989. (Part 2).—Continued

(Thousand persons, except percent)

Geographical Unit	Bashkir No.	Bashkir %	Belorussian No.	Belorussian %	Mordvin No.	Mordvin %	Chechen No.	Chechen %	German No.	German %	Other No.	Other %
Chuvash Republic	0.3	0.0	2.2	0.2	18.7	1.4	0.2	0.0	—	—	9.6	0.7
Central Chernozem economic region	—	—	21.6	0.3	1.2	0.0	1.6	0.0	—	—	85.9	1.1
Belgorod	—	—	5.1	0.4	—	—	—	—	1.1	0.0	15.0	1.1
Voronezh	—	—	6.3	0.3	1.2	0.0	1.6	0.1	1.1	0.1	26.5	1.1
Kursk	—	—	3.4	0.3	—	—	—	—	—	—	14.6	1.1
Lipetsk	—	—	3.3	0.3	—	—	—	—	—	—	12.8	1.0
Tambov	—	—	3.5	0.3	—	—	—	—	—	—	17.0	1.3
Povolzhkiy economic region	26.8	0.2	75.2	0.5	321.2	2.0	33.6	0.2	63.1	0.4	766.5	4.7
Astrakhan	—	—	4.0	0.4	4.9	0.2	7.9	0.8	—	—	169.0	17.0
Volgograd	—	—	16.1	0.6	—	—	11.1	0.4	28.0	1.1	107.5	4.1
Penza	—	—	3.0	0.2	86.4	5.7	—	—	—	—	15.8	1.0
Samara	7.5	0.2	19.9	0.6	116.5	3.6	—	—	10.6	0.3	73.4	2.2
Saratov	—	—	17.8	0.7	23.4	0.9	6.0	0.2	17.1	0.6	146.0	5.4
Ulyanovsk (Simbirsk)	0.2	0.1	4.6	0.3	61.1	4.4	—	—	1.8	0.1	18.5	1.3
Republic of Kalmykia (Khalmg Tangch)	—	—	1.3	0.4	0.2	0.1	8.3	2.6	5.6	1.7	159.2	49.3
Republic of Tatarstan	19.1	0.5	8.4	0.2	28.9	0.8	0.3	0.0	—	—	76.1	2.1
North-Caucasus economic region	1.7	0.0	95.2	0.6	14.1	0.1	828.1	5.0	64.1	0.4	2,292.8	13.8
Krasnodar Kray	0.2	0.0	37.4	0.7	7.4	0.1	0.2	0.0	31.8	0.6	460.6	9.1
Adygeya SSR	—	—	2.7	0.6	0.5	0.1	—	—	1.8	0.4	115.4	26.7
Other Krasnodar Kray	—	—	34.7	0.8	6.8	0.1	0.2	0.0	29.9	0.6	345.2	7.5
Stavropol' Kray	—	—	14.7	0.8	4.7	0.1	14.5	0.6	13.2	0.5	213.7	8.9
Rostov	0.2	0.0	38.0	0.9	0.3	0.0	17.2	0.4	7.5	0.2	165.2	3.8
Republic of Dagestan	—	—	—	—	0.7	0.0	57.9	3.2	—	—	118.7	6.6
Kabardino-Balkar Republic	—	—	2.0	0.3	0.2	0.0	0.7	0.1	8.6	1.1	479.7	63.7
Karachayevo-Cherkess SSR	—	—	1.3	0.3	0.3	0.0	0.5	0.1	—	—	212.8	51.3
North-Ossetian SSR	—	—	1.8	0.3	0.5	0.0	2.6	0.4	3.1	0.5	410.5	64.9
Chechen-Ingush Republic	—	—	—	—	—	—	734.5	57.8	—	—	196.7	15.5
Urals economic region	1,194.9	5.9	114.0	0.6	150.5	0.7	0.6	0.0	147.1	0.7	1,262.6	6.2
Kurgan	17.5	1.6	5.6	0.5	1.6	0.1	—	—	2.6	0.2	28.9	2.6
Orenburg	53.3	2.5	10.8	0.5	68.9	3.2	—	—	47.6	2.2	139.6	6.4
Perm'	52.3	1.7	18.8	0.6	4.2	0.1	—	—	15.3	0.5	201.7	6.5
Komi-Permyat AO	0.1	0.1	1.2	0.8	0.1	0.0	—	—	—	—	97.1	61.2
Other Perm'	52.2	1.8	17.6	0.6	4.1	0.1	—	—	15.3	0.5	104.6	3.6
Sverdlovsk (Yekaterinburg)	41.5	0.9	28.9	0.6	15.5	0.3	—	—	31.5	0.7	130.2	2.8
Chelyabinsk	161.2	4.5	29.1	0.8	27.1	0.7	—	—	39.2	1.1	84.8	2.3
Republic of Bashkortostan	863.8	21.9	17.0	0.4	31.9	0.8	0.2	0.0	11.0	0.3	156.0	4.0

Region												
Udmurt Republic	5.2	0.3	3.8	0.2	1.4	0.1	0.4	0.0	—	—	521.4	32.5
West Siberian economic region	47.8	0.3	113.2	0.8	42.3	0.3	4.7	0.0	416.5	2.8	565.5	3.8
Altay Kray	—	—	11.6	0.4	7.3	0.3	—	—	126.9	4.8	43.6	1.7
Kemerovo	4.4	0.1	19.3	0.6	13.9	0.4	—	—	48.0	1.5	62.7	2.0
Novosibirsk	—	—	13.1	0.5	4.4	0.2	—	—	61.5	2.2	56.2	2.0
Omsk	—	—	11.0	0.5	2.8	0.1	4.6	—	134.2	6.3	113.3	5.3
Tomsk	2.3	0.2	9.1	0.9	2.6	0.3	2.8	0.1	15.5	1.6	33.9	3.4
Tyumen'	41.1	1.3	49.1	1.6	11.2	0.4	1.0	0.2	29.6	1.0	183.4	5.9
Khanti-Mansiysk AOkr	31.2	2.4	27.8	2.2	7.1	0.6	0.8	0.2	8.9	0.7	85.2	6.6
Yamalo-Nenetsk Republic	6.8	1.4	12.6	2.5	2.0	0.4	0.8	0.1	3.2	0.6	58.7	11.9
Other Tyumen'	3.1	0.2	8.7	0.7	2.1	0.2	0.3	0.0	17.5	1.3	39.5	3.0
Republic of Gorny Altay	—	0.0	—	—	0.1	0.1	—	0.0	0.8	0.4	72.3	37.9
East Siberian economic region	12.7	0.1	74.1	0.8	25.2	0.3	—	—	66.0	0.7	882.1	9.6
Krasnoyarsk Kray	5.0	0.1	29.9	0.8	11.7	0.3	—	—	43.0	1.2	676.9	18.8
Taymyr AOkr	0.2	0.3	0.7	1.3	0.2	0.3	—	—	0.8	1.5	10.6	19.0
Evenki AO	0.1	0.4	—	—	0.1	0.2	—	—	—	—	6.1	10.6
Other Krasnoyarsk Kray	4.8	0.1	29.2	0.8	11.5	0.3	—	—	42.2	1.2	660.2	24.7
Irkutsk	3.9	0.1	25.7	0.9	6.8	0.2	—	—	7.6	0.3	133.0	18.7
Ust-Ordynsk Buryat AOkr.	0.1	0.1	—	—	0.1	0.2	—	—	—	—	51.9	4.7
Other Irkutsk	3.8	0.1	25.7	1.0	6.7	0.1	—	—	7.6	0.3	81.1	38.2
Chita	2.1	0.2	9.2	0.7	1.9	0.1	—	—	2.0	0.1	90.8	3.0
Aga Buryat AOkr	0.2	0.3	—	—	0.1	0.1	—	—	—	—	44.6	6.6
Other Chita	1.9	0.1	9.2	0.7	1.9	0.1	—	—	2.0	0.2	46.3	57.8
Buryat SSR	0.9	0.1	5.3	0.5	1.3	0.1	—	—	2.1	0.2	266.9	3.6
Republic of Tuva	0.2	0.1	—	—	0.3	0.6	—	—	—	—	205.4	25.7
Republic of Khakasia	0.5	0.1	3.9	0.7	3.2	0.4	—	—	11.3	2.0	75.9	66.6
Far Eastern economic region	8.6	0.1	92.5	1.2	32.2	0.4	0.1	—	17.3	0.2	719.7	13.4
Primor Kray	—	—	22.0	1.0	9.2	0.5	0.1	—	4.2	0.2	49.7	9.1
Khabarovsk Kray	0.3	0.0	20.4	1.1	8.2	0.4	—	—	4.4	—	85.0	2.2
Yevreysk AO	0.3	0.1	2.1	1.0	0.8	0.5	0.2	—	—	0.3	14.9	4.7
Other Khabarovsk Kray	0.0	0.0	18.3	1.1	7.4	0.4	0.5	—	4.4	0.2	70.1	7.0
Amur	2.7	0.3	18.0	1.7	2.5	0.5	—	—	2.3	—	30.7	4.4
Kamchatka	0.1	0.0	0.4	0.1	2.4	0.2	—	—	1.0	0.2	34.5	2.9
Koryak ASR	0.1	—	0.4	1.0	0.1	0.5	—	—	—	—	11.1	7.3
Other Kamchatka	—	0.3	0.0	0.0	2.2	0.2	—	—	1.0	—	23.4	27.7
Magadan	0.3	—	10.4	1.9	1.4	0.2	—	—	—	0.2	45.0	5.4
Chukotsk ASR	—	0.3	3.0	1.9	1.0	0.8	—	—	—	—	21.4	8.1
Other Magadan	1.0	—	7.4	1.9	0.4	0.3	0.1	—	1.2	0.2	23.6	13.1
Sakhalin	4.2	0.1	11.4	1.6	5.6	0.4	0.1	0.0	4.1	0.4	51.7	6.0
Republic of Sakha (Yakutia)	—	0.2	9.9	0.9	3.0	0.3	0.0	0.0	—	—	423.1	38.7
Kaliningrad	—	—	73.9	8.5	3.5	0.4	0.5	—	—	—	41.2	4.7

TABLE 22b. The Nine Largest Nationalities in Ukraine, 1989. (Part 1).

(Thousand persons, except percent)

Geographical Unit	Total Population	Ukrainian		Russian		Jewish		Belorussian		Moldovan	
		No.	%	No.	%	No.	%	No.	%	No.	%
U.S.S.R.	285,742.5	44,186.0	15.5	145,155.5	50.8	1,378.3	0.5	10,036.3	3.5	3,352.4	1.2
UKRAINE	51,452.0	37,419.1	72.7	11,355.6	22.1	486.3	0.9	440.0	0.9	324.5	0.6
Donets-Dnieper economic region	21,691.7	14,050.3	64.8	6,762.3	31.2	141.5	0.7	220.5	1.0	10.7	0.0
Dnepropetrovsk	3,869.9	2,769.6	71.6	935.7	24.2	50.1	1.3	49.5	1.3	—	—
Donetsk	5,311.8	2,693.4	50.7	2,316.1	43.6	28.1	0.5	76.9	1.4	—	—
Zaporozh'ye	2,074.0	1,308.0	63.1	664.1	32.0	14.4	0.7	18.4	0.9	—	—
Kirovograd	1,228.1	1,047.0	85.3	144.1	11.7	—	—	9.7	0.8	10.7	0.9
Lugansk	2,857.0	1,482.2	51.9	1,279.0	44.8	—	—	33.5	1.2	—	—
Poltava	1,748.7	1,536.6	87.9	179.0	10.2	—	—	9.5	0.5	—	—
Sumy	1,427.5	1,220.5	85.5	190.1	13.3	—	—	—	—	—	—
Khar'kov	3,174.7	1,993.0	62.8	1,054.2	33.2	48.9	1.5	22.9	0.7	—	—
Southwestern economic region	22,140.3	19,337.4	87.3	1,737.2	7.8	186.2	0.8	53.5	0.2	84.5	0.4
Vinnitsa	1,920.8	1,725.8	89.9	112.5	5.9	26.2	1.4	—	—	—	—
Volyn'	1,058.4	1,001.3	94.6	46.9	4.4	—	—	—	—	—	—
Zhitomir	1,537.6	1,306.1	84.9	121.4	7.9	21.7	1.4	—	—	—	—
Zakarpat'ye	1,245.6	976.7	78.4	49.5	4.0	—	—	—	—	—	—
Ivano-Frankovsk	1,413.2	1,342.9	95.0	57.0	4.0	—	—	—	—	—	—
Kiev	4,506.6	3,592.9	79.7	704.6	15.6	107.6	2.4	37.4	0.8	—	—
Kiev city	2,572.2	1,863.7	72.5	536.7	20.9	100.6	3.9	25.3	1.0	—	—
Kiev oblast	1,934.4	1,729.2	89.4	167.9	8.7	7.0	0.4	12.1	0.6	—	—
L'vov	2,727.4	2,464.7	90.4	195.1	7.2	14.2	0.5	—	—	—	—
Rovno	1,164.2	1,085.7	93.3	53.6	4.6	—	—	16.1	1.4	—	—
Ternopol'	1,164.0	1,126.4	96.8	26.6	2.3	—	—	—	—	—	—
Khmel'nitskiy	1,521.6	1,374.7	90.4	88.0	5.8	—	—	—	—	—	—
Cherkassy	1,527.4	1,381.7	90.5	122.3	8.0	—	—	—	—	—	—
Chernigov	1,412.8	1,292.1	91.5	96.6	6.8	—	—	—	—	—	—
Chernovtsy	940.8	666.1	70.8	63.1	6.7	16.5	1.8	—	—	84.5	9.0
Southern economic region	7,620.0	3,999.2	52.5	2,856.1	37.5	106.1	1.4	98.4	1.3	161.2	2.1
Krym ASSR	2,430.5	625.9	25.8	1,629.5	67.0	17.7	0.7	50.1	2.1	—	—
Nikolayev	1,328.3	1,003.6	75.6	258.0	19.4	11.9	0.9	14.5	1.1	16.7	1.3
Odessa	2,624.2	1,432.7	54.6	719.0	27.4	69.1	2.6	21.3	0.8	144.5	5.5
Kherson	1,237.0	936.9	75.7	249.5	20.2	7.4	0.6	12.6	1.0	—	—

TABLE 22b. The Nine Largest Nationalities in Ukraine, 1989. (Part 2).

(Thousand persons, except percent)

Geographical Unit	Bulgarian		Polish		Hungarian		Rumanian		Other	
	No.	%	No.	%	No.	%	No.	%	No.	%
U.S.S.R.	373.0	0.1	1,126.3	0.4	171.0	0.1	146.0	0.1	79,817.7	27.9
UKRAINE	233.8	0.5	219.2	0.4	163.1	0.3	134.8	0.3	675.6	1.3
Donets-Dnieper economic region	34.6	0.2	—	—	—	—	—	—	471.8	2.2
Dnepropetrovsk	—	—	—	—	—	—	—	—	64.9	1.7
Donetsk	—	—	—	—	—	—	—	—	197.2	3.7
Zaporozh'ye	34.6	1.7	—	—	—	—	—	—	34.5	1.7
Kirovograd	—	—	—	—	—	—	—	—	16.7	1.4
Lugansk	—	—	—	—	—	—	—	—	62.2	2.2
Poltava	—	—	—	—	—	—	—	—	23.6	1.3
Sumy	—	—	—	—	—	—	—	—	17.0	1.2
Khar'kov	—	—	—	—	—	—	—	—	55.7	1.8
Southwestern economic region	—	—	151.8	0.7	155.7	0.7	129.8	0.6	304.1	1.4
Vinnitsa	—	—	8.4	0.4	—	—	—	—	47.9	2.5
Volyn'	—	—	—	—	—	—	—	—	10.2	1.0
Zhitomir	—	—	69.4	4.5	—	—	—	—	18.9	1.2
Zakarpat'ye	—	—	—	—	155.7	12.5	29.5	2.4	34.2	2.7
Ivano-Frankovsk	—	—	—	—	—	—	—	—	13.3	0.9
Kiev	—	—	10.4	0.2	—	—	—	—	53.6	1.2
Kiev city	—	—	10.4	0.4	—	—	—	—	35.5	1.4
Kiev oblast	—	—	—	—	—	—	—	—	18.1	0.9
L'vov	—	—	26.9	1.0	—	—	—	—	26.4	1.0
Rovno	—	—	—	—	—	—	—	—	8.8	0.8
Ternopol'	—	—	—	—	—	—	—	—	11.0	0.9
Khmel'nitskiy	—	—	36.7	2.4	—	—	—	—	22.1	1.5
Cherkassy	—	—	—	—	—	—	—	—	23.3	1.5
Chernigov	—	—	—	—	—	—	—	—	24.1	1.7
Chernovtsy	—	—	—	—	—	—	100.3	10.7	10.3	1.1
Southern economic region	165.8	2.2	—	—	—	—	—	—	233.2	3.1
Krym ASSR	—	—	—	—	—	—	—	—	107.2	4.4
Nikolayev	—	—	—	—	—	—	—	—	23.7	1.8
Odessa	165.8	6.3	—	—	—	—	—	—	71.8	2.7
Kherson	—	—	—	—	—	—	—	—	30.5	2.5

TABLE 22c. The Six Largest Nationalities in Belarus, 1989.

(Thousand persons, except percent)

Geographical Unit	Total Population	Belorussian		Russian		Polish	
		No.	%	No.	%	No.	%
U.S.S.R.	285,742.5	10,036.3	3.5	145,155.5	50.8	1,126.3	0.4
BELARUS	10,151.8	7,904.6	77.9	1,342.1	13.2	417.7	4.1
Brest	1,449.0	1,199.5	82.8	145.9	10.1	31.7	2.2
Vitebsk	1,409.9	1,119.5	79.4	213.9	15.2	25.3	1.8
Gomel'	1,667.8	1,338.1	80.2	210.4	12.6	—	—
Grodno	1,163.6	702.2	60.3	124.3	10.7	300.8	25.9
Minsk	3,181.7	2,493.4	78.4	481.6	15.1	51.7	1.6
Minsk city	1,607.1	1,154.0	71.8	325.1	20.2	18.5	1.1
Minsk oblast	1,574.6	1,339.4	85.1	156.5	9.9	33.2	2.1
Mogilev	1,279.8	1,051.9	82.2	166.0	13.0	—	—

Geographical Unit	Ukrainian		Jewish		Lithuanian		Other	
	No.	%	No.	%	No.	%	No.	%
U.S.S.R.	44,186.0	15.5	1,378.3	0.5	3,067.4	1.1	80,792.7	28.3
BELARUS	291.0	2.9	111.9	1.1	7.6	0.1	76.9	0.8
Brest	60.6	4.2	—	—	—	—	11.3	0.8
Vitebsk	26.1	1.9	12.7	0.9	—	—	12.4	0.9
Gomel'	68.6	4.1	31.8	1.9	—	—	18.9	1.1
Grodno	23.4	2.0	—	—	—	—	12.9	1.1
Minsk	82.8	2.6	39.1	1.2	—	—	33.0	1.0
Minsk city	53.2	3.3	39.1	2.4	—	—	17.1	1.1
Minsk oblast	29.6	1.9	—	—	—	—	15.9	1.0
Mogilev	29.4	2.3	18.4	1.4	—	—	14.1	1.1

TABLE 22d. The Ten Largest Nationalities in Moldova, 1989.

(Thousand persons, except percent)

Geographical Unit	Total Population	Moldovan		Ukrainian		Russian		Gagauz		Bulgarian	
		No.	%	No.	%	No.	%	No.	%	No.	%
U.S.S.R.	285,742.5	3,352.4	1.2	44,186.0	15.5	145,155.5	50.8	198.0	0.1	373.0	0.1
MOLDOVA	4,335.4	2,794.7	64.5	600.4	13.8	562.1	13.0	153.5	3.5	88.4	2.0
Chisinau city	714.9	366.5	51.3	98.2	13.7	181.0	25.3	6.2	0.9	9.2	1.3
Moldova excluding Chisinau	3,620.4	2,428.3	67.1	502.2	13.9	381.1	10.5	147.3	4.1	79.2	2.2

Geographical Unit	Jewish		Belorussian		Gypsy		German		Polish		Other	
	No.	%	No.	%	No.	%	No.	%	No.	%	No.	%
U.S.S.R.	1,378.3	0.5	10,036.3	3.5	262.0	0.1	2,038.6	0.7	1,126.3	0.4	77,636.1	27.2
MOLDOVA	65.7	1.5	19.6	0.5	11.6	0.3	7.3	0.2	4.7	0.1	27.4	0.6
Chisinau city	35.7	5.0	6.4	0.9	—	—	—	—	—	—	11.8	1.6
Moldova excluding Chisinau	29.9	0.8	13.2	0.4	11.6	0.3	7.3	0.2	4.7	0.1	15.6	0.4

TABLE 22e. The Nine Largest Nationalities in Lithuania, 1989.

(Thousand persons, except percent)

Geographical Unit	Total Population	Lithuanian		Russian		Polish		Belorussian		Ukrainian	
		No.	%	No.	%	No.	%	No.	%	No.	%
U.S.S.R.	285,742.5	3,067.4	1.1	145,155.5	50.8	1,126.3	0.4	10,036.3	3.5	44,186.0	15.5
LITHUANIA	3,674.8	2,924.3	79.6	344.5	9.4	258.0	7.0	63.2	1.7	44.8	1.2
Vil'nyus city	576.7	291.5	50.5	116.6	20.2	108.2	18.8	30.3	5.3	13.3	2.3
Lithuania excluding Vil'nyus	3,098.1	2,632.7	85.0	227.8	7.4	149.8	4.8	32.9	1.1	31.5	1.0

Geographical Unit	Jewish		Tatar		Latvian		Gypsy		Other	
	No.	%	No.	%	No.	%	No.	%	No.	%
U.S.S.R.	1,378.3	0.5	6,648.8	2.3	1,459.0	0.5	262.0	0.1	72,423.0	25.3
LITHUANIA	12.3	0.3	5.1	0.1	4.2	0.1	2.7	0.1	9.8	0.3
Vil'nyus city	9.1	1.6	—	—	—	—	—	—	7.7	1.3
Lithuania excluding Vil'nyus	3.2	0.1	5.1	0.2	4.2	0.1	2.7	0.1	2.2	0.1

TABLE 22f. The Ten Largest Nationalities in Latvia, 1989.

(Thousand persons, except percent)

Geographical Unit	Total Population	Latvian		Russian		Belorussian		Ukrainian		Polish	
		No.	%	No.	%	No.	%	No.	%	No.	%
U.S.S.R.	285,742.5	1,459.0	0.5	145,155.5	50.8	10,036.3	3.5	44,186.0	15.5	1,126.3	0.4
LATVIA	2,666.6	1,387.8	52.0	905.5	34.0	119.7	4.5	92.1	3.5	60.4	2.3
Riga city	910.5	331.9	36.5	430.6	47.3	43.6	4.8	43.6	4.8	16.7	1.8
Latvia excluding Riga	1,756.1	1,055.8	60.1	475.0	27.0	76.1	4.3	48.5	2.8	43.8	2.5

Geographical Unit	Lithuanian		Jewish		Gypsy		Tatar		German		Other	
	No.	%	No.	%	No.	%	No.	%	No.	%	No.	%
U.S.S.R.	3,067.4	1.1	1,378.3	0.5	262.0	0.1	6,648.8	2.3	2,038.6	0.7	70,384.3	24.6
LATVIA	34.6	1.3	22.9	0.9	7.0	0.3	4.8	0.2	3.8	0.1	27.9	1.0
Riga city	7.0	0.8	18.8	2.1	—	0.0	—	—	—	—	18.2	2.0
Latvia excluding Riga	27.6	1.6	4.1	0.2	7.0	0.4	4.8	0.3	3.8	0.2	9.7	0.6

TABLE 22g. The Ten Largest Nationalities in Estonia, 1989.

(Thousand persons, except percent)

Geographical Unit	Total Population	Estonian		Russian		Ukrainian		Belorussian		Finns	
		No.	%	No.	%	No.	%	No.	%	No.	%
U.S.S.R.	285,742.5	1,026.6	0.4	145,155.5	50.8	44,186.0	15.5	10,036.3	3.5	67.0	0.0
ESTONIA	1,565.7	963.3	61.5	474.8	30.3	48.3	3.1	27.8	1.8	16.6	1.1
Tallinn city	499.4	233.7	46.8	207.5	41.6	24.2	4.8	13.8	2.8	3.4	0.7
Estonia excluding Tallinn....	1,066.2	729.6	68.4	267.3	25.1	24.1	2.3	14.0	1.3	13.2	1.2

Geographical Unit	Jewish		Tatar		German		Latvian		Polish		Other	
	No.	%	No.	%	No.	%	No.	%	No.	%	No.	%
U.S.S.R.	1,378.3	0.5	6,648.8	2.3	2,038.6	0.7	1,459.0	0.5	1,126.3	0.4	72,620.1	25.4
ESTONIA	4.6	0.3	4.1	0.3	3.5	0.2	3.1	0.2	3.0	0.2	16.6	1.1
Tallinn city	3.6	0.7	—	—	—	—	—	—	—	—	13.2	2.6
Estonia excluding Tallinn..	1.0	0.1	4.1	0.4	3.5	0.3	3.1	0.3	3.0	0.3	3.4	0.3

TABLE 22h. The Ten Largest Nationalities in Georgia, 1989.

(Thousand persons, except percent)

Geographical Unit	Total Population	Georgian		Armenian		Russian		Azeri		Osset	
		No.	%	No.	%	No.	%	No.	%	No.	%
U.S.S.R.	285,742.5	3,981.0	1.4	4,623.2	1.6	145,155.5	50.8	6,770.4	2.4	598.0	0.2
GEORGIA	5,400.8	3,787.4	70.1	437.2	8.1	341.2	6.3	307.6	5.7	164.1	3.0
Tbilisi city	1,246.9	824.4	66.1	150.1	12.0	124.9	10.0	18.0	1.4	33.2	2.7
Abkhaz ASSR	525.1	239.9	45.7	76.5	14.6	74.9	14.3	—	—	—	—
Adzhar ASSR	392.4	324.8	82.8	15.8	4.0	30.0	7.7	—	—	—	—
South Ossetian AO	98.5	28.5	29.0	—	—	2.1	2.2	—	—	65.2	66.2
Republic territories	3,137.9	2,369.8	75.5	—	—	109.2	3.5	287.9	9.2	63.7	2.0

Geographical Unit	Greeks		Abkhazian		Ukrainian		Kurds		Jewish [2]		Other	
	No.	%	No.	%	No.	%	No.	%	No.	%	No.	%
U.S.S.R.	358.0	0.1	105.0	0.0	44,186.0	15.5	153.0	0.1	1,394.3	0.5	78,418.0	27.4
GEORGIA	100.3	1.9	95.9	1.8	52.4	1.0	33.3	0.6	24.6	0.5	56.9	1.1
Tbilisi city	21.7	1.7	—	—	16.1	1.3	30.3	2.4	13.5	1.1	14.8	1.2
Abkhaz ASSR	14.7	10.8	93.3	17.8	11.7	2.2	—	—	—	—	14.1	2.7
Adzhar ASSR	7.4	1.9	—	—	5.9	1.5	—	—	—	—	8.4	2.1
South Ossetian AO	0.0	0.0	—	—	—	—	—	—	—	—	2.6	2.6
Republic territories	56.5	1.8	—	—	18.3	0.6	—	—	7.0	0.2	225.5	7.2

TABLE 22i. The Ten Largest Nationalities in Azerbaijan, 1989.

(Thousand persons, except percent)

Geographical Unit	Total Population	Azeri		Russian		Armenian		Lezgin		Avar	
		No.	%	No.	%	No.	%	No.	%	No.	%
U.S.S.R.	285,742.5	6,770.4	2.4	145,155.5	50.8	4,623.2	1.6	466.0	0.2	601.0	0.2
AZERBAIJAN	7,021.2	5,805.0	82.7	392.3	5.6	390.5	5.6	171.4	2.4	44.1	0.6
Baku city	1,794.9	1,184.2	66.0	295.5	16.5	180.0	10.0	38.1	2.1	—	—
Nakhichevan ASSR	293.9	281.8	95.9	3.8	1.3	1.9	0.6	—	—	—	—
Nagorno-Karabakh AO	189.1	40.7	21.5	1.9	1.0	145.5	76.9	—	—	—	—
Republic territories	4,743.3	4,298.3	90.6	91.1	1.9	63.2	1.3	133.2	2.8	43.3	0.9

Geographical Unit	Ukrainian		Tatar		Jewish		Talysh		Turks		Other	
	No.	%	No.	%	No.	%	No.	%	No.	%	No.	%
U.S.S.R.	44,186.0	15.5	6,648.8	2.3	1,378.3	0.5	22.0	0.0	208.0	0.1	75,683.3	26.5
AZERBAIJAN	32.3	0.5	28.0	0.4	25.2	0.4	21.2	0.3	17.7	0.3	93.5	1.3
Baku city	18.3	1.0	24.3	1.4	22.3	1.2	—	—	—	—	32.2	1.8
Nakhichevan ASSR	—	—	—	—	—	—	—	—	—	—	6.4	2.2
Nagorno-Karabakh AO	—	—	—	—	—	—	—	—	—	—	1.0	0.5
Republic territories	—	—	—	—	—	—	20.9	0.4	—	—	93.3	2.0

TABLE 22j. The Seven Largest Nationalities in Armenia, 1989.

(Thousand persons, except percent)

Geographical Unit	Total Population	Armenian		Azeri		Kurd		Russian	
		No.	%	No.	%	No.	%	No.	%
U.S.S.R.	285,742.5	4,623.2	1.6	6,770.4	2.4	153.0	0.1	145,155.5	50.8
ARMENIA	3,304.8	3,083.6	93.3	84.9	2.6	56.1	1.7	51.6	1.6
Yerevan city	1,141.0	1,100.4	96.4	4.2	0.4	7.1	0.6	22.2	1.9
Armenia excluding Yerevan	2,163.8	1,983.2	91.7	80.7	3.9	49.0	2.3	29.3	1.4

Geographical Unit	Ukrainian		Assyrian		Greek		Other	
	No.	%	No.	%	No.	%	No.	%
U.S.S.R.	44,186.0	15.5	26.0	0.0	358.0	0.1	84,470.4	29.6
ARMENIA	8.3	0.3	6.0	0.2	4.7	0.1	9.7	0.3
Yerevan city	—	—	—	—	—	—	7.1	0.6
Armenia excluding Yerevan	8.3	0.4	6.0	0.3	4.7	0.2	2.5	0.1

TABLE 22k. The Ten Largest Nationalities in Kazakhstan, 1989.

(Thousand persons, except percent)

Geographical Unit	Total Population	Kazakh No.	%	Russian No.	%	German No.	%	Ukrainian No.	%	Uzbek No.	%
U.S.S.R.	285,742.5	8,135.8	2.8	145,155.5	50.8	2,038.6	0.7	44,186.0	15.5	16,697.8	5.8
KAZAKHSTAN	16,464.5	6,534.6	39.7	6,227.5	37.8	957.5	5.8	896.2	5.4	332.0	2.0
Aktyubinsk	732.7	407.2	55.6	173.3	23.7	31.6	4.3	74.5	10.2	0.8	0.1
Alma-Ata	2,098.8	658.9	31.4	957.5	45.6	81.4	3.9	64.1	3.1	7.6	0.4
Alma-Ata city	1,121.4	252.1	22.5	663.3	59.1	20.1	1.8	45.6	4.1	5.0	0.4
Alma-Ata oblast	977.4	406.8	41.6	294.2	30.1	61.3	6.3	18.5	1.9	2.6	0.3
East Kazakhstan	931.3	253.7	27.2	613.8	65.9	22.8	2.4	16.2	1.7	1.3	0.1
Gur'yev	749.0	504.0	67.3	170.5	22.8	2.5	0.3	13.9	1.9	1.5	0.2
Dzhambul	1,038.7	507.3	48.8	275.4	26.5	70.2	6.8	33.9	3.3	21.5	2.1
Dzhezkazgan	493.6	227.4	46.1	172.3	34.9	24.2	4.9	29.5	6.0	1.1	0.2
Karaganda	1,347.6	231.8	17.2	703.6	52.2	143.5	10.7	107.1	7.9	3.7	0.3
Kzyl-Orda	645.0	512.0	79.4	86.0	13.3	2.1	0.3	11.5	1.8	2.0	0.3
Kokchetav	662.1	191.3	28.9	261.8	39.5	82.0	12.4	55.6	8.4	0.4	0.1
Kustanay	1,222.7	279.5	22.9	534.7	43.7	110.4	9.0	118.0	9.6	1.3	0.1
Mangistausk	NA	NA	NA	NA	NA	NA	NA	NA	NA	NA	NA
Pavlodar	942.3	268.5	28.5	427.7	45.4	95.3	10.1	86.7	9.2	1.0	0.1
North Kazakhstan	599.7	111.6	18.6	372.3	62.1	39.3	6.6	38.1	6.3	0.4	0.1
Semipalatinsk	834.4	432.8	51.9	300.5	36.0	44.1	5.3	19.5	2.3	0.1	0.0
Taldy-Kurgan	716.1	360.5	50.3	235.3	32.9	35.3	4.9	12.2	1.7	1.3	0.2
Turgay	NA	NA	NA	NA	NA	NA	NA	NA	NA	NA	NA
Ural'sk	629.5	351.1	55.8	216.5	34.4	4.6	0.7	28.1	4.5	0.4	0.1
Tselinograd	1,002.8	224.8	22.4	447.8	44.7	123.7	12.3	94.5	9.4	1.7	0.2
Chimkent	1,818.3	1,012.3	55.7	278.5	15.3	44.5	2.4	33.0	1.8	285.0	15.7

Geographical Unit	Tatar No.	%	Uygur No.	%	Belorussian No.	%	Koreytsy No.	%	Azeri No.	%	Other No.	%
U.S.S.R.	6,648.8	2.3	263.0	0.1	10,036.3	3.5	439.0	0.2	6,770.4	2.4	45,371.4	15.9
KAZAKHSTAN	328.0	2.0	185.3	1.1	182.6	1.1	103.3	0.6	90.1	0.5	627.2	3.8
Aktyubinsk	16.9	2.3	—	—	4.7	0.6	—	—	1.6	0.2	22.0	3.0
Alma-Ata	37.3	1.8	144.6	6.9	10.5	0.5	16.1	0.8	23.3	1.1	97.5	4.6
Alma-Ata city	27.3	2.4	40.9	3.6	7.5	0.7	16.1	1.4	5.0	0.4	38.6	3.4
Alma-Ata oblast	10.0	1.0	103.7	10.6	3.0	0.3	—	—	18.3	1.9	58.9	6.0
East Kazakhstan	8.9	1.0	—	—	4.6	0.5	—	—	0.8	0.1	9.1	1.0
Gur'yev	10.1	1.3	—	—	2.8	0.4	3.8	0.5	5.2	0.7	34.6	4.6
Dzhambul	16.6	1.6	—	—	4.0	0.4	13.4	1.3	11.7	1.1	84.8	8.2
Dzhezkazgan	10.3	2.1	—	—	6.8	1.4	—	—	1.4	0.3	20.6	4.2
Karaganda	45.8	3.4	—	—	31.0	2.3	11.5	0.9	3.7	0.3	65.9	4.9
Kzyl-Orda	5.9	0.9	—	—	2.7	0.4	12.2	1.9	0.6	0.1	10.0	1.5
Kokchetav	11.5	1.7	—	—	17.2	2.6	—	—	0.8	0.1	41.5	6.3
Kustanay	27.8	2.3	—	—	35.4	2.9	—	—	4.6	0.4	111.1	9.1
Mangistausk	NA	NA	NA	NA	NA	NA	NA	NA	NA	NA	NA	NA
Pavlodar	20.2	2.1	—	—	12.3	1.3	—	—	2.0	0.2	28.6	3.0
North Kazakhstan	15.9	2.7	—	—	7.1	1.2	—	—	1.0	0.2	14.0	2.3
Semipalatinsk	19.1	2.3	—	—	4.5	1.2	—	—	0.9	0.1	13.0	1.6
Taldy-Kurgan	10.0	1.4	30.5	4.3	1.8	1.2	13.6	1.9	1.5	0.2	14.1	2.0
Turgay	NA	NA	NA	NA	NA	NA	NA	NA	NA	NA	NA	NA
Ural'sk	12.7	2.0	—	—	5.1	0.8	—	—	0.8	0.1	10.2	1.6
Tselinograd	24.3	2.4	—	—	28.7	2.9	—	—	2.9	0.3	54.3	5.4
Chimkent	34.6	1.9	—	—	3.5	2.9	11.4	0.6	27.0	1.5	88.4	4.9

TABLE 22I. The Ten Largest Nationalities in Uzbekistan, 1989.

(Thousand persons, except percent)

Geographical Unit	Total Population	Uzbek		Russian		Tajik		Kazakh		Tatar	
		No.	%	No.	%	No.	%	No.	%	No.	%
U.S.S.R.	285,742.5	16,697.8	5.8	145,155.5	50.8	4,215.4	1.5	8,135.8	2.8	6,648.8	2.3
UZBEKISTAN	19,810.1	14,142.5	71.4	1,653.5	8.3	933.6	4.7	808.2	4.1	467.8	2.4
Andizhan	1,721.3	1,507.0	87.5	44.7	2.6	24.5	1.4	—	—	24.9	1.4
Bukhara	1,622.5	1,227.0	75.6	133.2	8.2	50.9	3.1	91.1	5.6	36.8	2.3
Dzhizak	NA	NA	NA	NA	NA	NA	NA	NA	NA	NA	NA
Kashkadar'ya	1,595.8	1,399.2	87.7	37.6	2.4	79.9	5.0	—	—	21.2	1.3
Namangan	1,470.9	1,252.2	85.1	27.2	1.9	130.0	8.8	—	—	15.2	1.0
Samarkand	2,281.9	1,764.0	77.3	113.5	5.0	209.2	9.2	8.2	0.4	35.0	1.5
Surkhandar'ya	1,249.9	993.2	79.5	37.8	3.0	160.8	12.9	—	—	17.0	1.4
Syrdar'ya	1,297.9	923.5	71.2	88.4	6.8	58.9	4.5	71.4	5.5	33.9	2.6
Tashkent	4,203.7	1,985.8	47.2	1,015.2	24.1	104.5	2.5	297.0	7.1	235.4	5.6
Tashkent city	2,060.2	910.3	44.2	701.3	34.0	14.9	0.7	30.6	1.5	129.2	6.3
Tashkent oblast	2,143.5	1,075.5	50.2	313.9	14.6	89.6	4.2	266.4	12.4	106.2	5.0
Fergana	2,141.7	1,735.0	81.0	123.8	5.8	114.5	5.3	—	—	32.7	1.5
Khorezm	1,012.3	957.6	94.6	12.2	1.2	—	—	14.2	1.4	7.8	0.8
Karakalpak ASSR	1,212.2	397.8	32.8	19.8	1.6	—	—	318.7	26.3	—	—

Geographical Unit	Karakalpak		Crimean Tatar		Koreytsy		Kyrgyz		Ukrainian		Other	
	No.	%	No.	%	No.	%	No.	%	No.	%	No.	%
U.S.S.R.	424.0	0.1	272.0	0.1	439.0	0.2	2,528.9	0.9	44,186.0	15.5	57,039.3	20.0
UZBEKISTAN	411.9	2.1	188.8	1.0	183.1	0.9	174.9	0.9	153.2	0.8	692.6	3.5
Andizhan	—	—	9.8	0.6	—	—	70.4	4.1	—	—	40.1	2.3
Bukhara	15.7	1.0	3.4	0.2	3.2	0.2	—	—	12.9	0.8	48.2	3.0
Dzhizak	NA	NA	NA	NA	NA	NA	NA	NA	NA	NA	NA	NA
Kashkadar'ya	—	—	7.2	0.4	—	—	—	—	—	—	50.7	3.2
Namangan	—	—	11.6	0.8	—	—	16.2	1.1	—	—	18.4	1.3
Samarkand	—	—	36.5	1.6	8.1	0.4	—	—	14.2	0.6	93.2	4.1
Surkhandar'ya	—	—	—	—	—	—	—	—	—	—	41.0	3.3
Syrdar'ya	—	—	19.0	1.5	16.7	1.3	29.3	2.3	—	—	56.6	4.4
Tashkent	—	—	78.4	1.9	120.2	2.9	10.1	0.2	86.5	2.1	270.6	6.4
Tashkent city	—	—	13.5	0.7	44.0	2.1	—	—	60.0	2.9	156.4	7.6
Tashkent oblast	—	—	64.9	3.0	76.2	3.6	10.1	0.5	26.6	1.2	114.3	5.3
Fergana	—	—	22.8	1.1	—	—	43.6	2.0	11.1	0.5	58.2	2.7
Khorezm	—	—	—	—	—	—	—	—	—	—	20.5	2.0
Karakalpak ASSR	389.1	32.1	—	—	9.2	0.8	—	—	—	—	77.5	6.4

1102

TABLE 22m. The Ten Largest Nationalities in Kyrgyzstan, 1989.

(Thousand persons, except percent)

Geographical Unit	Total Population	Kyrgyz		Russian		Uzbek		Ukrainian		German	
		No.	%	No.	%	No.	%	No.	%	No.	%
U.S.S.R.	285,742.5	2,528.9	0.9	145,155.5	50.8	16,697.8	5.8	44,186.0	15.5	2,038.6	0.7
KYRGYZSTAN	4,257.8	2,229.7	52.4	916.6	21.5	550.1	12.9	108.0	2.5	101.3	2.4
Bishkek city	619.9	141.8	22.9	345.4	55.7	10.4	1.7	34.3	5.5	13.6	2.2
Dzhalal-Abad	NA	NA	NA	NA	NA	NA	NA	NA	NA	NA	NA
Issyk-Kul'	658.1	520.1	79.0	95.6	14.5	5.1	0.8	7.7	1.2	—	—
Naryn	NA	NA	NA	NA	NA	NA	NA	NA	NA	NA	NA
Osh	1,996.8	1,192.1	59.7	126.1	6.3	520.5	26.1	18.4	0.9	—	—
Talas	NA	NA	NA	NA	NA	NA	NA	NA	NA	NA	NA
Chuysk	NA	NA	NA	NA	NA	NA	NA	NA	NA	NA	NA
Republic territories	983.0	375.6	38.2	349.4	35.5	14.1	1.4	47.5	4.8	80.4	8.2

Geographical Unit	Tatar		Kazakh		Dungane		Uygur		Tajik		Other	
	No.	%	No.	%	No.	%	No.	%	No.	%	No.	%
U.S.S.R.	6,648.8	2.3	8,135.8	2.8	69.0	0.0	263.0	0.1	4,215.4	1.5	55,803.7	19.5
KYRGYZSTAN	70.1	1.6	37.3	0.9	36.9	0.9	36.8	0.9	33.5	0.8	137.5	3.2
Bishkek city	17.0	2.7	8.9	1.4	2.6	0.4	11.0	1.8	—	—	34.8	5.6
Dzhalal-Abad	NA	NA	NA	NA	NA	NA	NA	NA	NA	NA	NA	NA
Issyk-Kul'	4.4	0.7	6.9	1.1	—	—	4.3	0.7	—	—	13.8	2.1
Naryn	NA	NA	NA	NA	NA	NA	NA	NA	NA	NA	NA	NA
Osh	39.2	2.0	10.8	0.5	—	—	10.8	0.5	31.9	1.6	46.8	2.3
Talas	NA	NA	NA	NA	NA	NA	NA	NA	NA	NA	NA	NA
Chuysk	NA	NA	NA	NA	NA	NA	NA	NA	NA	NA	NA	NA
Republic territories	9.5	1.0	18.4	1.9	30.4	3.1	10.6	1.1	—	—	47.0	4.8

TABLE 22n. The Ten Largest Nationalities in Tajikistan, 1989.

(Thousand persons, except percent)

Geographical Unit	Total Population	Tajik		Uzbek		Russian		Tatar		Kyrgyz	
		No.	%	No.	%	No.	%	No.	%	No.	%
U.S.S.R.	285,742.5	4,215.4	1.5	16,697.8	5.8	145,155.5	50.8	6,648.8	2.3	2,528.9	0.9
TAJIKISTAN	5,092.6	3,172.4	62.3	1,197.8	23.5	388.5	7.6	72.2	1.4	63.8	1.3
Gorno-Badakhshan AO	160.9	143.9	89.5	0.3	0.2	3.2	2.0	0.1	0.1	10.8	6.7
Dushanbe city	601.5	235.4	39.1	62.8	10.4	194.7	32.4	24.6	4.1	—	—
Kulyab	619.1	525.1	84.8	78.6	12.7	8.1	1.3	1.6	0.3	—	—
Kurgan-Tyube	1,044.9	616.1	59.0	333.8	31.9	35.2	3.4	8.7	0.8	—	—
Khudzhand	1,554.1	884.9	56.9	486.2	31.3	100.5	6.5	26.1	1.7	18.1	1.2
Republic territories	1,112.1	766.9	69.0	236.2	21.2	46.7	4.2	11.1	1.0	30.8	2.8

Geographical Unit	Ukrainian		German		Turkmen		Koreytsy		Kazakh		Other	
	No.	%	No.	%	No.	%	No.	%	No.	%	No.	%
U.S.S.R.	44,186.0	15.5	2,038.6	0.7	2,729.0	1.0	439.0	0.2	8,135.8	2.8	52,967.7	18.5
TAJIKISTAN	41.4	0.8	32.7	0.6	20.5	0.4	13.4	0.3	11.4	0.2	78.5	1.5
Gorno-Badakhshan AO	—	—	—	—	—	—	—	—	—	—	2.7	1.6
Dushanbe city	21.3	3.5	13.7	2.3	—	—	6.6	1.1	1.1	0.2	41.3	6.9
Kulyab	—	—	—	—	—	—	—	—	—	—	5.6	0.9
Kurgan-Tyube	—	—	9.5	0.9	17.8	1.7	—	—	6.6	0.6	17.2	1.6
Khudzhand	8.3	0.5	—	—	—	—	—	—	—	—	30.0	1.9
Republic territories	—	—	—	—	—	—	—	—	—	—	20.3	1.8

TABLE 22o. The Ten Largest Nationalities in Turkmenistan, 1989.

(Thousand persons, except percent)

Geographical Unit	Total Population	Turkmen		Russian		Uzbek		Kazakh		Tatar	
		No.	%	No.	%	No.	%	No.	%	No.	%
U.S.S.R.	285,742.5	2,729.0	1.0	145,155.5	50.8	16,697.8	5.8	8,135.8	2.8	6,648.8	2.3
TURKMENISTAN	3,522.7	2,536.0	72.0	333.9	9.5	317.3	9.0	87.8	2.5	39.2	1.1
Ashkhabad city	403.2	205.4	50.9	130.2	32.3	3.8	1.0	2.6	0.6	7.2	1.8
Mary	811.8	658.5	81.1	56.5	7.0	—	—	16.4	2.0	8.3	1.0
Tashauz	696.6	428.0	61.4	7.3	1.1	219.8	31.6	27.7	4.0	—	—
Chardzhou	732.8	551.9	75.3	56.1	7.7	85.3	11.6	8.3	1.1	11.0	1.5
Balkan	NA	NA	NA	NA	NA	NA	NA	NA	NA	NA	NA
Republic territories	878.3	692.7	78.9	83.8	9.5	—	—	32.7	3.7	8.3	0.9

Geographical Unit	Ukrainian		Azeri		Armenian		Beludzh		Lesgi		Other	
	No.	%	No.	%	No.	%	No.	%	No.	%	No.	%
U.S.S.R.	44,186.0	15.5	6,770.4	2.4	4,623.2	1.6	29.0	0.0	466.0	0.2	50,301.0	17.6
TURKMENISTAN	35.6	1.0	33.4	0.9	31.8	0.9	28.3	0.8	10.4	0.3	69.0	2.0
Ashkhabad city	11.0	2.7	10.0	2.5	18.3	4.5	—	—	—	—	14.7	3.6
Mary	7.3	0.9	—	—	—	—	28.0	3.4	—	—	36.8	4.5
Tashauz	—	—	—	—	—	—	—	—	—	—	13.7	2.0
Chardzhou	—	—	—	—	—	—	—	—	—	—	20.2	2.8
Balkan	NA	NA	NA	NA	NA	NA	NA	NA	NA	NA	NA	NA
Republic territories	10.7	1.2	13.8	1.6	6.4	0.7	—	—	7.8	0.9	22.0	2.5

Source: *Natsional'nyy Sostav Naseleniya SSSR, Perepis' Naseleniya, 1989.* 1991, pp. 28–140.
Data may not sum to total due to rounding. In addition, data may not sum to the reported total of a specific nationality, because in some oblasts the population of that nationality is not reported, though this number would be very small (often less than 50 people and always less than 1 percent of the total population for that particular oblast).
NA Data not available.
—Zero or negligible.
[1] People of Dagestan (POD). The People of Dagestan is not a nationality in and of itself, rather it is a group of nationalities consisting of a large number of sub-groups, for less than ten of which separate population totals are listed in preliminary Soviet census reports. The largest are the Avars (544 thousand people in Russia and 601 thousand in the entire former USSR), Dargin (353 and 365), Kumyks (277 and 282), Laks (106 and 118), Lezgians (257 and 466), Nogai (74 and 75), and Tabasaran (94 and 98). The total given here represents the sum of the reported populations of those seven groups plus the Aguly (18 and 19), Rutul'tsy (20 and 20), and Tsakhury (7 and 20).
[2] The Jews category shown in the Georgian table includes Georgian Jews that were listed as a separate nationality in the 1989 Soviet census. They comprised about 58 percent of the total Jewish population in Georgia, but only about 1 percent of the total Jewish population in the U.S.S.R.

C. ETHNICITY AND EMPLOYMENT

One concern in most of the newly independent states is the effect of emigration on the labor force. Often, Russians or other non-titular nationalities were sent into republics to run particular enterprises or industries; most typically Russians were given supervisory roles and higher paying positions. The most systematic and complete set of data we have on the role of local ethnic groups in the economies of each republic is a table of titular employment shares by sector of the economy. These data (see Table 23) show the proportion of employment in the major state sectors (excluding collective farms and private activity) comprised by the titular nationality. For comparison we have also shown that titular share of total population and the relationship between the population share and employment shares. The ratio of employment share to population share indicates whether the titular nationality is disproportionately over- or under-represented in a given sector. Ratios less than 100 indicate under-representation; over 100, over-representation. As we indicated elsewhere, nationality should not be equated with citizenship or loyalty, but these data suggest the general magnitude of this potential problem.

In the majority of the republics, the people of the titular nationality are under-represented in industry, construction, and science, while being over-represented in agriculture, trade, education, and government. The opposite trend exists within Russia. There, Russians have a higher proportion than their overall state sector share in such high-paying sectors as industry, transport and communications, and science. Where wages are below the state sector average (agriculture and education), they are under-represented. Many of the low-paying jobs that Russians do not occupy are held by indigenous nationalities within Russia.

These patterns are particularly pronounced in the Central Asian republics. In sectors such as construction, industry, and science, wages were 27, 10, and 8 percentage points above the average state sector wage, respectively. In these sectors, the titular nationality constituted 10 to 40 percentage points less than their share of the overall state sector. On the other hand, in state agriculture, wages were 3 percentage points less than the state sector average and the titular shares were 17 to 68 percentage points higher than their overall state sector shares.

Armenia's uniqueness as the most ethnically homogeneous republic is reflected in the statistics cited here. Armenians make up 93.3 percent of the republic's total population and 93 percent of the state sector and industry. Armenians make up more than 93 percent of such high-paying sectors as transport and communications, trade, and science, but make up only 85 percent of the low-paying agricultural sector.

MAP 2. RUSSIANS IN THE FORMER SOVIET UNION, 1989

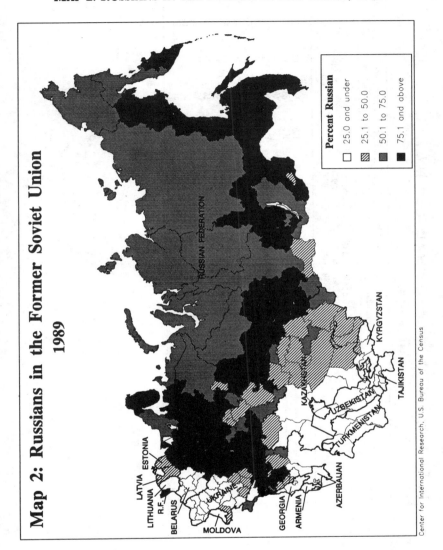

Map 2: Russians in the Former Soviet Union
1989

Percent Russian

☐ 25.0 and under

▨ 25.1 to 50.0

▧ 50.1 to 75.0

■ 75.1 and above

RUSSIAN FEDERATION

KYRGYZSTAN

TAJIKISTAN

KAZAKHSTAN

UZBEKISTAN

TURKMENISTAN

AZERBAIJAN

LATVIA

ESTONIA

LITHUANIA

R.F.

BELARUS

UKRAINE

MOLDOVA

GEORGIA

ARMENIA

Center for International Research, U.S. Bureau of the Census

TABLE 23. Employment of Titular Nationalities by Sector of the Economy, 1987.

(Percent of sectoral total)

Economic Sector	Russian Federation Titular Share:		Ukraine Titular Share:		Belarus Titular Share:		Moldova Titular Share:		Lithuania Titular Share:	
	of Sectoral Employment	Compared to Total Population	of Sectoral Employment	Compared to Total Population	of Sectoral Employment	Compared to Total Population	of Sectoral Employment	Compared to Total Population	of Sectoral Employment	Compared to Total Population
Total population, 1989	82	100	73	100	78	100	65	100	80	100
State sector, total	82	100	70	96	78	100	59	91	76	95
Industry	83	101	68	93	77	99	48	74	71	89
Agriculture	75	91	79	108	89	114	79	122	84	105
Transportation and communications	85	104	71	97	78	100	54	83	67	84
Construction	78	95	69	95	76	97	52	80	81	101
Trade and public dining	84	102	73	100	81	104	55	85	79	99
Housing—communal economy and non-productive personal services	85	104	68	93	77	99	51	78	80	100
Health, physical culture, and social security	83	101	68	93	76	97	62	95	80	100
Education	81	99	74	101	74	95	58	89	84	105
Culture and art	83	101	70	96	72	92	56	86	83	104
Science and scientific services	85	104	59	81	58	74	37	57	64	80
Government	83	101	73	100	74	95	51	78	86	108

TABLE 23. Employment of Titular Nationalities by Sector of the Economy, 1987.—Continued

(Percent of sectoral total)

Economic Sector	Latvia Titular Share:		Estonia Titular Share:		Georgia Titular Share:		Azerbaijan Titular Share:		Armenia Titular Share:	
	of Sectoral Employment	Compared to Total Population	of Sectoral Employment	Compared to Total Population	of Sectoral Employment	Compared to Total Population	of Sectoral Employment	Compared to Total Population	of Sectoral Employment	Compared to Total Population
Total population, 1989	52	100	62	100	70	100	83	100	93	100
State sector, total	48	92	59	95	72	103	78	94	93	100
Industry	38	73	43	69	61	87	69	83	93	100
Agriculture	69	133	84	135	77	110	90	108	85	91
Transportation and communications	38	73	47	76	68	97	74	89	96	103
Construction	46	88	61	98	70	100	73	88	95	102
Trade and public dining	49	94	62	100	70	100	78	94	94	101
Housing—communal economy and non-productive personal services	45	87	67	108	77	110	76	92	89	96
Health, physical culture, and social security	53	102	67	108	77	110	88	106	97	104
Education	59	113	71	115	85	121	80	96	97	101
Culture and art	75	144	84	135	84	120	79	95	94	104
Science and scientific services	42	81	67	108	77	110	60	72	94	101
Government	56	108	72	116	78	111	78	94	96	103

TABLE 23. Employment of Titular Nationalities by Sector of the Economy, 1987.—Continued

(Percent of sectoral total)

Economic Sector	Kazakhstan Titular Share:		Uzbekistan Titular Share:		Kyrgyzstan Titular Share:		Tajikistan Titular Share:		Turkmenistan Titular Share:	
	of Sectoral Employment	Compared to Total Population	of Sectoral Employment	Compared to Total Population	of Sectoral Employment	Compared to Total Population	of Sectoral Employment	Compared to Total Population	of Sectoral Employment	Compared to Total Population
Total population, 1989	40	100	71	100	52	100	62	100	72	100
State sector, total	33	83	61	86	41	79	54	87	59	82
Industry	21	53	53	75	25	48	48	77	53	74
Agriculture	52	130	76	107	69	133	63	102	81	113
Transportation and communications	28	70	55	77	35	67	57	92	48	67
Construction	21	53	50	70	26	50	48	77	54	75
Trade and public dining	29	73	66	93	34	65	61	98	65	90
Housing—communal economy and non-productive personal services	23	58	55	77	30	58	56	90	53	74
Health, physical culture, and social security	38	95	64	90	46	88	50	81	62	86
Education	43	108	69	97	43	83	58	94	67	93
Culture and art	42	105	63	89	46	88	56	90	70	97
Science and scientific services	25	63	39	55	27	52	31	50	48	67
Government	40	100	57	80	42	81	51	82	51	71

Sources: *Trud v SSSR*, 1988. 1989, pp. 20–23; *Natsional'nyy sostav naseleniya SSSR, 1989.* 1991, pp. 9–19.

D. INTER-ETHNIC INSULARITY AND CONFLICTS

Most of the newly independent states have made their titular language the official language of their country. Therefore, it is not surprising to hear reports that Russian speaking people are now having difficulty communicating with those who have adopted the titular language. This is due to the inability of Russians to speak the native language, the outright discrimination against Russian speakers, or more likely, a combination of both. These factors have been contributing to the emigration of Russians (as well as other non-titular nationalities).

In 13 of the 15 republics of the former Soviet Union, 97 percent or more of the people of the titular nationality spoke the titular language as either their first or second language (Table 24). Only Ukrainians (94.7 percent) and Belorussians (89.7 percent) had lower shares of their populations that spoke the native language.

Although all Russians in the Russian Federation spoke the titular language (Russian), less than half of the Russians who lived elsewhere in the Soviet Union as of 1989 spoke the titular language of their adopted homes. This was especially true in Central Asia despite the fact that Russians accounted for significant proportions of the local population. Consider Kazakhstan with a 38 percent Russian population and Kyrgyzstan with a 21 percent Russian population, but only 0.9 and 1.2 percent who could speak the titular language, respectively. To some extent, this language gap may indicate how a large community can avoid assimilation because it has the critical economic and political mass to remain independent.

TABLE 24. Language Capability, 1989.

(Percent)

Geographical Unit	Titular Speaking Titular Language	Titular Speaking Russian Language	Russians Speaking Titular Language	Russians Speaking Russian Language
Russian Federation	100.0	—	—	99.6
Ukraine	94.7	71.7	34.3	99.5
Belarus	89.7	80.2	26.7	99.7
Moldova	97.1	57.6	11.8	98.9
Lithuania	99.8	37.6	37.5	99.8
Latvia	98.7	68.3	22.3	99.7
Estonia	99.6	34.6	15.0	99.4
Georgia	99.8	32.0	23.7	99.9
Azerbaijan	99.6	32.1	14.4	99.5
Armenia	99.8	44.6	33.6	100.0
Kazakhstan	98.8	64.2	0.9	99.9
Uzbekistan	99.0	22.7	4.6	100.0
Kyrgyzstan	99.6	37.3	1.2	99.9
Tajikistan	99.4	30.5	3.5	99.9
Turkmenistan	99.4	28.3	2.5	

Source: *Natsional'nyy Sostav Naseleniya SSSR, Perepis' Naseleniya, 1989.* 1991, pp. 28–140.
—Not applicable.
Language capability is the percent of the population reported in the 1989 census who are either claiming the language as mother tongue or otherwise able to communicate freely in it as a second language.

Table 25 shows the proportion of students who were educated in the titular language of their republic in the 1990–91 school year. Column 2 compares the titular share of the population (column 6) to the share of the population which attends general-education schools conducted in the titular language (column 1). Above 100 indicates that there are proportionally more students attending titular language general-education schools than there are people of that titular nationality in the population as a whole.

A few explanatory notes are needed for this table. A share above 100 does not mean that all of the students of the titular nationality attended those schools. Very often the secondary school aged titular population accounted for a different share of that population group than the entire titular population would for the total population of their republic. This is particularly true in the Central Asian republics where young people of the titular nationality have disproportionately higher shares of the population than the titular nationality does for the population as a whole. In addition, not all students that attended titular language institutions were of the titular nationality.

Though the titular populations of all the republics had 89 percent or more who spoke the titular language, several did not have the same proportions attending schools where that language was taught. In three of the republics, less than half of the students that attended primary schools were taught in the native language of the republic. The three Baltic republics, on the other hand, had significantly above average shares of the population that attended native language higher education institutions.

TABLE 25. Share of Students Receiving Instruction in Titular Language in the 1990-91 School Year.

(Percent)

Geographical Unit	General-Education Day Schools		Vocational Technical Schools	Specialized Secondary Schools	Higher Education Institutions	Titular Share of Population in the Republic (1989 Census)
	Share	Ratio				
	(1)	(2)	(3)	(4)	(5)	(6)
Russian Federation	98.1	120	99.9	99.6	98.8	81.5
Ukraine	47.9	66	32.9	21.1	15.2	72.7
Belarus	20.8	27	0.0	0.2	0.4	77.9
Moldova	60.2	93	61.7	44.9	45.0	64.5
Lithuania	N/A	100 [1]	84.4	88.1	90.7	79.6
Latvia	53.2	102	54.9	49.9	56.0	52.0
Estonia	63.0	102	57.0	65.4	79.8	61.5
Georgia	68.8	98	75.9	87.8	85.7	70.1
Azerbaijan	86.1	104	82.8	87.7	77.3	82.7
Armenia	86.9	93	96.7	98.1	81.7	93.3
Kazakhstan	32.3	81	16.4	8.7	13.6	39.7
Uzbekistan	78.1	109	79.7	71.1	65.1	71.4
Kyrgyzstan	55.7	106	49.2	18.0	23.4	52.4
Tajikistan	67.2	108	66.1	38.2	48.2	62.3
Turkmenistan	76.6	106	58.0	17.1	23.6	72.0

Source: *Vestnik Statistiki, No. 12, 1991.* 1991, p. 47.
N/A Data not available.
This table shows the percent of students for each republic and each type of educational institution who are attending schools which use the titular language for that republic.
[1] Column 2 ratio has been estimated for Lithuania because data for students in general-education day schools are not available.

Historically, the objective of nationality policy of the U.S.S.R. was the elimination of all nationality problems and conflicts. This goal was never achieved, and the current social, economic, and political changes that are developing only aggravate existing controversies. Many of the ethnic tensions erupting today are extremely complicated problems rooted in the distant past.

Table 26 presents a list of actual and potential sources of interethnic conflicts in the republics of the former Soviet Union. Combined with Map 3, this table shows the location, the classification, and a brief description of each dispute. Some of these disputes are rather minor, such as the provision of special national status for the city of Daugavpils (conflict number 3), while others are major conflicts, such as the warfare in and around Nagorno-Karabakh (conflict numbers 121-125). The following information is used with permission of the International Boundaries Research Unit at the University of Durham.

1113

MAP 3. TERRITORIAL DISPUTES IN THE FORMER U.S.S.R.

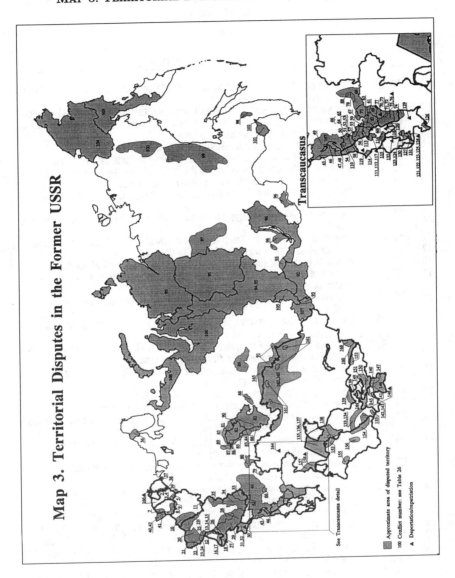

Source: Kolossov, Glezer, Petrov. *Ethno-Territorial Conflicts and Boundaries in the Former Soviet Union.* 1992.

TABLE 26. Territorial-Ethnic Disputes on the Territory of the Former Union of Soviet Socialist Republics, 1991.

(as of December 8, 1991)

No.	Type [1]	Proposal or Event
1	A2, B1	Creation of a Narva republic in north-eastern Estonia, its secession from Estonia and its reunification with Russia
2	A1	Restoration of the boundary between Estonia and Latvia to its pre-1941 position
3	B1	Provision of special national status for the city of Daugavpils
4	A1	Transfer of the Daugavpils district to Belarus
5	A1	Transfer of an area of south-eastern Latvia to Belarus
6	B1	Creation of a Polish autonomous national territory in south-eastern Lithuania
7	A1	Secession of the city of Klaipeda and the former Memel region from Lithuania
8	A1	Transfer of an area of south-eastern Lithuania to Belarus
9	A1	Transfer of parts of the Belorussian oblasts of Vitebsk, Grodno and Minsk to Lithuania
10	B1	Creation of a Western Polesye autonomous territory in the borderlands of Belarus and Ukraine
11	A1	Transfer of an area in the south-east of the Gomel oblast (Russia) to Ukraine
12	A1	Transfer of an area in northern Moldova to Ukraine
13	A1	Return to Ukraine of the Moldovan territory on the east bank of the Dniestr river
14	B1, B2, B5	Creation of a Dniestr Moldovan republic and its secession from Moldova or its inclusion in Moldova on a federal basis
15	B2	Creation of a Dniestr republic within the 1924–1940 boundaries of the Moldavian ASSR.
16	B2, B5	Creation of a Gagauz republic and its secession from Moldova or its inclusion in Moldova on a federal basis
17	B1, B5	Secession of southern Bessarabia (Budzhak) from Moldova and Ukraine and the creation of a federation of Budzhak and Gagauzia
18	B1	Creation of a Bulgar autonomous territory in southern Bessarabia on the borderlands of Ukraine and Moldova
19	A1	Transfer of northern areas of Zhitomir oblast (Ukraine) to Belarus
20	B1	Creation of a Galician autonomous territory in western Ukraine
21	B1, B2, B5	Creation of a Transcarpathian republic and its secession from Ukraine or inclusion in Ukraine on a federal basis
22	B1	Creation of a Hungarian national district in the south-western part of the Transcarpathian oblast (Ukraine)
23	B1	Creation of a Rumanian autonomous territory in the north-eastern part of Transcarpathian oblast (Ukraine)
24	B2, B5	Creation of an autonomous territory in Northern Bukovina and its secession from Ukraine or inclusion in Ukraine on a federal basis
25	A1	Transfer of a Ukrainian section of northern Bessarabia to Moldova
26	A1	Transfer of the north-western part of the Odessa oblast (Ukraine) to Moldova
27	A1	Transfer of the Ukrainian part of southern Bessarabia (Budzhak) to Moldova
28	B1, B4, B5	Creation of a Novorossiya republic in the southern Ukraine and its secession from Ukraine or inclusion in Ukraine on a federal basis
29	B1, B4	Creation of an independent state of Novorossiya including four southern oblasts of Ukraine
30	C2	Repatriation of Crimean Tatars to the Crimea
31	B2	Creation (restoration) of the Crimean Tatar republic
32	A2, B3	Secession of Crimea from Ukraine, its return to Russia or its inclusion in the Union as a sovereign member
33	B1, B4, B5	Secession of eastern oblasts from Ukraine as an independent unit or their inclusion in Ukraine or in Russia on a federal basis
34	B1, B4, B5	Creation of a Donetsk-Krivoy Rog republic in eastern Ukraine as an independent state or its inclusion in Ukraine on a federal basis

TABLE 26. Territorial-Ethnic Disputes on the Territory of the Former Union of Soviet Socialist Republics, 1991.—Continued

(as of December 8, 1991)

No.	Type [1]	Proposal or Event
35	B1, B4, B5	Creation of a Sloboda (Slobozhanskaya) republic and its inclusion in Ukraine on a federal basis
36	A1	Return to Karelia of the southern part of Murmansk oblast
37	A1	Return to Estonia of the borderland area of Leningrad (St Petersburg) oblast (Russia)
38	A1	Return to Estonia of the borderland districts of Pskov oblast (Russia)
39	A1	Return to Latvia of the borderland areas of Pskov oblast (Russia)
40	A1	Transfer of the Kaliningrad oblast (Russia) to Lithuania
41	B1	Creation of a Polish autonomous territory in the Kaliningrad oblast of Russia
42	B1, B2	Creation of a German republic (in Russia) on the territory of the Kaliningrad oblast (East Prussia until 1945)
43	A1	Transfer of the south-western part of the Rostov oblast to Ukraine
44	B2	Creation (restoration) of a Cossack republic on the territory of the former Region of the Don Army (Oblast Voyska Donskogo) in Russia
45	B1	Creation of a Greek republic in the coastal areas of the Krasnodar region (Russia)
46	B3	Creation of an Adygeya republic and its secession from the Krasnodar region (Russia)
47	A1	Transfer of coastal areas of the Krasnodar region to Adygeya
48	A1	Transfer of the southern part of Greater Sochi to Georgia
49	B2	Creation (restoration) of a Cossack republic on the territory of the former Kuban oblast
50	B2	Creation (restoration) of the autonomous Cherkess republic
51	B2	Creation (restoration) of the autonomous Karachay republic
52	B3	Proclamation of the Karachayevo-Cherkess republic and its secession from the Stavropol region
53	B1	Creation of an Abazin republic and its secession from Karachayevo-Cherkess
54	B1	Creation of a Zelenchukso-Urupsky territorial Cossack district and its transfer from Karachayevo-Cherkess to the Stavropol or Krasnodar region
55	B2	Creation (restoration) of the Kabardin republic as an autonomous unit
56	B2	Proclamation of a Balkar republic within the Russian Federation
57	B4	Creation of a Kabardino-Cherkess republic
58	B4	Creation of a Karachayevo-Balkar republic
59	A1	Transfer of part of North Ossetia with the town of Mozdok to Kabardino-Balkar
60	A1	Transfer of the eastern part of North Ossetia to Chechen-Ingush
61	A1, B2	Creation (restoration) of an independent (autonomous) Ingush republic, including eastern districts of North Ossetia
62	B2	Creation (restoration) of an independent Chechen republic (Nokhchi-Cho)
63	B2	Creation of a Cossack autonomous area in the Sunzhensky district of Chechen-Ingush
64	B4	Creation of a united Cherkess to include Cherkess, Kabarda, Adygeya and coastal districts of the Krasnodar region
65	B4	Creation (restoration) of a Gorskaya (Mountainous) republic to include Chechen-Ingush, North Ossetia, Kabarda and Cherkess
66	B4	Creation of a Caucasian Peoples Confederation and its secession from Russia and Georgia
67	B2	Creation (restoration) of a Cossack republic on the territory of the former Terek oblast
68	B2	Creation of a Nogaisko-Terskaya Cossack autonomous oblast
69	B1	Creation of a Nogay republic in eastern districts of the Stavropol region and northern Dagestan
70	B1	Creation of a Kumyk republic (within Russia) in the central part of the Dagestan lowlands

TABLE 26. Territorial-Ethnic Disputes on the Territory of the Former Union of Soviet Socialist Republics, 1991.—Continued

(as of December 8, 1991)

No.	Type [1]	Proposal or Event
71	B1	Creation of an Avar republic in the central and western parts of mountainous Dagestan
72	B1	Creation of a Darghin republic in the eastern part of mountainous Dagestan
73	B1, B5	Creation of a federative republic of Dagestan
74	B1	Creation of a republic of Lezghistan in the borderlands of Dagestan and Azerbaijan as part of the Russian Federation or as an independent state
75	C2	Repatriation of Ingush in the suburban district of North Ossetia
76	C1	Deportation and flight of Cossacks from the Sunzhensky district of Chechen-Ingush under the pressure of Chechen nationalism
77	C2	Return of Chechen-Akkins to western Dagestan
78	A1	Transfer of the western part of the Volga delta to Kalmykia
79	B1	Creation of a Volga-German republic on the former Kapustin Yar military range on the lower Volga
80	B2	Creation (restoration) of the Volga-German republic
81	B3	Secession of Tatarstan from the Russian Federation
82	B4	Reunification of Tatarstan and Bashkortostan in a single republic of Bashtatarstan
83	A1	Transfer of the south-western part of Bashkortostan to Tatarstan
84	B2	Creation of a Tatar autonomous area in Bashkortostan
85	A1	Creation of a "Greater Tataria" to include Tatarstan and considerable areas of all the adjoining republics and oblasts
86	B2	Creation of a Russian-speaking Zakamskaya republic and its secession from Tatarstan
87	B1	Creation of a Chuvash autonomous area in Tatarstan
88	B2	Creation of Tatar autonomous areas in the Astrakhan, Yekaterinburg, Samara, Tyumen, and Chelyabinsk oblasts of Russia
89	A1	Revision of the boundaries of Chuvash with Tatarstan and the Ulyanovsk and Nizhegorodsk oblasts
90	A1	Transfer of territory in the south-east of the Udmurt Republic, with the town of Votkinsk, to the Perm oblast
91	B1	Creation of German national districts in the Altay region and the Omsk and Novosibirsk oblasts of Russia
92	B2	Restoration of the Tuva people's republic as an independent state
93	A1	Transfer of the eastern part of Gorno-Altay and the southern part of Irkutsk oblast to the Tuva republic
94	B1	Creation of a Russian national district in the central and southern parts of the Krasnoyarsk region
95	B1	Creation of a Yenisey republic in eastern Siberia to include Evenki AO, Taymyr AOkr and the Russian national district
96	B2	Creation (restoration) of a Buryat-Mongol republic
97	B1	Creation of a Mirny autonomous district in Yakutia
98	B1	Creation of a Nanay national autonomous district on the lower Amur
99	A1	Transfer of part of the Khabarovsk region to Yakutia
100	A1	Transfer of part of Magadan oblast to Yakutia
101	B3	Proclamation of a Jewish republic and its secession from the Khabarovsk region
102	A1	Secession of four districts from the Jewish autonomous oblast
103	B3	Proclamation of a Koryak republic and its secession from Kamchatka oblast
104	B3	Proclamation of a Chukotsk republic and its secession from Magadan oblast
105	B3	Proclamation of a Khakass republic and its secession from the Krasnoyarsk region
106	B3	Creation of a Yamalo-Nenets republic
107	B3	Proclamation of a Gorno-Altay republic and its secession from the Altay region
108	B3	Proclamation of a Nenets republic

1117

TABLE 26. Territorial-Ethnic Disputes on the Territory of the Former Union of Soviet Socialist Republics, 1991.—Continued

(as of December 8, 1991)

No.	Type [1]	Proposal or Event
109	B1	Creation of the Republic of Rus including all the Russian oblasts and regions (without national-territorial formations)
110	A2, B3	Secession of Abkhaz ASSR from Georgia and its transfer to Russia or its transformation into an independent republic
111	B3	Creation of a South Ossetian autonomous republic within Georgia
112	B3	Abolition of the South Ossetian autonomous territory
113	A2, B3, B4	Secession of South Ossetia from Georgia, reunification of South Ossetia and North Ossetia, inclusion of a united Ossetia in Russia or its establishment as an independent state
114	B3	Abolition of the Adzhar autonomous area
115	A1	Transfer of a southern section of Georgia (Dzhavaketia) to Armenia
116	A1	Transfer of a southern section of Georgia to Azerbaijan
117	C1	Deportation and flight of Ossets from South Ossetia
118	C1	Deportation of Avars from Georgia
119	C2	Return of Georgian Turks to their historical homeland in Meskhetia (Georgia)
120	A1	Transfer of a north-western section of Azerbaijan to Georgia
121	A2, B3	Secession of Nagorno-Karabakh from Azerbaijan, its transfer to armenia or its direct control by the Russian Federation or its inclusion in the Union as a republic
122	A2	Transfer of Nagorno-Karabakh to Armenia
123	A1, B3	Creation of an autonomous (independent) Nagorno-Karabakh republic to include the former Nagorno-Karabakh autonomous oblast and the abolished Shaumyanovsky district of Azerbaijan
124	B2	Restoration of the Shaumyanovsky district of Azerbaijan
125	B3	Abolition of the Nagorno-Karabakh autonomous oblast
126	B1	Creation of a Talysh autonomous territory in Azerbaijan
127	B1	Creation (restoration) of a Kurdish autonomous area in Azerbaijan
128	C1	Deportation and flight of Armenians from Nagorno-Karabakh
129	C2	Return of Armenians to central and north-western districts of Azerbaijan
130	C1	Deportation and flight of Armenians from western border districts of Azerbaijan
131	A1	Transfer of southern districts of Armenia to Azerbaijan
132	C2	Return of Azeris to northern and north-eastern border districts of Armenia
133	A1	Transfer of the Zeravshan, Kashkadar'ya and Surkhandar'ya oases from Uzbekistan to Tajikistan
134	A1	Transfer of the Zeravshan oasis of Uzbekistan to Tajikistan
135	B3	Secession of Karakalpak ASSR from Uzbekistan
136	A2	Transfer of Karakalpak ASSR to Kazakhstan
137	A2	Transfer of Karakalpak ASSR to Russia
138	A1	Transfer of part of the Amu Darya delta of Karakalpak ASSR to the Khorezm oblast of Uzbekistan
139	C1	Mass flight of Meskhetian Turks as a result of massacres in 1989
140	A1	Transfer of the high-mountain pastures of the southern (Tajik) slopes of the Alay and Zaalay ranges to Kyrgyzstan
141	A1	Transfer of the upper reaches of the Surkhob valley to Kyrgyzstan
142	A1	Transfer of the northern sections of Karateghin to Kyrgyzstan
143	C2	Repatriation of Kyrgyz to Karateghin and the upper reaches of the Zeravshan (Tajikistan)
144	A1	Transfer of parts of the Tajik section of the Fergana basin to Uzbekistan
145	A1	Transfer of the upper reaches of the Zeravshan to Uzbekistan
146	B3	Secession of Gorno-Badakhshan from Tajikistan
147	A1, B1	Creation of a Kyrgyz autonomous territory in the northern Pamir of Tajikistan or the transfer of this territory to Kyrgyzstan

TABLE 26. Territorial-Ethnic Disputes on the Territory of the Former Union of Soviet Socialist Republics, 1991.—Continued

(as of December 8, 1991)

No.	Type [1]	Proposal or Event
148	C1	Flight of Armenians from Tajikistan as a result of the February 1990 pogroms in Dushanbe
149	A1	Transfer of the Batken district of Osh oblast (Kyrgyzstan) to Tajikistan
150	A1	Transfer of the high-mountain pastures of the northern (Kyrgyz) slopes of the Alay and Zaalay ranges to Tajikistan
151	A1	Transfer of part of the Kyrgyz section of the Fergana basin to Uzbekistan
152	A1	Transfer of northern districts of Kyrgyzstan adjacent to Lake Issyk-kul to Kazakhstan
153	A1	Transfer of a section of the Tashauz oasis (Turkmenistan) adjacent to the Amu Darya to Uzbekistan
154	A1	Transfer of the middle Amu Darya oasis (Turkmenistan) to Uzbekistan
155	B1	Creation of a Kurdish autonomous area in Turkmenistan
156	B1	Creation of a Beludzhian autonomous area in Turkmenistan
157	A1	Transfer of part of the Mangistausk peninsula (Kazakhstan) to Turkmenistan
158	C2	Repatriation of Turkmen to Mangistausk
159	A1	Transfer of lands between the Syr-Darya and Arys rivers from Kazakhstan to Uzbekistan
160	A1	Transfer of the northern slopes of the Transily Alatau mountains and the Kungey-Ala-Too district of Kazakhstan to Kyrgyzstan
161	B1	Creation of German national-territorial areas in northern Kazakhstan
162	B1	Creation of an autonomous republic in the Russian-speaking areas of northern Kazakhstan
163	A1	Transfer of northern Kazakhstan to Russia
164	C1	Flight of Caucasian nationalities from western Kazakhstan as a result of ethnic conflicts in summer 1989
165	A1	Transfer of districts in the southern Urals and south-western Siberia to Kazakhstan
166	C2	Deportation from Latvia of that section of the non-Latvian population which entered the republic after 1940
167	B2	Creation (restoration) of a Shepsugh national district in the Krasnodar region or under the direct control of the Russian federal authorities
168	B1	Creation of an Uyghur autonomous territory in Kazakhstan

Source: Kolossov, Glezer, Petrov, *Ethno-Territorial Conflicts and Boundaries in the Former Soviet Union.* 1992, pp. 41–51.

[1] Each conflict has a key number denoting its location on the map of the Soviet Union displayed in Map 3. This is followed by a code number allocating each conflict to one or more of the following categories:
A. BOUNDARY CHANGES
    A1—a change in the position of a boundary line
    A2—the transfer of a national-political unit from one former union republic to another
B. CHANGES IN THE STATUS OF TERRITORIAL UNITS
    B1—the creation of new national-political units
    B2—the restoration of previously existing national-political units
    B3—a rise or fall in the status of a national-political unit
    B4—the reunification of two or more units
    B5—the acquisition by a territorial unit of the status of a member of a federation
C. RESETTLEMENT OF ETHNIC GROUPS
    C1—deportations
    C2—repatriations.

V. THE ECONOMY

A. MACRO-ECONOMIC INDICATORS

Measuring economic performance has many dimensions. In the following discussion, we will concentrate on a few measures which have implications for overall levels of well-being in society. These are the same macroeconomic indicators which have historically been the yardsticks against which western democracies have judged the stewardship of their top leaders: GNP levels and growth, productivity, inflation, and unemployment.

Since the early 1950s, policymakers world-wide have been proclaiming that economic growth is an important social objective. The principal rationale for using economic growth as a goal is that a constantly rising real income is necessary to maintain a high level of employment and to improve living standards. Countries with low growth rates have trouble absorbing new job entrants or resolving competing claims for shares of national income. While this study adopts the convention of using GNP and its growth to explore economic development and other issues, it must be emphasized that western reconstructions of GNP are flawed at the union level and even more problematic at the republic level. For this reason, some attempt is made to provide a range of estimates and a context for interpreting the underlying physical reality.

Table 27 presents current ruble and current dollar estimates for GNP in 1990. As in any measurement exercise involving national accounts, there is always some uncertainty about the degree of precision. This is especially true for the republics of the former Soviet Union. Still, the official Goskomstat numbers, the CIR estimates, and the Intelligent Decision Systems (IDS) estimates of GNP in current rubles all track one another fairly closely in nominal terms. Consistency in this regard increases our confidence in assessing the relative size of the different republican economies. Unanimity disappears when dollar measurements are produced. Interim procedures used by the World Bank and Noren result in estimates which can diverge by more than 200 percent. [15]

Such a wide disparity is not unexpected given the long history of controversy about the true value of the ruble. This problem will be addressed in the future through the use of ICP Project purchasing power parities. In Table 28 the standard of living, as measured by ruble GNP per capita, is derived and then used to rank the repub-

---

[15] The World Bank estimates use synthetic atlas conversion factors to establish the ruble-dollar exchange rate. The second set of dollar estimates was provided by James Noren, private consultant. They follow in the tradition of CIA research on purchasing power parity price ratios used to measure U.S. and Soviet consumption, investment, and defense. His ruble-dollar conversion factors were applied to the nominal CIR estimates to arrive at the numbers reported in the table. For a more complete discussion of this latter methodology see "U.S. and U.S.S.R.: Comparisons of GNP" by Imogene Edwards, Margaret Hughes, and James Noren, JEC *Soviet Economy in a Time of Change* vol. 1 pp. 369–401, 10 October 1979.

Russian economists have also estimated GNP in dollars. One set of estimates that can be compared with those given here are those computed by Boris Belotin, an economist in the Institute of World Economy and International Relations (Moscow). His results for 1990 (billion dollars) were: Russia—1,061.5; Ukraine—277.6; Belarus—67.0; Uzbekistan—76.0; Kazakhstan—101.0; Georgia—38.0; Azerbaijan—23.0; Lithuania—29.0; Moldova—17.5; Latvia—21.0; Kyrygstan—16.0; Tajikistan—17.5; Armenia—26.0; Turkmenistan—17.0; Estonia—14.0. Another respected Russian economist compiled dollar estimates but used constant 1985 prices; therefore his results cannot be compared with those given here (see Ilarionov, *Voprosy Ekonomiki*, Nos. 4–6, 1992, pp. 122–143).

TABLE 27. Gross National Product, 1990.

Geographical Unit	CIR (Bil. Rubles)	Official (Bil. Rubles)	IDS (Bil. Rubles)	World Bank (Bil. $US)	Noren (Bil. $US)	World Bank ($ per capita)	Noren ($ per capita)
	(1)	(2)	(3)	(4)	(5)	(6)	(7)
U.S.S.R.	1,061	1,000	1,085	830	2,784	2,870	9,623
Russian Federation	661	626	660	509	1,688	3,430	11,382
Ukraine	168	165	180	130	451	2,500	8,690
Belarus	42	40	44	32	111	3,110	10,777
Moldova	13	13	15	11	33	2,390	7,500
Lithuania	13	13	15	12	35	3,110	9,459
Latvia	12	12	12	10	31	3,590	11,481
Estonia	7	8	8	7	20	4,170	12,500
Georgia	16	15	16	12	43	2,120	7,818
Azerbaijan	17	15	16	12	43	1,640	5,972
Armenia	10	10	10	8	25	2,380	7,576
Kazakhstan	45	45	48	44	133	2,600	7,917
Uzbekistan	33	32	36	28	98	1,340	4,780
Kyrgyzstan	9	8	9	7	25	1,570	5,682
Tajikistan	8	7	8	6	21	1,130	3,962
Turkmenistan	7	7	9	6	22	1,690	5,946

Sources: 1) Column 1: Center for International Research, "Gross National Product Accounts of the Newly Independent States of the Former Soviet Union 1987–1990," December 1992. 2) Column 2: Official estimates *Ibid.* p. 3. 3) Column 3: Intelligent Decision Systems estimates, *Ibid.* p. 3. 4) Columns 4 and 6: World Bank estimates, see "Measuring the Incomes of Economies of the Former Soviet Union," December 1992, pp. 3–4. 5) Columns 5 and 7: Estimates provided by James Noren, private consultant.

lics. Since these are ruble figures, international comparisons cannot be made. The fact that Russia ranks first, putting it above the Baltic republics, may seem somewhat surprising. But we remind the reader that GNP is a more inclusive measure than personal consumption and covers such things as expenditures on investment and the military.[16] For purposes of comparison, welfare as measured by the PQLI (Physical Quality of Life Index) and the HDI (UN Human Development Index) are computed and their implied rankings for the republics juxtaposed against the ruble counterparts. While the use of the PQLI or HDI, in theory, permits the analyst to see beyond the monetary veil, these measures rely on reported data sets (life expectancy, infant mortality rates, levels of literacy etc.) which are known to be flawed in the Soviet case. This is immediately apparent in the case of Georgia, where both the PQLI and HDI indices place the republic in first position because of reported life expectancy. There is little firm evidence to support the claims of extraordinary longevity in the Caucasus, notwithstanding American commercials showing spry centenarians testifying to the benefits of eating yogurt. Thus, completely unambiguous domestic and international comparisons are still not possible, and the reader must be content with looking for points of substantial consistency between the various monetary and physical rankings (Ukraine, Belarus, Kazakhstan, Kyrgyzstan and Turkmenistan).

Time series data recording the growth of republic GNP in constant prices, to our knowledge, have never been estimated. Nevertheless, approximations to these growth rates can be developed

---

[16] Military expenditures, in particular, are disproportionately concentrated in a few republics, notably Russia and Ukraine.

TABLE 28. Standard of Living Indicators, 1990.

Geographical Unit	GNP (Rubles Per Capita)	Ranking Per Capita GNP	PQLI Index	PQLI Ranking	HD Index	HD Index Ranking
	(1)	(2)	(3)	(4)	(5)	(6)
U.S.S.R.	3,669					
Russian Federation	4,459	1	0.976	11	0.55	8
Ukraine	3,233	6	0.983	6	0.60	7
Belarus	4,037	4	0.986	4	0.73	3
Moldova	2,911	9	0.973	14	0.22	15
Lithuania	3,597	5	0.987	3	0.63	5
Latvia	4,263	3	0.979	8	0.63	5
Estonia	4,381	2	0.980	7	0.66	4
Georgia	2,947	8	0.993	1	0.87	1
Azerbaijan	2,308	11	0.984	5	0.44	9
Armenia	3,121	7	0.990	2	0.74	2
Kazakhstan	2,704	10	0.975	12	0.41	10
Uzbekistan	1,629	14	0.978	10	0.37	11
Kyrgyzstan	1,955	13	0.974	13	0.33	12
Tajikistan	1,526	15	0.979	8	0.33	12
Turkmenistan	2,022	12	0.961	15	0.26	14

Sources: 1) Column 1: CIR estimates. 2) Column 3: Physical Quality of Life Index (PQLI). The PQLI is a composite index which combines measures of infant mortality, life expectancy at age 1, and literacy percentage rates. CIR has used weighted male-female life expectancies and adjusted adult literacy rates in performing the calculation. 3) Column 5: Human Development Index (HDI). The HDI uses three variables: life expectancy, literacy, and the log of real GDP in the calculation were CIR estimates. For columns 2, 4, and 6 the index is computed by CIR using official Soviet data or CIR reconstruction, as appropriate.

from information on real GNP growth at the all union level and synthetic measures of real per capita GNP at the republic level. Growth rates vary from under 1 percent per year (Armenia) to over 3 percent (Georgia), but on average cluster in the 2 percent range (Table 29).

Implicit in the discussion of economic growth is the fact that the development of an economy can follow several different paths. In the absence of resource constraints, the simplest way to increase GNP is to augment the stock of factor inputs—that is, retain existing technique but increase the scale of usage of land, labor, and capital. Such an approach characterizes the traditional Stalinist model of growth on the extensive margin. Alternatively, one can make better use of current levels of resources and/or promote policies for technological change. This is referred to as growth on the intensive margin. To the extent that a country adopts this latter strategy, the sacrifice that society endures is less than what would follow from a strictly resource-augmenting approach.

Despite the fact that Soviet plans for extensive margin growth were imposed union-wide, a republic level search for differences in efficiency is meaningful because factors of production have historically been non-homogeneous and their utilization, non-uniform. Table 29 reports total factor productivity trends for the period 1980–1988. These numbers should be interpreted with caution because they are based upon the synthetic growth rates reported earlier, and because they assume that a Cobb-Douglas production func-

1122

tion adequately describes the laws of technology. [17] Nevertheless, one observes that the calculated growth in factor productivities varied by republic, and significantly, was uniformly negative. Put differently, it took more resources to produce a unit of output toward the end of the decade than it did in the beginning. The clear implication is that future increases in the standard of living are going to be difficult to secure unless there is substantial restructuring of the labor force and capital stock.

TABLE 29. Growth and Productivity, 1980–1988.

Geographical Unit	Annual Average GNP Growth	Annual Growth in Total Factor Productivity
Russian Federation	2.08	−0.88
Ukraine	1.67	—
Belarus	2.77	−0.17
Moldova	2.08	—
Lithuania	2.86	—
Latvia	1.95	—
Estonia	1.96	—
Georgia	3.02	—
Azerbaijan	2.88	−0.4
Armenia	0.89	−1.88
Kazakhstan	2.24	−0.62
Uzbekistan	1.70	—
Kyrgyzstan	2.57	−0.17
Tajikistan	2.88	−0.66
Turkmenistan	2.73	−1.3

Sources: 1) Real growth in GNP is derived from All-Union GNP estimates in constant prices ("Measures of Soviet Gross National Product in 1982 Prices," JEC, November 1990, pp. 57, 72) and per capita GNP information based on estimates using the methodology developed by Gertrude Schroeder. 2) To calculate total factor productivity, both labor and capital stock growth rates were combined using their respective output elasticities and then deducted from the corresponding GNP growth rate.
— Insufficient data to calculate factor productivity.

GNP, measured from the end-use side, can be decomposed into price and quantity data. Analysis of these series, in turn, can shed light on underlying questions of economic stability. Before Gorbachev, questions about the instability of the Soviet economy were largely dismissed. Empirical work supported Soviet claims that the business cycle was primarily a capitalist disease; however, by 1990, *perestroika* had unleashed the forces of inflation and unemploy-

[17] For purposes of calculating dynamic efficiency, a Cobb-Douglas production function exhibiting constant returns to scale is assumed. Both capital and labor output elasticities are calculated as the geometric means for the endpoint years 1980 and 1988. Finally, a capital charge of 12 percent is applied to the deflated capital stock when estimating payments to that factor of production.

ment. These developments set the stage, in part, for the August 1991 coup.

People concerned about measuring the impact of inflation on economic performance may want to construct price deflators which allow nominal GNP to be converted into real GNP. Table 30 provides preliminary estimates of the magnitudes involved based on official Goskomstat data. Before interpreting these numbers, a caveat is in order since coverage and interpretation are not well understood. Greater reliability and precision can be expected once the calculation of western style consumer and producer price indices is fully under way. As of the end of 1992, fewer than half of the republics have adopted the standardized procedures for making these calculations, and none have officially released the results. Having said this, it appears that republic level retail price inflation rates ranged between 80 and 244 percent during 1991. At the same time, wholesale industrial prices may have increased by 120 to 288 percent.

TABLE 30. Inflation Rates, 1991.

Geographical Unit	Official Retail Prices Goskomstat	Official Wholesale Prices Goskomstat
Russian Federation	90.4	138.1
Ukraine	84.2	125.4
Belarus	80.3	151.1
Moldova	98.0	130.0
Lithuania	216.4	NA
Latvia	244.3	155.9
Estonia	211.8	187.6
Georgia	90.0	NA
Azerbaijan	87.3	137.9
Armenia	90.7	120.0
Kazakhstan	84.0	172.4
Uzbekistan	82.2	147.4
Kyrgyzstan	181.0	288.0
Tajikistan	83.5	163.0
Turkmenistan	84.6	205.0

Sources: 1) Georgia: *The World Factbook 1992*, Central Intelligence Agency, Washington, D.C. 2) All other republics: *Economic Review Series*, International Monetary Fund, 1992.
NA Data not available.

People investigating labor force issues may want to track how changes in the output of goods and services drive (un)employment magnitudes. Again, there are problems interpreting the published data. Until the last months of the Soviet period, unemployment was not officially acknowledged. However, since then all republics have begun developing such statistics and corresponding employment policies. The most recent data, for August 1992, show that unemployment in 9 of the 11 commonwealth countries (Ukraine and Turkmenistan figures are not available) was increasing rapidly (Table 31). As of this date, 374,700 unemployed people were registered at job placement centers. From a labor force of 103.9 million

(December 1991) this translates into an unemployment rate of 0.36 percent. This figure is certainly too low because the process to register officially as unemployed is difficult, protracted, and causes many of those out of work to refrain from signing up.

TABLE 31. The Number of Officially Unemployed Registered at The Employment Office for 1992, CIS Countries.

(Thousands)

Geographical Unit [1]	January	February	March	April	May	June	July	August
Russian Federation	69.2	93.1	118.4	151.0	176.5	202.9	248.0	294.2
Belarus	2.6	3.4	4.2	5.1	5.8	7.1	9.7	12.2
Moldova	—	0.2	0.3	0.4	0.4	0.6	0.9	1.2
Azerbaijan	4.9	5.5	7.0	7.9	7.2	7.2	6.8	6.6
Armenia	—	—	—	6.1	8.9	14.5	20.8	29.3
Kazakhstan	4.5	6.7	9.2	11.8	13.6	15.8	19.6	22.4
Uzbekistan	—	—	—	—	—	—	1.4	2.1
Kyrgyzstan	0.2	0.3	0.5	0.7	0.8	0.8	1.1	1.2
Tajikistan	—	—	—	0.5	1.3	3.5	3.6	5.5

Source: Commonwealth of Independent States, Goskomstat Data Base, CIR.
[1] Data on Ukraine and Turkmenistan not available.

Table 32 indicates that once duration requirements (three months) are met, the number of people designated as officially unemployed could jump substantially. There are also problems in interpreting these unemployment rates because the Soviet definition of labor resources does not correspond to the western concept of the labor force. [18] Finally, international comparisons are confounded by the fact that the reference period (one year) is rather long and thus forces the use of the concept "usually active population" as opposed to "currently active population." Until these and other defects are remedied, it is probably best to look at underlying trends rather than absolute levels.

TABLE 32. The Number of Non-Working People Asking for Job Placement Assistance from the Employment Office for 1992, CIS Countries.

(Thousands)

Geographical Unit [1]	January	February	March	April	May	June	July	August
Russian Federation	473.0	552.6	617.7	695.4	742.3	779.9	842.7	904.3
Belarus	19.7	22.1	26.5	32.5	37.0	41.7	46.9	52.5
Moldova	—	14.2	14.5	18.1	19.9	19.9	20.0	23.6
Azerbaijan	12.5	14.3	16.0	17.9	18.6	19.4	20.7	22.8
Armenia	—	—	—	8.2	12.4	19.1	27.5	35.2
Kazakhstan [1]	53.0	55.0	57.0	59.0	60.0	61.0	63.0	65.0
Uzbekistan	214.4	158.0	153.5	134.2	119.2	98.9	11.9	14.6
Kyrgyzstan	5.6	5.8	6.8	7.7	7.8	8.01	8.11	8.31
Tajikistan	8.4	11.3	15.1	17.8	20.8	22.8	24.7	26.8

Source: Commonwealth of Independent States, Goskomstat Data Base, CIR.
[1] Data on Ukraine and Turkmenistan not available.
[2] Estimated.

---

[18] The Soviet concept of labor resources includes housewives and students. Both of these categories are excluded from the western definition.

B. PRIVATIZATION

For nearly the entire Soviet period, virtually all economic activity was controlled by the state (the most significant exception being small private agricultural or garden plots). The reforms begun by Gorbachev in the mid-1980s allowed for an increase in legal private and cooperative activities. Consequently, the new economic organizations' (excluding the state sector and long-standing collective farms) share of the labor force grew considerably in recent years, from 5 percent in 1989 to an estimated 19 percent in 1991. [19] Tables 33 and 34 provide background data.

Sales by new forms of cooperatives rose rapidly, from less than 400 million rubles in 1987 to more than 60 billion rubles in 1990 (Table 35). In 1990, Russian cooperatives generated 64 percent of all cooperative sales. Employment in private enterprise [20] over the entire period has also increased, although less dramatically than the increase in sales (Table 36). In 1990, 673.8 thousand people were employed in private enterprise, about half of whom were in Russia.

---

[19] This assumes that employment in the collective farm sector remains at 8.4 percent of the work force (as in 1989).

[20] Private sector employment covers the following three sectors: the peasant farm economy, private subsidiary agriculture, and individual labor activities. It comprises all those persons who work without affiliation. Note the peak reached in 1988.

TABLE 33. Employment by Form of Property, 1989.

Geographical Unit	Total	State	Collective Farms	Cooperatives	Private Agriculture	Other Private Labor
U.S.S.R.	100.0	86.2	8.4	2.2	3.0	0.2
Russian Federation	100.0	88.7	5.4	4.4	1.3	0.2
Ukraine	100.0	82.5	13.6	1.9	1.8	0.2
Belarus	100.0	84.9	12.6	1.3	1.0	0.2
Moldova	100.0	80.9	10.8	6.3	1.2	0.8
Lithuania	100.0	81.5	11.2	4.1	1.1	2.1
Latvia	100.0	86.1	10.4	2.1	0.9	0.5
Estonia	100.0	87.8	10.1	1.6	0.3	0.2
Georgia	100.0	78.7	9.9	4.8	6.1	0.6
Azerbaijan	100.0	77.8	11.0	2.2	8.6	0.4
Armenia	100.0	81.3	4.0	8.3	5.4	0.9
Kazakhstan	100.0	91.6	3.4	2.4	2.4	0.2
Uzbekistan	100.0	70.0	13.8	2.4	13.6	0.2
Kyrgyzstan	100.0	74.4	10.1	4.5	10.8	0.2
Tajikistan	100.0	65.5	13.2	1.8	19.4	0.1
Turkmenistan	100.0	62.4	22.3	1.1	14.1	0.1

Sources: *Norodne Gospodarstvo Ukrainskoi RSR*, 1990, p. 51.; *Statisticheskiy Yezhegodnik Kazakhstana*, 1990, 1991, pp. 53, 54; *Statisticheskiy Yezhegodnik Kazakhstana*, 1990, (Part II), p. 97; *Narodnoye Khozaystvo Tadzhikskoy SSR, 1990*, p. 22; *Statisticheskiy Yezhegodnik Latvii, 1990*, pp. 29–30; *Narodnoye Khozaystvo Belorussii, 1990*, p. 36; *Narodnoye Khozaystvo Uzbekskoy SSR, 1990*, p. 23; *Narodnoye Khozaysto RFSSR, 1989*, pp. 107–108; *Narodnoye Khozaystvo SSSR, 1989*, p. 47; *Narodnoye Khozaystvo Armyanskoy SSR, 1988*, p. 17; *Narodnoye Khozaystvo Azerbaizhanskoy SSR, 1988*, p. 27; *Respublika Moldova v Tsifrakh, 1990*, pp. 66–67; *Narodnoye Khozaystvo Latvii, 1989*, p. 39; 1989 economic progress reports.

TABLE 34. Employment by Form of Property, 1991. [1]

Geographical Unit	Total	State	Leased Enterprises	Joint Stock Company	Concerns, Associations	Social Organizations	Joint Ventures	Collective Farms and Cooperatives	Private
U.S.S.R.	100.0	72.6	6.8	0.7	1.0	0.9	0.2	13.3	4.5
Russian Federation	100.0	76.3	8.0	1.1	0.6	0.9	0.2	10.4	2.5
Ukraine	100.0	69.0	5.6	0.3	2.2	1.1	0.1	18.5	3.2
Belarus	100.0	70.3	6.4	0.4	2.0	1.1	0.2	17.8	1.8
Moldova	100.0	54.2	7.0	0.1	1.8	1.0	0.2	25.8	9.9
Lithuania	100.0	NA	NA	NA	NA	NA	NA	NA	NA
Latvia	100.0	NA	NA	NA	NA	NA	NA	NA	NA
Estonia	100.0	NA	NA	NA	NA	NA	NA	NA	NA
GEORGIA	100.0	NA	NA	NA	NA	NA	NA	NA	NA
Azerbaijan	100.0	67.6	2.5	0.4	0.1	3.3	—	16.4	9.7
Armenia	100.0	77.1	1.2	0.4	0.7	0.8	—	9.9	9.9
Kazakhstan	100.0	75.5	9.0	0.2	1.7	0.7	0.1	8.8	4.0
Uzbekistan	100.0	62.4	3.0	0.2	0.7	0.3	0.1	17.3	16.0
Kyrgyzstan	100.0	66.0	2.8	0.1	0.7	0.8	—	15.1	14.5
Tajikistan	100.0	57.6	4.7	0.1	0.5	0.6	—	16.3	20.2
Turkmenistan	100.0	55.7	0.7	—	—	0.2	—	26.2	17.2

Source: Heleniak and Velkoff, "Unemployment and the Transformation of the Labor Force in the Former Soviet Union." 1992, p. 28.

NA Data not available.

— Zero or negligible.

[1] Economic organizations have not yet been defined. These include: leased enterprises (state and collective farm enterprises that have been leased, usually to the employees), joint stock companies (state enterprises in which shares have been sold), concerns and associations (associations of enterprises which have been bonded together to operate outside the ministerial structure), social organizations (foundations or charity organizations), joint ventures (enterprises jointly owned with foreign persons or entities).

TABLE 35. Sales by Cooperatives, 1987–90.

(Million rubles)

Geographical Unit	1987	1988	1989	1990
U.S.S.R.	349.7	6,060.6	40,339.1	67,313.0
Russian Federation	168.2	3,325.8	24,874.5	42,801.3
Ukraine	47.8	900.6	5,152.7	7,938.0
Belarus	11.2	143.1	891.1	1,497.5
Moldova	7.0	158.1	1,055.3	1,575.1
Lithuania	12.7	118.2	651.6	1,056.3
Latvia	9.7	190.5	1,078.8	2,040.9
Estonia	8.3	101.6	384.6	976.6
Georgia	19.6	204.0	986.4	1,739.7
Azerbaijan	8.1	69.0	383.6	336.4
Armenia	15.1	223.3	779.6	1,322.7
Kazakhstan	11.5	275.4	1,592.8	2,678.7
Uzbekistan	19.6	229.3	1,782.5	2,181.0
Kyrgyzstan	4.0	63.5	255.7	318.3
Tajikistan	4.2	35.3	279.3	524.8
Turkmenistan	2.7	22.9	190.6	325.7

Source: *Narodnoye Khozyaystvo SSSR, 1990.* 1991, pp. 58–59.

TABLE 36. Employment in Private Enterprises.

(Thousand persons)

Geographical Unit	1987	1988	1989	1990
U.S.S.R.	427.2	734.2	672.6	673.8
Russian Federation	194.1	346.5	328.4	342.7
Ukraine	79.1	133.3	125.1	118.6
Belarus	16.7	27.6	24.6	26.1
Moldova	12.6	15.5	15.0	15.3
Lithuania	28.4	49.4	40.4	33.4
Latvia	10.9	19.5	14.9	14.9
Estonia	6.3	11.2	6.5	6.5
Georgia	13.5	21.2	18.1	16.1
Azerbaijan	8.1	11.0	10.1	8.4
Armenia	10.8	23.6	15.6	17.8
Kazakhstan	15.4	25.1	25.6	25.1
Uzbekistan	20.7	32.2	29.5	28.6
Kyrgyzstan	3.9	6.9	7.0	8.5
Tajikistan	3.1	6.4	6.8	6.2
Turkmenistan	3.6	4.8	5.0	5.6

Source: *Narodnoye Khozyaystvo SSSR, 1990.* 1991, p. 65.
People employed in private enterprises may also have been employed in another sphere of the economy.

TABLE 37. Private Enterprise by Type of Activity in the First Half of 1990.

(Percent share of employment in private enterprises)

Geographical Unit	Total	Handi-crafts	Serv-ices	Social-cultural	Artistic	Other
U.S.S.R.	100.0	62.8	24.5	6.1	1.2	5.4
Russian Federation	100.0	63.6	22.0	8.0	0.5	5.9
Ukraine	100.0	63.4	26.0	5.1	1.1	4.4
Belarus	100.0	54.2	27.7	3.9	1.4	12.8
Moldova	100.0	55.1	38.0	3.3	1.9	1.7
Lithuania	100.0	78.6	11.0	2.9	4.2	3.3
Latvia	100.0	58.3	17.8	12.6	7.9	3.4
Estonia	100.0	72.6	19.5	6.4	1.2	0.3
Georgia	100.0	47.0	38.6	6.5	4.4	3.5
Azerbaijan	100.0	33.0	55.0	10.1	1.4	0.5
Armenia	100.0	70.2	27.6	1.9	—	0.3
Kazakhstan	100.0	52.4	33.8	4.1	0.7	9.0
Uzbekistan	100.0	71.3	19.2	1.8	0.4	7.3
Kyrgyzstan	100.0	47.5	49.4	1.7	—	1.4
Tajikistan	100.0	69.9	12.7	1.8	—	15.6
Turkmenistan	100.0	49.0	48.5	1.5	—	1.0

Source: *Press-vypusk, #150, 1991.* 1991, p. 7.
— Zero or negligible.

C. NATURAL RESOURCES

RUSSIAN FEDERATION

Russia has some of the world's largest reserves of a wide variety of natural resources. Fuel deposits are, arguably, the most valuable. According to some western estimates, the former U.S.S.R. held approximately 8 billion tons of proven oil reserves (6 percent of the world's reserves) and produced about 20 percent of world output. Ninety percent of this output is attributable to the Russian Federation. Within the latter's territory, West Siberia is presently the largest producing area, accounting for some 70 percent of output. Some of the best known producing areas include: Tyumen' and the Urals-Volga area (with large centers at Samarska Luka, Tuimazy, Yshimbaev, and Perm).

Russia has huge proven natural gas reserves, which at 34 trillion cubic meters (1990) constitute a significant share of the world's total. The fields are located primarily in Siberia (60 percent of production), in the European part of Russia, and around the Sakhalin Islands. Historically, development of the giant west Siberian fields-Tyumen', Uregenoy, Yamburg, and Yamal has been hampered by a lack of investment in infrastructure and equipment. Despite these difficulties, Russian natural gas output was 608 billion cubic meters in 1990 (about one-fifth of world output).

Total proven recoverable coal reserves amount to some 202 billion tons with an additional 100 billion tons of lignite. Major deposits are found in: the Kuznetsk Basin, the Kansk-Achinsk Basin (lignite), the Pechora Basin, the South Yakutian Basin, and the Moscow Basin.

Other fuel resources include: peat (producing areas concentrated around Moscow-Gor'kiy though used from St. Petersburg to Novosibirsk), oil shale (small producing areas near St. Petersburg and scattered in Siberia), wood (throughout northwest Russia and Siberia).

Russia also has great wealth in metals: iron, manganese, chromite, nickel, platinum, and gold. The former U.S.S.R. possesses the largest iron ore resources in the world with 50–60 billion tons having an average iron content of 38 percent (low by world standards). There are an additional 200 billion tons rated as being of potential ore grade. Major deposits are found in the Kursk magnetic anomaly located south of Moscow in the central black earth zone, and on the Kola peninsula.

Finally, there are millions of acres of commercially valuable forest and wood products. Despite these riches, exploiting their full potential has been hampered by physical and administrative problems. Further development will depend on large infusions of capital equipment and skilled manpower.

UKRAINE

The most important industrial activity in Ukraine is heavy metallurgy based on the rich mineral resources of the Donets-Dnieper Region, specifically on the coal from the Donetsk Basin (Donbass) and the iron ore at Krivoy Rog, 300 kilometers to its west. The Donets Ridge contains the Donbass, the oldest center of coal production in the former Soviet Union, with its ample and varied supplies of coal, including quality coking coal. The relative importance of Donbass coal declined over the years as newer Soviet fields were exploited in West Siberia (Kuzbass), Kazakhstan (Karaganda, Ekibastuz) and the Pechora Basin (Vorkuta), but the Donbass still produced, in 1990 (although at increasingly greater costs), a quarter of the total coal mined in the former U.S.S.R., and nearly 40 percent of the coking coal. The location of high-grade iron ore at nearby Krivoy Rog, which was producing half of the iron ore in the U.S.S.R., facilitated the growth of the country's largest metallurgy complex in the large, integrated iron and steel plants of both the Donbass and Krivoy Rog regions. Ukraine's self-contained ferrous metallurgy industry also makes use of a wide variety of other local Donets-Dnieper minerals, such as mercury, salt, limestone, and especially manganese (used to harden the finished steel). The area around the city of Nikopol', lying on the Dnieper between Donetsk and Krivoy Rog, contains one of the world's major deposits of manganese, with an estimated 40 percent of the reserves of the former Soviet Union.

Mineral and energy resources are rather limited in the Southwest Region. There are deposits of magnesium salt and potash in the Carpathian foothills which form the basis of a potash fertilizer facility at Kalush. Important sulfur beds are mined in the region of Rozdol on the drained marshy floodplain of the Dniester. Soda ash and high quality sands provide the raw materials for a glass making and building industry, although timber production is limited. Power produced by thermal electric stations using local sources of peat (in Poles'ye), coal (in the L'viv-Volyn' region), oil (Drogobych), and natural gas (at Dashava), are supplemented by the oil and natural gas imported from Russia. Additional electric energy is provided by hydroelectric power stations on the Dnieper at Kiev and Kanev, and the nuclear reactors at Rovno, Khmel'nitskiy, and Chernobyl'.

The South Region is not strong in mineral or industrial resources. There is low-grade iron ore mined at Kerch', which is beneficiated locally before being shipped across the Sea of Azov to the Azovstal iron and steel works in Zhdanov. Impurities collected during the beneficiation process are used in the manufacture of fertilizers, sulfuric acid, and cement.

BELARUS

Belarus is not well-endowed with non-agricultural raw materials. Historically, peat has been the only major industrial resource found on the territory of Belarus. Until the 1960s, when a local source of oil was developed, two-thirds of the fuel burned by the republic's thermal-electric power stations was peat. It is estimated that Belarus contained about 50 percent of the Soviet Union's reserves and, in 1989, produced 60 percent of the total peat in the U.S.S.R. (The former Soviet Union contained an estimated 60 percent of the world's reserves). In 1963 a major potash deposit was opened up at Soligorsk in the Starobin area of south-central Belarus, and a large mill was built to produce potassium salts and fertilizers. Approximately one-third of all Soviet potassium fertilizers were produced from the Soligorsk reserves, which also include deposits of magnesium and rock salts.

Oil deposits were discovered near the town of Rechitsa in southeastern Belarus in the early 1960s and, although production pales in comparison to the vast West Siberian production, it is of considerable local importance for the oil-poor western regions of the former U.S.S.R. Other industrial resources found in Belarus include the quartz sands of the Gomel' region (the basis for the manufacture of high-quality glass), pottery clays found near Brest, building materials (limestone and cement rock), phosphorites, and low-quality oil shales, iron ore and lignite.

The timber reserves of Belarus are not great; nevertheless, the wood products industries remain strong, producing such products as high-quality sawn (pine) timber suitable for woodworking and veneering, paper and cellulose, and wood-based chemicals.

MOLDOVA

Moldova is lacking in both energy and mineral resources, and relies on agricultural-related endeavors for the bulk of its industrial production. The republic is nearly totally dependent on outside sources for its fuel and most consumer durables. A natural gas pipeline from the Shebelinka fields in Ukraine passes through Moldova on its way to Bulgaria, providing household fuel for the capital city and the raw material for some nitrogenous fertilizer production. A large thermal plant (based on imported Donets coal) at Dnestrovsk (42 kilometers southeast of Tiraspol') provides most of the republic's electricity. Some hydropower installations on the Dniester River, near Dubossary, and on the Reut River supply power to local industrial centers.

Heavy industry is poorly developed, with the exception of the building materials industry, based on indigenous sources of granite,

chalk, and cement rock in the Dniester valley, northwest of Ryb-
nitsa, and some gypsum in the extreme north near Lipkany. Some
fertilizer production also takes place from phosphorite deposits in
the north.

LITHUANIA

Prior to the opening of the first hydropower plant on the Ne-
munas River near Kaunas in 1959, and the arrival of the natural-
gas pipeline in 1961, Lithuania relied for fuels on the republic's
substantial peat resources, supplemented by long-haul coal. The
widespread peat sources are located convenient to most of Lithuania's major cities, although peat now provides less than 5 percent
of the total fuels consumed (down from 25 percent in 1960). In 1968,
oil was discovered east of Klaipeda at the city of Gargzdai, but production, which began in 1990, remains insignificant despite high
initial expectations. Plans to put a third nuclear reactor into operation at Ignalina, the Baltic republics' only major atomic facility,
was cancelled in response to popular opposition following the Chernobyl' disaster. Lithuania today imports three-quarters of its
energy needs.

Lithuania is poor in mineral resources except for certain raw
materials used in the building and construction industry such as
limestone and clay (used for the production of lime and cement),
sands and gravel (for glass and concrete production), dolomite, and
chalk. Lumbering also furnishes raw materials for the buildings industry, as well as for woodworking plants and paper mills.

LATVIA

Latvia is not rich in useful mineral resources, and is highly dependent on outside sources for energy and industrial raw materials. Imported natural gas provides for the majority of Latvia's
energy needs. Latvia also receives electricity transmitted from the
shale-fueled power complex in northeastern Estonia and the gas-fed
electric plant at Elektrenai in Lithuania. Peat is the only local
combustible material of any importance, and prior to the construction of the first gas pipeline (1962), peat-burning thermal power
plants provided the majority of Latvia's heat and electricity. Latvia
also relies more heavily than the other Baltic states on hydroelectricity; the Daugava River's power plants provide over one-third of
the total electricity consumed. The only significant industrial resources found in Latvia are certain widely dispersed raw materials
useful in construction such as: dolomite, limestone, gypsum, clay,
gravel, and sand.

ESTONIA

Estonia is the most industrialized of the three Baltic states and
probably had the highest standard of living in the Soviet Union.
While hardly resource-rich, Estonia is better endowed with mineral
resources than are the other two Baltic republics. Estonia is a net
importer of fuels such as natural gas, oil, and coal, but does have
rich oil shale deposits which accounted for over 83 percent of all
Soviet (1989) production. With more than 50 percent of its energy
demand supplied by shale, Estonia was the only republic of the

former U.S.S.R., and in fact the only political entity in the world, where oil shale is the major source of energy. Most of the oil shale is found in the northeastern part of Estonia, near the cities of Narva and Kokhtla-Jarve. Estonia produces large amounts of peat as well, and in 1989 accounted for 5 percent of the total Soviet production. There is a uranium mining and concentrating facility at Sillimae, 15 miles west of Narva, along with a fertilizer plant which uses local phosphorite deposits.

Estonia also has an historically well-developed but presently declining building materials and furniture industry based on its production of lime, cement, and lumber. Despite the fact that forests cover a large portion its land territory, Estonia still imports much of its timber.

GEORGIA

The interior of Georgia has some relatively minor deposits of lignite (Akhaltsikhe and Tkibuli) and coking coal (Tkvarcheli, in Abkhazia), petroleum (at Kazeti in the Shiraki steppe east of Tbilisi), and a variety of other resources ranging from peat to marble. The manganese deposits at Chiatura are among the largest and richest in the world, and during the 1980s were producing about a third of annual Soviet production (prior to World War I the Chiatura output accounted for half of the world's manganese trade). Georgia also has considerable hydropower resources, especially on the Rioni River and its tributaries, the Inguri, the Kodori, and the Bzyb. These western rivers account for three-quarters of the total hydropower capacity, with the eastern Kura, Aragvi, Alazani, and Khrami accounting for the rest. Dozens of hydroelectric power stations, integrated with the republic's thermal power plants, served as the basis for the region's industrial development. Nevertheless, Georgia's energy requirements have been increasingly met by imported natural gas since the construction of pipelines from the North Caucasus and Azerbaijan in the 1960s.

There is some nonferrous metals production based on the lead, zinc, and copper ore deposits at Kvaisi (in the mountains of South Ossetia) and Madneuli (southwest of Tbilisi). Georgian manganese, along with several nonmetallic minerals ranging from talc (at Tsnelisi, southwest of Tskhinvali in South Ossetia) to barite (at Madneuli and at Iri, in the upper Rioni Valley) to gumbrin (near Kutaisi) supply a variety of local industries.

AZERBAIJAN

Petroleum is the Transcaucasus' single most important resource, and Azerbaijan's industrial economy is based almost entirely on Caspian Sea oil. Specifically, the oil is found where the Kura depression adjoins the eastern end of the folds of the Greater Caucasus. Exploitation began in the 1860s and, by the turn of the century, the Baku field was producing half of the world's petroleum. Although Baku's production has since been dwarfed, first in the 1950s by the Volga-Urals field (the "Second Baku") and then in the 1970s by West Siberian oil and gas, petroleum and petroleum-related industries remain crucial to the local economy. Smaller oil fields occur near the mouth of the Kura River, and there is natural gas at Bakhar, 40 kilometers southwest of Baku. Most of the oil is shipped by tanker from Baku or sent via pipeline to the refinery at Batumi on the Georgian Black Sea coast. In addition to thermal energy, hydropower is utilized at the Mingechaur dam and reservoir complex on the Kura River. This is a multi-purpose scheme for involving hydroelectricity, irrigation, flood protection, and river transportation. Fisheries are also important and the Caspian Sea sturgeon is the source of some of the world's finest caviar.

ARMENIA

Armenia has plentiful amounts of hydroelectric power. Most rivers in Armenia are short and turbulent with numerous rapids and waterfalls ideal for hydroelectric power. Many of the major hydropower stations in Armenia are located on the Razdan (formerly Zanga)- the only river outlet of Lake Sevan (a large body containing over 39 cubic kilometers of water). The Voroton River, in the southeast, has also become an important hydropower source. At the initial stages of industrialization, the creation of a power base utilizing the hydroelectricity from these stations was of decisive importance. By the 1960s, however, thermal power continued to account for most of the energy produced in Armenia, and the republic still remains heavily dependent on energy and fuel imports.

Armenia's mining industry is focused on nonferrous metallurgy, primarily copper (around the city of Kafan in the Zanzegur mountains of the southeastern panhandle), molybdenum (Dastakert, Agarak), and associated lead-zinc ores. Limestone, pumice, and volcanic building materials such as obsidian, are mined primarily in the Armenian west. Armenia also has some gold deposits in the area of the Zod pass, near Lake Sevan.

KAZAKHSTAN

Kazakhstan has a diverse and rich mineral base, containing mineral fuels, iron ore, nonferrous metals, and nonmetallic ores. In 1989, Kazakhstan accounted for 10 percent of the total ferrous ore production in the Soviet Union, nearly 20 percent of its coal, and a healthy share (5–10 percent) of the associated finished steel products. The Karaganda coal basin, which began production the 1930s in conjunction with the development of the Magnitogorsk steel mills in the southern Urals, is one of the country's major suppliers of coking coal. Because the Karaganda coal has a high ash content and most of it (approximately two-thirds of production) is not of coking quality, it must be mixed with richer coal from the Kuzbass in West Siberia before it can be used in blast furnaces. Ekibastuz, to the northeast of Karaganda, began coal production in the 1950s and became the Soviet Union's third largest producer, behind the Kuzbass and the Donbass (Karaganda remains #3 in coking coal production). The brown coal of this basin is of generally poor quality (high ash content) but it is cheaply extracted through open cast (strip) mining. It is both shipped and used locally, in both cases primarily for the production of electricity in thermal power plants.

Iron ore found in Kustanay Oblast (Rudnyy, Lisakovsk, Kachar) supplies foundries in Magnitogorsk and other Urals iron and steel plants, mills in the Kuzbass, and integrated iron and steel producing complexes at Karaganda and Temirtau. More than 5 million tons of steel per year are produced from these ores. Copper ores are found in East Kazakhstan Oblast, on the northern shore of Lake Balkash at Kounradskiy and East Kounradskiy, and at Dzhezkazgan. The latter had the largest reserves of all sites located within the former Soviet Union. East Kazakhstan, in the foothills of the Altay Mountains, has Kazakhstan's greatest hydroelectric power potential and is its principal center of non-ferrous metallurgy. Lead, zinc, copper, gold, silver, cadmium, and other non-ferrous metal ores are found in the region east of the upper Irtysh River. The latter's waters provide the hydropower for smelting and refining these ores. Chimkent in southern Kazakhstan was the Soviet Union's major center for lead smelting, using local ores and concentrates from Central Asia. Nearby, the Kara Tau Mountains between Chimkent and Dzhambul have a large supply of phosphate rocks which provide the raw material for a superphosphate plant at Dzhambul, phosphate furnaces in Chimkent, and fertilizer plants in Central Asia and Togliatti (on the Volga River in Russia).

Deposits of bauxite are found in Turgay at Arkalyk and Krasnooktyabr'skiy. These provide the ores for the alumina and aluminum plants at Pavlodar and Ust'-Kamenogorsk. Salts are produced at the town of Aralsulfat at the northeastern tip of the Aral Sea, and the asbestos complex of Dzhetygara in the Aktyubinsk region of northwestern Kazakhstan is the country's second largest producer (after the town of Asbest in the Urals). The Soviet Union's first chrome-ore concentrator went into operation in 1974 in the Mugodzhar Hills city of Khromtau, whose deposits produced over 80 percent of the Soviet's total chromite. (The Soviet Union was the world's leading producer of chromite, a significant portion of which was exported, including some to the United States).

Kazakhstan contains domestic sources of oil, gas, and hydropower, although most of its energy needs are still met through thermal power production. Oil is found in the Emba (Gur'yev) fields along the northern shore of the Caspian and further south, at Tengiz (considered a major future source of high-sulfur oil), and in the desert area of the Mangyshlak Peninsula. The Mangyshlak deposits are substantial, but output is hindered by technical problems caused by the high paraffin content of the crude oil. Some natural gas is also produced in conjunction with the Mangyshlak oil, but most is fed into the pipeline system connecting Central Asia with European Russia. While water and hydropower are in short supply, a number of important hydroelectric projects have been constructed. The Bukhtarma and Ust'-Kamenogorsk dams on the upper Irtysh River support the non-ferrous metallurgy exploitation and refining of East Kazakhstan, while the Kapchagay Dam on the Ili River north of Alma Ata and the Chardara Dam on the Syr Dar'ya River in the south are also major producers of electricity for a variety of regional industrial enterprises.

Fisheries are an important branch of the Kazakh economy, and are concentrated on the northeast coast of the Caspian Sea. The shallowness and consequent high water temperature of the northern portion of the Caspian, coupled with the presence of a large amount of organic materials discharged by the Volga and other rivers, have made this one of the richest fishing areas of the former U.S.S.R. Most common fish types include sturgeon, salmon, herring, and carp.

UZBEKISTAN

In terms of energy resources, Uzbekistan is sufficiently endowed with coal, natural gas, oil, and hydroelectric potential to meet its internal demands. Uzbekistan also has commercially valuable deposits of minerals and metals. Akhangaran is known primarily for its cement and alumina plants. The city of Almalyk concentrates, smelts, and refines local ore deposits of copper, zinc, lead, tungsten and molybdenum. Gold is found at Muruntau in the Kyzylkum Desert and in the Chadak area of the Fergana Valley, on the southern slopes of the Kurama Mountains; this latter region (along with the parallel slopes of the Chatkal range to the north), is also the site of uranium mining and concentrating. Fluorspar, the principal fluorine-bearing mineral, is found at Toytepa, halfway between Almalyk and Tashkent. Finally, Uzbek marble (notably Gazgan marble from the Nuratau range in northern Samarkand Oblast) is of high quality and was used in the facades of the Moscow subway system.

KYRGYZSTAN

Until the development of the Angren field in Uzbekistan in the late 1950s, Kyrgyzstan was the major source in Central Asia for subbituminous (brown) coal, needed for supplying the steam power stations in the Fergana Valley. Most of Kyrgyzstan's coal mines were situated on the southern fringe of the Fergana Valley until the later discovery of important deposits of bituminous coal on the northeast fringe and at Dzhergalan east of the Issyk-Kul' near the Chinese border. Additional scattered brown coal reserves are found in places such as Min-Kush, west of Lake Song-Kyel, and at Kadzhiksay at the southern shore of Issyk Kul'.

Despite Kyrgyzstan's large coal reserves, half of the total electricity used in the republic comes from hydropower. In the postwar period, hydropower production, based on a series of dams constructed along the Chu irrigation canal in the Chu Valley, served manufacturing industry around Bishkek. Since then, major hydroelectric projects have been developed on the Kokomeren and Susamyr headwaters of the Naryn River, at Toktogul' and Uchkurgan on the Naryn River itself, at Kayrakkum on the Syr Dar'ya (supports Tashkent), and on the Atbashi River 40 kilometers southwest of Naryn city in southeastern Kyrgyzstan.

Oil and natural gas production is of limited importance. What little there is comes mostly from the Mayli-Su fields along the eastern margins of the Fergana Valley. A gas pipeline reaches from Mayli-Su south to Osh; another pipeline brings gas from the Bukhara fields to Bishkek, where it is used to generate electricity and to serve as an industrial raw material.

Kyrgyzstan was an early center for the mining of nonferrous metals, and was the leading producer in the Soviet Union of antimony and mercury ores, which are often found in conjunction with lead-zinc and fluorspar, respectively. Principal deposits are found along the northern foothills of the Turkestan-Alay mountain range, which extends along the southern margins of the Fergana Valley, and on the southern slopes of the Chatkal Range (Terek-Say, Sumsar) at the Valley's northern fringe. Kyrgyzstan was also one of the Soviet Union's leading producers of uranium. Most uranium production is now concentrated at the town of Min-Kush in the Tyan'-Shan Mountains. From this locale, it is trucked for processing to a mill at Kosh-Tegirmen in the Chu Valley, west of Bishkek. The mountains of Kyrgyzstan also contain deposits of tungsten, molybdenum, indium, sulphur, and arsenic. A rich deposit of tin, a mineral commodity which is in scarce supply in the region, is being developed at Sary-Dzhaz in Issyk-Kul' Oblast.

TAJIKISTAN

Tajikistan was noted primarily for its handicraft industries, semi-nomadic herding, and limited cotton production until Soviet rule brought with it industrial enterprises, mining, and irrigated agriculture. Most Tajiks today remain farmers or herders, but abundant hydroelectric power and minerals extracted from the mountains brought significant changes to the structure of the Tajik economy. Over 90 percent of electricity produced in Tajikistan is hydropower, provided by a series of dams and reservoirs. The major hydropower complexes are located on the Vakhsh ("mad" in Tajik) River. Its two largest are at Nurek, which was the highest dam in the former Soviet Union, and the Golovnaya Dam at Rogun, just 85 kilometers northeast of Nurek. The Kayrakkum Dam on the Syr Dar'ya River forms a reservoir referred to as the Tajik Sea, with its "Druzhba Narodov" ("Friendship of Nations") hydropower station primarily serving the needs of the Fergana Valley in neighboring Uzbekistan.

The availability of hydroelectric power attracted industries that were oriented toward cheap energy. One of the principal industrial consumers of Vakhsh River hydropower is an electrochemical complex at Yavan which produces sodium chloride, magnesium chloride, chlorine, etc. based on local deposits of salt, dolomite, and limestone. The minerals industry northeast of Leninabad is dependent on the Kayrakkum hydropower station for its energy.

Although of negligible value compared to hydropower, the major thermal fuel mineral in Tajikistan remains brown coal. There are also some deposits of petroleum, in the south at Kichek-Bel' in the Vakhsh Valley near the Afghan border and at Ravat, in north central Tajikistan. Natural gas is extracted from the fields of Kyzyl-Tumshuk on the lower Vakhsh, and from several small gas fields (Komsomol, Shaambary, Andygen) near Dushanbe.

Tajikistan is fairly rich in both metallic and nonmetallic mineral resources, including non-ferrous metal concentrates and polymetallic and rare metal ores. There are deposits of lead-zinc ores, molybdenum, copper, arsenic and bismuth, tin, tungsten, vanadium, and some radioactive ores (uranium at Taboshar) on the southern slopes of the Kurama Range, northeast of Leninabad. Nonmetals mined throughout the republic include common salt, carbonates, fluorite, arsenic, quartz, asbestos, precious and semiprecious stones. The Zeravshan and Gissar Ranges contain a number of valued minerals such as antimony and mercury. Gold is mined southeast of Garm and in the Pamirs.

TURKMENISTAN

Among Turkmenistan's mineral resources, its natural gas deposits (third largest in the world) are the most important. Most of the gas is found in the heart of the country, at the Shatlyk field west of the city of Mary. Petroleum is mined near the area of Nebit-Dag and on the Cheleken peninsula (an island which became attached to the mainland due to the lowering of the level of the Caspian Sea), and a new oil field has also been discovered at Yolotan, south of the city of Mary. Turkmenistan is largely self-sufficient in energy resources.

Turkmenistan also possesses significant deposits of sulfur (the third largest in the world) in the Kara-Kum Desert. Other mineral deposits include potassium, sodium chloride, and an extensive mirabilite (sodium sulfate) site on the Kara-Bogaz-Gol. Ozecerite, iodine, and bromine are found on the Cheleken peninsula; salt is in the Balkhan range, north of Nebit-Dag; and polymetallic ores are spread throughout various regions of the republic.

D. LABOR FORCE AND EMPLOYMENT

More than three-fifths of the former Soviet labor force was concentrated in four sectors: industry, construction, education, and agriculture (Table 38). At the all-union level, industry accounted for the largest share of employment. In 1990, 31.2 percent of the all-union labor force was employed by industry, followed by 10.8 percent in construction, 9.9 percent in education, and 9.7 percent in agriculture.

While these sectors as a whole were almost always the key employers in each of the former republics, their individual shares and rank orders varied in several instances. In three largely agrarian republics (Azerbaijan, Turkmenistan, and Uzbekistan), industry accounted for a smaller share of the labor force than agriculture. By way of contrast in Russia, agriculture ranked sixth in employment, behind industry, construction, transport and communications, education, and trade and distribution.

TABLE 38. Labor Force by Sector, 1990 (except where noted).

(Total in thousands, breakdown in percent)

	U.S.S.R.	Russian Fed.	Ukraine	Belarus	Mol- dova	Lithua- nia	Latvia	1989 Estonia	Georgia	Azerbai- jan	1989 Arme- nia	Kazakh- stan	Uzbekis- tan	Kyrgyz- stan	1989 Tajikis- tan	1989 Turk- menistan
Total (thousands)	112,936	63,878	19,470	4,851	1,415	1,853	1,094	811	2,763	2,800	1,363	6,434	6,227	1,253	1,159	854
Percent shares:																
Industry [a]	31.2	32.9	35.3	42.2	27.7	30.0	31.5	32.0	31.0	26.0	39.0	21.1	16.1	22.7	18.6	20.0
Agriculture [b]	9.7	8.3	7.1	19.3	14.8	18.5	8.0	12.0	25.0	32.6	19.0	18.6	326	17.9	17.9	41.1
Forestry	0.3	0.4	NA	NA	0.3	0.4	0.6	0.9	NA	NA	NA	0.2	0.1	0.2	NA	NA
Construction	10.8	11.0	9.7	NA	8.2	11.3	9.0	9.9	NA	NA	NA	11.4	8.9	10.2	12.3	NA
Transport and communication	9.0	9.1	8.9	7.1	7.7	5.7	9.2	8.4	7.0	7.2	7.0	10.7	6.3	7.4	8.0	7.1
Trade and distribution	8.7	8.7	9.0	7.4	9.7	8.2	10.8	9.0	7.0	6.2	6.0	8.2	6.9	8.5	8.2	6.3
Housing	4.4	4.6	4.5	NA	3.2	NA	5.3	4.5	NA	NA	NA	4.0	2.6	3.0	3.5	NA
Health, physical culture, and social security [c]	6.7	6.2	7.4	17.3	7.8	5.9	7.0	6.1	20.0	20.4	21.0	6.8	7.3	7.7	8.2	18.6
Education	9.9	9.0	9.4	NA	12.4	NA	9.3	12.0	NA	NA	NA	11.5	13.6	14.2	15.1	NA
Credit and insurance	0.6	0.6	0.7	NA	0.7	0.6	0.6	0.5	NA	NA	NA	0.6	0.4	0.6	0.5	NA
Management [d]	1.4	1.4	1.5	2.2	1.7	1.5	1.6	2.1	2.0	2.2	2.0	1.6	1.3	1.6	1.7	2.5
Other branches	7.2	7.9	6.6	4.5	5.7	17.9	7.0	2.6	8.0	5.4	6.0	5.4	4.1	6.0	5.9	4.4

Sources: *Narodnoye Khozyaystvo USSR, 1990. 1991*, pp. 100, 101; *Narodnoye Khozyaystvo RSFSR 1990. 1991*, p. 110; *Narodne gospodarstvo Ukrainskoi RSR u 1990 rotsi, 1991. 1992*, p. 53; *Narodnoye Khozyaystvo Byelorusskoy SSR 1990. 1991*, pp. 37–38; *Narodnoye Khozyaystvo Uzbekskoy SSR 1990. 1991*, pp. 23–25; *Statisticheskiy Yezhegodnik Kazakhstana. 1991*, pp. 55–58; *Republic of Georgia: A Short Economic and Statistical Survey. 1992*, p. 5; *Azerbaijan Republic: A Short Economic and Statistical Survey. 1992*, pp. 3–4; *Statisticheskiy Yezhegodnik Litvy 1991. 1992*, pp. 28–29; *Respublika Moldova v Tsifrakh. 1991*, pp. 73–74; *Narodnoye Khozyaystvo Latvia 1990. 1991*, pp. 66, 68; *Statistika Yezhegodnik Kyrgyzstana 1990. 1991*, pp. 98–100; *Narodnoye Khozyaystvo Tajikistan 1989. 1990*, pp. 23–24; *Narodnoye Khozyaystvo Armyanskoy SSR 1988. 1989*, p. 16; *Narodnoye Khozyaystvo Turkmenistan 1989. 1990*, pp. 25–26; *Statisticheskiy Yezhegodnik Estonii 1990. 1991*, pp. 236–237.

NA Data not available.

[a] Data for Belarus, Georgia, Azerbaijan, Armenia, and Turkmenistan include construction.

[b] Data exclude employment on collective farms and private subsidiary enterprises. Employment on collective farms (11.9 million in 1990—*Narodnoye Khozyaystvo USSR, 1990. 1991*, p. 451) exceeds employment on state farms (10.9 million). See "Estimates and projections of the Labor Force and Civilian Employment in the USSR: 1950 to 2000," CIR Staff Paper No. 45, 1988, for further detail. Data for Ukraine, Belarus, Georgia, Azerbaijan, and Armenia include forestry.

[c] Data for Belarus, Georgia, Azerbaijan, and Turkmenistan include education, science, and the arts.

[d] Data for Belarus, Georgia, Azerbaijan, and Turkmenistan include credit and insurance.

E. SECTORAL ISSUES

1. INDUSTRY

Given their preference for rapid economic growth and military parity with the West, the leaders of the Soviet Union chose industry to spearhead the drive for economic development. The program was instituted nationwide, but its effects were felt differentially across republics both in terms of output and income. The most industrialized region of the former union, on a per-capita basis (Table 39), the Baltic republics, had the highest living standards. Conversely, the former republics with the lowest living standards (primarily Central Asia) were also the least industrialized. Russia, which comprised the industrial core of the former Soviet Union, tended to be somewhat more industrialized than the union as a whole and produced the majority of many types of industrial output (Tables 41a–o and Figures 4 and 5).

TABLE 39. Per Capita Industrial
Output, 1986.

Geographical Unit	Index (U.S.S.R. = 100)
U.S.S.R.	100.0
Russian Federation	114.9
Ukraine	103.0
Belarus	125.5
Moldova	84.3
Lithuania	127.8
Latvia	139.9
Estonia	137.7
Georgia	73.0
Azerbaijan	61.8
Armenia	82.9
Kazakhstan	58.0
Uzbekistan	46.8
Kyrgyzstan	57.1
Tajikistan	42.5
Turkmenistan	43.1

Source: Diamond and Kisunko, *Food Consumption in Recent Years in the Former Republics of the USSR.* Center for International Research, U.S. Bureau of the Census, 1992, p. 23.

According to our most recent estimates, industrial output grew modestly during the early 1980s (1.9 percent annually during 1980–1985), peaked in 1987 (3 percent), and then declined in each of the three subsequent years (Table 40). By 1990, industrial output for all former republics for which data are available (all except Moldova) was in decline. The most severe annual decline occurred in Lithuania, where industrial production fell 4.8 percent.

Heavy industry dominated the manufacturing sectors of the economy. Over 70 percent of industrial output, in value added terms, was produced by the following sectors: machinery (33.9 per-

TABLE 40. Estimation of Industrial Growth Rates by
Republic, 1981–90.

(Percent)

Geographical Unit	1981–1985 (average annual)	1986	1987	1988	1989	1990
U.S.S.R.	1.9	2.4	3.0	2.7	-0.6	-2.8
Russian Federation	1.6	2.6	2.6	2.5	-0.7	-2.9
Ukraine	1.5	2.0	2.5	3.1	-0.4	-2.8
Belarus	3.5	5.0	5.4	5.4	2.4	-0.5
Moldova	4.3	4.9	5.6	2.3	2.8	1.0
Lithuania	2.8	2.5	7.1	4.8	2.8	-4.8
Latvia	1.7	1.2	4.2	1.3	0.4	-2.2
Estonia	1.0	1.3	2.6	1.2	-1.2	-2.9
Georgia	2.7	0.8	1.8	1.8	NA	NA
Azerbaijan	2.9	-0.1	2.6	-0.2	NA	NA
Armenia	4.7	3.7	4.3	-3.1	NA	NA
Kazakhstan	2.5	3.7	3.4	2.7	0.3	-3.5
Uzbekistan	3.6	4.4	3.0	2.6	1.0	NA
Kyrgyzstan	2.2	3.5	-0.2	11.0	1.3	-3.6
Tajikistan	3.1	1.6	5.6	6.9	-2.4	NA
Turkmenistan	2.3	2.4	4.0	0.9	1.7	NA

Source: Diamond and Kisunko, *Slavic and Eurasian Republics: Food Consumption in Recent Years in the Former Republics of the USSR.* U.S. Bureau of the Census: 1992, pp. 37–44.
NA—Data not available.

cent), fuels (12.2 percent), metallurgy products (9 percent), power (8.1 percent), and chemicals (7.8 percent) (Figure 6).

RUSSIAN FEDERATION

The majority of manufactured goods in the former Soviet Union are produced in Russia. Figure 4 displays this dominance with a small, but representative, sample of the output shares of important industrial and consumer products. Russia has substantial capacity to produce machinery, steel, chemicals and petrochemicals, construction materials, light industrial products, and processed foods. The largest share of enterprises are located in the Central economic region, producing 23 percent of Russian industrial output. Smaller shares of industrial output are produced in the Urals (16 percent), and the Volga region (11 percent).

UKRAINE

Ukraine is also an important producer of consumer products, as well as the equipment and armaments for national defense. The former republic is administratively divided into three industrial regions: the Donets-Dnieper, the Southwest, and the South. Heavy industries of the Donets-Dnieper Region include: mining equipment, machine tools and instruments, agricultural machinery, diesel locomotives, electric motors, transformers and large turbo-alternators. Light industries are also well-developed, particularly those based on local agricultural resources in the northern oblasts. In the Southwest region, the chemical industry produces fertilizers, toxic sprays, synthetic fibers, plastics, and synthetic rubber. The region also features industries specializing in electronics and radio engineering, cameras, medical equipment, agricultural machinery, and machine tools. Among processed food industries, sugar beet refining is most important. In the South Region, large-scale engineering concerns produce farm equipment, lathes, and road-building equipment. The light and processed food industries are dominated by fruit and vegetable canneries, vegetable oil pressing, distilleries and wineries, along with some textile production.

BELARUS

The industrial sector in Belarus is dominated by industries that were developed after the destruction of World War II. Machine-building factories produce heavy-duty trucks, tractors, electrical machinery, agricultural machinery, peat cutting machinery, instruments, lathes, and machine tools. Another increasingly important industry in Belarus is chemicals. It is linked with the oil refineries at Mozyr and Polotsk and with the potash deposits at Soligorsk. Synthetic fiber plants in Mogilev and Grodno produced nearly 30 percent of the total Soviet output of chemical fibers and knits (polyesters and polyamide fibers). Belarus textile mills produce linen, woolen, cotton, and silk fabrics. Food processing is widespread, and includes milk-processing, butter and margarine manufacturing, and fruit and vegetable canning.

MOLDOVA

Moldova is lacking in both energy and mineral resources, and relies on agricultural-related endeavors for the bulk of its industrial production. Machine-building industries in some of the larger cities produce tractors for orchards and vineyards, refrigerators, and personal computers. Most of Moldova's light industry (textiles and apparel) and processed food industry is related to the processing of agricultural commodities. The latter includes fruit and vegetable canning, meat packing, wine making, flour milling, vegetable-oil extraction, tobacco processing, and sugar refining.

LITHUANIA

Post-war industrialization led to the development of a manufacturing industry based on machine building, consumer durables, minicomputers, and electric motors. Vil'nyus produces agricultural equipment, electric motors, and radio equipment. The former capital of Kaunas is the center of the transport industry, with rail shops, metal works, as well as textile, furniture, and chemical industries. Klaipeda is home to the pulp and paper industries and is a producer of superphosphate fertilizers and ocean-going vessels (and is the center of the fishing industry). Canning facilities, meat-packing plants, and tanneries are widespread, while sugar and flour milling are located at Marijampole and Panevezys.

LATVIA

Latvia's rapid industrialization following incorporation into the Soviet Union transformed the economy from one based on light industries, processed food industries, and timber and paper industries to an economy based more on machinery, electrical engineering, and chemical and petrochemical production. Latvia's industrial economy produces electric and diesel trains and minibuses, plastics, chemical reagents, pharmaceuticals, paper and lumber, furniture, relatively high quality electronic and consumer goods such as stereo equipment and radio sets (17.1 percent of all those produced in the U.S.S.R. in 1990), and textile products.

ESTONIA

Estonia is the most industrialized of the three Baltic states. Plastic and petrochemical processing industries, which have developed along the route of the natural gas pipeline emanating from Russia, are key components of Estonia's industrial economy. Kokhtla-Jarve is the center of Estonia's oil and gas distillation and nitrogenous fertilizer production. Estonia also has an historically well-developed but presently declining building materials and furniture industry based on its production of lime, cement, and lumber. The machine building sector is characterized primarily by the production of electronic and engineering equipment. The textile industry (predominantly cotton) employs over half of Estonia's light industry labor force and produced some of the highest quality knit and woven fabrics in the Soviet Union.

GEORGIA

Georgia's heavy industry sector is small and dependent on other regions for much of its raw materials. There is a modest iron and steel industry based largely on imported sources of coking coal and iron ore. Nonferrous metals production is limited to the lead, zinc, and copper ore deposits at Kvaisi (in the mountains of South Ossetia) and Madneuli (southwest of Tbilisi). The machine-building industry, centered in the largest cities (Tbilisi and Kutaisi), produces a diverse range of products, from electric railway locomotives, heavy vehicles, and earth-moving equipment to lathes and precision instruments. The chemical industry provides mineral fertilizers, synthetic materials and fibers, and pharmaceutical products. Light industry produces cotton, wool, and silk fabrics, as well as clothing. The processed food industry produces dairy products, tea, wine, brandy, champagne, tobacco, and canned foods.

AZERBAIJAN

Azerbaijan's industrial sector is based on its Caspian Sea oil resources. However, over the years, more diversified, albeit related, pursuits have supplemented oil extraction. These include petrochemicals production, oil refining, and the manufacture of specialized equipment such as turbo-drills, pipes, compressors, and storage tanks. Sumgait is the center of ferrous metallurgy, in addition to being a leader in the production of mineral fertilizers, herbicides, synthetic rubber, and plastics. Light industries (such as textile manufacturing and footwear) and food processing are distributed throughout most of the cities in Azerbaijan.

ARMENIA

Armenia has a variety of industries, including chemicals, nonferrous metals, mechanical engineering, electrical power machines, precision instruments, electronics, textiles, and clothing. Machinery and light industries have been developed primarily in the three largest cities, Yerevan, Kumayri (formerly Leninakan), and Kirovakan (the latter contains a major sugar refinery). Chemical products, such as synthetic rubber and plastics, are produced at Yerevan, Kirovakan, and Alaverdi. Light industry specializes in the production of woolen, silk, and cotton fabrics; knitted goods and clothes; carpets; and footwear. The processed food industry prepares farm products primarily for domestic consumption, and produces high-quality wines and cognacs, and canned fruits and vegetables for export.

KAZAKHSTAN

Industrial production in Kazakhstan is dominated by heavy metallurgy and petrochemical production based on its rich domestic mineral resources. Nevertheless, there is a good deal of associated manufacturing at these heavy industrial complexes, and light industry can be found in most large cities. The countryside surrounding Alma-Ata supports the city's fruit-preserving, meat packing, leather-making, and wine and tobacco factories. Engineering, machine building and textiles are also of local importance. The Karaganda region produces construction and mining machinery, chemicals, cement, and foodstuffs. The Aktyubinsk and East Kazakhstan oblasts are the major regions for nonferrous metallurgy. Petrochemicals, fertilizers, and pharmaceutical production takes place in the cities of Chimkent, Dzhambul, Aktyubinsk, and Pavlodar. Textile (cotton) and food industries (meat packing, sugar, and flour milling) are located throughout Kazakhstan, primarily in the cities of Chimkent, Semipalatinsk, Petropavlovsk, Ural'sk, Kustanay, Kokchetav, and Taldy-Kurgan. Gur'yev and Pavlodar are the major centers of oil refining. Tselinograd manufactures agricultural and transport equipment and processes grain, and Kzyl-Orda is important for its large pulp and cardboard mill, which utilizes reeds growing in the mouth of the nearby Syr-Dar'ya River.

UZBEKISTAN

In Uzbekistan, heavy industrial development also began in earnest after World War II. Uzbekistan is the primary producer of machinery and heavy equipment in Central Asia, and has been the main Soviet producer of machinery for cotton cultivation, harvesting, and processing. Uzbekistan's heavy industry also produces machines for irrigation projects, road construction, and the textile industry. The chemical industry is closely associated with the production of nitrogenous and phosphate fertilizers needed for cotton production. Light industry in Uzbekistan is dominated by the processing of agricultural raw materials, cotton fabric, and silk. Among the processed food industries, there are wineries and tobacco factories, as well as fish processing.

KYRGYZSTAN

The major emphases in Kyrgyzstan's industry have been on manufacturing as well as light and food industries that utilize local agricultural raw materials. Heavy industry is primarily limited to the production of agricultural machinery, particularly that designed for the former republic's rugged terrain. The food industry includes several large sugar processing factories as well as meat and vegetable canneries (Bishkek, Dzhalal-Abad, Osh). Emphasis also is given to the primary processing of cotton and other fiber crops. In light industry, woolens, silk fabric, and leather goods are produced.

TAJIKISTAN

Abundant hydroelectric power and minerals extracted from the mountains during the Soviet era boosted industrialization in highly agricultural Tajikistan. The availability of hydroelectric power (producing over 90 percent of Tajikistan's electricity) attracted aluminum, chemicals, and other industries that are oriented toward cheap energy (such as the electrochemical complex at Yavan which produces sodium chloride, magnesium chloride, chlorine, and other chemicals, using local deposits of salt, dolomite, and limestone).

The manufacturing, engineering, and metalworking industries produce significant amounts of output for the domestic economy. Loom production is geared toward local textile manufacturing; power transformers and cables are manufactured for electricity transmission; and various types of machinery are produced for agricultural purposes. The machinery plant at Dushanbe also manufactures turbines and other equipment for hydroelectric installations.

The light and processed food industries are important components of Tajikistan's economy. The former republic has more than a dozen cotton ginning plants and mills. Light industry includes cotton processing, as well as the manufacture of knitted goods and footwear, sewing, and tanning. The processed food industry engages in fruit canning, wine making, tobacco processing, and the production of cottonseed-oil.

TURKMENISTAN

Turkmenistan is only minimally industrialized, with a smaller percentage of the total labor force being employed in industry than in any former Soviet republic. Among the manufacturing industries, the textile branch is the leading producer. Cotton ginning and milling, silk spinning (located at Chardzhou and Ashkhabad), wool washing (at Mary), and carpet weaving are important industries. There are chemical plants located at Chardzhou and Ashgabat, and a small automotive and agricultural machine industry in Ashkhabad. The food processing industry is small but expanding, and consists primarily of flour milling, cottonseed-oil extraction, meat packing, fruit canning and drying, and fish processing.

TABLE 41a. Russia: Production and Extraction of Selected Industrial Products and Resources, 1985–90.*

Product	1985	1986	1987	1988	1989	1990	1990 % of U.S.S.R.
FUEL-ENERGY							
Electric power (billion kWh)	962	1,002	1,047	1,066	1,077	1,082	63
Oil (including gas condensate) (mil tons)	542	561	569	569	552	516	90
Natural gas (billion tons)	462	503	544	590	616	641	79
Coal (mil tons)	395	408	415	425	410	395	56
Peat (mil tons)	8	11	4	10	8	5	46
Oil shale (mil tons)	6	5	5	5	5	5	NA
METALLURGY							
Cast iron (mil tons)	57	60	61	62	62	59	54
Steel (mil tons)	89	92	93	94	93	90	34
Finished rolled metal products (mil tons)	63	64	66	66	66	64	57
Steel pipes (mil tons)	12	12	12	13	13	12	61
Iron ore (mil tons)	104	106	108	109	107	107	97
MACHINERY							
Metal-cutting lathes (mil rubles) **	11,658	1,831	1,755	1,952	2,121	1,994	62
Forge-press machines (mil rubles)	435	435	391	405	433	454	65
Computers (billion rubles)	2	2	2	3	3	4	NA
Medical equipment (mil rubles)	623	680	713	777	840	1,097	70
Oil equipment (mil rubles)	194	206	203	213	188	192	81
Chemical equipment (mil rubles)	616	627	598	658	667	675	63
Agricultural machinery (mil rubles)	2,125	2,272	2,381	2,345	2,111	2,143	48
Radios (1000 units)	15,747	5,601	5,120	4,984	5,561	5,760	63
Televisions (1000 units)	4,773	4,579	4,152	4,370	4,465	4,717	45
Refrigerators & freezers (1000 units)	3,453	3,461	3,432	3,492	3,594	3,774	58
Electric Vacuum cleaners (1000 units)	3,131	3,301	3,427	3,725	3,997	4,470	77
Washing machines (1000 units)	3,271	3,503	3,823	4,110	4,501	5,419	69
CHEMICAL AND FORESTRY							
Mineral fertilizers (mil tons)	17,304	17,712	18,454	19,071	17,506	15,979	50
Pesticides (1000 tons)	215	213	208	201	162	111	54
Sulfuric acid (mil tons)	12	13	13	13	12	13	48
Soda ash (w/o potash) (mil tons)	3,755	3,793	3,726	3,649	3,547	3,240	74
Caustic soda (mil tons)	2,171	2,332	2,359	2,413	2,324	2,258	76
Chemical fibers and yarn (1000 tons)	725	747	739	734	731	673	46
Synthetic resins & plastics (mil tons)	3,013	3,208	3,257	3,382	3,391	3,258	59
Medicinal products (mil rubles)	1,905	2,056	2,177	2,291	2,422	2,522	64
Lumber (mil cubic m)	257	272	278	280	270	242	92
Sawn lumber (mil cubic m)	80	83	83	85	82	75	82
Paper (1000 tons)	5,030	5,205	5,243	5,334	5,344	5,240	85
Cardboard (1000 tons)	2,877	3,025	3,148	3,249	3,140	3,085	73
CONSTRUCTION MATERIALS							
Cement (mil tons)	79	81	83	84	85	83	60
Construction bricks (billion units)	22	23	23	24	24	25	53
Soft roofing materials (mil sq. m)	1,068	1,127	1,113	1,139	1,114	1,075	58
Asbesto-cement shingles (mil std. units)	4,637	4,838	4,938	5,028	5,033	4,966	55
Window glass (mil sq. m)	146	156	153	155	150	130	61
LIGHT INDUSTRY							
Cotton fabric (mil sq. m)	5,514	5,597	5,700	5,779	5,821	5,624	72
Wool fabric (mil sq. m)	433	438	451	461	471	466	66
Linen and hemp-jute fabric (mil sq. m)	611	631	641	643	639	603	67
Silk fabric (mil sq. m)	970	994	1,044	1,078	1,084	1,051	51
Stocking-hosiery goods (mil pairs)	760	782	814	833	848	872	40
Knitted goods (mil units)	689	701	714	733	759	769	40
Shoes (mil pairs)	361	366	366	369	378	385	46
PROCESSED FOODS							
Granulated sugar (1000 tons)	3,642	3,981	3,997	3,945	4,216	3,590	30
Meat (industrial production) (1000 tons)	5,334	5,755	6,106	6,445	6,621	6,642	51
Animal fats (1000 tons)	721	764	786	809	820	833	48
Vegetable oil (1000 tons)	775	1,012	959	1,080	1,127	1,159	35
Canned goods (all types) (mil cans)	7,058	7,418	7,732	7,913	8,214	8,207	40
Confectionery goods (1000 tons)	2,268	2,368	2,475	2,594	2,737	2,869	55

Source: *Narodnoye Khozyaystvo RSFSR v 1990 g.* 1991, pp. 143, 145–147, 373, 375–379, 380, 385, 500–1, 506, 508, 510. *Narodnoye Khozyaystvo SSSR v 1990 g.* 1991, pp. 395, 397–399, 401, 403–405, 408, 410–417, 420–423, 517–522.
Abbreviations: kWh—kilowatt hour; m—meters; mil—million; NA—not available; sq.—square; std.—standard.
* Reported data rounded to nearest whole number.
** Including metal-cutting lathes for agricultural repair shops.

TABLE 41b. Ukraine: Production and Extraction of Selected Industrial Products and Resources, 1985-90.*

Product	1985	1986	1987	1988	1989	1990	1990 % of U.S.S.R.
FUEL-ENERGY							
Electric power (billion kWh)	272	273	282	297	295	298	17
Oil (including gas condensate) (mil tons)	6	6	6	5	5	5	1
Natural gas (billion cubic m)	43	40	36	32	31	28	3
Associated gas (billion cubic m)	1	1	1	1	1	1	NA
Coal (mil tons)	189	193	192	192	180	165	23
METALLURGY							
Marketable iron ore (mil tons)	120	120	118	116	110	105	44
Cast iron (mil tons)	47	49	47	47	47	45	41
Steel (1000 tons)	54,971	56,646	56,287	56,461	54,807	52,622	34
Rolled ferrous metals (mil tons)	45	47	47	48	47	45	35
Finished rolled ferrous metals (mil tons)	38	39	39	40	40	39	34
Steel pipes (mil tons)	7	7	7	7	7	7	33
MACHINERY							
Precision instruments (billion rubles)	1,156	1,237	1,268	1,387	1,446	1,466	25
Metal-cutting tools (1000 units)	31	28	28	29	32	37	24
Stamping & pressing equipment (units)	10	10	10	10	11	11	26
Coal-cleaning equipment (units)	1,027	967	796	867	877	847	84
Tractors (1000 units)	136	140	131	131	116	106	21
Tractor plows (1000 units)	103	107	99	98	99	89	49
Radios (1000 units)	291	299	395	432	574	777	8
Televisions (1000 units)	3,067	3,178	3,110	3,434	3,572	3,774	36
Refrigerators & freezers (1000 units)	743	752	745	843	882	903	14
Electric vacuum cleaners (1000 units)	789	815	864	904	905	1,073	19
Washing machines (1000 units)	372	390	457	533	651	788	10
CHEMICAL AND FORESTRY							
Mineral fertilizers (mil tons)	5	6	6	6	5	5	15
Sulfuric acid (1000 tons)	4,125	4,125	4,221	4,339	4,267	5,011	18
Calcinated soda (1000 tons)	1,161	1,240	1,325	1,340	1,263	1,120	26
Caustic soda (1000 tons)	500	492	489	494	472	445	15
Chemical fibers & yarn (1000 tons)	165	177	188	192	191	179	12
Synthetic resins & plastics (1000 tons)	722	781	797	829	840	827	15
Paper (1000 tons)	299	309	320	343	353	369	6
Cardboard (1000 tons)	520	554	549	567	543	543	13
CONSTRUCTION MATERIALS							
Cement (1000 tons)	22,444	23,069	23,193	23,533	23,416	22,729	17
Soft roofing materials (mil sq. m)	303	298	300	302	300	282	15
Construction bricks (mil units)	8,952	9,271	9,451	10,006	10,425	10,481	23
Asbesto-cement shingles (mil std. bricks)	1,361	1,387	1,401	1,431	1,467	1,463	16
Reinforced concrete assemblies (1000 sq. m)	21,513	22,075	22,867	23,744	23,931	23,284	16
LIGHT INDUSTRY							
Cotton fabric (mil sq. m)	534	539	557	558	567	565	7
Wool fabric (mil sq. m)	67	66	68	71	74	72	10
Linen fabric (mil sq. m)	96	100	100	103	105	98	11
Silk fabric (mil sq. m)	283	289	294	300	300	283	14
Stocking-hosiery goods (mil pairs)	388	398	405	415	428	443	21
Knitted goods (mil units)	320	328	335	347	355	351	18
Shoes (mil pairs)	186	187	187	191	194	196	23
PROCESSED FOODS							
Granulated sugar (1000 tons)	6,247	6,660	7,579	6,131	7,014	6,786	54
Meat (1000 tons)	2,357	2,519	2,615	2,731	2,793	2,762	21
Animal fats (1000 tons)	390	407	421	440	441	441	25
Vegetable oil (1000 tons)	846	876	971	1,047	1,078	1,070	33
Canned foods (mil cans)	3,978	4,738	4,833	4,808	4,891	4,832	24
Confectionery goods (1000 tons)	924	951	992	1,033	1,075	1,111	21

Source: *Ukrayins'ka RSR u tsifrakh u 1990 r.*, 1991, pp. 147–150; *Narodne hospodarstvo Ukrayins'koyi RSR u 1990 r.*, 1991, pp. 294, 296–297, 299, 300, 302–308, 313–318; *Narodnoye khozyaystvo SSSR v 1990 g.*, 1991, pp. 395–399, 401, 403–405, 408, 410–417, 420–423, 517–522.
Abbreviations: kWh—kilowatt hour; m—meters; mil—million; NA—not available; sq.—square; std.—standard.
* Reported data rounded to nearest whole number.

TABLE 41c. Belarus: Production and Extraction of Selected Industrial Products and Resources, 1985–90.*

Product	1985	1986	1987	1988	1989	1990	1990 % of U.S.S.R.
FUEL-ENERGY							
Oil (including gas condensate) (1000 tons)	2,019	2,028	2,041	2,056	2,075	NA	NA
Natural gas (mil cubic m)	243	257	269	279	293	NA	NA
Associated gas (mil cubic m)	243	257	269	279	293	NA	NA
Electric power (billion kWh)	33	36	38	38	39	40	2.3
Peat briquettes (1000 tons)	2,102	2,287	2,240	2,346	2,341	2,071	NA
METALLURGY							
Steel (1000 tons)	813	1,095	1,091	1,109	1,105	1,112	0.7
Finished rolled ferrous metals (1000 tons)	264	510	533	663	685	720	0.6
Cast iron water pipes (1000 tons)	130	131	135	136	136	137	NA
Rolled ferrous metals (mil tons)	0	1	1	1	1	1	0.5
Products from metal powder (tons)	3,148	4,535	5,114	6,183	6,806	NA	NA
MACHINERY							
Metal-cutting machines (1000 units)	24	22	18	16	15	15	9.7
Stamping & pressing machines (units)	762	957	890	984	781	1,135	2.7
Tractors (1000 units)	96	98	100	100	101	101	20.3
Corn combines (1000 units)	24	26	25	20	11	10	31.3
Elevators (1000 units)	9	11	12	11	14	14	36.8
Radios (1000 units)	712	723	726	798	882	979	10.7
Televisions (1000 units)	886	987	1,064	1,040	1,102	1,302	12.4
Refrigerators & freezers (1000 units)	657	666	682	704	718	728	11.2
Motorcycles (1000 units)	230	234	216	227	231	225	20.6
CHEMICAL AND FORESTRY							
Mineral fertilizer (1000 tons)	5,972	6,340	6,584	6,715	6,268	6,000	18.9
Chemical fibers & yarn (1000 tons)	338	373	402	437	450	453	30.7
Sulfuric acid (1000 tons)	1,194	1,171	1,186	1,185	1,179	1,177	4.3
Lumber (1000 cubic m)	6,278	6,609	6,727	6,962	6,805	6,154	2.3
Sawn lumber (1000 cubic m)	3,074	3,221	3,293	3,320	3,325	3,082	3.4
Paper (1000 tons)	189	190	204	203	204	198	3.2
Cardboard (1000 tons)	222	226	227	238	230	219	5.2
CONSTRUCTION MATERIALS							
Cement (1000 tons)	2,119	2,141	2,204	2,266	2,283	2,258	1.6
Wall materials (mil std. bricks)	2,871	3,057	3,271	3,482	3,649	NA	NA
Construction bricks (mil std. units of bricks)	1,997	2,102	2,193	2,300	2,310	2,348	5.1
Soft roofing materials (mil sq. m)	137	137	138	138	139	140	7.6
Asbestos-cement sheets (mil std. sheets)	369	376	390	402	442	451	5.0
Reinforced concrete materials (1000 sq. m)	6,010	6,258	6,748	7,188	7,430	7,407	5.1
LIGHT INDUSTRY							
Fabric (mil cubic m)	451	457	478	501	512	511	4.0
Stocking-hosiery (mil pairs)	165	166	169	170	174	175	8.1
Knitted goods (mil units)	137	137	141	148	154	169	8.8
Shoes (mil pairs)	44	45	45	47	45	47	5.6
PROCESSED FOODS							
Meat (1000 tons)	728	778	835	884	900	889	6.9
Cheese (1000 tons)	49	51	54	58	62	65	7.3
Granulated sugar (1000 tons)	335	346	368	354	354	347	2.8
Vegetable oil (1000 tons)	20	19	21	23	25	26	0.8
Animal fats (1000 tons)	126	143	158	162	158	159	NA
Canned foods (mil std. cans)	660	694	702	747	790	789	3.8
Confections (1000 tons)	168	170	174	182	188	173	3.3

Source: *Narodnoye Khozyaystvo SSSR v 1990 g.*, pp. 395–399, 401–408, 413–416, 420–422, 520–522; *Narkhoz Belorusskoy SSR in 1990*, pp. 193–194, 210–211; *Promyshlennost' SSSR*, 1990, p. 156.
Abbreviations: kWh—kilowatt hour; m—meters; mil—million; NA—not available; sq.—square; std.—standard.
* Reported data rounded to nearest whole number.

TABLE 41d. Moldova: Production and Extraction of Selected Industrial Products and Resources, 1985–90.*

Product	1985	1986	1987	1988	1989	1990	1990 % of U.S.S.R.
FUEL-ENERGY							
Electric power (billion kWh)	17	18	17	17	17	16	0.9
METALLURGY							
Steel (1000 tons)	210	538	685	713	685	712	0.5
Finished rolled ferrous metals (1000 tons)	85	393	481	512	486	578	0.5
MACHINERY							
Large electrical machines (units)	3,380	3,360	3,199	3,242	3,151	3,389	7.3
Alternating current electrical motors (1000 kWt)	877	799	811	816	845	665	1.5
Tractors (1000 units)	11	12	12	13	12	10	2.0
Power transformers (1000 kVA)	407	449	441	402	394	416	0.3
Centrifugal pumps (1000 units)	107	106	92	103	85	79	NA
Auto-trailers (1000 units)	35	35	36	38	32	21	NA
Washing machines (1000 units)	291	301	325	310	280	298	3.8
Refrigerators and freezers (1000 units)	200	194	162	156	204	133	2.1
CHEMICAL AND FORESTRY							
Pharmaceutical products (1000 rubles)	12	13	13	14	14	23	—
Lumber** (1000 cubic m)	142	143	146	165	148	134	—
Synthetic resins & plastics (1000 tons)	16	16	16	16	16	18	0.3
Sawn timber (1000 cubic m)	348	360	323	338	338	298	0.3
Wood-particle boards (1000 sq. m)	91	96	99	101	105	NA	NA
CONSTRUCTION MATERIALS							
Cement (1000 tons)	1,232	1,955	2,209	2,361	2,258	2,287	1.7
Reinforced concrete assemblies (mil sq. m)	2	2	2	2	2	2	1.4
Construction bricks (mil units)	218	233	233	240	237	236	0.5
Asbestos cement shingles (mil std. units)	166	168	172	174	163	177	2.0
Wall materials (mil std. bricks)	832	867	858	827	827	805	1.2
LIGHT INDUSTRY							
Fabric (all types) (mil sq. m)	166	175	196	211	224	244	1.9
Stocking-hosiery goods (mil pairs)	40	40	40	41	41	44	2.1
Knitted goods (mil units)	64	63	64	67	68	66	3.4
Shoes (mil pairs)	18	20	21	22	23	23	2.8
PROCESSED FOODS							
Granulated sugar (1000 tons)	414	409	387	374	446	436	3.5
Meat (1000 tons)	219	232	219	237	246	258	2.0
Animal fats (1000 tons)	24	25	27	29	29	27	1.6
Vegetable oil (1000 tons)	108	110	116	115	118	126	3.9
Canned goods (all types) (mil std. cans)	1,586	1,955	1,987	1,823	1,748	1,814	8.8
Confectionery goods (1000 tons)	62	65	60	71	71	70	1.3

Source: *Respublika Moldova v tsifrakh 1990*, pp. 107–111, 199–201; *Narkhoz SSSR in 1990*, pp. 395–399, 403–407, 410–417, 520–522.

Abbreviations: kVA—kilovoltampere; kWh—kilowatt hour; m—meters; mil—million; NA—not available; sq.—square; std.—standard.

—Zero or negligible.

* Reported data rounded to nearest whole number.

** Including commercial lumber.

TABLE 41e. Lithuania: Production and Extraction of Selected Industrial Products and
Resources, 1985-90.*

Product	1985	1986	1987	1988	1989	1990	1990 % of U.S.S.R.
FUEL-ENERGY							
Electric power (billion kWh)	21	22	23	26	29	28	1.6
Peat (1000 tons)	136	192	128	172	130	60	0.3
METALLURGY							
Steel (1000 tons)	7	7	8	8	7	7	—
MACHINERY							
Metal-cutting tools (1000 units)	28	22	19	13	13	9	—
Precision instruments (mil rubles)	137	147	153	162	171	158	2.7
Agricultural machinery (mil rubles)	73	70	74	74	72	64	1.8
Electric welding equipment (1000 units)	72	72	72	75	77	78	NA
Electric meters (1000 units)	3,301	3,320	3,420	3,631	3,612	3,177	NA
Alternating current electric motors (1000 units)	444	483	474	475	441	415	4.8
CHEMICAL AND FORESTRY							
Mineral fertilizers (1000 tons)	747	796	819	791	632	483	1.5
Sulfuric acid (1000 tons)	440	441	440	430	512	412	1.5
Chemical fibers and yarn (1000 tons)	14	14	14	14	14	11	0.8
Lumber (1000 cubic m)	1,991	2,008	2,092	2,129	2,070	1,913	0.7
Sawn lumber (1000 cubic m)	934	755	985	1,006	938	776	0.8
Paper (1000 tons)	120	120	120	123	117	101	1.6
Cardboard (1000 tons)	145	146	146	146	139	117	2.8
CONSTRUCTION MATERIALS							
Cement (1000 tons)	3,383	3,388	3,394	3,405	3,410	3,359	2.4
Construction bricks (mil units)	1,028	1,018	1,040	1,101	1,121	1,100	2.4
Soft roofing materials (mil. m)	46	45	45	41	47	31	1.7
Asbesto-cement shingles (mil std. units)	106	107	108	114	114	114	1.3
Window glass (mil sq. m)	4	4	3	4	4	3	1.5
LIGHT INDUSTRY							
Cotton textile fabric (mil sq. m)	121	123	127	117	98	99	1.3
Wool fabric (mil sq. m)	22	22	22	22	23	22	3.1
Linen fabric (mil sq. m)	29	29	30	30	31	28	3.1
Silk fabric (mil sq. m)	41	41	42	42	52	40	1.9
Stocking-hosiery goods (mil pairs)	99	100	102	103	105	82	3.8
Knitted goods (mil units)	61	62	61	62	62	59	3.0
Shoes (mil pairs)	11	11	11	11	12	12	1.4
PROCESSED FOODS							
Granulated Sugar (1000 tons)	222	238	239	239	239	159	1.3
Meat (1000 tons)	397	410	420	433	447	432	3.3
Animal fats (1000 tons)	72	75	77	78	78	74	4.2
Vegetable oil (1000 tons)	2	0	0	0	1	1	—
Canned goods (all types) (mil std. cans)	327	343	373	405	423	369	1.8

Source: *Statisticheskij Yezhegodnik Litvy, 1990 g.* p. 167; *Narodnoye Khozyaystvo SSSR v 1990 g.* pp. 395, 397-399, 401-405, 408, 410-417, 420-423, 517-522; *Promyshlennost' SSSR,* 1990, pp. 150, 167, 196.
Abbreviations: kWh—kilowatt hour; m—meters; mil—million; NA—not available; sq.—square; std.—standard.
—Zero or negligible.
* Reported data rounded to nearest whole number.

TABLE 41f. Latvia: Production and Extraction of Selected Industrial Products and Resources, 1985–90.*

Product	1985	1986	1987	1988	1989	1990	1990 % of U.S.S.R.
FUEL-ENERGY							
Electric power (billion kWh)	5	5	6	5	6	7	0.4
Peat (1000 tons)	400	536	214	367	419	253	2.3
METALLURGY							
Steel (1000 tons)	550	567	568	559	555	550	0.4
Rolled ferrous metals (1000 tons)	823	836	849	848	795	731	0.6
MACHINERY							
Electric lamps (mil units)	66	58	56	43	38	34	1.5
Potato harvesting machines (units)	2,062	1,000	1,410	1,401	1,104	18	0.3
Autobuses (units)	15,230	14,663	17,106	17,580	17,034	17,100	19.7
Agricultural fertilizing machines (units)	27,688	27,186	26,079	25,419	21,501	13,113	28.4
Agricultural milking equipment (units)	29,515	31,265	29,496	32,238	25,051	21,796	41.5
Radios (1000 units)	1,570	1,908	1,871	1,762	1,486	1,567	17.1
CHEMICAL AND FORESTRY							
Mineral fertilizers (1000 tons)	169	186	185	176	188	180	0.6
Detergents (1000 tons)	1	1	2	2	2	2	0.1
Chemical fibers and yarn (1000 tons)	50	51	52	52	51	48	3.3
Synthetic resins & plastics (1000 tons)	35	37	38	40	38	34	0.6
Varnish and paint (1000 tons)	54	53	50	53	53	47	1.3
Lumber (1000 cubic m)	2,387	2,457	2,497	2,517	2,333	2,123	0.8
Sawn lumber (1000 cubic m)	866	921	946	1,024	825	789	0.9
Paper (1000 tons)	167	160	145	153	138	107	1.7
Cardboard (1000 tons)	10	8	21	10	10	11	0.3
CONSTRUCTION MATERIALS							
Cement (1000 tons)	787	868	843	825	776	744	0.5
Window glass (1000 sq. m)	3,525	4,189	4,187	4,156	3,846	2,982	1.4
Construction bricks (mil units)	377	411	450	447	466	472	1.0
Asbestos cement shingles (mil std. units)	99	103	103	97	94	86	1.0
Linoleum (1000 sq. m)	6,740	6,958	7,412	7,599	7,813	6,476	4.1
LIGHT INDUSTRY							
Cotton textile fabric (mil sq. m)	61	61	61	59	56	49	0.6
Wool fabric (mil sq. m)	16	16	16	16	16	15	2.1
Linen fabric (mil sq. m)	19	20	19	20	20	14	1.6
Silk fabric (mil sq. m)	26	28	28	28	28	26	1.2
Stocking-hosiery goods (mil pairs)	76	77	78	78	79	74	3.4
Knitted goods (mil units)	45	44	42	43	43	40	2.1
Footwear (all types) (mil pairs)	26	26	27	26	25	21	2.4
PROCESSED FOODS							
Granulated Sugar (1000 tons)	249	240	248	243	248	230	1.8
Meat (1000 tons)	243	250	257	264	259	234	1.8
Animal fats (1000 tons)	45	46	47	47	47	44	2.5
Vegetable oil (1000 tons)	8	9	9	12	13	14	0.4
Canned goods (all types) (mil std. cans)	456	480	477	495	504	467	2.3
Confectionery goods (1000 tons)	48	50	52	54	56	55	1.0

Source: *Narodnoye Khazyzystvo Latvii v 1990g.* pp. 213–219, 254, 255; *Narodnoye Khozyaystvo SSSR v 1990g.* pp. 395, 397–399, 401, 403–408, 410–417, 420–423, 517–522.
Abbreviations: kWh—kilowatt hour; m—meters; mil—million; sq.—square; std.—standard.
* Reported data rounded to nearest whole number.

1151

TABLE 41g. Estonia: Production and Extraction of Selected Industrial Products and Resources, 1985-90.*

Product	1985	1986	1987	1988	1989	1990	1990 % of U.S.S.R.
FUEL-ENERGY							
Electric power (bil. kWh)	18	18	18	18	18	17	—
Gas from oil shales (mil cubic m)	193	150	121	NA	NA	NA	NA
Peat (1000 tons)	430	778	500	752	872	648	0.1
Peat briquettes (1000 tons)	150	217	169	208	216	201	NA
Oil Shales (mil tons)	26	25	25	23	23	23	NA
METALLURGY							
Steel (1000 tons)	12	12	12	12	11	10	—
Products from metal powder (tons)	232	234	215	199	177	NA	NA
Cast iron (1000 tons)	34	33	32	26	19	NA	NA
Cast steel (1000 tons)	6	6	6	6	4	NA	NA
MACHINERY							
Excavators (1000 units)	2	2	2	2	2	2	—
Agricultural machinery for crops (mil rubles)	NA	NA	NA	NA	NA	15	—
Livestock equipment (mil rubles)	NA	NA	NA	NA	NA	10	—
Alternating current electric motors (1000s)	286	301	284	248	215	NA	NA
VRG, SRG power cable (1000 km)	8	8	8	11	13	NA	NA
CHEMICAL AND FORESTRY							
Mineral fertilizers (1000 tons)	244	256	257	245	214	216	—
Sulfuric acid (1000 tons)	616	654	653	654	552	NA	NA
Lacquers and enamels (tons)	3,806	3,806	4,063	3,831	3,437	NA	NA
Detergents (1000 tons)	35	37	37	40	41	NA	NA
Timber production (1000 cubic m)	2,108	2,126	2,136	2,122	2,004	1,279	—
Sawn lumber (1000 cubic m)	668	708	666	675	585	500	—
Paper (1000 tons)	90	95	90	95	92	77	—
Cardboard (1000 tons)	4	4	5	5	5	5	—
CONSTRUCTION MATERIALS							
Cement (1000 tons)	1,094	1,118	1,161	1,200	1,129	938	—
Construction bricks (mil units)	255	251	244	254	263	NA	NA
Soft roofing materials (mil sq. m)	36	37	37	38	32	NA	NA
Asbestos cement shingle (mil std. sheets)	72	73	73	75	72	69	—
Window glass (1000 sq. m)	2,297	2,339	1,948	1,855	1,892	1,638	—
Wall materials (mil std. bricks)	581	655	627	670	728	693	—
Reinforced concrete assemblies (1000 sq m)	943	977	1,039	1,056	995	889	—
LIGHT INDUSTRY							
Cotton textile fabric (mil sq. m)	198	199	195	192	188	NA	NA
Wool fabric (mil sq. m)	8	8	8	8	8	NA	NA
Linen fabric (mil sq. m)	11	11	11	12	11	NA	NA
Silk fabric (mil sq. m)	9	9	9	11	11	NA	NA
Stocking-hosiery goods (mil pairs)	16	16	17	17	17	19	—
Knitted goods (mil units)	22	23	23	23	24	23	—
Shoes (mil pairs)	6	6	7	7	7	7	—
Skis (1000 pairs)	939	951	965	986	1,031	NA	NA
Matches (1000 boxes)	972	798	810	800	801	NA	NA
Furniture (mil rubles)	174	176	186	204	189	223	—
PROCESSED FOODS							
Meat (1000 tons)	179	180	185	186	187	165	—
Animal fats (1000 tons)	32	33	34	32	31	29	—
Canned goods (mil std. cans)	337	339	343	355	355	324	—
Confectionery goods (1000 tons)	48	49	51	53	54	51	—
Macaroni (1000 tons)	6	6	7	7	6	6	—

Source: *Lithuania, Latvia, Estonia; Statistical Abstract*, 1991, pp. 84–89, 92, 98, 116; *Narodnoye Khozyaystvo Estonskoy SSR in 1987*, p. 112; *Narodnoye Khozyaystvo Estonskoy SSR in 1988*, pp. 100, 168; *Promyshlennost' SSSR*, 1990, p. 168. Abbreviations: kWh—kilowatt hour; m—meters; mil—million; NA—not available; sq.—square; SRG—translates to Medium Distribution Flexible; std.—standard; VRG—translates to Highest Distribution Flexible.
—Zero or negligible.
* Reported data rounded to nearest whole number.

TABLE 41h. Georgia: Production and Extraction of Selected Industrial Products and Resources, 1985–90.*

Product	1985	1986	1987	1988	1989	1990	1990 % of U.S.S.R.
FUEL-ENERGY							
Electric power (billion kWh)	14	15	15	15	16	14	0.8
METALLURGY							
Manganese (1000 tons)	2,743	2,183	2,085	1,839	NA	NA	NA
Steel (1000 tons)	1,441	1,440	1,445	1,451	1,429	1,315	0.9
Rolled ferrous metal (mil tons)	1	1	1	1	1	1	0.9
Finished rolled ferrous metal (mil tons)	1	1	1	1	1	NA	NA
Steel tubes (1000 tons)	524	515	510	517	504	NA	NA
Cast iron (1000 tons)	1	1	1	1	1	NA	NA
MACHINERY							
Metal cutting tools (1000 units)	3,089	2,701	2,469	2,309	NA	NA	NA
Precision Instruments (mil rubles)	37	43	47	56	NA	NA	NA
Agricultural machinery (mil rubles)	10	10	9	7	NA	NA	NA
Tower cranes (units)	561	656	578	611	NA	NA	NA
Alternating current electric motors, under 100 kWt (1000 units)	260	284	307	277	NA	NA	NA
CHEMICAL AND FORESTRY							
Mineral fertilizers (1000 tons)	114	84	155	157	155	NA	NA
Paint and varnish (1000 tons)	57	61	66	64	NA	NA	NA
Chemical fibers and yarn (1000 tons)	28	36	37	40	38	NA	NA
Timber Production (1000 cubic m)	357	357	377	345	304	155	0.1
Sawn timber (1000 cubic m)	545	471	544	557	531	541	0.6
Paper (1000 tons)	40	35	28	29	28	27	0.4
Cardboard (1000 tons)	59	59	58	58	47	NA	NA
CONSTRUCTION MATERIALS							
Construction bricks (mil units)	308	304	306	305	271	NA	NA
Soft roofing materials (mil sq. m)	78	90	85	87	60	NA	NA
Asbestos cement shingle (mil std. sheets)	37	36	30	26	35	NA	NA
Cement (1000 tons)	1,576	1,544	1,481	1,351	1,530	1,290	0.9
Reinforced concrete assemblies (1000 cubic m)	2,139	2,219	2,327	2,159	NA	NA	NA
LIGHT INDUSTRY							
Fabric (mil sq. m)	122	122	131	137	123	111	0.9
Cotton fabric (mil sq. m)	58	60	59	60	45	34	0.4
Wool fabric (mil sq. m)	8	7	9	10	10	10	1.4
Silk fabric (mil sq. m)	46	43	48	51	48	46	2.2
Stocking-hosiery goods (mil pairs)	31	32	33	33	32	30	1.4
Knitted goods (mil units)	56	56	58	60	56	52	2.7
Shoes (mil pairs)	17	18	18	18	17	17	2.0
PROCESSED FOODS							
Granulated Sugar (1000 tons)	50	52	50	53	32	34	0.3
Meat (1000 tons)	105	109	106	100	98	77	0.6
Animal fats (1000 tons)	1	2	2	1	1	1	0.1
Vegetable oil (1000 tons)	11	10	15	12	9	14	0.4
Canned goods (mil cans)	744	845	798	950	727	695	33.8
Confectionery goods (1000 tons)	64	65	67	69	66	NA	NA

Source: *Narodnoye Khozyaystvo SSSR v 1988 g.* pp. 459–469, 470–472; *Narodnoye Khozyaystvo SSSR v 1989*, pp. 375, 399; *Narodnoye Khozyaystvo SSSR v 1990*, pp. 395–399, 401–408, 411–417, 420–422; *Narodnoye Khozyaystvo Gruzinskoy SSR v 1988 g.*, pp. 209–213, 216; *Promyshlennost' SSSR*, 1990, pp. 149, 150–155, 185, 196–199, 208, 223–229, 244–249, 252; *Tovary narodnogo potrebleniya*, 1991, p. 80.

kWh—kilowatt hour; m—meters; mil—million; NA—not available; sq.—square; std.—standard.
* Reported data rounded to nearest whole number.

TABLE 41i. Azerbaijan: Production and Extraction of Selected Industrial Products and Resources, 1985-90.*

Product	1985	1986	1987	1988	1989	1990	1990 % of U.S.S.R.
FUEL-ENERGY							
Electric power (billion kWh)	21	22	23	24	23	23	1.3
Oil (including gas condensate) (1000 tons)	13,142	13,321	13,804	13,741	13,159	NA	NA
Natural gas (mil cubic m)	14,067	13,580	12,523	11,827	11,112	NA	NA
Associated gas (mil cubic m)	2,988	2,845	2,608	2,686	2,457	NA	NA
METALLURGY							
Ferrous ores (mil tons)	1	1	1	1	1	NA	NA
Steel (1000 tons)	853	830	857	840	820	703	0.5
Rolled ferrous metals (mil tons)	1	1	1	1	1	1	0.4
Steel tubes (1000 tons)	582	541	566	604	584	NA	NA
Products from metal powder (tons)	228	231	341	445	417	NA	NA
MACHINERY							
High-voltage apparatus (mil rubles)	17	17	19	17	NA	NA	NA
Low-voltage apparatus (mil rubles)	20	26	25	30	NA	NA	NA
Agricultural equipment (mil rubles)	25	24	24	19	NA	NA	NA
Livestock equipment (mil rubles)	7	8	8	8	NA	NA	NA
Electric welding equipment (1000 units)	34	30	26	26	NA	NA	NA
Alternating current motors (1000 units)	390	404	406	407	NA	NA	NA
Compressors (units)	5,723	6,245	6,270	5,011	NA	NA	NA
CHEMICAL AND FORESTRY							
Mineral fertilizers (1000 tons)	306	305	313	320	275	NA	NA
Sulfuric acid (1000 tons)	782	839	872	846	NA	NA	NA
Caustic soda (1000 tons)	227	235	245	236	NA	NA	NA
Sawn lumber (1000 cubic m)	280	244	247	211	157	126	0.1
Tires (1000 units)	1,666	1,587	1,592	1,483	NA	NA	NA
Lumber (1000 cubic m)	7	5	4	4	4	4	—
CONSTRUCTION MATERIALS							
Cement (1000 tons)	1,253	1,279	1,290	1,220	1,058	990	0.7
Wall materials (mil std. units of brick)	1,392	1,436	1,523	1,465	1,454	NA	NA
Construction bricks (mil units)	117	120	126	136	141	NA	NA
Asbestos cement shingle (mil std. sheets)	112	100	116	92	85	NA	NA
Window glass (1000 sq. m)	5,448	6,375	6,838	5,683	5,413	NA	NA
LIGHT INDUSTRY							
Fabric (mil sq. m)	189	167	189	185	170	151	1.2
Cotton fabric (mil linear m)	167	139	160	151	144	NA	NA
Wool fabric (mil sq. m)	12	12	12	13	12	NA	NA
Silk fabric (mil linear m)	35	32	36	35	33	NA	NA
Stocking-hosiery goods (mil pairs)	42	44	44	44	43	38	1.8
Knitted goods (mil units)	41	42	43	43	42	37	1.9
Sewn goods (mil rubles)	382	379	382	375	399	NA	NA
Shoes (mil pairs)	23	24	24	20	17	15	1.8
PROCESSED FOODS							
Meat (1000 tons)	77	86	87	87	82	62	0.5
Dairy products (1000 tons)	220	232	236	239	224	NA	NA
Animal fats (1000 tons)	5	5	5	6	5	4	0.2
Vegetable oil (1000 tons)	55	57	58	50	50	41	1.3
Canned goods (mil cans)	620	642	790	845	729	668	3.2
Confectionery goods (1000 tons)	95	97	104	106	111	NA	NA

Source: *Narodnoye Khozyaystvo Azerbaijan SSR 1988*, pp. 256, 258-259, 275; *Narodnoye Khozyaystvo SSSR v 1990g.* pp. 395, 397-398, 401, 412-414, 416-417, 420, 472; *Promyshlennost' SSSR*, 1990, pp. 136-147, 151, 206-208, 248.
Abbreviations: kWh—kilowatt hour; m—meters; mil—million; NA—not available; sq.—square; std.—standard.
—zero or negligible.
* Data rounded to nearest whole number.

TABLE 41j. Armenia: Production and Extraction of Selected Industrial Products and Resources, 1985-90.*

Product	1985	1986	1987	1988	1989	1990	1990 % of U.S.S.R.
FUEL-ENERGY							
Electric power (mil kWh)	14,911	14,520	15,209	15,305	12,137	10,000	0.6
METALLURGY							
Steel (1000 tons)	6	6	6	6	3	4	—
Products from metal powder (tons)	396	428	512	458	494	NA	NA
MACHINERY							
Alternating current generators under 100kV (1000s)	66	67	59	58	NA	NA	NA
Alternating current generators over 100 kV (1000s)	2	2	1	1	—	—	—
Air and gas compressors (units)	5,723	6,245	6,270	5,011	NA	NA	NA
Electric welding equipment (units)	1,364	1,510	1,760	1,779	NA	NA	NA
Electric lamps (millions)	186	187	165	146	NA	NA	NA
Alternating current electric motors (1000s)	985	984	1,050	857	NA	NA	NA
Power transformers (mil kVA)	7	7	5	6	NA	NA	NA
CHEMICAL AND FORESTRY							
Mineral fertilizers (1000 tons)	81	78	77	39	NA	NA	NA
Sulfuric acid (1000 tons)	169	183	186	155	NA	NA	NA
Chemical fibers and thread (1000 tons)	14	15	15	15	11	NA	NA
Sawn lumber (1000 cubic m)	100	105	115	108	93	87	0.1
Lumber (1000 cubic m)	6	6	6	6	6	6	—
Paper (1000 tons)	15	15	15	15	11	8	0.1
CONSTRUCTION MATERIALS							
Wall materials (mil std. units)	883	922	920	791	893	NA	NA
Construction bricks (mil units)	0	0	0	0	NA	NA	NA
Asbesto-cement shingle (mil std. units)	79	92	86	63	74	NA	NA
Reinforced concrete (1000 cubic m)	1,421	1,549	NA	NA	NA	NA	NA
Cement (1000 tons)	1,665	1,735	1,759	1,680	1,639	1,466	1.1
LIGHT INDUSTRY							
Fabric (mil cubic m)	129	136	130	117	63	58	0.5
Cotton fabric (mil linear m)	123	130	123	107	35	NA	NA
Wool fabric (mil linear m)	5	5	5	5	4	NA	NA
Silk fabric (mil linear m)	14	14	15	15	18	NA	NA
Stocking-hosiery goods (mil pairs)	90	96	109	111	49	64	3.0
Knitted goods (mil units)	97	98	106	106	91	86	4.4
Sewn goods (mil rubles)	650	678	673	657	550	NA	NA
Shoes (mil pairs)	18	20	21	20	18	19	2.2
PROCESSED FOODS							
Granulated Sugar (1000 tons)	23	28	28	25	NA	NA	NA
Meat (1000 tons)	70	74	75	75	69	59	0.5
Animal fats (1000 tons)	0	1	1	1	1	1	—
Vegetable oil (1000 tons)	7	8	9	7	8	6	0.2
Canned goods (all types) (mil cans)	494	475	478	489	413	267	1.3
Confectionery goods (1000 tons)	41	45	47	47	48	NA	NA
Cheese (1000 tons)	27	27	27	28	25	NA	NA

Source: *Narodnoye Khozyaystvo Armyanskoy SSR in 1988*, pp. 167-168; *Narodnoye Khozyaystvo SSSR v 1988*, pp. 408-410; *Narodnoye Khozyaystvo SSSR v 1989*, pp. 397-399, 404-406; *Narodnoye Khozyaystvo SSSR v 1990*, pp. 395, 403, 405, 410-416, 420-421; *Promyshlennost' SSSR*, 1990, 132, 188, 199, 206, 208, 215-219, 226, 250.

Abbreviations: kWh—kilowatt hour; kV—kilovolt; kVA—kilovoltampere; m—meters; mil—million; NA—not available; sq.—square; std.—standard.

—Zero or negligible.

* Reported data rounded to nearest whole number.

1155

TABLE 41k. Kazakhstan: Production and Extraction of Selected Industrial Products and Resources, 1985–90.*

Product	1985	1986	1987	1988	1989	1990	1990 % of U.S.S.R.
FUEL-ENERGY							
Electric power (mil kWh)	81,263	85,094	88,490	88,417	89,657	87,379	5.1
Oil (including gas condensate) (1000 tons)	22,839	23,681	24,461	25,516	25,388	25,820	4.5
Natural gas (mil cubic m)	5,456	5,824	6,311	7,134	6,710	7,114	0.9
Coke (1000 tons)	31,040	32,298	32,023	32,199	30,286	NA	NA
Coal (mil tons)	131	138	142	143	138	131	18.6
METALLURGY							
Cast iron (1000 tons)	4,932	4,890	4,797	4,940	5,279	NA	NA
Steel (1000 tons)	6,155	6,496	6,555	6,766	6,831	6,753	4.4
Finished rolled ferrous metals (1000 tons)	4,188	4,566	4,580	4,874	5,013	4,899	4.4
Iron ore (mil tons)	23	24	24	24	24	24	10.1
Manganese ore (1000 tons)	84	87	111	140	152	169	2.0
MACHINERY							
Metal-cutting equipment (units)	2,848	2,630	2,155	2,214	2,307	2,578	1.6
Stamping & pressing equipment (units)	1,295	1,249	1,139	1,161	1,205	1,173	2.8
Instruments (mil rubles)	79	81	82	91	90	77	1.3
Rolled equipment (mil rubles)	20	20	18	20	20	22	8.0
Excavators (units)	1,877	1,843	1,045	570	528	710	1.9
Bulldozers (units)	13,670	14,504	15,220	14,810	15,308	13,328	35.9
Agricultural machines (mil rubles)	366	389	399	323	228	215	6.0
Livestock equipment (mil rubles)	111	127	137	146	156	135	5.3
CHEMICAL AND FORESTRY							
Mineral fertilizer (1000 tons)	1,430	1,520	1,603	1,737	1,705	1,656	5.2
Sulfuric acid (1000 tons)	1,671	1,850	2,008	2,063	1,896	3,151	11.6
Caustic soda (1000 tons)	58	38	58	61	63	65	2.2
Synthetic resins & plastics (1000 tons)	178	180	194	182	203	215	3.9
Tires for autos & agricultural machines (1000 units)	1,452	2,010	2,313	2,697	2,450	2,633	3.9
Chemical fibers and yarn (1000 tons)	21	24	23	22	21	17	1.2
Cellulose (1000 tons)	41	49	49	51	53	45	0.6
Paper (1000 tons)	11	1	2	3	3	2	—
Lumber (1000 cubic m)	2,035	2,022	2,138	2,143	2,000	1,760	0.5
CONSTRUCTION MATERIALS							
Cement (1000 tons)	7,549	8,066	8,349	8,446	8,650	8,301	6.0
Asbestos-cement shingles (mil std. units)	643	652	668	681	691	722	8.0
Construction bricks (mil units)	1,947	2,055	2,268	2,354	2,468	2,285	5.0
Reinforced concrete assemblies (mil cubic m)	6,575	6,824	7,535	7,747	7,717	7,504	5.2
LIGHT INDUSTRY							
Fabric (mil sq. m)	289	300	288	324	330	326	2.6
Cotton fabric (mil sq. m)	133	136	120	147	150	151	1.9
Wool fabric (mil sq. m)	29	28	30	33	34	34	4.9
Stocking-hosiery (mil pairs)	77	77	78	81	83	88	4.1
Knitted goods (mil units)	100	102	105	108	123	127	6.6
Sewn goods (mil rubles)	1,215	1,202	1,212	1,264	1,289	1,344	4.6
Shoes (mil pairs)	32	33	33	34	35	37	4.3
PROCESSED FOODS							
Meat (1000 tons)	665	807	848	869	946	899	6.9
Granulated sugar (1000 tons)	337	342	349	314	377	320	2.6
Cheese (1000 tons)	29	30	30	33	35	35	4.0
Vegetable oil (1000 tons)	74	76	80	85	92	95	2.9
Confectionery good (1000 tons)	221	229	236	244	255	259	4.9
Canned foods (mil std. cans)	391	447	449	468	448	442	2.1

Source: *Statisticheskiy yezhegodnik Kazakhstana v 1990*, pp. 284–299, 345–349; *Narodnoye khozyaystvo SSSR v 1990*. pp. 395–423, 517–522.
Abbreviations: kWh—kilowatt hour; m—meters; mil—million; NA—not available; sq.—square; std.—standard.
—Zero or negligible.
* Reported data rounded to nearest whole number.

TABLE 41I. Uzbekistan: Production and Extraction of Selected Industrial Products and Resources, 1985-90.*

Product	1985	1986	1987	1988	1989	1990	1990 % of U.S.S.R.
FUEL-ENERGY							
Electric power (billion kWh)	48	52	55	51	56	56	3.3
Oil (including gas condensate) (1000 tons)	1,978	2,178	2,305	2,436	2,673	2,810	0.5
Natural gas (billion cubic m)	35	39	40	40	41	41	5.0
Coal (1000 tons)	5,250	5,983	5,030	5,470	6,239	6,477	0.9
Coal briquettes (1000 tons)	142	139	143	139	136	129	2.2
METALLURGY							
Steel (1000 tons)	927	976	1,044	1,016	1,080	1,015	0.7
Finished ferrous sheet metal (1000 tons)	694	786	905	806	896	955	0.9
MACHINERY							
Tractors (1000 units)	26	27	26	23	24	23	4.7
Cotton harvesters (1000 units)	9	9	8	8	6	5	100.0
Excavators (units)	1,576	1,548	1,536	1,587	794	900	2.4
Turbine pumps (1000 units)	11	12	10	8	9	9	0.7
Spinning machines (units)	1,603	1,704	1,318	1,498	1,615	1,539	46.6
Electric overhead travelling cranes (units)	1,467	1,510	1,525	1,524	1,455	1,412	24.1
CHEMICAL AND FORESTRY							
Mineral fertilizer (1000 tons)	1,546	1,764	1,929	2,045	1,900	1,762	5.6
Sulfuric acid (1000 tons)	2,302	2,457	2,495	2,642	2,390	2,188	8.0
Synthetic resins & plastics (1000 tons)	124	146	158	160	164	155	2.8
Pesticide (1000 tons)	29	31	36	45	48	41	19.8
Chemical fibers & yarn (1000 tons)	38	42	46	49	51	53	3.6
Synthetic detergents (1000 tons)	124	146	158	160	164	155	10.3
Paper (1000 tons)	25	26	25	26	26	26	0.4
Carton (1000 tons)	55	55	56	56	56	51	1.2
Sawn lumber (1000 cubic m)	466	424	511	494	563	556	0.6
CONSTRUCTION MATERIALS							
Cement (1000 tons)	5,287	5,425	5,512	5,583	6,194	6,385	4.6
Asbesto-cement tile (mil std. units)	425	438	436	445	430	441	4.9
Construction bricks (mil units)	1,875	1,923	1,998	2,047	2,163	2,169	4.7
Reinforced concrete assemblies (mil cubic m)	6	6	7	7	6	6	4.4
LIGHT INDUSTRY							
Fabric (mil sq. m)	621	639	694	749	762	763	6.0
Cotton fabric (mil sq. m)	353	363	408	454	468	469	6.0
Silk fabric (mil sq. m)	142	133	135	138	145	144	6.9
Stocking-hosiery (mil pairs)	64	73	81	96	114	113	5.3
Knitted goods (mil units)	61	77	96	106	110	105	5.4
Sewn goods (mil rubles)	1,019	1,058	1,097	1,200	1,322	1,399	4.8
Shoes (mil pairs)	35	36	39	42	44	47	5.5
Carpets (1000 sq. m)	5,586	5,894	5,960	6,511	7,122	8,095	7.0
PROCESSED FOODS							
Meat (1000 tons)	232	243	253	266	277	261	2.0
Fish catch (1000 tons)	27	28	27	26	26	27	0.3
Cheese (1000 tons)	2	2	2	2	2	2	0.2
Vegetable oil (1000 tons)	451	508	510	498	513	514	15.7
Animal fats (1000 tons)	11	14	15	16	16	16	0.9
Confections (1000 tons)	165	169	173	191	205	219	4.2
Canned foods (mil std. cans)	882	1,060	1,135	1,211	1,163	1,133	5.5

Source: *Narodnoye Khozyaystvo Uzbek SSR in 1989,* pp. 225–229; *Narodnoye Khozyaystvo Uzbek SSR in 1990,* pp. 187, 208–210, 214–220, 286, 289; *Narodnoye Khozyaystvo SSR v 1988,* pp. 408, 468, 469; *Narodnoye Khozyaystvo SSR v 1990,* pp. 405–423, 471–472, 476, 484–487.
Abbreviations: kWh—kilowatt hour; m—meters; mil—million; sq.—square; std.—standard.
* Reported data rounded to nearest whole number.

1157

TABLE 41m. Kyrgyzstan: Production and Extraction of Selected Industrial Products and Resources, 1985-90.*

Product	1985	1986	1987	1988	1989	1990	1990 % of U.S.S.R.
FUEL-ENERGY							
Electric power (mil kWh)	10,500	14,200	9,348	14,230	15,116	13,370	0.8
Oil (including gas condensate) (1000 tons)	190	190	186	177	165	155	—
Natural gas (mil cubic m)	115	106	112	105	105	96	—
Coal (mil tons)	4	4	4	4	4	4	0.5
METALLURGY							
Steel (1000 tons)	7	6	6	5	3	3	—
MACHINERY							
Metal-cutting equipment (units)	1,382	1,355	1,224	1,104	1,311	1,342	0.9
Stamping & pressing equipment (units)	512	450	452	241	335	317	0.8
Instruments (mil rubles)	35	36	36	39	41	38	0.7
Press-welding machines (units)	512	450	452	241	335	317	0.8
Livestock equipment (mil rubles)	75	74	67	69	66	59	2.3
CHEMICAL AND FORESTRY							
Carton (1000 tons)	10	9	8	8	7	NA	NA
Lumber (1000 cubic m)	7	7	7	7	7	6	—
Sawn lumber (1000 cubic m)	225	205	205	255	228	202	0.2
CONSTRUCTION MATERIALS							
Cement (1000 tons)	1,209	1,272	1,311	1,380	1,408	1,387	1.0
Asbesto-cement shingles (mil std. units)	103	134	146	157	174	178	2.0
Wall material (mil std. bricks)	529	565	572	589	668	819	1.2
Construction bricks (mil units)	463	524	527	542	619	649	1.4
Reinforced concrete assemblies (1000 sq. m)	1	1	1	1	1	1	0.9
LIGHT INDUSTRY							
Fabric (all types) (mil sq. m)	137	138	133	141	150	134	1.1
Cotton fabric (mil linear m)	101	100	92	99	112	NA	NA
Wool fabric (mil linear m)	7	7	8	8	8	NA	NA
Silk fabric (mil linear m)	12	11	13	13	13	NA	NA
Stocking-hosiery (mil pairs)	24	25	27	29	33	34	1.6
Knitted goods (mil units)	18	19	19	20	21	20	1.1
Sewn goods (mil rubles)	229	233	244	253	278	293	1.0
Shoes (mil pairs)	11	11	11	12	12	12	1.4
PROCESSED FOODS							
Meat (1000 tons)	106	126	131	144	133	114	0.9
Granulated sugar (1000 tons)	282	433	435	378	415	380	3.0
Cheese (1000 tons)	6	6	6	6	6	6	0.7
Vegetable oil (1000 tons)	12	13	14	14	15	14	0.4
Animal fats (1000 tons)	12	13	13	13	14	13	0.7
Confections (1000 tons)	40	42	44	48	54	59	1.1
Canned foods (mil. std. cans)	106	143	140	175	161	147	0.7

Source: *Statisticheskiy yezhegodnik Kyrgystana 1990*, Part 2, pp. 240-248, 250-251, 319-320; *Narodnoye Khozyaystvo Kyrgyzskoy SSR in 1988*, pp. 146-149, 152-155, 188; *Narodnoye Khozyaystvo SSR v 1990g.* pp. 395, 397-399, 401, 403-408, 410-417, 420-423.
Abbreviations: kWh—kilowatt hour; m—meters; mil—million; NA—not available; sq.—square; std.—standard.
—Zero or negligible.
* Reported data rounded to nearest whole number.

TABLE 41n. Tajikistan: Production and Extraction of Selected Industrial Products and Resources, 1985–90.*

Product	1985	1986	1987	1988	1989	1990	% of U.S.S.R. 1989	% of U.S.S.R. 1990
FUEL-ENERGY								
Electric power (mil kWh)	15,700	13,566	15,862	18,800	15,300	18,100	0.9	1.0
Oil (including gas condensate) (1000 tons)	387	367	322	271	190	NA	—	NA
Natural gas (mil cubic m)	303	292	280	235	195	NA	—	NA
Coal (1000 tons)	516	660	593	673	515	NA	0.1	NA
METALLURGY								
Steel (1000 tons)	5	6	7	6	5	· 5	—	—
MACHINERY								
Metal-cutting machines (1000 units)	6	6	6	7	5	NA	3.2	NA
Textile industry equipment (mil rubles)	10	10	10	9	9	NA	1.2	NA
Technological equipment for trade and public dining (mil rubles)	23	26	26	28	30	NA	4.8	NA
Agricultural machines (mil rubles)	8	10	10	10	12	NA	0.3	NA
Power transformers (1000 kVA))	2,572	2,610	2,783	2,708	2,820	NA	1.8	NA
CHEMICAL AND FORESTRY								
Mineral fertilizer (1000 tons)	88	83	87	85	88	NA	0.3	NA
Caustic soda (1000 tons)	55	67	70	61	58	NA	1.8	NA
Varnish and paint (tons)	6,569	6,652	6,760	7,242	8,115	NA	0.2	NA
Rubber footwear (1000 pairs)	6	6	6	7	7	NA	—	NA
Sawn lumber (1000 cubic m)	121	134	127	140	187	96	0.2	0.1
CONSTRUCTION MATERIALS								
Cement (1000 tons)	1,080	1,102	1,194	1,109	1,110	1,067	0.8	0.8
Asbestos-cement sheets (mil std. units)	NA	8	42	41	88	NA	1.0	NA
Wall material (mil std. bricks)	315	327	313	325	320	NA	0.5	NA
Construction bricks (mil std. units)	305	317	303	314	309	NA	0.7	NA
Reinforced concrete assemblies (mil cubic m)	1,067	1,133	1,192	1,206	1,169	NA	0.8	NA
Soft roof material (mil sq. m)	10	10	11	11	11	NA	0.6	NA
LIGHT INDUSTRY								
Fabric (mil sq. m)	184	185	191	213	217	208	1.7	1.6
Cotton fabric (mil sq. m)	108	107	109	123	129	NA	1.6	NA
Silk fabric (mil sq. m)	65	66	68	77	76	NA	3.5	NA
Wool fabric (mil sq. m)	1	2	2	2	2	NA	0.3	NA
Non-woven fabrics (mil sq. m)	11	10	12	11	10	NA	NA	NA
Stocking-hosiery (mil pairs)	33	36	37	40	45	60	2.1	2.8
Knitted goods (mil units)	13	13	15	16	16	16	0.8	0.8
Sewn goods (mil rubles)	277	264	257	259	290	NA	1.0	NA
Shoes (mil pairs)	10	10	10	10	11	11	1.3	1.3
PROCESSED FOODS								
Meat (1000 tons)	59	64	65	65	66	61	0.5	0.5
Cheese (1000 tons)	3	3	3	3	3	NA	0.3	NA
Vegetable oil (1000 tons)	88	92	92	92	93	80	2.9	2.5
Animal fats (1000 tons)	6	6	6	6	6	6	0.3	0.3
Confections (1000 tons)	40	40	43	48	54	NA	1.1	NA
Canned foods (mil std. cans)	301	333	346	350	374	309	1.8	1.5

Source: *Narodnoye Khozyaystvo Tajik SSSR v 1989*, pp. 205–207, 210–213; *Narodnoye Khozyaystvo Tajik SSSR v 1987*, pp. 67–70; *Narodnoye Khozyaystvo USSR v 1990*, pp. 395–398, 403–408, 410–417, 420–421, 519–522.

Abbreviations: kVA—kilovoltampere; kWh—kilowatt hour; m—meters; mil—million; NA—not available; sq.—square; std.—standard.

—Zero or negligible.

* Reported data rounded to nearest whole number.

TABLE 41o. Turkmenistan: Production and Extraction of Selected Industrial Products and Resources, 1985–89.*

Product	1985	1986	1987	1988	1989	1989 % of U.S.S.R.
FUEL-ENERGY						
Electric power (billion kWh)	11	12	13	13	15	0.8
Oil (including gas condensate) (1000 tons)	6,029	5,943	5,812	5,747	5,751	0.9
Natural gas (mil cubic m)	83,193	84,707	88,135	88,303	89,921	11.3
METALLURGY						
Steel (1000 tons)	2	2	2	2	2	—
MACHINERY						
Oil equipment (1000 rubles)	1,593	2,039	767	1,167	2,181	0.9
Turbine pumps (units)	811	798	802	753	870	0.1
Chemical equipment (1000 rubles)	152	142	243	271	476	—
Exhaust fans for water-cooling towers (units)	2,422	2,306	1,957	1,997	2,016	NA
Electrical wires (1000 km)	8	8	7	8	8	NA
Radio wires (1000 km)	2	8	9	12	8	NA
Technological equipment for trade and public dining (mil rubles)	6	7	7	8	8	1.3
CHEMICAL AND FORESTRY						
Mineral fertilizer (1000 tons)	119	162	204	192	182	0.5
Pesticides (tons)	211	168	247	246	241	0.1
Pharmaceutical (mil rubles)	14	16	16	16	15	0.4
Synthetic detergents (1000 tons)	27	27	28	26	29	2.0
Household soap (1000 tons)	8	8	10	11	12	1.6
Sawn lumber (1000 cubic m)	55	50	64	59	65	0.1
CONSTRUCTION MATERIALS						
Cement (1000 tons)	1,005	1,024	1,066	1,110	1,057	0.8
Asbesto-cement shingles (mil std. units)	62	66	68	70	69	0.8
Asbesto-cement pipes and muffs (mil std. pipes)	1,482	1,664	1,710	1,661	1,707	NA
Wall materials (mil std. bricks)	446	480	534	562	603	0.9
Construction bricks (mil units)	379	410	450	483	528	1.1
Reinforced concrete assemblies (1000 cubic m)	102	102	115	118	114	0.1
LIGHT INDUSTRY						
Fabric (mil sq. m)	40	47	47	51	54	0.4
Cotton fabric (mil sq. m)	23	26	27	27	28	0.3
Wool fabric (mil sq. m)	3	3	3	3	3	0.4
Silk fabric (mil sq. m)	8	8	9	9	10	0.4
Stocking-hosiery (mil pairs)	5	5	10	18	20	0.9
Knitted goods (mil units)	10	10	11	11	11	0.6
Sewn goods (mil rubles)	172	180	180	191	195	0.7
Shoes (mil pairs)	5	5	5	6	5	0.6
PROCESSED FOODS						
Meat (1000 tons)	38	40	41	41	45	0.3
Cheese (tons)	827	830	773	865	944	0.1
Vegetable oil (1000 tons)	88	94	97	107	108	3.3
Animal fats (tons)	3,571	3,737	3,880	3,966	4,378	0.3
Confections (1000 tons)	23	23	26	29	33	0.6
Canned foods (mil std. cans)	54	56	55	75	80	0.4

Source: *Narodnoye Khozyayztvo Turkmenskoy SSR v 1989 g.*, pp. 193–197, 200–201; *Narodnoye Khozyayztvo SSSR v 1988 g.*, p. 382; *Narodnoye Khozyayztvo SSSR v 1990 g.*, pp. 395–423, 520–522.
Abbreviations: kWh—kilowatt hour; m—meters; mil—million; NA—not available; sq.—square; std.—standard.
—Zero or negligible.
* Reported data rounded to nearest whole number.

1160

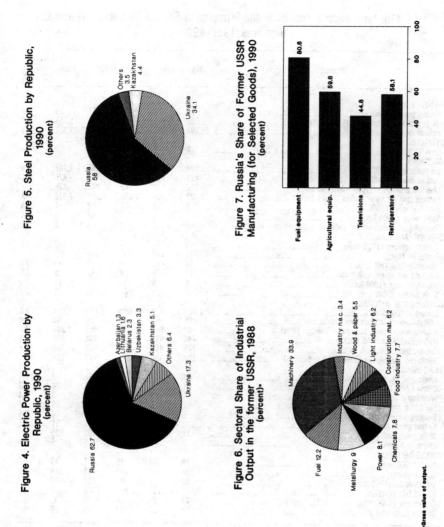

Figure 4. Electric Power Production by Republic, 1990 (percent)

Russia 62.7
Azerbaijan 1.3
Lithuania 1.6
Belarus 2.3
Uzbekistan 3.3
Kazakhstan 5.1
Others 6.4
Ukraine 17.3

Figure 5. Steel Production by Republic, 1990 (percent)

Russia 58
Others 3.5
Kazakhstan 4.4
Ukraine 34.1

Figure 6. Sectoral Share of Industrial Output in the former USSR, 1988 (percent)*

Machinery 33.9
Industry n.e.c. 3.4
Wood & paper 5.5
Light industry 6.2
Construction mat. 6.2
Food industry 7.7
Chemicals 7.8
Power 8.1
Metallurgy 9
Fuel 12.2

*Gross value of output.

Figure 7. Russia's Share of Former USSR Manufacturing (for Selected Goods), 1990 (percent)

Fuel equipment 80.8
Agricultural equip. 59.8
Televisions 44.8
Refrigerators 58.1

Source: *Narodnoye Khosyaystvo SSSR v 1990g.*, *Narodnoye Khosyaystvo RSFSR v 1990g.* and other official statistics of former republics.

2. TRANSPORTATION

The former Soviet Union's freight transport network relies upon railroads to provide the largest share of transport services. Measured in ton-kilometers, railroads carried 47 percent of freight traffic in 1989, with another 37 percent of freight being transported via pipeline (Table 42).

TABLE 42. Freight Traffic by Mode, 1989.[1]

(Million ton-kilometers)

Geographical Unit	Total	Rail	Pipeline	Sea	River	Truck	Air
U.S.S.R.	8,322,668	3,851,700	2,944,400	991,200	239,487	292,561	3,320
Russian Federation	NA	2,557,000	1,351,000	531,000	220,848	71,000	NA
Ukraine	1,071,136	497,300	199,600	285,700	11,848	76,588	100
Belarus	105,105	81,734	—	—	2,084	21,242	45
Moldova	22,306	15,632	—	—	260	6,393	21
Lithuania	NA	21,749	NA	NA	170	8,113	19
Latvia	NA	21,132	NA	65,156	302	2,394	25
Estonia	36,762	7,609	—	24,378	5	4,761	9
Georgia	80,944	12,671	91	61,214	—	6,937	30
Azerbaijan	NA	NA	NA	NA	—	9,425	NA
Armenia	NA	NA	—	—	—	4,713	NA
Kazakhstan	482,985	409,573	22,320	—	3,857	47,147	88
Uzbekistan	77,227	58,600	200	—	—	18,357	70
Kyrgyzstan	6,403	113	—	—	113	5,812	365
Tajikistan	16,435	11,174	—	—	—	5,229	32
Turkmenistan	NA	NA	—	—	—	4,450	324

Source: *Narodnoye Khozyaystvo SSSR v 1990g.* pp. 586, 587; *Transport i svyaz', 1990*, p. 41; SNG and Avista databases.
[1] 1989 data are used because 1990 data are lacking for several republics.
NA—Data not available.
—Zero or negligible.

However, despite their central role in transport, the railroad's share of transport services declined from 53 percent of freight traffic in 1980 to 47 percent in 1990. At the same time, the pipeline's share of freight increased from 28 percent to 37 percent. As of 1990, pipeline traffic was fairly evenly divided between petroleum (45 percent) and natural gas (55 percent).

Despite the length and density of the highway system (Tables 43 and 44), automotive transport plays a very limited role in freight transport. [21] For the most part, trucks are used for short hauls within cities and inter-modal transshipment. Long distance trucking is constrained by a variety of factors, such as a skeletal road network, antiquated trucks that are often in disrepair, a lack of well-equipped auto repair facilities (whose work is hampered by shortages of spare parts and lubricants), limited supplies of special-function vehicles, and insufficient materials-handling capability (to transfer cargo between transport modes). These shortcomings increase demand for rail services and prevent the economy from offering a more responsive transport system.

Automotive transport plays a more significant role in moving passengers. In 1989, buses carried 43 percent of this type of traffic, while railroads transported 36 percent (Table 45). Roughly 20 per-

---

[21] Although the road system is more extensive in terms of network length (Tables 43 and 44), the rail system is far more intensively used, with an annual average of 15.3 million ton-kilometers being carried by each kilometer of the rail network, compared to 0.2 million ton-kilometers per kilometer of roads.

TABLE 43. Transport Network: Railroads &
Highways, 1990.

(Thousand kilometers)

Geographical Unit	Railroads	Highways
U.S.S.R.	148.9	1,838.1
Russian Federation	87.2	879.1
Ukraine	22.8	273.7
Belarus	6.0	98.0
Moldova	1.2	20.0
Lithuania	3.0	45.0
Latvia	2.4	59.5
Estonia	1.0	30.3
Georgia	2.0	34.0
Azerbaijan	2.0	37.0
Armenia	0.8	11.3
Kazakhstan	14.5	189.0
Uzbekistan	3.0	78.0
Kyrgyzstan	0.4	30.3
Tajikistan	0.5	29.9
Turkmenistan	2.1	23.0

Source: *Narodnoye Khozyaystvo SSSR v 1990g.*
pp. 620–623.

TABLE 44. Density of Transport Network:
Railroads & Highways, 1990.

(Kilometers per 1000 sq. km.)

Geographical Unit	Railroads	Highways
U.S.S.R.	7	82
Russian Federation	5	51
Ukraine	38	453
Moldova	34	593
Lithuania	47	683
Latvia	37	922
Estonia	23	672
Belarus	29	472
Georgia	29	488
Azerbaijan	23	427
Armenia	28	379
Kazakhstan	5	70
Uzbekistan	7	174
Kyrgyzstan	2	153
Tajikistan	3	209
Turkmenistan	4	47

Source: *Narodnoye Khozyaystvo SSSR v 1990g.*
pp. 620–623; *Demograficheskiy Yezhegodnik SSSR.* 1990,
pp. 7–13.

cent of passenger traffic is moved by air. This latter mode was especially important for people travelling to remote areas where road connections were marginal or non-existent.

1163

TABLE 45. Passenger Traffic by mode, 1989.[1]

(Billion passenger-kilometers)

Geographical Unit	Total	Rail	Bus	Air	River
U.S.S.R.	1,125.5	410.7	480.4	229.0	5.4
Russian Federation	682.9	270.1	261.2	147.0	4.7
Ukraine	179.3	73.2	90.0	15.4	0.6
Belarus	41.4	16.5	19.1	5.8	—
Moldova	7.3	1.7	4.9	2.4	—
Lithuania	13.3	3.5	7.4	2.4	—
Latvia	14.6	5.4	5.9	3.3	—
Estonia	7.3	1.6	4.5	1.3	—
Georgia	NA	NA	8.5	5.3	—
Azerbaijan	16.8	2.0	7.2	4.9	—
Armenia	NA	NA	3.8	5.5	—
Kazakhstan	67.1	18.9	35.4	12.7	0.1
Uzbekistan	34.9	4.0	19.9	11.0	—
Kyrgyzstan	NA	NA	5.3	3.7	—
Tajikistan	9.8	0.8	3.8	5.2	—
Turkmenistan	NA	NA	3.5	3.3	—

Sources: *Narodnoye Khozyaystvo SSSR v 1990.* 1991, pp. 591, 595–596; *RSFSR v Tsifrakh v 1990g.* 1991, p. 235; *Narodne Gospodarstvo Ukrainskoi RSR u 1990 rotsi.* 1991, pp. 424; *Narodnoye Khozyaystvo Byelorusskoy SSSR v 1990g.* 1991, pp.–267–268; *Narodnoye Khozyaystvo Uzbekskoy SSR v 1990g.* 1991, p. 326; *Statisticheskiy Yezhegodnik Kazakhstana 1990.* 1991, p. 390; *Georgia v Tsifrakh, 1990.* 1991, p. 20; *Statisticheskiy Yezhegodnik Litviy, 1990.* 1991, p. 230; *Respublika Moldova v Tsifrakh, 1990.* 1991, p. 253; *Narodnoye Khozyaystvo Turkmenskoy SSR, 1989.* 1990, pp. 275–278; *Statisticheskiy Yezhegodnik Estonii, 1990.* 1991, p. 225; SNG and Avista databases.

[1] 1989 data are used due to insufficient republic level data for 1990.

NA—Data not available.

— Zero or negligible.

Data may not sum to total due to rounding.

F. FOREIGN ECONOMIC RELATIONS

Foreign trade (embracing both trade with former Soviet republics, as well as with foreign countries) was a critical outlet for extracted raw materials and an important source of modern technology for the country's aging manufacturing sector. The former Soviet Union's substantial oil and gas reserves permitted massive exports to Central and Western Europe (Tables 46a–o). At the same time, trade between the former republics was fostered by long-standing Soviet industrial and agricultural policies aimed at producing rapid economic and military growth. [22]

The former Soviet republics relied heavily upon inter-republic trade. Most former republics exported roughly one-third of their domestic production of industrial goods and imported a similar proportion of domestic consumption of industrial products (Table 47). Predictably, in Russia, due to the considerable size of its domestic economy, foreign trade in most products provides a smaller share of domestic consumption and claims a smaller share of domestic production than in most of the smaller republics. Yet, Russia's key role in energy trade is revealed in the 1989 data showing that fully one-third of its oil and gas production was exported to other former republics or abroad.

For the former Soviet Union as a whole, inter-republic trade accounted for the vast majority of foreign trade, 80 percent of exports and 64 percent of imports, expressed in domestic prices (Table 48). The former U.S.S.R.'s orientation in foreign trade changes somewhat when valued in foreign trade prices (roughly world market prices). Inter-republic trade's share of total exports decreases to 74 percent, while its share of imports increases to 73 percent.

Differences in the method of valuation significantly alter the balance of trade. When determined in domestic prices, the former Soviet Union was a net importer in 1989, with a trade deficit of 59,572 million rubles. But in foreign trade prices, the trade deficit declines to just 1,483 million rubles.

---

[22] In the former Soviet Union, international trade was largely conducted through a state monopoly system, in which offical Foreign Trade Organizations (FTOs) were "middlemen" between domestic producers and users and international markets. The FTOs operated in two price systems. Transactions in the domestic market were conducted in domestic prices and trade abroad was conduted in negotiated (generally world market) prices. Taking advantage of the Soviet price system allowed the FTOs to generate huge profits for the state in the conduct of international trade. This system also generated two sets of foreign trade accounts. Transactions on the world market were recorded in "foreign trade rubles," which were transactions prices coverted to rubles according to official exchange rates. These data were regularly reported in the official Soviet trade yearbook. A separate set of accounts was maintained in domestic prices. Data in domestic prices were almost never reported prior to 1989. Even before the dissolution of the Soviet Union, each republic became concerned with its balances of trade with the other republics and with the rest of the world. To address these concerns, the U.S.S.R. statistical office compiled a set of input-output tables with complete foreign trade vectors for both inter-republic and international trade valued in both domestic and foreign prices. These vectors were estimated using the assumption that relationships between foreign and domestic prices derived for the Union at a 110-sector level were applicable to each of the republics without adjustment. The data from this exercise were not formally published but were released by the statistical office. They form the basis of the data used in the section.

TABLE 46a. Foreign Trade: Russian Federation, 1989.

(Million rubles)

Trade Component	Total		Inter-republic		International	
	Exports	Imports	Exports	Imports	Exports	Imports
A. IN DOMESTIC PRICES						
Total	109,606.9	144,266.6	75,066.9	70,668.1	34,540.0	73,598.5
Industry	105,615.4	132,441.0	72,146.0	65,003.0	33,469.4	67,438.0
Power	662.6	538.0	546.6	538.0	116.0	—
Oil and gas	18,046.4	2,216.3	9,235.3	1,689.0	8,811.1	527.3
Coal	1,166.7	463.9	469.8	291.2	696.9	172.7
Other fuel	2.8	11.0	1.4	11.0	1.4	—
Ferrous metallurgy	7,449.9	8,271.0	5,980.7	6,238.4	1,469.2	2,032.6
Nonferrous metallurgy	5,102.6	3,242.7	3,158.6	1,626.0	1,944.0	1,616.7
Chemicals & petrochemicals	11,515.0	12,081.9	9,091.1	5,911.7	2,423.9	6,170.2
Machinery	37,997.1	48,094.0	26,364.9	20,971.7	11,632.2	27,122.3
Wood and paper	7,634.7	2,058.7	3,837.1	516.3	3,797.6	1,542.4
Construction materials	1,411.2	1,415.5	1,251.8	779.7	159.4	635.8
Light industry	8,179.7	28,367.2	7,297.1	12,506.6	882.6	15,860.6
Processed foods	4,072.5	23,718.2	2,808.6	12,766.7	1,263.9	10,951.5
Industry n.e.c.	2,374.2	1,962.6	2,103.0	1,156.7	271.2	805.9
Agriculture	792.4	9,207.5	468.1	3,357.4	324.3	5,850.1
Other	3,199.1	2,618.1	2,452.8	2,307.7	746.3	310.4
B. IN FOREIGN TRADE PRICES						
Total	140,922.8	108,462.5	88,353.8	59,738.3	52,569.0	48,724.2
Industry	137,089.0	101,898.4	85,547.9	56,091.3	51,541.1	45,807.1
Power	1,000.6	812.4	825.4	812.4	175.2	0.0
Oil and gas	43,988.2	4,227.8	22,240.9	3,250.9	21,747.3	976.9
Coal	1,061.7	526.7	427.5	265.0	634.2	261.7
Other fuel	2.9	14.1	1.8	1.1	1.1	0.0
Ferrous metallurgy	8,385.2	10,012.0	6,672.8	7,341.0	1,712.4	2,671.0
Nonferrous metallurgy	7,805.8	3,972.1	4,823.0	2,340.8	2,982.8	1,631.3
Chemicals & petrochemicals	8,707.8	8,767.8	6,902.7	4,455.7	1,805.1	4,312.1
Machinery	53,288.1	52,111.5	34,599.0	26,815.3	18,689.1	25,296.2
Wood and paper	4,847.8	1,341.6	2,454.1	321.6	2,393.7	1,020.0
Construction materials	1,419.2	1,157.3	1,239.9	807.4	179.3	349.9
Light industry	2,418.4	8,211.9	2,046.2	4,298.2	372.2	3,913.7
Processed foods	1,860.6	9,195.8	1,293.1	4,254.8	567.5	4,941.0
Industry n.e.c. [1]	2,302.7	1,547.4	2,021.5	1,114.1	281.2	433.3
Agriculture	346.1	3,948.4	231.9	1,308.4	114.2	2,640.0
Other	3,487.7	2,615.7	2,574.0	2,338.6	913.7	277.1

Source: Goskomstat USSR.
— Zero or negligible.
[1] Not elsewhere classified.

TABLE 46b. Foreign Trade: Ukraine, 1989.

(Million rubles)

Trade Component	Total		Inter-republic		International	
	Exports	Imports	Exports	Imports	Exports	Imports
A. IN DOMESTIC PRICES						
Total	48,061.7	54,539.6	40,466.7	39,970.9	7,595.0	14,568.7
Industry	46,030.6	52,387.1	38,688.8	38,954.3	7,341.8	13,432.8
Power	659.2	177.7	160.2	177.7	499.0	—
Oil and gas	863.2	4,381.4	368.4	4,320.5	494.8	60.9
Coal	858.0	371.9	275.8	293.4	582.2	78.5
Other fuel	—	2.2	—	2.2	—	—
Ferrous metallurgy	8,088.1	2,892.9	6,257.9	2,511.7	1,830.2	381.2
Nonferrous metallurgy	964.7	2,188.2	917.7	2,008.4	47.0	179.8
Chemicals & petrochemicals	3,943.6	5,883.3	3,131.9	4,476.3	811.7	1,407.0
Machinery	18,163.9	18,045.8	15,913.3	14,199.9	2,250.6	3,845.9
Wood and paper	446.3	1,933.1	379.2	1,528.7	67.1	404.4
Construction materials	709.1	507.8	678.3	424.3	30.8	83.5
Light industry	2,674.4	9,694.1	2,501.3	5,600.7	173.1	4,093.4
Processed foods	7,789.8	5,057.8	7,315.3	2,342.0	474.5	2,715.8
Industry n.e.c. [1]	870.3	1,250.9	789.5	1,068.5	80.8	182.4
Agriculture	1,494.5	1,409.3	1,430.4	290.6	64.1	1,118.7
Other	536.6	743.2	347.5	726.0	189.1	17.2
B. IN FOREIGN TRADE PRICES						
Total	47,816.8	53,432.0	39,129.3	44,196.1	8,687.5	9,235.9
Industry	46,402.0	52,034.8	37,964.1	43,276.9	8,437.9	8,757.9
Power	995.4	268.3	241.9	268.3	753.5	—
Oil and gas	1,474.1	10,702.2	636.6	10,632.2	837.5	70.0
Coal	780.7	385.9	250.9	267.0	529.8	118.9
Other fuel	—	2.8	—	2.8	—	—
Ferrous metallurgy	9,486.4	3,307.9	7,372.5	2,818.6	2,113.9	489.3
Nonferrous metallurgy	1,461.3	3,227.9	1,388.9	3,066.1	72.4	161.8
Chemicals & petrochemicals	2,961.5	4,439.8	2,406.2	3,428.9	555.3	1,010.9
Machinery	23,397.2	21,252.2	20,237.8	17,785.4	3,159.4	3,466.8
Wood and paper	292.0	1,261.4	253.2	1,000.4	38.8	261.0
Construction materials	711.8	471.8	680.3	419.0	31.5	52.8
Light industry	958.8	2,706.4	885.6	1,655.8	73.2	1,050.6
Processed foods	3,028.2	2,897.3	2,839.6	919.7	188.6	1,977.6
Industry n.e.c. [1]	854.6	1,110.9	770.6	1,012.7	84.0	98.2
Agriculture	836.1	601.3	814.6	138.7	21.5	462.6
Other	578.7	795.9	350.6	780.5	228.1	15.4

Source: Goskomstat USSR.
—Zero or negligible.
[1] Not elsewhere classified.

TABLE 46c. Foreign Trade: Belarus, 1989.

(Million rubles)

Trade Component	Total		Inter-republic		International	
	Exports	Imports	Exports	Imports	Exports	Imports
A. IN DOMESTIC PRICES						
Total	20,301.5	19,347.7	18,310.4	14,834.4	1,991.1	4,513.3
Industry	19,775.0	18,250.7	17,812.8	14,349.0	1,962.2	3,901.7
Power	54.7	147.2	33.4	147.2	21.3	—
Oil and gas	1,497.7	1,849.8	1,311.1	1,846.3	186.6	3.5
Coal	—	70.1	—	55.8	—	14.3
Other fuel	0.9	1.1	—	1.1	0.9	—
Ferrous metallurgy	190.3	1,371.9	172.1	1,309.5	18.2	62.4
Nonferrous metallurgy	73.5	422.9	72.8	411.2	0.7	11.7
Chemicals & petrochemicals	2,649.0	2,454.6	2,227.4	1,987.3	421.6	467.3
Machinery	8,870.7	6,571.9	7,892.9	4,972.5	977.8	1,599.4
Wood and paper	508.2	480.2	455.0	396.7	53.2	83.5
Construction materials	246.2	283.2	235.7	257.5	10.5	25.7
Light industry	3,678.5	2,605.9	3,567.5	1,547.4	111.0	1,058.5
Processed foods	1,610.2	1,699.3	1,567.6	1,142.6	42.6	556.7
Industry n.e.c. [1]	395.1	292.6	277.3	273.9	117.8	18.7
Agriculture	283.1	891.6	263.4	283.1	19.7	608.5
Other	243.4	205.4	234.2	202.3	9.2	3.1
B. IN FOREIGN TRADE PRICES						
Total	18,749.7	20,230.3	16,546.6	17,359.0	2,203.1	2,871.3
Industry	18,396.3	19,524.6	16,211.4	16,968.0	2,184.9	2,556.6
Power	82.6	222.3	50.4	222.3	32.2	—
Oil and gas	2,555.2	5,250.2	2,251.5	5,246.2	303.7	4.0
Coal	—	72.5	—	50.8	—	21.7
Other fuel	0.7	1.4	—	1.4	0.7	—
Ferrous metallurgy	222.9	1,556.4	200.7	1,474.9	22.2	81.5
Nonferrous metallurgy	113.9	641.5	112.8	633.2	1.1	8.3
Chemicals & petrochemicals	2,081.7	1,778.5	1,718.2	1,450.8	363.5	327.7
Machinery	10,643.5	7,570.8	9,388.0	6,176.3	1,255.5	1,394.5
Wood and paper	315.8	340.8	285.5	286.2	30.3	54.6
Construction materials	223.7	268.0	214.1	252.4	9.6	15.6
Light industry	1,020.0	746.2	974.3	479.1	45.7	267.1
Processed foods	799.4	804.2	780.8	432.7	18.6	371.5
Industry n.e.c. [1]	336.9	271.8	235.1	261.7	101.8	10.1
Agriculture	98.5	471.3	91.8	159.4	6.7	311.9
Other	254.9	234.4	243.4	231.6	11.5	2.8

Source: Goskomstat USSR.
—Zero or negligible.
[1] Not elsewhere classified.

TABLE 46d. Foreign Trade: Moldova, 1989.

(Million rubles)

Trade Component	Total		Inter-republic		International	
	Exports	Imports	Exports	Imports	Exports	Imports
A. IN DOMESTIC PRICES						
Total	5,456.4	6,611.5	5,186.4	5,191.5	270.0	1,420.0
Industry	5,089.5	6,175.8	4,822.7	4,883.2	266.8	1,292.6
Power	114.2	16.2	26.3	16.2	87.9	—
Oil and gas	—	519.6	—	519.6	—	—
Coal	—	129.1	—	128.6	—	0.5
Other fuel	—	—	—	—	—	—
Ferrous metallurgy	63.3	322.1	56.1	310.8	7.2	11.3
Nonferrous metallurgy	—	181.3	—	154.7	—	26.6
Chemicals & petrochemicals	197.6	711.2	195.5	588.9	2.1	122.3
Machinery	1,033.4	1,861.0	983.1	1,610.4	50.3	250.6
Wood and paper	112.6	261.5	109.3	223.6	3.3	37.9
Construction materials	60.3	150.7	59.7	119.2	0.6	31.5
Light industry	1,182.7	1,274.4	1,148.7	704.3	34.0	570.1
Processed foods	2,182.7	604.0	2,101.5	364.6	81.2	239.4
Industry n.e.c. [1]	142.7	144.7	142.5	142.3	0.2	2.4
Agriculture	322.0	216.6	319.4	90.3	2.6	126.3
Other	44.9	219.1	44.3	218.0	0.6	1.1
B. IN FOREIGN TRADE PRICES						
Total	2,844.0	5,904.9	2,612.2	5,105.7	231.8	799.2
Industry	2,711.8	5,553.2	2,481.4	4,832.9	230.4	720.3
Power	172.4	24.5	39.7	24.5	132.7	—
Oil and gas	—	870.7	—	870.7	—	—
Coal	—	117.8	—	117.0	—	0.8
Other fuel	—	—	—	—	—.	—
Ferrous metallurgy	77.6	370.0	68.7	355.5	8.9	14.5
Nonferrous metallurgy	—	258.7	—	239.8	—	18.9
Chemicals & petrochemicals	161.3	529.8	159.5	438.8	1.8	91.0
Machinery	1,115.1	2,239.7	1,071.5	2,027.3	43.6	212.4
Wood and paper	64.0	172.2	62.5	148.2	1.5	24.0
Construction materials	56.7	132.1	56.0	110.7	0.7	21.4
Light industry	381.0	348.9	367.5	204.0	13.5	144.9
Processed foods	554.0	355.7	526.5	164.6	27.5	191.1
Industry n.e.c. [1]	129.7	133.1	129.5	131.8	0.2	1.3
Agriculture	85.5	126.7	84.9	48.8	0.6	77.9
Other	46.7	225.0	45.9	224.0	0.8	1.0

Source: Goskomstat USSR.
—Zero or negligible.
[1] Not elsewhere classified.

TABLE 46e. Foreign Trade: Lithuania, 1989.

(Million rubles)

Trade Component	Total		Inter-republic		International	
	Exports	Imports	Exports	Imports	Exports	Imports
A. IN DOMESTIC PRICES						
Total	6,325.2	7,351.6	5,850.0	5,789.0	475.2	1,562.6
Industry	6,017.8	6,916.6	5,549.9	5,603.4	467.9	1,313.2
Power	201.2	93.2	201.2	93.2	—	—
Oil and gas	484.8	1,009.9	322.2	1,009.2	162.6	0.7
Coal	—	30.0	—	30.0	—	—
Other fuel	1.7	—	—	—	1.7	—
Ferrous metallurgy	32.4	332.8	28.9	310.8	3.5	22.0
Nonferrous metallurgy	8.5	163.1	8.4	156.9	0.1	6.2
Chemicals & petrochemicals	428.6	851.1	406.7	713.7	21.9	137.4
Machinery	1,966.4	2,492.2	1,848.5	2,120.4	117.9	371.8
Wood and paper	276.9	209.5	238.0	194.8	38.9	14.7
Construction materials	79.7	94.6	73.3	80.6	6.4	14.0
Light industry	1,476.9	1,052.9	1,445.8	647.4	31.1	405.5
Processed foods	1,008.8	499.4	926.6	163.7	82.2	335.7
Industry n.e.c. [1]	51.9	87.9	50.3	82.7	1.6	5.2
Agriculture	203.8	313.9	196.6	65.0	7.2	248.9
Other	103.6	121.1	103.5	120.6	0.1	0.5
B. IN FOREIGN TRADE PRICES						
Total	4,818.5	8,090.3	4,322.4	7,170.6	496.1	919.7
Industry	4,649.1	7,789.0	4,155.4	7,005.9	493.7	783.1
Power	303.8	140.7	303.8	140.7	—	—
Oil and gas	785.4	2,324.6	522.0	2,323.8	263.4	0.8
Coal	—	27.3	—	27.3	—	—
Other fuel	1.3	—	—	—	1.3	—
Ferrous metallurgy	27.4	383.1	23.7	355.3	3.7	27.8
Nonferrous metallurgy	13.2	247.6	13.0	243.2	0.2	4.4
Chemicals & petrochemicals	306.0	638.1	291.5	539.1	14.5	99.0
Machinery	2,004.8	3,148.3	1,876.7	2,832.3	128.1	316.0
Wood and paper	177.1	139.4	154.8	130.5	22.3	8.9
Construction materials	73.3	84.9	67.5	76.2	5.8	8.7
Light industry	436.4	288.3	424.2	182.5	12.2	105.8
Processed foods	473.8	287.3	433.3	78.4	40.5	208.9
Industry n.e.c. [1]	46.6	79.4	44.9	76.6	1.7	2.8
Agriculture	64.9	179.4	62.6	43.2	2.3	136.2
Other	104.5	121.9	104.4	121.5	0.1	0.4

Source: Goskomstat USSR.
—Zero or negligible.
[1] Not elsewhere classified.

TABLE 46f. Foreign Trade: Latvia, 1989.

(Million rubles)

Trade Component	Total		Inter-republic		International	
	Exports	Imports	Exports	Imports	Exports	Imports
A. IN DOMESTIC PRICES						
Total	5,413.2	6,030.0	5,039.3	4,520.2	373.9	1,509.8
Industry	4,900.5	5,598.4	4,589.9	4,323.5	310.6	1,274.9
Power	80.8	121.6	80.8	121.6	—	—
Oil and gas	6.0	486.8	6.0	485.7	—	1.1
Coal	—	26.4	—	2.6	—	23.8
Other fuel	—	0.2	—	0.2	—	—
Ferrous metallurgy	117.0	347.0	102.0	333.0	15.0	14.0
Nonferrous metallurgy	14.2	137.8	13.8	135.6	0.4	2.2
Chemicals & petrochemicals	693.0	700.8	682.5	618.3	10.5	82.5
Machinery	1,518.4	1,822.8	1,403.7	1,501.5	114.7	321.3
Wood and paper	147.6	159.4	119.3	139.8	28.3	19.6
Construction materials	83.0	93.4	79.9	87.6	3.1	5.8
Light industry	875.4	872.8	851.9	455.5	23.5	417.3
Processed foods	1,196.2	692.8	1,089.2	313.3	107.0	379.5
Industry n.e.c. [1]	168.9	136.6	160.8	128.8	8.1	7.8
Agriculture	142.8	355.9	101.9	123.9	40.9	232.0
Other	369.9	75.7	347.5	72.8	22.4	2.9
B. IN FOREIGN TRADE PRICES						
Total	4,412.7	5,640.2	4,148.6	4,747.2	264.1	893.0
Industry	3,994.9	5,374.8	3,768.8	4,602.4	226.1	772.4
Power	122.0	183.6	122.0	183.6	—	—
Oil and gas	9.7	809.7	9.7	808.4	—	1.3
Coal	—	38.5	—	2.4	—	36.1
Other fuel	—	0.3	—	0.3	—	—
Ferrous metallurgy	137.2	406.3	122.8	387.8	14.4	18.5
Nonferrous metallurgy	22.0	211.5	21.4	209.9	0.6	1.6
Chemicals & petrochemicals	525.4	497.9	516.7	438.3	8.7	59.6
Machinery	1,943.1	2,294.0	1,829.4	2,023.0	113.7	271.0
Wood and paper	93.9	111.5	78.0	99.0	15.9	12.5
Construction materials	65.1	88.3	62.2	85.9	2.9	2.4
Light industry	290.9	235.9	280.7	131.4	10.2	104.5
Processed foods	618.6	372.7	567.3	112.0	51.3	260.7
Industry n.e.c. [1]	167.0	124.6	158.6	120.4	8.4	4.2
Agriculture	46.9	187.8	31.4	69.8	15.5	118.0
Other	370.9	77.6	348.4	75.0	22.5	2.6

Source: Goskomstat USSR.
—Zero or negligible.
[1] Not elsewhere classified.

TABLE 46g. Foreign Trade: Estonia, 1989.

(Million rubles)

Trade Component	Total		Inter-republic		International	
	Exports	Imports	Exports	Imports	Exports	Imports
A. IN DOMESTIC PRICES						
Total	3,123.4	3,817.9	2,903.3	3,230.5	220.1	587.4
Industry	2,906.3	3,564.0	2,690.4	3,106.4	215.9	457.6
Power	118.6	24.0	118.6	12.6	—	11.4
Oil and gas	8.0	266.9	8.0	266.9	—	—
Coal	—	10.3	—	9.9	—	0.4
Other fuel	16.9	0.2	14.5	0.2	2.4	—
Ferrous metallurgy	11.4	123.3	5.9	118.2	5.5	5.1
Nonferrous metallurgy	8.3	92.6	8.3	92.2	—	0.4
Chemicals & petrochemicals	323.5	540.9	316.3	494.1	7.2	46.8
Machinery	560.7	1,128.2	538.7	1,054.2	22.0	74.0
Wood and paper	132.0	92.7	113.1	85.1	18.9	7.6
Construction materials	28.2	51.5	26.9	47.8	1.3	3.7
Light industry	877.5	739.7	830.0	534.3	47.5	205.4
Processed foods	756.6	415.9	650.5	316.3	106.1	99.6
Industry n.e.c. [1]	64.6	77.8	59.6	74.6	5.0	3.2
Agriculture	35.1	185.1	31.5	56.8	3.6	128.3
Other	182.0	68.8	181.4	67.3	0.6	1.5
B. IN FOREIGN TRADE PRICES						
Total	2,084.1	3,486.6	1,959.3	3,192.3	124.8	294.3
Industry	1,888.7	3,305.9	1,765.9	3,099.7	122.8	206.2
Power	179.1	40.5	179.1	19.0	—	21.5
Oil and gas	13.0	447.2	13.0	447.2	—	—
Coal	—	9.6	—	9.0	—	0.6
Other fuel	20.5	0.3	18.7	0.3	1.8	—
Ferrous metallurgy	13.8	137.7	6.9	131.2	6.9	6.5
Nonferrous metallurgy	12.9	143.2	12.9	142.9	—	0.3
Chemicals & petrochemicals	234.7	403.4	230.0	371.8	4.7	31.6
Machinery	622.5	1,574.6	594.2	1,514.9	28.3	59.7
Wood and paper	72.3	61.7	63.5	56.8	8.8	4.9
Construction materials	29.2	46.2	28.2	45.1	1.0	1.1
Light industry	275.9	236.2	257.7	182.8	18.2	53.4
Processed foods	350.0	134.4	302.1	109.5	47.9	24.9
Industry n.e.c. [1]	64.8	70.9	59.6	69.2	5.2	1.7
Agriculture	11.0	108.5	9.8	21.7	1.2	86.8
Other	184.4	72.2	183.6	70.9	0.8	1.3

Source: Goskomstat USSR.
—Zero or negligible.
[1] Not elsewhere classified.

TABLE 46h. Foreign Trade: Georgia, 1989.

(Million rubles)

Trade Component	Total		Inter-republic		International	
	Exports	Imports	Exports	Imports	Exports	Imports
A. IN DOMESTIC PRICES						
Total	6,084.2	6,469.0	5,718.8	4,888.3	365.4	1,580.7
Industry	5,789.3	6,008.1	5,427.6	4,587.6	361.7	1,420.5
Power	31.9	49.9	19.7	49.9	12.2	—
Oil and gas	68.0	360.1	5.0	359.8	63.0	0.3
Coal	7.0	17.7	7.0	17.7	—	—
Other fuel	—	0.2	—	0.2	—	—
Ferrous metallurgy	375.6	443.3	314.4	429.6	61.2	13.7
Nonferrous metallurgy	47.5	105.6	42.8	94.1	4.7	11.5
Chemicals & petrochemicals	343.4	543.8	336.0	479.6	7.4	64.2
Machinery	869.4	1,522.0	822.0	1,363.4	47.4	158.6
Wood & paper	53.1	244.4	52.9	209.6	0.2	34.8
Construction materials	33.0	148.0	33.0	133.9	—	14.1
Light industry	1,284.9	1,287.2	1,244.7	710.0	40.2	577.2
Processed foods	2,572.9	1,142.1	2,447.6	601.8	125.3	540.3
Industry n.e.c. [1]	102.6	143.8	102.5	138.0	0.1	5.8
Agriculture	190.4	358.0	186.9	197.9	3.5	160.1
Other	104.5	102.9	104.3	102.8	0.2	0.1
B. IN FOREIGN TRADE PRICES						
Total	3,452.8	5,475.6	3,096.2	4,792.2	356.6	683.4
Industry	3,301.0	5,133.7	2,945.3	4,556.6	355.7	577.1
Power	48.1	75.3	29.7	75.3	18.4	—
Oil and gas	110.2	739.6	8.1	739.3	102.1	0.3
Coal	6.4	16.1	6.4	16.1	—	—
Other fuel	—	0.3	—	0.3	—	—
Ferrous metallurgy	455.8	513.0	380.5	495.6	75.3	17.4
Nonferrous metallurgy	51.6	151.5	44.3	143.3	7.3	8.2
Chemicals & petrochemicals	243.7	409.0	238.6	367.0	5.1	42.0
Machinery	1,166.9	1,956.5	1,098.8	1,821.8	68.1	134.7
Wood and paper	36.7	150.3	36.5	131.2	0.2	19.1
Construction materials	35.3	145.5	35.3	139.7	—	5.8
Light industry	428.2	373.2	410.2	232.4	18.0	140.8
Processed foods	624.3	464.9	563.2	259.2	61.1	205.7
Industry n.e.c. [1]	93.8	138.5	93.7	135.4	0.1	3.1
Agriculture	45.4	233.0	44.8	126.8	0.6	106.2
Other	106.4	108.9	106.1	108.8	0.3	0.1

Source: Goskomstat USSR.
—Zero or negligible.
[1] Not elsewhere classified.

1173

TABLE 46i. Foreign Trade: Azerbaijan, 1989.

(Million rubles)

Trade Component	Total		Inter-republic		International	
	Exports	Imports	Exports	Imports	Exports	Imports
A. IN DOMESTIC PRICES						
Total	7,122.9	5,189.8	6,674.9	3,794.3	448.0	1,395.5
Industry	6,656.3	4,895.3	6,221.8	3,728.6	434.5	1,166.7
Power	40.3	23.4	40.3	23.4	—	—
Oil and gas	988.8	293.9	886.1	292.4	102.7	1.5
Coal	—	6.0	—	6.0	—	—
Other fuel	—	—	—	—	—	—
Ferrous metallurgy	91.6	288.2	88.5	206.0	3.1	82.2
Nonferrous metallurgy	113.8	91.4	102.2	91.3	11.6	0.1
Chemicals & petrochemicals	609.6	501.5	601.0	407.1	8.6	94.4
Machinery	1,118.2	1,271.5	1,012.3	1,104.5	105.9	167.0
Wood and paper	22.4	131.1	22.4	99.2	—	31.9
Construction materials	45.7	123.2	45.6	111.3	0.1	11.9
Light industry	1,651.6	982.9	1,479.1	620.0	172.5	362.9
Processed foods	1,858.5	1,052.1	1,828.5	642.3	30.0	409.8
Industry n.e.c. [1]	115.8	130.1	115.8	125.1	—	5.0
Agriculture	321.3	280.2	312.6	51.8	8.7	228.4
Other	145.3	14.3	140.5	13.9	4.8	0.4
B. IN FOREIGN TRADE PRICES						
Total	4,990.5	4,234.1	4,589.9	3,545.0	400.6	689.1
Industry	4,743.3	4,086.4	4,350.2	3,502.6	393.1	583.8
Power	60.9	35.3	60.9	35.3	—	—
Oil and gas	1,663.1	757.7	1,496.7	756.0	166.4	1.7
Coal	—	5.5	—	5.5	—	—
Other fuel	—	—	—	—	—	—
Ferrous metallurgy	107.4	347.2	103.6	241.1	3.8	106.1
Nonferrous metallurgy	175.9	139.6	157.9	139.5	18.0	0.1
Chemicals & petrochemicals	453.1	391.3	447.3	327.5	5.8	63.8
Machinery	1,145.1	1,402.3	1,039.1	1,260.1	106.0	142.2
Wood and paper	12.4	82.3	12.4	6.3	—	76.0
Construction materials	38.3	106.6	38.2	103.5	0.1	3.1
Light industry	559.9	265.7	478.2	171.9	81.7	93.8
Processed foods	411.4	429.9	400.1	278.9	11.3	151.0
Industry n.e.c. [1]	115.8	123.0	115.8	120.3	—	2.7
Agriculture	98.6	132.4	97.1	27.5	1.5	104.9
Other	148.6	15.3	142.6	14.9	6.0	0.4

Source: Goskomstat USSR.
—Zero or negligible.
[1] Not elsewhere classified.

TABLE 46j. Foreign Trade: Armenia, 1989.

(Million rubles)

Trade Component	Total		Inter-republic		International	
	Exports	Imports	Exports	Imports	Exports	Imports
A. IN DOMESTIC PRICES						
Total	3,691.2	4,897.9	3,597.8	3,842.0	93.4	1,055.9
Industry	3,658.8	4,692.4	3,566.3	3,747.2	92.5	945.2
Power	12.2	13.3	12.2	13.3	—	—
Oil and gas	—	407.0	—	407.0	—	—
Coal	—	15.2	—	15.2	—	—
Other fuel	—	0.1	—	0.1	—	—
Ferrous metallurgy	19.1	283.6	18.5	280.5	0.6	3.1
Nonferrous metallurgy	112.1	140.5	107.4	91.2	4.7	49.3
Chemicals & petrochemicals	337.7	385.2	328.7	311.6	9.0	73.6
Machinery	860.9	1,005.2	826.6	918.4	34.3	86.8
Wood and paper	17.7	135.5	17.7	87.7	—	47.8
Construction materials	38.3	98.1	37.9	78.1	0.4	20.0
Light industry	1,426.9	1,107.3	1,399.8	798.7	27.1	308.6
Processed foods	640.9	945.6	626.9	595.4	14.0	350.2
Industry n.e.c. [1]	193.0	155.8	190.6	150.0	2.4	5.8
Agriculture	9.9	199.5	9.1	88.8	0.8	110.7
Other	22.5	6.0	22.4	6.0	0.1	—
B. IN FOREIGN TRADE PRICES						
Total	2,364.7	3,693.8	2,291.8	3,211.9	72.9	481.9
Industry	2,338.2	3,556.3	2,265.5	3,154.0	72.7	402.3
Power	18.4	20.1	18.4	20.1	—	—
Oil and gas	—	714.5	—	714.5	—	—
Coal	—	13.8	—	13.8	—	—
Other fuel	—	0.1	—	0.1	—	—
Ferrous metallurgy	22.9	325.5	22.2	321.5	0.7	4.0
Nonferrous metallurgy	126.1	156.4	118.8	121.4	7.3	35.0
Chemicals & petrochemicals	267.1	269.2	261.6	221.0	5.5	48.2
Machinery	978.2	1,048.7	939.5	981.9	38.7	66.8
Wood and paper	9.6	84.1	9.6	55.3	—	28.8
Construction materials	44.1	77.2	43.7	71.3	0.4	5.9
Light industry	532.9	314.8	521.6	236.6	11.3	78.2
Processed foods	146.6	393.2	140.3	260.9	6.3	132.3
Industry n.e.c. [1]	192.3	138.7	189.8	135.6	2.5	3.1
Agriculture	2.6	130.7	2.5	51.1	0.1	79.6
Other	23.9	6.8	23.8	6.8	0.1	—

Source: Goskomstat USSR.
—Zero or negligible.
[1] Not elsewhere classified.

TABLE 46k. Foreign Trade: Kazakhstan, 1989.

(Million rubles)

Trade Component	Total		Inter-republic		International	
	Exports	Imports	Exports	Imports	Exports	Imports
A. IN DOMESTIC PRICES						
Total	9,094.0	17,569.0	8,201.2	14,570.7	892.8	2,998.3
Industry	7,730.6	16,948.9	6,861.6	14,214.7	869.0	2,734.2
Power	223.5	370.8	223.5	370.8	—	—
Oil and gas	875.0	1,446.8	860.1	1,443.2	14.9	3.6
Coal	311.5	154.6	311.5	154.6	—	—
Other fuel	—	0.7	—	0.7	—	—
Ferrous metallurgy	1,077.0	1,039.7	888.7	976.6	188.3	63.1
Nonferrous metallurgy	790.5	272.2	492.0	251.8	298.5	20.4
Chemicals & petrochemicals	1,121.1	1,703.0	967.8	1,577.0	153.3	126.0
Machinery	836.5	5,358.7	790.0	4,753.6	46.5	605.1
Wood and paper	25.9	988.0	25.6	904.7	0.3	83.3
Construction materials	145.4	313.2	143.5	285.2	1.9	28.0
Light industry	1,625.0	3,113.2	1,495.1	1,849.2	129.9	1,264.0
Processed foods	617.5	1,871.3	582.2	1,346.5	35.3	524.8
Industry n.e.c. [1]	81.7	316.7	81.6	300.8	0.1	15.9
Agriculture	1,146.0	457.5	1,122.8	193.6	23.2	263.9
Other	217.4	162.6	216.8	162.4	0.6	0.2
B. IN FOREIGN TRADE PRICES						
Total	9,405.9	16,631.3	8,409.8	15,075.5	996.1	1,555.8
Industry	8,427.1	16,282.5	7,439.5	14,822.6	987.6	1,459.9
Power	337.5	559.9	337.5	559.9	—	—
Oil and gas	2,454.3	3,180.6	2,405.3	3,176.5	49.0	4.1
Coal	283.5	140.7	283.5	140.7	—	—
Other fuel	—	0.9	—	0.9	—	—
Ferrous metallurgy	1,228.9	1,177.0	1,002.2	1,087.0	226.7	90.0
Nonferrous metallurgy	1,172.9	399.6	710.3	378.1	462.6	21.5
Chemicals & petrochemicals	833.5	1,364.1	732.1	1,284.8	101.4	79.3
Machinery	1,146.3	6,555.7	1,074.4	6,021.7	71.9	534.0
Wood and paper	19.4	600.9	19.2	552.5	0.2	48.4
Construction materials	169.3	278.5	166.9	267.3	2.4	11.2
Light industry	422.2	906.5	364.4	600.0	57.8	306.5
Processed foods	290.7	820.0	275.2	463.6	15.5	356.4
Industry n.e.c. [1]	68.6	298.1	68.5	289.6	0.1	8.5
Agriculture	749.1	170.6	741.4	74.9	7.7	95.7
Other	229.7	178.2	228.9	178.0	0.8	0.2

Source: Goskomstat USSR.
—Zero or negligible.
[1] Not elsewhere classified.

TABLE 46I. Foreign Trade: Uzbekistan, 1989.

(Million rubles)

Trade Component	Total		Inter-republic		International	
	Exports	Imports	Exports	Imports	Exports	Imports
A. IN DOMESTIC PRICES						
Total	10,169.3	14,158.3	8,541.6	12,046.0	1,627.7	2,112.3
Industry	9,154.7	13,140.2	7,582.2	11,275.4	1,572.5	1,864.8
Power	213.9	186.8	212.8	186.8	1.1	—
Oil and gas	645.6	1,031.6	624.4	1,029.7	21.2	1.9
Coal	8.1	41.9	8.1	41.9	—	—
Other fuel	—	0.2	—	0.2	—	—
Ferrous metallurgy	111.5	676.1	111.5	655.7	—	20.4
Nonferrous metallurgy	468.1	424.5	464.5	413.5	3.6	11.0
Chemicals & petrochemicals	893.7	1,110.6	833.4	973.7	60.3	136.9
Machinery	1,190.1	3,552.6	1,104.2	3,323.7	85.9	228.9
Wood and paper	35.0	724.9	35.0	666.6	—	58.3
Construction materials	69.0	227.6	69.0	216.2	—	11.4
Light industry	4,658.9	2,761.3	3,300.5	1,855.9	1,358.4	905.4
Processed foods	795.3	2,155.5	762.3	1,669.4	33.0	486.1
Industry n.e.c. [1]	65.5	246.6	56.5	242.1	9.0	4.5
Agriculture	757.2	661.1	703.6	413.7	53.6	247.4
Other	257.4	357.0	255.8	356.9	1.6	0.1
B. IN FOREIGN TRADE PRICES						
Total	7,754.1	12,460.0	6,821.8	11,519.0	932.3	941.0
Industry	7,288.8	11,637.6	6,368.2	10,878.1	920.6	759.5
Power	323.0	282.1	321.3	282.1	1.7	—
Oil and gas	1,297.3	2,218.6	1,263.0	2,216.4	34.3	2.2
Coal	7.4	38.1	7.4	38.1	—	—
Other fuel	—	0.3	—	—	—	—
Ferrous metallurgy	134.3	755.4	134.3	729.9	—	25.5
Nonferrous metallurgy	689.6	622.1	684.0	614.3	5.6	7.8
Chemicals & petrochemicals	588.9	820.9	550.8	725.2	38.1	95.7
Machinery	1,772.1	4,304.6	1,633.2	4,109.8	138.9	194.8
Wood and paper	18.7	426.7	18.7	395.0	—	31.7
Construction materials	64.7	213.7	64.7	209.6	—	4.1
Light industry	2,074.7	765.3	1,397.4	546.9	677.3	218.4
Processed foods	254.9	952.5	239.6	775.6	15.3	176.9
Industry n.e.c. [1]	63.2	237.3	53.8	234.9	9.4	2.4
Agriculture	201.3	450.9	191.6	269.5	9.7	181.4
Other	264.0	371.5	262.0	371.4	2.0	0.1

Source: Goskomstat USSR.
—Zero or negligible.
[1] Not elsewhere classified.

TABLE 46m. Foreign Trade: Kyrgyzstan, 1989.

(Million rubles)

Trade Component	Total		Inter-republic		International	
	Exports	Imports	Exports	Imports	Exports	Imports
A. IN DOMESTIC PRICES						
Total	2,600.2	4,296.0	2,549.0	3,361.6	51.2	934.4
Industry	2,478.2	4,021.8	2,433.0	3,183.3	45.2	838.5
Power	80.2	28.6	80.2	28.6	—	—
Oil and gas	11.0	324.6	11.0	324.6	—	—
Coal	22.4	32.2	22.4	32.2	—	—
Other fuel	—	—	—	—	—	—
Ferrous metallurgy	10.5	172.8	8.5	167.8	2.0	5.0
Nonferrous metallurgy	141.9	99.2	124.1	91.2	17.8	8.0
Chemicals & petrochemicals	24.3	409.2	24.3	349.2	—	60.0
Machinery	951.0	1,089.4	945.9	1,019.5	5.1	69.9
Wood and paper	4.5	136.3	4.5	128.7	—	7.6
Construction materials	17.1	71.5	16.7	67.0	0.4	4.5
Light industry	660.1	894.7	650.1	559.8	10.0	334.9
Processed foods	528.9	692.0	519.0	344.2	9.9	347.8
Industry n.e.c.[1]	26.3	71.3	26.3	70.5	—	0.8
Agriculture	101.6	183.4	95.7	88.1	5.9	95.3
Other	20.4	90.8	20.3	90.2	0.1	0.6
B. IN FOREIGN TRADE PRICES						
Total	2,196.8	3,706.4	2,154.3	3,091.6	42.5	614.8
Industry	2,142.1	3,490.7	2,101.3	2,935.3	40.8	555.4
Power	121.1	43.2	121.1	43.2	—	—
Oil and gas	35.2	546.8	35.2	546.8	—	—
Coal	20.4	29.3	20.4	29.3	—	—
Other fuel	—	—	—	—	—	—
Ferrous metallurgy	12.6	187.3	10.5	180.9	2.1	6.4
Nonferrous metallurgy	172.6	122.8	148.4	117.1	24.2	5.7
Chemicals & petrochemicals	19.3	313.5	19.3	268.8	—	44.7
Machinery	1,386.1	1,258.2	1,378.2	1,203.4	7.9	54.8
Wood and paper	2.7	83.5	2.7	79.2	—	4.3
Construction materials	15.6	65.7	15.2	64.0	0.4	1.7
Light industry	157.8	276.6	155.6	193.6	2.2	83.0
Processed foods	176.1	496.8	172.1	142.4	4.0	354.4
Industry n.e.c.[1]	22.6	67.0	22.6	66.6	—	0.4
Agriculture	33.0	123.2	31.4	64.3	1.6	58.9
Other	21.7	92.5	21.6	92.0	0.1	0.5

Source: Goskomstat USSR.
— Zero or negligible.
[1] Not elsewhere classified.

TABLE 46n. Foreign Trade: Tajikistan, 1989.

(Million rubles)

Trade Component	Total		Inter-republic		International	
	Exports	Imports	Exports	Imports	Exports	Imports
A. IN DOMESTIC PRICES						
Total	2,527.0	3,930.2	2,176.2	3,249.3	350.8	680.9
Industry	2,385.4	3,661.4	2,040.3	3,059.6	345.1	601.8
Power	46.1	82.6	46.1	82.6	—	—
Oil and gas	13.2	299.9	13.2	299.9	—	—
Coal	3.6	12.5	3.6	12.5	—	—
Other fuel	—	—	—	—	—	—
Ferrous metallurgy	3.5	116.3	3.5	108.1	—	8.2
Nonferrous metallurgy	443.1	242.7	302.2	192.4	140.9	50.3
Chemicals & petrochemicals	114.7	367.2	114.0	310.2	0.7	57.0
Machinery	248.9	931.9	242.5	864.0	6.4	67.9
Wood and paper	7.4	126.3	7.4	110.4	—	15.9
Construction materials	33.0	69.6	32.9	65.7	0.1	3.9
Light industry	1,233.7	768.7	1,040.4	484.9	193.3	283.8
Processed foods	234.5	568.1	230.8	455.0	3.7	113.1
Industry n.e.c. [1]	3.7	75.5	3.7	73.9	—	1.6
Agriculture	81.4	189.7	75.7	110.7	5.7	79.0
Other	60.2	79.1	60.2	79.0	0.0	0.1
B. IN FOREIGN TRADE PRICES						
Total	1,804.0	3,376.2	1,483.0	3,046.0	321.0	330.2
Industry	1,720.7	3,165.0	1,400.7	2,889.2	320.0	275.8
Power	69.6	124.7	69.6	124.7	—	—
Oil and gas	40.0	505.4	40.0	505.4	—	—
Coal	3.3	11.4	3.3	11.4	—	—
Other fuel	—	—	—	—	—	—
Ferrous metallurgy	4.0	128.0	4.0	117.4	—	10.6
Nonferrous metallurgy	676.8	350.6	458.4	297.9	218.4	52.7
Chemicals & petrochemicals	84.0	269.4	83.5	230.8	0.5	38.6
Machinery	280.5	1,123.6	273.6	1,072.8	6.9	50.8
Wood and paper	4.0	73.6	4.0	64.9	—	8.7
Construction materials	33.9	67.2	33.8	65.9	0.1	1.3
Light industry	446.0	212.1	353.5	144.5	92.5	67.6
Processed foods	74.9	228.3	73.3	183.7	1.6	44.6
Industry n.e.c. [1]	3.7	70.7	3.7	69.8	—	0.9
Agriculture	20.6	131.3	19.6	77.0	1.0	54.3
Other	62.7	79.9	62.7	79.8	—	0.1

Source: Goskomstat USSR.
—Zero or negligible.
[1] Not elsewhere classified.

1179

TABLE 46o. Foreign Trade: Turkmenistan, 1989.

(Million rubles)

Trade Component	Total Exports	Total Imports	Inter-republic Exports	Inter-republic Imports	International Exports	International Imports
A. IN DOMESTIC PRICES						
Total	2,659.4	3,333.4	2,418.2	2,743.9	241.2	589.5
Industry	2,425.9	3,150.3	2,197.4	2,611.5	228.5	538.8
Power	69.6	9.6	69.6	9.6	—	—
Oil and gas	745.1	100.0	743.0	100.0	2.1	—
Coal	—	6.6	—	6.6	—	—
Other fuel	—	—	—	—	—	—
Ferrous metallurgy	3.4	102.4	3.4	83.9	—	18.5
Nonferrous metallurgy	5.2	9.6	5.2	9.5	—	0.1
Chemicals & petrochemicals	152.3	230.4	151.5	209.4	0.8	21.0
Machinery	39.4	1,042.0	38.5	949.4	0.9	92.6
Wood and paper	0.3	137.0	0.3	124.9	—	12.1
Construction materials	24.2	59.0	24.1	54.2	0.1	4.8
Light industry	1,299.1	696.6	1,076.0	453.3	223.1	243.3
Processed foods [1]	86.6	621.8	85.1	477.9	1.5	143.9
Industry n.e.c. [1]	0.7	135.3	0.7	132.8	—	2.5
Agriculture	132.5	84.3	127.6	33.6	4.9	50.7
Other	101.0	98.8	93.2	98.8	7.8	—
B. IN FOREIGN TRADE PRICES						
Total	2,590.5	2,866.7	2,466.7	2,595.3	123.8	271.4
Industry	2,443.6	2,716.3	2,330.4	2,480.5	113.2	235.8
Power	105.1	14.5	105.1	14.5	—	—
Oil and gas	1,477.7	162.0	1,474.3	162.0	3.4	—
Coal	—	6.0	—	6.0	—	—
Other fuel	—	—	—	—	—	—
Ferrous metallurgy	3.4	114.9	3.4	91.1	—	23.8
Nonferrous metallurgy	8.1	14.8	8.1	14.7	—	0.1
Chemicals & petrochemicals	151.2	174.4	150.7	160.2	0.5	14.2
Machinery	40.6	1,500.8	40.0	1,427.4	0.6	73.4
Wood and paper	0.3	77.8	0.3	71.2	—	6.6
Construction materials	24.5	54.2	24.4	52.4	0.1	1.8
Light industry	600.6	209.1	492.5	149.9	108.1	59.2
Processed foods	31.4	256.8	30.9	201.4	0.5	55.4
Industry n.e.c. [1]	0.7	131.0	0.7	129.7	—	1.3
Agriculture	42.3	51.4	41.5	15.8	0.8	35.6
Other	104.6	99.0	94.8	99.0	9.8	—

Source: Goskomstat USSR.
—Zero or negligible.
[1] Not elsewhere classified.

TABLE 47. Ratio of Exports and Imports to Domestic Production and Use, 1989.

(Percent)

Component	Russian Federation				Ukraine				Belarus				Moldova				Lithuania			
	Inter-republic		International		Inter-republic		International		Inter-republic		International		Inter-republic		International		Inter-republic		International	
	Exports	Imports	Exports	Imports	Exports	Imports	Exports	Imports	Exports	Imports	Exports	Imports	Exports	Imports	Exports	Imports	Exports	Imports	Exports	Imports
Industry	9	8	4	8	23.0	25.0	19.0	19.0	35.0	29.0	4.0	8.0	36.0	33.0	—	2.0	32.0	30.0	9.0	7.0
Power	2	2	—	1	18.0	5.0	3.0	3.0	3.0	11.0	2.0	—	6.0	5.0	21.0	—	32.0	18.0	—	—
Oil and gas	17	4	16	1	20.0	99.0	5.0	40.0	42.0	53.0	6.0	15.0	—	84.0	—	—	33.0	67.0	17.0	—
Coal	5	4	8	2	11.0	6.0	4.0	4.0	—	60.0	—	—	—	85.0	—	—	—	81.0	—	—
Other fuels	—	3	—	—	—	6.0	—	4.0	—	1.0	1.0	—	—	—	—	—	—	—	8.0	8.0
Ferrous metallurgy	12	12	3	4	48.0	23.0	32.0	17.0	34.0	78.0	4.0	4.0	39.0	77.0	5.0	3.0	15.0	63.0	2.0	4.0
Nonferrous metallurgy	12	6	7	6	69.0	97.0	43.0	60.0	80.0	93.0	1.0	3.0	—	84.0	—	14.0	69.0	94.0	1.0	12.0
Chemicals & petrochemicals	19	12	5	13	24.0	31.0	25.0	31.0	51.0	47.0	10.0	11.0	46.0	63.0	2.0	13.0	58.0	63.0	3.0	8.0
Machine building and metalworking	14	10	6	13	41.0	37.0	28.0	25.0	49.0	36.0	6.0	12.0	38.0	47.0	2.0	7.0	45.0	46.0	3.0	2.0
Wood and paper	11	2	11	5	5.0	18.0	7.0	22.0	22.0	20.0	3.0	4.0	22.0	35.0	1.0	6.0	28.0	25.0	5.0	2.0
Construction materials	4	8	—	2	9.0	6.0	8.0	5.0	11.0	12.0	—	1.0	10.0	17.0	—	4.0	8.0	9.0	1.0	2.0
Light industry	6	9	1	11	4.0	9.0	11.0	19.0	36.0	17.0	1.0	12.0	38.0	23.0	1.0	18.0	40.0	20.0	2.0	13.0
Food industry	2	4	1	8	7.0	7.0	16.0	6.0	16.0	12.0	7.0	6.0	43.0	11.0	2.0	7.0	22.0	4.0	—	9.0
Industry n.e.c.[1]	7	2	1	3	11.0	14.0	10.0	13.0	15.0	16.0	—	1.0	17.0	17.0	1.0	—	4.0	6.0	—	—
Agriculture	—	2	—	4	1.0	1.0	3.0	1.0	2.0	2.0	—	4.0	6.0	2.0	2.0	2.0	3.0	1.0	—	4.0

TABLE 47. Ratio of Exports and Imports to Domestic Production and Use, 1989.—Continued

(Percent)

	Latvia				Estonia				Georgia				Azerbaijan				Armenia			
	Inter-republic		International		Inter-republic		International		Inter-republic		International		Inter-republic		International		Inter-republic		International	
	Exports	Imports	Exports	Imports	Exports	Imports	Exports	Imports	Exports	Imports	Exports	Imports	Exports	Imports	Exports	Imports	Exports	Imports	Exports	Imports
Industry	33.0	29.0	2.0	9.0	32.0	35.0	3.0	5.0	35	29	2	9	36.0	24.0	3.0	8.0	21.0	20.0	1.0	5.0
Power	37.0	47.0	—	—	37.0	6.0	—	5.0	5	13	3	—	8.0	5.0	—	—	2.0	3.0	—	—
Oil and gas	6.0	84.0	—	—	9.0	76.0	—	—	1	57	19	—	35.0	16.0	4.0	—	—	14.0	—	—
Coal	—	9.0	—	83.0	—	61.0	—	2.0	13	27	—	—	—	59.0	—	—	—	78.0	—	—
Other fuels	—	1.0	—	—	7.0	—	1.0	—	—	15	12	—	—	—	—	15.0	—	100.0	—	1.0
Ferrous metallurgy	53.0	79.0	8.0	3.0	20.0	83.0	18.0	4.0	59	72	8	10	26.0	38.0	1.0	—	5.0	46.0	2.0	15.0
Nonferrous metallurgy	90.0	98.0	3.0	2.0	98.0	99.0	—	—	75	82	1	7	33.0	32.0	4.0	12.0	35.0	27.0	1.0	8.0
Chemicals & petrochemicals	63.0	56.0	1.0	8.0	66.0	71.0	2.0	7.0	49	54	2	5	66.0	51.0	1.0	6.0	36.0	33.0	1.0	3.0
Machine building and metalworking	41.0	40.0	3.0	9.0	39.0	54.0	2.0	4.0	32	42	—	5	36.0	37.0	4.0	8.0	30.0	31.0	—	3.0
Wood and paper	17.0	19.0	4.0	3.0	19.0	15.0	3.0	1.0	11	32	1	5	7.0	23.0	—	2.0	6.0	20.0	—	11.0
Construction materials	16.0	17.0	1.0	1.0	7.0	11.0	—	1.0	4	13	2	1	7.0	15.0	—	13.0	6.0	11.0	1.0	3.0
Light industry	31.0	16.0	1.0	15.0	44.0	31.0	3.0	12.0	37	21	1	17	42.0	22.0	5.0	10.0	40.0	25.0	—	10.0
Food industry	27.0	9.0	3.0	11.0	28.0	16.0	5.0	5.0	43	14	2	13	38.0	16.0	1.0	1.0	13.0	12.0	—	7.0
Industry n.e.c.[1]	17.0	14.0	1.0	1.0	10.0	12.0	1.0	1.0	15	19	1	1	22.0	24.0	—	5.0	37.0	31.0	—	1.0
Agriculture	3.0	3.0	1.0	5.0	3.0	5.0	—	11.0	5	5	—	4	7.0	1.0	—	—	—	2.0	—	2.0

TABLE 47. Ratio of Exports and Imports to Domestic Production and Use, 1989.—Continued

(Percent)

	Kazakhstan				Uzbekistan				Kyrgyzstan				Tajikistan				Turkmenistan			
	Inter-republic		International		Inter-republic		International		Inter-republic		International		Inter-republic		International		Inter-republic		International	
	Exports	Imports	Exports	Imports	Exports	Imports	Exports	Imports	Exports	Imports	Exports	Imports	Exports	Imports	Exports	Imports	Exports	Imports	Exports	Imports
Industry	15.0	26.0	2.0	—	24.0	32.0	5.0	5.0	29	32	1	8	30.0	38.0	5.0	7.0	35.0	37.0	4.0	8.0
Power	13.0	19.0	—	—	20.0	18.0	—	—	29	12	—	—	23.0	35.0	—	—	28.0	5.0	—	—
Oil and gas	29.0	41.0	—	—	35.0	47.0	1.0	—	17	86	—	—	18.0	83.0	—	—	56.0	14.0	—	—
Coal	24.0	13.0	—	—	13.0	44.0	—	—	25	33	—	—	22.0	49.0	—	—	—	59.0	—	—
Other fuels	—	12.0	—	—	—	91.0	—	—	—	—	—	—	—	—	—	—	—	—	—	15.0
Ferrous metallurgy	37.0	42.0	8.0	3.0	37.0	76.0	—	2.0	30	88	7	3	21.0	83.0	—	6.0	14.0	68.0	—	1.0
Nonferrous metallurgy	14.0	8.0	8.0	1.0	45.0	42.0	—	1.0	47	41	7	4	58.0	59.0	27.0	16.0	63.0	75.0	—	6.0
Chemicals & petrochemicals	32.0	44.0	5.0	3.0	43.0	45.0	3.0	6.0	25	72	—	12	42.0	59.0	—	11.0	55.0	59.0	—	6.0
Machine building and metalworking	11.0	40.0	1.0	5.0	25.0	49.0	2.0	3.0	48	48	—	3	32.0	60.0	1.0	5.0	8.0	63.0	—	6.0
Wood and paper	2.0	42.0	—	4.0	6.0	50.0	—	4.0	3	43	—	3	6.0	45.0	—	6.0	—	52.0	—	5.0
Construction materials	5.0	10.0	—	1.0	3.0	10.0	—	1.0	4	15	—	1	9.0	16.0	—	6.0	6.0	12.0	—	1.0
Light industry	21.0	22.0	2.0	15.0	31.0	21.0	13.0	10.0	30	24	—	14	39.0	22.0	7.0	13.0	52.0	31.0	11.0	16.0
Food industry	6.0	12.0	—	5.0	11.0	20.0	6.0	6.0	21	13	—	13	15.0	24.0	—	6.0	7.0	27.0	—	8.0
Industry n.e.c.[1]	6.0	19.0	—	1.0	6.0	22.0	1.0	—	5	13	—	—	2.0	29.0	—	1.0	1.0	73.0	—	1.0
Agriculture	6.0	1.0	—	1.0	5.0	3.0	—	2.0	7	6	—	7	3.0	4.0	—	3.0	4.0	1.0	—	2.0

Source: Goskomstat USSR.

Interrepublic and international export/import values in domestic prices divided by domestic production and domestic use, respectively; expressed in percent. Domestic use equals domestic production minus exports plus imports.

[1] Not elsewhere classified.

TABLE 48. Foreign Trade: Former U.S.S.R., 1989.

(Million rubles)

Geographical Unit	Total foreign trade		Inter-republic trade		International trade	
	Exports	Imports	Exports	Imports	Exports	Imports
A. IN DOMESTIC PRICES						
U.S.S.R.	242,236.5	301,808.5	192,700.7	192,700.7	49,535.8	109,107.8
Russia	109,606.9	144,266.6	75,066.9	70,668.1	34,540.0	73,598.5
Ukraine	48,061.7	54,539.6	40,466.7	39,970.9	7,595.0	14,568.7
Belarus	20,301.5	19,347.7	18,310.4	14,834.4	1,991.1	4,513.3
Moldova	5,456.4	6,611.5	5,186.4	5,191.5	270.0	1,420.0
Lithuania	6,325.2	7,351.6	5,850.0	5,789.0	475.2	1,562.6
Latvia	5,413.2	6,030.0	5,039.3	4,520.2	373.9	1,509.8
Estonia	3,123.4	3,817.9	2,903.3	3,230.5	220.1	587.4
Georgia	6,084.2	6,469.0	5,718.8	4,888.3	365.4	1,580.7
Azerbaijan	7,122.9	5,189.8	6,674.9	3,794.3	448.0	1,395.5
Armenia	3,691.2	4,897.9	3,597.8	3,842.0	93.4	1,055.9
Kazakhstan	9,094.0	17,569.0	8,201.2	14,570.7	892.8	2,998.3
Uzbekistan	10,169.3	14,158.3	8,541.6	12,046.0	1,627.7	2,112.3
Kyrgyzstan	2,600.2	4,296.0	2,549.0	3,361.6	51.2	934.4
Tajikistan	2,527.0	3,930.2	2,176.2	3,249.3	350.8	680.9
Turkmenistan	2,659.4	3,333.4	2,418.2	2,743.9	241.2	589.5
B. IN FOREIGN TRADE PRICES						
U.S.S.R.	256,207.9	257,690.9	188,385.7	188,385.7	67,822.2	69,305.2
Russia	140,922.8	108,462.5	88,353.8	59,738.3	52,569.0	48,724.2
Ukraine	47,816.8	53,432.0	39,129.3	44,196.1	8,687.5	9,235.9
Belarus	18,749.7	20,230.3	16,546.6	17,359.0	2,203.1	2,871.3
Moldova	2,844.0	5,904.9	2,612.2	5,105.7	231.8	799.2
Lithuania	4,818.5	8,090.3	4,322.4	7,170.6	496.1	919.7
Latvia	4,412.7	5,640.2	4,148.6	4,747.2	264.1	893.0
Estonia	2,084.1	3,486.6	1,959.3	3,192.3	124.8	294.3
Georgia	3,452.8	5,475.6	3,096.2	4,792.2	356.6	683.4
Azerbaijan	4,990.5	4,234.1	4,589.9	3,545.0	400.6	689.1
Armenia	2,364.7	3,693.8	2,291.8	3,211.9	72.9	481.9
Kazakhstan	9,405.9	16,631.3	8,409.8	15,075.5	996.1	1,555.8
Uzbekistan	7,754.1	12,460.0	6,821.8	11,519.0	932.3	941.0
Kyrgyzstan	2,196.8	3,706.4	2,154.3	3,091.6	42.5	614.8
Tajikistan	1,804.0	3,376.2	1,483.0	3,046.0	321.0	330.2
Turkmenistan	2,590.5	2,866.7	2,466.7	2,595.3	123.8	271.4

Source: Goskomstat USSR.

BIBLIOGRAPHY

Anderson, Barbara and Brian Silver. Infant Mortality in the Soviet Union; Regional Differences and Measurement Issues," *Population and Development Review*, Vol. 12, No. 4, 1986, pp. 705–738.

Central Intelligence Agency. *The World Factbook 1992*. Washington, D.C.: U.S. Government Printing Office, 1992.

Departament statistiki Estonii. *Statisticheskiy yezhegodnik Estonii, 1990*. Tallinn, Olion, 1991 (p. 150)

Departament statistiki Latvii. *Statisticheskiy yezhegodnik Latvii, 1990*. Riga, Avots, 1991 (p. 136).

Departament statistiki Litvy. *Statisticheskiy yezhegodnik Litvy, 1991*. Vil'nyus, Informtsentr, 1992 (p. 150).

Derkomstat Ukrainy. *Ukrains'ka RSR u tsyfrakh u 1991 r.* Kiev, Tekhnika, 1991 (p. 156).

Diamond, Douglas and Gregory Kisunko. *Slavic and Eurasian Republics: Food Consumption in Recent Years in the Former Republics of the USSR*. Washington, D.C.: U.S. Bureau of the

1184

Census, Center for International Research, 1992. (Draft report)

Edwards, Imogene; Margaret Hughes, James Noren. "US and USSR: Comparisons of GNP," in U.S. Congress, Joint Economic Committee. *Soviet Economy in a Time of Change*, Vol. 1, pp. 369–401. Washington, D.C.: U.S. Government Printing Office, 10 October 1979.

Goskomstat Armyanskoy SSR. *Narodnoye khozyaystvo Armyanskoy SSR v 1988 godu. Statisticheskiy yezhegodnik.* Yerevan: Ayastan, 1990.

Goskomstat Azerbaydzhanskoy SSR. *Azerbaijan Republic: A Short Economic and Statistical Survey,* Moscow, Informatics, 1992 (p. 149).

————. *Narodnoye khozyaystvo Azerbaydzhanskoy SSR v 1988 g.* Baku: Azerneshr, 1989.

Goskomstat Belorusskoy SSR. *Narodnoye khozyaystvo Belorusskoy SSR v 1989 g. Statisticheskiy yezhegodnik.* Minsk: Belarus', 1990.

Goskomstat Estonskoy SSR. *Narodnoye khozyaystvo Estonskoy SSR v 1987 godu. Statisticheskiy yezhegodnik.* Tallin: Eesti Raamat, 1988.

————. *Narodnoye khozyaystvo Estonskoy SSR v 1988 godu. Statisticheskiy yezhegodnik.* Tallin: Olion, 1989.

Goskomstat Gruzinskoy SSR. *Narodnoye khozyaystvo Gruzinskoy SSR v 1987 godu. Statisticheskiy yezhegodnik.* Tbilisi: Sabchota Sakartvelo, 1988.

————. "Republic of Georgia: A Short Economic and Statistical Survey." Moscow, Informatics, 1992 (p. 149)

Goskomstat Kazakhskoy SSR. *Statisticheskiy yezhegodnik Kazakhstana.* Alma-Ata, Kazinform, 1991.

————. *Statisticheskiy yezhegodnik Kazakhstana v 1990 g.* Alma-Ata, Kazinform, 1991 (pp. 136, 149, 161).

Goskomstat Kirgizskoy SSR. *Narodnoye khozyaystvo Kirgizskoy SSR v 1988 godu. Statisticheskiy yezhegodnik.* Frunze: Kyrgyzstan, 1989.

————. *Statisticheskiy yezhegodnik Kyrgyzstana,* 1990. Frunze, Kyrgystan, 1991 (pp. 150, 171).

Goskomstat Latvii. *Narodnoye khozyaystvo Latvii v 1989 godu. Statisticheskiy yezhegodnik.* Riga: Avots, 1990.

Goskomstat Moldova. *Respublika Moldova v tsifrakh. Kratkiy statisticheskiy sbornik, 1990. Chisinau, n.p., 1991.*

Goskomstat RSFSR. *Chislennost' naseleniya RSFSR, po dannym Vsesoyuznoy perepisi naseleniya 1989 goda.* Moscow: Informtsentr RSFSR, 1990.

————. *Ekonomicheskoye polozheniye Rossiyskoy Federatsii, 1991.* Goskomstat RSFSR: Moscow, 1992.

————. *Narodnoye khozyaystvo RSFSR v 1989 godu. Statisticheskiy sbornik.* Moscow: Finansy i statistika, 1990.

————. *Narodnoye khozyaystvo RSFSR v 1990 godu. Statisticheskiy yezhegodnik.* Moscow: Finansy i statistika, 1991.

1185

_____. *Pokazateli sotsial'nogo razvitiya avtonomnykh respublik, krayev i oblastey RSFSR.* Goskomstat RSFSR: Moscow, 1990.

_____. *Sotsial'no-ekonomicheskoye razvitiye Rossiyskoy Federatsii v 1991–92 gg.* Goskomstat RSFSR: Moscow, 1992 (p. 187).

Goskomstat SSSR. *Byudzhety rabochikh, sluzhashchikh i kolkhoznikov v 1975–1988 gg.* Goskomstat SSSR: Moscow, 1989.

_____. *Chislennost' naseleniya soyuznykh respublik po gorodskim poseleniyam i rayonam na 1 yanvarya 1991 g.* Goskomstat USSR: Moscow, 1991.

_____. *Demograficheskiy yezhegodnik SSSR, 1990.* Goskomstat SSSR: Moscow, 1990.

_____. *Itogi Vsesoyuznoy perepisi naseleniya 1979 goda.* Tom I. *Chislennost' naseleniya SSSR, soyuznykh i avtonomnykh respublik, krayev i oblastey.* Moscow: Informtsentr, 1989.

_____. *Narodnoye khozyaystvo SSSR v 1988 godu. Statisticheskiy yezhegodnik.* Moscow: Finansy i statistika, 1989.

_____. *Narodnoye khozyaystvo SSSR v 1989 godu. Statisticheskiy yezhegodnik.* Moscow: Finansy i statistika, 1990.

_____. *Narodnoye khozyaystvo SSSR v 1990 godu. Statisticheskiy yezhegodnik.* Moscow: Finansy i statistika, 1991.

_____. *Naseleniye SSSR, 1988. Statisticheskiy yezhegodnik.* Moscow: Finansy i statistika, 1989.

_____. *Naseleniye SSSR. Perepis' naseleniya, 1989.* Moscow, Goskomstat SSSR, 1990.

_____. *Naseleniye SSSR. Perepis' naseleniya, 1989.* Moscow, Goskomstat RSFSR, 1990.

_____. *Natsional'nyy sostav naseleniya SSSR. Perepis' naseleniya, 1989.* Moscow, Goskomstat, 1991.

_____. *Okhrana zdorov'ya v SSSR. Statisticheskiy sbornik.* Moscow: Finansy i statistika, 1990.

_____. *Press-vypusk.* No. 16, No. 33, No. 230, No. 251, No. 358, No. 440. Moscow, Informtsentr, 1990.

_____. *Press-vypusk.* No. 150. Moscow, Informtsentr, 1991.

_____. *Promyshlennost'. Statisticheskiy sbornik.* Moscow: Informtsentr, 1991.

_____. *Statisticheskiy press-byulleten'.* Moscow: Informtsentr. No. 21, 1990.

_____. *Transport i svyaz', 1990.* Moscow, Finansy i statistika, 1991 (p. 182).

_____. *Sotsial'noye razvitiye SSSR.* Moscow, Goskomstat SSSR, 1990.

_____. *Torgovlya, 1990.* Moscow, Goskomstat SSSR, 1991.

_____. *Tovary narodnogo potrebleniya.* Moscow: Informtsentr, 1991.

_____. *Trud v SSSR. Statisticheskiy sbornik.* Moscow: Finansy i statistika, 1988.

_____. *Uroven' obrazovaniya naseleniya SSSR. Perepis' naseleniya, 1989.* Moscow, Goskomstat SSSR, 1990.

_____. *Vozrast i sostoyaniye v brake naseleniya SSSR. Perepis' naseleniya 1989.* Moscow, Goskomstat SSSR, 1990.

———. *Zhilishchnyye usloviya naseleniya SSSR*. Moscow: n.p., 1990.

Goskomstat Tadzhikskoy SSR. *Narodnoye khozyaystvo Tadzhikskoy SSR v 1987 godu. Statisticheskiy yezhegodnik*. Dushanbe: Irfon, 1988.

———. *Narodnoye khozyaystvo Tadzhikskoy SSR v 1989 godu. Statisticheskiy sbornik*. Dushanbe: Irfon, 1991.

Goskomstat Turkmenskoy SSR. *Narodnoye khozyaystvo Turkmenskoy SSR v 1989 godu. Statisticheskiy sbornik*. Ashkhabad: Turkmenistan, 1990.

Goskomstat Uzbekskoy SSR. *Narodnoye khozyaystvo Uzbekskoy SSR v 1989 g. Statisticheskiy yezhegodnik*. Tashkent: Uzbekistan, 1990.

———. *Narodnoye khozyaystvo Uzbekskoy SSR v 1990 g*. Tashkent: Uzbekistan, 1991.

Heleniak, Timothy and Victoria Velkoff. "Unemployment and the Transformation of the Labor Force in the Former Soviet Union." Washington, D.C., U.S. Bureau of the Census, Center for International Research, 1992 (p. 137).

International Monetary Fund. Economic Review Series. Washington, D.C.: International Monetary Fund, 1992. (Series of individual reports featuring the republics of the former Soviet Union.)

Kingkade, W. Ward. "The Demographic Development of the Soviet Nationalities: Post Mortem." in *Migration, Population Structure, and Redistribution Policies*. (ed., Edvin Goldscheider.) Boulder, Westview Press, 1992 (p. 78).

Kolossov, V. A., O. Glezer and N. Petrov. *Ethno-Territorial Conflicts and Boundaries in the Former Soviet Union*. Durham, UK: University of Durham, International Boundaries Research Unit, 1992, pp. 41–51.

Kurtzweg, Laurie. *"Measures of Soviet Gross National Product in 1982 Prices."* U.S. Congress, Joint Economic Committee. Washington, D.C.: U.S. Government Printing Office, November 1990.

Lithuanian Department of Statistics, Latvian Department of Statistics, and Estonian Deparment of Statistics. *Lithuania, Latvia, Estonia, Statistical Abstract*. Vilnius, 1991.

Lithuanian Department of Statistics. *Lithuania's Statistics Yearbook, 1990*. Vilnius, Lietuvos Ukis, 1991 (p. 167).

Minstat Ukrainskoi RSR. *Narodne hospodarstvo Ukrains'koi RSR u 1990 r*. Kiev, Tekhnika, 1991 (pp. 136, 149, 156).

Socio-Economic Data Division, International Economics Department, The World Bank. "Measuring the Incomes of the Economies of the Former Soviet Union." Washington, D.C.: December 1992.

Tretyakova, Albina and Barry Kostinsky. "Gross National Product Accounts of the Newly Independent States of the Former Soviet Union, 1987–90." Washington, D.C.: U.S. Bureau of the Census, Center for International Research, 1992.

U.S. Congress, Joint Economic Committee. "Measures of Soviet Gross National Product in 1982 Prices." Washington, D.C., Government Printing Office, Nov. 1990 (p. 133).

Vestnik statistiki, No. 12, 1991.

World Development Report, 1989 (p. 60).

O